ACM 1998 CONFERENCE

ON COMPUTER SUPPORTED

COOPERATIVE WORK

PROCEEDINGS

CSCW 98

COMPUTER SUPPORTED COOPERATIVE WORK

Sponsored by ACM's Special Interest Groups on Computer-Human Interaction (ACM SIGCHI) and GroupWare and GroupWork (SIGGROUP)

SEATTLE, WASHINGTON

NOVEMBER 14-18, 1998

The Association for Computing Machinery
1515 Broadway
New York New York 10036

ACM ISBN: 1-58113-009-0

Additional copies may be ordered prepaid from:

ACM Order Department
PO Box 11405
New York, NY 10286-1405

Phone: 1-800-342-6626
(US and Canada)
+1-212-626-0500
(all other countries)
Fax: +1-212-944-1318
E-mail: acmhelp@acm.org

ACM Order Number: 612980
Printed in the USA

From the Conference Co-Chairs

Computer Supported Cooperative Work has established itself as a research forum without an umbrella organization or primary academic home discipline. A successful series of North American and European conferences, a journal, and a series of books demonstrate that this multi-disciplinary approach has a major contribution to make to the design, use, and understanding of technology in social contexts.

Saul Greenberg and Christine Neuwirth, the Program Co-Chairs, describe the contents of this volume. As an archival resource, this Proceedings will be the most enduring legacy of the conference. It is appropriate to thank here the many who have made the conference a success; without their work this contribution to scholarship would not have appeared.

Accordingly, we thank the Program and Conference Committee members, including our vendors. Technology makes conference organizing easier, but it is still an extraordinary collective effort. We thank SIGCHI, SIGOIS, and the staff of ACM who have supported this conference unflaggingly.

We are grateful to the Conference Benefactors: Smart Technologies, Lotus Development Corporation, and Microsoft; our Sponsors: MITRE and Sun Microsystems; and our affiliate The Boeing Company for their very significant contribution to the conference.

Steven Poltrock

The Boeing Company

Jonathan Grudin

University of California

Conference Committee

Conference Co-Chairs

Steve Poltrock, The Boeing Company

Jonathan Grudin, University of California, Irvine

Technical Program

Demonstrations
Beth Hetzler, Pacific Northwest National Laboratory

Doctoral Colloquium
Gary Olson and Judy Olson, University of Michigan

Panels
M. Lynne Markus, Claremont Graduate School

Tora Bikson, RAND Corporation

Papers
Christine Neuwirth, Carnegie Mellon University

Saul Greenberg, University of Calgary

Tutorials
Thomas Finholt, University of Michigan

Mark Ackerman, University of California, Irvine

Video
Steven Whittaker, ATT Labs-Research

John Tang, Sun Microsystems

Steve Harrison, Xerox PARC

Hideaki Kuzuoka, University of Tsukuba

John Patterson, Lotus Development Corporation

Steve Benford, University of Nottingham

Saul Greenberg University of Calgary

Workshops
Paul Dourish, Xerox PARC

Mike Robinson, University of Jyväskylä

Randy Trigg, Xerox PARC , (PDC Liaison)

Operations:

A/V & Computing Support
Steven Russert, Randy Groves and Chris Esposito, The Boeing Company

Electronic Publishing
Scott Mainwaring, Interval Research

Local Arrangements
Debra Dubrow and Gayna Williams, Microsoft

Proceedings
David Durand, Boston University, Dynamic Diagrams

Publications
George Engelbeck and Chris Bussler, The Boeing Company

Registration
Steve Anderson, Lawrence Livermore National Labs

Student Volunteers
Christine Halverson, IBM, TJ Watson Research Center

Gail Rein, Xerox Corporation

Eileen Kupstas, University of North Carolina

Treasurer
Keith Lash, The Boeing Company

Liaisons:
ACM: David Riederman, ACM

Asian: Ken-Ichi Okada, Keio University

Australian: Simon Kaplan, University of Queensland

European: Gloria Mark and Norbert Streitz, GMD

Latin American: Hugo Fuks, Catholic University of Rio de Janeiro

PDC: David Levinger, Rensselaer Polytechnic Institute

SIGCHI: Austin Henderson, Rivendel Consulting

SIGGROUP: Dirk Mahling, University of Pittsburgh

Consultants

Conference Management & Registration
Stephanie Benjamin and Tina Nathan, Convention Services Northwest

Publications & Graphic Design
Bob Meador, RMB Vivid

From The Papers Co-chairs

Welcome to CSCW'98, the Seventh Conference on Computer-Supported Cooperative Work.

One of the hallmarks of the CSCW conferences has been a commitment by the CSCW community to defining "computing research" as consisting of an integration of behavioral and technological research. The CSCW'98 Technical Program continues a tradition of bringing together researchers from behavioral and technical disciplines – including anthropology, communications, computer science, education, engineering, graphics, human-computer interaction, management and information systems, media/multimedia, political science, social psychology and sociology – to integrate research results and chart new research directions.

In the pages of the proceedings, you will find papers addessing a wide range of outstanding research issues in computer-support for cooperative work. These research issues include:

- More adequate conceptualizations of key theoretical concepts (e.g., "awareness;" "organizational memory")
- Architectures to support group activity more effectively (e.g., scalable, reliable protocols across heterogeneous platforms; rapid, end-user construction of collaborative applications and run-time change of coordination policies)
- Development of innovative prototypes and techniques designed to solve or mitigate problems that users experience with current systems (e.g., mitigation of users' sense of intrusiveness in video systems) and their evaluation
- Development of new technologies (e.g., mobile computing, tele-manipulation, wearable computers) and identification of requirements for their use in collaborative work
- Studies of work that result in the identification of new research problems and design requirements for CSCW architectures and applications (e.g., identification of potential collaborative partners)
- Better frameworks and empirical measures/metrics that predict collaborative success (e.g., the amount of communication and the perception of communication overload and their relationship to successful project outcome)
- New models of the social and organizational effects of technology (e.g., factors influencing computer-mediated conversations among hundreds of people)

Paper acceptance continues to be highly competitive. From 220 papers submitted for CSCW'98 from all over the world, we selected the 41 papers included here, for an acceptance rate of 19%. Each paper submission had at least 3 Reviewers plus one Associate Chair who also read and reviewed it.

Our heartfelt gratitude to the volunteers who made the technical program possible and shaped it: to the 20 Associate Chairs, who flew for the full-day Program Commitee Meeting from as far away as Australia, Europe, Canada, and Japan, and to the just over 60 Paper Reviewers, for their diligent effort in reading about 12 papers per person and writing reviews for them; and to the Members of the Demonstration, Panel, Tutorial, Video, and Workshop Committees. And our tremendous thanks to Lotus Development Corporation for supporting our use of a CSCW tool, Domino/Lotus Notes, as part of our reviewing process; the use of the tool allowed us to expand the reviewing pool and made it easier to communicate with reviewers internationally. Many thanks also to Scott Mainwaring, the CSCW'98 Electronic Publishing Chair, whose efforts enabled us to use the Web site to communicate with the authors about requirements for their submissions, and to David Durand, who put together these Proceedings.

We hope that you enjoy the CSCW'98 conference and that you will take this opportunity to meet colleagues from other disciplines in order to continue building the CSCW community and its commitment to a greater understanding of the requirements for, the development of, and the effects of innovative technologies in collaborative work.

Sincerely,

Saul Greenberg

University of Calgary, Canada

Christine M. Neuwirth

Carnegie Mellon University, USA

Papers Committee

Co-chairs

Saul Greenberg University of Calgary
Christine Neuwirth Carnegie Mellon University

Associate Chairs

Mark Ackerman, University of California, Irvine
Tora Bikson, RAND Corporation
Georgio DeMichelis, DSI, University of Milan
Gerardine DeSanctis, Duke University
Paul Dourish, Xerox PARC
Keith Edwards, Xerox PARC
Thomas Finholt, University of Michigan
Hiroshi Ishii, MIT Media Lab
Simon Kaplan, The University of Queensland
Sara Kiesler, Carnegie Mellon University
Robert Kraut, Carnegie Mellon University
Alison Lee, IBM TJ Watson Research Center
Ken-Ichi Okada, Keio University
John Patterson, Lotus Development Corporation
Atul Prakash, University of Michigan
Mike Robinson, University of Jyväskylä
Chris Schmandt, MIT Media Lab
Norbert Streitz, GMD-IPSI
John Tang Sun, Microsystems, Inc.
Steve Whittaker, ATT Labs – Research

Reviewers

Anne Anderson, University of Glasgow
Liam Bannon, University of Limerick
Victoria Bellotti, Xerox PARC
Jeanette Blomberg, Xerox PARC
Sara Bly, Sara Bly Consulting
John Bowers, Royal Institute of Technology and University of Manchester
Andy Cockburn, University of Canterbury
Mauricio Cortes, Bell Labs, Lucent Technologies
Kevin Crowston, Syracuse University
Prasun Dewan, University of North Carolina at Chapel Hill
JD Eveland, California School of Professional Psychology
Robert Fish, Panasonic Information and Networking Technologies Lab
Geraldine Fitzpatrick, The University of Queensland
Richard Furuta, Texas A&M University
Jolene Galegher, Carnegie Mellon University
Andreas Girgensohn, FX Palo Alto Laboratory
Natalie Glance, Xerox Research Centre Europe
Irene Greif Lotus Development Corporation
Rebecca Grinter, Bell Labs, Lucent Technologies
Carl Gutwin, University of Saskatchewan
Jörg Haake, GMD-IPSI
Steve Harrison, Xerox PARC
Will Hill, AT&T Labs - Research
Debby Hindus, Interval Research Corporation
Scott Hudson, Carnegie Mellon University
Ellen Isaacs, Electric Communities
Barbara Katzenberg, Ellora Software, Inc.
Hideaki Kuzuoka, University of Tsukuba
Paul Luff, King's College, London
Wendy Mackay, University of Paris-Sud
Allan MacLean, Xerox Research Centre Europe
Marilyn Mantei-Tremaine, Drexel University
John Mariani, Lancaster University
Gloria Mark, GMD-FIT
Susan McDaniel, University of Michigan
Thomas Moran, Xerox PARC
James Morris, Carnegie Mellon University
Elizabeth Mynatt, Xerox PARC
Hideyuki Nakanishi, Kyoto University
Gary Olson, University of Michigan
Judy Olson, University of Michigan
Francois Pacull, Xerox Research Centre Europe
Wolfgang Prinz, GMD-FIT
James Pycock, Xerox Research Centre Europe
Paul Resnick, University of Michigan
Matthias Ressel, Swiss Bank Corporation
Tom Rodden, Lancaster University
Mark Roseman, TeamWave Software
Jane Siegel, Carnegie Mellon University
Markus Sohlenkamp, COSA Solutions Standard-software GmbH
Dan Shapiro, Lancaster University
Kjeld Schmidt, Technical University of Denmark
Gareth Smith, Lancaster University
David Stotts, University of North Carolina at Chapel Hill
Lucy Suchman, Xerox PARC
Loren Terveen, AT&T Labs - Research
Konrad Tollmar, The Royal Institute of Technology
Jozsef Toth, University of Pittsburgh
Jennifer Watts-Perotti, Eastman Kodak Company
Terry Winograd, Stanford University
Volker Wulf, University of Bonn
Nicole Yankelovich, Sun Microsystems, Inc.
JoAnne Yates, MIT Sloan School of Management

Additional paper reviews by:

Lee Sproull, School of Management, Boston University, Scott Brave, MIT Media Lab, Paul Yarin, MIT Media Lab, Fiorella DeCindio, University of Milano, Milano Italy, Christine Halverson, IBM T.J. Watson Research Center, Charlotte Linde, Institute for Research on Learning, M. Lynne Markus, Claremont Graduate School, Kevin Schlueter, Telepresence Systems Inc, Canada, Michael Travers, IBM T.J. Watson Research Center, Susan Brennan, SUNY Binghamton, Doug Terry, Xerox PARC, Samuli Pekkola, University of Jyväskylä, Finland.

Contents

Supporting customer and health-care service workers

Infrastructures for collaboration (1)

Mirrors to the future: New interaction paradigms

Infrastructures for collaboration (2)

Shared visual spaces

Primitives for building flexibile groupware systems

Asynchronous communication

From single-display groupware to mobility

Finding and sustaining relationships

Social filtering, social influences

Supporting design activity: Observations and requirements

Panels

Conference program summaries

OfficeWalker: A Virtual Visiting System Based on Proxemics

Akihiko Obata **Kazuo Sasaki**

Fujitsu Laboratories Ltd.
64 Nishiwaki, Ohkubo-Cho, Akashi 6748555, Japan
+81 78 934 8250
obata@flab.fujitsu.co.jp ksasaki@flab.fujitsu.co.jp

ABSTRACT

We propose an interaction model for video mediated communication systems that support informal communication among distributed groups. We focused on two issues raised in previous research, the problem of intrusiveness that occurs when a caller glances at a recipient prior to conversation, and the failure of facilitating unintended interactions with unexpected partners. The proposed model addresses these problems by introducing "interactional distance" among users. We developed our prototype system that embodied this model, and examined these problems by conducting a user experiment. We confirmed that the problem of intrusiveness was reduced, and unintended interactions were partially supported.

Keywords

Informal communication, video, awareness, glance, privacy

INTRODUCTION

There is much interest for system that use video connections to facilitate informal communication among members of distributed organizations that occurs effortlessly among people in proximity. Several literatures demonstrated the importance of informal communication for collaborative work. Kraut, et al. pointed out the role of informal communication for generating collaborative relationships [11]. Issac, et al. reported that people get essential information mainly through informal communication [10]. It is widely reported that most interactions in the working environment take place when people meet each other by chance [12][21]. Numerous experiments have been conducted to evaluate video communication as a technology for supporting informal communications [4,5,6,7,13,19,20]. These systems used video links for checking availability of recipients prior to conversations, and as triggers of unintended interactions. However, many problems remain unsolved with these systems.

In this paper, we first review issues raised in previous research, and focus on two problems, the problem of intrusiveness that occurs when a caller glances at a recipient prior to conversation, and the failure of facilitating unintended interactions with unexpected partners. Then, we propose an interaction model that would solve these problems by introducing "interactional distance" among users in the network.

People usually communicate with others from a distance that is appropriate to their mutual relationship. We claim that the problem of intrusiveness is caused by eliminating the sense of distance that affords appropriate behavior and social norms. Glancing at a recipient prior to a conversation from the same distance as that used when starting a conversation urges the recipient to respond.

The sense of distance as conveyed by 3D images [3,14] is meaningless when recipients are not getting involved in activities of the virtual world. We tried to introduce the sense of distance into the network by creating public places and private places. A caller approaches a recipient from a public place instead of directly intruding into the private place of the recipient. Encounters in public places may afford behaviors like greeting each other, or simply ignoring, but do not afford any social imperative to start a conversation. A caller also has the opportunity to encounter the neighbors of a recipient in these public places.

We present our prototype system, called OfficeWalker, which incorporates this model, and we also examine the problem of intrusiveness and the behavior of unintended interactions over the network. We conclude this paper with a discussion of what we learned from our experiment, and point out issues for future study.

OVERVIEW MODEL VS. HALLWAY MODEL

Previous research methodologies can be classified into an overview and a hallway model. Overview model systems [4,6,13] simulate a virtual room by providing a matrix of slowly scanned continuous video images of each member. User experiments provided anecdotal evidence of unintended interactions in these systems [6]. However, some people feel uncomfortable about having their video image broadcast without knowing who is watching, since these systems do not notify who is currently looking at a user [13,19]. Overview model systems are appropriate for tightly coupled collaboration groups, but might not be suitable for large scale organizations. In addition, support for unintended interactions is available only to members that were predefined as collaborators. Users can not receive serendipitous information from unexpected partners.

On the other hand, hallway model systems [5,7,19,20] simulate visits to remote private offices through virtual hallways by providing a function for "glance" prior to conversations. These systems do not require to predefine collaborators and are applicable to large organizations, but have other problems. CRUISER [5,7] provides the glance function by opening a 3-second audio-video link with a recipient from which either of the participants can decide to start a conversation. To maintain privacy, the audio-video link is reciprocal. However, experimental results revealed that CRUISER's method for initiating conversations was abrupt and intrusive. The screen suddenly displayed the image of the caller, compelling conversation even when this was not welcome [7]. Besides, some users were worried about possibly interrupting activities of recipients by glancing into their offices. Sometimes, this resulted in a reluctance to use the system [5]. Montage introduced a fade-in video effect to reduce the perception of abruptness. However, users commented that a glance was still more of an interruption than someone walking down the hallway and looking into the room [19,20].

In the cases of the CRUISER [7] and Montage [20] experiments, the rates of calls resulting in conversations were very high; 54%, and 25%, respectively. Considering the rate by which employees were in their offices (10% and 13%, according to the observation of two engineers by Bellotti et al. [1]), almost of the calls in the CRUISER and Montage experiments might result in conversations when recipients were in their offices as the telephone calls do.

Another problem raised in the hallway model is the failure to supporting unintended interactions. Video links for supporting a glance function might reduce the psychological barriers to start conversations, but can't support unintended interactions with unexpected persons. CRUISER [7] provides a random connection service called "autocruise", which simulates encounters in hallways for supporting such unintended interactions. However, the experiment of using CRUISER[7] showed that few "autocruises" actually resulted in conversations. In addition, many users disliked this feature since they perceived it as intrusive.

INTERACTION MODEL

We decided to base our new system design on the hallway model, as the overview model systems can not support unintended interactions with unexpected partners. In this section, we propose an interaction model that would solve the problem of intrusiveness that commonly exists in hallway model systems, while also providing opportunities for unintended interactions with unexpected persons by introducing the sense of distance among people in the network.

Behaviors afforded by physical distance

The problem of intrusiveness, which is inherent to hallway systems, might be caused by breaking down appropriate behaviors and social norms afforded by real world settings. Bellotti, et. al [2] claimed that the breakdown of social norms and practices was partly due to inadequate feedback about what information one is broadcasting and an inability to control one's accessibility from others. We claim here that such a breakdown also occurs due to a lacking sense of distance among users in the network.

Hall [8] argued that people possess unspoken proxemics rules that specify the amount of distance that is perceived as appropriate in daily relationships and the kinds of situations in which either closeness or distance is proper. Hall categorized four zones in terms of appropriate distances for conversation: the zone of intimacy, personal distance, social distance and the public zone. Nishide [15] further categorized the distances into the following five zones according to the possibilities for starting a conversation:

1. The zone of exclusion, which ranges from body contact to a distance of about 50 cm. Others are generally not allowed to enter this zone. Usual conversations do not occur at this distance.
2. The zone of conversation, which ranges from approximately 50 cm to 150 cm. In this zone, conversations take place. Formal conversations occur in a range more than 80 cm. When this zone is entered, a conversation is mandatory.
3. The zone of proximity, which ranges from approximately 1.5 m to 3 m. This is the zone to approach a recipient for a conversation. However, it is possible to enter this zone without starting a conversation for the time being.
4. The zone of mutual recognition, which ranges from approximately 3 m to 20 m. It is possible to recognize acquaintances and their facial expression at this distance. Greetings usually occur in this zone. Ignoring acquaintances is difficult when the range from 3 m to 7 m is entered.
5. The zone of recognition, which ranges from approximately 20 m to 50 m. It is possible to recognize acquaintances, but greetings rarely occur in this zone.

The ranges which are listed in literatures of proxemics vary for different environments and circumstances. However, it is probably true that there are several categories of distance that afford different behaviors such as starting conversations, greeting, or ignoring. We claimed that the problem of intrusiveness encountered with previous hallway model systems was caused by breaking down the sense of distance. Glancing at a recipient while being in the same distance as for starting conversations might urge the recipient to respond to it, and leads to the impression of intrusiveness. The random video connection service of CRUISER, which simulates encounters in a hallway, might place together two users in the zone for conversations too abruptly. It does not provide a distance in which it is possible to ignore each other.

Proxemics over the network

How is it possible to create the sense of distance in a communication environment that has the goal to eliminate the distance? Is the solution to provide a virtual world using 3D computer graphics like in Massive [3], DIVA [3], and FreeWalk[14]? Hallway model systems construct a hybrid world which integrates virtual spaces and physical spaces [9]. Recipients of communication are not always confined to virtual spaces. They are sometimes getting involved in activities in a physical space as well. The sense of distance constructed by 3D images is meaningless if the recipients aren't looking in and getting involved in the activities in virtual spaces.

We tried to introduce the sense of distance in the hybrid world by providing public and private places, as well as by varying the amount of information exchange between a caller and a recipient according to the phases of communication. When a caller visits a recipient, the caller approaches the recipient from a public place instead of directly jumping into the private place of the recipient. Encounters in public places may afford behaviors of greeting each other, or just simply ignoring. Contrary to this, encounters in private places put people in a situation where it is awkward to ignore each other and conversations are mandatory.

The sense of public-ness or private-ness of a place is developed by how people use this space. Public places are used by anonymous people, while private places are used by specific persons. Figure 1 shows the concept of our proposed interaction model. A place for informal communication consists of a public place that is shared by neighbors as a hallway, and private places, that are used by these neighbors as their offices. The hallway is provided in a virtual space on the network, while the private offices are located in physical spaces. Neighbors can be defined independently from their physical locations. The virtual hallway and the physical offices are interconnected by virtual doorways that are provided by the computer terminals of the network.

When a caller wishes to initiate a conversation with a recipient, the caller virtually visits a virtual hallway that is shared by virtual neighbors of the recipient, instead of visiting the recipient's private place directly. The caller can see the private offices of the virtual neighbors as well as that of the recipient from a distance. A questionnaire which was answered by 29 members of our laboratories showed that taking video images at a distance and together with other people drastically decreased the number of persons who felt uncomfortable [18]. The experiment of NYNEX porthole [13] also suggested this effect of placing a camera at a distance.

When a caller visits a recipient's virtual hallway, the recipient and the neighbors can also see the caller's video image from their virtual doorways. In this phase, the recipient does not know who the recipient of the caller is, and there is therefore no social need to respond to the caller even when the recipient recognizes the caller. The caller can wait till the recipient is available without interrupting the activities of the recipient when the recipient looks busy.

After the caller decides to contact the recipient, the caller approaches the private place of the recipient. The caller and the recipient can see each other on closer view. The recipient is notified that the caller is at their doorway. Staying at this distance for a while without having a conversation is uncomfortable for both of them, which is in contrast to the situation at the distance before approaching.

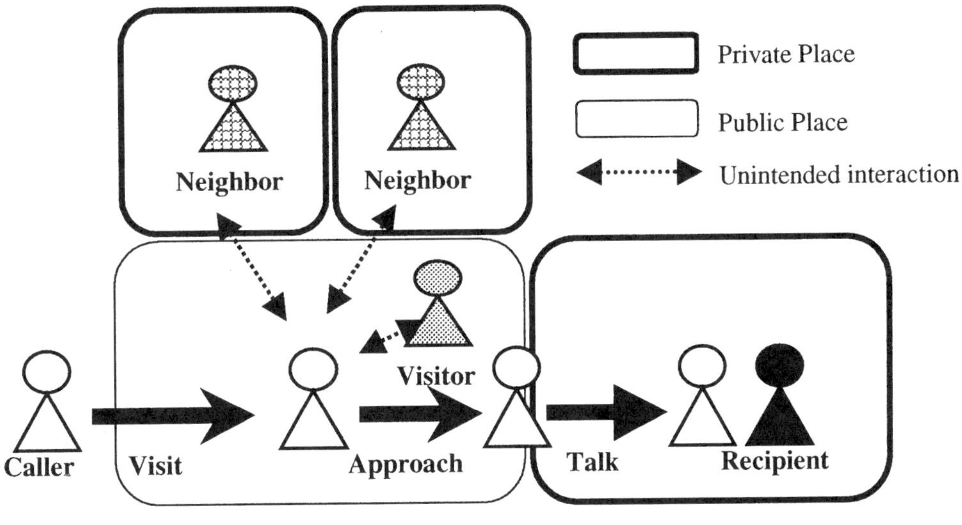

Figure 1. Interaction model

The recipient is under pressure to suspend such current activities as talking with others. The caller can also not wait a long time at this distance that the recipient becomes available. The caller needs to decide whether to interrupt the recipient, or give up the attempt to initiate a conversation for a short time. According to the observations of Whittaker, et. al [21], callers wait for a verbal sign or visual orienting sign of attention from the recipient, otherwise, they just launched into interaction when the recipient is engaged in activity. Establishing a short-term audio link might be required in this phase, as well as a video link. After either caller or recipient decided to talk, high quality audio and video links are established. Data links for shared objects might be added during the conversation.

Unintended interactions with neighbors

The proposed interaction model that introduced the sense of distance also can support unintended interactions with virtual neighbors, as well as solve the problem of intrusiveness. When a caller visits the virtual hallway of a recipient, the caller might talk with a virtual neighbor of the recipient, especially when the recipient is not available. In the same way, some of the virtual neighbors might initiate conversations with the caller while the caller is waiting in the virtual hallway that the recipient becomes available. Moreover, it is possible to talk with virtual visitors who happen to visit the same hallway. As these opportunity for unintended interactions are provided in public places, the problem of intrusion may not occur as in the random connection service provided by previous hallway model systems [5,7] that directly connected two users for conversations.

We observed how frequently unintended interactions occurred with neighbors of recipients by setting up camcorders with fish eye lenses in our laboratory. We took videos of four subjects for four hours. The four subjects worked side by side but were separated by low partitions. There were 18 visitors during the time when the video was recorded. Visitors talked to the neighbors of recipients in 40% of the visits, after and during the period while the visitors talked to their recipients. Besides, the subjects initiated conversation with persons who were passing by their workplace by chance 14 times during the recording period of the video.

OFFICEWALKER

User interface

Based on the proposed interaction model, we implemented a prototype system called OfficeWalker. The client software of OfficeWalker runs on personal computers with Windows95, a voice modem, TCP/IP network, and a video capture camera for taking a close view of the user. The system also needs server systems for managing the status of virtual hallways, and server systems with video capture devices for taking distant views of users.

When starting OfficeWalker, a window for the virtual hallway that is connected to the user's physical office is displayed as shown in Figure 2. The virtual hallway window shows slowly scanned video images of the user's virtual neighbors (in the upper three child windows), and of virtual visitors who are currently visiting the virtual hallway (in the lower two child windows). These images are taken from cameras with distant views unless one of the participants selects the approach command (The 'approach' command is described later). The user's video image is also presented as one of the neighbors in the virtual hallway.

Neighbors can be defined independently from their physical location. The current version of OfficeWalker has, however, a limitation on the possible neighbor relationships. The neighbor relationship is defined as a group: If A is a neighbor of B and C, B and C must be neighbors to each other, even though B and C might not be neighbors in the real world.

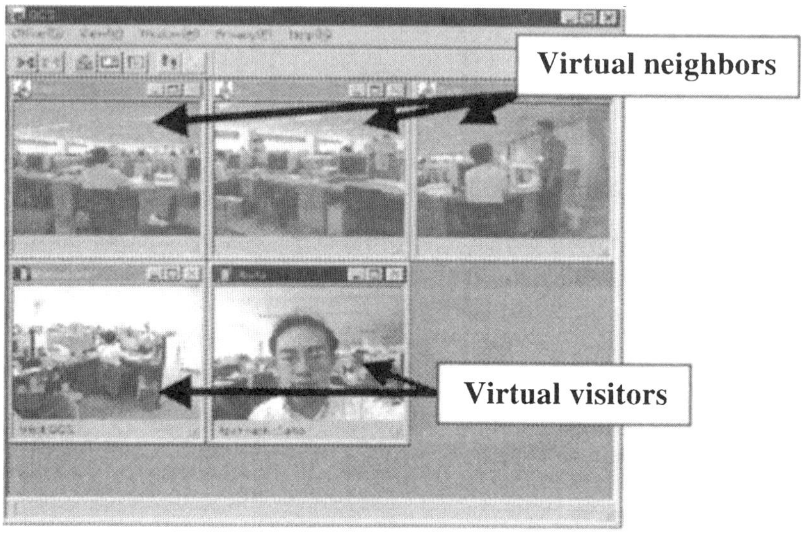

Figure 2. User Interface

Each child window shows the current communication status on its status bar, the user's name and an icon which distinguish between neighbors and visitors on its title bar, as well as a slowly scanned video image of the user. Video images are usually refreshed once per minute, but they are refreshed once per second when a user activates a child window by clicking the title bar, or when a new child window is created for a new visitor. These refresh rates are continued only for 10 seconds so as to reduce the traffic on the network.

All video links are reciprocal so as to protect privacy. A user's neighbors and visitors can also see video images of the user. When the user closes the virtual hallway window, the neighbors and visitors can not see the user any longer. This action simulates closing the virtual door that connects a user's physical office and the virtual hallway. When other users of the hallway close their virtual doors, the sign "not started" is displayed in their child windows instead of their video images.

When users want to communicate with a neighbor or a visitor in the virtual hallway, they need to select a communication tool from the menu that appears when clicking the right mouse button in the child window of a recipient. The menu provides the following communication tools: "approach", "talk", "electronic mail", "shared whiteboard", and "application sharing".

The approach command is useful when the recipient is engaged such activities as talking with others. When the "approach" command is selected, video images of the recipient change from a distant view to a closer view. In the same way, the video image of the caller in the recipient's computer is changed from a distant view to a closer view as well. The recipient is notified that the caller is at their doorway (the lower right child window in Figure 2). This might require the recipient to respond, but does not immediately interrupt the recipient's activity. Contrary to this, the "talk" command immediately interrupts the activities of the recipient by placing a phone call. The current version of the "approach" command does not provide an audio link for sending verbal signs to decide whether to talk, as the quality of audio transmission over a computer network is poor. Instead, we provided a "knock" command as a cue for starting conversation. The caller and the recipient can send knocking sounds by clicking on the respective child windows.

The "shared whiteboard" command can be used to send message-tag like messages as well as for sharing drawings and images with a remote partner. When the user selects the 'shared whiteboard', windows for a shared whiteboard are created both on the side of caller and recipient without the need for an acknowledgement by the recipient. It is possible to use the shared whiteboard for leaving messages when recipients are absent.

To talk to a member outside the user's hallway, the user needs only to select a recipient from the directory. Then, the user can virtually visit the hallway connected to the recipient's private office. A window for the recipient's hallway is created on the user's computer as shown in Figure 3. It shows video images of virtual neighbors and visitors, as well as of the recipient. At the same time, a child window that shows the video image of the user is created in the hallway as a virtual visitor. Virtual neighbors and visitors in the hallway are notified of the visit. In this phase, it is still unknown who is the recipient of this visit, and there is therefore no social need to respond. The recipient can continue with current activities.

After the user decided to initiate conversation, a communication tool can be selected from the menu that appears when the user clicks the right mouse button in the child window of a recipient as described previously. The caller can also communicate with other users in the hallway in this way.

Figure 3. Visiting other hallway

Usage scenarios

In this section, we describe a scenario of unintended interactions that are possible with OfficeWalker.

Bob, the manager of the Planning division, is concerned about the progress of project X. He virtually visits Tom who is responsible for the project X by clicking on Tom's name in the directory. The virtual hallway connected to Tom's office is displayed. The video image of Tom shows he is talking with his superior. Bob decides to wait in the virtual hallway. Steve, a neighbor of Tom, notices that Bob has appeared as a virtual visitor in his hallway window. He guesses that Bob is waiting for that Tom becomes available. Steve selects the 'talk' command from the menu displayed in Bob's child window, and starts a conversation with Bob. While Bob is talking with Steve, Bob notices that Tom has finished his conversation with his respective superior. Bob suspends the conversation with Steve and selects instead the "talk" command for Tom.

USER EXPERIMENT

Subjects

Ten employees of Fujitsu Limited in Kawasaki and of Fujitsu Kyusyu Communication Systems Limited in Fukuoka participated in our experiment. Kawasaki and Fukuoka are more than 1000 km apart from each other. They collaborate on designing digital switching systems and promoting the sales of these systems. Five employees work on design, of which three are located in Kawasaki and two in Fukuoka. The other five employees work on sales promotion, two in Kawasaki, and three in Fukuoka. All participants are acquainted with each other. Their neighbor relationships are defined by working group rather than location according to the wishes of the participants.

Measures

We examined the following questions about OfficeWalker by our user experiment:

How much is the problem of intrusiveness reduced?

We examined the intrusiveness of OfficeWalker by observing the rate for how much of virtual visits resulted in conversations with recipients. As described earlier, almost all visits in the previous hallway model experiments might result in conversations when the recipients were in their office at that time. We expected that a larger percentage of OfficeWalker visits would not result in conversations even when recipients were available. We used a video-logging feature for taking video images of recipients at times when callers visited so as to monitor the availability of recipients.

How frequently do unintended interactions with virtual neighbors and visitors occur?

We evaluated the frequency of unintended interactions by logged data of user commands that resulted in conversations with virtual neighbors and visitors. We also examined how much of these interactions started with greetings and social conversations. Subjects were asked to select among the following nine conversation categories after each call; "scheduling meetings and tasks", "assigning tasks", "reporting work status", "querying information", "solving problems", "making decision", "discussing non-workplace related topics", and "greeting".

Does OfficeWalker lead to an increase in communication frequency?

Evaluating the effect of a system on communication frequency is fairly difficult. A method that compared communication behaviors in the three phases, "before system introduction", "with the system", and "after removing the system" was used in previous research [20]. It may include a lot of noises: Communication behavior might change not only due to the effect of the system, but also due to changes in project phase, and due to the Hawthorne effect. However, we cannot simply discard this method.

We set up the period of the experiment by consulting with the participants. Some of them recommend to use a short time period for the experiment as communication frequency might vary with phases of their projects. We decided to set up the period for the experiment as follows: one week before introducing the system, two weeks of using the system, and another one week after removing the system.

We proposed that participants would use electronic phone directory software for controlling a voice modem, so that we would get log data of phone calls. However, some of the participants rather prefer to keep records by taking a note after each call, as they were accustomed to making phone calls by the one-touch-dial feature provided in their phones. Therefore, we decided that the participants would keep records by themselves each time they made calls to other participants in the week before installing, and the week after removing OfficeWalker. The nine communication categories and the name of all participants were listed on checklists. The participants had to mark the appropriate field. During the phase of using OfficeWalker, the participants were asked to select the communication categories after finishing their conversations in the dialog box that appeared after issuing the 'talk' command.

We were concerned about the Hawthorne effect according to which the behavior of users would change because of the novelty of the new application in our experiment. In the version of the experiment, the subjects were asked to make phone calls by conventional telephones after they selected the "talk" command. We cannot remove the influence of the Hawthorne effect on the frequency of looking at remote partners, however, we were at least able to evaluate the effect of glancing on the frequency of phone calls. The frequency of calls measured by above method might be unreliable since the participants sometimes failed to mark checklists. However, we assume that these noise-effects would occur approximately at random during each phase of the test.

Experimental system

For our experiment, we used an experimental version of OfficeWalker that runs in connection with the World Wide Web system, and added a logging feature and an automatic questionnaire collection function to the original version of OfficeWalker. Figure 4 shows the experimental version of OfficeWalker. User commands were logged, such as clicking the name of a member in the directory for visiting other virtual hallways, clicking on a title bar of a child window to change the refresh timing of the video rate (we used the term "visit", and "activate" for convenience), and clicking communication tools. Video still images of recipients were sampled when users issued the "visit", "approach" or "talk" command.

The experimental version of OfficeWalker did not have the feature of changing from a distant view in video images to a closer view. Instead, the message "approaching!" was shown in the child window of a caller when the users select the "approach" command. The reason for developing the experimental version of OfficeWalker based on web systems is that this system was not only intended for research. The experimental version of OfficeWalker was developed by the courtesy of Fujitsu Kyusyu Communication Systems Limited.

Figure 4. Web browser version.

RESULT

Usage

Figure 5 shows the average frequency of phone calls that were accepted, and the usage of OfficeWalker per person and day during the four weeks period of the experiment, excluding Saturdays and Sundays. Unfortunately, we could not get the checklists from three of the participants, as our explanation of the experiment procedure was insufficient. Figure 5 shows the average frequency per person and day for seven participants. When participants were on business trips or took days off, we counted the frequency values as missing value. In figure 5, the "visit" and the "activate" line show the frequency of visiting the other virtual hallway and activating the child window of remote partners respectively. We excluded logging data of commands for participants in the same location. The total number of accepted phone calls were as follows: 8 calls in the week before introducing the system, 37 calls during the two weeks using the system, and 26 calls in the week after we removed the system. There were a total of 154 instances for visiting the other virtual hallway, and 692 instances of activating child windows. The "electronic mail", the "shared whiteboard", the "application sharing", and the "approach" commands were invoked 5, 6, 1, and 10 times, respectively.

Intrusiveness

Many visits in our experiment did not result in conversations even when the recipient seemed available. We examined 85 randomly sampled video snapshots from 154 visits. There were 39 instances of visits in which recipients were in their offices. Within these visits, recipients seemed available in 33 instances, and they were on their phone in 6 instances. There were no instances in which recipients were with other guests. Only 18% (6 instances) of the visits that occurred when recipients seemed available resulted to conversation.

We asked the participants why they did not make calls even when their recipients appeared available. A few of the participants commented that they gave up their intend for conversation as the recipient looked busy. However, many participants answered that they had used the system only to see the current situation of their recipients and hadn't intended to communicate with them. One of the participants commented that he had just tried to use the system because of its novelty.

From these results, we concluded that the proposed interaction model at least allows callers to freely glance at a recipient without having any important communication issues, and that the glance mechanism did not compel conversation with recipients.

Unintended interactions

We evaluated the frequency of unintended interactions between the two work groups by looking at the logged data. We did not evaluate the frequency of unintended interactions that occurred in the same group, as it was impossible to estimate this only from the logged data. As a result, we found that unintended interactions occurred to some extent, however, they occurred much more seldom than observed in real world settings and in different patterns.

From a total of 154 visits, 16 resulted in conversations. Twelve of these resulted in conversations with the original recipients, three resulted in conversations with neighbors of recipients, and one resulted in a conversation that was initiated by a neighbor of a recipient. There was no instance of conversations among virtual visitors. These results mean that 25% of the conversations between the two groups were unintended interactions.

The frequency of unintended interactions in real world settings is much higher than in the results of our experiment. Kraut, et. al estimated that 52% of the conversations they studied were unintended interactions [12]. Our observation of real world settings as described in an earlier section also showed frequent interactions between persons who are passing a workplace by chance. In contrast, there was only one instance of initiating a conversation with a virtual visitor, although the logged data indicate that there were more instances of participants intentionally looking at virtual visitors by activating their child windows (32 instances).

The observation of real world settings showed different patterns of unintended interactions compared to the experiment. In our real world observation, visitors talked to neighbors as well as their recipients. In contrast, there were no instances where callers talked to virtual neighbors after or before talking to their recipients. They might just have talked to other recipients for a related task. In addition, there were no instances where conversations were categorized as "greetings", or "non-workplace related topics". All conversations were categorized as "asking questions", "reporting work status", or "scheduling meetings and tasks".

The above results suggest that unintended interactions that are categorized as spontaneous interaction did not occur in our experiment. Kraut et. al [12] categorized unintended interactions into opportunistic interactions, that were anticipated by one party but occurred only when the parties happened to see each other by chance, and spontaneous interactions, that were not anticipated by either party. They estimated 21% of interactions were opportunistic, and 31% of the interactions were spontaneous among a total of 117 studied conversations. Spontaneous interactions typically occurred in front of vending machines and were started by greetings or social conversations. Norms of politeness require exchanging greetings encountering acquaintance [12]. Contrary to this, ignoring virtual visitors in the same virtual hallways is easy and not considered impolite. OfficeWalker might have failed to provide appropriate distance for facilitating spontaneous interactions.

Transition of communication frequency

As shown in Figure 5, the frequency of accepted phone calls appeared to increase during the first a few days of using OfficeWalker, as we expected. However, the frequency declined after a few days of using OfficeWalker, and climbed to a higher rate a few days after removing OfficeWalker than recorded before using OfficeWalker. We found that the decline in using OfficeWalker after a few days was due to the fact many of the participants went on business trips. The average frequencies of accepted phone calls in the three periods were 0.25, 0.70, and 0.76 per person and day, respectively. An analysis of variance (ANOVA) showed that there was no significant difference depending on whether OfficeWalker was used ($F(1,103) = 0.9$). Only one participants of the test answered that the frequency of calls had increased slightly by introducing OfficeWalker. We were not able to obtain evidence that would show that video had facilitated frequent interaction among remote partners.

Interestingly, we found that the frequency of accepted phone calls per day and person was highly correlated with the frequency of virtual visits ($r(7)=0.82$, $p<0.01$) and the frequency of activating child windows for refreshing video images ($r(7)=0.89$, $p<0.01$) after we excluded the first day of introducing OfficeWalker from the calculation. As previously described, many participants commented that they often glanced at their remote colleagues without having any special intention for communication, and the rate of visits that resulted in conversation was very low. Nevertheless, the frequency of accepted phone calls was highly correlated with the frequency of using OfficeWalker. We can not make any definite conclusions about this relationship only based on this data. However, this data might suggests that just looking at video images of co-workers without any special intention for communication trigger conversations.

We also examined the transition of communication categories during the three periods. The results suggest that OfficeWalker might have the effect of facilitating questions. Figure 6 shows the average frequency of each communication category during the three phases. When the participants in the test didn't select any of the nine categories, we classified these conversations as "others".

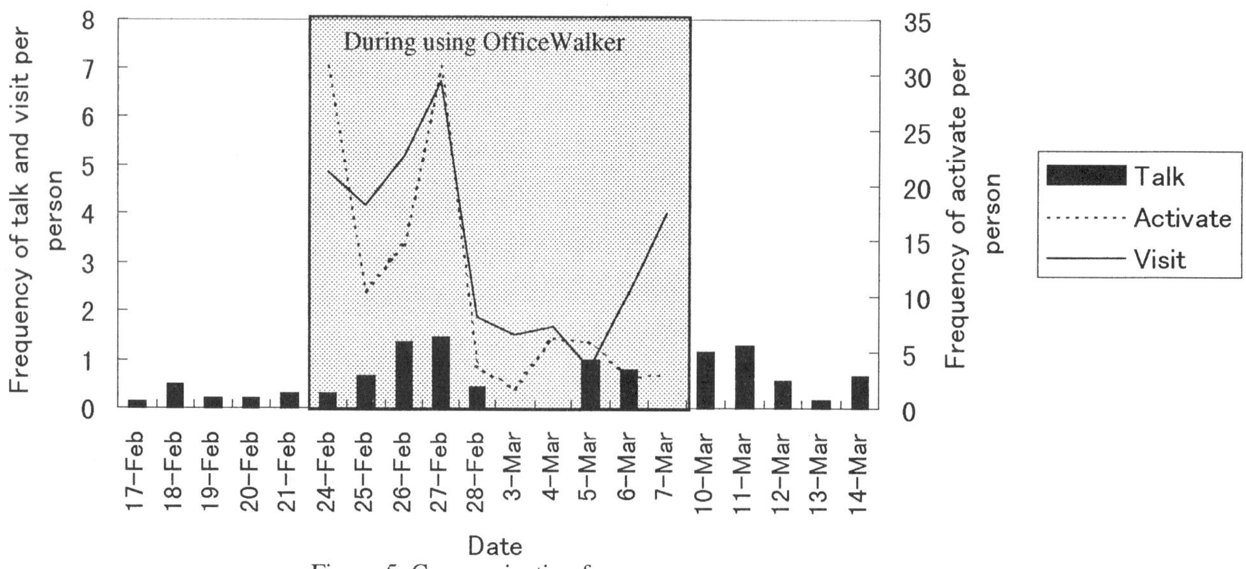

Figure 5. Communication frequency

We allowed selecting multiple categories, however, all participants selected only one category for each call. As you can see, the number of the category of "asking questions" increased drastically only during the phase OfficeWalker was used. The frequency of "asking questions" per person and day was 0.41 when OfficeWalker was used and 0.17 when OfficeWalker was not used. ANOVA results showed that there was a significant difference between the two phases ($F(1,103) = 4.22$, $p<0.05$). The other categories did not show significant differences between using and not using OfficeWalker when the level of significance was equal to 0.05. However, the number for the category of 'reporting work status' increased drastically after removing OfficeWalker, as shown in Figure 6. ANOVA results showed a marginally significant difference between using and not using OfficeWalker ($F(1,103) = 3.16$, $p<0.10$). This might have occurred as many of the participants took business trips from Feb 28 to Mar 7.

Contrary to our expectations, the use of OfficeWalker did not increase conversation of the categories "non-workplace topic" and "greeting". There were no instances where these categories were recorded during the experiment. There were a few instances of highly complicated conversations in such categories as "generating ideas", "making decisions", and "solving problems". Most conversations were simple. The shared whiteboard and application sharing features were invoked between the remote offices only six times, and one time, respectively. In addition, these connections were used in phone conversations in only one instance. It is likely, that this feature was used to send short message-tag like messages, or for the purpose of testing this new feature. The low frequency of using the provided shared whiteboards and the application sharing feature might be related to the fact highly complicated conversations were rare.

CONCLUSION

We proposed an interaction model that introduces "interactional distance" among users in the network by creating public places and private places. With this system, a caller approaches a recipient from a public place instead of directly jumping into the private place of the recipient. We conducted on user experiment using OfficeWalker that embodied this model so as to examine the problem of intrusiveness and how much the system can support unintended interactions between virtual neighbors. We confirmed that the problem of intrusiveness was successfully reduced. Glancing at recipients did not interrupt the activities of these recipients or forced them to respond. The participants were also able to glance at recipients without reluctance. Sometime, they had a look at recipients without having any special communication intentions. In addition, OfficeWalker partially supports unintended interactions with virtual neighbors. Among the interactions that occurred between the two groups, the design team and the sales team, 25% were unintended interactions.

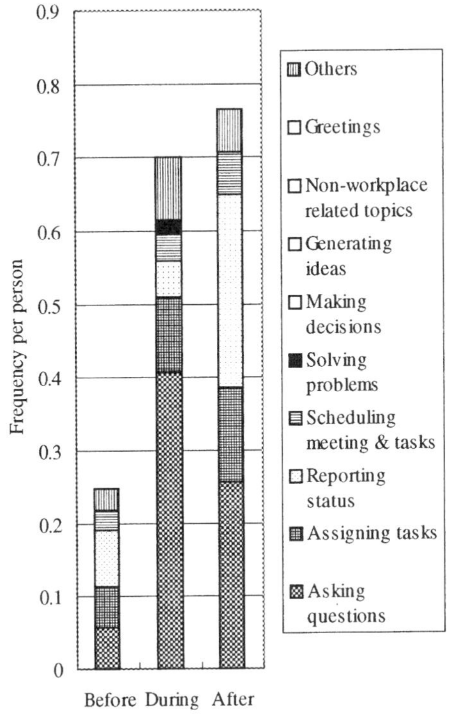

Figure 6. Transition of communication categories.

On the other hand, OfficeWalker did not have the effect to increase the frequency of communications, which was contrary to our expectations. Unintended interactions with virtual neighbors occurred much more seldom than the frequency of these interactions in real world settings and in different patterns. The participants of the test seemed only to talk with virtual neighbors, when these neighbors were alternative recipients of a related task. There were no instances where callers talked to virtual neighbors after or before talking to their recipients. Greetings and social conversation never occurred during the experiment, while they usually occur in the real world. The participants rarely initiated a conversation with virtual visitors.

These problems might be attributed to the same reason as previously discussed in this paper. It appears that we were successful in creating the perception of distance that was sufficient for glancing at recipients without interrupting their activities. However, we failed to create a distance that would be appropriate for greeting and social conversations. The participants recognized other persons in the same virtual hallway, but easily ignored each other. Nishide [15] categorized this distance as the zone of recognition. It is possible to recognize acquaintances, but greetings rarely occur in this zone. We failed to create the sense of distance for the zone of mutual recognition, where it is possible to recognize acquaintances and their facial expressions, and exchange greetings.

Lack of unintentional interface is probably the main reason of the failure. Users are required to issue the "approach" command intentionally to send a signal to a particular person, while eye-gaze is appeared almost unconsciously. Intentional messages might also urge the recipients to respond to it. In addition, users are required to establish an audio link by the "talk" command, while there is no need to establish an audio link in real world settings. Embodiment of unintentional interface is an important issue for future studies.

Virtual hallways in the current implementation of OfficeWalker are almost like a virtual room [17]. Virtual hallways consist of closed spaces where nobody just passes by. If the number of neighbors is small and they have a tight collaborative relationship, the perception of public-ness of a virtual hallway might be decreased. Strangers would probably hesitate to enter such a private virtual hallway. On the other hand, the neighbors might feel the impression of intrusiveness if strangers entered the hallway. How we define virtual neighbors could be another important issue for future studies.

Results of this experiment suggested that glancing at partners without having any special communication intention might possibly trigger conversations. This result encourages us to continue exploring the possible use of video links for supporting unintended interactions instead of using symbols that represent merely the status of a user.

ACKNOWLEDGEMENT

We would like to thank Yoshiharu Sato, and Hideo Ueno of Fujitsu Kyusyu Communication Systems Ltd. for developing the experimental version of the OfficeWalker system. We especially thank the ten users of Fujitsu Ltd. and Fujitsu Kyusyu Communication Systems Ltd. We also thank anonymous reviewers for insightful comments on the draft version of this paper.

REFERENCE

1. Bellotti, V., and Bly, S., Walking away from desktop computer: distributed collaboration and mobility in a product design team. Proc. CSCW'96, ACM, 1996, 209-218
2. Bellotti, V., Design for Privacy in Ubiquitous Computing Environment. Proc. ECSCW'93, 1996, 77-92
3. Benford, S, Greenhalgh,C., Bowers, J., Snowdon, D., and Fahlen, L., User Embodiment in Collaborative Virtual Environments, Proc. CHI'95 (Denver CO, May. 1995), ACM, 242-249
4. Borning, A., and Travers, M. Two approaches to casual interaction over computer and video networks. Proc. CHI'91, 1991, ACM, NY, 13-19
5. Cool,C., Fish,R., Kraut,R, and Lowery,C., Iterative design of video communication systems. Proc. CSCW'92 (Toronto, Oct. 1992), ACM, 25-32
6. Dourish,P., Bly,S., Portholes: Supporting awareness in a distributed work group. Proc. CHI'92 (Monterey CA, May 1992), ACM, 541-547
7. Fish,R. ,Kraut,R., Root,R., and Rice,R., Evaluating video as a technology for informal communication. Proc. CHI'92 (Monterey CA, May 1992), 37-48
8. Hall, E.T., The hidden dimension. Doubleday, New York, 1966
9. Harrison, S., and Dourish, P., Re-Place-ing Space: The roles of place and space in collaborative systems, Proc. CSCW'96 (Boston MA. Nov. 1996), ACM, 67-76
10. Isaacs,E., Tang,J., and Morris,T., Piazza: A Desktop Environment Supporting Impromptu and Planned Interactions. Proc. CSCW'96 (Boston MA, Nov. 1996), ACM, 315-324
11. Kraut,R., Egido,C., and Galegher,J., Patterns of Contact and Communication in Scientific Research Collaboration. in Galegher,J. and Kraut,R. (Eds.), *Intellectual teamwork: Social and technological foundations of group work.* , Lawrence Erlbaum Association, NJ, 1990, 149-171
12. Kraut,R.E., Fish,R.S., Root, R.W. & Chalfonte, B.L., Informal communication in organizations: Form, function, and technology. in S.Oskamp & S.Spacapan (Eds), *People's Reactions to Technology*, Sage Publications, London, 1990,145-199
13. Lee, A., Girgensohn, A., and Schlueter, K. NYNEX Portholes: Initial User Reactions and Redesign Implications, Proc. GROUP'97 (Phoenix, Arizona, Nov. 1997), ACM, 385-394
14. Nakanishi, H., Yoshida, C., and Ishida, T., FreeWalk: Supporting Casual Meetings in a Network, Proc. CSCW'96 (Boston MA. Nov. 1996) ACM, 308-314
15. Nishide, K., Distance between a human and a human (Architecture design based on Human psychology and behaviors ①), Architect and Business, 1985, 5, 95-99 (in Japanese)
16. Obata, A., Sasaki, K., Sato, Y. and Ueno, H. Group-Oriented method of interaction for Informal Communication. CSCW'96 Short Paper(Boston MA, Nov. 1996), ACM, 1996, 3-4
17. Roseman, M., and Greenberg, S., TeamRooms: Network places for collaboration, Proc. CSCW'96 (Boston MA. Nov. 1996), ACM, 325-333
18. Sasaki, K. and Obata, A. Study on virtual proximity service using video communication, Proc. IPSJ conference (March, Tokyo), 1996, 6, 313-314 (in Japanease)
19. Tang,J., Rua,M., Montage:Providing Teleproximity for distributed groups, Proc. CHI'94 (Boston MA, April, 1994), ACM, 37-43
20. Tang,J., Isaacs,E., and Rua,M., Supporting distributed groups with a Monatage of lightweight interactions. Proc. CSCW'94 (Chapel Hill NC, Oct. 1994), ACM, 23-34
21. Whittaker,S., Frohlich,D., and Dary-Jones,O., Informal workplace communication: what is it like and how might we support it? Proc. CHI'94 (Boston MA, April 1994), ACM, 131-137

Evaluating Image Filtering Based Techniques in Media Space Applications

Qiang Alex Zhao, John T. Stasko
Graphics, Visualization, and Usability Center
Georgia Institute of Technology
Atlanta, GA 30332-0280 USA
{azhao, stasko}@cc.gatech.edu

ABSTRACT

Media space applications that promote informal awareness in an organization confront an inevitable paradox: the shared video connections between offices and rooms that promote informal awareness also can rob individuals of privacy. An important open problem in this area is how to foster awareness of colleagues while minimizing the accompanying loss of privacy. One proposal put forward is to filter the communicated video streams rather than broadcasting clear video. Such a scheme may facilitate awareness while helping to alleviate some aspects of the privacy loss. In this article, we describe several image filtering techniques that provide awareness in informal group communication applications while blurring the details of an individual's activities, thus potentially preserving more privacy. We describe studies to quantitatively and qualitatively assess the degrees of awareness and accuracy that these filtering techniques provide.

KEYWORDS

Informal group awareness, privacy, video, image filter, media space, real-time groupware

INTRODUCTION

Using real-time audio and video transmission together with other human-computer interface techniques, media space applications provide virtual human-to-human interaction spaces to people at physically separated locations [3]. In addition to supporting planned, formal interactions, great efforts have been made to support casual, informal group communications in media spaces [4, 5, 13]. In the synchronous communication realm, where events occur at nearly the same time, co-located informal group interactions are often implicit and serendipitous [9]. For example, an important conversation between two colleagues might be caused by merely "bumping into" each other. One simple method to support informal interactions beyond physical proximity is to continuously provide awareness information such as video and audio signals to the entire group rather than on an explicit, by-request basis. It is then up to the user to determine if a remote participant in the media space is available, and whether it is appropriate to start a conversation or not.

This continuous-access requirement poses a difficult problem in media space applications: how to balance awareness and privacy. On one hand, users must have access to awareness information about other users. Guided by social protocols, this awareness information provides the context that people utilize to start interactions. For example, a person may need someone's presence to remind him or her of the possibility and appropriateness for interaction.

On the other hand, disclosing awareness information about oneself inevitably compromises the individual's own privacy. How much privacy is compromised may vary, however. Privacy is a complex issue and has many aspects. Particular dimensions of privacy include [2]:

- Knowing where an individual is, i.e. "tracking";
- Hearing what someone is saying;
- Recording and manipulating audio, video, and other information without consent of the user;
- Identifying what someone is doing, that is, their "activity";
- Identifying who is meeting with a person;
- Seeing details of someone's actions, for example, watching as they change clothes to go play tennis;
- Seeing how someone looks, what their mood is, what they are wearing, etc.

Clearly, these are just a few of the possible privacy issues that a person may encounter. Further amplifying the complexity of the privacy issue is the fact that different people have widely varying levels of concern in this regard. Nonetheless, opening a constant video view into an individual's office as done in some media space applications probably compromises all these dimensions of privacy. So then, how can one promote awareness while minimizing people's feelings of the loss of privacy?

CSCW 98 Seattle Washington USA
Copyright ACM 1998 1-58113-009-0/98/11...$5.00

One proposed approach to this issue is to use abstract, iconic representations of users instead of video [1, 7, 14]. However, it is still debatable whether sacrificing the relatively richer contextual information in video images is necessary [11].

Another proposed approach is to transmit modified video data instead of raw video at low frame rates. For example, media space software may slowly transmit lower-than-ordinary resolution video images so that remote users are able to sense the presence of the owner of the video and her movement, but they are less likely to recognize the details in the video. High resolution, high frame-rate video might be reserved for users engaged in focused interactions.

Clearly, the use of modified video addresses only some of the dimensions of privacy. Individuals still may feel "tracked" and this approach does nothing with the audio channel. Modified video may help blur the details of an individual's activities, however, thus helping to protect privacy in the latter four of the privacy dimensions listed above.

For example, consider the case of a person who changes clothes in his or her office to go running, and who forgets to "turn off" the video feed of the media space office-share application. The use of a modified, altered video feed might blur the images enough such that the images could be transmitted and the person would not feel that her privacy was violated. Similarly, modified video might show that a person is meeting someone else in her office, but determining the identity of that other person may be impossible.

Image filters are natural candidates for transforming video images. After images are captured by a hardware device and before they are transmitted to other parties, image filters can change the contents of the images. Examples of image filters that hide details include a blurring filter, an edge-detection filter, and so on. Depending upon which filter is used in a video stream, users receiving the video may perceive more or less information about the person who is present in the video.

Each of the image filtering techniques obscures details to a certain degree while providing some level of presence information. However, it is not obvious how these image filtering techniques compare against each other, and whether they can give the user the flexibility of controlling presence and clarity.

The focus of this paper is to evaluate the effectiveness of several filtering techniques for communicating status and supporting presence. We sought to understand how well video-filtering techniques convey or hide details of the images' contents, that is, who is present and what they are doing. First, we describe several image filters to introduce the reader to the set of techniques. Next, we describe a comparative study to evaluate how well the different filtering techniques suppress identity and activity in the video. Finally, we describe a prototype media space application that supports these different filtering modes and that has been deployed locally. We provide early user experiences with the system and describe how people have been using it.

IMAGE FILTERING BASED TECHNIQUES

Generally, the more clear that a transmitted video image is, the more an observer will be able to perceive details in the image. An ideal media space application would convey only the details necessary to promote awareness and the intended use of the tool, while suppressing other details. Such an ideal application probably never will exist, but our goal was to understand how different image filtering techniques may or may not convey status details such as identity and activity.

The NYNEX Portholes system uses blur filters to process video images before making them available on the network [10, 11]. A blur filter usually refers to a process that averages neighboring pixels in an image to produce a new, blurry image. Repeated applications of a blur filter produce incrementally blurrier images. A NYNEX Portholes user can control the cloudiness parameter of video images of her being transmitted to other users.

Other filtering techniques already exist and are worth considering. Specifically, we have been experimenting with the following image filters: a pixelization filter, an edge-detection filter, a shadow-view filter and one of its variations. To illustrate the differences among these techniques, we present images shot from the same scene using the different filters (Figure 1-a is a regular image not processed by any image filters).

Pixelization Filter

A simple pixelization filter divides an image into a grid of eight-pixel wide by eight-pixel high blocks. Then within each block, the filter calculates the average intensity and color values, and assigns them to all the pixels in that block. The effect is that the result image appears to be made of many uni-color squares, and some details in the original image are lost (Figure 1-b).

Edge-Detection Filter

An edge-detection filter produces a new image that only includes edges in the original image (Figure 1-c). An edge is a boundary of sudden intensity changes. A pixel is likely to be on an edge if at that location, the maximum rate of intensity change per unit distance in all directions is great. A simple way to compute an approximation of edges in an image is to apply the Sobel operators to the original image [6].

Shadow-View Filter

The shadow-view filter [8] assumes that the camera position and orientation do not change. At a user-specified time, usually when the field of view of the camera is empty, the filter saves the image of the scene as background. After the background image is taken, the algorithm compares live video images against the background image. If there is something that comes into the scene and does not appear to be part of the background, the live video image should differ than the saved background image. Therefore, the shadow-view filter records average intensity changes in the grid of eight pixel by eight pixel blocks to create a new image: for each eight-by-eight pixel block in image space, if the intensity change is small, the filter copies the block of data in the background image to the corresponding position in the new image; if the intensity change is greater than a threshold, the filter copies a pixelized representation of this block in the background image to the new image. In addition, if the changed block in the background image is dark, the filter brightens its pixelization in the new image. Likewise, if the block is bright, the filter darkens it. The resulting synthesized image is then transmitted instead of live video, giving the visual effect of a ghostly shadow of the new object (Figure 1-d).

(a) unfiltered image

(b) pixelized image

(c) edge-detected image

(d) shadow image

(e) live-shadow image

Figure 1. A regular image (a) and the images resulting from the application of four different filtering techniques (b)–(e)

The shadow-view algorithm saves the intensity changes of each block with regard to the background image and reduces them periodically. It brightens or darkens each changed block according to the combined amount of new and old changes. This process effectively produces a vague motion trail of the "shadow" in the scene. The motion trail gradually fades away if the object or person in the scene remains motionless.

Global illumination changes, occurring for example when a light is turned on, can cause false motions in the images. One solution is to pre-process each image with a blur filter then followed by a histogram equalization filter [6] to lessen the effect of lighting change. Another option is to provide the user with an easy way to re-take the reference image. For example, after the user issues the reset command, the application pauses, letting the user to leave the field of view of the camera, then the program takes a snapshot of the new scene as the new reference image.

Live-Shadow Filter

While hiding some level of details, the shadow-view may not be sufficient to provide enough awareness information about the user. Under normal conditions, a viewer could have problems recognizing the moving object in shadow-filtered video. If instead of darkening or brightening the pixelizations of changed blocks in the background image, we blend them with pixelized blocks of the most recent live video image, the resulting image exposes more information about the current scene. This variation of this shadow-view algorithm is thus called the "live-shadow" technique (Figure 1-e).

One simple way to think about the shadow algorithms is that they are like pixelizers for objects that move or are alien to the usual background scene which itself is presented unmodified.

We were curious about how these different image filters might affect the utility of a media space application. Understanding and assessing the effectiveness of the image filtering techniques include evaluating how much detail one can perceive from watching a sequence of filtered video images, and comparing this with the amount of information needed to communicate status.

Use of the Portholes system [4] showed that in a media space environment, people often are interested in other people's presence, availability, and interruptability. This kind of information can sometimes be inferred from seemingly unsubstantial artifacts in the environment. For example in a private office, if the occupant is on the telephone or talking with a guest, it is usually impolite to interrupt her. Depending on her work habits, an empty office with the door open may signal that she is around and will return soon.

In our study, we sought to learn how well people could interpret a scene viewed through the different image filters. For example, could a viewer detect the presence of a person in the video? If so, could they identify the person and/or the person's activity? If the viewers can recognize the activities in the video streams, they can probably infer availability and interruptability information. This recognition, however, also potentially conveys private information. Conversely, if viewers cannot recognize and identify activity without contextual clues such as whose office it is, a bit more of the individual's privacy may have been preserved. Though in this case, one must check whether the original purpose of the viewer has been fulfilled, such as determining whether a person is available or interruptible.

QUANTITATIVE STUDY

We conducted a study to help evaluate the effectiveness of the specific image filters in delivering information about a remote space. This was done by showing filtered video segments to users, then determining whether the users could perceive awareness-related information correctly.

We recruited five students as actors in preparing the videos for user testing (Figure 2). The individuals were chosen so that all were moderately similar in appearance (males, relatively short hair, no glasses, and white shirt), thus simulating a type of worst-case scenario for identification purposes.

For each of the actors, a portrait picture was taken, then a series of video segments were shot. The office set up for filming the video included a table, a workstation with a monitor, a camera, and two chairs. The camera was placed next to the monitor, facing the primary chair where a user of the workstation would likely sit, with a glance of the doorway. The image of an actor's head occupied roughly one-ninth of the total image area in the video.

We filmed video segments of each actor performing four different but typical office activities: looking at a computer monitor at eye level, talking on the phone, meeting with a second actor while facing away from the camera (the second actor sat further away from the camera so the subjects would know which to identify), and flipping through a magazine on his lap. We also recorded a special video segment of an office without any occupants, in which the door was open and an actor passed by the doorway. Each video segment lasted 15 seconds to leave enough footage for editing. Then each segment was processed through the four filters: the pixelizer, the edge detector, the live-shadow filter, and the shadow-view filter. Finally, five seconds of the most representative portion of each processed video segment was saved to disk, along with the unfiltered version.

Figure 2. The five student actors

Subjects with adequate or corrected vision participated in the study. Before each set of tests, a subject was given the five portrait images of people possibly in the video streams. We showed five randomly selected warm-up video segments with brief verbal explanations prior to the formal tests to allow the subject to become familiar with the different filters, and to help reduce misinterpretations.

The subjects in the study viewed twenty-one video clips in a session (five actors doing each of the four activities plus the one empty room clip). Each subject viewed the same order of these actor-activity-pairing segments. The image filter utilized on the video clip and the image size (80 by 60 pixels or 320 by 240 pixels) of the clip were varied randomly, however. For each video segment, we asked the subject questions according to the decision tree in Figure 3.

Results

Twenty people participated in the study. All of the subjects except one were unfamiliar with the student actors in the videos. The exception only knew one of the five actors very well. Some of the subjects may have seen some of the actors before, but they did not know the actors personally.

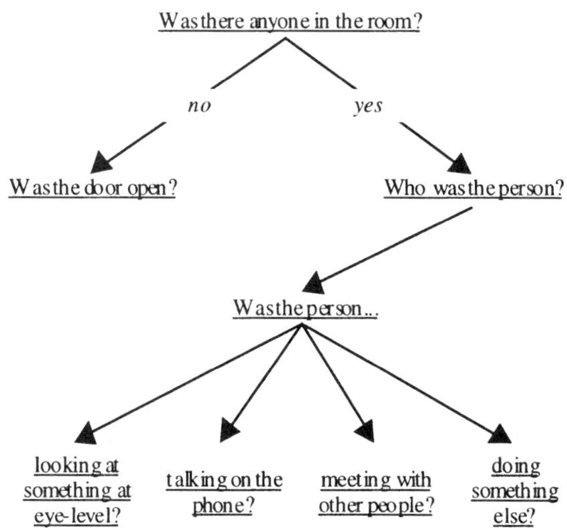

Figure 3. Decision tree for asking questions

Regardless of the image filter used, all of the subjects responded correctly to the empty room scene and noted that the door was open. In less than one percent of all trials with an actor present, a subject identified the room as being empty. This occurred because the actor was not moving much and the shadow-view filter was used, transforming the actor semi-transparent. However, in all these cases, subjects did guess correctly that the door was closed.

The chart in Figure 4 lists the correct activity recognition totals and percentages for the different image filters. Note that this is cumulative data summed over all different actors and activities. Note how all the filters supported high activity recognition levels (90% and up) except for the shadow-view filter. With it, subjects identified the correct activity about 60% of the time with both image sizes. The data is also broken out in Figure 5 according to the different activities (for simplicity, the chart for the empty room scene is not shown).

The chart in Figure 6 lists the correct actor identification totals and percentages for all the different image filters. Again, this data is summed over all actors and activities. The data is broken out by activity in Figure 7.

Note how identity was uniformly more difficult to recognize than activity (Figure 6 vs. Figure 4). As occurred for activity recognition, the shadow-view filter again exhibited the lowest correct actor identification percentages. Here, however, the other filters exhibited correct actor identifications below the 90% level found in activity recognition. The live-shadow filter showed a marked difference between the two correct recognition rates, particularly at the small image size (95% correct activity recognition vs. 53% correct actor recognition). This may be important for an application seeking to transmit activity information while suppressing individual identification, such as a view into a common area, for example a departmental copy-machine room. If an application seeks to suppress both actor and activity information while still conveying whether an individual is present, clearly the shadow-view filter would be the best.

Finally, the chart in Figure 8 lists the totals and percentages for a correct identification of *both* actor and activity in the same scene for all the different filters.

Please note that our research, and this study in particular, did not directly address the tie between the conveyance of particular types of information (identity, activity, presence, etc) and the more subjective, personal notion of the loss of privacy. This study simply assessed how effective the different image filters were at conveying or suppressing different types of information over a video stream. However, it should not be difficult to imagine how changes in the information conveyed could affect the notion of more or less privacy being surrendered.

In the next section, we describe the deployment of a simple media space application armed with these different filtering

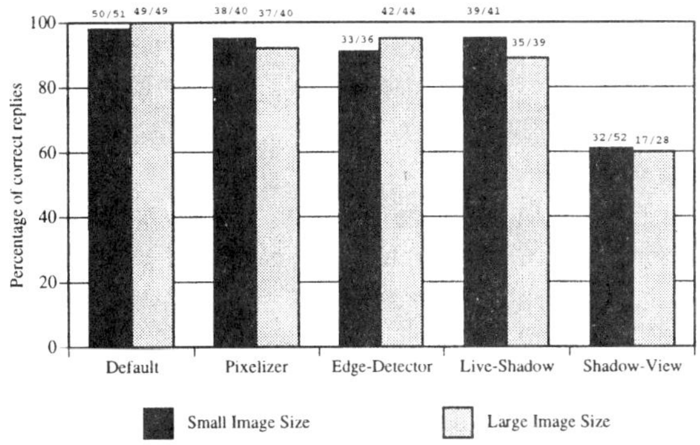

Figure 4. Activity recognition (collapsed across all different actors and scenes)

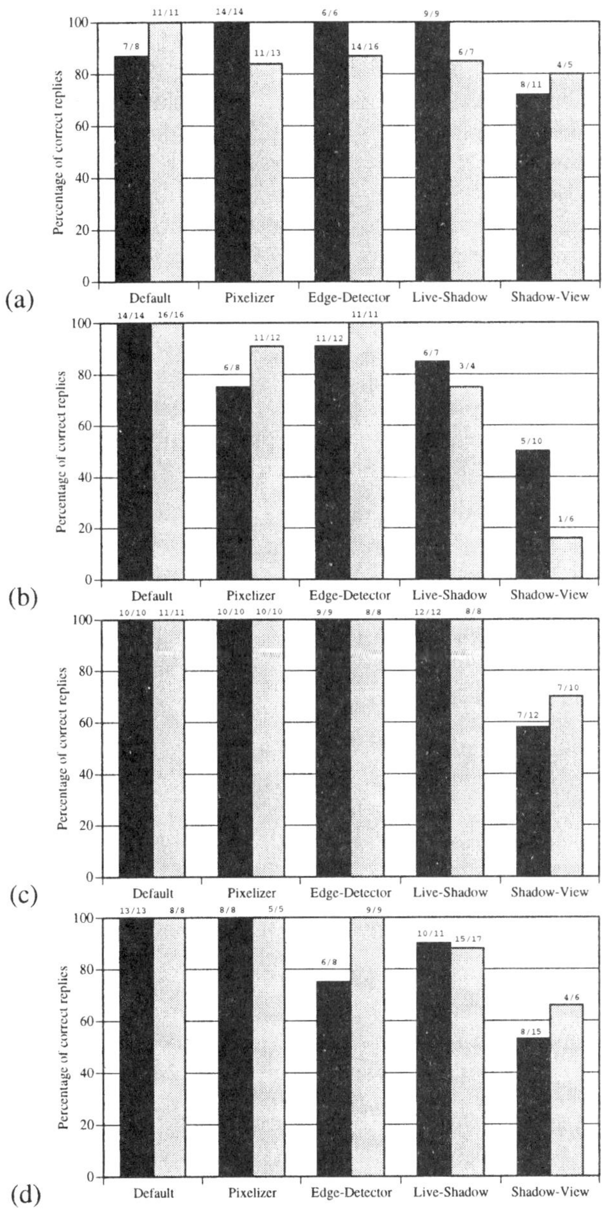

Figure 5. Activity recognition: charts (a)-(d) represent the computer scene, the phone scene, the meeting scene, and the magazine scene, respectively

tools, as a way of gauging individuals' views on the effectiveness of the image filtering techniques in video space applications.

QUALITATIVE STUDY

In order to acquire more subjective data about the use of different video techniques in a casual group awareness system, we prototyped a video space application based on a modified version of "vic" [12], a popular Internet video conferencing tool.

On start up, the program displays a collection of thumbnail images (80 by 60 pixels) of available video sources in a video space (Figure 9). By clicking on the "Capture" button, the user can start or stop capturing and transmitting video from the camera connected to his or her computer. The "Options" pull-down menu allows the user to switch among the different image filtering modes plus the no filtering mode, and built-in static image-notes such as "at a meeting" or "do not disturb". It was important to us to allow a user to select the video filter being used to broadcast her signal to all other users. This menu also has an option to pop up the control panel, which allows the user to fine tune parameters of the transmission, such as the video capture hardware device to use, the frame- and bit-rate bounds, etc. The "Members" button pops up a participant list that shows everyone known to the current video session, including those not sending a video stream. This participant list also allows the local user to choose which video streams to receive and which video streams to ignore.

If the user clicks on a thumbnail image, a larger window of the same video source pops up. The size of this window varies depending on the type of hardware its source uses, but is usually close to 320 by 240 pixels. This larger view also includes other information about the video sources, such as a text note posted by its owner, frame rate and other statistics (Figure 10).

Adding the image filters accounted for a majority part of the modifications done to the original vic. Besides the previously described four images filters, we added an "Activity Only" mode as an extreme in providing the least amount of information about a user. In this mode, a bar chart of overall image intensity differences was transmitted instead of video (similar to that in [11]).

Other modifications to the original vic are mostly user interface related. For example, the original vic displays transmission statistics of each video source along with the thumbnail video images in the main application window. When this tool is used in a media space setup, the statistical information is less frequently needed in the main display area. To keep the top-level application window small and well utilized, we moved statistical information displays to the detail windows associated with individual video sources.

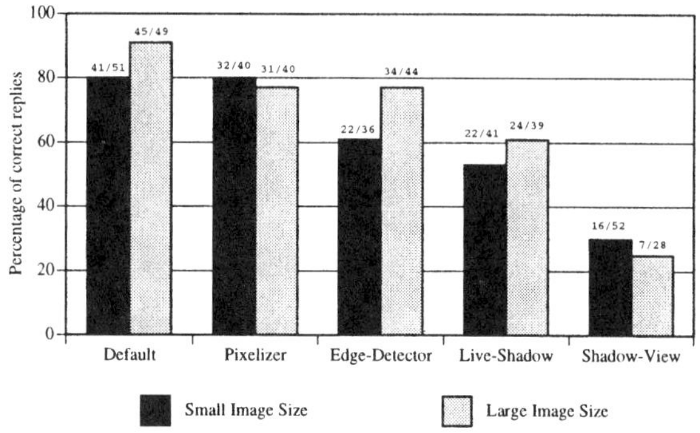

Figure 6. Actor identification (collapsed across all different actors and scenes)

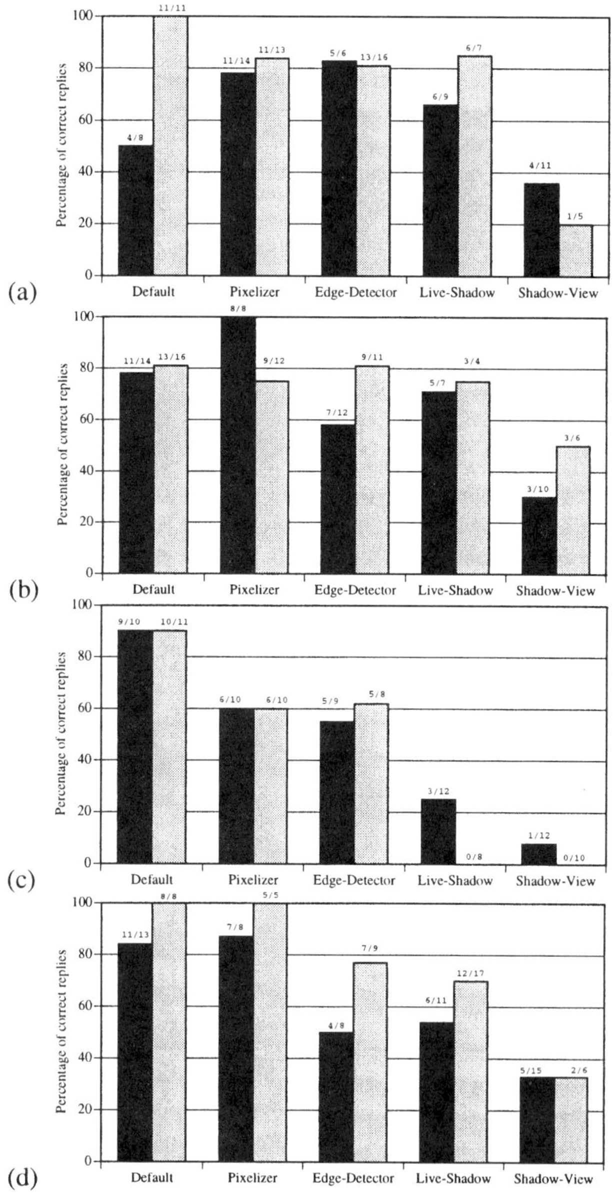

Figure 7. Actor identification: charts (a)-(d) represent the computer scene, the phone scene, the meeting scene, and the magazine scene, respectively

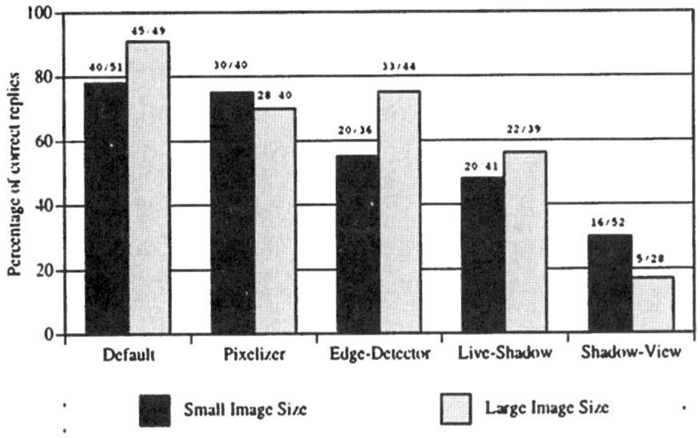

Figure 8. Accuracy levels in correctly identifying both activity and actor

Usage Feedback

We set up a special media space called the "Electric Lounge". A number of volunteers within the local community participated in this study and connected to the Electric Lounge using our enhanced system. However, due to video capturing equipment shortage and user on-line time variations, the number of simultaneous users in the Electric Lounge ranged from four to about ten.

Initially, users had a little trepidation about participating in the Electric Lounge. Fairly quickly, however, users became accustomed to having the video space application running.

Figure 9. The main display area of the prototype video space application

As curiosity and novelty wore off, people tended to forget about the video space when working on other tasks, even if the videos were visible on the desktop. They used the video space to check the status of other people with whom they interacted. Sometimes the users would glance the gallery of video images to get a vague sense of what was happening in the virtual proximity. They also preferred to use the Electric Lounge to express some information about themselves, such as "not in office right now" or "do not disturb", rather than leaving the video space by quitting the application.

From informal interviews, we found that the possibility of identifying someone in a filtered video changed with familiarity level. For example, someone familiar with the user might be able to guess if she was in a pixelated video based on shirt color, or hairstyle, or the geometry of her face. Especially in a tightly related group of people with frequent collaborations, identifying the person in the video was not difficult because people were extremely familiar with each other, and the video thumbnails were labeled. In this case, people could reliably judge the availability and interruptability of other users by watching filtered videos, even if the details of the activity in a video were not available. Without being able to recognize most of the gestures, people used the Electric Lounge many times to watch a remote office and wait for the guest in the room to leave before making a visit or placing a call.

We also observed that users did not often change among the different filters broadcasting their signal. People tended to choose one filter and stayed with it. The shadow and live-shadow views were seldom used, usually because they involved a background setup process. The pixelization filter was often chosen – it seemed to convey a reasonable level of information while also blurring fine-grain details. The "Activity Only" bar chart filter was virtually never used.

Several users suggested that they might not be interested in what the background looked like, and it could be made even blurrier than the foreground. To test out this idea, we added a fifth image filter, the "mosaic" filter (Figure 10). Instead of using a background, the mosaic filter kept a two dimensional array of intensity change values calculated from consecutive video images. It periodically lowered the recorded intensity change levels to gradually lessen the effects of old intensity changes. Before each image redraw, the mosaic filter painted blocks that had motion in higher resolution and static blocks in lower resolution. Effectively, the mosaic filter serves as a form of pixelizer with fine-grain pixelization in areas of motion and coarse-grain pixelization in static areas. Since the mosaic filter was implemented after we started the evaluation studies, we do not have any quantitative data or user comments about this filter yet.

CONCLUSION

This article describes studies to evaluate the effectiveness and utility of different image filtering techniques used in

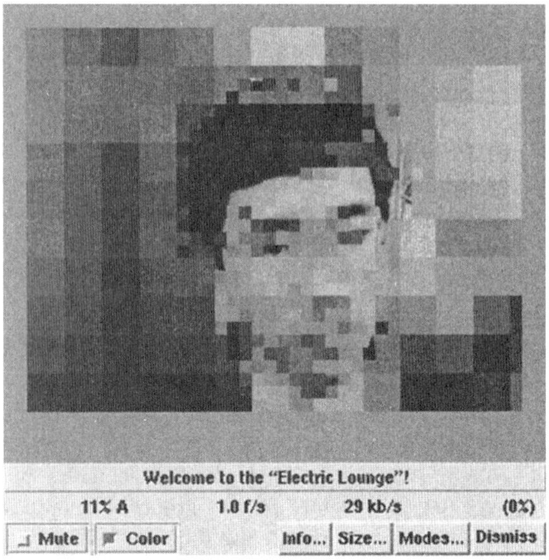

Figure 10. The close-up view of one video source (video image shown as processed by the new "mosaic" filter)

media space applications. We described a number of existing filtering techniques, and introduced two new methods. We believe that these techniques can be useful tools for software designers to help control interpersonal access in media space applications. In addition, we presented a study to quantitatively assess the ability of these different filters to convey or suppress activity, identification, and presence information over a video stream. Further, we presented a video space application that utilizes these filtering techniques, and we discussed early user feedback on the program.

ACKNOWLEDGEMENTS

We wish to thank Richard Catrambone for helpful discussions on the analysis of the data. We also thank everybody who participated in the studies, and the vic team for making the source code publicly available.

REFERENCES

1. Ackerman, M., and Starr, B. *Social Activity Indicators: Interface Components for CSCW Systems.* In UIST'95 Conference Proceeding, 159-168. ACM, 1995.
2. Bellotti, V. *What You Don't Know Can Hurt You: Privacy in Collaborative Computing.* In HCI'96 Conference Proceeding, British Computer Society. Springer-Verlag, 1996.
3. Bly, S. A., Harrison, S. R., and Irwin, S. *Media Spaces: Bringing People Together in a Video, Audio, and Computing Environment.* Communications of the ACM, Vol. 36, No. 1, 28-47. ACM, January 1993.
4. Dourish, P., and Bly, S. *Portholes: Supporting Awareness in a Distributed Work Group.* In CHI'92 Conference Proceeding, 541-547. ACM, 1992.
5. Fish, R. S., Kraut, R. E., Root, R. W., and Rice, R. E. *Video as a Technology for Informal Communication.* Communications of the ACM, Vol. 36, No. 1, 48-61. ACM, January 1993.
6. Gonzalez, R. C., and Woods, R. E. *Digital Image Processing.* Addison-Wesley, 1992.
7. Greenberg, S. *Peepholes: Low Cost Awareness of One's Community.* In CHI'96 Conference Companion, 206-207. ACM, 1996.
8. Hudson, S. E., and Smith, I. *Techniques for Addressing Fundamental Privacy and Disruption Tradeoffs in Awareness Support Systems.* In CSCW'96 Conference Proceeding, 248-257. ACM, 1996.
9. Kraut, R. E., Fish, R. S., Root, R. W., and Chalfonte, B. L. *Informal Communication in Organizations: Form, Function, and Technology.* In Oskamp, S., and Spacapan, S. (Eds.) People's Reactions to Technology in Factories, Offices, and Aerospace, The Claremont Symposium on Applied Social Psychology, 145-199. Sage Publications, 1990.
10. Lee, A., Girgensohn, A., and Schlueter, K. *NYNEX Portholes: Initial User Reactions and Redesign Implications.* In GROUP'97 Conference Proceeding, 385-394. ACM, 1997.
11. Lee, A., Schlueter, K., and Girgensohn, A. Sensing Activity in Video Images. In CHI'97 Extended Abstracts, 319-320. ACM, 1997.
12. McCanne, S., and Jacobson, V. *vic: A Flexible Framework for Packet Video.* In Multimedia'95 Conference Proceeding, 511-522. ACM, 1995.
13. Tang, J. C., Isaacs, E., and Rua, M. *Supporting Distributed Groups with a Montage of Lightweight Interactions.* In CSCW'94 Conference Proceeding, 23-34. ACM, 1994.
14. Wax, T. *Red Light, Green Light.* In CSCW'96 Conference Companion, 1-2. ACM, 1996.

Interlocus: Workspace Configuration Mechanisms for Activity Awareness

Takahiko Nomura
Knowledge Design Initiative
Fuji Xerox Co., Ltd.
2-17-22 Akasaka, Minato-ku
Tokyo, 107-0052, Japan
+81 3 3585 3211
Takahiko.Nomura@fujixerox.co.jp

Koichi Hayashi, Tan Hazama
Corporate Research Labs.
Fuji Xerox Co., Ltd.
430 Sakai, Nakai-machi,
Kanagawa 259-0157, Japan
hayashi.koichi@fujixerox.co.jp
hazama.tan@fujixerox.co.jp

Stephan Gudmundson
Dept. of Computer Science
University of British Columbia
201-2366 Main Mall
Vancouver, B.C. V6T 1Z4,
Canada
stephang@netinfo.ubc.ca

ABSTRACT
This paper describes the concept of *activity awareness*, which enables workspace awareness without employing shared workspaces, and our framework for supporting activity awareness. Activity awareness extends the concept of asynchronous workspace awareness to provide asynchronous progress notifications and collective perspectives on related activities. Our framework adopts the temporally threaded workspace model, which tracks an activity in each individual's workspace by storing a sequence of snapshots of their workspace, and uses workspace configuration mechanisms to provide awareness functions. We then present Interlocus, an implementation of the framework in the WWW environment.

Keywords
shared workspace, awareness, common information space, contextual information sharing, World Wide Web

INTRODUCTION
As the Internet extends the sphere of communication over the network, the concept of shared workspace has begun to engage public attention [2,6,12,13]. Internet-based communication tools enable people to work in new and flexible ways. When working collaboratively, people may not be close in space or organizational hierarchy. People can work at home without commuting to the office. They can also work with colleagues from other departments or even other companies. Further, it enables groups to take more dynamic forms, which leads to an organizational structure based on goal-oriented lightweight projects. Virtual companies often have this structure. Although email and remote filing systems have been central figures in networked collaboration, shared workspaces have come into the limelight because of their useful features.

The shared workspace is a concept from groupware systems that provides workers with a virtual space in which they execute collaborative tasks by sharing and exchanging information. Since a shared workspace keeps track of the state of tasks, workers are aware of who is doing what [9,10]. Gutwin and Greenberg analyzed various types of awareness between users in shared workspaces and coined the term *workspace awareness* [4,5]. Workspace awareness provides workers with perspectives on the current state of their collaborative work. It can help members to proceed in their tasks by succinctly presenting the states of concurrent activities, hinting at upcoming events, and indicating when to start communication with others. Workspace awareness falls into 2 types: synchronous and asynchronous. While synchronous awareness enables real-time collaboration distributed over space, asynchronous awareness enables collaboration distributed over time, as well as space. GroupDesk [3] and BSCW [1,8,14] support asynchronous workspace awareness, which involves informing workers of what has changed in the workspace since their last session. Asynchronous workspace awareness allows shared workspace systems to support flexible and dynamic work styles.

The recent progress of hardware and software technology has made shared workspace technology more accessible to common users. BSCW, for example, provides a sophisticated WWW-based shared workspace, which can be used by anyone who can access the Internet. Meanwhile, the progress of technology enhances each worker's computing environment and thus enables workers to perform their jobs without depending on a common, centralized information space. In a small laptop computer, one can store all the necessary documents for performing their job. Moreover, they can even publish their data to enable colleagues to share the documents. Workspace awareness works effectively when user activity directly and instantly affects the state of the shared workspace. As workers become less dependent on the shared workspace for sharing documents and doing their jobs, workspace awareness in the centralized, separate shared workspace becomes less reliable.

Furthermore, the progress of communication technology has allowed a richer variety of forms of collaboration. When a worker does her/his individual job, it affects

CSCW 98 Seattle Washington USA

several other activities in an organization at the same time, formally or informally, tightly or loosely. For example, when a researcher designs a novel system, s/he might collaborate closely with colleague researchers and programmers while drafting the functional specification, and formally report the necessary information to her/his supervisor. S/he might also informally discuss the system concept with researchers in the field, and investigate the business potential with marketing staff. S/he might further maintain loose contact with engineers in the field for exchanging technical information. If we use shared workspaces for such concurrent collaboration, we would have to manage a set of interrelated shared workspaces for a single activity. It would be tedious for workers to prepare such workspaces and maintain them properly. Each workspace has special requirements based on the nature of the collaboration. For example, the events of interest to a co-researcher are different from the events of interest to a supervisor. Also, relevant activities are occasionally discovered several months into the project, which makes it inconvenient to establish a shared workspace. As the shared workspaces that workers must maintain become more complicated, workspace awareness becomes less convenient.

The above deficiencies of workspace awareness are caused by limitations on the range of awareness. Although most activities in an organization are collaborative, they often include both individual and collaborative parts. Most documents necessary for a collaborative task are prepared in an individual environment and exchanged periodically with others. Since a shared workspace only concerns itself with explicit and intentional collaborative actions, important documents can remain hidden in individual environments. Therefore, as individual activities increase in importance, workspace awareness based on shared workspace becomes less reliable and less convenient. For providing necessary awareness about related activities, we need a new awareness framework that covers individual activities involved in a collaborative work process.

In this paper we present a concept of *activity awareness*, which extends workspace awareness in a shared workspace to include awareness among interrelated individual activities. Like conventional workspace awareness, activity awareness gives workers indications of what has happened to and what is happening to related activities. Instead of using a shared workspace, we extend the *temporally threaded workspace* model proposed in [7] to provide activity awareness. This model represents activities based on the implicit information space that workers maintain while executing the task. We further introduce workspace configuration mechanisms to provide awareness of related activities by forming a view of activity progress or a collective activity perspective.

In the following sections, we first define activity awareness, and introduce an activity awareness framework based on individual workspaces. We also illustrate *Interlocus*, an experimental implementation of our framework, by explaining a fictitious collaborative work process. We then discuss our framework by comparing our proposal with related work. Finally, we suggest some future directions.

ACTIVITY AWARENESS

Activity awareness gives workers indications of what is going on and what has been going on in related activities. Activity awareness extends the concept of asynchronous workspace awareness to cover interrelated activities in individual workspaces. Activity awareness consists of a representation of individual activities, the dynamic awareness scope, asynchronous progress notification, and a collective activity perspective.

Representation of individual activities defines a computer-manageable object corresponding to an individual activity. We use the word *activity* as a human process to achieve some specific goal, such as writing a paper on awareness of workspace or analyzing information on the Internet search services. In contrast, a shared workspace represents the current state of a group activity. It lacks the ability to represent individual work. It indicates each member's actions done inside the workspace and ignores the actions done outside. Further, a shared workspace is designed to represent the latest or recent states rather than the whole process of an activity, which includes changes of states from the beginning to end of the activity.

Dynamic awareness scope is the set of individual activities corresponding to a single collaborative task. While executing a collaborative task, members exchange information within the awareness scope. Each individual activity may be included in more than an awareness scope, as a result, each individual task may affect several collaborative tasks. For a single collaborative task, several awareness scopes may be prepared and changed dynamically depending on stages or the workers' roles within the work process. In contrast, a shared workspace defines a single awareness scope for each collaborative task by defining the members of the task. To prepare different scopes, for each role it provides limited facilities to control access rights for each member.

Asynchronous progress notification provides workers with information on the latest state of and changes to related individual activities within an awareness scope. In contrast, a shared workspace holds the latest state and changes made within the shared space only. If a member fails to put the latest work from her/his own information space into the shared space, the shared space's state does not correctly indicate the correct state of the collaborative task.

Collective activity perspective provides a summarized view of activities in an awareness scope. To understand and manage a collaborative task, members have to get overviews on the relationship and states of individual activities. By presenting the result and operations of each activity in a shared space, it helps members succinctly understand the latest state and changes on the group activity.

In the following section, we present a framework for activity awareness based on individual workspaces instead of shared workspaces.

ACTIVITY AWARENESS FRAMEWORK

In this section, we first describe our representation of individual activities, based on the temporally threaded workspace model. We then introduce additional structure into individual workspaces and access control for dynamically defining the awareness scope. Then, we present the workspace configuration mechanisms for *contextual what's new* and *collective view*. The contextual what's new provides asynchronous progress notification; the collective view provides collective activity perspective.

Activity Representation Based on Temporally Threaded Workspaces

The temporally threaded workspace model is for maintaining individual workspaces corresponding to specific activities. In this model, the concept of activity is defined as the human process of changing document spaces to achieve some specific goal. It does not deal with predetermined classes of activities, such as writing, discussing, and planning. Writing a specific document, discussing a specific topic, and planning a specific product are all examples of activities. We use this characterization of activity because we intend to provide activity awareness across a wide range of knowledge workers' activities, including ad-hoc tasks. Since this model uses the word document in wider sense, it is adaptable for most asynchronous collaboration based on shared information space. Document includes any information recorded on some media, like memos on paper or recorded telephone conversations, as well as electronic files of word processor data.

The temporally threaded workspace model records the progress of an activity as a chronological thread of snapshots of a workspace. A workspace is a spatial environment, employing the familiar desktop metaphor, for organizing the set of documents and tools used for carrying out an activity. The latest snapshot of a workspace represents the worker's present state in the associated activity. Workspace threads enable workers to restart at a past stage of the activity, to reuse documents from their own or others' past activities, and to see the progress of their own or others' activities.

Activity Domain. An *activity domain* in this model is an information space in which workers execute tasks collaboratively. An activity domain is defined as a set of *workspace threads* connected by a set of *links.* Figure 1 illustrates the relationships among the objects in an activity domain. Each worker has more than one workspace, each of which is used for a specific activity. A workspace thread binds only one worker as the owner, who can edit the workspace and thus further the thread. Thus, an activity domain consists of interrelated workspaces of the different workers involved in the activity. The activity domain determines the maximum scope of activity awareness for the collaborative task.

Workspace Thread. A workspace thread records an activity as a sequence of changes to the set of documents and tools on the user's graphical workspace. A thread is defined as a set of *snaps* bound with their creation times.

Snap. A snap (short for snapshot) represents the state of an activity at a given time. Snaps are used for both current and recorded workspace states. Thus, the terms "current snap" and "workspace" are interchangeable. A snap records the position of each document and tool placed on the graphical workspace. A snap is defined as a set of *anchors* and anchor position pairs.

Anchor. An anchor is a spatial element on the graphical workspace that references an external document or tool relevant to the activity. An external document may be a page in the WWW with which the worker performs the activity. Anchor is defined as a name, image, and locator triple. A name is a string briefly describing the document, possibly within the context of the workspace. An image is a graphical spatial element that expresses the characteristics of the referenced document or region. A locator is a reference to the external document. A URL is an example of a locator. This model does not suppose anything about the management of the documents referenced by the locators. There are three types of anchors: icons, regions, and curtains. The differences are illustrated in later sections.

Link. Workspace threads may be related to each other by links. We provide two types of links: reference links and continuation links. These links are used to determine the scope of awareness.

Activity Domain Construction. An activity domain is designed to grow based upon actions performed in the graphical workspace. A workspace thread usually displays the latest snap in the thread, to maintain coherence. The latest snap includes the set of anchors related to the current state of the user's activity. It reminds the user what s/he should do, and helps to keep the activity on track. Implicit or explicit operations executed on the graphical workspace become triggers for recording a snap, creating a new workspace, or defining links between threads.

Workspace Configuration. This model allows users to create new snaps by synthesizing more than one workspace thread. Since the temporally threaded workspace model records snaps as a set of anchors, users can create new snaps by applying set-based functions, such as union and subtraction. We define functions for activity awareness as synthesized views generated by specific combinations of basic set-based operations.

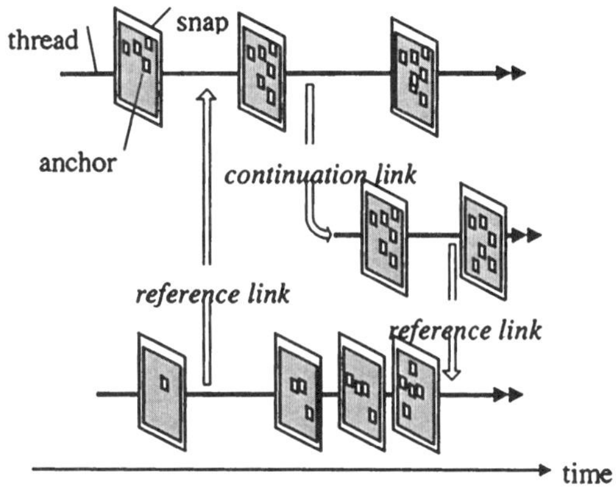

Figure 1: Temporally threaded workspaces

Note that this model only manages references to documents and applications to allow a wide variety of document sharing styles (e.g., publishing from personal web server or storing centralized document database). For actual usage for collaborative work, some complementary system for managing document contents and versions is needed.

Dynamic Awareness Scope

To control scopes of awareness, we introduce mechanisms for determining which activities are related to a collaborative task and for access control, which is used to filter information in activity based on the member's role in the collaboration.

To determine activities related a collaborative work, we introduce a mechanism that collects activities by traversing links between workspace threads. Both reference and continuation links may be used for determining the scope of awareness. A reference link implies that a certain activity is related to another activity. In other words, while performing a certain activity, a worker needed to reference the other activity. The reference link also records the last time that the source thread was referenced from the destination thread. A continuation link indicates that one activity was spawned from another activity. In other words, while performing some activity, a worker started a subtask by creating a successive new workspace thread. The structure formed by continuation links becomes a tree.

These links roughly determine the awareness scope for the set of tasks that reference each other or composite tasks that consist of several subtasks. Since the links are defined based on user actions on the graphical workspace, the awareness scope changes dynamically. Initially the scope of awareness is calculated automatically by traversing links from a given workspace thread. Users may select specific links to restrict the scope.

By using dynamic awareness scopes, each activity may be included in more than one collaborative task. It implies that members of the dynamically determined collaborative scope may view individual workspaces for different purposes. Moreover, each collaborative task has several roles, e.g., supervisor or colleague, each of which has different access requirements. Therefore, we need control scopes of sharing information in each workspace.

We introduce three levels of workspace access: owner, observer, and coworker; we also introduce a spatial access restriction facility called a curtain. The owner of workspace is the worker who created the workspace. Coworkers are individuals who are in close collaboration and are therefore allowed to view all of the details of the individual's workspace. Observers are workers who are in formal, loosely coupled, or ad-hoc collaboration and are allowed to see only a limited level of detail of the workspace. Curtains are used to divide the information on a workspace into areas for tight collaboration and areas for more general publishing.

Each workspace thread specifies only one worker as the owner and an arbitrary number of workers as observers and coworkers. Only the owner of a workspace can edit the workspace. The owner can place curtains on the workspace to restrict observer access. A curtain is a type of anchor that occupies a region in the two-dimensional workspace. Any anchors in a curtain region are hidden from observers, but are accessible to the owner and coworkers (Figure 2).

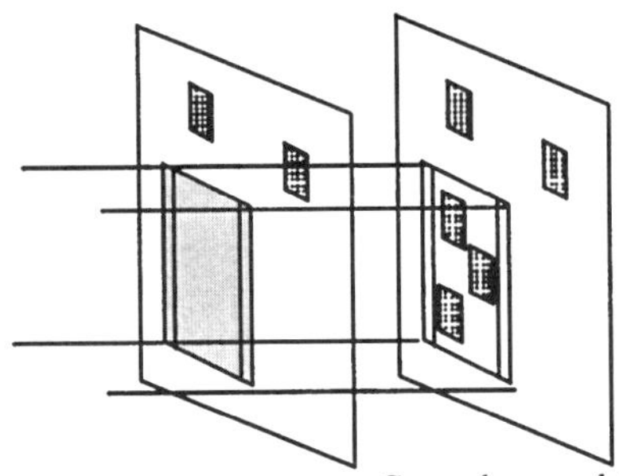

Figure 2: Access control imposed by curtains

A worker who is not the owner (i.e. observers, coworkers, or people who have no access rights) is prohibited from modifying the workspace at all. These access restrictions affect the synthesized views that provide awareness functions.

Asynchronous Progress Notification

To notify people of progress in related activities asynchronously, we introduce the *contextual what's new* function. This function provides a synthesized view that shows the changes to the workspace since the user last accessed it.

The scope of awareness of this function is the set of workspace threads connected by reference links to the user's workspace thread. For each referenced thread, this function subtracts the last snap that the user referenced from the current snap. These sets of anchors are then united with the current snap of the user's workspace to produce the final snap. (Figure 3)

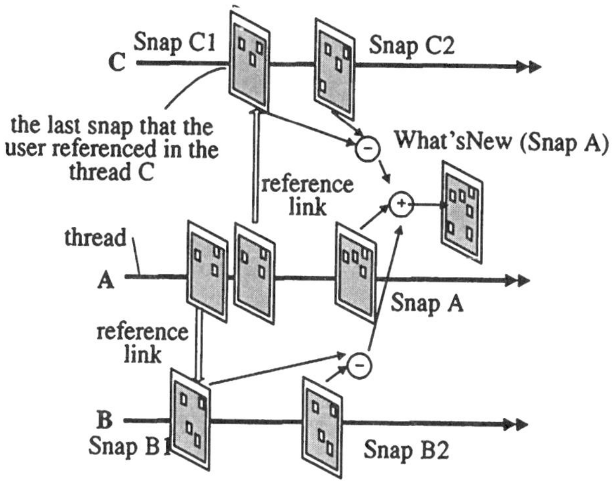

What'sNew (Snap A) = union (Snap A, subtract (Snap B2, Snap B1), subtract(Snap C2, Snap C1))

Figure 3: Contextual what's new function

The temporally threaded workspace model monitors every worker's actions to construct the activity domain. For example, removing anchors from the current snap, switching the current snap to a past snap, or ending the session all cause the workspace state to be recorded automatically, extending the workspace thread. Since the operations on each individual workspace immediately affect the latest snap, and synthesized views are dynamically generated, the contextual what's new function provides the correct progress of the related activities.

Collective Activity Perspective

To present a summarized view of activities related to a collaborative task, we introduce the collective activity view function. This function provides a synthesized view for collaboration, in place of a shared workspace.

The scope of awareness of this function is a set of workspace threads connected by a link to the user's workspace thread. This function is simply the union of the latest snap of each linked workspace thread. The access control specified in each workspace affects the synthesized view.

For example, if a user, who is working on thread A, would like to merge with thread B, s/he can create a collective view by traversing a continuation link (Figure 4). The collective view makes it easier to monitor the progress of coworkers.

Furthermore, the user can construct a synthesized view by taking the union of the newest snapshot of thread B and the current snap of her/his thread. The synthesized view presents a virtual shared workspace, which works as if they had prepared a shared workspace before starting the collaboration. The owners of these workspace threads can see the changes that the others make, and proceed with her/his own work with minimal attention to the others' activities. In this way, this collective activity perspective function makes workers aware of what is happening in the related individual activities.

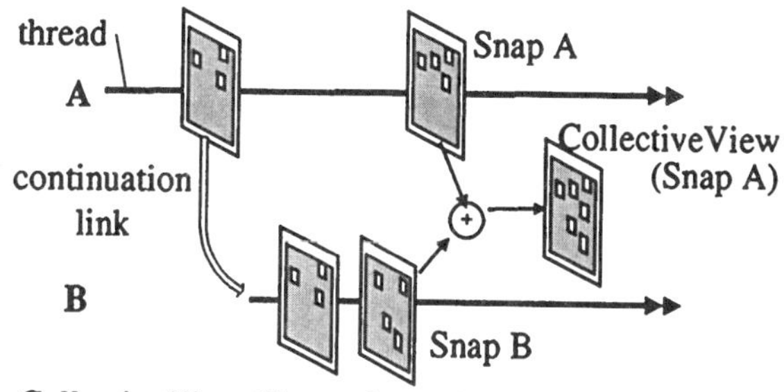

CollectiveView (Snap A) = union (Snap A, Snap B)

Figure 4: Collective activity view function

INTERLOCUS SYSTEM

In this section, we present Interlocus, a client/server system based on temporally threaded workspace model. The system is implemented with Java.

Interlocus consists of *Locus server* and *Interlocus clients.* The Locus server maintains objects and supports operations for realizing the temporally threaded workspaces. Since the Interlocus client is implemented as a Java applet, users can use Interlocus within most standard WWW browsers on several computing platforms. The server and client communicate with RMI.

User Interface

The Interlocus client provides a two-dimensional desktop metaphor with chronological tracking. The Interlocus client's user interface presents combined spatial and time frame information, and allows users to operate on snapshots from other workspaces to synthesize a collective workspace view within their collaboration context.

A novel feature of the Interlocus client is the user interface of the *activity view*, which presents a spatial-temporal view of a workspace thread. This tool consists of the *spatial frame* and the *time line frame.* The spatial frame displays anchors on a two-dimensional space. It describes the relations among a set of anchors. Figure 11 shows an example of an activity view. In this spatial frame (Figure 11-a), there are three types of anchors: 6 icons, 2 regions, and 1 curtain. In our application of the desktop metaphor, an icon is a small image, which references a document or an application. A region image is a larger image that provides an area where icon anchors can be placed. In this example, the left image containing 3 icons ("Overall Spec", "Schedule", and "Required Spec") is a region. A curtain looks similar to a region, except that it has "poles" at the left and right edges. In this example, the center image containing 1 icon ("Project Manager") is a curtain. The set of these anchors represents the state of the workspace, reflecting the state of the activity. In the spatial frame, users can add, remove and move anchors, and access documents via anchors.

The time line frame (Figure 11-b) presents the snaps comprising the workspace thread. By selecting one of the snap symbols, the activity view switches to the state corresponding to the selected snap. The example of Figure 11 presents 10 snaps at March 25 and 3 snaps at March 27. The black snap indicates that the snap is being displayed in the spatial frame. Figure 11 shows an example of an activity view providing a synthesized view. The symbol of the synthesized view is also represented by the same snap symbol in the time line frame. The 6 gray snap symbols, which represent other people's snaps used during a workspace configuration operation, are also displayed in the time line frame.

Example of Activity Awareness

Figure 5 shows an example of fictitious scenario of concurrent collaboration for writing specifications for a prototype. The main cast is Mr. A, who is in charge of designing the server/client system. Ms. B is his supervisor. Mr. C and Ms. D are Mr. A's coworkers.

At first (Figure 5: A-1), Mr. A discusses the overall specification of the system with his supervisor, Ms. B. Figure 6 shows that Mr. A prepares a workspace for designing the system, which consists of 2 icons referencing documents and 3 regions representing the structure of the workspace. After Mr. A makes Ms. B an observer of the workspace, Ms. B duplicates the snap of the workspace, with which her new workspace thread begins, to share information with Mr. A's workspace thread. At that time, Interlocus automatically generates a continuation link from Mr. A's workspace thread to Ms. B's one to indicate a task-subtask relation between them.

After discussing the overall specifications with Ms. B, Mr. A makes Mr. C and Ms. D coworkers in the workspace, asking Mr. C to design the client and Ms. D to design the server. Then, they each construct continuation workspace threads by duplicating the current snap of Mr. A's workspace thread. Two continuation links, from Mr. A's workspace to each of their workspaces, are created automatically. After that, Mr. A can reference their workspaces any time by traversing these continuation links. Figure 7 shows Mr. C's workspace for designing the client specifications (Figure 5: C-2), and Figure 8 shows Ms. D's workspace for designing the server (Figure 5: D-3).

At time t_4 in Figure 5, Mr. A wishes to synthesize his own thread with Mr. C's, and Ms. D's into a collective view (Figure 5: A-4). The collective view is shown in Mr. A's activity view, as illustrated in Figure 9. The snap contains all of the anchors included in the latest snaps in the three threads. The time line frame in Figure 9 shows a merged thread that consists of three workspace threads, with the snaps sorted by creation time. It makes Mr. A aware of what Mr. C and Ms. D have done, while Mr. C and Ms. D can proceed with their work concurrently. Mr. A, Mr. C, and Ms. D are concurrently writing detailed specifications, and they sometimes (e.g., when one person requests, when a specified event occurs, or once every 10 minutes) check the collective view. In this way, the collective view, which consists of Mr. A's, Mr. C's, and Ms. D's workspaces, is provided by the workspace configuration mechanism.

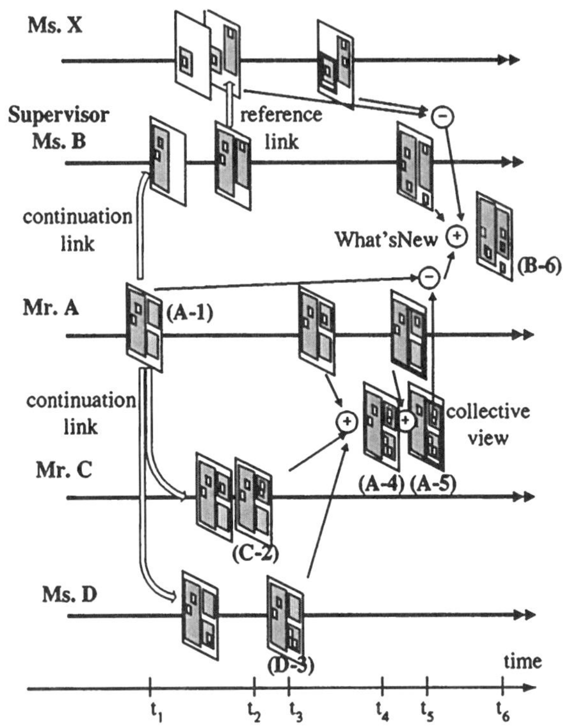

Figure 5: Example of concurrent collaborations

At time t_5 (Figure 5: A-5), Mr. A puts a curtain over all of his coworkers' newly added anchors. This restricts the observer's view, since there are several drafts that need not be reported. Once Mr. A considers the specifications satisfactory, he moves the anchor ("Required Spec") outside of the curtain to present the document. In this example, since his supervisor is an observer and the others are coworkers, the curtain restricts only the supervisor's view. The team members can use the area under the curtain to share ongoing drafts and referential documents that need not be reported formally. The access restrictions imposed by curtains allow Mr. A to change the structure of the workspace easily, even after the collaboration started.

Next, we will illustrate the contextual what's new function. Ms. B also supervises another team leader (Ms. X in Figure 5), so Ms. B's thread is connected by a reference link to Ms. X's. When Ms. B turns her attention to Ms. X's work at time t_6 in Figure 5, she uses the contextual what's new function to synthesize selected workspace threads. In this case, Interlocus makes another synthesized view (Figure 5: B-6) by synthesizing Ms. B's thread, Ms. X's thread, and Mr. A's collective view (Figure 5: A-5). Therefore, she can quickly find the newly added document icons in Mr. A's and Ms. X's workspaces. Note that the icons in the curtain region of Mr. A's workspace are not present in the synthesized snap for Ms. B.

Figure 11 shows a more complicated example. Besides the region for collaborating with Mr. A, Ms. B uses a curtain to define an area for doing her own job and a region for monitoring the progress of Ms. X. Figure 11 indicates newly created documents from Mr. A's and Ms. X's workspaces by highlighting the icons. She gets two

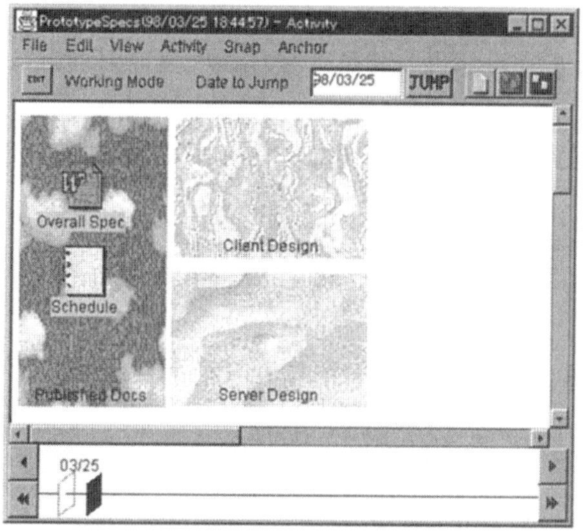

Figure 6: Mr. A's initial workspace (A-1)

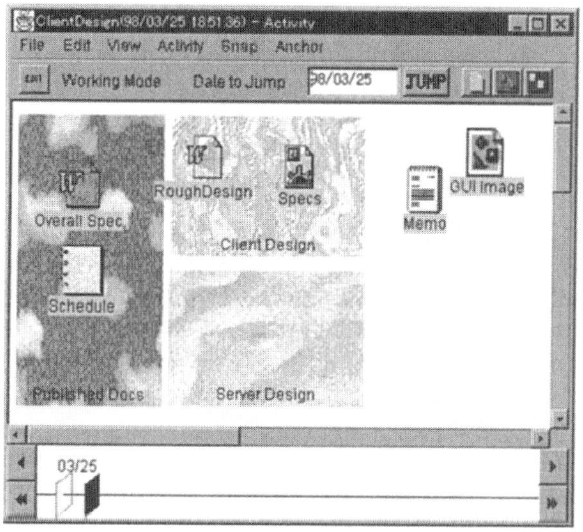

Figure 7: Mr. C designs the client (C-2)

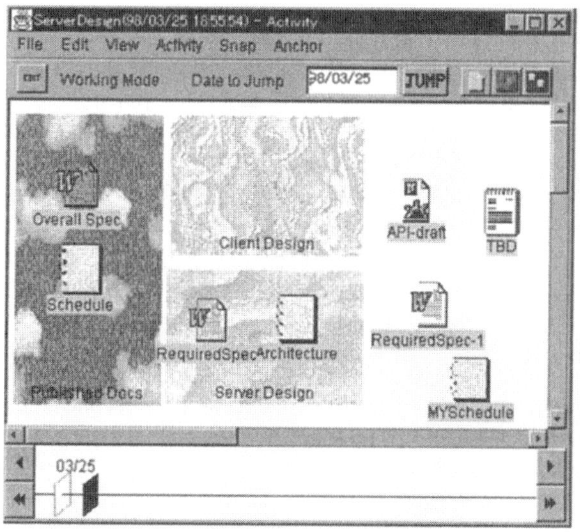

Figure 8: Ms. D designs the server (D-3)

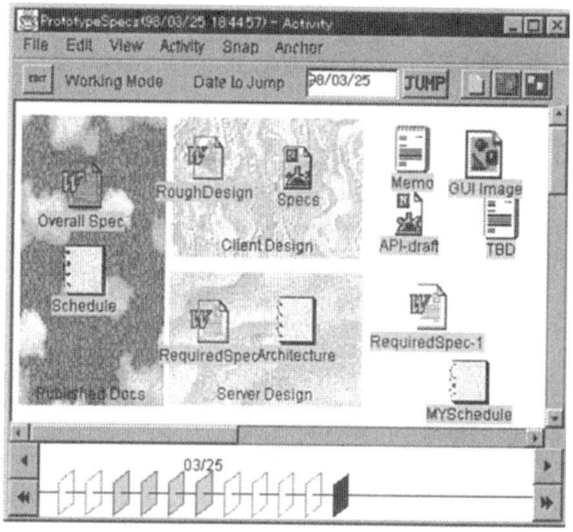

Figure 9: Mr. A gets a collective view (A-4)

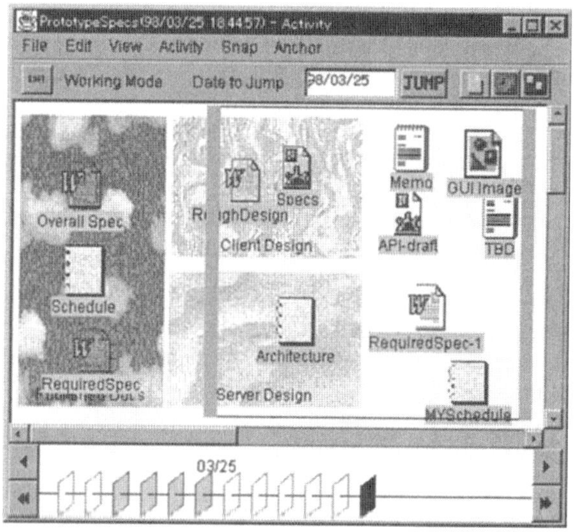

Figure 10: Mr. A puts a curtain (A-5)

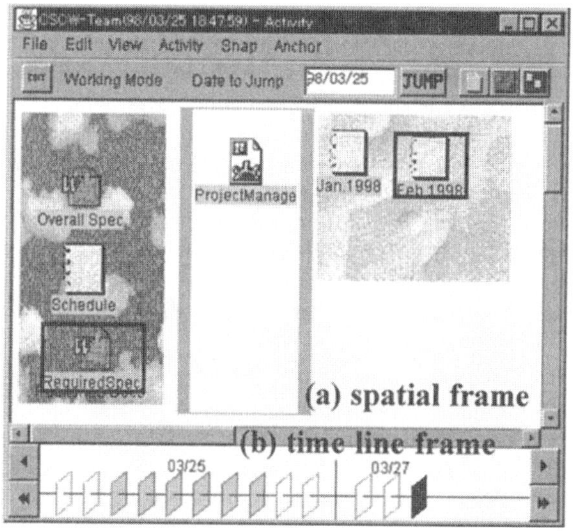

Figure 11: Ms. B gets the contextual what's new (B-6)

anchors: one is "Required Spec" from Mr. A's workspace and the other is "Feb.1998" from Ms. X's workspace.

If Ms. B allows them to access the snap (except for the area under the curtain), Mr. A could see reports from Ms. X's team and come across important information like bugs in the development environment they both use. In this way, even though they did not plan to collaborate with each other, they can become aware of related activities through Ms. B's workspace thread.

In this example, the access control function makes Ms. B aware of important changes in Mr. A's collective view (Figure 5: A-5). This demonstrates that the function controls the scope of her awareness. Although Interlocus provides only individual workspaces, the collective view function provides a shared information space (Figure 5: A-4) for Mr. A, Mr. C, and Ms. D. Furthermore, the contextual what's new function notifies Ms. B of what is going on and what has been going on in the scope of her awareness (i.e., Mr. A's and Mr. X's threads).

Mr. A did not prepare any shared workspaces, but only one individual workspace for an activity. Nevertheless, he can be aware of his team members' progress, and make his supervisor aware of selected changes. Furthermore, Mr. A can become aware of changes in related activities, even though the workers did not plan to collaborate. In this way, the collective view function, and the contextual what's new function realize the key functionality of activity awareness.

DISCUSSION

Comparison to Previous Work

In this section, we describe how our framework relates to existing groupware systems. We discuss the similarities and differences between our awareness concept, implementation of awareness, and representation of activities.

We introduce the novel concept of activity awareness and an implementation. This concept is an extension of asynchronous type of workspace awareness, which has been investigated by Gutwin and Greenburg. The unique feature of our concept is that it defines awareness between activities included in a collaborative task without employing shared workspaces. Instead, we introduce representation of individual activities and method for determining the awareness scope. Since our approach deals with individuals' workspaces directly, our implementation can provide asynchronous progress notification using the contextual what's new function. Meanwhile, to provide a summarized view of collaborative activities, which is a key feature of shared workspaces, we introduce the collective view function.

The TeamRooms system [11] provides a shared workspace, which maintains the execution progress of each applet in the workspace and a set of documents. Furthermore, they support awareness within the shared workspaces by tracking each member's telepointer and scrollbar. Users can collaborate with generic communication tools (e.g., a chat tool and a shared whiteboard) and specific tools (e.g., task lists, an outliner, and so on). However, the system focuses on a single workspace, so the user is not aware of what happens in other workspaces. Furthermore, since the system does not keep track of the collaboration history, a worker does not know what has happened in the workspace before s/he arrived.

The BSCW system provides shared workspaces in the WWW. A BSCW workspace maintains a set of documents and records actions performed against documents in the space. In the BSCW system, one must prepare a workspace before starting a specific collaboration to share an organized document space. The notable functionality of BSCW is a workspace awareness feature that records what has happened lately in each document space, as well as the current status of the space. It further provides a view to help workers catch up with other coworkers by showing actions that have occurred since s/he last accessed the space. However, the awareness scope is static. The awareness function notifies the events either in a specific folder or all folders that the worker can access.

Like our framework, the GroupDesk system is intended to provide awareness functions within a space of inter-related activities. GroupDesk is a shared workspace system that further offers the functionality of workflow systems. It supports two types of asynchronous awareness. The first, called interest contexts, makes users aware of the changes related to their predefined interests. The second, called event distribution, supports awareness of the changes to related workspaces (e.g., included in the same workflow). Like BSCW, although the system records the event history (e.g., opening the document, editing the document) to make users aware of what has been changed, it is difficult to comprehend the past states and understand why the change happened.

Wang and Haake [15,16] provide groupware systems based on the concept of *Activity Spaces* that represent task-specific hypermedia spaces. Like the temporally threaded workspace model, their model defines an activity space by using a hypermedia structure: links, nodes, pages, and media objects. This model is designed to support dynamic collaborative tasks, which include unstructured, semi-structured, and structured parts. Based on this model, their prototype system CHIPS provides shared workspaces that manage shared information spaces for collaborative activities. It adopts an issue-based decision making scheme to represent the internal structure of an activity.

The primary difference between our framework and other groupware systems is the model for recording past contexts. Shared workspaces maintain the current states of workspaces and the action histories separately. Interlocus manages both the current and past states in the same way. Therefore, our framework can provide a clearer view of the whole activity (from the start to the end) and allows users to explore the past snaps of activities.

Representation of Collective Activity Perspectives

At present we have completed the main functions of Interlocus and started daily use. As for activity awareness functions, however, we have just started trials for refining the design of the functions.

Since we adopted the temporally threaded workspace model as a basis for realizing activity awareness, we inherit the two-dimensional interface for workspaces. For the activity awareness functions, the idea that an activity domain consists of a set of workspace threads is central, but the two-dimensional nature of the workspace is not. We could provide activity awareness functions for list-based workspaces, like BSCW.

The use of two-dimensional design of workspaces provides both advantages and disadvantages. As an advantage, the two-dimensional interface is easy to change the structure, and also easy for observers to understand. For example, a combination of region images can guide coworkers in using the space. In the example presented earlier, Mr. A established three regions (see Figure 6). Then, Mr. C and Ms. D arranged their new anchors according to these regions (see Figures 7, 8, 11). By using region images in this way, workspaces are more organized after synthesizing workspace threads into a collective view. This way of establishing structure is more flexible than using workspaces where the structure must be defined beforehand.

On the other hand, we have to be concerned about the placement of icons when merging several workspaces. It is quite common for icons from one workspace to overlap with icons from another workspace. Since each worker places regions and icons according to their individual workspace structure, the placement of these icons on a synthesized snap might be misleading. For example, an icon from one person's workspace might appear in a region of an observer's workspace with a different meaning.

To avoid clutter in the collective view, we are investigating several functions to control merging snaps. These functions enable users to specify the position and visibility of each anchor when overlapping.

Group Workspaces vs. Individual Workspaces

We represent all of the activities in the organization as workspace threads. Since both personal operations and group collaborations are important in our daily work, we need a workspace model that can represent both personal and group workspaces. We see two approaches to represent all the types of activities: the enhanced personal workspace approach and the enhanced group workspace approach. We have tried to represent all activities based on the personal workspaces on each personal computer, which is the former approach, because we think it is difficult to keep workers motivated to maintain group workspaces appropriately.

Our model has the advantage of lower maintenance, since each worker maintains only her/his workspaces for performing her/his work. On the other hand, it requires a more complicated access control model. In this paper we have presented an authorization model and curtain concept, but this model does not sufficiently support more complex structures. It seems effective to introduce grouping or inheriting functions, but it is not desirable because we wish to avoid assuming a static organizational structure.

FUTURE WORK

In this paper we focus on asynchronous awareness in order to support a more flexible work style that enables us to work distributed in time, as well as space. Although this paper illustrates only asynchronous awareness using workspaces, the possibility of applying activity awareness to synchronous workspace awareness is worth investigating. Activity awareness, which consists of a representation of individual activities, dynamic awareness scope, asynchronous progress notification, and a collective activity perspective, can be extended to support synchronous awareness. The mechanisms of dynamic awareness scope and collective activity perspective would also be useful features for synchronous awareness.

Further, we would like to investigate a possibility of extending the range of collaborative work. The activity awareness and temporally threaded workspace models allow information exchanges between activities distant in time or space. It could be used to perform collaborative work with past activities whose members have already retired, or collaborative work in which no worker had intended to work collaboratively.

CONCLUSIONS

Using places or rooms as metaphors for session management is a solid idea to keep several people who are distributed over space concentrating on a collaborative task. Furthermore, workspace awareness has made the place or the room more realistic. However, the widespread adoption of the WWW requires workspace awareness to support more flexible awareness, whose scope may change dynamically based on the user's activity. In this paper, we introduce the concept of activity awareness to provide this extended workspace awareness for our own activities, which may transcend several electronic workspaces. We further illustrate a prototype, Interlocus, which provides individual workspaces based on temporally threaded workspace model and the activity awareness function using workspace configuration mechanism.

The framework of workspace configuration for activity awareness presented in this paper could be a starting point for exploring awareness based on workers' activities in the WWW.

ACKNOWLEDGMENTS

We would like to thank a number of colleagues at the Corporate Research Laboratory in Fuji Xerox for their fruitful discussion. In particular, we thank Makoto Takeoka, Sunao Hashimoto, Hiroki Ishida, and Akifumi Sekijima for their contributions to this work.

REFERENCES

1. Bentley, R., Appelt, W., Busbach. U., Hinrichs, E., Kerr, D., Sikkel, S., Trevor, J. and Woetzel, G., Basic Support for Cooperative Work on the World

Wide Web, in International Journal of Human-Computer Studies: Special issue on Innovative Applications of the World Wide Web, Spring 1997, (C)Academic Press.

2. Dourish, P., Bellotti, V., Awareness and Coordination in Shared Workspaces, CSCW'92, 1992.
3. Fuchs, L., Pankoke-Babatz, U., Prinz, W., Supporting Cooperative Awareness with Local Event Mechanisms: The GroupDesk System, ECSCW'95, 1995.
4. Gutwin, C., Greenberg, S., Workspace Awareness, CHI 97 Workshop on Awareness in Collaborative Systems, http://www.cpsc.ucalgary.ca/projects/grouplab/papers/97-StudyingAwareness.CHIWorkshop/gutwin.html, 1997.
5. Gutwin, C., Rosenman, M., and Greenberg, S., A Usability Study of Awareness Widgets in a Shared Workspace Groupware System, CSCW'96, 1996.
6. Harrison, S., Dourish, P., Re-Place-ing Space: The Roles of Place and Space in Collaborative Systems, CSCW'96, 1996.
7. Hayashi, K., Nomura, T., Hazama, T., Takeoka, M., Hashimoto, S., Gudmundson, S., Temporally-threaded Workspace: A Model for Providing Activity-based Perspectives on Document Spaces, Hypertext'98, 1998.
8. Horstmann, T. and Bentley, R., Distributed Authoring on the Web with the BSCW Shared Workspace System, in ACM Standards View, Spring 1997, (C)ACM Press.
9. Mark, G., Fuchs, L., and Sohlenkamp, M., Supporting Groupware Conventions through Contextual Awareness, ECSCW'97, 1997.
10. Rodden, T., Populating the Application: A Model of Awareness for Cooperative Applications, CSCW'96, 1996.
11. Roseman, M., Greenberg, S., TeamRooms: Network Places for Collaboration, CSCW'96, 1996.
12. The WORLDS Project, Orbit-Gold, http://www.dstc.edu.au/worlds/Prototypes/OrbitGold.html.
13. Tolone, W.J., Kaplan, S.M., and Fitzpatrick, G., Specifying Dynamic Support for Collaborative Work within WORLDS, COOCS'95, 1995.
14. Trevor, J., Koch, T. and Woetzel, G., MetaWeb: Bringing synchronous groupware to the World Wide Web, ECSCW'97, 1997.
15. Wang, W., Haake, J., Supporting user-defined activity space, HyperText97, 1997.
16. Wang, W., Haake, J., Flexible Coordination with Cooperative Hypermedia, HyperText98, 1998.

The Long and Winding Road: Collaborative IT and organisational change

Helena Karsten
University of Jyväskylä
Department of Computer Science and Information Systems
P.O.Box 35, 40351 Jyväskylä, Finland
eija@jytko.jyu.fi

Matthew Jones
University of Cambridge
The Judge Institute of Management Studies
Trumpington Street
Cambridge CB2 1AG, United Kingdom
mrj1@eng.cam.ac.uk

ABSTRACT
The role of collaborative information technology in organisational changes continues to be a source of controversy in the CSCW literature. We report organisational changes in a Finnish computer consultancy accompanying the introduction and use of Lotus Notes over a period of three years. The case shows that collaborative information technologies, such as Lotus Notes, are capable of supporting a variety forms of organisation. The uptake and use of Notes appeared to be more strongly influenced by aspects of the organisational context, internal social structure and the users' capabilities – in this case economic recession, changing foci of control and the role changes in the company – than by any intrinsic logic of the technology.

Keywords
Small business, professional service organisations, organisational change, collaboration, collaborative information technology, Lotus Notes

INTRODUCTION
The role of collaborative information technology (CIT) in organisational changes has been the focus of both scholarly and practical discussions throughout the 1990s. One aspect of this debate has been the relationship between CIT and organisational culture. Initially, it was suggested [9, 20], that the introduction of CIT would, of itself, give rise to more collaborative organisational relations. Following a number of studies questioning this simple deterministic relationship [18, 25, 39] the argument was revised to suggest that CIT can be expected to give rise to increased collaboration only if the organisational culture supports it. A much quoted study is one by Orlikowski [25], where she states that Lotus Notes is unlikely to engender collaboration if the organisational culture is competitive or individualistic, but rather it will be used to promote individual aims. This statement has been interpreted in commercial literature (eg. [15]) to mean that Notes will engender collaboration in organisations where the culture supports collaboration.

CSCW 98 Seattle Washington USA

A second aspect of the debate has been the literature on new organisational forms [8, 21]. Here it is argued that the complexity and turbulence of current economic conditions requires new, flexible and responsive forms of organisation, characterised by flattening of hierarchies (eg. [27]), teamwork (eg. [22]), and decentralisation of decision-making authority (eg. [2]). Such developments are seen to imply more collaborative organisational relations [10, 14, 21]. One type of organisation that is seen as particularly suited to these new forms [32] is knowledge-based, professional service organisations (PSOs) such as management and technical consultancies, many of which have invested heavily in CIT [4, 28].

Although much of this literature makes little reference to the contribution of information technologies to these organisational transformations, there is a third strand of the debate which ascribes it a central role. Thus Applegate [1] argues that "information technology is a critical component that is both driving the change and enabling survival". In many cases this is not seen to be attributable specifically to CIT, but to characteristics of information technology in general, such as its capacity to 'informate' work practices [40], to collect, analyse and disseminate information [5] and to facilitate intra- and interorganisational communication and coordination [35]. Being specifically geared towards coordination and communication, however, collaborative information technologies would seem significantly implicated in such developments.

From a number of perspectives, therefore, arguments may be traced, linking collaborative information technologies with organisational change. Unfortunately, although it provides many anecdotes of successful transformation, much of the literature on collaborative information technology is relatively short-term and offers little information on the process by which change occurs. The few notable exceptions to this include work by Ciborra and colleagues [6]; Ngwenyama [23]; Orlikowski [26]; and Ruhleder, Jordan and Elmes [34]. Even though detailed in their analysis of the collaborative technology and changes in work, these do not focus on change at the organisational level, and are generally of limited duration. More longitudinal studies of the use of collaborative information technologies in specific firms would thus seem to be required to examine such processes. In this paper we therefore consider in detail the organisational changes related to the introduction and use of collaborative information technology (specifically Lotus Notes) in a Finnish computer consultancy over a period of three years.

THEORY AND METHODS

The aim of this paper is to develop an understanding of the role of Notes in organisational change in the consultancy. As Van de Ven & Poole [38] argue, contextualist, ideographic methods are appropriate in studying such organisational processes. Pettigrew [30] suggests that such methods can also help to link theory and practice by focusing on events in their natural settings, exploring phenomena at vertical and horizontal levels and over time, and by encouraging systematic description of the properties and patterned relationships of the process.

The research thus adopts a subjectivist ontology which sees the organisational context and processes as being socially constructed through the interaction of the different meanings of the various human actors involved. The primary data was therefore the perceptions of the members of CCC as revealed in interviews and through their actions and interactions during the course of the study. The data were validated by comparison between different sources. Rather than seeking to use triangulation to identify a single, "true" interpretation of events, however, differences were seen as sites of contested meaning to be explained.

Data collection took place over a period of three years between spring 1992 and early 1995 using observation, interviews and analysis of company documents, and Notes databases. One of the authors was given access to the Notes discussions and records of other Notes use (excluding the contents of private email messages) and attended several Board and consultants' meetings. This was supplemented by regular interviews with all organisational members, approximately every 7-10 months. Access was also provided to the minutes of the meetings and other memoranda. Some aspects of potentially significant informal interaction were not accessible, however, as casual exchanges and quick decisions were likely to take place unexpectedly, at irregular intervals, in a variety of locations.

The data obtained from these sources were then used to construct a case description focusing on organisational level changes over the three-year period. This was then iteratively analysed by the authors to construct a common interpretation. Where necessary the case description was revised to provide more detail on critical events. This iterative analysis, involving several rounds of comparison of the authors' independent interpretations of the case decription, was intended to provide validation of the themes and patterns identified and to promote convergence towards a common understanding. It was not assumed, however, that this would lead to either a completely shared, or final, definitive analysis, since the differences in the authors' experience and interest could not be eliminated from their perceptions and interpretation itself was seen as an ongoing, emergent process.

In contrast to the idealised model of "grounded theory" [11] in which the researcher allows themes to emerge without any preconceptions, the analysis was focused on changes in the organisation over the study period and was recognised to have been unavoidably influenced by the authors' prior knowledge of theories of organisational transformation. The approach was therefore not primarily exploratory, but directed towards the collection of qualitative evidence that might support or question popular theories of the role of collaborative information technologies in organisational change.

This study also differs from previous analyses of collaborative information technologies in a number of important respects. First, in contrast to some of the well-known ethnographic studies of IT such in [3, 13, 37], the focus is upon intangible knowledge work rather than material work practices. It may also be contrasted with ethnographies of knowledge work (eg. [19, 33, 36]), in being focused on the management of work rather than the work practices themselves. This study is also distinctive in terms of the duration of the study (three years, compared to, typically, three months or less) and its level of analysis which addresses changes at the level of a specific organisation, rather than individual work practices or across organisations. Finally, compared to evaluative studies of Notes, such as [12, 31], the aim is to understand the relationship between Notes and organisational change rather than to assess the appropriateness of Notes to specific tasks.

CASE DESCRIPTION

1986 – Spring 1992: Growth and stability

Collegiate Computer Consulting Inc. (CCC) is a small computer consultancy company in the Helsinki region. As a company, it does not have a clear image nor a firm position in the market but it is best known through the consultants, who are recognised experts in their areas. Each consultant has her or his own customers and area of specialty, which vary widely from, for example, IT management consulting to designing computer networks to developing specialist graphics programs. The consultants usually do projects for computing departments of large companies, software houses or IT companies. In 1991, when it was at its largest, the company had 14 consultants, but the number decreased to 10 during the recession of 1992-3.

The company was founded in 1986 by four senior members of the Finnish computing profession: Mr Bank, Mr Law, Mr Credit and Mr ComputerService (the Founding Fathers), with the idea of giving young talents an opportunity to be independent entrepreneurs while protected by the 'umbrella' of a limited liability company. The company was designed to provide a marketing front, basic administrative services, and contact with colleagues, while the consultants would work as independents.

Thus officially, CCC is a limited liability company, for legal and taxation reasons, with employees (here, the consultants and administrative staff), one of whom acts as a managing director (MD). The shares are owned by the Founding Fathers and the active and past consultants. A board of directors (the Board) is elected by the shareholders' annual meeting and it is responsible for the management of the company and the adequate organisation of its operations. According to law, the managing director is in charge of the company's day-to-day management in accordance with instructions and orders laid down by the Board. The Founding Fathers have been members of the Board of CCC from the beginning and their influence has remained significant over the years.

About one year after the company was started it hired its first MD to whom the Board gradually transferred management responsibilities. This MD had had a long career in computer consultancy which gave him a wide range of contacts. He saw himself as a resource in marketing and sales and spent a major proportion of his time as an IT management consultant. In CCC, he adopted a democratic management style, encouraging expression of opinions, discussion and responsibility for one's own actions, although his long experience meant that his own views were often highly influential.

The work of the consultants was usually carried out in the customer sites or in their home offices. There were shared desks in the company offices, with rent charged to their users. Consultants who had few projects thus tended not to have a desk, to save on costs. Those who worked in the company offices tended to participate more in company management, as the files and documents were more accessible to them. The others usually visited about once a week to collect mail and exchange gossip, in addition to attending meetings.

From 1986 to 1992 the consultants held bi-weekly meetings to exchange information on projects and customers, to make decisions on company-level matters such as investments and to reach consensus on contested issues such as the fees for administration. Not all consultants participated in these meetings, feeling that as they worked independently anyway they did not need to coordinate their work with that of their colleagues and that the administration took care of the 'umbrella' functions. However, as share-owners, most of the consultants took an interest in its management. Thus the consultants came to form a majority of the Board members and by summer 1992 almost all active consultants had been voted onto the Board by shareholders' meetings.

Although the Board was kept informed and made sure of the legal functioning of the firm, it seldom intervened in the daily workings of the company which was left to the MD and a secretary. The MD, however, minimised this task. The consultants managed their projects themselves, either alone or through their meetings. Then, when growth of the firm lead to the hiring of a financial assistant in 1989, the MD left much of the routine daily management of the firm to her. This role rapidly became very important due to the amount of information that passed through her desk.

Summer 1992 - Spring 1993 Recession

Lotus Notes was introduced to the company during late spring 1992 [16]. The main uses intended for Notes were twofold. Some consultants wanted to include it in their repertoire of software tools, used in customer projects. Within the company, Notes was to be used to communicate about administrative and professional issues; to share information, especially on customers and projects; and to coordinate marketing and sales efforts. Its acquisition was noted by the Board. The Founding Fathers paid little attention to this acquisition, however, as they thought that it was a operational decision to be made by the consultants. Each consultant paid for his or her own program licence and thus the cost for the company was insignificant.

A number of applications were developed during summer 1992 by a consultant (Arto) interested in developing Notes expertise (see Table 1). He also maintained the user accounts. The network and server infrastructure had been built earlier that year and it was maintained by another consultant (Sten), a network specialist. As the users were computer professionals, they could solve most of the problems by themselves. The small amount of support that was required was given by Arto and Sten, who then would use this experience in their customer projects. The first five users were Arto and Sten, the financial assistant, the secretary, and one consultant who had moved to another part of the country and needed a means to transfer files.

The introduction of Notes coincided with the resignation of the first MD although he continued to work as a part-timer until September 1992 and to serve on the Board until summer 1993. Mr Credit took over as a part-time MD, but still left much of the daily management to the consultants and the financial assistant. He also played little part in the Board and consultants' meetings and decisions continued to be taken collectively. Mr Credit saw his main task as MD as improving the efficiency of the administration, cutting costs and creating a uniform practice for project bids and agreements.

The Finnish economy had entered a severe recession in 1991 [24] and the effects of this began to be felt in CCC in spring 1992, as their customers had problems in paying for projects. During autumn 1992, the recession deepened, fewer and fewer projects were won, and CCC faced severe financial problems. While the company was searching for a new full-time MD, the Board acted as the main decision making body. Financial issues were excluded from the consultants' meetings, and during winter 1992-3, as there was

Database/application	Main uses	Monthly use
Customers	Maintain customer contact information	85
BusinessBase	Enter project leads, won and lost projects, project information, main project events such as negotiations with customers.	69
Discussion	Main discussion forum for the company, a wide range of topics	15
Bulletins	Company bulletin board. It also contained discussions.	42
Meetings	Meeting agendas and minutes of both Board and consultants' meetings, with links to the appropriate documents (eg. a strategy memo discussed over several meetings)	18
Mail	Electronic mail within CCC (external electronic mail separate)	22
Other minor applications	Examples include weekly *PC* and *Mac News* from a news service, *Technical Bulletins*, company *Library Catalogue*, company *Software Catalogue*, *Squash Ranking* list, *Forms*, frequently used *Texts*.	typically < 8

Table 1: The initial applications in CCC, installed during summer and autumn 1992, and their use after autumn 1993 (average monthly reads and writes per person).

very little to report in terms of projects, they were usually short or not held. Three consultants left during the winter and the financial assistant was kept very busy juggling the finances of the company.

The financial situation reached its lowest point in January and February 1993 when at one time only one consultant had work. Because of the crisis the Board demanded that all consultants should get involved in sales and marketing. Notes was presented as a means for coordinating this effort. In particular, the customer database had become out-dated and all consultants were required to identify their clients and update contact information in the Notes *Customer* database whether they were users or not, thus giving them an exposure to it. Sten set up a work station in the office for this and Arto gave hands-on support.

The dire straits also brought tension and distrust to the company. Many consultants commented that even when an agreement was reached during a meeting, it was not always acted upon, as each consultant only looked after her or his own interests. There were also some disputes with customers over verbal contract agreements. Thus a discussion on the need for more formal procedures in both contracts and company management ensued.

Spring 1993 - Spring 1994 New growth

In March several projects, mainly from old customers, were won and the situation changed dramatically. In April, a new MD was appointed and he soon showed his skill by winning new customers and projects for CCC. Together, these changes meant that that by summer 1993 everybody was working again.

While all the Notes applications developed so far were in operation, the amount of use remained minor until August 1993 when Arto made user accounts for all consultants – whether they had requested it or not. He and Sten also helped to set up modem connections for mobile users. Several consultants started using Notes in September and by November all were regularly scanning the active databases on a daily basis. Most of the use was either from home, via a modem, in the evening or, for those in the office, scanning the unread entries several times a day.

The main use of Notes was to log customer contacts and project events in the *Customer* and *BusinessBase* databases. This was done selectively, however. For example two consultants commented that they still maintained their own files and only entered into Notes those project ideas, calls for proposals, and contacts they thought would be useful to others. The financial assistant had for a time maintained her lists of projects, but when the Notes use spread, she slowly relinquished this and subsequently her coordinator role.

Notes was also used to store meeting agendas and minutes in the *Meetings* database (although the benefit of this was decreased by having several writers for the minutes, with different styles and timetables for posting them); to post company bulletins in *Bulletins* and to discuss everything from setting up a squash game to buying a new server, in several discussion applications, of which the main one was called simply the *Discussion*. The discussions were floating in a rather free form and comments could be found not only discussion databases but also in *Bulletins* and *Meetings* databases. The final decisions were still made in mainly Board meetings or, in some minor cases, by the MD. *Electronic mail*[1] was used in one-to-one communication but only three consultants used it heavily. Table 1 shows the monthly average usage of these applications per user.

The new MD introduced new ways of reporting to the Board meeting which impressed the members. With this, he changed the role of the financial assistant from the source and presenter of all information to that of assisting in compiling his reports. A third blow to the financial assistant was when the MD brought out into the open the consultants' discontent with the administration and in particular the slow pace with which the financial assistant carried out some of her duties. With the still persisting financial prob-

[1] Outside email services were used for external mail and Notes was connected to Internet only in 1995.

lems, the company could no longer afford a secretary, thus doubling the financial assistant's work load. All this came to a head during a shareholders' meeting in June where the work of the administration was criticised. The Board also criticised the MD, however, for not keeping a close enough eye on the management of the firm. One of the results was that the MD requested setting up two small Notes applications to support administrative tasks: *Billing*, to log future income from current projects to plan expenditure and to enter annual budgets; and *Hours*, for logging time spent on each project. Their monthly usage stabilised quite rapidly to around 28 and 33 reads-plus-writes per consultant.

During spring and summer 1993 there was much discussion of the roles of the Board and consultants' meetings. The MD stated that he saw very little need or use for the consultants' meeting since almost everybody was a member of the Board and proposed moving decision-making power to himself and the Board. In October it was decided that the consultants meetings should be held once a month before the Board meeting. In December, all money-related issues were also transferred to the Board meetings. In February 1994 the Board further downgraded the consultants' meetings' status by deciding that it should only make recommendations and offer opinions while the Board and the MD would make and carry out decisions. As a result, there were no consultants' meetings during spring 1994, but more and more discussions between the consultants were held in Notes and also informally, face-to-face. Several consultants observed that much of the internal debate in CCC was now conducted through Notes and that Notes also provided most of the information and coordination formerly conveyed during their meetings.

During summer and autumn 1993 several consultants brought up the need to redefine some of the "ground rules" of the company, such as guidelines for written contracts, salary calculations or investment funding. With the changes of MD, the Board found that it lacked relevant information about legal and contract issues. In November 1994, it was therefore decided that the MD should prepare an overview of current practices. He did this by preparing a plan to develop administration, cost accounting and the roles of the Board, consultants and the MD. A task group was then set up to write the ground rules and to gather opinions about them. The senior consultant in charge of this group (Sten) built a Notes database (*GroundRules*) to bring together the relevant laws, regulations and old practices and this was made available for discussion in January 1994.

The MD emphasised the need to have few good customers and demonstrated this by winning large projects from two or three major companies that gave work to most of the consultants. This idea was carried further in August 1993 when the Board discussed, at his initiative, the possibility of joint work with a major software house. Negotiations with several software houses were carried out by Mr Bank and the MD and reported to the Board in particular at the January 1994 meeting. A number of the consultants were concerned that this would amount to a takeover. The one consultant who was not a Board member therefore sought to attend the meeting to hear the discussion and was permitted to stay only after a reprimand by the Chair. Some of the consultants who were opposed to the terms of the agreement drafted their own suggestions for a more equal relationship, but these were not approved by the larger company. The negotiations ended, however, without any agreement.

Having won a major project for himself in November 1993 the MD had actually moved to the client's offices and only visited CCC occasionally after Christmas 1993. He finally left the company at the end of March 1994 (when the restraint on competition by his former employer had lapsed). Although he gave no reasons for leaving, he reappeared some months later as a leading consultant for an affiliate of one of the software houses with whom CCC had earlier been in negotiations.

Spring 1994 - Winter 1995 New stability

In early 1994 CCC was therefore again looking for a new MD. A senior consultant who had joined the firm in October 1993 was asked by the Board to take on the job. He accepted, but having no prior management experience he relied heavily on the help of the more senior partners in the firm. His management style, however, was seen as much more democratic and easy-going than the previous MD and during his first consultants' meeting as MD, he brought up the need for the consultants to work as a team and organised a series of team-building exercises over the summer.

Criticism of CCC's administration continued during the spring, however. The financial assistant took a long leave in the spring and then left the company in May 1994. Administrative tasks were therefore either not done or were taken care of by the secretary, or consultants. Thus during the interim between the departure of the previous MD and the new one becoming familiar with the firm, there was no central control of CCC's finances. The first Board meeting with the new MD discussed this at length and made a decision to transfer more items of the daily management from the administration – the financial assistant and MD – to the Board and demanded clearer financial statements. They also decided to speed up the streamlining of accounting.

In April 1994 a new Board was elected. Due to the decline in consultant numbers, and in order to clarify responsibilities and make decision-making faster, only three consultants (Arto, Sten and Mikko) and two Founding Fathers (Mr. Bank and Mr Law) were elected. The new MD had the right to attend meetings but had no vote. He was also given specific guidance by the Board. During its first meeting the Board outlined three long-term tasks for itself: developing a business strategy, controlling investments, and overseeing the consultants' profit centres. The Board also identified a number of priorities including continuing the work on developing clearer ground rules and reorganising the administration.

The three consultant Board members became key players in CCC's management: acting as a communication channel with their colleagues (both directly and via Notes); providing the experience and background that the new MD and even to some extent Mr. Bank, the chairman, lacked; and through their involvement in the various task groups for reforming company management.

Initially only a few consultants participated in the *Ground-Rules* discussion database in Notes, but during the summer and autumn, there were several lively exchanges on decision-making, management of the firm and CCC's business plan in which most active consultants took part. These issues were also discussed informally and in meetings, but the main points of the argument were entered into Notes. These discussions helped all participants gain an appreciation of the main management issues in CCC.

During 1994 Notes came to be relied upon more and more. For example the MD used *BusinessBase* and *Billing* information directly for Board meetings. He also made sure that minutes were put onto Notes soon after the meeting. For their part, the consultants responded by making sure that databases were kept up-to-date and that newcomers also maintained these standards. The consultants regained their decisionmaking power by discussing and agreeing on issues in Notes databases. Several joint investments were also planned in Notes, and carried out with or without the official blessing of the Board. This happened by the initiator of the investment presenting the issues and asking for reaction from everybody. The discussion with clarifying information would then continue until nobody opposed the investment, in much the same manner as the earlier consultants' meetings. Moreover, as projects tended to take consultants to customer sites more than before, Notes became important as a means of keeping in touch. Informal face-to-face meetings or phonecalls between consultants remained important however, particularly for minor decisions, where, as the MD described it, Notes was "too democratic."

With the increasing skills of the new MD and the return of better economic conditions during autumn 1994 the Board began to relinquish control of day-to-day management and again took a more supervisory role. The streamlining of the administration also meant that it ran more smoothly with the result that the September Board meeting agreed to transfer some tasks back to the MD leaving the Board to focus on the strategy of the firm, the ground rules discussion, and the few outstanding recession-related problems.

OVERVIEW OF KEY PHASES

The history of CCC during the period 1992-1995 may be seen as consisting of a number of phases based on changes in economic conditions and in circumstances inside the firm (see Table 2). The original culture of the company before the adoption of Notes was democratic and its form decentralised, with each consultant pursuing their own interests and approach. The first MD, while a charismatic leader with considerable personal authority, also adopted a consensual management style in which the consultants largely managed themselves and in which the day-to-day management was devolved to the FA. The success of this approach (although perhaps never tested under adverse conditions) helped to set a standard by which later organisational changes would be assessed.

The recession, which coincided with the introduction of Notes, changed the situation of the company drastically. As a stop-gap leader, Mr Credit saw his main task as sorting out the administrative system while letting the consultants continue to run the projects for themselves. Notes was used to support marketing efforts but with meagre results. Although Mr. Credit's administrative improvements may have helped to delay the financial crisis brought on by the economic recession, this approach ultimately did not prove sustainable, and the Board decided that it was necessary for it to take control. As a consequence of this and the small number of active projects, consultants own managing and coordinating activities almost ceased.

Phase	Growth & Stability 1986 - August 92	Recession Sept 92 - March 93	New Growth April 93 - March 94	New Stability March 94 - January 95
Main decision making body	consultants	Board	MD	Board and consultants. Consultants make decisions with the help of Notes.
Control of consultants	self	Board, FA	MD, Board	Consultants control each other via Notes, self, Board and MD.
Control of MD	self, (Board)	Board, FA	Board, (consultants)	Board, esp. consultant members
Communication	Consultants meetings and informal situations	informal situations, some Notes use	Board meetings, Notes, informal situations	Extensive use of Notes, Board meetings, informal situations.
Planning and control	FA keeps a list of projects and prospects.	List of projects and prospects kept in Notes (in partial use).	Most projects and prospects kept in Notes (everybody reads but not all update).	Almost all projects and prospects kept in Notes (everybody reads and updates, at least selectively)

Table 2. Phases of CCC

This process was then extended by the second full-time MD who further centralised powers to the Board and officially downgraded the role of the consultants' in managing the company. Having impressed the Board by his success in winning contracts and in improving reporting mechanisms he was also able to persuade them to transfer many key management responsibilities to himself, thus trying to introduce hierarchy and formalized culture to the firm. The consultants, however, maintained their own social networks, with the help of Notes, among other aids. Differences between the consultants and the MD came to a head around the negotiations with the larger software house, leading eventually to his resignation.

Looking again for a new MD, CCC turned to one of their own consultants. His approach was much more democratic and emphasised collaboration. His inexperience, together with the departure of the financial assistant and concerns about financial control, however, lead to the Board again becoming much more actively involved in day-to-day management. Coupled with the streamlining of the Board membership and the non-voting status of the new MD, control thus appeared to be yet more centralised. The use of Notes databases for discussion and for reporting of Board meetings, however, actually enabled wider, if more indirect participation and the restoration of something of the original consensual management approach. This increased participation and the skills gained by both the consultants and the new MD were recognised by the Board in deciding to relinquish management and financial responsibilities to the MD and the consultants together. Thus at the end of the study period, the consultants collaborated in managing the company to a much greater extent than during any previous time. Also their collaboration in running the projects had increased.

DISCUSSION

Overall, therefore, the number of Notes users and the range of activities in which Notes was used, increased steadily over the period 1992-1995 (Table 3). By November 1993 all ten consultants had formed a regular usage pattern and the level of Notes use had stabilised at about 250 database accesses per day. This neat picture, however, may be seen to suggest a series of discrete phases of the diffusion of Notes in CCC, rather than the more gradual and uneven spread observable in practice, and disguises a number of individual variations in enthusiasm and attitudes towards Notes use.

The neat progression of phases is also rather misleading in relation to the character of the organisational change processes. As Ciborra [7] argues, organisational change may best be understood not as a succession of discrete and independent forms, but as an accretion of different designs upon the sedimented relics of earlier formative contexts. In this respect organisational change may be seen as less like the replacing of an old car with a new model, and more like the extension, refurbishment or rebuilding of an old house. Even if in some cases the old structure is demolished, elements may remain, whether as hard-core for the foundations of the new or perhaps as an odd fireplace, doorway (or even a whole room as in the case of the Lloyds building in London) fitted into the new design.

In terms of organisational culture, we can see a move from independent culture, via a period of general resignation during the deep of the recession, to formalized and then to collaborative culture. However, we cannot say that collaborative information technology increased collaboration. Rather, the different aspects of the applications, the organisational information space [17], and the communication possibilities were used by the consultants and the management both to support their current activities and to explore alternative ways of working, including collaboration.

In seeking explanations for these changes in CCC we may identify both context and content elements [29]. The economic conditions, the changes in the management style, the changes in consultant's role and work practices, in addition to the specifics of the process, as outlined here, may be identified as crucial in the changes.

Activity	1986- August 1992	September 1992 - March 93	April 1993 - March 1994	March 1994 - January 95
scanning for leads	MD and each consultant	consultants, also Founding Fathers at times	MD and each consultant	each consultant
marketing and sales	slowly arising need, MD and each consultant	consultants, also Founding Fathers at times	MD and each consultant	each consultant with MD's support
managing projects	consultants	consultants, guidelines by Mr Credit	consultants, supervised by MD	consultants
general management	MD, FA & secretary from 1989	FA	MD and FA	Board, then MD, secretary
strategic management	MD, Board, consultants	Board, consultants	MD, Board	Board and consultants

Key to shading

No Notes support	Some Notes support	Routine Notes support	Significant/Innovative Notes support	Entirely supported by Notes

Table 3. Activities, responsibilities and Notes usage in CCC.

The economic conditions

The effect of economic conditions – especially of the recession – on organisational change in CCC was felt in two main ways. Firstly on the availability of slack resources in the system to compensate for the high costs of communication in participative management; and secondly on staff morale, which influenced their ability to resist changes that deleteriously affected their autonomy. The recession also forced CCC to undertake a re-appraisal of its aims and practices, the "ground rules" debate, ultimately with apparently beneficial results.

It should be emphasised that while the economic conditions were clearly significant in their effect on CCC, they should not be regarded as an objective, external force, but were subject to differing interpretations by different actors, some of whom were able to draw on these to support particular developments. Thus the second MD was able to legitimate his attempts to impose a more centralised form and formal culture by appealing to economic necessities and to prove his analysis of economic conditions correct through his success in winning contracts from large companies. The perception of the Finnish recession as particularly affecting large companies using mainframes, who were seen as having over-invested in IT, was also used to support the move towards developing client-server expertise and to the perception of Notes expertise as a potential source of revenue.

Management Style

The effect of the MD's management style was perhaps most evident in the way in which the various phases of organisational change coincided with changes in organisational leadership. The second MD's failure to achieve legitimacy for his position through the "ground rules" debate, however, or to get his way on the negotiations with the larger software house, illustrated that, despite the formal marginalisation of the consultants and the economic conditions which encouraged their acquiescence, they were able to draw on their social network (in part through the use of Notes) to prevent any significant loss of their independence and decision-making power.

For management, Notes served primarily a support role. Rather than pushing CCC towards either greater participation, decentralisation and team-working, or centralisation, specialisation and formal management structures, Notes appeared adaptable to either approach depending on the prevailing management style. This was the case both in terms of the types of applications that were developed, but also the ways in which these were used.

For example, the second full-time MD's concern with centralisation and improving administration lead to the introduction of the small administrative databases. At the same time, though, the *GroundRules* database in Notes lead to a relatively free and wide-ranging debate that allowed the consultants to reassert their influence. It was not simply a matter, however, of the administrative applications increasing managements' surveillance of the consultants or the increased ability of consultants working away from the office to monitor and participate in the debate. The administrative databases, in addition to the *Customers* and *BusinessBase* databases, also made the consultants' work more visible to each other and hence could support more collegial management, while the *GroundRules* database was seen, at least initially by the second full-time MD, as a means of pushing through his ideas about how CCC should be run. Even individual applications were thus open to appropriation in different ways.

Consultants' roles and work practices

The consultants modified their roles as their skills expanded, as their discourse about the firm became visible, as their participation increased in volume and involvement, and as their work became more visible. All these were much influenced by Notes. Although some of these developments, especially participation and visibility, were planned, others arose opportunely and as unexpected consequences of Notes use.

Increased skills

At the start of the recession, the key skills that it was expected the consultants needed to acquire were in marketing and sales and this was one of the reasons for CCC buying Notes. The management changes also drew attention to the need to build 'organisational memory' of company practices [17].

As Notes use grew, however, consultants acquired other skills. For example, the availability in Notes of meeting minutes allowed those not present to keep themselves informed, while information on taxes and secretarial problems meant that all staff became aware of day-to-day management issues. Notes also enabled the consultants to participate in establishing CCC's "ground rules". Consequently, those consultants who were most active in contributing to the Notes discussions acquired considerable knowledge of practical management of a small firm. This was recognised by the other consultants when electing their representatives to the Board in 1994 and by the third full-time MD in his reliance on these consultants in managing the firm.

Debating the nature of organisation

Notes was used also to open up debate about the nature of CCC as a company. This was influenced by economic conditions and by personnel changes. The second full-time MD, for example, promoted the view that CCC should become an efficient, professional bureaucracy and was able to recruit the support of the Board in negotiating collaboration with the major software house. His position proved unsustainable, however, in the face of the consultants' alternative vision. Their resistance was facilitated by the *GroundRules* database in Notes which provided both a practical model of participation and a forum for developing a common position.

Wider participation

As Notes use spread and more and more of the discussions and information was provided through it, the role of the consultants gradually changed from that of independents towards being more active participants. Thus, despite the consultants' face-to-face meetings becoming fewer and shorter, Notes enabled those who worked away to remain involved, and even those who had traditionally been either quiet or absent from the meetings, began giving their input, at first just commenting on discussions and then later initiating them. By the end of the study period the importance of Notes was such that some consultants referred to their firm as the virtual CCC.

Not all the company's management operated through Notes, however. Most of the work of the Board, for example, was not directly accessible, as the Founding Fathers had no Notes accounts. As the willingness of the consultants to accede to the reduction in the size of the Board illustrates, though, it appeared that they felt sufficiently confident of their ability to monitor and influence decisions through Notes that the high level of direct participation they had sought under the second MD was no longer necessary.

Visibility

Notes also affected organisation in CCC through increased mutual visibility. While initially some consultants had reservations about making details of their work available to colleagues, when the benefits, such as improved coordination and recruitment of assistance, became evident, more and more projects were entered and maintained in *BusinessBase*. This lead to increased horizontal coordination and eventually to a degree of horizontal integration through an increase in joint projects. The application also assisted vertical coordination, by providing a project history which could be consulted if a project had to be transferred to another consultant. Some consultants extended this, providing project content documentation, including working documents, as well as the project management documentation. This visibility was not strongly enforced, however, and consultants were still able to act independently if they wished.

CONCLUSIONS

Although the establishment of a consensual management style and more collaboration in projects at CCC might seem to support the arguments for the role of collaborative IT in the promotion of increased integration, the case has a more complex story to tell. Firstly, the collaborative approach supported by the third full-time MD was not so much a new way of managing work, as a return to CCC's early management form, albeit now supported electronically, enabling participation by consultants working at client sites (and by those who preferred not to attend meetings).

If we look at the process of organisational change over the course of the study period, however, it would seem that there was not one "ideal type" of managing work, but that other ways proved, at least temporarily, suited to the consultancy environment. Thus, had we reported the process of CCC's organisational transformation at another point in time, another story could have been told. As this emphasises moreover, we cannot assume that by the end of the study period the practices of managing work at CCC stabilized and culture and that further changes would not occur in future. However, the period of three years does seems to have been long enough to show clearly distinguishable changes in the organisation. The negative findings on the effects of Notes on levels of collaboration of authors such as Vandenbosch and Ginzberg [39], who expected to observe significant developments over the course of a nine-month study, may thus be accounted for. The complex changes evoked by collaborative technology such as Notes may require substantially longer to emerge, even in a relatively small and flexible organisation, such as CCC. Such effects also depend on complex processes of learning and adaptation, the duration of which cannot be easily foreseen.

As far as Notes is concerned, the CCC case would seem to show that such collaborative information technologies are capable of supporting a variety of ways to manage work and that individual applications are capable of appropriation by organisational members in quite different ways. Thus this study challenges the view that collaborative information technology can support collaboration (or indeed work in general) only if the organisational culture is collaborative. The uptake and use of Notes in our case appeared to be more strongly influenced by aspects of the organisational context and internal social structure – in this case the recession, the changing foci of control and the role changes in the company – than by any intrinsic logic of the technology.

REFERENCES

1. Applegate, L.M., Managing in an information age: transforming the organization for the 1990s, in *Transforming Organizations with Information Technology*, R. Baskerville, O. Ngwenyama, S. Smithson, and J. DeGross, Eds. 1994, North-Holland: Amsterdam. 15-94.
2. Bowen, D.E. and Lawler, E.E., The empowerment of service workers: what, why, how and when? *Sloan Management Review*, 1992(Spring): 21-39.
3. Bowers, J., Button, G., and Sharrock, W. Workflow from within and without: Technology and cooperative work on the print industry shopfloor. in *ECSCW'95*. 1995. Stockholm, Sweden: Kluwer: 51-66.
4. Caldwell, B., *Informationweek 500: Making IT a group effort*, in Information Week. September 18, 1995. 170-173.
5. Child, J., Information technology, organization, and the response to strategic challenges. *California Management Review*, 1987(Fall): 33-50.
6. Ciborra, C., Ed. *Groupware & teamwork: Invisible aid or technical hindrance?* 1996, Wiley: Chichester.

7. Ciborra, C., The platform organization: Recombining strategies, structures, and surprises. *Organization Science*, 1996. 7(2): 103-118.

8. Drucker, P., The coming of the new organization. *Harvard Business Review*, 1988. 66(Jan-Feb): 35-53.

9. Dyson, E., *Why groupware is gaining ground*, in Datamation. March 1, 1990. 52-56.

10. Eccles, R.G. and Crane, D.B., Managing through networks in investment banking. *California Management Review*, 1987. 30: 176-195.

11. Glaser, B. and Strauss, A., *The discovery of grounded theory*. 1967, Chicago: Aldine Publishing Co.

12. Haley, B. and Watson, H.J., Using Lotus Notes in EISs. *Information Systems Management*, 1996. 13(1): 38-44.

13. Heath, C. and Luff, P. Collaborative activity and technological design: task coordination in London Underground control rooms. in *ECSCW'91, The Second European Conference on Computer-Supported Cooperative Work*. 1991: Kluwer: 65-80.

14. Heydebrand, W.V., New organizational forms. *Work and Occupations*, 1989. 16(3): 323-357.

15. Hummingbird, *The Intranet: Implementation of Internet and Web technologies in organizational information systems*. 1996, Hummingbird Communications Ltd.

16. Karsten, H., Converging Paths to Notes: In Search for Computer-based Information Systems in a Networked Company. *Information Technology and People*, 1995. 8(1): 7-34.

17. Karsten, H., Relationship between organizational form and organizational memory: An investigation in a professional service organization. *Journal of Organizational Computing and Electronic Commerce, Special Issue on Organizational Memory Systems*, forthcoming.

18. Kling, R., Cooperation, coordination and control in computer-supported work. *Communications of the ACM*, 1991. 34(12): 83-88.

19. Mambrey, P. and Robinson, M. Understanding the role of documents in a hierarchical flow of work. in *GROUP'97: International ACM SIGGROUP Conference on Supporting Group Work: The Integration Challenge*. 1997. Phoenix, Arizona, USA: ACM: 119-127.

20. Marshak, D.S., The Notes phenomenon: the industry reacts to Lotus Notes. *Office Computing Report*, 1992. 15(12): 3-24.

21. Miles, R. and Snow, C., Organizations: New concepts for new forms. *California Management Review*, 1986. 28: 62-73.

22. Mills, Q., *Rebirth of the Corporation*. 1991, New York: Wiley.

23. Ngwenyama, O., *Groupware, social action and organizational emergence: On the process dynamics of computer mediated distributed work*. 1997. Working paper. Virginia Commonwealth University: Richmond, VA, USA.

24. OECD, *Developments in Individual Countries: Australia, Austria, Belgium, Denmark, Finland*, in OECD Economic Outlook. 1992. 88.

25. Orlikowski, W.J., Learning from Notes: Organizational issues in groupware implementation. *The Information Society*, 1993. 9(3): 237-250.

26. Orlikowski, W.J., Improvising organization and transformation over time: A situated change perspective. *Information Systems Research*, 1996. 7(1).

27. Ostroff, F. and Smith, D., The horizontal organization. *McKinsey Quarterly*, 1992(1): 148-168.

28. Ouellette, T., *Some consultancies don't do as they say*, Computerworld. 1996. 30(23): 75.

29. Pettigrew, A.M., Context and action in the transformation of the firm. *Journal of Management Studies*, 1987. 24(6): 649-670.

30. Pettigrew, A.M., Longitudinal field research on change: theory and practice. *Organization Science*, 1990. 1(3): 267-292.

31. Press, L., Emerging dynabase tools. *Communications of the ACM*, 1994. 3(3): 11-13.

32. Quinn, J., *The Intelligent Enterprise*. 1992, New York: Free Press.

33. Ruhleder, K., Reconstructing artifacts, reconstructing work: from textual edition to on-line databank. *Science, Technology and Human Values*, 1995. 20: 39-64.

34. Ruhleder, K., Jordan, B., and Elmes, M.B. Wiring the "new organization": Integrating collaborative technologies and team-based work. in *Academy of Management Annual Conference*. 1996

35. Sproull, L. and Kiesler, S., *Connections: New ways of working in the networked organization*. 1991, Cambridge, MA, USA: MIT Press.

36. Star, S.L. and Ruhleder, K., Steps toward an ecology of infrastructure: design and access for large information spaces. *Information Systems Research*, 1996. 7(1): 111-134.

37. Suchman, L. Centers of coordination: A case and some themes. in *NATO Advanced Research Workshop on Discourse, Tools and Reasoning*. 1993. Lucca, Italy

38. Van de Ven, A.H. and Poole, M.S., Methods for studying innovation development in the Minnesota Innovation Research Program. *Organization Science*, 1990. 1: 313-335.

39. Vandenbosch, B. and Ginzberg, M., Lotus Notes and collaboration: Le plus ca change... *Journal of Management Information Systems*, 1997. 13(3): 65-81.

40. Zuboff, S., *In the age of the smart machine*. 1988, New York: Basic Books.

Considering an Organization's Memory

Mark S. Ackerman
Information and Computer Science
University of California, Irvine
Irvine, CA 92697 USA
ackerman@ics.uci.edu
http://www.ics.uci.edu/CORPS/ackerman.html

Christine Halverson
IBM, T.J. Watson Research Center
P.O. Box 704
Yorktown Heights, NY 10598 USA
+1 914 784 7751
krys@watson.ibm.com

ABSTRACT
The term *organizational memory* is due for an overhaul. Memory appears to be everywhere in organizations; yet, the term has been limited to a few uses. In this paper we examine what memory in an organization really is. Based on an ethnographic study of a telephone hotline group, this paper presents a micro-level analysis of a hotline call, the work activity surrounding the call, and the memory used in the work activity. We do this analysis from the viewpoint of distributed cognition theory, finding it fruitful for an understanding of an organization's memory.

Keywords
Organizational memory, knowledge management, collective memory, group memory, information sharing, distributed cognition, CSCW, computer-supported cooperative work

INTRODUCTION
The term *organizational memory* has been overworked and confused. Burdened with the requirement to reuse experience, the term organizational memory obscures and ignores critical functions of the organization's memory. Instead, only some forms of memory have been considered. Unfortunately, while these forms have been most visible, they are also the most likely to be corrupted by the extension of the metaphor from cognitive science's physical-symbol-system model (also called the information processing model) to social groupings.

In this paper we wish to address this failure. We are therefore primarily interested in exploring where memory exists within an organizational setting, rather than focusing on particular memory augmentations. To do this we present a micro-level analysis of a domain that we find to be overflowing with organizational memory -- a telephone helpline for personnel issues. We take an ethnographic based approach for data collection and base our analysis in distributed cognition theory [9, 13, 17].

The paper begins with a brief overview of the organizational memory literature. We follow this with a description of the field site and data collection. Before beginning the detailed analysis, the next section provides a brief overview of distributed cognition theory. This is followed with a detailed analysis of a hotline call, progressively describing the call, the work activity surrounding the call, and the memory used in the work activity. The paper concludes with a discussion of the implications for organizational memory research.

EXAMINING MEMORY IN AN ORGANIZATION
Organizational memory, as a literature, has been rife with varying, and occasionally competing, definitions and elaborations. Little of the literature rests on empirical examinations of organizational memory within a context of use. Walsh and Ungson, in their review article [22], note that:

> Despite the general use of the term organizational memory, it is not clear that we have understood the concept or its implications for the management of organizations. To date, a myriad of unexamined conjectures has defined a concept that has even served as a basis for prescriptive management advice. (pp. 84-85)

Indeed, the need for systematic work to examine organizational memory is even more pressing than for many other organizational concepts. Organizational memory as a concept, especially at a grand level, has a number of theoretical problems. For example, an organization is hardly a single, unified entity, as the metaphor implies. An organization's memory must be socially constructed, maintained, and directed.

Generally, papers theorizing about organizational memory often theorize at a very grand scale, not relying on empirical data. Walsh and Ungson do distinguish a number of general components of organizational memory. They include people, archives, organizational procedures, organizational structures, and culture. (We assume here that their omission of internal archives, such as computer data-

CSCW 98 Seattle Washington USA

bases and paper files, was an oversight.) Walsh and Ungson's paper is not empirical, and does not cite any empirical studies.

Other theoretical studies also lack an empirical base. Huber [11] argues that support for organizational learning and memory would be useful, but does not distinguish clearly what concretely constitutes organizational memory. Stein and Zwass [21], while acknowledging the need for empirical studies, nonetheless rely on an information-processing model of the organization, again at a very grand scale. Smith [19] uses a similar model.

Most studies of organization memory have largely focused on the technology systems designed to replace human and paper-based memory systems. While many of these studies (e.g., [1], [15], [5]) have examined memory systems in use, the studies have nonetheless been limited. They often rely on narrow definitions of organizational memory or organizational tasks, and more importantly, they have been limited to particular, usually prototype, systems in use.

This paper does not argue for abandoning or ignoring organizational memory as a concept. Despite the conceptual problems, there is something arresting about the idea or metaphor of organizational memory, as Bannon and Kuutti state:

> ...that such a concept is appealed to across a wide range of studies, even if its definition is disputed, is testimony to the fact that even if people cannot agree on what exactly the term means, there must be some set of issues that can be subsumed under its umbrella that people feel are important and worth discussing. ([4], pp. 156-157)

Instead, as we have above, this paper argues for resting an analysis of organizational memory on an empirically derived analysis. It is important that this analysis result from a study within an organizational field setting; that is, within a context of everyday use. As Bannon and Kuutti go on:

> What is surprising is that there has been little focus among the various disciplinary groups concerned with organizational memory on the details of how organizations actually develop and use organizational memories.... ([4], p. 164)

Indeed, one might argue that system construction must be founded upon empirically determined insights about organizational memory – instead of just building blindly.

This study, then, is an empirical examination of memory in an organizational setting. Because of the state of the literature, and the circumstances of the setting, we believe that a descriptive examination that allows both a micro-scale analysis alongside a more comprehensive overview will be most useful. We have necessarily restricted our examination to a very small scale of operation in order to more clearly explore the nature of organizational memory, and we used distributed cognition theory as a theoretical framework that is useful for examining small-scale social activities and arrangements.

SETTING AND DATA COLLECTION

The following analysis is based on field observations of a telephone hotline group (here called HLG) at a well-established company, CyberCorp, headquartered in Silicon Valley. The study took place over a period of 18 months, and included a variety of data collection methods including direct observation, video, semi-structured interviews, and social network analyses. Originally, the field study was concerned with the design and use of an organizational memory system and HLG was merely the user group. However, HLG was noticeably interesting in its own right, and the study quickly turned to an examination of HLG itself.

HLG specializes in answering human resource questions, primarily about benefits and personnel policies for the company's thousands of employees. Here we describe and analyze one of the calls captured on video. This call involves Joan[1], one of the hotline representatives. Joan is a full-time agent. She had been at CyberCorp for five years and at HLG for one year.

Joan, like all of the agents, works in a cubicle that is open to a central corridor (figure 1). Like many control room settings (e.g., [18]), the cubicles are close enough to easily hear the activities of other agents. Her chair, like the other agents, faces away from the corridor between the cubicles and towards the windows.

Joan faces two monitors, where she uses a number of software packages. The telephone to the right of her monitors is another computational system that plays a role in Joan's

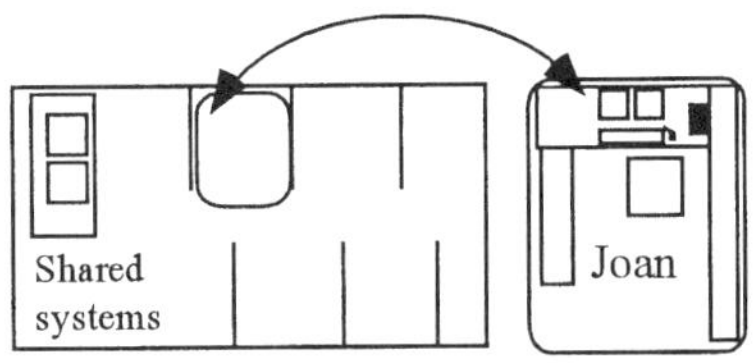

Figure 1: Joan's workplace. The left-hand portion shows how the cubicles are related to each other, as well as the shared terminals. The right is a larger picture of Joan's office.

work. These computational systems and software will be discussed at length below.

HLG, and telephone hotlines in general, are good places to study memory in an organization, because their operation is so information intensive. HLG agents must start forming their answer within 45 to 60 seconds after the start of the call, while simultaneously listening to the caller's elaborations and information. Many answers came directly from the hotline member's memory; hotline questions tend to be repetitive. Yet, there is also a great need for external memory sources: Facts must be double-checked, new

[1] All participants and their individual attributes have been disguised for publication.

questions arise, some questions recur only sporadically or seasonally, while some answers become obsolete with new conditions.

We believe that the distributed cognition framework [6, 9, 10, 13, 17] provides several advantages for studying phenomena of this kind. The next section provides a brief overview of distributed cognition theory and its utility for analyzing organizational memory.

DISTRIBUTED COGNITION

Given the acknowledged range of components which comprise organizational memory [22], it would be useful to have a theoretical framework that allows us to examine how all those components work in concert. Distributed cognition provides both the framework and the theoretical language to analyze this system.

First of all, distributed cognition theory frames the problem in terms of examining a functional system as a cognitive system. The first task in a distributed cognition analysis is to identify how a functional system works, good and bad [17]. Functional operation is decomposed into smaller units of analysis that make sense with respect to the particular system. In some cases this may be a straightforward task decomposition, while other systems may call for a more event driven segmentation. Once this smaller unit is observed and detailed with respect to a particular task, distributed cognition provides a theoretical language to analyze how that function is achieved. This language addresses artifacts, human actors, and organizational and social structures on an equal theoretical footing. With this we can begin to understand how technologies currently fit a system's operation. By extension we can speculate about how changes in technologies might affect future operations. We believe that looking at the phenomena of organizational memory is well supported by taking this essentially cognitive view of a system, and in our interpretation, giving it a certain social twist.

What distributed cognition shares with other cognitive models is an identification of the informational input entering a system. Whether a computational or cognitive system, we want to know how information is represented and how these representations are transformed, combined and propagated through that system in order to produce the system's observable behavior. (See figure 2.)

Once the function of a system has been analyzed into its component representational states and processes, the analyst uses that information to reconstruct a story of the functioning of the system. This allows an analysis with respect to the context of use within an organization. For example, our study of HLG shows a plethora of *information* is both available and necessary. In some cases the required information is easily accessible, while in others it must be located or uncovered. In any case, information must be monitored, managed, and communicated in order to do the job. In the next section we try to give the sense of how such a description is built out of the more detailed

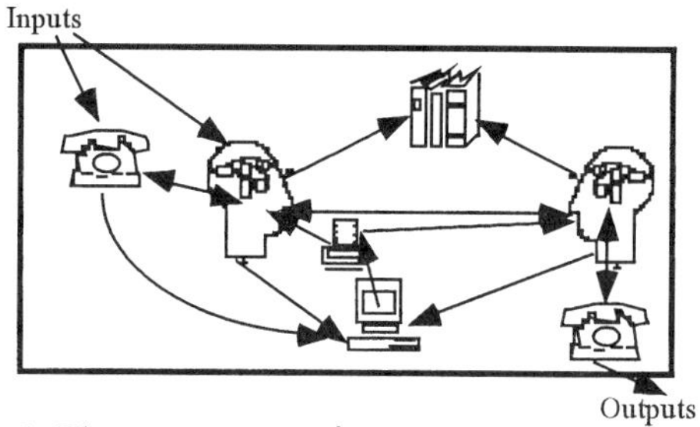

Figure 2. The components in the system are analyzed as media in a particular state that is interpreted by some agent. The heavy lines between the components represent the *processes* that progress the mapping.

analysis. Then in the remainder of the paper we will discuss the analysis at the higher level.

Applying distributed cognition to HLG

A functional human system such as HLG has the property that many of the system properties are directly observable. We can bound the portion of the system to be analyzed, based on the observed function. Within this unit we expose information about the task, its resources and organization.

In the case of HLG, the cognitive system's purpose is to answer or solve the caller's problem. The caller can be seen as the input to this system, and her question is a representational state traveling via the material media of the phone to one of the HLG agents. For each call the unit of consideration may vary. Figure 3 shows how we might initially *bound* the system to include the caller, Joan, the telephone, and other materials (or *resources*) available to Joan.

While her use of the telephone is an indicator of where the process is occurring, it does not completely define the limits of the task. In general, the functional system is observed to be bounded by physical, resource, and temporal limits.

Jumping back to a higher level, an examination of Joan's cubicle shows there are many other available resources. Depending on the type of query Joan can use a variety of on-line resources. In addition there are a myriad of yellow post-it notes stuck to every possible surface, and as our call

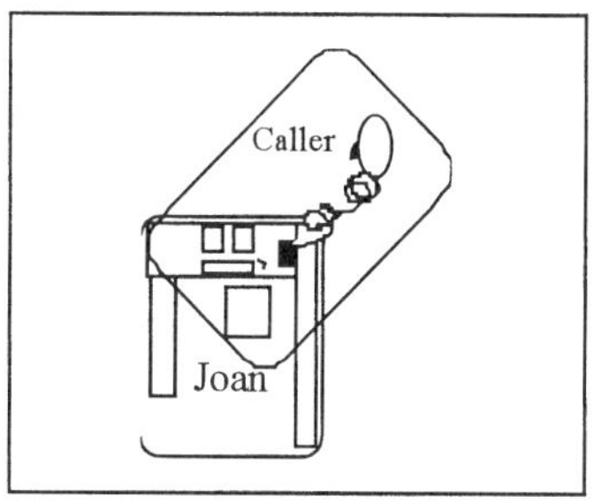

Figure 3. The unit of analysis for a particular call can be roughly bounded based on the trajectory identified by the telephone as a mediating device between Joan and the caller.

example shows, the resources of other people should not be ignored. In addition, her employee benefits book, this day, lies atop assorted papers on her right "shelf." Pages of quickly required information, such as telephone numbers, are tacked to her left wall, and neatly stacked project files, color coded, for her spare moments are on the left "shelf."

Delving further we can observe much of the system processing as it involves transitions between humans and artifacts. We are able to record the representational state, the material media on which it is instantiated, as well as the processes that transform it. An advantage of the distributed cognition framework, to be drawn upon below, is its commitment to a unit of analysis defined in relation to the complex phenomena being observed. As Hutchins shows in *Cognition in the Wild* (1995), the information processing in a navigation team varies with the context and circumstances. Solo watch standing involves the interaction of one individual with various artifacts, structured via well-established procedures and routines. In contrast, the high tempo activity of entering a harbor requires the effort of several people, again in coordination with specialized tools and with each other. While the overall "intelligent behavior" exhibited by the system is the same, the means change.

In the case of HLG, our analysis shows how the work of the system is organized and reorganized to meet changing needs. An important part of understanding this is knowing all the possible resources and following their use through a variety of situations.

Our analysis shows the agent's similarity and differences with respect to other agents. Some are more dependent on the employee handbook, notebooks of frequently needed information, and other collections of materials. HLG members used a variety of information systems, including multiple databases and electronic documents. They also consulted a number of paper documents, manuals, post-it notes, telephone lists, scribbled messages, and the like. Very critically, they also used one another as information sources, bridging social and cognitive worlds, as well as technical and domain understanding. We adopted Hutchins' distributed cognition framework precisely because it provides a mechanism that can be used to bridge these worlds.

CORRECTING A DATABASE ENTRY

Below is a transcript from videotape of an HLG call. A walkthrough of this call will use distributed cognition to unpack the working of organizational memory. We reproduce and discuss the beginning of this call at length; later we will summarize sections of the call to be more concise. Because of privacy reasons, only one side of the exchange was taped.

Answering the Phone

The first four turns of the call are routine, but even so they demonstrate critical aspects of the organization's memory. The call begins with Joan's standard opening. Turn 1 consists of Joan greeting the caller, and acknowledging that the caller was forced to hold for some period of time. While the telephone system automatically routed a call to her as soon as she finished the previous call, the caller was forced to wait for an available agent. Turn 2 acknowledges the caller's request. In this case an employee has called because a benefits provider does not show her as receiving their benefit. This benefits provider, Eye and Vision Associates (EVA), will not process the employee's claim (or rather, allow the employee to purchase eyeglasses at a discount) until this is corrected.

1	HR Helpline. This is Joan. Thanks for holding. (Joan nods slowly to herself.)
2	You called EVA directly? I'll find out what our system shows for you. Oh I see. Oh, so right, right...yeah.... (Encouragingly) Let me do this. (In an aside tone) The system is being very slow, so it'll take a second to get a new record up for you.

The employee says that she called EVA directly and that EVA did not show her as having coverage. Joan must then check whether the employee, Michelle, actually showed coverage within the CARL database: This database, built from payroll data, shows the employee benefits for each employee in CyberCorp.

At the end of turn 2, Joan starts a new call-tracking record in the CAT (CAll Tracking) system for the new call, closing out the old one that she had not quite finished. Turn 3 is more complex, as Joan does several things simultaneously. She asks for the relevant information, namely the caller's employee number. Joan has now opened a new CAT record for the call and checked the employee phone list for the caller. She double-checks the employee's social security number for later use with the CARL database. As she is confirming the employee information with the caller, Michelle, she is also typing the information into the call-tracking record. She also writes Michelle's social security number on a piece of scrap paper, because she must go to the CARL terminal to look up the employee data. When she is finished obtaining and double-checking this information, she asks Michelle to hold, knowing that the next step will take a minute or two.

3	I'm sorry. Oh what a shame. Well you know, these funny things. (More officially) What is your employee number?
4	Okay, what I'm going to do is, I'm going to check the, uh, the CARL. Is this Michelle? Let me check your social security number is the one I have, 1-8-2-4-zero-7-3-5-5. Okay, what I'm going to do is to check the system and find out what your coverage is, and if it's not showing...coverage on CARL, uh, then we'll, hmm, we'll have to do something else, okay? Hold just a second, Michelle

At the end of turn 4, Joan goes to the CARL terminal, which is physically in another location behind her cubicle. (There are separate terminals for two different employee databases, and part of Joan's routine is selecting the correct database.) She types, looking at the piece of scrap paper, and pulls up the appropriate record. This takes 23 seconds. After obtaining the data, she visibly pauses and stares abstractedly at the ceiling.

Many Small Memories

We will proceed with the rest of the call below, but even the first four turns show many cognitive, social, and institutional arrangements in the organization's memory. In her execution Joan uses not one monolithic memory, as many technocentric models would have it. Instead, she uses many small memories.

To recap, the call was triggered by the telephone system's short-term memory of the group's activity. The system state shows that Joan's station is free, and the call falls to her. Hearing the caller's information, Joan uses her own short-term memory as she then types that information into the CAT record. (For convenience, other uses of Joan's short-term memory are omitted here.)

Joan then takes the information in CAT and reproduces it onto a piece of paper, creating a mobile form of memory. She appears not trust to her own memory, but resorts to something that can help her reconstruct the circumstances of the call. She then types the information from the paper into the CARL system. CARL is a typical type of organizational memory, a corporate database with employee records. Joan places the CARL output onto the paper again.

Within just these three turns, Joan has used three separate software systems (CAT, the employee phone list, and CARL), the telephone system, and scratch paper, all of which maintain representational state for Joan, the group, or both. Figure 4 below graphically displays the order of processing of those memories; it consists largely of transferring information from memory to memory in order to answer the query. Within what is so far a very structured process, Joan's cognitive work consists largely in knowing which memories to trigger. Little processing is done on the actual information.

Although we present the flow of representations in Figure 4 as an individual process, there are actually multiple group and organizational processes occurring. In distributed cognition theory, expanding the boundaries of the analysis is required as we enlarge the relevant task in order to understand a memory's use in its full organizational context. This will become clearer at the end of the call, when Joan indexes the call-tracking record and changes the telephone state, but at this point, Joan is already embedded within these processes. For example, Joan uses CAT, the call-tracking system, seemingly as a short-term memory aid. Its major use, however, is to provide other agents with the ability to reconstruct the history of a caller's problem. In addition to maintaining a history of calls for the group, the CAT program also creates transformed, longer-term memory in the form of statistics, based on the indexing done by the agent (later) during her wrap-up period. These statistics are used by management to govern the group's future behavior, as has been typical in organizations since the late nineteenth century [23, 24]. The telephone system, in addition to being a primitive form of group memory that coordinates and paces the HLG agents' activities, also creates summary statistics for the group and the organization as a whole.

To recap, even within these four turns, Joan uses many discrete memories. Sometimes the memory used is individual and private; sometimes it is group and public. But all of these memories must be used together seamlessly (or nearly so) to create an organizational product (the product being not only the solution to the call but all of the institutional arrangements surrounding it). The density and connectedness of memories used as resources in this environment are remarkable.

The call, of course, continues past Joan's finding the employee's record. Next Joan must determine what to do with the facts she has uncovered.

Handling an Exception

As mentioned, Joan pulled up Michelle's record within the CARL database. After this, Joan visibly paused and stared at the ceiling. As will be seen below, Michelle should have EVA coverage according to her CARL record; yet, EVA shows no such coverage. Presumably, Joan is trying to figure out what to do about this unusual discrepancy.

After five seconds, she begins a conversation with one of the senior telephone agents who had been wrapping up her call. In turns 5 through 15, Joan asks the senior agent, Nichole, how to proceed.

Joan appears in turns 5 through 15 to be trying to under-

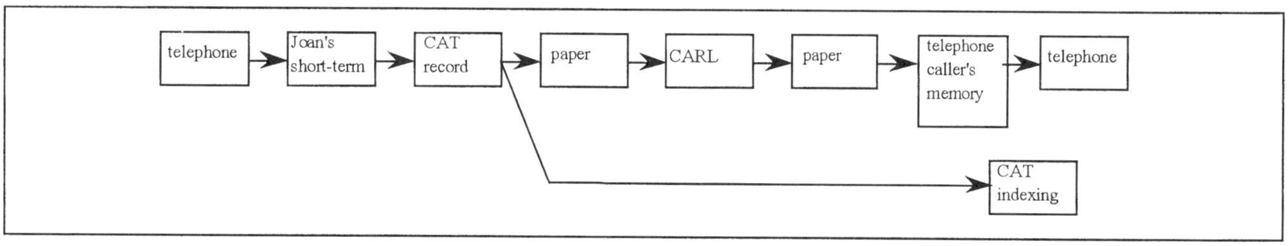

Figure 4. The flow of representational states in the first 4 turns of Joan's call.

stand whether to escalate the problem to the benefits group. Organizationally, the HRG is dependent on other groups to handle more complicated or complex situations; these are called *escalations*. The senior agent confirms that she should escalate, and tells her what information is necessary to properly create the escalation. (In the following, the angle brackets <> indicate a section of the tape that was indistinct. The slashes \ / and / \ indicate overlapping conversational areas on the tape; a = sign indicates that there was no appreciable pause between the two words.)

5	Joan	Nikki, can I get your...
6	Nichole	Uh, huh. (Nichole nods her head and walks towards Joan.)
7	Joan	If this employee, uh, called EVA and they say they show no coverage for her, but she's showing, showing active on CARL. She's has confirmed no problems, but what should I do as far as the referral?
8	Nichole	Call, call them [EVA] yourself and find out what they want.
9	Joan	Okay.
10	Nichole	Then escalate it to the <Benefits>. EVA is asking for this information on this (indistinguishable). (Official tone, as though acting out a scenario) We show it as having such-and-such. That way /we\
11	Joan	\Okay./ Okay, /I\
12	Nichole	\can/ tell <them>... what EVA is looking for.
13	Joan	I can tell the employee it's showing there's not, shouldn't be a problem, so=
14	Nichole	=we're trying to fix it.
15	Joan	I'm trying to get a <feel> for it. Thanks, Nik.

Nichole tells Joan, then, to escalate the problem to the Benefits group and to obtain from EVA what they need to resolve the problem. Joan walks away from Nichole at the end of this interaction, and returns to her seat.

Organizing the Work and Organizational Boundaries

We showed earlier how Joan's processing was dependent on many small memories, including her own. However, solving a problem may not be dependent solely on an individual's cognition and the artifacts (memory or otherwise) within the environment. These turns show how Joan's work is socially organized as well as the role of memory in that organizing.

Unlike ship navigation [12, 13] or air traffic control [7-9] with their standard operating procedures, HLG has fewer pre-specified routines. Yet, as Pentland [16] observed in his study of a software hotline and as Katzenberg et al. [14] observed in hospital situations, the HLG group has developed a set of informal routines that can be combined flexibly to solve a large range of problems. Indeed, the HLG manager repeatedly mentioned during the study that he was trying to balance flexible diagnosis and service with transaction efficiency. There were numerous minor task reallocations during the study period as the group attempted to juggle the two demands and build their repertoire of small routines.

In this case, Joan has a routine to uncover a discrepancy between what an employee wishes to have for benefits and what he or she currently has – she looks it up. Joan can then explain that discrepancy as well as potential solutions to the employee. The discrepancy, however, between the internal CyberCorp databases and the benefit provider's database is not routine. Joan later demarked the situation as neither usual nor unusual, and as such, one without a given routine.

Instead, Joan relies on Nichole. Nichole was considered the "expert" on more obscure situations; HLG agents would often pose difficult questions to Nichole. Like Hutchins' Navy navigation crew, the HLG is organized such that the more senior agents have served in all simpler positions. (The HLG roles are less differentiated than are those for shipboard navigation, but the coverage of experts' knowledge over novices' tasks is the same.) In addition, Joan liked asking questions of other agents as a way of obtaining needed information, so this interaction suited her information seeking style. The intent of many organizational memory systems would be to replace Nichole but without losing the supposedly reusable information. Instead, many exceptions may be better serviced by task experts; this exchange is extremely short. We will discuss this trade-off space further below.

The production is divided not only among group members but among groups as well. Relaxing the boundaries of the task shows Joan's work is also connected organizationally across other group's processes. There are two larger tasks that are invoked in these turns.

First, Joan and HLG are dependent on another organizational group to maintain the database used to verify an employee's benefits. Considering the call more broadly demonstrates the important set of organizing arrangements required to imbue and inscribe the memory with authenticity and veracity [3]. The HLG agent relies on the payroll group for the correctness of the information, when they create and maintain an employee record, which serves as a boundary object [20]. Joan knows none of the details of the record's creation or maintenance; almost all of the context has been lost. She does not know whether there are problems with the employee's employment or whether there are extenuating circumstances. Indeed, it is assumed that the CARL database is more authoritatively correct than the employee database (maintained by the accounting department), since CARL is more authoritative for deducted benefits.

In addition, escalations are problematic organizationally because there is a fine line between taking action inappropriately or incorrectly and between wasting the other group's time. In fact, there was a fair amount of tension between the Benefits group and HLG. HLG felt that Benefits looked down on them for not knowing the Human Resources (HR) subject area sufficiently, and HLG agents wished to be regarded as professionals. Indeed, HLG perceived themselves as the future of the HR profession, as did the CyberCorp management. But this was a future unwanted by most of Benefits, since hotline work was perceived by the Benefits professionals as leading to HR deskilling in CyberCorp. Therefore, inappropriate escalations sometimes furthered political tensions. Since escalations were always to some extent problematic, the procedures around them often shifted during the study, thus the need for the question to Nichole.

Playing a Hunch

In the next segment of the call, Joan returns to her chair, reconnects her telephone headset, and begins to speak with Michelle again. Procedurally, all Joan must do is to tell Michelle that she will call EVA and escalate the problem. However, this is derailed by a side discussion over Michelle's incorrect telephone number.

16	Michelle, when you spoke with the folks at EVA, what, what is it that they said to you?
17	Okay, because you do in mine. ...So I don't know what the situation is.
	[Segment of the call deleted; Joan is dealing with Michelle's phone number.]

In the omitted portion of the transcript, Michelle reports that she cannot seem to correct her telephone number in the employee phone list, even though she has tried many times. She discusses this at some length with Joan, asking her to change it. At first analysis, the incorrect telephone number appeared to be extraneous to this call, but it is an interesting side conversation. The employee, having found someone to correct her employee records, now asks Joan to correct her telephone number in all CyberCorp databases. We believe that to Michelle, it appears that she has found the person that is in charge of correcting the appropriate memory, whether it is her telephone number or her benefits status. Joan cannot, because the responsibility for changing something so seemingly mundane as a telephone number lies with another group. In the actual production, there are distinct organizational boundaries to the memories. To the organizational member, however, these boundaries are arbitrary and frustrating.

Joan continues with her explanation of the escalating process (as it needs to be seen by the employee). However, this is derailed several times by a side discussion about obtaining an electronic form for EVA. This side discussion triggers off a recollection and hunch in Joan.

24	Okay, what we'll do is, I'm going to call EVA (voice rising in question tone) directly and find out what the situation is, and, uh, it's possible they might need some other information that the benefits department can provide for them, but either way, you'll get a call back from somebody by the end of the day tomorrow and let you know what the status is, uh, go ahead...
25	Oh. (surprised) I can request a form for you, but the, the thing is if I request the form and for some reason they don't have coverage for you they're going to reject it. So what I'll do is I'll do two things. Uh, EVA, did you, did you call the 800 number? Did you call, did the hotline direct you to that number?
26	Right
27	Oh, I see. Well, you know what? I think I remember this happening once before, Michelle, and since my system showed that, that the employee that called was covered, they said, okay, I'll put that in the system and we'll go ahead and send the form out ... so who knows? Did...
	[Segment of the call deleted; Joan and Michelle discuss Michelle's address for the EVA form.]

Finally, Joan ends the call with the employee. Interestingly, Joan has formulated a plan of action that attempts to solve the problem, rather than following Nichole's advice literally. In this, she uses Nichole's statements as advice to formulate her own activity, rather than a requirement.

At the end of her conversation with the employee, Joan turns to the camera and explains the call. In the time that it takes Joan to explain the situation, she pulls up EVA's telephone number (using a computerized rolodex program) and dials the call. In fact, she appears to end her explanation when the call is connected. In the final section of the call, Joan convinces the EVA agent that Michelle is a CyberCorp employee and that she should have EVA benefits. (This has been compressed for space reasons.)

	You don't [show her on your system]? No. Is it, is it possible for me to, to uh, verify she's on our (rising, questioning) system? And you can go ahead and send the form to her? Excellent. I have an address (rising, questioning), if that would help you?

After finishing her call with the EVA agent, Joan wraps up by indexing the call in the CAT system and then signaling to the phone system that she is ready for a new call.

At the end of the call, one might surmise that Joan now has a new routine, calling EVA directly and getting an employee her benefits. She could assume that this kind of transaction is routine, since the EVA agent treats it as relatively straightforward. However, as Joan says: "I think I remember this happening once before." There is no reason to suppose that this will not be recreated again from a very hazy human memory.

We next turn to a discussion of the call as a whole and its implications for organizational memory.

CONTEXT VS. CONTEXTUALIZING

The term "context" is often used as a catchall to denote the wealth of organizational and cultural knowledge one effortlessly brings to bear in a given situation. Joan shows in this call that she has knowledge of how her world works and that this knowledge is necessary for getting her work done. Within the call, she displays an understanding of her limitations, the range of knowledge within HLG, Nichole's role, and the complex relationship of HLG to Benefits and to EVA.

If one were primarily interested in implementing a technocentric view of organizational memory or knowledge management, with their immediate emphasis on capture and reuse, one might assume that all Joan needs is more information, whether in a computer system or on paper. Instead, the story is more complex. We see Joan moving seamlessly through this real setting with its many process states, using the memories and other artifacts that she judges to be critical to finishing her task. To understand her use of memory resources in accomplishing this, however, it will be important to tease apart the concurrent use of contextualization, decontextualization, and recontextualization in obtaining a solution to the situation.

The Missing Bark

The need for context, and Joan's contextualization of the environment, is revealed in the order and access of various resources. As with Sherlock Holmes' famous hound, the interesting thing about this call is all of the things that did not happen. Joan did not stumble or falter, searching for her next step. She needed help in the face of a breakdown, but she carefully and quickly determined a resolution. In her selections, she showed an enormous understanding of her environment and the role of artifacts and people within it.

On the other hand, Joan did not use paper or on-line documents to formulate her plan of action for this situation. The key was not that detail was missing from the on-line sources. If this were so, the solution would be indeed to add even more information on-line. To the contrary, the key to Joan's lack of use is the overwhelming amount of detail available. Since an HLG agent must have an answer within 45-60 seconds, it is impossible to sift through megabytes of information. A search with terms "EVA" or "enrollment" might turn up dozens of documents. Even if the retrieval is ranked (i.e., the search engine evaluates the likelihood of fit), the agent does not have the time to consider the retrieved materials.

The information use that does occur is situated. Joan does not view all sources equally. She went to Nichole, rather than to another agent. She avoided one database for another. She relied on her own memory. Like the other agents, Joan considers some sources as authoritative. Sources have different costs, psychological or financial, associated with their access. She selects and chooses resources in her environment, according to her immediate understanding of the situation.

Memories as Boundary Objects

In a distributed cognition view, an organization's memory consists of many states, instantiated by people and artifacts, all within a single system allowing the participants to get their work done. To solve Michelle's problem, the process apparently is losing contextual information in many places – from payroll to HLG, from Nichole to Joan, from HLG to Benefits, from Joan to Michelle (in explaining the process), from Joan to the EVA representative, and finally from Joan to the CAT record.

Some of these differentiations correspond to boundaries with respect to the propagation of representational state and its re-interpretation. These boundaries often correspond with organizational divisions. Three of the four individuals involved in the call are all employees of CyberCorp. However, their different roles imply different meanings for the same representations. For the caller Michelle, Joan is the expert at HLG who will solve her problem. Pushing the notion of social boundaries to its extreme, even though Joan and Nichole are in the same department, Nichole's acknowledged expertise creates a boundary, and thus different contextualizations between her and Joan. A comparison of these boundaries with the propagation of representations through the processing of the call illustrates how the cognition involved (i.e., the use of memory) is constrained by social arrangements.

As representational state propagates across individuals, inter-organizational, and intra-organizational boundaries, it must necessarily lose some of its context. As Star [20] points out, boundary objects in an organization work because they necessarily contain sufficient detail to be understandable by both parties, but at the same time, neither party must understand the full context of use by the other. As boundary objects, artifacts and other potential resources are given to other people or in this case, stored for later use by others. This requires the information to be decontextualized. Otherwise, the secondary users will drown in unnecessary, unhelpful, or conflicting data. (One may also wish to hide or obscure some institutional and social arrangements from the other group.) As an example, the payroll records are necessarily standardized and stripped of much informational content before they can be given to groups such as HLG. Decontextualization, and perhaps commodification, must be expected by those who will try to use the memory.

To reuse a memory, the user must then recontextualize that information. The information, if not supplied by the same individual, must be reunderstood for the user's current purposes. Elsewhere we have written about the recontextualization problem in organizational memory systems [2], but the call shows that a difficulty, or even outright inability, in recontextualization, would make the memory useless or nearly so. For example, reused information must be imbued with attributes of veracity, authenticity, and even status [3]; it must be provided with everyday organizational context.

Joan understands that the CARL database record is authoritative; she knows enough of its meaning within HLG's context. Joan also knows she can ignore Nichole's advice, based on her understanding of HLG, Benefits, and EVA. Rather than adopt Nichole's advice – find out what EVA wants and then escalate – Joan proceeds to convince EVA herself that Michelle is an employee.

The Complexity of Reuse

Obviously reuse is possible. Joan's call showed many memories reused by Joan, other members of the group, and the organization as a whole. We have also shown that these memories can be rearranged and reused in different ways, depending on the production that is required.

The above sections, however, cautioned that the informational requirements for reuse are not trivial. For reuse, decontextualized information must be recontextualized sufficiently by the secondary user, according to his or her purposes. This is most likely to be done within a familiar process with little time lapse [2]. In distributed cognition terms, the cost of reuse is most likely to be borne where the traffic or the processing utility is highest – within heavily used or high payoff processes.

The problem with reuse, then, is the coexisting requirement for contextualization, decontextualization and recontextualization. To use information as a memory, one must remove the detail that provides context, making the information into a boundary object. However, at the same time one must consider how others will use it later as a resource in their processes; otherwise, subsequent users of the memory will not be able to properly recontextualize it.

On the other side, based on their understanding of their own situations, users of a memory must determine what contextual aspects of that memory are important and whether they have changed. This determination may be nearly impossible, given people's limited view of an organization as well as the decontextualization of the information. Users must then decide how their differing context should effect their use of the memory, and finally they must absorb the memory into their current situation. The simpler the memory, the more likely this all can occur.

CONCLUSIONS

This study has many limitations. Because of page restrictions, only a single call was presented here. The representativeness of HLG and its activities could be argued. Yet, within the limits of a single ethnographic record, we have tried to show that:

- There is no such thing as <u>an</u> organizational memory, as the metaphor attempts to invoke. We have tried to show how a supra-individual memory, using several people and many artifacts, works. This analysis also showed the utility of distributed cognition in understanding such a supra-individual memory.

This simple call and the distributed cognition analysis exposed a number of interesting aspects of this organization's memory. The procedure involved nine different memory states, and the human agent either translated among representational states or reconstructed memory states. We also showed that:

- Even this simple example was a not-so-very simple case of distributed memory. Memories were complexly distributed, interwoven, and occasionally overlaid. They were sometimes the province of the individual (e.g., Joan's scratch notes) or the group (e.g., the call-handling procedure embedded in the telephone system). But, often enough, the memory that served as individual memory also had a definition as a group and even an organizational memory.
- While knowledge management largely restricts itself to viewing organizational memory to repositories of experience "objects" that are magically reusable, we have tried to show in this paper that it is more fruitful to consider organizational memory as both object and process. Memory is both an artifact that holds its state and an artifact that is embedded in many organizational and individual processes.

  The container metaphor is easier to consider computationally, but it is extremely limited organizationally. The distributed cognition view of a network of artifacts and people, of memory and of processing, bound by social arrangements, provides a deeper and ultimately more usable understanding of organizational life. It describes how memory as representational states can be both separated from organizational actors and necessarily bound to their actions and understandings.
- There is a tension in creating new memory artifacts between seamlessness and flexibility that cannot be easily resolved. In the last stage of the call, Michelle wants her phone number changed; she does not want to hear about the organizational boundaries that prevent Joan from doing so. On the other hand, we have argued here that small memories can be most easily decontextualized and recontextualized; they will serve most flexibility and may be of the most utility.
- Finally, there are many examples in this environment

demonstrating the reuse of memory. However, information to be used as memory is valuable only when it can be contextualized, decontextualized, and recontextualized at the proper time. Moreover, the proper context to capture is dependent on how the information will be used as a memory resource in the future and the ability of the users to recontextualize the information.

Acknowledgements

This paper has benefited greatly from conversations with many people, including Ed Hutchins, Jonathan Grudin, John King, Kate Ehrlich, Tom Gruber, Tom Malone, John Quimby, Charlie Osborne, Lorne Olfman, Gerhard Fischer, John Hughes, Kari Kuutti, Leysia Palen, Yvonne Rogers, Liam Bannon, and Kjeld Schmidt. Thanks also to the participants at the 1996 HCIC, ECSCW95 organizational memory, and ECSCW97 Fringe Event workshops.

This project has been funded, in part, by grants from National Science Foundation grant (IRI-9702904), NASA (NRA-93-OSSA-09), and the UC MICRO program. The UCI research group, Dave McDonald, Jack Muramatsu, Wayne Lutters, and Keri Carpenter, also contributed to this understanding of organizational memory.

We would also like to thank Clare-Marie Karat, John Karat, Wendy Kellogg and John Vergo for their support at IBM.

References

1. Ackerman, M. S. Augmenting the Organizational Memory: A Field Study of Answer Garden. Proceedings of CSCW'94, 1994: 243-252.
2. Ackerman, M. S. Definitional and Contextual Issues in Organizational and Group Memories. Information Technology and People, 1996, 9(1): 10-24.
3. Anderson, R. and W. Sharrock. Can Organisations Afford Knowledge? Computer Supported Cooperative Work, 1993, 1(3): 123-142.
4. Bannon, L. J. and K. Kuutti. Shifting Perspectives on Organizational Memory: From Storage to Active Remembering. Proceedings of HICSS-29, 1996: 156-167.
5. Conklin, J. and M. L. Begeman. gIBIS: A Hypertext Tool for Exploratory Policy Discussion. Proceedings of CSCW '88, 1988: 140-152.
6. Flor, N. V. and E. Hutchins. Analyzing Distributed Cognition in Software Teams. In Koenemann-Belliveau, J., T. Moher and S. Robertson (ed). Empirical Studies of Programmers: Fourth Workshop. Ablex, Norwood, NJ, 1992.
7. Halverson, C. A. Analyzing a Cognitively Distributed System: a Terminal Radar Approach Control. Cognitive Science. 1992.
8. Halverson, C. A. Distributed Cognition as a Theoretical Framework for HCI. University of California, San Diego, Department of Cognitive Science, 94-03, 1994.
9. Halverson, C. A. Inside the Cognitive Workplace: New Technology and Air Traffic Control. Cognitive Science. 1995.
10. Hazlehurst, B. Computation and cognition in the cockpit. 1990.
11. Huber, G. P. A Theory of the Effects of Advanced Information Technologies on Organizational Design, Intelligence, and Decision Making. 1990, 15(1): 47-71.
12. Hutchins, E. The Technology of Team Navigation. In J. Galegher, R. K., and C. Egido (ed). Intellectual Teamwork: Social and Technical Bases of Cooperative Work. Lawrence Erlbaum Associates, Hillsdale, NJ., 1988.
13. Hutchins, E. L. Cognition in the Wild. MIT Press, Cambridge, MA., 1995.
14. Katzenberg, B., F. Pickard and J. McDermott. Computer Support for Clinical Practice: Embedding and Evolving Protocols of Care. Proceedings of CSCW'96, 1996:
15. Morrison, J. Team Memory: Information Management for Business Teams. Proceedings of HICSS-26, 1993: 122-131.
16. Pentland, B. T. Making The Right Moves: Toward a Social Grammar of Software Support Hot Lines. PhD. Thesis, MIT, 1991.
17. Rogers, Y. and J. Ellis. Distributed cognition: an alternative framework for analysing and explaining collaborative working. Journal of information technology., 1994, 9: 119-128.
18. Seifert, C. M. and E. L. Hutchins. Error as opportunity: learning in a cooperative task. Human-Computer Interaction., 1992, 7: 409-435.
19. Smith, J. B. Collective Intelligence in Computer-based Collaboration. Lawrence Erlbaum Associates, Hillsdale, NJ, 1994.
20. Star, S. L. The Structure of Ill-Structured Solutions: Boundary Objects and Heterogeneous Distributed Problem Solving. In Gasser, L. and M. Huhns (ed). Distributed Artificial Intelligence. Morgan Kaufmann, San Mateo, 1989.
21. Stein, E. W. and V. Zwass. Actualizing Organizational Memory with Information Systems. Information Systems Research, 1995, 6(2): 85-117.
22. Walsh, J. P. and G. R. Ungson. Organizational Memory. The Academy of Management Review, 1991, 16(1): 57-91.
23. Yates, J. Control through Communication: The Rise of System in American Management. John Hopkins Press, Baltimore, 1989.
24. Yates, J. For the Record: The Embodiment of Organizational Memory, 1850-1920. Business and Economic History, 1990, 19: 172-182.

Diaries at Work

Mikko Kovalainen, Mike Robinson
Department of Computer Science
University of Jyväskylä
PO Box 35, SF-40351, Jyväskylä, Finland
+358-14-606048/603095
mipeko@cs.jyu.fi, mike@cs.jyu.fi

Esa Auramäki
Solution Garden Ltd.
Ylistönmäentie 24
Fin-40500, Jyväskylä, Finland
+358 50 5498614
esa.auramaki@solutiongarden.fi

ABSTRACT

Brief critiques of organisational memory as "thing" are presented, and an alternative conceptualisation as artefact mediated process is offered. Within this frame, the paper gives an account of usage of a simple electronic artefact within a process industry: specifically an Electronic Diary on the factory floor of a large modern papermill. Analysis of 3,500 entries made in a year illustrates the multifaceted use of the Diary. These show that Diary entries constitute dialogues within and between work-shifts, and partially with other organisational levels. The dialogues share some properties — "talking out loud" and "overhearing" — with work coordination in face-to-face situations.

Keywords

Organisational memory, papermill, CSCW, overhearing, peripheral awareness

INTRODUCTION

Papermills are gigantic and complex machines, incorporating much state-of-the-art technology. As part of a larger project to provide CSCW support for factory floor workers in Process Industries [2], electronic diaries were substituted for paper diaries. One design aid was a conception of organisational memory as "artefact mediated process". The electronic Diary has been introduced on one production line, to support factory floor management of the paper production process. There is now more than a year of experience with, and daily use of the Diary. Since use is voluntary, the simple fact of 3,500 entries leads us to believe the Diary is felt to be useful to the workers. Analysis of the Diary entries indicates the main value is, as intended, as process rather than record. Specifically, the entries constitute, and are valued because they constitute a dialogue.

Comments are answered by other workers, often on other shifts. Sometimes this dialogue extends over many weeks. Some comments are not answered. In a formal or a workflow system, this would be a failing. We believe that such "hanging comments" can be analysed as an achievement.

CSCW 98 Seattle Washington USA

We will later argue that Diary entries are analogous to "talking out loud" and "overhearing" in a face-to-face context [9, 13]. This enables others to maintain a "peripheral awareness" of events and activities of others that would otherwise be invisible. From this basis they can orientate their actions within a wider context. It is of the nature of talking out loud that the talking is *unaddressed*, and does not call for specific responses — although it can evoke them. Diary entries follow this pattern, with the interesting difference that they radically extend the spatio-temporal boundaries of the overhearing.

The usefulness of the Diary on the factory floor led to an interest in it from Shift Supervisors and Departmental Managers. Access to the Diary is now extended from the original 35 factory floor workers (plus 2 managers) to more than 100 people including 13 managers. CSCW literature leads us to believe that such sharing of "dialogue" between levels, especially when sharing was not part of the original design brief, may lead to problems, and/or to changes in behaviour. Most communities of practice (e.g. police [1], medical practitioners [10], economists [8]) take care that internal notes, on-the-fly records, etc. do not pass outside the community, since this can lead to a conflict. In the papermills, Diary sharing between levels has not (yet) led to problems. This is explicable in the current situation, but there are no guarantees for the future.

A previous publication on papermills [2] noted that there were several reasons why paper diaries were not much used, and workers expressed doubts about electronic diaries. One of the reasons was the Grudin [7] principle that they would create extra work without obvious benefit. Another was doubt about who would see the entries. The main use of the paper diary was as a shift foreman's Log, and as part of the material for morning meetings. The process of dealing with "challenges" and "special situations" (papermill workers prefer not to talk about "problems") involves much intuition and divination — a "feel" for the appropriate action is a consequence of a long period of experience with *this* machine.

"The basis for the man in the paper mill is the instinct how to run the machine and it should never be forgotten. You must always use common sense. ... have your wits about you and also the ability to control the process as a whole."

[interviewee][2]

In the midst of a host of statistical reporting and monitoring devices, workers deal with complex inter-related nests of probabilities and unknowns. Writing down what might look like guesses about a situation for scrutiny by management was felt to be problematic in several ways:

"publishing" is perceived to have a risk and a price

"... something remains in permanent view: what opinions I had, what I have thought. Then you take a risk ..."

and

"You get really pissed off one night and then you write it down in the morning that this bloody thing happened again, and then you come to work in a couple of days and there it is, the thing that you wrote, at the bottom of the paper."

nor is clear what to write down

"... nobody writes self-evident things there because we have had this feeling that all of the things that we write are being read there in the office. Then they think, what the fuck is person A doing, is he suffering from dementia because he is writing down obvious things."

[all from interviewees — ibid.]

Auramäki et al.[2] then listed some design points for an electronic version of the diary. The original computer based information systems had been designed for the benefit and use of management, and were systematically deficient in supporting the *ad hoc* information needs of production workers. The systems included helpful material such as procedures, trends, cases, but were generally difficult or time consuming for crews to search. The position was taken that an application (the Diary) should be designed specifically for production workers. At the least, it would need a more appropriate structure, the ability to conduct a full text search, and support for the construction of "local categories" to support local organisation of relevant material. The idea was to meet the Grudin [7] principle that those keeping the Diary should be the ones to benefit from it, and also to remove the fear of management scrutiny. Another benefit of the redesigned electronic Diary would be that it could be read and written from different points on the shopfloor. Workers would not have to walk round to the foreman's box. In the event, this turned out to be a crucial factor in facilitating the use of the Diary as dialogue, which forms the central theme of this paper.

ORGANISATIONAL MEMORY IN PROCESS INDUSTRIES

'Organisational memory' was not used in workplace analysis and design in process industries because it has any outstanding advantage over other available concepts. It was utilised because it provided a common ground between the researchers and the workers and managers. In discussions, it was picked up and re-used (adopted) much more than other CSCW ideas. Its ordinary language vagueness, its blurring of the distinction between object and person, artefact and process was an advantage in the free discussion of issues. Nevertheless, when it came to design, the various, often contradictory ideas involved had to be teased out.

Many definitions of organisational memory can be found in CSCW literature. Conklin [6] suggests "record of an organization that is embodied in a set of documents and artefacts". Kim [12] offers "includes everything that is contained in an organization that is somehow retrievable" and "collects shared and stored understandings and beliefs and forms the basis for organisational sense-making and social construction of reality". Walsh & Ungson [18] suggest "stored information from an organisation's history that can be brought to bear on present decisions", and Stein [17] "means by which knowledge from the past is brought to bear on present activities, thus resulting in higher organisational effectiveness". Walsh & Ungson[18] also discuss various "bins" into which organisational memory may be dumped: (individuals; culture; transformation logics (e.g. procedures); organisational structures; ecology (e.g. buildings), external archives (e.g. previous employees, reports), to which Stein [17] add information systems.

Auramäki et al. [2] state that Kim's conceptualisation provides the fit best constellations of concerns in the mills, which centre on paper breaks, appropriate and timely action, and (lack of available) organisational memory to help with this. They give as a working definition: *Everything (whether document, artefact, ecology, logic, person, or experience) that is somehow retrievable and helps with organisational sense-making and resolving troubles.* They emphasise that the experience or information needed is not ready-to-hand — making it present-to-hand is the achievement. This perspective, locates organisational memory in process rather than any specific artefact, was utilised for Diary design. This is very similar to the position taken by Bannon [3], where the tempting reifications inherent in the very concept of organisational memory are critiqued. One of their conclusions is that

"organisational memories that simply consist of some passive capturing, storage, and eventual re-play of information will have very limited if any use for the practical accomplishments of activities within an organisation"

We concur with this critique, and agree that process is central. The Diary facility to organise and reorganise information in "local categories" relevant to the workers themselves is our embedded functionality that allows the move from passive storage to active structuring. We also believe that these experiences can be generalised, and that it is possible to define organisational memory as a special sort of process: "artefact mediated process". In general this means that, while organisational memory is essentially a context dependent process and activity, it implicates, co-opts, and needs material artefacts. More particularly, these artefacts are formatted in the sense that documents are formatted [11] although they certainly need not be documents. They can be any sort of artefact provided they are ready-to-hand when needed cf. Walsh & Ungson's (1991) buildings which are ready-to-hand during activity, "formatted", and can be "inscribed" in various ways.

SOME THINGS YOU NEED TO KNOW ABOUT PAPER MILLS

They are gigantic, unbelievably expensive, extremely noisy, mind blowingly complicated, and each one is unique. Paper and papermills are a cornerstone of the Finnish economy. Let us expand the description a little.

Size varies, and can be up to 120m long, or 150m. if the workspaces for the rolls of paper are included. They are up to 9 m. wide, and 6m. high. It takes time to walk round them, and other workers are often out of sight.

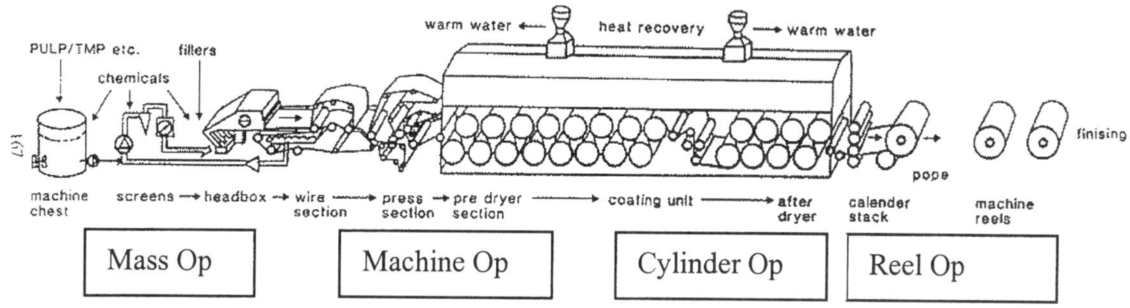

Fig. 1: Papermachine Layout adapted from Norros [14]

Cost: Capital is measured in hundreds of millions of dollars, with many implications for the workprocess. Shift work is normal, since 24 hour production is needed to repay investment. The cost, including lost sales, of downtime can be $20,000 per hour — so there is a major incentive to keep the machine running come what may. Machines are only halted for servicing during the Christmas break. At other times it is cheaper and more effective to wait for a breakdown, and then carry out servicing and replacements in parallel with other repairs.

Days are divided into three shifts. The usual pattern of shift work for each worker is 3 morning shifts, followed by 3 day shifts, followed by 3 night shifts, followed by 5 days off. Again, this has implications for the type of support that is needed.

Noise, together with sheer size and difficulty in seeing others, mean that communication between workers on the same shift is often difficult. The noise is partly a result of the dramatic speed of production. In our case and [2] a 5m. wide stream of paper runs through the machine at 1,300m per minute or 78 kilometers per hour. Speeds on other machines can be much higher. Paper breaks, the main topic of [2], can be correspondingly dramatic. The paper is not paper as it is normally known, but a sludge of varying degrees of wetness (depending on the stage in the process). Holes and other defects can start to appear in the paperstream, and fast compensatory actions are necessary to prevent it getting out of control — with consequential downtime cost, not to mention mess.

Complicated: papermills are fundamentally a set of interlinked big machines (See Fig. 1) with all the bearings, rods, connectors, pumps, gaskets, cylinders, drive belts etc. associated with mechanical devices. The most important "conveyor belt" — the one which carries the paperstream — is termed "the wire". In addition, much of the machine is controlled, monitored, calibrated, and adjusted by a multitude of electronic devices and computers. A paper machine (depending on age and design) may incorporate up to 50 logic and process control computers (the latter are used extensively in fault diagnosis by production crews); it may have as many as ten, fixed-position, on-line video cameras. The images are used directly in control, and the tapes for post mortems on particularly "challenging" or "special" situations.

Unique: Each machine is configured differently, and has its own history of "updates" — changes, modifications, and improvements (e.g. more sophisticated control computers, new sensors). This means that experience with *this* machine is critical for fluent control. Training and experience with other machines is not enough. Experience, length of service, and intuition are accordingly highly valued by both workers and managers. Another factor that adds to the importance of experience and intuition is that (as opposed to e.g. oil refining) the state of the production process can be, and is directly perceived (seen, heard, smelt, tasted). Experience and intuition resist *a priori* categories. Informality and potential to generate "local categories" were designed into the Diary with this in mind.

Some other things: Papermill management is essentially hierarchical, with reporting going upwards. An important tool of management is the "morning meeting", where challenges and special situations are reviewed, production levels monitored, and new activity and purchases initiated. The original paper diary was an information instrument for morning meetings, and the electronic diary continued to fill this role. This was one reason why the Diary diffused from the factory floor to management levels.

TRANSITION FROM PAPER TO ELECTRONIC DIARY

The transition was based on a cooperation between the researchers and the process control professionals. The design was a cooperative effort between workers in an oil refinery, a superintendent and foreman from the paper mill, and the research group. The design was piloted in the oil refinery, and a refined prototype used in the paper mill on one production line. All 35 production line staff received about 4 hours training each, including Windows, Lotus Notes, and the electronic diary. The feedback from the training was positive. This was reflected in a quick transition to "real" use of the application. The paper diary was abandoned soon after.

The main features of the paper *shift foreman's diary* were

It contained free-form information about "interesting" events, plus a lot of factual and numerical data.

The left page was reserved for memos to others and the right page for diary entries

Only the shift foreman and superintendent made entries in the diary

Other workers could read it in the shift foreman's office.

The design principles for the electronic *Diary for production* are

It offers both an overview of what is going on, and different perspectives can be taken (e.g. to show views from specific roles, such as Mass operator)

Most workers in any shift can make entries to the electronic diary

The emphasis in the electronic diary design (and in use) is in recording "soft" information (such as interesting events and experiences)

All workers in any shift and also some daily workers have access to the diary

The electronic diary is more structured (specific roles, headlines) than the paper diary.

A report of the 24 last hours is offered (and used e.g. in the morning meetings)

Full-text search facilities are provided to support the use of "local categories".

See Figs. 2 & 3 for screenshots showing overview of the diary entries (with alternative view buttons) and the Diary itself.

There are several other practical differences between the manual and paper diaries. The entries in the manual diary were hard to read because hand writing varies enormously. The indexing in the manual diary depended on the person. Often they recorded some headlines such as date and shift and some hard data such as machine speed. The date appeared in different places and sometimes only the shift identification was recorded. Searching and combining entries to give different perspectives in the paper diary was almost impossible. The data in paper diary was also much harder, including many quasi-tables of numbers and times, although this was not systematic. After starting the electronic diary, most of the hard data was hived off to the machine operator's report.

An important observation on the comparative paper/electronic entries is that people's names appear often in the paper diary, while in the electronic diary they are very rare — unaddressed notes are the norm. Another interesting observation concerns the diffusion of the application to roles not taken into account in the design. The diary has not been substituted for other reports used in process control. Hard data is still recorded and presented in reports from different roles.

USE OF THE DIARY

Casual inspection of the Diary shows its use as factual record. Although there are many other records of similar data, the diary is useful because it allows *salient* factual/numerical data to be highlighted. *Salient to whom*? The answer to this question illustrates the core function of the diary in the work process. The data that is highlighted by appearing in the diary is salient to those concerned with the hour by hour and day by day operation of the mill. In general, neither we, the researchers, nor the author of the entry can put an exact boundary on this group. It may be those in the same shift; it may be those in adjoining shifts; or even distant shifts. It may include managers. And, in general, even if we knew the boundaries of the group, neither we nor the author of the entry would know which individual the data was salient to. The relevant group boundary and the relevant individual are defined if and when they respond to, or take some other action in the light of the entry. For this reason the diary entries are *unaddressed* — and the addressing is completed by the response, not by the author. This indicates that the Diary is a vehicle for a very special type of dialogue, different from face-to-face conversation and different from email exchanges where most utterances are addressed to specific others.

A fairly typical Diary entry follows, where the process of addressing is completed by a response from the next shift. The second entry responds to the first and completes a small dialogue.

17.5.97 morning, shift foreman, finishing:

Sensor problem in PL72.....Night shift will make the next trim. Then we will see does the fault occurs again.

17.5.97 evening, shift foreman, finishing:

Making trim on PL72 went fine.

The visibility of this process of responding to comments led us to the above re-interpretation of the meaning of factual/numerical entries. They appear to be factual records, but are not[1]. Unlike databases, where criteria of generality

[1] Apparently factual records and databases also have great variability in use. The machine and Mass operators collect data on specific numerical values separately from the Diary. This data could easily be collected automatically, and in any event is never used by anyone! Discussion revealed that the value is in the smell. The two workers have to visit various different points of the machine to collect the data — and would probably not make these systematic visits without the need to collect the data.

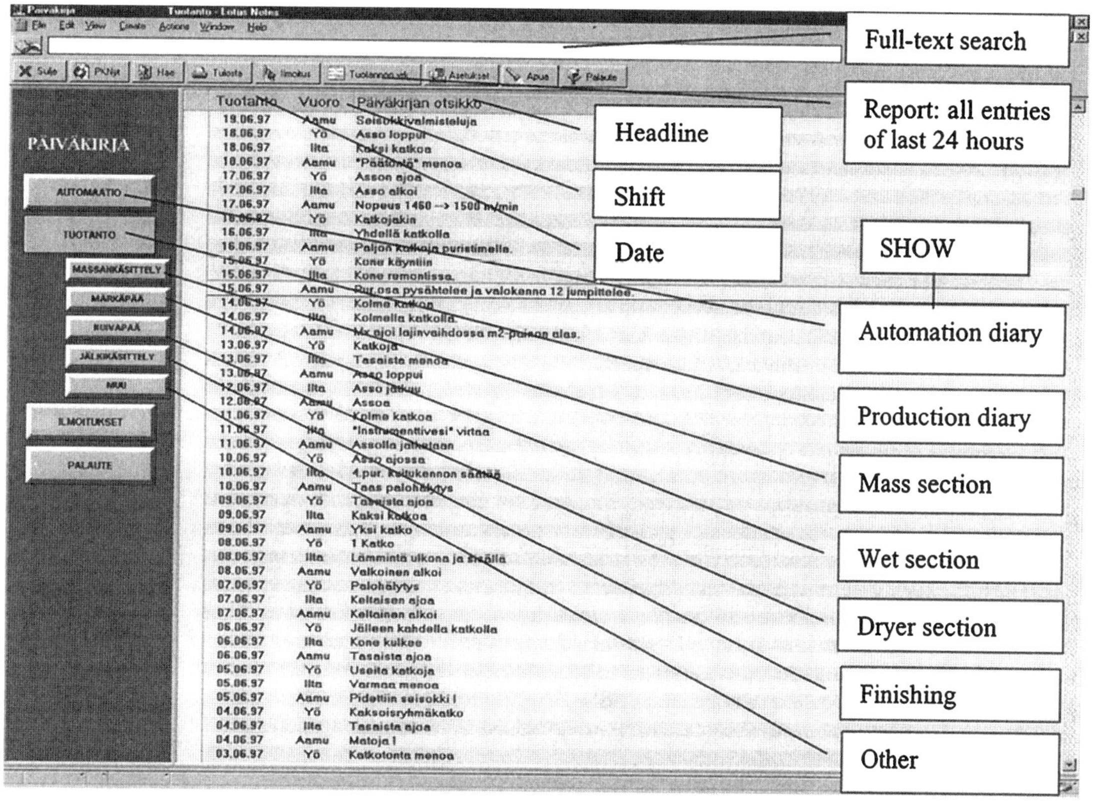

Figure 2. Screenshots showing overview of the diary entries (with alternative view buttons)

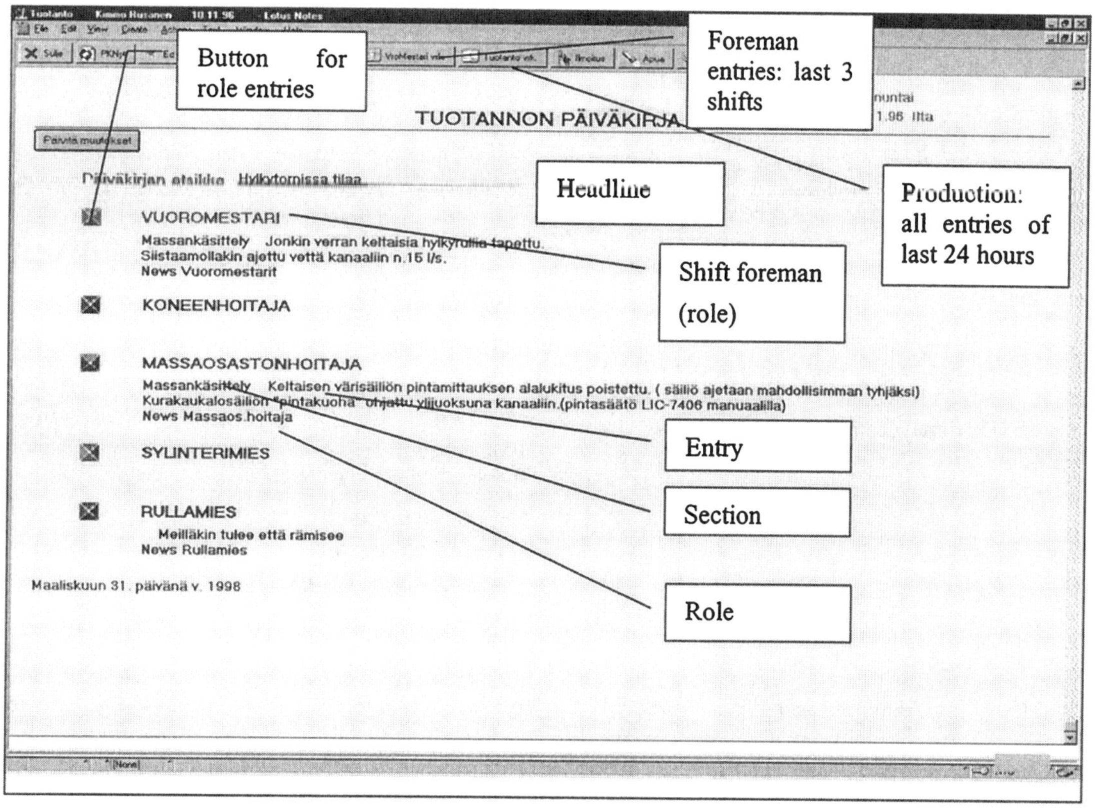

Figure 3. The shift diary

and completeness are important, Diary entries (fact or comment) are structured by *salience*. Their meaning comes from being embedded in a particular context, and is not available outside this frame. Diary entries (factual and comment) are part of a dialogue, and as such are only implicitly addressed — even the workers themselves do not have a *clear* idea of who in particular they are addressing[2]. Nevertheless, it would not be possible to select the salient "facts" to include or emphasise without a good idea of who constitutes the audience.

This drew out attention to the precedent for this type of dialogue that can be found in the work of Heath and Luff [9, 13] as "talking out loud" and "overhearing". Basically, this is the phenomena where one worker will, apparently eccentrically, talk to herself while performing her job. She may describe the actions she is taking with respect to e.g. controlling the movement of trains; which train has been diverted; possible consequential problems (another train on the wrong schedule?); who she is trying to phone. She may describe her own actions with screens or keyboards or other local equipment. She may leave speakers open so conversations with others can be overheard. Her talking-out-loud is not specifically *addressed* to others, but Heath and Luff suggest it is *designed* to be *overheard*. The colleagues who overhear may then take supportive, or collaborative action without specifically being asked to do so. Or, depending on their own pressures and workload, they may not. Either way, they have *peripheral awareness* of the overall working context because of the talking out loud. Such informal processes are noted to be essential for collaboration and coordination, and have been found in numerous other studies e.g. [4]

Diary entries are very similar to a text version of talking out loud. The difference is that the spatial and temporal scope of the talking and overhearing are extended. The Diary entries also reflect other features of talking out loud, appropriately modified for the text medium. Emotions and humour are used freely, reinventing such email forms as CAPS., multiple !!!!! and ???, truncated and incomplete sentences, 'bad' language, etc.

At this point we can also note that making a change to the process without recording it in the Diary is "frowned upon" i.e. the system is completely voluntary, but there is social pressure to use it. This may have something to do with dialogue conventions. More likely the social pressure arises because use of the diary does result in smoother working and fewer paperbreaks, because there is competition between the production lines,— and there is a *bonus* that depends on production levels.

Lastly we need to note the difficulties of translating the Diary entries from Finnish to English — which are orthogonal languages with neither word roots nor grammar in common. Compounding this, the entries mix abbreviation (as mentioned, workers do not feel called upon to write complete sentences) with jargon, specialist technical terms, and local slang.

Diary as Overview

We have seen that millworkers' shifts involve 9 days on and 5 days off. It has now become normal for workers returning from days off to "catch up" on those days from the Diary. This did not happen with the paper diary, and is attributed the salience of the entries highlighted, and to the increased ease of displaying the last few days. The practice of gaining an "overview" seems confined to factory floor workers, and is not followed by managers.

Dialogues within shifts

Dialogues within and between shifts both illustrate the recognisably conversational nature of exchanges.

10.11.96 *evening, shift foreman, mass section:* Some yellow rolls have been wrecked

Mass operator, mass section: The locking of yellow ink drum has been removed (it will run until its empty) ...

Roll person: It is rattling along here too

Dialogues between Shifts

Dialogues between shifts are usually brief conversations not spanning more than a few days, as illustrated below. Small dialogues within and between shifts constitute the vast majority of entries. Two examples are:

23.5.97 *night, finishing:* Wall side brakes of the packing machine 'taittari' broken. New parts needed. Repair for morning shift

24.5 *morning, finishing:* Wall side brakes of the packing machine 'taittari' repaired first thing. Working well.

8.6 *night, wet section:* The retention pump for X was...blocked. Shift maintenance were busy working in other departments. Repair for morning.

9.6 *morning, other:* Gasket of retention pump for X3...is broken. Ordered new, will be changed tomorrow.

10.6 *morning, wet section:* Gasket of retention pump for X3 was changed and pump works.

Hanging Entries

Hanging entries are those to which there is not response when a response might be expected. These form a small minority of the Diary entries, but have theoretical significance, as will be discussed below. Four examples follow.

A) 5.5.97 *night, wet section:* Problems in making PL 72 trim, system announced a transfer problem, ...sensor is defective, to do in morning shift.

B) 1.6.97 *morning, finishing:* Inside part of PL 72 safety gate falls too quickly. Whipping for night shift ('whipping' translates approximately as 'beat the bushes and see what comes out')

While making the visits they see, hear, feel, smell and taste the machine, sensing impending problems that may be invisible to numerical monitoring or virtual surveillance.

[2] This was contrary to our initial expectation — probably deriving from our familiarity with email — that production workers *would* address each other through the Diary, probably by name, with notes, details of "challenges" and requests for action.

C) 26.4.97 *night, dryer section:* Pneumatic post blocked about 2 pm, we noticed it two hours later. Shift repair group have to check. Did you manage to fix it?

D) 12.5.97 *night, mass section:* ...rising over two (about 2.3%) but no foam in wirewell. Foam blocking solid 58 -> 60 ml/min. Is it necessary to check calibration?

Hanging Entries: Discussion

As the examples show, these are entries that are unadressed or generally aimed at other groups, as notes, questions, or requests. The key property is that they are not "answered". It is usual to regard such unfulfilled requests as a "bad thing". A similar phenomenon would be the many entries regarding malfunction (nuisance, delay, irritation) with on the Reject Carrier (*see later*). An abstract and structured view of management and computer system design regards this level of repetition as unnecessary, inefficient, and time wasting. A down-to-earth manager might look at the entries and say the same. The socially plausible and computer embeddable Language Action Theory [19, 20] was designed precisely to avoid such unanswered requests. Requests *should* be met with promises (or at least with counter offers or rejections), and promises *should* be monitored for completion within specific time frames. At some levels (legal, contractual, schematics of project management) these views are sensible. However, we believe it is a mistake — and counterproductive — to try to *discipline* all work in these terms. One size does not fit all. Hanging entries illustrate one interesting way in which one class of work process has developed a frame of effective working that depends precisely on the ability not to respond.

We have already discussed Diary dialogues as analogous to "talking out loud" and "overhearing" in face-to-face work situations demanding tight coordination e.g. plane or train control rooms. Talking out loud enables others to maintain an awareness of events and phenomena that would otherwise be invisible, and to orientate their actions, directly or indirectly, to situations that would otherwise be wider than their perceptions. It is of the nature of talking out loud that the talking is unaddressed, and does not call for specific responses — although it frequently evokes them. Diary entries generally follow this pattern. There are two differences. First, as noted, entries radically extend the spatio-temporal boundaries of the overhearing. Second, they are more laid back. Papermill work can be as pressured and time critical as train control, but textual overhearing is not used for such tight, live coordination. It is used, appropriately, for those things that are troublesome or important — but not critical this very second.

The talking out loud paradigm differs from, and provides an alternative to the Language Action perspective, which is largely based on an e-mail paradigm. Email requests are generally specifically addressed to a single person — who of course may not respond. Nevertheless, because a specific person is addressed, there is a reasonable expectation, based on conversational experience, that there will be a response. LA Theory was intended to bring the two into line, with improvements.

We suggest that there is a whole class of notes, questions, or requests that are not specifically addressed. Diary entries are often (but not always) of this type.

Although correctly identifying the "core of organization" as "networks of recurrent conversations", the LA perspective makes a further, implicit assumption that such conversations will be channeled through a computational medium (without this implicit assumption the postulated development of a network of commitments does not make much sense). Against this, researchers have pointed to the layered nature of technology e.g. [15] Newer technologies are overlaid on, and are used in addition to, but do not replace older technologies. Moreover, work involves fluid transitions between media (phone, fax, face to face, Internet) as convenient and appropriate. Discussions with papermill workers reveal that many (but by no means all) "hanging entries" are part of a dialogue that has been concluded by other means. Completions (where there are completions) may be made in conversations, by workers simply seeing that something has been done, in morning meetings, and in other ways.

Discretion is what makes the difference between jobs that are done by people, and tasks that can be automated or subject to routinised 'commitments'. Discretion involves at least a sense of priority, and intuitions about what can be safely ignored or even forgotten. Complaining out loud (i.e. in the Diary) about the irritating delays caused by the sporadic malfunctioning of the Reject Carrier fits generally with the priorities of uninterrupted maximum production. Not taking any notice of, or making a special effort to respond via the Diary fits with the priorities of discretion: there are other more important things to be getting on with at this moment.

In brief, hanging entries reflect the effectiveness (not the inefficiency or lack of discipline) of the moment-to-moment management of the paper production process. Unaddressed Diary comment is a useful form of coordination, allowing both discretion and completion through other media. Although a very simple artefact, the use of the electronic Diary draws our attention to an area that has not been much investigated in CSCW: the role of unaddressed comment in extended spatio-temporal contexts.

Extended Dialogue

Extended dialogues again form a small minority of Diary entries, but, like hanging entries, indicate important aspects of Diary use. Extended dialogues are revealed both to the researchers and to the millworkers by the use of the 'search' facility. This gives a perspective that is different from the adjacent day or adjacent shift perspective normally used when making entries, or when "catching up". It enables sets of dialogues about the same issue to be seen together. In the examples the Reject Carrier and the Packing Machine are the search terms. These two terms (many other more obscure ones are used by workers) are "local categories" — and are not anticipated in formal reporting sheets. In this sense, the dialogues are part conversation, part organisational memory. Later comments can (but are often not) made in the light of the whole history. The most noticeable aspect of the extended dialogues is the repetition of the same issue. This will be conceptualised later as redundancy rather than inefficiency. Repetition does not indicate failure to deal with a challenge, but a continuing *opportunity* to deal with something that is irritating, but not critical for continuing production.

Example 1: Reject carrier problems in SIISTAAMO (The De-inking Mass Plant)

24.4.97 *night shift, mass section:* Reject carrier triggered it's relay once in SIISTAAMO

4.5 *morning, other:* Reject carrier stops once in a while

9.5 *evening, mass:* Headline: Reject carrier to be repaired. Another part of the reject carrier's chain wheel fell off the carrier through the hole made in the cover. It looks like staying there a while. New wheel installed and production in SIISTAAMO started at 5 pm.

15.5 *evening, mass:* Reject carrier stopped twice at the beginning of the shift. Warm bilgefilter looks pink, reason unknown. A lot of foam again.

16.6 *evening, mass:* In SIISTAAMO reject carrier drum often triggers it's relay.......... God knows why?

23.6 *night, wet:* Two breaks took 20 minutes in all. In SIISTAAMO the rejectcarrier triggered its relay again, why doesn't someone find the fault?

24.6 *night, other:* Hasn't anyone found the fault on the reject carrier's fibre drum. TWICE acknowledged relay. (*acknowledge means to switch off the alert triggered by the relay*) It needs: A MUCH BIGGER ENGINE AND A MUCH BIGGER RELAY. This problem seems to getting worse. Maybe the relay could be brought closer to the store carrier filling pit, so it would be quicker to acknowledge.

25.6 *night, other:* RECORD: Reject carrier's relay acknowledged 4 times

26.6 *morning, other: One* part fell off the rejectcarrier.

26.6 *night, other:* Proposition for investment: if this reject carrier can't be repaired, you buy a new carrier

27.6 *night, mass:* Reject carrier triggered its relay once

28.6 *morning, wet:* The bearing nest bolts near the switch side cylinder located on the upper side of the reject carrier in SIISTAAMO's recycling paper stock are loose, can turn by hand. 'TISURIT' tightened the bolts. Lets see if the reject carrier will trigger the relay again.

29.6 *morning, other:* The reject carrier has not triggered its relay after tightening the bearing nest bolts near the switch side cylinder located on the upper side of the reject carrier in SIISTAAMO's recycling paper stock** (** *ironic use of cut-and-paste*)

29.6 *night, mass:* Reject carrier triggered once.

30.6 *morning, other:* Reject carrier's relay triggered once in SIISTAAMO

30.6 *night, mass:* SIISTAAMO: Reject carrier's relay triggered 4 times

A similar extended dialogue was seen over problems with the packing machine glue pump, brake disintegration, relay, and 'jumping ram' over six months. This generated 22 entries between January and May '97, and the dialogue continues at the time of writing.

COMMENTS ON THE FACTORY FLOOR DIALOGUES

Most diary entries are similar to dialogue in the sense that one note demonstrably responds to one or more others, amplifying, repeating, or completing it. They are similar to dialogue in their use of humour, slang, and agrammatical emphases (CAPS etc.) They differ from spoken dialogue, where (from Conversation Analytic accounts) the individual utterances of one person are not necessarily complete semantic entities. They may contain interjections from others which alter their original course, or they may be completed by others. The completion may be agreed by the original speaker, even if different to the one that would have followed without the other-completion. [5]. This does not appear to happen in the Diary, where most entries are complete, in the sense of being comprehensible on their own. This is partly a courtesy of using a text medium. It also reflects the nature of talking out loud, where more completeness is often provided (e.g. a question *and* its answer) than would be the case in conversation.

The overall usefulness of the Diary is illustrated by a minority of entry types — hanging entries and extended dialogues. Both illustrate the ways in which diary use is similar to talking out loud and overhearing. The extended dialogues illustrate the way in which 'search' enables the use of local categories (not previously anticipated) to construct perspectives that are part conversation, part organisational memory. Together these illustrate a mode of computer mediated workplace coordination that is very different from structured or workflow modes.

DIALOGUES WITH LEAKY BOUNDARIES

The Diary, although fully operational, is an experimental system. There were no protocols on entitlement to access. As the Diary became extensively used and mentioned in conversation, many others became interested and asked for access. One interesting aspect of this was that the workers using the Diary became known as the factory experts on the use of Lotus NOTES, since they were using the Diary daily. Other groups with more formal systems began to request help. Diary access extended from the original 35 factory floor workers and 2 managers to more than 100 people including 13 managers. The diffusion from the original groups of factory floor workers is shown in the following table.

Initial Period (Operators & managers of Paper Machine 7)

C=Read/Write/ Manage Access; D=Wrote or Read paper diary

A:Role	B: No.	C	D
Shift foreman	5	W	W
Machine, Mass, Cylinder, Roll operators	20	W	R
Instrument ops, Electricians	10	W	
Production Superintendent	1	M	W
Production Manager	1	W	R
System Designer	1	M	

Totals 35 workers, 2 managers, 1 IT Support

Second Period (SIIST & Previous Manual Users join)

Leader PM7, Dist. Leaders Automation & Mechanical	4	W	W
Automation & IT managers	2	R	
Development Engineer, Deputy Superintendent	2	W	
De-inking control room	10	R	
System Designer	2	M/R	

Totals 45 workers, 9 managers, 4 IT Support

Third Period (Managers & Pre-Maintenance join)

Automation Engineer, Superintendent SIIST, Service Director	3	W	
Dept. Leader SIIST	1	R	
Pre-maintenance	1	R	

Totals 47 workers, 12 managers, 4 IT Support

Last Period (Cutting & Stores workers join)

Cutting & Stores	40+5	R	

Totals 92 workers, 12 managers, 4 IT Support

The reasons for the diffusion were mixed. One was tradition. The original paper diary was one information instrument amongst many (e.g. Foremen's' End of Shift Reports, numerous statistical reports) for morning meetings. The Diary printout continued to fill this role. Being one amongst many documents, it is not subject to any special scrutiny. The difference in content (far fewer statistics, more issues) was compensated by a another, properly statistical record of paperbreaks etc. introduced at the same time as the Diary. Another reason was function. Some individuals felt their work would benefit from the information in the Diary. One was curiosity. In part the diffusion happened because the Shift Supervisor had commissioned the research and Diary, amongst other software support. He was keen to show the success of the initiative by "selling" it to other users and audiences. Nevertheless, this sort of access permission was not just cosmetic. Logs show the files are opened frequently by individuals joining later in the process, and not directly working with the production line.

As noted earlier, CSCW literature leads us to believe that sharing the Diary with management could lead to problems. Informal remarks, complaints, reminders, etc. involving the use of informal and local categories, of jargon, slang, and humour [10] are not *formatted* to be understood outside the context of the work shifts. They do not provide overview of the work to outsiders, and may even be styled to prevent it. But they may appear to provide an audit-trail — and one which disadvantages the authors. The anxieties expressed by workers at the design stage of the electronic Diary mainly concern the visibility of *ad hoc*, free comments to management (*see quotes in Intro*). The 'hanging entries' in particular, with the repetition of the same issue (e.g. the packing machine challenges) invite the attempt to impose a more disciplined Language Action type of system — which in terms of real work effectiveness would be counter-productive.

A second danger is that managers may (and in practice did) request a different, standardised format for the Diary. This is understandable, as they wish to use it for agenda, reporting, or statistical purposes. Such an (externally imposed) standard format would work against, or prevent informality and the use of discretion in entering *salient* observations with local currency. It would also contradict the design principle of "local categories" — and hence local usefulness which underpins the shopfloor popularity of the Diary.

Why, so far, does diffusion not create problems (although potential problems may lurk on the horizon)? There appear to be several reasons. First, paper production workers and managers are a specialised and fairly tightly knit community of practice. There is a long induction period, and managers are generally familiar with the day to day difficulties and fixes used to avoid paperbreaks and maintain production. Less social distance means less "misreading" and misunderstanding of local terms and categories.

Second, managers in practice do not write to the Diary, even though many of them do have write permissions. This may be because the Diary labels for making entries are role specific (See Fig. 3). It is also logical, as managers are not in a position to directly observe the machines, or to add first hand data. Several use the diaries as part of their data for "morning meetings" (where problems and issues arising on specific shifts are discussed on a daily basis). In terms of our analytic frame, managers take part in a different but related dialogue using the Diary as a resource. There are some entries that appear to be addressed to the morning meetings (e.g. 26.6 *night shift*: *Proposition for investment: if this reject carrier can't be repaired, you buy a new carrier*). However, in general, the morning meeting dialogue has a separate purpose, different participants and rhythm from the factory floor dialogue.

Thirdly, the artefact has not been changed to accommodate the new audience. It would be here that the greatest risks lie. It is difficult to imagine how highlighting and salience, 'talking out loud and overhearing' — and hence use — could survive a reformatting into pre-defined categories.

Fourthly, it may be that the current format of the Diary (within its community of practice) enables it to work as a boundary object [16], and that there are advantages in reaching a wider audience to workers as well as to managers.

CONCLUSION

Organisational memory, as explored here, is neither artefact nor process, but artefact mediated process. The Diary is best understood in this way: artefact mediated process where the predominant form is an unaddressed entry. This can be understood in terms of "talking out loud" and "overhearing", but extends the spatio-temporal ambit of this face-to-face work practice. The special type of dialogue constituted by unaddressed entries included "hanging entries" — those to which there is no response — and extended and repetitive dialogues. This is analysed as a merit rather than a defect of work process coordination. Generally these forms of unaddressed, textual material suggest an alternative modality of computer support to explicit structured communication.

The diffusion of such factory floor dialogue to other audiences, such as managers, proved unproblematic in this case. Nevertheless, in general, there are reasons to expect unlimited access to such dialogue to be problematic. Future developments of applications to support unaddressed dialogue will need to consider issues of boundary management carefully.

REFERENCES

1. Ackroyd, S., *et al.*, *New Technology and Practical Police Work*. 1992, Milton Keynes: Open University Press.

2. Auramäki, E., Mike Robinson, Anne Aaltonen, Mikko Kovalainen, Arja Liinamaa, & Taina Tuuna-Väiskä. Paperwork at 78 k.p.h. in *CSCW'96*. 1996. Boston: ACM.

3. Bannon, L. and K. Kuutti. Shifting Perspectives on Organisational Memory: From Storage to Active Remembering. in *Proc. of 29th. Annual Hawaii International Conference on System Sciences (HICSS-29)*. 1996: IEEE Computer Press, Los Alamitos.

4. Bentley, R., *et al.*, Ethnographically-Informed Systems Design for Air Traffic Control, in *Proceedings of ACM CSCW'92 Conference on Computer-Supported Cooperative Work*. 1992. p. 123-129.

5. Bowers, J. and J. Pycock. Talking through Design: Requirements and Resistance in Cooperative Prototyping. in *CHI'94: Celebrating Independence*. 1994. Boston, MA. April 24-28 1994: ACM.

6. Conklin, J., Capturing Organizational Memory, in *Groupware '92*, D. Coleman, Editor. 1992, Morgan Kaufmann. p. 133-137.

7. Grudin, J., Why groupware applications fail: problems in design and evaluation. *Office: Technology and People*, 1989. **4**(3): p. 245-264.

8. Harper, R., *Inside the IMF: An Ethnography of Documents, Technology, and Organisational Action*. Computers and People, ed. B.R.G. A.Monk. 1998, San Diego: Academic Press.

9. Heath, C. and P. Luff, Collaborative Activity and Technological Design: Task Coordination in London Underground Control Rooms, in *ECSCW '91. Proceedings of the Second European Conference on Computer-Supported Cooperative Work*, L. Bannon, M. Robinson, and K. Schmidt, Editors. 1991, Kluwer Academic Publishers: Amsterdam. p. 65-80.

10. Heath, C. and P. Luff, Documents and Professional Practice: 'bad' organisational reasons for 'good' clinical records, in *Proceedings of the ACM 1996 Conference on Computer Supported Cooperative Work*, M.S. Ackerman, Editor. 1996, ACM: NY. p. 354-363.

11. Hughes, J., *et al.*, Paperwork and its lessons for database systems, in *The Design of Computer-Supported Cooperative Work and Groupware Systems*, D. Shapiro, M. Tauber, and R.Traunmüller, Editors. 1994, Elsevier Science: Amsterdam.

12. Kim, D., The link between Individual and Organizational Learning. *Sloan Management Review*, 1993(Fall 1993).

13. Luff, P., Computers and Interaction: The Social Organisation of Human-Computer Interaction in the Workplace, in *Department of Sociology*. 1997, University of Surrey.

14. Norros, L. Conceptual Mastery of Work. in *XIII European Annual Conference on Human Decision Making and Manual Control*. 1994. Espoo, Finland, June 13-14: VTT Automation & Technical Research Centre of Finland.

15. Reder, S. and R.G. Schwab, The temporal structure of cooperative activity, in *CSCW 90, Proceedings of the Conference on Computer-Supported Cooperative Work, Los Angeles, CA, October 7-10, 1990*. 1990, ACM Press: New York. p. 303-316.

16. Star, S.L. and J.R. Griesemer, Institutional Ecology, 'Translations' and Boundary Objects: Amateurs and Professionals in Berkeley's Museum of Vertebrate Zoology, 1907-39. *Social Studies of Science*, 1989. **19**: p. 387-420.

17. Stein, E. and V. Zwass, Actualizing Organizational Memory with Information Systems. *Information Systems Research*, 1995. **6**(2).

18. Walsh, J. and G. Ungson, Organizational Memory. *Academy of Management Review*, 1991. **16**(1).

19. Winograd, T. A language/action perspective on the design of cooperative work. in *CSCW '86. Proceedings. Conference on Computer-Supported Cooperative Work*. 1986. Austin, Texas, December 3-5, 1986: ACM, New York, N.Y.

20. Winograd, T. and F. Flores, *Understanding Computers and Cognition: A New Foundation for Design*. 1986, Norwood, New Jersey, Ablex Publishing Corp. 207.

Operational Transformation in Real-Time Group Editors: Issues, Algorithms, and Achievements

Chengzheng Sun
School of Computing and Information Technology
Griffith University
Brisbane, Qld 4111, Australia
scz@cit.gu.edu.au
http://www.cit.gu.edu.au/~scz

Clarence (Skip) Ellis
Department of Computer Science
University of Colorado
Boulder, CO 80309-0430, USA
skip@colorado.edu
http://www.cs.colorado.edu/~skip/Home.html

ABSTRACT

Real-time group editors allow a group of users to view and edit the same document at the same time from geographically dispersed sites connected by communication networks. Consistency maintenance is one of the most significant challenges in the design and implementation of these types of systems. Research on real-time group editors in the past decade has invented an innovative technique for consistency maintenance, called operational transformation. This paper presents an integrative review of the evolution of operational transformation techniques, with the goals of identifying the major issues, algorithms, achievements, and remaining challenges. In addition, this paper contributes a new optimized generic operational transformation control algorithm.

Keywords

Consistency maintenance, operational transformation, convergence, causality preservation, intention preservation, group editors, groupware, distributed computing.

INTRODUCTION

Real-time group editors allow a group of users to view and edit the same text/graphic/image/multimedia document at the same time from geographically dispersed sites connected by communication networks. These types of groupware systems are not only very useful tools in the areas of CSCW [5], but also serve excellent vehicles for exploring a range of fundamental and challenging issues facing the designers of real-time groupware systems in general. One such issue is consistency maintenance of shared documents under the constraints of short response time, and support for free and concurrent editing in distributed environments [17].

Research on real-time group editors in the past decade has invented an innovative technique for consistency maintenance, under the name of operational transformation, which was pioneered by the GROVE (GRoup Outline Viewing Editor) system in 1989 [3]. Since then, several research groups have independently extended the operational transformation technique in their design and implementation of these types of systems. Major representatives in this area include the REDUCE (REal-time Distributed Unconstrained Cooperative Editing) system [14, 15, 16, 17], the Jupiter system [11], and the adOPTed algorithm [13]. This paper will present an integrative review of the evolution of operational transformation techniques, with the goals of identifying the major issues, algorithms, achievements, and remaining challenges. In addition, this paper will contribute a new optimized generic operational transformation control algorithm. This paper will focus exclusively on transformation-based consistency maintenance algorithms. For discussion of alternative consistency maintenance techniques, such as turn-taking, locking, serialization, and transactions, the reader is refereed to [5, 7, 8, 10, 17].

The rest of this paper is organized as follows: First, some basic concepts and terminologies are introduced. Then, the operational transformation algorithm in the GROVE system is reviewed to see where the original work was started and what problems were left unsolved. Next, the problems with the original GROVE transformation algorithm are analyzed, and three different approaches to solving them are discussed one by one, including the REDUCE approach, the Jupiter approach, and the adOPTed approach. Furthermore, a new optimized generic operational transformation control algorithm is proposed. Finally, the paper is concluded with a summary of the major achievements so far and remaining challenges for future research.

PRELIMINARIES

In this section, some basic concepts and terminologies are introduced. Following Lamport [9], we define a causal (partial) ordering relation on operations in terms of their generation and execution sequences as follows.

Definition 1: Causal ordering relation "$\rightarrow$"
Given two operations O_a and O_b, generated at sites i and j, then $O_a \rightarrow O_b$, *iff*: (1) $i = j$ and the generation of O_a *happened before* the generation of O_b, or (2) $i \neq j$ and the execution of O_a at site j *happened before* the generation of O_b, or (3) there exists an operation O_x, such that $O_a \rightarrow O_x$ and $O_x \rightarrow O_b$. □

Definition 2: Dependent and independent operations
Given any two operations O_a and O_b. (1) O_b is *dependent* on O_a *iff* $O_a \rightarrow O_b$. (2) O_a and O_b are *independent* (or *concurrent*), expressed as $O_a \parallel O_b$, *iff* neither $O_a \rightarrow O_b$, nor $O_b \rightarrow O_a$. □

To illustrate, consider a real-time group editing session with three sites, as shown in the time-space graph of Figure 1.

CSCW 98 Seattle Washington USA

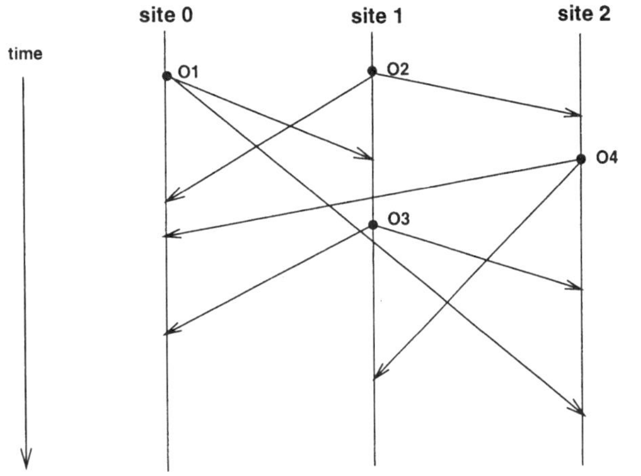

Fig. 1. A scenario of a real-time group editing session.

There are four editing operations in this scenario: operation O_1 generated at site 0, operations O_2 and O_3 generated at site 1, and operation O_4 generated at site 2. It is assumed in this scenario that an operation is executed immediately at the local site, then propagated to remote sites and executed there upon their arrival. The arrows in the graph represent the propagation of operations from the local site to remote sites. Each vertical line in the graph represents the activities performed by the corresponding site. At site 1, for example, O_2 is executed first, followed by O_1, O_3, and O_4.

According to Definitions 1 and 2, there are three pairs of dependent operations in this scenario: $O_1 \rightarrow O_3$, $O_2 \rightarrow O_3$, and $O_2 \rightarrow O_4$ because the execution of O_1 happens before the generation of O_3, the generation of O_2 happens before the generation of O_3, and the execution of O_2 happens before the generation of O_4. Moreover, there are three pairs of independent operations in this scenario: $O_1 \parallel O_2$, $O_1 \parallel O_4$, and $O_3 \parallel O_4$ because for any pair, neither operation's execution happens before the other operation's generation. As will be seen in the following discussion, several fundamental inconsistency problems are embedded in this scenario. Moreover, the seemingly simple independence relationship among operations in this scenario is actually quite intricate, and has given significant technical challenges to the design of correct operational transformation algorithms [17].

THE GROVE APPROACH

To achieve good responsiveness and avoid a single-point of failure in the system, a replicated architecture has been adopted by GROVE: the shared documents are replicated at the local storage of each participating site. An (update) operation is executed on the local replica of the shared document immediately after its generation, then broadcast to remote sites for execution (after some delay and transformation).

Divergence and causality-violation problems

Suppose remote operations are executed upon their arrival and in their *original form*, two inconsistency problems which may occur in a concurrent editing session have been identified in GROVE: one is divergence, and the other is causality-violation.

For example, consider the scenario shown in Fig. 1. The four operations arrive and are executed in the following orders: O_1, O_2, O_4, and O_3 at site 0; O_2, O_1, O_3, and O_4 at site 1; and O_2, O_4, O_3, and O_1 at site 2. If operations are not commutative, final editing results would not be identical among cooperating sites. This problem is called *divergence*. Clearly, the divergence problem should be prohibited for applications where the consistency of the final results is required.

Moreover, since each cooperating site generates and broadcasts operations without synchronization, operations may arrive and be executed in an order different from their natural causal order. As shown in Fig. 1, operation O_3 is generated after the arrival of O_1 at site 1, so $O_3 \rightarrow O_1$. However, since O_3 arrives before O_1 at site 2, the execution of O_3 before O_1 may result in an undefined operation O_3, which refers to a nonexistent context to be created by O_1, or a confused user at site 2, who observes the *effect* in O_3 before observing the *cause* in O_1. This problem is called *causality-violation*. Out of causal order execution should be prohibited for applications where a synchronized interaction among multiple users is required.

Consistency correctness criteria

Based on the identification of the two inconsistency problems, the GROVE consistency correctness criteria were defined by the following two properties:

1. **Convergence property**: copies of the shared document are identical at all sites at quiescence (i.e., all generated operations have been executed at all sites).
2. **Precedence property**: if one operations O_a causally precedes another operation O_b, then at each site the execution of O_a happens before the execution of O_b.

In search of a solution where the only constraint on execution order is the causal ordering among operations, GROVE invented the late well-known distributed OPerational Transformation (dOPT) algorithm. GROVE's solution consists of two components: one is the state-vector timestamping scheme for ensuring the precedence property, and the other is the dOPT algorithm for ensuring the convergence property. The basic idea of the dOPT algorithm is that when an operation satisfies the precedence condition for execution, it is transformed against independent operations in the Log (which saves all executed operations in the order of their execution) in such a way that executions of the same set of properly transformed independent operations in different orders produce identical document states, thus ensuring the convergence property.

A transformation property

To ensure convergence, the dOPT algorithm requires the transformation function T to satisfy the following condition: For any two independent operations O_a and O_b, suppose that $O'_a = T(O_a, O_b)$, and $O'_b = T(O_b, O_a)$, it must be that

$$O_a \circ O'_b \equiv O_b \circ O'_a$$

where "$\equiv$" means the two sequences of operations $O_a \circ O'_b$ and $O_b \circ O'_a$ are *equivalent* in the sense that when applied on the same input document state they produce the same output document state.

In addition to the above formally specified condition, GROVE also recognized there were some circumstances, in which the transformation function should achieve an effect which is *non-serializable*. For example, suppose O_a and O_b are two independent (character-wise) *delete* operations referring to the same position, then T must ensure only one character is eventually deleted no matter in which order O_a

and O_b are executed. This non-serializable effect is, however, not captured by the above formal condition for T.

A sketch of the dOPT algorithm

The transformation function T relies on the semantics of the editing operations and hence is application-dependent. The dOPT algorithm, however, is generic and takes care of selecting operations for transformation and determining the transformation order. The basic control structure of the dOPT algorithm is simple: Given a causally ready operation O, the dOPT algorithm scans the Log to transform O against any operation in the Log which is independent of O; then the transformed O, denoted as EO (i.e., the execution form of O), is executed and saved in the Log. The dOPT algorithm is sketched below.

```
dOPT(O, Log) {
   EO = O;
   for (i = 1; i <= n; i++) {
       if (Log[i] || O)
       then EO = T(EO, Log[i]);
   }
   Execute EO;
   Append EO at the end of the Log;
}
```

An unsolved dOPT puzzle

In [3] (Fig. 4 in Section 6: Discussion of Correctness), one scenario was identified, where the dOPT algorithm could not ensure convergence. This scenario[1] is re-displayed in Fig. 2.

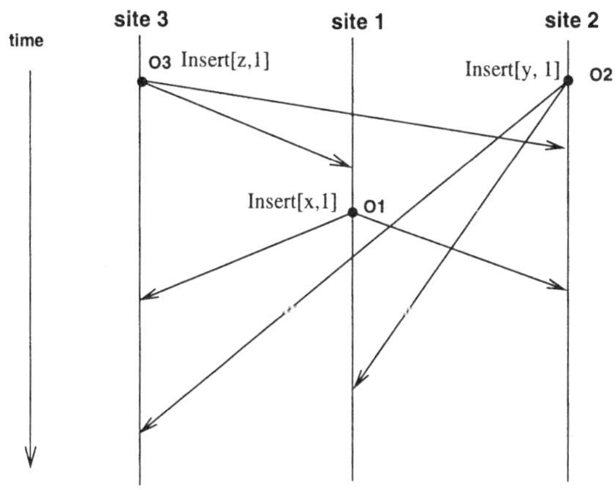

Fig. 2. The mixed priority example, in which the dOPT algorithm failed to ensure convergence.

Suppose the GROVE transformation function uses the following *priority rule*: when two insert operations have the same position parameter, the position of the operation with a *lower* priority (i.e., smaller site identifier) will be shifted[2]. According to the generic dOPT algorithm and the application-dependent transformation function in [3], the operation transformation and the final document states at the three sites are as follows (assume the initial document is empty).

[1]In fact, the scenarios in Fig. 2 can be obtained by removing O_2 from the scenario illustrated in Fig. 1.

[2]It should be noted that this priority rule is actually opposite to the one used in the definition of transformation function T_{11} in [3]. This change is necessary to correctly illustrate the problem the GROVE designers really intended to illustrate.

At site 3, O_3 first inserts "z" into the document[3]. When O_1 arrives, it inserts "x" in front of "z" to get a document with "xz". Finally, when O_2 arrives, since $O_2 \parallel O_3$ and $O_2 \parallel O_1$, it is first transformed against O_3 and becomes $O_2' = Insert[y, 2]$ due to its lower priority than O_3; then it is transformed against O_1 and becomes $O_2'' = Insert[y, 3]$. After the execution of O_2'', the document contains "xzy"[4]. At site 1, the process of operation transformation and the final result are the same as that at site 3. At site 2, O_2 first inserts "y" into the document. When O_3 arrives, it has to be transformed against O_2 since $O_3 \parallel O_2$, but no change has been made to O_3 due to its higher priority than O_2. After the execution of O_3, the document contains "zy". Finally, when O_1 arrives, it has to be transformed against O_2 since $O_1 \parallel O_2$. The transformation of O_1 against O_2 will produce $O_1' = Insert[x, 2]$ due to its lower priority than O_2. O_1' does not need to be transformed against O_3 since $O_3 \rightarrow O_1$. After the execution of O_1', the document contains "zxy", which is not identical to "xzy" at sites 3 and 1.

The problem illustrated in Fig. 2 is fundamental to the correctness of operational transformation approach. As correctly pointed out in [3], this problem could not be fixed by simply reversing the priority rule, since this patch works in this case but fails in other rather similar cases. In search of a correct solution to this problem, the simple-minded priority scheme (using a single site identifier) was thought to be root of the problem, thus a sophisticated (and complicated) priority scheme (using a list of site identifiers) was proposed in [3]. This new priority scheme did not prove to be successful in solving the problem, thus leaving one unsolved puzzle to the groupware research community.

The innovative idea of maintaining consistency by operational transformation, as well as the unsolved dOPT puzzle, has been a major inspiration and stimulation to a number of research groups in the area of real-time groupware systems. In fact, several research groups [1, 11, 13, 17], have independently re-discovered that the dOPT algorithm did not work whenever an operation is concurrent with two or more dependent operations, and different approaches have been proposed to fix it. In the following sections, three alternative approaches will be discussed, including the REDUCE approach [14, 15, 17] using an *1-dimensional* data structure for keeping track of executed operations, the Jupiter approach [11] using a *2-dimensional* data structure for maintaining executed operations, and the adOPTed approach [13] using a *N-dimensional* data structure (where N is number of cooperating sites in the system) for maintaining executed operations.

THE REDUCE APPROACH

REDUCE follows GROVE in adopting a fully distributed and replicated system architecture. A linear *History Buffer* (HB), which is the same as the Log in GROVE, is used to keep track of all executed operations. In addition, a garbage collection scheme was devised to remove useless operations from the HB [17].

[3]In this paper, the sequence of characters in a text document are referred to (or addressed) from 1 to the end of the document.

[4]It should be pointed out that this result is different from what was presented in [3].

The intention-violation problem

Apart from divergence and causality-violation problems, one special kind of inconsistency problem – *intention-violation* – has been identified in REDUCE [14].

To illustrate, consider the two independent operations O_1 and O_2 in the scenario shown in Fig. 1. At site 0, O_2 is executed on a document state which has been changed by the preceding execution of O_1. Therefore, the subsequent execution of O_2 may refer to an incorrect position in the new document state, and result in an editing effect different from the O_2's *intention*, which is defined as the editing effect which could be achieved by applying O_2 on the document state from which O_2 was generated [14].

For example, assume the shared document initially contains the following sequence of characters: "ABCDE". Suppose $O_1 = Insert[\text{"12"}, 2]$, which intends to insert string "12" at position 2, i.e., between "A" and "BCDE"; and $O_2 = Delete[2, 3]$, which intends to delete the two characters starting from position 3, i.e., "CD". After the execution of these two operations, the *intention-preserved* result (at all sites) should be: "A12BE". However, the actual result at site 0, obtained by executing O_1 followed by executing O_2, would be: "A1CDE", which clearly violates the intention of O_1 since the character "2", which was intended to be inserted, is missing in the final text, and also violates the intention of O_2 since characters "CD", which were intended to be deleted, are still present in the final text. A serialization protocol might be used to ensure that all sites execute O_1 and O_2 in the same order to get an identical result "A1CDE", but this identical result is still inconsistent with the intentions of both O_1 and O_2.

It is important to recognize that intention violation is an inconsistency problem of a different nature from the divergence problem. The essential difference between divergence and intention violation is that the former can always be resolved by a serialization protocol, but the latter cannot be fixed by any serialization protocol if operations were always executed in their original forms.

A consistency model

Due to the distinction of the intention-violation problem from the divergence problem, one additional consistency correctness criteria – intention-preservation – was proposed in REDUCE [14]. The REDUCE correctness criteria for consistency maintenance has been defined in the form of a consistency model as follows.

Definition 3: A consistency model

A cooperative editing system is consistent if it always maintains the following properties:

1. **Convergence**: when the same set of operations have been executed at all sites, all copies of the shared document are identical.
2. **Causality-preservation**: for any pair of operations O_a and O_b, if $O_a \rightarrow O_b$, then O_a is executed before O_b at all sites.
3. **Intention-preservation**: for any operation O, the effects of executing O at all sites are the same as the intention of O, and the effect of executing O does not change the effects of independent operations.

□

To support the three properties of the consistency model, REDUCE adopted the same state-vector timestamping scheme as that in GROVE for achieving causality-preservation (or precedence in GROVE's terminology). With the distinction of intention-preservation from convergence, two separate schemes were devised for supporting these two different properties: an *undo/do/redo* scheme for achieving convergence, and an operational transformation algorithm for achieving intention-preservation.

To achieve convergence, a total ordering relationship "$\Rightarrow$" among operations is defined [14]. However, operations are allowed to be executed in any order as long as their causality is preserved. When a new operation O is causally-ready for execution, (1) **undo** operations in the *HB* which totally *follow* O to restore the document to the state before their execution; (2) **do** O; and finally (3) **redo** all operations that were undone from the *HB*. It should be noted that the *undo/redo* operations involved in this scheme are *internal* operations, rather than *external* operations initiated from the user interface [12]. Therefore, the undo/do/redo scheme should be implemented in such a way that only the final result (instead of the intermediate ones) produced at the end of the undo/do/redo process is reflected on the user interface.

Transformation pre-/post-conditions

Since transformation functions in REDUCE are not responsible for ensuring convergence, they are not required to satisfy the same condition as in GROVE. In REDUCE, when operation O_a is transformed against operation O_b, it is required that the effect of the transformed operation O'_a on the document state that contains the impact of O_b should be the same as the effect of O_a on the document state that does not contain the impact of O_b. This type of transformation is called *Inclusion Transformation* (IT), since it transforms an operation O_a against another operation O_b in such a way that the impact of O_b is effectively included. The GROVE transformation functions can be regarded as a kind of inclusion transformation. Most importantly, it was recognized that the correctness of this inclusion transformation relies on the condition that both O_a and O_b are defined on the same document state [17], so their parameters are comparable and can be used to derive a proper adjustment to O_a. Failing to recognize and to ensure this condition is the root of the unsolved dOPT puzzle.

In search of a correct and sophisticated solution to intention-preservation, REDUCE introduced another type of transformation, called *Exclusion Transformation* (ET), which transforms O_a against another operation O_b in such a way that the impact of O_b is effectively excluded from O_a [17]. For example, O_4 and O_1 are independent operations but generated from different documents states, as shown in Fig. 1. When O_4 arrives at site 0, it is incorrect to simply transform O_4 against O_1. Instead, exclusion transformation should be applied on O_4 against its causally preceding operation O_2 to produce O'_4 in such a way that O_2's impact on O_4 is excluded. Consequently, O'_4 effectively shares the same document state with O_1, and then can be applied with the inclusion transformation against O_1.

To capture the required relationship between operations for *correct* transformation, the notion of operation *context* is introduced. The context of a document state is the sequence of operations executed on the initial document state to arrive at the current document state. Given an operation O, the *definition context* of O, denoted as $DC(O)$, is the context of the document state on which O is defined; and the *execution context* of O, denoted as $EC(O)$, is the context of the document state on which O is to be executed. The intention of an operation can be preserved if its definition context matches its execution context, i.e., $DC(O) = EC(O)$.

REDUCE uses two primitive transformation functions – $IT(O_a, O_b)$ and $ET(O_a, O_b)$ – to make an operation's definition context equivalent to its execution context. For specifying pre-/post-conditions of the transformation functions, two context-based relations are defined below (Note: a context is expressed as an operation list in the rest of the paper).

Definition 4: Context equivalent relation " $\sqcup$ "
Given two operations O_a and O_b, O_a and O_b are *context-equivalent*, i.e., $O_a \sqcup O_b$, *iff* $DC(O_a) = DC(O_b)$. □

Definition 5: Context preceding relation "$\mapsto$"
Given two operations O_a and O_b, O_a is *context preceding* O_b, i.e., $O_a \mapsto O_b$, *iff* $DC(O_b) = DC(O_a) + [O_a]$ (where "+" expresses the concatenation of two lists). □

With the context-based relations, the pre-/post-conditions of the two transformation functions are specified as follows.

Specification 1: $IT(O_a, O_b) : O'_a$
1. Precondition for input parameters: $O_a \sqcup O_b$.
2. Postcondition for output: $O_b \mapsto O'_a$, and the effect of O'_a in $DC(O'_a)$ is the same as the effect of O_a in $DC(O_a)$. □

Specification 2: $ET(O_a, O_b) : O'_a$
1. Precondition for input parameters: $O_b \mapsto O_a$.
2. Postcondition for output: $O_b \sqcup O'_a$, and the effect of O'_a in $DC(O'_a)$ is the same as the effect of O_a in $DC(O_a)$. □

The design of a pair of IT/ET functions for string-wise operations, which satisfy the specified post-conditions, can be found in [16, 17].

The GOT control algorithm

To ensure transformation pre-conditions a Generic Operational Transformation (GOT) control algorithm has been devised [17]. Taking a causally-ready operation O and its execution context $EC(O)$ (i.e., the current contents of the HB) as input parameters, the GOT control algorithm uses the IT/ET functions to transform O into EO (the execution form of O) such that $DC(EO) = EC(O)$.

Three cases have been distinguished and handled differently in the GOT control algorithm, as illustrated in Fig. 3. In this example, we assume $EC(O) = HB = [EO_1, EO_2, EO_3]$.

Case 1 : All operations in $EC(O)$ are causally preceding O. It must be that $DC(O) = EC(O)$, so that $EO = O$ (no transformation is performed).

Case 2 : Operations causally preceding O are listed in $EC(O)$ before operations independent of O. Since $EO_1 \to O$, $EO_2 \parallel O$, and $EO_3 \parallel O$, by transforming O against EO_2 and EO_3 in sequence, we get EO such that $DC(EO) = EC(O)$.

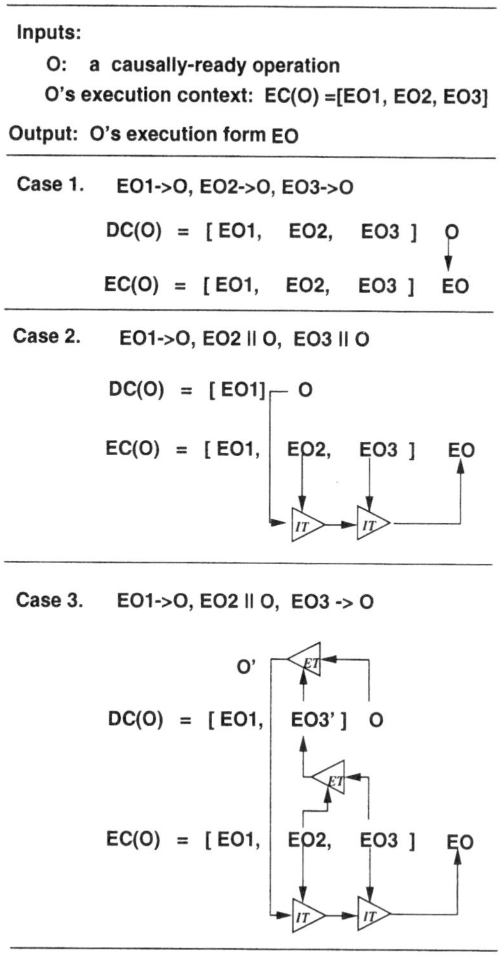

Fig. 3. Three cases analysis and handling by the GOT control algorithm

Case 3 : At least one causally-preceding operation is positioned after an independent operation in $EC(O)$. This is the case that the dOPT algorithm failed to handle correctly. Since $EO_1 \to O$, $EO_2 \parallel O$, and $EO_3 \to O$, it must be that $DC(O) = [EO_1, EO'_3]$, where EO'_3 is the original form of EO_3 when O was generated. Transforming O directly against any operation in $EO(O)$ would violate the pre-conditions for IT/ET functions. The strategy taken by the GOT algorithm is as follows: (1) apply exclusion transformation on EO_3 against EO_2 (both EO_3 and EO_2 are available in $EO(O)$) to obtain EO'_3, (2) apply exclusion transformation on O against EO'_3 to get an intermediate O'; and finally (3) apply inclusion transformation on O' against EO_2 and EO_3 in sequence, we get EO such that $DC(EO) = EC(O)$.

To describe the GOT algorithm, a few notations need to be introduced: Given a list of operations L, $L[i, j]$ denotes a sublist of L containing the operations from EO_i to EO_j inclusively; and L^{-1} denotes the reverse of L. $LIT(O, L)/LET(O, L)$ is used to denote the application of IT/ET function on operation O against a list of operations in L in sequence from left to right.

Algorithm 1: GOT(O, L): EO
O: a causally-ready operation
L: the list of operations $[EO_1, EO_2, ..., EO_m]$ in $EC(O)$.

EO: the execution form of O.

1. Scan $L[1, m]$ from left to right to find the first operation EO_k such that $EO_k \parallel O$. If no such an operation is found, then **return** $EO := O$.
2. Otherwise, scan $L[k+1, m]$ to find operations causally preceding O. If no single such operation is found, then **return** $EO := LIT(O, L[k, m])$.
3. Otherwise, let $L_1 = [EO_{c_1}, ..., EO_{c_r}]$ be the list of operations in $L[k, m]$ which are causally preceding O.
   (a) Get $L'_1 = [EO'_{c_1}, ..., EO'_{c_r}]$ as follows:
      i. $EO'_{c_1} := LET(EO_{c_1}, L[k, c_1 - 1]^{-1})$.
      ii. For $2 \leq i \leq r$,
         $O_t := LET(EO_{c_i}, L[k, c_i - 1]^{-1})$;
         $EO'_{c_i} := LIT(O_t, [EO'_{c_1}, ..., EO'_{c_{i-1}}])$.
   (b) $O' := LET(O, L_1'^{-1})$.
   (c) **return** $EO := LIT(O', L[k, m])$.

□

It can be shown that the pre-conditions required by the transformation functions are always guaranteed by the GOT control algorithm. Therefore, if the post-conditions are always ensured by the transformation functions, then the GOT control algorithm will transform O into EO, so that the execution of EO on $EC(O)$ will preserve the intention of O. To achieves both intention-preservation and convergence, the GOT control algorithm has been integrated with the undo/do/redo scheme to form an undo/transform-do/transform-redo scheme [17].

A solution to the dOPT puzzle

In this section, we show how REDUCE solves the dOPT puzzle. We assume, without losing generality, the total ordering relationship "$\Rightarrow$" among the three operations in Fig. 2 is: $O_3 \Rightarrow O_1 \Rightarrow O_2$. Also, we assume the the REDUCE transformation function $IT(O_a, O_b)$ uses the following *shifting rule*: if both O_a and O_b are insertions and have the same position parameter, the position of O_a will be shifted. This shifting rule is consistent with the priority rule used in GROVE.

Under REDUCE, the operation transformation and the final document states (i.e., "xzy") at sites 3 and 1 are the same as they are under GROVE. The situation at site 2, however, is different: O_2 first inserts "y" into the document. Next, when O_3 arrives, O_2 has to be undone since $O_3 \Rightarrow O_2$. Then O_3 is executed as is, and O_2 is inclusively transformed against O_3 (according to $O_3 \parallel O_2$ and Case 2 in the GOT algorithm) to become $O'_2 = Insert[y, 2]$ according to the shifting rule. After the execution of both O_3 and O'_2, the document contains "zy". Finally, when O_1 arrives, O'_2 has to be undone since $O_1 \Rightarrow O'_2$. Then O_1 is executed as is (since $O_3 \rightarrow O_1$), and O'_2 is inclusively transformed against O_1 (according to $O_2 \parallel O_1$ and Case 2 in the GOT function) to become $O''_2 = Insert[y, 3]$. After the execution of O''_2, the document contains "xzy", which is identical to the document state at sites 3 and 1, and the intentions of all three operations are preserved. In this particular example, the exclusion transformation is not used, but in more complex scenarios, such as the one shown in Fig. 1, exclusion transformation is needed (see [17]).

THE JUPITER APPROACH

The Jupiter collaboration system was developed at Xerox PARC [11]. Since Jupiter has already had a central server for maintaining the states of objects (e.g., White-board, text documents, etc.) in the shared persistent virtual world, it is natural to use this central server for supporting consistency maintenance of shared objects as well. The Jupiter consistency maintenance algorithm was derived from the dOPT algorithm. The most interesting part of the Jupiter approach is the adaptation of the dOPT optimistic algorithm to an environment with multiple replicated clients sites *plus* one centralized server site.

In Jupiter, the shared documents are replicated at all cooperating client sites, which is the same as in GROVE. The difference is that the shared documents are also maintained at the central server and communications happen only between a client and the server (i.e., a 2-way communication). When an updating operation is generated at a client site, it is immediately executed at the local client site (for fast response to user actions), and then propagated to the central server. The server first transforms the incoming operation if necessary, then executes the transformed operation on its copy of the shared document, and finally broadcasts the transformed operation to all other client sites. Upon receiving an operation propagated from the central server, a client site may transform this operation if necessary, and then executes it on the local copy of the document. This star-like topology of communication eliminates the concern for ensuring causality (i.e., causality-violation never occurs). It also substantially simplifies the operational transformation control algorithm.

To achieve convergence, the Jupiter transformation function is required to satisfy the same property as that required by the dOPT algorithm. However, Jupiter uses a 2-dimensional *state space* graph, instead of a linear Log/HB, to keep track of all possible operation transformation paths to guide the selection of right operations for transformation. The Jupiter algorithm ensures that any pair of operations involved in a transformation must have originated from the same starting state in the state space graph, which is essentially the same as ensuring the *context equivalent* precondition by the GOT algorithm in the REDUCE approach. Therefore, the Jupiter algorithm is able to correct the dOPT algorithm under the condition that only 2-way communications are allowed in the system. An alternative approach to correcting the dOPT algorithm for the 2-way communication special case can be found in [1].

THE ADOPTED APPROACH

The adOPTed algorithm adopted the same correctness criteria from GROVE for consistency maintenance: convergence and precedence (i.e., causality-preservation). It also followed GROVE in using a fully distributed and replicated architecture. What is different in the adOPTed algorithm is that it requires an additional property for transformation functions to satisfy. Given two operations O_a and O_b, let $O'_a = T(O_a, O_b)$, and $O'_b = T(O_b, O_a)$, the transformation function T is required to possess the following two properties:

Transformation Property 1 (TP1) :

$$O_a \circ O'_b \equiv O_b \circ O'_a$$

Transformation Property 2 (TP2) : For any O,

$$T(T(O, O_a), O'_b) = T(T(O, O_b), O'_a)$$

TP1 is the same as that required by the dOPT algorithm and the Jupiter algorithm, but TP2 is new in the adOPTed algorithm. TP2 ensures that the transformation of operation O along different paths will yield the same resulting operation. These two properties can be illustrated by using a directed graph, called *interaction model* [13], as shown in Figure 4.

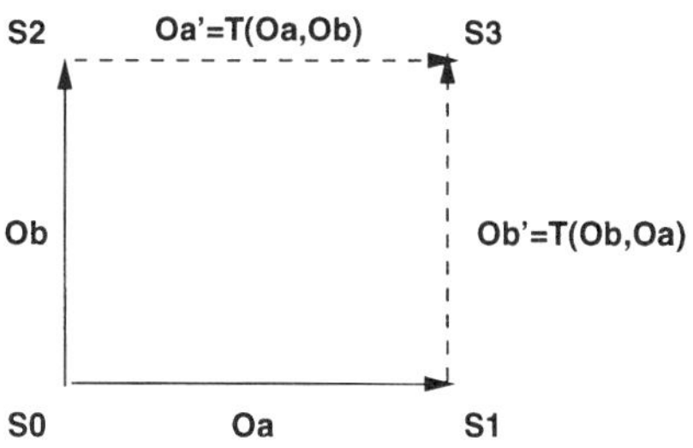

(a) Transformation property 1: : Oa o Ob' $\equiv$ Ob o Oa'

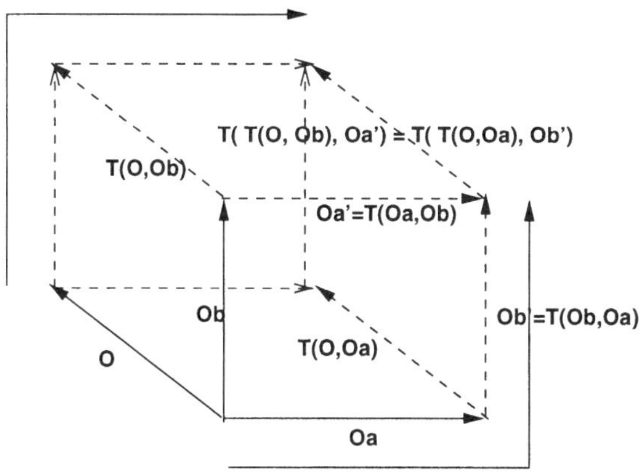

(b) Transformation property 2: T(T(O, Oa), Ob') = T(T(O,Ob), Oa')

Fig. 4. Interaction model illustration of transformation properties.

The vertices of the interaction model graph are labeled by document states, and the edges are labeled by operations. For example, the four vertices of the square in Figure 4-(a) are labeled by four document states: S_0, S_1, S_2, and S_3, respectively; the two solid edges are labeled by two original operations: O_a and O_b, respectively; and the other two dashed edges are labeled by two transformed operations: $O'_a = T(O_a, O_b)$, and $O'_b = T(O_b, O_a)$, respectively. Essentially, TP1 ensures the unique vertices labeling, whereas TP2 ensures the unique edge labeling in the interaction model graph. It has been shown in [13] that TP1 and TP2 are the necessary and sufficient conditions for ensuring convergence in systems which allow N-way communication (where N is the number of cooperating sites).

The adOPTed algorithm used an N-dimensional interaction model graph to keeps track of all valid paths of operation transformations. The N-dimensional interaction model graph can be viewed as a generalization of the *2*-dimensional state space in the Jupiter algorithm, and it also plays the same role in guiding the selection of the right path and right operations for transformation. The adOPTed algorithm ensures that any pair of operations involved in a transformation are defined on the same document state.

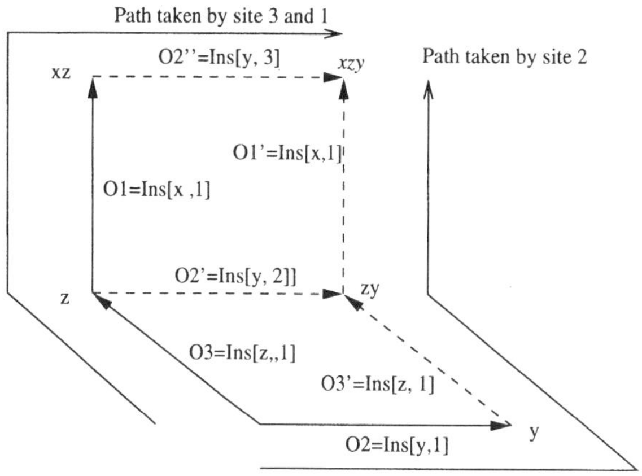

Fig. 5. The adOPTed solution to the dOPT puzzle

Using the adOPTed algorithm and the same transformation function T_{11} from GROVE, the solution to the dOPT puzzle can be illustrated in Figure 5. At sites 3 and 1, the operation transformation and execution follow the same path: O_3 and O_1 are executed as is, but O_2 is transformed against O_3 and O_1 in sequence, resulting in $O'_2 = Ins[y, 2]$, then $O''_2 = Ins[y, 3]$ (In the meantime, the adOPTed algorithm also produces $O'_3 = Ins[z, 1]$, and $O'_1 = Ins[x, 1]$, which are of no use at sites 3 and 1). The execution of O_3, O_1, and O''_2 in sequence results in the final document state "xzy". At site 2, a different path in the interaction model graph is taken. First, O_2 is executed as is. When O_3 arrives, it is transformed against O_2 to become $O'_3 = Ins[z, 1]$. Meanwhile, the adOPTed algorithm also transforms O_2 against O_3 to produce $O'_2 = Ins[y, 2]$, and both O'_3 and O'_2 are maintained at proper positions in the interaction model graph. When O_1 arrives, the adOPTed algorithm searches the interaction model graph to find the right operation O'_2 (instead of O_2, which was used in the dOPT algorithm) for transformation to get $O'_1 = Ins[x, 1]$. In the meantime, the adOPTed algorithm also produces and maintains $O''_2 = Ins[y, 3]$ at site 2 (O''_2 is of no use in this example). The execution of O_2, O'_3, and O'_1 in sequence results in an identical document state "xzy".

AN OPTIMIZED ALGORITHM: GOTO

Without requiring TP1 and TP2, the GOT control algorithm, integrated with the undo/do/redo scheme [17], is the only known solution for achieving both intention-preservation and convergence. An interesting question is: what could the GOT algorithm achieve if TP1 and TP2 are satisfied by IT/ET functions? In this section, we will answer this question and propose a new optimized GOT control algorithm.

To take advantage of the two additional post-conditions TP1 and TP2, we modify the original context-based relations in Definitions 4 and 5 as follows: replace the *equal* sign "=" with the *equivalence* sign "$\equiv$". Obviously, the equal relation "=" between operation contexts is a special case of the equivalence relation "$\equiv$". With this generalization of context-based relations and the extension of pre-/post-conditions for IT/ET functions, we found that the original GOT control algorithm can ensure both intention-preservation and convergence, without integrating with the undo/do/redo scheme or using a multi-dimensional graph. The verification of this claim can follow similar reasonings as used in [13], which is, however, beyond the scope of this paper.

Moreover, the two additional post-conditions TP1 and TP2 can be employed to optimize the GOT control algorithm by reducing the number of IT/ET transformations. The optimized algorithm, named as GOTO (GOT Optimized), resembles the original GOT algorithm in handling the first and the second cases (see Fig. 3). For the third case, the handling is different. In addition to performing transformations on the definition context of O, we also perform transformations on the execution context of O to make the two contexts equivalent. This can be achieved by executing the following two steps:

1. Transform execution context $EC(O)$ into such an *equivalent* $EC(O)'$ that all operations causally preceding O are positioned before independent operations in $EC(O)'$. Let $EC(O)' = EC(O)'.left + EC(O)'.right$, where $EC(O)'.left$ is the sublist of causally preceding operations, and $EC(O)'.right$ is the sublist of independent operations.
2. Apply the inclusion transformation on O against the list of independent operations in $EC(O)'.right$. The transformation pre-condition is satisfied because $EC(O)'.left \equiv DC(O)$.

The question now is: how to transform $EC(O)$ into such an equivalent $EC(O)'$?

By using *IT* and *ET* functions, the *Transpose* function is defined to transform and swap two operations in an execution context.

Function 1: $Transpos(O_a, O_b) : O_b', O_a'$

{
  $O_b' := ET(O_b, O_a)$;
  $O_a' := IT(O_a, O_b')$;
  return (O_b', O_a');
}

The pre-condition for O_a and O_b is: $O_a \mapsto O_b$. The post-condition for O_a' and O_b' is: $O_b' \mapsto O_a'$. Based on the Transpose function, function $LTranspose(L)$ is defined, which transforms and circularly shifts the list of operations in L.

Procedure 1: $LTranspose(L)$

{
  for (i = $|L|$; $i > 1$; i- -)
    $(L[i-1], L[i]) := Transpose(L[i-1], L[i])$;
}

According to TP1 and TP2, and the definition of *Transpose*, it must be that $L \equiv L'$, where L' is the list of operations after calling $LTranspose(L)$.

As an example, the handling of case 3 by the GOTO algorithm is shown in Fig. 6. In this example, we can transpose EO_2 and EO_3 in $EC(O)$ by calling $Transpose(EO_2, EO_3)$, so that an equivalent execution context $EC(O)' = [EO_1, EO_3', EO_2']$ can be obtained. Then, since $DC(O) \equiv [EO_1, EO_3']$, we can apply an inclusion transformation on O

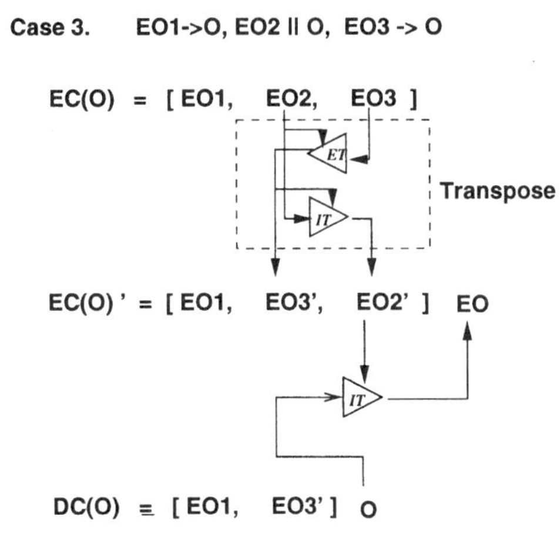

Fig. 6. The handling of mixed independent and dependent operations by the GOTO control algorithm

against EO_2' to get EO, such that $DC(EO) \equiv EC(O)'$. To transform O into EO in this example, three IT/ET transformations (one Transpose function costs one IT and one ET transformations) are needed under the GOTO control algorithm, whereas four IT/ET transformations are needed under the GOT control algorithm.

Algorithm 2: GOTO(O, L): EO

O: a causally-ready operation

L: the list of operations $[EO_1, EO_2, ..., EO_m]$ in $EC(O)$.

EO: the execution form of O.

1. Scan $L[1, m]$ from left to right to find the first operation EO_k such that $EO_k \parallel O$. If no such an operation is found, then **return** $EO := O$.
2. Otherwise, scan $L[k+1, m]$ to find operations causally preceding O. If no single such operation is found, then **return** $EO := LIT(O, L[k, m])$.
3. Otherwise, let $L_1 = [EO_{c_1}, ..., EO_{c_r}]$ be the list of operations in $L[k, m]$ which are causally preceding O.
   (a) For $1 \le i \le r$:
       $LTranspose(L[k+i-1, c_i])$;
   (b) **return** $EO := LIT(O, L[k+r, m])$.

□

It can be shown that the pre-conditions required by the transformation functions are always guaranteed by the GOTO control algorithm. Therefore, if the post-conditions, including TP1 and TP2, are always ensured by the transformation functions, then the GOTO control algorithm will transform O into EO, so that the execution of EO on $EC(O)$ will preserve the intention of O and ensure convergence.

CONCLUSIONS AND FUTURE DIRECTIONS

Many people have experiences of using various editors. Not so many people have recognized that there would exist many interesting research issues in an editor when used in a real-time collaborative context. Even less people have come to learn that some research issues in real-time group editors, such as consistency maintenance, would be so challenging that a decade exploration would not be enough to exhaust their research potential. In this paper, we have reviewed a number of major operational transformation algorithms for consistency maintenance in real-time group editors, including the dOPT algorithm, the GOT algorithm, the Jupiter algorithm, and the adOPTed algorithm, and have proposed a new optimized transformation control algorithm – the GOTO algorithm. In this concluding section, we summarize the major achievements in the past decade on the transformation-based consistency maintenance techniques and point out the major open issues for further exploration.

Major achievements

Three inconsistency problems – divergence, causality-violation, and intention-violation – have been identified and explored. Particularly, the non-serializable intention violation problem has been distinguished from the serializable divergence problem. Corresponding to these three problems, consistency correctness criteria consist of three properties: convergence, causality-preservation, and intention-preservation. It is useful to integrate these three properties in a consistency model, which effectively specifies what consistency has been promised to the system users and what properties must be supported by the underlying system algorithms.

The discovery of the necessary transformation pre-conditions has been a significant step toward the design of correct transformation control algorithms. The notion of operation context is very useful in capturing the required relationship between operations for correct transformation. Alternative approaches to ensuring transformation pre-conditions include the GOT/GOTO control algorithms working on an 1-dimensional history buffer, the Jupiter algorithm working on a 2-dimensional state space graph, and the adOPTed algorithm working on a N-dimensional interaction model graph.

Two types of transformation functions have been proposed: inclusion and exclusion transformations. For algorithms that use a multi-dimensional data structure to keep track of operations in their original, intermediate, and executed forms, such as the Jupiter and adOPTed algorithms, only inclusion transformation is needed. For algorithms that use an 1-dimensional history buffer to save operations in their executed form only, such as the GOT and GOTO algorithms, apart from inclusion transformation, exclusion transformation is needed to recover operations' original and intermediate forms from their executed forms.

The identification of proper transformation post-conditions has played a crucial role in the design of both the generic transformation control algorithms and application dependent transformation functions. By requiring context-based post-conditions, the GOT control algorithm can achieve intention-preservation. The context-based post-conditions, however, do not capture the conditions for ensuring convergence, so the GOT control algorithm must be integrated with an undo/do/redo scheme to achieve convergence. In essence, undo/redo can also be viewed as a kind of transformation, which is performed directly on the document states rather than on the operations. By requiring TP1 only, the Jupiter algorithm can achieve convergence in systems which are restricted to 2-way communication. By requiring both TP1 and TP2, the adOPTed algorithm achieves convergence in systems which allow N-way communication. Neither TP1 nor TP2, however, captures the conditions for ensuring intention-preservation, so intention-preservation has been *implicitly* handled by transformation functions in the dOPT algorithm, the Jupiter algorithm, and the adOPTed algorithm. By requiring both TP1 and TP2, in addition to the context-based post-conditions, the GOT control algorithm alone is able to achieve both intention-preservation and convergence. By performing transformations on both definition and execution contexts, the GOTO algorithm is able to optimize the GOT algorithm by reducing the number of transformations.

Open issues and future directions

The correctness of the whole operational transformation scheme relies on the satisfaction of both transformation pre-conditions and post-conditions. Lots of work have been done on the design of correct generic transformation control algorithms to ensure transformation pre-conditions. However, not much work has been done on the design of application-dependent transformation functions which could really ensure transformation post-conditions [16]. We have learned that TP1 and TP2 have to be satisfied by transformation functions in order to ensure convergence, but we know little about how to verify whether an existing transformation function really satisfies TP1 and TP2. In fact, as illustrated in [17], some seemingly correct transformation functions do not really satisfy TP1 and TP2. More serious attention should be given to the design of transformation functions to better understand the intrinsic interactions (in the form of pre-/post-conditions) between transformation functions and transformation control algorithms.

Research should also be directed toward formal specification and verification of operational transformation concepts, properties, and algorithms. This formalization and verification is necessary for rigorously proving the correctness of the algorithms and for analyzing and improving the time and space complexities of existing algorithms. In [1], a Calculus for Concurrent Update (CCU) has been derived from the dOPT algorithm as a tool for the purpose of formal modeling and verification of consistency-preserving operational transformation. The *Team Automata* [6] is another mathematical model for describing the interaction of a groupware system components. More work needs to be done in developing and applying innovative theoretical tools to verify operational transformation algorithms and systems.

Future research should distinguish and explore two types of consistencies: one is *syntactic* consistency, which is concerned with whether all sites have the same view of the shared objects, regardless of whether the common view makes sense in the application context; and the other is *semantic* consistency, which is concerned with whether all sites have the same view of the shared objects, as well as whether the common view makes sense in the application context. There may exist many levels of syntactic consistency and semantic consistency in a particular application context. Previous work has mainly explored issues related to syntactic consistency. Particularly, the term *intention* as defined in [14, 17] and used in this paper has captured only a small piece of the much richer meaning of intention from the human user's perspective. This brings up interesting areas of research concerned with characterization and preservation of the human user's intentions in collaborative contexts, or *group intentions*. It may be infeasible for the system alone to automatically determine the human group intentions for different groups with divergent group goals. The system, however, could and should have mechanisms to help the group users decide their group intentions and resolve their conflicts. In general, we advocate a groupware system design paradigm, which builds a sufficient amount of generic supporting *mechanism* into the system, but leave the high level collaboration *policy* decisions up to the system users. A good groupware system should be easily tunable by its users for supporting various collaboration needs [2, 10].

A lot of efforts have been putted on achieving the shortest response time (as short as single user editors), but not much research has been done on notification policy – when and how to make local updates public to achieve global consistency. Alternatives to notifying remote sites immediately after executing an operation at the local site include periodic notification, notification on demand, greying out the screen to tell user that the displayed information is out-of-date, etc. Future research should be conducted on mechanisms for supporting alternative notification policies and their applicability in different application environments.

Operation granularity is another unexplored issue. Current transformation algorithms are only capable of handling fine-grain primitive operations, such as *Insert* and *Delete*. Useful editors, however, must offer to the end user higher level compound operations, such as *Move*, and *Replace*. On one hand, the system needs additional mechanisms to support coarse-grain compound operations as an atomic sequence of primitive operations while still ensuring consistency properties. The richer semantics of the compound operations, on the other hand, could help the system to better understand and preserve the user's intentions.

A number of prototype group editors have been built in the past by various research groups for testing the feasibility of transformation-based consistency maintenance algorithms, and for investigating system design and implementation issues. GROVE has been used in several real groups for a variety of design activities to evaluate the system from users perspective and to gain usage experience [4, 5]. Since then, however, little has been reported on using this type of system in real-life collaborative environments to study the user's working modes in using the system, and to conduct statistics analysis of conflicts. Much more research efforts should be directed toward better understanding the potential effects of this type of system on people, their work and interactions.

Although all the transformation-based consistency maintenance algorithms and functions were designed in the context of text editing, many of them are actually quite general and potentially applicable in other domains of group editing. It would be interesting and useful to apply operational transformation in graphics/image/multimedia editors to further validate the generic algorithms and to gain more insights in the design and application of these types of systems. Even techniques used in transforming a sequence of characters could potentially be applicable in other real-time groupware systems, which allow concurrent insertion/deletion of any sequence of objects with a linearly ordered relationship. Moreover, operational transformation has been found very useful in supporting user-initiated collaborative undo operations [12, 13].

Consistency maintenance is a fundamental issue in many areas of computing systems, including operating systems, databases systems, distributed shared memory systems, and groupware systems. Research on real-time group editors, as a special class of distributed systems supporting human-computer-human interactions, has drawn inspirations from traditional distributed computing techniques (e.g., causal/total ordering of events, state-vector timestamping, serialization, etc.), and has also invented the non-traditional operational transformation technique to address its special issues, such as intention-preservation. The generalization and application of this unique operational transformation technique to other areas of distributed computing and CSCW is an exciting direction for future exploration.

References

[1] C. V. Cormack: "A calculus for concurrent update," Research Report CS-95-06, Dept. of Computer Science, University of Waterloo, Canada, 1995.

[2] P. Dourish: "Consistency guarantees: exploiting application semantics for consistency management in a collaborative tookit," In *Proc. of ACM Conference on Computer Supported Cooperative Work*, pp. 268-277, Nov. 1996.

[3] C. A. Ellis and S. J. Gibbs: "Concurrency control in groupware systems," In *Proc. of ACM SIGMOD Conference on Management of Data*, pp.399-407, 1989.

[4] C. A. Ellis, S. J. Gibbs, G.L. Rein: "Design and use of a group editor," In *Engineering for Human-Computer Interaction*. G. Cockton, Ed., North-Holland, Amsterdam, 1990, pp.13-25.

[5] C. A. Ellis, S. J. Gibbs, and G. L. Rein: "Groupware: some issues and experiences," *CACM 34(1)*, pp.39-58, Jan. 1991.

[6] C. A. Ellis: "Team Automata for Groupware Systems," In *Proc. of ACM Conference on Supporting Group Work*, pp.415-424, Nov. 1997.

[7] S. Greenberg and D. Marwood: "Real time groupware as a distributed system: concurrency control and its effect on the interface," In *Proc. of ACM Conference on Computer Supported Cooperative Work*, pp. 207-217, Nov. 1994.

[8] A. Karsenty and M. Beaudouin-Lafon: "An algorithm for distributed groupware applications," In *Proc. of 13th International Conference on Distributed Computing Systems*, pp. 195-202, May 1993.

[9] L. Lamport: "Time, clocks, and the ordering of events in a distributed system," *CACM 21(7)*, pp.558-565, July 1978.

[10] J. Munson and P. Dewan: "A concurrency control framework for collaborative systems," In *Proc. of ACM Conference on Computer Supported Cooperative Work*, pp. 278-287, Nov. 1996.

[11] D. Nichols, P. Curtis, M. Dixon, and J. Lamping: "High-latency, low-bandwidth windowing in the Jupiter collaboration system," In *Proc. of ACM Symposium on User Interface Software and Technologies*, pp. 111-120, Nov. 1995.

[12] A. Prakash and M. Knister: "A framework for undoing actions in collaborative systems," *ACM Transactions on Computer-Human Interaction*, 4(1), pp.295-330, 1994.

[13] M. Ressel, D. Nitsche-Ruhland, and R. Gunzenbauser: "An integrating, transformation-oriented approach to concurrency control and undo in group editors," In *Proc. of ACM Conference on Computer Supported Cooperative Work*, pp 288-297, Nov. 1996.

[14] C. Sun, Y.Yang, Y. Zhang, and D. Chen: "A consistency model and supporting schemes for real-time cooperative editing systems," In *Proc. of The 19th Australasian Computer Science Conference*, pp. 582-591, Melbourne, Jan. 1996.

[15] C. Sun, X. Jia, Y. Zhang, and Y. Yang: "A generic operation transformation scheme for consistency maintenance in real-time cooperative editing systems," In *Proc. of ACM Conference on Supporting Group Work*, pp. 425-434, Nov. 1997.

[16] C. Sun, D. Chen, X. Jia: "Reversible inclusion and exclusion transformation for string-wise operations in cooperative editing systems," In *Proc. of The 21st Australasian Computer Science Conference*, pp.441-452, Springer-Verlag, Perth, Feb. 1998.

[17] C. Sun, X. Jia, Y. Zhang, Y. Yang, and D. Chen: "Achieving convergence, causality-preservation, and intention-preservation in real-time cooperative editing systems," *ACM Transactions on Computer-human Interaction*, 5(1), March 1998, pp.63-108.

Operation Transforms for a Distributed Shared Spreadsheet

Christopher R. Palmer and Gordon V. Cormack
Department of Computer Science
University of Waterloo
Waterloo, Ontario
{crpalmer,gvcormack}@plg.uwaterloo.ca

ABSTRACT

The Distributed Operation Transform (dOPT), proposed by Ellis and Gibbs, is used to define concurrently updatable shared objects. Ellis and Gibbs give the operation transforms that define a simple shared text editor supporting single character insertions and deletions on a linear buffer. We report here on the construction of operation transforms for a more sophisticated groupware application: a shared spreadsheet. We identify a set of abstract operations that characterize the operations on a spreadsheet. Using Cormack's Calculus for Concurrent Update, which extends and corrects dOPT, we give the transforms on these operations necessary to define a shared spreadsheet. We use the transforms to build a shared version of `sc`, the Unix spreadsheet due to Gosling.

KEYWORDS

Groupware, Operation Transforms, Distributed Spreadsheets

INTRODUCTION

We are concerned with asynchronous distributed groupware, in which any copy of a replicated object can be updated at any time, and each update is then propagated to all copies. Asynchronous distributed groupware offers responsiveness and freedom from locking or check-in/check-out procedures even with slow or part-time connectivity. The challenge is to deal with concurrent updates to different copies of the object.

As a simple example, consider a simple text object with the initial value "xyz". The update *insert "a" after the first character* is applied to one copy, with a resulting value of "xayz". Before this update is propagated the update *insert "b" after the second character* is applied to another copy with a resulting value of "xybz". If the updates were propagated naively, the update *insert "b" after the second character* would be applied to the first copy, while the update *insert "a" after the first character* would be applied to the second copy. The end result would be that the two copies would be inconsistent, containing "xabyz" and "xaybz" respectively.

Operation transforms, proposed by Ellis and Gibbs [4], modify concurrent updates as they are propagated so as to ensure that, in the end, all copies are consistent. For the example above, the update *insert "b" after the second character* would, when applied to the other copy, be transformed to *insert "b" after the third character* with the end result that both copies would have the value "xaybz".

To date, operation transforms have been defined only for very simple groupware objects like the example above. Defining operation transforms for a spreadsheet represents a more significant challenge. Our purpose in tackling this problem is twofold: first, a shared spreadsheet is a useful groupware object in its own right; second, its definition allowed us to explore the methodology of defining more complex groupware objects using operation transforms.

OPERATION TRANSFORMS

We use the notation of Cormack's Calculus for Concurrent Update (CCU) [3], which corrects and formalizes the dOPT algorithm of Ellis and Gibbs.

To define a replicated object we begin with an ordinary sequential object; that is, a store and a set of update operations. We then specify the meaning of the concurrent application of every pair of update operations. From these definitions the meaning of all possible combinations of concurrent and sequential updates is automatically derived.

Consider two update operations f and g. Their concurrent meaning is defined as follows. First, an arbitrary but *canonical* consistent order is placed on all operations. Second, a new operation f/g is defined that preserves the meaning of f although a concurrent appli-

CSCW 98 Seattle Washington USA

e	$\rightarrow$	@function(e_1, ..., e_n)
e	$\rightarrow$	cell
e	$\rightarrow$	range
e	$\rightarrow$	literal
cell	$\rightarrow$	[rowref, colref]
range	$\rightarrow$	{cell, cell}
rowref	$\rightarrow$	row | :row
colref	$\rightarrow$	col | :col

Figure 1: Spreadsheet Expressions

cation of g has intervened. Third, a new operation $g\backslash f$ is defined that has the same effect as if a concurrent application of g had intervened before f. That is, g followed by f/g must have exactly the same effect as f followed by $g\backslash f$. Formally, for every state X of the object and any pair of updates f and g, $f/g(g(X)) = g\backslash f(f(X))$.

We use the text object from the previous section as an example. Suppose

$f =$ *insert "a" after the first character*
$g =$ *insert "b" after the second character*

we may define

$f/g = f\backslash g =$ f
$g/f = g\backslash f =$ *insert "b" after the third character*

In this case f/g and $f\backslash g$ are identical but this is not always the case.

If we choose

$f =$ *insert "c" after the first character*
$g =$ *insert "d" after the first character*

then / and \ must be different; one valid definition is:

$f/g =$ *insert 'c' after the second character*
$f\backslash g =$ *insert 'c' after the first character*
$g/f =$ *insert 'd' after the second character*
$g\backslash f =$ *insert 'd' after the first character*

The definitions can be shown to be valid because g followed by f/g always has the same effect as f followed by $g\backslash f$ (that is, *insert "dc" after the first character*). On the other hand, f followed by g/f has the same effect as g followed by $f\backslash g$ (that is, *insert "cd" after the first character*). Which sequence is used depends on the canonical ordering chosen for f and g.

Further details of CCU and an algorithm to implement replicated objects appear elsewhere [2]. Other algorithms correcting the Ellis and Gibbs algorithm have been proposed [1, 7, 8].

A SPREADSHEET MODEL

Spreadsheets provide sophisticated features for manipulating numeric and textual data. Data is organized in a tabular format with rows and columns of data. Each entry in the spreadsheet table contains data which may include functions of the other entries in the table. To make it easier to duplicate sections of a spreadsheet, including their computation, a special *copy* operation copies entries and updates the formula. These features may be implemented in terms of a few primitives. The set of operations we define are sufficient to model Gosling's `sc`; other spreadsheets, such as `Excel` or `1-2-3`, are similar. Before defining the operations, we need to formalize the store of the spreadsheet.

The store of a spreadsheet is a two-dimensional array of *cells*, a one-dimensional array of default formats, and a set of name bindings.

Each cell contains a value, a formula, and a format. The value of a cell is the result of evaluating its formula, and the format controls the manner in which the value is displayed. Details of the values and formats are unimportant in this discussion. The syntax of a formula is shown in figure 1. Formulas consist of literal values, functions, cell references, and range references. A cell reference denotes the row and column of some other cell. Each row and column denotation may be *fixed* or *relative*. A *fixed* row or column denotation (preceded by a colon in the syntax) is not changed if the formula is copied to another cell. A *relative* row or column denotation is adjusted when the formula is copied so that the relative distance between the formula and the denoted cell is unchanged. For example, if a formula containing a *relative* column denotation were copied two positions to the right, the column denotation would be incremented by 2. A range reference comprises two cell references that specify the upper left and lower right corner of a rectangular area in the spreadsheet.

Seven primitive operations are sufficient to capture all updates on the store: set, format, insert, delete, copy, define, and undefine:

set(cell, value) - Replace the contents of the cell at location *cell* with *value*. In `sc`, *value* is a triple $< l, e, f >$ where l is a potentially empty string label and e is either a numeric or string based expression. Expressions are defined in figure 1. Cell specific formatting information is stored in f.

format(column, format) - Replace the formatting information for the *column* with the new formatting information *format*.

insert(row, nr, col, nc) - Insert rows and/or columns by adding *nr* rows before *row* and adding *nc* columns before *col*. All cell references will be updated to ensure that they continue to point to the same cell regardless of how the cell may have been moved by the insert.

delete(row, nr, col, nc) - Delete *nr* rows beginning with

A spreadsheet is a pair $S = < C, F >$ where C is 2 dimensional array of cells, F is a 1 dimensional array of column formats and a cell is the triple $< l, e, f >$. Let C have size $maxr$ rows and $maxc$ columns.

set($[r, c]$, $value$) is
  $C[r, c] = value$

format(c, f) is
  $F[c] = f$

copy($[fr, fc]$, $[tr, tc]$, $< l, e, f >$) is
  $C[tr, tc] = < l, cfix(e), f >$

delete(row, nr, col, nc) is
  FOR all $1 \leq c \leq maxc$ and $1 \leq r \leq maxr$:
    $C[row, c] = dfix(C[row, c])$
  $C[row..maxr - nr, 1..maxc] =$
    $C[row + nr..maxr, 1..maxc]$
  $C[1..maxr, col..maxc - nc] =$
    $C[1..maxr, col + nc..maxc]$
  maxr = maxr - nr
  maxc = maxc - nc

insert(row, nr, col, nc) is
  FOR all $1 \leq c \leq maxc$ and $1 \leq r \leq maxr$:
    $C[r, c] = ifix(C[r, c])$
  $C[row + nr..maxr + nr, 1..maxc] =$
    $C[row..maxr, 1..maxc]$
  $C[row..row + nr - 1] =$ empty
  $C[1..maxr, col + nc..maxc + nc] =$
    $C[1..maxr, col..maxc]$
  $C[1..maxr, col..col + nc - 1] =$ empty
  $F[col + nc..maxc + nc] = F[col..maxc]$
  $F[col..col + nc - 1] = default$
  maxr = maxr + nr
  maxc = maxc + nc

Figure 2: Spreadsheet Definitions

row and nc columns beginning with col. As with the *insert* operation, all cell references will be updated. Cell references into the deleted region will be left unchanged.

$copy(src, dest, value)$ - Copy the cell at position src, which contains $value$, to $dest$ updating the relative references in $value$ as it is copied. We require that the $value$ of the cell begin copied be attached to this operation to facilitate the concurrent semantics.

$define(name, range)$ - Create a mapping from a name to a specific range of the spreadsheet.

With auxiliary functions:
$cfix(< l, e, f > = < l, cfix(e), f >$ where
$cfix(e)$ is
  $cfix(literal) = literal$
  $cfix(@f(e_1, ..., e_n)) = @f(cfix(e_1), ..., cfix(e_n))$
  $cfix(\{cell_1, cell_2\}) = \{cfix(cell_1), cfix(cell_2)\}$
  $cfix([r, c]) = [r', c']$
  where
    $r' = r$ (isfixed(r))
    $r' = max(r + (tr - fr), 0)$ (isrel(r))
    $c' = c$ (isfixed(c))
    $c' = max(c + (tc - fc), 0$ (isrel(c))

$dfix(< l, e, f > = < l, dfix(e), f >$ where
$dfix(e)$ is
  $dfix(literal) = literal$
  $dfix(@f(e_1, ..., e_n)) = @f(dfix(e_1), ..., dfix(e_n))$
  $dfix(\{cell_1, cell_2\}) = \{dfix(cell_1), dfix(cell_2)\}$
  $dfix([r, c]) = [r', c']$
  where
    $r' = r$ $(r < row)$
    $r' = r - nr$ $(r \geq row + nr)$
    $c' = c$ $(c < col)$
    $c' = c - nc$ $(c \geq col + nc)$

$ifix(< l, e, f > = < l, ifix(e), f >$ where
$ifix(e)$ is
  $ifix(literal) = literal$
  $ifix(@f(e_1, ..., e_n)) = @f(ifix(e_1), ..., ifix(e_n))$
  $ifix(\{cell_1, cell_2\}) = \{ifix(cell_1), ifix(cell_2)\}$
  $ifix([r, c]) = [r', c']$
  where
    $r' = r$ $(r < row)$
    $r' = r + nr$ $(r \geq row)$
    $c' = c$ $(c < col)$
    $c' = c + nc$ $(c \geq col)$

Figure 3: Auxiliary Spreadsheet Definitions

$undefine(name, range)$ - Remove a mapping from a name.

Figure 2 contains a formal definition of the primitive operations, excluding $define$ and $undefine$. Figure 3 contains the auxiliary definitions used to define these operations. The definitions encode the actual implemented semantics of `sc` and they have not been modified in any way to facilitate the definition of their corresponding concurrent semantics.

The set and $format$ definitions merely update the data structures. It is worth noting that set and $format$ are actually updating different data structures. $copy$ defines a mapping, $cfix$, to update the expression be-

$$\begin{aligned}
&\textbf{format}(c_1,\ f_1)\ /\ \textbf{format}(c_2,\ f_2) = \\
&\quad \text{format}(c_1,\ f_1) \\
&\textbf{format}(c_1,\ f_1)\ \backslash\ \textbf{format}(c_2,\ f_2) = \\
&\quad \text{format}(c_1,\ f_1) \qquad (c_1 \neq c_2) \\
&\quad \text{ident} \qquad (c1 = c2) \\
&\textbf{format}(c,\ f)\ /\ \textbf{set}([r,c],\ v) = \\
&\quad \textbf{format}(c,\ f)\ \backslash\ \textbf{set}([r,c],\ v) = \\
&\qquad \text{format}(c,\ f) \\
&\textbf{format}(c,\ f)\ /\ \textbf{copy}([r,c],\ [r',c'],\ v) = \\
&\quad \textbf{format}(c,\ f)\ \backslash\ \textbf{copy}([r,c],\ [r',c'],\ v) = \\
&\qquad \text{format}(c,\ f) \\
&\textbf{format}(c,\ f)\ /\ \textbf{delete}(fr,nr,fc,nc) = \\
&\quad \text{ident} \qquad (fc \le c < fc+nc) \\
&\quad \text{format}(c,\ f) \qquad (c < fc) \\
&\quad \text{format}(c-nc,\ f) \qquad (c \ge fc+nc) \\
&\textbf{format}(c,\ f)\ \backslash\ \textbf{delete}(fr,nr,fc,nc) = \\
&\quad \textbf{format}(c,\ f)\ /\ \textbf{delete}(fr,nr,fc,nc) \\
&\textbf{format}(c,\ f)\ /\ \textbf{insert}(fr,nr,fc,nc) = \\
&\quad \text{format}(c,\ f) \qquad (c \le fc) \\
&\quad \text{format}(c+nc,\ f) \qquad (c > fc) \\
&\textbf{format}(c,\ f)\ \backslash\ \textbf{insert}(fr,nr,fc,nc) = \\
&\quad \textbf{format}(c,\ f)\ /\ \textbf{insert}(fr,nr,fc,nc)
\end{aligned}$$

Figure 4: Semantics of **format**

$$\begin{aligned}
&\textbf{set}([r,c],\ v)\ /\ \textbf{format}(c,\ f) = \\
&\quad \textbf{set}([r,c],\ v)\ \backslash\ \textbf{format}(c,\ f) = \\
&\qquad \text{set}([r,c],\ v) \\
&\textbf{set}([r_1,c_1],\ v_1)\ /\ \textbf{set}([r_2,c_2],\ v_2) = \\
&\quad \text{set}([r_1,c_1],\ v_1) \\
&\textbf{set}([r_1,c_1],\ v_1)\ \backslash\ \textbf{set}([r_2,c_2],\ v_2) = \\
&\quad \text{ident} \qquad ([r_1,c_1] = [r_2,c_2]) \\
&\quad \text{set}([r_1,c_1],\ v_1) \qquad ([r_1,c_1] \neq [r_2,c_2]) \\
&\textbf{set}([r,c],\ v_1)\ /\ \textbf{copy}([sr,sc],\ [dr,dc],\ v_2) = \\
&\quad \text{set}([r,c],\ v_1) \\
&\textbf{set}([r,c],\ v_1)\backslash\textbf{copy}([sr,sc],\ [dr,dc],\ v_2) = \\
&\quad \text{ident} \qquad ([r,c] = [dr,dc]) \\
&\quad \text{set}([r,c],\ v_1) \qquad ([r,c] \neq [dr,dc]) \\
&\textbf{set}([r,c],\ v)\ /\ \textbf{delete}(fr,\ nr,\ fc,\ nc) = \\
&\quad \textbf{set}([r,c],\ v)\ \backslash\ \textbf{delete}(fr,\ nr,\ fc,\ nc) = \\
&\qquad \text{ident} \qquad (fr \le r < fr+nr \text{ or } fc \le c < fc+nc) \\
&\qquad \text{set}(dfix([r,c]),\ dfix(v)) \qquad \text{(otherwise)} \\
&\textbf{set}([r,c],\ v)\ /\ \textbf{insert}(fr,\ nr,\ fc,\ nc) = \\
&\quad \textbf{set}([r,c],\ v)\ \backslash\ \textbf{insert}(fr,\ nr,\ fc,\ nc) = \\
&\qquad \text{set}(ifix([r,c]),\ ifix(v))
\end{aligned}$$

where *dfix* and *ifix* are defined in figure 2.

Figure 5: Semantics of **set**

ing copied in the manner alluded to above. *insert* and *delete* use the auxiliary functions *ifix* and *dfix* respectively to update all of the cells in the spreadsheet. Once the cells have been corrected, they are copied to perform the actual insertion or deletion.

define and *undefine* are easily defined, but are omitted for brevity. They are implemented by a simple dictionary data structure, and the cell references associated with defined names must be adjusted using *ifix* or *dfix* as the result of *insert* or *delete* operations.

CONCURRENT SEMANTICS

To implement the CCU algorithm for a distributed shared spreadsheet, we must define the two transformations, / and \, for all pairs of update operations. That is, we must define $5 \times 5 = 25$ of each transformation. The exact mathematical details of the transforms are shown in figures 4 through 9.

The transformations for *copy* concurrent with *insert* or *delete* are sufficiently complex that a proof that the CCU condition holds is provided. The remaining definitions are easily verified; we concentrate our attention on explaining and clarifying the formal definitions. It is important to see that the transformations "make sense". It is always possible to define transformations that are consistent (on any concurrent update, simply initializing the store defines a set of concurrent semantics that will be consistent). It's not possible to quantify the meaning of the transformations. Instead, as we present the transformations, we will try to make the rationale clear. It is interesting to note that the majority of the transformations are fairly simple yet they will be combined with the CCU algorithm to handle all possible sets of concurrent updates to the spreadsheet.

Semantics of *format*

Concurrently storing a value into a cell is independent of changing the format of a column. If we refer to the model of the spreadsheet, we see that these two operations neither access nor modify any common data structures. As such, we may also perform *format* operations regardless of any *set* operations that occur concurrently. The same situation applies with *copy* operations.

On the other hand, two different *format* operations are not necessarily independent. If they are applied to different columns then they actually are independent. If two format operations apply to the same column, we need to resolve them in such a manner as to ensure consistency. The only reasonable solution is to guarantee that in the final state, exactly one of the two format operations will "win" over the other. To do this, we make use of the total order defined by CCU. We say that one format after another format always wins. To achieve consistency, we say that one format before an-

For any of $format$, set or $copy$ with any arguments, say α:

$\mathbf{delete}(fr, nr, fc, nc) \ / \ \alpha = \mathbf{delete}(fr, nr, fc, nc) \setminus \alpha = \text{delete}(fr, nr, fc, nc)$

$\mathbf{delete}(fr_1, nr_1, fc_1, nc_1) \ / \ \mathbf{delete}(fr_2, nr_2, fc_2, nc_2) =$

$\quad \text{delete}(frow(fr_1), frow(fr_1 + nr_1) - frow(fr_1), fcol(fc_1), fcol(fc_1 + nc_1) - fcol(fc_1))$

$\quad$ where $frow(r) = r'$ and $fcol(c) = c'$ as:

$$
\begin{array}{ll}
r' = r & (r < fr_2) \\
r' = fr_2 & (fr_2 \leq r \leq fr_2 + nr_2) \\
r' = r - nr_2 & (r > fr_2 + nr_2) \\
c' = c & (c < fc_2) \\
c' = fc_2 & (fc_2 \leq c \leq fc_2 + nc_2) \\
c' = c - nc_2 & (c > fc_2 + nc_2)
\end{array}
$$

$\mathbf{delete}(fr_1, nr_1, fc_1, nc_1) \setminus \mathbf{delete}(fr_2, nr_2, fc_2, nc_2) =$

$\quad \text{delete}(fr_1, nr_1, fc_1, nc_1) \ / \ \text{delete}(fr_2, nr_2, fc_2, nc_2)$

$\mathbf{delete}(r_1, nr_1, c_1, nc_1) \ / \ \mathbf{insert}(r_2, nr_2, c_2, nc_2) =$

$\quad \text{delete}(irow(r_1), irow(r_1 + nr_1)\text{-}irow(r_1), icol(c_1), icol(c_1 + nc_1) - icol(c_1))$

$\mathbf{delete}(r_1, nr_1, c_1, nc_1) \setminus \mathbf{insert}(r_2, nr_2, c_2, nc_2) =$

$\quad \text{delete}(r_1, nr_1, c_1, nc_1) \ / \ \text{insert}(r_2, nr_2, c_2, nc_2)$

$irow(row) = row'$ and $icol(col) = col'$ where:

$$
\begin{array}{ll}
row' = row & (row < r_2) \\
row' = row + (nr_2) & (row \geq r_2) \\
col' = col & (col < c_2) \\
col' = col + (nc_2) & (col \geq c_2)
\end{array}
$$

Figure 6: Semantics of **delete**

other format is nullified if they are operating on the same column.

Finally, if a format is concurrent with a deletion operation, we simply need to look at the three possible cases. First of all, we may have deleted only rows or the columns being deleted may be to the right of the format operation. In this case, the format operation may safely be applied independently of the deletion. Second, it may be the case that the column being formatted has been concurrently deleted. In this case, we nullify the format operation because it may not be reasonably applied to some other column. Finally, if columns are deleted to the left of the formatted column, the format operation must be transformed to the left by the number of columns that were actually deleted. The same analysis applies for insertions except that the format must be translated to the right.

Semantics of *set*

set and *format* operations are similar in that they both update data structures and they are independent. Two *set* operations occurring concurrently is analogous to two concurrent *format* operations since only one operation can "win". Thus, we use the combination of before and after definitions to declare one of the two operations the winner. We have defined the semantics of a *set* operation that occurs concurrently with a *copy* in a similar fashion.

Finally, if a *set* operation occurs concurrently with a *delete*, we have exactly the same three cases as we saw in the *format* semantics. However, we must take care to apply the same transformation to the expression that is being stored. The *set* operation is transformed into an operation that can be applied after the deletion has occurred to give a common state. This state is the same as having applied the *set* operation followed by the deletion which models what would seem "normal" given that the two operations were applied concurrently to a common initial state. Similar semantics apply for a concurrent insertion of rows and columns.

Semantics of *delete*

The previous two sets of transformations have modeled the concurrent *delete* requests to logically occur after their concurrent counter-parts. This is reflected in the concurrent semantics defined in figure 6. For any of *format*, *set* or *copy*, we simply apply the *delete* untransformed.

All that remains is to define the meaning of two concurrent *delete* operations. We will discuss the deletion of rows (deletion of columns is similar). The first observation is that the order of two deletions does not mat-

$$
\begin{array}{ll}
\mathbf{copy}([s_r,s_c],[d_r,d_c],v)\ /\ \mathbf{format}(c,f) = & \\
\quad \mathbf{copy}([s_r,s_c],[d_r,d_c],v)\ \backslash\ \mathbf{format}(c,f) = & \\
\quad\quad \text{copy}([s_r,s_c],[d_r,d_c],v) & \\
\mathbf{copy}([s_r,s_c],[d_r,d_c],v_1)\ /\ \mathbf{set}([r,c],v_2) = & \\
\quad \text{copy}([s_r,s_c],[d_r,d_c],v_1) & \\
\mathbf{copy}([s_r,s_c],[d_r,d_c],v_1)\ \backslash\ \mathbf{set}([r,c],v_2) = & \\
\quad \text{ident} & ([r,c] = [d_r,d_c]) \\
\quad \text{copy}([s_r,s_c],[d_r,d_c],v_1) & ([r,c] \neq [d_r,d_c]) \\
\mathbf{copy}([s_{r_1},s_{c_1}],[d_{r_1},d_{c_1}],v_1)\ / & \\
\quad \mathbf{copy}([s_{r_2},s_{c_2}],[d_{r_2},d_{c_2}],v_2) = & \\
\quad\quad \text{copy}([s_{r_1},s_{c_1}],[d_{r_1},s_{r_1}],v_1) & \\
\mathbf{copy}([s_{r_1},s_{c_1}],[d_{r_1},d_{c_1}],v_1)\ \backslash & \\
\quad \mathbf{copy}([s_{r_2},s_{c_2}],[d_{r_2},d_{c_2}],v_2) = & \\
\quad\quad \text{ident} & ([d_{r_1},d_{c_1}] = [d_{r_2},d_{c_2}]) \\
\quad\quad \text{copy}([s_{r_1},s_{c_1}],[d_{r_1},d_{c_1}],v_1) & ([d_{r_1},d_{c_1}] \neq [d_{r_2},d_{c_2}]) \\
\mathbf{copy}([s_r,s_c],[d_r,d_c],< l,e,f >)\ / & \\
\quad \mathbf{delete}(fr,\ nr,\ fc,\ nc) = & \\
\quad\quad \text{ident} & (fr \le d_r < fr + nr, \\
 & \ fc \le d_c < fc + nc) \\
\quad\quad \text{copy}([drow(s_r),dcol(s_c)],[drow(d_r),dcol(d_c)], & \\
\quad\quad\quad < l, dfix(e), f >)(\text{otherwise}) & \\
\mathbf{copy}([s_r,s_c],[d_r,d_c],v)\ \backslash & \\
\quad \mathbf{delete}(fr,\ nr,\ fc,\ nc) = & \\
\quad\quad \text{copy}([s_r,s_c],[d_r,d_c],v)\ /\ \text{delete}(fr,\ nr,\ fc,\ nc) & \\
\mathbf{copy}([s_r,s_c],[d_r,d_c],< l,e,f >)\ / & \\
\quad \mathbf{insert}(fr,\ nr,\ fc,\ nc) = & \\
\quad\quad \text{copy}([irow(s_r),icol(s_c)],[irow(d_r),icol(d_c)], & \\
\quad\quad\quad < l, ifix(e), f >) & \\
\mathbf{copy}([s_r,s_c],[d_r,d_c],v)\ \backslash & \\
\quad \mathbf{insert}(fr,\ nr,\ fc,\ nc) = & \\
\quad\quad \text{copy}([s_r,s_c],[d_r,d_c],v)\ /\ \text{insert}(fr,\ nr,\ fc,\ nc) &
\end{array}
$$

Figure 7: Semantics of **copy**

$$
\begin{array}{ll}
crow(r) = r & (\text{isfixed}(r)) \\
crow(r) = r + d_r - s_r & (\text{isrel}(r)) \\
ccol(c) = c & (\text{isfixed}(c)) \\
ccol(c) = c + d_c - s_c & (\text{isrel}(c))
\end{array}
$$

$$
\begin{array}{ll}
dfix(literal) = literal & \\
dfix(@f(e_1,...,e_n) = @f(dfix(e_1),\cdots,dfix(e_n)) & \\
dfix(\{cell_1,cell_2\}) = \{dfix(cell_1),dfix(cell_2)\} & \\
dfix([r,c]) = [r',c'] & \\
\text{where} & \\
\quad r' = r + drow(crow(r)) - crow(r) + delta\_r(r) & \\
\quad c' = c + dcol(ccol(c)) - ccol(c) + delta\_c(c) & \\
\quad \text{where} & \\
\quad\quad delta\_r(r) = (d_r - s_r) - (drow(d_r) - drow(fr)) & \\
 & (\text{isrel}(r)) \\
\quad\quad delta\_c(c) = (d_c - s_c) - (dcol(d_c) - dcol(fc)) & \\
 & (\text{isrel}(c)) \\
\quad\quad delta\_r(r) = 0 & (\text{isfixed}(r)) \\
\quad\quad delta\_c(c) = 0 & (\text{isfixed}(c))
\end{array}
$$

$$
\begin{array}{ll}
ifix(literal) = literal & \\
ifix(@f(e_1,...,e_n) = @f(ifix(e_1),\cdots,ifix(e_n)) & \\
ifix(\{cell_1,cell_2\}) = \{ifix(cell_1),ifix(cell_2)\} & \\
ifix([r,c]) = [r',c'] & \\
\text{where} & \\
\quad r' = r + irow(crow(r)) - crow(r) + delta\_r(r) & \\
\quad c' = c + icol(ccol(c)) - ccol(c) + delta\_c(c) & \\
\quad \text{where} & \\
\quad\quad delta\_r(r) = -(d_r - s_r) + (irow(d_r) - irow(fr)) & \\
 & (\text{isrel}(r)) \\
\quad\quad delta\_c(c) = -(d_c - s_c) + (icol(d_c) - icol(fc)) & \\
 & (\text{isrel}(c)) \\
\quad\quad delta\_r(r) = 0 & (\text{isfixed}(r)) \\
\quad\quad delta\_c(c) = 0 & (\text{isfixed}(c))
\end{array}
$$

$irow(row)$ and $icol(col)$ are defined in figure 6.

Figure 8: Auxiliary Definitions for **copy**

ter. We need only define the semantics to transform a *delete* operation to reflect the change in context caused by a previously applied, concurrent, deletion. There are four cases. First, the previously applied *delete* may have only deleted rows below the new *delete* request at which point the new request may be applied untransformed. Second, the previous deletion may have been entirely above the current deletion. In this case, we need to translate the deleted area up by the number of rows previously deleted. The last two cases deal with overlapping deletions. If the previous deletion deleted all of the rows being deleted by the new deletion, it may be transformed into an identity function. Alternatively, if they truly overlap, we need to translate the first row to be deleted to be the first row in the deleted range that remains and we need to reduce the number of rows to be deleted by the number of overlapping rows.

This will result in deleting exactly those rows that at least one of the deletions had requested. The transformation has been slightly condensed by merging the last two cases knowing that, if the deletion has been subsumed, then we will have $frow(fr_1 + nr_1) = frow(fr_1) = fr_2$ and consequently no rows will be deleted.

The situation is somewhat simpler when handling a concurrently applied insertion of rows and/or columns. If we are applying a deletion of rows after a concurrent insertion has been applied, we may need to transform the position of the deletion or we might need to transform the number of rows being deleted. If the insertion occurs in the middle of the deleted area, we need to delete all of the original rows plus the number of rows that were inserted. On the other hand, if the insertion occurs above the deletion, we need to translate the deletion by the number of rows that were inserted. It is never possible for the insertion to overlap with a deletion.

Semantics of *copy*

The definitions of the concurrent semantics for the *copy* operation are presented in figures 7 and 8. The *copy* and *format* operations are independent and consequently no transformation is required. Before discussing the other transformations, it is worth commenting on the *value* argument on the *copy* operation. If some site receives a $set([r,c],v)$ operation and processes it before a concurrent $copy([r,c],[r',c'],v')$, the receiving site will no longer have access to the original value of the cell. Thus, we have preserved the value being copied.

A *copy* that occurs concurrently with a *set* or a *copy* is treated identically. One operation will be the "winner" and we model this to be consistent with the model applied for the *set* semantics. It should be noted that this is not the only possible definition. It might be appealing to rely on the total order. That is, we may choose to care whether or not the source cell of the *copy* operation was updated before or after the *copy* in the total order. If the source was modified then we would transform the *copy* operation to use this new value. Our alternative definition is possible and may actually make the most mathematical sense. However, we felt that users would generally choose to *copy* a cell because the contents were of interest. It is not necessarily true that the new contents would be of interest. To be fair, it should be noted that this is merely the preference of the authors and either definition is likely acceptable.

We have previously chosen to model a *copy* operation that is concurrent with a *delete* operation by conceptually applying the deletion after the copy has taken place. The *copy* transformations must be defined to be consistent with this model. This transformation is not obvious and was actually mathematically derived. The first part of the transformation transforms the source and destination cells of the *copy* operation exactly as was done with *set* and *format* operations that occur concurrently with a *delete*. The problem lies in transforming the expression so that when the *copy* algorithm is applied to the *transformed* source and destination cells in a spreadsheet in which the *delete* has already occurred, the resulting formula will be the same as the formula arrived at by performing the operations in the reverse order. A careful analysis of the transformations will reveal that insertions are handled identically except for a difference in sign (and that insertions may never nullify the *copy*).

We provide a proof that the CCU condition holds for the definition (for any spreadsheet). The manipulation at the end of the proof makes clear the relationship between *delta_r* and *crow* in the definition.

Theorem 1 (Correctness of *copy/delete*)
If
cpy = copy($[sr, sc]$, $[dr, dc]$, v) and
del = delete(fr, nr, fc, nc)
then $cpy/del(del(S)) = del\backslash cpy(cpy(S))$ for any spreadsheet S.

Proof: By definition, $del\backslash cpy(cpy(S)) = del(cpy(S))$. Let cpy/del = copy($[sr', sc']$, $[dr', dc']$, v'). There are two conditions that we must verify. First, that $[dr', dc']$ is the same destination cell as in $del(cpy(S))$. We have previously outlined this argument. Applying the delete operation moves the cell $[dr, dc]$ to $[dr', dc']$. By definition of $drow$ and $dcol$, that is $[dr', dc'] = [drow(dr), dcol(dc)]$.

The second condition is more difficult. We must verify that if $[r, c]$ is a cell reference in v which becomes $[r'', c'']$ by the sequence $del/cpy(cpy(S))$ then $cpy/del(del(S))$ will also result in a reference of $[r'', c'']$. Let $[r', c']$ be the transformation of $[r, c]$ as specified in cpy/del. Let fix be the transformation function used in the definition of $copy$. We will show that $fix(r') = r'' = drow(crow(r))$. For simplicity, we assume that $dr' - sr' + r \geq 0$. If this is not the case, intermediate results will contain negative cell references but when the final *copy* operation is applied this will be caught and handled correctly.

If r is a fixed reference then *copy/delete* defines $delta\_r(r) = 0$ and *copy* defines $fix(r) = crow(r) = r$. Thus, $fix(r') = r' = r + drow(crow(r)) - crow(r) = r + drow(r) - r = drow(r) = drow(crow(r)) = r''$. That is, fixed references are transformed correctly.

If r is a relative reference then, when applying cpy/del, by the definition of fix, we have:

$$\begin{aligned}
\text{fix(r')} &= \text{r' + dr'-sr'} \\
&= \text{r' + drow(dr) - drow(sr)} \\
&= \text{(r + drow(crow(r)) - crow(r) +} \\
&\quad\ \text{dr-sr - (drow(dr)-drow(sr))) +} \\
&\quad\ \text{drow(dr) - drow(sr)} \\
&= \text{r + drow(crow(r)) - crow(r) + dr-sr} \\
&= \text{drow(crow(r))}
\end{aligned}$$

Finally, a similar argument holds to show that column references are preserved under the two transformations. Thus, $cpy/del(del(S)) = del\backslash cpy(cpy(S))$ for any spreadsheet S. □

Semantics of *insert*

As with deletions, insertion is not affected by any operation other than a concurrent *insert* or a concurrent *delete* operation. We discuss only the row based operations while the column based analysis is similar.

If a concurrent *delete* has been applied, we will have to transform the *insert* request. If the area being deleted covers the insertion point then we will nullify

For any of *format*, *set* or *copy* with any arguments, say α:

$$\textbf{insert}(fr,\ nr,\ fc,\ nc)\ /\ \alpha = $$
$$\quad \textbf{insert}(fr,\ nr,\ fc,\ nc)\ \backslash\ \alpha = $$
$$\quad \text{insert}(fr,\ nr,\ fc,\ nc)$$

$$\textbf{insert}(r_1, nr_1, c_1, nc_1)\ /\ \textbf{delete}(r_2, nr_2, c_2, nc_2) =$$
$$\begin{array}{ll} \text{ident} & (r_2 \leq r_1 < r_2 + nr_2, \\ & c_2 \leq c_1 < c_2 + nc_2) \\ \text{insert}(0,\ 0,\ idcol(c_1),\ nc_1) & (r_2 \leq r_1 < r_2 + nr_2) \\ \text{insert}(idrow(r_1),\ nr_1,\ 0,\ 0) & (c_2 \leq c_1 < c_2 + nc_2) \\ \text{insert}(idrow(r_1),\ nr_1,\ idcol(c_1),\ nc_2) & \\ & (\text{otherwise}) \end{array}$$

$$\textbf{insert}(r_1, nr_1, c_1, nc_1)\ \backslash\ \textbf{delete}(r_2, nr_2, c_2, nc_2) =$$
$$\quad \text{insert}(r_1, nr_1, c_1, nc_1)\ /\ \text{delete}(r_2, nr_2, c_2, nc_2) =$$
$$\textbf{insert}(r_1, nr_1, c_1, nc_1)\ /\ \textbf{insert}(r_2, nr_2, c_2, nc_2) =$$
$$\quad \text{insert}(irow(r_1),\ nr_1,\ icol(c_1),\ nc_1)$$
$$\textbf{insert}(r_1, nr_1, c_1, nc_1)\ \backslash\ \textbf{insert}(r_2, nr_2, c_2, nc_2) =$$
$$\quad \text{insert}(r_1, nr_1, c_1, nc_1)\ /\ \text{insert}(r_2, nr_2, c_2, nc_2) =$$

$idrow(row) = row'$ and $idcol(col) = col'$ where:

$$\begin{array}{ll} row' = row & (row < r_2 + nr_2) \\ row' = col - nr_2 & (row \geq r_2 + nr_2) \\ col' = col & (col < c_2 + nc_2) \\ col' = col - nc_2 & (col \geq c_2 + nc_2) \end{array}$$

$irow(row)$ and $icol(col)$ are defined in figure 6.

Figure 9: Semantics of **insert**

the insert. Note, however, if the insertion occurs after the last row being deleted, it will still occur. That is, if we insert after row 2 and concurrently someone deletes row 2, the insertion will not be nullified. Otherwise, if the deletion applied to rows above the insertion point, we will translate the insertion point by the number of rows deleted.

If we have concurrently applied another *insert* operation, we need only transform the insertion point. That is, if the previously applied insertion was above or at the same insertion point of the operation that we want to apply, we must translate this new operation by the number of rows inserted. Otherwise, the *insert* operation is untransformed.

IMPLEMENTATION ISSUES

A prototype distributed shared spreadsheet was developed based on the public domain spreadsheet `sc`. The most difficult part of the implementation was the development of the concurrent semantics. By examining the behaviour of `sc`, we convinced ourselves that the set of operations we have proposed is sufficient to model the actual implementation. Once the model and concurrent definitions were developed, it was necessary to integrate them into `sc`. The integration was time consuming but simple. Any code that updated the spreadsheet had to be examined. The code was modified to make the appropriate core function calls. These core functions generate network packets that are distributed to all other sites as notifications.

In addition to changing the low level details of `sc`, care had to be taken to ensure that network traffic was handled correctly. Whenever the system blocks waiting for user input, network packets are read. If the user is in the process of entering a command (for example, writing an equation to store in a cell), remote updates are disabled and the network packets are simply queued. Whenever the user is idle, network packets are received and processed along with any packets that were queued. This automatically provides the required atomicity for aggregate operations and provides a rational interface. If remote updates were constantly being processed, it would be nearly impossible to write an expression because the underlying spreadsheet would be a moving target.

Communication is done using the TCP protocol. It is possible to implement lost packet detection directly using the CCU algorithm (see [2] for details). Switching to UDP based network protocols is an avenue for improvement in the current implementation.

The CCU algorithm is used to process the updates. No changes are required to the CCU algorithm and the transforms are implemented exactly as specified (using a suitable encoding of expressions and operations).

The initial prototype was used and an interesting flaw was noticed and corrected. When storing a value in the spreadsheet, a special case arises when the destination cell is outside of the current spreadsheet boundaries. There may be a high transmission delay (for example, when some site is not connected to a network). When transmission delays are low, this problem is easily corrected manually by the users involved. If two users decide to add new information to the spreadsheet, they will invariably start changing the cells at the bottom or the right side of the spreadsheet. CCU and our transformations will consistently declare the updates made by one of the two users the "winner" over the other set of updates. That is, one user will lose their data. This is a case in which the concurrent semantics do not match the intention of the users. The problem is corrected by inserting a row whenever a value is stored outside of the spreadsheet boundaries. Making this change to the system guarantees that the two sets of updates will be reflected in the spreadsheet.

This example reinforces the fact that an implementation and user trial is essential. The model and concurrent semantics were provably correct but an oversight in the meaning of an update seriously reduced the usefulness of the spreadsheet.

CLASSIFYING TRANSFORMATIONS

It would be desirable to be able to classify all of the possible transformations in order to partition them into related groups. This eases the process of deriving the transformations and simplifies the task of verifying their validity. It is, of course, not possible to define such a taxonomy. Instead, we extract from our concurrent semantics four basic classes of transformations which seem to apply to specific types of functions. The basic classes are pairs of functions that commutate, bully functions, masking functions and functions that affect the relative position of updates.

Commutative Functions When two functions commute, it is trivial to handle the concurrent semantics. This is exploited in [6] to reduce the number of operations that must be undone. For an operational transformation system, it involves an identity transformation. That is, if f and g commute, we define $f/g = f\backslash g = f$ and $g/f = g\backslash f = g$.

Bully Functions Closely related to the commutative functions, there are functions which always "win" against other functions. These functions are very much like the commutative functions except that the relationship holds in only one direction. It may not matter whether or not we have concurrently applied some function, g, when we apply the bully function f. In the spreadsheet, the *delete* function was a bully function. The transformations are simply $f/g = f\backslash g = f$. There is no natural analogy to a text buffer for these types of functions. However, if you consider a text buffer augmented with a locking operation, the locking operation is a bully function [5].

Masking Functions Masking functions are those for which the earlier (conflicting) applications do not contribute to the final state of the object. For example, if two users set the value of a cell concurrently, it is only the last update that affects the final state of the spreadsheet. Making use of the total order, these transformations are of the form:

```
f(x1,y1) / g(x2,y2) = f(x1,y1)
f(x1,y1) \ g(x2,y2) =
   ident      (x1 = x2)
   f(x1,y1)   (x1 != x2)
```

Masking functions will generally be idempotent functions (functions such that $f(f(x)) = f(x)$). As a special case of the concurrency, two users may generate the same request and this will behave like an idempotent function.

Relative Functions Relative functions are functions which change the relative context in a simple, linear fashion. In terms of the spreadsheet, deletions offset row and column references. In terms of either a text buffer or a spreadsheet, update operations are relative to insertions and deletions. Typically there are up to three possible cases to handle. First, the operation may be nullified (e.g. inside the deleted region). If the operation is not nullified then it will either be offset by the relative change or it will be preserved.

CONCLUSIONS

An operation transformation algorithm, CCU, was used to develop a shared, distributed, spreadsheet. This spreadsheet has semantics which are considerably more complex than known operation transformation based systems. The concurrent semantics that were developed maintain a reasonable interpretation of the user's original intention. None of the semantics were modified to ease the definition of their corresponding concurrent semantics.

Due to the nature of an operation transform system, local changes to the spreadsheet may always be applied. As these changes are assumed to be distributed over a potentially unreliable network, a highly fault tolerant system has been developed. Every node is able to operate in isolation and thus the system is immune to network outages and any number of nodes may fail without affecting those that remain.

The defined transformations fall largely into four general classes. The nature of these transformation classes has been identified to provide a general framework that will assist others attempting to design large scale transformation based systems.

All transformations were based on a model of the public domain spreadsheet sc. A spreadsheet abstract data type was proposed and formal semantics were defined for the core components of this model.

REFERENCES

1. David Cheriton and Dale Skeen. Understanding the limitations of causally and totally ordered communication. In *Proceedings of the 14th Symposium on Operating Systems Principles*, pages 44–57, Asheville, NC, December 1993.

2. Gordon V. Cormack. A calculus for concurrent update. Technical Report CS-95-06, University of Waterloo, 1995.

3. Gordon V. Cormack. A calculus for concurrent update (abstract). In *Proc. ACM Symposium on Principles of Distributed Computing*, 1995.

4. C.A. Ellis and S.J. Gibbs. Concurrency control in groupware systems. In J. Clifford, B. Lindsay, and D. Maier, editors, *Proc. ACM SIGMOD Int. Conf.*

on Management of Data, pages 399–407, Portland, OR, June 1989. ACM SIGMOD Record, **18**:2.

5. Lin Hu. Handling lock operations in distributed real-time cooperative editing systems. Technical Report TR-96-12, RMIT, Melbourne, Australia, 1995.

6. Alain Karsenty and Michel Beaudouin-Lafon. An algorithm for distributed groupware applications. In *Proc. 13th IEEE Int. Conf. on Distributed Computing Systems*, pages 195–202, Pittsburg, PA, May 1993. Los Alamitos, CA: IEEE Comp. Soc. Press.

7. Matthias Ressel, Doris Nitsche-Ruhland, and Rul Gunzenhäuser. An integrating, transformation-oriented approach to concurrency control and undo in group editors. In *ACM Computer-Supported Cooperative Work*. ACM, November 1996.

8. Chengzheng Sun, Xiaohua Jia, Yanchun Zhang, Yun Yang, and David Chen. Achieving convergence, causality-preservation and intention- preservation in real-time cooperative editing systems. In *ACM Transactions on Computer-Human Interactions*, New York, NY, 1998. To be published.

Responsiveness and Consistency Tradeoffs in Interactive Groupware

Sumeer Bhola* sumeerb@cc.gatech.edu

Guruduth Banavar† banavar@watson.ibm.com

Mustaque Ahamad* mustaq@cc.gatech.edu

ABSTRACT

Interactive (or Synchronous) groupware is increasingly being deployed in widely distributed environments. Users of such applications are accustomed to direct manipulation interfaces that require fast response time. The state that enables interaction among distributed users can be replicated to provide acceptable response time in the presence of high communication latencies. We describe and evaluate design choices for protocols that maintain consistency of such state. In particular, we develop workloads which model user actions, identify the metrics important from a user's viewpoint, and do detailed simulations of a number of protocols to evaluate how effective they are in meeting user requirements.

Keywords: Replication, Consistency, Response Time, Performance Evaluation, Workload.

INTRODUCTION

Traditional interactive groupware, like chat, whiteboards, and text editors are becoming commonplace. In the future, we expect complex groupware like engineering CAD (Computer Aided Design), and DIS (Distributed Interactive Simulation) to be widely available. The interactive nature of such applications requires that the effect of a user's action is seen by himself as well as other users in a timely manner. However, the problem of providing quick response is becoming increasingly difficult as groupware is deployed in a wide-area distributed environment like the Internet, where high communication latencies are common. End-users are increasingly accustomed to direct manipulation user interfaces, which typically require response times of 50-100*ms*. However, due to the fundamental limitation of the speed of light, the round-trip delay to the far side of the planet is at least 200*ms*. In mobile wireless computers, intermittent connectivity can also cause large delays. As a consequence of these limitations, groupware systems have been exploring ways to provide interactive responsiveness independent of network latency.

The interactions across distributed collaborating users are supported by shared state. There is general agreement that replication of shared state has the potential to reduce response time for actions that manipulate this state, since a user's action can be executed on her local replica. In addition, it can reduce bandwidth requirements by batching of user actions [4], and provide fault tolerance. However, state replication leads to the problem of replica consistency due to the possibility of different ordering of updates at different replicas.

We assume a model in which the shared state is composed of a set of objects which are fully replicated at all the collaborating processes/users (A process is an instance of a groupware application running at a certain site). These objects are modified through *updates* that are *issued* by the collaborating processes. An update is a code fragment which can read and write a subset of the shared objects in a set, and is guaranteed to execute *atomically* at each replica. This model eliminates the need for groupware applications to explicitly use locks to achieve atomicity, and permits more flexibility in employing different consistency protocols. More details of the model and the motivation for it can be found in [3].

The protocols that are used by current groupware systems to order updates consistently at all replicas fall into two broad categories: *pessimistic* and *optimistic*. Pessimistic protocols usually delay the execution of an update until it is ordered consistently at all processes. An optimistic protocol allows a locally issued update to be executed immediately. The immediate execution of an update corresponding to a user action provides response time that is independent of communication latency between processes. However, there is a possibility that optimistic assumptions turn out to be false since two conflicting updates can be executed in different orders at different replicas. When this happens, updates have to be undone, and then redone in the *correct* order to get a consistent replica state (or updates can be transformed, as in dOpt [7]). This may cause surprise to the user, which we call *jitter*.

Optimistic protocols in some form have been used in many groupware research prototypes and protocols like dOpt [7], ORESTE [9], COAST [14], DECAF [16] and Villa [4]. However, there is no real quantitative evaluation, like measuring the response time and jitter, of these protocols. In this paper, our goal is to understand and evaluate certain de-

*College of Computing, Georgia Institute of Technology, Atlanta, GA 30332.

†IBM T. J. Watson Research Center, Yorktown Heights, NY 10598.

CSCW 98 Seattle Washington USA

sign choices for optimistic and pessimistic protocols in interactive groupware. We identify two contrasting classes of consistency protocols: *Dependent* and *Independent* and examine a pessimistic consistency policy for the former, and both optimistic and pessimistic policies for the latter. The two classes differ in how updates are timestamped to determine a global order, and how they commit updates. Commit is important in pessimism to determine when an update can be executed, and in optimism to know when an update will not need to be undone. To capture conflicts between updates of different users, we define two types of *contention*, *Object-level* and *Real*, which affect the behavior of these protocols. In particular, the following are the main contributions of this paper.

- We extend the user interaction model for graphical interfaces to include the concept of a *lookahead threshold*, which models the ability of the user to continue input actions while the previous actions are being executed. We use this to motivate why the issuing and execution of updates should be decoupled, and to develop a general model of user behavior for the synthetic workloads.
- We develop a detailed simulation of a protocol from each of the Independent and Dependent protocol classes. The simulations allow communication latency to be varied, and assign a cost to update execution and undo. They are driven by adaptive synthetic workloads, which allow control over parameters like the *lookahead threshold* and the amount of contention. The parameter values we use are motivated by real application scenarios. Metrics such as response time mean and standard deviation, stall count and stall time, message overhead and jitter count are used to understand the tradeoffs when choosing one of the protocols.

The benefits of quantitative evaluation are many. From a research viewpoint it can identify the weaknesses and strengths of current protocols, which can affect the direction of future research in consistency protocols. It can also be a tool for application developers to choose the appropriate protocol for their applications.

The next section describes the interactivity requirements in more detail and introduces the *lookahead threshold*. Subsequently, we describe the two consistency protocols we evaluate and how they are affected by contention. We then discuss the synthetic workloads, how they map to certain application scenarios, and motivate the metrics important for the evaluation. Next, we discuss the main results and how they can be used to choose the appropriate protocol for a certain situation. We then describe related work and conclude.

INTERACTIVITY REQUIREMENTS

In this section we give a more concrete definition of the interactivity requirements for groupware. For this, we build upon the considerable amount of research already done in single user graphical interfaces (for a good introduction see Collins [6], Shneiderman [15]).

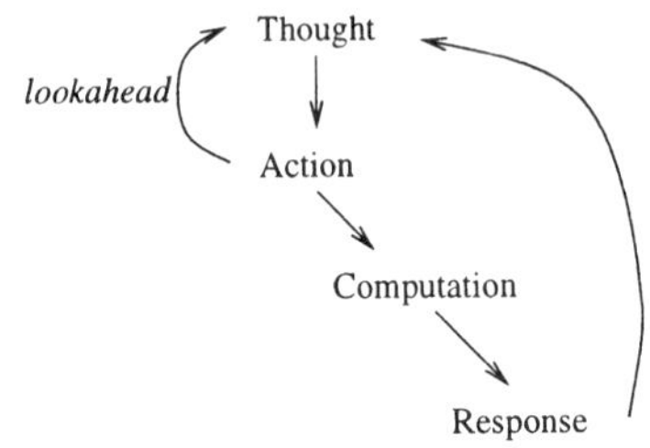

Figure 1: Extended human interaction model

The time interval between a user's input action and its response seen by the same user is the *Response Time* (RT). The key problem in interactive groupware is to keep the RT low enough so as to not differ significantly from single-user applications. This problem is made difficult because state consistency must not be overly compromised to achieve an acceptable RT.

User to User Time (UUT) is the time interval between a user's input action and its effect seen by a remote user. It is also important to minimize this quantity for interactive groupware, but this may not be as critical as low RT. However, in some scenarios, e.g., two users in the same virtual room involved in a war game, it is important to keep the ratio of UUT to RT small. The choices examined in this paper impact both UUT and RT, but our evaluation does not measure the impact on UUT.

The typical model used for user interaction is a cycle of *thought-action-computation-response*. The computation and response part of this cycle is responsible for the RT. This includes, translating the user *action* into an *update* on the shared state, and execution of this update on the local replica. Card [5] classifies tasks into categories based on the timing of this cycle. *Perceptual tasks* take less than 50-100ms and the user handles them without conscious processing. An example of this is tracking the motion of the mouse pointer.

Due to the very short duration of perceptual tasks, users do not necessarily wait for response from the previous task before going onto the next task. In terms of the human interaction model, we propose that tasks have a *lookahead threshold* (shown in Figure 1), which represents the number of actions that the user is willing to issue before the response to the first one is required. The lookahead threshold for perceptual tasks is expected to be non-zero. As tasks become longer duration this threshold will drop to zero. We now discuss the impact of a non-zero lookahead threshold.

Synchronous versus Asynchronous Processing

A non-zero threshold does not affect most single-user applications, in which RT is totally dependent on local processing. But in groupware, RT may depend on communication latency. This implies that a process can start computing the

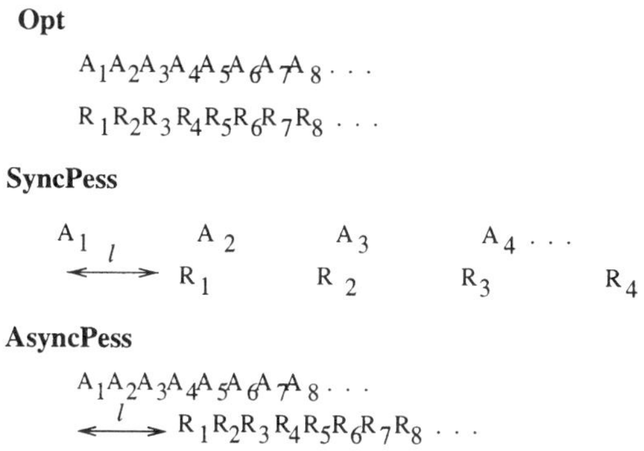

Figure 2: Some Action-Response Patterns

Protocol	Acceptable l (ms)	Unacceptable l (ms)
SyncPess	50	80
AsyncPess	140	240

Table 1: Response Time Expectations

next user action, if available, before the previous one has executed on the local replica. This asynchrony allows pipelining of the computation required for locally issued actions. Contrast this with a synchronous processing model, in which the process does not begin computing the locally issued action, until the previous action by it has executed on the replica.

To evaluate the impact of synchronous versus asynchronous processing, as seen by the end-user, we use a consistency protocol in which every update is sent to a central server, which totally orders all the updates. The optimistic policy will execute the update locally, before it is sent to the central server and therefore RT is independent of the network latency. The pessimistic policy waits till the update is returned by the central server, so RT, say l, depends on the round trip communication latency with the server. These policies can be combined with asynchronous or synchronous processing, to give four choices, SyncOpt, AsyncOpt, SyncPess, and AsyncPess. As synchrony or asynchrony has no impact when we execute optimistically, we are only left with three cases. Figure 2, shows some action-response patterns for the three cases. A_i is the instant when the computation on a user action begins and R_i is the instant when the response is seen locally.

We did an expert evaluation with two tasks, drawing lines and drawing free hand curves, to find the appropriate response time values. Optimism is the perfect case for response time, and we observed that the inter-action (most of the actions were mouse drag events) time was between 20-40ms — clearly a perceptual task. We then asked the experts to provide the minimum l values at which they started noticing the delay in response (acceptable), and when it became very irritating (unacceptable). These are tabulated in table 1. We can see that AsyncPess, which utilizes lookahead to pipeline computation, has a much higher unacceptable latency, implying that lookahead does occur, and can be utilized by the consistency protocol. On the other hand, even a response time of $80ms$ is unacceptable for SyncPess.

More detailed and rigorous user studies using more tasks are necessary to understand how the type of task affects these numbers. However, this preliminary result, which shows the significant effect of lookahead, motivates us to use an asynchronous processing model in the rest of the paper. Also, it shows that the value of the threshold can be an important factor when evaluating consistency protocols.

CONSISTENCY PROTOCOLS

The previous section discussed responsiveness. There is also a competing requirement, that of maintaining state consistency. We choose protocols that are representative of well-known protocols. A more comprehensive description of the design space of consistency protocols for interactive groupware is given in [3].

The shared state is composed of a set of objects that are fully replicated at all the processes in the collaboration. User actions are translated into *updates* by the process, which are then *issued* to the consistency protocol[1]. Each update can read and write a number of objects in the set. The system ensures that an update seems to execute *atomically* at a given replica i.e. reads and writes of two updates do not interleave. Also, as the *lookahead threshold* can be greater than zero, a process can issue updates even when its previously issued updates have not yet been executed locally.

Each update goes through the following stages: issue, timestamp at the source process, disseminate update with the timestamp to all replicas, execute at each replica. The timestamps define a *partial order* on all the updates issued by all processes. A total order is not essential as concurrent updates could be accessing different objects, and do not need to be ordered. The partial order must satisfy the *convergence criterion* i.e. any execution order of the updates that respects this partial order results in the same replica state. A pessimistic protocol always respects this partial order, while an optimistic protocol may have to reorder execution (using undo,redo), when it notices that it has violated the partial order. An update is said to have *committed* at a replica, when all the updates before it in the partial order have been received and executed. Therefore, a pessimistic protocol only executes an update after it has committed.

Other than the optimistic, pessimistic choice, a key aspect in which consistency protocols differ is: does the timestamp of an update depend on the objects accessed by it? The protocols for which the timestamp is independent of access are referred to as *Independent* protocols, and the one we use generates a total order using Lamport clocks [10]. With the optimistic policy, this protocol is similar to the ORESTE [9] protocol, except that our updates can read and write multiple objects. The other class is *Dependent* protocols, and the

[1] Sometimes referred to as the 'system'.

one we consider uses a 2-phase timestamping strategy (like 2-phase locking [2]). The update is executed at the source, and using the access information provided by the update as it executes, the source timestamps it. The motivation behind the use of dependent protocols is that they can generate a weaker ordering. Also, it is possible to commit an update even if some processes are not communicating with others. This is not possible with the Independent protocol using Lamport clocks, as before committing an update, a process needs to be sure that the clocks of all processes are greater than the timestamp of that update. However, dependent protocols may need to communicate with other processes while timestamping, so it slows down dissemination of updates. Fast dissemination is important for optimistic protocols, so we will only consider pessimistic execution with this protocol.

Before discussing the protocols, we define two pairs of read, write sets (r_1, w_1), (r_2, w_2) to be *conflicting* if and only if $r_1 \cap w_2 \neq \emptyset$ or $w_1 \cap w_2 \neq \emptyset$ or $w_1 \cap r_2 \neq \emptyset$.

Independent Protocols

These protocols use a Lamport clock at each process, which is incremented whenever a local update is issued, and is used along with the process number, to timestamp the update. These timestamps define a total order on all the updates. The update is then multicast to every process (including the source). Clocks are also modified whenever a timestamped remote update/message is received, using the usual modification rules. Every update received by a process is put in an uncommitted queue sorted in increasing order of timestamp. Each process also maintains a vector of timestamps which are estimates of the clock values of other processes (inferred from the messages received from those processes), and the minimum value in this vector is used to decide when an update in the uncommitted queue can commit. A committed update is removed from the queue. A timestamped heartbeat message is sent out by a process if it has not sent a message in a while, to ensure liveness of commit.

In the *optimistic* protocol (`optInd`), a process (say p) immediately executes all received updates. For each uncommitted update (say e), it also maintains the access sets (R_e, W_e) of the last time that update was executed. This information is changed whenever an update is undone and then redone. Suppose p receives an update u, which should have been ordered before a set of updates E, which it has already executed. To conform with the total order, p should undo E, however it is somewhat lazy. It first executes u, and if its access sets (R_u, W_u) *conflict* with R_e, W_e for any $e \in E$, some of the updates in E need to be undone.

For the *pessimistic* protocol (`pessInd`), updates are only executed after they commit, therefore no detection of conflicts is necessary.

Dependent Protocol

This protocol (`Dep`) uses locks, which are associated with mutually exclusive subsets of the objects. The larger the subset, coarser is the lock granularity. A lock has a version number, and the version numbers form a continuous sequence of integers starting with 0. These version numbers are used to timestamp updates associated with that lock, and this timestamp is used to order these updates. For example, suppose the current version number of lock A is 3, and lock B is 1. Then if user Alice issues an update (say u) which requires both lock A and B, then after acquiring both locks, this update will be timestamped with ((A,4),(B,2)). After timestamping, the locks are released, this update is multicast to others, and also inserted in the local uncommitted queue. Update u will be removed from this queue and executed only when update(s) with timestamps (A,3) and (B,1) have been executed. Note, that locks are only useful for timestamping, and are not required for committing an update. In our simulation of this protocol, we did not want to choose a specific lock management protocol, so we made a simplifying assumption. We assume that the process requesting the lock is omniscient and knows who last requested that lock. Therefore, it can send the lock request directly to that process, which eliminates the need to forward lock requests. To ensure no contradictory ordering information, locks that are acquired to timestamp an update are not released until the update is fully timestamped. This is similar to the 2-phase locking scheme used in databases.

Contention and Semantic Information

Due to social protocols mediating between users, in most collaboration scenarios where users are issuing actions concurrently, the concurrency is itself not a problem. However, it can cause problems for the consistency protocols. Also, social protocols do not guard against conflicts between concurrent updates when updates can have far-reaching indirect effects (like in some CAD scenarios), or when conflicts are deliberate (like in some multi-player games).

We define two kinds of contention which impact how these protocols perform. *Object-level Contention* (OC) between two concurrent updates occurs when their access sets (the read,write sets when they are executed in a total order that respects the partial order generated by the consistency protocol) are *conflicting*. Object-level contention limits the concurrency for `Dep` and can cause undos in `optInd`. Object-level contention between two updates does not imply that it was *really* necessary for the consistency protocol to order them. Therefore, we need to define a concept of *Real Contention* (RC). Informally, real contention between updates implies that if the ordering between them was removed from the partial order generated by the consistency protocol, that partial order would no longer satisfy the convergence criteria. Finally, in this paper we assume that when two updates with real contention are optimistically executed in the wrong order by `optInd`, and then corrected, it causes surprise to

Parameters	Text Editing	Engineering
N (number of users)	4	4
threshold	$0, 1, 2, 3$	3
update interval(ms)	$(400, 200)$	$(100, 50)$
numUpdates	1000	1000
latency (ms)	$100, \ldots, 1000$	$30, \ldots, 300$
heartbeat multiple	$1, 2, 3, 4$	3

Table 2: Parameter Values

the user, and we call this *jitter* in the user's interface (or view, in MVC terminology). Note, that in `optInd`, undo and redo is completely local and potentially very fast. By using techniques like double buffering we can hide the intermediate states of the view when undoing and redoing updates, and hence the user is not impacted by object-level contention which is not real. However, it is important to understand whether semantics of the shared state can be used to detect object-level contention that is not real, so that `Dep` can relax the partial order.

Note that we can conceptually split objects into multiple objects, and can then provide access information for these smaller objects. However, the lock (or object) granularity may not match the dynamic division of work the participants in a collaboration agree upon. Techniques like multi-granularity locking [2] can increase concurrency, but there are two problems which may limit improvements, or even worsen the situation. Firstly, in scenarios we consider with data-dependent access patterns, the granularity of what will be accessed by an update is not known beforehand, and so too many locks may be acquired. Secondly, having many locks may reduce the locality of acquiring locks by a process. For example, in the first sequence lock table given in [12], which can be used for text editors, insertion of every consecutive character causes a new lock to be acquired. Despite this, multi-granularity locking is a promising technique, and how to adapt it for timestamp-ordering protocols and its performance in a distributed environment needs more investigation, but is outside the scope of this paper.

Another scenario of OC which is not RC occurs when objects represent some physical entity, and there are physical constraints between them. For example, for collision detection in DIS, updates to the position of every entity require reading the positions of other entities in the neighborhood. However, the read value is discarded whenever collisions haven't occurred. In this case, the commutativity of two updates cannot be detected without knowing the state on which they will be executed.

EVALUATION SETUP

Workload

One of the main problems in evaluating the consistency protocols is that user input (both *what* is input, and *when* it is generated), can change with varying response time. We are not aware of any traces of user interaction with complex groupware that we can use to evaluate these protocols. As a first step in real evaluation of such protocols we construct adaptive distributed synthetic workloads. These workloads are adaptive in that they use the lookahead *threshold* to change the timing of the user input based on the response seen. A threshold of 0 means that a process does not issue a new update until the previous one has been locally executed i.e. each process only has 1 outstanding request at any time. Therefore a threshold of t means that a user can have $t+1$ outstanding requests, and we assume that the user stalls until the current lookahead falls below $t + 1$. An alternative user model, in which the number of stalls are minimized by using the past response time information to increase the inter-update interval, may be more appropriate in certain situations, but is outside the scope of this paper. A uniform distribution with a certain *(mean, range)* is used to model the *inter-update interval*. *numUpdates* is the total number of updates issued by each process and *latency* is the one-way communication latency between processes. The *heartbeat multiple* gives the inter-heartbeat interval for the `Ind` protocols as a multiple of the *latency*.

The key characteristic of a workload is the number and type of objects in the shared set, and the access patterns of the updates issued by each process. We use two realistic collaboration scenarios to motivate these characteristics.

Text Editing N users are editing a document which is divided into sections, each of which is modeled as a shared object. Assume that `Dep` uses a lock per section. Depending on the situation, each user is editing his own section, or two users are editing different parts of the same section. To capture this behavior we use a parameter h, where h=*0* implies no contention of any sort, while h=*1* means that there is object-level contention between pairs of users. There is *no* real contention. The values of the other parameters are given in table 2.

Engineering Design This scenario considers shared objects hierarchically arranged in a tree. This can occur in the design of a complex physical model, like the example in [1], or the design of key-frames for animation of an articulated model (example in [3]).

Although it can be scaled to higher N values, we illustrate it with N=*4*. All the vertices in figure 3 represent shared objects. The leaf vertices represent primitive models which are combined hierarchically to create more complex models. Two models with the same parent model constrain each other, and therefore a write of one has to read the other. For example, an update which writes model 5 must read model 4. In this scenario, each process reads and writes two primitive models. For example, process P_1 reads and writes model 10 and model 11. With a certain probability p, a write of a model at level i, results in a write of its parent at level $i + 1$.

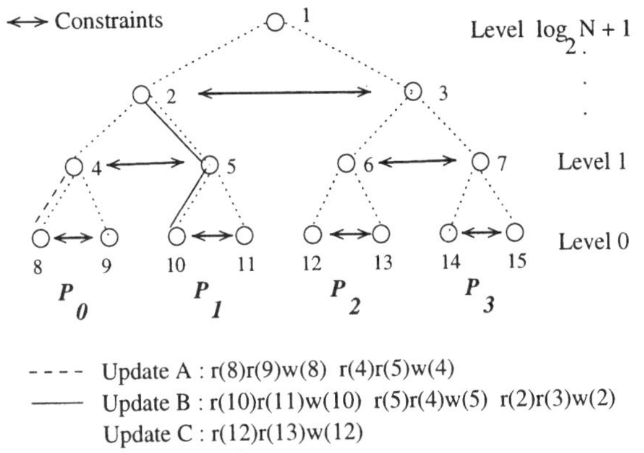

Figure 3: Forest Workload

Also, we can control the number of levels in the workload i.e. a maximum level of 2 means that there are 14 model objects, with model 2 and 3 not constraining each other. The number of the highest level is denoted by $h + 1$. The value of h controls the maximum possible object-level contention (max-OC), and is either 1 or 2. We simulate `Dep` with two lock granularities. For `DepCoarse`, there is one lock for each tree in the forest, and therefore we use $N/2^h$ locks. For `DepFine`, two siblings of a parent share a lock. As no locks are required for level $h + 1$, we optimize by only having $N/2^k$ locks for level k where $k < h + 1$. As children of the same parent share a lock, and every process moves from the bottom to the top when acquiring locks, there is no possibility of deadlock. p controls how much of the max-OC is realized (relative-OC), and is varied between $0.0, 0.2, \ldots, 1.0$. In figure 3, with *h*=2, only updates A and B cause object-level contention, while A and C, or B and C will contend in `DepCoarse`. The values of the other parameters are given in table 2.

Performance Metrics

We consider the following metrics.

1. Response time (mean and standard deviation) : Along with a low mean, a low deviation is also important to avoid user surprise due to wide variation in response time.

2. Local commit time (mean and standard deviation) : For the pessimistic protocols the commit time is the same as the response time. A low commit time is also good for an optimistic protocol as it reduces the possibility that an update may be undone a long time after it was initially performed.

3. Jitter Count : A subset of the local rollbacks/undos cause jitter. Note that rollbacks in `optInd` are completely local.

4. Number of messages of each type : Important for measuring the communication cost of the protocols. Other than the messages to disseminate the updates, which are the same for each protocol, the *extra messages* for `optInd, pessInd` are due to heartbeat messages, and those in `Dep` are due to lock request and reply messages.

5. Stalled count and Stalled time : Stalled count measures the number of times the user had to stall because the previous *threshold* + 1 updates had not been locally performed. Stalled time is the mean time for which the user stalled.

6. Total execution time : Measures how long the users took to finish their tasks.

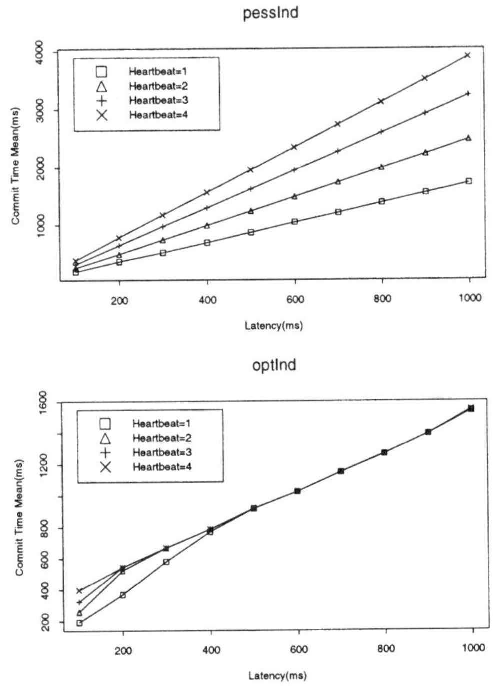

Figure 4: Commit time vs. Latency. Threshold=0

RESULTS

We simulated the protocols with both the text editing and engineering design workload. In this section we summarize some of the interesting results.

Text Editing

Due to the large number of parameters, we highlight the effect of the *threshold* and *heartbeat multiple* and then fix their values to reasonable levels. A scatter plot of the commit time versus the threshold, for all the protocols, showed that it was *usually* not affected by the lookahead threshold value. This may be expected as the threshold value affects when an update is issued, but should not affect the commit time of an already issued update. However, when *threshold=0* for `pessInd`, the commit time was sometimes much larger than when *threshold* > 0. Also, it was much larger than the

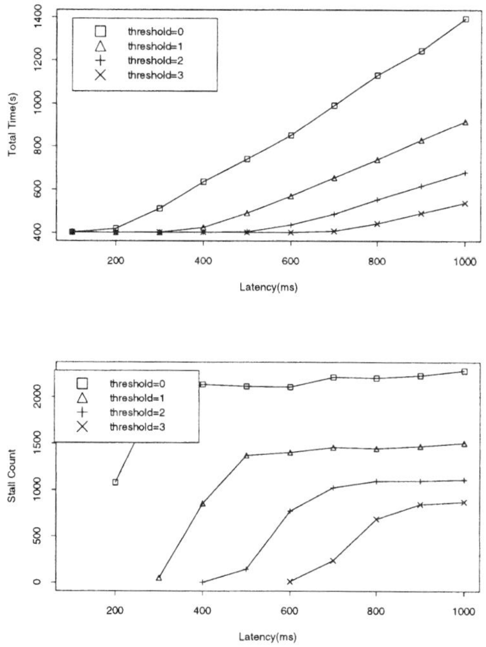

Figure 5: Total time and Stall count for Dep,h=1

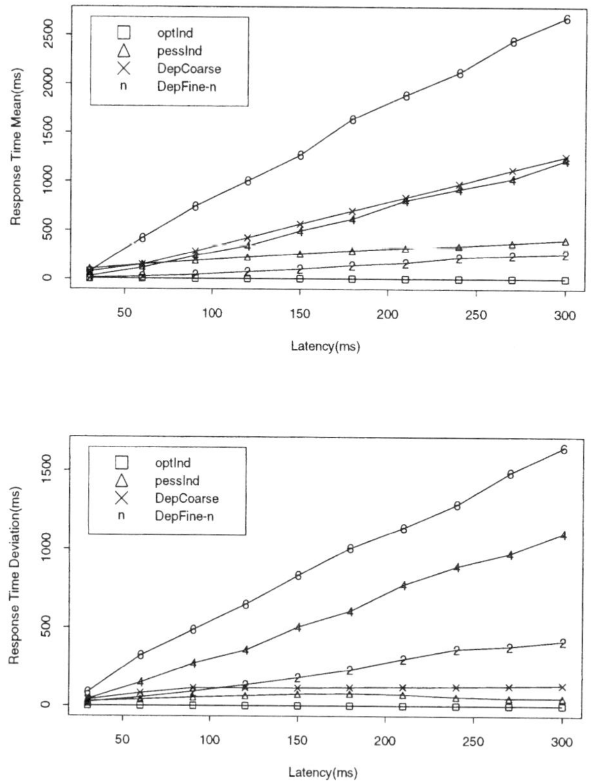

Figure 6: Responsiveness vs. Latency. h=2

commit time for optInd with *threshold=0*. To explain this, figure 4 shows the effect of heartbeat multiple and latency on commit time for pessInd and optInd when *threshold=0*. For optInd, the effect of heartbeat frequency decreases as latency is increased. This is because the inter-update interval is much lower than the latency so heartbeats are not really needed. However, as pessInd executes updates pessimistically, it stalls after issuing each update, and hence heartbeat messages are very important to pick up the slack in message frequency. It can be seen that with *heartbeat=1* the commit is almost as fast as that of optInd, however in this case the number of heartbeat messages was of the order of the total number of updates. This gives us the following observation.

Observation 1 *When* threshold=0, *increasing the heartbeat rate decreases the response time and total time for* pessInd *significantly. However,* optInd *is unaffected by heartbeat rate at high latencies.*

Next, we looked at how threshold affected the total time of the task. As expected, it did not affect optInd, and Dep when *h=0*, but had a strong effect on pessInd, and Dep when *h=1*. Figure 5 shows the effect of threshold and latency on Dep when *h=1*. As expected, the total time for the task decreases with increasing threshold value. Increase in total time with latency is due to increasing number of stalls (up to a certain maximum, dependent on the threshold value) and increasing time for each stall. For *threshold=3*, no process stalls until *latency=600ms* and therefore the total time taken remains constant until then.

Observation 2 *In a task with a high value of threshold, the user can perform well even at high latencies, because of the lower total number of stalls and the smaller mean time for each stall.*

The results pertaining to varying contention are better examined in the engineering design experiments.

Engineering Design

We fixed the *threshold=3* and *heartbeat=3*. With no max-OC, i.e. *h=0*, the performance of optInd and DepCoarse is equivalent, as neither communicates with other processes before executing a local update. Similarly, when $h = 0 \vee p = 0$, i.e. there is no OC, optInd and DepFine are equivalent. In figures 6 to 9, DepFine-n refers to the DepFine protocol when $p = 0.n$. The values of p, h have no effect on pessInd. In the following observations, *low* max-OC refers to *h=1*, *high* max-OC to *h=2*, *low* relative-OC to $p = 0.2, 0.4$ and *high* relative-OC to $p > 0.4$. We first examine metrics in which p, h do not affect optInd[2].

Figure 6, shows that pessInd gives a lower response time than DepCoarse beyond a latency of $60ms$. DepFine with $p \leq 0.2$ is better than pessInd, however it dete-

[2] Although undo and redo do impact these metric values, the effect was insignificant.

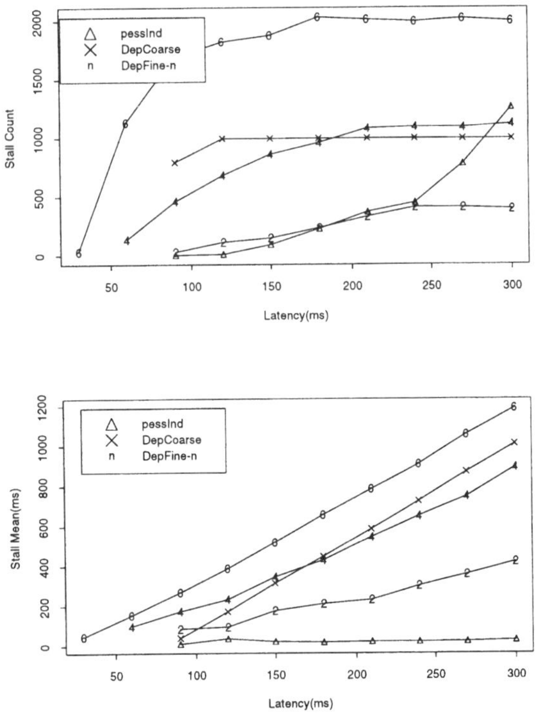

Figure 7: Stall vs. Latency. h=2

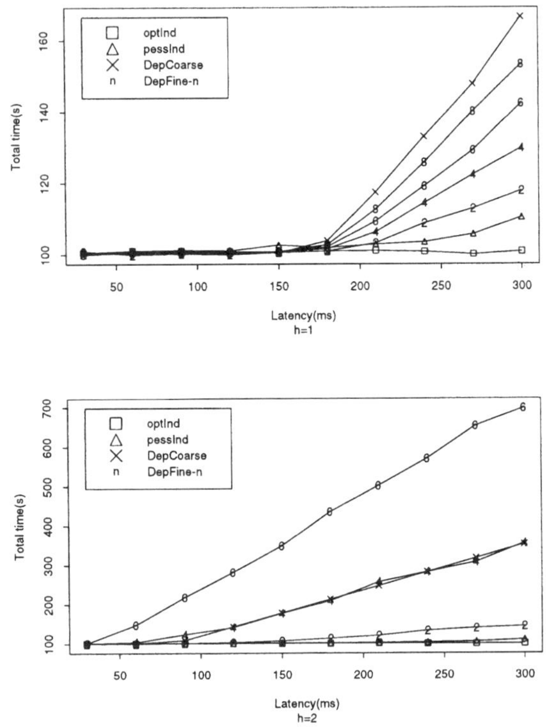

Figure 8: Total time vs. Latency

riorates quickly with increasing p. In fact, for $p > 0.4$, `DepFine` performs much worse than `DepCoarse`, because it is acquiring multiple locks in sequence for every update, while `DepCoarse` only acquires one lock of coarser granularity. This gives us the following observation.

Observation 3 *When max-*OC *is high and relative-*OC *is low,* `DepFine` *has lower mean response time than* `DepCoarse` *and* `pessInd`*. However, with high relative-*OC, `DepFine` *can have higher mean response time than* `DepCoarse` *and* `pessInd`*, and this difference increases with increasing latency.*

Looking at the standard deviation of response time, we see that it is lower for `pessInd` than both `DepCoarse` and `DepFine`. Also, the deviation for `pessInd` and `DepCoarse` is relatively independent of latency, even though the variation in latency is increasing with increasing mean latency. This can be attributed to the average of many independent random variables having a lower deviation than each of them alone. However, with $p = 0.2$, `DepFine` has a higher deviation than both `DepCoarse` and `pessInd`, even at very low latencies, because for each update it may have to acquire anywhere between 1 and 3 locks.

Observation 4 *Even with high max-*OC *and low relative-*OC, `DepFine` *can have a higher response time deviation than* `DepCoarse` *and* `pessInd`*, and this difference increases with increasing latency.*

Figure 7 shows how the stall count and mean vary with latency. The stall count of `optInd`, `DepCoarse` with *h=0*, and `DepFine` with *p=0* is zero. The stall count for `pessInd` rapidly increases after *latency=240ms*, because the lookahead can no longer suppress the effect of the latency. However its stall mean is relatively stable and is around $25ms$. In our user model, in which the user stalls when her lookahead exceeds the threshold, the relative importance of stall count and stall mean needs to be investigated i.e. does the user want to wait more number of times or wait longer each time. The stall count for `DepCoarse` stabilizes at $N * numUpdates/(threshold + 1)$.

Observation 5 *The stall count of the* Dep *protocols is limited by the* threshold, *while that of* `pessInd` *keeps increasing with latency. However, the mean time for the stall is independent of latency for* `pessInd`*, but keeps increasing for the* Dep *protocols.*

Figure 8 shows how the total time varies with latency with *h=1,2*. Even though the response time mean for `pessInd` was usually higher than the Dep protocols at low contention, the total time does not show this. This is because the lower stall mean of `pessInd` compensates.

Observation 6 *For low max-*OC *and* $latency \leq 180ms$*, the choice of the protocol has negligible effect on the total time taken to perform a task. However, with high max-*OC *and low relative-*OC*, the* Dep *protocols can perform significantly worse than the* `Ind` *protocols.*

Note that we have not modeled the increasing errors, or user

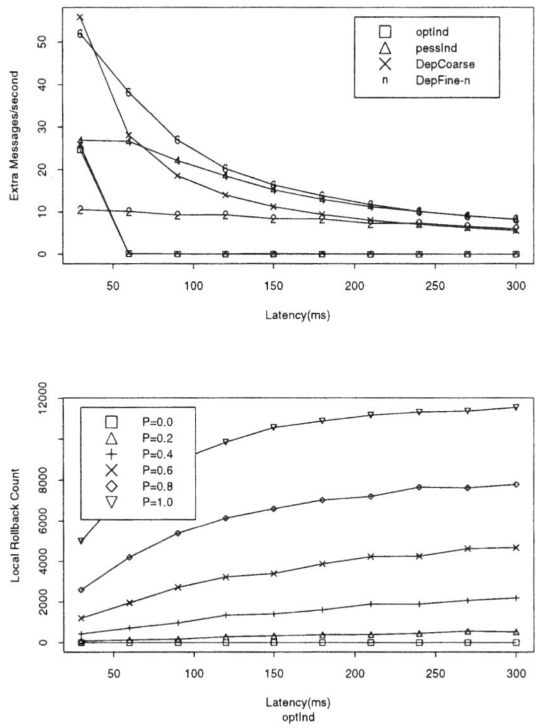

Figure 9: Extra Messages, Rollback count. h=2

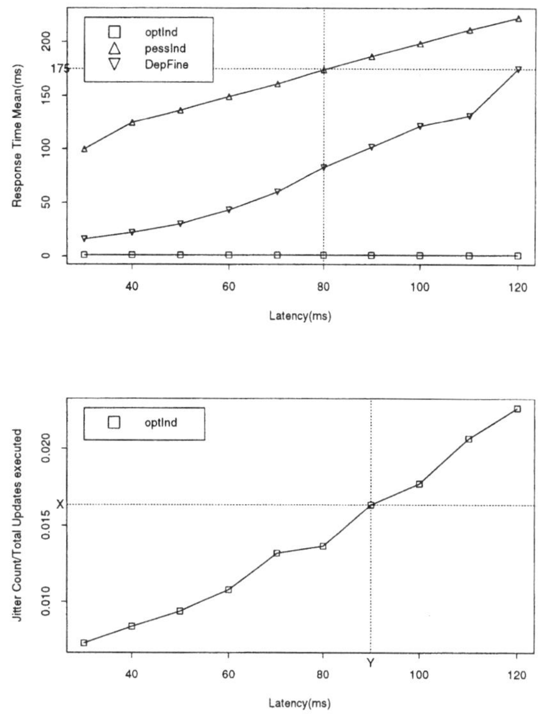

Figure 10: Protocol comparison. h=2,p=0.3

frustration that may occur when response time increases beyond a certain value. Therefore, acceptable response time values for the task need to be considered along with this total time information when choosing a protocol.

From figure 9, we can see how many extra messages are sent per second, by each of the protocols. For the `Ind` protocols at a very low latency, the heartbeat interval ($3 * latency$) is lower than the inter-update interval, so a lot of extra heartbeat messages are sent. Otherwise, the `Ind` protocols have 0 extra messages. The extra messages for the `Dep` protocols slowly decline as latency increases, as the total time to perform the task is increasing. Also, the same figure gives the number of rollbacks/undos for `optInd` as the latency and relative-OC increases. Note that how many of these rollbacks cause jitter is very dependent on the collaboration scenario. However, the amount of jitter that is tolerable, is a very important factor in determining whether `optInd` is useful for a certain collaboration scenario.

Discussion

An important question is, given the scenario, how do we apply the preceding information to decide which protocol to use. We illustrate with an example. Suppose we know that *h=2,p=0.3*, that the latency can vary between $30ms$ and $120ms$, and 50% of the rollbacks cause jitter. Figure 10 shows the mean response time for `optInd, pessInd, DepFine`, and the fraction of the total updates executed which caused jitter, which we call the *jitter fraction*. If the maximum tolerable jitter fraction is greater than 0.022, `optInd` is clearly the best because of its instantaneous response. If the maximum tolerable jitter fraction is a value x, less than 0.022, we have a choice to make. Let y be the latency value corresponding to this value x. We can use `optInd` when the latency is less than y, and then dynamically switch to `pessInd`. This can be easily done because the choice to switch from `optInd` to `pessInd` and vice versa can be made *locally* by each process. However, if we also cannot tolerate a mean response time greater than $175ms$, we will have to use `DepFine` beyond a latency of y. As it is hard to dynamically switch between the `Dep` and `Ind` protocols without coordination between all the processes, which may not be possible, we may then have to use `Dep` for the whole collaboration.

RELATED WORK

Greenberg and Marwood [8] qualitatively discuss the impact of different concurrency control schemes, including optimistic and pessimistic protocols, on certain collaboration scenarios. They observe that social protocol between participants make conflicts rare, and in many cases it is possible for users to notice conflicts and manually repair them. For the next generation of collaborative applications, we expect that conflicts usually occur due to secondary effects of user actions, for example, automatic constraint evaluation in engineering design, and collision detection in distributed interactive simulation. In such scenarios, conflicts will be more common, and we cannot expect the user to manually fix the state.

For replicated state, two types of consistency protocols have typically been used. Explicit locking approaches use locks for atomicity and concurrency control, like DistView [13]. Ordering based approaches need an associated commit protocol. The `Ind` protocol is similar to ORESTE [9]. DECAF [16] uses a primary copy commit protocol in which an update issuing process only needs to talk to the primary copy processes for the update to commit. A protocol in which the primary copies assign timestamps can also be constructed, and the `Dep` protocol is a dynamic variation of this, in which the primary copies can move.

Finally, there has been some studies to understand how poor response time affects human performance for single user tasks. MacKenzie and Ware [11] use a simple target acquisition task in which the user has to move the mouse cursor into a rectangular target. Their user studies show significant increase in both the time to perform the task, and the error rate, as response time is increased.

CONCLUSION

We have described and evaluated design choices for consistency protocols in interactive groupware deployed in a wide-area distributed environment. For such high latency environments, the concept of a *lookahead threshold* for user actions is very important for a real evaluation of protocols. This models the users ability to issue a number of actions without waiting for the first action to complete. We have described two classes of protocols that can be used to consistently execute the user updates at all replicas. With a novel workload model, we have evaluated these protocols along a number of dimensions and have discussed how to use the observed metric values to choose the appropriate protocol.

Although it is very important to quantitatively evaluate consistency protocols, the evaluation problem is incredibly hard. Firstly, it involves construction of workloads for a large class of applications and different usage scenarios for these applications. These workloads need to be adaptive like a user i.e. they should change according to the behavior of the system. Secondly, it is important to formally or informally validate these workloads, otherwise the results might be misleading. Thirdly, the relative importance of the metrics is not well understood and nor is the design space of such protocols. The answers to some of these questions are obviously highly dependent on the user. Therefore, it is important to get enough insight from the evaluation data, so that a very high-level interface can be offered to the user to tune the behavior of the protocols at run-time. This also brings up the question, can we dynamically switch between protocols at run-time? The goal of this paper is not to provide a definite answer to all these questions, but to start us down the path of finding the answers.

ACKNOWLEDGEMENTS

This research was supported in part by an IBM fellowship and NSF grant CCR-9619371. We would also like to thank the reviewers for their insightful comments.

REFERENCES

1 C. Bajaj and V. Anupam. Collaborative multimedia in scientific design. *IEEE Multimedia*, 1(2):39–49, 1994.

2 P. A. Bernstein, V. Hadzilacos, and N. Goodman. *Concurrency Control and Recovery in Database Systems*. Addison-Wesley, 1987.

3 S. Bhola and M. Ahamad. The design space for data replication algorithms in interactive groupware. Technical Report GIT-CC-98-15, College of Computing, Georgia Institute of Technology, 1998.

4 S. Bhola, B. Mukherjee, S. Doddapaneni, and M. Ahamad. Flexible batching and consistency mechanisms for building interactive groupware applications. In *Proceedings of the 18th ICDCS*, 1998.

5 S. Card, T. Moran, and A. Newell. *The Psychology of Human-Computer Interaction*. Lawrence Erlbaum Associates, 1983.

6 D. Collins. *Designing Object-Oriented User Interfaces*. Benjamin/Cummings Publishing Company, 1995.

7 C. A. Ellis and S. J. Gibbs. Concurrency control in groupware systems. In *Proceedings of the ACM SIGMOD'89*, pages 399–407, 1989.

8 S. Greenberg and D. Marwood. Real time groupware as a distributed system: Concurrency control and its effect on the interface. In *Proceedings of the Fifth ACM Conference on Computer Supported Cooperative Work (CSCW)*, 1994.

9 A. Karsenty and M. Beaudouin-Lafon. An algorithm for distributed groupware applications. In *Proceedings of the 13th ICDCS*, pages 195–202, 1993.

10 L. Lamport. Time, clocks, and the ordering of events in a distributed system. *Communications of the ACM*, 21(7):558–565, July 1978.

11 I. S. MacKenzie and C. Ware. Lag as a determinant of human performance in iteractive systems. In *INTERCHI'93 Proceedings*, 1993.

12 J. Munson and P. Dewan. A concurrency control framework for collaborative systems. In *Proceedings of the 6th ACM CSCW*, 1996.

13 A. Prakash and H. S. Shim. Distview: Support for building efficient collaborative applications using replicated objects. In *Proceedings of the 5th CSCW*, 1994.

14 C. Schuckmann, L. Kirchner, J. Schummer, and J. M. Haake. Designing object-oriented synchronous groupware with COAST. In *ACM CSCW'96*, 1996.

15 B. Shneiderman. *Designing the User Interface: Strategies for Effective Human-Computer Interaction*. Addison-Wesley, 2nd edition, 1992.

16 R. Strom, G. Banavar, K. Miller, A. Prakash, and M. Ward. Concurrency control and view notification algorithms for collaborative replicated objects. *IEEE Transactions on Computers*, 47(4):458 – 471, April 1998.

Designing for the Dynamics of Cooperative Work Activities

Jakob Bardram
Aarhus University, Computer Science Department
Ny Munkegade bldg. 540, 8000 Aarhus C., Denmark
bardram@daimi.aau.dk

ABSTRACT
CSCW seems to have a persistent problem of understanding the nature of "cooperative work". This paper argues that this problem is a direct result of not looking at the dynamic aspects of work – i.e. that cooperative work is not one thing, but different things at different times and in different places. Based on Activity Theory the paper gives a conceptual frame for understanding the dynamics of collaborative work activities, and argues that the design of computer support should view cooperative breakdowns not as a problem but as an important resource in design. These arguments are based on empirical studies of healthcare work and the design of a computer support for planning and scheduling operations and other activities within a hospital.

Keywords
Cooperative work, dynamics, Activity Theory, design, healthcare

INTRODUCTION
This paper is about the nature of "cooperative work". Explicitly, it addresses the *dynamics* of cooperative work, such as when cooperation breaks down, changes over time, and is perceived differently by different actors involved. Understanding the dynamics of cooperative work is extremely important as a way to understand how to design computer systems supporting cooperative work. If computer technology does not take into account support for the dynamic development, change, and breakdown in cooperation the system fails. This has been shown in numerous workplace studies [3, 6, 12, 22, 23]. Actually, the implicit assumption in many of the ethnographic studies made within the realm of CSCW is to study the dynamics, and especially the breakdowns, in cooperative work as a way to understand the 'normal' flow of work (c.f. [6, 23]). Unfortunately, the dynamics of cooperative work has not explicitly been addressed within CSCW. Questions like "how does cooperation develop and change over time?, "what is cooperation anyway? – can we identify different types of cooperation?", "and if so – how, when, and why does one type of cooperation transform into another?", "why does cooperation sometimes break down, and how do people recover from such breakdowns?", and "why is the same work viewed as cooperation in one situation and as competition in another?" are extremely important, yet unanswered questions in our attempts to support cooperative work by computer technology.

This paper takes a theoretical starting point in understanding the dynamics in cooperative work, and provides a conceptual frame for identifying, analyzing, and hence designing for cooperative work. The paper builds on extensive workplace studies within the Danish healthcare sector. Based on this empirical basis the dynamics in hospital work is analyzed and discussed, and computer support for the dynamics in cooperative work is discussed with a booking and scheduling systems as the focal point.

THE NOTION OF COOPERATIVE WORK IN CSCW
Before turning to the framework and the hospital case, let us shortly consider the background for the present discussion.

The Notion of "Cooperation" in Cooperative Work
By now – 14 years after Greif and Cashman's workshop in 1984 – it still seems like the research field of CSCW struggles with the issue of what CSCW exactly means. Bannon [1] argues that the term CSCW seems to be an "umbrella term" covering a loose agglomeration of communities. Hence, browsing through the proceedings of the different CSCW conferences and the journal, we find papers on a wide variety of issues, such as workflow technologies, groupware, ethnographic workplace studies, participatory design, labor issues, group psychology, etc. Even though this in itself might not be a problem – this diversity of background might even be advantantageous, as argued by Bannon [1] – it still leaves problems in fostering an internal and external discourse of ideas that we want to dedicate the term CSCW for. Because we do have a pretty good idea of what is meant by "computer support" this confusion lies in an understanding of what we mean by "cooperative work". And, as argued by Bannon and Schmidt [2], as long as we intend to support "it" with computers, it probably would be a good idea to know what we are talking about, as certainly at present the label "cooperative work" seems to be applied to just about anything.

CSCW has been identified with the increasingly commercial interest in "Groupware" and thereby identifying cooperative work with group work (c.f. [13]). However, narrowing down the definition of cooperative work by using

CSCW 98 Seattle Washington USA

the psychological notion of a group with its social psychological characteristics such as norms, roles, group pressure, and conformity, does not seem to quite encompass the intent of the CSCW field. Generally, a group is defined as a relatively small ensemble of people, who interact and communicate closely and who share the same goal. The notions of cooperation solely through communication and of a shared goal are dubious, however. As a description of the medical trajectory of a patient, the medical record fosters cooperation across departmental and professional boundaries without intense communication, and the cooperative process of decision making in a surgical department's managerial group is a very differentiated process involving the interaction and trade-offs between multiple goals, preferences, values, incentives, and inclinations. By focusing on the positive aspects of how people carry out work together, such as cooperation, collaboration, and commitment, instead of the difficult aspects, such as competition, conflict, and control, the field of CSCW has been criticized for being limited in its understanding of cooperative work [14]. When looking into the organization of hospitals, an important aspect of work coordination includes the conflicts between work goals and motivations for coordination activities [23].

The Notion of Dynamics in Cooperative Work

Trying to conceptualize "cooperative work" needs however to address the dynamics of this work. Without mentioning it explicitly, it seems as if such dynamic aspects of cooperative work play a major, but implicit role in many of the investigations of cooperative work done within CSCW. Let me illustrate this with three examples.

A central debate within CSCW concerns the notion of workflow systems. Many of the ideas of workflow systems came out of the office automation movement, viewing office work as routine work ready for rationalistic automation efforts. Hence, workflow systems embed standard operating procedures for routinely handling office work, and have as such been viewed as the assembly line of the office. The well-known work of Wynn and Suchman [22], however, has shown that office work – even in the most routine cases – is cooperatively handled in an ad hoc manner within the cooperative work ensemble, where operating procedures do not in any sense control the flow of work. This notion of work is widely accepted within CSCW and helps distinguish the field from the former field of office automation. But the 'survival' of workflow systems, and their commercial success, still gives credit to its advocates' argument that much work is characterized by routine that can be coordinated effectively by formal procedures and scripts for action. This tension points to a need for understanding that cooperative work is not one or the other, but might be both routine and cooperation at the same time. In this sense, concepts like routine, cooperation, conflicts, etc. might be viewed not as distinct categories of work, but as different *aspects* of the same work effort.

The conceptualization of cooperative work within the framework of Coordination Mechanism [21] makes an analytical distinction between "cooperative work" and "articulation work", the later being the work actors do, caused by their interdependency, in order to coordinate, schedule, mesh, integrated, etc., their cooperative work. Hence, articulation work is an overhead to the cooperative work. However, this view does not incorporate any dynamic understanding of work in the sense that what is cooperative work in one situation might be articulation in another, and vice versa. This is nicely put by Bødker and Mogensen [7] when they, based on an analysis of the cooperation between a labor inspection officer and his secretary, conclude that "one woman's job is another man's articulation work" – i.e. that the same work from one perspective is viewed as coordination of the 'real work', and from another perspective is viewed as the work *per se*.

The dynamics of cooperative work over time is also particular important in understanding work. Several sociological studies of the introduction of computer technology have adopted a "before-after" scheme of investigating the impact on the work practices (e.g. [6, 12]). These studies have tried to provide information about how work groups develop, function, and change over time. Often cooperative work can only be understood by studying the temporal unfolding of the work practices involved. In some cases, cooperation is temporarily initiated in response to the requirement within an organization (e.g. task-force groups). In other cases, in emergency situations at hospitals for instance, cooperation can have a more spontaneously instantiation and course. And in still other cases, cooperation has a quasi-permanent character like in project teams and, finally, cooperation is in many cases of a permanent character within fixed organizational roles and responsibilities.

Hence, cooperative work seems (at least) to be dynamic across types of interaction, actors, and time; what might be close cooperation in one situation might be routine in the next; what is coordination for one actor is the work of another, and cooperative efforts are constantly initiated and finalized over time. Hence, a framework trying to conceptualize cooperative work activities needs to address such dynamics in work.

The Notion of Breakdowns in Cooperative Work

Closely tied to the notion of dynamics in cooperative work is the notion of a breakdown in the flow of work. This notion of cooperative breakdowns has been a foundation for most of the sociological research done within CSCW and has been common to most of the workplace studies. Attention has been paid to studies of how people manage the contingencies inherent to cooperative work and the methods they apply in order to recover from different breakdowns in the flow of work. The classic study of Suchman [22], for instance, investigates how purchasing staff worked together to solve a problem of an incomplete invoice, and Symon et al. [23] focus on hospital staff's numerous deviations from 'normal' cooperative work and their coping strategies, as a method to understand cooperation and conflicts within hospitals. Moreover, several CSCW studies have, not surprisingly, paid special attention to cooperative breakdowns caused by the introduction of computer technology. For instance, how the smooth flow of work at a print shop is disrupted by the introduction of computers [6] and how general practitioners in the

UK encounted several breakdowns in their work, when a new computer-based medical record was introduced [12].

The notion of cooperative breakdowns in work hence exists as an important, but often unarticulated background for much of the work done in CSCW. The intent of this paper is to address the dynamics in cooperative work arising from such breakdowns and view such breakdowns as important places to look for an understanding of cooperation. The importance of understanding cooperative breakdowns, however, lies in the importance of supporting such breakdowns in the design of computer technology. Failures and problems with cooperative computer technology, as the ones mentioned above, arise precisely when the computer artifact leaves no support for handling breakdown situations in the flow of work. Hence, we need to study and understand cooperative breakdowns in order to design for recovery from them.

THEORIZING THE DYNAMICS OF COOPERATIVE WORK

As a social psychological theory focusing on the developmental transformations and dynamics in collective human work activity, Activity Theory seems to provide appropriate conceptualizations, suited for analyzing cooperative work, its dynamic transformation, and the importance of cooperative breakdowns.

Activity Theory[1]

The fundamental unit of analysis in Activity Theory (AT) is the *human activity*, carried out by an active subject. Every activity is specific and activities are distinguished from each other by their respective *objects*. It is the activity's object that gives it a specific direction, i.e. is the *objective* of the activity. The notion of object in AT is not limited to physical entities; the prestigious position as a neurosurgeon is an example of an ideal and culturally defined object, and becoming a neurosurgeon can hence be an objective for a medical intern. Human activities are always embedded within a socio-cultural context of other humans and work activities thus always take place within some community of practice. AT describes cooperation as a *collaborative activity*, with one objective, but distributed onto several actors, each performing one or more *actions* according to the overall and shared objective of the work. The relationship between the individual's work activity and the work activities of his fellow workers is subject to a division of work and is regulated by different more or less explicit rules and norms – e.g. that the surgeon can use nurses to assist the operation but not the anesthesiologist [8].

Human activity is always mediated by artifacts. These artifacts have been adopted and developed in ways so that they can mediate certain activities within a community of practice and an artifact hence becomes an intrinsic part of this community. For example, the surgical instruments used within a surgical department are mediators for operating on a patient, and they have been developed and specialized according to many years of experiences within the practice of the specific surgical speciality. Vygotsky extended the notion of mediation by artifacts to include psychological artifacts. Examples of more psychological artifacts used at surgical departments are the different operating procedures, heuristics, individual and collective experiences, medical concepts and scientific results and methods. Vygotsky emphasized signs and language as psychological artifacts mediating activity directed toward other humans. A psychological artifact is subject to the same socio-cultural rules of development as any other artifact.

Levels of a Collaborative Activity

AT identifies a three level hierarchical structure of a collaborative activity [9]: co-ordinated, co-operative, and co-constructive collaborative activity.

The *co-ordinated* aspect of work captures the normal and routine flow of interaction. In co-ordinated work the various actors are gathered together to act upon a common object, but their individual actions are only externally related to each other. Individuals are following their scripted roles, each concentrating on the successful performance of their assigned actions. The script is coded in written rules, in plans, in schedules, or in tacitly assumed traditions and norms. These scripts coordinate the participants' actions as if from behind their backs, without being questioned or discussed [9]. In this sense the actors are passive participants – not active subjects, but "wheels in the organizational machinery" [15]. Co-ordination ensures that an activity is working in harmony with its surrounding activities. Characterizing the relationship among the activities as *external* means that each actor might actually be working together to achieve a common object, e.g. treatment of a patient, but they do not relate to the common objective of their activity. The subjects only realize the whole of the activity from the point of view of their individual activity.

By *co-operative* collaborative work is meant a mode of interaction in which the actors, instead of each focusing on performing their assigned actions and roles, they focus on a common object and thus share the objective of the collaborative activity. With regard to the common object, each actor has to balance his own actions with the actions of his partners, and it might even be necessary to influence his partners' actions, with regard to achieving the common task.

In co-operative activity the object is stable and generally agreed upon. However the means for realizing the activity might not be present or known. Such means are primarily the script revealing a distribution of the activity onto several actions and actors, and the mediating artifacts. This does not mean that the artifacts necessarily have to be constructed (fabricated) as such. It merely means that an artifact is not recognized as a mediator in the action but merely exist as an object in the world. As a part of realiz-

[1] Some central references to Activity Theory are Leontjev [16], Engeström [8]. Kuutti [15] has introduced Activity Theory in the field of CSCW and several inspirations for using Activity Theory in the design of computer systems can be found in the book edited by Nardi [18]. Further elaboration on the use of AT as a foundation for CSCW research and design is presented in [5].

ing a cooperative activity these means have to be established, i.e. finding an appropriate distribution of the activity and finding appropriate artifacts that can be turned into mediating tools.

The important difference between coordinated and cooperative work is the sharing of the objective, which enables the participants in the distributed activity to relate to each other and make corrective adjustment to their own and other's actions according to the overall objective of the collective activity. In this sense the participants are active subjects within the collaborative activity.

In a hospital, for example, the collaboration between the ward and the kitchen concerning the food for patients can take form as both coordinated as well as cooperative work. If the kitchen only responds to the requests from the ward, without taking into consideration the motive of the healthcare professionals of treating the patient, we talk about coordinated work activities. However, if the kitchen shares the motive of treating the patient with the ward we talk about cooperative work. In the later case, the sharing of the motive enables the kitchen to adjust their activity not only to the request but also to the overall motive. Hence, if the ward orders the normal dinner for a patient with a cardiological illness and the kitchen knows that the menu is rather fat, the kitchen staff is able to make an ad hoc correction of the request or contact the ward to discuss whether this is a good diet according to the overall motive of treating the patient.

By *co-constructive* collaborative activity is meant interactions in which the actors focus on re-conceptualizing their own organization and interaction in relation to their shared objects. Both the object and the script are re-conceptualized, as is the interaction between the participants [9]. At this level of collaborative activity the object of work is not stable – or is not even existing – and therefore has to be collectively constructed, i.e. co-constructed. The community asks questions like: "What is the meaning of this problem in the first place? Why are we trying to solve it – and who benefits from its solution? How did the problem emerge – who created it and for what purpose? Is the objective still relevant or has the whole activity become obsolete?"

Transitions to the co-constructive level of collaboration are seldom in the ongoing flow of daily work actions [9]. Attempts to re-organize and re-construct work typically take place on an organizational level. For instance, by introducing the concept of "Patient Focused Hospitals" at one of the hospitals involved in the project, the patient treatment and care was being re-conceptualized from a rational administrative-economic model of patient treatment organized around separated departments to a more holistic and systemic oriented model of patient treatment organized around teams of healthcare professionals.

In the analysis of collaborative activities according to these three levels it must be emphasized that an activity cannot be said to exist on one level alone. The levels of coordination, co-operation, and co-construction are *analytical distinctions* of the same collaborative activity. This means that an analysis of even the most routinized work, seemingly only realized as coordinated individual actions, must also be analyzed in terms of co-operation and co-construction. Hence, the routinized work has been constructed by someone at some point of time as a way to achieve some common object through cooperation. There are examples of work actions that seem totally without purpose and without any reasonable objective – for instance, filling out forms in a bureaucracy. But this does not mean that the levels of cooperation and co-construction do not exist. It only means that the common objective and the means for work have achieved a tacit status within an organization. To fully analyze a cooperative work activity, we therefore need to look at it from a *cultural-historical perspective* in order to reveal its different components and how the common object, the means for work and the use of these means are established within a community over time.

Dynamic Transformation between the Levels of Collaborative Activities

Central to the notion of hierarchical levels of an activity is the notion of dynamic transformation between the levels. The transformations are tied to the stability of the means of work and the object of work. Basically, the upward transformation is caused by reflections on the means for doing the work or reflections on the object of work itself. Such reflections can be sparked either because of a *breakdown* or by deliberate *shift of focus*. The downward transformation is caused by resolving contradictions and problems, and re-embodying the resolution in the lower level. The dynamics are illustrated in figure 1.

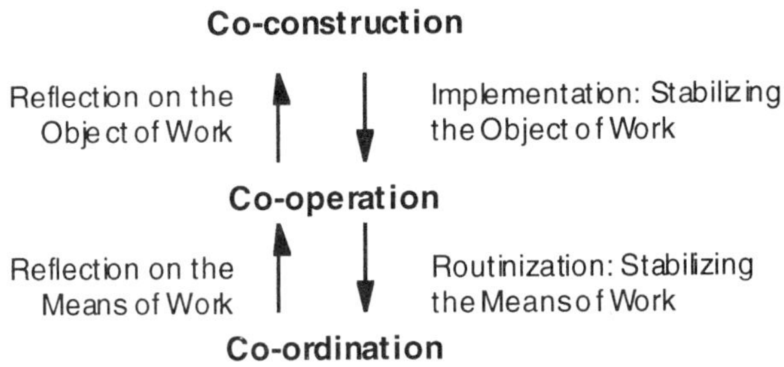

Figure 1: The Dynamics of Cooperative Work

Reflection on the means of work: The coordinated flow of work, where each actor relates only to the externalized actions of his fellow actors, relies on stable means of work – i.e. stable scripts, rules, and artifacts. However, these means of work might need to be cooperatively re-established according to the object of work – either because of a *coordination breakdown* or because of deliberate re-conceptualization of the way the work is achieved currently. At a hospital, for example, most requests for X-ray examinations were routine cases (e.g. simple X-ray picture of the skeleton), done merely based on the information written at the requisition. In some problematic cases, however, a closer cooperation between the physician and the radiologist was necessary in order to establish exactly what kind of radiology examination would provide the best means of establishing a exact diagnosis.

Routinization works in the opposite direction by re-establishing co-ordinated work where the means for collaboration are stabilized, i.e. the way that collaborative actions are distributed within a community, the rules guiding the work, and the mediating tools realizing the actions. In this transformation it is essential to ensure that everybody knows their part of the script and how to coordinate their work with others. For example, introducing new requisition forms or computer-based systems are new means of work, and hence need to be incorporated in the co-ordinated flow of routinized work.

Reflection on the object of work: Co-ordinated and co-operative work relies on a stable work objective. Transformation to the co-constructive level of collaboration is necessary when the objective becomes unstable within the collaborating ensemble – as a result of either a *cooperation breakdown* or because of deliberate re-conceptualization of the object of work. At hospitals, for instance, cooperation breakdowns often occur due to limited resources or conflicting motives. For example, balancing the needs for patient treatment, administration, and the obligation to conduct research can cause breakdowns in the cooperation at a hospital. Such breakdowns cause a department to re-conceptualize their objects of work and try to resolve conflicting motives and viewpoints among the employees.

Implementation: Stabilizing such controversies in the co-construction of a common objective is essential, if the object is to be realized. Answering a question like "what are we doing, and why?" needs to be resolved before the cooperation can proceed. This implementation process stabilizes the common objective of the activity. For example, the degree to which the individual physician should attend to the social background of the different patients was often a matter of balancing such concerns with the limited amount of resources in terms of physicians, nurses, beds, radiology timeslots, money, etc. When a common objective is stabilized it is ready to be shared by the participants in the community. This creates the need for communicating and ensuring commitment to this common objective.

The Role of Theory in CSCW

After having presented these basic tenets of AT, we are now equipped with some analytical concepts, which can help us address the core questions raised in the beginning of the paper. We have expanded our concepts on cooperative work to include co-ordinated as well as co-constructive work, and we have provided concepts for analyzing and understanding the dynamics inherent to cooperative work, including breakdowns.

But before turning to the hospital case, it might however be appropriate to shortly discuss the role of theory within a design discipline, such as CSCW. Activity theory views theories (including itself) as special kinds of artifacts (c.f. [18]). This implies that a theory is to be judged upon its contribution to a systematic expansion of possible actions within a particular practice. The crucial question is not whether the theory provides an 'objective representation' of reality, but whether the particular practice in question can be *informed* – in the original sense of the word of 'give character or form to' – by using the general propositions of the theory. Hence, the relevant question to ask is whether the practices concerning the design of computer support for cooperative work have been, or can be, informed by the presented activity theoretical framework, and in what way. The aim of the rest of the paper is to demonstrate, that the framework has helped inform the analysis and design made within the hospital project, and hence hopefully can inform other design endeavors as well.

THE SAIK-PROJECT

Due to the centralized and specialized nature of modern medical work, one of the main problems within Danish hospitals today is to coordinate distributed patient treatment. The purpose of the SAIK[2] project was to investigate how coordination and planning of patient care happens today – both with and without computer support – and based on these investigations to reveal how coordination can be supported by computer technology. The PATIENT SCHEDULER (see figure 3) is a prototype that illustrates how work within a hospital can be coordinated by computers within and between departments. The methods for data collection involved workplace studies based on traditional qualitative methods; qualitative interviews, participative observations of daily work at the hospitals, and studies of different documents, records and other tools (c.f. [19]). The data analysis was done by transcribing interviews, by drawing different rich pictures of the flow of documents within the hospital and by writing detailed scenarios describing the current work practice. Field studies were made in 5 hospitals. Two of these hospitals were incorporated in the participatory design process of the PATIENT SCHEDULER, applying techniques such as future workshops, cooperative prototyping session, and organizational games (c.f. [10]).

The following analysis of the dynamics in work is based on investigations of, and design in cooperation with, a surgical department for urinary surgery, named U (a pseudonym). Department U consists of a surgical clinic with 6 operating rooms, an outpatient clinic, 3 wards, a uroscopy laboratory, and the secretariat containing a planning office. At U the PATIENT SCHEDULER (PS) was designed to support the planning and scheduling of operation, and to support the request and booking of examination at other departments, e.g. at radiology and at different laboratories. For each operation a *patient appointment* is made in PS, to which is allocated different *resources*, such as a surgeon, a team of nurses, an operating room, etc. For each resource a *calendar* can be shared among different users with different levels of access rights. If certain types of appointments are made frequently – for instance a certain type of operation – an *appointment template* can be made, saved, and re-used in later cases. These templates can be combined into a *program*, which is a collection of templates needed in a particular treatment. A program can for instance consist of the necessary radiology examinations, the operation itself, and subsequent intensive care treatment. When the schedule has been made it can be used in the coordination of work at the surgical clinic and different status colors can

[2] SAIK is a Danish abbreviation for "Collaborative Informatics in Clinical Practice."

be attached to each operation in order to reveal the state-of-affairs for each operation. PS also supports easy re-scheduling if changes to the plan have to be made during the day.

ANALYZING THE DYNAMICS OF COLLABORATIVE ACTIVITIES

In this section we shall analyze the highly cooperative activities surrounding the operation of a patient based on the framework presented above. We shall not focus on the activity of operating a patient as such, but concentrate on the activities, which ensure that the operations can be successfully achieved – such as planning, scheduling, synchronization, and coordination of the numerous actors involved in the operations. The section seeks to show how the presented framework can inform the analysis of cooperative activities, by conceptualizing, and thereby identifying, different aspect and dynamics of cooperative work.

We shall analyze three important examples of the dynamic transitions between the levels of a collaborative activity. The examples are labeled A, B, and C and are illustrated in figure 2.

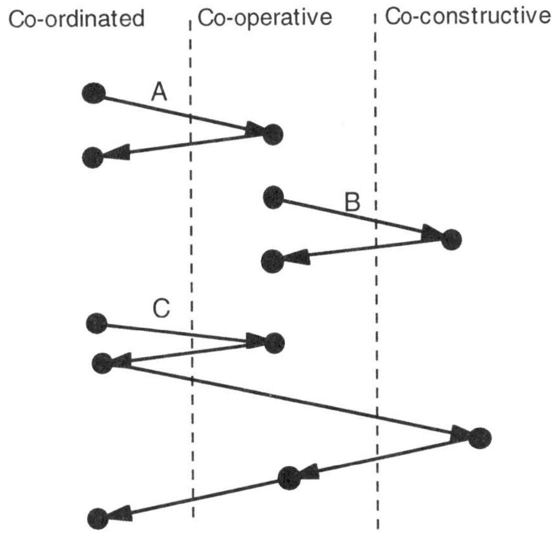

Figure 2: Examples of Dynamic Transitions

A: Transition from co-ordinated work to co-operation and back

The routine flow of operations at U is co-ordinated based on the operation schedule, which reveals which patients to operate when, where, and by who (i.e. surgeon, anesthesiologist, and scrub nurses). Based on this schedule, the head nurse is responsible for synchronizing the different operations and the actions involved in each. For instance, ensuring that the patient, the anesthesiologist, the surgeon, and the intensive care unit are "ready at the right place at the right time". This coordination is extremely important, ensuring that the operations are done in a continuous rhythm, leaving the surgical staff in the operating room to concentrate on the operation itself.

However, during the day unforeseen difficulties and constraints arises – e.g. complications during an operation, patients not being ready for operation, and illness among staff. Such co-ordination breakdowns imply that relevant staff engage in a co-operative problem solving activity trying to accommodate the problems. When a solution to the problem has been reached it is routinized back into the normal co-ordinated flow of work. This is typically done by re-scheduling the operations, creating a new schedule to be used as a coordinator, or is done by re-allocating e.g. scrub nurses to other operating rooms.

The creation of the schedule is done by the "operation planner" (a secretary), who schedules the operations based on a referral letter from the general practitioner and a "dispersal note" from the surgeon in charge of the admission of patients. The operation planner schedules a suitable time for the operation, taking into consideration all the constraints that have to be considered in the different cases; e.g. ensuring a vacant bed at one of the wards, that the appropriate radiology and laboratory examinations can be made in time for the operation, and finding a time for the operation according to the surgeon's other commitments. Hence, normal planning of operations takes place as co-ordinated work where both the means for work and the object of work is stable. The object of work is stable in the sense that the operation is prescribed via the referral letter. The means are stable in the sense that a strict division of work among departments, occupational groups, and individuals exists: there are fixed rules and norms for how to schedule certain types of operations and to put others on the waiting list, and standard artifacts exists to mediate this scheduling (the operation book, the telephone, etc.). In these routine cases the operation planner could do most of the planning herself.

Not infrequently, however, the operation planner cannot create an operation plan for a patient that meets all the constraints – often there are simply not enough resources available at U or at the radiology department within the time frames set up by the surgeon. Therefore the planner needs to engage in a co-operative effort with the surgeon in order to find another acceptable plan based on his knowledge about the operation and her knowledge of the resource constraints within the hospital. This type of cooperation has been institutionalized within U in the so-called "Wednesday meeting". Here the head surgeon in charge of scheduling operations, the head nurse of the wards, and the operation planner meets once a week to co-operatively schedule all the 'hard cases' that the operation planner has not been able to schedule on her own, and any free time-slots are filled in with patients from the waiting list.

B: Transition from co-operative work to co-construction and back

Because the surgical staff needs to concentrate on the operation, transitions to the co-constructive level of collaboration are rare in the daily flow of operations – the surgeon and the nurse do not start questioning the purpose of operations while the patient is on the table! However, transitions to co-construction did happen occasionally at the surgeons' morning conference. The morning conference at U was the primary place for co-operation among the surgeons, and between the surgeons and the radiologists, who participated in the conference. The cooperation was primarily focused on the different operations and patients, but also more general concerns for the way the work was done at U were addressed. And sometimes this was questioned loudly. For example, the distribution of available operation rooms among surgeons gives room for conflicts, because their professional career is closely connected to the operations they are performing. Also the issue of lack of resources at radiology was often raised (the radiologist being there) with the arguments that the cost of a simple radiology examination is incomparable with the extensive cost of postponing an operation. Radiology was asked to rearrange their allocations in order to comply to the demand for examinations.

The resolution to such co-construction of the object of work has subsequently to be implemented in the collaborative activity of scheduling operations. Hence, if U managed to get more radiology resources allocated, this allocation was to be incorporated in the operation planner's scheduling tools (the booking book and her knowledge of available resources at radiology). It is often also the case that such allocations are dedicated to special operations, or even surgeons, and this decision similarly needs to be implemented in the collaborative work of scheduling. Similarly, the operation planner needs to know the distribution of operating rooms among surgeons.

C: Expanding co-ordinated work through co-construction

A frequent complaint from the scrub nurses was that the operation schedule was too optimistic. Caused by the inevitable contingencies arising in such delicate work, operations often took longer than scheduled, hence leading the surgical team to work overtime. This turned out to be a bigger problem for the nurses than the surgeons, the former having a more rigid segmentation between working and leisure time (c.f. also [24]). This problem was well-known within the department, and before our investigations were initiated, several attempts had been done to cooperatively settle these problems. Especially the Wednesday meeting was a forum for this cooperative effort into making more 'valid' schedules. The problem nevertheless persisted. As a part of the participatory design process in the SAIK project, we therefore initiated a co-constructive workshop with the purpose of addressing this particular problem [4]. This workshop revealed several rather deeply rooted problems that lead to the overall problem of too optimistic schedules. For example, the fact that neither of the persons involved in the Wednesday meeting ever actually saw how their schedules were carried out, and the lack of institutionalized channels of feedback to the scheduling team and the operation planner, were identified as fundamental causes of the problem. Moreover, the problem was deeply rooted in the department's organizational culture and politics. Hence, the surgeons' conception of the job of the operation planner was that she was planning "on behalf of them" and that she therefore primarily had to comply to their concerns. Furthermore, each surgeon was allowed to schedule "his own patients", which often was done without the necessary understanding of the overall picture, again leading to too tight schedules. An often heard phrase was that a "patient needed to be squeezed into the schedule."

These problems were identified during the workshop and solutions were constructed and decided upon. For example, in the future the head nurse from the surgical clinic was invited to the Wednesday meetings too, and the operation planner was to be moved from the secretariat to the clinic, in this way being able to see how "her" plans actually played out. Moreover, a new organizational rule was established: no one was allowed to schedule operations after a 'one-week-deadline' on their own, but had to consult the operation planner, having her to do it. This rule, however, was bound to fail if it was not implemented correctly; a surgeon does not take orders from a secretary. Therefore, a considerable effort went into a cooperative implementation of these new ways of scheduling operations, involving all relevant personnel. After this co-operative effort, the new way of scheduling was to be routinized into new standard ways of scheduling, and the operation planner had to become accustomed to sitting at the highly hectic clinic rather that in the more silent secretariat.

A point to be emphasized in this example is that even though this co-constructive collaborative effort might seem removed from the scheduling itself, it becomes essential to view it as a part of the same activity, exactly because it helps us improve the scheduling activity. And helping improve collaborative activities (also by applying computer technology), is definitely a goal of CSCW.

DESIGNING FOR THE DYNAMICS OF COLLABORATIVE ACTIVITIES

The first and foremost conclusion to be drawn from the present understanding of collaborative work activities is to design for supporting the different levels of collaboration, and design for supporting the dynamic transformation of the work between the levels – once identified.

Communication is the primary way in which collaborative activities are accomplished by humans in a social setting, whether focused on coordination, cooperation, or co-construction and re-conceptualization. This explains that computer-based communication technology – such as electronic mail and conference systems – is the most successful category of CSCW application to date [11]. However, problems with communication technologies do emerge. Robinson [20] notes that the main complaint against the Coordinator has been that it seems to exclude negotiation, or – to put in our words – that it does not support a transition to the co-constructive level of collaboration.

However, the object of work is often not solely communicative; work cannot be achieved by just talking about it. Therefore, computer technology needs to support both the instrumental as well as the communicative aspects of work – both the 'doing' and the 'talking'. Hence, the second conclusion to be drawn is to integrate support for different levels of collaboration within support for the object of work as such. These two conclusions can be illustrated by some examples taken from the PATIENT SCHEDULER. Figure 3 shows a screenshot.

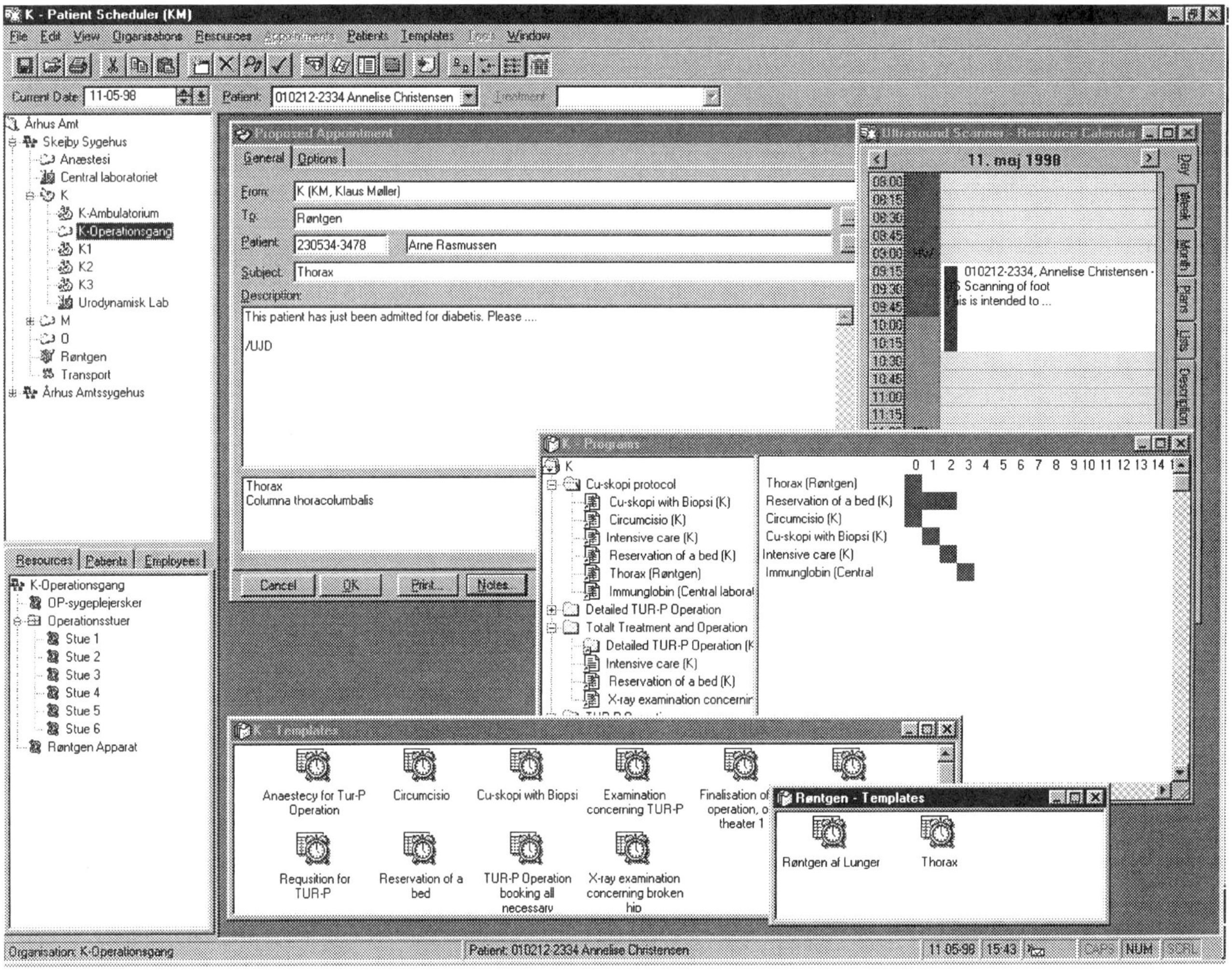

Figure 3: The PATIENT SCHEDULER. 'K' is a surgical department, and 'Røntgen' means Radiology.

Coupling communication with the object of work

Initially the PATIENT SCHEDULER only supported the creation of one operation plan, which implied that the plan could not be changed during its execution – i.e. during the operations. However, based on the analysis of the dynamic re-scheduling of operations due to diverse contingencies arising in the work (see example A), this design had to be changed. Therefore, the PATIENT SCHEDULER was re-designed to support the transition to the co-operative level of coordinating the operations by allowing ad hoc re-scheduling during execution. Furthermore, support for asynchronous communication through message notes was introduced into the design as a way to communicate to others the need or reason for changes to the plan.

Example A also described the case of the operation planner and the surgeon engaging in a co-operative effort aiming at finding a satisfactory operation plan for a patient. One of the main problems at U was that when the operation planner got stuck, and hence needed to cooperate with the surgeon, the surgeon was often operating and thus inaccessible. Asynchronous communication, as in electronic mail, would be a solution to this problem. However, after some initial experiments with using the notes as email, this suggestion was abandoned; notes detached from the concrete case, as described in the referral letter and other relevant documents, simply did not provide enough information to foster any cooperation. The notes in the PATIENT SCHEDULER were hence extended to be attachable to the different cases and operations. Of course these notes did not influence the accessibility of the surgeon, but they did provide a more flexible way of coupling communication with the case in question (i.e. the object of work).

Cooperation through sharing the object of work

The main prerequisite for engaging in cooperative problem solving is to share the objects of work, as e.g. illustrated in the hospital kitchen example. Basically, the PATIENT SCHEDULER has been designed to support sharing as much as possible. By sharing their resource schedules radiology gives the surgical department an opportunity to cooperatively plan their operations not only according to their own concerns, but also according to the distribution of examinations at radiology. Similar with other departments. Consequently, by sharing resource schedules, U and radiology has the shared basis for establishing a more optimal (in the sense optimal for both parts) plan through cooperation and communication.

In a similar way the operation schedule used in the coordination of work at the clinic can be shared. This makes for considerable ease in the daily cooperation among the many people involved in operating patients. By just monitoring the progress of operations, as evident in different status colors and changes to the schedule, the distributed staff can coordinate their work according to the operations, i.e. according to this representation of the object of work. Hence, the ward can start preparing the next patient for operation when they see the previous has been marked 'finished' on the schedule and the surgeon can see when the patient has been anesthetized and postpone his entrance to the operation room till then.

Supporting co-construction of the object of work

Analyzing the activity of scheduling and coordinating operations 'all the way up' to the co-constructive level (example B and C) also helped us initiate design actions directed towards supporting this level. This was, however, not at all trivial. It quickly turned out that supporting co-constructive activities – answering question concerning the overall objectives of operating patients in Denmark – were out of the scope of the project. However, what could be designed for was to provide input to such co-constructive activities. One of the main problems of 'invalid' operation schedules (see example C) was the lack of some accurate information on the average duration of an operation according to the involved staff, especially the surgeon. Therefore, the discussion involved in the co-constructive workshop became meaningless without just some sense of valid information on the object of work, i.e. information on how much delay each operation had compared to the schedule. Hence, an important feature in the design of PATIENT SCHEDULER was to save both the schedule and the actually completion of the operations, which later provided the data for making comparison and statistical information on average operation time, etc.

This example hence illustrates the importance of incorporating a concern for the three levels of any cooperative activity in the design of CSCW technologies, even though they might not be supported as such.

Supporting 'downward' transitions between levels of collaboration

The examples above show how the PATIENT SCHEDULER supports the 'upward' transition between the levels of collaborative activity. However, supporting the 'downward' transition – i.e. implementation and routinization – is equally important. A particularly severe difficulty at the hospital, and one of the reasons for the recurrent nature of some of the presented problems, was to implement the decisions made in these co-constructive sessions. In the co-construction of the cooperation between U and radiology (example B), there is a need for implementing the allocations decided upon, and in the example of co-constructing the scheduling activity towards more 'valid' schedules (example C), there is a need for routinizing the new scheduling practice. The PATIENT SCHEDULER supports the former through timeslot allocations on shared resource calendars, and the later through the creation and use of templates and programs for operations. Hence, when an allocation of radiology examinations to U has been decided upon, this decision can be implemented in the PATIENT SCHEDULER, and the operation planner and the surgeons can start using these allocations without the tiresome negotiation with radiology in each case. Creating a template for an particular operation for a particular surgeon helps routinize the creation of fair schedules, because the template reveals (among other things) the average time used by this particular surgeon to perform this particular operation. This can of course be changed if the surgeon and the operation planner co-operatively decide that more or less time is needed in a concrete case.

CONCLUSION

This paper has argued for the need for addressing the dynamics of cooperative work and provided a theoretical solid framework for doing so. This framework identifies three basic levels of any collaborative activity – coordinated, co-operative, and co-constructive collaborative activity – and the dynamic transitions between these levels in terms of reflections and/or breakdowns, implementation, and routinization. The paper has argued that this framework helps conceptualize, and thereby analyze and design for cooperative work and its inherent dynamic nature. This point was illustrated through an empirical case of designing computer support for coordinating surgical operations within Danish hospitals. The framework helped us understand the dynamic nature of cooperative work, and to design computer systems, which view cooperative breakdowns not as a problem but as an important aspect of all work and therefore as an important resource in the design of such technologies.

The two main conclusions concerning design of computer support for cooperative work are to (i) support collaborative work activities at all three levels, and the dynamic transition between the levels, and (ii) integrate this support for dynamic cooperation in the support for the object of work. Hence, support for co-construction of the planning and scheduling activity at department U should be integrated in the support for scheduling and planning as such.

A final conclusion to be drawn from this conceptual understanding of cooperative work and the presented study in the hospitals is that external intervention from e.g. action researchers or consultants can provide the platform for a development and co-construction of a working community. Moreover, the design of computer systems supporting some particular work-practice within an organization is essentially a co-construction of that work practice, and demands, as such, a concern for implementing and routinization to be viewed as a part of the same design effort.

ACKNOWLEDGMENTS

The work done in the SAIK-project is funded by the Danish Academy of Technical Sciences (ATV), Kommunedata, and the University Hospital for Århus County. I am grateful to all personnel at the hospitals for their participation in the project. Thanks to Susanne Bødker for helpful comments and critiques along the way, and to Olav Bertelsen for proof reading.

REFERENCES

1. Bannon, L. (1993): CSCW: An Initial Exploration. In *Scandinavian Journal of Information Systems*, vol. 5, pp. 3–24.
2. Bannon, L. and Schmidt, K. (1991): CSCW: Four Characters in Search of a Context. In J. Bowers and S. Benford (Eds.): *Studies in Computer Supported Cooperative Work*, Amsterdam, North-Holland, pp. 3–16.
3. Bardram, J. E. (1997a): I Love the System – I just don't use it! In *Proceeding of GROUP'97, ACM Conference on Supporting Group Work*, Phoenix, Arizona, USA, New York: ACM Press.
4. Bardram, J. E. (1997b): Organisational Prototyping: Adopting CSCW Applications in Organisations. In *ACM SIGGROUP Bulletin*, December, vol. 8, no. 3, pp. 41–45.
5. Bardram, J. E. (1998*): Collaboration, Coordination, and Computer Support: An Activity Theoretical Approach to the Design of Computer Supported Cooperative Work.* Ph.D. Thesis, Daimi PB-533, Århus: Århus University.
6. Bowers, J., Button, G., and Sharrock, W. (1995): Workflow from within and without: Technology and Cooperative Work on the Print Industry Shopfloor, In *Proceedings of the Fourth European Conference on CSCW, Stockholm, Sweden*. Kluwer Academic Publishers, pp. 51–66.
7. Bødker, S. and Mogensen, P. (1993) One woman's job is another man's articulation work. In *CoTech WG4: Developing CSCW Systems: Design Concepts.*
8. Engeström, Y. (1987): *Learning by Expanding: An activity-theoretical approach to developmental research*, Helsinki: Orienta–Konsultit Oy.
9. Engeström, Y., Brown, K., Christopher, L., Gregory, J. (1997): Coordination, Cooperation, and Communication in the courts. In Cole, M., Engeström, Y., and Vasquez, O. (Eds.) *Mind, Culture, and Activity*, Cambridge: Cambridge University Press.
10. Greenbaum, J. & Kyng, M. (Eds.) *Design at Work: Cooperative Design of Computer Systems*, LEA, Hillsdale NJ.
11. Grudin, J. and Poltrock, S. (1997): Computer-Supported Cooperative Work and Groupware. In *Advances in Computers*, vol. 45, pp. 269–320.
12. Heath, C. and Luff, P. (1996): "Documents and Professional Practice: 'bad' organisational reasons for 'good' clinical records", In *Proceedings of the Conference on CSCW, Boston, Massachusetts USA*. ACM, pp. 354-363.
13. Johansen, R. (1988): *Groupware. Computer Support for Business Teams*. Reading, Mass., Addision-Wesley.
14. Kling, R. (1991): Cooperation, Coordination and Control in Computer Supported Cooperative Work, *Communication of the ACM*, vol. 34, Dec. 1991, pp. 83–88.
15. Kuutti, K. (1991): The concept of activity as a basic unit of analysis for CSCW research, In *Proceedings of the Second European Conference on CSCW, Amsterdam.* Kluwer Academic Publisher, pp. 249–264.
16. Leontjev, A. (1978): *Activity, Consciousness, and Personality*, Prentice-Hall, Englewood Cliffs, NJ.
17. McGrath, J. and Arrow, H. (Eds.) (1996): Special issues on: Time, Technology, and Groups. In *Computer Supported Cooperative Work*, vol 4, no. 2–3.
18. Nardi, B. A., (ed.) (1996): *Context and Consciousness: Activity Theory and Human-Computer Interaction.* Cambrigde, MA: MIT Press.
19. Patton, Michael Quinn. (1990): *Qualitative Evaluation and Research Methods, 2nd edition.* Newbury Park: SAGE.
20. Robinson, M. (1991): Double-level Languages and Cooperative Working. In *AI & Society*, vol. 5, pp. 34–60.
21. Schmidt, K. and Simone, C. (1996): Coordination mechanisms: Towards a Conceptual Foundation of CSCW Systems Design, *Computer Supported Cooperative Work* , vol. 5, pp. 155–200.
22. Suchman, L. (1983): Office Procedures as Practical Action: Model of Work and System Design. *ACM Transaction on Office Information Systems*, vol. 1, pp. 320–328.
23. Symon, G., Long, K., and Ellis, J. (1996): The Coordination of Work Activities: Cooperation and Conflict in a Hospital Context, *Computer Supported Cooperative Work*, vol. 5, pp. 1–31.
24. Zerubavel, E. (1979): *Patterns of Hospital Life: A Sociological Perspective*. Chicago, University of Chicago Press.

Collaborative Customer Services Using Synchronous Web Browser Sharing

Makoto Kobayashi*, Masahide Shinozaki*, Takashi Sakairi*, Maroun Touma, Shahrokh Daijavad**, and Catherine Wolf****

*IBM Research, Tokyo Research Laboratory
1623-14, Shimotsuruma, Yamato
Kanagawa 242-8502, Japan
{mkobaya, sinozaki, sakairi}@jp.ibm.com

**IBM Thomas J. Watson Research Center
30 Saw Mill River Rd.
Hawthorne, NY 10532 USA
{touma, shahrokh, cwolf}@us.ibm.com

ABSTRACT

In this paper, we describe our experiences in designing two applications for synchronous web browser sharing in the context of Web-based collaborative customer service. Real-world business requirements were the key factors that dictated the design and architecture of these collaborative applications and as such, constitute the foundations for the paper.

KEYWORDS

CSCW, Synchronous Web browser sharing, Web-collaboration customer services, Collaboration architecture

INTRODUCTION

The ever-growing accessibility of the Web, both in public spaces and at home, is making it the sole user interface to the information highway. Consequently, many businesses have started to deliver their services over the Web. These services, however, are currently limited to primarily asynchronous, self-operational modes of interaction with the business Web servers.

For complicated transactions and inexperienced users, self-service may not be sufficient. In addition, for marketing and sales, there may be no substitute for a good salesperson. Thus, there is value in combining asynchronous access to products and services over the Web with synchronous, human assistance when needed. In order to provide better service to customers, increase sales, and differentiate their Web-based services from the competition, a number of businesses are starting to explore means of integrating live customer service into their Web sites.

A crucial component of this new mode of interaction is a mechanism to utilize the Web browsers as shared virtual workspaces, coupled with some form of human-human interaction between the customer and the customer service representative (to be referred to as an agent). This human-human interaction might take the form of a voice conversation, video conferencing, or text chat.

Various approaches have been tried for synchronous browser sharing, for example, GroupWeb [9], CoWeb [10], and CoReview [11], but their main focus has been on group work, rather than on the customer-agent type of interaction. There are also some commercial services which are starting to address this specific area, for example, WebLine [19], interactiveAnswers [3], and Click'nConnect [12]. However, utilizing synchronous Web browsing in a real environment is still in its infancy, and many problems need to be solved before this technology reaches its potential.

In this paper, we analyze the requirements for Web-based collaborative customer service based on our experiences in developing two banking applications. These two applications were developed in partnership with two different banks. While the two applications shared the overall goal of providing human assistance to customers on demand, they differed in a number of respects. These differences in requirements resulted in rather different architectures. In the following pages, the applications, requirements and resulting architectures will be described.

The first application had the goal of providing live support for complicated bank transactions, in particular, real-time personal loan application and crediting, in a kiosk environment. Two critical requirements for the kiosk application were:

- Asymmetric collaboration—The agent needed to be able to control operations at the customer side.
- Excellent performance—The system had to have consistently high performance under relatively narrow bandwidth conditions.

CSCW 98 Seattle Washington USA

The second application had the goal of providing assistance to home banking customers using existing self-service web pages for their personal banking. Two critical requirements of this application were:

- Security—The system had to provide support for the secure Web access protocol over the Internet.
- Dynamic web pages—The system had to handle dynamic pages, such as those that contained individual account information.

While the critical requirements for the two applications reflect the needs of our banking partners, they are representative of the requirements for kiosk banking and home banking more generally.

Common Requirements

Three major requirements were found to be common to the two applications: (1) Reuse of existing assets—This includes reuse of the existing bank Web pages in the collaboration environment with little or no modification, and the use of standard Web browsers without modification. (2) Synchronization of browser screen content during a collaborative session. (3) Tools to facilitate interaction in the shared web page, such as telepointers and annotation capabilities on top of the browser window.

In addition to these common requirements, there are significant unique requirements associated with each application. In each application section, the requirements are discussed in detail followed by sections on the architecture. We will conclude the paper by a discussion of related work and future work.

WEB-COLLABORATION BANKING KIOSK

The Web-collaboration banking kiosk aims to bring the bank's business processes, executed now at their branch offices, into the network environment so that a smaller, centralized group of bank agents and experts may effectively cover a large number of customers at kiosks.

It is designed to specifically serve two purposes: one is to support the complicated business transactions for the customers; an important one for our banking partner was real-time personal loan application and crediting. In this transaction, the customer needs to fill in and make selections on many items on the application form. The customer must also scan in personal identification, such as a driver's license, through the scanner attached to the kiosk. The agent helps the customer when necessary and checks that all the information provided by the customer is sufficient and valid to complete the loan application.

The other purpose is to provide the kiosk customers the general help for any page, such as for bank products, services, and branch location maps, as well as on how to work with loan simulation programs, at the customer's request. It should be noted that this information is used in common with what the bank provides over the Internet, though the actual page layout is slightly different to suit the kiosk screen size.

In order to save communication costs, kiosks are not always connected to the bank's network. They are connected through an ISDN 1B (64 kbps) channel up to the network only when the data communication is necessary. For this disconnect operation mode, the kiosk has its own copy of contents locally. Since the contents do not change frequently, the daily batch download for the updated pages was sufficient.

Unlike the home banking case, the connection is directly made to the call center Intranet; therefore, the security issues inherent to the open Internet environment need not be considered here.

An ISDN line, separate from the data communication channel, is used when the H.320 video conference communication is required between the customer and the agent.

Scenario of Use

The touch-panel kiosk screen is divided into two non-overlapping sections. One is the main panel where the Web page is shown. The other section is a control panel, including a ten-key pad for the numeric input, the video conference window which is normally hidden, and the "Call Agent" button.

Most of the time, the kiosk is self-operational; the customer navigates the HTML pages, and works, for example, with a loan simulation program. The customer can request help at any page shown in the main panel by clicking the button in the control panel. When this button is clicked, the kiosk connects up to the bank Intranet through ISDN, and an agent in the call center is assigned to the request. The agent's page is synchronized to the customer's, including the current form contents, such as text field and button values supplied by the customer. A video conferencing connection is established between the customer and agent at the same time.

Once the collaborative session is started, the agent can communicate with the customer using the telepointer and ink annotation directly on the page, type into fields and select buttons on a form, scroll, and navigate to other pages when necessary.

For the real-time personal loan application, the collaborative session is automatically started when the customer comes to the loan page, and the video conference session is also started. After filling in and selecting options for several pages, the customer is requested to scan in personal identification using the scanner attached to the kiosk terminal. The scanned images are converted into GIF files, and transmitted to the call center's Web server, so that both the customer and the agent can see them as Web pages. When necessary, the agent can control the scanner operations, which are simple but can sometimes be cumbersome for inexperienced users.

The agent checks the scanned images and tells the customer, if anything is wrong with a document, using the telepointer and ink annotations on the scanned image. When the agent has confirmed all the supplied information is adequate, then a loan expert in a third location is asked to make the credit decision on this customer in real-time.

Requirements

In order to realize the banking kiosk system described above, we identified the following key requirements on our synchronous Web browser sharing:

- The system should be able to reuse bank Web pages and work with standard browsers.
- The collaboration session should be able to start seamlessly on demand at the customer's request.
- The agent should be able to control or take over the customer's operations for complicated business transactions.
- The system should perform well under the narrow network bandwidth.

Each of these requirements is described in detail below.

Standard HTML Pages and Existing Web Browsers

The bank had already invested in large number of HTML pages with lots of Java applets and JavaScript for its Internet services, such as the loan simulation pages and attractive pages with animated presentation features. It was mandatory that these assets be reused in the kiosk system with no or minimal modifications.

It was also necessary that existing Web browsers could be used. Though a customized browser could be developed in the kiosk environment, unlike the home banking case, a popular Web browser is obviously a better choice. Since the browser capabilities are evolving very fast, a special browser tailored for synchronous page sharing could easily become obsolete, and the bank's HTML pages utilizing the latest browser features could not be reused without modifications.

Seamless Browser Sharing on Demand

The synchronization should start *on-demand* and be *seamless*. The current browser window that the customer is working in the self-operation mode needs to be used continuously in the collaborative session. Especially, the form values the customer has input before the session started, should not go away and need to be re-entered.

For this, the URL, form values, and the window scroll position are obtained from the kiosk and replicated on the agent PC when the session is started, establishing the so-called What You See Is What I See (WYSIWIS) mode. From there, both the customer and the agent can continue to work using synchronized navigation and collaborative form input, as well as using the telepointer and ink annotation for specifying the position in the page.

While WYSIWIS is the main mode of synchronization, it is also necessary that this mode can be relaxed at times, as discussed in [16]. In the banking kiosk, for example, the agent needs to temporarily switch off the URL synchronization on the shared browser, do a private search, and then synchronize on the page found. Since the agent PC screen is occupied by various information, opening another browser window for a private search was not preferred.

Asymmetric Collaboration

In the customer-agent relationship, the collaborative interaction on the shared page needs to be *asymmetric* [2]; the agent should be able to take the lead in support of the customer or prevent inexperienced customers from making erroneous operations. For example, only the agent is allowed to click the link to go to other pages, while both can type in the form fields on the shared page and scroll the window.

Another type of asymmetry required is for device control. The kiosk terminal is equipped with a printer and a scanner, while the agent PC is not. In the collaborative session, the agent's operations on the shared pages that control these devices should be effective only at the kiosk side.

Low Bandwidth Performance

The kiosk terminals are connected to the bank Intranet with ISDN, but only with the bandwidth of 64 kbps. The bandwidth is even more limited for general Internet access, like home banking applications described later. For the kiosk, excellent performance was required with the 64 kbps bandwidth. If the collaborative interaction is not very responsive, customers may become frustrated and walk away.

Architecture

The architecture for the web collaboration banking kiosk was driven by the need for the agent to control the collaboration and also by the need for fast performance. We, therefore, adopted a replicated architecture, where each of the kiosk terminals and the agent PCs has its own Web browser process and status synchronization mechanism. The solution we developed to meet these requirements as well as the others listed above is described here.

External Browser Control

Existing Web browser synchronization is achieved by providing an independent module for accessing and controlling the browser from outside. As shown in Figure 1, the external control process, called *WebShare*, is running at each node, watching the behavior of its corresponding browser through two interfaces: the browser client API and the message queue of the browser provided by the window system. When a change is detected through either of these interfaces, *WebShare* transmits the information to the other side, where the change is reflected to the browser through the corresponding interface.

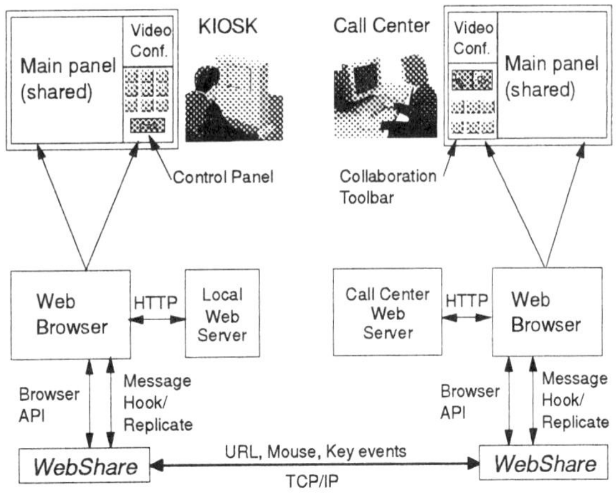

Figure 1. Web-Collaboration Kiosk Architecture

For example, when the browser window is scrolled at one side, the window scroll event is generated and is put into the message queue by the window system. Then the event is detected by *WebShare* through the hooking of the message queue. The scroll command with the position parameters is now transmitted to the other side, and then put into the message queue by *WebShare* on that side. Finally, the browser window is scrolled by executing the scroll event in its message queue, as if the operation is done locally.

WebShare is built on top of our multiparty real-time collaborative platform, called *CollaborationFramework* [15]. In the current banking kiosk application, it is used in the peer-to-peer mode, but the application can be extended, such as to the customer-agent-supervisor three-way collaboration.

Browser Synchronization on Demand

WYSIWIS features with seamless, on-demand synchronization, as illustrated in Figure 2, are achieved in the following approaches:

- URL synchronization

URL synchronization utilizes three functions in the browser client API: URL load request, URL query request, and event notification on URL change. The URL change is caused either by a user operation or a program within the page. When it occurs, a URL change event is notified, associated with the URL name string and the window or the frame ID into which the URL is being loaded. *WebShare* gets this event and transmits the string to the other side, where the browser is forced to load the same URL into the corresponding window or the frame, using the URL load function. This method is often referred to as URL sharing.

On-demand URL synchronization is achieved by first querying the URL at the kiosk, and then loading it at the agent, when the collaborative session is initiated.

Since the kiosk has its own local Web server, the customer sees the HTML page loaded locally, while the agent sees the same page from the Web server in the call center Intranet.

- Form synchronization

Each form element is internally represented as its corresponding window system's control object, like a text field and a button object. Operations on an element are detected by hooking the events in the message queue. Every window control object provides a way for querying and setting the current status, so the status is queried by *WebShare*, transmitted to the other site, and then set to the corresponding object there.

There can be multiple instances of the same object type in a form. For example, a form may contain multiple text fields, and they need to be distinguished from each other, so that the matching text fields can be synchronized in the customer's and agent's browsers. This matching is executed by analyzing the window tree consisting of the control objects when the HTML loading is completed.

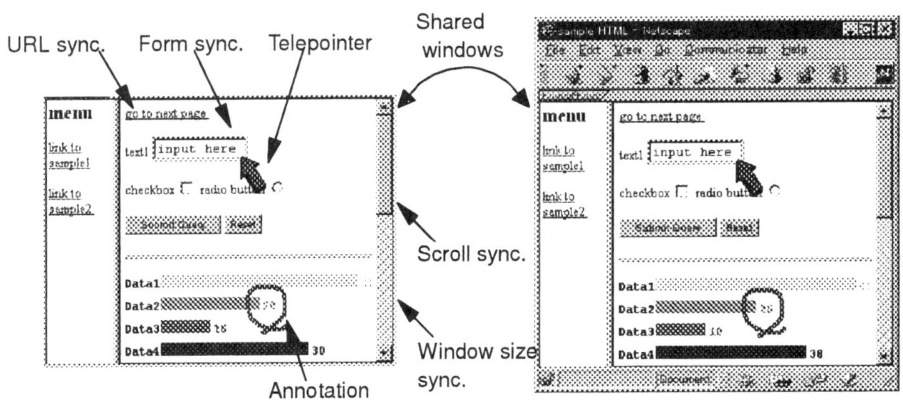

Figure 2. Features of Browser Synchronization

- Window size and scroll synchronization

In order to make the telepointing and the ink annotations meaningful, the scrolling and sizing of browser windows need be synchronized, since the text area in the HTML page is by default formatted on the browser window width.

Synchronization on these properties is again achieved by hooking and setting the events of the corresponding window handle of the window or frame structure in the window system's message queue.

- Integrated collaboration tools

The telepointing and the ink annotation over the browser window is achieved by detecting the mouse cursor movements in the window message queue. When detected, they are drawn directly in the window system's graphic context, while the operation is sent to the other site to be reflected. Each user can operate his or her own telepointer and annotation simultaneously.

Java API for Collaboration Control

We provided an API on *WebShare* for achieving relaxed WYSIWIS and asymmetric collaboration features over the shared browsers. Specifically, the API includes:

- Session control functions, including initiating and terminating the collaborative session,
- Synchronization control functions, including start and stop of synchronization on URL, form contents, scroll position, and size, of the specified browser window,

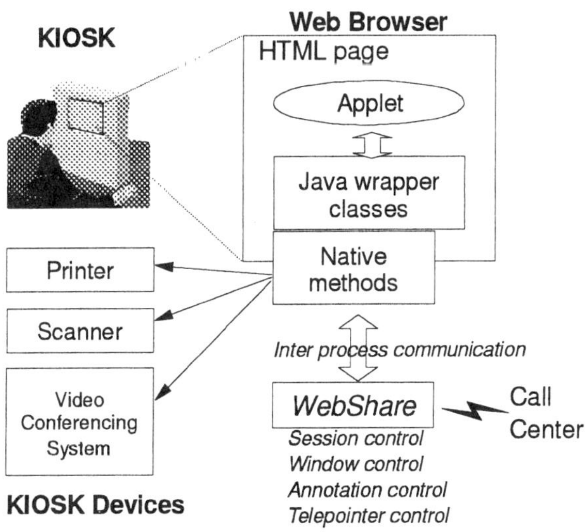

Figure 3. Collaboration control through Java API

- Input control functions, including enabling and disabling the input on URL links, form elements, scrolling, and sizing of the specified browser window, and input mode switching between normal, annotation, and telepointing modes.

In order to make the API accessible from HTML pages, we provided "Java wrappers" which run on the Java virtual machine in the browser process and communicate with *WebShare* through the inter-process communication mechanism. The relationship among HTML pages with Java applets (can be JavaScript as well), Java wrappers, and *WebShare*, is illustrated in Figure 3.

HTML pages written to this API are called *collaboration-aware* pages, and three kinds are used in the system: collaborative applications, the kiosk control panel, and the collaboration toolbar.

- Real-time personal loan application and crediting is a collaborative application, explicitly asking an agent to get involved into the transaction. The JavaScript codes embedded in HTML pages displayed in the main panel drive the collaboration mode and flow as the transaction proceeds.
- The kiosk control panel is a browser window and displaying its own collaboration-aware page. It contains a "Call Agent" button which triggers the JavaScript for initiating the collaborative session, specifying the main panel as the target window. Therefore, the collaboration can start on any *collaboration-unaware* page the customer is currently looking at in the main panel.
- In both above, the collaboration capability is set to the mode defined by the logic. The collaboration toolbar on the agent screen, yet another browser window showing an aware HTML containing a set of icons, is used for manually overriding these default settings of the main panel.

WEB-COLLABORATION HOME BANKING

The second application for which synchronous collaboration features were designed is web-based online banking. Online banking is currently offered by almost every major banking institution in the United States. It allows banking customers to access their accounts using a web browser. The customers usually dial into their favorite Internet Service Provider (ISP) access point using dial-up modem connections. After signing on to the bank's Web site, they may conduct various banking transactions such as verifying account balances, transferring money between accounts, or paying bills electronically.

The Web collaboration home banking system was designed to meet several objectives:

- To help inexperienced Web users feel more comfortable with Web-based online banking by providing a convenient way to get immediate assistance

- To provide a means for customers and agents to work together using both the shared Web workspace and voice to resolve problems
- To provide a channel for the agent to market products and services to customers by "pushing" pages to the customer during a collaboration session

Scenario of Use

In a typical scenario, a customer, John Lee, accesses the Internet from home using a low bandwidth connection of 56 Kbps or less. He browses the bank's promotional pages or accesses personalized account pages using a secure protocol. While doing so, John comes across a document inviting him to click on a "call us" button to talk to an agent at the call center regarding any question he might have. He clicks on the button which starts a process at the Web server to identify a customer service representative to take the call. During this time, a new browser window appears on the John's screen asking him to wait until a customer service representative is found to take the call. The search process interfaces with the Automatic Call Distribution (ACD) system at the call center to identify an available agent. In most cases, the agents assigned to take Internet calls will have T1 connections or better giving them a total bandwidth of 1.5 Mbps or higher to access the bank's Web site. Once an agent is identified, the customer browser window is restored and the agent's Web browser displays the same document that John was looking at when he clicked. The document content could be a form, a table, or any HTML 3.2 compliant document. Once connected, the agent and/or the customer can point to, highlight or annotate sections of the document while talking and interacting with each other. In addition, either can go to a different URL and the other one will follow.

Requirements

From the previous scenario, we can clearly identify the following business requirements:

• As a tool for collaboration over the Web, the system functions for customer-agent interaction should be built around the Web browser (refer to the kiosk section on this point).

• As a business tool, the system should allow collaboration over existing Web applications and allow seamless transition between self-service and collaboration modes.

• The system should provide support for dynamic and personalized pages as well as static pages.

• The system should provide support for secure protocols, predominantly used in home banking transactions conducted over the open Internet.

• Because of network delays and the asymmetrical configurations of the connections between the customer and the agent, the system should provide means for all participants to be aware of the state of the system and each others actions.

Support for Existing Applications

As in the case of the banking kiosk, it is highly desirable to allow collaboration over existing HTML pages. In addition to the benefits of supporting existing applications described in the kiosk section, there are other reasons to support such collaboration for home banking. Our goal was to add collaboration as an incremental enhancement to an existing Web site.

For home banking it is necessary for the customer and agent to collaborate on pages external to the bank Web site. For example, our banking partner had a link on their Web site to an investment service. It would not be feasible to ask the owners of every linked page to modify their Web pages to allow collaboration. However, the value of collaboration would be diminished if customers and agents were not able to collaborate on these pages. Therefore, there was a requirement to enable collaboration initiated from the bank's Web pages to continue onto other sites.

Home banking customers may become familiar with the banking pages they use. Another benefit of supporting collaboration on existing applications is that it allows the customer to make a smooth transition from working with familiar pages in a self-service mode to working with these pages in an interactive collaborative mode.

Support for Dynamic Pages

To provide a complete solution, unaware HTML document sharing should apply to dymanic as well as static Web pages.

Static documents are widely used for marketing and product information. They may contain animated objects and simple HTML forms, but, for the most part, they are text based and present the same generic information regardless of the user's identity or the configuration of the client who requests the information. The information is usually self contained and stored on the Web server file system and is accessible using simple HTTP requests. It is possible for all participants in a collaboration session to have knowledge of the request and be able to simultaneously issue the request to view and interact with the same document. This URL sharing approach, which was adequate for the banking kiosk, is not applicable to the dynamic document sharing required in the home banking case.

Dynamic documents are generated by a process that executes on the Web server. These could be cgi-bin, server side Java or JavaScript applications. The corresponding HTTP request specifies one or more parameters that are: specific to the user such as a user login id; specific to the session such as a session key assigned by the server following a successful identification of the user; or specific to the request such as the amount of money to transfer in a financial transaction. The request parameters are usually included as part of the HTTP request URL or as part of the HTTP request body.

The request parameters could include data that are private to the user and cannot be shared with other users in a collaboration session without compromising the system security. Such is the case, if the data include a user id and password that give the user access to his or her bank account information.

The request parameters could also include personal preferences information that is stored on the user's workstation in the form of a cookie, and difficult to share among participants in a collaboration session without knowing where and how the browser stores the information.

Dynamic documents could also be the result of a request that uses a POST method. In general, POST methods are used to modify the state of the supporting database. The submit button for example, on a fund transfer form would initiate a process that modifies the account balance before generating the HTML response that displays the result of the operation. If the customer needs to share the resulting document with a customer service representative, it should be possible to do so without having the agent's browser issue a duplicate of the same request since it would corrupt the database and generate a different result.

In order to view the same resulting document, all the participants in a collaborative session should be able to share the *content* of the HTTP response without prior knowledge of the corresponding HTTP request. This is also referred to as content sharing. It requires the presence of a server process or a proxy that can store the HTTP response and forward it to all participants in the collaboration session.

Support for Secure Protocols

Online banking applications use the HTTPS protocol exclusively to protect the privacy and security of the data being exchanged between the customer and the server. Using this protocol, the content of the customer's request as well as the resulting response document are encrypted using a dynamically generated session key that is only known to the Web server and the Web browser within the context of the transaction itself.

During a collaboration session, the customer might want to share with the agent a document that is natively encrypted using the HTTPS protocol. Sharing the document should not expose the system to security attacks by a third party.

Collaboration and Awareness Tools

Since the customer accesses the Internet using a Web browser, our goal was to enhance the standard browser functions to include collaboration.

During collaboration, the agent and the customer should be aware of the state of the system as well as of each other's actions and the result of these actions on the remote participant's screen. This is required in order to coordinate their conversation with what they are both seeing.

When a new document is requested, the agent needs to know when the customer's browser has finished downloading and displaying the document. Since the customer and agent access the Internet at substantially different connection speeds, they will most certainly receive the document at different points in time.

In order to coordinate text entry, when either the customer or agent selects an edit box in an HTML form, the other should be aware of this action.

If the agent is using a pen-like function to highlight sections of the document, the agent should be able to determine when the ink appeared on the customer's window.

Architecture

The solution implemented for Web-based collaborative home banking was driven by the need to support the HTTPS protocol and the need to support dynamic pages. These requirements caused us to adopt an architecture consisting of a collaboration server and a client plug-in. This client-server architecture is clearly different from the peer-to-peer architecture of WebShare in the kiosk application; however, many of the components illustrated in Figure 2 have the same manifestation on customer and agent screens in the kiosk and home banking applications. This discussion will focus on the significant differences between the two approaches.

In the home banking application architecture, the collaboration server acts as an Internet proxy for the application Web server, as illustrated in Figure 4. It receives a request from the client and routes it to the application Web server. For each user, it creates a local cache of the URLs visited. When the customer clicks to talk to an agent, the collaboration server routes the request to the ACD to select an agent to take the call. The ACD then returns a session Id that is used by both the customer and the agent to register with the collaboration server to establish a data collaboration session. When the agent registers to participate in a session with a customer, the agent's Web browser is 'served' a copy of the document the customer is looking at.

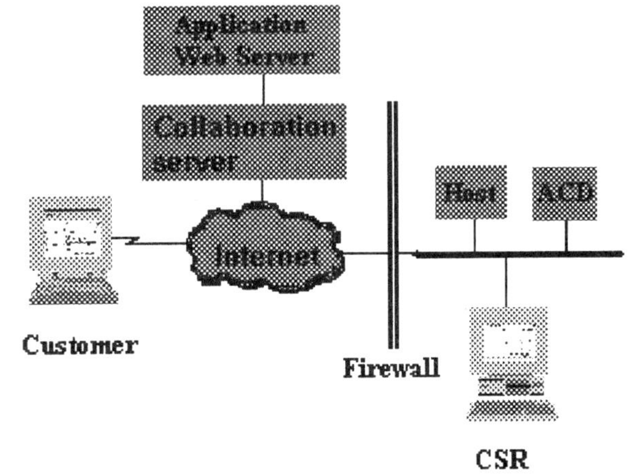

Figure 4. Home Banking Application Architecture

This is accomplished by having the plug-in on the agent PC issue a reload of the browser window. Upon receiving the request to reload, the collaboration server redirects the request to a copy of the URL cache it maintains for the customer.

During a collaborative session, when a customer issues a request to access a specific URL, the collaboration server retrieves the URL document from the application Web server, sends the response to the customer's browser and serves a copy of the document to the agent's Web browser as well. Similarly, if the agent initiates the request, the result is served to the customer as well. This design handles dynamic pages and by allowing the customer and the agent to share the results of a specific URL request without sharing the request itself.

A secure HTTPS request is processed in the same way as a non-secure HTTP request, except for the additional secure socket connection between the collaboration server and the application Web server. Upon receiving an HTTPS request from the customer, the collaboration server creates a matching HTTPS request and sends it to the application Web server. When the response is received, it is sent to the customer using the secure socket connection already established for the original request. The agent is also served a copy of the document using yet another HTTPS session. In total, three cascading HTTPS sessions are required.

In addition to the browser window synchronization, the collaboration server acts as a communication server allowing local events, such as remote pointer location, mouse clicks or pen annotation to flow between the customer and the agent residing on opposite sides of the corporate firewall.

The client plug-in implements most of the features described in the kiosk section for monitoring and replication of mouse and keyboard events on the user's PC.

In addition, it implements a set of features for increased user awareness of the system state and the session participants' actions and intended actions. Figure 5 is a screen dump of a Netscape window showing the system status indicators, the edit box corners and the changing color ink

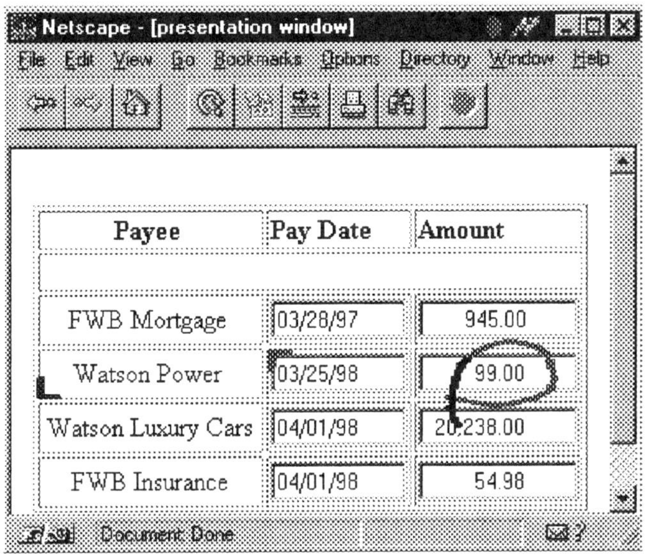

Figure 5. An Illustration of Awareness Tools in the Home Banking Application

The status indicators includes an icon indicating whether or not the current window is being shared with the remote participant, and an LED in the window title bar that can have one of 2 colors, green or red, indicating whether the document has finished loading on the remote participant's screen. The edit box corners are color-coded to represent the customer and agent (the remote telepointer and ink are also color-coded). They appear when a participant selects an edit box, and indicate to the remote participant that the first participant intends to modify the content of the selected field. The ink is first drawn using a neutral color, such as black or white, then turns to the customer's color (blue) or agent's color (red) when the corresponding segment coordinates are received and drawn on the remote screen.

RELATED WORK

Various approaches have been tried for synchronous Web browser sharing.

CoReview [11] takes the centralized approach, where only a single browser process is running and shared by participating sites, combining Mosaic with XTV [1]. Using NetMeeting [13]'s general application sharing for browser synchronization could be regarded as a centralized approach as well. It can simply share the existing Web browsers and HTML pages. A problem with this approach is that it requires larger bandwidth than the replicated approach we took, as analyzed in [8, 4], so it may not run sufficiently fast in the low bandwidth typical in the Internet. Another problem is that it is bound to the strict WYSIWIS mode, which is not appropriate to the customer-agent collaboration model.

GroupWeb [9] and GroupScape [6] chose to build their own browsers on top of their collaborative platforms (GroupKit [14] and Clock [7]). A benefit with this approach is that a sophisticated collaboration can be achieved, such as telepointing even in the relaxed WYSIWIS mode. However, a *collaboration-aware* browser is not preferable in the general case, since the customers have already installed their browsers of choice, and it is also difficult for a customized browser to keep up with the fast pace of browser improvements.

CoWeb [10] replaces the HTML form elements with shared Java applets at the CoWeb server, so that the existing HTML pages can be synchronized. However, in general cases, we found it difficult to parse the HTML for replacement with equivalent Java applets when the JavaScript changes dynamic behavior of these elements, such as setting the event handler after the page is loaded.

There is another approach in Internet-based synchronous collaboration, which is based on the shared Java framework such as DECAF [17], Promondia [5], and MetaWeb [18]. This approach enables more sophisticated object sharing, such as asymmetric views on distributed model objects, but it requires more development effort compared to reusing standard HTML pages.

STATUS OF APPLICATIONS

The two banking applications described in this paper have been implemented and are either operational (kiosk) or about to go to pilot testing (home banking).

The Web-collaboration banking kiosk was implemented with Windows NT as the operating system and Netscape Navigator as the Web browser, both at the kiosk and the call center workstations.

About 90% of the total 2,800 HTML pages stored in the kiosk are collaboration-unaware pages, and these pages can be shared between the customer and the call center agent on-demand, including the partially filled form contents. The rest are collaboration-aware pages, including the real-time personal loan application and new bank account opening transactions, where JavaScript accesses and controls the session and input capabilities of WebShare. The system has been in operation since April 1997, starting at two locations and lately extended to seven.

The home banking application targets Windows95 customer machines with Netscape Navigator as the browser and is about to go into a pilot test with selected bank customers. The changes required to pre-existing target applications on the bank Web server in order to add collaboration were minimal. In fact, the only changes were trivial adding of icons to start the collaboration session. Integration with the computer-telephony integration (CTI) software currently used in the call center operation of the bank has been achieved in order to timeshare agents who will receive both normal 800 number service calls initiated using a phone and calls initiated from the Web.

CONCLUSION AND FUTURE WORK

In this paper, we described the requirements and architecture of two banking applications for synchronous browser sharing between customers and agents. The emphasis of the paper was on the business requirements for each application, and how these requirements were translated into the corresponding architectures for the two applications. Most of the innovations and features which differentiate our work from existing related work are due to the fact we faced real business requirements.

The future of this work is in two parallel directions. In one direction, a common architecture is sought to address the largest possible set of real-world applications in web-based customer service. In the second direction, the applications will move forward to make integration with both existing Web server and call center operations more seamless.

ACKNOWLEDGMENTS

Many people, both within IBM and outside IBM, have contributed to realizing these projects. The authors are especially grateful to Research members, Tetsu Fujisaki, Tong-Haing Fin, and Shuang Chen, who have directly contributed to the architecture of synchronous Web browser sharing, and to Alison Lee for comments on earlier drafts of this paper. Discussions with other Research team members were also invaluable.

REFERENCES

1. Abdel-Wahab, H., and Feit, M. A., XTV: A Framework for Sharing X Window Clients in Remote Synchronous Collaboration, in Proceedings of the IEEE Tri-Comm'91 Communications for Distributed Applications & Systems (April 1991), 159-167.
2. Ando, F., Nakajima, A., and Furui, Y., An Information Kiosk with Asymmetric Collaboration, in Proceedings of the Seventh International Conference on Human-Computer Interaction (August 1997) 1, 591-594.
3. AT & T, interactiveAnswers Express Service. Available at http://www.iaexpress.com

4. Crowley, T., Milazzo, P., Baker, E., Forsdick, H., and Tomlinson, R. MMConf: An Infrastructure for Building Shared Multimedia Applications, in Proceedings of the ACM Conference on Computer Supported Cooperative Work (October 1990), 329–342.

5. Gall, U., Promondia: A Java-Based Framework for Real-Time Group Communication, in the Web, in Proceedings of the Sixth International World Wide Web Conference (April 1997).

6. Graham, T. C. N., GroupScape: Integrating Synchronous Groupware and the World Wide Web, in Proceedings of INTERACT'97 (July 1997), 547-554.

7. Graham, T. C. N., Urnes, T., and Nejabi, R., Efficient Distributed Implementation of Semi-Replicated Synchronous Groupware, in Proceedings of the Ninth Symposium on User Interface Software and Technology (November 1996), 1–10.

8. Greenberg, S., and Roseman, M., Groupware Toolkits for Synchronous Work, Research Report 96/589/09, Department of Computer Science, University of Calgary (1996).

9. Greenberg, S., and Roseman, M., GroupWeb: A WWW Browser as Real Time Groupware, in ACM SIGCHI'96 Conference on Human Factors in Computing System, Companion Proceedings (April 1996), 271-272.

10. Jacobs, S., Gebhardt, M., Kethers, S., and Rzasa, W., Filling HTML Forms Simultaneously: CoWeb - Architecture and Functionality, in Proceedings of the Fifth International World Wide Web Conference (May, 1996), 1385-1395.

11. Maly, K. J., Abdel-Wahab, H., Mukkamala, R., Gupta, A., Prabhu, A., Syed, H., and Venuru, C. S., Mosaic + XTV = CoReview, in Proceedings of the Fourth International World Wide Web Conference (December 1995).

12. MCI Communications Corporation, Click'nConnect. Available at http://www.mci.com

13. Microsoft Corporation, NetMeeting. Available at http://www.microsoft.com

14. Roseman, M., and Greenberg, S., Building Real-Time Groupware with GroupKit, A Groupware Toolkit, ACM Transactions on Computer-Human Interaction, 3, 1 (1996), 66 - 106.

15. Sakairi, T., Shinozaki, M., and Kobayashi, M., CollaborationFramework: A Toolkit for Sharing Existing Single-User Applications without Modification, in Proceedings of the Third Asia-Pacific Computer and Human Interaction (July 1998).

16. Stefik, M., Bobrow, D. G., Foster, G., Lanning, S., and Tatar, D. WYSIWYS Revised: Early Experiences with Multiuser Interfaces, ACM Transactions on Office Information Systems, 5, 2 (1987), 147–167.

17. Strom, R., Banavar, G., Miller, K., Prakash, A., and Ward, M., Concurrency Control and View Notification Algorithms for Collaborative Replicated Objects, in Proceedings of the Seventeenth International Conference on Distributed Computing Systems (May 1997), 194-203.

18. Trevor, J., Koch, T., and Woetzel, G., MetaWeb: Bringing synchronous groupware the World Wide Web, in Proceedings of the European Conference on Computer Supported Cooperative Work (September 1997).

19. WebLine Communications Corporation, WebLine. Available at http://www.webline.com

Talking to Customers on the Web: A Comparison of Three Voice Alternatives

Qiping Zhang*, Catherine G. Wolf, Shahrokh Daijavad**, Maroun Touma****

*University of Michigan/CREW
701 Tappan Street
Ann Arbor, MI 48109-1234 USA
qiping@umich.edu

**IBM Thomas J. Watson Research Center
30 Saw Mill River Rd.
Hawthorne, NY 10532 USA
{cwolf,shahrokh,touma}@us.ibm.com

ABSTRACT

This paper describes an empirical study that compared three alternatives for voice communication in conjunction with Web page collaboration for customer service. Two of the technologies used a single phone line for both voice and data transmission. These technologies were internet telephony and Simultaneous Voice and Data (SVD), a protocol which allows the voice to be routed over the public telephone network, rather than the internet. The study found that SVD was superior to internet telephony in terms of a number of behavioral and subjective measures of conversational interaction. The study also found that task time using internet telephony was 45% greater than with SVD, making the former a costly alternative in terms of human time.

Keywords

Voice communication, internet telephony, Web, customer service, usability, collaboration

INTRODUCTION

Businesses worldwide are increasingly making use of the Web as a channel for product sales and service. The products may be quite expensive (as in new automobiles) and the services may be quite complex (as in retirement planning). While many transactions are carried out without direct human-human interaction, in other instances human assistance is required. In addition, businesses are beginning to realize the importance of human-human contact in establishing and maintaining the customer relationship [4], and are seeking ways to do this over the Web.

Several years ago, we began a project to enable collaborative customer service over the Web [14]. Our goal is to allow customers and service/sales representatives to collaborate synchronously on web pages using both voice and data sharing (including screen-sharing, joint navigation, forms fill-out, remote pointers and pen annotation).

The importance of voice communication for a variety of collaborative tasks was documented in a landmark study by Chapanis [3] which found that modes of communication that included voice were much faster than those that did not. In the CSCW community, there have been a number of compelling demonstrations of the power of voice communication plus collaboration in a shared workspace for a number of tasks e.g. [1, 9]. The benefits of adding a shared workspace to voice were systematically explored in an experiment comparing voice communication only to voice plus a shared workspace [12]. This study found benefits for voice plus the shared workspace compared to voice only for a demanding text editing task and a graphical task.

More recently, a number of researchers have designed applications and architectures to support a variety of forms of collaboration on web pages e.g. [5, 6, 11]. These research efforts did not address the issue of voice communication, most likely assuming that the participants would talk to each other using an independent telephone call.

We cannot, however, assume that consumers at home will have a second phone line to use for voice, in addition to the one used for their internet connection. Consequently, the issue of how to provide voice communication over the same phone line as the internet connection is important for collaborative customer service over the Web. This paper describes an empirical study that compared the usability of three approaches to voice communication in conjunction with web page collaboration: two of the technologies used a single phone line for voice and data; the other required a second phone line and can be considered a baseline condition.

We will discuss these three approaches with a focus on the potential benefits and liabilities of each approach, and then discuss our empirical evaluation.

One approach to voice communication for collaborative customer service over the web is to use internet telephony. With this approach, both voice and data are routed through the internet. This approach has the benefit of not requiring the consumer to have a second telephone line, since voice and data packets are transmitted over a single phone line. It also avoids the necessity for the business to pay for a phone call to the consumer, required in the second line solution. However, the voice (as well as data) is subject to delay as it is transmitted over the internet. The delay may be as long as several seconds, depending on the number of nodes in the path and the amount of data being transmitted at the same time as the voice. As research to be discussed has shown, delay can have detrimental effects on communication. In addition to the delay problem, internet telephony voice may sound choppy. The reason for choppy voice is that voice packets may be lost just like other data packets during transmission. Lost data packets are usually compensated for by retransmission of data and buffering at either end, however, this adds to the voice delay. Smaller size buffers designed not to add excessive delay to voice may run out of voice packets causing gaps. Microsoft's NetMeeting and Netscape's Conference both use internet telephony for voice [16, 17].

A second alternative, Simultaneous Voice and Data (SVD) developed at IBM, transmits voice and data over a single telephone line to an access point where the voice is separated from the data. The voice is transmitted separately over the public telephone network and the data is routed over the internet. This approach has the benefit of requiring only a single phone line. In addition, the voice has low latency since it is not transmitted over the internet. Because of the need to conserve bandwidth, SVD voice quality may not be equivalent to a second phone line. Of perhaps greater importance from a business perspective, this new approach requires special software at the access point to separate the voice and data. Thus, customers must use only those internet service providers who have this new capability.

The third alternative, the second line approach, is to call the customer back on a second phone line (the baseline condition in our study). According to this approach, when the customer clicks on an icon to establish a collaborative session with a customer service representative, the phone number for the second line (not in use for the internet connection) is sent to the business's call center via the web server. This approach has the benefit of providing high quality telephone voice with no latency. No special hardware or software is needed by the consumer. However, it requires the customer to have a second phone line available for the call back. It also requires the business to pay for a phone line for the outgoing call. An example of this approach is the product Webline by Webline Communications [18].

From a usability perspective, the factors that may affect the acceptability of these three voice alternatives for customer service are delay and voice quality. Most of the previous work on the effects of delay on communication has been done in the context of audio-video conferencing or audio-only communication. Several early studies of audio-only communication found that delays in the range of 600-1200 msec produced small, but measurable effects on communication, such as more simultaneous speech, interruptions and awkward pauses [2, 7, 8]. A study of video conferencing found that with a half-duplex audio system (i.e. only one side at a time can talk and be heard) and delays of 840 msec, users perceived there to be more simultaneous speech, more interruptions and had a more difficult time hearing people at the other location than with delays of 330 or 0 msec [13]. However, there were no effects on measures of objective task performance. Not much seems to be known about the subjective or behavioral effects of voice delays of several seconds. At some point on the latency continuum, one might expect the interaction to cease to be conversational.

It is not obvious how the presence of the shared web page and the opportunities for interaction in this shared space might modulate the voice quality and delay effects (or conversely, how the benefits of the shared space might be affected by voice quality and delay). Compared to audio-only communication, the shared web page might provide an additional channel to ground the conversation, thus mitigating the effects of voice delay and poor voice quality. On the other hand, if the voice is significantly delayed relative to the web page and interactions on the page (i.e. pointer movement, typing), users might become confused. Similarly, if voice arrives before data, as is possible in the second line alternative, there may also be confusion. This was found to be the case in a retrospective analysis of Cognoter, which suggested that delays in seeing a shared document relative to hearing spoken comments impeded communication [10].

The current study addressed several questions:

- Are there differences in users' perceptions of the voice communication using the three alternatives? How acceptable is each alternative?
- Are there differences in users' behaviors with the three alternatives? Specifically, are there differences in the number of instances of simultaneous speech, the need for clarification or repetition, and the duration of the interaction?

- Do the three voice alternatives affect users' perceptions of the value of data collaboration or their general assessment of the system?

Because we anticipated that the amount of data transmitted concurrently with voice might affect the answers to these questions, one task used in the study required a relatively low amount of concurrent data transmission, while the other involved a relatively high amount of concurrent data transmission.

From a practical perspective, the study reported here contributes new knowledge about the acceptability of two single-line alternatives for collaborative customer service over the Web. This information can be weighed along with business considerations described earlier in deciding when each alternative is appropriate. From a research perspective, this study provides insights concerning the effects of voice delay and quality on users' interaction patterns and perceptions for problem-solving in a shared workspace.

METHOD

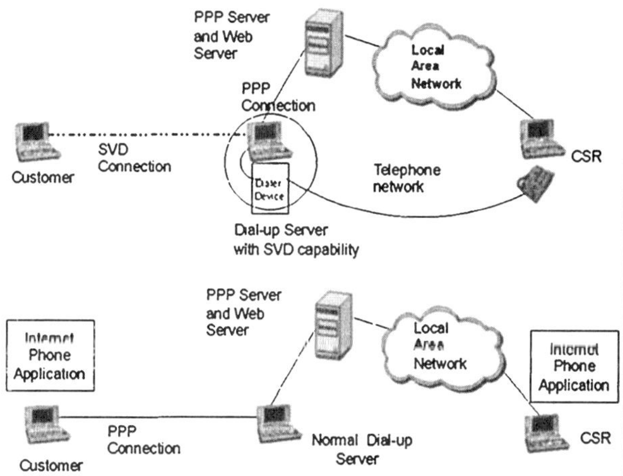

Figure 1a. SVD configuration, 1b. IP Configuration

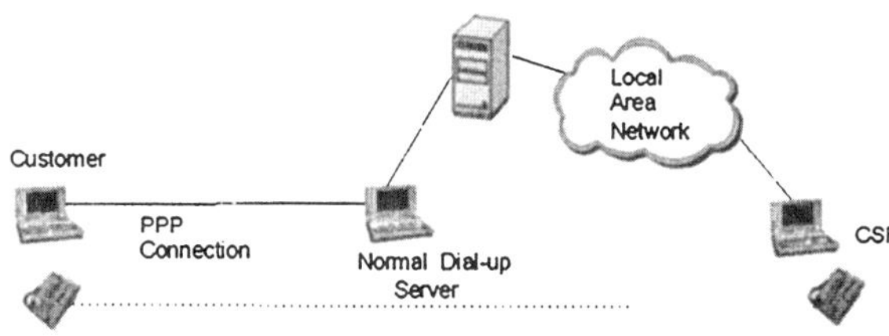

Figure 1c. Second Line Configuration

Apparatus and Setting

Two IBM Thinkpads (760) in two separate rooms were used for the experiment: one for the customer service representative (an experimenter), the other for the customer (a participant). On the customer side, a video camera recorded the shared screen and the customer's and service representative's voices.

The additional components of the system included a web server, a PPP server and a computer playing the role of a dial-up server, which separated voice from data for the SVD condition and simply passed the data to the PPP server for the two non-SVD conditions. In all three voice conditions, the customer reached the web server using a dial-up connection. To minimize equipment use, the web server ran on the same machine as the PPP server. The service representative was connected to the web server over a local area network (LAN). See Figs. 1a-c for a diagram of the three configurations tested.

The modem speed for the customer's dial-up connection was 14.4 kbps. In the SVD condition, 9.6 kbps of the bandwidth were allocated to voice. This corresponds to the use of the GSM/VQ codec for voice compression/ decompression.

Design

A 3x2 mixed factor design was used in the experiment. The three voice collaboration conditions were varied between participants, and the two data level conditions were varied within participants.

In all conditions, a participant took the role of a customer while one of two experimenters took the role of a customer service representative. The two experimenters were evenly distributed among three voice conditions.

Voice Collaboration

Condition 1 (Internet Phone, IP): In the IP condition, the voice and data coming from two separate Internet Protocol applications were combined and routed over a telephone line to the PPP server. Since the service representative's machine was on the same LAN and ring as the PPP server, the voice packets went between customer and service representative machines with only "two hops" in between (the dialup server and the PPP server in Fig. 1b). This two-hop connection represents an excellent connection in terms of latency contributed by the internet. In the IP condition, both service representative and customer communicated through microphones and speakers attached to their computers. The roundtrip delay for voice in this condition varied from about 400 msec to several seconds, depending on the amount of data being transmitted concurrently with the voice. The internet telephony application used was Bamba [15] which proved to be very competitive in our initial comparison tests with other commercially available internet telephony applications.

Condition 2 (Simultaneous Voice and Data, SVD): In the SVD condition, voice and data were combined by the customer's computer using a proprietary protocol and transmitted over a telephone line to the dial-up server where the voice was separated from the data. The voice was routed over the telephone network to the service representative's telephone. The customer used the computer's microphone and speaker for communication and the service representative used the telephone. The roundtrip delay for the voice was about 200-250 msec in this condition.

Condition 3 (Second Line): In the Second Line condition, voice communication was over a second, independent telephone line. Data communication was over a dial-up modem connection as in the other two conditions. The customer used a speakerphone for the voice communication. There was essentially no voice delay for this condition, since it was a regular telephone connection.

Data Collaboration

The same web collaboration application (CLIVE) was used with all conditions. This application permits shared web page viewing and navigation, remote pointer/cursors that allow each party to interact with the web page (e.g. scroll, click buttons, etc.) and see the other person's pointer/cursor, ink annotation that allows each party to mark on the page using the mouse, and, joint text entry using the keyboard. The data path was the same for all conditions.

Data Level and Tasks

Each subject completed two tasks. Both tasks required the customer to collaborate with the service representative to get auto insurance information from an auto insurance web site (designed by us for the purposes of this study). One task was designed to mainly involve conversation with some typed and mouse input to a form on a web page (low data condition). The other task required conversation but also involved the downloading of large images on two pages (high data condition). One image was 55.9 kbytes and the other was 73.3 kbytes. These task conditions allowed us to assess the effects of data volume on the acceptability of the three voice conditions. Specifically, since the data volume can affect voice delay markedly with IP voice communication, we were interested in how data volume would affect the acceptability of IP condition.

Participants

A total of 36 participants (22 male, 14 female) took part in the experiment, with 12 participants randomly assigned to each condition. All participants were recruited from the IBM T.J. Watson Research Center. Thirty-two were IBM employees and four were office temporary employees.

Participants were screened to meet requirements for age (18-65), language fluency (speak English as first language or have proficiency which is about the same as a native speaker of English), use of Netscape (exclude those who never use Netscape) and expertise in web technology (exclude professionals working in the area of web technology).

The age distribution was: 18-25 (15), 26-35 (7), 36-45 (11), 46-56 (3). Most of the participants (33) used Netscape daily; only 3 used Netscape weekly. The occupations included manager (3), researcher (5), engineer (7), programmer (4), secretary (7), student (10)). There were no significant differences in participants'' age, gender, frequency of Netscape use, or occupation across the three conditions.

The IBM employees were given a lunch voucher worth up to $10 for their participation and the office temporaries were paid.

Procedure

All three conditions used the same procedure.

First, participants were given written instructions for task 1, in which they assumed that they just bought a new car and wanted to buy auto insurance, keeping their premium as low as possible with adequate protection. They were told they would need to contact the service representative in order to complete the task.

Then they were shown the auto insurance web site. Before beginning the tasks of interest, participants completed an "application form" task designed to familiarize them with the web site. When ready, the participants clicked on a button labeled "Contact Agent" to establish the voice and data sharing session with the service representative. In the first task (low data condition), the customer asked the representative several questions suggested in the instructions in order to accomplish the goal of buying adequate auto insurance while keeping the premium as low as possible.

After the first task, participants were asked to fill in questionnaire 1. They then started the second task (high data condition), which required the representative to download several large images in order to answer the customer's questions. Finally, participants filled in questionnaire 2.

The experimenter used the remote pointer and ink annotation in both tasks. The participants were also able to use the pointer and ink annotation, but were not required to do so.

Measures

Questionnaires and behavioral coding were used to assess several aspects of the session.

Questionnaire 1 contained items to assess perception of voice communication. Questionnaire 2, given after the second task, contained these same items, plus questions to assess perception of data collaboration, and overall evaluation of the system.

The communication behavior coding is a relatively objective measurement of *voice interaction.* The following behavior categories were coded using the videotapes.

- Delayed Response—A delayed response was coded when the response to the customer's statement or question arrived after he/she had started to discuss another topic. For example, immediately after asking about the total cost, the customer may have received an answer to an earlier question about what is covered under collision insurance. Such delayed responses may disrupt the flow of conversation. Since the video recording was made from the customer side, this category includes only delayed responses as perceived by the customer.
- Simultaneous Speech—An instance of simultaneous speech was scored whenever the speech of the customer and service representative overlapped in time. This category includes all temporally overlapping speech as recorded from the customer side, regardless of whether the onsets and offsets of the speech were synchronized.
- Repeated Clarification—A repeated clarification was coded when the customer had to repeat what was said. Only repeated clarifications or requests for clarifications from the customer to the service representative were coded. For example, the customer might ask, What did you say?"
- Task time—The length of time it took to complete the high and low data tasks were measured separately. When both data and voice connection were established, "start" was coded for that task. When customers expressed that they had asked all their questions, "end" was coded for that task.

RESULTS

Questionnaire results

Audio communication

The questions related to audio communication were designed to assess ease of speech interaction and voice quality. Table 1 shows the participants' ratings on each question on a seven point scale with 1=strongly disagree, 7=strongly agree. Each question was analyzed using a 3 x 2 MANOVA analysis across three conditions (SVD, IP, 2 line) and data level (low vs high).

Summary

First, the results show a main effect of voice condition in all the questions related to ease of speech interaction and voice quality ($p<.05$). In general, SVD was perceived as significantly better than IP on measures of ease of speech interaction. Participants rated the Second line condition more favorably than either the SVD or IP condition on most measures of speech interaction and voice quality. There were no measures for which participants rated the IP condition more favorably than the SVD condition.

Second, the MANOVA analysis showed an effect of data level for two voice quality questions. However, there was also a voice condition x data level interaction for these questions.

An interaction between the effects of voice condition and data level was found for four voice quality questions. These interactions were largely due to the IP condition receiving significantly less favorable ratings for the high data condition than for the low data condition.

Comparison of SVD and Internet Phone

Participants gave SVD significantly better ratings than IP in terms of ease of speech interaction. As Table 1 indicates, SVD received better ratings than IP for both the low and high data conditions in terms of:

- Frequency of interruptions (Question 2)
- Responsiveness of service representative (Question 12)
- Voice delay (Question 14)
- Presence of long pauses in the conversation (Question 16)
- Frequency of simultaneous speaking (Question 17)

SVD was superior to IP for the high data condition for the questions which assessed:

- Ease of hearing the service representative (Question 7)
- Ease of talking to the representative through the computer (Question 8)

In absolute terms, the mean rating for SVD for the ease of speech interaction questions tended to be on the favorable side of the seven-point scale, while the mean ratings for IP were slightly on the unfavorable side of the scale.

There were no significant differences between SVD and IP on measures of voice quality.

Comparison of SVD and Second line (baseline condition)

The Second line condition was significantly better than SVD for many of the questions on ease of speech interaction and perception of voice quality (11 out of 14 questions for the low data condition and 8 out of 14 questions for the high data condition). There was no consistent pattern of superiority for the Second Line condition (e.g. better evaluations for ease of speech interaction or voice quality questions).

Question #		Low Data			High Data		
		SVD	IP	2 Line	SVD	IP	2 Line
	Ease of speech interaction						
2	I was often interrupted	2.42	4.17	1.67	3.08	4.75	1.58
7	It was easy to hear the customer service representative	5.25	5.83	6.58	5.83	4.00	6.67
8	It was easy to talk to the customer service representative through the computer.	5.25	4.75	6.67	5.67	4.25	6.50
12	The representative seemed to respond right away.	5.08	3.58	6.17	5.33	3.00	6.33
14	The voice was often delayed in the conversation.	3.17	5.58	1.42	4.00	5.83	1.33
16	There were long pauses in the conversation.	3.58	5.25	1.83	3.33	5.67	2.08
17	We were often talking at the same time.	3.42	4.75	2.00	2.75	4.75	1.75
	Voice quality						
3	I was satisfied with the voice quality.	5.08	5.83	6.42	4.92	3.75	5.92
4	In general, the incoming voice was good.	5.17	5.82	6.50	4.92	3.83	6.00
9	The incoming voice faded in and out.	3.92	3.17	1.33	3.75	4.17	1.33
10	The incoming voice seemed to break up.	4.33	3.50	1.50	4.42	4.75	1.50
11	The incoming voice was not loud enough.	2.67	2.67	1.58	2.33	3.00	1.50
13	The voice quality was as good as a normal telephone call.	3.50	4.83	6.42	4.08	2.92	6.50
15	There was too much noise.	4.17	3.08	1.58	4.25	4.00	1.33

Table 1 Means for Audio Communication Questions (1 = strongly disagree, 7 = strongly agree)

Comparison of Internet Phone and Second line (baseline condition)

Similar to the comparison between Second line and SVD, Second line was significantly better than IP on almost all the questions on ease of speech interaction and voice quality (11 of 14 questions for the low data condition, and 14 of 14 for the high data condition).

Effects of low data and high data tasks on perceived voice quality

There was a significant interaction effect between data level and condition on several measures of voice quality due to the lower rating of quality for the IP condition on the high data task compared with the low data task. This effect was found for the following:

- Satisfaction with voice quality (Question 3)
- Agreement that "incoming voice was good" (Question 4)
- Comparison of voice quality with a normal telephone call (Question 13)
- Noise (Question 15)

On every measure of ease of speech interaction and voice quality, the direction of change between low and high data tasks for the IP condition was towards a less favorable rating for the high data task. For the SVD and Second line conditions, there was no consistent pattern.

Data collaboration

At the end of the session, participants answered several questions about the data collaboration. As shown in Table 2, participants in all three conditions were aware of the other side (average score all above 5 with 1=strongly disagree and 7=strongly agree), thought it is useful to share the screen with the service representative during the conversation (all average scores are above 5), and noticed the sharing tool. ANOVA analyses showed no significant differences across the three voice conditions.

	SVD	IP	2 Line
1. In general, I knew what the customer service representative was doing.	5.92	5.75	5.67
2. It is useful to share the screen with the customer service representative compared to just a telephone conversation.	6.25	5.08	5.83
3. I noticed there was a window labeled "sharing tool" on the screen.	0.83	0.75	1.00

Table 2 : Means for Data Collaboration Questions

General evaluation

At the end of each task, the participants were given several questions intended to assess the helpfulness and efficiency of the interaction. At the end of the session, the participants were given several additional questions intended to assess their overall reaction to using the system (see Table 3). There were no significant differences across three conditions for any of these questions, although the IP voice condition was non-significantly lower than the other two on all six questions.

	SVD	IP	2 Line
Evaluation after tasks			
1. I felt the conversation was helpful.	5.92	5.04	5.75
2. This is an efficient way to get information from a customer service representative.	6.13	5.08	5.63
3. It took less time than I expected to find the best insurance plan.	5.75	5.17	5.33
Overall evaluation			
1. The system is easy to use.	5.92	5.50	6.00
2. I felt in control of the system.	5.00	4.67	5.00
3. The conversation is natural.	5.58	4.58	6.00

Table 3: Means for General Evaluation Questions

Communication behavior coding results

The behavior coding results shown in Table 4 support the findings from the questionnaire. ANOVA and additional t-tests were conducted on task time, frequencies of the three behavior categories (delayed response, simultaneous speech, and repeated clarification) for the three voice conditions and two data levels.

	Low Data			High Data		
	IP	SVD	2 Line	IP	SVD	2 Line
Task Time	14.35	9.77	10.65	9.82	6.87	5.77
Delayed Response	7.00	0.92	0.00	4.42	0.33	0.00
Simultaneous Speech	8.00	3.50	0.67	4.08	1.50	0.58
Repeated Clarification	2.83	2.25	0.75	2.33	0.92	0.33

Table 4: Means for Behavior Categories (task time in minutes)

There were significant main effects of voice condition and data level on task time ($p<.01$). IP took approximately 45% more time than SVD and Second line in both low data and high data tasks. There was no difference between SVD and Second line for the task time measure.

There was also a significant effect for voice condition for the other three behavior measures ($p<.01$). There were significantly more instances of delayed responses and simultaneous speech for the IP condition than for either the SVD or Second line condition for both data levels ($p<.05$). In addition, IP was worse than SVD in terms of the number of repeated clarifications for the high data level. There was also significantly more simultaneous speech in the SVD condition compared to the Second line condition for both data levels. Further comparisons between these two conditions revealed that the difference in the number of delayed responses was significant for the high data condition; the difference in the number of repeated clarifications was significant in the low data condition.

Comments from participants

From participants'' comments on the questionnaire and by talking with them after the experiment, we found that some participants adapted their speaking style to the constraints of the voice channel, such as waiting for the representative's response, or avoiding talking while images were being loaded when the voice was delayed.

Many customers complained that it took too long to load images in all three voice conditions. However, customers still enjoyed the ability of being able to talk to a real people and share the same visual information over the Web. Some commented that the visual indicator that provided feedback for the synchronization status of Web pages helped avoid confusion due to the temporal asynchrony between voice and data.

DISCUSSION

Like previous research, our study found that voice delay affected users' perceptions of ease of speech interaction. The IP voice condition, which had the greatest delay, was perceived least favorably on measures of ease of speech interaction; the Second line condition, with no delay, was perceived most favorably and SVD, with about 250 msec delay, was perceived as intermediate between these two. This is a particularly strong finding, given that the voice condition was a between subjects factor so participants could not make comparisons among the three voice options. In absolute terms, both the SVD and Second line conditions had mean ratings on the positive side of the rating scale, whereas the IP condition had mean ratings on the negative side.

A high level of concurrent data transmission exacerbated the unfavorable perceptions of IP voice. In particular, perceived voice quality suffered as the flow of voice packets was interrupted and delayed by the data.

The behavioral results tended to support the perception of participants. There were more instances of simultaneous speech and delayed responses for IP voice compared with SVD for both the high and low data conditions and more repeated clarifications for IP voice than for SVD in the high data condition.

Perhaps the most striking behavioral result was for task time. The task time for IP voice was about 45% longer than for SVD and the Second line alternative. There were no differences between task times for SVD and Second line. The fact that there was no difference in task time between SVD and Second line, in spite of the fact that there were measurable objective and subjective effects of delay in the SVD condition, suggests that the large increase in task time for IP voice may not be due solely to the added transmission time. We suggest that the magnitude of the voice delay for IP voice created communication problems that took time to recover from.

For SVD, the delay was perhaps not great enough to seriously disrupt communication and thus affect task time.

The perceived value of data collaboration did not seem to be affected by the voice alternatives. There was little evidence of confusion due to temporal asynchrony between the arrival of voice and data. Given that the data as well as voice packets suffer delay in the IP condition, the typical asynchrony between voice and data was undoubtedly less than the absolute delay (we have not attempted to measure the asynchrony). For the SVD and Second line conditions, voice typically preceded data. The lack of confusion for these conditions may have been due in part to the effectiveness of several awareness mechanisms that provide feedback to the users about when an action, such as loading a web page, was complete on the other side.

It is rather interesting that although the IP voice condition had lower mean ratings on measures of general evaluation of the system, the effect of voice condition was not statistically significant for these measures. One might interpret this lack of significant differences due to voice condition as evidence that the speech interaction and voice quality effects, although measurable, have little impact on the overall effectiveness or usability of the system. From another perspective, one must be cautious in generalizing from participants' evaluations in this experiment to attitudes of real users. It is reasonable to assume that participants' communication behavior and their perception of the voice interaction were not unduly influenced by the artificial nature of the experiment. On the other hand, evaluations of efficiency, helpfulness and other general aspects of the system might be different if users were attempting a real task of their own on their own time. We will learn which of these hypotheses is correct as we gain experience with real customers and service representatives.

This study has a number of implications for collaborative Web-based customer service. When a second line is available for an immediate callback to the customer, this voice alternative is preferable in terms of voice quality and speech interaction. Of the two single line alternatives, SVD's better interaction characteristics may be particularly important for interactions which involve sales, or discussion of complicated material, where delayed responses, need for repeated clarification and awkward conversational interaction may be very detrimental to both the customer's and business's purposes. This is particularly true if the collaboration is likely to involve concurrent transmission of large amounts of data.

From a business perspective, the finding that the task time with IP voice was about 45% greater than with SVD or Second line is a very serious liability. Labor is usually the most expensive component in a call center, and prolonging the customer-service representative interaction by even a few seconds per call can add up to millions of dollars a year. It is possible, however, that for simple, brief inquiries which do not involve concurrent data transmission IP voice may be acceptable for web-based customer service. As bandwidth to the home increases and internet telephony technology advances, IP voice will become acceptable for more purposes.

This study is the first reported empirical assessment of different voice alternatives for collaborative customer service over the Web. It has practical value in providing information to help businesses evaluate the pros and cons of each alternative. It contributes to our knowledge of the effects of voice delay and quality on users' interaction patterns and perceptions. These insights can be used to guide the design of the underlying technology.

ACKNOWLEDGEMENTS

We gratefully acknowledge the assistance of Evan MacDonald and Frank Jania who played the role of the customer service representative. We would like to thank Judy Olson, Gary Olson and Huahai Yang for the insightful comments on an earlier draft.

REFERENCES

1. Bly, S. (1988). A use of drawing surfaces in different collaborative settings. *Proceedings of CSCW 88*, 250-256.
2. Brady, P.T. (1970). Effects of Transmission Delay on Conversational Behavior on Echo-Free Telephone Circuits. *The Bell System Technical Journal*(January), 115-134.
3. Chapanis, A. (1975). Interactive human communication. *Scientific American, 232*, 36-42.
4. Conway, K.D. (1998). Building customer relationships in the electronic age: Technology Solutions Company.
5. Graham, T.C.N. (1997). GroupScape: Integrating synchronous groupware and the World Wide Web. *Proceedings of INTERACT97*, 547-554.
6. Greenberg, S., & Roseman, M. (1996). GroupWeb: A WWW browser as real time groupware. *CHI 96 Conference Companion*, 271-272.
7. Klemmer, E.T. (1967). Subjective Evaluation of Transmission Delay in Telephone Conversations. *The Bell System Technical Journal, 46*(July-August), 1141-1147.
8. Krauss, R.M., & Bricker, P.D. (1967). Effects of Transmission Delay and Access Delay on the Efficiency of Verbal Communication. *The Journal of the Acoustical Society of Amercia, 41*(2), 286-292.
9. Stefik, M., Foster, M., Bobrow, D., Kahn, K.L., & K. & Suchman, L. (1987). Beyond the chalkboard: computer support for collaboration and problem solving in meetings. *Communications of the ACM, 30*, 32-47.

10. Tatar, D., Foster G., & Bobrow, D. (1991). Design for conversation: lessons from COGNOTER. *International Journal of Man-Machine Studies, 34*, 143-160.
11. Trevor, J., Koch, T., & Woetzel, G. (1997). MetaWeb: Bringing synchronous groupware to the World Wide Web. *Proceedings of ECSCW97*, 65-80.
12. Whittaker, S., & Geelhoed, E. (1993). Shared workspaces: how do they work and when are they useful? *International Journal of Man-Machine Studies, 39*, 813-842.
13. Wolf, C.G. (1982). Video conferencing: delay and transmission considerations. *Teleconferencing and Electronic Communications: applications, technologies, and human factors*, 184-194.
14. Wolf, C.G., Chen, S., Daijavad, S., Fin, F., Fujisaki, T., Roffman, E., & Touma, M. (1996). Collaborative interfaces for customer service. *CSCW 96, Videos, Demonstrations and Short Papers*, 21-22.
15. Bamba (1998) See http://www.alphaworks.ibm.com/bamba for more information.
16. Microsoft (1998) See http://www.microsoft.com/netmeeting for more information.
17. Netscape (1998) See http://home.netscape.com/comprod/products/communicator for more information.
18. Webline (1998) See http://www.webline.com for more information.

Out of this world: an extensible session architecture for heterogeneous electronic landscapes

Jonathan Trevor, Tom Rodden, Gareth Smith
Department of Computing, Lancaster University
Lancaster, Lancs. LA1 4YR, U.K.
+44 1524 65201
{jonathan, tom, gbs}@comp.lancs.ac.uk

ABSTRACT
The growth in interest in virtual environments in CSCW has focused on co-operation within these environments. Little consideration has been given to how users manage these environments and their movement between them. In this paper we present a session management architecture that supports the management of virtual environments. The developed architecture is built upon the HTTP protocol and is sufficiently general to allow it to support a range of CSCW application. We present the architecture and its use to support both virtual environments and more generic cooperative applications.

Keywords
CSCW, session management, e-scape, HTTP, servlet, Java

INTRODUCTION
Over the last few years a large number of systems to support on-line virtual worlds and collaborative virtual environments have started to emerge. These include 3D virtual environments such as: MASSIVE[15]; DIVE[8]; AlphaWorlds [1]; Blaxxun[4]; 2D graphical systems such as the Palace[26]; and textual virtual environments such as MUDs[9]. The large number of these systems and their rapid development is impressive. However, the diversity of these systems is also problematic - particularly given the generally insular philosophy adopted by these systems.

Users seeking to exploit these cooperative environments are currently faced with worlds that are simultaneously massively interconnected *within* each system and yet isolated *between* systems. It is not unusual for users to face problems of managing the interconnection between many different worlds in virtual environments supported by a single system. Users are equally likely to become frustrated by the closed nature of these systems and the inability to seamlessly move between environments supported in different worlds. This is despite the development of world modelling standards such as VRML [28] which focus on the visualisation of these virtual environments.

CSCW 98 Seattle Washington USA

This paper seeks to directly address two frustrations for the users of online virtual environments:

- The problem of managing the growing scale and complexity of virtual environments.
- The problem of supporting heterogeneity of environments and the inability to provide links between environments supported by different classes of system.

To further understand these issues we have undertaken an ethnographic study of users moving between virtual environments in an interactive art museum [7, 27]. This study highlighted the need to support user orientation by allowing access to information about environments prior to entering them.

In this paper we present an architecture that allows such information to be made public. The architecture provides an extensible approach to managing on-line virtual environments sessions. In the rest of this paper we outline the developed architecture and demonstrate its use to provide access and connectivity between different virtual environments. In doing so we aim to provide a set of management services that exist *independently* of any single virtual environment and allow users to exploit information about the nature of these environments when they use them.

FROM SPACE TO LANDSCAPE
Core to the development of our supporting infrastructure is provision for the formation of large-scale *electronic landscapes* through the interconnection of different virtual environments. The notion of electronic landscapes is predicated on a vision of social information systems for the citizen. The assumption is that the increased growth of accessible distributed infrastructures (such as the World Wide Web) will result in distributed information spaces capable of supporting social forms of interaction. What is required however is a shift from our current considerations of these virtual environments as closed entities to a more open arrangement of these worlds.

The formation of electronic landscapes builds upon work in HCI and CSCW on the use of spatial metaphors to represent information and action in electronic systems. This work is rooted in the use of a 'room' based metaphor to allow the presentation of information [16]. From these early approaches we have seen concepts of spatial arrangement exploited in the development of desktop conferencing systems such as Cruiser [21] and more generally in the work of Mediaspaces [14].

The development of co-operative systems in CSCW has also seen a growing application of concepts drawn from spatial arrangements. These include the development of *groupkit* to *teamrooms* [22], the emergence of the *wOrlds* system [13] and the use of a notion of places to support infrastructure [20]. This notion of using concepts of space has considered equally amending existing physical spaces to form augmented spaces populated by electronically sensitive physical artefacts [18], and virtual spaces into which users project their presence [2]. Our particular interest is in the formation of on-line electronic landscapes that are both large scale and distributed in nature.

Extending virtual environments

The work reported here seeks to extend the work currently being undertaken in a number of initiatives that address the development of shared online virtual environments. This work has its history in Muds and Moos [9] but has more recently turned to the use of VR technology to visualise a space shared by multiple individuals.

Virtual environments have been used to support a number of different forms of cooperation. For example, several descriptions of virtual conferencing [15] and collaborative information visualisation and retrieval systems [6] exist in research literature. The work of these systems to promote and support co-operation within them has become a major area of CSCW research with the emergence of a cooperative virtual environments research community.

Proponents of shared virtual environments suggest that they support social interaction in ways that go beyond the limitations of technologies such as videoconferences, 'mediaspaces' or shared desktops. It has also been claimed that appropriately designed shared virtual environments enable users to sustain mutual awareness about each other's activities [5]. This research work is complemented by the continuing efforts of a number of organisations that provide access to shared virtual environments via the Internet [25]. Of these AlphaWorld, Worlds Away, The Palace and Blaxxun are some of the best known and they all suggest that these environments will become increasingly accessible. Similarly the VRML 3.0 ("Living Worlds") suggests support for simultaneously shareable worlds. This diversity and increased access further motivates the need for a consideration of the structure and support of these environments.

Overcoming limits of existing systems

While a number of different systems postulate the view of large-scale virtual environments populated by many users, their view of the world tends to be closed within the worlds supported by a single system. While VRML [28] offers some sense of standardisation it still does so with a focus on issues of visualisation and presentation rather than offering a wider consideration of virtual environments. It is clear that a number of systems will continue to coexist, each exploring particular approaches in supporting virtual worlds.

A model common to most virtual environments is the partitioning of space into discrete components linked by some form of porthole or gateway. Users traverse the environment by using these gateways to move between worlds. However, while this partitioning allows large scale virtual environments to be constructed it also hides the details of these different worlds from users as these separate worlds do not provide any external information about their nature. This partitioning into isolated closed worlds causes a number of real problems for users.

- **Support for heterogeneity is limited** in that each virtual environment is closed and does not provide external access to information about the environment.
- **Browsing collaborative virtual environments is difficult** as no information on the nature of these environments is available without entering the environment and using the supporting application.
- **Seeing how currently inhabited virtual environments are is difficult** as few environments provide on-line access to information about who is currently connected. Again those few that do provide this information require users to enter the environment to get it.
- **Configuring and launching environments is difficult** and currently requires some considerable knowledge of the detailed nature of the application.
- **Understanding the nature of the environment is difficult** as users are seldom provided with cues that allow them to orient to the particular characteristics of the environment.

Currently users are left to manage the information needed to address these problems and there are no techniques that allow different forms of virtual environments to be knitted together in a seamless manner. This paper presents the development of an architecture that allows such information to be managed externally to the environment, and provides facilities that allow both users and applications to access and exploit meta-information about environments. The core to the development and support of this meta-information is the notion of an e-scape.

THE NOTION OF AN E-SCAPE

The development of an architecture that allows a range of virtual environments to coexist and be reasoned about is dependent on the notion of an electronic landscape (or e-scape). An e-scape is any electronic world where sets of properties that provide an indication of the nature of the environment are made public. Thus an e-scape provides support for the development of applications and virtual environments that join virtual environments together.

The current architecture provides facilities for an extensible set of environments' properties to be maintained. In addition to these user-defined properties each e-scape has a core set of properties that aim to convey the nature of the virtual environment.

The E-scape Properties

The set of properties suggested here arise from considering the use of a range of virtual environments and a series of empirical studies of interactive art installations in a Multimedia art museum [7]. This study demonstrated difficulties users encountered when moving between differing environments. The study suggested the need to promote the "learnability" of an environment by providing cues about the nature of these environments [27].

The problem with attempting to generalise, summarise and capture the nature of an environment or e-scape as distinct properties is that many of these are subjective and difficult to quantify. In addition, how do the notions of the person responsible for externalising and providing this type of meta-data about e-scapes correspond to others? An equally problematic factor in trying to categorise properties of e-scapes is the range of possible types, from 1D text based Moos to 3D virtual worlds.

Our approach to this essentially thorny issue relies on providing a small set of properties with limited scales. The properties explicitly do not aim to categorise environments in any absolute sense or build some form of taxonomy but to provide users with a "rough idea" of the e-scape. As a result we allow a simple indicative scoring (typically with a small range of values) to be used for each property and can be considered as analogous to the summary icons often used in reviews and guidebooks. We fully expect these properties to change and evolve over time as our understanding of the nature of these environments grows.

Structural Indicators

Our first sets of properties consider the structure of the space and the nature of this structure. These environment properties describe the basic contents and nature of the world.

Dimensionality	how many dimensions is the environment presented in (typically 1, 2 or 3)
Orientation	does the e-scape provide cues for how users should orient themselves inside it (like a city) by providing a ground plane, or can the e-scape be viewed from any position (as in planet based environments)
Physical Laws	how many "physical" laws does the e-scape enforce - can the users collide with other objects in the environment or can they be passed through, is there gravity etc.

Abstractness and Urbanity

These properties aim to convey the extent to which the world represents a facsimile of existing physical environments or is an artificial environment. Rather than make this an explicit choice that a world must be either abstract of a facsimile we allow to complementary scales to reflect a range of different arrangements.

Abstractness	how abstract are the objects in the environment, e.g. do they represent database data or web page content
Urbanity	how urban is the layout of the environment, are things laid out like as a town or a city

Scale and Complexity

This set of properties seeks to convey the scale and complexity of an environment to allow users entering it to understand the extent of the environment.

Size	how big the e-scape is in terms of the scale used internally within the environment
Complexity	how dense or complex is the e-scape in terms of the objects within it.
Connectivity	is the e-scape connected to a number of other e-scapes or is it self-contained with no external connections
Population	how multi-user is the e-scape – or is it single user.
Media	does the e-scape provide a rich tapestry of media that can be exploited, such as video and audio, or is it limited to only text

Persistence Indicators

This set of properties conveys the extent to which the environment remembers events and actions, and is likely to change between visits.

Stability	does the e-scape grow and evolve or is a walkthrough which doesn't change very much
Remembrance (or memory)	when users make changes to objects in the e-scape, are these permanent or will they be reset the next time the user visits

THE GENERAL ARCHITECTURE

The e-scape session architecture builds on three separate services to provide support for electronic landscapes.

- **A User Profile Service** that maintains information about users and their relation to e-scapes.
- **An E-Scape Registry Service** that allows different environments to register as e-scapes by making meta-information about the environment publicly available.
- **A Personal E-Scape Service** that runs at each client that interprets and locally manages e-scape information.

The main aim of the e-scape session service is to provide support for the management of large-scale electronic landscapes that are both open and accessible by a wide community of users. In addition, the principal pattern of communication needed for establishing e-scape sessions is client-server. As a result of these two requirements we have adopted the HTTP protocol as the supporting mechanism for transporting requests and replies. In addition, since most of the interaction itself does not require any immediate active feedback between the services we can also exploit HTML to provide general management interfaces for the different services. Our use of these two standard and widely adopted protocols has many advantages [10] not the least of which is that of deployment and access to a large established community of users. The general arrangement of these services is shown in Figure 1

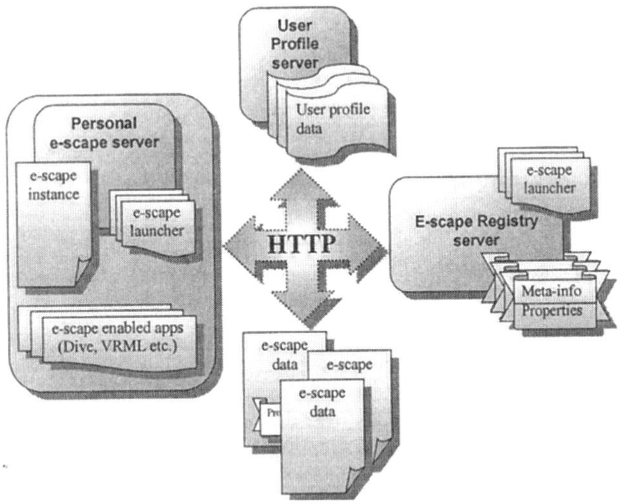

Figure 1 The e-scape session architecture

This arrangement exploits a distinction between the model used to record details of the e-scape and the means by which this is launched. The architecture of most virtual environments systems maintains a separation between a centralised world model that is shared and a local client that manages interaction. The e-scape architecture exploits this separation by providing appropriate launchers for different types of virtual environment.

USER PROFILE SERVER

The User Profile Server maintains information about the users of e-scapes and allows this information to be made shared with other users when necessary. When first created a user profile contains only a few values:

- The *name* of the user, e.g. Jonathan Trevor.
- An *alias* for the user, e.g. Jonathan.
- *Personal e-scape server* URL.
- An authentication *password.*

The e-scape service allows these profiles to be extended to allow additional information to be maintained as needed. Once created the profile can be extended by the user or anyone with sufficient access (see below). Each profile supports any number of additional name-value pairs. To aid access these pairs are stored in a similar way to the Windows95/NT registry within a hierarchy of folders, where each folder can have many name-value pairs and other folders. The server allows access to information in these folders through normal HTML and can be modified through HTTP GET and POST requests. The amount of information made accessible for each user profile depends on the access rights of the application or user accessing the server. Figure 2 shows the details of Jonathan's user profile.

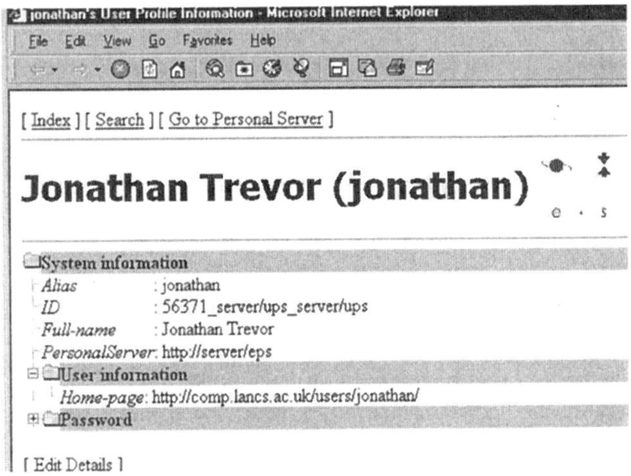

Figure 2 A user profile

The architecture allows many different instances of the user profile server to be running simultaneously. Each server maintains zero or more user profiles and each e-scape user can only have one profile at one server (although the profile may move during its lifetime between profile servers). For example, both Tom and Jonathan may have their profiles stored at the URL http://server/ups, but Jam has his profile at http://anotherserver/ups. The general location transparent access provided by the HTTP protocol allows for large-scale global federation of these servers and means we can exploit the general scalability provided by the Internet.

E-SCAPE REGISTRY SERVER

The registry service is responsible for maintaining all the meta-information associated with an e-scape. This information is added to a server when users and/or developers register an e-scape with the server. The registration of the meta-information associated with the e-scape includes both management information and a set of general properties of the e-scape. Initial registration is simply a case of filling in an HTML form. The server maintains associated e-scape information including:

- the *location* of the actual e-scape data
  This is typically a URL giving the location of an access point to the shared world.
- a *description* of the e-scape
  This provides a textual overview of the nature of the world.
- a *snapshot* of the e-scape
  This provides a view of the e-scape and can be either a 2D image or a sample 3D VRML world. This could make use of some form of 3D thumbnails [12].
- Current *users* of an e-scape
  The registry maintains a list of users currently connected to an e-scape.
- the *type* of e-scape, (e.g. Dive, VRML2, Quake etc.)
  These are normally specified in terms of mime-types

allowing the appropriate launcher to be initiated by the personal e-scape server held locally.

- any other *name-value pairs.*
  In a similar manner to the user profile service, any number of name-value paired parameters may also be added to the meta-information and structured into a folder hierarchy.
- the e-scape *properties.*
  These provide a general indication of the nature of the environment. These are held as a series of name value pairs for the general properties of the environment.

Similarly to the profile servers, the e-scape session architecture allows any number of e-scape registry servers which each server can be accessed through single URL, e.g. http://server/ers.

Presenting e-scapes

Once the meta-information about an e-scape is on the server, users are free to search and browse it. This can be done using a range of different interfaces. The simplest of these is the HTML interface provided by the server, as shown in Figure 3. Searching can be based on matching arbitrary name-value pairs in an e-scape's registration information, or may rely on the fixed fields like the e-scape's name, type or properties.

In this simple interface users are presented with a link at the bottom of each page of information about an e-scape that allows the user to start and join the e-scape on their local machine. This is done using a URL that causes the browser to execute a HTTP request (with appropriate parameters) to the user's Personal E-scape server.

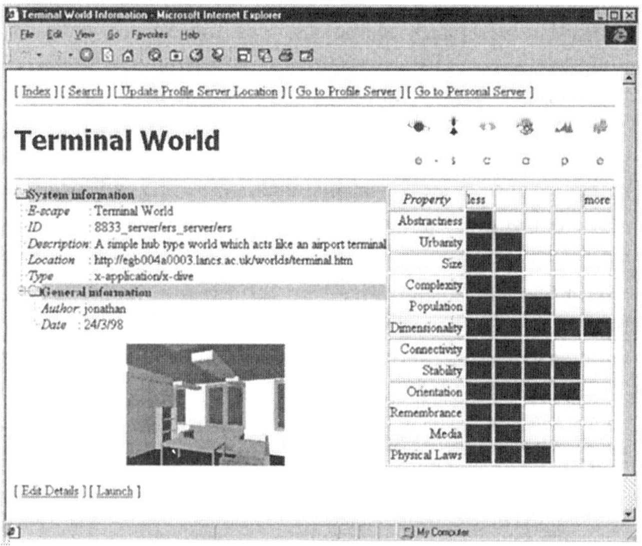

Figure 3 A registered e-scape

Other presentations of the information in the registry are possible and alternative displays can be constructed from the e-scape properties. This includes the generation of appropriate virtual environments that provide access to the local information. Environments and e-scapes can also access registered information to present it as annotations on gateways to these worlds [7], allowing users to gain an idea of what to expect before actually travelling to the new world (figure 4).

Figure 4 Annotated gateways to other e-scapes

In addition to providing a source of meta-information concerning available e-scapes, each registry server also contains a set of "*Launcher*" Java classes. These classes can be transported from the registry server to the user's local machine in a similar way to applets being fetched to a local browser. The launcher classes provide wrappers that allow e-scapes to be set-up and started.

Finally, each e-scape registry server automatically exports its location onto several Web search engines and contains an editable list of URLs to other known e-scape registry servers (on other machines). This linking of registries allows users to perform searches across a uniform federation of servers. Because URLs are location independent, browsing users can easily find themselves seamlessly moving from registry server to registry server. Each e-scape may only be registered with one server at once and facilities are provided to migrate the registration information between servers.

PERSONAL E-SCAPE SERVER

Each e-scape user requires a personal e-scape server to be running on their local machine. Again, the server is manipulated through HTML pages it provides and can be accessed from a single URL, e.g. http://server/pes. This standard interface allows users to configure, access and manage the information in the Personal e-scape server.

The personal server also presents an active interface that provides a graphic display of the properties of e-scapes the user inhabits. This interface is written in Java to overcome the static nature of HTML pages. Without such an interface remote servers would have to be repeatedly polled for the information to see if it has changed. Figure 5 shows the Personal E-scape Server Java GUI. This interface is analogous to the use of awareness widgets in other cooperative systems in that it keeps the users aware of the nature of the environment they are currently using.

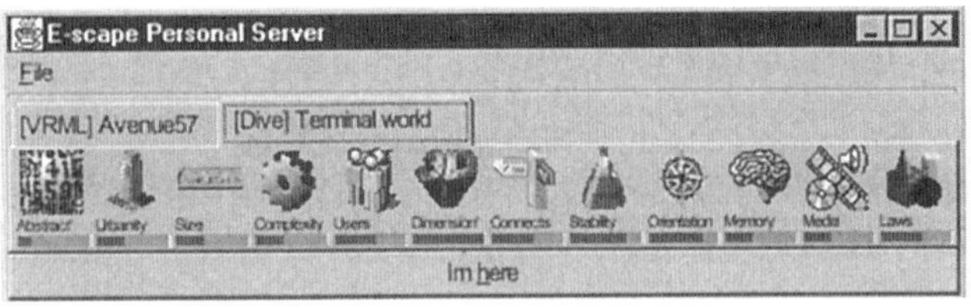

Figure 5 Java Personal E-scape Server Interface.

Accessing E-scapes

In addition to providing a dynamic indication of the nature of the environment being inhabited the personal e-scape server manages the local launching of applications that start and interface to virtual environments. In order to use the different types of e-scape on their local machine, the applications which can provide access to those e-scapes must obviously also be installed. For example, a Dive world requires a local Dive viewer and supporting processes, a VRML97 world requires a VRML97 capable browser, a Quake map requires the Quake game and so on.

These applications need to be started in different ways, take different parameters, require the data about their e-scape locations to be present locally or remotely, and so on. To overcome this problem we use the notion of *e-scape launchers* which can be fetched from remote launcher repositories (i.e. the e-scape registry server) as required. Once made available locally, each launcher may need to be configured further (with the location of the e-scape application for example). Such configuration is performed again through standard HTML via the personal e-scape server. Once suitably configured, each launcher can store this information locally to be reused later. Figure 6 shows an example of the configuration interface presented by the Dive launcher on NT4.

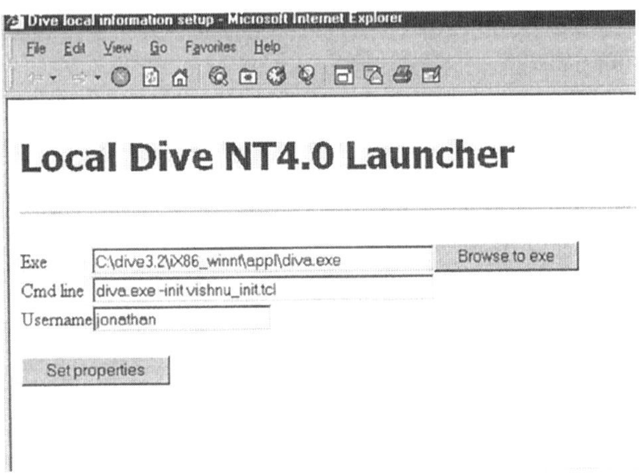

Figure 6 A launcher configuration screen

In addition to launching particular types of e-scape on the local machine, a launcher is responsible for augmenting the basic virtual environment application with e-scape aware features. E-scape aware applications can make public certain users' activities. For example it can detect a user leaving the e-scape (e.g. by quitting the application); entering a new e-scape. It can also extract the e-scape properties from the e-scape itself. Each of these actions will cause the launcher to perform a callback to the personal e-scape server which instantiated it, which can then act on the action (by fetching the properties of the new e-scape etc.).

Finally, each launcher may provide functionality for querying and maintaining registered e-scape information prior to launch through the registry. This includes checking the current users list is correct or getting the status of the remote multi-user server.

ACCESS CONTROL AND IDENTIFICATION

The e-scape session architecture employs a hierarchical access control scheme for data similar to the access control scheme used by the Macintosh file system. Each folder of information in the user profile server and the e-scape registry service is protected with an access control list, and each entry in that list contains an e-scape or user identifier and the permissions they have.

Each user and e-scape in the session architecture is allocated a unique identifier by the user profile server / e-scape registry service which first registers it. This identifier is a combination of an increasing value (maintained locally at the server in question), the URL of the server which first registered the entity, and the URL of the current server the user / e-scape information can be found at. In addition to creating this identifier, the registering server also creates a password for the user / e-scape and a locally associated alias which can be used instead of the full identifier in conjunction with the servers URL. For example, Jonathan could be registered at the user profile server with an identifier of "56371_server/ups_server/ups", with a password of "secret" and an alias of "jonathan". Jonathan can then authenticate himself at any when accessing any instance of the three types of server by providing either his identifier and password, or his alias, password and location of his current user profile server.

Each entry in a folders access control list dictates what operations can be performed on information in the folder by a particular identity. The set of allowable operations which can be specified are:

- Read (R) – the names and values of the name-value pairs can be read
- Write (W) – the values of the name-value pairs can be modified
- Create/Delete (C) – new name-value pairs can be created or removed
- Access (A) – these access rights can be modified

An e-scape obtains its current password and identifier through its e-scape launcher, which in turn receives this information from the e-scape registry that executes the launch command on the user's personal server.

Examples of the default access rights for new user profile and a new e-scape registration can be seen in Figure 7, where "8833_..." is the identifier for e-scape XYZ and "56371_..." is the identifier for Jonathan. Note that the creator of the e-scape registration, in this case Jonathan, is automatically inserted into the e-scape details access list. This allows the registering user to modify the details of the e-scape at a later time if necessary.

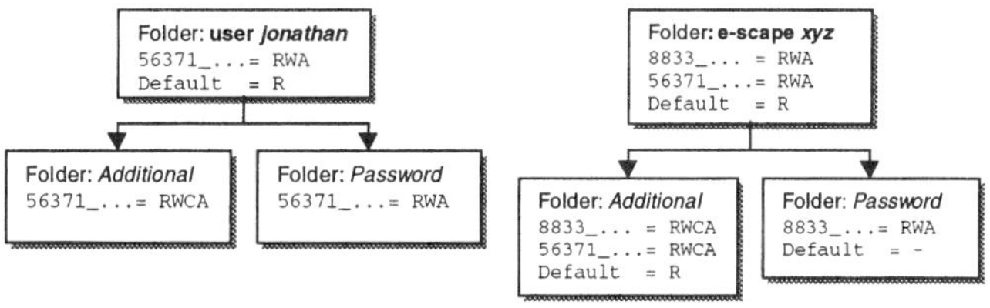

Figure 7 Default access rights for a newly created profile and e-scape

Top level folders have a special property which means that name-value pairs can never be created or deleted from them, i.e. the 'C' permission can never be set on a user. This stops users from deleting the main "system" allocated pairs, like the e-scape type. In addition, if Read access is not given on the contents of a folder then the folder itself is hidden.

IMPLEMENTATION

The e-scape session architecture has been implemented using Java servlet technology, which communicates through HTTP requests and responses. Each of the servers described above is a distinct servlet. Java servlets provide CGI-like functionality and can be embedded behind any appropriate Web server but offer several advantages over the more traditional CGI approach. First, servlets are loaded and embedded in the actual server itself. This means that each servlet is persistent and state is stored between requests. Secondly, each request does not require any forking of processes to deal with the request, making servlets very fast.

In addition, the combined use of Java, HTTP and HTML to support the architecture allows each server to run on a variety of operating systems and hardware, but also to be accessed from any computer with a standard web browser.

Finally, because Java inherently supports transportable code, its is relatively simple to provide for the notion of launchers which are transparently fetched and executed locally from remote servers - which allows the types of e-scape supported by the session architecture to grow and expand as required.

Example: Launching an e-scape

In order to demonstrate the responsibilities and inter-relation of the various e-scape services, consider the following example where a user locates and enters a Dive e-scape. If it not already running the user starts their personal e-scape server running on their machine. The user opens a web browser and enters the URL for a registry server. The registry server asks the user for the URL of their user profile before prompting for their username and password. Users do not need to keep providing the name of their profile server as once the information has been provided it is stored within a cookie, which can be passed automatically by the web browser the next time the user wants to log onto the server. The profile server authenticates the identity of the user and provides an overview of the registered e-scapes. In the default HTML display it provides a page listing the e-scapes registered on the server. The user refines the list by entering a search for e-scapes of type "x-world/x-dive" and clicks on one of the returned links to display the information about the e-scape (see Figure 3 above).

The e-scape is then started by clicking on the "Launch" link at the bottom of the page. This executes a GET request to the URL of the user's personal server, whose address will have previously been fetched by the registry server using the profile cookie. The GET request carries with it several pieces of information, the:

- *name* of the e-scape, e.g. "Patio area"
- *URL* of this registry server, e.g. http://server/ers
- *type* of the e-scape, e.g. x-escape/x-dive

Upon receiving the request, the personal e-scape server checks its local launchers for any which can handle the Dive e-scape type. If more than one launcher could potentially deal with the e-scape then the user is offered a choice, and the process is repeated. In this example however, no launchers are able to start the e-scape. Therefore the personal server contacts the registry which sent the request and asks for any launchers that have been registered which can handle this type. Again, if more than one registered launcher could deal with the type the user would make a selection through an HTML form. Once a remote launcher has been identified, the Dive launcher, the personal server downloads the relevant Java classes to the local machine and fetches all of the e-scape information from the originating registry (the e-scape properties, location URL etc.). It then instantiates the launcher with this information and registers itself to receive the launcher callbacks relating to the status of the e-scape. In addition, the launcher is added to the personal server's list of currently executing launchers.

As this is the first time the Dive launcher has been instantiated locally on this machine, it doesn't know if or where Dive is installed. Therefore, the launcher returns an HTML page to the personal server requesting this information (Figure 6 above). Once the user has filled in the form the launcher records it locally for use the next time the user launches a Dive e-scape, and proceeds to start the e-scape. The final HTML reply by the launcher is actually an HTTP re-locate request which returns the user's browser to the initial information screen on the registry server with the "Launch" button.

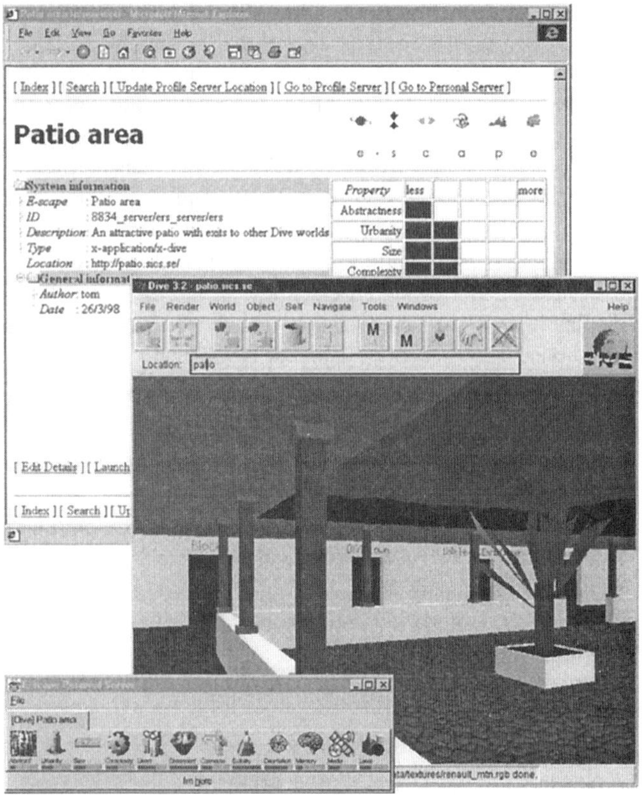

Figure 8 A Dive world with the properties display

The Dive launcher starts Dive by executing the Dive executable in a separate process with several different command line arguments which tell Dive where the world is (the URL), the name of the current user and so on. Once the process executes, the "started" callback is executed on the personal server that displays the e-scape properties (figure 8) and contacts the originating registry server to say the user is currently in the e-scape. The launcher enters a wait loop for the Dive process terminating. The Dive application will then run with the user inside the e-scape. When the user finally quits Dive, the launcher instance will signal the "stopped" callback on the personal server. The server then removes the properties for the e-scape from the display and contacts the e-scape registry to remove the user from that e-scape.

In this simplified example, the Dive launcher provides the most rudimentary e-scape aware wrapping of the application it starts (Dive). This type of "process" wrapping is available in all cases, whether the e-scape is a VR system or a text editor. However, the real Dive launcher connects to the Dive Client Interface and monitors the user's current Dive world. If the user exits the original e-scape to another Dive world, the Dive launcher can detect and signal this. If the new world is also a known e-scape on the registry server then the personal server can move the user appropriately and display a new set of property icons.

A BROADER CONSIDERATION OF E-SCAPES

Although this paper has considered e-scapes as 3D collaborative virtual environments, e-scapes are not limited to that domain. Any application that has some sense of user engagement and which externalises meta-information about itself can be considered as an e-scape. The ability to externalise properties of the application allows our architecture to integrate a diverse set of applications particularly those that exploit some form of spatial metaphor. These include the use of rooms by Teamrooms [22] and locales by wOrlds[13].

The architecture and protocol is intended to be sufficiently open to allow developers to integrate most CSCW applications. This builds upon the approach to session management suggested by Intermezzo [11] where properties of the application are separated from policy issues controlling sessions. In our case the ubiquitous nature of the HTTP protocol set allows us to move beyond the language specific approach suggested by Intermezzo. To further illustrate this point the following section considers how a session based CSCW application that does not adopt a spatial approach could be integrated in to the supporting session manager as an e-scape.

INTEGRATING EXISTING SYSTEMS

Many existing shared user interface systems, such as GroupKit [23], SOL [24], Rendezvous [17], and MMM [3] implement some form of session management environment to control invocation; provide a selection of possible applications to be launched; indicate the number of users; and so on. Often the underlying session management systems provide these services in a similar manner For example, MMM provides a 'Home Area', which is a control panel that links the user to the underlying system, which is external to any applications. This is similar to the *Access Point* of Rendezvous, the *Registrar* (and *Registrar Client*) of GroupKit, and the *User Panel* of SOL.

As in the case of virtual environments although systems exploit a similar model each one tends to adopt an individualistic approach. Most notably, each system uses component tools that are only supported by the registration service of that system. This makes using tools drawn from different systems in unison difficult. For example, to use the GroupKit shared drawing tool alongside the network management tool of SOL, requires each user to access both GroupKit's Registrar *and* SOL's User Panel to manage each of the two tools independently. If shared applications from a range of different CSCW systems are used simultaneously, the number of session management tools presented to a user can become distracting.

A much more preferable solution to this disparate arrangement is some form of unified registration service that can offer users a single interface. To illustrate the use of the e-scape architecture to realise this approach, consider the GroupKit architecture shown in Figure 9.

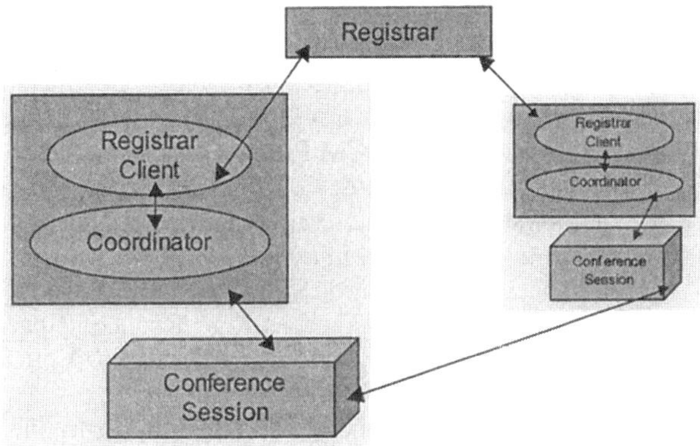

Figure 9 The GroupKit Architecture

The Registrar Client and Coordinator present the GroupKit session management user interface to the user. Upon start-up the Registrar Client is provided with the location of the Registrar itself. It is the Registrar Client/Coordinator process that enables users to view current conference sessions (e.g., a collaborative drawing tool) and their participants, or initiate new sessions of a tool. The Registrar is a common process that coordinates information held by registrar clients. Conference sessions communicate directly with each other, to maintain consistent application specific state. Hence, a normal situation is that a user's display will consist of a single Registrar-Client/Coordinator window and one or more Conference session windows. These are tied to the services provided by GroupKit and are not designed to be incorporated into other applications.

To promote easier integration with other environments we can consider GroupKit as one example of an e-scape. To do this we replace the Registrar and Coordinator service with the e-scape session architecture. In this case users would register and access the e-scape server through a web browser. All e-scape sessions will then be available to a user through a single interface.

A separate "x-escape/x-groupkit" type identifies GroupKit applications registered with the service. Launching a GroupKit application causes the user's personal server to execute the appropriate e-scape launcher. As with the Dive example above, the launcher updates the participant list for the new session by adding the new user to it. Other users wishing to join the same GroupKit application may locate and join it through the e-scape registry server. Here the active session is displayed, along with the current participants.

In essence, the use of the e-scape session architecture can provide collaborative applications with a unified session manager and interface. Moreover, the use of enhanced e-scape launchers to start and join application sessions enables extra meta-information to be gathered from each of these sessions. This information can be made available through the registry entry for that session. For example, information such as 'idle time' or the current type of tool being used (pen, eraser, rectangle etc.) for each user may be made public. In addition to allowing this information to be browsed, supplementary services can easily access and process this information through simple HTTP commands.

FUTURE WORK

The basic session architecture supports the migration of code to provide appropriate functionality required for launching different types of e-scape. This can be extended to promote the personal e-scape server as a framework for "plug-in services" to be downloaded and incorporated. Because these plug-ins are connected to the personal server they automatically gain access to e-scape session data. Such information can be exploited to enable cooperative services, the simplest of which would be chat facilities between the personal-servers.

Since each launcher makes any application e-scape aware, they can provide information concerning the implicit connections between e-scapes. For example, if a user moves through several Dive worlds, connected via Dive portals, the Dive launcher can record the paths and connections traversed by a user. This information can be used later to provide an overview of the connections between different e-scapes, or a history of a user's progress.

More generally, the session architecture is extendable to allow a more diverse set of usage information to be kept. The use of simple name-value pairs means that any application specific information can be made externally available and maintained between sessions. This allows us to support a range of different temporal operations. What these are and how they might be supported remains a matter of some further investigation based on the usage of the architecture.

CONCLUSION

In this paper we have introduced the notion of an "e-scape". An e-scape is any electronic world where sets of properties are made public that provide an indication of the nature of the environment. This publicity allows the development of applications and virtual environments that join these virtual environments together.

A session management system was presented that supports users accessing a range of different virtual environments or e-scapes. To promote scalability and accessibility the developed architecture is built upon the HTTP protocol. This allows us to realise a simple yet robust architecture that allows people to encode meta-information about environments - virtual or otherwise. This arrangement provides support for a heterogeneous set of connected environments through the notion of environment launchers.

The architecture makes a clear separation between the management of these environments and the users' connections with these environments, and the activities of users within them. Such activities and interactions of users are the responsibility of the environment itself. The architecture focuses on the issues of support and management needed to move these environments from isolated research prototypes to accessible everyday systems.

ACKNOWLEDGMENTS

This work was funded under Esprit Basic Research Grant 25377, "eSCAPE: electronic landSCAPEs".

REFERENCES

1. Alphaworlds, http://www.alphaworlds.com
2. Benford, S., Bowers, J., Fahlen, L., Mariani, J, Rodden. T, Supporting Cooperative Work in Virtual Environments. *The Computer Journal*, 1995. 38(1).
3. Bier, E., Freeman, S., MMM: A User Interface Architecture for shared editors on a single screen, *Symposium on UI software and Technology,* (Hilton Head, South Carolina, 1991), ACM Press, 79-86
4. Blaxxun, http://www.blacksun.com/
5. Bowers, J., Pycock, J., O'Brien, J., Talk and Embodiment in Collaborative Virtual Environments, in *Proc. CHI'96*, ACM Press
6. Brodbeck D., Chalmers M., Lunzer A., Cotture P.: Domesticating Bead: Adapting an Information Visualisation System to a Financial Institution. in *Proc. Information Visualization '97 (*Phoenix, AZ, October 20-21, 1997), 73-80.
7. Büsher, M., O'Brien, J., Hughes, J.: Interaction and Presence in Shared Electronic Environments: fieldwork at ZKM. In Escape Deliverable 1.1 (chapter 4), ISBN1-86220-052-1, Lancaster University, 1998, 93-111. Available from http://escape.lancs.ac.uk/
8. Carlsson, C., Hagsand, O. DIVE: A Multi User Virtual Reality System, in *Proc. IEEE VRAIS*, (September 1993), 394-400
9. Curtis, P., Dixon, M, MUDS grow up: Social Virtual Reality in the Real World, *in Proc. of IEEE Computer Conference*, (January 1994).
10. Dix, A., Challenges for Cooperative Work on the Web: An Analytical Approach, *CSCW: The Journal of Collaborative Computing*, 6, 2-3, 1997, 135-156.
11. Edwards, K. Session Management for Collaborative Applications, in *Proc. CSCW'94* (Chapel Hill, North Carolina, October 22-26, 1994). ACM press. 323-330
12. Elvins, T., Nadeau, D., Schul, R., Kirsh, D. Worldlets: 3D Thumbnails for 3D Browsing, to appear in *Proc. CHI'98* (Los Angeles, CA, April 18-23, 1998), ACM Press.
13. Fitzpatrick, G., et al, Physical Spaces, Virtual Places and Social Worlds: A study of work in the virtual, in *Proc. CSCW'96* (Boston, MA, Nov.16-20, 1996), ACM Press. 334-343.
14. Gaver W., The Affordances of Media Spaces for Collaboration, in *Proc. CSCW'92* (Toronto, Canada, Oct.31-Nov.4, 1992), ACM Press. 17-24.
15. Greenhalgh, C., Benford, S. MASSIVE: A Virtual Reality System for Tele-conferencing, to appear in *ACM Trans. on Computer Human Interfaces*
16. Henderson, A.J., and Card, S.A., Rooms: The Use of Multiple Virtual Workspaces to Reduce Space Contention, *ACM Transactions on Graphics*, Vol. 5, No. 3, (July 1985), ACM Press.
17. Hill, R., Brink, T., Rohall S., Patterson, J., Wilner, W., The Rendezvous architecture and language for constructing multiuser applications, *ACM Trans. on Computer-human Interaction,* Vol. 1 No. 2, (June 1994), ACM Press, 83-125
18. Ishii, H., Ullmer, B., "Tangible Bits: Towards Seamless Interfaces between People, Bits and Atoms," in *Proc. CHI '97*, ACM press, 234-241
19. Living Worlds, http://www.livingworlds.com
20. Patterson, J.F et al., Notification Servers for Synchronous Groupware, in *Proc. CSCW'96* (Boston, MA, Nov.16-20, 1996), ACM Press. 122-129
21. Root, R.W., Design of a Multi-Media Vehicle for Social Browsing, in *Proc. CSCW'88* (Portland, Oregon, September 26-28, 1988), ACM Press. 25-38
22. Roseman, M., Greenberg, S, TeamRooms: Network Places for Collaboration, in *Proc. CSCW'96* (Boston, MA, Nov.16-20, 1996), ACM Press. 325-333
23. Roseman, M., Greenberg, S., GroupKit. A groupware Toolkit for building Real-Time Conference Applications, in *Proc. CSCW'92* (Toronto, Canada, 1992), ACM Press, 43-50
24. Smith G., Rodden, T. SOL: a toolkit for cooperative interfaces, *International Journal of Human Computer Studies (IJHCS).* No 42. 1995. Academic Press Limited. 207-234
25. The Contact Consortium, http://www.ccon.org/
26. The Palace, http://www.thepalace.com
27. Trevor, J., Büsher, M., O'Brien, J., Hughes, J., Rodden, T., Mariani, J.: Developing a framework for e-scapes. In Escape Deliverable 1.1 (chapter 5), ISBN1-86220-052-1, Lancaster University, 1998, 113-136. Available from http://escape.lancs.ac.uk/
28. VRML97, International Standard ISO/IEC 14772-1:1997, "the Virtual Reality Modeling Language "

Ubiquitous Collaboration via Surface Representations

Dan R. Olsen Jr., Scott E. Hudson, Matt Phelps, Jeremy Heiner, Thom Verratti
Human Computer Interaction Institute
Carnegie Mellon University
Pittsburgh, PA 15213
{dolsen, hudson}@cs.cmu.edu

ABSTRACT

Essential prerequisites to asynchronous work with shared artifacts include things such as an ability to effectively communicate information, an ability to understand the actions of collaborators, and an ability to integrate work from others. Systems designed to support ubiquitous collaboration – collaboration that can scale to communities the size of the Internet – face a number of important challenges in providing these prerequisites. For example, when the set of potential collaborators becomes large, and collaborative media becomes richer, simple interoperability of application programs quickly becomes a difficult issue. Further, various market pressures, along with the rapid growth of a diverse Internet, will, for the most part, make these problems worse rather than better.

This paper considers a new strategy for asynchronous collaboration that is designed to support large-scale, ubiquitous, collaboration through shared artifacts. This strategy is based on *human consumable surface representations* – representations of information that are designed to be directly understood by people. Printing on paper is an important example of such a representation. In the work presented here, we concentrate on 2D images or pictures (what will be called *pictorial surfaces*, or simply *surfaces*) as one such representation. A prototype system that supports surface-based collaboration will be described. This system supports a collaborative process inspired by paper-based collaborations, and is designed to demonstrate concepts of surface representations as a first step towards ubiquitous collaboration.

Keywords: Asynchronous collaboration, ubiquitous collaboration, shared artifacts, pictorial surfaces.

INTRODUCTION

In the developed world we rarely question our ability to reach someone on the telephone, and knowing the phone number we never question whether their phone equipment is compatible with ours. FAX machines are not as ubiquitous as telephones but offer similar advantages. Knowing a FAX number we are almost completely assured that the documents can be received. One rarely asks if the FAX machines are compatible. Email has also reached nearly this stature (so long as we stick to simple text-only messages). The most ubiquitous collaborative medium of all is paper. Assuming a shared language, information placed on paper will communicate with the people that receive the paper. The technology itself doesn't fail – pencils and pens are always compatible with the paper medium.

Unfortunately, these ubiquitous characteristics are generally not found in computer-based collaborative tools. With the exception of text-based email and web documents (so long as the latest extensions are avoided), most digital media suffers from a high rate of communications failure. Even programs such as Microsoft Word, with its current relatively pervasive adoption, fail regularly in their ability to communicate between collaborators. The versions are incompatible, the source and destination machines are incompatible or some configuration is incompatible.

The traditional approach to providing ubiquity has been to attempt to create standards and have them be widely adopted. However, there are important market and other pressures, which makes standardization very difficult, and which drive systems towards incompatibility and divergence. In particular, in most computer-based systems, there is a tension between standardization and the adoption of new features – standardization normally limits the ability to add new features. Because feature sets differentiate products, this generally runs counter to the business interests of those who produce the systems. As a result, standards are inherently difficult to create, and even harder to hold fixed over time.

The successful examples of the telephone, FAX, and, to a lesser extent, text-only email, share a common feature. They are each centered around an end representation of information which is designed to be directly or nearly directly consumed by a person (in these cases, audio, 2D images or pictures, and simple text, respectively). Since human perceptual capabilities are not rapidly changing, the use of a human consumable end representations dramatically reduces the pressure for new features, and allows other market forces to push towards convergence and compatibility.

In this paper we propose an alternative approach to asynchronous collaboration based on human consumable surface representations, in particular 2D pictorial surfaces.

We believe that this general approach offers the chance to create systems capable of supporting truly large-scale ubiquitous collaboration. However, the use of surface based collaboration also presents some new challenges. To illustrate several of the specific concepts needed to overcome these challenges, a prototype system employing some of these concepts is also discussed.

Model-based collaboration

Most systems proposed for supporting asynchronous collaboration work on the basis of transmitting or sharing objects, often objects directly from underlying data models. This brings with it the assumption that all collaborators use applications that are compatible with the particulars of those objects. In fact most systems assume that all collaborators will use compatible versions of the same collaborative application (in the synchronous realm see for example [1,2,3]). Within the application, changes are managed so as to prevent divergence among multiple collaborators [4] or are merged later in a reconciliation phase that ranges from fully automatic [5] through manual user-based processes [4] (a good discussion of this part of the design space can be found in [6]). This approach is fundamentally fragile in at least three ways.

The first, and most basic problem, is one of compatibility. Suppose a group of N people decide that they will collaborate regularly using application A. Every time application A upgrades to a new version all members of the group must upgrade together or the collaborative fabric is damaged (and of course software developers *must* upgrade their software to remain profitable). When N grows to the size of a Fortune 500 company this is very problematic and requires corporate investment and coercion to maintain compatibility. If N grows beyond the bounds of a single organization, managing the compatibility problem becomes essentially impossible.

A second problem with model-based collaboration is out-of-band communications. Not all collaborative messages involve actual changes to application data. Messages of the form "awkward wording", "inconsistent with spec" and "make sure Mark understands" frequently occur. Each of these statements is essentially meaningless away from the specific information artifact to which they refer, but can rarely be encoded in the application model. They are statements about the collaboration itself and thus outside of the information encoded by the application. A collaborative medium first and foremost must communicate whatever the participants want to communicate whether the application developers thought of it or not. Model-based approaches are weak in this regard.

Finally, the vast majority of applications do not support representations of change in their models. In an asynchronous setting it is important to be able to understand the actions of others, but without an explicit representation of changes, this is very difficult to directly support.

Although some of the problems of model-based collaboration could be overcome over time, we feel that some of them – particularly relating to compatibility – are intrinsic, and will be very difficult to ever fully overcome because of basic market forces. This makes the prospects for truly large scale and ubiquitous collaboration dim.

To address this problem, the work presented here will consider changing the basis of collaboration from a model-based one, to a surface-based one. This brings with it a number of new research challenges, some of which have yet to be addressed. However, despite these new challenges, we believe that surface-based collaboration offers a chance for achieving truly ubiquitous collaboration that will be difficult or impossible to achieve with conventional model-based approaches.

The next section will consider a collaborative process that can be used as the basis for our tools. The use of paper, then conventional model-based media, and finally surface representations for this process will then be considered. Next, specific technological support for the surface collaboration process will be discussed along with change tracking and visualization mechanisms. Finally a summary and discussion of future work will be provided.

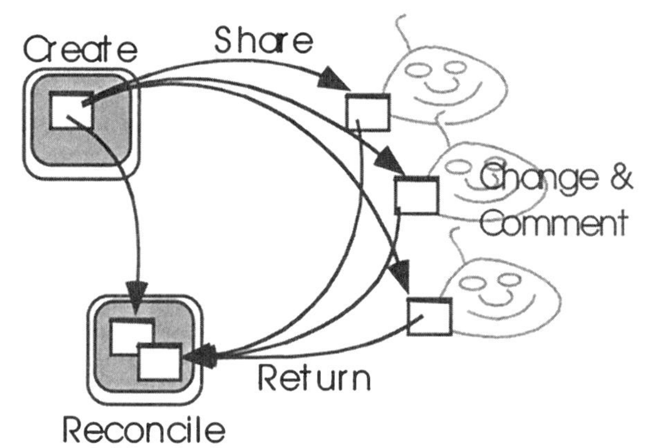

Figure 1 - A collaborative process

A COLLABORATIVE PROCESS

Figure 1 illustrates a simple and common collaborative process that we will use as a guide for the specific tools described in this paper. In this process, someone first produces an information artifact (like this paper for example). The artifact is then shared with the other collaborators (e.g., co-authors) who change and annotate the artifact using some set of collaborative tools. These changes and notes are then gathered together by one of the collaborators and the changes, notes and comments are reconciled into a new version of the artifact. This process may be repeated several times. A variant of this process is where the problem is subdivided into pieces with different participants taking responsibility for a piece. The process on each piece is then similar to that described with an added step at the end of assembling the whole and working through several cycles on the full artifact.

This process of artifact change and reconcile is not the only way in which asynchronous collaborative work is done, and is certainly not the only approach to digital collaboration. This process, however, is a very common and powerful one, and the one on which our tools are based.

Fragile points

This process imposes a number of requirements. If any of them are not met then the process tends to break down. First, the artifact must be communicated in a form that all collaborators can understand and manipulate. Secondly, all collaborators must possess technology that is compatible with the communication medium and is readily usable for making changes and comments on the artifact. The return medium must be able to communicate both changes and out of band meta-comments. Lastly, there must be sufficient information at the reconciliation step to indicate what has changed and by whom.

In addition to these technological requirements there are user requirements. Consider for a moment the case where one has an infinite support budget and a perfect operating system such that all possible versions of all possible applications were available instantly on a personal workstation. In such a world collaborative communication using the files of any application would always work technologically. However, this environment would still tend to fail collaboratively, because users could be forced to learn a new interface with each new type of message. The user learning burden would be tremendous. This is equivalent to saying "to receive a FAX from someone, you must know how to operate the sending FAX machine". Ubiquitous collaboration cannot stand on an architecture that requires users to learn a different conversational interface for every new type of message. The collaboration interface must be application independent, and must be under the control of message recipients not message senders.

PAPER-BASED STRATEGY

We can first look at the most ubiquitous technology for implementing our collaborative process – printing on paper. A recent study of work at the International Monetary Fund [7] showed that when people work alone they regularly use personal computers to create documents. However, when two or more people are involved in the work, paper is the dominant collaborative medium and computing almost completely disappears. There are non-technical reasons for this but even on technical grounds this is a powerful indictment of digital system support for collaborative work.

Paper offers the ubiquity that is so important in collaboration. As a means for communicating among people, paper always succeeds when all parties are literate and speak the same language. Any information artifact can be printed onto paper and transmitted. Anyone with a pencil or pen can make changes and annotations of any kind. The changes clearly stand out from the original information. Finally, the technology and user knowledge required to collaborate with paper is independent of any application or application domain.

There are, however, fundamental deficiencies with paper as a collaborative medium. If the artifact is large, the possibility of loosing changes becomes great. The ability for collaborators to get a clear overview of the artifact and of any changes is severely hampered. Big changes, such as the insertion of more material than can be scratched in the margins, are a problem. Reconciling the changes created by multiple collaborators is very difficult. The primary problem lies in the static nature of paper. As changes are made to an artifact, they cannot be directly merged with what has already been done. All of these deficiencies are overcome with digital media but the fragility issues must be dealt with first.

MODEL-BASED DIGITAL COLLABORATION

An alternative to the use of paper is to use the file formats of computer applications – the most common and direct form of model-based collaboration. Use of the applications themselves is very attractive because each application is tuned to providing flexible and powerful support for the needs of the particular artifact in question. This directly addresses most of the deficiencies of paper.

The model-based approach, however, fails in most of the areas where paper has its strengths. The model-based approach requires that all participants use compatible software. As has already been discussed, this compatibility requirement will not scale to Internet sized collaboration spaces. The lack of representations of what has changed also hinders collaboration. Without such representations, the application model cannot serve well in the RETURN step of Figure 1. Most applications also lack the means of finding and presenting changes in a manner that facilitates the RECONCILE step. In addition, the application model only rarely supports the meta-comments that are required for a collaborative conversation. Finally, the application specific approach also forces a learning burden on collaborators, which is not appropriate.

DIGITAL SURFACES

Our approach to collaboration based on human consumable surfaces is designed to achieve a high level of ubiquity, as found in media such as paper, while still offering the advantages of computer media.

We arrived at the notion of surface collaboration, by examining collaborative media that have achieved ubiquity. For example, the value of paper as a collaborative technology lies primary in the fact that almost any information can be encoded as a 2D picture. Such pictures provide visual input to the highest bandwidth and most precise human sensory system. The appropriate digital surface is an encoding for 2D pictures. Note that FAX succeeds because it draws directly on the value of 2D images as a surface representation. Similarly, telephony, while actually implemented with a very complex digital system, can achieve ubiquity because at its end points it uses the well-defined human consumable representation of audio. Further ubiquity can be maintained in the long term because there are few forces pushing to "enhance" this media in qualitative ways.

Email and the web have also achieved some level of ubiquity. However in these cases, where the media diverges from simple (near-)surface representations we can already see ubiquity being eroded. For example, email really only works for ubiquitous communication when messages are limited to ISO-Latin text. As soon as richer forms are included the probability of successful communications drops precipitously. Similarly, the ubiquity of the web is being challenged as new and competing feature sets, and new media are being introduced. Strenuous formal and informal standardization efforts may prevail to retain ubiquity in the web, but it will continue to be a struggle.

The "consumption by humans" requirement for surface collaboration is key. It flows directly from the collaborative need to communicate among people. Collaboration is not a system to system communication problem; it is a human to human communication problem. At some level, all collaborative systems must have surface representations. Further, because they are consumed by people with very similar (and unchanging) basic perceptual properties, they are intrinsically much more stable. The market and usage forces for surface representations tend to converge to a very small number of forms rather than diverge.

For example, after all these years, Postscript is still at version 2. The primary reason for such stability is the constancy of the human sensory and language systems. It is, for example, difficult to find a 2D image encoding that cannot be rendered in Postscript. Since Postscript can render nearly any image discernable to human beings there is little market advantage in proposing an alternative. A similar argument can be made about audio formats. Once a certain threshold in sampling rate and dynamic range is reached, the differences in audio encodings become irrelevant to human users.

The stability of digital surfaces and their application independence supports the development of consistent collaborative tools based on the surface representation. In this work we have focused on 2D pictures as our surface representation. We chose pictures because they subsume the information presentations of graphical user interfaces and because text-only and audio surface collaborations are already well served. 2D pictures can encode the preponderance of human knowledge and they subsume text as a representation of information. Pictures therefore form a very powerful collaborative medium. In this research we are looking at picture representations and tools that facilitate the collaboration process without forfeiting all of the ubiquity properties that pictures inherit from paper.

SYSTEMS FOR PICTURE-BASED COLLABORATION

Our work on picture-based collaboration is being done as part of the ICIE (Information Collaboration Interaction Environment) project. The overall goals of this project are to develop infrastructure, both interactive and architectural, for interfaces that support the work of multiple active agents. Such agents are either human or software but are all working in the same problem space. A fundamental approach in this work is to exploit the information inherent in the displayed images of graphical applications. In earlier work we have developed a general architecture for applications to provide semantic information as part of the rendering process. Using this information we have developed a general multi-agent application independent highlighting mechanism [8] which is used in this paper to point out where changes have occurred.

As background, in ICIE, semantic information is organized in trees where each branch of the tree is labeled with an attribute identifier and an object type. This information, combined with the actual graphics being rendered, forms the foundation for our tools that work with pictorial surface information. While this particular structure is unique to the ICIE system it is generic in nature, and as we will see provides a mechanism for representing surfaces which are derived from other structures.

Of particular importance to the work here is the concept of a *reference*. In ICIE systems, a basic reference is simply a list of attribute identifiers that defines a path from the root of the display down to the object being referenced. A more general case is the union of such paths which allows a reference to identify a set of objects. The ICIE highlight mechanism takes a reference and an ICIE application and will highlight those objects on the screen that are designated by the reference.

In ICIE, a pictorial surface is represented as a tree of graphical objects. There are objects for all of the drawing primitives found in the Java 1.1 (AWT) drawing model (We are currently developing surfaces based on the much richer Java 1.2 drawing model (*Java2D*) that will provide greater compatibility with Postscript). The branches of this tree are labeled with the semantic attribute and type information with the leaves being objects for drawing primitives. For surfaces that are imported from outside of ICIE, the tree is in the worst case reduced to a flat list of primitive graphical objects.

THE ICIE COLLABORATIVE PROCESS

In ICIE collaborative information artifacts are represented as ICIE pictorial surfaces. The collaborative process starts with some application in which someone creates an information artifact. The way in which such applications integrate with our collaboration architecture depends on whether the application was constructed for the ICIE environment or is an existing application outside the environment. All existing applications have the ability to print and in most systems they can print to a Postscript file. We provide a Postscript to surface translator which can make an ICIE pictorial surface via the system print mechanism.

Note that we have chosen Postscript as one of our primary surface representation because it is rich, fairly ubiquitous, application independent, and representative of computer-based drawing capabilities. It may eventually be possible to work with even lower-level representations (such as images). However, at this stage of our work, that has not been necessary, nor would it be particularly fruitful.

Surfaces created via the print stream do not have any embedded structure to provide identifier or type information. As will be shown later, this lack of embedded structure makes the collaboration tools harder to implement. Our long-term research plans include automatic discovery of semantic structure by analyzing the geometry. This will make the ICIE collaborative architecture more robust.

Capturing ICIE surfaces

If an application has been implemented for ICIE then the pictorial surface can be captured directly from the application. ICIE systems are based on the subArctic user interface toolkit [9]. In subArctic, like nearly all user interface toolkits, graphical applications must be able to respond to requests to redraw any part of the display. Drawing is performed by a recursive traversal of an internal tree that represents the interface, passing in an object that represents access to drawing operations on the screen. When we wish to capture a surface we create a new subclass of this drawing object which, instead of drawing on the screen, captures the drawing methods and writes them out as a surface file. In this way the application need not know about the collaborative architecture (although they may provide additional assistance if they do).

Capturing all of the drawing calls gives us unstructured surfaces of essentially the same type as we get via Postscript. However, to provide enhanced editing, it is helpful to have small amounts of the additional semantic information about what objects and types of objects are being drawn. As discussed elsewhere [8] we have augmented the drawing interface with three additional methods:

```
GroupStart(String Name, String Type)
GroupStart(int Index, String Type)
GroupEnd()
```

The GroupStart methods identify a name or index and a type for an object to be drawn. This information is application dependent and opaque to the ICIE system. GroupEnd is called when the drawing of an object is complete. The collaborative tools do not attempt to understand the names, types or indices. They only use the information to understand the hierarchic structure of the drawing. In addition, the collaborative tools use the uniqueness of the names and indices as the basis for naming objects within a reference.

We have chosen this particular augmentation of the drawing process because it is very simple and because we believe that similar information can be extracted from raw flat surfaces (although we are still working on the algorithms supporting that effort). In particular, adding these calls to the drawing methods of an application is very straightforward. There is no restructuring of the code required and the information is taken directly from whatever application model is being used without change. These calls are used to impose a tree structure on the drawing primitives written out to the surface.

The structure information embedded in the surface forms the basis for the references that ICIE uses to refer to objects displayed on the screen. This information is also used in the *deltas* that ICIE generates which describe changes to the surface. By using the application's names and indices, the collaboration tools can work with ICIE applications to highlight parts of the original application that have been changed or annotated by collaborators.

Sharing

Sharing with collaborators is implemented in terms of pictorial surface files either captured from the drawing of an ICIE application or from the print stream. These files can be distributed to collaborators in a variety of ways including email attachments, shared disk space or the web. There are already proposals for notification of sharing and changes developed by others [10]. We assume that such work can be applied to surface files as easily as any other data.

Collaborative editor

When a collaborator receives a shared surface they must be able to view and edit the surface. This is done via a collaborative editor. The collaborative editor can edit any drawing. Our current implementation functions as a standard drawing editor which understands the grouping structure of the surface.

If the sharing is performed via any pictorial representation and there are generally available editors for that representation, then the ubiquity goals that we set for collaborative tools have been achieved. For example an application could print to Postscript and collaborators could then use Freehand or some other Postscript editor as their collaborative editor. The return information could then be a modified Postscript file. PDF could serve a similar purpose. Other than enforcing Postscript or PDF as the communications medium there is no restriction on the applications that can be used or the editors that each collaborator can use. Because the medium is pictures, the collaborators are free to make any necessary changes and to make any meta-comments. The ubiquity and flexibility goals have been achieved. The goal of independent tool choice for each collaborator has also been achieved.

There are two important problems, however, with this simplistic approach to collaborative surfaces. The first is a painful editing model based purely on drawings, and the second is no support for the reconciliation step. At present we provide robust implementation solutions for the second of these problems, but only pointers to work to address the first. A challenge for the full success of the surface-based collaboration paradigm will be the eventual development of complete solutions for both these problems.

Editing in a drawing program

The editing provided by drawing tools is generally too cumbersome for most collaborative situations. Consider for example editing this paper where each line or each word is a separate text primitive. In the case of each line, word wrapping is ineffective as is flowing text up and down the page. If the primitives are words then simple editing of a line is painful as other words on the line must be manually moved to make room for new additions or for deletions.

Name	Room	Phone
Dan	1223	x2323
Fred	3233	x7872
Lloyd	1212	x2321

Figure 2 - Picture of a table

A second example is the picture of a table shown in Figure 2. If one was to edit this information inside of an address book application, adding an additional row after Fred would cause the outside box to resize and would move Lloyd down by the height of 1 row. In addition, a new line between the added entry and Lloyd would be drawn. Any text entered in the new row would align correctly and have the correct font. All this would be handled automatically by the application because the application model only stores the Name, Room and Phone. The other graphical information is a product of the rendering process. If this same information is edited in a drawing editor, the movement of Lloyd's row, the resizing of the border, the drawing of the new line and the alignment and font of any text must be done by hand by the user. This is an unpleasant experience.

The problem is that when the application model is rendered as graphical primitives a great deal of the application structure is lost. The fundamental assumption of most drawing tools is that each primitive is independent of all others. The only exceptions to this are tools with explicitly created constraints or temporary alignment and grouping behaviors. In the word processing and table examples the individual pieces are not independent. All words on a line share the same baseline. There is a well-defined spacing relationship between lines of text. By enforcing such relationships automatically the word processor becomes a powerful tool for editing text. Similarly there is great structure in the table which is automatically maintained by the application.

Because applications know the structure of the information that they are visually presenting, they provide the user with a great deal of support in manipulating that information. A collaborative editor that does not know such structure cannot provide an equivalently facile editor for the information. Encoding such information in the collaborative editor, however, would violate our ubiquity and universal compatibility goals.

Note however, that the desired structure information is not missing from the drawings, it is simply not directly encoded. Almost any reader of this paragraph immediately understands that all words are on the same baseline, lines are right and left justified and are evenly spaced. For a human, such structure is clearly encoded in the picture itself. Similarly, humans can pick up on the relationships encoded in the table. Recognizing that such structure is implicit in the surface, it is therefore possible to rediscover that structure and exploit it in a collaborative editor.

The embedded structure information for ICIE applications tells us which graphical primitives and sub-objects are grouped together. This information also tells us which groups are of the same type and therefore should have similar structure. This sharply reduces the complexity of the structure discovery problem. This information does not tell us what the geometric relationships should be between the graphical primitives. It also does not tell us which of the primitives are static decorations (lines between table rows) and which contain substantive information (the actual room numbers).

Fortunately, our prior work on Inductive Groups [11] provides an initial framework for discovering and exploit such regular relationships among geometric primitives. While Inductive Groups and the collaborative editor prototype have not yet been integrated into an implementation, Inductive Groups do provide a solid algorithmic basis for solving the problem, and we believe that they provide a solid foundation for finding the structure we need to provide usable editors. Rather than fully addressing this first issue at this stage of our work, we have chosen instead to work on the less well understood problem of support for reconciliation.

Supporting reconciliation

When a collaborator makes changes to a surface representation, the reconciliation phase must be able to understand what those changes were. The reconciliation step is all about understanding change and presenting it to the user. A simple drawing editor, such as Freehand, can only output a new pictorial surface. It is then up to the person doing reconciliation to search through the new surface, compare it to the application's data and find the changes by hand. An alternative is to compare the initial surface to each changed surface and compute a difference list (or simply *diff*). This is a common technique in textual surface tools. Such text differencing forms the basis of the Prep tool [12] and is found in Microsoft Word's Revisions... feature. An acceptable diff algorithm for 2D pictures, however, has not yet been developed. Pixel by pixel compares are possible but not acceptable solutions. If a paragraph of text shifts down by 1, there will be lots of pixel differences generated down the page but the actual change is quite localized.

Rather than tackle the picture differencing problem directly (which will be part of future work), we have modified our collaborative editor so that it tracks the changes that are made and reports them as *deltas*. These deltas are essentially a "patch" that encodes the necessary information to transform one data structure into another. We use them to represent the changes from the original surface into the new surface created by the collaborator's edits. By having the collaborative editor generate descriptions of changes, the reconciliation phase is greatly simplified. Because the collaborative editor is still fundamentally a picture editor there is little difference between edits that change the underlying information and edits that place meta-comments on the information.

Information return

As with the sharing process we have ignored the actual transmission and notification processes as topics well explored by others. The key information passed back from the collaborative editors, however, is not a surface but the delta or change to the surface. It is assumed that all collaborators, including the users that created the original information, possess a copy of the original surface. What everyone needs is information about everyone else's changes. These changes are encoded in the deltas.

Reconciliation

The reconciliation phase takes the deltas generated by the collaborators and compares them with the original surface or the original application. What would be of great value is if the surface deltas could be automatically transformed into changes to the original application. Take for example the changes to the table Figure 2 that are shown in Figure 3. Both of the changes consist of simple text edits which modify the numbers. One can conceive of a tool that could translate these edits into simulated mouse-clicks and key events that would drive the application to make the desired changes. There are several problems with this auto-reconcile approach.

Name	Room	Phone
Dan	1263	x2323
Fred	3233	x7872
Lloyd	1212	x2322

Figure 3 - Changes to a table

The first problem is the creation of robust algorithms that can transform surface deltas into input events that will work on any application. In the case of text editing this is possible because the editing events are fairly standard. For other surface changes the transformation is not generally as straightforward. A second problem is that of the interplay among multiple changes. When information is inserted or deleted, mimicking the layout changes so that input events for subsequent changes occur in the right place is problematic. A third problem is inherent in the concept of surface collaboration. The collaboration editors are purposely general purpose without application knowledge encoded in them. Collaborators are explicitly freed from learning the workings of the original application. This is a key strength of surface collaboration. The problem is that collaborators who do not know the original application can make changes that are inconsistent with the functioning of that application. If such surface changes are automatically translated, the translations will often be wrong.

The last problem is that surface deltas frequently contain not only underlying changes but meta-comments about the process. These, of course, should not be automatically translated into changes in the application. They were intended for other humans, not for the application. Suppose that the original application was an advertising layout tool. It would be impossible for any algorithm to discern between changes to the advertising copy and comments to the creators. The final problem is that there may be conflicts among the collaborators as to what changes should be made. Some such conflicts can be automatically resolved but others require human intervention. These issues have been explored in [13].

Rather than struggle with the problems of automatic update and conflict resolution, our reconciliation tools focus on highlighting the changes and conflict among changes in a way that simplifies reconciliation by a human being. We believe that ultimately it is more effective to provide automatic aids to human reconciliation than to seek application independent auto-reconciliation algorithms.

Summary of ICIE's collaborative process

To perform a collaboration, information is created using any application. The application data is transformed into a pictorial surface either via the print stream or directly via display capture in ICIE. The surface is transmitted to collaborators over the Internet. The collaborators may use any collaborative editor of their choice provided the tool can accept pictorial surfaces as input and generate surface deltas as output. The creation of sophisticated intelligent collaborative editors is left as an open problem. The deltas are transmitted to the reconciliation phase where the changes and their conflicts are highlighted for a user to resolve them.

DELTAS

The algorithmic heart of ICIE's collaborative architecture is the delta representation. Deltas were developed as a general representation of editing changes on any data structure that can be represented as a labeled tree. The change representation is designed to be application independent and to support reasoning about changes.

The delta data model

The fundamental assumptions are that the entire data model is a tree rooted at some node, and from any node there are zero or more branches to value or to other nodes. Each branch represents an attribute of the node and is either labeled with a name or a zero-relative integer index. The named attributes are assumed to have no particular order nor is it assumed that there is any uniformity or constraint upon which named attributes are attached to a given node. The actual underlying data may have such constraints (i.e. students have only name, id-number, and age attributes) but the delta system ignores such application specific requirements. The indexed attributes always start with zero and are assumed to be consecutive. The model here is of a zero-relative, variable length, one-dimensional array. Such a tree can be constructed directly when the GroupStart / GroupEnd mechanism described above is used, or could be extracted from a flat structure.

Assuming this labeled tree as the underlying data model, any object or value in the tree can be uniquely identified by a sequence of names or indices that specifies a path from the root to the desired object or value. This is exactly the same as the referencing model discussed earlier. This is exactly the kind of model that is created by the GroupStart and GroupEnd calls in ICIE's rendering architecture. Based on the indices of the primitive drawing objects and the labels supplied by the GroupStart calls, any object in the surface can be named by a path from the root of the surface.

If we assume that the table represented in Figure 2 consists of records numbered 0 through 2 and fields with their appropriate names, the path to the first change in 3 would be [0 Room]. There is a surface question as to how each field is drawn. If each field of a record is drawn by first drawing the text and then drawing the vertical bar to the right of the field, then each field contains two primitives of which the first is the text string. The path to the actual text strings being changed in Figure 3 are respectively [0 Room 0] and [2 Phone 0].

Basic edits

A basic delta consists of a path to an object or value to be changed, terminated by one of the three basic edits. The basic edits are Set, Insert and Delete. Using these three operations, any tree can be modified into any other tree and therefore any pictorial surface into any other surface.

Set

The set operation simply specifies that the referenced object should be changed to a new value. The set operation can be used to create new attributes simply by naming an attribute that did not previously exist and setting it to a value. The new value can be any new object. The Set operation also can encode the old value before the Set is applied. This allows the Reverse of the Set or an Undo to be computed from the Set operation.

As an example, the first change in Figure 3 can be encoded as

[0 Room 0 (set old: "1223" new: "1263")].

The second change is encoded as

[2 Phone 0 (set old: "x2321" new: "x2322")].

Insert

The purpose of the Insert is to add new elements into a sequence of indexed elements. This is exactly the kind of edits that occur in lists and lines of text. An Insert specifies a path to some indexed attribute and then specifies one or more new values to be inserted at that index. All existing attributes with an equal or higher index have their indices increased to make room for the inserted attributes. Insert is used to add rows to tables like Figure 2 or to add new graphics primitives to a pictorial surface.

Delete

The Delete specifies a number of attributes to be removed starting at some index. The result is to decrease the indices of attributes with higher numbers than those removed. A Delete can also carry with it the old values of the attributes that were deleted. This is necessary to support the Reverse operator described below.

Basic operators

Our deltas so far only specify simple atomic changes. There are several operations defined on deltas. The ones of interest in this paper are Concatenate, Reverse, Touched and UpdateRef.

Concatenate

All deltas can be combined together using the Concatenate operator. A key issue in Concatenate is that Inserts and Deletes change indices as part of their functions. The expression (A Concatenate B) assumes that delta B was created after delta A and therefore all indices in B are relative to the state of the model after A has been applied. The role of Concatenate is to work all of this out so that users of deltas need not worry about it.

Reverse

The Reverse operator will transform a delta into its inverse. If the delta D will convert X into Y then D.Reverse() will convert Y into X. Reverse can be used to compute Undo operations as well as other functions that require reasoning backwards through a change history.

Touched

The Touched operator computes a reference to all objects that are changed by a delta. If the delta D converts X into Y then D.Touched() will compute a reference to all nodes and values in X that are modified by D. The Touched operator is very important in our reconciliation tools.

UpdateRef

The UpdateRef operator will take a reference into an object that existed before a delta is applied and compute a new reference to the appropriate nodes after the delta is applied. Because deltas change indices and remove nodes the UpdateRef operator is important in working out what has happened to objects after some delta has been applied.

RECONCILIATION

The reconciliation tool is key to our architecture. The goals of the tool are to assist a user in integrating the comments and changes made by collaborators with the information in the original application. The basic tasks for such a user are to 1) find all of the changes and comments, 2) compare the changes to the previous state, 3) make judgements about what changes should actually be done, and 4) make the selected changes. To facilitate these tasks the ICIE reconciliation tool uses a side-by-side display showing what has been changed and where the changes have occurred. This layout is shown in Figure 4. This screen shot is taken from a comparison of a calendar application with a surface of the calendar that has been modified by a collaborator.

On the left hand side we see the original calendar with two appointments highlighted, the first on Tuesday Jan, 20 and the second on Thursday Jan, 29. On the right hand side is the new surface that has been edited by a collaborator. Only the Tuesday, Jan 20 appointment is highlighted where the label for the appointment has been changed. The Jan 29 appointment is missing. The collaborator has moved the appointment to another day in the following month.

Both sides of the reconciliation look very gray and have little visual contrast. This is due to ICIE's highlighting architecture. ICIE has the ability to highlight any visible object that is identified by a reference, regardless of its appearance or the background it appears over. This works by blending non-highlighted objects with gray to reduce their contrast and then bordering highlighted objects with colored regions to focus visual attention. For more details on how ICIE can highlight any application see [8]. For our purposes we only need to know that ICIE can take a reference, produce a highlight for that reference in any ICIE application and can compute a rectilinear region occupied by that reference.

Given a delta D that the user is trying to understand we can compute various references that will draw the user's attention to relevant information. The references to be highlighted in the original (left side) surface computed as D.Touched(). To compute the references for changes in the new version's (right side) we compute D.Reverse().Touched(). Using these two references, ICIE produces the appropriate highlights.

The change to Jan, 20 is readily located and understood. The Jan, 29 change is a problem because the change is not visible in the current view. Changes which involve large movements of information (out of the current view) are difficult for user's to locate and understand. ICIE provides two mechanisms for understanding such changes. They are awareness widgets and reference following.

There are currently two types of awareness widgets in ICIE, horizontal and vertical *awareness bars*, and a *radar view* that presents the full surface. Each is a projection of the referenced regions from the full surface (including off-screen portions) onto a small indicator area. Clicking on any of the awareness widgets will immediately scroll the surface to display the selected area.

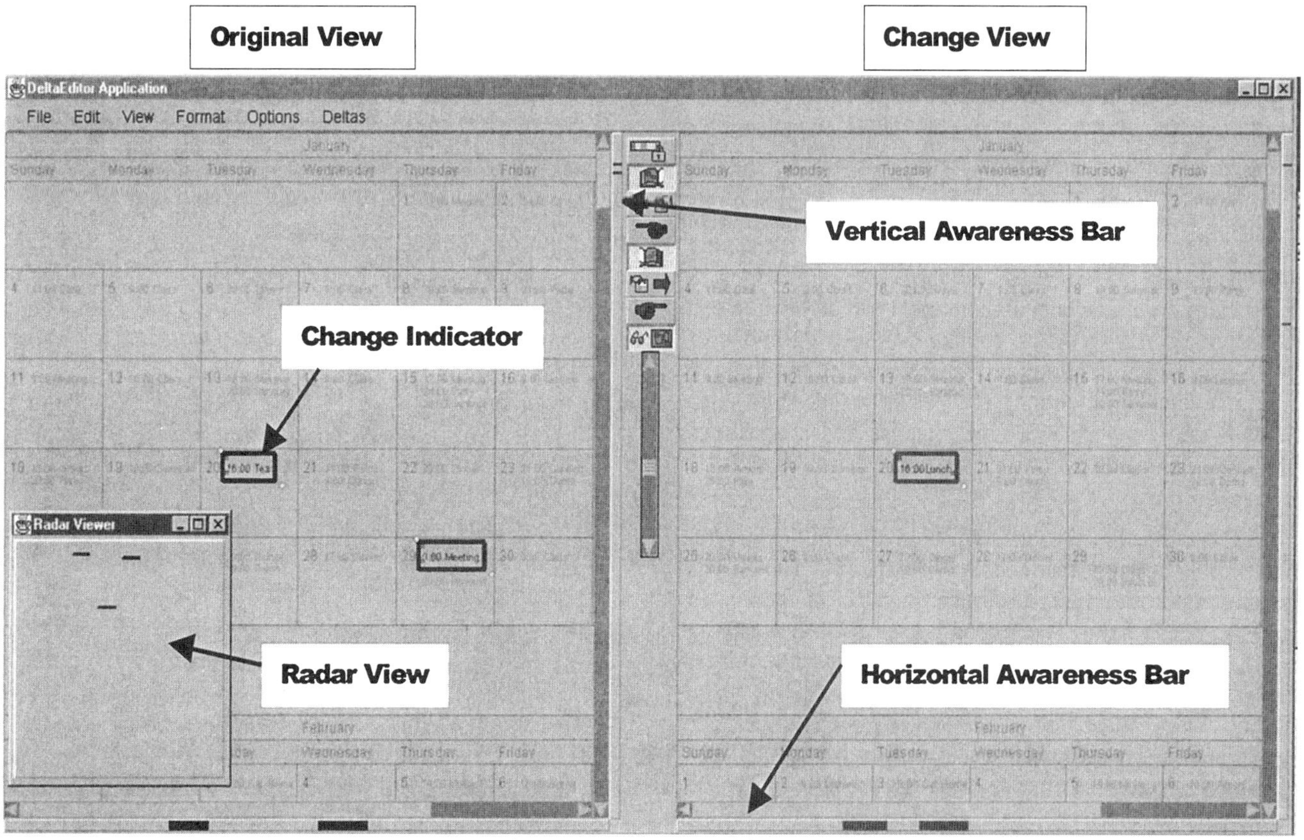

Figure 4 - ICIE reconciliation tool

In the calendar example the horizontal awareness bars are not very interesting. However, the vertical awareness bars clearly show that in the original (left side) the highlights are clustered near the top but in the changed surface there is a highlight farther down.

The awareness widgets are good for getting a sense of where all of the changes are clustered and they give single-click navigation to the highlighted area. They are not particularly good for determining where particular changes have actually occurred. Take for example the Thursday Jan, 29 highlight in the original. The user looks to the new surface and sees no corresponding highlight and the relevant appointment is gone. It is unclear if the appointment was deleted or moved. The user could scan all of the changes to find the appointment on another day. This, however, is a painful process even with the assistance the awareness widgets. Reference following solves this problem. Reference following is where a user selects any object in the original (left), which generates a reference to that object. They then select the Follow (right pointing finger) icon and the corresponding reference in the new surface is computed. For a reference R and the delta D computation is D.UpdateRef(R). The new reference is then highlighted in the new surface (right) and the awareness widgets will show exactly where it is. If the appointment had been deleted instead of moved, no highlight would appear in the new surface.

SUMMARY

By using pictorial surfaces as the medium for collaborative communication we achieve an independence from specific applications. This leads to a more stable collaborative architecture that can realistically scale to communities of the size of the Internet. This collaborative model allows each collaborator to independently choose and learn their own set of collaborative tools. This will facilitate the competitive development of such tools just as telephone services and email software have developed. Reasoning about change, as encoded in the deltas, provides a foundation for the reconciliation tools which facilitate a user's understanding of the comments and suggestions of collaborators. The resulting references are then fed through ICIE's general highlighting architecture to allow users to identify, track and consider the changes and suggestions that have been made.

FUTURE WORK

For this architecture to be fully effective there are several pieces of technology that need to be explored. The first is the automatic structure discovery in surfaces generated from the print stream. The second is that intelligent editing based on the structure and regularities in a surface is critical to the usability of this approach. Lastly there needs to be more work done on interactive techniques for reconciliation. The deltas are a rich descriptive source from which a variety of change presentation techniques can be developed and explored.

ACKNOWLEDGEMENTS

This work was supported in part by grants from DARPA and Microsoft Corporation.

REFERENCES

[1] Schuckmann, C., Kirchner, L, Schummer, J., and Haake, J. M., "Designing Object-Oriented Synchronous Groupware With COAST", Computer Supported Cooperative Work (CSCW '96), November 1996.

[2] Prakash, A., and Shim, H. S., "DistView: Support for Building Efficient Collaborative Applications using Replicated Active Objects", Computer Supported Cooperative Work (CSCW '94), October 1994.

[3] Roseman, M., and Greenberg, S., "GroupKit: A Groupware Toolkit for Building Real-Time Conferencing Applications", Computer Supported Cooperative Work (CSCW '92), November 1992.

[4] Munson, J., and Dewan, P., "A Concurrency Control Framework for Collaborative Systems", Computer Supported Cooperative Work (CSCW '96), November 1996.

[5] Edwards, W. K., "Policies and Roles in Collaborative Applications", Computer Supported Cooperative Work (CSCW '96), November 1996.

[6] Dourish, P., "Consistency Guarantees: Exploiting Application Semantics for Consistency Management in a Collaboration Toolkit", Computer Supported Cooperative Work (CSCW '96), November 1996.

[7] Sellen, A. and Harper, R., "Paper as an Analytic Resource for the Design of New Technologies" Human Factors in Computing Systems (CHI '97), March 1997.

[8] Olsen, D., Boyarski, D., Verratti, T., Phelps, M., Moffett, J., and Lo, E., "Generalized Pointing: Enabling Multiagent Interaction" Human Factors in Computing Systems (CHI '98), April 1998.

[9] Edwards, W.K., Hudson, S., Rodenstein, R., Smith, I., and Rodrigues, T., "Systematic Output Modification in a 2D UI Toolkit", *Proceedings of the ACM Symposium on User Interface Software and Technology*, October 1997.

[10] Patterson, J. F., Day, M., and Kucan, J., "Notification Servers for Synchronous Groupware", Computer Supported Cooperative Work (CSCW '96), November 1996

[11] Olsen, D. R., and Deng, X., "Inductive Groups", ACM Symposium on User Interface Software and Technology, UIST '96, (1996).

[12] Neuwirth, C. M., Chandhok, R., Kaufer, D. S., Erion, P., Morris, J., and Miller, D., "Flexible Diff-ing in a Collaborative Writing System", Computer Supported Cooperative Work (CSCW '92), November 1992.

[13] Edwards, W. K. "Flexible Conflict Detection and Management in Collaborative Applications", ACM Symposium on User Interface Software and Technology (UIST '97), October 97.

Rapidly Building Synchronous Collaborative Applications By Direct Manipulation

Guruduth Banavar, Sri Doddapaneni, Kevan Miller, and Bodhi Mukherjee
IBM TJ Watson Research Center
30 Saw Mill River Road, Hawthorne, NY 10532, USA
{banavar, dsp, klm, bodhi}@watson.ibm.com

ABSTRACT

Existing GUI builder technology supports building user interfaces for interactive applications via direct manipulation. However, it is notoriously difficult to build the underlying data sharing and application logic for multi-user synchronous collaborative applications. This paper describes a collection of very high-level software components, built using the JavaBeans component standard, that enables domain experts and application designers to rapidly build *entire* collaborative applications via visual programming – drag-and-drop, customization and wiring. Our component suite supports conference setup, awareness, data sharing, media streaming, access synchronization, and temporally coordinated media and event streams. We illustrate that the task of building non-trivial multi-user applications using this approach is significantly simplified.

Keywords

Rapid Application Development, Visual Programming, Software Components, Java Beans, Client-Server Synchronous Collaboration

INTRODUCTION

As the use of distributed applications is becoming more widespread in today's networked world, the relevance of synchronous collaboration is sharply increasing. Users in a number of application domains are seeking synchronous collaboration capabilities within their applications. The requirements of this broad range of applications are diverse enough that a "one size fits all" approach to building applications is no longer satisfactory. Our experience suggests that rapid turnaround of customized collaborative applications is critical to meet this increased demand for synchronous collaboration.

There are several advanced tools to rapidly construct the GUI part of applications via direct manipulation. However, building the distributed application logic for multi-user applications is notoriously difficult. This part of applications typically involve software components running on separate computers, communicating and synchronizing with each other, sharing data as needed, and managing user information. To get rapid turnaround, it is necessary to design programming tools that hide this complexity under clean, easy-to-use interfaces so that application domain experts and GUI designers are able to rapidly put together the underlying distribution logic of applications within a visual builder environment.

Most applications needing synchronous collaboration capabilities also need a variety of other capabilities, such as a sophisticated GUI, database access, workflow services, etc. It is thus necessary to provide synchronous collaboration capabilities as components that can interoperate with components provided by other vendors. Furthermore, the component set needs to be extensible so that new reusable components can be added as the need arises.

This paper describes a component suite for synchronous collaboration that meets the above requirements. The suite consists of easy-to-use visually programmable components that expose the functionality of a server-based synchronous collaboration infrastructure. The component suite supports conference setup, user awareness, typed data sharing, application synchronization, and synchronized event and media (audio and video) streams. The visual component suite is backed up by a high-level API that can be used both to write extension "scripts" as well as to author new visually programmable components.

The breadth of functionality exposed by our component suite is motivated by classes of applications which, in our experience, have been the most sought after. These include applications such as customer support, distance learning, and data visualization. At a minimum, these applications need support for conference management, data sharing, and media streaming. In addition, many applications require support for synchronized streams

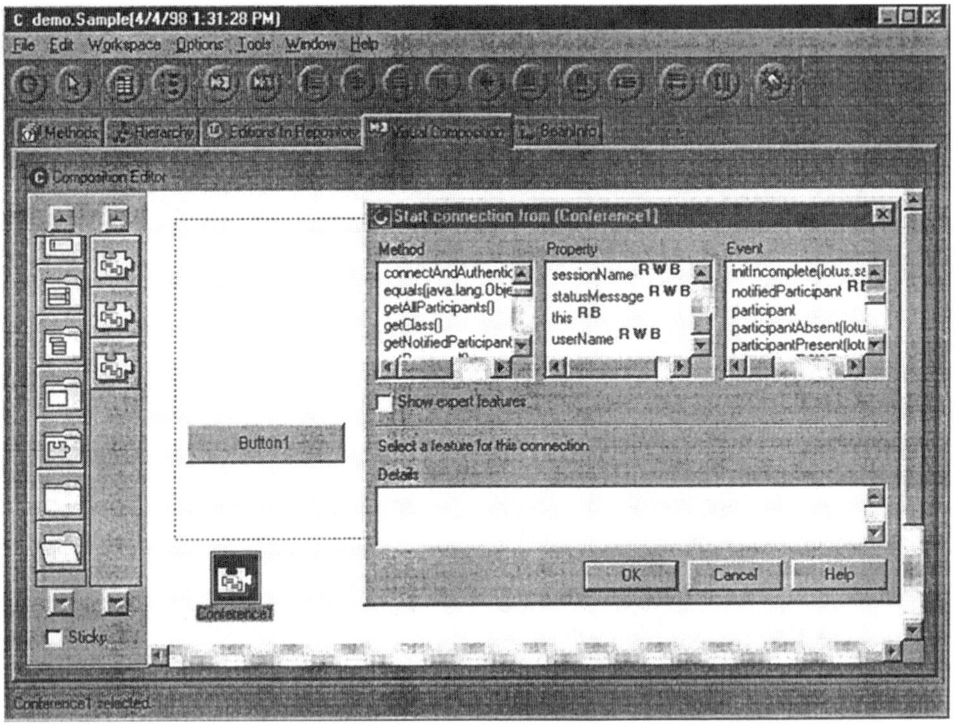

Figure 1: A JavaBean and its features shown in a visual builder tool.

(of data, audio and video) since the latency of streams can vary significantly. For example, in a typical foil presentation application, where a presenter shows a sequence of annotated foils accompanied with audio and video to a distributed group of attendees connected on the Internet, it is important that a specific annotated foil is displayed on a participant's screen only when the participant receives the audio and video describing the displayed foil.

It is difficult to justify that our component suite, or any other component suite for that matter, is "complete". We have chosen to implement a component suite that meets the requirements of classes of applications that, based on our previous experience with toolkits [16, 5], are popular and generally considered useful. More importantly, however, our component suite is *extensible*, since it is built as a layer that exposes a subset of the functionality supported by a sophisticated underlying system called Live. As a result, new components can be built as and when the need arises.

Our component suite is realized using the JavaBean component standard [17], since it allows our components to be used with existing tools and to interoperate with complementary componentry supplied by other vendors. A JavaBean is a component (an instance of a Java language class) that exposes a set of customizable *properties*, fires a set of *events*, and supports a set of *methods*. Collectively these are referred to as *features*. A JavaBean visual builder tool, such as IBM VisualAge for Java (see Figure 1), uses either implicit syntactic design patterns (as specified by the JavaBean standard) or explicit description (via a BeanInfo class) to infer the features supported by a JavaBean. The tool allows programmers to drag and drop Beans onto a programming canvas, customize the properties of Beans, and connect events generated by Beans to methods supported other Beans.

A well-designed JavaBean suite for building multi-user programs should satisfy two primary criteria. First, it should be at a high level of abstraction so that programmers do not get bogged down by the details of multi-user distributed programming. This criterion can be satisfied by similarly designed (textual) Java APIs as well. However, the second and more important criterion is that it should allow programmers to put together sophisticated applications within a uniform visual programming model for both GUI and underlying logic so that in most cases, they do not have to deal with the details of a general purpose programming language like Java.

In this paper, we show examples of several classes of synchronous collaboration applications that can be easily built using our component suite. As a detailed illustration, the following section describes how to build a poor man's buddy list and messaging program. Following that, we describe the basic concepts supported by the system whose API was used to implement our component suite. The next section details the component

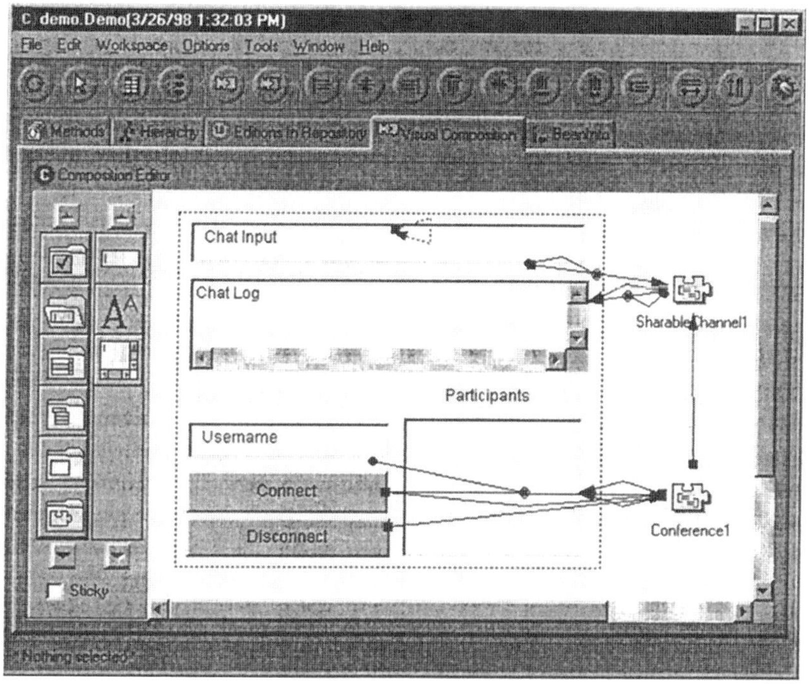

Figure 2: The complete sample application.

suite itself and illustrates how to build applications such as a shared editor with floor control, a remote presentation and archival application, and an application with invitation functionality. We then discuss issues, point to related work, and conclude.

A SAMPLE APPLICATION BUILDING SCENARIO

In this section, we illustrate building a simple, yet non-trivial, collaborative application[1] that supports:

1. Conference setup – logging in to a collaboration server and joining a named session,
2. Participant awareness – maintaining awareness of other users who are currently in the session, and
3. Chat – interacting with other users in the session by sending chat messages to them.

The entire visual program for this application, including the GUI *and* the distributed application logic, shown in Figure 2. To build this application, the programmer performs three kinds of operations: (a) drag and drop the necessary components onto the programming canvas, (b) customize the properties of components as necessary, and (c) wire events generated by some components to the methods supported by others to realize the application logic.

[1]This application is a much simplified version of several commercially available "instant messenger" type programs.

Notice that the programming canvas in Figure 2 is divided into two parts – the area inside the dashed line corresponds to the main GUI window of the application being built, whereas the area outside can consist of non-GUI components or other popup GUI components (e.g., dialogs). In this application, several GUI components such as Buttons, TextFields, a List, and a TextArea have been dropped onto the GUI part of the programming canvas. In addition, two non-GUI components that support collaboration, Conference and SharableChannel, have also been dropped onto the non-GUI part of the canvas. The Conference component supports conference setup and awareness and the SharableChannel component supports chat.

At design-time, some of the properties of the components shown in the figure are customized as follows:

- Properties of the Conference component related to the server and session, such as serverHostName, serverPortNumber, and sessionName are set to the appropriate values.
- The property of the SharableChannel component which controls the name under which the channel will be shared at the server, sharingName, is set to a string value.
- And, of course, the label properties of the GUI Buttons and Label components are set to the desired values.

Other properties, such as the userName property of the Conference component, are set at run-time via the wiring logic described below.

The application logic is realized by connecting the components together by specifying how events generated by some components should trigger methods supported by other components. Events are generated when significant state changes happen to components. For this application, the connections are made as follows:

Conference Setup:

1. When the Button labeled "Connect" is pressed (actionPerformed event),
   (a) set the userName property of the Conference component to the value of the TextField component labeled "Username", and
   (b) call the *connectAndAuthenticate* method of the Conference component.
2. When the Button labeled "Disconnect" is pressed (actionPerformed event), call the terminate method of the Conference component.

Participant Awareness:

3. When the Conference component generates the participantPresent event, call the addItem method of the List component. Make the printable name of the participant a parameter to the method.
4. Correspondingly, when the Conference component generates the participantAbsent event, call the remove method of the List component.
5. When the Conference component generates the terminateComplete event, clear the participant list by calling the removeAll method.

Chat:

6. When the enter key is pressed in the TextField labeled "Chat Input" (actionPerformed event),
   (a) call the post method of the SharableChannel component with the current value of the TextField as the parameter,
   (b) reset the value of the TextField in preparation for the next input.
7. When the eventOcurred event is fired by the SharableChannel component,
   (a) call the append method of the TextArea component with the current event data of SharableChannel as the parameter,
   (b) add a newline to the TextArea
8. Finally, when the authenticateComplete event of the Conference component is fired, the startSharing method of the SharableChannel is called with the Conference component as the parameter.

To a first approximation, that is the entire design phase of this application. Of course, some more work is required to make it production quality, i.e., more robust and prettier. These functions are supported by our component suite, however, what is shown here will suffice for this illustration.

At run-time, the user types in the username and presses "Connect". At that point, the Conference component performs an authentication protocol with the given server and if successful, joins the user to a session with the given name. The Conference components of the other users joined to the same session will then generate a participantPresent event, resulting in the new user being added to their participant list. When authentication has completed, the Conference component generates the authenticateComplete event to the local application, upon which the SharableChannel component is shared under its provided sharingName. Since the applications at all user sites are using the same sharingName for their chat channels, the channels are all bound together so that an event posted to any one of them will be delivered to all the others. Eventually, when a user hits the "Disconnect" button, that user will leave the session at the server, and a participantAbsent event is generated at all other user sites.

More sophisticated application examples built using our full component suite are shown in a later section that describes the component suite. The underlying system that supports the functionality of our component suite is described in more detail in the following section.

SYSTEM ARCHITECTURE

Table 1 summarizes the breadth of functionality supported by our component suite. However, in order to understand how these components work, it is necessary to understand the underlying system infrastructure. Our components are built using the API exposed by a client-server synchronous collaboration infrastructure, named *Live*. Each of our components exposes a carefully chosen subset of the functionality supported by the Live system. This section describes the main concepts supported by the Live system, and the following section describes how the individual components expose the system's functionality.

The Live system supports a centralized server-based architecture that offers several benefits. First, it allows latecomers in an ongoing collaborative session to easily access the current state of shared objects. Second, the server acts as a communication hub between clients, allowing clients that are behind firewalls to communicate with each other. Finally, the server can be used to make objects persistent across successive collaborative sessions.

As shown in Figure 3, the Live server supports object sharing within a number of named sessions. Before ob-

Category	Components	Description
Conference Setup	Conference	Server connection/disconnection, authentication, session joining/leaving, participant awareness
Invitation	Invitation	User-to-user invitation, private session setup
Data Sharing	SharableInt, SharableFloat, SharableText, SharableTextBuffer, SharedFloatTable, ...	Data replication
Event Sharing	SharableChannel	Ordered delivery of event objects
Access Synchronization	SharableToken	Floor control
Media Streaming	SharableAVStream, AVRecorder, AVPlayer	Sharing audio and video streams, recording live and playback of live and stored media
Event Streaming	SharableEventStream	Temporally synchronized delivery of shared event data
Archiving	EventArchive, MediaArchive	Storage and retrieval of streamed media and events
Utility GUI components	FoilFlipper, AwarenessFilter, ...	In support of commonly used applications

Table 1: The collaborative component suite.

jects can be shared, a named session must be created at the server. Client applications can then join the session to share system provided sharable objects on an object-by-object basis. Sharable objects include:

- high-level stateful objects such as strings, floats, arrays and vectors which are replicated, i.e., automatically maintained to be consistent when shared,
- sharable media stream objects (for audio and video) and their corresponding players and recorders,
- stateless objects such as channel objects which support ordered delivery of arbitrary application defined event objects, and event streams which can be temporally synchronized with other (media or event) streams, and
- token objects which provide support for application defined synchronization to control concurrent access to shared objects.

Applications can compose shared objects in arbitrary ways using aggregate shared objects such as arrays and vectors.

Dynamic sharing and unsharing of objects. Live supports dynamic sharing and unsharing of sharable objects by allowing clients to manipulate objects without connecting, then synchronize their state after connecting or reconnecting. A client application may begin by creating sharable objects and work with them locally without sharing them. When ready to share an object, the client can `join` a session and perform a `share` operation, which makes a copy of the object at the server under a global sharing name. A second client can share that object by creating a local object of the same type and performing a share operation using the same global sharing name. (The global sharing name may be agreed upon a priori by the applications, or the available sharing names may be dynamically retrieved from the server.) The second client may choose whether to reinitialize its local object with the current shared state from the server's copy or to send its local state to the server.

At any point, a client may perform an `unshare` operation to stop sharing its copy of an object. At this point, the object is decoupled from the server and the client application may continue local processing if desired, or share the object under a different sharing name.

Sharing structured objects. Individual objects can be shared as described above on an object-by-object basis. However, when a structured object such as an array or a vector is shared, all its contained objects are automatically shared. These contained objects may themselves be arrays or vectors, allowing easy sharing of arbitrarily deep structures of data. Any operation on structured shared objects, such as inserts and removes, are automatically replicated by the system at other shared copies.

Consistency model. Once sharing is set up, operations (writes, inserts, removes) performed on a local copy of a sharable object by any client are synchronously propagated to the server's copy and to the copies of other clients that are sharing the object. This means that if the shared object is stateful, the system will automatically keep the state of all copies of the object synchronized. Concurrent operations on client copies are applied in the order in which they arrive at the server.

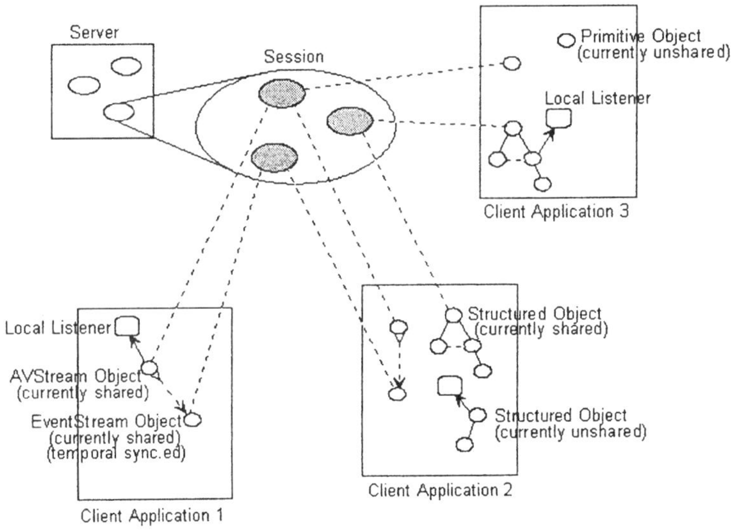

Figure 3: System architecture.

All client copies of sharable objects are guaranteed to see updates in this server applied order.

Streaming and temporal synchronization. Media streams (audio and video) are shared exactly like other sharable objects. An application that requires temporal synchronization of data with a media stream can use an event stream object. This object synchronizes notification of events to its listeners [6] with the media stream (called as reference stream). When such a temporal event stream is shared, events posted to a local copy of the stream are time stamped relative to the reference media stream. The event is then propagated to the copies of other clients that are sharing the stream. A local copy of the stream buffers the event until the time stamp of the event is current relative to the reference media stream being played in the client's copy of the application. The event is then delivered to the application. Events in a stream are strictly ordered by the server.

Session persistence. The default kind of sessions maintained by the Live server is non-persistent, i.e., the server creates the session when the first client joins the session and destroys it after the last client leaves the session. An application can also create a persistent session if it is necessary for shared objects to persist across collaborative sessions, even after the last client leaves the session. Within such a session, a subsequent joiner will be able to access the shared objects left behind by a previous session. Clients using persistent sessions are responsible for explicitly cleaning up server stored copies of shared objects.

Awareness. Finally, Live also supports awareness at two levels: (1) who else is joined to a particular session, and (2) among those who have joined a session, who else is sharing a particular object.

COLLABORATIVE COMPONENT SUITE

The salient features of all our components (shown in Table 1) are described here, using examples to illustrate uses. As can be seen in the table, nearly all of the components provided are non-visual in nature, i.e., they do not have a GUI representation. Our goal has been to provide components which support the necessary collaboration capabilities, and which can interoperate with the GUI components provided by other vendors. Programmers can combine our components with third-party GUI components and can create composite components, as described later.

Conference Setup

The Conference component enables an application to join and leave a session and monitor who else has joined the session. The Conference component connects to the Live server using the server properties (server host name and port number), authenticates using the user properties (user name and password), and joins a session with the given session name property. Once setup is complete, the Conference component generates events that can help an application track the other users in the session.

An application can use multiple Conference components to participate in multiple collaborative sessions, potentially on different servers. Also, the same Conference component can be used to join a different session after leaving a particular session.

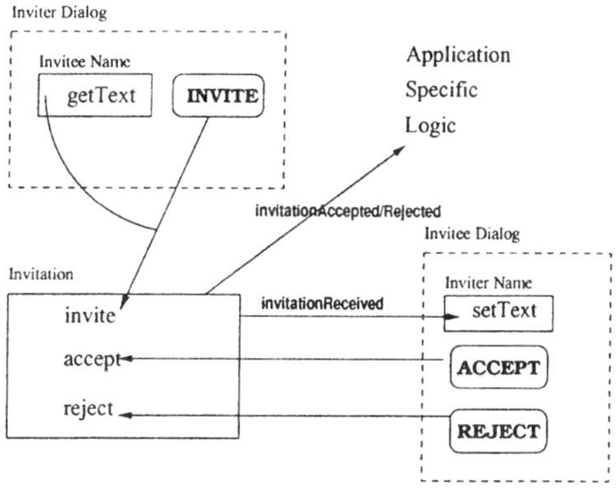

Figure 4: Example use of the Invitation component.

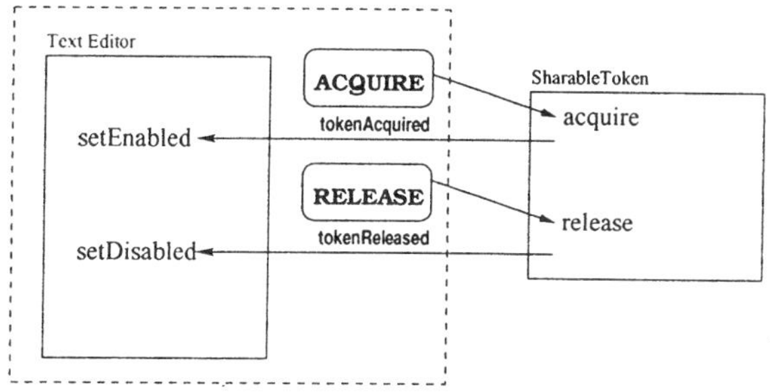

Figure 5: A shared editor with floor control.

Invitation

Invitation components are used to invite one or more participants within a collaborative session to participate in a new activity. The activity might, for example, include joining a new collaborative session or sharing a SharableChannel (known only to the inviter and invitees) to exchange private information. Invitees only learn the specifics of the new activity after they have "accepted" an invitation.

Invitation application. Figure 4 illustrates how an Invitation component can be used to trigger a new activity between two participants in a Conference. In this example, an Inviter Dialog is used to initiate some activity defined by the application. Reception of an invitation causes an Invitee Dialog to be displayed at the Invitee. Via this Invitee Dialog, the user may either accept or reject the invitation. The response from the invitee is communicated back to the Invitation component at the inviter. This response triggers an InvitationAccepted or InvitationRejected event which is used to drive additional application logic, such as starting a new activity as described above.

Data and Event Sharing

Several components are provided to support sharing stateful objects between the participants in a conference. Components that are shared under the same sharingName property are maintained to be consistent by the Live system.

Stateful components include primitive data types such as SharableString, Float, Int, Boolean, which are built using the corresponding constructs of the underlying Live system. Components that support "aggregate" shared data include SharableTextBuffer and SharableFloatTable. SharableTextBuffer supports an array of Strings to be shared between users – such a component can be used to build a sharable editor as shown in the example in the following section. A SharableFloatTable is a two dimensional array of sharable floats that can, for example, be used to build a spreadsheet.

SharableChannel components are stateless. An event posted to a SharableChannel is sent to all SharableChannels in the conference shared under the same sharingName property.

Access Synchronization

SharableToken components may be used to perform application specified synchronization, such as floor control. A SharableToken may be acquired synchronously or asynchronously. Once acquired, no other participant can acquire the SharableToken until it has been released. By using SharableTokens, applications can prevent concurrent access to shared state.

Floor control application. Figure 5 illustrates how a SharableToken component can be used to synchronize access to a shared editor. In this example, a tokenAcquired event will cause the shared editor to be enabled for editing. A tokenReleased event will cause the shared editor to be disabled.

Media Streaming

Several beans are provided to record, playback, and share streamed media, i.e., continuous media data such as audio and video. The primary media streaming component is SharableAVStream, which is shared in a manner similar to other shared objects, via a sharing name at the server. At any point, one of several shared streams can be the source of the media data and the others can be sinks (a SharableToken component can be used to dynamically control the single source).

Within a particular application, an AVRecorder component can be designated as the input source for a SharableAVStream (via the registerSource() method). The AVRecorder component captures and encodes realtime audio and full-motion video. Similarly, any number of AVPlayer components can be registerd as sinks of a SharableAVStream. AVRecorder and AVPlayer support a property for selecting the media type: audio, video or both. All the above components share a common format for the media data.

A sample use of media streaming components is illustrated in the following section.

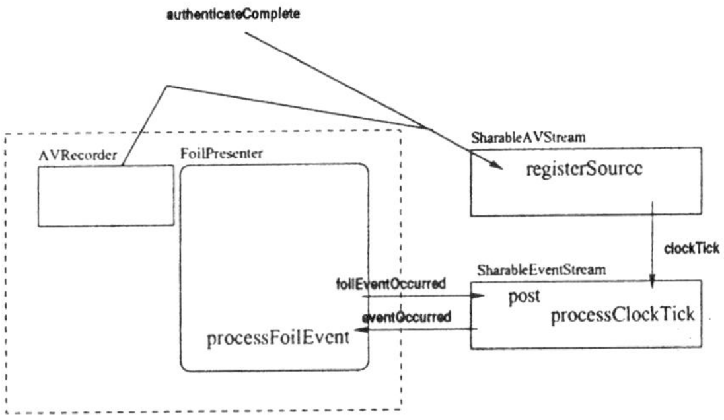

Figure 6: Foil presenter application.

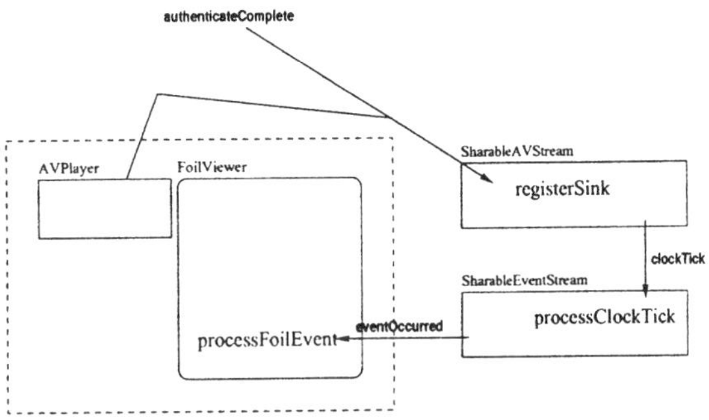

Figure 7: Foil receiver application.

Event Streaming and Temporal Synchronization

A SharableEventStream component is different from a SharableChannel in that the stream supports events that can be temporally synchronized with other streams, be it event or media streams. Events posted to an event stream are time stamped with reference to a clock ticks generated by a "clock provider" component. In most applications, a SharableAVStream is usually the clock provider, but a dedicated clock service component, called SystemClockProvider, is also provided for those applications which do not use a media stream[2]. A clock provider component generates a clockTick event at regular intervals, and this can be connected to the processClockTick method of SharableEventStream components.

Remote foil presentation application. Figures 6 and 7 illustrate the use of SharableEventStream and SharableAVStream components, in which we show how to build a remote foil presentation application where remote users are able to see a foil presentation synchronized with audio playback.

In this example, the presenter's application is built differently from the viewers' application. We use the GUI components, FoilPresenter and FoilViewer, for the presenter and the viewers respectively. In the presenter's application (Figure 6), the AVRecorder component captures and encodes the presenter's voice into audio data and streams it to the SharedAVStream. Occasionally, the FoilPresenter GUI component posts foil flip events to the SharableEventStream. These events are time-stamped using the clock provided from the SharableEventStream and sent to all sites sharing the SharableEventStream. At remote viewer sites (Figure 7), the events are re-synchronized with the audio and delivered to FoilViewer GUI components along with the audio streamed to the AVPlayer component.

[2]For example, an application which generates chess move events and associated commentary events will need to be temporally synchronized.

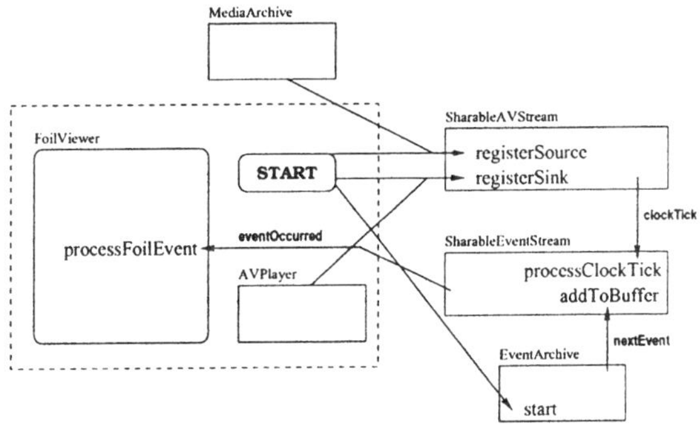

Figure 8: Archive playback application.

Archiving

The EventArchive component provides services that include storing and retrieving the contents of an event stream to a local or a network file. Similarly, the MediaArchive component supports storing and retrieving of a media stream to a file. These components can be used as the source or the target of events generated from a SharableEventStream, depending on whether the events are being stored or retrieved. These components have a property called URL which is used to specify the name of a local file or a network file.

Stored foil presentation application. Figure 8 shows an application similar to the one presented above, except that the source of the presentation is an archived file. In this application, a SharableEventStream component uses a EventArchive component to receive events reconstructed from the data stored in a file. Similarly, a SharableAVStream receives its audio stream from a stored MediaStream component.

Composite Components

There are many instances when certain groups of components are normally used together. A common example is a visual (GUI) component and its non-visual underlying model, e.g., a TextField, a SharableText, and a SharableToken may together form a SharableTextField component that may be directly embedded within sharable forms. Similarly, the session setup and awareness part of the application in Section is a common piece in many applications. JavaBean tools such as IBM VisualAge for Java supports creating *composite* components from a collection of simple ones and exposing only selected features from the embedded components.

DISCUSSION

Programming multi-user applications using a visual component suite such as ours is comparable to programming using a very high level API in a conventional programming language. The conceptual ease of programming in both cases is a result of the high level of abstraction and the hiding of many distributed programming concerns. Design time and run time are still distinct, although the visual programming cycle may be considerably more iterative. The main advantage of a using visual component suite such as ours is that users have a uniform programming model for both GUI and underlying logic and they do not have to learn the details of a general purpose programming language.

In our opinion, the approach of sharing deep structure (model) objects as opposed to surface structure (view) objects makes it easier to program multi-user applications, especially when the application is asymmetric for different user roles. Once the programmer decides on the (potentially small) set of objects to share, building the applications themselves for each user role will be considerably similar to building single user applications.

In our experience, it has been important to back up our JavaBean suite with the high level Java programming framework (exposed by Live), both for extensibility and for occasional scripting. Bean programmers should normally be able to find most of the functionality they need within the Bean suite. However, it may sometimes be the case that programmers need to write "scripts" using a Java programming API in order to get a variation on the pre-defined functionality of Beans, or to get around limitations in the Bean programming models supported by visual builder tools.

Limitations of Current JavaBean Tools

Currently available JavaBean builder tools leave much to be desired to be truly effective application building environments.

- *Limited connection models.* The builder tools which we evaluated did not allow properties of an event to be passed as a parameter on a method call. This and other limitations in the connection models increased the complexity of our JavaBean components.
- *Lack of polymorphism support.* The builder tools do not offer visual support for polymorphism. This either requires non-visual programming on the part of the application builder or increased complexity in the design of the JavaBean components. See connections 6(a) and 7(a) in the sample application given earlier.
- *Debugging and incremental refinement.* Debugging applications built using a visual builder can be a difficult and non-intuitive task. Tools for visualizing program execution and for incremental refinement of large programs will be needed as in the ClockWorks environment [7].

Implementation Status

The underlying Live system is completely implemented in Java and is being directly used for building a variety of applications including collaborative help desk, financial data management, and distance learning applications. The Live system minus streaming is publicly available under the name Shared Data Objects [9]. Most of the components described in this paper have been built and are being actively illustrated in prototype applications to customers. A typical one-hour demonstration of this suite consists of building a simple application and modifying it on-line based on audience requests.

RELATED WORK

Our component system is designed to enable a wide variety of collaborative applications to be built. The focus of our effort has been on providing JavaBean components which provide collaborative functionality in such a way that they can be visually manipulated to easily build collaborative applications.

Visual Obliq[3, 4] is a system for building collaborative applications. Written using the Obliq language and the FormsVBT extensions to Obliq, Visual Obliq provides the visual componentry for creating the GUI for collaborative applications. However, unlike our system, Visual Obliq requires collaborative functionality to be specified textually by the programmer via widget callbacks.

ViewSoft Internet[18] is a rapid application development environment for building thin-client, server-based, java client applications. The ViewSoft programming environment is a proprietary builder which creates C++ code which runs on a server and Java code which runs on a client. Unlike ViewSoft Internet, the Live system does not require the server to be pre-configured for a Live collaborative application. Also, the ViewSoft system is well-suited for dealing with symmetric applications (all instances of collaborating client applications have equivalent GUI appearances and capabilities), but, unlike our components, does not easily support asymmetric applications (collaborating applications with different GUI appearances or capabilities).

There are several systems which provide collaborative implementations of the Java AWT package. One example is Remote AWT[14]. These systems propagate AWT input events from remote sites to a central site which processes the input events. AWT output events are propagated from the central site to all remote sites. In this manner, collaborative AWT systems are similar to shared windowing systems such as shared X server[1] and shared applications in NetMeeting[11]. With these architectures, it is impossible to support asymmetric applications.

There are many toolkits which provide infrastructures for building collaborative applications, including DECAF[16, 2], Coast[15], Villa [5] and NSTP[12]. Many of the underlying concepts of the Live system have been derived from earlier work on DECAF and Villa. Although these systems provide support for basic collaborative functionality, they do not provide any support for visually building collaborative applications.

Our prototype implementation uses IBM Bamba technology for audio and video streaming [8]. Temporal synchronization of multimedia types provided by our infrastructure is similar to that provided by RealMedia [13] and NetShow [10] platforms. However, our focus in this paper is on providing higher level support, via visual builders, for integrating collaborative applications with multimedia components.

CONCLUSION

It is widely accepted that the GUI part of multi-user synchronous applications is best built via direct manipulation of GUI components. However, most existing GUI builders require that the application logic underlying the GUI, such as callback code, is implemented using a textual distributed programming language, often at a low level of abstraction. The complexity of this task precludes users such as domain experts and GUI designers from rapidly putting together prototype applications during the GUI building phase. Textual programming APIs may be designed to support high-level programming, however, users will then need to learn new skills (a new programming language) in addition to the direct manipulation GUI paradigm.

This paper presents a collection of very high-level software components that can be used within a visual builder environment to rapidly build a large space of multi-user synchronous collaborative applications. Based on our experience, we believe that our component suite supports most of the requirements of applications that are being sought in a variety of application domains. We illustrate in this paper how to build several representative applications using our component suite. Finally, the underlying system supports a high-level programming model in a traditional programming language, Java, for building new components as well as to augment applications built visually.

Acknowledgements. We gratefully acknowledge useful comments by the anonymous referees.

REFERENCES

1 H.M. Abdel-Wahab and M.A. Feit. *XTV: A Framework for Sharing X Window Clients in Remote Synchronous Collaboration* In Proc. IEEE Tricomm '91: Comm. for Distributed Applications and Systems, Apr. 1991.

2 Guruduth Banavar, Kevan Miller, and Michael Ward. *Adaptive Views: Adapting to Changing Network Conditions in Optimistic Groupware.* in Proceedings of the Second IASTED Conference on Parallel and Distributed Systems (Euro-PDS '98), Vienna, July 1998.

3 Kirshna Bharat and Mark H. Brown. *Building Distributed, Multi-User Applications by Direct Manipulation.* in Proc. of the ACM Symposium on User Interface Software and Technology (UIST'94), November 1994, pages 71-81.

4 Krishna Bharat and Luca Cardelli. *Migratory Applications.* in Proc. of the ACM Symposium on User Interface Software and Technology (UIST'95), November 1995.

5 Sumeer Bhola, Bodhi Mukherjee, Sri Doddapaneni, and Mustaque Ahamad. *Flexible Batching and Consistency Mechanisms for Building Interactive Groupware Applications.* in Proceedings of the International Conference on Distributed Computing Systems, IEEE, May 1998.

6 Sri Doddapaneni, Sumeer Bhola, Kumar Keeranoor, and Bodhi Mukherjee. *Villa++: A Framework for Synchronous Multimedia Collaboration.* in preparation.

7 T.C. Nicholas Graham, Catherine A. Morton and Tore Urnes. *ClockWorks: Visual Programmig of Component-Based Software Architectures.* in Journal of Visual Languages and Computing. Academic Press, pp. 175-196, July 1996.

8 IBM Corp. *Bamba.* www.alphaworks.ibm.com/ Bamba.

9 IBM Corporation. *Shared Data Objects.* www.alphaworks.ibm.com/ formula/ sdo.

10 Microsoft Corp. *NetShow SDK.* www.microsoft.com/ netshow.

11 Microsoft Corp. *NetMeeting.* www.microsoft.com/ netMeeting.

12 John Patterson, Mark Day, and Jakov Kucan. *Notification Servers for Synchronous Groupware.* in Proc. of ACM Conference on Computer Supported Cooperative Work, November, 1996.

13 Progressive Networks. *RealMedia.* www.realmedia.com.

14 Zvi Rosberg, Eran Gal, Yosef Moatti, and Eyal Zangi. *Remote AWT for Java.* www.alphaworks.ibm.com/ formula/ remoteawtforjava.

15 Christian Schuckmann, Lutz Krichner, Jan Schummer, and Jorg Haake. *Designing Object-Oriented Synchronous Groupware With Coast.* in Proc. of ACM Conference on Computer Supported Cooperative Work, November, 1996.

16 Robert Strom, Guruduth Banavar, Kevan Miller, Atul Prakash, and Michael Ward. *Concurrency Control and View Notification Algorithms for Collaborative Replicated Objects.* IEEE Transactions on Computers, Volume 47, Number 4, April 1998.

17 Sun Microsystems. *The JavaBeans Specification.* www.javasoft.com/ beans.

18 ViewSoft, Inc. *ViewSoft Internet.* www.viewsoft.com.

HyperMirror: Toward Pleasant-to-use Video Mediated Communication System

Osamu Morikawa
National Institute of Bioscience and Human-Technology,
1-1 Higashi, Tsukuba, Ibaragi 305-8566,Japan
+81-298-54-6775
morikawa@nibh.go.jp

Takanori Maesako
Faculty of Human Sciences,
Osaka University,
1-2 Yamadaoka, Suita, Osaka 565-0871, Japan
+81-6-879-8136
maesako@mcgyver.hus.osaka-u.ac.jp

ABSTRACT

We designed HyperMirror to provide a new video image that presents an attractive, highly understandable communication environment, rather than imitating face-to-face communication. The HyperMirror environment enables all participants to feel they are sharing the same virtual space. Participants communicate using images meeting the condition "What I See Is What You See" (WISIWYS). Both local and remote participants appear together on a shared video wall, and all things on the wall -- even those out of reach -- become appear to come within reach. Participants sharing the screen tend to act as if they are in the same room.

Keywords

HyperMirror, WISIWYS, mirror image, awareness, video conference, telepresence , interpersonal communication

INTRODUCTION

Communication can be roughly divided into two cases -- one emphasizing information transfer/exchange and one focusing on communication space sharing. Information transfer/exchange has been mainstream in attempts to develop or improve existing videophones and video conferencing systems. For such information systems to become widely disseminated in the general population, however, it is also important to consider the sharing of a communication space -- an environment in which people can enjoy conversation itself with friends and family. The telephone, for example, was originally developed to transfer/exchange information, but its subsequent, widespread population was due primarily to the recognition that it also could bring people together to share communication space.

Despite attempts at sophistication and popularization, videophones and video conferencing systems are being used in only a few limited applications. This suggests problems with the technology that prevent it from being accepted more widely -- in sharp contrast to the immediate, explosive spread of the cell phones and portable phones that are the second-generation in telephone applications. Our purpose is to clarify this problem with videophones and video conferencing systems in communication space sharing and to suggest a possible solution.

WHY DID PEOPLE EMBRACE THE TELEPHONE SO ENTHUSIASTICALLY?

A study by Yoshida et al. [28] showed that college students in and around Kyoto-Osaka (effective response: 549) cited the following reasons for the phone's popularity : speed, available anytime, available anywhere, no visual information about the other end, and easier way to say what we want than in face-to-face conversation. They also cited the following disadvantages: no visual information about the other end and difficulty in conveying subtle emotion. How interesting that no visual information about the other end becomes both an advantage *and* disadvantage !

The above study suggests that the telephone provides its own conversation environment rather than a substitute for face-to-face conversation -- in short, people have found a new way to communicate using voice alone. Why has this proven to be so appealing ?

Conveying voice alone, the telephone does not let people share a physical world --individuals at either end share a mutual, voice-only world in which the same sound information is provided to both speaker and listener(Fig.1). Voice alone limits other forms of information, but is complete enough to make this sound-only world acceptable

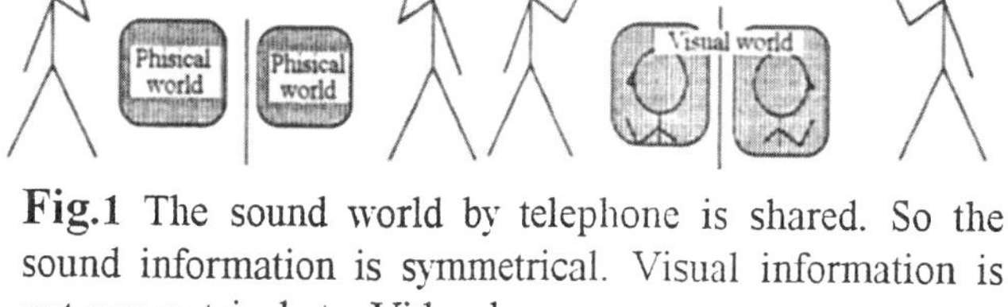

Fig.1 The sound world by telephone is shared. So the sound information is symmetrical. Visual information is not symmetrical at a Videophones

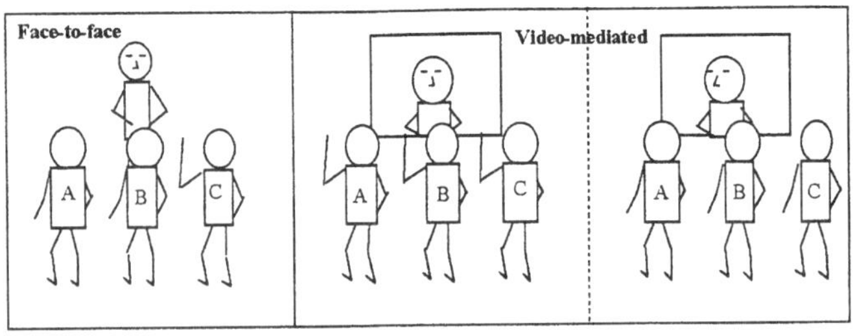

Fig.2 "Mona Lisa effect" by video medium

-- and very widely so.

PROBLEMS WITH CONVERSATIONAL VIDEO ENVIRONMENT

The video conversation environment provides other forms of information -- images -- in addition telephone functions. If possible, most people would probably like to see as well as hear people at the other end. Displaying faces on a screen, however, raises a new problem. Despite its apparently familiar presentation of a face, but it also conveys dissonant information, for example, about gaze direction.

"Gaze Direction"

Gaze direction, important to communication, serves at least five functions[10] -- regulating the conversation flow, providing feedback on how communication is perceived by the viewer, communicating facially evident emotion, communicating the nature of the interpersonal relationship, and preventing the input of excess information.

The video conversation system determines the speaker's image by the position relative to the camera. This image is interpreted much the same way by most people, independent of position -- a type of Mona Lisa effect in which a person passing in front of the famous face feels that those eyes are following them[1][17][19](Fig.2). It is not possible to direct the speaker's gaze to only one person with more than one listener present -- in other words, the speaker's gaze cannot be interpreted by all listeners as "face-to-face".

As Gaver[3] and Sellen[22] observed using a simple video conversation system having both video and audio channels, information on the gaze direction could not be used as effectively in video conversation, as in face-to-face conversation.

Simultaneously, however, at least a few participants understood, based on the situation, that the speaker intended to talk "to them" even though the gaze was not always face-to-face, or, in other words, did not always allow direct, mutual eye contact between speaker and listener.

Dourish et. al [2] observed similar phenomena.

> "Looking into the camera" provides feedback to the speaker that the listener is, indeed, paying attention. To develop a greater awareness of mutual gaze patterns, however, the speaker must learn to recognize when the listener's gaze is directed at the video monitor and, hence, that the listener is paying attention. The desired understanding of "eye contact" is replaced by the understanding of "being looked at".

Gestures

Communication does not, however, limit itself to facial expression, of course. Gestures are highly important, for example. This understanding has lead researchers to enlarge displayed area to include gestures. A study by Heath [6][7], showed that it becomes harder to understand gestures transmitted by video, even though the viewer is clearly communicating a readiness to listen or an indication of understanding. To compensate, people tended to exaggerate their gestures, which made things worse and did not add to the progress of conversation. Their study even reported a case in which gestures indicating a readiness to start conversation were not understood even when watching the screen.

We do not know yet why gestures are not conveyed smoothly. It may be because gestures are understood as interaction to be interpreted together with environmental information, rather than as something to be directly interpreted for its own meaning alone (Fig. 3).

Pointing

In current video conversation systems, we can point to objects in our own surroundings, but not to those in the viewer's space. This prevents such common gestures related to the relative positions of the speaker and listener as "come closer" or "move farther away". It also prevents "touch" gestures of physical interaction, such as patting the other person's shoulder or shaking hands.

Common Resources

In face-to-face conversation, we share objects in our surroundings -- like reading someone's note and appending additional information. With video as it is now, a speaker can show the viewer a note, but not to see a note from the viewer or write anything on that note

Fixed Viewpoint

In face-to-face conversation, we watch something interesting by turning toward it, approach closer, perhaps move it somewhere else. Video conversation viewers have

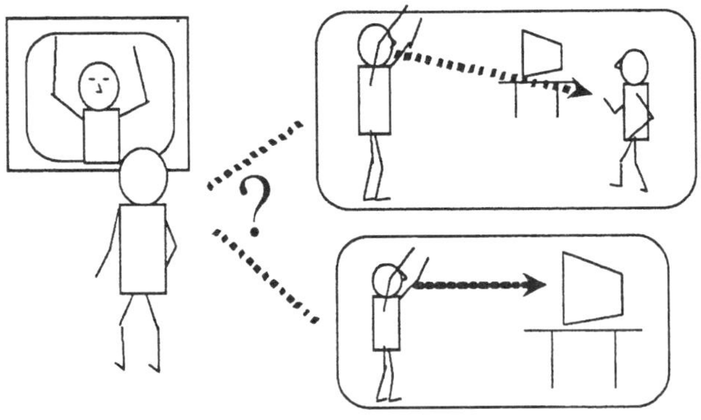

Fig.3 Disregarded exaggerated gestures at videophones.

no such freedom. The communicator also faces restrictions limited camera-view display area, no freedom of movement.

IMPROVED VIDEO CONVERSATION SYSTEMS

These problems are, in short, caused by the wide gap between the spontaneous desires of users when video became available and the functions actually provided by the video conversation system. Since then, many reports have reviewed these lacks and proposed solutions.

To support multiple eye contact, Sellen et al.[22] developed a system using a Hydra Unit in which a camera, display, microphone, and speaker are integrated compactly. The display is small and the camera is located just above it, almost maintaining eye contact. The small display makes the speaker look smaller, removing the feeling that life-size images give. To make participants feel more like they are sharing the environment, Okada et al.[21] developed MAJIC life-size display.

Tang's VideoDraw [25] stresses the importance of common resources in communication. Limiting communication to collaborative drawing, the system displays users' faces and the related drawing image--a canvas and users' hands. This makes pointing and other gestures meaningful. Tang's translucent VideoWhiteBoard [26] displays silhouettes of the whiteboard and those writing on it, sacrificing face display but enabling users to recognize each other by silhouette. Ishii's ClearBoard [9], for another example, makes facial expressions observable using a transparent board.

These methods still leave participants physically separated, fixed and able to work only near the screen. Their only sharable space is the two-dimensional canvas.

Kuzuoka, et al.[12] helped realized gaze awareness using three-dimensional objects on a desk that serves as a common resource and creating images as if two people face each other across the desk. This is a special case of face-to-face communication.

Another approach to these problems creates a "virtual" video conversation environment rather than imitating face-to-face communication.

In Ishii's TeamWorkStation[8], common communications resources are actual objects on a table. Images are displayed combined on the tables of all participants, together with their hands. Wellner's DigitalDesk[27] features a fusion of these table and hand images with computer graphics to create common communications of resources: These systems achieve communication by having participants manipulate objects and use gestures.

With Bruce Blumberg's ALIVE system[14] and Sommerer's MIC Exploration Space[23], participants are not actually seen, but are displaced similar to "avatars", who use objects in the display, such as electronic pets and electronic plants. Participants view their own as computerized graphics as they communicate with objects in the computer by gesture.

Kazuoka's GestureCom [13] gives the viewer camera control. This eliminates fixed viewing. Participants being imaged can determine the direction the camera is facing, enabling them to know what is being viewed. This produces a new gaze direction effect differing from the face image.

Yet other systems focus on relative user position. "Virtual Self" icons,--a sort of "avatar"--for example, represent users in electronic virtual space. By manipulating icons with mice, etc., users communicate directly within the same virtual space, called InterSpace [24], MASSIVE [4], and GreenSpace [15].

The reality of the participant's presence in the same room, however, is very different from face-to-face communication because icons, --not users themselves--are located in the same space.

Krueger's VideoPlace[11] displays the silhouettes of full torso or hands of the participants. Gestures are then used to communicate. As can be guessed, feeling of being in the same space as other participants is stronger than in previous examples. Because these are silhouettes, however, information and the like cannot be used interactively.

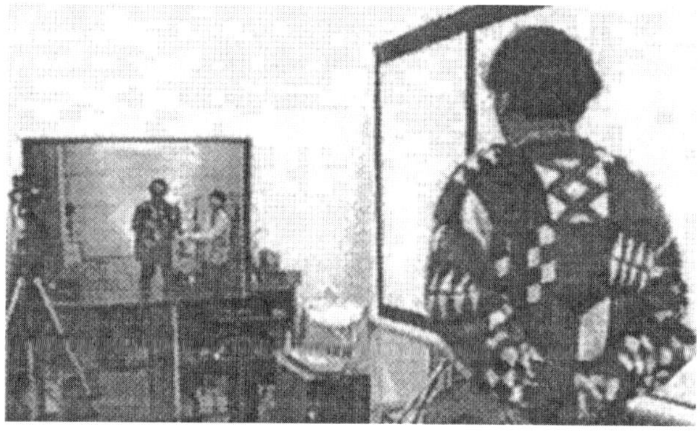

Fig.4 An Example of HyperMirror conversation.

HYPERMIRROR

HyperMirror proposes a solution that enables all participants to be project into the same room--but not by imitating face-to-face communication. This system takes into account limitations-with telephones, the "voice-only" fact-and eliminates dissonance by making communication itself easy through careful delineation of the communication space.

Even with existing video conversation systems, of course, the endlessly inventive human can create coping strategies-simulating eye contact by watching the camera and cuing return contact by watching a monitor--using gaze direction information in a way suitable for video. Unfortunately, existing video conversation systems are not the best way to do this because it takes too long to adjust to the "strange" communication environment. What we need is to design an environment enabling new, easier or more natural strategies that do not distort other parts of daily interaction.

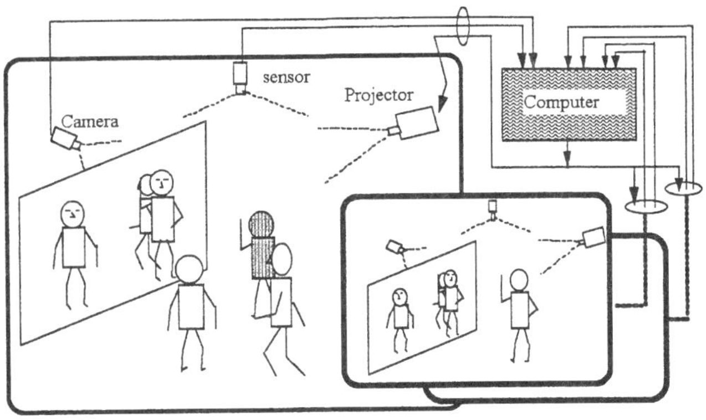

Fig.5 An example of HyperMirror system.

Better Understandability

HyperMirror [16] enables participants to communicate using the same "video wall"--making it "What I See Is What You See" (WISIWYS). More than just two communications sites, can be set up with users in front of the system, eliminating headgear and other interfaces. Images are mirror reflections projecting users on a single screen--in the same room--regardless of physical location. HyperMirror image does not separate communicators and viewers: it puts them all in the same space. .

This WISIWYS-ness lets HyperMirror users monitor, transmit, and create images as they like, making it easy to present objects, point to those belonging to others, and indicate things in shared space.(Fig.6)

HyperMirror Pointing

In face-to-face communication, each user views others at a slightly different angle, preventing common physical image information from being identical, in the strictest sense, for all viewers. This difference is most easily understood by attempting to point to beyond-reach objects, such as mountains.

Advantages of Reflected Image Display

People hardly ever see themselves face to face except in mirrors. Reflected images are more familiar to most than nonreversed video--or "normal"--images. People move more naturally when they can see their reflection. To tap a person next to you on the shoulder, you move naturally when you can see your reflection because it is like what you see in the mirror.

Psychological subjective evaluations related to embarrassment, affinity, etc., in showing people both reflections and normal images showed that most people were more comfortable with their reflections[18].

Creating a Relaxed Communication Environment

In face-to-face communication, eye contact occurs when people sitting across a table from each other look straight ahead into each other's eyes--a normal environment--to achieve eye contact. In such a case, if there is no eye contact, it has been avoided intentionally, creating strain that may be a factor preventing people from enjoying conversation.

Sometimes two people who are close sit at a 90-degree angle to relax and enjoy a conversation. They do not have straight-ahead eye contact. Eye contact is purely intentional--communication is relaxed because the lack of eye contact is not considered rude, yet it is easy to make eye contact when desired.

In HyperMirror communication, people are side by side on a screen but look straight at each other. Due to difficulty in transmitting gaze direction information in video image, eye contact is not so intense when looking at others on a screen. As a substitute for face-to-face eye contact, you can turn to the person on the screen and move synchronously with them. This provides relaxed communication much as in the seated, 90-degree angle case (Fig.7).

Fig.6 HyperMirror Pointing.

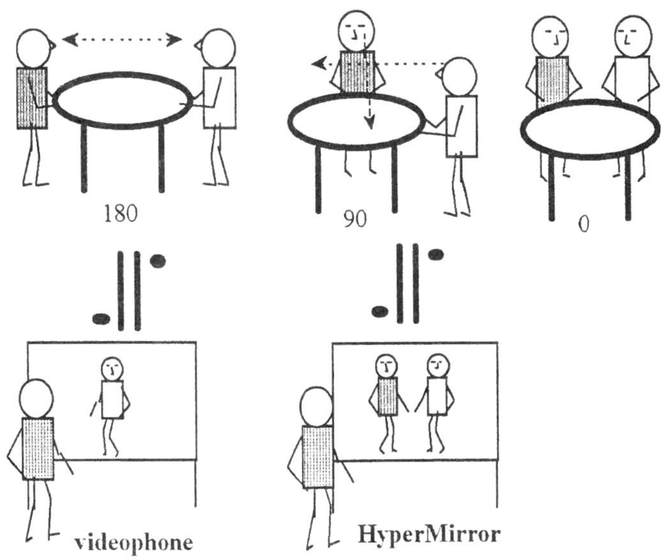

Fig.7 Relaxed conversation environment

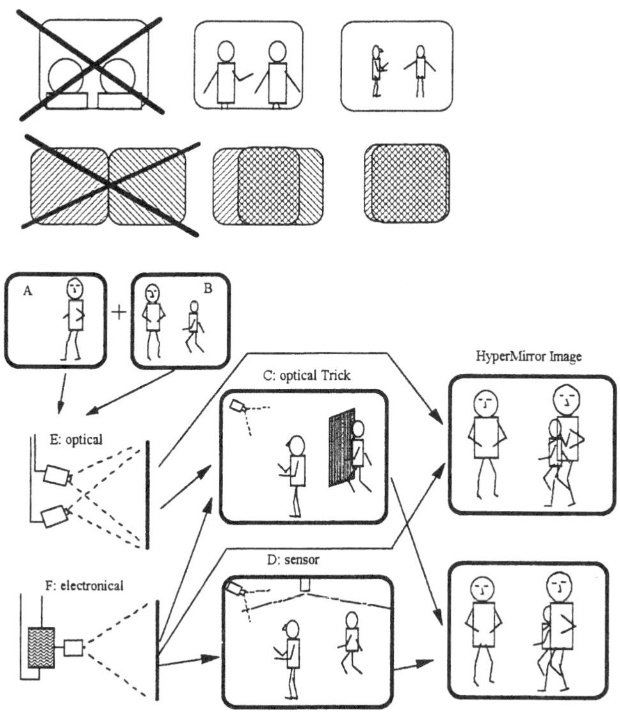

Fig.8 Variables of methods of making a HyperMirror image. HyperMirror requests to cover the upper half of the body, and to have overlapping area.

HYPERMIRROR HARDWARE

HyperMirror system implementation must consider parameters such as displayed body area, display size, and image resolution. If whole-screen resolution is fixed, enlarging the displayed body area results lowers resolution. Such critical parameters influence overall system performance.

In a preliminary experiment, we found necessary to cover an area large enough to display fingers unless elbows are akimbo, although conventional Videophones cover only the face. Life-size display was preferable, although reduced display showed no problem in practical use. We also found that the displayed size, vertical position, and colors are more important than the accuracy of absolute display size.

Basically, any participant can be displayed anyplace on the screen, although limiting movable areas showed no problem in practical use. We also found in the preliminary experiment that overlapping adjacent participants appropriately--shoulder to shoulder, at least--is necessary. Otherwise, participants are separated by invisible "window frame", destroying the HyperMirror advantage.

We must then determine how to synthesize images--either electronically or optically. Optical synthesis usually uses double projection(Fig.8-E and Fig.9). Some optical tricks also give display priorities to component images picked up at each end. Electronic synthesis enables optical tricks and sophisticated image processing in synthesizing images. Position sensors, for example, can be used to automatically judge which component images should be displayed on the top of the screen where multiple component image overlapped. This enables a more natural image to synthesized [23].

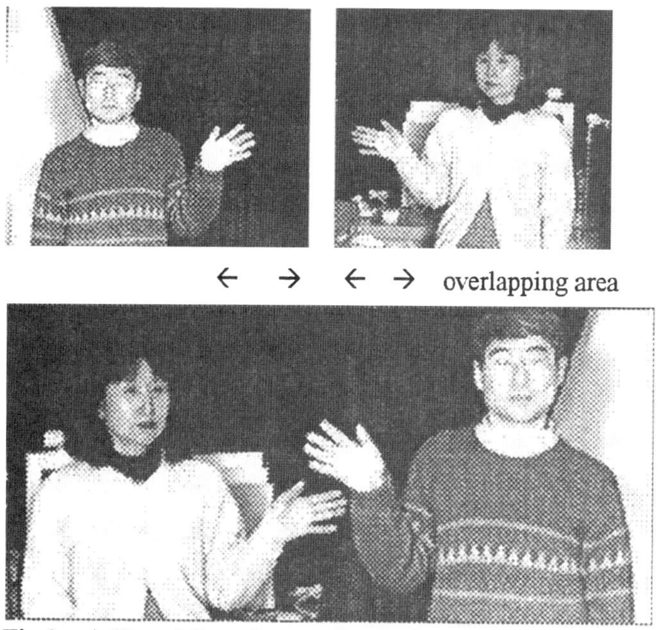

Fig.9 A HyperMirror image of optical version.

EXPERIMENT

Adding Self-Reflection to Displayed Participants

HyperMirror display reduces the psychological distance between the viewer and other participants. A psychological test was conducted to confirm this effect [18].

In the experiment, three types of display conditions are set up: (a) no display of the viewer, (b) display of the viewer as in a mirror image or photo on the left side of the screen and as a normal, nonreversed image on the right, (c) the viewer on the left side of the screen and the mirror image on the right. The experiment lets participants subjectively evaluate where they think others are located or the screen in relation to them in communications and the degree of strength of the presence at that position.

Subjects included 13 men and 12 women aged 10 to 50 years. The test was conducted in groups of three or four persons under the condition that the persons in the group

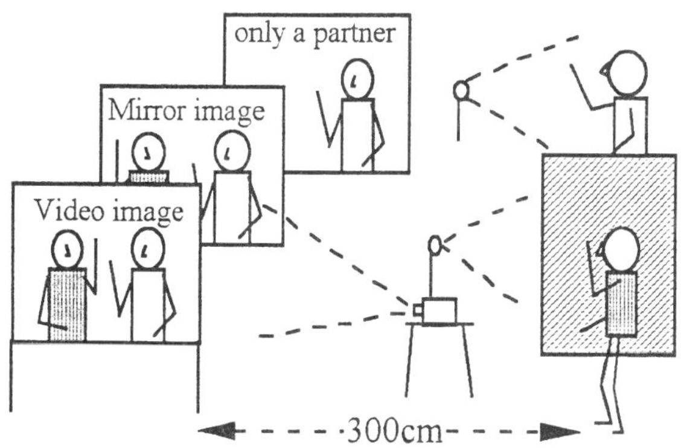

Fig.10 Details of Experiment.

were strangers.

Detail of Experiment

A screen 90 cm high and 120 cm wide was installed upright 90 cm above the floor, and adjusted until participants were displayed life-sized at actual height. Projectors were placed 170 cm away from the screen and 90 cm above the floor. A camera was mounted on a projector. Subjects were 300 cm from the screen. The camera and screen had resolution compatible with NTSC television signals. Using two projectors, we created a synthesized image representing the subject and other participants in the same room (Fig.10).

We set up two situations. Participants basically did not move much in one situation, but interacted by shaking hands, etc., in the other situation. Each was evaluated both with and without previously instructing the actual participant positions. This yielded 12 (3 x 2 x 2) cases.

In each case, subjects were asked to fill in a form showing the location of each participant based on their feeling, marking 1 for right-front-of-screen, 4 for next right, etc. For "realism", the level of feeling was reported using 5 levels form, 5 for "extremely strong" to 1 for "weak." We told subjects it was not unusual to feel the presence of a participant in more than one place, such as both on the screen and to their right simultaneously, and asked them to mark what they really felt. After each experiment under different conditions, we also had subjects comment freely about comfort in talking, any noticed events, and any other impressions. The reply form also included a category such as "uncertain location" for subjects who felt a presence but could not determine where it was.

Prediction

Visual information, existing knowledge, and varied feedback were provided to recognize the position of other participants [20].

If the subject's reflection is not displayed, "screen data" is derived from visual information and "specified position" from knowledge about participant positions. Because it is usually abnormal for one person to be in two places at once, subjects try to solve this contradiction, but this action was stopped early on by our guidance, so it was predictable that two positions would be selected by many.

If the subject's reflection is displayed, the presence of nearby participants is perceived because seeing the reflection provides feedback and images are displayed on the same screen. Interacting through the screen shows subject reactions immediately, again providing feedback for motion and the perception of the presence of others when an interaction succeeds. Perception also differs depending on which image--normal or reflected--is displayed. A subject recognizing the screen as a mirror is more likely to select "around me" with smaller displacement when reflections are displayed.

When actual participant positions are not taught, no knowledge contradicts visual and feedback information, resulting in more subjects selecting "screen" or "around me", as responses. (Fig.11)

Results

Our results were almost as predicted. Reality of presence was evaluated highest at the screen itself, followed by specified actual positions. We calculated the average reality of presence with an evaluation 0 set to nonselected position (presence not felt). Results indicate that displaying a subject's reflection raises the reality of presence nearby except for "actual position not taught and interaction instructed", in which case a significant difference was seen (Student's t-test with a significance level of 5% or lower).

In "actual position taught and interaction instructed" combined with the subject's reflection, reality of presence was highest--2.58-at the right of the subject, higher than in specified actual position--1.88-- and on the screen--1.92--. When a normal image was displayed, reality of presence nearby was low and toward right on left, indicating that normal images did not effectively reduce the reality of presence in specified actual position or on the screen (Fig.12).

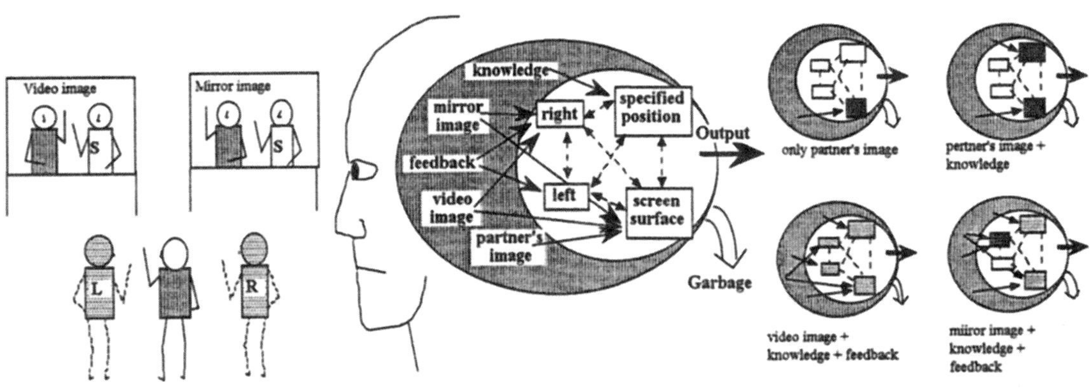

Fig.11 Prediction of experiment. There is a partner on the right of me in the screen, and s/he is on the side of raising my hand. (Video image condition)

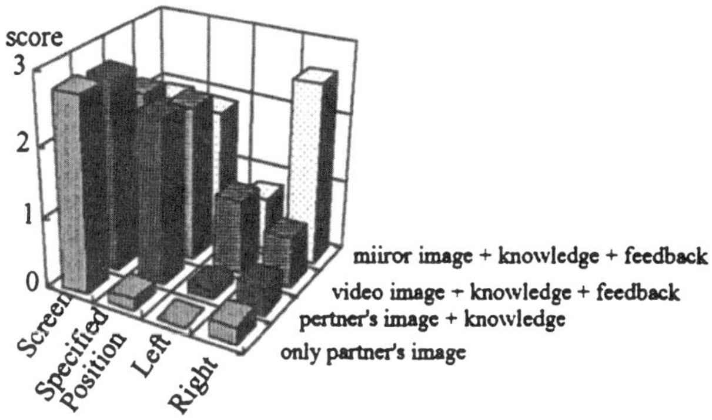

Fig.12 Results of experiment

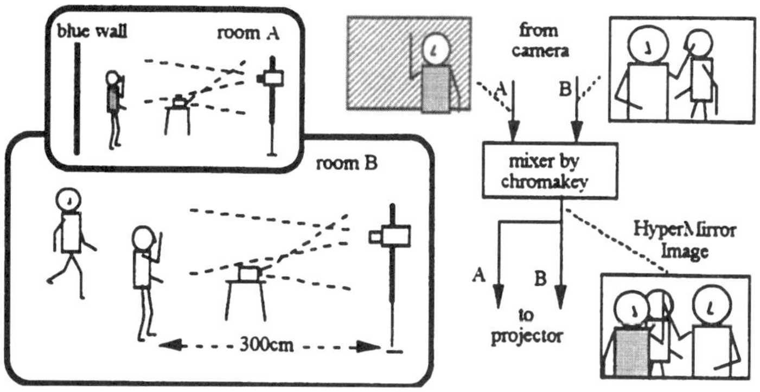

Fig.13 the HyperMirror system used observation

Under "comments", one subject said "handshaking was easy in some cases and very difficult in others." We explained the difference between reflected and normal images and requested a handshake retry, after which the subject said "Handshaking is easy and my hand extends unintentionally when the reflection is displayed"--probably using a mirror-image metaphor in recognition.

OBSERVATIONS ON SYSTEM USE

The observation of communications using HyperMirror led to some interesting behavior.

HyperMirror Hardware Used Observation

As mentioned in the discussion of HyperMirror hardware, the HyperMirror system offers many possible variations on how the combined image is created. The HyperMirror configuration for observation is shown in Fig.13. Two conversation sites are used. The video signal is NTSC and the composite screen is generated using chromakey. For chromakey synthesis, the wall of one of the sites is blue. The sequence of screen synthesis of the two sites is predetermined, with the blue background taking priority. In screen overlapping display is always closer to the viewer, with no image hiding.

Hardware uses only commercially available products-no special equipment or off-the-shelf products.

Appearance of Socializing Due to Presence in Same Room

Some subjects excused themselves, quickened their steps slightly, or stooped down while they passed in front of other participants and changed their positions on the screen. Such behavior was not observed when they passed behind others.

Reflections displayed in a common HyperMirror communication image influence how subject act. They often grasped the image of other participants passively as though not actually relating or interacting in the case of a normal image. When a reflection was displayed, they respond at least to their own reflection. The HyperMirror environment gives no border between subjects and other participants, so they respond to the whole screen. It also affects how they recognize other participants and surrounding objects. The above behaviors appear to occur because a subject's reflection appears to interfere or interact with images of others.

Similar images are provided by Krueger's VideoPlace[11], which also displays participants in silhouette. The line of vision is expressed by body positioning.

Fig. 14 Examples of voluntary visual interactions. (Left) kicking man soon after shaking hands.(right)head patting man

Fig.15 An example of pointing. She will avoid from pointing man soon after this picture.

Gaze Direction Expressed by Body

With HyperMirror, gaze direction information accuracy of participants is low, since eye contact cannot be gained by looking straight ahead since the camera is located next to the screen. Nevertheless, users conversed smoothly, turning to the speaker on the screen and gazing at them in eye contact corresponding to face-to-face communication. In one case, a user tapped another person's shoulder on the screen in an attempt to start a conversation.

Uniformity

In many cases subjects talked to others through the HyperMirror image, not directly , even when physically in the same room. After such conversations, we asked them who was nearest to them during the conversation? Most people answered it was the person near them on the screen, not the person actually present in the same room. Thus, physical distance tends to be ignored.

This is probably because HyperMirror creates a reality of presence exceeding that of physical presence.

Personal Space

Each person has "personal" space feeling that causes discomfort if invaded. This space depends on the relationship to the person violating this space[5]. We observed with HyperMirror that users tried to keep far enough away in order to avoid invading personal space--evidence of the reality that users have in HyperMirror interaction.

Approaching the Camera for a Close-up

In a case details of the object in question could not be transferred to other participants due to low screen resolution, the person providing the information spontaneously help the object out toward the camera for a closer look. When doing so, they moved to keep from covering other people's faces. Other participants also

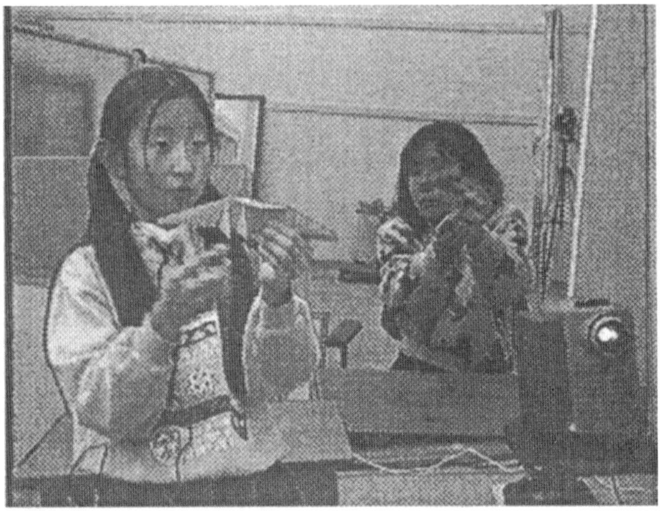

Fig.16 Approaching the Camera for Close-up.

moved to keep their faces visible. Everyone cooperated in creating an appropriate image for that moment (Fig.16).

From" That" to "This"

As mentioned, because HyperMirror uses WISIWYS, gestures are easier to communicate. Interestingly, the word subjects used to indicate objects, whether near or far, was "this" in all cases-meaning that objects seen on the screen had become close, at least psychologically, giving a sense of ability.

In dealing with distant or three-dimensional objects, communication is usually tried after changing objects into pictures or names (symbols) that are more easily handled. However, in HyperMirror, the object is automatically imaged that all participants can touch it.

Some users commented that pointing to objects in the air tires their hands and deprives them of actual "pointing" and that it is easier to point to objects by touching the blue background.

HYPERMIRROR-II

In the initial version of HyperMirror, all participants used reflection, so it was difficult to handle some objects, such as letters, maps, and drawings. To overcome this, HyperMirror-II displays the person as reflection and other participants as a normal image-although this is limited to two sites.

Except that images at each end are the reverse of the other, the system satisfies WISIWYS. With the self-displayed in reverse, the same function can be expected as in the previous version. Letters, maps, etc., displayed as reflections may cause confusion, however.

All objects displayed in reverse are present in real space where the user is. In other words, the user is able to obtain the normal images by looking at actual objects as required. In the previous HyperMirror version, an object pointed to on the HyperMirror screen was used in real space with no problem. Unfortunately, sufficient experiments have not been made with this new system to see if this is true. Further studies on HyperMirror-II, such as extraction and analysis of problems, will be made later.

Fig.17 A conversation using a map on HyperMirror-II

SITUATION FOR EFFECTIVE HYPERMIRROR USE

The feeling of being in the same room reduces psychological barriers between participants. Communication with HyperMirror offers a softer, "at-home" feeling. There are now more situations where this system is effective, even in business discussions. In interior decorating, parts assembly in schools and plants, and construction site, the site and content are closely related. HyperMirror is effective in situations where it is difficult to separate the two.

If the supervisor or customer cannot be present, they indicate their preferences looking at items being constructed. They can appropriately indicate points that are unsatisfactory and effectively communicate their detailed ideas to those doing the work. Because HyperMirror operates in real time, the contractor can make preferences known on site. Results then serve as a base when the contractor expresses ideas in more detail. It is also possible to instantaneous convey suggestions from the site to the contractor. Also, by switching to an idealized image, it is easier to exchange information required for conversation.

The result is a more complete, thorough exchange with a higher level of concreteness.

CONCLUSION

HyperMirror is effective in communication because it is easy to understand and has symmetry. Like with the telephone, what I see is also visible to others. This spontaneously creates a communication rule that objects visible only to me are excluded from conversation. If such objects must be mentioned, behavior such as explanations and close-up will be used spontaneously.

When we realize an object, we understand in relation to other objects, not alone. Self-image--that is, mirror reflection--is information most familiar to us. With a reflection displayed, we understand everything involved in conversation in the structure related to ourselves. Display of reflection also makes us aware of participation in conversations, giving a sense of responsibility to respond.

This system performs image processing to create HyperMirror images. Produced images are not present in reality, but the correspondence between images and the real world is very simple and understandable to most people. By making full use of the latest computer graphics, impressive images impossible in this world will be produced. It will also be possible to convert the image of a face looking at a screen to an image in the camera gaze direction. However, these applications are not priorities for fully implementing this system.

This is because the system design principle is that we fully utilize it based on a understanding of it. If it contains any obscurity, even slight, the reliability and value of video image information will be reduced to where communication cannot take place.

Back to the initial subject, telephones may not transmit images, but this does not deny their vast usefulness. We would like to view any inconveniences with HyperMirror as potential advantages, in the same way.

In comments by HyperMirror users, those living away from home viewed HyperMirror very favorably because it provided shared (although virtual) space. The system would best be set up as a public facility to avoid large numbers of unexpected anonymous visitors to a "home" setting. Some participants at a site with covered by thick blue paper felt that they had actually been "transferred" to real space where others were present. Others said that they would enjoy going hiking with friends via HyperMirror if they were hospitalized, for example.

We plan to continue future work with HyperMirror, and welcome your comments and suggestions.

REFERENCES

1. Anstis, S., Mayhew, J., Morley, T., "The perception of where a face or television 'portrait" is looking, American J. Psychology, 82, 474-489(1969)
2. Dourish, P., Adler, A., Bellotti, V. and Henderson, A., Your Place or Mine? Learning from Long-Term Use of Video Communication, Technical Report EPC-1994-105(1994)
3. Gaver, W., Sellen, A., Heath, C. and Luff P., One is not enough: Maltiple views in a media space. Proc. INTERCHI'93, 335-341(1993)
4. Greenhalgh, C. and Benford, S., Massive: A collaborative virtual enviroment for teleconferencing. ACM Transactions on Computer-Human Inteaction, 2.3, September1995, 239-261(1995).

5. Hall, E., The Hidden Dimension, (1970 In Hidaka, T., and Sato, N., trans. in Japanese), Misuzu Shobo(1966)
6. Heath, C. and Luff, P., Disembodied Conduct: Communication through video in a multi-media environment, Proc. CHI'91, 99-103(1991)
7. Heath, C. and Luff, P., Media Space and Communicative Asymmetries: Preliminary Observations of Video-Mediated Interaction", Human-Computer Interaction, 7(3), 315-346, (1992).
8. Ishii, H., TeamWorkStation: Towards a Seamless Shared Workspace, Proc. CSCW '90, 13-26,(1990).
9. Ishii, H. Kobayashi, M. and Grudin, J., Integration of Interpersonal Space and Shared Workspace:ClearBoard Design and Experiments, ACM Transactions on information Systems(TOIS), ACM, 11-4, 349-375(1993)
10. Kendon, A, Some functions of gaze direction in social interaction. Acta psychologica, 26, 22-63(1967)
11. Krueger, M., Artificial Reality II, Addison-Wesley Pub.(1991)
12. Kuzuoka, H. and Nakada, T., Assisting Remote Instruction Using Copied Reality.Advances in Human Factors/Ergonomics, 21B, 957-960(1997)
13. Kuzuoka, H., Kosuge, T. GestureCam:A video Communication System for Sympathetic Remote Collaboration. Proc. CSCW'94. 35-43(1994)
14. Maes, P., Blumberg, B., Darrell, T. and Pentland, A., The alive system: Full-body interaction with animated autonomous agents. ACM Multimedia Systems, 5:105-112(1997)
15. Mandeville, J. et al., GreenSpace: Creating a Distributed Virtual Environment for Global Applications, In Proceedings of IEEE Networked Virtual Reality Workshop(1995)
16. Morikawa, O. and Maesako, T., HyperMirror: a Video-Mediated communication system, CHI97 extended abstracts, 317-318(1997)
17. Morikawa, O., Difference of Gaze Perceptions Between on Face-to-face and on Video communication(in Japanese), Progress in Human Interface, 6, 13-20(1997)
18. Morikawa, O., Effects of displaying the reflected image of users(in Japanese), Proc. of the 14th Annual Meeting of the Japanese Cognitive Science Society, 240-245(1997)
19. Morikawa, O., Gaze Performance in Video communication, A bridged Proc. HCI International 97, 24-24(1997)
20. Morikawa. O., A human processing model for explaining the effects of media in communication (in Japanese), Information Processing Society of Japan SIG Notes, HI63-6, 41-47(1995)
21. Okada, K., Maeda, F. Ichikawa, Y., and Matsushita, Y., Mulyiparty Videoconferencing at Virtual Social Distance:MAJIC design, Proc. CSCW'94, 385-393(1994)
22. Sellen, A., Speech patterns in video-mediated conversations. Proc. CHI'92, 49-59(1992).
23. Sommerer, C. and Mignonneau, L., "MIC Exploration Space, " in Siggraph'96 Visual Proceedings, 17-17(1996).
24. Sugawara, S., et al., InterSpace: Networked Virtual World for Visual Communication, IEICE transactions on Information and Systems, E77-D(12), 1344-1349(1994)
25. Tang, J. and Minneman, S., VideoDraw: A Video Interface for Collaborative Drawing", ACM Transactions on information Systems(TOIS), ACM, 9-2, 170-184(1991)
26. Tang, J. and Minneman, S., VideoWhilteBoard: Video Shadow to Support Remote Collaboration", Proc. CHI'91, 315-322(1991)
27. Wellner, P., Interaction with the Paper on the DigitalDesk, Communication of the ACM, 36.7, (1993)
28. Yoshida, A., Kakuta, J., Research study on the communication by telephone in Japanese university students(in Japanese), Proc. of 8th Symposium on Human Interface, 643-650(1992)

Meme Tags and Community Mirrors: Moving from Conferences to Collaboration

Richard Borovoy, Fred Martin, Sunil Vemuri, Mitchel Resnick, Brian Silverman, and Chris Hancock
MIT Media Laboratory
20 Ames Street
Cambridge, MA 02139 USA
+1 617 253 0331
{borovoy, fredm, vemuri, mres, bss, ch}@media.mit.edu

ABSTRACT

Meme Tags are part of a body of research on GroupWear: a wearable technology that supports people in the formative stages of cooperative work. Conference participants wear Meme Tags that allow them to electronically share memes—succinct ideas or opinions—with each other. Alongside of the person-to-person transactions, a server system collects information about the memetic exchanges and reflects it back to the conference-goers in *Community Mirrors*—large, public video displays that present real-time visualizations of the unfolding community dynamics. This paper presents results from a proof-of-concept trial of the Meme Tag technology undertaken at a MIT Media Laboratory conference.

Keywords

groupware, name tag, community, meme, collaboration, wearable computing, infrared communication, interaction design

INTRODUCTION

A new type of collaborative technology, called GroupWear, supports people in the formative stages of cooperative work. We are specifically interested in the conference-type setting, where people united by a common interest meet to share ideas, renew friendships, and forge new collaborations.

Our work is partly motivated by the irony that as CSCW researchers, we spend a lot of time at conferences, yet we have seen little use of CSCW ideas or technologies to help make this time more productive. This may be because time spent interacting with others at conferences is not considered cooperative work: conference interactions are somewhat evanescent, and a shared agenda is often not articulated. However, we believe that the groundwork for meaningful and enduring collaborations can be laid at such events, and that this can be encouraged with appropriate technology.

CSCW 98 Seattle Washington USA

As a starting point for our research, we look to the wearable "paper and stick-pin" technology that is ubiquitous at every conference—the name tag. Judging by their popularity, name tags work very well as they are. Therefore, as we have developed our GroupWear Tags, we have been very careful not to break what was good about the name tag [2]. Our GroupWear Tags have two major capabilities that paper and stick-pin technology cannot support, however.

GroupWear Tags are about understanding relationships. While a normal name tag tells you something about its wearer, GroupWear tags can tell you something your relationship to the wearer. For example, the original GroupWear tags [1] offered two conversing people a simple measure of their agreement on a set of community-relevant issues. This type of relationship feedback can be an excellent "bootstrap" into a conversation for building a shared understanding with a new acquaintance.

GroupWear Tags are about understanding community. Our latest GroupWear tags, called Meme Tags (Figure 1), go further by helping people build a shared understanding of the whole conference community. In order for participants to build effective collaborations with others, they need to be able to understand the structure and dynamics of this community, and be able to locate themselves and others in it. People also need to be encouraged to more freely associate with a wider spectrum of individuals.

This paper presents a proof-of-concept trial of the Meme Tag technology undertaken at a conference at the MIT Media Laboratory. We start with an overview of the Meme Tag activity, a discussion of some of the design tradeoffs we had to make to support our goals, and some informal observations of the effectiveness of those choices. We then present a more focused analysis of some of the quantitative data we collected at this event, and what it suggests about redesigning part of the technology. We conclude with some plans for future work, including a detailed study of the impact of the Meme Tags on cooperative activity.

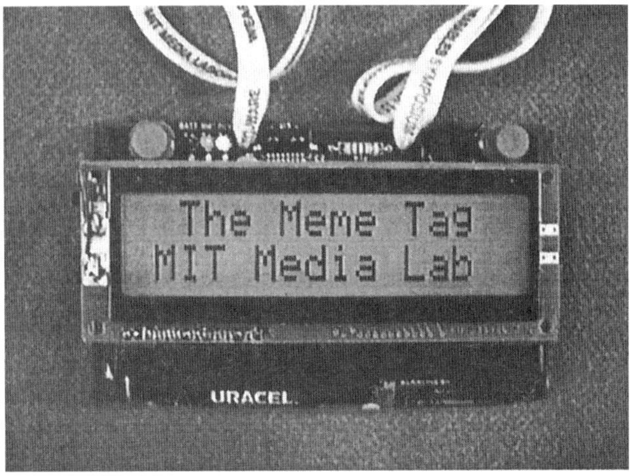

Figure 1: The Meme Tag. Worn around the neck, the Meme Tag includes a large, bright LCD screen, green and red pushbuttons (for accepting or deleting memes), a knob (not visible) for reviewing and choosing memes to offer, and a bidirectional infrared communications device.

THE MEME TAG EVENT

The Meme Tag event took place over a period of two days in October 1997. The event was designed to be a part of the MIT Media Lab's *Digital Life* (DL), *Things That Think* (TTT), and *News In the Future* (NIF) consortia sponsor meetings. Sponsors of the lab are invited to see work at the lab, visit with faculty and students, meet with other sponsors, and pursue collaborations. At the event, approximately 400 sponsors, faculty, and students congregated and were each given a Meme Tag, which also functioned as their name tag.

Richard Dawkins first introduced the term "meme" to suggest how ideas can spread and evolve through Darwinian selection [4]. In our use, a meme is an idea or opinion, expressed as a short piece text that spreads from person to person. The Meme Tag contains community-relevant memes that a participant has chosen.

Several weeks prior to the Meme Tag event, a web page was created to allow members of the Media Lab's extended community to submit memes. Approximately 400 memes were collected. A sample of approximately 200 of these were chosen and each Meme Tag was initialized with one random meme. We ensured that each of the 200 preselected memes was found on at least one tag. Table 1 presents a sampling of memes contributed both before and during the event.

Sample Memes
If brute force isn't working you're not using enough of it
We learn best from experience... preferably someone else's
Microsoft-Intel won't last long. Net computers are the future!!
History convinces more people than philosophy
The future is best seen through peripheral vision -- N.N.
Keyboards as we know them will disappear by the year 2010
Content is a commodity ... context is value added
Do not read the "Good Times" meme
Don't talk to me Talk to my agent
This meme good for one free dinner with Prof Michael Hawley
A witty saying... proves nothing. -- Voltaire

Table 1: Sample Contributed Memes. Memes were restricted to 64 characters each.

Once participants received their Meme Tags, they were free to roam about the Media Lab and exchange memes with fellow participants. In Figure 2, Bob and Nancy meet and their Meme Tags activate, lighting their screens. Bob's tag presents a new meme to Nancy, while Nancy's tag simultaneously presents a fresh meme to Bob. For example, Nancy's tag might say

```
Fresh meme for Bob:
  Computing should be about
  insight, not numbers
```

while Bob's tag displays

```
Fresh meme for Nancy:
  Make money fast --
  pass this meme to your friends!
```

If Bob likes the meme shown on Nancy's tag, he can press the green button on his tag, causing the meme to be replicated onto his. Similarly, if Nancy wants the message Bob's tag has shown her, she can capture it onto her tag. After the exchange, the Meme Tags become idle and do not distract from their subsequent conversation.

Figure 2: Meme Exchange. "Bob" and "Nancy," two conference-goers at the Media Lab consortia meetings, exchange memes.

In addition to subscribing to memes from other people, participants were able to author their own memes at a kiosk and add them to their tags (Figure 3). When a participant wearing a tag approached the kiosk, the kiosk recognized that a Meme Tag was near, and greeted the participant by name. From the kiosk, participants could then add a meme to their badge. Approximately 300 memes were added to the original set of 200 during the event.

Figure 3: Kiosk Usage. A participant authors a new meme and adds it to his tag.

Around the event, large-screen displays presented visualizations of how the memes spread throughout the community (Figure 4). These displays formed a "Community Mirror," where in real-time participants saw which ideas were most popular and which ones were dying out, as well as information about group dynamics, such as the "cliquishness" of the gathering.

These Community Mirrors also gave participants a sense of knowing what other participants knew. This facilitated the formative stages of interaction by providing people with additional common reference points for conversation. Figure 5 shows four of the ten different visualizations offered by the Community Mirror; these visualizations cycled in rapid succession continuously throughout the event.

Figure 4: The Community Mirror. A large-screen display shows a series of visualizations based on real-time interaction data, reflecting a representation of social activity back to event participants.

The final piece of the Meme Tag System was the Meme Server Database (Figure 6). In addition to storing all of the meme text and meme subscription information, the server also stored basic demographic information on each participant: gender, affiliation (sponsor, faculty, student), and consortium (DL, TTT, NIF). This information was used for the Community Mirrors as well as for our post-event data analysis.

Each time participants met, their Meme Tags created a record indicating who met and what memes were exchanged (or rejected). During the participants' conversation, the Meme Tags also invisibly shared records of all other conversations they knew about—that is, not only conversations in which they were involved, but conversations they learned about "through the grapevine" from other tags. Thus, each Meme Tag collected a sample of the conversation records from throughout the entire community.

When a participant visited a kiosk, the kiosk downloaded the interaction records and sent them to the Meme Server Database. Because each participant's Meme Tag contained a representative sample of conversation records from the entire group, only a fraction of the participants needed to visit kiosks in order for the Meme Server to collect a substantial portion of all conversation records. This decentralized mechanism allowed the Meme Server to collect live community data from purely local interactions.

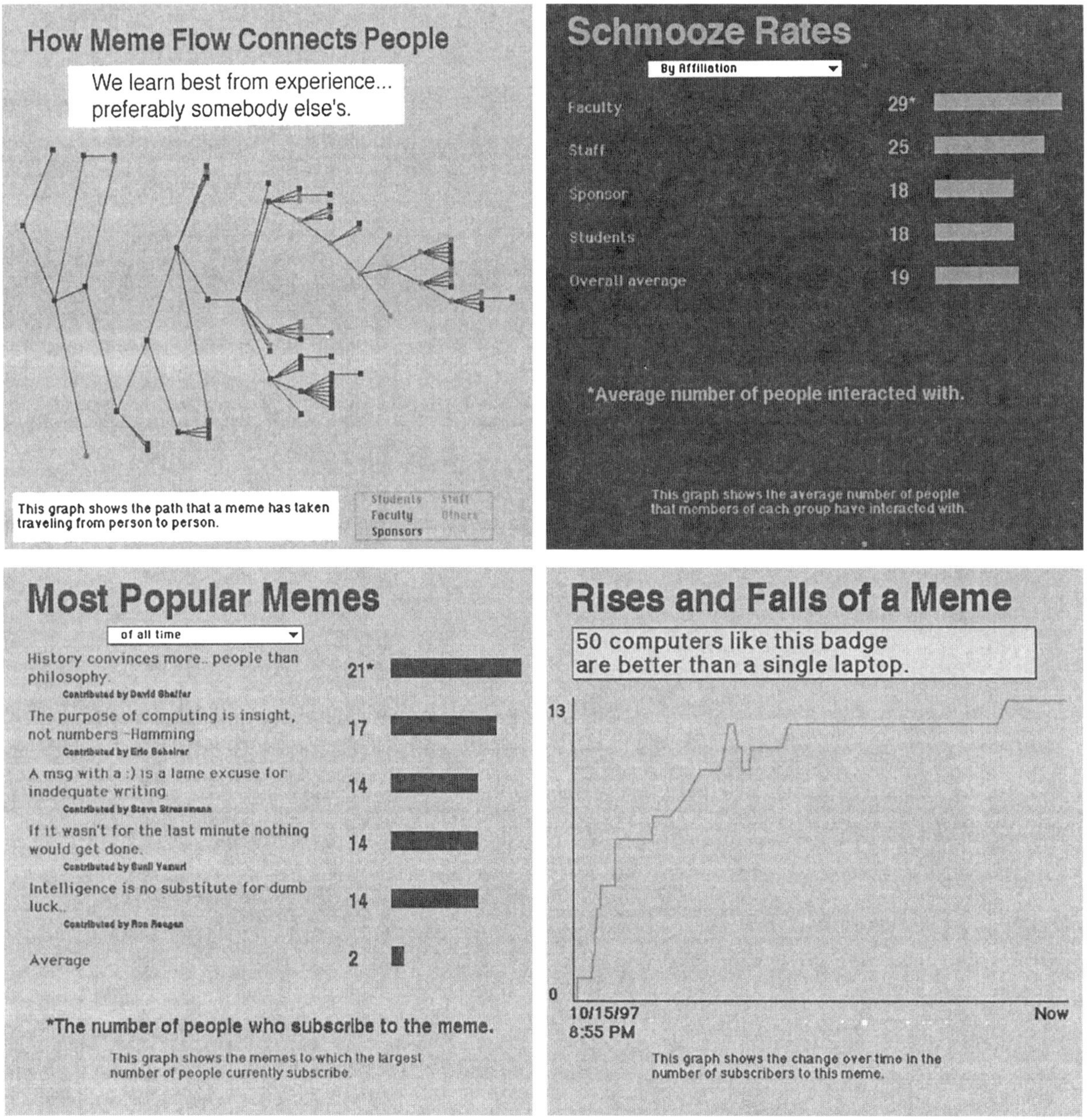

Figure 5: Four Examples of Community Mirror Visualizations.

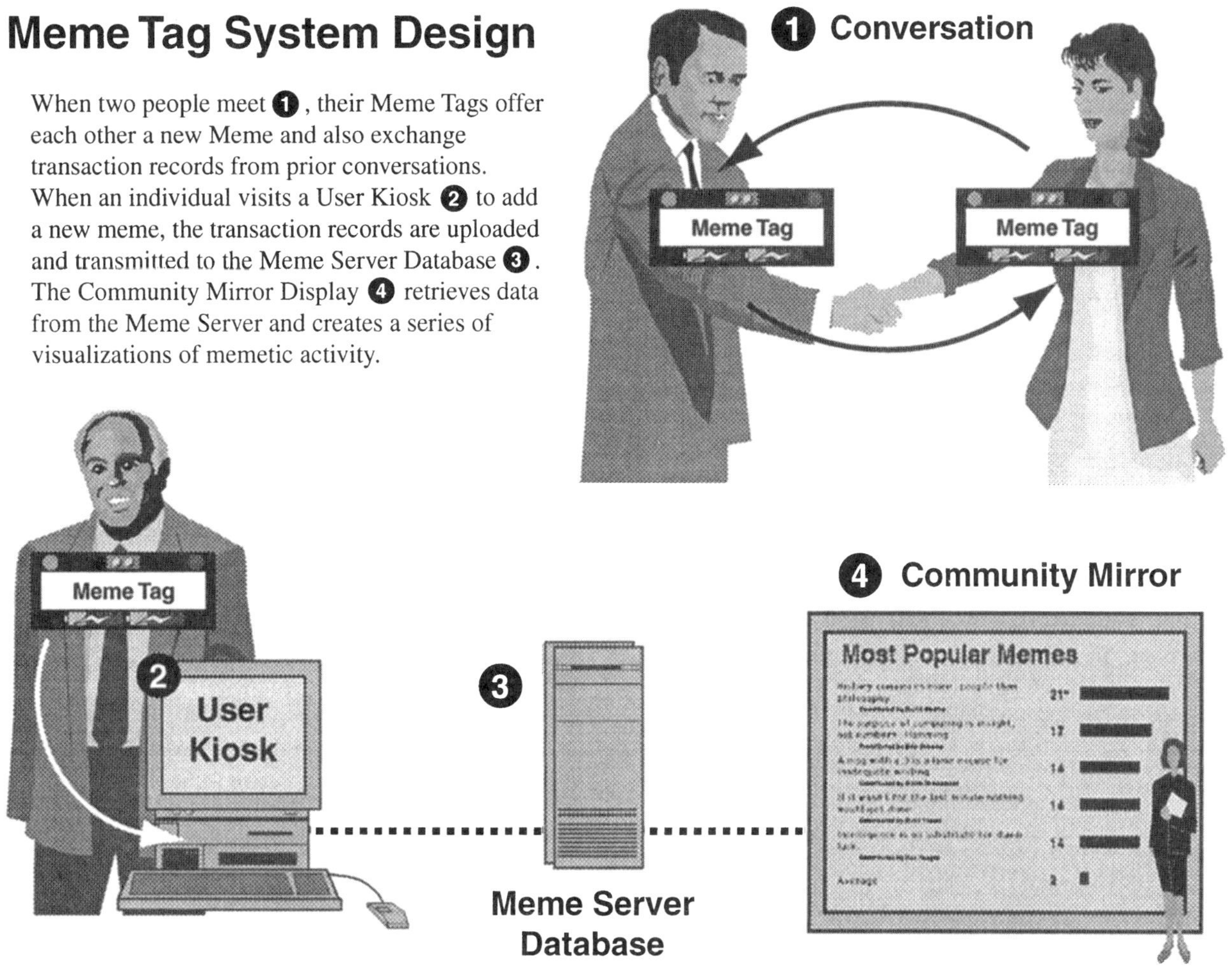

Figure 6: Meme Tag System Design.

RELATED RESEARCH

Our original GroupWear tags, called Thinking Tags, helped two conference participants build a shared understanding by showing them a measure of their agreement on some community-relevant issues [1]. At a Thinking Tag event, participants programmed their tags with answers to several multiple-choice questions. When two participants met, their tags flashed a green light for each question they agreed upon and a red light for each question they answered differently.

Unlike the design of the Meme Tag activity, Thinking Tag content had to be determined in advance of the event—there was no way for participants to add new issues as the event progressed. Also, the Thinking Tags did not have any support for visualizations of community activity like the Meme Tags' Community Mirrors.

Our GroupWear research continues the emerging CSCW trend toward support for the more informal, unstructured, and unplanned aspects of the collaborative process [10, 13]. Also, like the Xerox PARC work on Collab and LiveBoard, our research aims to augment face-to-face work [16, 7]. We have worked hard to weave the GroupWear tags into the social fabric of a normal conference, heeding Moran, et al's warning that the tools should not "inhibit or distort" people's natural collaborative activities [12]. To this end, we have insured "alignment" between GroupWear mechanics and normal group dynamics: when two people face each other at normal conversational distance, their tags interact; also, tag output is designed to be easily comprehensible within the time and space constraints of regular social interactions.

Unlike other research on face-to-face CSCW, GroupWear attempts to augment the collaborative work that goes on before collaborative work is formally acknowledged—before any project meetings have taken place, a team has been established, or a shared vision has been articulated. GroupWear technology is designed to help participants at a conference find like-minded individuals, and begin conversations that can lay the groundwork for further collaboration. Although people spend a lot of time engaged in this type of face-to-face activity, we know of no other technology designed to support it.

GroupWear Community Mirrors support a type of "social group awareness," another strong theme in CSCW research. Dourish and Bellotti's definition of awareness [6] is "the understanding of the activity of the others, which provides a context of your own activity." Community Mirrors do this by letting participants view their own social activity in the context of community dynamics (for instance, "The average person has met fifteen people, but I've spoken with only six"). We also extend the definition of awareness to include understanding of the knowledge and beliefs of others, in order to provide context for one's own knowledge and beliefs. Community Mirrors let participants examine the beliefs of others by allowing them to see statistics such as a particular meme's current popularity within the community.

Community Mirrors offer viewers knowledge of other people's knowledge (specifically, knowledge of the collective beliefs of a community), allowing them to serve as a partial solution to the "Mutual Knowledge Problem." Krauss and Fussell characterize this problem as the work communicating parties must do in "constructing their common cognitive environment—that is, ascertaining and representing the information that they and the other participants can (and will) assume to be known to all." [11]

Because Community Mirrors are displayed in full public view, and people can assume that most people have seen them, they reflect a gathering's common cognitive environment, in terms of a set of shared beliefs, and shared knowledge of these shared beliefs. This knowledge, shared by the community about the community, can then be a powerful resource for individual conversation. By locating themselves within this space, participants in a conversation can begin to build a more personal shared understanding that can lead to continued collaboration.

The Community Mirrors feed back visualizations of community dynamics in real-time to a co-present community. Real-time community visualizations have been previously explored for on-line communities [5]. Also, sociologists engaged in Social Network Analysis have produced many interesting representations of real-world community activity [15]. However, their representations were not available for the real-time consumption of their subject community.

DESIGN DECISIONS

During the design of the Meme Tag event, the object was to ensure that the activity and technology facilitated meaningful interaction between participants that could lead to further collaboration. All of the following design decisions follow from this purpose.

Tag Design

How many memes per tag

Though there were over 300 memes circulating during the event, the Meme Tags were restricted to hold a maximum of seven memes. This was not a technical restriction, since there was enough free memory in the Meme Tags to hold many more memes. Rather, we wanted participants to have a sense that the space on their Meme Tag was precious. By restricting the number of memes, people needed to be selective in accepting memes. (Participants could delete memes to make room for new ones they found more interesting.) Furthermore, by restricting space on the tags, we hoped to find interesting global trends in meme popularity.

Initializing tags with memes

In order to bootstrap the event, each tag was initialized with one meme. By seeding participants' tags with memes, people could start exchanging memes immediately without having to go to a kiosk to enter a new meme. However, it was extremely important that people feel a bond with their tags [2], which could be lessened by the presence of random content. Nevertheless, without a substantial pool of memes in circulation from the beginning, the activity might not have been able to get started. As a compromise, tags were initialized with exactly one random meme.

As another way to bootstrap the event, we placed large posters with Meme Tags attached to them. These special "Poster Tags" had several memes in them. Participants could walk up to the poster and receive a meme from the poster tag. In this way, people could easily seed their tags with memes of their own choosing before joining the social activity.

Meme Exchanges

Identity

As part of the design of the Meme Tag, two tags within infrared communications range start an exchange by displaying a greeting that included the name of the conversation partner. This was important because in a group of more than two people, it made clear which two Meme Tags were interacting by creating a visible connection between conversation partners.

Which Meme to Offer

After the greeting, each tag selected a meme to offer the other. We considered different methods for the Meme Tag to computationally determine which would be the best meme to offer in an exchange. Proposals included using a collaborative filtering algorithm to determine which among a given set of memes would be most relevant. After some debate, we concluded that meme selection would appear fairly arbitrary regardless of the method, since the interface could not reveal the selection process. The final design attempted to present persons with a meme from their conversation partner's tag that they had not seen before. As such, the choice of meme was based on both participants' history: one had subscribed to the meme, and the other had not yet encountered it.

In trial runs, some users wanted to evangelize a specific meme or carefully choose a particular meme for a colleague. So, a feature was added that would allow a user to offer a specific meme: by turning the knob on the tag to a specific meme, that meme would be offered in the subsequent exchange.

Double Interactions

To ensure that when a pair of tags finished an exchange, they did not start another one immediately, a feature was added that prevented a tag from initiating an exchange with the same tag twice in a row. However, in early user interface tests, people sometimes wanted to initiate a second session with the same person. The design was modified to allow people to reset their tags by pressing the red button. Though this overloaded the red button to mean both "delete a meme" and "reset the tag," the added feature proved valuable to power users.

Design of the Community Mirrors

Showing the whole meme

The purpose of the Community Mirrors was to convey a variety of information about the event in real time to event participants. Included within these displays were the actual text of the memes. In the initial design, the entire text of the meme was not displayed. We reasoned that if people had seen a meme on a Community Mirror before they encountered it from a fellow participant, the meme might be less intriguing and their reaction to it would be muted. However, participants found the displays confusing without the entire text of the meme. Therefore, we reversed this decision in favor of showing the entire meme in the Community Mirror and kiosks.

RESULTS

The focus of this pilot study was on getting the technology working, not on collecting detailed data on its use and impact. However, the data that the Meme Tags themselves collected tells us something about the success of the project. During the course of the event, the 400 participants collectively hit their green buttons to subscribe to a meme approximately 2000 times. Also, during the event, 147 different people took the time to go to a kiosk and author, on average, two new memes each. This data paints a picture of a gathering that was fairly engaged with the Meme Tag activity.

Unfortunately, due to a software bug, the Meme Tags relayed only about 45% of the transaction data to the server, where a transaction consisted of a meme offer between two people, a meme acceptance, or a meme deletion. Although we were disappointed with this outcome, we eventually came to regard the data glass as half full, rather than half empty. The networking algorithm we designed for the Meme Tags was complex, and this was our first opportunity to test it with a large group of people over an extended period of time. Furthermore, we could find no reason to believe there was any selection bias in the data that was captured. Therefore, we believe the Community Mirrors—and our further analysis here—were based on a representative sampling of the data.

In addition to the above quantitative data, we have a collection of informal observations and anecdotes relating to the impact of the Meme Tags.

Compellingness of a Meme Tag Personal Greeting

When one of the conference speakers concluded his speech and walked up the aisle to the exit, he purposefully shielded his tag with his hand. It seemed clear that this was to avoid the potentially awkward situation of his tag "striking up" an unwanted interaction with a member of the audience. Many people told us they found the Meme Tag introduction protocol—where a Meme Tag on a person you are facing lights up with a salutation that includes your name—extremely engaging, almost to the point of distraction. One person said that if they walked past someone and their tags inadvertently started to interact, it was hard to resist stopping and talking when he saw his name lit up on the other person's tag.

Of course, it is highly ironic that finding one's name on someone else's name tag is compelling. Conventional wisdom would say that this is the last thing anyone needs to see on someone else's name tag, since we all know our own names. There is something more important happening here. Part of the salutation's significance is that it demonstrates to Meme Tag viewers that what they are seeing has been created just for them. It hints at fulfillment of the childhood fantasy world that is totally constructed for one's own viewing pleasure.

More importantly, the Meme Tag personal salutation seemed to have the power to create what Goffman called a "focused interaction" between two people, which involves "individuals who extend one another a special type of mutual activity that can exclude others who are present in the situation" [9]. In fact, we designed the Meme Tag software to ensure that one Meme Tag would seek out a single other one, and exclude other tags in the vicinity. We did not want one person's tag starting an interaction with several others' tags at once, leading to multiple meme offers and subsequent confusion about which meme might be accepted by pressing the green button.

Goffman describes an elaborate human protocol for negotiating focused interactions, that includes such rituals as third party introductions of two people who have something in common. In some ways, the Meme Tags enacted this protocol by choosing two people in a group and lighting up their tags with memetic content drawn from one and personalized for the other. Whether this is too much power to give to a name tag is worthy of further consideration.

Technology as Fashion

Before anyone could use the Meme Tags to help form collaborations, we saw that they had to overcome a conceptual hurdle. Some people had a hard time dealing with the fact that although they were the ones wearing this small computer, its LCD screen was designed primarily to be viewed by other people. In fact, several Media Lab members demonstrated difficulty with this concept: in a brainstorming session on possible Meme Tag uses, they repeatedly suggested applications, such as using them as pagers, for which they were not well suited. Of course, Meme Tags are unusual in the world of technology, where pagers, PDAs, and cell phones that we carry are designed to be looked at primarily by us.

Over time, however, as participants looked at the tags of the others, they seemed to get more comfortable with the idea that their tag was meant for others to view. In fact, this is a communicative model with which we are all familiar: namely, fashion. Fashion is about wearing things that communicate something about us to others [3]. In some ways, the Meme Tag is another type of wearable display like a neck-tie, a piece of jewelry, or a

T-shirt with text on it. Of course, the Meme Tag has the special ability to change its appearance depending on who is viewing it. We believe people will become increasingly comfortable with this model of "interpersonalizable" hi-tech fashion.

Testimonials

We got a lot of feedback like the following part of an e-mail from one participant, who wrote asking if he could keep his tag after we asked sponsors to return them: "In all of the conferences that I have attended and produced, the meme tag is the most unique and high-tech solution to a low tech-problem: getting random people to connect and converse with each other." Other people also told us the Meme Tags helped them have meaningful interactions with others that they otherwise might not have.

We have little hard data on the impact of the Community Mirrors. We know that many people stood around and watched the displays as the visualizations streamed past. One faculty member reported talking to a sponsor who kept glancing over at the display. At one point, the sponsor suddenly stood up, pulled out a camera, and took a picture of the Community Mirror. He told the faculty member that one of his memes had made it to the "Most Popular Memes" list, and that he wanted to be able to show this to his friends at home. A much more thorough study of the impact of the Community Mirrors will be undertaken in a future study.

A NEXT GENERATION OF COMMUNITY MIRRORS

Designing the original Community Mirrors turned out to be a bootstrapping problem. Part of the reason for building the Meme Tags in the first place was that people—including ourselves—do not have good intuitions about community dynamics. Therefore, we were in the position of building visualizations for a data set that we could barely imagine. We relied on our intuitions and on relevant research [13] to come up with the first set of visualizations. Now, however, having run a large-scale event and collected a set of interaction data, we can propose a set of views based on interesting patterns in the data. The following sections sketch the content of some of these views, without presenting the specifics of the visualizations.

Insularity

During our work on GroupWear, one of the complaints we have heard is that organizations will go to great lengths to bring a diverse set of people together, only to see them interact with the small subset of people that they see every day. This pattern of behavior was evident in our Meme Tag data (Figure 7). The graph shows the amount of face-to-face interactions that occurred between members of the same group (i.e., sponsors, faculty, and students). Each group's data is displayed as the ratio between the number of interactions that occurred and the number that would occur if people were mixing randomly (i.e., without bias toward interacting with particular groups). Therefore, the line at 100% represents what the values would be if there were no insular bias. As one can see, sponsors have the smallest tendency toward insularity, while students have the largest—they are twice as likely to interact with another student as they would be if they mixed randomly.

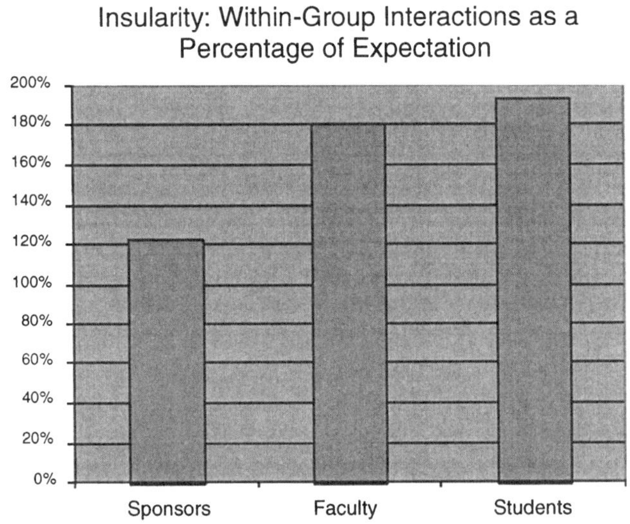

Figure 7: Insularity Between Groups.

Since insularity can have a negative impact on the initiation of useful new collaborations, we would like to highlight it in future GroupWear Community Mirrors. Of course, we are not trying to interfere with the Constitution's guaranteed right to freedom of association. There are times when people may want to be insular. However, research suggests that group behavior like insularity can occur despite the wishes of individual group members [14]. This could occur if people had a slight personal preference toward insularity, and no sense of how their actions were contributing to an undesirable trend. A Community Mirror could make this trend visible, helping people link their own choices to this otherwise invisible macro behavior. Furthermore, because of the public nature of the Community Mirror, insular groups will also be able to see that other people can see their behavior. This is in contrast to the perceived invisibility of individual interactions in a group situation. These two factors could contribute to a shift in an individual's perceived trade-off between insular and non-insular behavior. This matter will be taken up in future GroupWear research.

A word about statistical significance: The insularity bias is statistically significant, with $p<0.01$. However, it is important to keep in mind that these graphs are not meant to provide an after-the-fact, statistically significant sociological analyses of the event. Rather, they are leading us to design new visualizations whose significance will be rightfully determined by the participants who will be able to discuss them as they unfold in real-time at a future Meme Tag event.

Communities of Believers

Communities are partially constituted by the set of beliefs they hold in common [8]. Sub-groups within a community will share some beliefs, but divide on others. Identifying these "belief communities" at a conference gathering, and locating oneself and others within them, could be helpful for identifying potential collaborators, establishing common ground, and creating a sense of group identity.

By putting the memes into thematic categories, we were able to analyze various Media Lab groups' predisposition to subscribe to certain types of memes. This analysis is somewhat costly to include in the Community Mirror because it would require human attention during the progress of an event. For memes that were added during an event, someone—either the meme author or someone behind the scenes—would have to categorize them.

Many of the disparities between different groups' subscription rates to different types of memes were telling. For example, Figure 8 shows that *Digital Life* sponsors had a larger percentage of subscriptions than *Things That Think* sponsors to memes that sounded a cautionary note about technology (e.g., "New does not equal good. More does not equal better"). This is in keeping with the Digital Life Consortium's focus on looking at technology in a broader, human context, and not just liking it for its own sake. Both groups had roughly equal percentage of subscriptions to memes with explicit technical content, however, showing that Digital Life sponsors are certainly not technophobes. A Community Mirror that paired such graphs showing disparity and commonality between groups could be very powerful tool to help establish a shared sense of individual consortia identities in the context of a larger Media Lab identity. Once again, this shared understanding would be very useful starting point for collaborations.

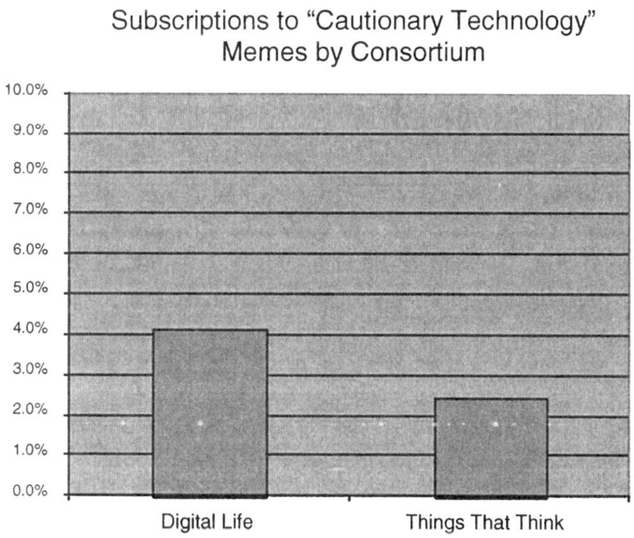

Figure 8: Cautionary Technology Subscriptions by Percentage of Total.

The variance in popularity of "Self-Referential" memes among different Media Lab groups was also revealing. These were memes that were explicitly about memes, or about the meme tag activity. Some examples were "This is not a Meme" and "Make money fast. Pass this meme to your friends." Figure 9 shows that sponsors found these memes less appealing than faculty, who in turn found them less interesting than students. This data supports the stereotype that sponsors prefer ideas that are about the real world, whereas academics are more interested in ideas about ideas and students appear to be the most invested in this kind of metaphysical contemplation. By presenting such a graph at a future event, we would hope people would think about these patterns and their relationships to them.

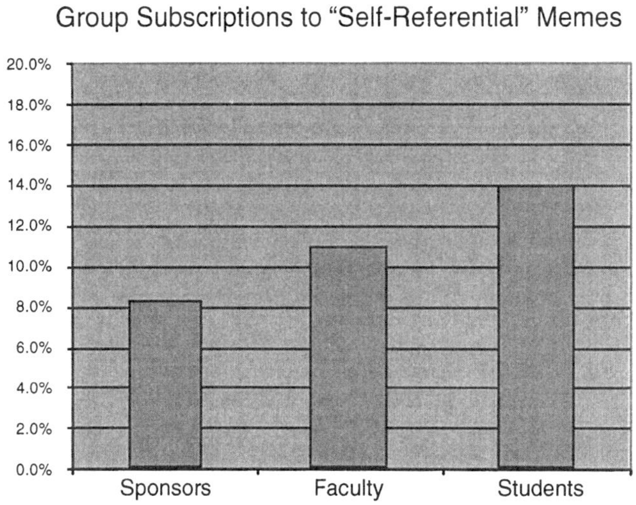

Figure 9: Group Subscriptions to Self-Referential Memes by Percentage of All Group Subscriptions.

Not all visualizations would perpetuate stereotypes. For example, although one might predict some gender differences in terms of memetic taste, the data does not support it. Categories such as "attempt at humor," "techie," "self-referential," "cautionary about technology"—any category we looked at—showed no significant gender-based preferences. Even if they had, however, what would it mean? We believe very strongly that the community in which these visualizations are embedded should determine their meaning. The real-time nature of these visualization is important because it keeps them within the "hermaneutic circle" of those participating in the event: they get to decide the significance of what they see, and whether it should impact their behavior.

CONCLUSION

Our informal observations suggest that the proof-of-concept trial of the Meme Tags was successful. People enthusiastically used the tags through both days of the event, and even through dinner on the first night. The Kiosks were in fairly constant use through both days, with people lining up to author memes that they hoped would reach the "big board" (the Community Mirror). Several people told us that the Meme Tags helped them feel comfortable about approaching people they otherwise would not have. Finally, although we asked for the tags back, many people asked to keep them as conversational props to explain the event to their colleagues.

We also found some flaws in the activity. Probably the most significant was people's seeming lack of attachment to the memes in their tags. Often, we saw that people did not really know what memes they owned. Also, the data showed that no memes really reached a "mass audience"—the maximum number of people that subscribed to any one meme was about forty (we cannot determine this exactly due to the previously mentioned data loss).

Rigorous study of the hypotheses discussed in this paper were beyond of the scope of our initial study. However, now that we have the technology operating and have seen its potential power, we are applying what we learned to the design of a more methodical study. While we will not vary the technology greatly, we are interested experimenting with a different context. We would like to see how the Meme Tags work at a more narrowly focused intellectual gathering, such as a small academic conference. We believe such an environment might offer a more focused meme pool, and result in stronger bonds between memes and participants. This should provide us with the opportunity to further test the impact of the Meme Tags and Community Mirrors on the early stages of collaborative activity.

ACKNOWLEDGMENTS

We are grateful for the contributions of Walter Bender, Michael Best, Vanessa Colella, Austina DeBonte, Judith Donath, Will Glesnes, Kwin Kramer, Lewis Neiboh, Andrew Lippman, Linda Lowe, Bakhtiar Mikhak, Carol Novitsky, Artemis Papert, Rebecca Prendergast, David Williamson Shaffer, Andrew Shalit, Sindhu Srinivas, Sean Sutherland, Deb Widener, and Florence Williams.

This project was funded in part by the Media Laboratory's Things That Think, News in the Future, and Digital Life consortia. Hewlett-Packard donated infrared transceivers used in each of the Meme Tags. Duracell Corp. donated several thousand AA alkaline batteries to power the event.

REFERENCES

1. Borovoy, R., McDonald, M., Martin, F., and Resnick, M. Things that blink: Computationally augmented name tags. *IBM Systems Journal 35*, 3&4.
2. Borovoy, R., Martin, F., Resnick, M., and Silverman, B. Name tags that tell about relationships. *CHI '98 Summary*, Los Angeles, CA, 1998.
3. Davis, F. *Fashion, Culture and Identity.* University of Chicago Press, Chicago, 1992.
4. Dawkins, R. *The Selfish Gene.* New York, Oxford University Press, 1976.
5. Donath, J. Visual who. Presented at the *ACM Multimedia '95*, San Francisco, CA, 1995.
6. Dourish, P. and Bellotti, V. Awareness and coordination in shared workshops. *Proceedings of Computer Supported Cooperative Work '92* (Toronto, CA 1992), ACM Press.
7. Elrod, S., Bruce, R., Goldberg, D., Halasz, F., Janssen, W., Lee, D., McCall, K., Pedersen, E. R., Pier, K., Tang, J., and Welch, B. Liveboard: A large interactive display supporting group meetings, presentations and remote collaboration. *Proceedings of CHI '92 Conference on Human Factors in Computing Systems*, Monterey, CA, 1992.
8. Fish, S. *Is There a Text in this Class?:The Authority of Interpretive Communities.* Harvard University Press, Cambridge, MA, 1980.
9. Goffman, E. *Behavior in Public Places: Notes on the Social Organization of Gatherings.* The Free Press, New York, 1963.
10. Isaacs, E., Tang, J., and Morris, T. Piazza: A desktop environment supporting impromptu and planned interactions. *Proceedings of Computer Supported Cooperative Work '96* (Cambridge, MA 1996), ACM Press, 315–324.
11. Krauss, R. and Fussell, S. Mutual knowledge and communicative effectiveness. In *Intellectual Teamwork: Social and Technological Foundations of Cooperative Work*, L. Erlbaum Associates, Hillsdale, NJ, 1990.
12. Moran, T. et. al. Evolutionary engagement in an ongoing collaborative work process: A case study. *Proceedings of Computer Supported Cooperative Work '96* (Cambridge, MA 1996), ACM Press, 150–159.
13. Nakanishi, H. et. al. Freewalk: Supporting casual meetings in a network. *Proceedings of Computer Supported Cooperative Work '96* (Cambridge, MA 1996), ACM Press, 308–314.
14. Schelling, T. *Micromotives and Macrobehavior.* Norton, New York, 1978.
15. Scott, J. *Social Network Analysis: A Handbook.* SAGE Publications, London, 1991.
16. Stefik, M., Foster, G., Bobrow, D., Kahn, K., Lanning, S., and Suchman, L. Beyond the Chalkboard: Computer support for collaboration and problem solving in meetings. *Communications of the ACM, 30 (1)*, 1987.

Tangible Interfaces for Remote Collaboration and Communication

Scott Brave, Hiroshi Ishii, and Andrew Dahley
MIT Media Laboratory
Tangible Media Group
20 Ames St., Cambridge, MA 02139
{brave,ishii,andyd}@media.mit.edu

ABSTRACT

Current systems for real-time distributed CSCW are largely rooted in traditional GUI-based groupware and voice/video conferencing methodologies. In these approaches, interactions are limited to visual and auditory media, and shared environments are confined to the digital world. This paper presents a new approach to enhance remote collaboration and communication, based on the idea of Tangible Interfaces, which places a greater emphasis on touch and physicality. The approach is grounded in a concept called Synchronized Distributed Physical Objects, which employs telemanipulation technology to create the illusion that distant users are interacting with shared physical objects. We describe two applications of this approach: PSyBench, a physical shared workspace, and inTouch, a device for haptic interpersonal communication.

Keywords

Tangible Interfaces, haptic interfaces, telemanipulation, force-feedback, physical presence

INTRODUCTION

For many years our conception of human-computer interaction has been focused on the Graphical User Interface (GUI) (Figure 1a). GUIs allow interaction with digital objects and online information through the generic screen, keyboard, and pointing device. Current systems for Computer Supported Cooperative Work (CSCW) are largely based on extensions of the GUI to a distributed multi-user context, providing distant users with shared access to online digital environments (Figure 1b). When direct communication between distributed users is desired, these systems are traditionally augmented with voice/video conferencing technologies.

In the real world, touch and physical manipulation play a key role in understanding and affecting our environment [12]. Traditional interfaces to the digital world, in contrast, largely fail to address our sense of touch and offer only the generic keyboard and pointing device as tools for indirect manipulation of digital objects.

CSCW 98 Seattle Washington USA

a) Graphical User Interface (GUI)

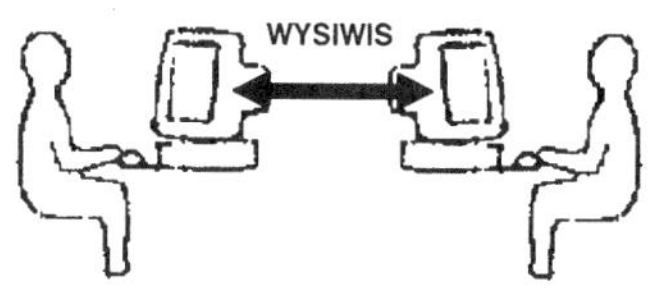

b) Real-time, distributed CSCW based on GUI

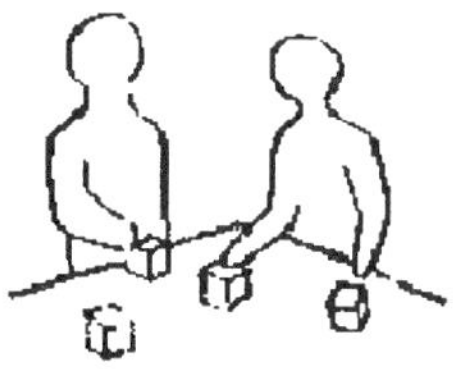

c) Tangible User Interface (TUI)

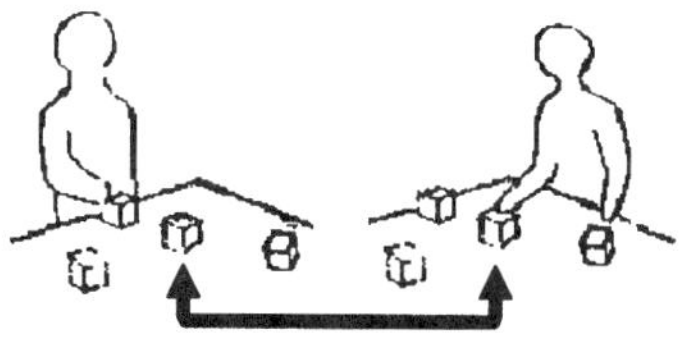

d) Real-time, distributed CSCW based on TUI

Figure 1. Interface Techniques for HCI and CSCW.

Physicality also plays an important role in interpersonal communication (consider the impact of a strong handshake or a nudge for attention). However, current GUI-based systems for distributed interactions, provide no means for this type of physical communication or awareness.

We have previously introduced Tangible User Interfaces (TUIs) as an alternative to the GUI that makes greater use of physical space and real-world objects as interface tools (Figure 1c) [8]. This paper presents an approach called Synchronized Distributed Physical Objects which enables the extension of Tangible User Interfaces into the space of distributed CSCW (Figure 1d). The goal is to enhance real-time remote collaboration and communication by bringing a greater sense of touch and physicality to distributed multi-user interactions. We describe two applications of this approach. PSyBench provides a generic shared physical workspace for distributed users. We present an early prototype of PSyBench, built from two motorized chessboards, and discuss relevant interface issues. We then present inTouch, which applies Synchronized Distributed

Physical Objects to create a "tangible telephone" for long-distance haptic communication.

Tangible Interfaces

Tangible Interfaces [8] represents a general approach to human-computer interaction that puts greater emphasis on physicality than traditional graphics-based interfaces. Illuminating Light [20] is one example of a Tangible Interface for optical design and layout (Figure 2). In this system, users directly arrange and manipulate physical objects representing lasers, mirrors, lenses, and other optical components on an augmented tabletop. The positions of these objects are recognized by the system and the behavior of the laser light is projected onto the table in the same physical space as the optical components. Users are thus able to make full use their hands and bodies in affecting the simulation, as well as use their spatial and kinesthetic senses in understanding the arrangements. Other examples of Tangible Interfaces include the metaDESK [18], Triangles [7], and mediaBlocks [19].

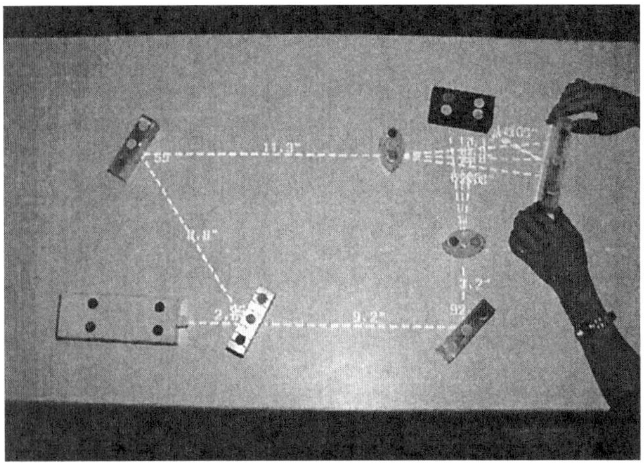

Figure 2. Illuminating Light, a Luminous-Tangible Interface for holography simulation.

A big advantage of Tangible Interfaces is that they support multi-user interactions well. Since a generic pointing device is not needed to mediate interactions, many users can interact with a Tangible Interface system in parallel. In Illuminating Light, for example, multiple users can simultaneously grab and manipulate the optical components to cooperatively create and explore simulated holography layouts.

An important next question is, how can such an object-based interface be used in a distributed context? One solution would simply be to give each *separate* space their own interface objects and then project a video capture of remote spaces onto the local setup, in a way similar to TeamWorkStation [10] (also see [13]). This may be unsatisfactory, however, as local users may want to manipulate objects in remote spaces, as well as in their own local space. Synchronized Distributed Physical Objects presents an approach that allows distant users to share physical objects across distance, enabling the extension of Tangible Interfaces into the space of distributed multi-user interactions.

SYNCHRONIZED DISTRIBUTED PHYSICAL OBJECTS

Imagine that you are an urban planner and are trying to design the layout of a new college campus with a remote colleague. You sit down at a table and place on it a blueprint of the area and a number of scaled models representing each of the landmarks you wish to arrange. Your remote colleague has the same blueprint and set of models and places them on her table. Using both hands, you begin to arrange the physical building models in the central campus. At the same time you are positioning and adjusting the central campus, you see the physical models representing the laboratory clusters moving around on your table in the are designated "east campus". Recognizing your remote colleague's struggle with fitting in all the lab buildings, from her frequent subtle yet unsuccessful tweaks, you grab two of the lab buildings and suggest a new arrangement by moving them to the other side of the campus. On her table, she sees the models move as you make the suggestion and then begins to move her gaze around the table space to get a few different views of the area and your changes.

The above scenario is representative of the Synchronized Distributed Physical Objects vision. Traditional CSCW systems have long allowed distributed users to share *digital* objects and environments (Figure 3a). Synchronized Distributed Physical Objects allow distant users to share *physical* objects and environments as well (Figure 3b).

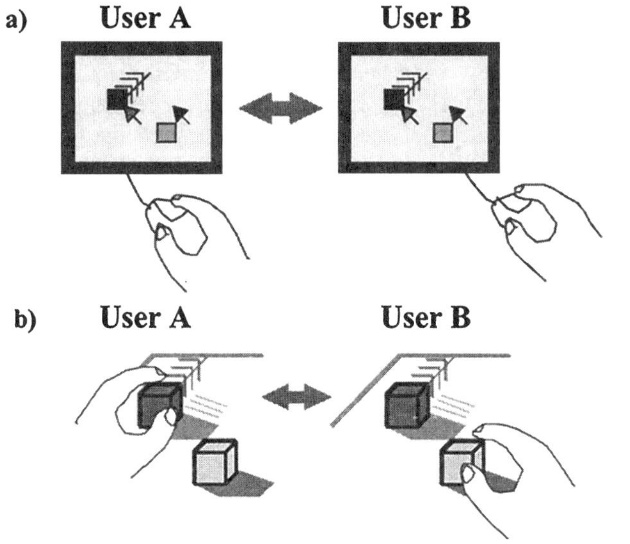

Figure 3. Distributed shared spaces. a) A shared digital space. b) A shared physical space.

A Synchronized Distributed Physical Object creates the illusion of a shared physical object across distance by physically synchronizing the states of distant, identical copies of an object, using telemanipulation technology.

Sensors (e.g. optical encoders, cameras) monitor the states of the distributed copies of a "shared" object and actuators (e.g. motors) are employed to synchronize those states. Thus, when a local user manipulates her local copy of a shared physical object, she is effectively manipulating all remote copies as well (Figure 3b). Distributed users can then share physical objects, able to both manipulate and see others' manipulation of the same objects.

Level of Synchronization

The level to which physical synchronization is implemented can be dictated by the dynamics of the intended application. Although ideally we would like the ability to tightly synchronize all aspects of a shared object (including 3D physical location and internal state), this is often not technically feasible or worthwhile. Depending on the application, it may be adequate--and perhaps even preferable--to synchronize only some physical aspects of the shared objects or relax the synchronization to a looser coupling.

PSyBench, for example, is intended as a generic platform for extending shared physical workspaces, such as Illuminating Light, into a distributed multi-user context. For these types of applications (the urban planning scenario described above is another example), synchronizing the 2D positions and orientations of objects only when they are on an augmented tabletop is reasonable. PSyBench also temporarily suspended synchronization if multiple users move the same objects at once. inTouch, on the other hand, a device for haptic interpersonal communication, exploits a much tighter coupling that maintains synchronization when multiple users simultaneously manipulate an object (Figure 4); however, synchronization is limited to one degree-of-freedom of three cylindrical rollers embedded with a base. This tight coupling provides a channel for direct physical communication between distant users.

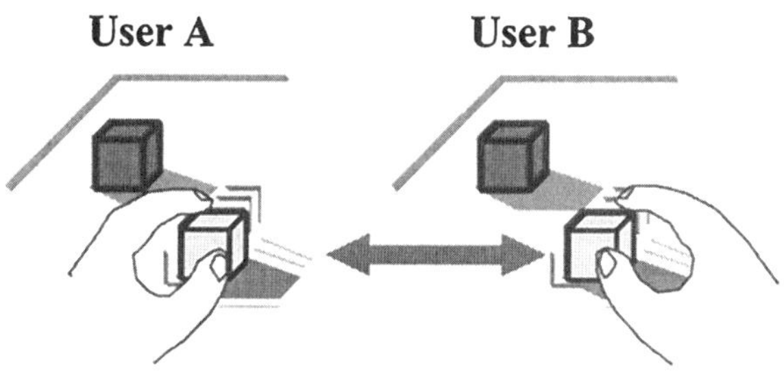

Figure 4. Synchronization of a shared physical object being simultaneously manipulated by multiple users.

PSYBENCH

PSyBench (Physically Synchronized Bench) employs the concept of Synchronized Distributed Physical Objects to provide a generic shared physical workspace across distance. The goal is to allow distributed users to cooperate in Tangible Interface applications, such as Illuminating Light, which are heavily based around physical objects. To do this, we turn each physical interface object into a Synchronized Distributed Physical Object so that it can be shared by distant users.

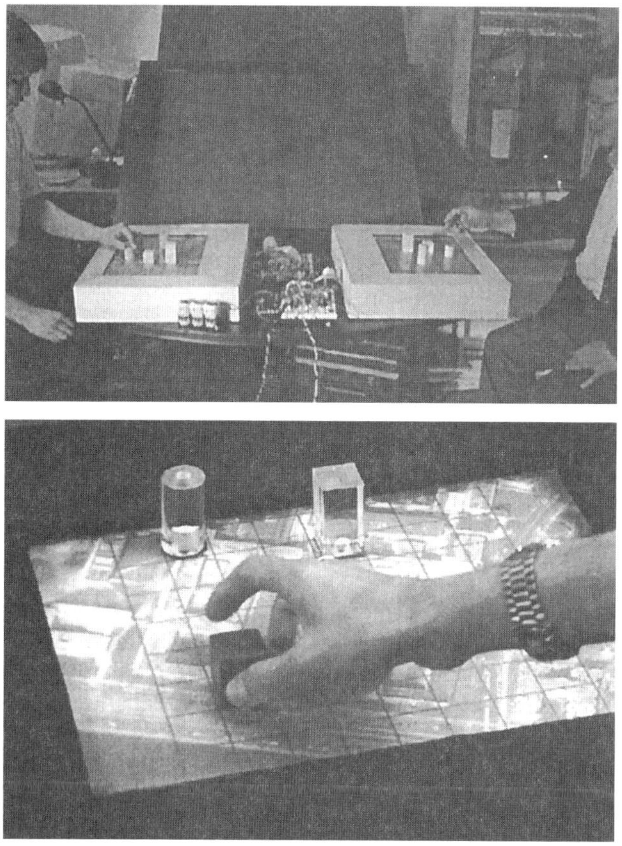

Figure 5. Early prototype of PSyBench.

An initial prototype of PSyBench is constructed from two augmented and connected motorized chessboards from Excalibur (Figure 5). Positions of objects on a ten-by-eight grid are sensed by an array of membrane switches. The objects have magnetic bases so that they can be moved using an electromagnet placed on a 2-axis positioning mechanism under the surface. Each board is outfitted with custom hardware, based around the PIC microprocessor, to handle the control and serial communication between boards. Figure 6 shows this system architecture.

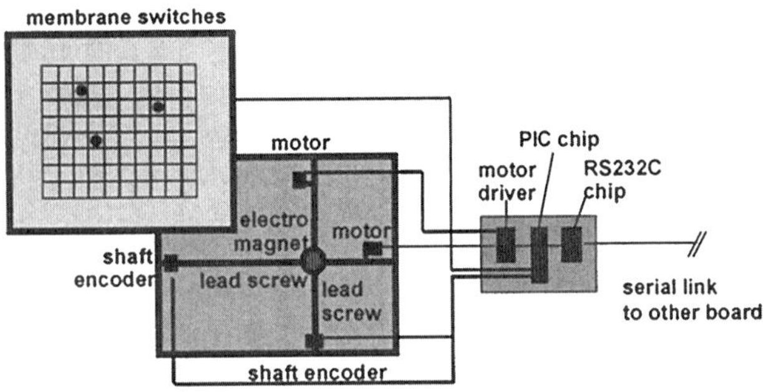

Figure 6. System architecture for PSyBench prototype.

This early prototype has obvious limitations; most notably, positioning is discrete and there is no mechanism for synchronizing the orientation of objects. However, the system has been extremely helpful in bringing to light many implementation issues, as well as design implications.

Tangible Presence

PSyBench primarily provides a means for geographically distant users to collaborate in a shared physical workspace, extending the benefits of Tangible Interfaces into a distributed CSCW context. Initial experiences with the prototype system, however, have suggested that PSyBench also presents a new form of "awareness" of the *physical* presence of remote collaborators. The actions of remote users are manifested in a physical and tangible way, as motion of grasped objects, that suggests form and movement of a motivating physical body. Much in the way that a player piano compels us to imagine a real body sitting at the piano bench with arms extending to the keys, the movement of objects on PSyBench, many initial users have commented, evokes strong feelings of physical presence.

This feeling is particularly compelling considering that the objects affected by remote users are not in some distant or removed space, but in the same space you yourself are sitting and acting in. Objects manipulated by distant users are the same objects that you can touch and feel with your hands; they may even get in your way or touch you as they move. In this way, the shared workspace of objects and your physical interpersonal space are seamlessly integrated, much in the way that ClearBoard integrates the two on a visual level [9].

Co-located Vs. Distributed Users

Another important property of PSyBench is that all users, be they local or remote, essentially interact with the workspace in the same way: by manipulating physical objects on the augmented table's surface. One major difference in person-to-person interactions between co-located and distributed users, however, is the lack of direct visual presence of remote users. Co-located users, for example, are able to see one another's hands moving toward an object before they begin manipulating it. This cue can provide an early means for avoiding the situation where two users try to grab the same object simultaneously. A similar situation arises if a user who has been moving an object pauses to think but still keeps his/her hand on object. In the described system, co-located users would be able to see this behavior, while distributed users would lack this visual cue.

We are currently experimenting with several options to address these issues including projecting a direct visual overlay of remote users' hands onto the table [13] and projecting more abstract representations of users' hands and/or object contact. Integration of more traditional video-conferencing techniques through table projection is also a possibility. One particularly interesting setup could be created if a wall was placed abutting one side of the table onto which a remote user's space was projected in a way similar to ClearBoard [9], providing both direct and task-oriented "gaze awareness" for distributed users.

INTOUCH

Touch is often recognized as a fundamental aspect of interpersonal communication. Whether a strong handshake, an encouraging pat on the back, a nudge for attention, or a gentle brush of a shoulder, physical contact can convey a vitality and immediacy at times more powerful than language. Touch can instantly indicate the nature of a relationship; it is sincere, immediate, and compelling. Yet while many traditional technologies allow communication through sound or image, none are designed for expression through touch. inTouch is a system for haptic interpersonal communication based on the concept of Synchronized Distributed Physical Objects.

Previous work in Telehaptic Communication

Although sparse, there have been a few projects that explore haptic interpersonal communication (or telehaptic communication). *Telephonic Arm Wrestling* [21] provides a basic mechanism to simulate the feeling of arm wresting over a telephone line. *Denta Dentata* [6] is an elementary "hand holding" device that communicates one bit of information over the phone line to activate a mechanism that can squeeze a user's hand. *Feather, Scent, and Shaker* [17] consists of a pair of linked "shaker" objects. Shaking one object causes the other to vibrate, and vice-versa. *HandJive* [5] is a pair of linked hand-held objects for playing haptic games. Each object has a joystick-like controller that can be moved vertically or horizontally. A horizontal displacement of the local object causes a vertical displacement in the remote object, and vice-versa. *Kinesthetic Constructions* [15] explores the application bilateral force-feedback to interpersonal communication. Schena describes a network of large modern sculptures distributed around the world where parts of each sculpture are hapticly connected to sculptures at other locations.

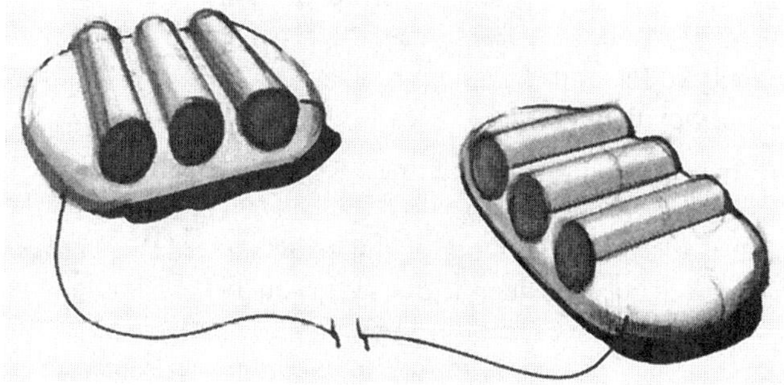

Figure 7. inTouch concept sketch.

inTouch Design

In the spirit of many of these explorations, inTouch provides a system for haptic interpersonal communication across distance. Of these other works, inTouch perhaps resembles the idea of *Kinesthetic Constructions* most closely in that the interaction is bilateral (fully integrated 2-way) and general (without a designated task space or connotation). As seen in Figure 7, inTouch consists of two hand-sized objects each with three cylindrical rollers embedded within a base. Employing the Synchronized Distributed Physical Objects concept, the rollers on each base are hapticly coupled such that each one feels like it is physically linked to its counterpart on the other base. To achieve the tight coupling necessary to allow simultaneous manipulation, inTouch employs bilateral force-feedback technology, with position sensors to monitor the states of the rollers and high precision motors to synchronize those states. Two people separated by distance can then passively feel the other person's manipulation of the rollers, cooperatively move the "shared" rollers, or fight over the state of the rollers, providing a means for expression through touch.

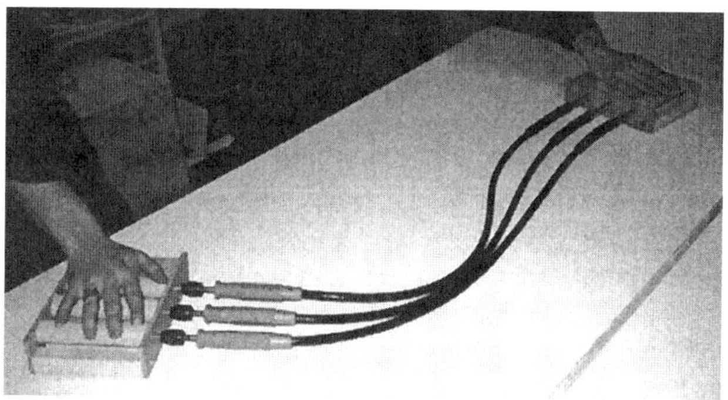

Figure 8. Mechanical mockup of inTouch (inTouch-0). Corresponding rollers are connected using flexible drive shafts.

Mechanical Mockup: inTouch-0

Figure 8 shows an early mockup of inTouch where corresponding rollers were actually mechanically connected using flexible drive shafts (see [1] for a discussion of this mockup as well as inTouch design decisions). This model was implemented in a graduate course on interface design, in October 1996, and was presented in class. Users often described the interaction as fun or playful, with one student relating the experience to when he and his sister would use a broom to play tug-of-war as children. Some remarked that the lack of ability to pass concrete information made the medium uninteresting, while others applauded the subtle and abstract nature of the interaction. This mechanical mockup can been seen as a benchmark for creating the distributed version, since it is this feeling of direct connection that we are aiming to simulate across distance.

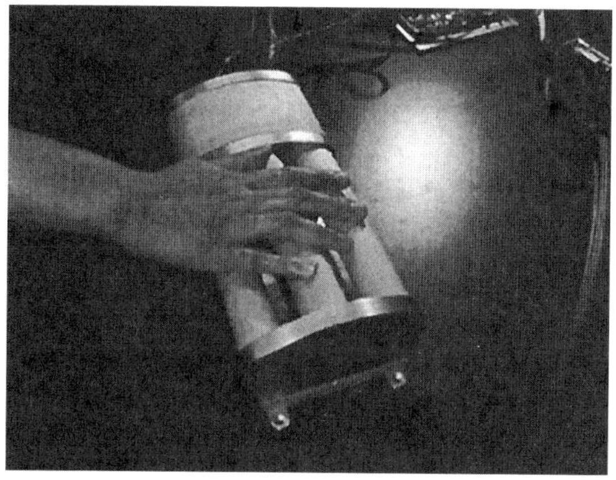

Figure 9. Prototype of inTouch where corresponding rollers are connected virtually, using force-feedback technology.

Standalone Prototype: inTouch-1

InTouch-1 was created next to implement the connection between rollers, virtually, using force-feedback technology (Figure 9). Ideally, the goal is to have virtually connected rollers that behave identically to the mechanically connected rollers in inTouch-0.

The system architecture for inTouch-1 is shown in Figure 10. Hewlett Packard optical position encoders were used to monitor the physical states of the rollers (positions were read directly, other values were interpolated) and high performance Maxon DC motors were used to synchronize those states. A 200MHz Pentium PC controlled all motor/encoder units (one unit for each roller) using Immersion Corporation's Impulse Drive Board 1.0 boards and 2-Axis Card 1.0 ISA cards.

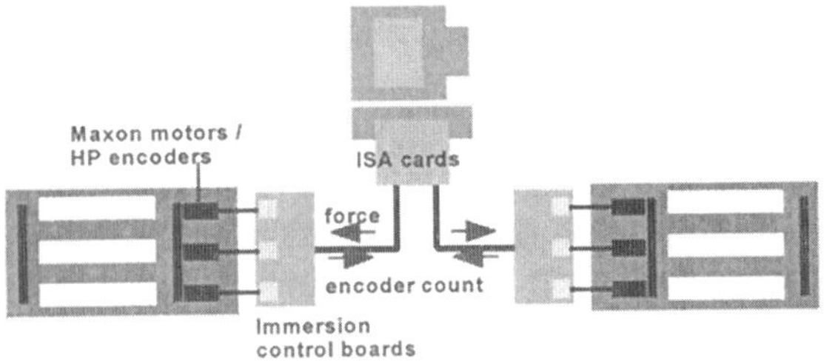

Figure 10. inTouch-1 system architecture (standalone prototype).

The control algorithm that ran on the host PC simulates a highly damped, stiff rotary spring between corresponding rollers. In other words, the algorithm looks at the difference in position of each pair of "connected" rollers and applies a restoring force, proportional to that difference, to bring the rollers together (see the Appendix for an in depth discussion of the control algorithm and optimization).

The first prototype of inTouch-1 was completed in March 1997, and has been demonstrated at sponsor meetings and at the 1997 Ars Electronica Festival, as well as tested internally. People who knew the previous version, inTouch-0, were surprised at how closely the interaction matched the mechanical mockup. In total, more than 500 people have tried inTouch, several of whom have made enthusiastic requests for the system to "keep in touch" with distant family and loved ones. Many people have indicated their belief that inTouch provides a means to be aware of a distant person's emotional state and sincerity, however, we have not yet formally tested this proposition.

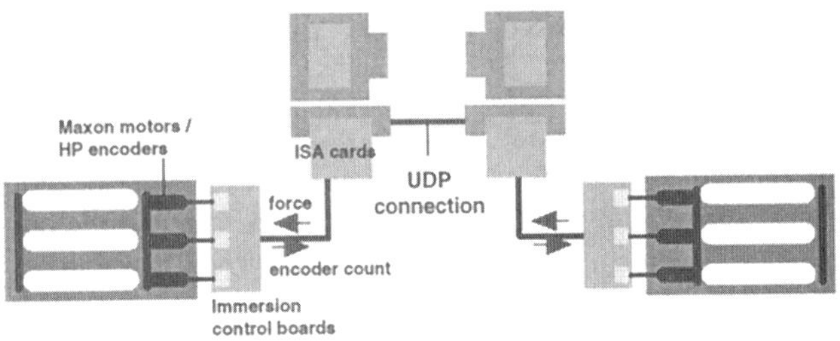

Figure 11. inTouch-2 system architecture.

Networked Prototype: inTouch-2

Our current prototype, inTouch-2, allows the virtual connection of inTouch-1 to be extended over arbitrary distance, using the Internet.

The system architecture for inTouch-2 is shown in Figure 11. The architecture is identical to that of inTouch-1 except that the two sets of three rollers run on separate host computers, distributed over a standard network. Positions and velocities of the local rollers are passed to the remote computer using User Datagram Protocol (UDP).

The basic control algorithm for the networked design is also the same as that for inTouch-1. Each computer simply calculates the forces to impart to its three rollers given the state of each local roller (received from the local control hardware) and the most recently received position and velocity of the corresponding remote roller (passed over the network by the other PC).

We have so far distributed inTouch-2 over the local area network in our building. At this distance, with a little modification to the control algorithm (see Appendix), inTouch-2 behaves identically to inTouch-1. Simulations of longer distances, and consequently longer network delays, have shown promise in extending inTouch over arbitrary distances (see Appendix).

FUTURE WORK

We designed the two prototypes illustrated in this paper, PSyBench and inTouch, as a means to explore a new design space for CSCW and demonstrate the potential of distributed Tangible Interfaces. Although still in the early stages, these explorations have raised a number of interesting and tough research questions. We are now focusing on the following three directions as our future work:

1) Developing robust and extendable platforms for Synchronized Distributed Physical Objects. For example, we are currently developing a larger table-sized version of PSyBench, which detects objects through a combination of machine vision and electromagnetic field sensing, and employs a larger magnetic positioning system for actuation.

2) Identifying collaborative applications which can take full advantage of shared physical objects, coupled with digital augmentation, and

3) Investigating the implications and appropriate applications of a haptic interpersonal communication link through experimentation and long-term user testing.

CONCLUSION

The personal computer has enabled distant users to work together by providing distributed access to shared digital environments. Limited by available interface technology, however, collaborations in these digital spaces often pale in comparison to the richness and facility of interactions in the physical world. In co-located situations, for example, collaborators often rely on the ability to interact with various shared physical objects and appreciate the physical co-presence with others. Traditional interfaces to the digital world, in contrast, tend to impoverish our sense of touch and limit our physical interactions to typing on a generic keyboard or manipulating a plastic mouse.

In this paper, we have introduced a concept called Synchronized Distributed Physical Objects, which poses a new approach to addressing this lack of physicality in GUI-based CSCW interfaces. We have introduced two prototype systems that begin exploration of this new design space for distributed multi-user systems. PSyBench allows distributed users to cooperate in a shared physical workspace, where the presence of remote users is manifested, tangibly, as the movement of shared physical objects. inTouch provides a "tangible telephone" to enable haptic interpersonal communication across distance.

What You See Is What I See (WYSIWIS) has long been a guiding principle for the design of shared *digital* spaces. Synchronized Distributed Physical Objects offer an extension of the WYSIWIS abstraction into the *physical* world. Synchronized Distributed Physical Objects can be seen first as Physical WYSIWIS, since all users will *see* other users' manipulation of the shared physical object. In implementations that use a tight coupling, such as inTouch, What You Feel Is What I Feel will also hold, since all users will be able to simultaneously manipulate and *feel* other users' manipulation of the shared object. As we have mentioned, the idealized notion of strict synchronization may need to be relaxed for technical and/or interface reasons, as is often true with WYSIWIS as well [16]. However, the general principle of Synchronized Distributed Physical Objects can be used as a guide in the design of distributed Tangible Interfaces.

ACKNOWLEDGMENTS

We would like to thank the many fellow Tangible Media Group members who have contributed ideas and time to this project. In particular, we thank Phil Frei for his continued and excellent work in building the mechanical part of inTouch (used in inTouch-1 and -2), Victor Su for his continued efforts in designing the electronics for a next-generation version of inTouch, and Colyn Bulthaup for his hard work in implementing the PSyBench prototype. We would also like to thank Paul Yarin and Wendy Plesniak for their comments on drafts of this paper. This work is funded in part by the National Science Foundation.

REFERENCES

1. Brave, S., and Dahley, D. inTouch: a medium for haptic interpersonal communication. *Extended Abstracts of CHI'97* (Atlanta GA, Mach 1997). ACM Press, 363-364.
2. Burdea, G.C. *Force and Touch Feedback for Virtual Reality*. John Wiley & Sons, Inc., New York NY, 1996.
3. Buxton, W. The three mirrors of interaction: a holistic approach to user interfaces. *Proceedings of Friend21 '91 International Symposum on Next Generation Human Interface* (Tokyo, Japan, November 1991). 25-27.
4. Buxton, W. Touch, Gesture & Marking. Chapter 7 in R.M. Baecker, J. Grudin, W. Buxton and S. Greenberg, S. (Eds.) *Readings in Human Computer Interaction: Toward the Year 2000*. Morgan Kaufmann Publishers, San Francsco CA, 1995.
5. Fogg, B.J., Cutler, L., Arnold, P., and Eisback, C. HandJive: a device for interpersonal haptic entertainment, in *Proceedings of CHI '98* (Los Angeles CA, April 1998), ACM Press. 57-64.
6. Goldberg, K., and Wallace, R. Denta Dentata, in *Visual Proceedings of SIGGRAPH '93*. ACM Press.
7. Gorbet, M.G., Orth, M., and Ishii, H. Triangles: Tangible Interfaces for manipulation and exploration of digital information topography, in *Proceedings of CHI '98* (Los Angeles CA, April 1998), ACM Press. 49-56.
8. Ishii, H., and Ullmer, B. Tangible Bits: towards seamless interfaces between people, bits and atoms, in *Proceedings of CHI '97* (Atlanta GA, Mach 1997), ACM Press, 234-241.
9. Ishii, H., Kobayashi, M., and Grudin, J. Integration of inter-personal space and shared workspace: ClearBoard design and experiments. in *Proceedings of CSCW '92* (Toronto, November 1992), ACM Press, 33-42.
10. Ishii, H. TeamWorkStation: towards a seamless shared workspace, in *Proceedings of CSCW '90* (Los Angeles CA, October 1990), ACM Press, 13-26.
11. Jackson, B., and Rosenberg, L. Force feedback and medical simulation, in Morgan, K., Satava, R., Sieberg, H., Mattheus, R, and Christensen, J. (Eds.) Interactive Technology and the New Paradigm for Healthcare (Amsterdam, January 1995), IOS Press, 147-151.
12. Johnson, M. *The Body in the Mind*. The University of Chicago Press, Chicago IL, 1987.
13. Krueger, M. K. *Artificial Reality II*. Addison Wesley Publishing, Reading MA, 1991.
14. Massie, T.H., and Salisbury, J.K. The Phantom haptic interface: a device for probing virtual objects, in *Proceedings of the 1994 ASME International Mechanical Engineering Congress and Exhibition* (Chicago IL) VOL DSC 55-1, ASME Press, 295 - 302.
15. Schena, B. Design of a Global Network of Interactive, Force-Feedback Sculpture. Master's Thesis in the Department of Mechanical Engineering, Stanford University, 1995.
16. Stefik, M., Bobrow, D. G., Foster, G., Lanning, S., and Tatar, D. WYSIWIS revised: early experiences with multiuser interfaces, in Baecker, R. M. (Ed.), *Readings in Groupware and Computer-Supported Cooperative Work, Assisting Human-Human Collaboration*. Morgan Kaufmann Publishers, Inc., San Mateo CA, 1993, 585-595.
17. Strong, R., and Gaver, B. Feather, Scent and Shaker: Supporting Simple Intimacy, in *Videos, Demonstrations, and Short Papers of CSCW '96* (Boston MA, November 1996), 29-30.
18. Ullmer, B., and Ishii, H. The metaDESK: models and prototypes for Tangible User Interfaces, in *Proceedings of UIST '97, User Interface Software Technology* (Banff, October 1997), ACM Press. 223-232.
19. Ullmer, B., Ishii, H, and Glass, D. mediaBlocks: physical containers, transports, and controls for online media, in *Proceedings of SIGGRAPH '98* (Orlando FL, July 998), ACM Press.

20. Underkoffler, J., and Ishii, H. Illuminating Light: an optical design tool with a luminous-tangible interface, to appear in *Proceedings of CHI '98* (Los Angeles CA, April 1998), ACM Press. 542-549.

21. White, N., and Back D. Telephonic Arm Wrestling, shown at *The Strategic Arts Initiative Symposium* (Salerno, Italy, Spring 1986). See http://www.bmts.com /~normill/artpage.html

APPENDIX A: CONCEPTUAL FRAMEWORK

This appendix illustrates the conceptual framework addressed in this paper in more detail (Figure 12). Current approaches to Human Computer Interaction are largely based on the Graphical User Interface. GUIs allow interaction with digital objects and environments through the generic screen, mouse, and keyboard. Traditional approaches to CSCW employ "What You See Is What I See" (WYSIWIS) to extend this approach into the area of distributed multi-user interactions, allowing distant users to interact in a shared digital space. When direct communication between users is desired, these systems are often augmented with traditional video/telephony.

Tangible Interfaces [8] provides an alternative to these traditional approaches that moves the focus of interaction off of the screen and into the physical world. The aim is to exploit the richness of the physical world while allowing users to make use of their spatial manipulation and perception skills. Examples of Tangible Interfaces for HCI include the metaDESK[18], mediaBlocks[10], Triangles[7], and Illuminating Light [20]. Because many users can manipulate the physical objects in a Tangible Interface simultaneously, Tangible Interfaces already begin to address issues of co-located multi-user interactions.

This paper has introduced Synchronized Distributed Objects as a way to extend the Tangible Interface approach into distributed CSCW. We have described PSyBench, a shared *physical* workspace over distance, as an application of this concept to shared workspace design. We have also considered applications to physical interpersonal space with inTouch, which allows distant users to communicate using their sense of touch.

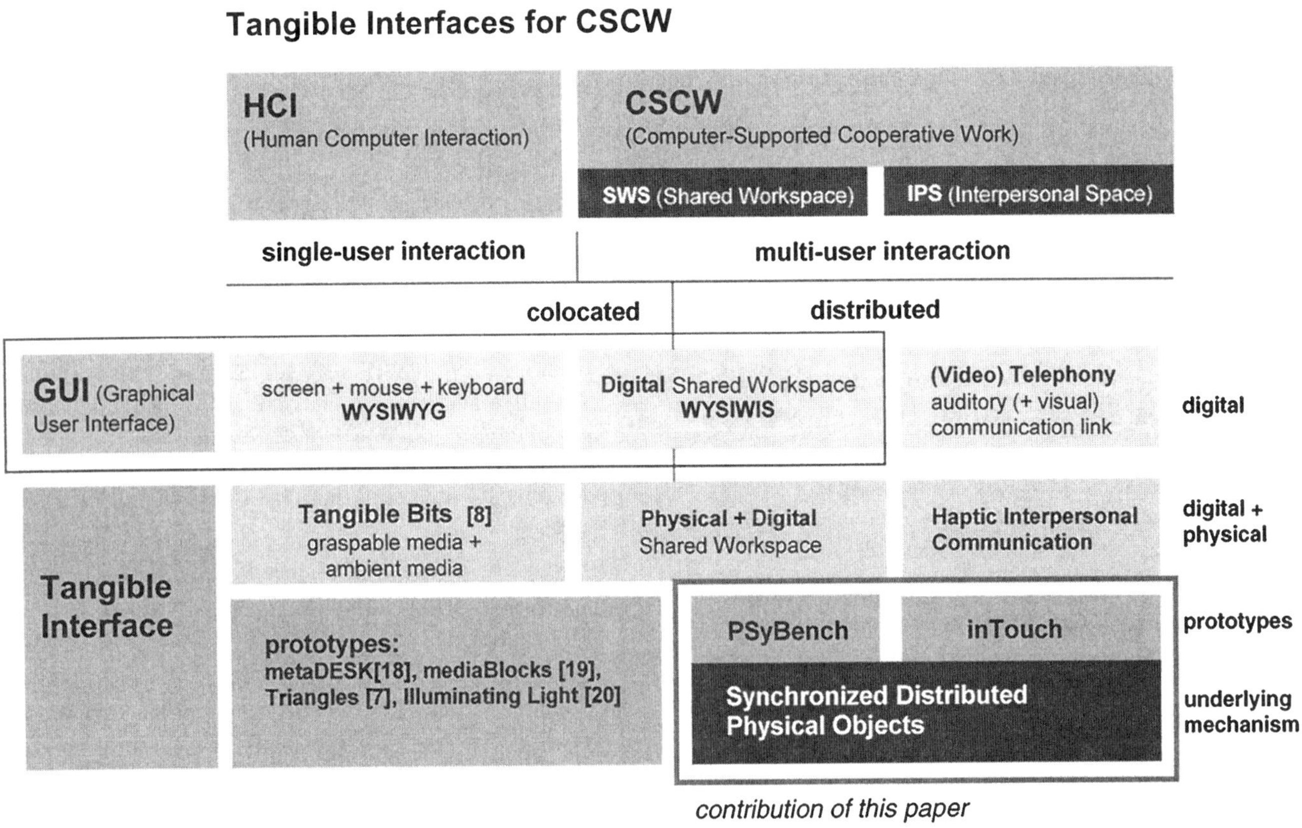

Figure 12. Conceptual framework addressed in this paper.

APPENDIX B: INTOUCH CONTROL ALGORITHM

This appendix describes the control algorithm used for inTouch-1 and inTouch-2 in greater detail.

inTouch-1: Standalone Prototype

As mentioned previously, the control algorithm connects corresponding rollers with a simulated, highly damped, stiff rotary spring. The equations to control a single pair of synchronized rollers is shown below:

$$\tau_0 = -K(\theta_0 - \theta_1) - B(\dot{\theta}_0 - \dot{\theta}_1)$$

$$\tau_1 = -K(\theta_1 - \theta_0) - B(\dot{\theta}_1 - \dot{\theta}_0)$$

$\theta_{0/1}$ = angular positions of the two "connected" rollers

$\tau_{0/1}$ = torque to exert on the corresponding roller

K = spring constant

B = damping constant

Since the system architecture uses only optical position encoders for sensing, angular velocity is interpolated from the ten most recent position readings. Rollover of theta is corrected for so that the rollers behave as expected. It should be noted that the algorithm is symmetrical, giving no roller any advantage over its partner roller.

Optimization

To simulate the direct mechanical connection of inTouch-0 as closely as possible, we would ideally like to set the spring constant (K) extremely high. This constant, however, is limited by the discrete nature of the control algorithm (discrete position encoding, force output, and update interval). Too high of a spring constant for the given parameters will result in unwanted vibration. The maximum torque value is also limited by the strength of the motors.

With the control algorithm running at an update rate of 1 kHz, a spring constant equivalent to ~23mNm/rad gave excellent response and no unwanted vibrations. The maximum output torque of 140nNm for the Maxon motors was also high enough to give an excellent feeling of connection. It should be noted that finite K and maximum torque allow connected rollers to be forced apart from their consistent state; however, doing so merely results in a high force attempting to restore both rollers to that consistent state without causing any harm to the mechanical or control systems. The damping constant, B, was set so that the system appeared to be near critically damped.

Synchronizing More Than Two Objects

A slight remanipulation of the control equations makes clear how to extend the algorithm to synchronize more than two objects:

$$\tau_0 = -2K(\theta_0 - \frac{\theta_0 + \theta_1}{2}) - 2B(\dot{\theta}_0 - \frac{\dot{\theta}_0 + \dot{\theta}_1}{2})$$

$$\tau_1 = -2K(\theta_1 - \frac{\theta_1 + \theta_0}{2}) - 2B(\dot{\theta}_1 - \frac{\dot{\theta}_1 + \dot{\theta}_0}{2})$$

The equations can now also be seen as applying a restoring force on each roller proportional to its offset from the average position of the two rollers. We could clearly now extend this to three rollers for example, but applying a restoring force on each of the three "connected" rollers proportional to its offset from the average position of the three.

inTouch-2: Networked Prototype

As stated earlier, the basic control algorithm for the networked design, inTouch-2, is the same as the algorithm for inTouch-1. Each computer simply calculates the forces to impart to its rollers given the state of each local roller and the most recently received position and velocity of the corresponding remote roller:

Computer 0 runs:

$$\tau_0[t] = -K(\theta_0[t] - \theta_1[t-D]) - B(\dot{\theta}_0[t] - \dot{\theta}_1[t-D])$$

Computer 1 runs:

$$\tau_1[t] = -K(\theta_1[t] - \theta_0[t-D]) - B(\dot{\theta}_1[t] - \dot{\theta}_0[t-D])$$

t = time

D = communication latency (delay)

UDP was chosen as the protocol for communication between distributed objects because it is faster than Transmission Control Protocol (TCP) and the system does not require the reliability of TCP. Absolute position is passed between computers so that a dropped value results in no real loss of data; current values can be assumed to be valid until new values are received. Values are passed between computers along with a count so that values received out of order (i.e. values received that have a lower count than the highest count received so far) are ignored.

Minimizing the Effect of Delay

We have so far distributed inTouch-2 over the local area network in our building (average one-way UDP delay ~2ms). With this small delay, the basic control algorithm described in the previous section works extremely well. Compared to the standalone prototype, inTouch-1, the one difference in performance is that there appears to be more friction on the rollers in the distributed setup. With inTouch-1, the rollers could spin freely (a moderate push would keep a roller spinning for several seconds), while with inTouch-2 the rollers were much harder to spin. The reason for this is that the communication delay causes the local control algorithm to see the remote roller a few steps behind where it really is. So if a user spins a local roller, even if the remote roller is trying to keep up, the local setup sees it as dragging behind, resulting in a resistive force. Our solution to this problem was simply to add prediction into the algorithm so that the local setup is always estimating the true position of the remote roller given the old information. In simulating longer delays, this solution worked well up to a delay of around 12ms (approximate average on-way UDP trip from MIT to University of Pennsylvania), again allowing rollers to spin freely.

Once the delay exceeds around 12ms, however, we begin to see unwanted oscillations in the system due to feedback. Analysis of collected data has shown that the system hits a "resonant" frequency dependent on the delay and other control parameters. A 40ms delay, with the parameters described earlier, for example, results in an unwanted oscillation at around 15Hz. Accurate prediction could alleviate this problem as well, but at these delays, noise in the system compromises the ability to predict accurately and attempting to do so also results in instability.

After recognizing that users rarely try to oscillate the rollers at higher than 5Hz, we decided to put a simple low-pass filter on the position information before it is passed over the network. This solution coupled with a decrease in the spring constant K to 1/3 its previous value stabilized the system up to a delay of 40ms (approximate average on-way UDP trip from MIT to Stanford University). We then added a small amount of prediction back in to alleviate unwanted drag.

Although we had to make the compromise of decreased responsiveness in the system by using a smaller spring constant, K, and a low-pass filter on positions, we were able to achieve very reasonable performance for a delay approximately representing communication across the United States. Since this was achieved with very crude prediction and low-pass filtering, it is likely that further system analysis and tailoring of the control algorithm could increase the allowable delay significantly.

COCA: Collaborative Objects Coordination Architecture

Du Li
Dept. of Computer Science
University of California, Los Angeles
Los Angeles, CA 90024
lidu@cs.ucla.edu

Richard Muntz
Dept. of Computer Science
University of California, Los Angeles
Los Angeles, CA 90024
muntz@cs.ucla.edu

ABSTRACT

Coordination policies vary from collaboration to collaboration and are even subject to evolution in different phases of the same collaboration. It is vital for collaborative systems to be flexible enough to accommodate changes to the coordination policies during development and the lifetime of the collaboration.

Motivated by previous work of separating coordination and computation, we propose COCA as a generic framework for developing collaborative systems and modeling the coordination policies. Participants explicitly adopt roles, and coordination policies are specified in terms of roles in a logic-based specification language. Policies are interpreted at runtime at each collaboration site by a COCA virtual machine. It is easy to change the coordination policies both during development and at runtime.

Keywords

CSCW, Groupware, Collaboration, Coordination Languages, Logic Programming, Distributed Systems

INTRODUCTION

Motivation

Social groups are governed by particular policies. To support group collaboration more effectively with the help of networked computer systems, these social policies must be somehow translated into rules in the supporting software, called *coordination policies*. Apart from rules for access control [18], concurrency control [7] and floor control [3], we also include as coordination policies the following design considerations commonly seen in the literature: process architecture and data distribution schemes, role and session constraints, exception handling, etc. Process architecture and data distribution schemes are often critical to the performance and functioning of the whole collaboration. A replicated scheme may increase availability and performance but requires more complicated control algorithms. A centralized architecture is easier to control, but it does not scale well and the central component often becomes the bottleneck and single point of failure of the whole system. Many collaborations have strict constraints over roles such as who can take which roles and how many participants can take a certain role. Many applications require flexible session control [6][8] to allow the participants to dynamically join and leave a session, to take multiple roles simultaneously, and to smoothly shift between different roles. Exception handling is critical in many applications to handle undesirable situations such as floor loss due to unexpected loss of the floor controller or network segmentation. Many social rules are better built into the software as mechanical protocols to ensure that they are followed by all the participants, while some others are better left to the participants as social protocols to obtain more flexibility [6][8]. This is opposed to traditional single-user or distributed systems in which human-computer interaction patterns are generally more predictable and can be governed by pre-coded mechanical rules.

Coordination policies are usually sensitive to the work style and organizational structure of individual groups. Different groups are often governed by different policies, and even the same group may need different coordination policies in different phases of its collaboration. Development of collaborative systems is typically heuristic in that the definition of coordination policies often involves intensive interactions between end users, developers and scientists from many fields. This is in contrast to a once-and-for-all solution that defines everything right from the beginning. With regard to this dynamic nature of collaborative systems, it is vital to start with a software architecture that is flexible enough to model collaborations and to accommodate the evolution of coordination policies both during the development of experimental systems and at runtime by the end users.

Over the past decade, the CSCW community has developed a number of experimental collaborative systems and commercial products. The traditional approach is to develop groupware in procedural languages, such as C/C++. Early collaborative systems were generally developed in this way on a per-application basis and much implementation effort was duplicated.

Later, designers extracted some of the basic services required by certain domain of groupware systems and provided them to the application developers in the form of groupware toolkits, such as GroupKit [17] and MASH [15]. Groupware toolkits usually provide a library of programming interfaces for building multi-user interfaces, and a few programming abstractions such as those for group communication and those for separating data views from representation and keeping them consistent. In this way, a lot of implementation work is avoided, but the coordination policies are still developed in procedural languages and built into all the involved computation modules. It is therefore still difficult to accommodate evolution of coordination policies either during development time or at runtime. Tools developed in this way are generally not compatible with each other and cannot interoperate. This results in a plethora of experimental systems while it is still hard for the users to find the right systems to meet their particular needs.

More recently, researchers [11] in coordination languages advocate separation of coordination and computation in the design of concurrent systems. This principle is echoed in the CSCW literature. Cortes [1] proposed a declarative language DCWPL, and Furuta [10] used a variant of Petri Nets, CTN or colored timed nets, respectively, to separate implementation of coordination policies from other computation components and specify coordination policies in a declarative way. Languages introduced therein vary in expressive power. Choices between them are usually a matter of individual taste or convenience. This approach can, or at least shows promise to, overcome the afore-mentioned problems of the traditional approach.

COCA and Its Contribution

We favor the idea of separating coordination and computation, and propose COCA (Collaborative Object Coordination Architecture) as a generic framework for developing evolvable collaborative systems. Based on IP multicast [2] as its group communication model, COCA provides the groupware developers a dual-bus collaboration architecture and a logic-based specification language for modeling coordination policies. We divide participants in a collaboration by roles, and define active rules for each role to guard its interactions with other collaborators. These policies are interpreted at runtime by the COCA virtual machine, a copy of which runs on each participant machine. This approach makes it convenient to make changes both during development and at runtime.

Compared to previous work, COCA has at least the following advantages. Firstly, coordination policies are explicitly and collectively specified instead of being scattered in all the involved components of a collaborative system. The policies are much more tractable to manage and evolve than they would otherwise. Secondly, development of other components such as the audio/video communication tools, is relatively simple and introduces no significant work over single-user scenarios. Many tools can even be incorporated from legacy systems with only minor work. The same tools can be used in many collaboration scenarios by only changing the coordination policies in the collaboration specification. Reusability of collaboration modules can be generally achieved. Thirdly, the language we propose is based on first-order logic and has a simple syntax and a clear semantics. The language is self-contained so that we do not need to constantly resort to procedural languages for more expressive power. Potentially we can develop tools to verify properties of the specification, detect possible inconsistencies and deadlock situations, and derive test cases from the specification. Additionally, COCA is a meta-architecture in the sense that it does not impose any process architecture or data distribution schemes, or any other coordination policies. The users have the full freedom to specify these policies with the aid of the language.

Organization of This Paper

We first compare COCA with the major related work. Then we describe the COCA architecture, and proceed to present the syntax and semantics of our specification language in a semi-formal manner. A simple example is elaborated in a progressive way. Current status of the COCA prototype is also discussed. Finally some conclusions are presented.

RELATED WORK

Reker etc. [16] attempted to use LOTOS [12] to specify a group drawing tool. LOTOS is a formal description technique used in specifying telecommunication systems. However, our observation is that LOTOS and other process algebra based formal methods are not convenient for specifying collaborations. In LOTOS, communicating components must be explicitly connected by parallel composition operators. This proved sufficient for some situations where communicating components are fixed and relatively small in number. But in many collaborative situations, only the participant types (namely the roles) are fixed, while the number of involved participants is large and fluid, the exact number cannot be determined at specification time. LOTOS is not directly convenient for specifying such situations. And even for small and fixed-population collaborative situations, LOTOS is also not always convenient. For example, in order to model situations where a process offers a value and several other processes accept it, LOTOS uses a multi-way synchronization which fails if even one process fails to synchronize at that point. Many collaborations can actually tolerate such exceptions by allowing processes that have received the value to proceed while ignoring or trying to re-transmit the lost data to processes which are temporally unavailable due to communication link delay or failure. We replace the parallel composition operators in LOTOS with the collaboration bus and the conference bus, synchronization among communicating components are achieved by explicit message passing.

Moses [13] was originally intended to make the Linda [11] communication safer by ensuring that the interaction of each process with the shared tuple space be managed by a controller. Each controller enforces a set of rules to capture the following two events: when a message is **sent** out by the local agent, and when one **arrive**s at this agent, the local control state is checked, transformation is possibly performed, then this message is either **forward**ed to the tuple space, or **deliver**ed to the local agent, or blocked according to the rule definition. Our work is different from Moses in the following ways: (1) we explicitly divide participants in a policy group by roles. Different roles are controlled by different set of rules rather than all participants governed by the same set of rules as in Moses. Messages can be directed to roles (fluid sets of participants) as well as individual participants. We further allow participants to dynamically join and leave a collaboration by taking and dropping roles, and support the dynamic modification of rules at runtime. (2) We borrowed the concept of "gate" from LOTOS to denote the points where our controller, the COCA virtual machine, interacts with its environment, and define active rules upon the arrival of messages at these gates. In this way, the controller can monitor messages arriving at multiple different gates instead of just one to and one from the tuple space as defined in Moses.

Our work is related to Trellis [10] and DCWPL [1] in that we all advocate separating implementation of the coordination part from other computation parts, so that the coordination policies can be specified in a more declarative way, interpreted at runtime, and allowing easy evolution of coordination policies. DCWPL is a scripting language which provides facilities for modeling and controlling access to shared artifacts. It allows definition of a fixed set of artifact attributes such as "Authorized", "MaxInstance", and trigger-like attributes such as "Preexecution", "Postexecution" etc. Even if we can presume that the set of attributes provided is sufficient to capture every possible artifact in all collaborations so that we do not need to extend the language under any circumstances, the problem is that whenever a policy or function is not directly available in the declarative language DCWPL, the user still needs to program it in a procedural language. In this way the declarativeness of the language is undermined. The language we propose in COCA, however, is self-contained. The users can specify whatever coordination policies they want without constantly resorting to a procedural language, assuming the tools have the required functionality. In this way the declarative feature is reserved.

Trellis [10] used a variant of Petri Nets, CTN or colored timed nets, to specify group interaction protocols. Trellis is a client/server architecture in which a centralized controller processes service requests from clients according to the specification. We argue a centralized architecture like Trellis may work well for small groups which primarily exchange textual messages. But for large groups with hundreds of participants, especially when multimedia data is widely communicated, it is not clear how it is modeled and handled in Trellis and what level of performance can be expected. It is also not clear, at least in the paper, how CTN models the collaboration of large groups whose participants are highly fluid, and how exceptions, such as floor loss and unexpected loss of the current floor holder, are handled in a Trellis specification.

Intermezzo [6] is also related in that it used the concepts of roles and policies in a manner quite similar to COCA. However, the difference between Intermezzo and COCA is evident. In Intermezzo, roles are limited to the definition of access control groups. COCA takes a more radical approach in which roles are used to specify coordination policies. Policies in COCA include not only access control, but also session control, concurrency control, floor control, etc. As a result, the language for defining roles and policies in Intermezzo is much simpler and limited in expressive power, as compared with the logic-based language in COCA.

COCA ARCHITECTURE

An important difference between groupware and traditional software is the critical need for an efficient and scalable group communication model. Early models were largely based on grouping of multiple point-to-point communications. A packet with **n** intended recipients must be delivered **n** times by the sender, regardless of the physical location of the involved parties. This approach incurs tremendous overhead on both the message senders and the communication paths, and latency increases with the size of the receiver population. Especially for time-critical data delivery, its performance is not acceptable. Deering [2] proposed IP multicast as a better solution to this problem. In this model, multicast messages are delivered along the minimum spanning tree built from the sender to all the receivers. Overlapping paths are utilized and scalability is achieved. Research and development of the MBone tools [9][14] reveals that IP multicast is an efficient model for group communication, both for delivery of time-critical media streams and for non-realtime messages.

We adopt IP multicast as the group communication model of COCA. The collaboration architecture we propose consists of the following three layers. The communication layer lies at the bottom providing basic multicast and unicast services. The application layer on the top runs the multimedia communication tools, session control tools, data presentation and manipulation interfaces, etc. The collaboration layer in the middle interprets the coordination policies and glues the other two layers together. Our work focuses on the collaboration layer and the COCA virtual machine realizes this layer. Similar to the Mbone tools, we utilize the notions of collaboration bus and conference bus, and view COCA as a dual-bus architecture. These two buses are an abstraction of the communication layer. The collaboration bus connects all the participants involved in the same collaboration together and provides the basis for them to communicate. The conference bus connects a local instance of the COCA virtual machine and the various collaboration tools and other computation modules at that site.

As an example, figure 1 and figure 2 give the COCA perspective of the software architecture of a typical classroom-type collaboration. In figure 1, the participants, such as a professor and multiple students, are connected by the collaboration bus. Figure 2 depicts the microscopic view of each participant: the COCA virtual machine connects the collaboration bus and the conference bus, monitoring and controlling information flows through it according to the policy specification. Collaboration tools such as the audio and video tools for communication, the presentation tool for showing slides, the whiteboard tool for drawing, and the floor control tool, are connected with the COCA virtual machine via the conference bus.

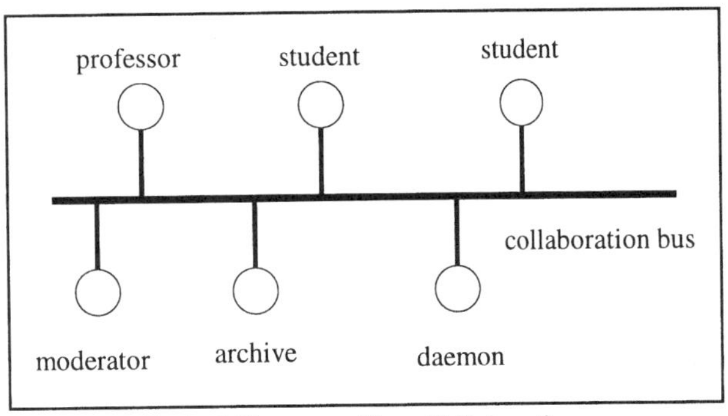

Figure 1. A Typical Classroom-Type Collaboration

In a classroom, the professor and the students usually follow different social rules. For example, in a lecture, the professor talks until there is a question, and then goes on after he or she answers the question. A student usually listens passively, and needs permission from the professor to talk. In collaborative systems, the rules which control who can speak at a time are translated into floor control policies. Different collaborations require different floor control policies. In a formal situation like the classroom, participants need to explicitly request the floor in order to talk, while in an informal conversation, participants may be free to speak without explicit control. We say the set of participants who are governed by the same set of coordination policies is playing the same **role**.

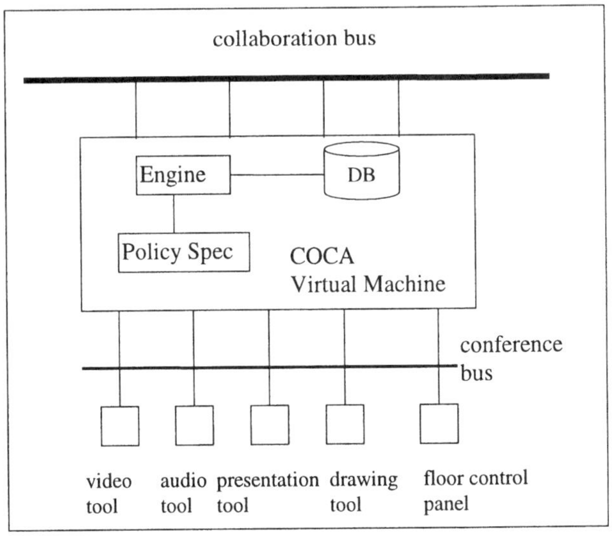

Figure 2. Microscopic View of Each Participant

In COCA, we explicitly divide participants into different roles, and specify their individual behavior and constraints in different sets of logic rules. Specifically in this example, in addition to a professor role and a student role, a moderator role can be defined to take care of floor control. An archive role can be defined to interact with an external database in order to control the storage and retrieval of messages or media streams communicated during a collaboration. A daemon role can be defined to perform session management tasks, such as controlling who can take which role, how a session is established and torn down. A participant may take multiple roles at the same time, drop a role and shift between different roles as the collaboration progresses, as long as it is allowed in the specification.

In the multimedia networking community, separate multicast channels are usually allocated to deliver media streams and control messages that have different quality of service requirements. In figure 2, we can assign separate multicast channels to deliver the audio/video streams, image streams, drawing commands, and floor control messages to and from different collaboration tools respectively. Therefore, the collaboration bus and the conference bus may each consist of multiple multicast channels and unicast connections. Note that channels in the collaboration bus and the conference bus may be multiplexed and thus are not necessarily mapped in a one-to-one manner. This is decided by the coordination policies. Following the conventions of LOTOS [12], we call the interfaces or service access points to these communication channels **gates**. When a media packet or message arrives at one gate, we may do some processing and then forward the same packet or new ones to other gates, or just block it. In this way, coordination messages are transmitted from the tools of one participant to those of the other participants. Conversely, from the perspective of the conference bus and the collaboration bus, we can also view the interfaces to a COCA virtual machine as gates. Then the COCA virtual machine, controlled by the coordination policies, appears to its environment as a software module with gates where the virtual machine and its environment communicate.

COCA SPECIFICATION LANGUAGE

Syntax and Semantics

We adopt the Prolog convention in our specification language. Prolog syntax and semantics apply wherever not otherwise stated. Variables begin in upper case, constants, functors and predicates begin in lower case. Anonymous variables are denoted by underscores. Comment lines start with double slashes "//".

[**Def**.1] A **term** is defined inductively as follows:
(1) A variable is a term
(2) A constant is a term
(3) If f is an n-ary function symbol and $T_1, T_2, \ldots, T_n$ are terms, then $f(T_1, T_2, \ldots, T_n)$ is a term (called a compound term), $n \geq 0$. For convenience, we sometimes use f/n to denote a functor f with arity n.

A special functor **self/0** is used in a COCA specification to denote the current participant. Each appearance of it is replaced at runtime with a structure which uniquely denotes the current participant, possibly including the user login name, IP address and the list of roles this participant is currently taking in a collaboration.

[**Def**.2] A **formula** is defined inductively as follows:
(1) if p is an n-ary predicate symbol and $T_1, T_2, \ldots, T_n$ are terms, then $p(T_1, T_2, \ldots, T_n)$ is a formula (called an atomic formula or more simply, an **atom**), $n \geq 0$. We use p/n to denote a predicate p with arity n.
(2) If T is a compound term, then the following are atomic formulas called database formulas (keywords **query**, **add** and **delete** are called database predicates).
- (2.1) **query** T: evaluates to true if T unifies with a term in the database.
- (2.2) **add** T: adds T to the database and evaluates to true.
- (2.3) **delete** T: deletes the first term unified with T from the database and evaluates to true if there is at least one unified term.

(3) if F is a formula, so is (**not** F).

[**Def**.3] A **literal** is an atom or the negation of an atom. A **positive literal** is an atom. A **negative literal** is the negation of an atom.

[**Def**.4] If A is a positive literal, $B_1, B_2, \ldots, B_n$ are literals, $n \geq 0$, then

A :- $B_1, B_2, \ldots, B_n$.

is a **Prolog rule**. Atom A is called the **head**, and $B_1, B_2, \ldots, B_n$ combined is called the **body** of this rule. We further require that rule heads can only be atoms defined by the first rule of **Def**.2.

To define a collaboration, we need to declare an optional collaboration bus which is used to connect all the participants in this collaboration. A collaboration bus is defined in the following form:

collaboration-bus { *<channel-declarations>* }

with at least one channel declaration. A channel declaration has the following form:

channel (*<channel name>*).

Channels declared in the collaboration bus are global to the whole collaboration.

Then one or more roles are defined each in the form below, where rules include Prolog rules defined above as well as COCA rules which will be defined later:

role *<role name>*
{
[**conference-bus** { *<channel-declarations>* } *]*
[<rules>]
}

A conference bus declaration is also optional. Rules are optional for each role. The conference bus is used for communication between the COCA virtual machine and the collaboration tools for each role. So channel names declared there are local to each role. Channels in the conference buses of different roles can use the same name without confusion. But communication channels in the same scope cannot use the same name, nor can they use role names.

We introduce predicate **isa**/2 to test if a given participant is currently taking a given role. Its first argument is either functor **self/0** or a bound variable denoting a participant, the second argument is the name of a role. A typical collaboration may require the definition of a special role "daemon". A participant taking the daemon role will become the session daemon and, in this role, controls who is allowed to take which roles, and also performs other session management related tasks. It is possible for a session to have multiple daemons, e.g. for availability and scalability. A session without a daemon role will be open to all, i.e., any participant can take any roles.

Following the convention of LOTOS, we use the term **gate** to denote a service access point to a communication channel. Role names can be used directly as channels without being explicitly declared in the collaboration bus. Gates usually use the same name as the communication channels.

[**Def**.5] Further, we adopt a convention of LOTOS (but with slight changes in syntax), and define the following **LOTOS formulas** as complementary to **Def**.2

(1) *gname* **!** (<*terms*>)

(2) *gname* **?** (<*terms*>)

"!" and "?" are called **offer** and **accept** in LOTOS respectively. The former sends out a list of terms through a gate named "*gname*", while the latter expects a list of terms at gate "*gname*".

In a LOTOS specification, it is permitted to use these two formulas together with parallel composition operators. In COCA, we use communication channels instead of parallel composition operators to connect components. To reduce confusion without harming expressive power, we only allow use of **offer** formulas in the rule body and replace the **accept** formulas with active rules. An active rule waits for certain event at a given gate and will be fired when the event unifies with the arguments of its head predicate. A LOTOS formulas mixed with **offer** and **accept** can be simulated by an automaton. We can easily rewrite the original formulas by keeping only the **offer** formulas in the rule body, recording state information in the database, and checking the database states in the active rules.

[**Def**.6] Currently, we define **COCA active rules** to include only the following forms:

(1) **on-arrive**(gate(<*gate name*>), ...) :- ...

(2) **on-take**(role(<*role name*>), source(< *term*>), ...) :- ..

(3) **on-drop**(role(<*role name*>), source(<*term*>), ...) :- ...

Rules of form (2) and (3) are only defined in the daemon role for the convenience of monitoring membership changes of the defined roles. Essentially, they are equivalent to on-arrive rules defined on the daemon gate, with role name and participant id, etc. as arguments. Functors gate/1, role/1, source/1, etc. are not treated differently from other functors if they are used elsewhere.

[**Def**.7] Thus we specify a collaboration in the following format:

> **collaboration** <*collaboration name*>
> {
> *[* **collaboration-bus**{ <*channel-declarations*> } *]*
> <*role-definitions*>
> }

As is illustrated in figure 2, the COCA virtual machine includes a reasoning engine and an internal database. The reasoning engine monitors events which arrive at gates according to the collaboration specification, firing the matched active rules, and performing the specified actions. The database maintains state information regarding the ongoing collaboration. All the database predicates defined in COCA are performed against this database. Thus COCA has two levels of concurrency. On a higher level, a number of participants taking roles from the same collaboration are working on a common task concurrently. They synchronize with each other through explicit message passing. On a lower level, execution threads of different active rules synchronize with each other via the internal database by explicitly querying and updating the database states.

EXAMPLE

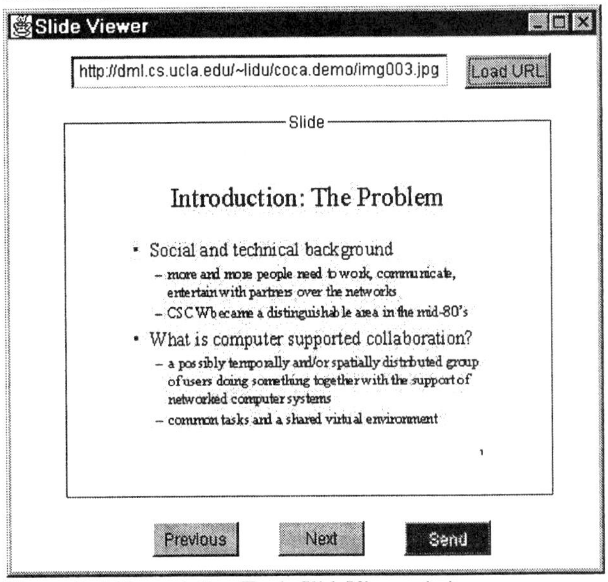

Figure 3. A Presentation Tool: SlideViewer (*sv*)

As shown in figure 3, SlideViewer (*sv*) is a simple but versatile tool for showing slides. It can be used in a single-user scenario and a number of multi-user situations. For instance, a distributed group can use it to plan a joint presentation, and a professor can use it for presentation to a class. When the user types in the address of a slide and presses the button "Load URL", a slide is loaded and displayed. The "Previous" and "Next" buttons are used to navigate between loaded slides. When used in a collaboration, the "Send" button is used to send the current slide to other participants. Meanwhile, *sv* receives and displays slides from other participants. Two gates are required for an *sv* to interact with its environment: one for receiving messages and one for sending out messages, respectively. We can specify coordination policies in order for the COCA virtual machine to talk with *sv* through those two gates. The *sv*'s engaged in a collaboration can be orchestrated to behave in many ways by specifying different coordination policies.

Let's start to specify the coordination policies in figure 4. Here we only define one role, the "chaotic slide viewer". The COCA virtual machines communicate with each other through the "remote" channel in the collaboration bus, and each exchanges messages with its local *sv* via the "local-in" and "local-out" channels in the conference bus. There are simply two active rules. One is defined for gate "remote": when a slide X with id URL arrives from some remote *sv*, it is forwarded to the local *sv* via gate "local-out". Another rule is defined for gate "local-in": when the local *sv* sends a slide X with id URL, it is delivered to other *sv*'s via gate "remote". This collaboration is chaotic because everybody can send out slides anytime and every slide received from other participants is displayed immediately. But this is not acceptable in a more formal collaboration like the classroom where the participants, the professor and the students, may require a more controlled interaction protocol. In this case we need to define a floor control policy to decide who can send out slides at any time.

```
collaboration "chaotic presentation"
{
  collaboration-bus { channel(remote). }

  role "chaotic slide viewer"
  {
    conference-bus {
      channel(local-in).
      channel(local-out).
    }

    on-arrive(gate(remote), id(URL), slide(X)) :-
      local-out !(id(URL), slide(X)).

    on-arrive(gate(local-in), id(URL), slide(X)) :-
      remote !(id(URL), slide(X)).
  }
}
```

Figure 4. Specification of a "chaotic presentation"

We redefine the two active rules of the "chaotic slide viewer" as shown in figure 5, and call the modified role "controlled slide viewer". Now, when a slide arrives from a remote *sv*, it is associated with a unique id of the sender, so that we can check if he or she is currently holding the "slide floor", to the best of our knowledge. Only if this is the case, is that slide forwarded to the local *sv*. And when the local *sv* wants to send out a slide to other participants, it is checked in the local knowledge base, if it is the current holder of the slide floor. If so, the participant id is sent with the slide as an additional term to other *sv*'s via gate "remote", otherwise it is simply thrown away. At this point, we can change the name of our collaboration from "chaotic presentation" to "controlled presentation".

```
on-arrive(gate(remote), id(URL), slide(X), source(Agent)) :-
        query held-by(slide-floor, Agent),
        local-out !(id(URL), slide(X)).

on-arrive(gate(local-in), id(URL), slide(X)) :-
        query held-by(slide-floor, self),
        remote !(id(URL), slide(X), source(self)).
```

Figure 5. Rules for the "controlled slide viewer" role

```
role moderator
{
        conference-bus {
            channel(cntrl-in).
            channel(cntrl-out).
        }

        on-arrive(gate(cntrl-in), grant(slide-floor, Agent)) :-
            grant-floor(slide-floor, Agent).

        grant-floor(slide-floor, self) :-
            not query held-by(slide-floor, _),
            add held-by(slide-floor, self),
            cntrl-out !(grant(slide-floor, self)),
            msg !(grant(slide-floor, self)).

        grant-floor(slide-floor, Agent) :-
            delete held-by(slide-floor, _),
            add held-by(slide-floor, Agent),
            cntrl-out !(grant(slide-floor, Agent)),
            msg !(grant(slide-floor, Agent)).

        on-arrive(gate(msg), request(slide-floor, Agent)) :-
            query held-by(slide-floor, self),
            cntrl-out !(request(slide-floor, Agent)).

        on-arrive(gate(cntrl-in), revoke(slide-floor, _)) :-
            delete held-by(slide-floor, _),
            add held-by(slide-floor, self),
            cntrl-out !(grant(slide-floor, self)),
            msg !(grant(slide-floor, self)).

        on-arrive(gate(msg), release(slide-floor, Agent)) :-
            query held-by(slide-floor, Agent),
            delete held-by(slide-floor, Agent),
            add held-by(slide-floor, self),
            cntrl-out !(grant(slide-floor, self)),
            msg !(grant(slide-floor, self)).
}
```

Figure 6. Specification of the moderator role.

In order to control the slide floor, we define a centralized control policy. This policy requires a moderator role that handles floor requests and grants the slide floor to one appropriate participant at a time. Aside from the moderator role, an aspirant role is specified to denote participants who will possibly request the slide floor. For simplicity, we require that only one participant can take the moderator role while any number of participants can take the aspirant role. The moderator and the aspirants use different floor control interfaces. The one used by the former allows the moderator to grant floor to one aspirant or revoke the floor from the current floor holder. The interface used by an aspirant, however, only allows the aspirant to request the floor and release it afterwards. In both cases, the floor control tools communicate with their environment at two gates: one for sending and one for receiving floor control commands respectively. To deliver the floor control messages among participants, we add one more channel "msg" to the collaboration bus. The moderator and each of the aspirants will exchange messages with their floor control tools through channels "cntrl-in" and "cntrl-out" declared in the conference bus.

The moderator role is defined in figure 6. Initially, the moderator grants the slide floor only to itself. When a message arrives at the "msg" gate requesting the slide floor, the local database is checked to see if the moderator itself is the current floor holder (which indicates whether the floor is free). If so, this request is forwarded to the floor control tool via gate "cntrl-out", leaving the decision to the moderator. When the moderator decides to grant the slide floor to some participant, a message will be received at the "cntrl-in" gate. Here we simply update the database and multicast such a decision to all other participants. When the moderator decides to revoke the floor from the current floor holder, or when a "release floor" message is received from the current floor holder, the moderator automatically takes the floor and its database is updated accordingly. We specify the aspirant role in figure 7 without further explanation.

```
role aspirant //who will possibly request the floor
{
    conference-bus {
        channel(cntrl-in).
        channel(cntrl-out).
    }

    on-arrive(gate(cntrl-in), request(slide-floor)) :-
            not query held-by(slide-floor, self),
            msg !request(slide-floor, self).

    on-arrive(gate(msg), grant(slide-floor, Agent)) :-
            grant-floor(slide-floor, Agent).

    grant-floor(slide-floor, Agent) :-
            not query held-by(slide-floor, _),
            add held-by(slide-floor, Agent),
            cntrl-out !(grant(slide-floor, Agent)).

    grant-floor(slide-floor, Agent)) :-
            delete held-by(slide-floor, _),
            add held-by(slide-floor, Agent),
            cntrl-out !(grant(slide-floor, Agent)).

    on-arrive(gate(cntrl-in), release(slide-floor)) :-
            query held-by(slide-floor, self),
            delete held-by(slide-floor, self),
            msg !release(slide-floor, self).
}
```

Figure 7. Specification of the aspirant role.

```
role daemon
{
    on-take(role(moderator), source(Agent)) :-
        not query role(moderator, _),
        add role(moderator, Agent).

    on-drop(role(moderator), source(Agent)) :-
        query role(moderator, Agent),
        delete role(moderator, Agent).
}
```

Figure 8. daemon role of the "controlled presentation"

As we require that one and only one participant can take the moderator role at anytime, we need to define a daemon role. In figure 8, when an Agent requests to take the moderator role, the database is checked to see if it is already taken by someone. If not, this request is granted and the database is updated. When a request is received to drop the moderator role, the database is used to verify that this message comes from the moderator.

Discussion

A problem with the above specification is that a late aspirant cannot receive any slide until the first "grant floor" message arrives. Many lightweight collaborations allow participants to join and leave at will. Besides, IP multicast is a best-effort yet unreliable delivery model. Control messages may be not received by all intended recipients or be received out of order. How to keep a consistent state among all the participants is important and challenging. In our example, one solution is to have the moderator periodically broadcast key state information such as who is the current floor holder. If the moderator is lost, another participant can take this role and grant the slide floor to itself. A similar algorithm can be found in the implementation of *wb* [9].

We can extend the coordination policies specified above in several ways. For example, we can replace the centralized floor control policy with other policies, like round robin, first come first served, etc. This can be done without changing the tool *sv*. We can also extend the specification by allowing participants to delete slides, modify the slide contents and add comments. Take slide modification for example, the following scenarios are possible: (1) every participant can modify every slide, (2) everybody can only modify his or her own slides, and (3) only a special participant can modify other participants' slides, and so on. But these extensions require that the presentation tools in use have corresponding functionality.

The concepts of collaboration and role defined above are similar to data type or class in traditional programming languages in the sense that they all imply certain constraints on the runtime behavior of their instances. The user can create instances of a pre-defined collaboration type, called **sessions**. Participants can take roles from a session in order to join, and later leave the session by dropping the roles they are enacting.

We have implemented a collaborative session directory tool, *csdr*, in order for the users to create and browse collaborative sessions and take roles from them. The session creator needs to provide the session name, session description, in the same manner as an MBone session is created. Additionally, the session type, namely the collaboration specification, must be provided. A list of all available roles will then be extracted from the definition.

The creator may make available to the potential participants all or part of the specified roles. Especially, IP addresses and port numbers of channels declared in the collaboration bus must be provided in order for the participants to actually communicate with each other. In this sense, we say that the collaborations specified are **relocatable**. Similarly, when the user takes a role from a session, the conference bus channels also need actual IP addresses (which are typically the same as that of the local host) and port numbers, for the COCA virtual machine and the collaboration tools to communicate. So the roles specified in COCA are also relocatable.

The COCA virtual machine, *cocavm*, has also been implemented. When a user creates a collaborative session with *csdr*, a *cocavm* process is started to take the daemon role and become the session daemon. If no daemon role is defined, this *cocavm* will take default actions when "take role" and "drop role" requests arrive, namely, simply pass the role specification to the participants without authentication or any other checking. When a participant takes a role from a session, a new *cocavm* process will be started on the participant's machine. A thread will be created for each gate used in the heads of the active rules defined for this role. When a message arrives at a gate, the first unified active rule is fired, and then the rest of the execution is just as a goal is proved in Prolog. The difference is that multiple such threads may be executing simultaneously if several messages arrive at different gates. Parallel threads running inside the same *cocavm* synchronize through database operations.

A few collaborations have been modeled. Coordination policies have been specified and collaboration tools including the aforementioned *sv* and floor control tools have also been the implemented. Currently we are working on multimedia collaboration tools. Other scenarios, such as collaborative editing and multi-user games will be tried in the near future.

CONCLUSIONS

Our approach is different from previous work in that we explicitly divide participants in the same collaboration into different roles, and specify the coordination policies by roles. At every collaboration site, the policies are managed in a separate process instead of being scattered through the involved system components. This separate process, called the COCA virtual machine, orchestrates the application tools as well as other computation modules to make a collaboration. The coordination policies can be implemented in any language. We favor a declarative language similar to Prolog for its simple syntax, clear semantics and expressive power. Moreover, the sound logic basis make it potentially possible to develop verification tools, which would be ruled out by use of a procedural language like C/C++ or a scripting language like DCWPL. Interpretation instead of compilation allows for easier implementation, flexible management, and dynamic changes to policies and roles at run time.

Predictably, a potential problem with COCA is performance. In the current implementation, all the messages and media streams to and from each collaboration participant will run through the COCA virtual machine. But this problem is not insurmountable. The coordination policies are interpreted by the COCA virtual machine for easier evolution. As the users and developers gradually find the appropriate coordination policies for their particular application, the final version of the policies can then be compiled. To ease this process, a tool can be developed to compile the final specification instead of interpreting it.

The point of our work is not to solve all the problems in collaboration, but to provide a testbed for further study of (1) how active rules can be used to specify coordination policies, and (2) how COCA can be used to model and develop collaborative systems and distributed systems in general. Our initial experience with COCA shows that this is a promising direction to go. However, COCA is not yet full-featured and many research issues still need further work. We list below several issues which we are currently investigating.

In order for the COCA virtual machine and a collaboration tool to talk with each other, they must speak the same protocol. It is important for a collaboration specifier to know what commands a tool sends out and what it accepts. We are attempting to somehow specify these protocols in a rather standardized way. LOTOS [12] seems a candidate model for this purpose since the users typically only care about the observable behavior of a collaboration tool and this is exactly what LOTOS is good at modeling. Heterogeneous tools could there be easily orchestrated in the same collaboration.

Many collaborations are structured. For example, in the classroom scenario, a class typically consists of a sequence of lecture sessions and ended by a final exam. The students may team up in a number of subgroups. These sub-activities are part of a larger collaboration. It is both of practical importance and theoretical challenge to model such situations.

The COCA virtual machines engaged in a collaboration observe all the events as well as the messages and media streams ever communicated. Storage structures and retrieval methods of such information differ from collaboration to collaboration. It is hard to have a database management system generic and convenient enough to support storage and retrieval of the collaboration results of all possible collaborations. In

COCA, however, we can define archive roles to route such information to external databases with possibly varied capabilities and to control the retrieval from them. Logic-based reasoning can be performed to support queries specific to individual collaborations. For example, a session can be defined as all the happenings between a session begin event and a session end event. Queries like "what did Paul say during this collaboration" can be answered by locating the events of "the audio-floor is granted to Paul" and "the audio-floor is released by Paul", and locating the audio streams observed during this period.

Last but not least, we temporarily adopt Prolog semantics as the operational semantics of our specification language. A number of complications result from the fact that we have language level support for group communication and database updates. Pure Prolog semantics no longer works well as those operations have side effects and the execution can not backtrack over them. We need to explore an appropriate formal semantics for our language. Research results from the logic programming community may be adopted, as such a formal semantics is also a problem there.

REFERENCES

1. Cortes, Mauricio and Mishra, Prateek. DCWPL: A Programming Language for Describing Collaborative Work. *ACM CSCW'96* Proceedings
2. Deering, S. Multicast Routing in Datagram Internetworks and Extended LANs. *ACM Trans. On Computer Systems*, 8, 2, May 1990
3. Dommel, H.-P. and Garcia-Luna-Aceves, J.J. Floor Control for Multimedia Conferencing and Collaboration. *ACM Multimedia'97*, 5, 1, Jan.1997
4. Dourish, Paul and Bellotti, Victoria. Awareness and Coordination in Shared Workspaces. *ACM CSCW'92* Proceedings, November 1992
5. Edwards, W. Keith. Session Management for Collaborative Applications. *ACM CSCW'94*, Oct.1994
6. Edwards, W. K. Policies and Roles in Collaborative Applications. *ACM CSCW'96* Proceedings
7. Ellis, C.A. and Gibbs, S.J. Concurrency Control in Groupware Systems. *ACM SIGMOD'89* Proceedings, Portland Oregon, 1989
8. Ellis, C.A, Gibbs, S.J. and Rein, G.L. Groupware: Some Issues and Experiences. *Comm. ACM*, 34, 1, January 1991
9. Floyd, S., Jacobson, V., Liu, S., McCanne, S., and Zhang, L., A Reliable Multicast Framework for Lightweight Sessions and Application-Level Framing. *ACM SIGCOMM'95* Proceedings
10. Furuta, Richard and Stotts, David. Interpreted Collaboration Protocols and Their Use in Groupware Prototyping. *ACM CSCW'94* Proceedings
11. Gelernter, David and Carriero, Nicholas. Coordination Languages and Their Significance. *Comm. ACM*, 35, 2, Feb.1992
12. Logrippo, L. Faci, M. and Haj-Hussein, M. An Introduction to LOTOS: Learning by Examples. Computer Networks and ISDN Systems, 23, 5, February 1992
13. Minsky, Naftaly and Ungureanu, Victoria. Regulated Coordination in Open Distributed Systems. *2nd Intl. Conference on Coordination Languages and Models*, Berlin, Germany, Sept.1997 Proceedings
14. McCanne, S. and Jacobson, V. vic: A Flexible Framework for Packet Video. *ACM Multimedia'95* Proceedings
15. McCanne, S., Brewer, E., Katz, R., etc., Toward a Common Infrastructure for Multimedia-Networking Middleware. Proc. *7th Intl. Workshop on Network and Operating Systems Support for Digital Audio and Video*, St. Louis, Missouri, May 1997
16. Rekers, J. and Sprinkhuizen, I. A LOTOS Specification of a CSCW Tool. *Proc. of Design of Computer Supported Cooperative Work and Groupware Systems*, Schearding, Austria, 1993
17. Roseman, Mark and Greenberg, Saul. Building Real-time Groupware with GroupKit, A Groupware Toolkit. *ACM SIGCHI'96*, 3, 1, March 1996
18. Shen, Honghai and Dewan, Prasun. Access Control for Collaborative Environments. *ACM CSCW'92* Proceedings, November 1992

Artefact: A Framework for Low-Overhead Web-Based Collaborative Systems

Jeff Brandenburg, Boyce Byerly, Tom Dobridge, Jinkun Lin, Dharmaraja Rajan, Timothy Roscoe
Persimmon I.T., Inc.
4813 Emperor Boulevard
Durham, NC 27703 USA
+1-919-941-9339
{jeffb,boyce,dobridge,jinkun,dsrajan,timothy}@persimmon.com

ABSTRACT

The Artefact framework is a tool for building collaborative applications that deliver HTML representations of an object-oriented application space to standard browsers. We present some aspects of Artefact's implementation, including HTTP enhancements to support synchronous collaboration, the decoupling of input and output in the interaction protocol, a lightweight general-purpose Java applet, and the user agents that bridge the gap between a browser and an application. We describe some of the characteristics that make it easy to create multi-user applications with Artefact, and illustrate this with a simple example application. Finally, we compare Artefact to some existing distributed application platforms.

KEYWORDS: Artefact, multi-user environments, CSCW, World Wide Web, groupware, collaboration, HTTP, CORBA, update protocols.

INTRODUCTION

The Internet and the World Wide Web have become ubiquitous and familiar platforms for communication. Public access points are becoming common in hotels, libraries and universities, and businesses often have at least low-speed access to Internet services. As access becomes affordable and widespread, more people are becoming comfortable with the conventions of Web-based interaction.

This familiarity and ubiquity makes Web browsers and protocols attractive as a platform for delivering access to many kinds of systems, including collaborative applications. A Web-based system can be used by salespeople or field engineers to interact with one another and their organization from remote locations, perhaps using borrowed equipment and software on other organizations' premises. It can also allow people outside an organization to interact with each other and with organization personnel for applications such as customer support.

Unfortunately, the Web does not make it easy to deploy highly dynamic interfaces, especially synchronous collaborative interfaces. The client-initiated nature of HTTP (HyperText Transfer Protocol) [5] makes it difficult to update information dynamically in response to remote events or the actions of other users. While Java and proprietary clients can solve these problems, they introduce new problems of cross-platform consistency and download delays. In particular, people who want to use an application only occasionally may be reluctant to install a large, specialized client; people who examine an application out of curiosity or mild interest may lose that interest after waiting several minutes for a large applet to download.

The Artefact project [22] represents our effort to address these limitations. Artefact provides an infrastructure for developing distributed object-oriented applications. Users can interact synchronously and asynchronously with multi-user applications through standard Web browsers, even over low-speed (14.4 Kbps or 28.8 Kbps) connections. Developers can use HTML, JavaScript, Java, Tcl, and C++ to define the appearance and behavior of objects.

A User's View of the Artefact System

Artefact uses the metaphor of a person moving within a set of rooms that contain objects such as other users, documentation, system resources, merchandise, or customized application programs. We chose this spatial model to facilitate relationships such as containment of items within others, connectedness between places, and partitioning of objects into different rooms. Spatial models provide numerous advantages, and are widely used in recent CSCW systems [28, 11, 16]. They provide a familiar mental model that facilitates problem solving and memory [6, 3] and allows salient relationships such as containment and connectedness to be expressed. (We rejected a fully spatial model that included exact object placement in a three dimensional space because of its increased demands on hardware, software and

CSCW 98 Seattle Washington USA
Copyright ACM 1998 1-58113-009-0/98/11...$5.00

network bandwidth.) The appearance, placement, and contents of rooms and objects are designed to be easily configurable by naive users, since the ability to customize the space is associated with successful spatial CSCW projects [9]. The set of connected rooms and their contents in an Artefact site is referred to as an *application space*.

The *Artefact User Agent* (AUA) is a software object that represents a person and provides on-line presence. The "page" a user views with a browser is actually his User Agent's perspective of a room, including any objects and other users in that room. A browser connected to an AUA displays a set of frames that comprise the AUA's view of the application space (an example is shown in Figure 1). The browser contacts the AUA through a single URL; as the AUA interacts with different applications, or moves to different rooms, the URL pointed to by the person's browser never changes.

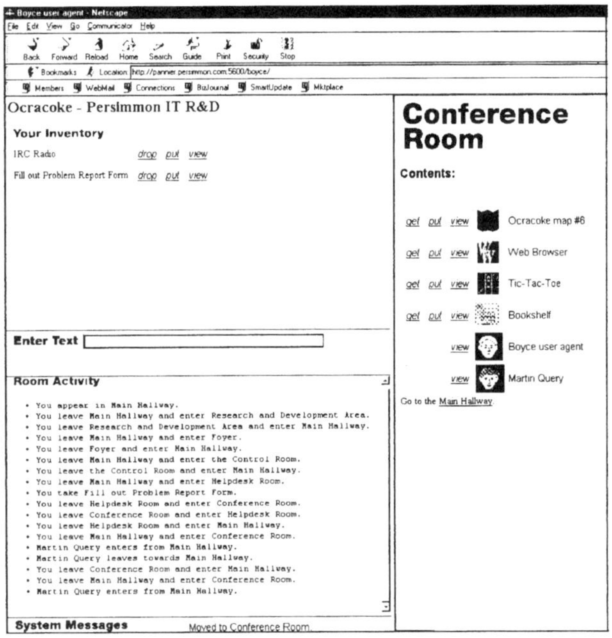

Figure 1: A browser connected to Artefact User Agent

The rightmost frame displays the room the AUA is currently in. Any objects that the room "contains" are reflected by icons, followed by short textual descriptions, displayed in this frame. For example, the room viewed in Figure 1 contains a map, a shared web browser, a TicTacToe game, and a bookshelf in addition to two AUA's. Exits to other rooms in the application space are displayed as part of the room; at the bottom of the frame is a link to "go to the Main Hallway." Clicking on an exit causes the AUA to move to a new room, updating the room frame to show the new location.

If the user has appropriate access permissions, he can examine objects displayed in the room ("view"), pick them up ("get"), or move them around ("put"). Clicking on the "view" button beside an icon opens a window displaying the application's user interface. Moving an object lets the user rearrange the Artefact application space, place an object into his personal space (much like putting an item into a shopping cart), or pass an object to another user. Whenever objects move in the application space, the system updates the appropriate frames of all users' views of the space.

An "inventory" frame for a particular AUA, shown on the upper left of Figure 1, displays the icons of objects that the user has picked up. These objects might represent resources he needs to manage, personalized documentation, communications devices, or items being purchased in an electronic commerce application.

The remaining three frames of the AUA screen, shown on the lower left quadrant of Figure 1, contain text-send and text-receive windows for online chat, and a messages line for the most recent status message. An administrator can customize the size, appearance and layout of all AUA frames as appropriate for specialized applications.

Application Programmer's View

For a site developer, Artefact provides a number of base classes of objects, such as:

- documents: web pages, files
- containers: briefcases, boxes, filing cabinets
- collaborative tools: whiteboards, shared browsers, address books, buddy lists
- autonomous agents: search bots, knowledge bots
- gateways: Internet Relay Chat (IRC) repeaters, SNMP monitors
- scriptable objects: JavaScript and Tcl interpreting objects

Objects can be declared and added on the fly by users familiar with HTML. Every object supports access control lists to allow fine-grained security controls.

In addition, Artefact provides a complete object-oriented SDK for developing customized application objects. Advanced developers can use C++ and Java to create new object classes; content developers, graphic designers, and casual programmers can use HTML, JavaScript and Tcl to specify object appearance and functionality without in-depth OOP experience. New components can be added to a running system with no interruption of service.

IMPLEMENTATION

Figure 2 shows an overview of Artefact's run-time architecture. This diagram shows all objects contained within a single Artefact server, but they could easily be deployed on separate servers, which could be running on different hosts. All Artefact objects communicate via the CORBA (Common Object Request Broker Architecture) standard [18], allowing applications to be distributed transparently across multiple servers and platforms. CORBA is an object-oriented, language-independent, platform-independent standard for exchanging data and method invocations over TCP/IP connections. This makes it easy to distribute application functionality across a number of hosts; in addition, CORBA provides facilities for on-demand server restart and connection re-establishment, which improves robustness in the face of program or communication failures.

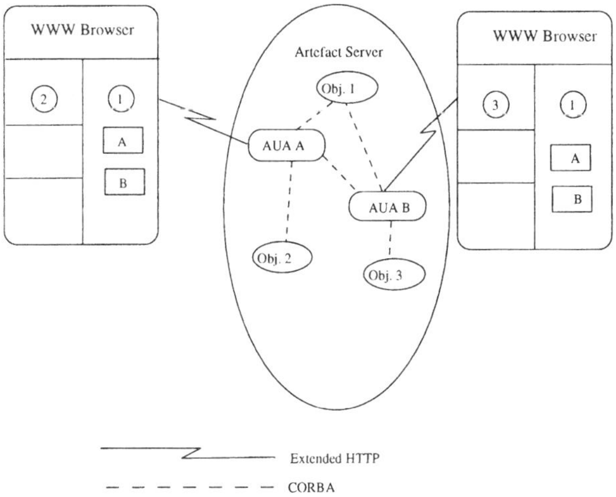

Figure 2: Artefact Architecture

The Artefact User Agent

The Artefact User Agent communicates with a web browser via HTTP. The AUA generates HTML that comprises the user's view of the objects in the application space. This allows a conceptually simple interface; users see the objects they are carrying, and those present in the room they occupy.

To begin using an Artefact application, a user connects to her own AUA. This is usually accomplished through a login process that validates the user's identity; the login facility can also return a cookie that serves as an authentication token for the rest of a session. Once the user is validated, the login process redirects the browser to a URL that encodes the identity of the user's AUA and the address of the server on which that AUA runs.

When the server receives an HTTP request for this URL, it examines the URL for the *marker*, or unique-within-the-server identifier, of the AUA. It then forwards the request to that AUA's request queue. The AUA replies to this initial request with a frame set; each frame in the set, in turn, loads its contents from another URL referring to the same AUA.

One of these frames loads a small *remote-control applet*. When this applet starts running, it establishes a TCP connection back to the AUA from which it was loaded. When the AUA determines that a frame's content has changed, it sends an *update request* along this connection; the request contains the frame's name, and the URL from which it should be loaded. When the remote-control applet receives the request, it uses the Java `showDocument()` method to make the browser reload the frame.

Besides controlling frames in the basic frameset, the remote-control applet can also open new windows. The AUA associates "view actions" with most objects; by selecting an object's "view" link, a user can open a separate view on that object. As it does with other frames, the applet updates this view dynamically as the viewed object changes.

AUAs manipulate other Artefact objects through CORBA method invocations. These methods allow an AUA to move from location to location, to move other objects, to obtain views of other objects, to send or broadcast messages, and to invoke object-specific actions. Since AUAs are first-class objects, other objects can also obtain a AUA's views or send it messages. An event-distribution protocol notifies objects when a change happens in their location, in their contents, or in an object they are explicitly observing.

The user interacts with the Artefact application through standard HTML input elements, such as links and forms. As with the initial frameset, the URLs associated with these elements refer to the AUA and its server. But when the user selects one of these elements – for example, when she follows a link – that request does not return an HTTP response; instead, the AUA interprets the request and performs the appropriate CORBA method invocations to carry it out, then reports the results through the update protocol.

Decoupling input and output

HTTP requests in Artefact are split conceptually into two types: *content requests* and *input events*.

Content requests return the contents of frames, and are generally initiated by the remote control applet, or by users clicking "reload." These requests are idempotent, which increases resilience and preserves a useful property of the WWW: one can always hit reload to update one's screen if something appears to go wrong.

Input events are caused by user activity, such as clicking a button in an application, closing a window, etc. These requests do not return any content themselves (they return an HTTP `No Content` message), but will generally result in an update notification being sent to the browser at some later time. In this way, input to application objects (including the user agent itself) and output to the screen from application objects are effectively decoupled.

Decoupling is an advantage for a developer writing a shared application object, since it separates the business of updating the appearance of the application object from that of sending that appearance to the screen. Communication between Artefact objects is also decoupled: each application object can be queried for its appearance at any time, and propagates events to other interested application objects (including user agents) when its appearance changes. The drawback of this approach is that it does not address the need for instant feedback to the single initiator of each input. In practice, this issue is often hidden by the latencies of the Web itself: by the time the browser has received the "no content" acknowledgment of the input, there is usually a resulting update notification already pending, and we can rely on the "loading document" animation of the browser to provide this feedback.

Decoupling output from input also reduces the potential for confusion in the face of reloads or repeated clicks. Reloading a frame (or the entire frameset) only refreshes the screen; it does not repeat any commands. Clicking multiple times on a link does submit multiple requests, but by using idempotent commands – for instance, by avoiding "toggle" commands in favor of "on" and "off" commands – we can create interfaces that respond predictably to these multiple commands.

For each frame of the user's browser, the AUA instantiates an *update protocol manager*. This manager handles HTTP requests for the content of the frame, regenerates its internal representation of the frame's contents when necessary, and sends update notifications back to the remote control applet in the browser. This protocol ensures that the frame is not "out of date."

In busy systems, when an AUA is in a room with many active objects, change events can arrive so quickly that they outrun the update mechanism. For example, if a user is connected over a 28.8Kbps link, and a room's view contains 3 Kbytes of HTML, the view cannot be updated more rapidly than approximately once per second. To avoid communication backlogs, the AUA batches updates. Between the time it sends an update message to the remote-control applet and the time it receives and services the resulting HTTP request, the AUA simply collects changes; only after the request is serviced does the AUA send a new update message. This protocol adapts to varying latency and available bandwidth, so the user always sees a relatively current view. This view may be delayed by the network latency between the AUA and the browser, or by the time needed to send the view's contents across the connection, but not by backlogged responses.

HTTP Usage and Enhancements

As we have shown in the preceding sections, we use a simple TCP connection to control frame updates, but all the traffic for requesting and returning frame contents is standard HTTP. We chose to use HTTP for several reasons:

- User expectations: from experience with the World Wide Web, users are familiar with browsers and how they work, and how transient network failures can affect responses. While we have changed the interaction model in Artefact from a document-retrieval paradigm to one closer to window system interaction, we have retained some features of the Web that users find reassuring (for example, the use of the "reload" button).
- Security configuration: HTTP is well understood by proxy servers and firewalls, simplifying network management within an organization. It is also much easier to validate an HTTP request than (for example) a CORBA invocation.
- Installed base: a sophisticated implementation of HTTP already exists in Web browsers, with access to a rich base of multimedia types.

HTTP itself is primarily a client-server, request-response protocol, with no provision for a server to send asynchronous updates to the user's screen. Some browsers do support a "server-push" facility, whereby the server sends a multipart MIME message to the browser, which displays each part in succession as it arrives. This approach does not work well for our purposes: it requires an open TCP connection for each frame of the display, and is not robust in the face of connection failures.

Server push also presents user-interface problems. While a push connection remains open, the browser appears to be constantly loading a document; this removes feedback that we have found useful in practice. Worse, Artefact "goes dead" when the connection to the browser is interrupted – for instance, when the user clicks the "stop" button.

It is possible to discard HTTP entirely and implement an entire user interface as a Java applet. While this approach supports sophisticated and fine-grained interaction, it entails other costs. Large Java applets are slow to load over a low-bandwidth connection. Once loaded, their performance and reliability can depend strongly on hardware speed, browser brand and version, Java runtime version, and even operating system version. Creating new object appearances and behaviors in Java is more complex than creating appearances in HTML, and developers with the necessary skills are currently in short supply.

Our update protocol avoids these problems. The remote-control applet is small (less than 10K), and it has no user interface at all; as a result, it loads very quickly even over a 28.8 Kbps link. It is quite reliable and portable: we have successfully used Artefact with versions 2.02, 3.0 and 4.0 of Netscape Navigator, and with Microsoft Internet Explorer 4.0. Every message sent by the browser to the AUA is a valid HTTP request; this makes it easy for us to validate requests at the server end, traverse proxy servers, and so forth. Finally, the update protocol updates only frames whose content has changed, and does so only as the content changes; this requires less bandwidth than schemes which update an entire page in response to any change.

EXAMPLE

Objects are created in Artefact by defining their behavior and appearance in an XML-like language called ADL (Artefact Definition Language). Figure 3 shows the complete definition of a very simple TicTacToe game in ADL.

The object is defined on the first line of Figure 3 by specifying a name (`TicTacToe`) for the object, together with a *class*, which specifies the underlying implementation to be used. In this case, the class is `TclObj`, which provides an interpreter in the popular embedded language Tcl [20] for controlling

```
<ARTEFACT CLASS="TclObj" NAME="TicTacToe">
<SHORT>TicTacToe board</SHORT>
<BEHAVIOR>
array set board ""
set curmove 0
proc onevent {} {
 global curmove board
 if { [event type] == "action" } {
  if { [event cmd] == "reset" } {
   unset board; array set board ""
   set curmove 0
  } else {
   set board([event cmd]) $curmove
   incr curmove
  }
  refresh
 }
}
proc cell { loc } {
 global curmove board
 if { [info exists board($loc)] } {
  if { [expr $board($loc) % 2] == 1 } { write "O" } else { write "X" }
 } else {
  writeaction "-" $loc
 }
}
proc tomove {} {
 global curmove
 if { [expr $curmove % 2] == 1 } { write "O" } else { write "X" }
}
</BEHAVIOR>
<HTML>
<HEAD><TITLE>TicTacToe</TITLE></HEAD>
<BODY>
 <CENTER>
 <H1>TicTacToe</H1>
 <P><SUBST EXPR="tomove"> to move.</P>
 <P><TABLE BORDER><TR>
  <TD><SUBST EXPR="cell 00"></TD>
  <TD><SUBST EXPR="cell 01"></TD>
  <TD><SUBST EXPR="cell 02"></TD>
 </TR><TR>
  <TD><SUBST EXPR="cell 10"></TD>
  <TD><SUBST EXPR="cell 11"></TD>
  <TD><SUBST EXPR="cell 12"></TD>
 </TR><TR>
  <TD><SUBST EXPR="cell 20"></TD>
  <TD><SUBST EXPR="cell 21"></TD>
  <TD><SUBST EXPR="cell 22"></TD>
 </TR></TABLE>
 <P><ACTION CMD="reset">Reset the board</ACTION>
 </CENTER>
</BODY>
</HTML>
</ARTEFACT>
```

Figure 3: Complete TicTacToe application definition in Tcl and ADL

how objects behave. The body of the definition contains two main sections: the `HTML` and `BEHAVIOR` elements.

The HTML section, occupying roughly the bottom half of Figure 3, defines static aspects of the object's appearance, using a superset of HTML 4.0. The use of HTML in this case allows us to make use of the considerable layout capabilities of modern Web browsers in creating the user interface for objects. More importantly, it provides a minimal learning curve for Web developers new to the Artefact system. New objects can be defined from many preexisting classes (for example, IRC gateways or SNMP monitoring objects) entirely using HTML.

The TicTacToe example shows the use of two elements not present in HTML 4.0: the `SUBST` and `ACTION` tags. The `SUBST` tag is used to substitute dynamic content provided by the implementation of the class. In the case of Tcl objects, the expression to be substituted is simply handed to the interpreter for evaluation, and so the expressions we see in the file are really Tcl command invocations.

The `ACTION` element is the simplest construct available for handling user input in the system. It is analogous to a conventional HTML anchor or link: if a user clicks on the area defined by the tag, the AUA interprets the request and invokes the object's `action()` method, passing as parameters the command string corresponding to the action (in this example the string "reset") and the identity of the user who caused the input. More sophisticated constructs are available for handling other user input features of HTML such as forms.

The `BEHAVIOR` element for scriptable objects, beginning on line 3 of the example shown in Figure 3, defines how the object behaves in response to the actions of other objects around it (including, but not limited to, human users). Artefact currently supports two classes of fully scriptable objects: TclObj, illustrated here, and a second based on a JavaScript/ECMAscript interpreter.

The `onevent` procedure is called for each event encountered by the object; in this case the only type of events we are interested in are "actions" (inputs) performed by users of this object. These correspond either to resetting the board, or clicking on an unoccupied cell in the board.

The other two Tcl procedures shown are called from the HTML section. The first, `proc cell`, generates an individual cell of the board, including generating a clickable area for cells which have not been filled in yet. The second, `proc tomove`, simply prints whose move is next. The view of the resulting object is shown in Figure 4.

Note that this fully shared, multiuser TicTacToe game is implemented in 27 lines of Tcl and 23 lines of HTML. Artefact's scripting API is event driven, and hides much of the complexity of the full C++ API to provide an easy to learn programming model which is well suited to rapid prototyping.

This example was stripped down for inclusion in this paper, but it does illustrate how much can be achieved with very little code. Floor control could be easily enforced by adding

Figure 4: How the TicTacToe application appears

additional Tcl code, but in this simple example social conventions, such as use of the chat or audio, would suffice. There is clearly room for improving the application cosmetically, for instance using graphics images rather than simply "X", "O" and "-"; this is simply a matter of enhancing the HTML portion of the object definition.

MORE COMPLEX CLIENTS

As previously discussed, Artefact allows site developers to declare an object using only an ADL file. In the simplest cases, these files do little more specify the object's Artefact class, its name, and HTML description.

Even though objects based on ADL files are sufficient in many situations, some applications require more fine-grained interaction. To support such applications, Artefact can serve as a "switchboard" for out-of-band communication among specialized applets or clients. As an example, we have built a shared whiteboard application that allows collaborators to simultaneously draw or type on a shared workspace.

The Whiteboard application differs from other Artefact applications based on a simple ADL definition file, in that much of its user interface is implemented in Java. When a user opens a Whiteboard object, the user's browser loads an applet from the Artefact server. The applet uses a conventional mouse- and keyboard-based interface to draw images or text. The applet also opens a TCP/IP socket back to its corresponding Artefact object. Through this socket, the applet sends drawing commands to the Artefact object which, in turn, broadcasts the commands to instances of the applet running in other users' browsers. In this way, all applets receive the drawing commands and update their drawing areas. Moreover, the drawing commands are stored persistently by the Whiteboard Artefact object; when other users later open the same Whiteboard, their applets get up-to-date images immediately. Finally, since the Whiteboard object that serves up the applets also serves as a central distribution point for update information, it overcomes the security restrictions which make it difficult for applets to communicate directly with one another.

The Whiteboard application shows that the Artefact framework is not limited to HTTP protocols and HTML documents, but allows a natural mechanism for out-of-band communications using a complex client. Artefact can easily support specialized user interface agents with Java applets or other browser plug-ins. These applications can bring extended capabilities to clients and applications that require them, while still benefiting from Artefact's persistence, access control, and event-handling mechanisms.

RELATED WORK

A number of commercial products now provide collaborative capabilities. Ding [1], ichat [10] and ICQ [14] provide text-based chat and "buddy list" functions; Netopia's Virtual Office [16], TeamWave [28] and eRoom [11] provide virtual office environments, with various combinations of synchronous and asynchronous communication features. For each of these products, users must either install a proprietary client program prior to using the system, or download a large, complex Java applet at the beginning of each session. These systems each provide a standard set of applications, with limited support for adding new object types or applications. All the systems appear to rely on centralized back-end servers for maintenance of shared state.

Previous academic collaborative systems have taken various approaches in distributing functionality. Systems may replicate state on each client, distribute state across clients, or maintain state in a central server.

DistView [23], COTERIE [13] and DIVA [26] replicate object state on each client. This approach yields good response time, since users interact with local copies of objects. However, replication increases client size and complexity, and can entail significant startup or installation overhead as the server propagates initial state information to clients.

Distributing system components to clients makes sense when a single client dominates the traffic to any given object. Again, local objects lead to excellent responsiveness, but impose heavier demands on clients. When clients must interact with remote objects, responsiveness suffers. Suite [4] was an early example of this approach; more recent examples include GroupKit [24], CommonPoint [19] and CBE [12].

Centralized systems support applications on a single server, with users accessing applications through relatively lightweight clients. Rendezvous [21], Jupiter [17] and TeamRooms [25] are examples of this approach. While clients are general-purpose within each system, they do not interoperate among different systems. CVW [27] does support a browser-based Java client, but this client is not publicly available, and it is unclear how large or complex the client is. (The client runs on UNIX and Windows, with a "very limited version" available for the Apple Newton, but not the Macintosh.) Habanero [15] represents a hybrid approach, in which servers may run remotely or on the same machine as a client; again, the Habanero client is not browser-based, and is quite large. Artefact differs from these systems in that it has a very thin client, yet has multiple distributed servers instead of a single monolithic one.

Systems in which clients interact with remote objects must cope with network latency and bandwidth restrictions. Artefact's basic structure is targeted at applications and communication modes in which sub-second latency is not critical. Instead of minimizing update latency, Artefact minimizes network traffic, batching updates to dynamically match available bandwidth and latency. For systems that must support more fine-grained mutual interaction among users, enhanced update protocols [7] can bring update performance close to the theoretical limits imposed by two-way latency.

CONCLUSIONS

Artefact's lightweight, HTML-based interface supports useful collaborative applications using standard browsers and low-bandwidth connections. We have created testbed applications implementing a virtual office and a problem ticket management system, and we have used these systems without modification with clients running under Solaris, Digital UNIX, Windows 3.1, Windows 95, Windows NT 4.0, and Macintosh System 7.5; from desktop and laptop machines, ranging from a 333-MHz DEC Alpha to a 40-MHz 68030; and over modem connections as slow as 14.4 Kbps. While the slowest systems and the slowest links do provide noticeably slower performance, sometimes taking several seconds to perform a single update, they still are responsive enough for text-based conversations and simple, non-graphics-intensive application interaction. Even on these slow systems, it takes less than twenty seconds to start up the Artefact frameset and update applet.

We have used the Artefact testbed applications to let users on both sides of the Atlantic interact with application objects. While the increased network latency does slow down responses, the subjective feel of the application remains quite good. The basic structure of Web browsers and protocols is designed to cope with potentially high latency and low bandwidth, and users with Web experience are familiar with the variations in performance that result. We have not done extensive quantitative tests on Artefact's performance as latency and bandwidth vary, but since Artefact uses the same protocols and presentation languages (HTTP and HTML) as the rest of the Web, we expect that its performance will scale in the same way.

Where more bandwidth and more powerful client machines are available, Artefact can use out-of-band techniques to support richer forms of interaction. We have already implemented a Java-based shared-whiteboard application, and an audio-connection facility, whereby users with LAN-based clients can hear other users whose AUAs are in the same virtual room. Similar support for video, and for large data objects such as medical images, has been planned.

We continue to work on enhancements of our windowing model to give the AUA more control over the user's display. Currently, the remote-control applet can open windows and detect when the user closes windows; a small amount of JavaScript also allows the applet to close windows itself. Further enhancements will give application objects more control over the size and appearance of their "view" windows, and add support for multiple frames within an object's HTML view.

As Artefact systems are deployed more widely, we will also investigate scaling issues. There are practical limits on the number of objects displayed in a room, the number of AUAs that can participate in a single linear thread of conversation, and the speed at which events can be propagated to a single browser. While our current applications bring users together in small groups, and thus remain well within those limits, techniques like those presented in [8] and [2] should allow us to support much larger numbers of simultaneously interacting users, for example in a "virtual auditorium".

REFERENCES

1. Activerse, Inc. *Ding! User's Guide*. Available from `http://www.activerse.com/ding/v10/docs/intro.htm`.

2. S. Benford, C. Greenhalgh, and D. Lloyd. Crowded collaborative virtual environments. In *Proceedings of ACM CHI '97 Conference*, pages 59–66., Atlanta, GA USA, 1997.

3. J.M. Clark and A. Pavio. Dual coding theory and education. *Psychological Review*, 3:149–210, 1991.

4. P. Dewan and R. Choudhary. Flexible user interface coupling in collaborative systems. In *Proceedings of ACM CHI '91 Conference*, pages 41–49, New Orleans, LA, USA, 1991.

5. R. Fielding, J. Gettys, J. Mogul, H. Frystyk, and T. Berners-Lee. Hypertext transfer protocol—HTTP/1.1. IETF Request for Comments No. 2068, January 1997.

6. A. M. Glenberg and M. A. McDaniel. Mental models, pictures, and text integration of spatial and verbal information. *Memory and Cognition*, 20(5):458–460, 1992.

7. N. T. C Graham, T. Urnes, and R. Nejabi. Efficient distributed implementation of semi-replicated synchronous groupware. In *Proceedings of ACM UIST '96*, pages 1–10, Seattle, WA, USA, 1996.

8. R. W. Hall, A. Mathur, F. Jahanian, A. Prakash, and C. Rasmussen. Corona: A communication service for scalable, reliable group collaboration systems. In *Proceedings of ACM CSCW '96*, pages 140–140, Cambridge, MA, USA, 1996.

9. S. Harrison and P. Dourish. Re-place-ing space: The roles of place and space in collaborative systems. In *Computer Supported Cooperative Work '96*, pages 67–77, Cambridge MA, 1996. ACM.

10. ichat, Inc. *Real-time Object Oriented Multimedia Server Administrator's Guide*, 2.1 edition, 1996.

11. Instinctive Technology, Inc. *eRoom*. Available from `http://www.instinctive.com`.

12. J. H. Lee, A. Prakash, T. Jaeger, and G. Wu. Supporting multi-user, multi-applet workspaces in CBE. In *Proceedings of ACM CSCW '96*, pages 344–353, Cambridge, MA, USA, 1996.

13. B. MacIntyre and S. Feiner. Language-level support for exploratory programming of distributed virtual environments. In *Proceedings of ACM UIST '96*, pages 83–94, Seattle, WA USA, 1996.

14. Mirabilis Ltd. *ICQ*. Available from `http://www.mirabilis.com`.

15. National Center for Supercomputing Applications. *The NCSA Habanero User's Guide*. Available from `http://www.ncsa.uiuc.edu/SDG/Software/Habanero/Docs/Environment/`.

16. Netopia, Inc. *Netopia Virtual Office*. Available from `http://www.netopia.com/software/nvo/win/overview.html`.

17. D. Nichols, P. Curtis, M. Dixon, and J. Lamping. High latency, low bandwidth windowing in the Jupiter collaboration system. In *Proceedings of UIST '95*, pages 111–120, Pittsburgh, PA, November 1995.

18. The Object Management Group. *The Common Object Request Broker: Architecture and Specification*, 1995. Available from `http://www.cs.wustl.edu/ schmidt/CORBA-docs/corba2.0.ps.gz`.

19. R. Orfali, D. Harkey, and J. Edwards. *The Essential Distributed Objects Survival Guide*, pages 297–312. John Wiley and Sons, 1996.

20. John K. Ousterhout. *Tcl and the Tk Toolkit*. Addison-Wesley, 1994.

21. J. F. Patterson, R. D. Hill, S. L. Rohall, and W. S. Meeks. Rendezvous: An architecture for synchronous multi-user applications. In *Proceedings of the Third Conference on Computer Supported Cooperative Work (CSCW '90)*, pages 317–328, Los Angeles CA USA, 1990.

22. Persimmon IT, Inc. *Artefact User's Guide*. Available from `http://artefact.persimmon.com`.

23. A. Prakash and H. S. Shim. DistView: Support for building efficient collaborative applications using replicated objects. In *Proceedings of ACM CSCW '94*, pages 153–164, Chapel Hill, NC, USA, 1994.

24. M. Roseman and S. Greenberg. Building real time groupware with GroupKit, a groupware toolkit. *ACM Transactions on Computer-Human Interaction*, 3(1):66–106, March 1996.

25. M. Roseman and S. Greenberg. TeamRooms: Network places for collaboration. In *Proceedings of CSCW '96*, pages 325–333, Cambridge, MA, 1996.

26. M. Sohlenkamp and G. G. Chwelos. Integrating communication, cooperation, and awareness: the DIVA virtual office environment. In *Proceedings of ACM CSCW '94*, pages 331–343, Chapel Hill, NC USA, 1994.

27. P. J. Spellman, J. N. Mosier, L. M. Deus, and J. A. Carlson. Collaborative Virtual Workspace. In *Proceedings of the International ACM SIGGROUP Conference on Supporting Group Work (GROUP'97)*, pages 197–203, Phoenix, AZ, USA, 1997.

28. TeamWave Software Ltd. *TeamWave Workplace*. Available from `http://www.teamwave.com/`.

Supporting Flexible Roles in a Shared Space

Randall B. Smith, Ronald Hixon, and Bernard Horan

Sun Microsystems Laboratories
901 San Antonio Rd. MV29-110
Palo Alto, CA 94303

+1 650 336 2620

{randall.smith, bernard.horan, ronald.hixon}@sun.com

ABSTRACT

We describe the support for roles in a shared space application and programming environment called Kansas. As in reality, the underlying physics of Kansas has no notion of role. However, roles are *supported* by two features of the system: the spatial character of Kansas (which enables different views for different users) and a capability system that filters user inputs. Spatial positions and capabilities can be easily changed, so the support for roles is dynamic, lightweight, and flexible. Our system is simple, and intentionally limited in scope.

KEYWORDS

Shared space, video, audio, virtual reality, roles.

INTRODUCTION

People in a group play various roles. Manager, intern, department chair, guest speaker, the woman who knows how the fax machine works, the guy who got the pizza, the person speaking now, the person capturing this on the whiteboard; roles can be formal or informal, long-lived or ephemeral. They can be bestowed by ceremony, or assumed with the invisibility of the taken-for-granted. But it is the interaction of minds that create and sustain a role: a role is a human construct. Even roles like "mother" or "father," which would seem to demand certain biological characteristics cannot be defined at any depth without appeal to social convention. The largely hands-off approach taken by nature seems to work fairly well for groups of humans: when there is confusion or concern about who is playing what role, it is generally good for a group to work it out as a social issue. If roles were encoded solely in human biology or in physical law, life might be simpler but certainly more stultifying.

However, roles can be at least partly *supported* by physical reality. For example, a speaker benefits from adopting a special position (center stage) with a particular spatial orientation (facing the audience). The note taker benefits from physical proximity to pen and paper, the piano player by proximity to the piano. These spatial positions and orientations are available to all, they are simply used at certain times by certain individuals as part of their role.

When it comes to computer supported cooperative work, it is perhaps natural to try to be helpful by supplying roles directly [2], [13], [14], [15]. Group dynamics can be difficult to proscribe, and individual activities can vary from group to group, from one context to the next. Consequently, most workers in this area realize that a system that prevents a group from modifying their roles can hinder rather than help. But roles can evolve in unexpected ways, even in the midst of a collaboration. More recently there has emerged a recognition for the importance of lightness and flexibility in the midst of a session. For example, Shen and Dewan [12], Dourish and Bellotti [1], and Edwards [2], all argue the importance of having a flexible system that can support dynamically changing ways of working. We suggest taking a lesson from reality, and supply a virtual physics that may partly support roles, but does not define them. Real world physicality was the model underlying the design of the Kansas system: a large, two dimensional world in which multiple users can slide about, coming together in groups, dispersing as individuals, moving between various display objects to build and/or use applications.

Roles are in general supported by a system's treatment of output and user inputs. Focus for the moment on the system's output to users. Different users will need to see and hear different things, based on the tasks associated with their role. In Kansas, we already have a mechanism in which different users see and hear different things based on their window size and placement in the larger Kansas world. As part of the need to support awareness (mutual comprehension of each other's position and activity in the world), we designed Kansas according to a principle we call WYSIWITYS (What You See Is What I Think You See), so that it is easy and natural to know who is seeing and hearing whom. We find we are able to support roles without violating the WYSIWITYS principle.

CSCW 98 Seattle Washington USA

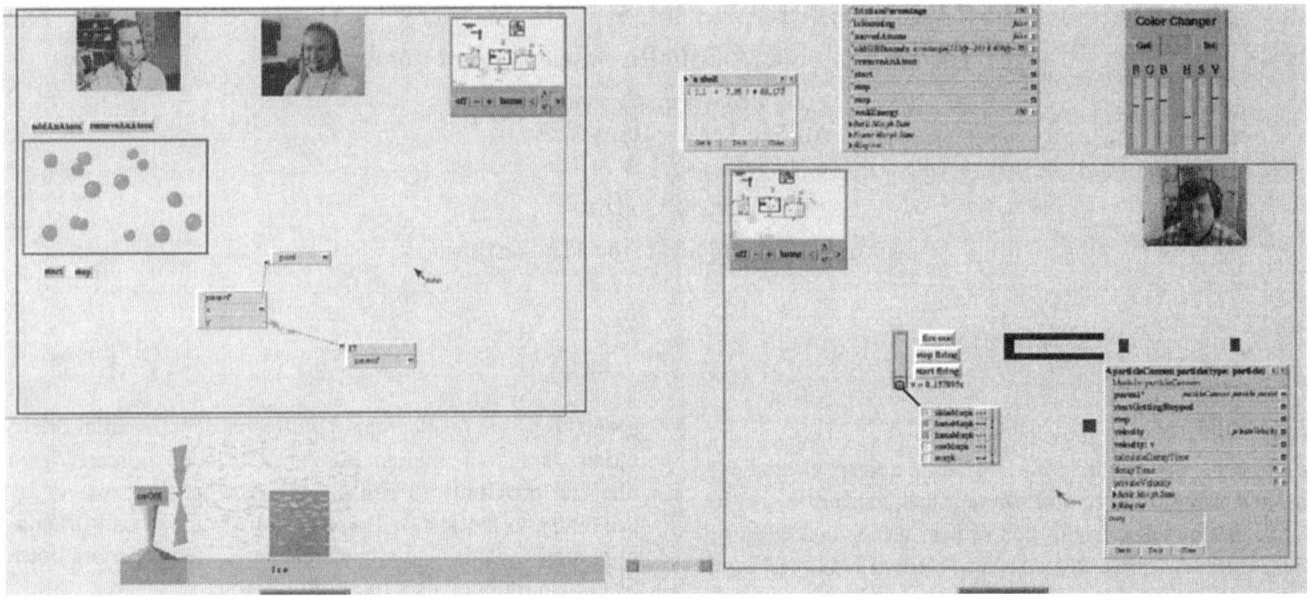

Figure 1. An overview of a portion of the Kansas space: Each user's window into the Kansas world is limited, and here we see the view bounds for three users. The two on the left are working together on an ideal gas simulation, while the user at the right has moved off on his own where he is programming another simulation. Each user has an image from a desktop video camera, and, as with any object in Kansas, it can be moved, directly embedded into other objects, or even reprogrammed as it runs. Also shown here are two radar views, objects that display a miniature overview of a larger portion of Kansas. Radar views have buttons for sliding the user over the Kansas surface.

Focus now on the system's treatment of user inputs. We found that by giving novice users all the user input functionality available to developers, we had unintentionally booby-trapped the world. (Kansas differs from reality in that it is more flexible: the "laws of physics" and even of arithmetic can be changed from within Kansas while it runs.) What is responsive and empowering for a developer can cause confusion and rude surprises for a novice. We somehow had to introduce something new, a system to filter various user inputs for the various kinds of users. But we wanted the system to be flexible and lightweight, disturbing the underlying democracy of our reality as little as possible.

The system we added is based on "capabilities." A capability governs one object's access to another. In our case, a capability govern's a user's access to an object on the screen. We take minimalist approach in our design: the capability system can in principle operate anywhere in the Kansas universe, with output as well as input, or with abstract data structures far from the user interface. However, we found it sufficient to use capabilities as filters on the inputs to the user interface. Furthermore, we employ a simple form of inheritance in the capability system: it mirrors that of the underlying language and we believe it gives expressive power without undue complication.

A capability is itself a display object, and so can be manipulated directly within the world. Because we normally use capabilities to govern access to user interface objects, the physical world metaphor is at play in this part of the system. A capability is loosely analogous to a key or tool that enables access to some tangible object or set of objects. (Unlike a tool however, we do not require that a capability be visibly "held" by the user in order to be effective.)

We will show how a user's capabilities can be changed with a few gestures, and we'll present several user interface mechanisms we've created for that purpose. Because one can move through space quiet simply and easily change one's capabilities, we are pleased that the resulting system is lightweight and flexible.

We are also happy that the physics of Kansas supports but does not delineate roles. Though a Kansas user may have a distinct location and unique input capabilities, any notion of role resides at the human, social level.

Two final comments: we are illustrating a system we feel is simple and limited, and the fact that it has worked in several real world settings gives us hope that supporting roles need not mire one in confusion, nor muck up an entire architecture. Secondly, we are using Kansas mainly for synchronous, small group interaction. Our support for roles in general, and our capability system in particular is not about providing security against malicious attack. Rather, we hope to show how these facilities alleviate user frustration and facilitate group work: we support roles to enhance usability.

KANSAS

Kansas is so named because it is a large flat space containing multiple people. Each user sees only their window's worth of Kansas, a foot or so wide: the entire Kansas space is actually larger than its real world counterpart, measuring millions of square miles, though it currently only supports small groups of a dozen or so users. A portion of the space is shown in Figure 1, where we can see three users. For each user, there is a *view bounds* rectangle, indicating within the larger world the limits of the user's viewport. Each user's mouse pointer is present as an object in the world, normally showing the user's name as a label. Kansas also supports audio and video among users. Some of the objects in the world can be video images from desktop cameras.

Users can slide their viewport across the Kansas surface, moving apart to work in isolation, or moving together for real-time collaboration. When left running for extended periods, a user can check into Kansas for a brief period of asynchronous work, or can rendezvous to meet others for synchronous group work. One might call an environment that is both synchronous and asynchronous "fully chronous."

In its default mode (with no capabilities) Kansas exhibits a kind of open, naive physics: any user can grab any object, press any button, or inspect and reprogram any object. Our reasoning was simply that social protocols are sufficient in most real-world situations, and we expect the intuitions one has about object ownership to carry over in to the virtual world of Kansas. These expectations proved correct in some ways; however, we did see problems arising from unintentional user actions, some of which had consequences that were hard to undo.

Self: Kansas as Programming Language

Kansas is unusually malleable. Kansas is essentially the programming environment for the dynamic object-oriented language Self [5],[18]. Objects can easily be reprogrammed even as the system is running. Kansas is itself written in Self, so its implementation can be changed while it is running.

Self is a quite pure and uniform object-oriented language. Everything is an object in Self, including collections, closures, and numbers. Furthermore, all computation happens by message passing. A Self object consists only of named slots containing references to other objects. A slot in an object can be activated by sending to that object a message matching the slot name. When a slot is activated, code found in the slot will be run, or an object stored directly in the slot will be returned. Consequently, all code in the system is unaware of whether a value is computed or stored. Edwards [2] emphasizes the utility of dynamic computability by providing role-related information with functions rather than with constants. With Self, one can change representations (from stored to computed) without having to change anything else in the system.

Self provides object-based inheritance. If a message does not match any slot in the object to which the message was sent, the lookup continues through any "parents" of the object. Parents are themselves simply Self objects. In Self, any object can be a parent. Though there are no classes in the conventional sense, objects that are used as parents tend to be the repository for shared state and behavior for use by their inheritance children.

We emphasize then that this is a very flexible world, and might be best thought of as a collaboration kit or a programming environment, as many different systems can and have been created from within Kansas.

Benefits and dangers of a dynamic environment

A fully chronous environment can benefit from being programmable as things are running. Because a fully chronous system needs to run nearly continuously, changes can be made while the system is in use. Also, a long running system accumulates important state: with dynamic programming it is not necessary to stop the world, recompile, start over, and somehow restore the state of the world.

Because a change to Kansas itself, or to something critical (like integer addition) can crash the world, we've devised a robust architecture involving monitoring processes and dynamic creation of a parallel reality called "Oz," as described in [3]. If Kansas can no longer run, the system creates Oz, and Kansans are transported into this world where they can visit an (emerald) debugger to collaboratively solve their problems with life in Kansas.

TWO EXAMPLES

Remote Physics Lab. This experience led us to introduce capabilities and it illustrates the utility of their flexibility. Groups of three or four remote high school students were each given their own piece of Kansas in which to operate a simulation,. The "instructor" (one of the authors) first explained how to use the environment, then "wandered about" to visit each student, clarifying the various phases of the simulated lab, answering questions, and occasionally adding a feature as requested by a student.

In our first trials, the students immediately started playing with buttons, popping up menus and flying around the Kansas space. Some default menu items can have unfortunate side effects in the world (such as deleting an object) so that, through simple curiosity as opposed to malicious intent, students would make a mess of things fairly quickly.

After introducing the capability system, we started the sessions with the students all in one place but with their mouse buttons essentially disabled. As the instructor explained each feature of the environment, he would incrementally enable a new capability so the students could try out and use the feature. The sessions became much more orderly. By the end of each session, the students had all the capabilities of the instructor, and, on one occasion, students came together on their own to combine their simulations, even inspecting objects at the Self language level to change some of the param-

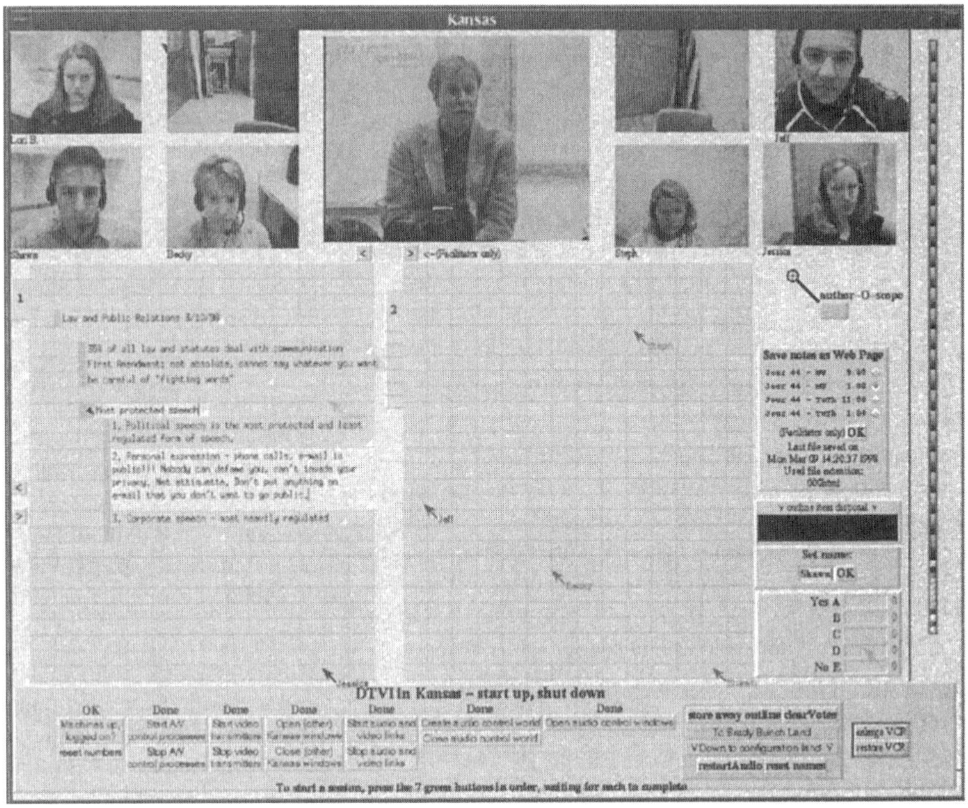

Figure 2. In this use of Kansas, five students and a facilitator watch a videotaped lecture (center) while taking collaborative notes. Because this is a persistent world it is critical that students are prevented from (and need not worry about) making accidental modifications. The facilitator's window (shown here) is slightly larger than that of each student, giving the facilitator access to some more widgets.

eters.

Note again that though we talk about roles, the system does not explicitly reify any such notion. There are only users, their mouse cursors, view bounds, and capabilities. Any kind of role object would seem to be more problematic than useful. Whereas initially the student role *is* very different from that of the instructor, by the end of the session, as far as the system is concerned, there is no difference.

DTVI. Kansas is being used in an experiment at California State University at Chico to test a learning paradigm called Distributed Tutored Video Instruction (or DTVI). In this usage, Kansas runs nearly continuously for months on end, and various student groups drop in for study sessions in which they view videotapes of lectures. This is part of a large multi-year study to compare the course grade performance of the DTVI groups with their co-present counterparts [10].

The DTVI students see each other through desktop video links, and (in our current version of the system) can take notes collaboratively by typing into an outliner tool (see Figure 2). Any student can type at any time, so note taking task division is worked out through informal verbal discourse. A facilitator is present to start and stop the videotape, keep the discussion on track, save the notes to a web page, and perform similar tasks having to do with administrative or system support.

The DTVI system is set up to support four different roles: student, facilitator, coordinator, and developer. The Kansas world as experienced by each role differs in the input and/or output in subtle ways. DTVI students are the most restricted, in that they can operate the fewest user interface widgets, and have slightly smaller viewports onto the Kansas surface. The facilitator needs to perform certain administrative and support tasks, while coordinators are able to do anything. The developer is similar to the coordinator, except that in practice the developer is typically at a large geographical distance across the internet, and so has no audio and video support.

Interestingly, we found it useful to let the facilitators manage some of their own capabilities, selectively enabling and disabling their own mouse buttons. We also prevent students from picking up and moving many of the objects on the main screen. With full capabilities, a student's accidental mouse click and release could move an object from a carefully placed location, wasting group time and generating frustration.

AWARENESS AND WYSIWITYS

To support multiple users adequately in synchronous environments, one must provide some form of mutual "awareness" of each other's presence, current activities, and potential actions [8]. Ideally, this awareness should be easily attained (e.g., through a shift of gaze) rather than through some slower, complex action requiring a conscious distraction, such as finding and pulling down a menu [1], [9].

An obvious way to take care of much of the need for mutual awareness is to build a WYSIWIS environment (What You

See Is What I See). Because all participants in a WYSWIS world see the same thing, (the same widgets, the same telepointing mouse cursors) the presence and actions of participants are pretty obvious. However, WYSIWIS environments are rather limiting, in that, for example, they prevent customized or private views [17]. Consequently, there has been an interest in how to provide awareness in "relaxed WYSIWIS" or even "non-WYSIWIS" environments.

We have designed Kansas to support a property called WYSIWITYS (What You See Is What I Think You See) [4]. WYSIWITYS can hold in a completely non-WYSIWIS environment. WYSIWITYS is a property of most everyday physical world settings. While together in an office conversation, you and I see largely different things: what is important is that I know what you are seeing, even though I do not directly experience your view myself. For example, I can tell from your position and direction of gaze whether or not my hand gestures are obstructed from you view. Such awareness greatly facilitates our conversation.

WYSIWITYS was a key discovery in earlier work of one author in the SharedARK world [7], [6], and WYSIWITYS was the motivation behind the design of the "Video Tunnel," a camera and monitor with half-silvered mirror [7]. (Using a video tunnel, A can read the apparent gaze direction of B to know about A's own visibility to B, much as A and B would interpret each other's gaze in the real world). What has become called "gaze awareness" is a special case of WYSIWITYS.

Because it is a deeply ingrained property of physical reality, WYSIWITYS tends to emerge naturally in virtual realities: In a multi-user VR, user A's avatar's direction of "gaze" essentially depicts to other users that part of the space that is visible to A. In shared worlds that support audio, one's voice can be made to drop off with virtual distance, helping clarify who you are hearing, and who can hear you.

But Kansas is not a conventional virtual reality because of its two-dimensional character and the lack of avatars. We therefore use the view bounds rectangle to designate that part of the space visible to each user. The telepointers further support mutual awareness: I know that if I highlight text in some text field that lies outside of your view bounds, you will not be able to see it. Finally, the radar view objects provide a miniature overview of a much larger portion of Kansas: users can discern the presence of quite distant collaborators in the small overview display. A miniature view bounds denotes their position, and the motion of tiny telepointers reveals their activity. (Gutwin and Greenberg demonstrate the effectiveness of radar views in [9]).

Audio volume level can be set to drop off with distance in Kansas, thereby supporting a natural intuition about mutual audibility, and the video images help make users aware of each other's presence and level of attention. Because the video windows are within the Kansas world, the view bounds make clear which image can be seen by whom.

Awareness and Roles

It is interesting to note how awareness and roles are intertwined. You might want others to be aware of your role.

A student's audio window:

The facilitator's window:

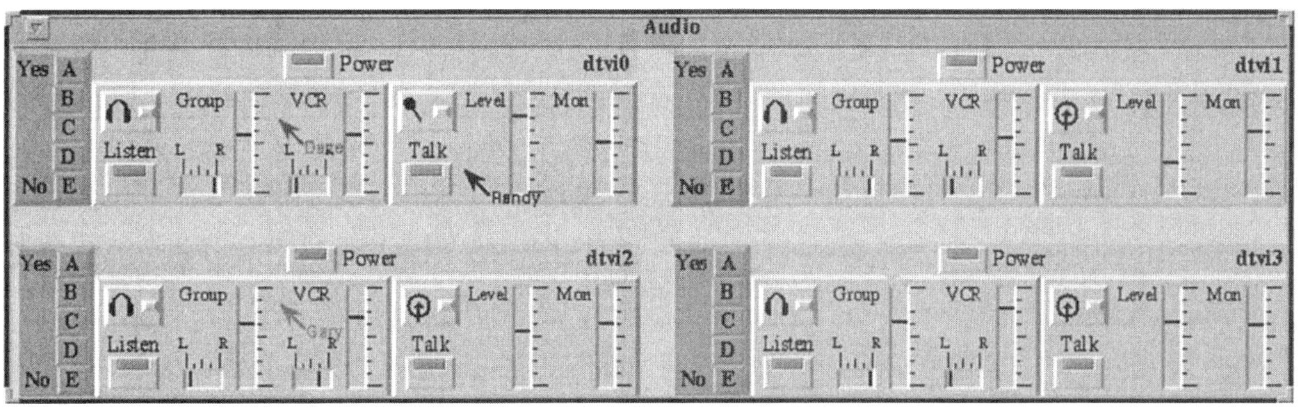

Figure 3. A large shared space can afford different views for different roles. The set of audio control panels for four users lie in a single shared world, though each participant sees only their own control panel: their view of the shared audio world is wrapped tightly about their own control. The facilitator, however, sees all four controls, and can help any one participant learn to use the widgets or make adjustments.

Conversely, as part of your role, you need to be aware of certain things. It is this latter category where we have found the spatial metaphor of Kansas to be particularly useful.

As an example, our DTVI users actually have two windows on the screen, the main window as depicted in Figure 2, and a small window containing an audio control widget, as shown at the top of Figure 3. The audio control lets each user adjust the stereo placement and volume of the sound sources, and the audio level of their own microphone. Naturally we want each user to be able to see and operate their own audio control, whereas depicting the controls of others is a waste of screen real estate. However, it's hard to balance one's own voice in the audio mix, so each microphone level can also be adjusted by the facilitator. Furthermore, if the facilitator can access your control, he or she can teach you how to operate the various buttons and sliders. or help you debug some audio problem. Thus the facilitator's role is supported by being able to adjust any audio control, while the student's role is supported by not having to worry about any controls but their own.

To support these goals, we laid out the audio controls in a rectangle isomorphic to the layout of video images in the main screen. The facilitator can see all of these controls in a single window. Each student, however, has a window exactly large enough to show only their personal control (see Figure 3). The audio control appears as a more-or-less conventional application, except that occasionally the facilitator's mouse cursor may sweep past. If the facilitator wishes, he or she can move a troublesome audio control aside, to replace it with another, or to give it to another user, perhaps to enlist their help in working with the control.

We utilize the main screen (featuring all the video windows) in a similar way: by giving the facilitator a slightly larger view, certain objects in the surrounding space can be accessed only by the facilitator. Because the students can neither resize nor move their viewport, these objects remain accessible only to the facilitator. (These objects are primarily controls that start and stop a session.)

Awareness is in a way only half of the story, dealing with the graphical or auditory output of the system. What about the other half, the users' inputs?

CAPABILITIES IN THE USER INTERFACE

Capabilities, Capability Tables, and Capability Sets

Capabilities were first conceived in the 1960's for use in operating systems (for a review see [16]). A more modern exposition of capabilities can be found in [11], which emphasizes the elegance and expressive power of capability-based security. Capabilities, because they can be passed from one object to another, allow for "delegation of authority," and can therefore solve problems that cannot easily be solved using an access control list mechanism.

A "capability" is an object representing the right to access some protected object. There are three objects in the story, some "protected object," some generalized "user" object wishing to access the protected object, and the capability object itself. In general, the user object maintains a collection of capabilities (the user's *capability set*). In normal capability usage, the capability not only stores the kind of access it represents, but it retains a reference to the protected object: ideally the capability is the only access the user has to the protected object. In object-oriented programming, the capability would be called a kind of "transparent forwarder," "encapsulator," or "facade" object.

But we are adding this capability system onto an existing user interface programming environment, so references to the objects we wish to protect are already being passed about in many different ways. Furthermore, we wish to use inheritance to allow a single capability to represent access to an entire (and possibly changing) family of objects. Finally, we are supporting a situation in which we are less concerned with protecting against security attacks at the language level, and more concerned with facilitating interaction within a group of humans. In our implementation, we reverse part of the above story so that the protected object retains a reference to capability C: when the user wishes some sort of access, the object can test to see if the user's capability set includes C. Objects may in general issue many different capabilities for different purposes, hence each object maintains a *capability table*, logically a dictionary (a collection of key-value pairs) in which each key is a descriptive string name ("edit text") and each value is a capabilities.

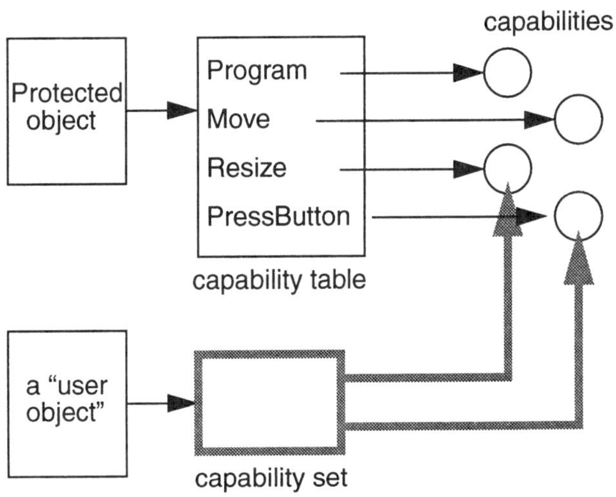

While the system we describe could be used by any of the Self objects in Kansas, we have found it sufficient to use capabilities within the user interface. It is only the displayable objects that have a capability table, and only "user objects" that have a capability set. Thus, if one wants to protect, say, some text file from being overwritten, one must do so through the user interface, installing capabilities in the widgets that enable such writing (such as a text editor). This might seem awkward, since all current and future text editors will need to maintain a capability table. However, as dis-

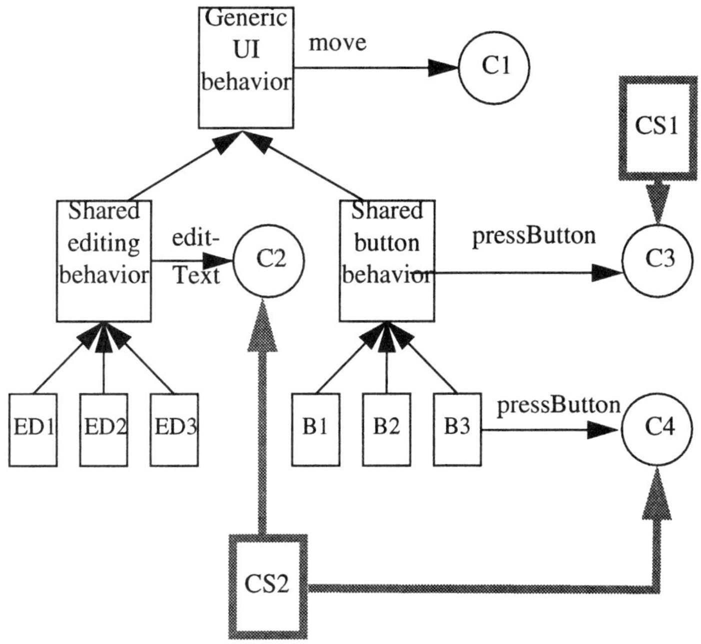

Figure 4. Objects may inherit their capabilities, which they use as access filters for various user interactions. Here are shown 4 capabilities (C1 ... C4) and two capability sets (CS1, CS2). For graphical simplicity, we just show labeled references to stand for capability table entries, so that, for example, C1 is stored under the string "move." The object within the user interface are in an inheritance hierarchy: depicted here is a simple case of three text editors (ED1...ED3) and three buttons (B1...B3). A user with capability set CS2 can edit text in any of the editors, but can press only one button, B3. A user with capability set CS1 can press only buttons B1 and B2. Notice that capability C4 has overridden C3, because it is stored under the same name in an inheritance parent of B3.

cussed below, user interface objects can inherit entries in their capability tables, and thus one capability placed sufficiently high up in the inheritance hierarchy can provide access protection for many objects.

A capability is itself a user interface object, and so it can appear on the screen and can be more literally passed around among users.

In practice we cache the key (the string under which the capability is stored in the capability table) within the capability itself. This key is useful as a label in the user interface to describe the kind of access the capability governs. However, when a protected object looks to see if a given capability is in its capability table, the comparison is made based on identity, *not* based on name.

Programming, and Lexical Access.

As a programmer, how does one access a capability? Normally one is writing code for a method in a user interface object such as a button, playing the role of the protected object. The programmer typically has a reference to some user interface event, provided as an argument to the method call. The programmer can access the entries in the button's capability table by sending to itself the message `capabilityAt(keyName)`. The other half of the problem is finding if this capability is in the user's capability set. In Kansas, every UI event (such as mouse move) has a reference to the user object from which the event originated, and hence its associated capability set can be queried to determine if it contains a certain capability. Furthermore, every thread retains a reference to the user interface event from which it originated, and one can always obtain a reference to the currently active thread in which one is running. Hence, if some event is not passed down the stack as an argument, the user who created the thread can be ascertained through the thread's originating event. These cases have proven adequate for our needs to date, although theoretically there are cases in which access to the appropriate event would have to be made available by construction of some new mechanism. Constructing new mechanism is no problem if everything in the underlying language is accessible for reprogramming, but of course it's not a realistic a option in general.

Inheritance

Every Self object can inherit from one or more other Self objects. References to these "parents," as they are called, are from specially marked slots known to the virtual machine. As previously mentioned, when a message is sent to some Self object, the object's slot names are searched to find one that matches the message name. If there is none, the objects parents slots are searched, and so on, until a match is found.

We have implemented the capability tables to mirror these semantics of message lookup. If a capability of a certain name (e.g.: "pressButton") is not found in an object's capability table, then the search continues in the capability table of the object's parent, and so on. In Figure 4, the object B3 inherits the "move" capability C1. Note however, that the "pressButton" capability C4 overrides the "pressButton" capability C3 in B3's parent. (Capabilities are matched based on identity, so C3 and C4 are different even though they are stored under the same name.)

Why must the "pressButton" capability of B3 override that of its parent? One could imagine a system in which *both* "pressButton" capabilities are present in B3. Such an "additive" inheritance would evoke the method combination rules enabled by "super" or "call-next-method" invocations in object-oriented programming languages. The override semantics we use seemed to us simplest, and allows us to easily express the notion of a "specially protected object" in an inheritance hierarchy. That is, if you want a user to be able to press all buttons except B3, give the user the widely inherited capability C3, and store a special "pressButton" capability in B3's capability table. Thus, with this use of inheritance we are able to get some of the benefits of "negative rights" as explained in [12]. (In a system with negative rights, giving a user a negative right on B3 would prevent the user from accessing B3).

With the uniform, object-oriented nature of the Self language that makes up the Kansas environment, we are in an ideal position to make use of inheritance for the other players in the capability story. Recall there are three objects at play: the protected object, the user object, and the capability itself. The capability table inheritance mechanism is associated with the protected object. Adding significant roles for the user object and/or for the capability would create a triple dimensional inheritance scheme. The implications of such a mechanism are discussed in [12]. However, we find the complexity of three simultaneous inheritance dimensions hard to comprehend, and are thankful we have so far not found it necessary to go down that path.

USER INTERFACES TO DYNAMIC CAPABILITY ACQUISITION

Here are some of the ways we have made capabilities accessible from the user interface. Recall, capabilities are themselves displayable user interface objects, and so can be incorporated into various applications as the world is running.

Capability Set Transfer Button: This has proven useful for our own use in giving demonstrations. We can start with the DTVI world (as illustrated in Figure 2) with some of us playing the role of student, and at least one playing the role of coordinator, with full capabilities in his capability table. In order to demonstrate collaborative programming, the coordinator carries this "copy my capabilities" button into a mutu-

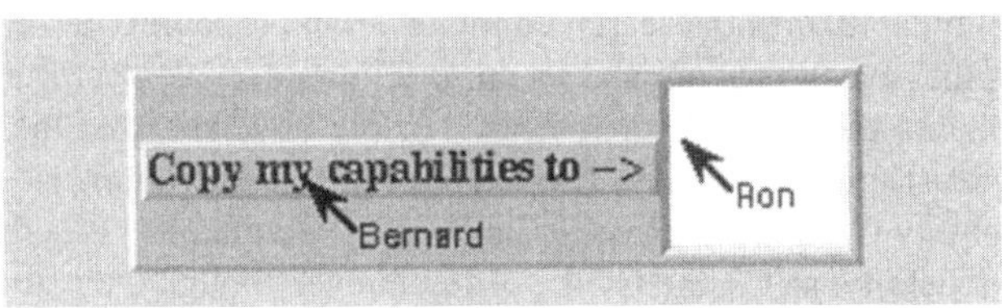

ally shared region of Kansas. The "students" then hover their mouse over the special white square while the facilitator presses the button. The students are given a copy of all the coordinator's capabilities, and are thus transformed into coordinators themselves. This button was graphically assembled while the world was running. It contains a single though lengthy expression, and so it was fairly easy for a Kansas/Self programmer to create.

Capability Tray: This was the interface we devised for the remote physics lab simulations. Because in this case we only used a small number of capabilities — enabled one at a time — an interface showing all the capabilities for each user seemed reasonable. The trays can be placed in a region of the world visible to the instructor but not to the students (by giving the instructor a slightly larger view bounds, or a view bound offset by a small amount). Dropping a capability in

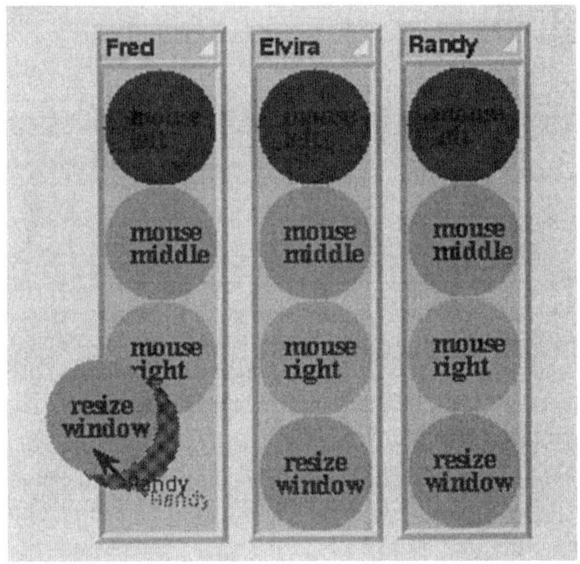

the tray causes it to be added to that student's capability set. Because each capability can be owned by only one tray, this may not be suitable for applications in which several users share a particular capability.

Small Computers: This is a session start-up mechanism through which the initial capability set can be established for each participant. The small computer represents a partici-

pant's host, including the capabilities that will be given to that participant if and when they are brought into Kansas. The functionality of the small computer is available in a pop-up menu. In this case the capabilities, though they are displayable objects, are held by language level references only, references reachable from the small computer objects.

Drop/Acquire a Capability: Kansas currently assumes each user has a three-button mouse, and the facilitators in the DTVI system are sometimes required to use pop-up menus that are triggered by the middle (or in rare cases, the rightmost) mouse button. Accidentally pressing and releasing these buttons when the mouse is over the wrong object can have unpleasant side effects (for instance, it could create new, large objects, resize the object, or it may delete the object from the Kansas world). Consequently we found our facilitators were nervous about accidentally sending the system off into some state from which it would be tedious and time consuming to recover. We therefore introduced a button which alternately enables or disables a user's mouse buttons. Press it once to acquire a capability, press it again to deposit the capability back in the world. We put two of these buttons in a part of the world reachable by the facilitator, one for the middle mouse button, one for the right. This is an ex-

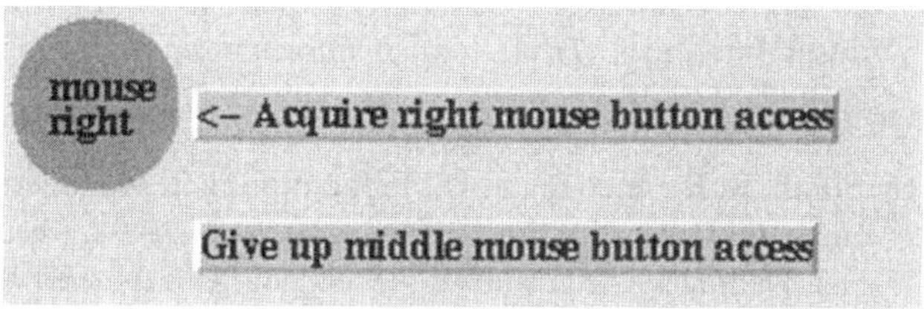

ample of a Kansas user intentionally modifying their own capabilities for the sake of usability.

The Infinite Tower of Gloves Metaphor: In Kansas, a mouse cursor is a regular display object, and we call it a "hand" since it is used for pressing buttons and carrying virtual objects about. Each hand has a capability set—a hand plays the role of the "user object" in the capability story. Each hand also has a "meta hand" which is normally invisible. By pressing the meta-escape key combination, a user's hand falls off, and their meta hand appears, coming to life. The original hand remains stationary and lifeless on the screen, though it can be manipulated as an ordinary Kansas object. By hovering over this discarded hand and pressing the shift-meta-escape key combination, a user can reabsorb the original hand, or *any* inanimate hand, for that matter.

Because each hand has its own capability set, different hands can represent different bundles of functionality. Users can run from one hand to the next, dropping this one to pick up that, much as one does with tools on a work bench. Or, one might come to think of these hands as gloves, each glove specialized for a different role.

Users can shed as many "gloves" as they wish, there is always more, so the illusion is that one is wearing an infinite number of gloves. This is perhaps the authors' favorite interface to changing capabilities, though interestingly, it is probably the least used. It requires those specially reserved keypresses, and it usually takes several gestures to affect a change (drop one glove, move to the other, pick it up). The other mechanisms we describe are more efficient.

CONCLUSIONS

The physics underlying reality does not define roles, though it supports them. We have tried to mirror this kind of support in the multi-user world of Kansas. We found that we can use the basic spatiality of Kansas to provide the necessary different views for different users. We have devised a capability system that operates on the user inputs to the interface. The capability tables used by protected objects follow an inheritance scheme that is simple, mirrors the underlying language Self, and has proven useful in providing the kinds of input filtering we need. The capability system is fairly simple to comprehend, allows for dynamic flexibility, and yet has proven sufficiently expressive to meet our needs.

If necessary we could extend the capability system to apply to graphical and auditory outputs as well as to user inputs, but our concern would be the resulting violation of the WYSIWITYS principle, which allows users to maintain an awareness of who sees what. It is interesting that, so far, we have been able to support roles without violating this principle.

Physical reality has provided some interesting metaphors for human computer interaction. Direct manipulation, the desktop metaphor, virtual reality: all have been at least moderately successful in providing users with a model that is quickly comprehended. We have again benefited by turning to physical reality, this time to find an understandable and flexible way to support roles within a group.

REFERENCES

1. Dourish, P., and Bellotti, V., Awareness and coordination in shared workspaces, in *Proceedings of CSCW '92* (Toronto Canada, October 1992), ACM Press, 107-114.
2. Edwards, K., Policies and roles in collaborative applications, in *Proceedings of CSCW '96* (Cambridge MA, November 1996), ACM Press, 11-20.
3. Smith, R. B., Wolczko, M., and Ungar, D., From Kansas to Oz: Collaborative debugging when a shared world breaks, in *Communications of the ACM 40*, 4, April 1997, 72-78.
4. Smith, R. B., What You See Is What I Think You See, in Proc. Conf. Computer-Supported Collaborative Learning, published as *SIGCUE Outlook 21*, 3, (Spring 1992), ACM Press, 18-23.
5. Smith, R.B., Maloney, J. and Ungar, D., The Self-4.0 User Interface: Manifesting a System-wide Vision of Concreteness, Uniformity, and Flexibility, in *Proc. OOPSLA `95*, (Austin Texas, October 1995) 47-60.
6. Gaver, W., Smith, R. B., O'Shea, T., Effective sounds in complex systems: the ARKola simulation, in *Proceedings of CHI `91* (New Orleans LA, April 1991), ACM Press, 85-90.
7. Smith, R.B., O'Shea, T., O'Malley, C., Scanlon, E., and Taylor, J., Preliminary experiments with a distributed, multimedia problem solving environment, in *Proceedings of EC-CSCW `90*, (Gatwick England, 1990) 19-34. Also appears in J. Bowers, S. Benford, eds., *Studies in*

Computer Supported Cooperative Work: theory, practice and design, Elsevier, Amsterdam, 1991, 31-48.

8. Gutwin, C. and Greenberg, S., Workspace Awareness for Groupware, in *CHI '96 Conf. Companion* (Vancouver, B.C., April 1996), ACM Press, 208-209.

9. Gutwin, C. and Greenberg, S., Effects of Awareness Support on Groupware Usability, to appear in *Proceedings of CHI'98* (Los Angeles, CA, April 1998), ACM Press.

10. Sepusic, M., Pannoni, R., Smith, R.B., Gibbons, J., Sutherland, B. and Dutra, J., Will virtual collaborative learning be effective?, *in preparation.*

11. Electric Communities' white paper on "Introduction to Capability Based Security" can be found at http://www.communities.com/company/papers/security/index.html

12. Shen, H., and Dewan, P., Access Control for Collaborative Environments, in *Proceedings of CSCW '92* (Toronto, Canada, October 1992), ACM Press, 51-58.

13. Neuwirth, C., Kaufer, D., Ravinder, C., and Morris, J., Issues in the Design of Computer Support for Co-authoring and Commenting, in *Proceedings of CSCW '90* (Los Angeles, CA, October 1990), ACM Press, 183-195.

14. Brothers, L., Sembugamoorthy, V., and Muller, M., ICICLE: Groupware for Code Inspection, in *Proceedings of CSCW '90* (Los Angeles, CA, October 1990), ACM Press, 169-181.

15. Kaplan, S., Tolone, W., Bogio, D., and Bignoli, C., Flexible, Active Support for Collaborative Work with Conversation Builder, in *Proceedings of CSCW '92* (Toronto, Canada, October 1992), ACM Press, 378-385.

16. Denning, P., *Fault-Tolerant Operating Systems, Computing Surveys 8,* 4 (December, 1976) 359-389.

17. Stefik, M., Bobrow, D., Foster, G., Lanning, S., and Tatar, D., WYSIWIS Revised: Early Experiences with Multiuser Interfaces. *Trans. Office Information Systems* 5, 2(1987), 147-167.

18. Smith, R. B., and Ungar, D., Programming as an Experience: the Inspiration for Self, in *proc. ECOOP'95*, (Aarhus, Denmark, August 1995). Proceedings published as G. Goos, J. Hartmanis, and J. van Leeuwen, (Eds.), *Lecture Notes in Computer Science, Vol. 952,* (1995) Springer, Berlin, 303-330.

Design for Individuals, Design for Groups: Tradeoffs Between Power and Workspace Awareness

Carl Gutwin
Department of Computer Science
University of Saskatchewan
Saskatoon, SK, S7N 5A9, Canada
+1 306 966-4886
gutwin@cs.usask.ca
www.cs.usask.ca/faculty/gutwin

Saul Greenberg
Department of Computer Science
University of Calgary
Calgary, AB, T2N 1N4, Canada
+1 403 220-6087
saul@cpsc.ucalgary.ca
www.cpsc.ucalgary.ca/~saul

ABSTRACT

Users of synchronous groupware systems act both as individuals and as members of a group, and designers must try to support both roles. However, the requirements of individuals and groups often conflict, forcing designers to support one at the expense of the other. The tradeoff is particularly evident in the design of interaction techniques for shared workspaces. Individuals demand powerful and flexible means for interacting with the workspace and its artifacts, while groups require information about each other to maintain awareness. Although these conflicting requirements present real problems to designers, the tension can be reduced in some cases. We consider the tradeoff in three areas of groupware design: workspace navigation, artifact manipulation, and view representation. We show techniques such as multiple viewports, process feedthrough, action indicators, and view translations that support the needs of both individuals and groups.

Keywords

Groupware design and usability, workspace awareness

INTRODUCTION

Many kinds of collaborative work involve both individual and shared activity (eg. [6,8,20]). In these *mixed-focus* situations, people frequently move back and forth between individual tasks performed in relative isolation and shared work undertaken with other members of the group. Even when working apart, though, people maintain a sense of the whereabouts and activities of the rest of the group. For example, when a group of people get together to plan a project, we might see people working individually on different sections, but keeping an eye on what the rest of the group is doing, and then joining one or more others to confer, coordinate, or give feedback.

When mixed-focus collaboration is to happen through synchronous distributed groupware, both the individual tasks and the shared activity present design requirements to the creator of the system. Unfortunately, these two sets of requirements often contradict or compete with one another [2,8,25]. Designs that are good for individual work often hinder group work, and designs that support the group often restrict the individual's interaction with the application. Groupware designers are left with a tradeoff between meeting the needs of individuals and meeting the needs of the group as a whole.

This tradeoff becomes particularly apparent as designers try to satisfy two design goals: support for individual control over the application, and support for *workspace awareness*—the up-to-the-moment understanding of how other people are interacting with a shared workspace [13,14,15]. Three situations illustrate the tension between these goals and serve as case studies in design: workspace navigation, artifact manipulation, and view representation.

Workspace navigation. Who should control where people move, the individual or the group? In single-user software, people move freely around the workspace to look at and manipulate the work artifacts that they need for their tasks. In group activity, however, collaboration is simplified when people see the same artifacts at the same time. This is a long-standing issue in groupware design: previous systems have generally favoured either the group (through strict WYSIWIS view sharing), or the individual (through relaxed-WYSIWIS sharing).

Artifact manipulation. Should manipulation techniques be designed to increase an individual's power and capability, or to provide the group with information about what is happening? The powerful interaction techniques of single-user systems often involve symbolic commands and indirect manipulation, which give little information to others about the author of the action, its occurrence, or its progress.

View representation. Should groupware systems allow each person to change the way in which the workspace is represented? Different representations can simplify individual work, but can greatly complicate communication between group members.

CSCW 98 Seattle Washington USA

In each of these situations, designers can choose to favour one side or the other. The ideal solution, however, would be to find a way around the tradeoff, and support both the needs of individuals and the needs of groups. Our goal in this paper is to explore the tradeoff in each of these three situations and present interface techniques that reduce the tension between individuals and groups.

Although ideal solutions are difficult to achieve, we have identified a set of techniques that provide individual users with flexible control and powerful interaction, while at the same time providing the rest of the group with workspace awareness information. In the next few sections, we explore the situations introduced above as case studies of design tradeoffs. We discuss ways of negotiating the problem and provide example solutions from systems we have built using GroupKit [19]. Before turning to these case studies, we look at the origins of the problem in more detail.

THE ROOTS OF THE PROBLEM

The tradeoff between individuals and groups is much more of an issue in groupware environments than it is in the physical world. In physical workspaces, the tradeoff is fixed by the properties of the environment—and fixed in such a way that groups can easily maintain awareness of one another. People have become used to the constraints of physical workspaces, and work practices have evolved to take advantage of them. Groupware workspaces, in contrast, are *synthetic environments* that do not have a fixed set of constraints. Designers must make explicit decisions about every aspect of the environment, from the way that things will look to the ways that users will interact with them. Because these decisions must be made, groupware designers must consider who will benefit and who will suffer from each choice.

There are three areas in particular where groupware workspaces differ from their physical counterparts. These differences stem both from the freedom described above and from the limitations imposed by current groupware input and display technology.

- Groupware systems show far less of the workspace than what can be seen in a physical environment.
- Manipulation techniques in virtual workspaces are not bound by the physical constraints that exist in physical workspaces.
- Virtual workspaces can represent and display artifacts in more ways than physical workspaces allow.

When a small group collaborates in a physical workspace, such as a tabletop or a whiteboard, people can see the entire workspace and everyone in it. Even when they are working on individual tasks, people can see others as they move and work. People interact with physical artifacts by directly manipulating them, which provides others with a great deal of information about the nature and progress of the activity. Physical workspaces also present a consistent representation of the artifacts to everyone in the group—that is, although perspectives may differ, everyone sees the same objects represented in the same way.

In computational workspaces, display resources are markedly reduced, and the flexibility of input devices is considerably less. However, there are fewer restrictions on interaction than there are in the real world. In fact, many single-user systems have mitigated the display and input shortcomings of computer environments by providing a wide range of powerful interaction techniques that would be impossible in the real world.

Each of these differences between physical and virtual environments creates tension between individual and group needs. The next three sections describe our specific encounters with the tradeoff in the areas mentioned above, and some of our solutions.

WORKSPACE NAVIGATION: FREEDOM TO MOVE

Groupware display devices are much smaller and offer much lower resolution than the normal human field of view. As a result, only a small part of the workspace is visible at a time, forcing people to look and work through a small viewport. This display constraint raises the following problem: when only a portion of the workspace can be seen at once, whose needs (the individual's or the group's) should be considered when deciding what to show?

There are two competing requirements. Group activity is simplified when collaborators can see the same part of the workspace, since they can see others' actions and the objects they are working on. Individuals, however, need to move around the workspace independently to see and manipulate the objects they need for their specific tasks.

In the past, synchronous groupware has favoured either groups or individuals. Early systems imposed "what you see is what I see" (WYSIWIS) view sharing (eg. [25]), where all participants' viewports looked at exactly the same part of the workspace. This approach ensures that people can stay aware of one another's activities, but is too restrictive for mixed-focus collaboration. Other systems implement relaxed-WYSIWIS view sharing, allowing people to navigate independently (eg. [26]). Unfortunately, when people look at different areas of the workspace, they are effectively blinded to the actions and events that go on outside their viewport, making the maintenance of awareness far more difficult.

The ideal solution would be to support both needs—show everyone the same objects, as in WYSIWIS systems, but also let people move freely around the workspace, as in relaxed-WYSIWIS groupware. One approach that makes this possible involves splitting the view of workspace into two viewports. The main viewport is under the control of the local user, and the smaller secondary viewport shows a different perspective on the workspace and provides workspace awareness information.

In earlier work (eg. [13,14,16]) we have introduced two types of secondary displays, overviews and detail views, that follow this approach. Overviews show the entire workspace in miniature, and show objects as they move or change. When the overview also displays each person's telepointer and the extents of their main view, it is called a radar view [24] (Figure 1c). Radar views make people's presence, location, and activities visible, regardless of where they are in the workspace. Detail views are secondary viewports that show more detail of another person's activity, but show less of the workspace than an overview. Detail views can show any part of the workspace, but we consider two configurations to be most applicable: the "over the shoulder view" (Figure 1d) and the "cursor's-eye view" (Figure 1e). These secondary views are described below and are illustrated in Figure 1.

To begin with, Figure 1a shows the entire workspace of a groupware concept-map editor. In this example, there are two people in the workspace: Carl is working at the left side of the workspace, and Saul is working at the right side. Figure 1b shows the application interface on Saul's screen, containing a main view and a secondary view. The main view shows the workspace at full size, and allows independent navigation. In the top left corner of Saul's main view (Figure 1b) is an inset radar view. The radar view is also shown separately in Figure 1c. The radar view shows each person's main view extents as a filled rectangle, and shows a miniature telepointer for each person. Although Saul can move freely, the radar view provides him with immediate information about Carl's location and activities.

The radar view in Saul's main view could be replaced by, or used together with, one of two detail views. First, an "over-the-shoulder" view shows a reduced version of another person's main view. The objects are shown smaller than full size, but are considerably larger than they would be in an overview. Figure 1d shows an over-the-shoulder view of Carl's work area. By adding this view to his interface, Saul can keep track of exactly what Carl can see. Second, a "cursor's-eye" view shows a small area directly around another person's mouse cursor. Although its extents are limited, the cursor's-eye view shows objects and actions in full size and full detail. A cursor's-eye view of Carl's cursor is shown in Figure 1e.

Tradeoff issues in workspace navigation

The use of secondary viewports allows individuals to move freely around the workspace, while still providing information about others' whereabouts and activities.

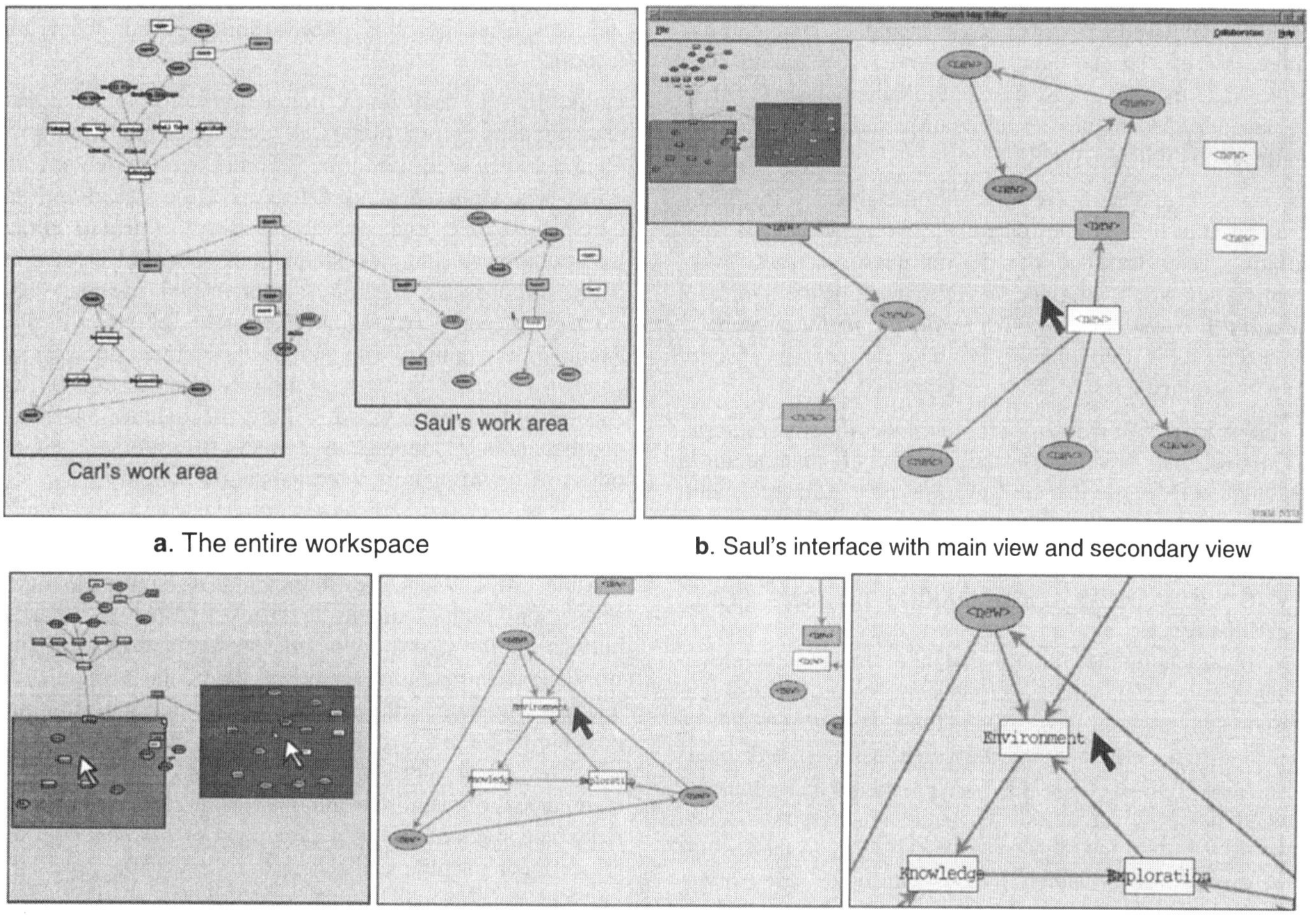

a. The entire workspace

b. Saul's interface with main view and secondary view

c. The radar view

d. Over-the-shoulder view of Carl's area

e. Cursor's-eye view around Carl's cursor.

Figure 1. Secondary viewports on the workspace.

Overviews and detail views release designers from the bind of having to give navigation control to either the group or the individual. However, this approach does not make the tradeoff go away, but simply shifts it to the window level rather than the application level. Designers must now trade off the amount of screen space allocated to the individual and group windows.

Nevertheless, it is now at least possible to form a compromise, and these compromises can be based on the specific needs of the task. Designing a usable system thus implies knowing what kinds of awareness information are important to the group activity, and how much detail about others' actions is needed to maintain awareness.

For example, the radar view in Figure 1b shows general locations and conveys basic actions and gestures, but takes up only a small amount of screen space. In previous evaluations of collaborative construction tasks (eg. [12,17]), overviews that used about an eighth of the main view were found to be valuable additions to the system, and a good use of screen space.

We have not evaluated detail views to the same extent, but it is clear that they would be used when awareness requirements are much more specific. Since they can only show information about one other person, multiple displays would be required for groups larger than two. This requires more screen space than an overview, reducing the allocation to the local user's individual tasks. Other visualization techniques, such as transparent overlays, could mitigate this problem (eg. [3]).

In sum, secondary views provide designers with finer-grained control over the tradeoff between individuals and groups. They translate the design question from 'who controls the whole interface' to 'how much of the interface is controlled by each party.' Knowledge of the awareness requirements in the collaborative task can provide insight into how to make a satisfactory compromise.

In the next section, we turn from the tradeoffs in navigation to those that arise from the design of manipulation techniques. At issue are the ways that people interact with workspace artifacts, and the ways that others in the group perceive those interactions.

SYMBOLIC MANIPULATION: MAKING ACTIONS MORE PERCEIVABLE

The manipulation techniques that a designer puts into a groupware system also introduce a tradeoff between individuals and groups. Techniques for manipulating objects often support either individual tasks or workspace awareness, but not both. Two aspects of these techniques are particularly important: the amount of power they provide the user, and their degree of visibility to the rest of the group. Unfortunately, these attributes are often related—more power for the user often also means less visual information about the action. Since the information produced by an action greatly assists others in maintaining workspace awareness, the groupware designer faces a problem: should manipulation techniques be designed to aid the individual or the group?

Before discussing solutions to the problem, we explain further what it means for an action to generate information. To begin with, consider manipulation in physical workspaces. In this environment, people act on objects through direct manipulation, which produces two kinds of information: consequential communication and feedthrough.

In *consequential communication* [22], the characteristic movements of an action communicate its character and content to others. For example, when a pilot reaches over and lowers the landing-gear lever, the action "not only controls the landing gear, but just as important, it acts as a natural communication between the two pilots, letting both know the action has been done." ([18], p. 142)

In *feedthrough* [5], the feedback produced when artifacts are manipulated provides others with clues about that manipulation. For example, when one pilot sees the landing-gear lever move, they can conclude that their partner is moving it, even when they cannot see the other pilot. Feedthrough is also commonly associated with auditory feedback: the sound of the landing-gear lever indicates what the other pilot is doing, just as the visual information does.

Unlike the physical world, interaction with computational environments is not limited to direct manipulation. In a computational workspace, the visibility of an action and the effort it requires depend entirely on the design of the system. At one end of the spectrum, (virtual) direct manipulation techniques simulate real-world interaction. They emphasise visibility, incremental action, and immediate and continuous feedback (eg. [23]). For example, dragging a file across the screen in order to change its parent directory is a direct-manipulation action. As in the real world, these techniques produce consequential communication and feedthrough, giving others in the group information about the action.

At the other extreme, symbolic manipulation techniques are commands that let users specify actions in powerful and flexible ways. They are shortcuts that emphasize rapid invocation and minimal feedback. Menu commands, buttons, toolbars, and keyboard shortcuts are examples of symbolic manipulation techniques. Symbolic manipulation lets users interact with artifacts in ways that are often not possible in the real world. While a good idea in single user systems, they produce almost no consequential communication, and their minimal feedback can drastically reduce people's ability to maintain awareness. Therein lies the designer's problem.

In addressing this situation, we start from the assumption that symbolic manipulation is here to stay—it is simply too useful to the individual. People who are used to these techniques would be unlikely to accept an increase in effort just to benefit the group. Our efforts, therefore, have been in considering how symbolic commands and indirect manipulation might be augmented to provide more information to the group.

Symbolic manipulation techniques have four drawbacks for group members trying to stay aware of one another.

- Symbolic actions may use interfaces like buttons and menus that are not a natural part of the shared workspace. Interaction with these interface objects happens outside the workspace, and so cannot be seen by others.
- Symbolic actions such as key commands have little or no visible representation in the workspace, and have few if any characteristic movements. Actions are therefore harder to see in the workspace, and are more likely to go unnoticed by others.
- Many symbolic actions are performed in similar ways (eg. select an object and execute a command), and so they are difficult to distinguish from one another.
- Symbolic actions can happen almost instantaneously, providing little warning of their occurrence and allowing little time for others to see and interpret them.

The problems can be addressed, however, by transforming the minimal information provided by these actions to a more visible form. This is the approach suggested by Segal [22]: "compensate for consequential information that is lost...by providing enhanced feedback from the system indicating what specific actions each operator is performing" (p. 411). Below, we discuss two approaches—process feedthrough and action indicators—that can make symbolic manipulation more obvious, more distinguishable, and more interpretable to others.

Process feedthrough

Some symbolic commands are invoked through interface widgets such as buttons, menus, or dialog boxes. These interfaces provide the local user with visual reminders of what can be done, as well as feedback indicating the action that is being composed. For example, buttons depress under a mouse click, and menus highlight the command currently underneath the cursor. Other users in a groupware system rarely see this feedback, for two reasons: first, it is considered to be part of the application rather than part of the workspace, and second, it is considered to be distracting to other users. Feedback from these interfaces, however, can help the group to determine what actions people are composing. When other people receive this information, it becomes *process feedthrough.*

As a simple example of process feedthrough, consider a button in the interface of a groupware application. When a person's cursor moves over the button, it becomes highlighted on all user's screens; when a person presses the button, it is shown being pressed on all screens. The highlight and the press give people a chance to interpret the action and determine what the other person is doing. If the button represents a particularly important action, the natural feedthrough can even be augmented to make it more visible. For example, the button could make a clicking sound when it is pressed, or use a more obvious highlight colour [11].

A second example involves process feedthrough for menus. Menus are a more complicated case than buttons, since they carry a greater risk of distracting others or even obscuring their work. To reduce this risk, we display only a portion of the feedback information that is visible to the local user. Figure 2 shows a group-visible popup menu as it appears on a local and a remote display. The menu can be shown in several different ways on other user's screens, each providing a different amount of process feedthrough. The first variant (Figure 2, right) shows the extents of the menu as an empty rectangle, and shows only the item that the remote user's mouse is currently over. This version is useful when a large menu would hide too much of the local user's view. The second variant (not shown) provides only minimal information. It does not show intermediate selections, but only the menu outline, and once the user has made a choice, what item was chosen.

Figure 2. A remotely visible popup menu, as it is seen locally (left) and remotely (right).

This technique can also be used with other kinds of symbolic commands. Figure 3 illustrates a group-visible dialog box used to change the properties of a workspace artifact. Again, reproducing the entire dialog on all screens would cause too much disruption, but we can provide a summary representation (Figure 3 right) that conveys the current state of activity.

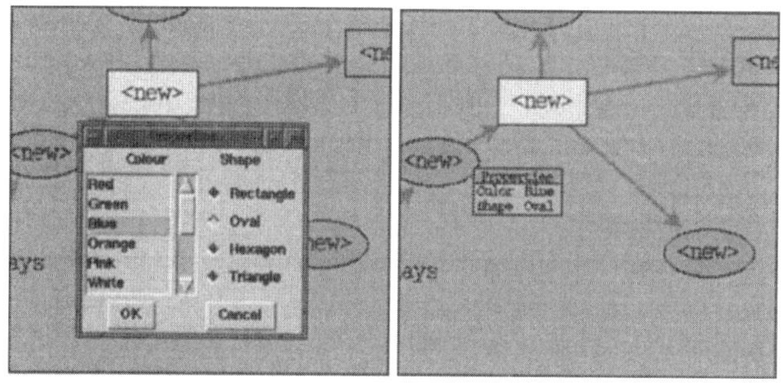

Figure 3. A group-visible dialog box, as seen locally (left) and remotely (right).

Providing process feedthrough shows how actions are being composed and invoked, but does not make the action itself more noticeable. When actions are hard to see, they can be augmented with artificial indicators, an approach we discuss next.

Action indicators and animations

Symbolic actions happen quickly and abruptly, making them hard to see and hard to interpret. For example, when someone presses the 'delete' key to remove a selected object, the operation is nearly instantaneous. In addition, since a keypress provides no process feedthrough, other users have little warning that the deletion is about to happen. When actions are invisible, our approach is to create an artificial signal for them; these signals (called *action indicators*) can be given a more perceivable workspace representation. Action indicators differ from process feedthrough in that they are tied to the action itself rather than to the process of selecting a command.

A deletion operation can be indicated in several ways. A simple solution is shown in Figure 4. When a node in this concept-map application is deleted using a keyboard command, the application draws a text flag on remote screens and displays it for a moment before removing the object. This technique gives the rest of the group information and time to interpret the sudden disappearance of the object from the workspace.

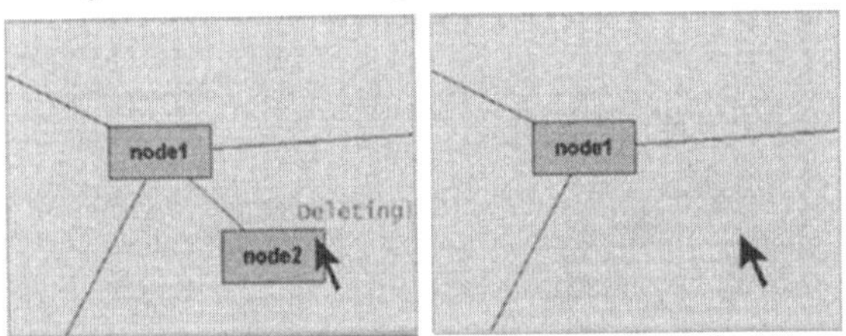

Figure 4. Symbolic delete indicator, during and after delete.

Although this solution is an improvement over no action representation, it still has a fairly high interpretation cost. A remote user has to see and read the indicator, and if several actions are represented the same way, distinguishing between them may still be a problem.

An alternate approach that can mitigate these problems is to have the artifact itself animate the action. When actions cause a visible change in the artifact, these changes can be made more perceptible even if the action is invisible. Figure 5 shows this approach in a concept-map system. When a node is deleted, it does not simply disappear, but swells up for a moment before gradually fading away (the supernova effect). Although the original delete action is still invisible, the effects of that action have been drawn out and made more noticeable.

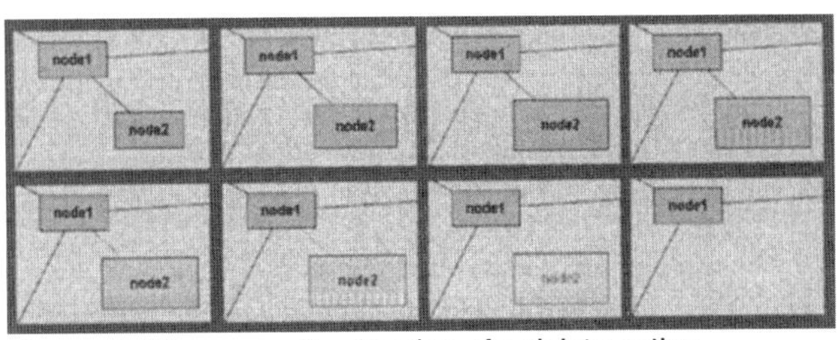

Figure 5. "Supernova" animation of a delete action.

The idea of animating actions builds on the observation of Ellis, Gibbs, and Rein [7] that others' actions are inherently more difficult to interpret than your own, so smooth animation of changes can aid interpretation. The extra step that we take is in inventing characteristic behaviours for the purpose of indicating action.

A final indication technique uses sound cues to indicate actions. Sound has the advantage of being perceptible even when the object is off-screen, and can be combined with the visual approaches described above. Different sounds can indicate different types of action, and can even convey the characteristics, progress, and location of the action (eg. [1,8,9]). For example, the system shown in Figure 5 plays a descending "whoosh" sound that fades away along with the visual representation of the deleted node.

Tradeoff issues in making actions perceivable

Process feedback shows people's actions as they invoke a symbolic command, and action indicators emphasize or embellish what happens after a command is executed. Either way, the idea is to draw out the action, make it more perceivable, and differentiate it from other actions. This approach allows the designer to provide symbolic manipulation techniques while still helping groups maintain awareness. However, as in the previous situation, these techniques introduce new decisions that the designer must balance in order to create a usable system.

Making actions more perceivable aids the maintenance of awareness, but as more visual information is displayed on the screen and more auditory information is played, the risk of distracting the individual increases. The question for the designer becomes one of making demands on people's attention: how much attention should people pay to the activities of the group, and how much should they pay to their individual activities? In past systems, the balance has been in favour of the individual, but it could clearly be swung too far to the side of the group as well.

As the above techniques show, the designer can control the way process and action are presented, and they can tailor this presentation to the demands of the task. It is clear that not all events can be shown just as they appear on the local user's screen; some large actions must be made smaller, and some small actions must be made larger. It may also be wise to give the user some control over these presentations, so that they can in essence say: "leave me alone, I'm trying to concentrate."

VIEW REPRESENTATION: POINTING AT THINGS

A third example of the tradeoff between individual and group needs involves the way the workspace and its artifacts are displayed on each person's screen. Groupware systems can display objects in different ways: for example, Figure 6 shows how a system might represent a hierarchy of objects as a tree or as an outline. Providing different representations can make individual tasks easier, but can also greatly restrict communication about the objects in the workspace. The designer must decide whether to assist individuals by allowing multiple representations, or to assist groups by restricting the workspace to a single consistent representation.

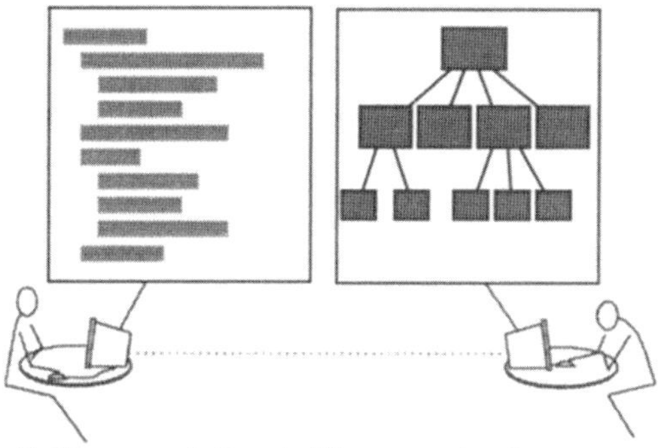

Figure 6. Representational differences in views

This problem does not occur in physical workspaces, where the appearance of an object is determined by its physical properties. In a groupware workspace, however, each person could change the way things look to suit their individual tasks and tastes. Individual tasks may benefit from different representations of the workspace that highlight particular aspects of the data or allow certain kinds of operations. Workspace awareness, however, is easier to maintain when people have a common representation.

We focus on two kinds of activity that are particularly important in collaboration: gestural communication and deictic reference. Both of these activities are ubiquitous in shared workspaces (eg. [22,27,28]). Deixis and gesture can only be interpreted correctly when they are seen in context—that is, when their relationships to the surrounding area of the workspace and nearby objects can be determined. With only one common representation of the workspace, this context is preserved for all the members of the group. As representations diverge, however, the surrounding context is quickly lost.

For example, consider the system shown above in Figure 6, where one person views a hierarchy as an indented text outline, and another person views it as a graphical tree. If one user circles a leaf node in the text view with their cursor, the gesture will be impossible to interpret in the tree view, since the corresponding leaves are different sizes and shapes, and are in different screen locations [11]. Similarly, the path along which the cursor is moved in the tree view has no meaningful analogue in the text view. Before considering whether these problems can be solved, we look at two simpler cases where representational differences are smaller.

The first case involves a concept-map editor that uses a fisheye view to represent the workspace (Figure 7). The fisheye distorts the spatial representation based on a focus point and a distortion factor [21]. However, in a relaxed-representation groupware system, each user can set their own focus point and level of distortion. When two fisheye views differ, telepointers no longer map to the correct locations in others' windows.

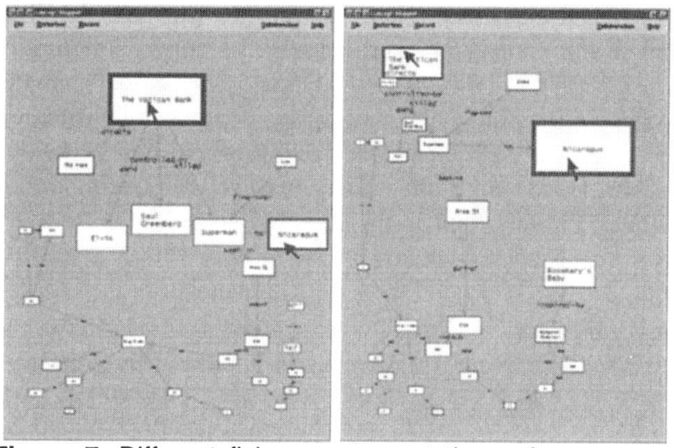

Figure 7. Different fisheye representations of a concept-map workspace.

This problem can be solved easily, since the two representations are related by a mathematical transformation. Telepointers can be placed in the correct location relative to the underlying workspace objects by determining the transformation from one fisheye function to the other [11]. In Figure 7, each cursor and its corresponding telepointer are in different screen locations, but in the same workspace location.

The second case introduces a larger disparity between views. Figure 8 shows two people's views of a shared web browser, where each person is using a different font. The font sizes cause lines to wrap differently on the two displays. Once again, if a telepointer simply tracks the screen location of a remote user's cursor, it will point at the wrong part of the text. In this case, there is no mathematical transformation relating the two views.

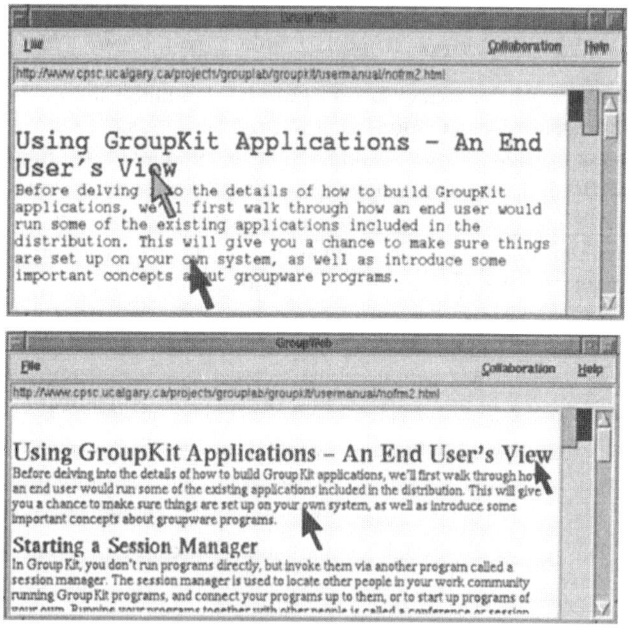

Figure 8. Two representations of a document in a shared web browser.

However, gestures can be put into their proper context by attaching the telepointer to the text location of the cursor rather than the screen location [4,10,11]. Movement is thus tied to the underlying representation, which is structurally equivalent in both views. These two cases provide strategies for conveying workspace awareness information (gestures and deictic references) even when representations differ. However, both cases involve relatively minor differences, and neither of the solutions work particularly well in the initial scenario of the system with a tree view and a text view (Figure 6). Cursor movement in this system could be tied to the common underlying structure, as described above. However, the granularity of the objects in the workspace is much coarser than in the web browser, and therefore only a broad indication of motion could be conveyed. This strategy would allow rudimentary pointing and deictic reference, but would not show gestures in enough detail. In addition, people would have to learn how to point 'properly' in this system, so that their actions could be correctly interpreted by others [11].

Tradeoff issues in view representation

View representation presents designers with more problems than do either of the previous two situations. Although we have found techniques for translating gestures across small differences in representation, larger disparities allow only crude solutions. It may be that meaningful discussions about objects in the workspace will require users to converge their views on a single common representation.

If this is the case, then knowing what representation others are using becomes useful knowledge, since initiating a conversation may only prove successful when views are similar. The over-the-shoulder display illustrated above in Figure 1d, which shows exactly what another person can see and how they see it, could be valuable for keeping track of view differences.

Finally, we have focused on gestural communication, but divergent representations also affect other kinds of activity. In particular, direct manipulation techniques lose their ability to convey information when representations diverge, since both feedthrough and consequential communication depend on workspace context for interpretation. Oddly, symbolic manipulation can provide better support for workspace awareness than direct manipulation in these cases, since the techniques introduced in the previous section (process feedthrough and action indicators) can be used regardless of representation.

DISCUSSION

The main conclusion of this research is that the needs of both individuals and groups can be met in groupware interfaces. In the three situations we considered (summarized in Table 1), we found that:

- control over workspace navigation can be tailored through multiple workspace viewports,
- manipulation techniques can provide both power and awareness information, and
- gestural communication can be preserved across some kinds of representational differences.

This success, however, must be received with two caveats. First, avoiding the tradeoff at one level often just moves it to a different level, albeit one that is more manageable. Second, the tradeoff appears in many guises in a groupware interface, and different situations allow different amounts of success in supporting both roles.

There are several other general issues underlying the tradeoff that require further thought. We consider four of these here: the importance of understanding the collaborative situation, the ways in which new technology can mitigate the tradeoff, the extra demands placed on the designer, and the difficulty of removing the tradeoff entirely.

Issue 1: Understanding collaboration

The designer's goal is to provide appropriate techniques for navigating, manipulating, and viewing the workspace. As the solutions above indicate, this goal is aided by knowing what information people require for effective collaboration, and how they gather that information from the environment. Unfortunately, there is not a great deal known about how people use environmental information when they work together. Furthermore, this knowledge is difficult to obtain. As Norman [18] says, "natural interaction is often invisible, unnoticed interaction...the problem is, it isn't always obvious just which parts [of the environment] are critical to

Situation	Tradeoff	Techniques
Workspace navigation	Individual freedom to move around the workspace vs. Consistent visual focus for the group	Split workspace views (radar, over-the-shoulder, cursor's-eye view)
Artifact manipulation	Individual power through symbolic actions vs. Awareness information produced through consequential communication and feedthrough	Process feedthrough, Action indicators and animations, Sound cues
View representation	Individual flexibility to tailor representations to individual tasks vs. The ability to point to and communicate about artifacts	Location transformations based on underlying representation

Table 1. Summary of tradeoffs and techniques

the social, distributed nature of the task, [and] which are irrelevant or detrimental" (p. 145). In our work, concentrating on the information that people need to maintain awareness has provided insight into new designs for interaction techniques [13]. Other analyses of collaborative situations will undoubtedly provide additional kinds of useful design knowledge.

Issue 2: The mixed blessing of improved technology

New and improved input and display devices will help designers avoid the tradeoff in some situations, but not in others. This is because only some of the design tensions between individuals and groups are caused by the limits of groupware technology—others are caused by the freedom designers have to invent interaction techniques that are impossible in the real world. For example, a system with a table-sized display would better approximate the large visual field of a physical workspace, and would reduce the problem of navigation control. However, large displays will do nothing to improve the perceptibility of actions, and will not help in translating between view representations. In fact, new technology will likely lead to even more powerful symbolic manipulation techniques and more flexible ways of changing representations. These new techniques will further complicate the designer's task of providing awareness information to the group.

Issue 3: Extra demands on the designer

Management of the tradeoff requires considerable additional work for the groupware designer. To produce an application that supports people both as individual users and as a group, the designer must investigate awareness requirements of the work situation, assess the capacities for feedthrough and consequential communication of each interaction technique and artifact representation, and augment the system using approaches like those described above. These tasks add to the complexity of a groupware system and to the time needed to design and build one. To mitigate this problem, software components should be made available to designers that support these groupware-specific needs. For example, we have added devices such as the radar view and the group-visible menu to the GroupKit toolkit [19], but much more could be done.

Issue 4: The difficulty of removing the tradeoff entirely

Although the solutions described above do successfully manage the tradeoff, they are imperfect in many ways. For example, radar views are small and provide limited resolution for perceiving actions and events; animations occur after the action itself has happened; and transformations of actions from one representation to another can end up looking clumsy. In some cases, further design and evaluation work on these devices will improve their usability, but in others we are left with few options, forcing us to accept an information environment that is better than the status quo but not as good as we would like.

CONCLUSION

We have explored a persistent problem in the design of synchronous groupware systems—the competing requirements of users as individuals and as members of a group. We examined the tradeoff as it applies to individual power and to the maintenance of workspace awareness. In three kinds of situations (workspace navigation, interaction with artifacts, and view representation), we described approaches that let a designer manage the tradeoff and support both individuals and groups. These approaches provide designers with an initial set of tools, but additional work on the issues underlying the tradeoff remains to be done. These efforts will move us closer to the goal of groupware that is flexible and powerful for the individual, and that also allows groups to interact smoothly and efficiently.

ACKNOWLEDGMENTS

Thanks to Steve Jones, Mark Apperley, and Mark Roseman for comments and discussions on these ideas. Thanks also to Intel Corporation and the National Science and Engineering Research Council of Canada (NSERC) for support in carrying out this research.

REFERENCES

1. Beaudoin-Lafon, M., and Karsenty, A., Transparency and Awareness in a Real-Time Groupware System. *Proceedings of UIST'92*, ACM Press, 1992.
2. Bellotti, V., Dourish, P., and MacLean, A. From users' themes to designers' DReams: Developing a design space for shared interactive technologies. Rank XEROX EuroPARC/AMODEUS Working Paper RP6-WP7, 1991. (Quoted in [6]).
3. Cox, D., Chugh, J., Gutwin, C., and Greenberg, S. The usability of transparent overview layers. *Companion Proceedings of the CHI'98 Conference on Human Factors in Computing Systems*, 301-302, ACM Press, 1998.
4. Dewan, P., and Choudhary, R., Flexible User Interface Coupling in Collaborative Systems. *Proceedings of the CHI '91 Conference on Human Factors in Computing Systems*, ACM Press, 1991.
5. Dix, A., Finlay, J., Abowd, G., and Beale, R., *Human-Computer Interaction*, Prentice Hall, 1993.
6. Dourish, P., and Bellotti, V., Awareness and Coordination in Shared Workspaces, *Proceedings of the Conference on Computer-Supported Cooperative Work*, Toronto, 107-114, ACM Press, 1992.
7. Ellis, C., Gibbs, S., and Rein, G., Groupware: Some Issues and Experiences, *Communications of the ACM*, 34(1), 38-58, 1991.
8. Gaver, W., Sound Support for Collaboration, *Proceedings of the Second European Conference on Computer Supported Cooperative Work*, 293-308, 1991.

9. Gaver, W., Smith, R., and O'Shea, T., Effective Sounds in Complex Systems: The ARKola Simulation, *Proceedings of the CHI'91 Conference on Human Factors in Computing Systems*, New Orleans, 85-90, ACM Press, 1991.

10. Greenberg, S. Collaborative Interfaces for the Web. In C. Forsythe, E. Grose and J. Ratner eds., *Human Factors and Web Development*, 241-254, LEA Press, 1997.

11. Greenberg, S., Gutwin, C., and Roseman, M. (1996). Semantic Telepointers for Groupware. *Proceedings of the OzCHI '96 Sixth Australian Conference on Computer-Human Interaction*, Hamilton, New Zealand, November 24-27.

12. Gutwin, C. and Greenberg, S. Effects of Awareness Support on Groupware Usability. *Proceedings of the CHI'98 Conference on Human Factors in Computing Systems*. Los Angeles, ACM Press, 1998.

13. Gutwin, C. *Workspace Awareness in Real-Time Distributed Groupware*. Ph.D. Dissertation, University of Calgary, Calgary. 1997. Available from www.cs.usask.ca/faculty/gutwin/publications/

14. Gutwin, C., Greenberg, S. and Roseman, M. (1996). Workspace Awareness in Real-Time Distributed Groupware: Framework, Widgets, and Evaluation. *People and Computers XI (Proceedings of BCSHCI'96)*, Eds. A. Sasse and R. Cunningham. August, London, 281-298, Springer-Verlag, 1996.

15. Gutwin, C., and Greenberg, S., Workspace Awareness for Groupware, *Companion Proceedings of the CHI'96 Conference on Human Factors in Computing Systems*, Vancouver, 208-209, ACM Press,1996.

16. Gutwin, C., and Greenberg, S., Workspace Awareness Support with Radar Views, *Companion Proceedings of the CHI'96 Conference on Human Factors in Computing Systems*, Vancouver, 210-211, ACM Press, 1996.

17. Gutwin, C., Roseman, M., and Greenberg, S., A Usability Study of Awareness Widgets in a Shared Workspace Groupware System, *Proceedings of the Conference on Computer-Supported Cooperative Work*, Boston, 258-267, ACM Press, 1996.

18. Norman, D., *Things That Make Us Smart*, Addison-Wesley, Reading, Mass., 1993.

19. Roseman, M., and Greenberg, S., Building Real-Time Groupware with GroupKit, a Groupware Toolkit, *ACM Transactions on Computer-Human Interaction*, 3(1), 66-106, ACM Press, 1996.

20. Salvador, T., Scholtz, J., and Larson, J., The Denver Model for Groupware Design, *SIGCHI Bulletin*, 28(1), 52-58, ACM Press, 1996.

21. Sarkar, M., and Brown, M., Graphical Fisheye Views of Graphs, *Proceedings of the CHI'92 Conference on Human Factors in Computing Systems*, 83-91, ACM Press, 1992.

22. Segal, L., Designing Team Workstations: The Choreography of Teamwork, in *Local Applications of the Ecological Approach to Human-Machine Systems*, P. Hancock, J. Flach, J. Caird and K. Vicente ed., 392-415, Lawrence Erlbaum, Hillsdale, NJ, 1995.

23. Shneiderman, B. The Future of Interactive Systems and the Emergence of Direct Manipulation *Behaviour and Information Technology* 1 (3): 237-256, 1982.

24. Smith, R., What You See Is What I Think You See, *ACM SIGCUE Outlook*, 21(3), 18-23, ACM Press, 1992.

25. Stefik, M., Foster, G., Bobrow, D., Kahn, K., Lanning, S., and Suchman, L., Beyond the Chalkboard: Computer Support for Collaboration and Problem Solving in Meetings, *Communications of the ACM*, 30(1), 32-47, 1987.

26. Stefik, M., Bobrow, D., Foster, G., Lanning, S., and Tatar, D., WYSIWIS Revised: Early Experiences with Multiuser Interfaces, *ACM Transactions on Office Information Systems*, 5(2), 147-167, 1987.

27. Tang, J., Findings from Observational Studies of Collaborative Work, *International Journal of Man-Machine Studies*, 34(2), 143-160, 1991.

28. Tatar, D., Foster, G., and Bobrow, D., Design for Conversation: Lessons from Cognoter, *International Journal of Man-Machine Studies*, 34(2), 185-210, 1991.

Fragmented Interaction: Establishing mutual orientation in virtual environments

Jon Hindmarsh[1], Mike Fraser[2], Christian Heath[1], Steve Benford[2] & Chris Greenhalgh[2]

[1]Work, Interaction & Technology Research Group
The Management Centre
King's College London
London W8 7AH, UK.
+44 171 333 4194(/4496)
{jon.hindmarsh, christian.heath}@kcl.ac.uk

[2]Communications Research Group
Department of Computer Science
University of Nottingham
Nottingham NG7 2RD, UK.
+44 115 951 4225(/4203/4221)
{mcf, sdb, cmg}@cs.nott.ac.uk

ABSTRACT

This paper explores and evaluates the support for object-focused collaboration provided by a desktop Collaborative Virtual Environment. The system was used to support an experimental 'design' task. Video recordings of the participants' activities facilitated an observational analysis of interaction in, and through, the virtual world. Observations include: problems due to fragmented views of embodiments in relation to shared objects; participants compensating with spoken accounts of their actions; and difficulties in understanding others' perspectives. Design implications include: more explicit representations of actions than are provided by pseudo-humanoid embodiments; and navigation techniques that are sensitive to the actions of others.

Keywords

Social Interaction, Virtual Environments, Media Spaces, Object-focused Work.

INTRODUCTION

It is increasingly recognised that changes in the structure of contemporary organisations will place corresponding demands on technology to provide support for distributed collaborative work [1]. The trend towards the disaggregation and globalisation of firms suggests that CSCW technologies will play an increasingly important part in supporting co-operation and communication amongst distributed personnel. Already, asynchronous text based systems, such as e-mail, Lotus Notes and the World Wide Web are flourishing within the business community. However technologies to support real time, distributed collaborative work have met with less success. Innovative systems such as media spaces and virtual environments have not as yet proved to provide satisfactory domains for collaborative work, and even their precursors, such as video-telephony and video-conferencing, have failed to have the impact that many envisaged. It has been argued that the relative weakness of such systems to support synchronous remote working, derives from their inability to assist individuals in working flexibly with documents, models and other workplace artefacts.

In this paper we build on workplace studies and media space research to develop and evaluate a Collaborative Virtual Environment (CVE) designed to support real time work and interaction with objects and artefacts. In particular, we wish to explore the extent to which the system provides participants with the ability to refer to and discuss features of the virtual environment. We also draw out the implications of our observations for developing more sophisticated support for distributed collaborative work.

BACKGROUND

In their wide-ranging investigation of organisational conduct, workplace studies have powerfully demonstrated how communication and collaboration are dependent upon the ability of personnel to invoke and refer to features of their immediate environment [e.g. 9, 12, 14]. Studies of settings such as offices and control rooms have shown that participants not only use objects and artefacts, such as documents, plans, diagrams, pictures and models, to accomplish their various activities, but to co-ordinate those activities, in real time, with the conduct of others. Indeed, it is found that many activities within co-located working environments rely upon the participants talking with each other, and monitoring each others' conduct, whilst looking, both alone or together, at some workplace artefact. An essential part of this process, is the individual's abilities to refer to particular objects, and have another see in a particular way, what they themselves are looking at [15]. These studies provide insights into the demands that will be placed on technologies that aim to provide flexible and robust support for remote working.

Interestingly, systems to support distributed collaboration are increasingly attempting to meet these needs. Rather than merely presenting face-to-face views, conventional video-conferencing systems are now often provided with a 'document camera', and media spaces are increasingly designed to provide participants with access to common digital displays or enhanced access to the others' domain [e.g. 13, 16, 19]. However, it is not clear that such systems provide adequate support for object-focused collaboration.

Our own earlier attempts to develop a media space to support variable access between participants and their respective domains or objects and artefacts have also met with limited success [cf. 8, 13]. In MTV II, an experiment undertaken with Bill Gaver, Abi Sellen and Paul Luff, we provided remote participants with various views of each other and their respective domains on three separate monitors, including a 'face-to-face' view, an 'in-context' view (showing the individual in the setting), and a 'desktop' view (allowing access to documents and other objects). Participants were asked to undertake a simple task which necessitated reference to objects in, and features of, each others' respective environment. Despite providing participants with visual access to the relevant features of each others' domains, participants encountered difficulties in completing the task. In general, individuals could not determine what a co-participant was referring to, and, more specifically, where, and at what, s/he was looking or pointing. This problem derived from participants' difficulties in (re)connecting an image of the other with the image of the object to which they were referring. The fragmentation of images - the person from the object and relevant features of the environment - undermined the participants ability to assemble the coherence of the scene [12]. This undermined even simple collaboration in and through the mutually available objects and artefacts.

In the light of these findings we decided to pursue a rather different solution - developing a collaborative virtual environment. Of course, CVEs enable participants to work with shared access to objects located in the virtual environment, whilst media spaces endeavour to provide participants with the opportunity to work on 'real, physical' objects. However, we believe that CVEs may provide a more satisfactory method of supporting certain forms of distributed collaborative work, especially those requiring reference to, and use of, objects. There is growing weight to this argument, given that CVE developers have recently devised techniques for integrating video views of physical locations and objects into virtual worlds [17]. In particular, it is felt that:

- even though the actual users are located in distinct physical domains, the CVE allows participants to share views of a stable and common virtual world consisting of the same objects and artefacts;
- the use of embodiments located in the virtual world, provides the participants with access both to the other, and to the other's actions and orientations in the 'local environment'. The embodiments can look and point at things and, thus, can be seen alongside the objects at which they are looking and pointing. In this way, and unlike media spaces, (representations of) participants are visibly 'embodied in', and 'connected to', the common world of objects.

Aside from exploring the extent to which a CVE might support object-focused collaboration, we are also interested in more general issues concerning how individuals interact and work with each other in virtual environments. Surprisingly, despite the substantial literature on communication in media space and parallel technologies, there is little analysis, either in CSCW or elsewhere, concerning the organisation of human conduct in collaborative virtual environments. Bowers et al. have begun to explore such issues, for instance by highlighting the interactional use of even simple embodiments [4] and by showing how actions within a CVE can relate to users' real-world conduct outside of it [5]. This paper, however, will consider how the visible properties of the virtual environment (i.e. objects others than the embodiments) feature in, and are often critical to the intelligibility of, the participants' actions and activities.

EXPERIMENTING WITH 'FURNITURE WORLD'

To investigate object-focused interaction in CVEs, we adapted a task from the previous studies of the MTV system [8]. Participants were asked to collaboratively arrange the lay-out of furniture in a virtual room and agree upon a single design. They were given conflicting priorities in order to encourage debate and discussion. The virtual room consisted of four walls, two plug sockets, a door, two windows and a fireplace.

The participants used Silicon Graphics workstations connected via an Ethernet, with speech being supported by headphones and a microphone. The CVE enabled movement, talk, pointing and object manipulation.

The Design of the Embodiment and Interface

Our application was developed using the MASSIVE-2 CVE [3]. However, we extended the capabilities of its default embodiment and simplified its default interface.

The Furniture World Interface

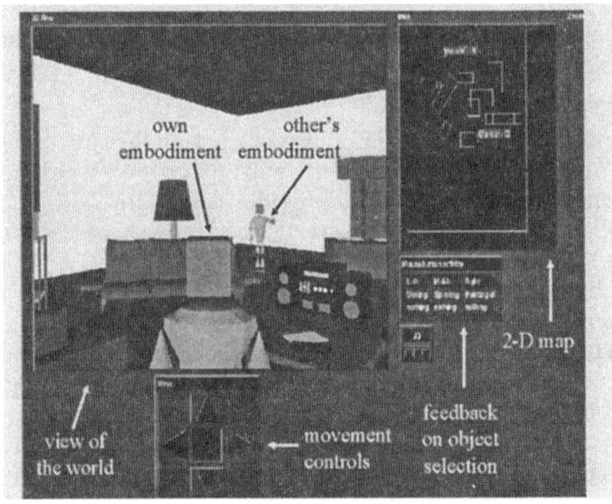

Our aim in revising the default embodiment was to support more easily the referencing of objects. The guiding principle behind our design was that the embodiment should broadly reflect the appearance of a physical body. Although photo-realism was not possible for performance reasons, this meant that the embodiment should be generally humanoid (i.e. have a recognisable head, torso and limbs). We adopted this approach because we felt that it is the most obvious choice and indeed, is one that has been widely adopted by CVE designers. One goal of our work was therefore to provide some insights as to the utility of pseudo-humanoid embodiments in CVEs.

Our embodiment supported pointing as a way of referencing objects. This was in addition to referencing them in speech or by facing them as were already supported by MASSIVE-2. A participant could choose to point at a target (an object or a general area of space) by selecting it with the right mouse button. Their embodiment would then raise its nearest arm to point at the target and would also incline its head towards it.

Participants could grasp and move objects by selecting them with the left and middle mouse buttons. The left button moved the object across the floor of the room and the right rotated it around its vertical axis. In order to simplify this particular design task, we removed the ability to lift objects off the floor and rotate them around other axes. This manipulation was also shown on the embodiment by raising an arm to point at the object and tilting the head towards it.

In addition, a connecting line was drawn between the embodiment and the object being moved. This connecting line was our only extension beyond normal physical embodiment. It was included to reflect the ability to manipulate objects at a distance in the CVE (e.g. without being within arm's length of them), as this is not a familiar experience in the physical world.

In addition to this embodiment design, we took several steps to simplify the user interface. Participants could only carry out a limited set of actions. These were: *looking* (i.e., moving about on the ground plane so as to adjust their viewpoint), *speaking*, *pointing*, and *grasping* to move objects. Other simplifications included:

- restricting movement to the ground plane only (i.e. no 'flying').
- using of an out of body camera view that showed one's own body in the foreground of the scene. This technique was initially introduced in the MASSIVE system to extend one's field of view and to provide feedback as to the state of one's embodiment [10]. When pointing at an object with a viewpoint situated through the embodiment's 'eyes', for example, it is not possible to see the 'arm' move. Thus the only feedback that pointing is in progress is through the reporting facility on the interface. An 'out of body' view allows participants to see their own embodiment pointing and grasping. The field of view provided in our application was 55 degrees horizontally and 45 degrees vertically, in order to minimise distortion on the desktop interface.

Data Collection

Six trials of two participants and two trials of three participants were performed. Most participants were students, twelve male and six female, with a broad mixture of previous acquaintance. None of them had a background in CVE technology. Each trial took about an hour and consisted of ten minutes for participants to get used to the system, approximately half an hour to perform the given task, and then to conclude, we interviewed them about their experience of using the system.

A VCR was used to record each participant's on-screen activity and audio from their perspective - their own voice in real time, plus the other participant's voice(s) with a delivery lag over the network. Depending upon network traffic, the lag varied from being almost negligible up to imposing a 1 second delay on sound and image. Video cameras simultaneously recorded the participants in the real world (see the photograph below) and contained audio from the participant in shot.

A User Being Filmed

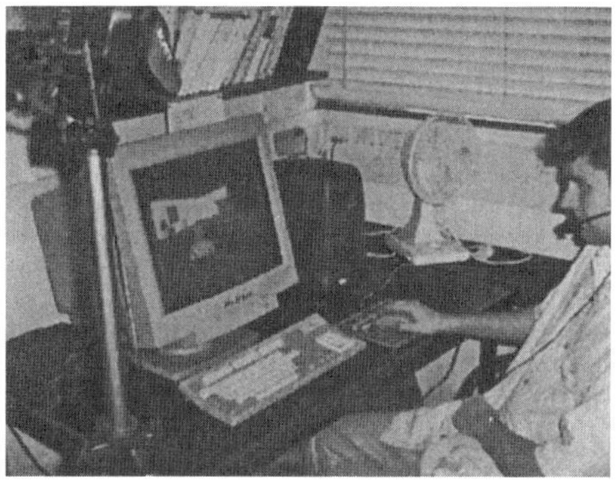

OBSERVATIONS

The participants found it relatively straightforward to accomplish the task asked of them. Unlike MTV, participants were not just making the technology work against the odds. In contrast, in this CVE they comfortably accomplished the desired task and even claimed to enjoy using the system. However, there are three key observations that would seem to have some import both for our understanding interaction in the CVE and for the development of distributed, shared workspaces:

- The image of the object is often 'fragmented' or separated from the image of the others' embodiment. This is primarily due to the narrow field of vision provided by the CVE (55°);
- Participants compensate for the 'fragmenting' of the workspace by using talk to make explicit actions and visual conduct that are recurrently implicit in co-present work;
- Participants face problems assessing and monitoring the perspectives, orientations and activities of the other(s) even when the other's embodiment is in view.

Fragmenting The Workspace

In this CVE (representations of) participants are located in a single, virtual domain. They are also given the ability to produce a very simple pointing gesture towards an object. This enables participants to use their virtual embodiments to indicate features within the common workspace. The following instance provides a simple example of how such gestures are used successfully to encourage another to look at an object with them.

As we join the action, Sarah and Karen are repairing a confusion over which table should be moved.

<u>Example 1: C20/2/98-14:29:45-VP:S</u>

K: It's this table I'm talking about. this one yeah? *((K Points))*

S: Yeah.

K: Can you see me point?

S: Yeah, it's the one in front of you isn't it.

Here is the view that Sarah has of Karen's embodiment, her gesture and the table:

Sarah's View[1]

Sarah is able to see Karen's gesture in relation to her surroundings. Moreover, she is able to see the point in relation to the relevant table. So, the ability to gesture is used as a successful resource with which to indicate an object in the world. The embodiment is located in the same domain as the referent, which enables the other to relate or 'connect' the gesture to the object referred to in the talk.

A key finding from the MTV experiments, and one that would seem to resonate with many media space and shared workspace technologies, is that object-focused discussions are rendered highly problematic due to the 'fragmentation' of different elements of the workspace. For example, with an utterance such as 'in that corner there', the recipient may be able to see the speaker's face, the speaker's gesture and the relevant object. However, these are rarely seen together in one scene. They are often presented in different parts of the recipient's world [12]. For instance, the object could be at their fingertips, whilst the speaker's face is presented on one video screen and the gesture on another screen. Participants find it problematic to re-assemble the relations between body and object. As a result, they find it difficult to retrieve the referent.

In this CVE, the gesture and referent can be seen alongside one another. Therefore, this type of fragmentation of the workspace is overcome, as shown in Example 1 above.

Interestingly, however, a new version of the 'fragmented workspace' emerges. The 55 degree field of view provided by the desktop CVE restricts participants' opportunities to see embodiments in relation to objects. When an utterance is produced, individuals are rarely in an immediate position to see the embodiment alongside the referred-to object. It turns out that it is critical that they do see them in relation to one another. So, they firstly turn to find the other's embodiment and then look for the object.

In Example 2, Sarah asks Karen about the "desk-thing" in the room. Before they can discuss where they might put the desk, they need some 25 seconds to achieve a common orientation towards it (square brackets indicate overlapping utterances; a dot in brackets indicates a short pause in talk):

---

[1]For this one experiment, we did not provide users with a view of their own embodiment.

<u>Example 2: C20/2/98-14:31:10-VP:K</u>

S: You know this desk-thing?

K: Yeah?

S: Can you see- what I'm pointing at now?

((K Turns to Find S))

K: Er I can't see you, but [I think-

S: [Its like a desk-thing.

K: Er-where've you gone? [heh heh heh

S: [Erm, where are you?

K: I've- th- I can see

S: Tur- (.) oh, oh yeah. you're near the lamp, yeah?

K: Yeah.

S: And then, yeah turn around right. (.) and then its like (.) I'm pointing at it now, but I don't know if you can see what [I'm pointing at?

K: [Right yeah I can see.

When Sarah asks if Karen can see what she is pointing at, Karen starts to look for Sarah's embodiment and her pointing gesture. She is actually facing the desk very early on in the sequence, but ends up turning 360°, via Sarah's gesture, to return to the very same desk.

In co-present interaction, when an individual asks a co-participant to look at an object at which they are pointing, that co-participant can usually see them in relation to their surroundings. They simply turn from the body of the other to find the referred-to object [15].

In this CVE, participants often do not have the other's embodiment in view during an utterance. They might turn out to have initially had the referent in view, but without seeing the object in relation to the pointing gesture, they have little information with which to assess if they are looking at the appropriate object; in other words, they may see a "desk-thing", but is it the right "desk-thing"? In some cases, then, they cannot be certain that they are looking at and discussing the same object without seeing that object in relation to the other's embodiment.

Participants find the relevant object by following a particular sequence. First they turn to find the gesture and then they use this as a resource to find the referent. Even in short and straightforward instances, participants can be seen to turn away from an object to find the other's gesture, only to subsequently return to face that object. Participants may, however, need to engage in an extensive search for their co-participant's embodiment before being able to see the relevant object.

These problems often arise because the other's embodiment is not visible at the onset of a new activity. However, misunderstandings can also arise when the others' embodiment *is visible*, but is again separated from the objects on which they are acting.

For example, in the following instance, Andre is turning around whilst suggesting possible design changes. He happens to rotate past Trevor's embodiment just as Trevor's virtual arm lifts up.

Example 3: B30/1/98-12:03:50-VP:A

```
A:  I think maybe the couch can go
    in front of the
    ((T's arm rises))
    -er fireplace.
    what you pointing at?
    ((A begins to rotate his view
    back towards T))
T:  Just moving the telly a bit.
A:  Oh right.
```

Andre curtails his own utterance in order to attend to the demands of Trevor's gesture and its potential relevance for him at this moment. Trevor is at the edge of his viewpoint, so he cannot see the objects toward which Trevor seems to be pointing, so he asks "what you pointing at?".

Andre's View

The act of pointing is represented by an arm lifting and the head tilting slightly. The act of moving an object is represented in the same way on the embodiment. The only difference is that when the object is being moved, a thin line is projected out from the embodiment to the object. When Andre sees the embodiment (and its gesture) in isolation from its surroundings, he sees Trevor pointing and recognises that it could be designed for him. Unfortunately, Trevor is just re-positioning the T.V., but the line from the virtual arm is not visible.

Seeing the embodiment in isolation from the specific object on which it is acting, leads Andre to misunderstand Trevor's actions. This misunderstanding disrupts the onset of the new activity, namely a discussion over where to place the couch.

In co-present environments, the local complex of objects and artefacts provides a resource for making sense of the actions of others. The production of action is situated in an environment and its intelligibility rests upon the availability of that environment [12].

However, participants in CVEs only encounter a fragment of the visible world. Separating an embodiment from the objects on which they are acting creates difficulties for participants. Indeed, their overall sense of action is impoverished. As they are rarely in a position to see both object and embodiment simultaneously, they have problems in relating the two. Critically, the sense of talk or action is based upon the mutual availability of that relationship.

Even when participants have a referred-to object in their view of the world, they need to see it in relation to the other's embodiment. Without seeing them together, they cannot be sure if it is the relevant object or not. In co-present interaction these resources are often simultaneously available. However, in this CVE participants have to follow a sequence of action to assemble the scene. First they must look for the other's embodiment, then they turn to find the object in relation to it.

Making The Implicit Explicit

The previous section highlights a problem related to the narrow field of view provided by the CVE. However, participants are sensitive to the possibility that the other is not in a position to see their embodiment or the objects on which it is acting. Therefore they use their talk to make explicit certain actions and visual conduct.

For example, in co-present interaction an individual may simply say 'what do you know about this?' alongside a gesture. Their co-participant can often turn quite easily to see what 'this' is and attend to the query. In such a way, the referential action and the projected activity can be conflated [15]; that is, the presentation of the object and the initiation of the activity (e.g. asking a question) can be one in the same.

In the CVE, participants tend to engage in a prefatory sequence in which the identity of the relevant object is secured before the main activity continues. Typical utterances include "The thing that I'd like this room to have is erm (.) you see the fireplace which is like (.) there?" or "See this sofa here?". The activity only progresses when the other has found the referred-to object.

So, participants are sensitive to and have ways of solving the problems of working in a 'fragmented' environment. However, these 'solutions' do damage to common patterns of working. An added sequence is inserted into the emergent activity.

A clear illustration is Example 2, in which a 25 second search for the desk takes place prior to a discussion about where it could be moved. This problem is compounded by the slow speed of movement in the CVE, preventing quick glances to find the other and the object. Interestingly, these referential sequences can last longer than the very activities that they foreshadow - for example, the length of time it takes to establish some common orientation towards an object or location can be much longer than the simple query that follows.

Unfortunately, the additional time involved to establish mutual orientation is not the critical concern. This prefatory sequence actually disrupts the flow and organisation of collaborative activities.

In co-present interaction, participants are able to engage in the activity at hand, whilst assuming that the other can see or quickly find the referent. Within the CVE, participants become explicitly engaged in, and distracted by, the problem of establishing mutual orientation. Indeed, it becomes a topic in and of itself.

In the CVE, participants cannot assume the availability of certain features of the world and so attend to making those features available to the other. Rather than debating where an object should be placed or whether to remove a piece of furniture altogether, participants are drawn into explicit discussions about the character of an object. It inhibits the flow of workplace activity and introduces obstacles into collaborative discussions.

Interestingly, in the case of three-party interaction, it takes just one participant to say that they can see the referent, for the speaker to proceed. Speakers drop their pointing gesture and move the activity on. Unfortunately, this can leave the third party struggling to find the object when the resources to find it (e.g. a gesture) have been taken away. They become restricted from participating in the emerging activity, or else they must interrupt the others to 'catch-up'.

As well as greater attention to reference, participants use their talk to make explicit the visual conduct of their embodiments.

In co-present interaction, when an individual points something out, they are able to see the movement of the other. That movement reveals if another is looking for the object and therefore engaged in this activity rather than some separate concern. It can also be used to establish whether they are in a position to see the relevant object.

In this CVE, often individuals are not able see their co-participant as they point something out. To compensate, their co-participants tend to 'talk through' what they are doing and what they can see.

Consider Example 4, in which Trevor points out the door to Andre.

Example 4: B30/1/98-12:02:20-VP:T

T: Th-the door's behind me.

A: Oh right.

T: Over here, can you see that?
((T points towards the door))

A: I'm coming *((A rotates))*

T: Hang on *((T re-positions gesture))*

A: Yeah, okay, I got the door.

In pointing out the door, Trevor turns around and cannot see Andre:

Trevor's View

Andre's talk reveals certain critical aspects of his conduct to Trevor. For example, although Trevor cannot see whether Andre is attempting to look for the door, Andre makes this available by saying "I'm coming".

Given that movement in the world is relatively slow, participants often display that they are trying to look for the gesture and that the other's actions are not being ignored. Often this is marked with phrases such as "Hang on, Hang on", "I *am* looking" or even "errr" noises to fill the gap in talk. These actions would normally be available visually, through the sight of the other's body movement.

When encouraging another to look at a particular feature of the local environment, participants attempt to design their referential actions for the other. In co-present interaction, they are even able to transform the course of a pointing gesture with regard to the emerging orientation of their co-participant(s) [15].

In this CVE, the problem for participants is that when they point to something, they often cannot see their co-participant(s). In co-present interaction, participants routinely configure a pointing gesture and then turn to view their co-participant's 'response' [15]. This CVE does not allow participants to point at something and simultaneously look elsewhere. Therefore, it is much harder for them to be sensitive to the movements and visual conduct of the others' embodiment. Their ability to design gestures or utterances to indicate an artefact is constrained.

This highlights a more general concern for participants engaged in collaborative work in CVEs. The organisation and co-ordination of much co-present work is facilitated by the ability to 'monitor' the activities of others. The narrow field of view, however, cuts out the visible features of many of those activities. So, participants' 'peripheral awareness' of the other is severely constrained.

The talk of participants does reveal features of their conduct. However, there is a much greater reliance on the talk than in everyday workplaces. Normally, individuals can rely upon the availability of the others' visual conduct and see that visual conduct with regard to workplace artefacts. Here participants cannot.

This leads to much cruder and less flexible practices for co-ordinating and organising collaborative work. Whereas they would normally be able to talk and simultaneously reveal other 'information' via visual conduct, almost all their actions must be revealed through talk.

Hidden Perspectives

These examples have shown that participants face problems when the other's embodiment is not visible in their window on the world. However, even when the other's embodiment is visible, troubles often emerge. In particular, certain idiosyncrasies of the technology 'hide' how embodiments are viewing, and acting in, the world.

In the following instance, Pete is explaining to Rick where the fireplace is located. As he does, both Rick's embodiment and the fireplace are visible on his screen.

Example 5: D30/1/98-15:54:25-VP:P

P: Do you reckon it might be better if we moved the T.V. over by the fireplace?

(.)

R: By the fireplace?

P: Yeah [in the cor-

R: [Is there a fireplace in here?

((R Rotates))

P: In the cor- yeah you're facing it now.

Although Rick has the fireplace in his view, he does not recognise it as a fireplace. So when he says "is there a fireplace in here?", he simultaneously begins to rotate to his right to look for it. Pete treats Rick's embodiment as still facing or at least able to see the fireplace ("you're facing it now"). Unfortunately, at the moment he says this, Rick's viewpoint is focused on the door to the right of the fireplace[2]. Compare their viewpoints below:

Pete's View **Rick's View**

This reveals a problem for participants in assessing what the other can see. Even though they may have the other 'on-screen', it is hard for them to ascertain what is visible on that other's screen.

In other cases, for example, participants assume the availability of their gestures, when the other is visible to them. Unfortunately, it turns out that the other cannot see them.

It may be that seeing a pseudo-humanoid form is confusing. This kind of embodiment may give participants a sense that it possesses a 'human-like' field of view, i.e. 180°. However, the users' field of view in this CVE is only 55°. Moreover, the CVE does not facilitate stereoscopic vision and the embodiments are often large virtual distances from their interlocutor(s). This exacerbates the problem, further concealing the other's perspective.

So, it is very difficult for participants to assess what the other might be able to see. This multiplies the problems raised in previous sections. It makes it far harder for participants to attempt to design actions for, and co-ordinate actions with, others. It is not simply that they need to get the other 'on-screen', because even then their sense of what the other is seeing is confused.

This issue also leads to problems with regard to the collaborative manipulation of objects - when one participant moves an object and the other directs that movement.

When participants move an object in the CVE, their embodiment does not turn with it. Therefore, if they need to move an object out of the range of their field of view, they have to move it in stages - to the edge of their viewpoint, drop it, turn and then move it again.

In Example 6, Mark and Ted are discussing where the standard lamp should be placed. Mark manipulates the lamp and Ted comments on his actions.

Example 6: A30/1/98-10:31:50-VP:M

M: Do you want the -er lamp moving?

T: Could do. see what it looks like.

M: Where d'ya want it put?

T: Erm- you decide

((pause as M moves the lamp))

T: That's right in front of the window, that's probably not so clever actually. over the other side, over here.

Mark drops the lamp and Ted suggests that this is an inappropriate position for it ("that's right in front of the window, that's probably not so clever").

The video data suggests that Mark has not completed the movement and that this is a first 'step' in the positioning of the lamp. However, the technology 'hides' this from Ted.

Mark's View as he Moves the Lamp

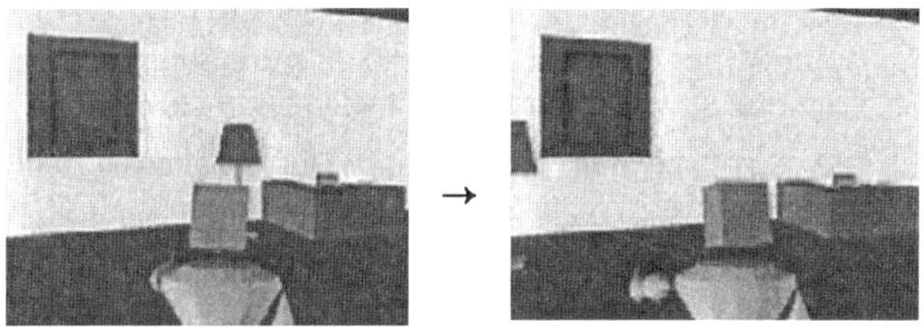

Ted cannot see how Mark is viewing and engaging with this activity. All he can see is the object being moved into an inappropriate position. So, he suggests an alternative.

Ted is prevented from getting a sense of how Mark views the lamp. He cannot see that the object is crossing the edge of Mark's window on the world. He is unaware that Mark cannot move the object further without first temporarily releasing it and turning around. In such a way, the 'boundary' of Mark's actions is hidden from Ted.

In everyday situations, if an individual finds an object to heavy or too awkward to carry, they can display the temporary nature of its setting-down through their visual conduct and demeanour. Bare virtual embodiments, on the other hand, conceal reasons for the placement of an object. Thus, the technology 'disrupts' access to the trajectory of moving objects. Objects that seem to have been placed once

[2] In this case the delivery lag is negligible. In other instances, however, the lag disrupts the notion that this is a stable, common environment. When an individual says "now", for example, the other may hear it up to a second later. Therefore, if one is commenting on the other's actions, the other may hear those comments in relation to different actions than they were produced for.

and for all, are often still on their way somewhere. This problematises an individual's ability to assess what the other is doing, how they are orienting to the world and how they are engaging with the objects in that world. The technology thereby conceals critical aspects of the ongoing activity.

So, although an embodiment and the relevant object may be visible on screen, the relations of one to the other may not be visible or available. Moreover, the action is visibly produced in a different light to which it is seen and understood. This is important, because it makes it difficult for an individual to imagine 'being in the other's position'. As a result it is difficult to assess the nature or trajectory of the other's actions. Thus, it is problematic for individuals to design and tailor their actions for co-participants, as they have little sense of how they are engaged in, or orienting to, the ongoing activity.

The orientations of the other in the world are hidden from view, which even leads to confusion about what they are doing. The technology distorts access to the common resources for working with others and making sense of their actions. Thus an individual's understanding of the activity at hand can be disordered by the technology.

PRINCIPAL ISSUES

The CVE undermines certain resources commonly used to organise and co-ordinate collaborative work. Although the system does not prevent task completion (indeed, far from it), it does set up a range of obstacles to collaborative working. In particular, the system:

- reveals features of the world in 'fragments', due to its narrow field of view. This often separates views of the other's embodiment from relevant objects. As a result, participants are provided with an impoverished sense of action. They cannot make sense of talk and activity without seeing (and seeking) the embodiment in relation to relevant features of the environment;
- forces participants to compensate for the problems of interacting in a 'fragmented workspace' by explicitly describing actions and phenomena that are unproblematically available in co-present interaction. In particular, referencing visual features of the world becomes a topic in and of itself, rather than being subsumed within the more general activity;
- reduces opportunities for participants to design and co-ordinate their actions for others. (Peripheral) awareness of the actions and orientations of the other is significantly undermined. Even when the other's embodiment is visible on-screen, the technology disrupts the resources used to make sense of an individual's activity.

For co-present interaction, Schutz suggested that we assume our different perspectives on the world and on an object are irrelevant for the activity at hand [18]. Individuals have a relatively sound understanding of what a colleague can see within the local workspace. Indeed, research suggests that individuals exploit their colleagues' visible orientations in order to initiate new activities or to collaborate on particular tasks [12, 14]. The technical constraints imposed by the CVE render such activities more problematic. This is likely to lead to more intrusive means of monitoring others' actions and interleaving activities with them. If CSCW technologies do not wish to impede the expedient production of work in the modern organisation, it is suggested that these issues are important for the design of systems to support synchronous remote working.

IMPLICATIONS

These observations lead us to conclude that certain technical issues should be addressed if CVEs are to provide more robust support for distributed collaboration. We propose that four key limitations have contributed to the phenomena noted above. These are:

- Limited horizontal field of view – it is difficult to simultaneously view the source (i.e. embodiment) and target of actions such as pointing and looking.
- Lack of information about others' actions – not all actions are explicitly represented on embodiments or target objects. Where they are, it may not be easy to distinguish between them.
- Slow movement – movement in CVEs may be clumsy due to problems of locating destinations, controlling the interface and system performance.
- Lack of parallelism for actions – the interface disallows some combinations of actions from being performed concurrently (e.g. moving and grasping; pointing and looking around).

Radical solutions to these problems might involve the use of immersive technologies such as head-mounted displays, wide-screen projection interfaces and CAVEs (purpose built rooms which can contain several users and where different views of a virtual environment are back projected onto some combination of the walls, floor and ceiling), as these may enable more rapid movement and a larger-field of view. However, these technologies introduce their own constraints, including poor resolution, high-cost, large space requirements and health and safety concerns. The use of immersive technologies is part of our on-going research and will be reported in future papers. Other potential solutions, such as fish-eye views [6], can be used to provide a widened, but visually distorted, field of view. However, in this paper we propose to explore two general areas for improving desktop CVE interfaces, as these remain the dominant access technology: improved representations of others' actions; and rapid navigation with respect to these actions. We conclude with some implications of this kind of 'quasi-experimental' research for naturalistic studies of the workplace.

More Explicit Representations Of Others' Actions

Given a limited field of view, it may be that the pseudo-realistic approach of showing actions solely by moving the source embodiment (e.g. raising an arm to show pointing) is too understated. Developers of 3-D spaces tend to represent actions on the source embodiment. However, the narrow field of view provided by this system makes it difficult for participants to relate embodiments to relevant objects. Therefore, there would seem to be a need to compensate by somehow 'embedding' the actions of an embodiment in the environment.

The source embodiment and target object are unlikely to be simultaneously in view. So, actions could be represented on the source, target and also in the surrounding environment. The latter might involve 'in-scene' representations such as drawing a connecting line between the source and target, or 'out of band' representations such as playing back an audio sample or labelling the action on the observer's view in the style of a head-up display.

Further, the solution should reveal not only which bodies and objects are 'related', but how they are related. With this emphasis, an observer can get a sense of the other's actions from seeing, 'in isolation', their embodiment, the object that is being acted upon or even the space between the two.

We propose that the designers of CVE applications should adopt a systematic approach to the representation of actions that involves the following steps:

- identify all possible actions - this includes actions such as looking and speaking as well as more explicit gestures, such as pointing.
- identify the targets of each action - some actions such as grasping an object address an explicit target whereas others such as speaking could be heard by a number of objects/embodiments located within a region of space.
- determine whether and how each action is represented on the source embodiment, target object(s) and in the surrounding environment. Also, make sure that these representations are consistent and distinguishable.

Retrospectively applying this approach to our initial design results in the following table.

Action	Targets	Represented on body?	Represented on targets?	Represented in env'ment?
Look	region	orientation	none	none
Speak	region	none	none	voice
Point	object or region	raise arm	none	none
Grasp	object	raise arm	may be seen to move	connecting line

The design table can be used as a tool to highlight potential problems that may be investigated further. Inspection of this table reveals several points with regard to our design. The raised arm was used to show both pointing and grasping. Only one action, grasping, could be seen on the target, and only then when it was actually being moved. Also, there were no representations of looking or pointing in the environment.

There are many potential solutions to these problems and a detailed re-design is beyond the scope of this paper. However, there is a general need to improve or enhance resources to support (peripheral) awareness of the other's actions. For example, consider the representation of *looking* in 'furniture world'. As noted previously, it is hard to tell what another person is able to see from the position and orientation of their embodiment alone. We could emphasise the portrayal of looking in several ways: by making the view frustrum visible as a wire-frame or by highlighting viewed objects in some way (perhaps using lighting or shadows). Even when the embodiment is not in view, this would increase an individual's opportunities to get a sense of the other's perspective. Individuals might then be able to design their own actions more sensitively for the other. We can extend this concern to other collaborative technologies (e.g. videoconferencing and media spaces) where the participant's field of view may differ from that expected by an observer.

It may be that other 'key' actions could be displayed in helpful ways. However, peripheral awareness need not be associated simply with visible resources. Audio signals could equally be used to make manifest certain actions. Currently, participants often reveal their movements to look for an object through talk (e.g. "I'm coming", "hang on, hang on", etc.). Therefore, it would be worth investigating if suitable sounds could helpfully be used to 'automatically' display such conduct.

There is a general aim to use 'realistic' or 'humanoid' embodiments within CVE design [e.g. 11]. Indeed, some may argue that the emboidments used in this experiment were not realistic enough and that this was the source of users' problems. However the findings would suggest that the straight-forward translation of human physical embodiments into CVEs (however detailed) are likely to be unsuccessful unless participants can also be provided with the perceptual capabilities of physical human bodies including a very wide field of view and rapid gaze and body movement. Indeed, to compensate for the curious views on, and possible behaviours within, virtual environments, more exaggerated embodiments are required to compensate. For instance, actions may best be represented across disparate features of the environment to enhance access to the sense of an action in the CVE.

Navigating With Respect To Others' Actions

Our second design issue concerns the speed of navigation. Here, we propose the adoption of a form of target-based navigation where the user is offered shortcuts for moving or turning towards relevant targets. Furthermore, in a co-operative application, the choice of targets should depend to a large part on other participant's actions.

For example, if an observer is looking at an embodiment that is pointing at an object, then the target of this point becomes a likely destination for the observer's next movement. Conversely, if they can see the target, then the source embodiment becomes a possible next destination. Such a mechanism would make it easier to glance back and forth between embodiments and the targets of their actions. We can consider more sophisticated techniques for selecting targets, perhaps taking account of the number of people who are acting on a target (e.g. looking or pointing at it).

Once suitable targets have been determined, they have to be presented to the user so as to enable their selection. For example, they might be offered as lists of names or icons on their display. Alternatively, the user might be given the ability to glance left or right so as to move to the nearest target in either direction.

The system also has to manage the users' movement to look at the target. Our proposal here is that this movement should involve an animated transition, both from the point of view of the user and of any on-lookers. This would attempt to preserve the fluidity of the co-operative interaction and maintain the users' overall sense and geography of the space.

More generally, we suggest that support for navigation, and co-participation, in CVEs could be oriented to the activities of others rather than with sole regard for the individual's current actions.

Implications For Studies Of Work

There is long-standing discussion in CSCW as to the ways in which social science, and in particular naturalistic studies of work, can inform the design and deployment of complex systems. Less attention is paid to the contribution of systems design to social science.

The materials discussed here raise some potentially interesting issues for studies of work and interaction. The analysis of interaction in CVEs, like earlier discussions of media spaces and MTV, point to critical, yet largely unexplicated aspects of collaborative work. In particular, they reveal, *par excellence*, how collaborative activity relies upon the participants' mundane abilities to develop and sustain, mutually compatible, even reciprocal, perspectives. Critically they also uncover the resources on which participants rely in identifying and dealing with incongruities that arise.

Whatever our sensitivities about using 'quasi-experimental' data, they provide, as Garfinkel suggests, 'aids to a sluggish imagination' [7]. They dramatically reveal pre-suppositions and resources which often remain unexplicated in more conventional studies of the workplace. Whilst we believe these pre-suppositions and resources are of some importance to sociology and cognate disciplines, it can also be envisaged how they may well influence the success or failure of technologies designed to enhance physically-distributed collaborative work.

ACKNOWLEDGEMENTS

We would like to thank Tony Glover, Paul Luff, Abi Sellen and Jolanda Tromp with whom many of these issues have been discussed and developed. This research has been supported by ESRC Grant No. R000237136.

REFERENCES

1. Barnatt, C. (1997) *Challenging Reality: In Search of the Future Organisation.* Chichester: John Wiley.
2. Benford, S. D. & Fahlen, L. E. A Spatial Model of Interaction in Virtual Environments, *Proc. ECSCW'93* , 1993, Kluwer Academic Publishers.
3. Benford, S. D., Greenhalgh, C. M. & Lloyd, D. Crowded Collaborative Environments, *Proc. CHI'97* (1997), ACM Press.
4. Bowers, J., Pycock, J. & O'Brien, J. Talk and Embodiment in Collaborative Virtual Environments, in *Proc. CHI'96* (1996), ACM Press.
5. Bowers, J., O'Brien, J. & Pycock, J. Practically Accomplishing Immersion: Cooperation in and for Virtual Environments, in *Proc. CSCW'96* (1996), ACM Press, 380-389.
6. Furnas, G.W. Generalized Fisheye Views, in *Proc. CHI'86* (April 1986), ACM Press.
7. Garfinkel, H. *Studies in Ethnomethodology*, Polity Press, Cambridge, 1967.
8. Gaver, W. W. et al. One is not enough: Multiple Views in a Media Space, in *Proc. INTERCHI '93* (April 1993), 335-341.
9. Goodwin, C. & Goodwin, M.H. Seeing as Situated Activity: Formulating planes. In Engeström, Y. & D. Middleton (eds.) *Communication & Cognition at Work.* Cambridge University Press, Cambridge, 1996.
10. Greenhalgh, C.M. & Benford, S.D. Virtual Reality Teleconferencing: Implementation and experience, in *Proc. ECSCW'95* (Stockholm, Sept. 1995).
11. Guye-Vuilleme, A. et al. Nonverbal Communication Interface for Collaborative Virtual Environments, in *Proc. CVE'98* (June 1998), 105-112.
12. Heath, C. & Hindmarsh, J. Les objets et leur environnement local. La production interactionnelle de réalitiés matérielles. *Raison Pratiques. Cognition et Information en Société*, 8, (1997), 149-176.
13. Heath, C., Luff, P. & Sellen, A. Reconsidering the Virtual Workplace. In Finn, K, Sellen, A. & S. Wilbur (eds.) *Video-Mediated Communication.* Lawrence Erlbaum, New Jersey, 1997.
14. Heath, C. et al. Unpacking Collaboration: The interactional organisation of trading in a city dealing room. *Computer-Supported Co-operative Work, 3* (1995), 147-165.
15. Hindmarsh, J. The Interactional Constitution of Objects. Unpublished Ph.D. thesis, U. of Surrey, 1997.
16. Kuzuoka, H., Kosuge, T. & Tanaka, M. GestureCam: A video communication system for sympathetic remote collaboration, in *Proc. CSCW'94* (1994), ACM Press, 35-43.
17. Reynard, G., Benford, S., Greenhalgh, C. & Heath, C. Awareness Driven Video Quality of Service in Collaborative Virtual Environments, in *Proc. CHI'98*, (LA, April 1998), ACM Press.
18. Schutz, A. *On Phenomenology & Social Relations.* U. of Chicago Press, Chicago, 1970.
19. Tang, J., Isaacs, E. & Rua, M. Supporting Distributed Groups with a Montage of Lightweight Interactions, in *Proc. CSCW'94* (1994), ACM Press, 23-34.

Exploring the design space for notification servers

Devina Ramduny, Alan Dix
School of Computing
Staffordshire University
Stafford ST18 0DG UK
+44 1785 353255
{D.Ramduny, A.J.Dix}@soc.staffs.ac.uk

Tom Rodden
Computing Department SECaMS
Lancaster University
Lancaster LA1 4YR UK
+44 1524 593823
tom@comp.lancs.ac.uk

http://www.soc.staffs.ac.uk/~cmtajd/topics/webarch

ABSTRACT
Issues of notification and awareness have become increasingly important in CSCW. Notification servers provide a notable mechanism to maintain shared state information of any synchronous or asynchronous groupware system. A taxonomy of the design space for notification servers is presented, based on theoretical results from status–event analysis. This generates a framework and vocabulary to compare and discuss different notification mechanisms to improve design. The paper shows that notification servers are often ideally placed to support impedance matching to give an appropriate pace of feedthrough to the user by allowing them to see changes to shared objects in a timely manner.

Keywords
Collaborative applications, feedthrough, awareness, status-event analysis, initiative, mediation, notification server, protocol, impedance matching

INTRODUCTION
An essential feature of collaborative interfaces is *feedthrough* – the ability of one person to see the effects of another's actions. This is important for 'functional' reasons as it allows each person to see an up-to-date version of the work; for 'coordination' by preventing inconsistent updates and finally for supporting general 'awareness' of other people at work. The first two have given rise to considerable work on algorithms for synchronous editing and for merging versions of asynchronously edited material. The last factor has instead always been an informal concern in CSCW, it has however recently been augmented by formal analysis of 'awareness' models [2,19]. This modelling approach has arisen largely because of work on virtual collaborative environments. Whereas the main objects of interest used to be documents or shared drawings, now they are the virtual locations and actions of the participants themselves. Both effective feedthrough of updates to shared data and up-to-date views of other participants require underlying computational mechanisms to distribute and inform about these updates.

There are therefore two main requirements, firstly, to access and update shared data and secondly, to know when that data has been updated. The former lies behind the design of shared data repositories, either bespoke systems designed for CSCW [4,13] or off-the-shelf databases and shared object stores. The latter requires notification mechanisms. Even if data is stored and accessed rapidly from a central location, it is of no use unless client programs know that it has changed and users' screens are updated accordingly. Notification mechanisms fulfil precisely this role – telling programs and people not about what has happened, but that it has happened. Without this, users may eventually see the changes that have occurred but at a timescale and pace that is not acceptable for the task at hand.

Each application that updates shared data can be responsible for notification, and consequently broadcast to all interested parties that the change has happened. However, as with peer-peer methods for data replication, this has a high overhead in both algorithm complexity and network load. For instance, every participating client program should know about all others in order to broadcast change information to them. Furthermore, the changes must be kept up-to-date as users join and leave the system. So, for just the same reasons that data stores are often centralised, there is a need for notification servers to keep track of interested parties and take over the task of propagating change information. Such notification servers may either be coupled closely with the data store, as is the case with some databases supporting triggered actions, or they may be entirely separate, knowing about the data but being decoupled from it.

Clearly, there are numerous ways in which notification services can be managed in a collaborative system and the central aim of this paper is to explore and clarify the design space for notification servers. We believe this is a timely point as the last few years have seen the beginnings of a

CSCW 98 Seattle Washington USA

literature on notification servers as entities in their own right. It is also clear that the development of the web has forced the issue in showing that data storage (in the form of web pages) may be separate from control issues (such as indexing). In our previous work, we have looked in a similar fashion at web-based CSCW architectures and at awareness models [18,19]. A structured analysis of design options is important in clarifying the similarities and differences between different example systems and in identifying new directions. It is also essential for the academic credibility of the discipline.

We begin this paper with a brief description of status-event analysis, an analytic framework developed to tackle various user interface issues, which we use as the basis for our subsequent analysis of notification servers. This foundation is essential as it enables us to ascertain that the options we consider do cover the design space. We use Status-Event analysis to examine the ways in which an agent in a system can become aware of a status change. This is then employed to look at the ways in which a notification server becomes aware of changes in the shared data and how it in turn makes this available to client applications. The ultimate purpose of a notification server is to provide effective user-level behaviour. We will finally look at how a notification server can provide impedance matching in order to achieve an appropriate pace of feedthrough for the users.

STATUS-EVENT ANALYSIS

Analytic techniques in Computer Science tend to focus on events as the locus of activity and control. This is natural given the discrete nature of computer systems. Also for user interfaces and collaborative systems it is a good way of describing input such as keystrokes, mouse clicks and network messages between remote applications. However, if we consider shared data in collaborative systems, the event-based models fit less well. The nature of shared data is that it persists; it doesn't just happen at a particular moment, it is always there. This is not the only phenomenon of its kind in user-interfaces; the position of a mouse and the contents of a screen are similar.

In fact, status-event analysis was developed some years ago to deal with such phenomena. It is a collection of semi-formal and formal techniques with a shared conceptual framework that includes aspects of both events and status. Status is used to describe all those occurrences which, like shared data, have a persistent value through time – events happen, status are.

Applications Of Status–Event Analysis

Status–event analysis has been applied in several contexts – from the analysis of issues in fine grained interaction [12] and auditory interfaces [5,6,9] to the specification of the complex behaviour of shared scrollbars in collaborative applications [1,10]. Status–event analysis is also the theoretical foundation of the Cameo [23] architecture which is used in the construction of CyberDesk [22], a Java based framework for dynamic integration of desktop applications. An important use of status–event analysis has been in the understanding of delays in user interfaces and collaborative systems [11,12]. The study of delay has centred around the idea of mediation and this will also be the key to an architectural understanding of notification mechanisms.

Key Concepts

The two central concepts in status–event analysis are obviously events (such as mouse click, beep, 6 o'clock) which occur at particular moments and status (shown by mouse position, screen, position of hands on the clock) which always have a value. In addition, we have to consider agents which respond to events and thereby modify the status.

A key feature of status–event analysis is the difference between the *actual event* and the *perceived event* for a particular agent. For example, the time may be six o'clock, but one may not notice it until a few minutes later when one looks at the clock. Similarly with notification servers, although events occur at certain places there may be a substantial delay before those changes are perceived.

Mediation

The most important aspect of status–event analysis for this paper is that of mediation. This is when some desired behaviour is achieved by interposing some additional agent or status entity. Consider the example of an electronic mail system – when a mail has arrived (an event) this is communicated to the user by a change of the screen icon (a status) [12]. The use of a status to mediate communication between agents is very common and in particular, it is the essence of shared data.

A second form of mediation occurs when a status–status relationship needs to be maintained [11]. For instance, when dragging a window across the screen with a mouse, the window must keep track of the mouse position. These relationships are typically maintained by a mediating agent which monitors the first status and then alters the second accordingly.

In both the case of agents communicating via status or an agent mediating a status–status relationship we face the same question: how does an agent become aware of a status-change?

Status Change Discovery

Let us reformulate the previous question. We have a status S and some agent A. An actual event occurs and the status S changes its value. What process occurs so that this can become a perceived event for the agent A?

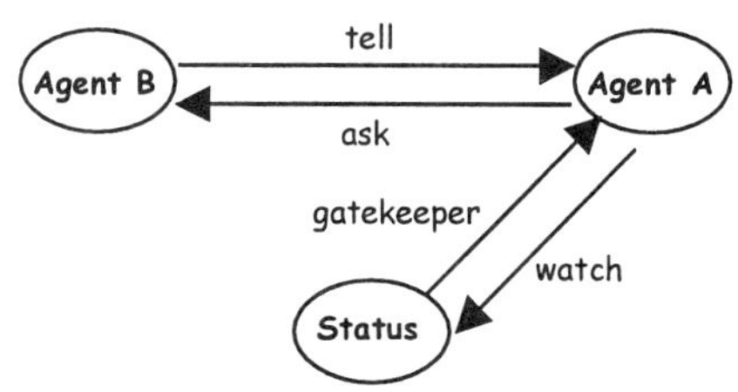

Figure 1 status-agent interaction

Figure 1 shows the alternative interactions by which agent A becomes aware of the status change. The critical point is that we are not interested in the flow of data that informs agent A of the new value of the status; instead it's simply the perceived event for agent A that a change has occurred.

Case 1 *watch*
Agent A can watch the status S. In a discrete system 'watching' means periodically *polling* the status.

A second question now arises: what event prompts the polling? This leads to 3 subcases:

- time driven – polling at fixed intervals
- demand driven – checking the status when it is needed
- spontaneous – caused by some unrelated event

The polling model of update is common in many client-server based applications where a local client needs to access some remote repository to refresh the local client's states. For example, in the case of groupware systems such as Lotus Notes[1] the system periodically accesses a remote server and updates the local client. At the moment of refresh, the user is informed of updates to the remote server.

Case 2 *told*
Agent A may be told by a second party agent B. This occurs in certain arrangements used in collaborative filtering where a user registers an interest in changes of a particular form. When the system updates a central repository the registered clients are told of changes that effect them.

Obviously we may then ask how does B know about the status change, again leading to two subcases:

- originator – B is the agent which caused S to change (B is packaged with S)
- mediator – B needs to find out itself, by one of the methods 1 – 4

Case 3 *ask*
Agent A asks the second party agent B. In this case we need to both ask what event prompts A to ask – leading to subcases as in case 1 and how B knows – leading to subcases as in case 2.

Perhaps the most notable example of this category is the logon process for computer conferencing system where an agent managing a centralised repository is asked to inform a new user of any alterations to the system. This is often presented as the number of unread messages.

Case 4 *gatekeeper*
The status is in some way active or is closely bound to an agent which 'knows' instantly when the status is changed. Such an agent can then tell A that S has changed.

This arrangement is usually employed in active databases in order to propagate the effects of changes. A similar technique is adopted in terms of the use of adaptors to underlying objects [21]. This paradigm is also applied in Suite [7] and other constraint based toolkits.

Source v/s Initiative

Figure 2 shows a source versus initiative matrix. Although the actual information resides in the status, we are particularly interested in the source as it holds the knowledge of any changes to the data. Initiative plays a key role in determining how changes of status are discovered.

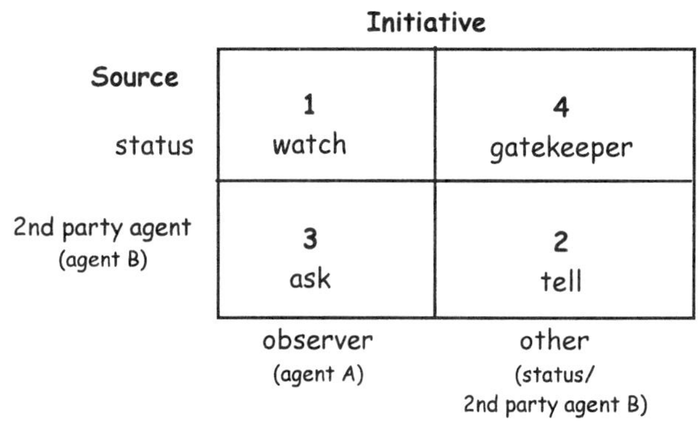

Figure 2 Source v/s Initiative

Both cases 2 and 3 involve a second party agent, but the difference between them is one of initiative. In case 2, it is the second party agent B which takes the initiative to find out about the status change while in case 3, the responsibility lies with the agent A itself. Therefore the difference between 'asking' and 'telling' is one of initiative. Similarly, in case 1 the initiative originates from agent A as it polls or watches the status but in case 4, the initiative comes from the status itself.

Given this arrangement we may then ask ourselves what prompts one to take the initiative. For example, in case 1 this leads to subcases such as it may be internal (most likely time driven), or it may be due to a third party agent (demand driven) or it may be spontaneous (either be time driven or demand driven).

This section has examined the status event arrangement that exists between an agent altering some status value and an observing agent interested in changes to this status value. While it is possible to construct systems that manage status updates by propagating all alterations at a per update level to others, it does however require a considerable overhead at the application level. The application is in fact responsible for managing all the updates as they occur. The overhead involved in this management is one of the core motivations for the research into notification (or awareness) services that provide a set of standard techniques for managing status changes. The following section will consider the status event issues involved in the development of these notification (or awareness) servers.

NOTIFICATION SERVERS AS MEDIATORS

A similar analysis for the cases of status change discovery will now be applied to notification servers in collaborative applications. For the sake of the following discussion, it is assumed that there is a centralised architecture with some

[1] Lotus Notes is a registered trademark of Lotus Development Corporation

sort of central database or information server and client applications on each user's workstation.

Consider the following scenario. A user updates some shared data and the changes are sent by the user's client application to the central server. How does another user's client become aware of the change in order to update the screen?

Although the client applications are likely to be identical on both workstations, they take different rôles in this scenario:

Active Client (AC) – on the workstation of the user who performs the change

Passive Client (PC) – on the workstation of the user who is observing

Since the client applications perform the updates and display the resulting changes, we will concentrate on the clients themselves rather than the users who will ultimately interact through them. Thus we are concerned with how the events about the changes to the information are propagated rather than how the information is displayed.

To structure our analysis, we will first examine the scenario when there is no notification server and look at the options which enable the passive client to discover the changes. Then we will look at any additional options required when the notification server is added.

Without a Notification Server

The agents of interest are the active client and passive client and the status is the shared data (figure 3).

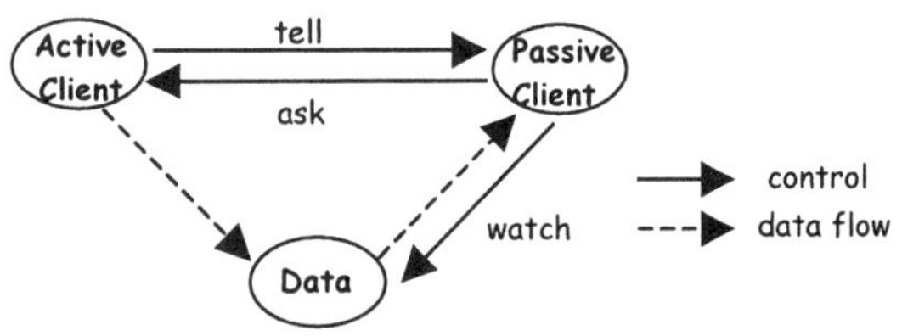

Figure 3 client-data interaction without notification server

In the previous section, we identified four cases of discovering status change. However, case 4 corresponds to the status having some closely allied gatekeeper agent and this acts as a type of notification server. Also, in cases 2 and 3 there is the possibility of a mediating agent; again this is the role of a notification server. Therefore we only need to consider the cases when the agent is the originator of the status change, namely the active client. Thus by direct application of the options from the status–event analysis we have the following options:

• passive clients polls the data (case 1)

This is the classic email arrangement where the responsibility lies with the client to interrogate the data and find out when changes have taken place.

• active client tells the passive client (case 2)

This arrangement is used in some forms of shared screen systems where screen updates are broadcast to all other clients. It is also adopted in multicast applications such as those used for virtual worlds[3].

• passive client asks the active client (case 3)

This situation is less common but normally occurs in shared screen systems where there is a designated master version of an application that is responsible for managing distribution of updates. Systems of this form include early versions of shared screen systems.

With a Notification Server

When a notification server (NS) is introduced, it acts as an intermediary between the active and the passive clients. This offers the benefits of managing the process and allowing support for more scaleable arrangements. The notification server facilitates distributed architectures including hybrid arrangements where the advantages of a replicated architecture in terms of local responses are combined with the propagation offered from a central awareness service.

In most cases both clients communicate with the notification server in various ways and we will consider each of them shortly. Essentially the active client informs the notification server of the update while the passive client seeks to be informed of updates. The notification server therefore removes the need for direct communication between the active client and the passive client. Also the notification server does not pass on the data to the clients. Instead the data repository fulfils this role. The notification server only mediates the control between the clients and the data. Events notifying changes to the underlying state information are basically sent between the clients and the notification server.

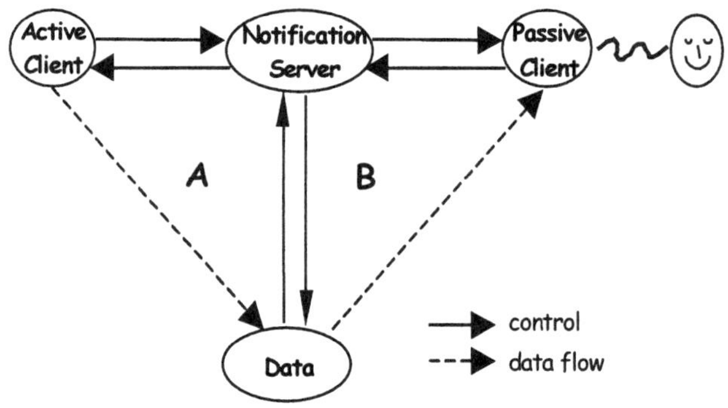

Figure 4 client-data interaction with notification server

Figure 4 shows the potential control flows between the clients and the notification server thus allowing the notification events to propagate through the system. It should be noted that not all of these control flows would be active in a particular system. By examining the combinations that may occur we will reach our taxonomy of the design space for notification servers.

Let us first consider the interaction between the notification server and the active client (figure 5). By applying the options discussed in the status-event analysis, the notification server is able to discover the stages of any change in the following ways:

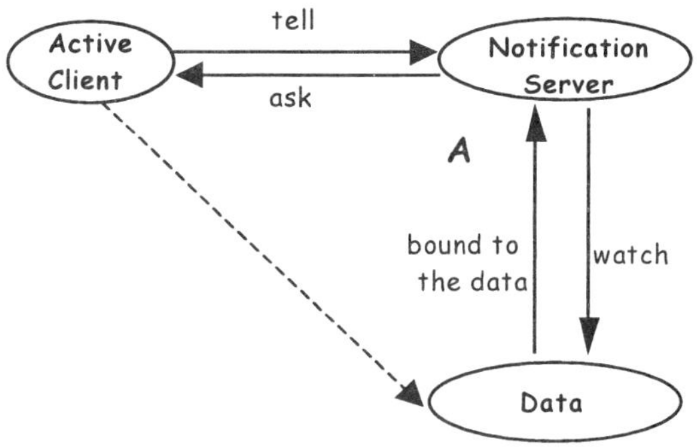

Figure 5 notification server communicating with active client and data store

• notification server polls the data (A1)

The responsibility lies with the notification server to monitor the data and detect any changes to the underlying data. This is often used in computer conferencing systems to provide some active propagation.

• active client tells the notification server (A2)

In this case the notification server is placed between the client and the data repository. This is similar to the technique used to develop shared X systems where a splitter was placed between the display and the underlying application [14].

• notification server asks the active client (A3)

This option is seldom used as it requires the notification server to ask the client if it seeks to make changes. However, with the development of mobile systems this arrangement is more likely to become significant as cellular architectures become more widely exploited.

• notification server is bound to the data (A4)

The Rendezvous [13] system adopts such an arrangement as it separates the abstract view from the data and uses some coupled mechanism to manage updates based on an encoding of constraints.

Once the change in the data has become a perceived event for the notification server, the latter must then relay that event to the passive client. The options are shown below.

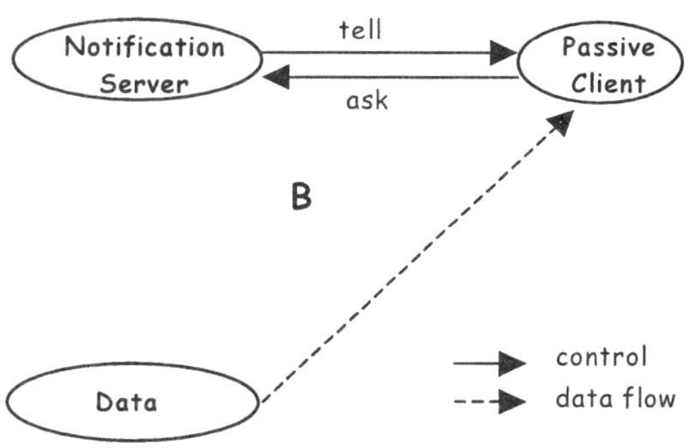

Figure 6 notification server relaying change passive client

Note that the figure does not show any explicit connection between the notification server and the data repository. Depending on the cases considered for A above, the link between the notification server and the underlying data may either be of a direct or an indirect nature.

• notification server tells the passive client (B2)

This is used by notification servers that are linked to window system where events can be sent directly to the client. The development of the push technology on the web also allows this to take place.

• passive client asks the notification server (B3)

This is the classic arrangement used in web based awareness mechanisms such as WAP [15].

It should be noted that since the notification server is acting as the intermediary, the options of having the passive client interacting with the data repository directly for changes (B1, B4) are ruled out.

TAXONOMY OF NOTIFICATION SERVERS

We saw that the notification server can find out about changes from the active client and the data store in 4 different ways (A1–A4). Furthermore, the notification server can communicate the updates to the passive client in 2 ways (B1, B2). We can represent these possibilities in a 4x2 matrix as shown in figure 7.

	B2 (NS $\rightarrow_{tells}$ PC)	B3 (PC $\rightarrow_{asks}$ NS)
A1 (AC $\rightarrow_{polls}$ NS)	....	....
A2 (AC $\rightarrow_{tells}$ NS)	....	....
A3 (NS $\rightarrow_{asks}$ AC)	....	....
A4 (NS ≡ Data)	....	....

Figure 7 (4x2) matrix

The above matrix is now populated by some example systems built using the respective protocol to produce the taxonomy of notification servers (figure 8).

		(NS-PC)	
		B2	B3
(AC-NS)	A1	desktop web crawler/ agents	pop server
	A2	pure notification server	certain MUDs
	A3		
	A4	NSTP [16]	awareness protocol [15]

Figure 8 notification server taxonomy

Note that in options A2 and A3 the notification server and the data repository are separate while in options A1 and A4, the notification server has some knowledge of the data. Let us now look at each of the systems on the matrix in turn.

A desktop web crawler looks for changes on some shared files on a web server (A1). As soon as some updates occur it generates a list and informs (B2) the clients about the changes, perhaps via an email message.

A POP server watches for the data (A1) but it is activated when it receives a request (B3) from the mail client. Unlike a web crawler which asks for changes in a spontaneous fashion, the event which drives polling in a POP server may either be time driven or demand driven. By default, a POP server does not perform any automatic notification. It is only triggered by a certain event from a mail client. Therefore a POP server only acts as a weak notification server.

Case A2-B2 can be seen as a pure notification server as the server is entirely separate from the data store. The server is told (A2) about the changes from the active client and it then notifies (B2) the users' clients about them. This is similar to, for example, the locking mechanism in the UNIX file system where applications explicitly request locks on remotely stored files from a special process, the lock daemon (file d). However, the lock daemon has no control over the files it is referred to and thus it is logically distinct from the file store.

Certain Web MUDs would be of type A2-B3. It would involve a low level client such as a Java applet running on a web page and a rapidly polling notification server at a web site. If someone visits that site and requests the page, this tells (A2) the notification server that the page is being visited. So when the applet next polls the server (B3) other users see an avatar appear or may hear a door clink.

In NSTP [16] the notification server is closely coupled to the shared data repository (A4). In the event of any updates, the notification server tells (B2) the clients about the changes in the shared state information.

The awareness protocol proposed by Palfreyman et al [15] is stateless and is based on a client making a request and the server sending back a reply. The shared data is the awareness of the presence and the locations of individuals in virtual space. Therefore the awareness server is bound to the shared data (A4) and clients have to explicitly query (B3) the server.

Note that row A3 of the matrix in figure 7 is empty. Both cases A3-B2 and A3-B3 are ineffective. Case A3-B2 is particularly inefficient as it implies that the passive client would constantly have to ask for changes from the notification server and the latter would then have to send a request to the active client.

However, we are more likely to have an A3-B2 scenario where the notification server can be partially stateless. The server will have an interest in the changes without being fully aware of them. Such a situation may arise in a mobile environment where the server needs to avoid contention on the demands.

Location of Notification Server

For the sake of this discussion we effectively assumed a centralised architecture in that we have been talking about a single notification server and data repository. However, this is a conceptual architecture and the physical location of notification servers need not be centralised. The notification server may sit remotely from the data or it can be packaged within the data. Indeed there may be no single physical entity corresponding to the notification server, instead the notification service may be spread over several physical components as shown in figure 9.

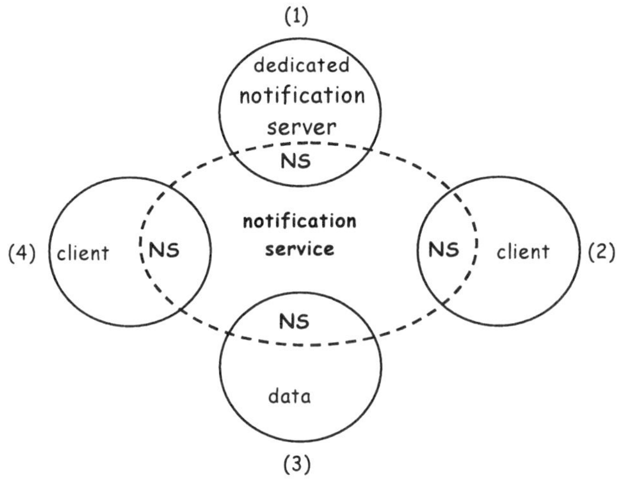

Figure 9 location of notification server

We can therefore identify 4 major options:

1. the notification server is *closely bound* to the data repository

Clearly, the notification server must reside in the same physical address space as the data store or the data must at least be part of the server. An example is a database supporting triggered actions. Instead of having the notification server explicitly asking for the changes, the data store informs the server about them.

2. the notification server and the data repository are *loosely coupled* together

In software engineering terms, the notification server is regarded as a separable component which may reside in the same physical address space as the data store but it which also sit somewhere else on the network.

3. a distributed *peer-peer* notification service

Often a conceptual notification server is realised as a software abstraction within the clients using peer-peer communication. An extreme example is AETHER [20], which percolates awareness information from node to node in a network thus effectively providing an emergent distributed notification service uniformly throughout the network.

4. a *hybrid* of the above

In practice, systems may include elements of all the above three options. For example, a single notification server may be running on the network but a notification service component may be integrated within each client in order to provide an effective application interface.

NOTIFYING USERS

We are interested in the timeliness of information by providing rapid feedback and appropriate pace of feedthrough to collaborative users; hence the need for an underlying notification server which will provide such a level of user awareness. Although the notification server may use a particular mechanism at the protocol level, the user may perceive it in a different way at the behavioural level.

Low level software may poll reasonably rapidly when the client talks to the notification server but at a higher level of abstraction, the server could actively send messages to notify users despite the fact that it received those messages via polling. For instance, a notification server may watch for changes in web pages and then email a list of updated pages to the users.

Similarly, if we compare the true push technology (based for example on a Java applet) with a browser refreshing web pages based on expiry time then from the user point of view they may appear little different. However, at a lower level, the applet is informed by the 'pushed server' while the browser polls after the expiry date.

Layering

To understand these complex interactions we return again to status-event analysis. In status-event analysis we find that the mode and the pace of interaction may change radically at different layers between the software, the hardware and the human parts of the system. Consider the scenario when a person decides to press on a keyboard. When a key is pressed, the wire changes to a high or low voltage (status) and as soon as the chip notices the change it causes an interrupt (event) at the lowest level which in turn is processed at higher levels.

Similarly, the interaction between the user and the passive client creates an extra layer of indirection. Let us look at Lotus Notes as an example. By default, Notes does not actively notify users when the database has changed. It puts a mark against the changed notes in a list view. It is only when the user explicitly looks at the relevant list view that he/she becomes aware of the change. At the user level this corresponds to case 3 (asking) but at the lower level, the Notes server informs the Notes client when changes occur (case 2) so that it can update its local structures.

Alternatively, many mail clients will periodically poll the server (case 3) but when they notice that mail has arrived they inform the user by popping up a dialogue box (case 2). Even when low level protocols do not directly support the desired user level behaviour it is possible to provide different types of notification although this may be less efficient, for instance in terms of network traffic.

We can use different layers between client-notification server and client-user in order to achieve the desired pace of interaction.

IMPEDANCE MATCHING

We have so far discussed the various scenarios when notification takes place and we will now consider the frequency of notification. So how often must the notification server send updates to the users? This will depend heavily on the desired pace of interaction.

The pace of interaction is the rate at which users interact with computer systems, the physical world and with one another. Three major factors influence the pace of interaction: the pace of communication channels, the pace of the shared task and the pace at which the users operate. Unlike bandwidth, which gives a measure of the amount of information that is transmitted, the pace of channels indicates the frequency of communication. A previous study [8] highlighted the problems which may arise when there is a mismatch between the communication channel and the cooperative task.

Collaborative participants not only interact individually with the system but also with other group members via the shared objects. As a result, it is important to see both the user's own updates (feedback) and the effects of other users' actions (feedthrough). Feedthrough is a form of awareness [18]; it is an awareness of the effects of group members actions, hence the changes that have occurred. By observing the intermediate steps and the way the changes happen, we can also infer the reasons why the changes take place. The pace of the feedthrough is directly affected by the pace of the interaction.

Pace Impedance

Collaborative users often have to work with a large number of shared objects and it is not always possible to maintain an appropriate rate of feedthrough for each object, even over fast networks. Indeed, if we do try to obtain a maximum rate of feedthrough for all objects the resulting network congestion and computational load would undoubtedly mean delays for all objects including the most salient and important. We clearly need some form of *impedance matching* between the active and passive clients.

Impedance matching can be achieved by simply reducing the rate at which the active client generates update messages. For example, a shared cursor need not broadcast changes after each pixel movement. However, impedance matching at the active client level is global – all passive clients will receive the same pace. This implies that the passive clients must further filter the event stream. Although this will achieve appropriate user level feedthrough, it still consumes network bandwidth and computational effort.

As the notification server acts as an intermediary, it can be used to adjust the pace of feedthrough. It does not necessarily have to forward the changes to the passive client at the same rate that it received it from the active client. Consequently, the pace between the active client and the notification server (side A of figure 4) may differ from that between the notification server and the passive client (side B).

In order to obtain the right pace and the right granularity of the changes the clients will have to negotiate with the notification server. For example, at a user level, mailing lists distribute messages to subscribed users each time they hit the server. In contrast, moderated lists may send digests to users each month.

Volume Impedance

In addition to pace impedance, the volume of data sent to users can be adjusted to make it more manageable. For example, some moderated lists send users a list of the contributions main headings and if someone is interested in a particular article then he/she sends a request. A similar example arises in Lotus Notes and bulletin board systems. The user sees some mark against changed items, but not the full text of changes until requested. In fact, in many such systems the entire text has already been downloaded. So this is a case of volume impedance matching between the passive client and the user. Impedance matching between the server and client can be found in some POP email clients where only the headers of large messages are downloaded until the text is actually requested.

Both pace and volume impedance matching can be seen as a form of quality-of-service [17]. However, whereas most QoS is concerned with achieving minimum standards of throughput, we are trying to limit it.

Implementation Issues

If the notification server is bespoke then it may have an in-built knowledge of the appropriate pace of feedthrough for impedance matching purposes. However, in general, the information as to what pace of low-level events is needed to achieve appropriate user-level feedthrough will not reside in the notification server, but must be communicated to it from the clients.

The frequency of updates may be controlled either explicitly by the user or may be built into the client application. For example, certain objects may be regarded as *active* and require almost instantaneous feedthrough to be effective, whereas other objects may be less active and the rate of notification can be reduced accordingly.

In order to enable the notification server to provide effective impedance matching, the client needs to use some form of protocol to inform the server of the required pace. However, this communication between the client and the server does not require the server to have any knowledge of the application semantics.

Because the server is delaying feedthrough to the clients, some form of event queues must be held at the server end before they are sent across to the clients. This lays an extra storage load on the server. It also means that when updates are sent they have the accumulated size of all the delayed messages. Ideally the server should be able to compress the event queues, for example the event queue:

```
insert(" hello" ), insert(" world" )
```

can be reduced to:

```
insert(" hello world" )
```

However this requires the server to have substantial knowledge about the events and the objects.

SUMMARY

We have taken a general model of status change discovery from status–event analysis and applied it to notification server architectures. This highlighted the similarities between the communication (A) from the active client to the notification server and (B) from the notification server to the passive client. Grounding our framework for notification architecture on this generic theoretical analysis gives us confidence in its coverage.

The status–event analysis also highlighted the important distinction between the knowledge of *what* has changed in shared data and the knowledge *that* it has changed.

This analysis allowed us to construct a taxonomy based on issues of source and initiative within the three way PC–NS–AC communication.

We also saw that a conceptually single notification server may be placed in various physical locations within a CSCW system and may even be distributed over several components. In the latter case it may be more appropriate to think of a notification service operating within the system as a whole.

Notification servers operate at a low-level within the computer system, but their purpose is to provide user-level behaviour in the form of feedthrough and awareness. We looked at the way that different categories of notification may be seen at different levels so that a client application may make use of non-optimal low-level notification services to achieve acceptable user-level behaviour.

A crucial behavioural issue is achieving the appropriate pace of feedthrough and awareness. The central mediating position of the notification server allows it to perform impedance matching and thus reduce network bandwidth and improve user-level notification.

In order to demonstrate some of the issues discussed in this paper, we are constructing an experimental notification server called 'Getting to Know' (GtK) within a distributed agent architecture that supports impedance matching. The notification server operates at the same location in the taxonomy as NSTP, but in a more loosely coupled fashion thus allowing a separation of concerns between notification and data.

It is essential in any design process to be able to effectively compare and discuss different design options. We believe that the framework provided in the paper begins such a design vocabulary for the implementation of notification services.

REFERENCES

1. Abowd, G. and Dix, A., Integrating status and event phenomena in formal specifications of interactive systems, in *Proceedings of SIGSOFT'94* (New Orleans, 1994), ACM Press, 44–52.

2. Benford, S. and Fahlén, L. A spatial model of interaction in large virtual environments. *Proceedings of ECSCW'93*, Kluwer Academic. (1993). pp. 109–124.
3. Benford, S., Bowers, J., Fahlén, L., Mariani, J, Rodden. T, Supporting Cooperative Work in Virtual Environments. *The Computer Journal, 38*, 1 (1995).
4. Bentley, R. Supporting Multi-User Interface Development for Cooperative Systems, *PhD Thesis* (University of Lancaster, UK, 1994).
5. Brewster, S.A. Providing a structured method for integrating non-speech audio into human-computer interfaces. *PhD Thesis* (University of York, UK, 1994).
6. Brewster, S.A., Wright, P.C. and Edwards A.D.N. The design and evaluation of an auditory-enhanced scrollbar, in *Proceedings of CHI'94* (Boston, Massachusetts, 1994), ACM Press, 173–179.
7. Dewan, P, A tour of the Suite user interface software, *in Proceedings of UIST'90* (1990), ACM Press, 57-65.
8. Dix, A.J. Pace and interaction, in *Proceedings of HCI'92: People and Computers VII*, (Sept. York, 1992), Cambridge University Press, 193–208.
9. Dix, A. and Brewster, S.A. Causing Trouble with Buttons, in *Ancillary Proceedings of HCI'94* (Glasgow, UK, 1994). Available at http://www.soc. staffs.ac.uk/~cmtajd/papers/ buttons94/
10. Dix, A. and Abowd, G. Modelling status and event behaviour of interactive systems. *Software Engineering Journal 11,* 6 (1996), 334–346.
11. Dix, A. and Abowd, G. Delays and Temporal Incoherence Due to Mediated Status–Status Mappings, *SIGCHI Bulletin 28,* 2 (1996), 47–49.
12. Dix, A., Finlay, J., Abowd, G., and Beale, R. *Human–Computer Interaction.* Prentice Hall (second edition 1998). Available at http://www.hiraeth. com/books/hci/
13. Hill, R.D., Brinck, T., Rohall, S.L., Patterson, J.F. and Wilner, W. The Rendezvous architecture and language for constructing multi-user applications. *ACM Transactions on Computer-Human Interaction, 1,* 2 (1994), 81–125.
14. Lauwers J.C. and Lantz K.A. Collaboration awareness in support of collaboration transparency: Requirements for the next generation of shared window systems, in *Proceedings of CHI'90* (Seattle, Washington, April 1990), ACM Press, 303–311.
15. Palfreyman, K. and Rodden, T. A Protocol for User Awareness on the World Wide Web, in *Proceedings of CSCW'96*, (Boston, Massachusetts, Nov. 1996), ACM Press, 130–139.
16. Patterson, J.F, Day, M. and Kucan, J. Notification Servers for Synchronous Groupware, in *Proceedings of CSCW'96* (Cambridge Massachusetts, 1996), ACM Press, 122–129.
17. Rada, R. *Interactive Media.* Springer-Verlag, New York (1995).
18. Ramduny, D. and Dix, A. Why, What, Where, when: Architectures for Cooperative Work on the World Wide Web, in *Proceedings of HCI'97*, (Bristol, UK, Aug. 1997), Springer-Verlag, 283–301.
19. Rodden, T. Populating the Application: A Model of Awareness for Cooperative Applications, in *Proceedings of CSCW'96*, (Boston, Massachusetts, Nov. 1996), ACM Press, 87–96.
20. Sandor, O., Bogdan, C and Bowers, J. Aether: an awareness engine for CSCW, in *Proceedings of ECSCW'97*, (Lancaster, UK, 1997), Kluwer Academic, 221–236.
21. Trevor J., Mariani J. Rodden T. The use of adaptors to support cooperative work, in *proceedings of CSCW'94* (Chapel Hill, North Carolina, Oct. 1994), ACM Press, 22–26.
22. Wood, A., A. K. Dey and G. D. Abowd (1997). CyberDesk: Automated Integration of Desktop and Network Services, in *Proceedings of CHI '97*, ACM Press, 552–553.
23. Wood, A. CAMEO: Supporting Agent-Application Interaction, *PhD Thesis* (University of Birmingham, UK, 1998).

Re-Coupling Tailored User Interfaces

Gareth Smith
Computing Department,
Lancaster University,
Lancaster, LA1 4YR,
UK
gbs@comp.lancs.ac.uk

Jon O'Brien
Sociology Department,
Lancaster University,
Lancaster, LA1 4YR,
UK
j.obrien2@lancs.ac.uk

ABSTRACT
The development of shared environments and displays has also seen the emergence of facilities to allow some form of subjective tailoring of shared interfaces. This paper considers the need to dynamically re-couple tailored interfaces as users become increasingly aware of each other. We present a general model to support awareness based re-coupling of shared interfaces and show its implementation in cooperative virtual environments and shared user interfaces.

Keywords
Shared user interfaces, awareness, collaborative virtual environments.

INTRODUCTION
The development of applications that support a number of interfaces across a community of users has played a prominent role in CSCW. Different researchers have investigated techniques and architectures to support the real time management of these interfaces. Research has focused on the development of facilities to coordinate and manage interaction across the different interfaces.

Early multi-user interface systems supported shared interfaces by presenting exactly the same image of the application to all users. This simple replication of the system's image secured a founding abstraction for multi-user interfaces: What You See is What I See (WYSIWIS). Experiences with these systems in the CoLab environment highlighted problems with the WYSIWIS approach [20], Stefik concluded that "*WYSIWIS (What You See is What I See) is too inflexible, if strictly interpreted, and must be relaxed to better accommodate important interactions in meetings*". Stefik suggested that the shared interfaces which conformed to the WYSIWIS abstraction should be relaxed along a number of dimensions. The notion of relaxed WYSIWIS provides each individual user with the ability to configure their shared user interface to best suit their working needs. User interface tailoring is now generally accepted in the areas of all user interface systems [9].

CSCW 98 Seattle Washington USA

A similar approach is emerging in the field of Cooperative Virtual Environments (CVEs). CVEs may be considered as shared *three dimensional* interfaces which provide a shared 3D space that may be populated by users and any type of three dimensional artefact. Generally, CVEs present the same shared data to each of the cooperating users, albeit from a different viewpoint, which is analogous to the use of strict-WYSIWIS in early 2D interfaces. That is, they lack a number of cooperative features such as interface tailoring. But, the lessons from work in the field of shared 2D user interfaces are being introduced into the area of 3D shared user interfaces. For example, a model to support individual *Subjective Views* of a shared 3D world has been presented [18], and implemented [19] within a publicly available CVE, the *Dive* system [4][5].

Shared user interface research has formed a solid theme of supporting the ability for users to tailor their user interfaces on an individual and group basis. However, different presentations of shared user interfaces, whether 2D or 3D, can cause problems in collaboration due to lack of 'common knowledge' and awareness between the collaborating parties and their activities [8]. This problem is also highlighted by [11], but is termed *workspace awareness* and defined as "*the up-to-the-minute knowledge a person holds about another's interaction with the workspace*". Therefore there is an operational trade-off between the benefits of interface tailoring and the amount of 'common knowledge' required to facilitate collaboration [7]. Generally, this fine tuning of user interface coupling between users is the responsibility of the users themselves. This activity is problematic as it is difficult for individual users to know the customised details of other users' interfaces.

This paper argues that user interface tailoring mechanisms provide individual users with different *static* user interfaces, which must be explicitly re-configured to aid in certain collaborative tasks. Additionally, the process of *user interface re-coupling* must be an automatic process without placing additional responsibility on the user. Rather, it should operate seamlessly, and re-configure the different shared user interfaces on the users' behalf.

MOTIVATION

The motivation for this work comes from a consideration of empirical studies of action within a CVE constructed in MASSIVE [10] as part of a previous project [2]. These ethnographic studies were carried out with the intention of exploring the ways in which users might make use of the CVE for interactional purposes, and subsequently making these findings available as a resource for the refinement of both user embodiments and the CVE itself. Much of this work focused on the interactional affordances of the user embodiments, and some mention was made of the use of alternative 'views' of the virtual world by users in order to achieve certain activity-specific practices most effectively. We include one particular extract here, as an example of the exploitation of 'freedom of viewpoint' along with a brief section of discussion of the action within the CVE, taken from [2].

> *CT suggests gathering in a circle. Some complaints... notoriously difficult to manage. Problems of orienting one's own embodiments to those of all others. Some attempts at first, people's embodiments run through each other.*
>
> *Someone from Site B explains that you can switch to a bird's eye view and see your own and other embodiments from directly above, much easier to orient embodiments in relation to others.*
>
> Initially users struggled to co-ordinate their position in relation to other users, before it was pointed out that they were able to 'leave' their embodiments and look down on them from above, making such co-ordination much more manageable. Here the ability to exploit the 'freedom' of viewpoint in MASSIVE contributed to the successful completion of a task by making all participants aware of the work of others. The example also indicates that the form which embodiment in a CVE should take (whether one 'looks out of' the blockie's eye or prefers an 'out of the body experience') is a contingent and activity specific affair

Of interest here for the purposes of this paper is not so much the fact that users exploited the 'freedom of viewpoint' in order to manage gathering in a circle within the CVE, but the *assumptions about the properties of the CVE* that provided for this strategy as one available to users for the mutual orientation of their embodiments towards one another. The viability of adopting such a 'bird's eye' view as a strategy of this kind is based upon a knowledge that all participants see the CVE as constituted in the same way: their *perspectives upon* the CVE may well be different (in this case they may not all share the same 'bird's eye' view, for example) but they all share the *same understanding* of the CVE as a space within which they are all embodied. This intersubjective consistency therefore allows for a range of activity-specific strategies for interacting within the CVE – participants can be sure that they share a given common intersubjective space upon which they are taking individual perspectives. Were this intersubjective consistency *not* to hold, and participants have radically different understandings of the underlying constitution and properties of the CVE, it would make no sense to adopt the 'bird's eye' view as a strategy for coordinating the position of one's embodiment with others, since one could not be sure that others would be experiencing the space within the CVE in an intersubjectively consistent way. In short, other objects and actions, not visible to the adopter of the bird's eye view may be constraining the action and interaction of those being viewed from above and hence the utility of this manoeuvre would disappear.

APPROACH

The notion of coupling in shared user interfaces is currently based on some form of derivation from a common interface. The common interface definition provides a basis for tailoring by users. Each user controls their own interfaces by altering their presentation of a common shared model. This model may be expressed as a user interface (as in SOL [17]) or a set of shared state (as in Rendezvous [13]). Essentially this approach means that each subjective view results in a separate branch within a derivation hierarchy from the common shared interface, see figure 1.

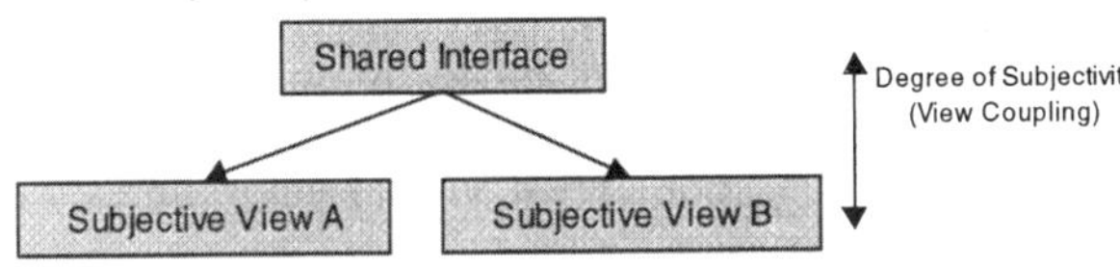

Figure 1. The subjective or personal view model

This traditional approach to developing subjective views means that each user has a separate perspective on the shared model. This separation of interfaces means that users can manage the local presentation of information and have personalised views of information intermingled with common elements. The problem we wish to address is the situation where we wish to bring these currently separate views together to allow users to share a greater common experience and to promote a greater degree of commonality by re-coupling elements of the interface.

Obviously one way to re-couple the separate interfaces is for users to revert to the common interface definition. However, this requires users to reconfigure their interface definition and is potentially rather costly. We wish to develop a low cost means of re-coupling these interfaces depending on the context of use. The approach we have adopted is based on the consideration that a user's subjective specification reflects their personal preferences, and should not have to be manually re-configured to suit transitory working conditions. Rather we wish to exploit an awareness of other users activities to automatically recouple their interfaces.

The core of our approach is the explicit identification of the awareness users have of each other. The knowledge of this awareness is combined with the subjective information specified for each user, to generate an *awareness sensitive subjective view*. Figure 2, depicts the process where the knowledge of a user's subjective view is combined with an *awareness map*, which describes the awareness other users have of each object, to create a new subjective view. This new subjective view is a second-generation subjective view derived from a combination of the users initial subjective configuration and the awareness map.

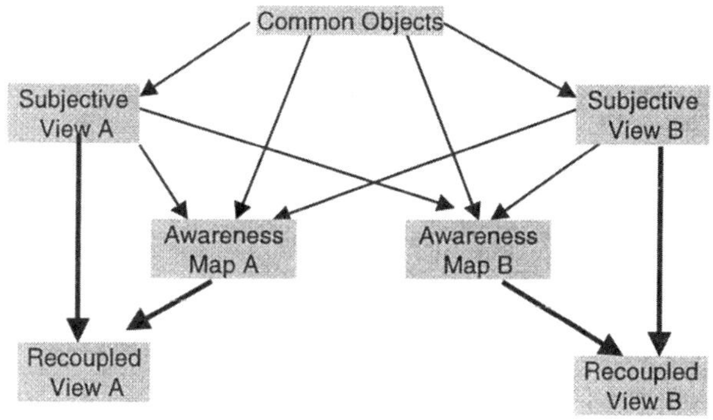

Figure 2. Generation of Recoupled-Subjective Views

An Awareness Model to support subjective views.

To develop these re-coupling mechanisms we build upon an existing awareness model [15] that describes the interactivity between users. We extend this model to allow it to be used to further manipulate user's subjective views of the common model. The extension creates an additional level of user interface control based on the common interface model and users' subjective preferences.

The awareness model provides a generalised approach for understanding shared objects and multiple users of cooperative systems. The benefit of this model is that it enables us to focus on the shared manipulation of objects, without being restricted to a particular cooperative system.

The key elements of the model are motivated by a spatial consideration of users populating a shared pool of objects. The core of the awareness model is the view of these shared spaces as a set of interconnected objects. The key concepts used to describe awareness in the model are *location, focus* and *nimbus.*

- *Location*: the object where the user is currently positioned
- *Focus*: a set of adjacent objects the user is interested in
- *Nimbus*: a set of adjacent objects that the user is affecting

It is possible for a user to have more than one position in this pool of objects and to have some form of aggregated focus and nimbus associated with them. Each of location, focus and nimbus can be considered as sets of objects. Figure 3 shows the general arrangement for a user 'Tom' in a pool of objects.

Using this model we can represent the objects where users are placed as sets of adjacent objects that can be used to determine how aware users are of each other. We wish to extend this model to allow us to describe the general mechanism of re-coupling independently of a particular user interface paradigm or implementation. In developing an extension of this model we seek to exploit the general nature of sets to develop an understanding of awareness across subjective world views.

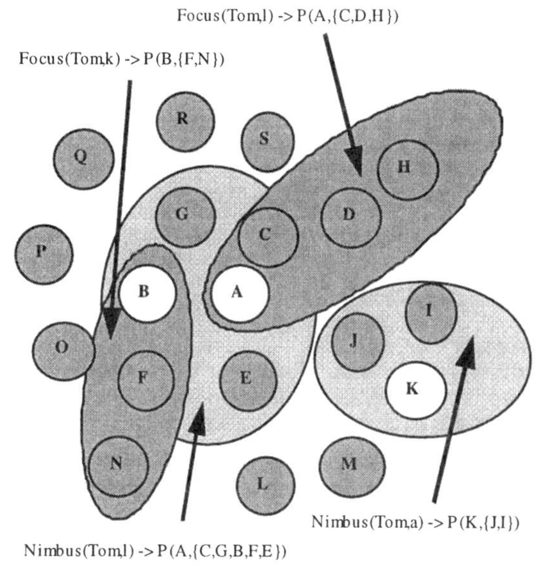

location(Tom) -> {B,A,K}
agg_nimbus(Tom) -> {C,G,F,E,J,I}
agg_focus(Tom) -> {C,D,H,F,N}

Figure 3. Location, aggregate focus and aggregate nimbus

The core of the awareness model is the use of simple sets to represent location, aggregate nimbus and aggregate focus and the comparison of these sets allows us to reason about awareness. For example, we can decide that we have an awareness strength measure by using a simple ratio of number of objects in the intersection of the focus and nimbus sets divided by the number of objects in the union of these sets.

$$\frac{|\,agg\_focus(u1) \cap agg\_nimbus(u2)\,|}{|\,agg\_focus(u1) \cup agg\_nimbus(u2)\,|}$$

Subjective Views of the Common Space

Our extension relies on understanding the particular derived views that an object has at any one moment in time and representing these within the model. This relies on the use of a *subjective pair* which shows that one object has been derived from another. This subjective pair linking a common object (o_c) and the subjective object for a particular user (o_u) is represented as:

$$S(o_c, o_u)$$
where $o_c \in O$ and $o_u \in O$ (O is the set of all objects)

For example, if a user has chosen a different presentation of a door, o_u represents that presentation, while o_c represents the default (original) presentation. We refer to the particular parts of the pair using a simple bracket notation. Where S is a subjective pair:

Common(S) is the common object
Subjective (S) is the subjective object

This pairing allows us to construct a *subjective space* (SS(O)) to represent the derivation of alternative views from the common set of objects. The subjective space can be represented as:

$SS(O) = \{ S(o_c, o_u) | o_c \in O, o_u \in O \}$

This merely collects all the objects that have different subjective presentations for a given user (such as the door in the above example). We can also refer to the these components collectively where SS is a subjective space:

Common_objects(SS) is the set of common objects
Subjective_objects(SS) is the set of subjective objects

A general function *SubjectiveModifier* is used to represent the decoupling of objects from the common space s:

$SubjectiveModifier: U \rightarrow SS(O)$

This simply states that the user **U** has a subjective space consisting of the set of pairings of a common object linked to the subjective object replacing it. That is, it defines SS(O) (the subjective space) for a given user.

This allows us to reason about both the user's common object space and the subjective object spaces presented to the user. To aid this we use a function *projected_space* that takes as parameters a set of objects and a subjective space. This function replaces the objects in the common space with their subjective counter parts:

$ProjectedSpace: SS(O) \rightarrow Op$

Where Op is the set generated by replacing all the common_objects with the corresponding subjective_objects, i.e. the set is 'flattened'. In the above example, the original presentation of the door is overwritten by the subjective presentation.

Let us illustrate this with a simple example. Consider two users Tom and Dick sharing a common space consisting of three different objects A, B, C. Now, Tom modifies object A to create A' and Dick modifies object C to create C' then both have subjective versions of the shared space. We can say that

SubjectiveModifier(Tom) = {S(A,A')}

and

SubjectiveModifier(Dick) = {S(C,C')}

We can also represent the two different versions of the shared space using the projected space function.

ProjectedSpace (SubjectiveModifier(Tom)) = {A',B,C}

and

ProjectedSpace (SubjectiveModifier(Dick)) = {A,B,C'}

So, in Tom's view, objects B and C are taken from the common view, whereas object A's presentation is a subjective one. Likewise, in Dick's view, objects A and B are taken form the common view, but object C is subjectively different.

Presenting the space

In developing our subjective view we also need to consider how a space is made available to users. Remember that we are considering users sharing a space constructed from sets of common objects and allowing an individualised projection of this common space by selectively replacing objects with alternatives. In addition to selecting replacement objects, we also support the (subjective) visual modification of these objects. To do this we again exploit a simple pair linking an object (o) and a view modifier (m) represented as:

V(o, m)
where $o \in O$ and $m \in M$

The set M is a set of *modification tokens* that instruct the application how to display an object to the user. This token is application specific and particular interpretations of the model may use it differently. For example, in a simple GUI it could consist of the tokens {*invisible, normal, shaded*} and these would be interpreted in displaying these objects.

The view pairing allows us to construct a *view space* (VS(O)) to represent a user's view of a set of objects. The view space can be represented as

$VS(O) = \{ V(o, m) | o \in O, m \in M \}$

This provides us with a means of applying the view modifiers to relevant objects (whether these objects are subjective or common). A user's view of a set of objects can then be represented by the function *Subjective_View* taking a set of objects and a user as a parameter:

$Subjective\_View: U \times O \rightarrow VS(O)$

We can demonstrate this in terms of the example used above. Consider now that user Tom sees his modified object A as *shaded* and the others as *normal*. In contrast Dick does *not see* A, sees object B as normal and his modified version of C as *shaded*. The following functions describe the subjective views for both Tom and Dick:

Subjective_View(Tom,{A',B,C}) =
{V(A', shaded),V(B, normal), V(C, normal)}

Subjective_View(Dick,{A,B,C'}) =
{V(A, invisible),V(B, normal), V(C', shaded)}

Note, in this example our modification tokens include shaded, normal and invisible.

Developing an Awareness Map

We can combine the common space and each user's subjective view to consider awareness. To do this we exploit an awareness pair that links objects (o) with an awareness modifier (a). This is represented as:

AP(o, a)
where $o \in O$ and $a \in A$

The set A is a set of *awareness modifiers* that indicate (for a given user) how aware they should be of a particular object. This is a product of considering the given user's awareness of other users and the (subjective) differences in each of their views of that object.

The generation of these awareness modifiers is determined by the detailed semantics of a particular application. For example, in a CVE an awareness modifier may involve the visibility of an object (invisible, transparent or normal), and the distance between users. Here, the awareness modifier of an object would be deemed to be high if it appeared normal (solid) in the display of a nearby user (likewise, it would be less, if that user moved away, or if the object was invisible).

It is obvious here that for each object we may have an awareness modifier for each of the users. Again it is dependent on the semantics of the system implementing the model to define the calculation which combines these values into a single awareness modifier. For example, later in this paper we describe how we choose the highest value awareness modifier (in a CVE implementation) to ensure that (for a group of users in close proximity) subjectively *invisible* objects appear, if they are visible in one or more of the users' displays.

We use these pairs to form an *awareness map AM(O)* for each user. The awareness map is represented as a set of these pairs.

$$AM(O) = \{ AP(o, a) | o \in O, a \in A \}$$

This general arrangement can be represented using the simple function map_awareness that generates a map for a given user:

map_awareness: U -> AM(O)

The user's awareness map shows how their subjective view should be altered. Each of the awareness modifiers indicate how the presentation should be altered to reflect the way in which other users are seeing the object. These modifiers are core to the development of a recoupled view of these objects.

Recoupling the views

At any given moment we can recouple different users' views by exploiting each user's awareness map and particular view. If we consider the display for a given user Tom, we can say the user (Tom) has a subjective view space (VS) represented as:

VS = Subjective_View(Tom, ProjectedSpace
(SubjectiveModifier(Tom)))

We can also say that the awareness map (AM) for this user can be represented as

AM = map_awareness(Tom}

A final function *display* combines these two sets to give a modified view space that can be presented to the user. This is of the form:

$$display: VS(O) \times AM(O) \rightarrow VS(O)$$

The display function applies, for each object, the resultant awareness modifier from the awareness map to their (subjective) view space (VS(O)), which modifies their view space to produce the re-coupled display.

This arrangement allows each user's subjective display to be modified to reflect the effects of other user's subjective displays. The awareness based recoupling of these subjective displays can exploit a range of different particular algorithms. The framework presented in this paper aims at being independent of the particular *policies* used to detail how two or more objects should be merged. These might range from the use of strength values to represent the view and awareness modifiers to the more complex re-coupling mechanisms offered by [12].

If many users are in close proximity and have very different views of a very complex space then the computational requirements of re-coupling each of the interfaces may potentially be high. However, in our experiences the proportion of objects in a user's display, which have been subjectively changed, is small. Additionally, the data held in a user's awareness map is mostly static (such as the subjective view specifications), hence reducing the number of calculations required. In implementations where computational demand is high however, the notion of an 'aura', from the spatial model [1] may be exploited. An aura is a computational boundary, which limits access to objects outside it, in much the same way as the nimbus limits a user's area of presence. In highly populated, complex environments it may be necessary to introduce an aura to the re-coupling model to limit the objects used to generate the awareness map. In this case, the objects furthest away from a user will not be re-coupled (assuming aura selection is based merely on distance from user).

In the following sections we consider the implementation of the re-coupling model in different types of shared user interface systems. These different implementations of the model provide two different interpretations of the model; within a Collaborative Virtual Environment, and a shared 2D user interface system.

IMPLEMENTING RE-COUPLING IN A CVE

Cooperative Virtual Environments (CVEs) support the population of generic 3D spaces by a number of users. Such systems include DIVE [4], dVS [6], and MASSIVE [10], and allow users to navigate through the shared space and interact with objects and other users. A central facility of CVEs is the presentation of the shared environment, where the shared world is rendered onto the user's display. In a number of these systems, each users' presentation of the same shared world may differ through the use of subjective views where the underlying world object is modified or replaced. Subjectivity is used in these systems in a number of different ways, for example, a user may wish to find the location of the church, or be shown the quickest path from the church to the museum. Both these queries can be visualised subjectively, as depicted in figure 4.

Figure 4. Highlighting locations of interest, by making other objects appear as transparent, and visualising paths between them.

Throughout, our discussion of the implementation an example scenario of engineering design (of aircraft) is used. Here two or more users inspect the internals of an aircraft, which normally contains a number of separate systems organised in close proximity. Figure 5 denotes such an area, where a section of the aircraft's hydraulics are located near some of the aircraft's electrical system.

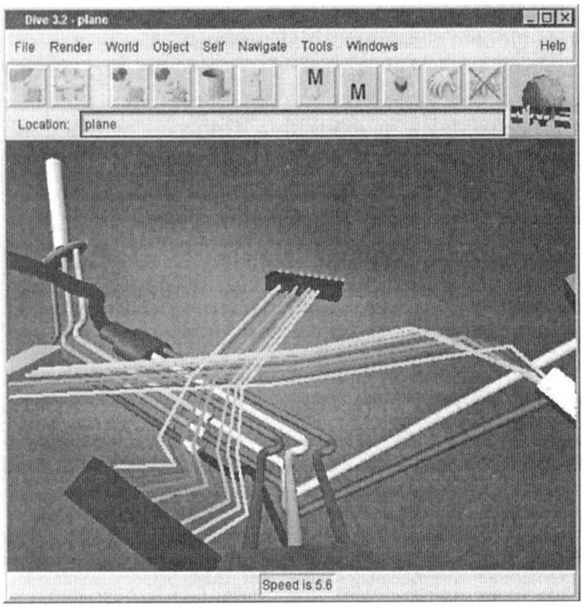

Figure 5. Inside the aircraft, a normal view

Using subjective views, each of the users' displays can be configured differently. This enables each engineer to concentrate on the objects most relevant to him or her. The CVE used in this example is Dive, which utilises the SOLVEN [18] model of supporting subjective views. This allows objects to have a number of alternative representations, and supports a range of modifiers which manipulate the visual aspects of the geometry. For example, a wireframe modifier will cause the object to be drawn in wireframe mode. This forms a matrix of representations against modifiers, as depicted in figure 6.

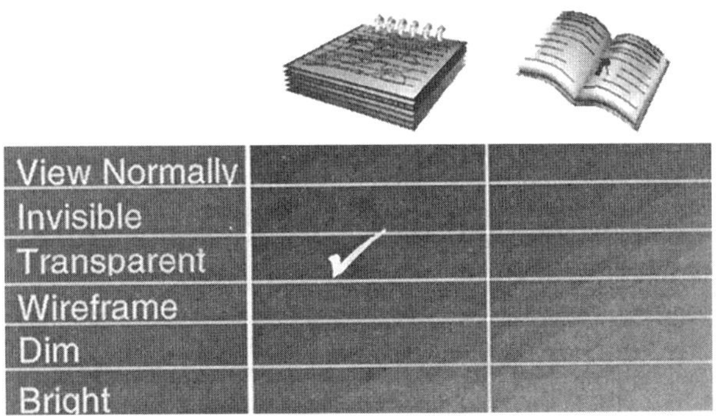

Figure 6. A view matrix of a book, showing two possible presentations and six modifiers.

In the above diagram, the user has chosen to represent a book in the style of a note-book (rather than a traditionally bound book), and that it should appear transparent. Using this model, users can selectively configure their interfaces.

In the engineering design example, each class of engineer may decide to remove the view of objects that are generally not relevant to them. Figure 7, depicts the isolated components that compose the subjective views of the hydraulics engineer and the electronics engineer.

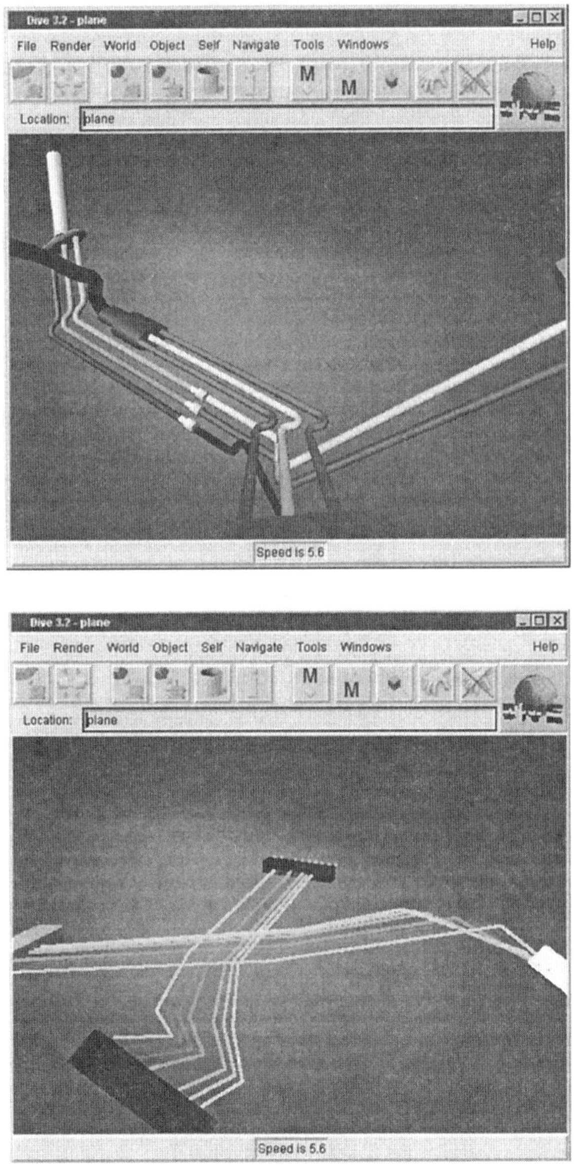

Figure 7. The hydraulic engineer's view and the electrician's view

When working on their individual tasks, their subjective views enable them to concentrate on their specialised domain. However when two or more users are working across a similar set of objects their different views can lead to communication and referential problems due to the lack of common knowledge. To overcome this, users involved would normally need to adjust their subjective specifications, requiring each to describe the state of their interface. In our case however, we can exploit the awareness of other users to allow a recoupling of these displays.

Mapping to the model

In this application of the general awareness driven recoupling model we exploit the following interpretations:

- The set of common objects maps to objects in the CVE
- Object replacements map to representations in the projected spaces.
- The view modifier tokens map to the modifiers in the SOLVEN model

Describing the Subjective views

Specification of the subjective views relies on the different display characteristics of the SOLVEN subjectivity mechanism. These display characteristics are mapped to *view modifier* tokens. We exploit a set of simple integer values to encode this information as shown in the following table:

Display Characteristic	View Modifier
Bright	*+1*
Normal	*0*
Dim	*-1*
Wireframe	*-2*
Transparent	*-2*
Invisible	*-3*

These values are used to represent the different presentations of objects in each user's display. In the case shown above we can consider each user's subjective display space as consisting of sets of subjective pairs linking objects to view modifiers. The subjective specification of the 'Wiring' and 'Hydraulics' objects for both the electronic engineer and the hydraulic engineer are detailed below:

Electronic Eng. Object	View Modifier
Wiring	+1 (bright)
Hydraulics	-3 (invisible)

Hydraulic Eng. Object	View Modifier
Wiring	-3 (invisible)
Hydraulics	0 (normal)

In the model this is represented as:

Subjective_View: (Elec_Eng,0) = { (Wiring, + 1), (Hydraulics,-3) }

Subjective_View: (Hydr_Eng,0) = = { (Wiring, -3), (Hydraulics,0) }

These two different subjective views now need to be recoupled to take account of each user's view and the awareness the users have of each other. What we seek to do here is develop a view that allows for some form of intersubjectivity where users are aware of the presence of others and what they may also be seeing. The basis of developing this coupled view is through the development of an awareness map for each user.

Developing an Awareness Map

The core to deriving the re-coupled view is an encoding of other users' awareness of each other. This is calculated in terms of the common object model and the different subjective views of other users. We use this information to form an *awareness map* made up of a pairing of shared objects and an awareness modifier. In the case of the CVE the awareness modifier is calculated using a field awareness method that exploits each user's nimbus on the common space, and the pre-defined view modifiers.

Using spatial awareness

The spatial awareness approach considers awareness by examining a user's nimbus in terms of which other users' nimbi are in collision with it. Then, the view modifiers from those users are interpreted and used along with the awareness measure to construct the original user's awareness map.

In our implementation, recoupling operates in a single direction (making objects *more* visible to a user). This reduces conflict when a number of users are in close proximity as the *most aware* (greatest number) value is chosen. Hence as a general rule, as more users, with different subjective settings, converge at a common location the more their displays loose their subjective values, and a more *common* interface is provided to each. To reason about awareness we use a visibility measure which is a percentage of how solid an object appears to users.

Consider the case depicted in figure 8. The subjective modifiers of a particular object have already been identified for three users. User C sees the object normally and it is invisible for Users A and B. The crossover of nimbi is used to calculate the awareness modifiers. User C affects User B's display making the object in that display 75% visible (or 25% transparent) and means that users B awareness map contains an awareness pair for the object encoding this.

In the case of our CVE development, the awareness calculation also considers the propagation of effects in building awareness maps. Before the arrival of User C, both User A and B did not see the object. However, now that User B can see this object it affects User A's display in the same way that User C affected User B. User A has their awareness map modified to indicate that the object can be made 15% visible as compared with User B's display. Hence the object in User A's display appears as 15% of 75%, which is 11% visible.

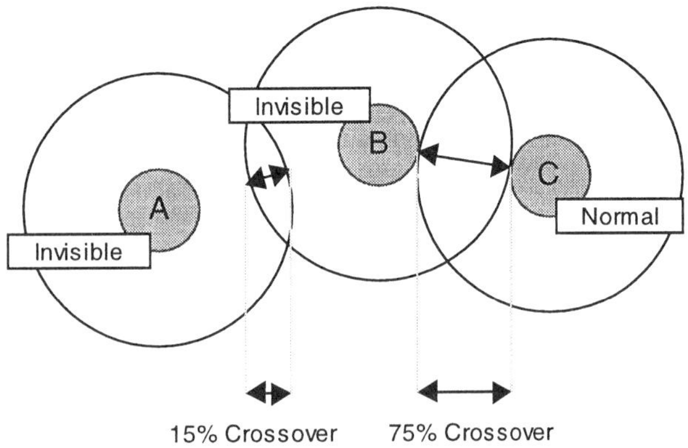

Figure 8. User C directly affects User B's display and indirectly affects User A's display

The awareness map for each user is modified to reflect changes in the environment. Consider the case where user C has moved closer to User A with a crossover of 60%, but the distances between Users A and B and Users B and C are unaltered. User A's awareness map is now directly affected by User C and User B. However, User B's impact on User A is to make the object 11% visible (through User C), and User C's impact on User A is to make the object 60% visible. Hence, the object in User A's awareness map is modified to make it 60% visibility (40% transparent), as our awareness mechanism chooses only the highest possible value.

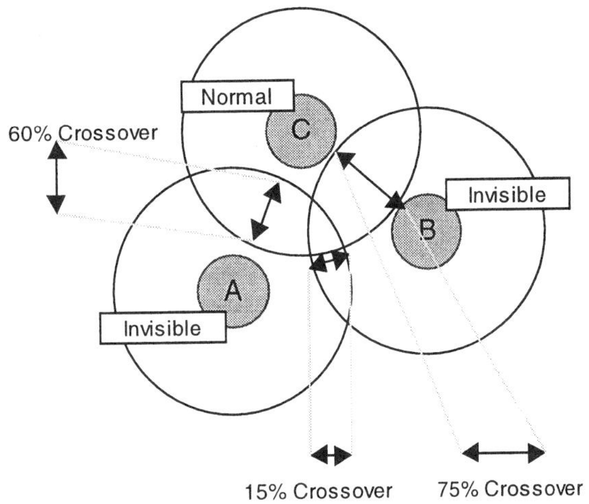

Figure 9. User C directly affects displays of Users A and B.

In some circumstances the re-coupling mechanism can cause unwanted disturbances, if this is the case it is possible for users to reduce the size of their nimbus (see figure 10), or switch it off completely. This provides a simple one-dimensional metric to control the amount of inter-subjectivity a user wishes to promote and receive. In certain conditions it may be advantageous to provide users with a range of different shaped nimbi to choose from. For example, in a meeting room scenario, it may be desirable to choose a forward only facing nimbus, emphasising the activities in the centre of the room while reducing those behind the users.

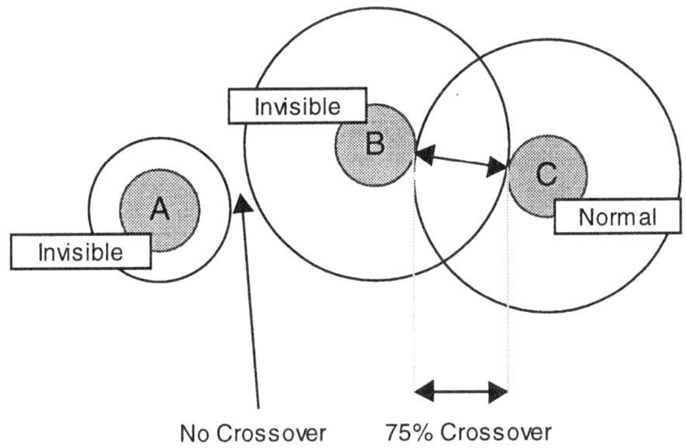

Figure 10. User A reduces the size of their nimbus to reduce intrusions from other users.

The recoupled displays

The object based awareness model detailed above is used to calculate an awareness map for each user. The re-coupling mechanism exploits the awareness map and generates the user's final display by combining the awareness map with their subjective view. This allows the displays to independently adjust themselves based on the users' awareness of each other.

The resulting view modification is some product of an object's existing modification (if any) and the awareness modifier. Our implementation operates in an increasing manner, in that objects should always become more visible through this mechanism. For example, in the electronic engineer's view the wiring is bright (+1), but is invisible (-3) in the hydraulic engineer's view. In the case of the electronic engineer the existing value is the maximum and is unaltered. In the case of the hydraulic engineer the view modifier (-3) can be less than that suggested by an awareness modifier. When it is greater, the final display is altered within the range [-3 ➔ +1].

The degree to which the user's view is changed is dependent on the awareness modifier value. In this implementation it is based on a percentage visibility of other users' view modifiers, see figure 11. The value of this visibility is linked to the overlap of nimbi and the view modification value for other users. This means that as the user overlap increases the percentage visibility will increase and this will be applied to the highest view modifier.

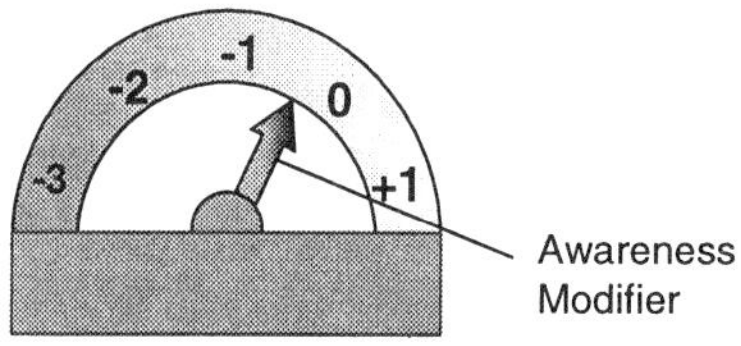

Figure 11. The selection effect of the awareness modifier

In the case of our example the electrical engineer has removed their view of the hydraulic system, but as the other engineer is aware of this system, it is reflected in the display of the electrician. Likewise the electrical system will appear in the display of the hydraulic engineer, see figure 12.

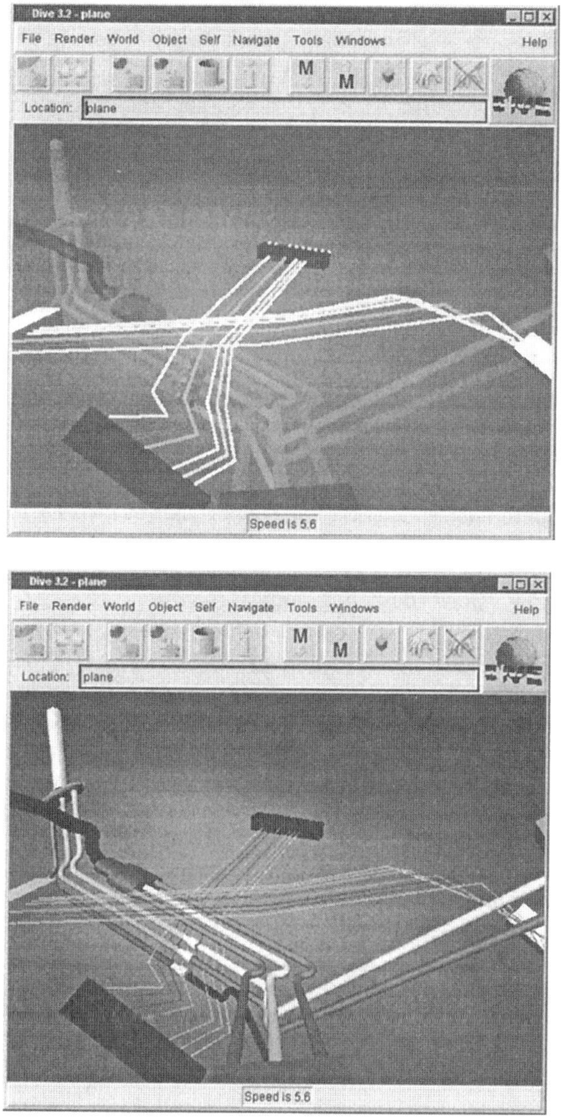

Figure 12. The common-subjective views of the electrician and hydraulics engineer.

Implementing Re-Coupling in non-3D environments

User interface re-coupling can be used to enhance shared user interfaces, other than those of 3D virtual environments. Many shared 2D user interface systems, such as SOL [17], Suite [3] and GroupKit [16] support individual user interface tailoring and a range of user interface coupling means. The notion of awareness based re-coupling can be introduced into these systems to both promote a common understanding throughout the potentially different interfaces, and aid in the promotion of awareness between the two users. Coupling in many shared 2D systems involves user interfaces with relaxed spatial constraints. That is, the location of objects on one user's display may be at another location on another's. Such user interface systems are problematic when telepointers are used to portray users' activities within the workspace [14]. A telepointer allows one user's mouse pointer to be replicated within the shared environment. As a user moves or points to an area within this environment, a representation of this user's pointer is replicated onto the other users' views. However, in a relaxed WYSIWIS scenario, when a user points at an object in their interface its coordinates may not be the same for all other users' interfaces, see figure 13. Hence for some users, the original user's telepointer may be gesturing at empty space. Thus the power of telepointing is lost, and produces meaningless gestures across the shared displays.

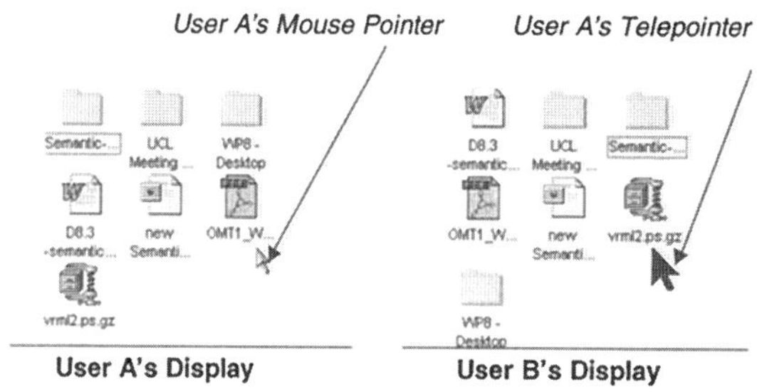

Figure 13. Problems of telepointers in relaxed WYSIWIS views

The re-coupling mechanism can be used to implement a non-spatial telepointing system. Rather than appear as a 2D pointer, the telepointer may be realised as an increased brightness (colours tend to white) in the objects that are visually important to other users. These objects may be gained by choosing those semantically close to the originating user's pointer by some consideration of awareness based on the window hierarchy [15]. For example, consider a simple control panel interface with three buttons. Each user's subjective view of the panel can be represented by the function:

Subjective_View (Tom, O)={ (open, 0), (*close'*, 0), (cancel, -1)}

Subjective_View (Jon, O)={ (open, 0), (close, 0), (cancel, 0)}

This states that Tom has the *open* button as normal, a different representation of the *close* button and an invisible version of the *cancel* button (in this case –1 represents invisible). Jon's display resembles the default presentation. Both subjective interfaces as depicted in figure 14.

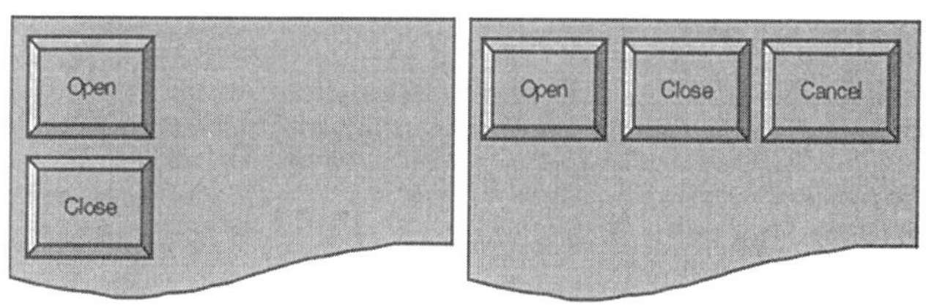

Figure 14. Two subjective interfaces.

The awareness map in this case considers these two users in close awareness given the common objects in both users' displays, and the proximity of their pointers to the closest object. For example, if two users are pointing near the open button in each of their displays (which may not be spatially linked in the two displays), their awareness values will rise.

Hence, as the user Tom becomes more aware of the user Jon, their user interfaces become more re-coupled. The re-coupling function ('display') defines the changes to each interface such that invisible objects appear, and objects that other users are aware of become brighter. Hence, in Tom and Jon's interfaces the open and close buttons appear brighter. The cancel button also appears a little brighter in Jon's display, but in Tom's display the (once) invisible button appears in a faded (dark or near background colour) fashion.

Figure 15. The re-coupled subjective interfaces.

CONCLUSIONS

This paper has considered the issues involved in users dynamically sharing interfaces that have been subject to some form of tailoring. We have argued the need to consider the provision of some form of intersubjectivity and suggested a means by which tailored user interfaces can be dynamically recoupled based on awareness. A general recoupling model was developed that builds upon our previous work in subjectivity and a general purpose model of awareness. This model was also implemented and demonstrated.

We believe that the model and framework is sufficiently general that it can be extended to consider different views of shared information. This allows us to develop tailored presentations of CSCW systems that can be recoupled in terms of different users' awareness of each other. The model leaves the particular views of the shared information and awareness mechanism used to drive the recoupling to the discretion of designers as these are very dependant on the particular semantics of the application.

ACKNOWLEDGEMENTS

Many thanks are due to colleagues at Lancaster University, especially Tom Rodden, and to Emmanuel Frécon from the Swedish Institute of Computer Science. This work was partly funded by the ACTS project COVEN (AC040).

REFERENCES

1. Benford, S. Fahlen, L. "A Spatial Model of Interaction in Large Virtual Environments". *Proc. ECSCW'93. Kluwer Academic Press.* Pp 109-124.
2. Bowers J. O'Brien J. Pycock J. "Practically Accomplishing Immersion: Co-operation in and for Virtual Environments". *Proc CSCW 96. ACM Press.* 380-389.
3. Dewan P. (1990). "A tour of the Suite User Interface Software". *Proc. of the 3rd ACM SIGGRAPH Symposium on User Interface Software and Technology.* October 1990. 57-65.
4. Carlsson C, Hagsand. (1993) "DIVE - Multi-User Virtual Reality System", *VRAIS '93, IEEE Virtual Reality Annual International Symposium.* 394-400
5. DIVE System. http://www.sics.se/dce/dive/dive.html
6. Division Ltd. (1993) "dVS Technical Overview, Version 2.0.4." (http://www.division.com)
7. Ellis C, Gibbs S, Rein G. "Groupware: Some Issues and Experiences". *CACM 34, 1 (1991),* 38-58.
8. Fussell S., KraussR "Coordination of knowledge in communication: Effects of speakers' assumptions about others' knowledge" *(1992) Journal of Personality and Social Psychology, 62,* 378-391.
9. Greenberg S. "Personisable Groupware: Accommodating individual roles and group differences". *Proceedings of ECSCW '91,. Kluwer Academic Press.* 17-31
10. Greenhalgh C., Benford S., "MASSIVE: a Collaborative Virtual Environment for Tele-conferencing", *ACM transactions on CHI, March 1995*
11. Gutwin, C. Greenberg, S. "Workspace Awareness for Groupware" *CHI'96 Conference Companion (Vancouver 1996),* 208-209.
12. Munson J, Dewan P. "A Flexible Object Merging Framework". Proceeding of *CSCW 94.. ACM Press.* pp231-242
13. Patterson, J. F., Hill, R. D., Rohall, S. L., Meeks, W. S. (1990). "Rendezvous: An architecture for synchronous multi-user applications", *Proceedings of CSCW '90,* October 7-10, Los Angeles, Ca., ACM Press, 1990. 317-328.
14. Rodham, K., Olsen, D., "Smart telepointers : maintaining telepointer consistency in the presence of user interface customization" *ACM Transactions on Graphics Vol.13, No. 3 (July 1994),* pp. 300-307.
15. Rodden T. "Populating the Application: A Model of Awareness for Cooperative Applications". *Proceedings of CSCW 96. Boston MA, USA. Nov.r 1996. ACM Press.* 87-96.
16. Roseman, M., Greenberg, S. "GroupKit. A Groupware toolkit for building Real-Time Conferencing Applications". *Proc CSCW '92. ACM Press.* 43-50
17. Smith, G., Rodden T. "SOL: A shared object toolkit for cooperative interfaces". *Int. J. Human-Computer Studies (1995) 42.*pp 207-234.
18. Smith G. "Cooperative Virtual Environments: lessons from 2D multi user interfaces". *Proc. Conf. Computer Supported Collaborative Work 1996 (CSCW '96). ACM Press.* Pages 390-398.
19. Smith G., Mariani J. "Using Subjective Views to Enhace 3D Applications". *ACM Symposium on Virtual Reality Software and Technology (VRST '97). ACM Press. Swiss federal Institute of Technology (EPFL), Lausanne, Switzerland. September 1997.* Pages 139-146.
20. Stefik M, Foster G, Bobrow D, Kahn K, Lanning S, Suchman L. "Beyond the chalkboard: Computer support for collaboration and problem solving in meetings". *CACM 30 (1), Jan 1987,* pp 32-47.

Flexible Meta Access-Control for Collaborative Applications

Prasun Dewan
Department of Computer Science
University of North Carolina
Chapel Hill NC 27599
+1 919 962 1823
dewan@cs.unc.edu

HongHai Shen
IBM Santa Teresa Lab
555 Bailey Ave
San Jose, CA 95141
+1 408 463 3843
honghai@us.ibm.com

ABSTRACT

Meta access-control, also called access administration, ensures that users do not make unauthorized access definitions. Such control in a collaborative system must support fine-grained protection, a flexible scheme for assigning access administrators, joint ownership of shared objects, multiple ownership semantics of varying complexity, delegation of access rights, and both shallow and deep revocation. It should also be easy to implement in a variety of applications, easy to use by users of varying sophistication with different protection needs, and offer a small set of features that can be incrementally learned. We have designed a new model to meet these requirements and implemented and used it in a generic, extensible collaborative system. We have also developed techniques for simulating a large variety of existing policies for meta access-control. In particular, we have developed an implementation-independent technique of indirect roles to support flexible delegation and revocation. In this paper, we identify requirements of meta access control, describe our model together with the techniques for using it, compare it with related work, give our experience with it, and evaluate how well it meets the requirements.

Keywords: Access control, collaboration, computer supported cooperative work, groupware, privacy, security,

INTRODUCTION

A protected system must answer two related questions: (a) *Basic Access-Control:* What kind of primitives should be provided to guard operations on the basic objects managed by the protected system? (b) *Meta Access-Control* or *Access Administration:* [1] How should the operation of specifying access-control itself be protected? Both issues have been addressed extensively in traditional protected systems such as operating systems and database systems. These systems offer access-control primitives such as access lists and capability lists to protect operations on the basic objects such as files and databases managed by them. They also support meta access-control primitives such as central administration and object ownership to control the specification of access definitions.

[1] We use the term "meta" instead of "administration" since it is more general and applies to computing concepts other than access control.

CSCW 98 Seattle Washington USA

Since these traditional models were developed, the area of collaborative applications has emerged. These applications allow users to collaborate, possibly in real-time, on some common task such as document editing, drawing, education, and software development. Like the traditional multiuser applications before them, these applications must offer both basic- and meta- access control. However, traditional protection mechanisms have not been designed to support these applications. While many aspects of these mechanisms can be reused for these applications, the support they offer is not flexible enough for this domain, for several reasons:

First, the set of shared operations offered by collaborative applications is much richer than that offered by traditional systems. These operations include not only the traditional read and write operations to manipulate shared application objects but also operations to couple distributed interaction objects of different users, and operations to change a large number of (potentially coupled) interactive attributes such as color, font, and indentation. The protection system, thus, must provide new ways to efficiently specify and store a large number of rights.

Second, the range of protected objects is much larger than in traditional systems. These objects include not only relational tables but also spreadsheet matrixes, hypertext documents, structured programs, and so on. The system is concerned, thus, not just with protection of a small number of large-grained tables but also possibly a large number of fine-grained objects. For instance, each comment in a program reviewed by a software inspection team can be owned by a different user and is thus a separate protection unit.

Third, there is great variability in the nature of specific collaborative applications. Some of these are traditional database-like applications allowing sharing only via the central application state, while others allow coupling among the state of different users. Among the latter group, some applications require users to couple all attributes of all interaction objects, others support coupling of only semantic data, and still others give users flexibility in what is coupled.

Finally, there is great variability in the kind of users who interact with a specific collaborative application. For instance, a chat program or a shared whiteboard may be used by a sophisticated military team to develop a highly secret plan or by a set of anonymous users to while away their idle time. The challenge for the protection system is to make users of the application aware of only those aspects of access control necessary to meet their security needs.

In our previous work [20, 6], we discussed how these challenges could be addressed for basic access control. In this paper, we do the same for meta access control. Both models have been implemented in the user-interface layer of the protected collaborative system, Suite. A more detailed discussion of some of these concepts can be found in the second author's thesis [19].

In the remainder of the paper, we shall refer to a user who can specify access rights as an *authorizer* or *administrator*. Moreover, we shall refer to rights to specify access-control as *meta rights* or *administration rights*.

Meta access control is more than merely the application of basic access-control schemes on access-control objects such as access lists, for at least two reasons. First, as we show in this paper, it is possible to automatically derive some meta access-control properties (such as implication relationships among meta rights) from basic access-control properties, thereby reducing the cost of specifying meta access-control. Second, and more important, meta access-control does not itself have a meta layer to protect it. If every layer of access control had a meta layer above it, then we would have infinite meta layers. To stop this recursion, meta access control must address several concepts such as ownership that do not arise in basic access control. Nonetheless, as will be seen in this paper, there is much to be gained by sharing concepts between basic and meta access control.

The rest of the paper is organized as follows. We first identify a set of meta access-control requirements for collaborative applications. Next we survey previous work on which our solution is based. We then motivate and describe our mechanisms. Next we evaluate them based on how well they meet the requirements. Finally, we present conclusions and directions for future work.

REQUIREMENTS

Based on previous work in traditional and collaborative systems, we have identified the following set of related meta access-control requirements:

- *Flexible authorizer assignment*: An authorizer assignment scheme determines which users are authorizered to give a meta right. The model should support the authorizer assignment scheme that is appropriate to the collaboration task. In particular, it should support as many of the existing authorizer policies as possible, including simple ones such as central administration and more complicated ones such as ownership. This requirement and the ones below are analogous to the goal in [20] and [3] of providing high-level support for a large range of policies for basic access-control. This principle must be extended to meta access-control.

- *Fine-grained meta rights*: As required by the least privilege principle [16], the model should allow authorizers to specify only those rights they need to perform their tasks. For instance, in a software inspection application, the chairman of a reviewing team may be in charge of distributing only the coupling rights, while a user interface specialist may be responsible for distributing only the formatting rights. In this scenario, these authorizers should not be able to specify all rights to the program being inspected - only those they need to perform their specialized task. Thus, the model should support fine-grained meta rights to allow their possessors to authorize arbitrary subsets of the rights in the system.

- *Joint ownership:* The model should be able to support the single-user ownership scheme supported in traditional systems. In addition, it should be able to support group ownership, for two related reasons. First, one user can create an object on behalf of a particular role. For instance, in a software development application, user `Bob` may create a function `common` on behalf of the `SoftwareDeveloper` role to allow every user who takes this role to be the owner of the function. Second, multiple users may contribute to the creation of elements of a complex object through collaboration. For example, two persons may work together to co-author a paper. If the paper is treated as a complex object, then it is meaningful that both persons jointly own the object. Thus, in the two cases above, multiple users may jointly own the object and each of them should have the privileges associated with ownership.

- *Flexible ownership semantics*: The exact meaning of ownership may vary depending on the application. In a classroom exam application, the teacher owns the exam in the sense that he creates it and is in charge of administrating all the rights the students should have. However, the "least privilege" principle requires that the teacher not have all the rights directly himself because the teacher is not taking the exam himself. On the other hand, in a software development application, the owner of a comment line should have all the rights associated with the line, including the privileges to transfer these rights.

- *Flexible delegation and revocation* The model should support the notion of access delegation [1] which allows the responsibility of an authorizer to be distributed among different parties. It should allow a user to delegate not only all of his privileges, but also a selected part of his privileges, and perhaps the authority to distribute these privileges further to others. Related to access delegation is the concept of revocation, which is an operation that undoes the effects of delegation [2], thereby providing a way to contain the spread of access rights. Two possible semantics of revocation can be defined: a) shallow revocation, which simply removes the previously granted right, and b) deep revocation, which recursively revokes rights from those to whom the grantee granted the right. The model should be able to support both of the above semantics.

To illustrate and motivate the above requirement in a collaborative application, consider again the example of a classroom examination. Assume that teacher, `Alice`, has delegated to her teaching assistant, `Cathy`, the right to distribute the coupling rights of the class and the right to further distribute these rights. We can envision two scenarios in which `Alice` may want to use both semantics of revocation to revoke the rights she delegated to `Cathy`. In the first scenario, `Alice` wants `Cathy` to help her only temporarily with the administration of the coupling rights. Once `Alice` has the time to handle the task herself, she would like to do it totally by herself to save her the effort required to coordinate with `Cathy`. In this situation, `Alice` requires the semantics of shallow revocation, since she would still want to keep what `Cathy` has done. In the second scenario, assume that `Alice` finds that some of the coupling administration by `Cathy` is not correct. In this situation, `Alice` needs the semantics of deep revocation, since she would like to undo all the administration work that `Cathy` has done.

- *Easy to use/High-level*: The model should be easy to use. A measure of ease-of-use is the amount of effort needed to to specify an access requirement. Therefore, the model should provide high-level constructs for specifying meta rights.
- *Easy to learn/Compact*: The model should be easy to learn. A measure of ease-of-learning is the number of features a user of the model must learn to specify the kind of access requirements he needs to make. Therefore, the model should be compact, that is, have few features. It should also be possible to learn the model incrementally.
- *Easy to implement/automation:* The model should be easy to implement - low-level implementation details should be automated for the programmer.

PREVIOUS WORK

Several previous works have identified techniques for meeting one or more of these requirements. These works include both traditional operating and database systems and recent collaborative systems that have addressed protection. In this section, we survey these works to lay the foundation for the subsequent section.

The *matrix model* provides a framework for describing protection systems. It was proposed by Lampson [13] and refined by Graham and Denning [10] for protection in operating systems. It defines three kinds of access-control entities: protected-objects - the entities to which access must be controlled; subjects - the entities whose access to objects must be controlled, and access rights - the operations subjects can perform on objects. The protection state of the system is represented by an access matrix A, with rows representing subjects, columns representing objects and A[s,o] denoting the access rights a subject s has over an object o. The access checking rule of the model states that a request by subject s for accessing object o is granted only if A[s,o] contains the requisite right.

To protect the access matrix itself, the model introduces the notion of *-rights. A *-right is defined for each regular access right and its holder has the privileges to grant the corresponding regular right. For example, the write *-right allows its holder to grant the write right to others. The model also supports the notion of ownership and defines rules allowing the owner of an object to grant both regular and *-rights to others.

Because the access matrix is usually sparse in practical situations, systems based on the matrix model seldom choose the matrix as the implementation data structure. Instead, for efficiency reasons, they usually use two common approaches to implement the basic matrix model: access control list (ACL) and capability list (C-list). The former stores the matrix by columns, i.e., associates each object with a list of (subject, right) pairs; while the latter stores the matrix by rows, i.e., associates each subject with a list of (object, rights) pairs, which are called capabilities. Several techniques, discussed below, have been devised to protect access-lists and capability-lists.

An example of an ACL-based system is Unix [14]. Like the access matrix model, it supports the notion of ownership, which can be changed by the superuser. Unix also allows a umask to be associated with any process. The value of the umask decides the default protection of a file when the file is created. In particular, it specifies the default right the owner has over a file. Unlike the access-matrix model, it does not support user-specified meta-rights. As a result, it supports coarse-grained meta access-control in that some users (the owner) can specify all rights to an object while others can specify none of them. Moreover, it does not support delegation in that users cannot give their rights to others. On the other hand, its meta access-control is simpler than that of the access-matrix model. It is perhaps for this reason that several systems including collaborative systems such as the Grove outline editor [8] and the Intermezzo collaboration infrastructure [7] have adopted its approach of associating a single authorizer with an object.

AFS [18] is a file system that provides an intermediate degree of flexibility. Like Unix, it associates a protected object (file/directory) with an access list and unique owner. However, unlike Unix, it also associates the object with a user-specified administration right. A user who has this right to an object can give all rights to the object (including the administration right) to other users by changing its access list. Moreover, a user who has the write right to a protected object can also change the access list of the object. Thus, AFS cannot prevent a writer of an object from administering it. As we saw earlier with the exam application, in some collaborative situations, this flexibility is important.

Guan et al [12] propose an extension to the classical matrix model that supports the notion of joint ownership. They provide a mechanism that allows multiple users to own an object. In addition, they associate conditions with objects that determine the access to them. A condition can be authority-based or quorum-based. An authority-based condition associates a user list (called control authorities) with an object, and specifies that before a right of an object is given out, the users appearing in the list must be present. A quorum-based condition, on the other hand, associates a number q with an object, and specifies that before a right is given out, at least q co-owners of the object must be present to meet the quorum q. This work also provides a set of primitives at the system level to support automation.

In all of the systems discussed so far, each object can have its own set of owners, and an owner of an object has all the rights to the object, including the right to grant these rights to other subjects. In an alternative approach, a central administrator is responsible for specifying the access definitions, but does not have direct rights himself. This approach is used by some database systems such as INGRES and collaborative systems such as RTCAL [17] that support an all-powerful conference chairman.

Yet another approach is to not support any distinguished owners/administrators. This approach is used in capability-based systems such as Hydra [22]. The designers of Hydra observed that "while ownership is a useful, perhaps even an important, concept for certain 'security' strategies, to include the concept at the most primitive level would be to exclude the construction of certain other classes of truly secure systems". As a result, Hydra and other capability-based systems discard the ownership concept and do not associate any ownership property with a protected object. Instead, these systems allow capabilities to protected objects to be passed to others. They associate a capability not only with rights to the referenced object but also a special "copy" right to the capability itself. Only a subject who possesses this meta right can pass a copy of the capability to others.

Capability-based systems have also supported revocation of delegated rights by supporting the concept of *indirect capabilities*. An indirect capability is a capability that references another capability. A request to perform an operation on an indirect capability results in a request to perform that operation on the referenced capability. Thus, from a holders point of view, it behaves like the referenced capability. However, the creator of such a capability can invalidate the capability by destroying the intermediate object.

System R [2] shows that it is also possible to support revocation in systems based on access-lists. It supports a complex revocation mechanism based on time stamps. Sikkel describes an access control scheme for the BSCW system [21]. It is based on our basic access-control model but was developed independently of our meta access-control model. Like our work, it uses the notion of user-groups to support delegation and revocation. However, it is not designed to meet all of the requirements listed above.

Finally, recent work by Bertino et al [3], which was done about the same time as this research, considers access administration in an inheritance-based system. The model distinguishes between strong authorizations, which cannot be overridden, and weak authorizations, which can be overridden. Giving an administration right to a user has the side-effect of also giving him a strong version of the corresponding regular right. Moreover, an administration right cannot be overridden to prevent situations in which a delegator's administration right has been overridden but not the administration rights of the delegates.

OUR APPROACH

We have developed a new model for supporting meta access-control designed to meet the requirements above. To meet the requirement of compactness, we have based it on the Suite model for basic access-control [20], thereby reusing several of the basic access-control primitives for meta access-control. Before we present the new primitives added for meta access-control, we briefly overview relevant aspects of basic access-control in Suite.

Basic Access-Control

Access-control in Suite is based on the access matrix model. Each application is associated with an access matrix, which protects the objects defined by the application. Suite predefines a large variety of rights, which include traditional semantic rights such as `ReadR` and `WriteR`; formatting rights such as `ColorR` and `FontR` (rights to change the color and font, respectively, of an object); and coupling rights such as `TransmitR` and `ListenR` (rights to send and receive, respectively, changes from other users).

Suite provides several forms of grouping and inference, in the three access-matrix dimensions of objects, subjects, and rights. Objects are grouped according to their structure (IS-PART-OF) and type (IS-A) relationships, and an access specification made for an object group is inherited by its members. A special object group, called the generic group (corresponding to class Object in Smalltalk and Java), unites all the objects of an application. Similarly, subjects are grouped into hierarchical user groups, also called roles, [2] and all rights associated with a role are inherited by its members. Finally, rights are grouped into logical categories such as

[2] In this paper, we use the term role and user group interchangeably. A user group in some systems such as [3] is simply a role from which a user cannot remove himself.

DataR (semantic rights), FormatR (formatting rights), CoupleR (coupling rights), and AllR (all rights), and an access specification made for a right group is inherited by all rights included in the right group. Besides this "include" relation, another relation, the "imply" relation [9], is defined among rights, which allows a powerful right such as WriteR to imply a weaker right such as InsertR. These grouping/inference mechanisms allow users to make high-level access specifications. For instance, a user can give all coupling rights to all section titles to all authors by simply giving the Author role the CouplingR right-group to the type ASectionTitle.

Suite provides several mechanisms/rules for resolving multiple inheritance allowed by the model. For instance, it allows users/applications to specify if type or structural inheritance should be given preference in the object dimension. Finally, it protects the operations for manipulating the groups and inference rules. For instance, it defines the right, AddMemberRoleR, which protects the operation to add a member to a role.

Thus, Suite supports an extended form of the access matrix. We now discuss the meta access-control primitives we have added to protect this access matrix.

Meta Rights

To meet the requirement of fine-grained meta-rights, like the access control model, we support fine-grained *-rights for the protection of access matrix entries. For each individual right R, we define an R* right that protects the value of R. A *-right is a first class right in that it can be inherited along all three dimensions. In particular it can be included in right groups and associated with imply relationships. Unlike the case in [3], a *-right does not imply the corresponding regular right so that we can support applications such as the classroom exam application mentioned earlier.

The meta and regular rights are linked in Suite in that the include and imply relationships among *-rights are automatically derived from the corresponding relationships among the regular rights. Observe that the semantic relationships among conventional non-* rights also exist among their corresponding *-rights. For the *imply* relationship, the capability to grant others the right to do a strong operation such as write means the capability to grant others the right to do a weak operation such as read. Therefore, from the "WriteR implies InsertR" relationship, we can draw a new relationship "WriteR* implies InsertR*". For the *include* relationship, we have grouped the *-rights into a tree hierarchy similar to the non-*-rights. Therefore the *include* relationship of non-*-rights is mapped into corresponding *-rights. For example, from "CoupleR includes TransmitR and ListenR", we can define "CoupleR* includes TransmitR* and ListenR*", and so on. We represent the above observation as the following two rules:

***-Right Inheritance Rule:** *The include relationships among non-*-rights are mapped to the *-rights, i.e.,* $include(R1, R2) \rightarrow include(R1*, R2*)$ *where R1 and R2 are non-*-rights.*

***-Right Implication Rule:** *The imply relationships among non-*-rights are mapped to the *-rights, i.e.,* $imply(R1, R2) \rightarrow imply(R1*, R2*)$ *where R1 and R2 are non-*-rights.*

Assigning Authorizers

The above discussion raises the question of "who should possess the *-rights?" This is called the authorizer problem. Although it is a policy issue specific to individual applications, we would like to provide system-level mechanisms to support these policies to meet the requirement of automation.

As surveyed in the previous section, there are currently several approaches to defining the authorizer in conventional systems. One approach is to use the concept of ownership. The creator of an object becomes its owner and has all the rights to the object, including the right to grant these rights to other subjects. This is the approach defined by the classical matrix model. In another approach, a central administrator is responsible for specifying the access definitions, but does not have direct rights himself. To meet the requirement of authorizer flexibility, we would like to provide mechanisms that are able to support all existing authorizer policies. One possible approach is to follow Hydra's design philosophy. That is, we can discard the concept of ownership and let individual applications decide who the authorizers are. This approach, though flexible, does not provide any built-in mechanisms to assist application developers in constructing their protection subsystems.

Our solution to the authorizer problem is to support the concept of ownership, while at the same time providing mechanisms that allow applications to tailor their needs individually. This is in the spirit of the classical matrix model. However, as will be described in more detail below, the two works are different in that we support flexible definition of ownership semantics, and support group ownership and dynamic change of ownership.

Semantics of Ownership

To define the exact semantics of ownership, we observe that ownership of an object usually denotes a set of special privileges. Therefore, instead of treating ownership as a concept totally alienated from other elements of the model, we treat it as a special right. The exact meaning of the right is defined by a set of "imply" relationships reconfigurable by individual applications. We use the following rule to define the semantics of ownership:

Ownership Semantic Rule: *Ownership is a special right defined by associating a set of imply relationships with the right.*

As will be discussed shortly, this rule combined with other ownership rules will enable us to simulate existing authorizer schemes.

Owner Specification

We have devised a set of rules to define owners of protected objects. We use the following rule to define the initial owner of an active object:

Ownership Initialization Rule: *A subject who starts an application owns all the initial objects defined within the application unless they have predefined owners. A subject who dynamically creates a new object owns that object.*

The above rule associates a single owner with a object since an operation such as insert that creates a new object dynamically is an atomic operation executed by a single user. To meet the requirements of joint-ownership, we associate an owner list with each object, whose contents can be changed dynamically. We use the following rule to define the semantics of an owner list:

Multiple Ownership Rule: *An initial owner of an object can add roles into or remove roles from its owner list. The owners of an object are users who take a role in the owner list.*

The above rule specifies that an initial owner, defined by the initialization rule, can dynamically change the owner list. In particular, the initial owner can add more subjects into the owner list and therefore allow joint-ownership by multiple users. For example, user `Bob` can create a function `common` on behalf of the `SoftwareDeveloper` group. After creating the function and becoming the initial owner, he can add `SoftwareDeveloper` to the owner list associated with the function `common`. As a result, user `John` also becomes an owner due to his membership in the `SoftwareDeveloper` group.

Because the owner list introduced above is defined over a shared object, it is a shared object itself and therefore should be a protected object according to the total mediation principle [16]. Therefore, we introduce a new right, called `OlistR`, which is used to protect the owner list. A subject is allowed to change an owner list only if it possesses `OlistR` to the object. In addition, we define a corresponding right, `OlistR*`. A subject is allowed to give `OlistR` only if it possesses `OlistR*`.

Allowing users to dynamically change ownership aggravates the specification problem. To illustrate, suppose `Bob` owns the function `Getvalue`, and every line of it. Later, `Bob` would like to add `John` as a co-owner of the function. If every line of the function is associated with an owner list consisting of `Bob`, it would be tedious and time-consuming for `Bob` to add `John` to all these owner lists one by one. In such cases, we observe that although the ownership initialization rule specifies that the creator of a object should own the object, it is unnecessary to actually store the owner into the owner list of the object if the creator also owns the object's parent. Instead, inheritance mechanisms can be used to infer the ownership of the child from its parent. For the above scenario, the owner lists of all lines created by `Bob` will be set to empty, and their owner lists, being empty, will be inherited from their structure parent, i.e., the function `Getvalue`. This approach makes it easy to change ownership. For instance, it would only be necessary for `Bob` to change the owner list associated with the function `Getvalue`. Like other forms of inheritance, it also saves space by eliminating information redundancy. It is possible that the creator of a parent may also create many of its children, in which case the saving of space for the owner lists of the children could be substantial.

The above discussion shows the usefulness of supporting inheritance of ownership list from structure parents. To ease the specification task, it is also useful to support inheritance from types. For instance, we can define the owner list associated with the type `Comment` of a program to contain only the role `Commenter`.

Because an object can belong to multiple object groups, conflicts can arise from inheriting an owner list from multiple object groups. To resolve the conflict, we adopt the existing approach in Suite to multiple inheritance because of its generality and flexibility. That is, we use the notion of inheritance directives ([4]) to resolve the conflicts. We have chosen `structure-first` as the default inheritance directive for the owner list because we expect this default setting to be frequently used by applications.

To summarize, we define the following ownership inheritance rule:

Ownership Inheritance Rule: *The owner list of an object o, if unspecified, is inherited from the object groups containing o that are chosen by the inheritance directive. In case of conflicts, the ownership list defined in the first object group chosen by the inheritance directive is used. By default, inheritance starts from structure object groups.*

Unlike [3], we allow overriding of inherited administration privileges, which in our system consist of owner lists and *-rights. The main reason is that, as mentioned before, the number of rights and objects in a collaborative system can be very large. For instance, Suite offers more than fifty predefined rights because of the large number of user-commands supported by the system, and these rights apply to each leaf-level data structure in a shared object. Each object is associated with an owner list and each right on the object is associated with a *-right. Overriding of owner lists and *-rights allows users to make exception-based specifications. For instance, it makes it easy to specify that Bob owns all procedures in a program except the one for which Mark is responsible. In the absence of this feature, we would have to explicitly give Bob ownership of all but one procedure in the program. Unlike [3], Suite can create potential "anomalies" wherein a delegator does not have the administration privileges that the delegates have. We believe these situations should be allowed to support the least privilege principle and our techniques discussed below should be used when controlled delegation is necessary.

Default Ownership Semantics

By default, we give users all rights to the objects they own:

Default Ownership Semantics: *By default, ownership implies OlistR, OlistR*, AllR, and AllR*.*

As we see below, we can support a variety of less permissive ownership policies by changing/overriding these semantics.

EVALUATION

In this section, we discuss how well the meta access-control model in Suite, together with the basic access-control model in Suite, satisfies the requirements we identified earlier.

Supporting Existing Authorizer Policies

The set of ownership rules defined above provides a flexible way to support existing authorizer policies. We discuss below how these policies can be simulated.

To simulate the conventional usage of ownership supported in Unix, we define "ownership implies DataR*." To simulate the INGRES- and RTCAL- like centralized administration approach, the application can grant the administrator role a positive `AllR*` over the generic group. In this way, the central administrator is responsible for specifying all the *-rights over all the objects.

To simulate the classical matrix definition of ownership, we define "ownership implies `AllR*`".

To simulate the other extreme of the authorizer solution, i.e., the Hydra approach, we define no imply relationship for the ownership right. In this way, even though an owner is defined for each object, there are no semantics associated with ownership and it entitles him no more and no less rights as the owner. This is useful in highly cooperative collaborations.

Supporting group ownership and letting the owner of an object change the owner list arbitrarily could be risky if an owner changes the owner list wantonly without considering its security consequences. Therefore, some applications may not want this feature. This approach, used in Unix, can be realized in our model by not defining our default implication, "ownership implies OlistR and OlistR*," thereby prohibiting the owner from changing the owner list or granting the right to do the operation.

Delegation and Revocation

We have described above an approach of using flexible ownership for access administration. It allows owners of an object to act as authorizers and dynamically change access definitions depending on ownership semantics. We now discuss how owners can distribute the above privileges to others through delegation and revocation. Delegation [1] is the ability of a user to distribute his privileges, including both *-rights and regular rights, to others. Related to access delegation is the concept of revocation, which is an operation that undoes the effects of delegation. As mentioned before, two possible semantics of revocation can be supported, namely shallow revocation and deep revocation:

- *Shallow Revocation:*

  If X grants r* or r to Y, then shallow revocation just removes r* or r from Y. If Y has granted r* or r to Y1, Y1 to Y2, ..., and so on, then the r* and r rights of Y1, Y2, ... are not affected. This semantics is simple to understand, easy to implement, and is used by most existing systems.

- *Deep Revocation:*

  Deep revocation, on the other hand, tries to completely undo the effects of right delegation by revoking the r and r* rights of Y1, Y2, ... in the above case. That is, a system supporting it must recursively revoke authorization from those to whom the grantee granted the right. It has been defined by Griffiths and Wade [11] formally as follows: Let (G1, G2, ..., Gi-1, Gi, Gi+1, ..., Gn) be the sequence of grants of a specific privilege on a given object by any user, where each Gj is the grant of a single privilege. If $i < j$, then Gi occurred earlier than Gj. If Ri denotes the revocation of Gi, then the authorization state of the system after (G1, G2, ..., Gi-1, Gi, Gi+1, ..., Gn, Ri) should be identical to (G1, G2, ..., Gi-1, Gi+1, ..., Gn).

We present below a series of increasingly complex approaches to supporting different kinds of delegation and revocation semantics so that users can pick the one that most directly meet their needs.

Total Delegation and Shallow Revocation: Taking and Leaving Roles

In the simplest case, a user A delegates all of his rights to another user B. To realize the above semantics in our model, we define a single-member role for each user. For every user X, its associated role(X) bears the same id as the user name, and by default has a member list containing only the user itself, that is, a user takes his own role. We further interpret the user id in the access matrix as its role id. To realize delegation, user A can add user B to the member list of Role(A), which initially contains only A itself. In this way, B will be able to receive A's rights through inheritance. Shallow revocation is the reverse process of removing B from the role.

*Partial Delegation and Shallow Revocation: Manipulating *-Rights of Direct Roles*

The above form of delegation and revocation, though simple, is not flexible. It does not allow users to grant and revoke selected rights. If what is desired is partial delegation and shallow revocation, then *-rights can be used. A user can distribute his *-rights to others by changing the associated access lists. To revoke one or more of these rights, he can just remove the corresponding *-right or regular right from the revokee, or alternatively, grant a negative *-right or regular right to the revokee. In comparison to the previous approach, this requires a separate action for each right group that is to be granted/ revoked - which is the cost of the additional flexibility afforded. In comparison to the next approach, it does not provide a general technique for recursively revoking rights given by the revokee.

Partial Delegation and Flexible Revocation: Indirect Roles

The implementation for supporting the total revocation semantics is non-trivial. As mentioned earlier, capability-based systems have used the concept of indirect capabilities to realize these semantics. ACL-based protection systems usually do not support total revocation because of the complexity and expense of the algorithm involved. The only exception known to us is System R, which records each delegation with time-stamps and uses these stamps to realize the revocation. Although the above two approaches all support deep revocation semantics, they are implementation dependent, that is, they depend on the particular data structures used to implement the access matrix. We describe below an approach to support the deep revocation semantics that is independent of the implementation of the access matrix and can be used by an ACL-based or capability-based system that supports protected hierarchical roles. More important, it does not require special primitives in the model designed solely for supporting deep revocation. It requires users to use the notion of indirect roles to delegate rights rather than grant the rights directly.

Here is a brief description of the algorithm. Suppose X wants to give Y0 the R right on object Obj, and allow Y0 to distribute the right to other subjects, say Y1, Y2, ...Yn. Instead of giving Y0 the R and R* right directly, X first creates a role S, and grants S a positive R right to Obj. To give Y0 the R right, X can add Y0 to the member list of S, thereby allowing Y0 to inherit the R right from S. To grant Y0 the right to distribute the R right, X can give Y0 the right, `AddMemberRoleR`, to S, thereby allowing Y0 to add into S more members who can inherit the R right from S. Furthermore, if X wants to allow Y0 to distribute the right to distribute the R right, X can grant Y0 the right, `AddMemberRoleR*`, to S, so that Y0 can grant the `AddMemberRoleR` to other subjects.

Now, X can realize complete revocation by simply removing the R right from S. Because the R rights of Y0, Y1, Y2, ..., Yn all depend on the access rights of role S, the above operation deprives Y1, ..., Yn's R rights too. In addition, it is also easy to realize shallow revocation by simply removing Y0 from the member list of S, and its `AddMemberRoleR` and `AddMemberRoleR*` rights of S. In this way, Y0's R right will be revoked, but Y1, Y2, ..., Yn's rights will not be affected.

To illustrate, let us return to the classroom examination scenario introduced in the requirements section. We mentioned that the teacher `Alice` delegates her coupling rights to teaching assistant `Cathy`, and later wants to revoke the delegation according to different revocation semantics depending on two possible scenarios. Instead of giving `Cathy` the `CouplingR` and `CouplingR*` directly, `Alice` can use the following process to realize the delegation of coupling rights. First, she creates a role `TrustedByAlice` and grants `TrustedByAlice` a positive coupling right. To give `Cathy` the coupling right, she adds `Cathy` to the member list of `TrustedByAlice`, thereby allowing her to inherit the positive coupling right. Furthermore, to give `Cathy` the right to transfer the coupling right to other parties, `Alice` can grant `Cathy` the right to add members into the role `TrustedByAlice`. Consequently, `Cathy` can further grant the coupling right to another user, `Bob`, by adding `Bob` to the member list of `TrustedByAlice`. To realize the deep revocation semantics, `Alice` can simply deny `TrustedByAlice` the positive coupling right she previously issued, thereby denying both `Cathy` and `Bob`'s coupling rights. On the other hand, `Alice` can realize the shallow revocation semantics by simply removing `Cathy` from the `TrustedByAlice` member list. We observe that although it is not necessary to realize our model using a capability list approach, the above indirect role approach is conceptually similar to the indirect capability approach in that they both use one level of indirection to grant a privilege rather than grant the privilege directly. Therefore, in both approaches, it is easy to realize deep revocation by simply removing the link of indirection,

In our current implementation of the revocation mechanism, an authorizer has to follow the above process manually in order to realize total revocation. It is possible to automate the above process to a single operation so that authorizers can have a simple and easy to use interface.

Other Requirements

We have discussed above how well our model meets the requirements of flexible authorizer, flexible ownership semantics, and flexible revocation/delegation. The requirements of fine-grained meta rights and joint ownership are directly met by fine-grained *-rights and ownership lists, respectively. Inheritance of ownership lists and the include and imply relationships among the meta rights support high-level specification. Given the number and complexity of requirements it meets, we believe the model is compact, introducing only three additional features for supporting meta access-control: meta rights, owner lists, and the owership rules. It is the composition of these features with basic access-control concepts such as roles and inheritance/imply rules that makes the model powerful. Moreover, the various defaults defined by the system allow these primitives to be learned incrementally. Finally, the model supports automation in that these primitives are supported automatically by the system.

By meeting these requirements, we have created a truly flexible system for supporting meta access-control in collaborative applications, which is confirmed by our preliminary experience with Suite.

Experience

We have used Suite to to create a variety of protected collaborative applications. We briefly describe these applications and how we met their meta access-control requirements.

We have developed a GROVE-like outline editor, which allows multiple users to edit outline items synchronously. The protected objects of the application are fine-grained outline items and their children. Each outline item is associated with an access control list. The owner of an item can change its access list, and decides whether the item is accessible to the owner only, to an enumerated set of users, or to all users. By default, the owner of an outline item has all rights to it while others have only the read right. In addition, the access definition of any child of an outline item is by default inherited from its structure parent. Since these meta-access needs are supported in our model by default, we made no meta-access specification in this application.

Another application we developed is a software inspection tool. The meta-access control policy used here is different. The creator of an object becomes its owner and has the data rights (read, insert, delete, and modify) over the object, and the rights to further transfer these rights. Multiple ownership is supported so that a group of users can jointly-own portions of a program. These two requirements are supported by replacing the default ownership implications with "ownership implies `DataR`, `DataR*`, `OlistR` and `OlistR*`." The chairman can change the name of the program to be inspected or give others the right to do so. Others can only read it. This is supported by giving the chairman the owner right of the program name, and others the `ReadR` right. Only the formatter can change the color, font, or title of the data in the program. Other participants can do so only under the permission of the formatter. This is supported by giving the formatter role the positive `FormatR` and `FormatR*` rights.

We have developed a Suite application to simulate the AFS protection policy. The `'a'` right of AFS is equivalent to the `AllR*` right of our model. The 'w' right is not equivalent to the `WriteR` right of our model because according to its semantics in AFS, it is used for both the `WriteR` and `AllR*` rights. Therefore, we define a new 'w' right and add a new *include* relationship: "w includes `WriteR` and `AllR*`."

We also changed the software development tool described here to support a programming contest application. In this application, participants form several teams to compete each other. The competition has two stages. In the first stage, each team is required to work out its solution to the contest problem without any collaboration outside of the team. In the second stage, after all the teams have submitted their programs, all the participants collaborate together to inspect and evaluate the solution of each team, adding comments if necessary.

In the first stage, the proctor is in charge of access administration, but has no modification rights to the programs being written. This is supported by giving the proctor role positive `ReadR` and `AllR*` rights over the generic group, and by removing the `AllR` and `AllR*` rights from the owners. In the second stage, after all the teams have submitted their solutions, a participant who inserts a comment line becomes its owner and is responsible for specifying the access definitions of the comment line. This is supported by re-enabling the rule "ownership implies `AllR` and `AllR*`."

Suite has been used to create other protected collaborative applications including a two-person talk, a mail tool, a Unix emulator, and a forensics library allowing pathologists to collaboratively solve cases [5]. All of these are prototype applications but they have given us useful insights regarding the flexibility, automation, and ease of use of the system. As illustrated by the discussion above, we have been able to meet the (basic and meta) access control requirements of these applications with very little effort. The number of access-control specifications made in these applications ranged from 1 to 27 lines. The exact code of some of these applications is given in [19].

However, we have found that it is easy to make mistakes when multiple access specifications are inherited by an object. The problem would have been reduced had we developed a graphical tool of the form discussed in [3] for viewing the current set of access specifications, discovering conflicts among them, and identifying paths along which a specification may be inherited. In most of our examples, we restricted ourselves to using a single inheritance-path.

Another usability criterion is the performance of the system. Our initial experiments, described in [19], show that access-control adds less than 6 milliseconds overhead, even when multi-dimensional inheritance is used. This overhead is not perceptible to the users and allows real-time collaboration.

CONCLUSIONS AND FUTURE WORK

This paper makes three main contributions. First, it identifies and motivates several meta access-control requirements that a protected collaborative system must meet. Second, it introduces several new meta access-control primitives, which include automatically-derived inheritance and imply relationships among fine-grained meta rights, joint ownership semantics defined by application-specified implications, and structural and type inheritance of user-overridable ownership lists. Finally, it shows how the model can be used to simulate a large variety of policies for meta access-control. In particular, it offers the implementation-independent technique of indirect roles to support flexible delegation and revocation. While our meta-access control concepts have been developed in the context of Suite text-editing operations, they are, in fact, independent of the exact operations to be protected, and thus apply to systems such as GroupKit [15] that support graphical user-interfaces. [3]

This work is only a first-step in flexible meta access-control for protected collaborative systems. While we know of no other system that offers all of the administration policies supported by our model, it does not directly support all existing policies. It does not automatically support the joint ownership semantics of Guan et al [12], which would require extending it with the authority- and quorum- based conditions of their model. These concepts can be implemented manually in Suite through the abstraction of programmer-defined access callbacks [19]. It also does not support the strong authorizations of [3], which would require adding a new inher-

[3]The same cannot be said for some of the Suite mechanisms for basic-access control such as the regular access rights, which are highly dependent on the Suite editing model.

itance directive that disallows overriding of inherited specifications. Further work is necessary to support missing existing policies and to identify and support additional useful policies.

So far these primitives have been used only by the authors of the paper for developing research applications. As more protected collaborative systems are developed and used, more extensive user studies need to be performed to evaluate if the model is truly flexible and easy to use and learn. This paper provides a basis for building such systems.

ACKNOWLEDGMENTS

We would like to thank the reviewers, whose comments improved the presentation of the paper. This research was supported in part by IBM, a Purdue Research Foundation Fellowship, by National Science Foundation Grants IRI-9408708, IRI-9508514, IRI-9627619, and CDA-9624662, and by DARPA/ONR grant N 66001-96-C-8507.

REFERENCES

1 M. Abadi, M. Burrows, and B. Lampson. A calculus for access control in distributed systems. *ACM Transactions on Programming Languages and Systems*, 15(4):706–734, Sept. 1993.

2 M. M. Astrahan. System R: relational approach to database management. *ACM TODS*, 1(2):97–137, June 1976.

3 E. Bertino, S. Jajodia, and P. Samarati. Supporting multiple access control policies in database systems. In *Proc. of IEEE Symposium on Security and Privacy*, May 1996.

4 P. Dewan. An inheritance model for supporting flexible displays of data structures. *Software – Practice and Experience*, 21(7):719–738, July 1991.

5 P. Dewan, K. Jeffay, F. D. Smith, J. B. Smith, D. Stotts, and W. Oliver. Early prototypes of the repository for patterned injury data. In *Proc. of Digital Libraries '95*, pages 123–130, June 1995.

6 P. Dewan and H. Shen. Access control for multiuser interfaces. *ACM Transactions on Computer Human Interaction*, 5(1):34–62, Mar. 1998.

7 K. Edwards. *Coordination Infrastructure in Collaborative Systems*. PhD thesis, Department of Computer Science, Georgia Tech. University, Atlanta, GA, Nov. 1995.

8 C. A. Ellis, S. J. Gibbs, and G. L. Rein. Design and use of a group editor. In *Proc. of IFIP WG 2.7 Working Conf. on Engineering for Human-Computer Interaction*, pages 13–28, 1989.

9 E. B. Fernandez, R. C. Summers, and T. Lang. Definition and evaluation of access rules in data management systems. In *Proc. of 1st International Conf. on VLDB*, pages 268–285, 1975.

10 G. Graham and P. Denning. Protection – principles and practice. *Proc. Spring Jt. Computer Conf.*, 40:417–429, 1972.

11 P. P. Griffiths and B. W. Wade. An authorization mechanism for a relational database system. *ACM TODS*, 1(3):242–255, Sept. 1976.

12 S.-U. Guan, H. Abdel-Wahab, and P. Calingaert. Jointly-owned objects for collaboration: Operating-system support and protection model. *Journal of Systems Software*, 16:85–95, 1991.

13 B. Lampson. Protection. In *Proc. 5th Princeton Symp. of Info. Sci. and Syst.*, pages 437–443. Reprinted in ACM Oper. Syst. Rev., Vol 8(1) pp. 18–24 (Jan. 1974), 1971.

14 D. M. Ritchie and K. Thompson. The Unix time-sharing system. *Communications of the ACM*, 17(7):365–375, July 1974.

15 M. Roseman and S. Greenberg. Building real-time groupware with GroupKit, a groupware toolkit. *ACM Transactions on Computer Human Interaction*, 3(1):66–106, 1996.

16 J. Saltzer. Protection and the control of information sharing in multics. *Communications of the ACM*, 17(7):388–402, July 1974.

17 S. Sarin and I. Greif. Computer-based real-time conferencing systems. *IEEE Computer*, 18(10):33–49, October 1985.

18 M. Satyanarayanan. Scalable, secure, and highly available distributed file access. *IEEE Computer*, 23(5):9–22, May 1990.

19 H. Shen. *Access Control for Collaborative Environments*. PhD thesis, Department of Computer Science, Purdue University, W. Lafayette, IN, Aug. 1994.

20 H. Shen and P. Dewan. Access control for collaborative systems. In *Proc. of ACM Conf. on CSCW*, pages 51–58, Nov. 1992.

21 K. Sikkel. A group-based authorization model for cooperative systems. In *Proc. of ECSCW'97*, pages 345–360, Sept. 1997.

22 W. Wulf, E. Cohen, W. Corwin, A. Jones, R. Levin, C. Pierson, and F. Pollack. HYDRA: The kernel of a multiprocessor operating system. *Communications of the ACM*, 17(6):337–345, July 1974.

The dynamics of mass interaction

Steve Whittaker, Loren Terveen, Will Hill, Lynn Cherny
ATT Labs-Research
180 Park Ave
Florham Park, NJ 07932 USA
+1 973 360 8339
{stevew,terveen,willhill,cherny}@research.att.com

ABSTRACT

Usenet may be regarded as the world's largest conversational application, with over 17,000 newsgroups and 3 million users. Despite its ubiquity and popularity, however, we know little about the nature of the interactions it supports. This empirical paper investigates *mass interaction* in Usenet. We analyse over 2.15 million messages from 659,450 posters, collected from 500 newsgroups over 6 months. We first characterise mass interaction, presenting basic data about demographics, conversational strategies and interactivity. Using predictions from the common ground [3] model of interaction, we next conduct causal modelling to determine relations between *demographics, conversational strategies* and *interactivity*. We find evidence for moderate conversational threading, but large participation inequalities in Usenet, with a small minority of participants posting a large proportion of messages. Contrary to the common ground model and "Netiquette" guidelines [8,10] we also find that "cross-posting" to external newsgroups is highly frequent. Our predictions about the effects of demographics on conversational strategy were largely confirmed, but we found disconfirming evidence about the relations between conversational strategy and interactivity. Contrary to our expectations, both cross-posting and short messages promote interactivity. We conclude that in order to explain *mass interaction,* the common ground model must be modified to incorporate notions of weak ties [5,6] and communication overload [11,18].

Keywords

Mass interaction, Usenet, conversation, newsgroups, common ground, moderation, FAQS, netiquette, empirical.

INTRODUCTION

Usenet may be regarded as the world's largest and fastest growing conversational application. In 1988 there were fewer than 500 newsgroups. Current estimates vary, but at the time of our data collection in Dec. 1996, there were over 17,000 newsgroups, with approximately 3 million users worldwide [7]. This growth has been achieved without any centralised organisation or governing body [9]. The ubiquity of Usenet and the fact that it supports conversations between hundreds or even thousands of participants, provides the opportunity to study what we term *mass interaction.* However, we currently lack basic data about Usenet interactions. The current paper analyses over 2.15 million messages produced by 659,450 people in 500 representative newsgroups collected over 6 months. We provide descriptive data about newsgroup demographics, communication strategies and interactivity. We then derive predictions from the *common ground* model of communication to test predictions about how these parameters interact.

Previous research on Usenet has tended to carry out small scale qualitative studies of specific newsgroups, their culture and their conversation [1,17]. While these studies have drawn attention to important phenomena, their specific focus means they cannot address general questions that are central to mass interaction such as the levels of communication between different newsgroups. They also cannot easily examine the effects on interaction of different demographic variables or communication strategies, in order to test specific communication models.

The current study attempts to redress the balance. We first present basic information from the 500 newsgroups about mass interaction addressing the following questions. What are the *demographics* of a typical newsgroup: how many people contribute and how often do they do so? Is participation roughly equal or are groups dominated by a few verbose individuals? A second set of questions concern *conversational strategies*. Do participants restrict their interactions to the current newsgroup or do they broadcast them widely to multiple groups (a phenomenon known as cross-posting)? How long is a typical message? Do most newsgroups have FAQs ("lists of frequently asked questions") and how often do they post them? Finally we can ask questions about *interactivity*: how deep is a typical conversational thread, and how often are attempts to initiate conversation successful?

CSCW 98 Seattle Washington USA
Copyright ACM 1998 1-58113-009-0/98/11...$5.00

We also tested how well the *common ground* communication theory [3] explains mass interaction. The scale of mass interaction, and the huge numbers of messages and participants, gives rise to two novel communication problems. The first of these concern how participants establish common ground in mass interaction. Common ground is a key principle of face-to-face conversation, and refers to the fact that participants must establish a degree of mutual knowledge for their conversational contributions to be understood [3]. Face-to-face conversations generally take place between dyads or small groups, however. So how can common ground be established when there is a huge set of conversational participants with potentially diverse perspectives? There are also issues concerning the stability of the newsgroup population. In some newsgroups, there is a core set of participants who repeatedly converse, allowing participants to become familiar with one another. This familiarity supports common ground, but how do conversations fare in newsgroups where the participants are constantly changing? Some newsgroups employ a strategy of moderation to address the problem of common ground. In a moderated group, all interactions are filtered by a small set of moderators who are knowledgeable about the goals and history of the newsgroup. Only messages that are relevant to the newsgroup's goals are allowed to appear. Our first set of hypotheses concern how the three *demographic* factors of newsgroup *size*, the *familiarity* of participants, and the effects of *moderation* affect common ground. We also investigate how these same factors affect *interactivity*. One measure of conversational interactivity is the extent to which a given conversational contribution depends on prior context [3,14]. By this definition, deeply threaded conversations are indicators of interactivity. We therefore looked at how demographic factors affect threading.

The second major communication problem arises directly from the difficulty of establishing common ground. Lack of common ground may mean that participants are inundated with postings that are redundant or irrelevant. For example, new participants who are ignorant of a newsgroup's goals or conversational history, may post questions that have been discussed before, or are largely irrelevant to the group's interests. We therefore investigated a second set of factors concerning people's *conversational strategies* in addressing redundancy and irrelevance. We tested the effects of three conversational strategies on interactivity: (a) FAQ production; (b) long messages; (c) low levels of cross-posting. These strategies are all derived from the notion of common ground. FAQs exemplify common ground by summarising prior discussions and providing information about newsgroup culture; cross-posting can be seen as a failure of common ground, representing participants' need to go outside the newsgroup for conversation; long messages can be taken as evidence for substantive discussions and hence established common ground. The common ground model would therefore predict that FAQ production, decreased cross-posting and greater message length should all increase interactivity. A second set of partially overlapping predictions about the effects of conversational strategy on interactivity, can be derived from the Netiquette guidelines (news.announce.newusers and news.answers). These are a set of prescriptive guidelines about effective communication strategies [8,10]. They tell users to be succinct ("avoid long postings"), avoid redundant or repeat postings ("read the FAQ"), and to avoid widespread posting of messages of only marginal relevance ("don't cross-post"). With the exception of succinctness, the Netiquette guidelines and common ground model make identical predictions about the effects of conversational strategies on interactivity.

To summarise, the paper first presents basic descriptive statistics for newsgroups: (a) *demographics* - size, familiarity and moderation; (b) *conversation strategies* - FAQ production, message length, and cross-posting; (c) *interactivity* - the extent of conversational threading. We then use predictions derived from the common ground model to test three further questions: (a) how the three demographic variables affect conversational strategy; (b) how demographic variables affects interactivity; (c) how conversational strategy affects interactivity. We conclude with a general characterisation of mass interaction and a discussion of how well the common ground model applies to mass interaction.

USENET ORGANISATION, DISTRIBUTION AND INTERACTION

There are several levels of structure in Usenet. Collections of messages are clustered into newsgroups, and newsgroups themselves are organised into hierarchies. Each hierarchy is intended to address different conversational topics. There are over a hundred different hierarchies but the majority of newsgroups belong to one of eight main hierarchies ("the big eight"). These eight are: *alt* for alternative topics; *comp* for computer issues; *humanities*; *misc* for miscellaneous discussions; *news* for discussions about Usenet; *rec* for recreational topics; *soc* for social issues; and *talk* for general conversations. Each hierarchy is then subdivided into more specific subhierarchies. The name of each newsgroup begins with the relevant main hierarchy, and terms of increasing specificity are added to this. Typical newsgroup names are rec.music.dylan and rec.music.beatles, where both newsgroups are part of the music subhierarchy within rec. Twelve percent of newsgroups are moderated, and moderation is reflected in the newsgroup name: soc.russian.culture.moderated. Newsgroup distribution also varies from site to site. Newsgroups are distributed through an informal network of servers, with the specific set of groups available at a given site being dependent on the particular site administration policy.

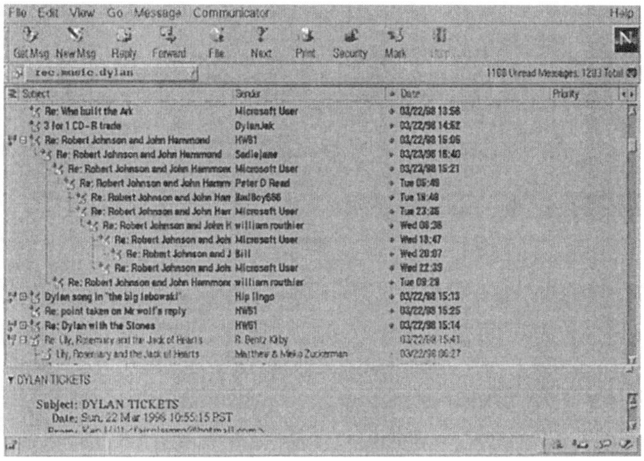

Figure 1: *Interaction and threading in rec.music.dylan*

A third level of structure within newsgroups is achieved by a mechanism that tracks conversational threads (see Figure 1). A conversation begins with an initiating post about a new issue or question ("Re: Robert Johnson and Don Hammond", posted by HW61) and any messages responding to the new posting will be linked to the message to which they respond. This is a conversational thread, i.e. a conversation consists of an *initiating post* along with various responses (if the posting elicits responses). There are also multiple levels of threading, so responding to an initial post is different from responding to a response to the initial post. For example, Figure 1 shows that the final message in the "Robert Johnson" thread (from william routhier) was actually a response to the second posting in that thread (from Sadiejane), as revealed by the line joining them. Most newsreading software organises messages according to threads, so users can view conversations in terms of the initiating post. They can also view the thread depth of a given message, i.e. whether it is an initiating post (depth of zero) a response an initiating post (depth of 1), and so on. Finally, cross-posting a message to multiple newsgroups is done by entering the names of additional newsgroups in the newsgroups field while composing a message.

DATA COLLECTION AND SAMPLING

We sampled from 26 different top-level categories, including seven of the "big eight" categories. We excluded various newsgroups for different reasons. We first excluded *alt* groups. Many server administrators have a policy of not distributing *alt* groups because of the tone and subject matter of many *alt* discussions. This makes *alt* groups less ubiquitous in terms of their distribution. *Alt* groups also differ from all other groups in their approval and creation process. We also excluded *humanities* groups because there are only a few groups (less than 10 worldwide that we have been able to find). We did not collect data for any *binaries* groups. These messages contain computer programs or images and we were only interested in textual messages, since we are studying conversation. For the same reason, we excluded *news*, **biz**, and **jobs** groups, because these groups are places for general announcements and advertisements, not conversation. We excluded regional groups, as our focus was on groups with global distribution.

This left us considering groups from the categories *comp, misc, rec, sci, soc*, and *talk*. From our newsfeed, we selected a stratified random sample of 500 newsgroups from these groups in proportion to their global occurrence, where the proportions were derived from a master list of 17,112 currently active newsgroups downloaded from uunet (ftp.uu.net). We selected only "active" groups, which we defined as those groups for which there were at least 180 messages over 6 months, equivalent to one message per day. A final selection criterion was moderation: the groups selected were representative of the overall level of moderation in Usenet.

We collected header information about each message in each of those newsgroups over a six month period, from July to December 1996. For each message we extracted various types of information including: the email address of the message poster; the date that the message was posted, the subject line of the message; message length (number of lines in the body of the message); and thread depth. In cases where messages were cross-posted we also gathered information about the newsgroups that the message was posted to.

We first present descriptive data about newsgroup *demographics, conversation strategies* and *interactivity*. We then outline specific hypotheses about the relations between these factors, and present a causal model testing these hypotheses.

DESCRIPTIVE RESULTS

Demographics

Table 1 shows demographic statistics for the 500 newsgroups. For each newsgroup, we calculated the total number of messages that people posted over the 6 month interval, and the number of different people who posted to that newsgroup. Overall levels of message traffic were high, with each group on average receiving 4299 messages (an average of 24 messages per newsgroup per day). In addition, each newsgroup attracted contributions from an average of 1319 different posters. Together these statistics provide evidence for mass interaction.

To calculate the *familiarity* of posters in a newsgroup, we used the criterion of repeat posting, i.e. whether a person posts more than once to a newsgroup. Our data show that in general a significant proportion of users are unfamiliar: 27% of messages are from "singleton posters" who only contribute to a newsgroup once. This raised the issue of whether newsgroups have participation inequality. Some participants must be contributing large numbers of messages, given: (a) the high proportion of singleton posters; and (b) that the mean level of contribution is 3.1 messages/poster. Figure 2 shows highly unequal levels of participation in each newsgroup. The right hand side of the graph shows that the majority of people post only a few times, while the left hand side reveals that there are a few people who post a large number of times. A final statistic bearing this out, is that a tiny percentage (2.9%) of posters in each newsgroup account for an average 25% of the total posts.

	DATA COLLECTED	MEAN
Demographics	Number participants	1319
	% messages from repeat posters	73
	Number messages	4299
Conversational Strategies	Message length	44
	% messages that were cross-posted	34
	% messages that were FAQs	0.4
Interactivity	Thread depth	1.8

Table 1: *Descriptive statistics for the 500 newsgroups over the 6 months of the study*

Conversational strategies

We found *cross-posting* to be prevalent. On average 34% messages in each newsgroup were addressed to at least one other group, and the average cross-posted message targetted 3.1 other newsgroups. Cross-posting was not specific either: newsgroups were highly inconsistent in the set of external groups they cross-posted to. Each newsgroup overall cross-posted to a mean of 272 distinct groups. To further investigate the precision of cross-posts, we calculated the mean number of cross-posts per distinct cross-posted group. Strong links between groups would lead to a large number of cross-postings to a small number of groups and hence a high mean. However the mean was 5.4. The absence of specific cross-posting argues against the view there are strong communication ties between specific newsgroups.

FAQs were detected automatically by an algorithm which searched subject lines for the words "FAQ" or "Frequently Asked Questions". It excluded certain other special cases such as subject lines including the word "re". FAQs are a common feature of newsgroups which is shown by the fact that 54% of newsgroups had FAQs, although less than 0.5% of messages were FAQs. We also calculated average *message length*, which was 44 lines.

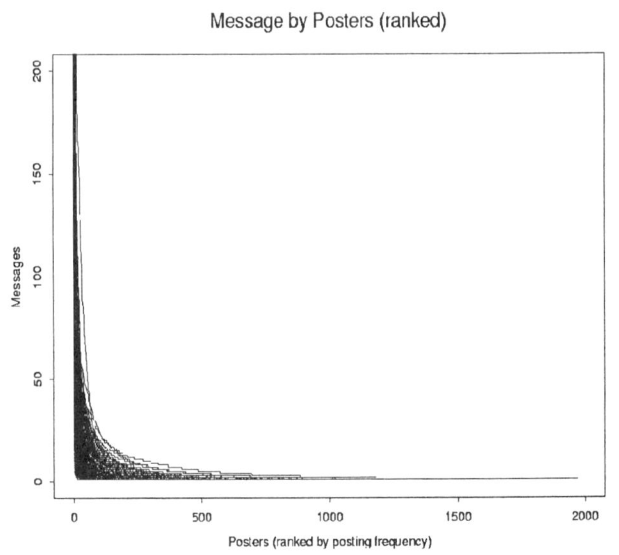

Figure 2: *Levels of individual participation within newsgroup*

Interactivity

Finally we looked at *interactivity*. The average thread depth is 1.8 messages, suggesting a typical exchange in which the average message refers to approximately two other messages. A substantial proportion of messages (33%) had two or more threads, indicating frequent extended conversations. We also calculated a complementary measure of interactivity, the number of initiating posts (those with zero references and thread depth of one). A high proportion of initiating messages would indicate repeated failures to start conversations, or a prevalence of conversational dead-ends. We found that initiating messages are highly prevalent, accounting for over more than 40% of messages. This suggests a view of Usenet in which it is hard to start a conversation. Once a conversation starts, however, then it seems to attract multiple contributions.

TESTING THE COMMON GROUND MODEL

We next use the common ground model to derive a specific set of predictions. Each of the conversational strategy variables of (a) increased FAQ production; (b) decreased cross-posting; (c) longer messages can be seen as an index of common ground. From our earlier arguments we would therefore expect *demographics* to affect common ground and hence *conversational strategies* in the following ways:

H1a,b,c: Newsgroups that are larger in *size* will have more difficulty establishing common ground, we would therefore expect them to have (a) fewer FAQs; (b) more cross-posting; and (c) shorter messages;

H2a,b,c: Newsgroups containing many repeat posters (i.e. people who are *familiar* with the newsgroup) will establish common ground more easily, they will therefore have (a) more FAQs; (b) less cross-posting; and (c) longer messages;

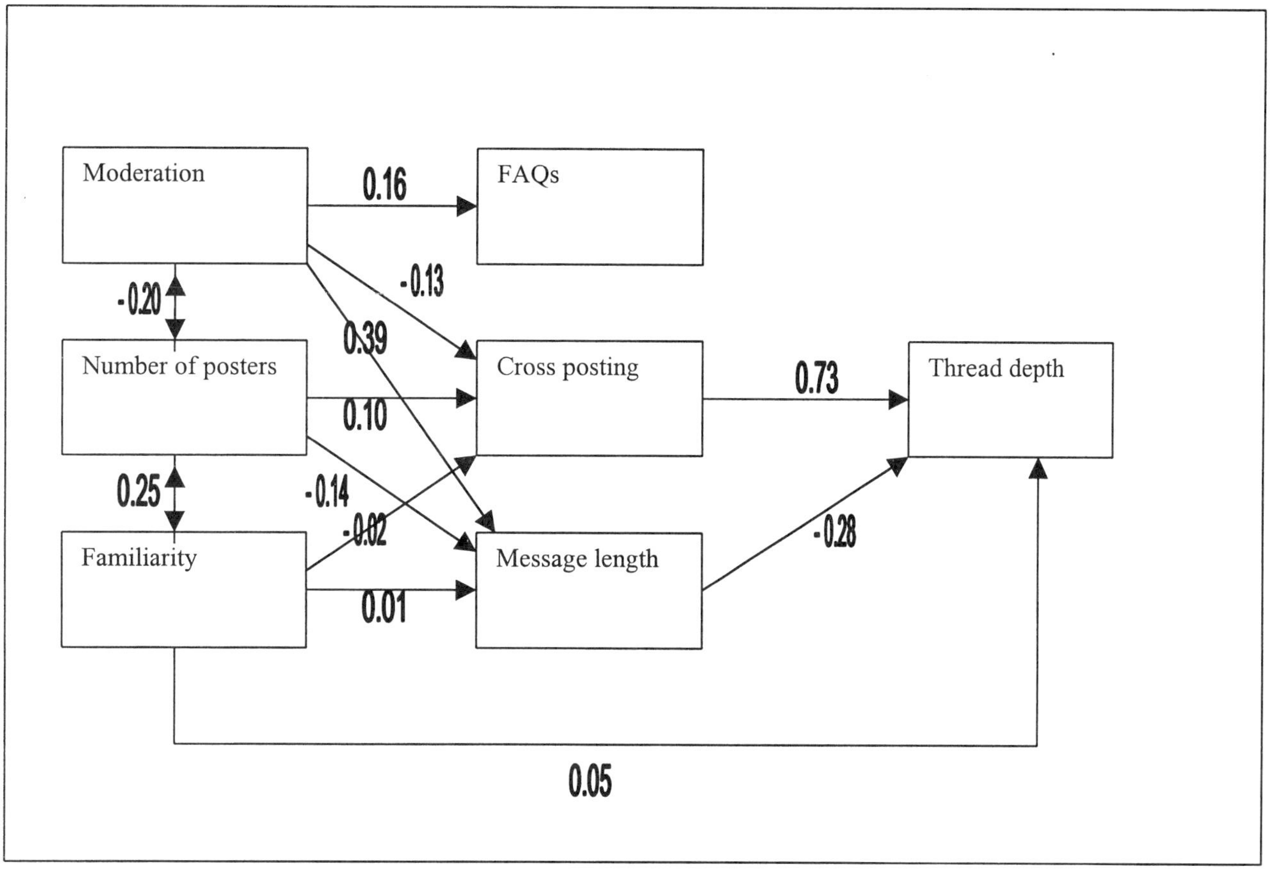

Figure 3: *Causal model showing effects of variables in structural equation analysis, for demographic, conversational strategy and interactivity variables*

H3a,b,c: *Moderated* newsgroups should more easily establish common ground, and hence have (a) more FAQs; (b) less cross-posting; and (c) longer messages;

We also expected *conversational strategy* variables to influence *interactivity.* If newsgroups can establish common ground through effective communication strategies, we should expect this to be manifested in terms of more *interactive conversation* as indicated by greater thread depth:

H4: Newsgroups with more FAQs will have greater interactivity as manifested by increased thread depth;

H5: Newsgroups with less cross-posting will have greater interactivity as manifested by increased thread depth;

H6: Newsgroups with longer messages will have greater interactivity as manifested by increased thread depth;

We should also expect *demographic* factors to have direct affects on *interactivity*:

H7: Newsgroups that are larger in *size* will have less interactivity as manifested by reduced thread depth;

H8: Newsgroups containing repeat posters (i.e. people who are *familiar* with the newsgroup) will have greater interactivity as manifested by increased thread depth;

H9: *Moderated* newsgroups will have greater interactivity as manifested by increased thread depth;

We tested these predictions using the following causal model, which was tested using a series of regression analyses [4]:

Demographics → Conversational strategies → Interactivity

The overall analysis involved two steps. In the first we regressed each of the *demographic* variables onto the *conversational strategy* variables to test H1-H3, and second we regressed all variables onto *interactivity* to test H4-H9. Where relevant, variables were normalised to allow for the fact that there were different numbers of messages and participants contributing to each newsgroup. For several variables (e.g. cross-posting) we experimented with different operationalisations (e.g. mean number of cross-posts/message, mean overall number of groups cross-posted to), choosing the operationalisation that best accounted for the variance in the regression equations.

Effects of demographics on conversational strategy

Figure 3 shows the results of three regressions of demographics on conversational strategy. The numbers on the arcs represent the standardised beta weights. For simplicity of presentation we show only significant relationships. Overall the models for each of the three factors was statistically significant. For message length ($F[3,496] = 41.3$, $p < 0.001$, $R^2 = 0.20$), for cross-posting ($F[3,496] = 11.3$, $p < 0.001$, $R^2 = 0.06$), and for FAQs ($F[3,496] = 5.89$, $p < 0.01$, $R^2 = 0.03$). We now discuss the specific predictions about the effects of each demographic factor. While *size* had no effect on FAQs (H1a), predictions concerning hypothesis H1b and H1c were confirmed: newsgroups that are larger in *size* have more cross-posting ($t = 2.2$, $p < 0.05$, $\beta = 0.10$) and shorter messages ($t = 3.2$, $p < 0.01$, $\beta = 0.14$). The familiarity predictions H2b and H2c were also confirmed: newsgroups containing more *familiar* contributors had less cross-posting ($t = 4.5$, $p < 0.001$, $\beta = 0.02$) and longer messages ($t = 2.4$, $p < 0.05$, $\beta = 0.01$), although again there was no affect of familiarity on FAQs, so H2a was not confirmed. Finally predictions H3a,b, and c were all confirmed. *Moderation* led to more FAQs ($t = 3.5$, $p < 0.001$, $\beta = 0.16$), reduced cross-posting ($t = 2.8$, $p < 0.01$, $\beta = 0.13$), and longer messages ($t = 9.5$, $p < 0.001$, $\beta = 0.39$).

Effects of demographics and conversational strategy on interactivity

The full model was very successful at predicting interactivity ($F[6,493] = 133.9$, $p < 0.001$, $R^2 = 0.62$). However, two of the predictions about the effects of conversational strategy on interactivity were disconfirmed. H5 predicted that newsgroups with less cross-posting will have greater interactivity, but in fact the less cross-posting there was in the group, the *less* the threading ($t = 23.3$, $p < 0.001$, $\beta = 0.73$). H6 predicted that newsgroups with longer messages will have greater interactivity, but in fact message length *reduced* interactivity ($t = 5.2$, $p < 0.001$, $\beta = 0.28$). There were no effects of FAQs on interactivity (H4).

Only one of the predictions about the effects of *demographics* on *interactivity* was confirmed, namely H8, newsgroups containing familiar contributors will have greater thread depth ($t = 16.2$, $p < 0.001$, $\beta = 0.05$). Neither H7 nor H9 concerning the effect of FAQs and size were validated.

CONCLUSIONS

We can draw a number of conclusions about mass interaction from this research. Although there are large numbers of people contributing to each newsgroup and large numbers of messages overall, the descriptive data show that the default mass interaction consists of a 43 line message referring to two previous messages. This indicates moderate but not large amounts of interactivity. This general view about interactivity should be tempered, however, by the fact that many attempts to initiate interaction were failures; over 40% of messages were initiating attempts. This suggests a problem of *conversational inertia*: it seems to be problematic to start a mass interaction but it is relatively easy to continue it once started.

We also found massive *participation inequalities* between different people in a given newsgroup. This is an important clarification of the view that the Internet is an egalitarian forum [9]. While it is true that anyone can post to a newsgroup, the descriptive data clearly show that conversations in newsgroups are dominated by a minority of highly verbose participants. Again this argues for a view that Usenet conversations do not strictly involve repeated levels of mass participation, as evidenced by the fact that 27% of messages are generated by people who only contribute once to the newsgroup. Overall these results suggest that as far as active posting is concerned, mass interaction may be a misnomer. Typical conversations involve only small numbers of posters, and newsgroups are often dominated by cliques of verbose contributors. This participation inequality contrasts with research on face-to-face interaction and video-mediated communication which has shown much more equal levels of participation [14]. Participation inequality may not have wholly negative outcomes, however. The majority of Usenet participants may well be satisfied with making infrequent contributions, posting only about issues that are important to them. Such peripheral participation may enable people to remain in the background, monitoring general conversations until they spot a topic of direct relevance, or they need to pose a question of their own. This type of background involvement has been observed to be beneficial in the case of corporate email [11] and interpersonal communication [12]. This form of participation has also been proposed as an important way for novices to learn about a novel topic [12].

While the conversational and participation data suggest a view in which conversation is carried out locally by a few participants, the cross-posting data suggest a slightly different perspective. It turns out that cross-posting is frequent, although it propagates potentially irrelevant messages and is thus contrary to both the common ground model and Netiquette guidelines. Cross-posting can also inform us about the relations between newsgroups. When people do cross-post, they are unspecific about the groups they cross-post to, as indicated by the fact that the average newsgroup cross-posted to over 200 others. This in turn argues against the view that there are tight conversational links between different newsgroups [15].

We also tested a number of predictions derived from the common ground model. These were mainly verified for the effects of demographics on common ground. The demographic variables of moderation, familiarity and smaller newsgroups all increased common ground as measured by increased message length and decreased cross-posting. The effects on FAQ production were less clear however. Only moderation increased FAQ production, with neither familiarity nor size having an effect. This view argues against the view that FAQs are a "defence mechanism" arising from participants' desire to instill consensus in diverse or rapidly changing user populations. Rather FAQs are most likely to arise under the orderly conditions induced by moderation.

What about the effects of demographics on interactivity? Here the common ground model fared much less well: only familiarity directly increased threading, with neither moderation nor size having an effect. Furthermore, and contrary to our expectations, cross-posting *increased* interactivity. This is counter to both the common ground view and the Netiquette guidelines: both of these contend that cross-posting should dilute conversational focus and hence reduce interactivity. This result is consistent, however, with a different perspective on large scale interaction, namely *weak ties* [5,6]. The positive effects of cross-posting on interactivity suggests that people exploit the mass distribution properties and diverse population of Usenet to go beyond a particular newsgroup to carry out their conversations. Combining the results about the effects of familiarity and cross-posting on interactivity indicates that there may be two complementary sets of circumstances that facilitate mass interaction. The first occurs when familiar participants share common ground and the second is where people seek out diverse perspectives by posting outside their newsgroup. Our final prediction about the effects of message length on interactivity was also disconfirmed: shorter messages actually promoted interactivity. How can we explain this? One possibility is consistent with communication overload [11,18]. Given the huge amounts of conversational traffic in Usenet, people are less likely to read, and hence reply to, long messages. Such an interpretation would be consistent with the Netiquette stricture ("avoid long postings").

Although moderation and FAQ production increased common ground, they had no effects on interactivity. Why was this the case? One reason why moderation does not increase threading may be that moderators increase conversational relevance by deciding that a new posting is tangential to the topic, and stopping the current thread. In doing so, however, they automatically reduce the amount of threading. A reason for the absence of expected conversational benefit of FAQs may be that FAQs have two contradictory effects. FAQs may promote conversation by providing access to information about group culture, conversational expectations and a precis of group conversational history. At the same time they may discourage newcomers from productively revisiting a previous conversation out of the mistaken belief that the topic has been exhausted. New research involving content analysis of FAQs and moderators' strategies is necessary to determine whether these suggestions are the case.

Our findings should also be qualified by a number of provisos. Our strictly quantitative analysis needs to be complemented by content analysis, as well as surveys of Usenet participants. The current analysis is silent about the effects of conversational content: which specific topics or conversational styles encourage large responses and which fail to elicit a response? What factors encourage or discourage flaming? What are people's reactions to flagrant examples of cross-posting? Surveys and interviews could also address people's attitudes to, and satisfaction with their Usenet interactions. Why do people contribute to certain discussions but not to others? How long do people lurk before they first post? And how is dominance viewed? Why do certain people post multiple messages and how are they perceived by others for doing so? Again some of these issues have been addressed in small scale studies, but more of this type of work is needed [1,17]. There are also issues about moderation and FAQ maintenance which are highly relevant for issues of group memory [2]: why do certain people take on the responsibility of moderating or maintaining FAQs, and what is their motive for doing so? Other issues that need to be addressed by content analysis include deliberate attempts to subvert Usenet conversation ("spamming, "trolling") or the generation of messages by artificial agents ("bots").

Finally there are issues concerning the use of thread depth to measure interactivity. One potential objection to using threading is it fails to include "backchannel" responses in email: Usenet users report that they sometimes reply to a public Usenet message privately in email. However, our interest here was in publicly observed mass interaction, and email conversations are not part of the public record. This argument also applies to the issue of "lurking", i.e. reading newsgroup messages without responding to them. While lurking may be a prevalent behaviour, again it leaves no public conversational trace. Finally there is the question of "flaming". Deeply threaded Usenet interactions sometimes result from emotionally charged and occasionally personally abusive exchanges. However this addresses the question of conversational content, an issue which we leave to future work.

What are the theoretical implications of these results? Our data show that while the common ground model provides a good account of the effects of demographics on conversational strategy, it is much weaker at predicting interactivity. Two major modifications need to be made in applying the common ground model to mass interaction. The fact that shorter messages promoted interactivity suggests that a model of *mass interaction* also needs to incorporate the notion of conversational overload: participants have to filter large numbers of messages to find relevant information, with the consequence that long messages may be ignored. Our finding that cross-posting benefits interaction indicates that the model needs to take account of the benefits of both familiarity and diversity. On the one hand common ground can promote consensus but conversations can grow stale through overfamiliarity of topics and people. On the other hand, a diverse population may stimulate interaction but their widely disparate perspectives may mean that no conversational progress can be made.

ACKNOWLEDGMENTS

We thank Marc Smith, Lyn Walker and Julia Hirschberg for comments on early versions of this work.

REFERENCES

1. Baym, N. Interpreting soap operas and creating community: Inside a computer-mediated fan culture, *Journal of Folklore Research*, 30, 143-176, 1993.
2. Berlin, L., Jeffries, R., O'Day, V., Paepcke, A., and Wharton, C., Where did you put it? Issues in the design and use of a group memory. In *Proceedings of CHI'93*, 33-30, 1993.
3. Clark, H. *Arenas of language use*. University of Chicago Press, Chicago, 1992.
4. Cohen, P. *Empirical methods for artificial intelligen*ce, Boston, MIT Press, 1995.
5. Constant, D., Sproull, L., and Kiesler, S. The kindness of strangers, *Organizational Science*, 7, 119-135, 1996.
6. Granovetter, M. The strength of weak ties. *American Journal of Sociology*, 78, 1360-1380, 1973.
7. Harrison, M. *The Usenet handbook*. O'Reilly, Boston, 1994.
8. Horton, M. (1993): Rules for posting to Usenet, news.misc,news.answers., FTP at rtfm.mit.edu.
9. King, J. Grinter, R and Pickering, J. The rise and fall of Netville. In S. Kiesler (Ed.), *Culture of the internet*. Erlbaum, NJ, 1997.
10. Kollock, P and Smith, M. Managing the Virtual Commons In S. Herring (Ed.) *Computer-Mediated Communication*, John Benjamins, Philadelphia, 1996.
11. Kraut, R. and Attewell, P. Media use in a global corporation. In S. Kiesler (Ed.), *Culture of the Internet*, Erlbaum, NJ., 1997.
12. Kraut, R., Fish, R., Root, B. and Chalfonte, B. Informal communication in organizations. In R. Baecker (Ed.), *Groupware and Computer Supported Co-operative Work*, 287-314, Morgan Kaufman, CA, 1992.
13. Markus, M. Towards a critical mass theory of interactive media. In J. Fulk and C. Steinfield (Eds.), *Organizations and Communication Technology*, Sage, CA, 1990.
14. O,Conaill, B., Whittaker, S., and Wilbur, S. Conversations over video conferences, *Human Computer Interaction*, 8, 389-428, 1994.
15. Smith, M. Measuring the social structure of the Usenet, Unpublished paper, University of California, Los Angeles, 1997.
16. Sproull, L., and Kiesler, S. *Connections*, Boston, MIT Press, 1991.
17. Sutton, L. Gender, power, and silencing in electronic discourse on Usenet, *Proceedings of the 20th Berkeley Linguistics Society*, University of California, Berkeley, 1994.
18. Whittaker, S. and Sidner, C. Email overload: exploring personal information management of email. In *Proceedings of CHI96,* ACM Press, NY, 1996.
19. Whittaker, S. Talking to strangers: an evaluation of the factors affecting electronic collaboration, In *Proceedings of CSCW96*, ACM Press, NY, 1996.

Envisioning Communication: Task-Tailorable Representations of Communication in Asynchronous Work

Christine M. Neuwirth
James H. Morris
Susan Harkness Regli
Carnegie Mellon University
Pittsburgh, PA 15213 USA
+1 412 268-8702
{jhm, cmn, shr1}@cmu.edu

Ravinder Chandhok
Geoffrey C. Wenger
Within Technology, Inc.,
Waynesburg, PA 15370 USA
+1 724 852-2599
{chandhok, wenger}@within.com

ABSTRACT

This paper reports on our efforts to improve interfaces for asynchronous communication in which a group is communicating to solve a problem. We report results from an observational study and an experiment and use them as a basis for drawing design requirements: task-tailorable representations, emergent representations, emergent sharing, public/private elements in a layout, incremental formalization, and asynchronous awareness. We describe an approach and prototype that embodies some of the key requirements.

Keywords

External representations, visualization, interfaces, incremental formalization, awareness, asynchronous communication, electronic mail, collaborative work

INTRODUCTION

Few would deny that external representations play an important role in many tasks. The relative difficulty of multiplying XLVII by LIV vs. 47 by 54 is a paradigm case; using pencil and paper while performing the multiplication steps vs. doing it "in your head" is another. Theories have been proposed and empirical research is accumulating in support of the view that external representations are not "merely" inputs and stimuli, but that the form of a representation influences what information is perceived, what processes are activated, and what structures are discovered [6, 7, 27, 31].

Our previous research examined the role of external representations in the writing process [23] and in communicating about artifacts (drafts of papers) [20, 21, 22]. In that research, we hypothesized that different external representations impose different information production and access costs, and demonstrated that such differences significantly affect the amount and nature of communication and the perceptions participants form of each other [19, 30]. In the research reported here, we focus on external representations for asynchronous communication in which a group is communicating to solve a problem (but not necessarily to create an artifact).

There are, of course, a great many differences between face-to-face and asynchronous communication [cf. 1, 17]. When people are dispersed in space and time, numerous aspects of communication are affected, including the sequencing of messages, the flow of communication, and the time required for a communication cycle (composing the message, editing, transmission, reception, feedback--acknowledgment of receipt--and reply).

We have chosen to concentrate on how to represent the state of the task. This is because one of the most basic properties of asynchronous communication is that the participants forget what is going on. As a result, they must depend much more on external representations than they would in a synchronous interaction. Thus, as we shall argue, the design and maintenance of a task-specific representation is crucial.

OUR APPROACH: TASK-DRIVEN DESIGN

The methodology we have employed in our approach is iterative design based on benchmark tasks:

- develop benchmarks tasks
- observe subjects performing the benchmark tasks, through laboratory studies and field tests, paying particular attention to difficulties encountered;
- develop prototypes intended to overcome these difficulties;
- measure and compare the performance of subjects completing the tasks with and without the aid of the prototype.
- revise the tasks and prototype based on the results of the comparison and repeat

In our work, we have attempted to design benchmark tasks that are simple enough to allow repeatable, controlled laboratory studies, yet complex enough to capture aspects of real-world tasks that impose "loads" on the system, loads that lead to problems surfacing.

Our work with a task called The Spoofer Identification Task will serve as an example of our approach. In this task, four subjects[1] act as System Administrators (SAs), each of whom administers a machine. Each of the SAs receives electronic mail messages that have obviously been forged or "spoofed" by users identifying themselves with fake user names or aliases (e.g., "The Phantom"). To identify the spoofers, the SAs have to use the message header information to find out where the message originated, and, for messages not originating on their own machine, find the SA who administers the machine and ask him/her to identify what users were logged in at the time a spoofed message was sent. By process of elimination, SAs eventually identify a spoofer as the only user logged in at all times when spoofed messages were sent from a particular alias.

Communication and problem-solving activities involved in the task include reading and analyzing spoofed messages, locating other SAs, developing a problem-solving strategy, requesting other people to do something for you (requesting other SAs to send login lists), processing people's replies (by comparing login lists to suspect lists and updating those lists), responding to others' requests to do things for them (analyzing logs in response to requests from other SAs for login lists), and deciding what information to share with others (sending the results from log analysis to other SAs who are attempting to identify a spoofer).

The task has properties designed to parallel real-world asynchronous communication tasks:

- It simulates a situation in which a person is receiving multiple messages regarding different tasks (finding the identity of any given spoofer represents a task; several spoofers are active at any given time). To be most effective, participants must assess the state of the various tasks and decide which task, given the state of affairs, it would be most strategic to work on next.
- Some messages can be dealt with relatively quickly (e.g., finding where the message was sent from and contacting the relevant administrator can be done in less than a minute provided the administrator's identity is known); other messages, however, require work before a response is possible (e.g., answering a request from another SA for information about who was logged in at a particular time). Thus, some messages cannot be dealt with immediately; the receiver must first do the work and get back to the sender. Participants forget to whom they still need to send answers and who has not gotten back to them.
- Some messages contain requests to do something for someone else whereas others are enabling messages that allow the participant to get more work done on his/her own tasks. Participants must decide on a strategy for balancing the work that will result in the most efficient overall solution.
- The situation changes over time (e.g., new tasks are added). The number of collaborators grows as the situation becomes more complex; participants must track down relevant collaborators and decide what information to share with them (e.g., should they share suspect lists with SAs who have just entered the situation).
- Participants develop a stable solution method and problem-solving routines, routines help them perform more reliably and fluently, only over time. As a result, their representation of the problem evolves and with it, their idea of how best to visualize the situation becomes more refined.

OBSERVATIONAL STUDIES

We conducted a series of observational studies of subjects engaged in the Spoofer Identification Task over several variants of the task. Participants were students, staff and faculty at Carnegie Mellon University and were paid for their participation. All were experienced email users, though not all were familiar with the email system used in the study (those unfamiliar with it were given hard copy documentation customized to explain all commands they would need). To avoid confounding with the load in their own inboxes, participants logged into special "system administration" email accounts when they worked on the task. We instructed them to try to login approximately once every two hours from 9-5 during the course of the study and work for about a half-hour during each session. Subjects could login more frequently and work longer if they desired and some did. Due to other time commitments (e.g., classes, other meetings), some subjects were delayed in their logins. For most of the task variants, the study lasted approximately two days before participants proposed a correct identification for the spoofer(s).

We recorded all participants' email communications, took notes and interviewed participants about their experiences. In general, participants reported finding the task challenging, engaging, and plausible. The observations reported here focus on those aspects of participants' performance that were most relevant to drawing our design implications.

[1] The Spoofer Identification Task can also easily be played with one actual subject and three subjects simulated by an experimenter. This structure allows the experimenter to simulate conditions such as an uncooperative collaborator, a system administrator with high needs for privacy, etc. As part of the Virtual Work Room project, we also developed a computer simulation program for network activity of *n* users and *m* spoofers to facilitate generation of realistic logs for The Spoofer Identification Task; this allows us to manipulate the complexity of the task. The Task and directions for using it are at http://muffin.hss.cmu.edu/vwr/web/index.html.

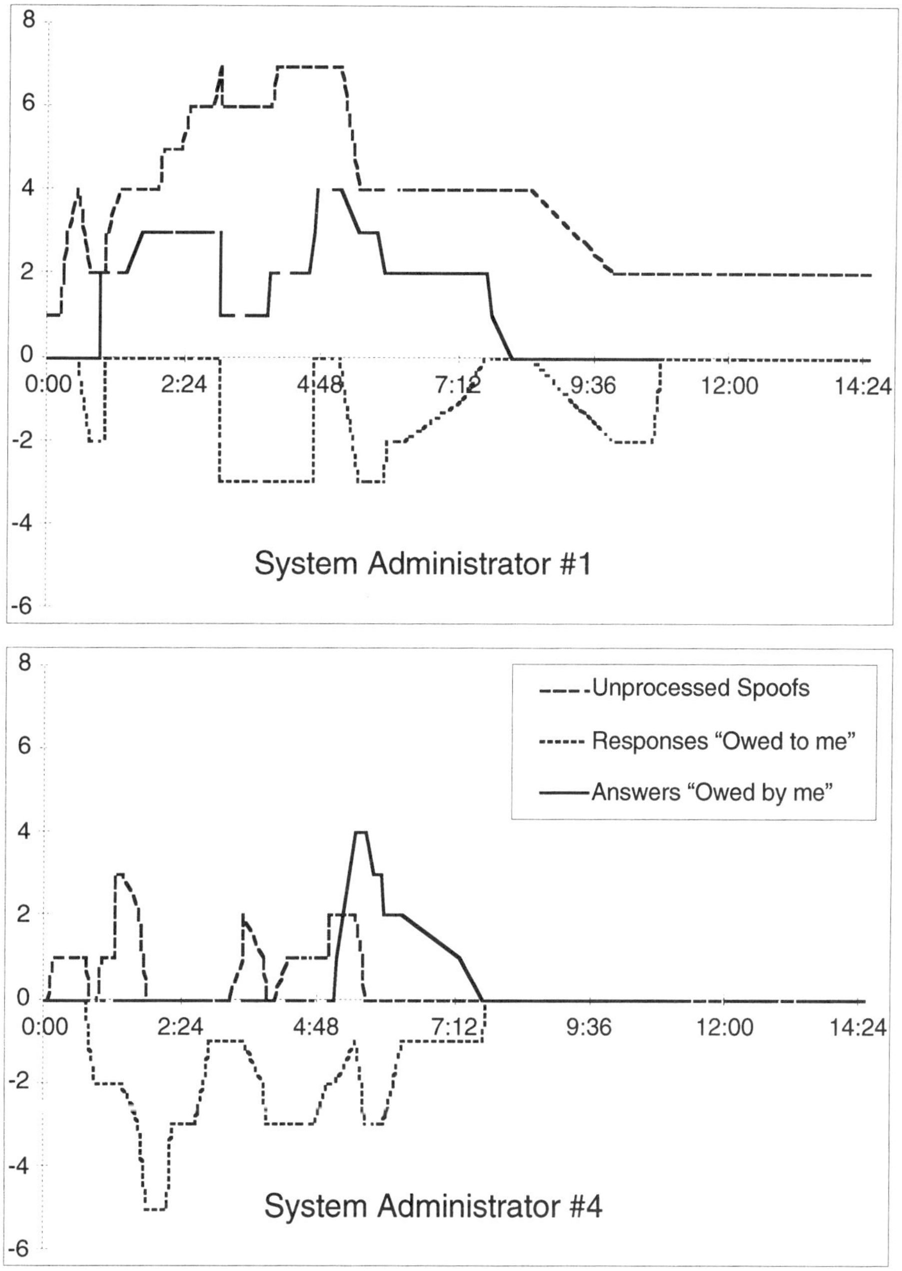

Figure 1: Patterns of Message Processing

Communication and Problem-Solving

Figure 1 depicts the patterns of messages for two of four participants over a two-day period[2] for one of our observational studies. "Unprocessed Spoofs" are spoofs that a participant received but for which he or she had not yet sent an email message to the relevant system administrator requesting login information; "Responses Owed to Me" is the number of messages the participant had sent to a relevant system administrator for which the participant had not yet received the requested information; "Answers Owed by Me" is the number of messages the participant had received that he or she had not yet answered by providing the requested information.

In general, participants developed a stable solution method and problem-solving routines by the end of the first day; these routines helped them perform more reliably and fluently, though not always more effectively. As can be seen in Figure 1, subjects varied in the problem-solving routines that they adopted. Some subjects (e.g., System Administrator #1) spent most of their time answering requests from other system administrators; others made it a practice to always process a spoof as soon as they received one (e.g., System Administrator #4). In terms of

---

[2] The x-axis represents hours in which subjects actually worked in the 2-day period; hours from 5pm to 9am in which no one worked have been elided.

minimizing the time it takes to solve the problem, the strategy of getting requests "off one's desk" is a better one, since another system administrator may have time to provide the answer, but cannot help if he or she doesn't know the spoof has occurred. Previous results from studies of co-located vs. distributed work would suggest that if these system administrators had been co-located, channels of informal communication may have facilitated the adoption of the more efficient strategy by all [cf. 17]. As it was, some subjects remained unaware of the more efficient strategy throughout the course of the task.

Look Ahead and Group Awareness

"Look ahead" refers to a problem-solving planner's activity of imagining and evaluating alternative sequences of actions before actually selecting an action. The basic idea is that for some tasks it is possible to do a complete "look ahead" at all alternatives sequences of actions and choose the best sequence of actions that leads to the goal. For other tasks it is not possible to do a (complete) Look ahead due to lack of information on which to base an evaluation function, task complexity, limited attention, or working memory limitations.

In contrast to group members who are aware of each others' work habits (e.g., Bob usually checks email in the morning), most subjects did not develop awareness of each other's patterns of work and few used this information to "Look ahead" in deciding what action to do next. One subject did, however, try to make use of the limited information that the "finger" command provides and expressed a desire to have more awareness about when other SAs were likely to be working to help him decide what to work on next. For example, if he knew that another SA was likely to log out in the next half hour, he might interrupt what he was currently doing in order to request information from him or her. The "finger" command, of course, is a primitive form of synchronous awareness (Is Bob working now?) but does not answer the question (What is Bob's typical pattern of work?). When people are co-located in an office, such information is more readily available. Support for richer awareness information from which patterns can be discerned is necessary to support efficient "look ahead" strategies in asynchronous communication.

Remembering the State of the Task

As messages accumulated, answers to key questions such as "Have I processed a spoof (i.e., sent an email to the relevant system administrator)?" "Who do I owe a response to?" "Who owes me a response?" and "Have I processed a response (i.e., updated the suspect list)?" were difficult for subjects to remember. The load of messages and related pieces of information became difficult to manage after an SA had received and begun processing approximately two messages from four different spoofing aliases.

Use of External Representations

Of particular interest is the fact that the representation afforded by the email system subjects used was apparently not adequate to represent the full context of the problem: most subjects used paper to keep track of their progress. Figure 2 depicts a task-specific representation typical of those invented by subjects. Some subjects used representations like the one illustrated to help them remember which machines had been spoofed at what times (the "To," "From," and "Time" columns), what work was outstanding (indicated in Figure 2 by a circle) and what work was completed (indicated in Figure 2 by a checkmark).

Note that the representation helps users visualize key parts of the situation "at a glance." These representations served as memory aids for subgoals and solution states, particularly because subjects worked at intervals–usually separated by a couple hours but as large as 18 hours–and had to reacquaint themselves with the situation each time they resumed work. Subjects using solely a chronological list of email messages with no notes reported that they paged through 10-20 messages at the start of the second day to recall what had taken place.

Some participants revised their paper representations over time as their understanding of the task (its scope, how to solve it and how best to represent it) improved; some participants reported that they were dissatisfied with their representations (e.g., the subject who produced Figure 2), but did not revise it because it was too time-consuming to recopy everything and produce a new one.

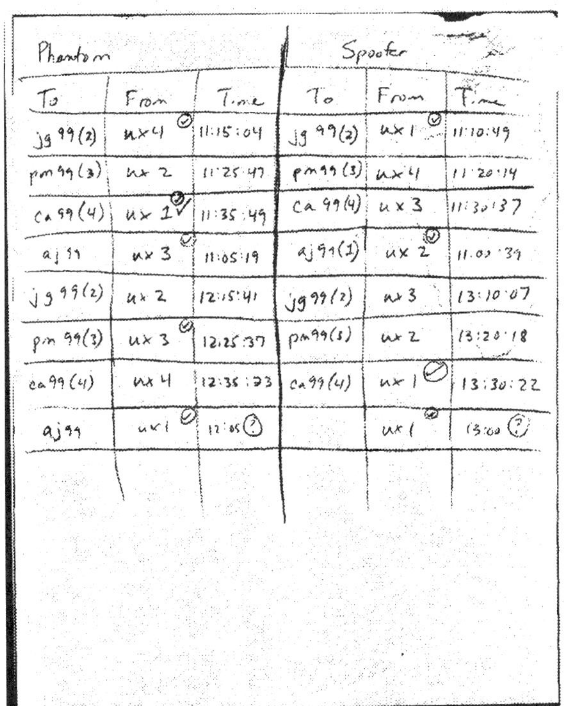

Figure 2. Task-specific representation

DESIGN IMPLICATIONS

During our observations of The Spoofer Identification Task, we formed the hypotheses that (1) subjects with a task-tailored external representation could determine more quickly at the start of a new session what had been done and what still needed to be done than subjects working with a basic chronological organization of email messages and (2) a system that supported task-tailorable representations would significantly improve task performance. Of course, like our subjects, users can always use paper, but paper is more difficult to share over distance and more difficult to revise as understanding of the task evolves. Users can also build such representations in a spreadsheet, but they would then loose the connection to their original messages. Other work has argued for the utility of retaining such connections [9].

Our observational studies and other studies in the literature suggest that next-generation asynchronous communication tools need to provide several key capabilities:

- Task-tailorable representations. The task representations that people build need to be task-specific; it is not possible for interface builders to create every potentially useful representation of information in advance. An effective interface must provide tools by which users can create new representations as needed without great effort or skill.
- Emergent representations. People's understanding of how to represent a task most effectively evolves with experience in the task. A system must allow people to modify representations easily.
- Emergent sharing. People may be well into a task before they discover that they should be working with others to solve a problem. A system must allow information to be selected and combined from multiple individual representations of the information created with heterogeneous systems.
- Public/private elements in a layout. People may want to make (parts of) their information (e.g., the suspect list) available to others in the group, either for viewing or updating, while still retaining its position in their own task representation.
- Incremental formalization. People vary in the sophistication with which they can compose agents that would automatically "place" communications appropriately in a layout automatically. Moreover, the overhead involved in formalizing may be too much for a task of short duration. A system must support informal expression of layout and direction manipulation as well as automated layout (cf. [4, 25]) as a way of supporting the ongoing refinement of candidate representations.
- Asynchronous awareness. If available, people can use awareness of others' activities to solve problems more effectively (e.g., Before I finish with task Y, I should send a request to this person because he/she typically logs in at this time of the day). A great deal of work has been directed toward providing awareness in synchronous systems [8]. Asynchronous systems similarly need to find ways to support awareness.

These capabilities are desirable in other situations besides asynchronous communication. Providing such capabilities for asynchronous communication, however, raises some special issues related to being able visualize dynamic data (e.g., recognizing new/unread messages in a layout; notification granularity for incoming messages, etc.).

Another issue concerns the cost of building and maintaining task-tailored representations. We felt that the cost would have to be offset by a big gain in task performance. Existing cognitive models of graphic and textual layouts are quite preliminary [2, 13] and did not easily lend themselves to predicting performance in advance, so we decided to run a study to measure changes in task performance using a task-tailored representation. We reasoned that it would be worthwhile developing a prototype system to support task-tailorable interfaces provided the performance gains were relatively large.

STUDY: HOW MUCH DOES A TASK-TAILORED REPRESENTATION HELP?

Conditions

Participants were randomly assigned to one of two conditions: Task-Tailored Interface and Chronological Interface. Based on the paper representations we had observed subjects using, we developed a task-tailored representation to support subjects doing The Spoofer Identification Task (Figure 3). The hypertextual task-tailored representation provides an affordance that the paper representations did not: subjects could have access both to the visual representation of situation and to the actual messages as background information. Highlighted text and check marks in this representation indicate active links to email messages.

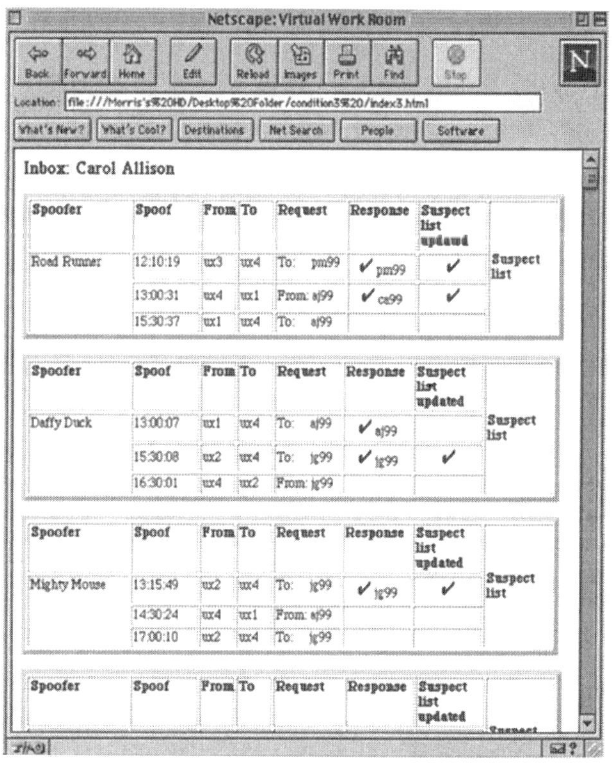

Figure 3: Task-Tailored

The control condition used a chronological list of email messages presented in the same browser as the experimental condition, with general characteristics of the user interface, including background color, font, and overall appearance kept constant (Figure 4).

Subjects

Subjects were twenty undergraduate students recruited from Carnegie Mellon University. Ten subjects completed each condition (Chronological/Task-Tailored); each was paid $10.00 for their participation in the experiment. All participants were highly familiar with email and used it daily.

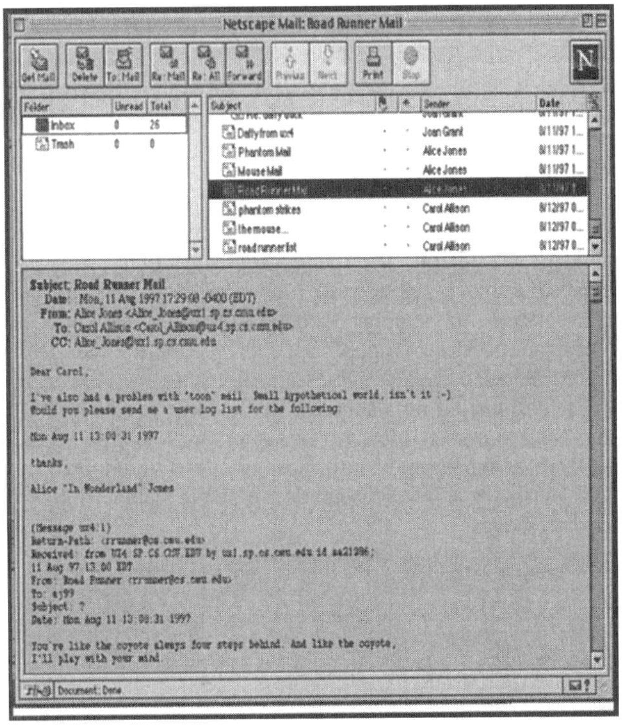

Figure 4: Chronological

Procedure

We wanted to focus on how well a subject could understand the state of a situation after returning from a long break between work periods, as occurs often in asynchronous communication situations. For example, a person completes some work on a project, saves it in a shared folder, and then returns to that folder to continue work after others have made new changes to the folder. To maximize the unfamiliarity of "forgetting" the situation and having to incorporate changes into one's understanding, we decided to simulate a turn-over situation in a workplace: when one shift passes on work to the next. Thus, we used subjects unfamiliar with the task, provided them with an introduction to the basic rules, and then told them they were participating in the following scenario:

The Game is in Progress

Four players have already been playing a game pursuing some spoofers. One of the players, Carol Allison, had to leave the game after the first day. Your task today will be to figure out what Carol knew when she left the game, and what you would have to do next if you were taking over for her. She has left you nothing but her email account to help you determine the current state of the situation. You'll have to use this account, set up as she created it, to answer some questions.

Before we start, you'll need some background information. First of all, the spoofers sending the email have been logged in to one of four different machines when sending the messages:

ux1.sp.cs.cmu.edu
ux2.sp.cs.cmu.edu
ux3.sp.cs.cmu.edu
ux4.sp.cs.cmu.edu

To find likely suspects, then, the system administrators of these machines have been exchanging lists of what users were logged into each machine at the time the spoofed email was sent.

Tasks and Measures

The tasks we asked subjects to complete were designed to test performance in figuring out what needs to be done, what responses are pending, and where crucial information is located. Performance on each of these tasks was timed by an experimenter, who told subjects exactly when to turn a page to read each question; the subjects were asked to say when they were ready to move on and the experimenter recorded the completion time. Answers were later scored for accuracy as well. Here is the exact text of the questions:

Your job is to find the answers to these three questions:

1) The system administrators were exchanging requests for lists of who was logged onto particular machines at particular times. Carol Allison was the system administrator for ux4, and she always kept copies of any responses she sent to other system administrators. Who did she owe lists to (i.e., who had asked her for lists but not received responses from her yet)?
2) Who owed Carol responses (i.e., which system administrators had not yet responded to a request for a list from ux4)?
3) The system administrators were afraid that they might have missed something in combining their user lists into a suspect list for the perpetrator who called himself The Phantom. You don't have to re-create the suspect list, but simply locate and print any user lists that Carol would have to examine to verify that the Phantom suspects were really all logged on at the time of the Phantom spoofs.

After competing all three tasks, subjects completed a subjective questionnaire.

Results and Discussion

Subjects using the task-tailored representation were able to determine more quickly what had been done and what still needed to be done than subjects who used only a basic chronological organization of email messages. Indeed, the amount of time was cut in half for two of the tasks with no difference in accuracy detected. Table 1 and 2 depict the means and standard deviations for time and accuracy in each of the two conditions.

It is worth noting that the majority of the time subjects spent in the task-tailored interface was used in interpreting the unfamiliar interface (we did not train them on the interface in advance). A separate test of a subject familiar with the interface indicated a time of around 30 seconds to do Task 1. Thus, the times we observed are probably upper bounds.

Task	Chrono-logical	Task-Tailored
1. To whom do I owe lists?	424.2 (173.2.)*	209.2 (66.3)*
2. Who owes me lists?	294.2 (62.1)**	125.1 (34.2)**
3. Where is Phantom data?	186.1 (65.0)	162.2 (70.9)

* $p < .01$, ** $p < .001$

Table 1: Means (S.D.s) for time in seconds.

Task	Chrono-logical	Task-Tailored
1. To whom do I owe lists?	2.00 (1.05)	2.20 (1.48)
2. Who owes me lists?	2.10 (1.29)	2.40 (.70)
3. Where is Phantom data?	2.00 (0.00)	1.10 (1.45)

Table 2: Means (S.D.s) for accuracy.

A supplementary analysis based on Lohse's [13] cognitive model of graphical perception helps to explain these results. For example, to answer the question "To whom do I owe lists?", the model predicts that the task-tailored interface requires 32 steps whereas the chronological representation requires 93. Interestingly, the model predicts that organizing the messages into folders, although not empirically tested in this study, would require 108 steps, thus performing worse than either of the other two interfaces.

PROTOTYPE

Given the relatively large performance gains, we decided it would be worthwhile to develop a prototype that allows users to organize messages into task-tailored interfaces like the one depicted in Figure 3, using a palette that offers both partial layout views and a range of layout primitives. Our goal is to provide a flexible, generative, direct-manipulation layout interface in which users can create a number of views, customize them on-the-fly, and map them to any messages they want to visualize.

In our approach, users are able to use direct manipulation to position and represent messages in a view onto a database (messages are pre-defined types in the database). The placement results in the messages being attributed with properties; users can remain unaware of those attributes if they just want to informally group messages. Users, however, can also name the attributes and use them to write simple rules (e.g., If an incoming message is a "Reply to the message in column x, put it in column y") to augment the direct manipulation capability with capabilities such as automatic filing (a la email filters).

To illustrate, imagine the following scenario:

Task-tailorable representations. Carol Allison, a system administrator in The Spoofer Identification Task, has a number of messages in her inbox. As she reads through them, she discovers she is being spoofed, as are other system administrators in the network.

She decides to represent the state of affairs by creating a view for these messages, chooses a tabular view from the layout palette, and decides to use the time the spoofs originated as an at-a-glance marker for the messages. She creates a column to represent this information and labels it as "Spoof." In her view of the spoofer message, she selects the time, 12:10:19, and drags and drops it into the first row in the column. Her action creates two effects: (1) the time is displayed in the cell and (2) the message is automatically linked to the text "12:10:19." (Figure 5).

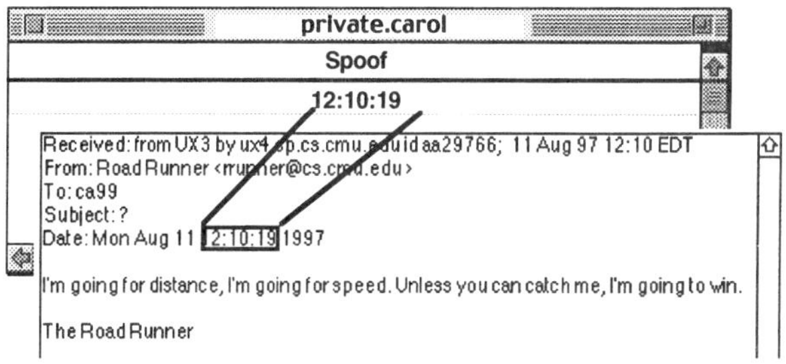

Figure 5. Creating a Column in a Tabular View

At this point, the system has attributed the message with attributes that simply indicate that it appears in a particular row and column. Carol can remain unaware of that attribution, but if she wishes to change the representation at a later time, she can group and name the implicit attribution and use it to create new views onto the messages.

Incremental formalization. Carol decides she'd like all new spoofs from this spoofer to be represented in one column, so she pops up a Column Specifier and writes a rule (From: Road Runner). Now all messages that are received "From: Road Runner" will appear in the column, with a default indicator for new and unread messages (Figure 6).

A second message, from Alice Jones, also contains the time of a spoof from Road Runner as an excerpt in the message body, so Carol selects the time information and drops it into a row. These actions result in the message from Alice being attributed with row/column attributes. The system does a union between messages that have been dropped into the column and the rule that specifies retrieval from the database.

Next, Carol creates a "Request To" column and selects "pm99" from the "To" field of the message she sent to Pat Mattis asking for login information and drops it into a row in this new column. Next, she creates a "Reply" field. She defines a rule that says "Messages in this column are

Replies to the previous column" and indicates that she would like the field to be represented as a check. Since she already has a message from Pat, a check appears in the column. In a similar way, she creates a "Request From" and "Reply" columns to represent the request from Alice Jones and her own reply. She grays rows in columns for which information is not expected (so she can better see the situation "at a glance"). Finally, she creates a column that spans all the rows and associates her Suspect List with those rows via a hypertext link in the last column.

Emergent representations. Later, Carol discovers that she is having difficulty remembering whether she updated the Suspect List, so she inserts a column "List Updated" and puts a check in the column whenever she updates the Suspect list in response to information.

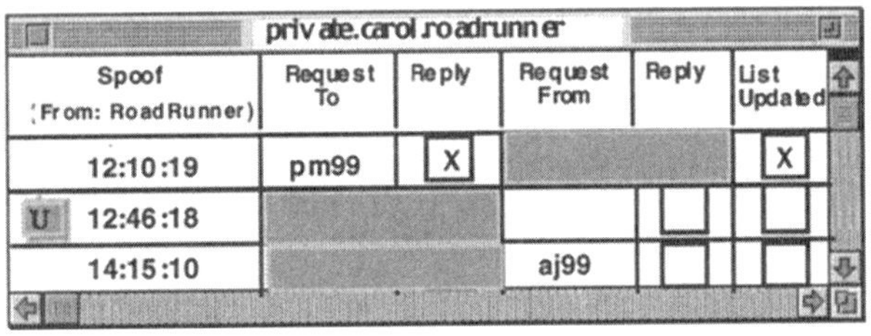

Figure 6. User-tailorable representation

Emergent sharing. Carol decides that it would be useful to share her Suspect List with other system administrators who are tracking down the spoofers, so she "publishes" the list to other SAs by renaming the list private.carol.roadrunner to SA.carol.roadrunner and inviting other SAs whom she knows are also working on the task to register and look at it.

To reduce the work in using parts of fields to represent messages and for manually putting messages in columns for which it is difficult to write simple rules that make use of system-represented attributes of messages, we are exploring the use of machine-learning techniques that allow training of agents that "look over the shoulder" of users and offer to automate recurring activities. These techniques are appropriate when the application involves repetitive behavior that is potentially different for different users [15].

RELATED RESEARCH

Numerous studies of asynchronous communication have been conducted (for an excellent review, see [17]). Most of the research has looked at the social-psychological effects of working face-to-face vs. communicating asynchronously. Other work on interfaces for asynchronous communication has focused on the social psychological effects of different interfaces [26]. Our research extends and complements previous work by focusing on the cognitive effects that user interfaces can have on asynchronous work. When people must work asynchronously, tools with effective interfaces can minimize the disadvantages and maximize the advantages of communicating across space and time. Both cognitive and social effects are relevant to measuring effectiveness.

Numerous field studies have been conducted on asynchronous communication [e.g., 10, 12, 14, 29]. Our work supplements those studies with formative observational and laboratory studies. We believe that all these types of study are essential in making progress in supporting asynchronous communication and plan to do a field study of our prototype.

Previous work on awareness has focused primarily on synchronous awareness. Gutwin et al. identify several types: workspace, organizational situation, informal, social, and structural and have done much work on synchronous workspace awareness [8]. The work reported here focuses on situation awareness (i.e., understanding the state of a dynamic system). We have also made a case for asynchronous workplace awareness and are actively working on representations of, for example, awareness of others intentions (Where are they going to be?).

In terms of interface and architecture, the work reported here is closely related to Oval [16], Object Lens [11] (and its precursor, Information Lens), systems which display values of selected fields from objects (e.g., messages) in a table or tree and support end-user programming of agents (e.g., email agents). Like Oval and Object Lens, our approach makes use of an object-oriented database that supports hypertext links. Our work extends this work by (1) separating the view of the object from the data in the object. This allows, for example, parts of a field or even a "check mark" to be used as a representation of a field; and (2) allowing direct editing of the object in the view rather than requiring the user to edit an *object type* or explicitly adding a field to an *object instance*. For example, in Object Lens, displaying messages in the "Response Received" column would require the user to create a new object type (e.g., a type "Message-for-which-a-reply-is-expected" as a subtype of the object type Message); if object instances already existed in the system that did not have the type, they would have to be retyped. In Oval, a user could edit an object instance directly by choosing Add Field from a menu; this would result in all instances of the object (and the object type) having the new field value.

In our system users are able to add a field by inserting a new column in the table and labeling it (e.g., "Response Received"). They can either place responses in the cells by direct manipulation (which adds a field to the message placed in the cell but not to the related message) or write a rule that says "If a message is a reply to the message in the previous column, put in this cell." We hypothesize that such direct manipulation will have two advantages: (1) users will be able to get the information they want represented without a great deal of overhead and thinking about types/subtypes, enabling users with minimal competence in conceptualizing types/subtypes to use the system (much as spreadsheet users may be unaware of computed values but still find a spreadsheet useful, cf. [18]); this was part of the motivation that Malone et al. [16] cite for moving from editing object types to editing object instances; and (2) for some problems, this representation will suffice and the added cost of defining such relationships for short-lived problems will be judged not to be worth the effort. By eliminating the requirement to always formalize representations, even for short-lived problems, we increase the likelihood that users will find the overall system cost-effective in terms of time and effort.

The architecture that allows direct manipulation by users draws upon work in incremental formalization [4, 25], especially an extensible set of attributes and relations that can take part in inheritance relationships. The use of such incremental formalization to create good external representations of the information was not a primary focus of those efforts.

Finally, the work we are doing is closely related to work in (semi-)automatic data visualization and we have been very influenced by the Sage/Visage systems [3, 24]. The Sage group has focused on providing excellent visualizations (i.e., conforming to principles of good graphic design) for quantitative data and they have explored automatic as well as user-tailorable visualizations of already attributed data. Our work has focused on providing visualizations for communication and on allowing users to interact with that data by adding attributes from within the view itself.

CONCLUSIONS AND FUTURE RESEARCH

We have demonstrated that a task-tailored representation can significantly improve task performance in an asynchronous communication task and argued that such representations would be useful generally.

We have only examined one aspect of task performance: reestablishing an understanding of the situation after time away from the task. The total cost, however, is a cost of building and maintaining, as well as using, a representation. Our next step is to test whether people can use task-tailorability of our prototype to easily build such representations for new, complex, and dynamic situations.

Moreover, time and accuracy are only one measure of performance in group work. We intend to do further studies to examine other cognitive issues (e.g., memory for the communication) and social issues (e.g., does being able to see "at a glance" who has not gotten back to you have a positive or negative effect on your perception of a person?) raised by our approach to asynchronous communication.

Assuming that our approach works, we plan to include an interface that allows users to browse previously created layout templates, use the template as a starting point and extend and customize the template as needed to visualize new situations [5, 28]. Our initial prototype provides only one layout type (a table). We are actively working on other layouts that can form the basis for good external representations of other communication tasks.

ACKNOWLEDGMENTS

This research was funded by ARPA, Contract Number N66001-96-C-8515. The authors would like to thank Anne Humphreys and Paul Erion, who also worked on the project.

REFERENCES

1. Bordia, P. (1997). Face-to-face versus computer mediated communication: A synthesis of the experimental literature. *The Journal of Business Communication, 34,* 99-120.
2. Chuah, M.C., John, B.E., & Pane, J. (1994). Analyzing graphic and textual layouts with GOMS: Results of a preliminary analysis. In *Proceedings of the CHI'94 Conference on Computer-Human Interaction* (pp. 323-324), April 24-28, Boston. ACM.
3. Chuah, M.C., Roth, S.F., Koljejchick, J., Mattis, J., & Juarez, O. (1995). SageBook: Searching Data-graphics by content. In *Proceedings of the CHI'95 Conference on Computer-Human Interaction* (pp. 338-345), May 7-11, Denver. ACM.
4. Haake, J., Neuwirth, C. M., Streitz, N.A. (1994). Coexistence and transformation of informal and formal structures: Requirements for more flexible hypermedia systems. In *Proceedings of the ACM European Conference on Hypermedia Technology (ECHT'94)* (pp. 1-12). Sep. 18-23, Edinburgh. Association for Computing Machinery.
5. Fischer, G. (1987). Cognitive view of reuse and redesign. *IEEE Software*, 60-72.
6. Gibson, J.J. (1966). *The senses considered as perceptual systems*. New York: Houghton Mifflin.
7. Gibson, J.J. (1979). *The ecological approach to visual perception.* New York: Houghton Mifflin.
8. Gutwin, C., Greenberg, S. and Roseman, M. (1996). Workspace awareness in real-time distributed groupware: Framework, widgets, and evaluation. In R.J. Sasse, A. Cunningham, and R. Winder (Eds.) *People and Computers XI* (pp. 281-298). Springer-Verlag.
9. Hofmann, M., Schreiweis, U., & Langendörfer, H. (1990). An integrated approach of knowledge acquisition by the hypertext system CONCORDE. In A. Rizk, N. Streitz, & J. André (Eds.) *Hypertext: Concepts, systems and applications*, pp. 166-179. Cambridge University Press, Cambridge, UK.
10. Kraut, R. E., Scherlis, W, Mukhopadhyay, T., Manning, J., Kiesler, S. (1996, Dec.) HomeNet: A field trial of residential Internet services. *Communications of the ACM.*
11. Lai, K., Malone, R., & Yu, K. (1988). Object Lens: A "spreadsheet" for cooperative work. *ACM Trans. on Office Inf. Systems, 6* (4), 332-353.
12. Licklider, J.C.R., & Vessa, A. (1978). Applications of information networks. *IEEE Proceedings, 66,* 1330-1346.
13. Lohse, G.L. (1993). A cognitive model for understanding graphical perception. *Human-Computer Interaction, 8,* 353-388.
14. MacKay, W.E. (1989). Diversity in the use of electronic mail: A preliminary inquiry. *ACM Transactions on Office Information Systems, 6* (4), 380-397.

15. Maes, P. (1994). Agents that reduce work and information overload. *Communications of the ACM, 37* (7), 31-40;146.

16. Malone, T.W., Lai, K., & Fry, C. (1994). Experiments with Oval: A radically tailorable tool for cooperative work. *ACM Trans. on Information Systems.*

17. McGrath, J.E., & Hollingshead, An. B. (1994). *Groups interacting with technology.* Sage Publications.

18. Nardi, B.A. & Miller, J.R. (1991). Twinkling lights and nested loops: distributed problem solving and spreadsheet development. *Int. J. of Man-Machine Studies, 34*, 161-184.

19. Neuwirth, C.M., Chandhok, R., Charney, D., Wojahn, P., Kim, L. (1994). Distributed collaborative writing: A comparison of spoken and written modalities for reviewing and revising documents. In *Proceedings of the CHI'94 Conference on Computer-Human Interaction* (pp. 51-57), April 24-28, Boston. ACM.

20. Neuwirth, C. M., Chandhok, R., Kaufer, D. S., Erion, P., Morris, J., & Miller, D. (1992). Flexible diff-ing in a collaborative writing system. In *Proceedings of the Fourth Conference on Computer-Supported Cooperative Work (CSCW '92)* (pp. 147-154). Baltimore, MD: Association for Computing Machinery. Reprinted in R. Rada (Ed.) (1996). *Groupware and authoring* (pp. 189-204). San Diego: Academic Press.

21. Neuwirth, C. M., Kaufer, D. S., Chandhok, R., & Morris, J. H. (1990). Issues in the design of computer-support for co-authoring and commenting. *Proceedings of the Third Conference on Computer-Supported Cooperative Work (CSCW '90)* (pp. 183-195). Baltimore, MD: Association for Computing Machinery.

22. Neuwirth, C. M., Kaufer, D. S., Chandhok, R., & Morris, J.H. (1994). Computer support for distributed collaborative writing: Defining parameters of interaction. In *Proceedings of the Conference on Computer-Supported Cooperative Work (CSCW '94)* (pp. 145-152). Oct. 22-26, Chapel Hill, NC. Association for Computing Machinery.

23. Neuwirth, C. M., & Kaufer, D. S. (1989). The role of external representation in the writing process: Implications for the design of hypertext-based writing tools. *Hypertext89 Proceedings* (pp. 319-341). Baltimore, MD: Association for Computing Machinery.

24. Roth, S.F., & Mattis, J. (1990). Data characterization for intelligent graphics presentation. In *Proceedings of the CHI'90 Conference on Computer-Human Interaction* (pp. 193-200), April. ACM.

25. Shipman, F.M. & McCall, R. (1994). Supporting knowledge-base evolution with incremental formalization. In *Proceedings of the CHI'94 Conference on Computer-Human Interaction* (pp. 285-291), April 24-28, Boston. ACM.

26. Sproull, L., Subramani, M., Kiesler, S., Walker, J.H., & Waters, K. (1996). When the interface is a face. *Human Computer Interaction*, 11, 97-124.

27. Suchman, L.A. (1987). Plans and siutated action: The problem of human-machine communication. New York: Cambridge University Press.

28. Trigg, R.H., & Bødker (1994). From implementation to design tailoring and the emergence of systematization in CSCW. In *Proceedings of the Conference on Computer-Supported Cooperative Work (CSCW '94)* (pp. 45-54). Oct. 22-26, Chapel Hill, NC. Association for Computing Machinery.

29. Whittaker, S. & Sidner, C. (1997). Email overload: Exploring personal information management of email. In Kiesler, S. (Ed.), *Culture of the Internet* (pp. 277-295). NJ: Lawrence Erlbaum Associates.

30. Wojahn, P., Neuwirth, C. M., Bullock, B. (1998). Effects of interfaces for annotation on communication in a collaborative task. In *Proceedings of the CHI'98 Conference on Computer-Human Interaction* (pp. 456-463). April 18-23, Los Angeles. ACM.

31. Zhang, J. (1997). The nature of external representations in problem solving. *Cognitive Science, 21* (3), 179-217.

Coordination, Overload and Team Performance: Effects of Team Communication Strategies

Susan R. Fussell, Robert E. Kraut, F. Javier Lerch, William L. Scherlis, Matthew M. McNally, and Jonathan J. Cadiz
Human-Computer Interaction Institute
Carnegie Mellon University
Pittsburgh, PA USA
+1 412 268 4003
sfussell+@andrew.cmu.edu; kraut+@andrew.cmu.edu

ABSTRACT

The goal of this paper is to identify the communication tactics that allow management teams to successfully coordinate without becoming overloaded, and to see whether successful coordination and freedom from overload independently influence team performance. We found that how much teams communicated, what they communicated about, and the technologies they used to communicate predicted coordination and overload. Team coordination but not overload predicted team success.

Keywords

Work groups, coordination, cognitive overload, electronic mail, computer-mediated communication, awareness devices

INTRODUCTION

For a work group to accomplish a task effectively, its members must coordinate their efforts in a very detailed way. Two ways groups can coordinate work are through team design and through communication. By design we mean the way teams structure their tasks and the tools they use to aid coordination [11]. By communication we mean the face-to-face meetings, electronic mail (email), file exchanges, and so forth that teams use to perform such tasks as negotiating their goals, making decisions, and providing one another task status information.

Although all teams use some degree of design and communication to coordinate their activities, to some extent these approaches are substitutes for each other. For example, when communication between team members is difficult, they often resort to increased division of labor to reduce their needs for communication [9]. However, sharp division of labor coupled with reduced communication is a poor choice for tasks characterized by high uncertainty, rapidly changing environments, poorly defined outcomes, and a substantial variety of problems to be confronted [8][14]. These conditions, however, characterize many tasks for which teams are used, such as managerial decision making, software engineering, and home contracting. Participants must communicate directly and extensively to coordinate successfully in these interdependent and uncertain tasks.

Imagine, for example, the top management team in a software company that must respond to an announcement from a competitor that the competitor is giving away a core product in order to build market share. The team must formulate and come to consensus on an initial strategy (e.g., give away the product too, bundle their product with those from other companies, seek anti-trust protection) so that they can all act in a unified way, monitor changes in the business environment, so that they can revise plans as needed, execute these plans, and maintain awareness of what one another is doing so that they do not duplicate or contradict each others actions. The danger is that the effort of communication and monitoring may overwhelm them and deflect them from actually doing work. It is difficult, for example, to craft a press release or lobby justice department officials if one needs to be continually discussing strategy with peers.

The goal of this paper is to identify the communication tactics that allow management teams to coordinate successfully without becoming overloaded and to see whether successful coordination and freedom from overload independently influence team performance. We examine how much teams communicate, what they communicate about, and the technologies they use in order to predict coordination and overload. We also examine the techniques they use to maintain awareness of what other team members are doing at a given point in time.

In addition to measuring team members' use of traditional technologies for maintaining awareness (e.g., group meetings and electronic mail), we provided them with two preliminary tools that were designed to increase awareness without increasing overload. An additional goal of this

CSCW 98 Seattle Washington USA
Copyright ACM 1998 1-58113-009-0/98/11...$5.00

study was to evaluate the usefulness of these tools and to draw implications for the design of a new generation of awareness tools.

Awareness

One function of within-team communications is to provide members with information about what their teammates are doing. When decisions and outcomes depend on integrating different team members' efforts, it is important for each member to know the status of the others' tasks—how near to completion the tasks are, preliminary results, and so forth.

The Impact of Technology on Awareness

When groups are co-located, members can maintain awareness by monitoring activities going on around them by, for instance, overhearing conversations between other team members [18]. For distributed work groups, maintaining awareness of others' activities is more difficult and requires some degree of technological intervention. The use of traditional technologies such as email among team members may affect both coordination and overload by allowing those members not directly involved in an exchange to be passively aware of the contents of that exchange. Passive awareness of what other team members are doing, provided by indirect participation in a communicative exchange (e.g., by carbon copying), should enable a team member to better coordinate his/her activities with the rest of the team. For example, several researchers have demonstrated that compared to people who do not use electronic mail, people who are heavy users are more likely to be able to keep up with the more variable aspects of their work environment, even if these are not the focus of their immediate work activities [12][16]. One reason is that electronic mail, through copies and distribution lists, is often sent to people who are only peripherally concerned with its contents.

Trade-offs Between Awareness and Overload

It is plausible, however, that passive awareness comes with the cost of increased information volume. By adding to team members' already large stream of incoming information, passive awareness information may consume too much of the team's attentional resources.

It may be possible to balance the tension between needs for greater information to improve coordination and needs for reduced information to conserve attentional resources. By providing information asynchronously and by aggregating it rather than providing it incrementally, one may reduce attentional demands without reducing the usefulness of the information. Kraut and Attewell [16], for example, show that people receiving asynchronous communication, like fax and email, report that it is much less intrusive than synchronous communication, like meetings or phone conversations. Because the receivers can fit asynchronous messages into their task schedules, an increase in volume of asynchronous messages leads to substantially less overload than an comparable increase in synchronous communication.

Aggregating information may be another technique to reduce the volume of information and amount of overload. For example, rather than presenting each message in order in a user's electronic mailbox, the databases used in several organizational memory systems consolidate all messages on a particular topic and provide an indicator to potential users of the volume of messages [17]. While there has been no explicit assessment of the effects of this technique on overload, it is plausible to assume that this technique consumes less attention than the alternative.

Research questions

We can summarize this discussion through several research questions:

What communication tactics allow teams to be better coordinated? Increased volume of communication in any modality may lead to better coordination. Because the interactivity improves communicators' ability to reach common ground, use of face-to-face communication may improve coordination more than use of electronic mail [1]. Because asynchronous communication reduces scheduling costs in communication, use of electronic mail may improve coordination most for distributed teams.

Topic of communication is also likely to influence coordination. One can broadly distinguish between discussions of substance—what work should be done—and process—how to do the work. Both of these may improve team coordination by clarifying for all team members what the team goals and procedures should be.

What communication tactics allow teams to reduce cognitive overload? Reduced volume of communication in any modality should reduce overload. Because it is asynchronous, use of electronic mail as a substitute for face-to-face communication should reduce overload.

Can well-designed awareness devices enhance team coordination without increasing overload? New awareness tools that follow certain design principles (aggregation of information, passive awareness, asynchrony) may lessen feelings of cognitive overload by reducing the heavy incoming stream of information a team member typically faces. In addition, passive awareness should enhance coordination by allowing team members to monitor or access information on an as-needed basis.

What, if any, are the effects of coordination and cognitive overload on objective and subjective team outcome measures? Although it is widely acknowledged that coordination improves performance and overload hinders it, these relationships, as well as trade-offs between coordination and overload, have rarely been examined in a naturalistic context in which all teams share the same tasks and goals and in which performance can be readily measured and compared using objective measures.

We investigated these four questions within the context of a business simulation, described in the next section.

THE MANAGEMENT GAME SIMULATION

All students in Carnegie Mellon University's (CMU) Graduate School of Information Administration must participate in a realistic business simulation called the *Management Game* ("Game"). In this simulation, five to six member teams are grouped into "nations" of four firms each; within each nation, firms compete with one another over the course of a simulated two-year business period condensed into 14 actual weeks.

During the simulation, teams must make decisions regarding the nature, production, distribution, and financing of their products (detergents). They must also, in a series of reports and presentations, present their companies' strategies to boards of directors consisting of actual business people, and they must trade shares of their own and other teams' companies in a simulated stock market. In addition to these routine business decisions, the game is punctuated by crises such as lawsuits and threats of work stoppages that call for rapid mobilization of effort and quick responses.

Team presidents are elected, but teams typically further divide their labor by assigning members to specific positions such as Chief Financial Officer and Marketing Strategist. Nonetheless, these individual tasks must be integrated in order for teams to make good decisions. Much of this integration process appears to result from the use of both synchronous communications (e.g., face-to-face meetings and telephone calls) and asynchronous, computer-mediated communications (e.g., email, electronic file sharing). Because team members generally have different work and class schedules, teams playing the Management Game tend to work in a distributed manner much of the time.

The Management Game thus combines the best features of both field and laboratory studies: it is a very realistic simulation; yet, it also provides sufficient control to allow meaningful comparisons between groups using different processes, employing different technologies, or varying on other measured dimensions. It is in the context of this simulation that we examined our research questions described above.

METHOD

Overview of Study

Teams of students participating in the Management Game interacted over the course of two seven-week periods. During this time, team process data was collected via three surveys, and team outcome data was obtained from objective sources. As part of the study, two awareness tools were introduced to Game participants and ratings of their usefulness by team members was obtained. In the remainder of this section we first describe the construction of the two awareness tools, then we describe the web-based surveys we administered, and finally we describe the outcome measures used in the study.

Construction Of Awareness Tools

In the context of the Management Game, a team member is likely to be interested in changes to the Game environment (e.g., changes to the firm's stock price), to his/her personal success (e.g., wealth in Game dollars), in the availability of teammates, in the status of others' tasks, and in changes made to shared artifacts such as documents and spreadsheets, among other things. We developed two simple awareness tools designed to address these informational needs without creating information overload: an email archiving system and an activity monitoring tool.

Although these two tools were somewhat primitive, they enabled us to evaluate the importance of several design principles for awareness tools. Both tools were designed to provide passive awareness of others' activities—that is, to make information available in such a way that it does not impose on the user's attentional resources—under the assumption that this will increase coordination and decrease cognitive overload. Both tools were also designed to be asynchronous in order to further reduce cognitive overload. Finally, the activity monitoring tool was designed to test a third design principle, namely, that by aggregating information sources such that multiple inputs are represented as a single flow of information and such that important changes to the environment can be readily identified, awareness tools can enhance coordination while reducing the overload associated with multiple information inputs.

Email Archive

The email archiving tool monitored a user's incoming email and automatically generated and filed copies of Game-related email into his or her email archive—a private collection of Game-related messages similar to an electronic bulletin board (bboard).

In order to evaluate the role of passive awareness on team process variables, we created two types of email archives. A "group archive" stored messages sent from any team member to any other team member and was readable by all members of a particular team. An "individual archive" was specific to each team member and contained all Game-related messages addressed to him or her. The functional difference between these two types of archives was that a team member using a group archive could browse all of the team's Game-related messages, even if he or she had not been directly addressed or copied when that message was originally sent, whereas a team member using an individual archive could only access messages he or she had received.

Activity Monitoring Tool

The activity monitoring tool, our first attempt at developing a tool that would monitor a variety of Game-specific information sources, provided team members with a personalized display of the state of several relevant team and personal variables. This tool was designed to help team members focus on the right information at the right time by providing background alerting services to indicate when important changes had occurred in the Game environment and by monitoring teammates, shared work objects, and information sources in the environment. The interface permitted users to customize the display by expanding or collapsing subsections to meet their informational needs. An example of an expanded interface is shown in Figure 1.

The activity monitoring tool was designed to monitor a set of heterogeneous inputs (e.g. new email count, firm price of a firm's shares on the simulated stock market, time since a collaborator was last seen, rate of change in personal net worth) and to map measures of these inputs onto a single visualization. That is, we aimed to design a tool that would tell a user if something "interesting" was happening in a variety of Game-related information domains in a single glance, regardless of differences in units of measurement used in these domains.

We chose to apply simple heuristics to map the raw inputs into an 8-point "interest" scale. Each input was then rendered with a graphic gauge that had seven slots arranged horizontally that could "light up"—a "0" on the interest scale would display zero lights, whereas a "7" would display seven lights (see Figure 1). The display updated itself every 15 minutes. Discussion of the heuristics will be presented in a more detailed presentation of the research.

Surveys

Game Survey

Participants completed web-based surveys at three points during the game: at the end of the first seven-week period, halfway through the second seven-week period, and at the end of the game. The second and third survey periods coincided with teams' second and third board presentations. The surveys contained a large number of questions addressing a number of aspects of team activity:

Media Importance. In the first survey, respondents were asked to rate the importance to their team of several communications modalities (face-to-face meetings, email, telephone, file exchange, and fax) on a scale of 1 (not at all important) to 5 (extremely important), and to indicate the frequency with which they used each of these modalities on a scale of 1 (never) to 6 (daily). Not surprisingly, frequency and importance ratings were very highly correlated (> .90) and to conserve survey space we retained only the importance ratings in the remaining two surveys.

Rated importance of face-to-face and telephone communications were highly and positively correlated, as were ratings for email and electronic file exchange. To

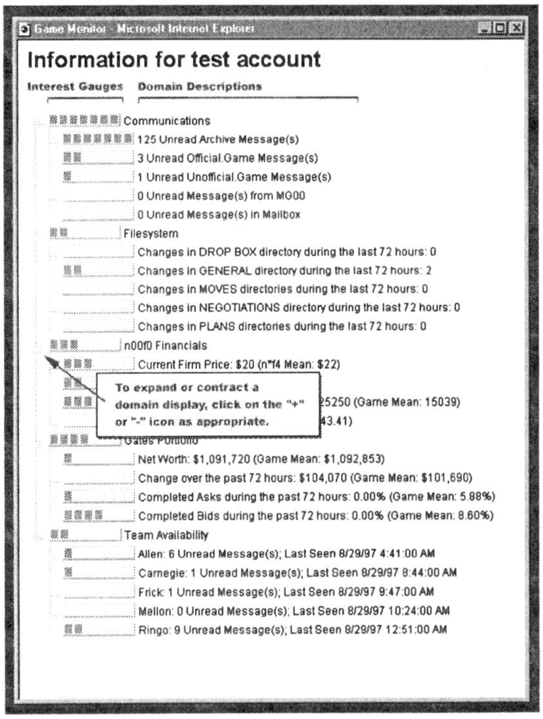

Figure 1. The Activity Monitoring Tool.

avoid multicollinearity, we selected Game teams' two primary communications modalities—synchronous face-to-face meetings and asynchronous email communication—to use in our analyses.

Topics of Communication. Respondents were asked to rate the frequency with which their team discussed six Game-related topics—financial strategy, product and product development, competitors, board presentations, Game rules, and team process—on a 6-point scale ranging from never to daily. Factor analyses of responses to these questions indicated two independent topic dimensions on which teams differed: strategy-focused discussion (strategy, product, competitors), and process-focused discussion (presentations, rules, team process). Teams' average scores on scales representing these two dimensions were used in our statistical analyses.

Team Process. The surveys contained a number of questions about team coordination (e.g., "Tasks were clearly assigned," "Team members had a clear idea of team goals"), and cognitive overload (e.g., "The pace of Game was overwhelming," "I received more information from my teammates than I could process"). Some of these questions were adapted from prior, standardized scales (e.g., [2][20]) and some were newly constructed for the current study. All responses were made using a 5-point scale ranging from strongly disagree to strongly agree. Scales for coordination and overload were constructed based on factor analyses and our knowledge of the item's author's original intent.

Awareness Tool Use. Surveys also included several questions concerning how often respondents used the email archiving and activity monitoring tools described below, and how important they judged these tools to be.

Outcome Measures. We used two measures of team performance in our analyses. Stock market price for a team reflected the judgment of all 277 Management Game participants of how well a team performed. Because stock prices rose rapidly over the course of the game, we used prices normalized across teams within each of the three survey periods. Board evaluation surveys were distributed to members of the board after each of the three board presentations. Because responses to all evaluation questions were highly inter-correlated, we used overall ratings, averaged across board members, to represent board evaluation scores.

Participants and Procedure

Participants consisted of 277 students, organized into 50 five or six member teams, who participated in the Management Game during the Spring and Fall of 1997. Of these teams, 39 consisted of full-time students and 11 consisted of part-timers.

The study took place over a period of approximately 14 weeks. During this time, teams made decisions about such managerial issues as what products they would sell to what markets ("Game moves"). These decisions changed the state of the Game environment and thus influenced their own and other teams' future moves. In addition, teams wrote three documents and made three oral presentations to their boards of directors. They also had to decide how to handle unexpected crises.

The email archive and activity monitoring device were introduced at separate times. Game teams who agreed to participate were randomly assigned to either the group or the individual archive condition. Archiving was introduced during Phase 1 to all teams who agreed to participate in the study. During Phase 2, we provided participating team members with the activity monitoring tool for a period of seven weeks.

Summary

By way of surveys and other measurement techniques we collected a large set of data that included control, work process, awareness tool, and outcome variables. We then trimmed down the full set of variables to reduce multi-collinearity. The final set of variables selected for use in our analyses is shown in Table 1.

RESULTS

In this section, we first describe the statistical techniques we used to test our hypotheses. We then present the results of structural equation modeling. Finally, we report additional analyses concerning the awareness tools we provided.

CONTROL VARIABLES
Firm starting position (Firms 1-4)
Number of members (5 or 6)
Student status (full-time vs. part-time)
WORK PROCESS
Topics of discussion (self-reported frequency)
Team process (task assignments, scheduling)
Team strategy (production strategy, competitors)
Media importance (self-reported)
Face-to-face meetings
Electronic communications
Team process measures (self-reported)
Self-reported coordination
Self-reported cognitive overload
TOOL USE
Awareness tool importance (self-reported)
Email Archive
Activity Monitoring Tool
Desired features for new awareness tools
TEAM PERFORMANCE
Firm stock price (objective)
Board evaluation (mean subjective evaluation)

Table 1. Measures used in statistical analyses.

Method of Analysis

Because the simulation is played over several weeks, we collected data at multiple points in time, allowing us to examine developmental processes and to test causal paths using panel designs and structural equation modeling.

Two types of regression analyses were used in the analyses reported below. Because the number and identity of members of each team who responded to the surveys differed from survey to survey, the equation used to analyze survey variables included only other variables that had been measured at the same point in time:

$$\text{Success of Team Process}_t = \text{Predictors}_t + \text{Controls}$$

In contrast, the two outcome measures were always analyzed by an equation of the following form:

$$\text{Performance}_t = \text{performance}_{t-1} + \text{Predictors}_t + \text{Controls}$$

This analysis looks at the effects of predictor variables (e.g., team coordination) on an outcome variable measured (e.g., firm stock price) while holding constant the initial value of the outcome variable and other control variables (e.g., team composition). Because the outcome variable is included on both the left and right sides of the equations, the analysis is equivalent to an analysis of change scores on the outcome, controlling for regression towards the mean, unreliability, contemporaneous covariation between the outcome and the predictor variables, and other statistical artifacts [4].

Structural Modeling of Team Processes and Outcomes

The model we report here tests the causal sequence illustrated in Figure 2. In this model, the first step involved regressing four communications variables (the two topics—strategy and group process—and the two modalities—face-to-face and email) onto users' ratings of the importance of the awareness tools (email archive and activity monitoring tool). Second, these six variables were regressed onto the two measures of team success—self-reported coordination and cognitive overload. Third, because firm price was set prior to each board meeting, we regressed the full set of variables plus standardized lagged firm price (that is, firm price at the time of the previous board meeting) onto current standardized firm price. Finally, we used all these variables plus lagged board evaluation (the evaluation from the previous board meeting) to predict current board evaluations. Because lagged variables were included in the equations, only data from the second and third survey could be included in the analyses.

All the regression equations also included the control variables listed in Table 1. However, because these variables seldom showed any significant effects on the dependent measures and because they were typically of little theoretical interest, results for these variables are not reported here unless they are especially strong and theoretically notable.

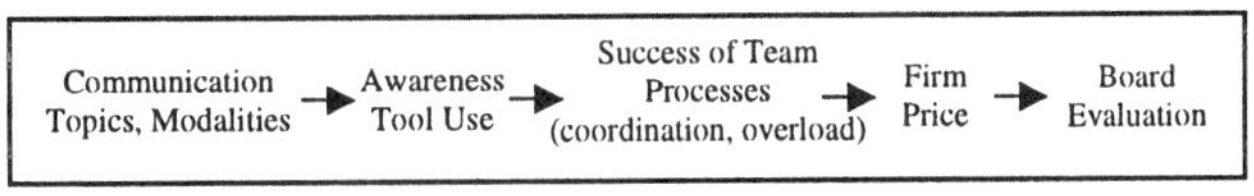

Figure 2. Causal path tested in regression analyses.

Step 1: Predicting Rated Importance of Awareness Tools.

Email Archive. The email archive was designed to enhance team coordination while reducing cognitive overload by storing messages in a convenient place. Game participants were not, however, forced to use their archives. Thus, this stage of our structural modeling examined the effects of communication content and modality variables on the rated importance of the email archiving system.

Not surprisingly, the more important teams rated email as a medium for their intra-team communications, the higher they rated the importance of the archive. The email archives were also rated as more important by teams consisting of full-time as opposed to part-time students. We had expected that part-time students would have more difficulty coordinating their schedules and therefore would value the archive more than full-time students. It is likely that this finding, which parallels the part-timers' somewhat lower ratings of the importance of email communications, stems from the difficulties part-time students have in accessing the CMU email system from off-campus.

The overall equation was quite successful at predicting archive use (F [9, 68] = 5.62, $p < .001$; $R^2 = .43$). The strongest predictor was student status ($t = 3.97$, $p = .001$; $\beta = .40$), followed by rated email importance ($t = 2.65$, $p = .01$; $\beta = .28$).

Activity Monitoring Tool. Our analyses found no significant predictors of the use of the activity monitoring tool, nor did we find that use of this tool affected any other variable in the equation. Thus, we have eliminated it from Figure 3 to make it easier to follow. We will discuss other analyses of activity monitoring tool use later in this paper.

Step 2: Predicting the Success of Group Processes

One of our major interests in this study was to examine the effects of team communication strategies (modality and content) and use of awareness tools on team coordination and feelings of cognitive overload.

Coordination. The frequency with which a team reported discussing issues regarding team strategy (marketing, competitors) was a good predictor of how well that team reported it coordinated its activity: The more time spent discussing strategy, the better coordinated the team. In contrast, increased discussion of team processes such as

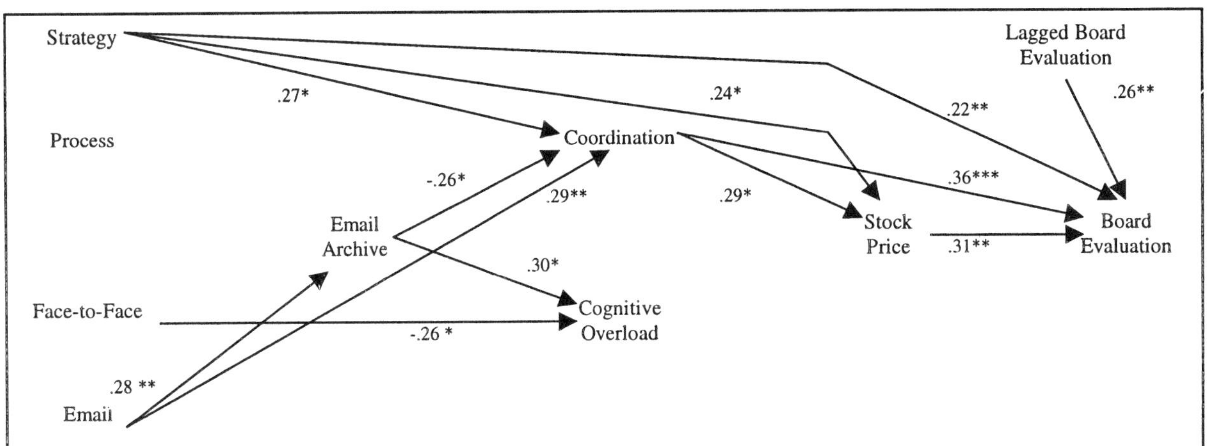

Figure 3. Direct and indirect effects of variables in structural equation analysis.

task assignment did not predict success of team coordination.

Email was also an important mechanism for increasing team coordination. The higher the rated importance of email (strongly correlated with the frequency of email use), the better coordinated the team. Contrary to our expectations, however, rated importance of face-to-face meetings did not predict coordination.

The complete set of variables in the equation was excellent at predicting self-reported team coordination (F [11, 64] = 4.92, $p < .001$; $R^2 = .46$). The best predictors were discussion of team strategy ($t = 2.46$, $p < .05$; $\beta = .27$), and rated email importance ($t = 2.62$, $p = .01$; $\beta = .29$). Use of the email archive was negatively associated with coordination ($t = -2.04$, $p < .05$; $\beta = -.26$), perhaps indicating that team members go back to look at older messages when coordination is poor.

Cognitive Overload. We had anticipated that most teams in this study would reported experiencing a significant amount of cognitive overload. However, most responses were in the intermediate range. Furthermore, contrary to our expectations, the extent of overload was negatively associated with rated importance of face-to-face communication. Because importance ratings were very highly correlated with self-reported frequency of use for each communication mode, these findings suggest that rather than overwhelming members' attentional resources, more frequent within-team communications may help clarify roles, keep others up to date on what one is doing, and otherwise provide information that helps a member complete his or her task.

In the full model, cognitive overload was significantly predicted by our independent measures (F [11, 65] = 2.06, $p < .05$; $R^2 = .26$). The strongest predictor variables were rated importance of face-to-face communications ($t = -1.97$, $p = .05$; $\beta = -.26$), and self-reported email archive use ($t = 1.99$, $p = .05$; $\beta = .30$).

Steps 3 and 4: Predicting Outcome Measures

Firm Stock Price. In predicting firm stock price, we included lagged stock price (the stock price just before the previous board meeting) to the variables already in the equation. The most important predictors of stock price were self-reported coordination and frequency of discussing strategic topics. Greater coordination and more frequent discussion of strategy probably have their effects on stock price by way of their effects on decision-making processes. Stock price was in large part a function of a teams profits, which in turn were based on agreement about product development, marketing, and competitors' strategies. It is conceivable that the goodness of a decision is improved when teams both know how to coordinate and integrate individual members' work activities and when all members understand team strategy.

Stock price was predicted well by the full model *(F* [14, 61] = 3.52, $p < .001$; $R^2 = .45$). The two primary predictors in this model were team coordination ($t = 2.10$, $p < .05$; $\beta = .29$) and discussion of strategy ($t = 2.00$, $p = .05$; $\beta = .24$). Although lagged price was highly correlated with current stock price, it was not a significant predictor of current stock price when all other variables were entered into the equation.

Board Evaluation. In the last stage of the analysis, we regressed all the previous variables plus lagged board evaluation (the evaluation from the preceding meeting) onto current evaluations. The results indicated that better board evaluation scores could be successfully predicted by higher values of two process variables—the success of team coordination and the extent to which teams discussed strategy—and of two outcome measures—lagged board evaluation and current stock price.

Better coordinated teams may receive better board evaluations because substantial coordination is required to integrate individual members' analyses for the written board reports and to create a unified oral presentation. Similarly, discussion of strategy, in addition to improving coordination, may allow teams to converge on a shared view of what they will present in their oral and written reports.

The full model was highly successful at predicting board evaluations (F [16, 58] = 6.01, $p < .001$; $R^2 = .62$). The most successful outcome-based predictors were lagged board evaluation ($t = 2.42$, $p = .05$; $\beta = .26$) and normalized current stock price ($t = 2.83$, $p = .01$; $\beta = .31$). The most successful process-based predictors were self-reported team coordination ($t = 2.97$, $p < .005$; $\beta = .36$) and frequency of strategy-related discussions ($t = 2.00$, $p = .05$; $\beta = .21$).

Further Analyses of Awareness Devices

In addition to assessing the role of the email archive and the activity monitoring tool within the context of structural equation modeling, we also performed analyses of awareness tool use in which we examined the effects of additional tool-specific variables. In this section we report on these additional analyses.

Email Archive

In the structural equations above, we did not distinguish ratings of email archive importance by teams in the group versus the individual archive condition. As noted above, in the group condition a team member could examine all email exchanges between teammates, regardless of whether he or she was one of the original recipients of those messages. In the individual archive condition, team members could only access email that they had sent or received.

We predicted that group archives would provide teams with more value than the individual archives because they enabled team members to monitor others' activities, through their email exchanges, on an as-needed basis. In contrast, the individual archive served essentially as an email filtering device—it organized information that the team member already had. We also predicted that archive importance would increase as the total number of messages exchanged between teammates increased.

We tested these predictions in a two (archive condition) by two (survey number) Analysis of Variance (ANOVA). An objective measure of the amount of within-team mail archived per day was used as a covariate, as the need for an archive is likely to increase as a function of email volume.

Consistent with our hypotheses, teams assigned to the group archive condition rated their archives as significantly more important than teams assigned to the individual archive condition (F [1, 73] = 9.74, $p < .005$). In addition, there was a strong effect of the covariate, email volume (F [1, 73] = 15.68, $p < .001$), indicating that regardless of archive condition, teams receiving more email placed greater value on the archive.

The Activity Monitoring Tool

As noted above, several types of information were presented in the activity monitoring tool's display: changes to shared documents and spreadsheets, to team members' whereabouts (e.g., when they last checked their email or logged on), to the team's financial status, and to the Game environment.

Respondents showed a clear preference for notifications about changes to their teams' finances and to the Game environment over information about others' availability or changes to shared documents and files. A two (study condition) by two (task-related vs. process-related information) ANOVA, with repeated measures on the second factor, showed a significant effect for type of information presented (F [1, 290] = 115.68, $p <$ .001). There was no effect of which type of the information was presented first nor a presentation condition by type of tool interaction. These results are paralleled by those when frequency of use rather than importance serves as the dependent measure.

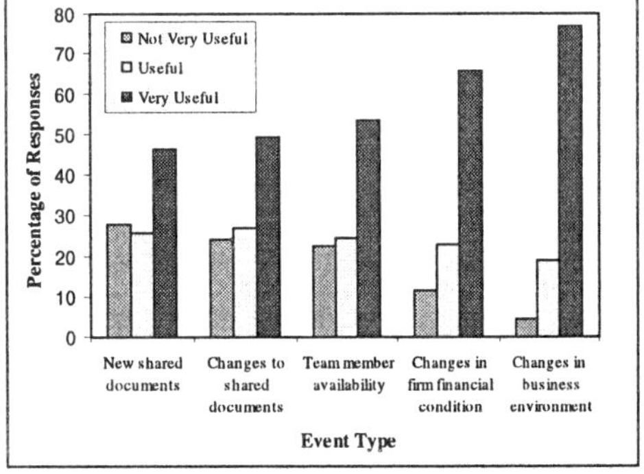

Figure 4: Rated usefulness of automatic notifications by event type

The means of the ratings, however, indicate that neither the team activity nor the Game environment monitoring were rated of high importance. Thus, the relatively low usage and ratings of our first awareness tools could stem from a lack of interest in such tools or from flaws in our first attempts to instantiate awareness tools (e.g., a poor interface, incorrect mappings of raw data to interest indicators).

Some indication that Game teams consider properly constructed awareness tools to be at least potentially helpful comes from responses to five questions we asked all students in the final survey. These questions asked respondents to rate how useful they thought it would have been if their team had been automatically notified about (a) new shared documents, (b) changes to existing documents, (c) the availability of team members, (d) changes to the financial condition of their firm, and (e) changes to the business environment that could impact their firm.

The results are shown in Figure 4. Consistent with ratings of the activity monitoring tool, there was greater interest in our developing future awareness tools for financial and Game environment information than for member availability and shared documents. One way to interpret these findings is that Game participants are in fact more interested in monitoring changes in finances and in the Game environment. However it is also possible that teams already had a notification system in place—email—for document changes and member availability. A casual examination of team members' email content revealed that a large proportion contained notifications about new and changed documents and spreadsheets and about team member availability. Few or none contained information about firm finances or the business environment. Instead, indications of interesting changes in these domains had to be actively sought (e.g., by logging onto the stock market simulation). Awareness tools, then, may benefit users when they provide passive awareness of information that previously had to be actively sought.

DISCUSSION

The results presented above provide us with some preliminary answers to the questions posed in the introductory section of this paper:

What communication tactics allow teams to be better coordinated?

Email was an important means by which teams in this study coordinated their activities. Although survey respondents rated the importance of each modality, not its frequency, the two were found to be so highly correlated in Survey 1 that we can infer that at least in part, the more email a team exchanges the better coordinated their activities will be.

Somewhat surprisingly, we found no evidence that face-to-face communication affected degree of coordination. This may be due to the extent to which teams worked in a distributed manner: because of members' different schedules, face-to-face meetings may simply have occurred too infrequently to allow for rapid coordination of effort. In addition, a substantial proportion of team emails were devoted to coordinating the face-to-face meetings themselves (time, location, agenda).

Choices about what to talk about and how often to talk about them also affected reported coordination. Teams that discussed issues related to their tasks and goals (here, their competitors activities and their products) were better coordinated. Discussion of process-related topics, however, did not appear to affect coordination.

One way to interpret these findings is that discussion of strategy helps team members develop a shared view or mental model of their team's goals and tasks [3][15]. This shared mental model may improve coordination because each team member understands how his or her tasks fit into the team's overall goals.

We are currently coding and analyzing within-team email content and type (question, statement, command, etc.) to help us further interpret our findings on team communications.

What communication tactics allow teams to reduce cognitive overload?

In this study, cognitive overload did not appear to be a function of any specific communication strategies. Self-reported overload levels were lower than we had anticipated and there was little variability across teams. There are several explanations. First, teams may experience different levels of information overload but they may adapt their behavior so that their current level of perceived cognitive overload is tolerable to them. Second, we may not be measuring cognitive overload correctly. Respondents rated their overload levels for the week prior to the survey and it is likely that they couldn't recall precisely how they felt during that time period.

Face-to-face communication had a direct effect on ratings of cognitive overload but interestingly, this effect was in the opposite direction than anticipated: the more communication, the less feelings of overload. We also found a nonsignificant effect in the same direction for email communications. These results may indicate that it is task demands rather than incoming communications that are responsible for feelings of cognitive overload. Alternatively, the results may be due to problems with our measure of overload.

Can well-designed awareness devices enhance team coordination without increasing cognitive overload?

Although we were unable to answer this question in the current study, we were able to identify properties that Game teams desire in future awareness tools. In general, team members find it natural to send one another notifications about their availability and changes to shared artifacts. What they desire is awareness tools that allow them to monitor exogenous changes in the Game environment—lawsuits, competitor actions, financial performance, and so forth.

Another reason teams may prefer notifications about the environment is that unlike the straightforward information provided by notifications of availability and changed artifacts, environmental information requires substantial processing before decisions may be made and/or actions may be taken based on this information.

These results suggest that awareness tools should focus extensively on monitoring and processing environmental information, at least within the domain we studied. The extent to which these results can be generalized to other types of work teams with other collaborative tasks is an issue for future research.

What, if any, are the effects of coordination and cognitive overload on objective and subjective team outcome measures?

Our analyses showed clearly that the better coordinated a team reported being, the better its performance both in the stock market and in board evaluations. Better coordinated teams may have had higher stock prices because smooth coordination allowed them to integrate their individual tasks easily and make good decisions about Game moves. Better coordinated teams also were able to write better documents and give better board presentations. These results, although expected, are important because they demonstrate a relationship between process and outcome that has not often been empirically established.

FUTURE DIRECTIONS

In our current work we are investigating the use of shared mental models as an underlying theoretical construct that explains many of our findings. For example, we found that discussion of team goals and strategies improved coordination and outcomes. It seems likely that this effect occurs because discussion of goals and strategies facilitates the development of shared mental models. These models, in turn, can be used by each team member to coordinate with the others and by teams as a whole to integrate their individual contributions resulting in better decisions (reflected in firm price) and board evaluations.

We also seek to understand the trade-offs and interactions between overload and the development of shared mental models. For example, it is possible that a high volume of communication during a period of frantic deadlines may make it more difficult for team members to achieve a shared mental model because there is too much information to attend to. Once in place, however, shared mental models may reduce feelings of overload by allowing team members to quickly categorize information, prioritize tasks, and distribute responsibilities. In other words, these models may help teams cope with information and decision environments that would otherwise lead to feelings of overload.

ACKNOWLEDGMENTS

This material is based on work supported by the Defense Advanced Research Projects Agency and administered by the Office of Naval Research under agreement number N66001-96-C-8506. The U.S. Government is authorized to reproduce and distribute reprints for government purposes notwithstanding any copyright annotation thereon. The views and conclusions contained herein are those of the authors and should not be interpreted as necessarily representing the official policies or endorsements, either expressed or implied, of the Defense Advanced Research Projects Agency or the U.S. Government.

REFERENCES

1. Brennan, S. B. (1998). The grounding problem in conversations with and through computers. In S. R. Fussell & R. J. Kreuz (Eds.), *Social and cognitive approaches to interpersonal communication*. Mahwah, NJ: Erlbaum.

2. Cammann, C., Fichman, M., Jenkins, Jr., D. & Flesh, J. R. (1983). Assessing the attitudes and perceptions of organizational members. In S. E. Seashore, E. Lawler, P. H. Mirvis, and C. Cammann (Eds.). *Assessing Organizational Change* (pp. 71-138). New York: John Wiley & Sons.

3. Cannon-Bowers, J. A., Salas, E., & Converse, S. A. (1993). Shared mental models in expert decision-making teams. In N. J. Castellan, Jr. (Ed.), *Current issues in individual and group decision making* (pp. 221-246). Hillsdale, NJ: Erlbaum.

4. Cohen J., & Cohen, P. (1983). *Applied multiple regression/correlation analysis for the behavioral sciences* (2nd ed.). Hillsdale, NJ: Erlbaum.

5. Dourish, P. and Bellotti, V. Awareness and coordination in shared workshops. In *Proc. of CSCW'92* (Toronto, Canada), ACM Press, 1992.

6. Dourish, P. and Bly, S. Portholes: Supporting awareness in a distributed work group. In *Proc. of CHI'92* (Monterey, California), ACM Press, 1992.

7. Fish, R. S., Kraut, R. E., and Chalfonte, B. L. The Video Window System in informal communications. In *Proc. of CSCW'92* (Toronto, Canada), ACM Press, 1992.

8. Galbraith, J. (1977). *Organizational design*. Reading, MA: Addison-Wesley.

9. Galegher, J., & Kraut, R. E. Computer-Mediated Communication and Collaborative Writing: Media Influence and Adaptation to Communication Constraints. In J. Turner & R. Kraut (Eds.), *CSCW '92: shared perspectives* (pp. 155-162). New York: ACM, 1992.

10. Gaver, W., Moran, T., MacLean, A., Lovstrand, L., Dourish, P., Carter, K. and Buxton, W. Realizing a video environment: EuroPARC's RAVE system. In *Proc. of CHI'92* (Monterey, California), ACM Press, 1992.

11. Hackman, J.R. (1987) The design of work teams. In J.W. Lorsch (Ed.), *Handbook of Organizational Behavior* (pp. 315-342). Englewood Cliffs, NJ: Prentice-Hall.

12. Huff, C., Sproull, L., & Kiesler, S. (1989) Computer communication and organizational commitment: Tracing the relationship in a city government. *Journal of Applied Social Psychology, 19,* 1371-1391.

13. Hutchins, 1991. The social organization of distributed cognition. In L. B. Resnick, J. M. Levine, & S. D. Teasley (Eds.), *Perspectives on socially shared cognition* (pp. 283-307). Washington, DC: APA.

14. Katz, R. & Tushman, M. (1978). Communication patterns, project performance, and task characteristics: An empirical evaluation in an R&D setting. *Organizational Behavior and Human Performance, 23*, 139-162.

15. Kraiger, K., & Wenzel, L. C. (1997) Conceptual development and empirical evaluation of measures of shared mental models as indicators of team effectiveness. In M. T. Brannick, E. Salas, & C. Prince (Eds.) *Team performance assessment and measurement: Theory, methods, and applications* (pp. 45-84). Mahwah, NJ: Erlbaum.

16. Kraut, R. E. & Attewell, P. (1997). Media use in a global corporation: Electronic mail and organizational knowledge. In S. Kiesler (Ed.) *Research milestones on the information highway*. Mahwah, NJ: Erlbaum.

17. Orlikowski, W. J. (1996). Improvising organizational transformation over time. A situated change perspective. *Information Systems Research.* 71, 63-92

18. Seifert, C. & Hutchins, E. L. (1992). Error as opportunity: Learning in a coooperative task. *Human-Computer Interaction*, *7*, 409-436.

19. Tang, J. C., Isaacs, E. A., and Rua, M. Supporting Distributed Groups with a Montage of Lightweight Interactions. In *Proc. of CSCW'94* (Chapel Hill, North Carolina), ACM Press, 1994.

20. Van de Ven, A. H., Delbecq, A. L., & Koenig, R., Jr. (1976). Determinants of coordination modes within organizations. *American Sociological Review, 41*, 322-338.

Collaboration Using Multiple PDAs Connected to a PC

Brad A. Myers **Herb Stiel[1]** **Robert Gargiulo**

Human Computer Interaction Institute
School of Computer Science
Carnegie Mellon University
Pittsburgh, PA 15213
bam@cs.cmu.edu
http://www.cs.cmu.edu/~pebbles

ABSTRACT

The Pebbles project is creating applications to connect multiple Personal Digital Assistants (PDAs) to a main computer such as a PC. We are currently using 3Com PalmPilots because they are popular and widespread. We created the "Remote Commander" application to allow users to take turns sending input from their PalmPilots to the PC as if they were using the PC's mouse and keyboard. "PebblesDraw" is a shared whiteboard application we built that allows all of the users to send input simultaneously while sharing the same PC display. We are investigating the use of these applications in various contexts, such as co-located meetings.

Keywords: Personal Digital Assistants (PDAs), PalmPilot, Single Display Groupware, Pebbles, Amulet.

INTRODUCTION

There are certain kinds of meetings, including design reviews, brainstorming sessions, and organizational meetings, where a PC is used to display slides or a current plan, and the people in attendance provide input. When a PC is used as part of the presentation, often different people will want to take turns controlling the mouse and keyboard. For example, they might want to try out the system under consideration, to investigate different options, or to add their annotations. With standard setups, they will have to awkwardly swap places with the person at the PC.

We observed that at most meetings and talks, attendees do not bring their laptops, probably because they are awkward and slow to set up, the batteries may not last long enough, and there is a social stigma against typing during meetings. Today, however, many people are taking notes on their "Personal Digital Assistant" (PDA), such as a PalmPilot or a Windows CE device. A *PalmPilot* is a small PDA from 3Com with a 3¼ inch diagonal LCD display screen which is touch sensitive, and a small input area for printing characters using a special alphabet (see Figure 1). PalmPilots are small, they turn on instantly, the batteries last for weeks and notes are taken by writing silently with a stylus. With the new palm-size PCs from Microsoft just starting to be available, this type of device will become even more ubiquitous. Since many people are already using a PDA, we developed a set of applications to explore how these could be used to allow everyone to provide mouse and keyboard input to the PC without leaving their seats. We call this the "Remote Commander."

Once the PDAs are connected to the PC, many other intriguing applications become available. In addition to the Remote Commander, we also created a shared drawing program, named PebblesDraw, that allows everyone to draw simultaneously. In creating PebblesDraw, we had to solve a number of interesting problems with the standard widgets such as selection handles, menubars and palettes. Since this is a *Single Display Groupware (SDG)* application, all users are sharing the same screen and therefore the same widgets. Palettes, such as those to show the current drawing mode or the current color, normally show the current mode by highlighting one of the items in the palette. This no longer works if there are multiple people with *different* modes. Furthermore, the conventional menubars at the top of the window or screen are difficult to use in multi-user situations because they may pop up on top of a different user's activities. The conventional way to identify different users is by assigning each a different color, but in a drawing program, each user might want to select what color is being used to draw, causing confusion between the color identifying the user, and the color with which the user will draw. We therefore developed a new set of interaction techniques to more effectively support Single Display Groupware.

This research is being performed as part of the *Pebbles* project. Pebbles stands for: **P**DAs for **E**ntry of **B**oth **B**ytes and **L**ocations from **E**xternal **S**ources.[2] This paper summarizes the PalmPilot's features, and then describes the first two applications: Remote Commander, which allows the PalmPilots to control the PC, and PebblesDraw, which allows multiple people to draw at the same time.

CSCW 98 Seattle Washington USA

[1] Current address: Herbert Stiel, Oracle Corporation, 500 Oracle Parkway, M/S 6op7, Redwood Shores, CA 94065.

[2] The "bytes" refers to the characters and the "locations" refers to mouse points that are sent from the PalmPilot down to the PC.

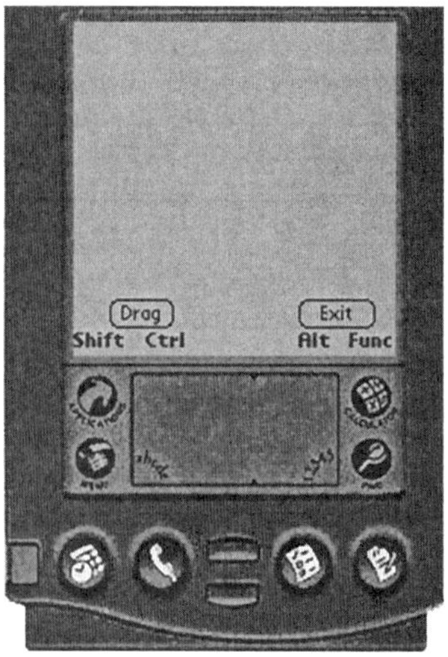

← Display and input area, currently running the Pebbles Remote Commander application

← Labels for the application buttons.

← Input area for "Grafitti" text input.

← 4 round application buttons, and 2 "up-down" arrow keys in the center.

Figure 1. One version of the 3Com PalmPilot running the Pebbles Remote Commander application.

RELATED WORK

Most previous CSCW approaches for multiple users in the same room use expensive and special-purpose hardware or specially constructed meeting rooms. For example, the Xerox CoLab [21] and the Univ. of Arizona's electronic meeting room [16] had computers for each person built into special tables. Another previous approach was the Xerox Liveboard [8], which originally supported multiple cursors operating at the same time, but when produced commercially, only supported one person with one cursor at a time. Liveboards proved to be too expensive to be widely used. The Tivoli system [18] supports up to three people using pens simultaneously on the LiveBoard. We believe that much of the software used with these previous technologies can be reproduced using a set of PalmPilots and a single PC, which will be much cheaper and easier to configure.

The Xerox ParcTab [24] project investigated using small hand-held devices continuously connected through infrared (IR) communication. Most of the PARC building was wired with special IR transceivers to make the ParcTabs work. The ParcTab screen was 128x64 pixels and had a few hard-wired buttons and a touch-sensitive screen, which supported the Unistrokes [9] gestural alphabet. The ParcTab was used to investigate some aspects of remote cursors, and informal voting about how well the speaker was doing, but due to problems with the IR, they found that multiple people simultaneously using the devices in the same room did not work well.

MMM [4] (Multi-Device, Multi-User, Multi-Editor) was one of the first Single Display Groupware (SDG) environments to explore multiple mice on a single display. MMM handled up to three mice. MMM had a single tool palette and color palette, and a separate "home area" to show each user's name, current color, and drawing mode. MMM only supported editing of text and rectangles, and used color to distinguish between the users.

The term "Single Display Groupware" was coined by Stewart et. al. [23]. Stewart's KidPad [22] is a SDG environment for kids, where multiple mice are connected to a Unix computer. It uses "local tools" [2] on Pad++, where each tool does exactly one thing (for example, there is a crayon tool). This model is easier for kids than conventional palettes, but it does not have any global state (so, for example, there is no concept of a selection). Therefore, KidPad does not face many of the issues addressed in our Pebbles work. Background studies showed that children often argue and fight when trying to share a single mouse [22], but when using separate mice, cooperated more effectively. Another SDG effort is the COLT toolkit [5], which explores some limited kinds of user interactions and showed that children will stay more focused on their tasks when each child has their own mouse and they simultaneously manipulate the same object together.

Other groups are studying the use of PalmPilots in various settings, where they are *not* connected to a PC. For example, NotePals synchronizes people's independent notes after a meeting [7], and Georgia Tech's "Classroom 2000" project [1] is studying the use of PalmPilots in classrooms.

THE PALMPILOT

The PalmPilot (http://palmpilot.3com.com/) is a small inexpensive hand-held "Personal Digital Assistant" (see Figure 1) formerly sold by USRobotics (which was bought by 3Com) and also now sold by IBM as the "WorkPad." The PalmPilot sold over one million units in its first 18 months, and many people in our academic community are using them to take notes in meetings. Although our research is using PalmPilots because they are easy to program and popular, the research would equally apply to any PDA. We will soon port the software to palm-size PCs running Microsoft Windows CE.

One of the most important reasons the PalmPilot is so popular is that it connects very easily to a PC (and also to a Macintosh or Unix workstation) for synchronization and downloading. Each PalmPilot is shipped with a cradle and wire that connects to a computer's standard serial port. Software supplied with the PalmPilot will synchronize the data with the PC. It is also easy to load new applications into the PalmPilot. Pebbles takes advantage of this easy connection to a PC.

The main display of the PalmPilot is a 160x160 pixel LCD panel, with 4 levels of gray (but most applications treat it as monochrome). The screen is touch sensitive, so text and graphics can be selected and drawn. A small stylus which fits into the PalmPilot case is usually used for this, but a finger can also be used for pointing and gestures. Textual characters are entered in the area at the bottom using special gestures called "Graffiti," which is a stylized alphabet that is designed to be easier for the PalmPilot to recognize accurately. Almost all letters and symbols are entered with a single stroke, which approximates the upper or lower case way the letter is drawn. Most people seem to be able to learn the gestures in about 15 minutes. There is also an on-screen keyboard. In Pebbles, we are taking advantage of the fact that people have *already* learned these gestures, and are comfortable with the operation of the PalmPilot since they are already using it for many daily activities.

REMOTE COMMANDER

The first application from our Pebbles project is the *Remote Commander*. This allows strokes on the main display area of the PalmPilot to control the PC's mouse cursor, and for Graffiti input to emulate the PC's keyboard input. The important point is that this works with *all existing* PC applications, without requiring any modifications to the applications themselves. For example, multiple people can use PowerPoint, Word, Excel, Illustrator, etc., from their PalmPilots.

We believe in distributing the results of our research, to help collect useful feedback and aid in technology transfer. The first version of the Remote Commander software was released for general use on February 17 (see http://www.cs.cmu.edu/~pebbles) and was downloaded about 3000 times in the first six weeks. The current version works with Windows 95 or NT, and current versions of the PalmPilot.

In designing this application, we wanted to make sure that it would fit in with the PalmPilot style. Therefore, it needed to be natural and non-intrusive. It should be easy to switch between using the Remote Commander and using other PalmPilot applications, and it should take advantage of the Graffiti gestures that the users had already learned. We also had to deal with the PalmPilot's limitations: a small, gray-scale screen, and a fairly slow processor. Furthermore, the users' focus should normally be directed to the PC's screen, so it should be possible to operate the Remote Commander without looking at the PalmPilot, just as the mouse can be used without looking.

In the current version of Remote Commander, we rely on social protocols to control whose turn it is, which is not difficult since everyone is in the same room. Everyone's inputs are mixed together. We decided that a more formal "floor control" mechanism would obstruct the fluid sharing and collaboration that is typical in meetings. This is supported by experience and informal experiments with other groupware systems [10].

Example Uses

When designing the Remote Commander, we had a number of uses in mind. The first is as discussed above: for multiple people in a meeting to take turns controlling the mouse and keyboard. Remote Commander is designed to support meetings where everyone is in the same room. (Remote participants might use other CSCW applications, such as Microsoft NetMeeting.) Remote Commander might be used so different people can have a turn controlling an application, to support multiple annotations on a work product, or so everyone can enter their personal data into a shared document. Having a single, shared visual display is important for coordination and collaboration [17], and people will take turns or all work together on these displays. A second use for Remote Commander is to support small, informal meetings. These arise when two or three people are discussing something that is running on a PC, such as a demo situation, or for small impromptu design and debugging discussions.

Another use for the Remote Commander might be any time that a single user would rather have a stylus for input instead of a mouse, for example in situations when freehand drawing or writing is desired. The PalmPilot digitizer can even read the stylus through a sheet of paper, so Remote Commander can support the tracing of small drawings. Of course, if tracing was frequently needed, the user would probably purchase a "real" tablet, but again we are taking advantage of technology the user might already have for a task they might do occasionally.

PalmPilot Module

There are two modules of the Remote Commander — one which runs on the PalmPilot and the other runs on the PC, and these two are connected using serial cables.

Moving the Cursor

Figure 1 shows the Remote Commander application running on the PalmPilot. The large blank upper area is used to represent the mouse. Moving the stylus (or your finger) across the screen of the PalmPilot moves the cursor on the PC. Through experimentation, we arrived at a system which provides good control.

The current design uses relative coordinates. This is analogous to the small touchpad on some laptops, like the Macintosh PowerBook. Movement across the PalmPilot screen is mapped to an incremental movement across the PC's screen, so the actual position where you put down the stylus is not important; just how far it is moved from the initial position.

Originally, we tried directly mapping the 160x160 pixels of the PalmPilot to the 1024x768 pixels (for example) of the PC, using absolute coordinates. Thus, tapping in the upper left of the PalmPilot screen would move the cursor to the upper left of the PC screen. However, this did not work at all. Since each pixel on the PalmPilot represented about 6 pixels on the PC, and since characters are often less than 6 pixels wide, this made it impossible to select individual characters. Furthermore, the positions reported by the PalmPilot digitizer are very jittery, varying by 1 or 2 pixels in all directions when the stylus is kept still, so the cursor jumped all over the PC's screen.

The jittery coordinates coming from the PalmPilot were still a problem when we switched to relative coordinates, making it difficult to position the cursor accurately. Looking at other applications running locally on the PalmPilot, such as various sketching programs, we noticed that the jittery values were not limited to our program, but seem to be a property of the device. Therefore, we added filtering of the positions. After experimenting with various algorithms and parameters, the best behavior resulted from collecting the last 7 points returned by the PalmPilot, and returning the average as the current point. This removes most of the jitter without adding too much lag. This filtering starts over each time the stylus comes in contact with the PalmPilot, and the array of the last 7 points is initialized with the initial point. This allows points to be provided immediately when the stylus comes in contact with the surface. We also added extra acceleration to the PalmPilot output so one swift movement across the PalmPilot screen would move entirely across the PC's screen.

Mouse Buttons

Another issue concerns emulating the mouse buttons. As with a touchpad, the stylus of the PalmPilot must be in contact with the surface in order to move the cursor, so a different method is needed to signal pressing of the mouse buttons. This is not a problem for applications which run on the PalmPilot itself, since the screen displays the objects that the user wants to point at, and there is no need for a separate cursor.

We provide three different ways to signal pressing a mouse button. First, tapping on the blank area of the PalmPilot screen with the stylus causes the Remote Commander program to send a click event (down press followed by a release) of the left mouse button to the PC. A double-click can easily be sent to the PC by double-tapping. A tap is determined by a press and release at the same place. Since Windows, and now Macintosh system 8, allow menus to stay up when clicked on, this is an easy way to select items in menus and to push on-screen buttons. User experience with this tapping is mixed. It appears to take practice to be able to tap without moving, and novices seem to draw little lines when they want to tap. On the other hand, others seem to tap by accident, possibly due to some bounce of the stylus on the surface, or when trying to draw small items. We will continue to investigate adjusting the parameters to see if we can eliminate these problems.

In many cases, it is also necessary to *drag* with the button held down. "Dragging" is when the mouse button is pressed somewhere, then the mouse is moved, and the button is released at a different point. To support dragging, we first added a "Drag" button to the Remote Commander screen (see Figure 1). Pressing on this Drag button starts the dragging by sending a left down event. The user can then move the stylus. Pressing on the Drag button again will end the drag by sending the button-up event. Experience suggests that the Drag button is not a particularly good idea, because people frequently make *mode errors*, where they forget whether the mouse button is pressed or not, and end up drawing a line when they planned to just move the cursor, and vice versa.

We added a third way to signal pressing of the mouse buttons, which proved to be the most successful way to drag. This uses the up and down physical buttons in the center bottom of the PalmPilot (shown in Figure 1 and at right). We use the up button for the left mouse button, and the down button for the right, which is similar to the way many laptops handle the mouse buttons. It is easy to hold the PalmPilot so that the thumb of the non-dominate hand (e.g. left hand) can work the buttons while the dominate hand (e.g. right hand) draws with the stylus. Experience shows that people do not have much trouble coordinating their two hands for this task. Unfortunately, the up and down buttons on the new PalmIII version are harder to use. We will be investigating the support for "tap-drag" as on some touchpads, where users can tap and quickly start dragging to signal a press and drag. Unfortunately, this has many usability problems so experimentation will be necessary to see if it is useful and to fine-tune the parameters.

Emulating the Keyboard

Writing characters in the Graffiti area of the PalmPilot will send those characters to the PC as if they were typed at the keyboard. Capital letters and punctuation marks work in the normal way for Graffiti. The PalmPilot comes with a built-in on-screen keyboard, which people often use especially for the obscure punctuation symbols for which they may not have memorized the Graffiti gestures. Unfortunately, this keyboard does not have all the special keys found on the PC keyboard, like F1 and ESC, so we had to create our own on-screen keyboard. Just like the regular PalmPilot keyboard, you pop-up the Remote Commander's keyboard by tapping the stylus inside the "abc" area (also labeled "abcde" on some PalmPilots) at the bottom left of the Graffiti area. This brings up the screen shown in Figure 2, on which you can tap the desired keyboard key. To dismiss the keyboard, tap in the "abcde" area again, or tap the "Done" button of the keyboard at the bottom right, or use the Menu command when the keyboard is displayed. The small area above the keyboard is still available to make mouse movements or taps.

The "Shift," "Ctrl" and "Alt" keys on the on-screen keyboard modify the characters hit on the keyboard, and will also modify Graffiti characters and mouse clicks. For example, to do a SHIFT-CLICK of the mouse, you can tap the "Shift" area on the keyboard and then tap the stylus in the upper area.

Because SHIFT, CONTROL and ALT clicking is so common, we wanted to provide more convenient methods for doing this, so we allow the four physical "application buttons" at the bottom of the PalmPilot (see Figure 1) to be used as SHIFT, CONTROL and ALT and FUNCTION.

Little labels above the keys show the assignment of the buttons, as shown in Figure 1. Since these buttons normally allow the user to quickly switch to a different PalmPilot application, the use of these buttons as shift keys can be turned off with a Remote Commander menu command, if desired.

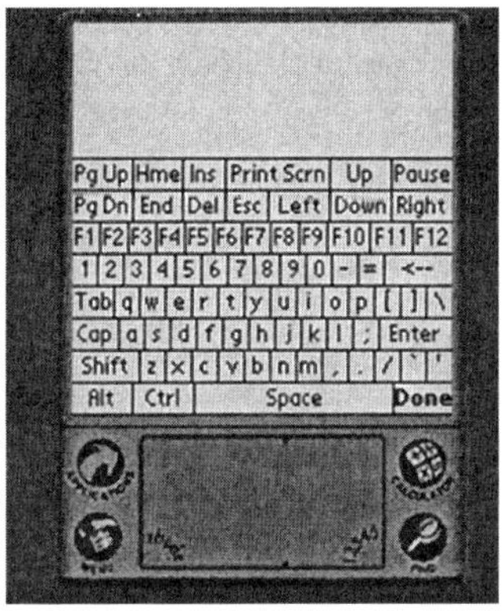

← Click in the "abcdef" area to get this keyboard.

Figure 2. The Remote Commander's on-screen keyboard.

The FUNCTION button allows Graffiti characters to send all the special PC keyboard keys. We defined a mapping of letters to the function keys so the user never needs to pop up the keyboard. For example, holding down the function button while making the **1** gesture sends F1, using FUNCTION-**e** sends ESCAPE, etc.

Connecting the PalmPilot with the PC

To use the PalmPilot to control the PC, they need to be connected to each other. Our goals for the connection technology include: minimal interference with the use of the PalmPilots, continuous connections while users are writing on the PalmPilots, multiple PalmPilots operating at the same time in the same room, and minimal power consumption.

Ideally, we would use some sort of wireless technology. The most popular short-range wireless technology is infrared (IR), but this has many problems for our application. For example, the IR built into the new PalmIII version of the PalmPilot appears to transmit for only about 1 meter, and it must be aimed at the receiver (in the same way that a TV remote control must be aimed at the TV). Only one PalmIII device can be operated in the same area at a time (because they interfere with each other), and the IR will require a lot of battery power, so you would not necessarily want to use it for long periods of time. The designers of the ParcTabs [24] had to go to enormous lengths to make the IR work in those devices, including installing multiple transmitters on each ParcTab, receivers on the ceilings of every room, and an elaborate software protocol to deal with multiple transmissions. They still reported problems, especially with multiple people trying to transmit at the same time. We hope that future IR technologies, like IRDA level 3, will resolve these problems for the PalmPilot.

Another wireless possibility is radio. There is a wireless modem for the PalmPilot for about $500, and Bell Atlantic offers wireless Internet service for about $50/month for each PalmPilot. This seems too expensive to use in our Remote Commander. Other radio-based options may soon be available, such as the "BlueTooth" local-area radio network (http://www.bluetooth.com).

In the meantime, we are using a wired solution, which has the advantage of being flexible, inexpensive, and easy to set up. It lets us explore the various user interface and systems issues, and is practical for use today.

The Remote Commander currently assumes the devices are connected using the built-in serial ports of the PalmPilot and the PC. The easiest way to do this is to simply use the cradle provided with the PalmPilot. However, using the PalmPilot while it is in the cradle is quite clumsy, so instead, we usually use the HotSync cable sold by 3Com, which does a nice job of staying attached to the PalmPilot without getting in the way. It is also inexpensive.

In order to connect *multiple* PalmPilots to a PC at one time, the PC needs multiple serial ports. For desktop PCs, there are many cards available which provide multiple serial ports. The one we found costs about $400 for 8 ports. For laptops, we found the QSP-100 PCMCIA card [19] which provides 4 ports (see Figure 3) and costs about $500. Most laptops have 2 PCMCIA slots, so this allows up to 8 serial ports using two cards in the laptop. The cards self-configure under Windows95 and use a sequence of COM ports.

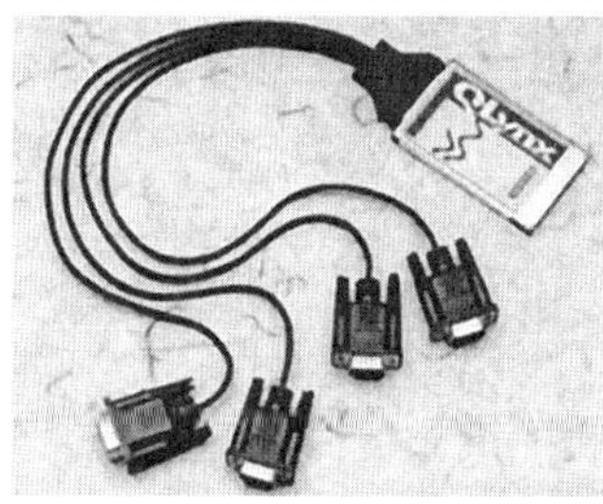

Figure 3. Quatech QSP-100 PCMCIA card.

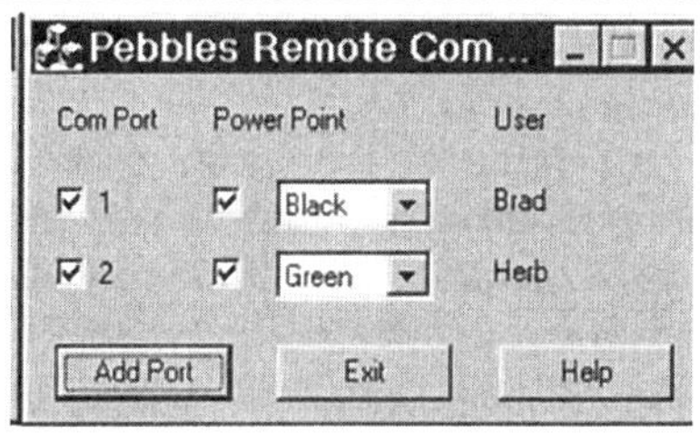

Figure 4. The PC module of the Remote Commander.

PC Module

The PC module of the Remote Commander is fairly simple. It takes the characters and mouse movements reported by the PalmPilot module and inserts them into the Windows input event queue, as if they were regular mouse and keyboard events. The user interface for the PC module is shown in Figure 4. Clicking on the "Add Port" button brings up a dialog box in which a serial port number can be typed, and a user name specified. The "PowerPoint" widgets in the middle are discussed in the next section. The Remote Commander can handle as many users as there are serial ports on the PC. In the future, we may try to make this module more self-configuring, by having the program automatically check for PalmPilots on the PC's serial ports.

PowerPoint version

Of course, Remote Commander can interface with *any* existing Windows application, because it just emulates the regular mouse and keyboard. However, we want to experiment with adapting *existing* applications so they are more amenable to *joint* use by multiple people in the same room.

As an experiment, we added a special feature for using the Remote Commander with Microsoft PowerPoint (versions 7.0 or 97SR-1). In presentation mode in PowerPoint, normally clicking the mouse will change to the next slide, but if you go into "pen" mode, then you can draw on top of the slides in various colors. When the PowerPoint checkboxes in the middle of the Remote Commander are selected (see Figure 4), then whenever the user drags on the PalmPilot end, Remote Commander will send out codes to set the color of the pen to that user's color. For example, in the case of Figure 4, whenever Brad drew on a slide using the PalmPilot, the ink would be black, and Herb's drawings would be green (see Figure 5). Remote Commander picks unique colors for each user, but users can change their colors by using the menu shown in Figure 4.

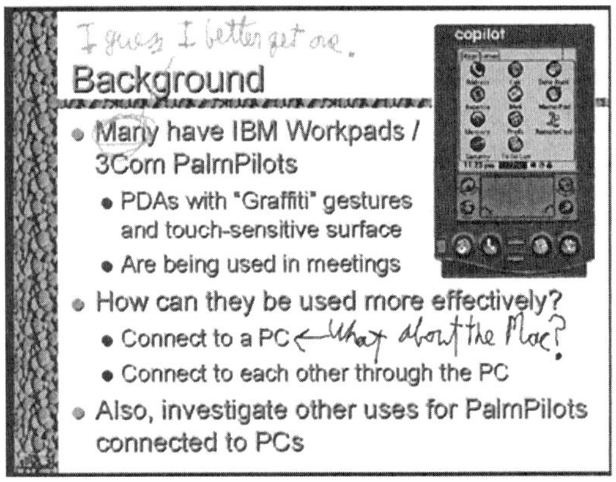

Figure 5. PowerPoint screen showing some annotations entered using Remote Commander from two PalmPilots.

It is important to emphasize that we achieved this without *any* modifications to PowerPoint – Remote Commander just uses the standard commands available from PowerPoint. The color change commands are sent before each mouse drag event (down press) to make sure that the color is set correctly for each user.

An observation while using this feature in early versions of Remote Commander was that, not surprisingly, users often made *mode errors* where they forgot to turn the PowerPoint mode off when switching applications. Remote Commander would then send the PowerPoint change-color commands to the current application, which would do various incorrect actions. For example, it was not possible to un-check the PowerPoint mode in the Remote Commander PC module because the color change commands would cause the module to quit! Therefore, we added more checking to try to detect whether the front-most window is really a PowerPoint presentation and only if so, does Remote Commander send the color-change commands.

In the future, we would like to investigate special versions of Remote Commander for other applications. For example, Microsoft Word allows the color of the text to be changed. Although Word lacks built-in keyboard commands to change the color, it would be easy to build special styles or macros to change the color, assign keyboard commands to these, and then have the Remote Commander execute these commands before each keystroke. Then, each user's input would appear in a different color. Similar techniques could be used for Excel, Paint, and many other tools. This is a very versatile capability that would allow gesturing and annotation on top of many different applications, without the need to change the applications themselves. Eventually, it might be better and more robust to use OLE integration to control the applications, instead of sending special text as commands.

Experiences with Remote Commander

When we use the Remote Commander in meetings, we find that people initially "fiddle around" by moving the mouse even when they are not planning to do anything, which interferes with other people's attempts at real work. The result is that someone will tell another to stop sending input. This problem seems to disappear with practice, but if we want to address it, Greenberg recommends having a timeout period so that one person automatically keeps the floor until there is a delay of (say) 3 seconds since their last action. At that point, it becomes a first come, first served for the next person who tries to input to the shared surface [10].

The feedback from the users who have downloaded the Remote Commander has been quite positive, and we have received many nice compliments. Some substantive suggestions from users that we have included in the new version include key repeat when the user holds the stylus over an on-screen keyboard key, adding acceleration for cursor movement, and supporting "Paste" in the PalmPilot module so text typed into other PalmPilot applications, like Memo, can be easily entered into the PC. Ideas from users still under investigation include the ability to support turning the PalmPilot upside down or sideways, so the physical buttons would be in a more natural position (but Graffiti would not work in these orientations), and to have the cursor on the PC continue moving when the stylus is pegged at the side of the PalmPilot screen. We will continue to gather feedback and ideas from the users and our own experience with Remote Commander.

PEBBLESDRAW

In addition to Remote Commander, we built another application, called PebblesDraw, to explore allowing *all* users to have their *own* cursors. PebblesDraw is a multi-cursor drawing program that is analogous to other "shared whiteboard" applications, with one important difference: here all the users share the *same* display. Thus, PebblesDraw qualifies as Single Display Groupware. PebblesDraw is implemented using the Amulet toolkit [15] on the PC.

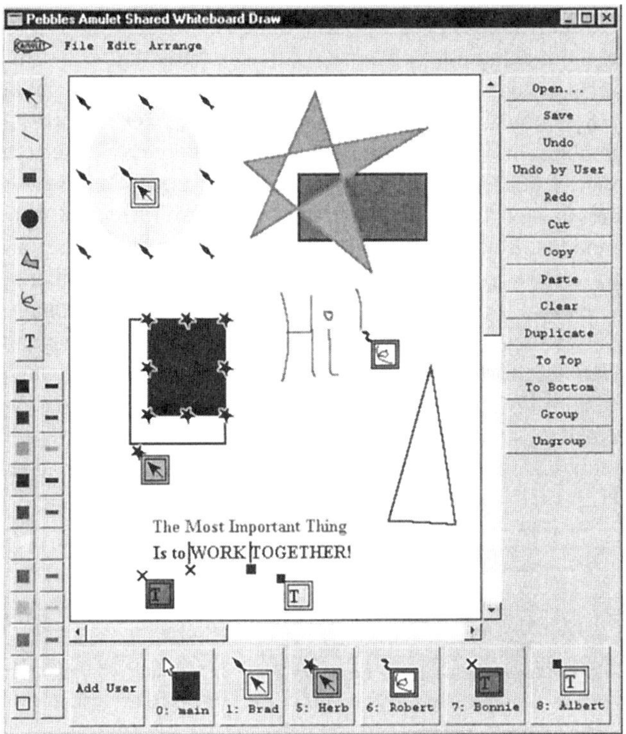

Figure 6. First version of PebblesDraw.

The initial design for PebblesDraw is shown in Figure 6. Clicking on the "Add User" button at the bottom allows the name, serial port number and the shape for that user to be entered. All active users are shown along the bottom of the window. At the left are the conventional drawing and color palettes. At the right is a button panel that contains the most common commands.

In creating this application, we discovered a number of important issues not addressed by previous SDG applications. In particular, the standard widgets, like selection handles, palettes, and pull-down menus, do not work for multiple users. Previous SDG systems had little state information associated with each user. For example, in KidPad [23] there are no selections. Tivoli [18] supports only a few pen widths. MMM [4] only dealt with up to 4 users. We wanted to support more of the choices available in typical drawing programs so a more general mechanism was required. In addition, we wanted the interaction style to be similar to conventional direct manipulation applications, so it would be familiar.

The problem with conventional selection handles is that they do not show which user has the object selected. One goal for PebblesDraw is that each user's actions are independent. Each user therefore must have their own separate selection handles. Most previous SDG applications, such as MMM [4], assign each user a color. Since PebblesDraw allows each user to select a color that will next be drawn, we thought using color-coding would be confusing for a drawing editor. In fact, the developer of KidPad [23] reported that using color as feedback was not a good idea because kids had difficulty with it. COLT [5] also used a color to identify people, and reported running into trouble with one color-blind user.

For all these reasons, we assign each user a *shape*. The model was a game like Monopoly where each person picks a shape as their piece. The same shape is used as the user's cursor, and to show the user's selection, to show the text editing position, and to mark the user's commands in the undo history. We designed a set of shapes that could be easily distinguished when they are very small (11x11 pixels). We also needed each shape to have a pointy part at the upper left, so it would be clear how to use them to point at objects. The complete set of the current icons is shown in Figure 7.

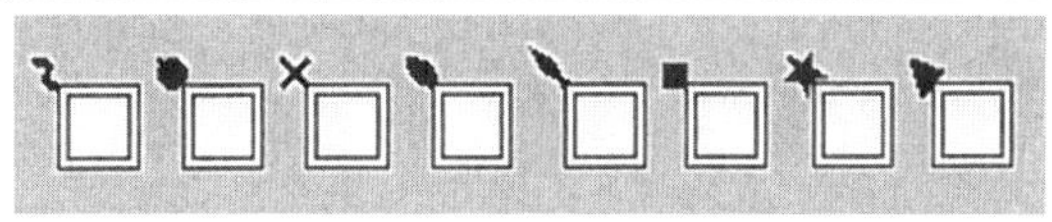

Figure 7. The current set of cursors for PebblesDraw.

When a user executes an operation, it will only operate on that user's selected objects. Thus, in Figure 6, if Brad does a cut, only the yellow oval will be affected. Currently, multiple people can select the same object at the same time. The cursor shapes are designed so users can always see that the object is multiply selected, although it can be difficult to tell by which users. The operations have the expected result if two people manipulate on the same object at the same time. In the future, we might want to disallow multiple people selecting the same object if this proves too confusing. Alternatively, we might make it easier to see which users have the object selected. For example, since there happen to be eight handles around an object and we support up to eight shapes, an obvious idea is to divide the handle positions among all the users who have this object selected. However, this might confuse users into thinking that they can only change the object's size from the handles that have their shape. Further studies of these issues are planned.

The problem with the standard design for palettes is that the currently selected tool is displayed in the palette itself (see Figure 8), which does not work if different users can have different modes. If one user is drawing a red circle at the same time that another is typing blue text, how would that be shown? Most CSCW applications are for multiple machines and assume that each user can see their own private copy of the palettes on their own separate displays, so this is not an issue. The MMM palettes did not show any state information and showed each user's current modes only in the home areas. The Tivoli project [18] mentioned this problem with palettes, but apparently provided no feedback as to the users' modes.

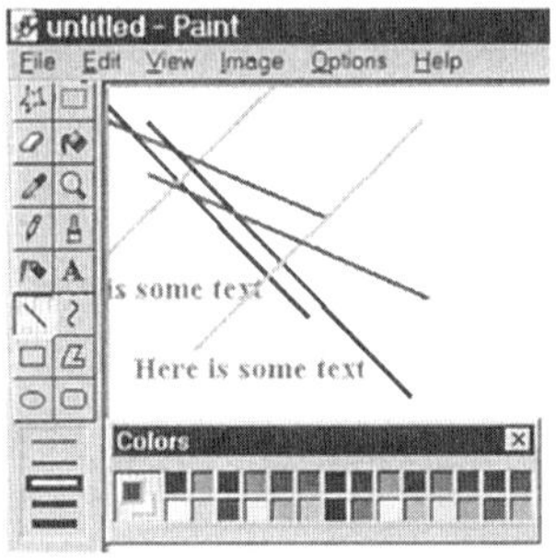

Figure 8. As a single-user application, Microsoft Paint can show the current tool (line tool), the current line style (medium) and the current colors (red line and white fill) in the palettes.

To solve this problem, we provide the feedback for all the user's modes both in that user's cursor as well as in the picture for that user at the bottom of the window. The bottom row corresponds to the home areas in MMM, but we feel that having the modes also in the user's cursor will be less confusing and will require less eye movement. Clicking on a item in a palette (at the left of Figure 6) copies that mode into the user's cursor and home area. Notice that the palettes do not show a current mode. Instead, the current tool is shown in the center of the box attached to the cursor, the line color is shown in the outline of the box, and the fill color is shown inside the box. In Figure 6, Herb is using the star cursor. He is currently in select mode, and is growing the blue rectangle. Brad is also in select mode, and has the yellow oval selected. Robert is drawing a freehand shape. Both Bonnie and Albert are editing the second row of text. Each user's text input cursor has that user's icon hanging from it, so users can simultaneously edit text and still know where they are working. Other multi-display CSCW systems have used this kind of "overloaded" cursor to show the status of the various users [11].

Another issue relates to drop-down and pop-up menus. The problem is that the menu for one user might pop up on top of where a different user is working, especially for the large menus typical in today's applications. Therefore, we try to minimize the use of pop-ups, so a button panel allows the most common operations to be performed without using a pop-up menu (see Figure 6).

Another issue is graying out of illegal items. Since only one user at a time can use the drop-down menus, it makes sense for the items in those menus to gray out as appropriate for that user. For example, if Bonnie has nothing selected, then if she would use the drop-down menus, the commands that require a selection would be grayed out. However, the button panel of commands (at the right of Figure 6) is always visible. Therefore, it does *not* work for items to be grayed out, because some commands will be valid for one user but invalid for another user. Therefore, we had to modify all the operations to make sure that they did something reasonable, like beep or display an error message, if they were invoked when they were not valid for the current user. The previous implementation of these commands in Amulet assumed that since they would be grayed out, they could never be invoked when not valid. Another idea is to gray out the illegal items after a user starts interacting with the widget, since other users are locked out until the first user finishes.

Gestural input is a quick and easy way to give commands without using a tool palette. With a gesture, the *path* of the input device is used to interpret the meaning. Like Tivoli [18], PebblesDraw supports *gestural* input. For example, in PebblesDraw, making an "L" shape while pressing the right mouse button (or the bottom PalmPilot arrow button) creates a new rectangle no matter what the current selected mode is. Making a circular shape with the right mouse button down creates a circle. Other gestures support entering lines and text, deleting objects, and undo. The advantages of gestures are that the user does not have to keep going back and forth to the palette to change tools, and the single gesture defines both the operation to perform, and the parameters such as how big the object should be. The gesture recognizer is trainable, so new gestures can be easily added [12].

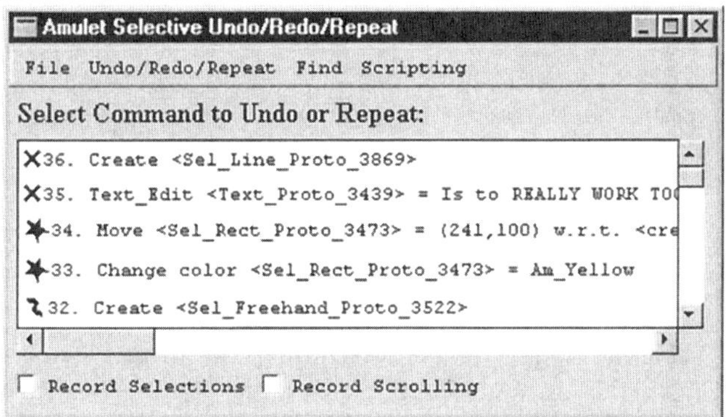

Figure 9. Undo dialog box [14] for PebblesDraw where each command is marked with the shape for the user who performed it.

The undo dialog box for Amulet was augmented to annotate each command with the shape for the user who executed it (see Figure 9). The normal Undo command undoes the last executed command no matter who executed it. The Undo-by-User command undoes the last command of the user who executes this undo command. This takes advantage of Amulet's selective undo mechanism [14] which can undo any previous operation if it still makes sense. For example, in Figure 9, if Herb (who is using the star shape) performs undo-by-user, it will skip over Bonnie's commands and undo the Move of a rectangle (command # 34). If that rectangle had been deleted by a different user, then Herb's attempt to do undo-by-user would just beep, since his last command could not be undone. Of course, regular undo is always possible. Multi-user undo has been previously studied in various systems, such as GINA [3].

The implementation architecture that supports PebblesDraw is based the Amulet toolkit [15]. Briefly, the part of the Remote Commander that accepts input from the serial ports and then converts it into events is linked in with Amulet's low-level input handling. Instead of inserting these events into the regular Windows input stream, as for the regular Remote Commander, Amulet was augmented to directly accept multiple, parallel streams of input. The Amulet behavior objects (called "interactors") and widgets were augmented to accept a *user-id* parameter. If the user-id is a particular user's id, then this widget is reserved for use by only that user. Each user in PebblesDraw has a separate selection handles widget using this mechanism. Special values for the user-id slot include *"anyone,"* which means everyone can use this widget, even simultaneously, and *"one-at-a-time,"* which means that whoever starts using this widget gets to finish their interaction and other users cannot use it until the first user is finished. *One-at-a-time* is the default, and the buttons, palettes, scroll bars and menus are all marked as *one-at-a-time*.

We envision PebblesDraw as being used to allow multiple users to create or annotate drawings at the same time. To make it more useful as an annotation tool, images can be read in and annotations added on top. The annotations can be saved, read and further edited. For example, Figure 10 shows PebblesDraw being used by 3 people to annotate a plan on a map.

STATUS AND FUTURE WORK

The first version of the Remote Commander was released for general use, as mentioned above, and the second version along with PebblesDraw will be released shortly. One important area for further research is to more formally evaluate the Pebbles applications.

We have many exciting ideas for future work for other applications which might benefit from multiple PDAs connected to a PC. We are currently working on a Chat program, so that one PDA user can write a note that will be seen on one or more other PDAs. This might be useful for passing side notes in a meeting. Another application might support voting, which could either be formal secret or role-call votes, or the informal "how is the speaker doing" style of votes that were done for the ParcTab [24].

Another project in progress is joint work with Alex Waibel to use his NPen++ handwriting recognizer [13] with the PalmPilot. NPen++ is much more accurate than previous attempts (like the Apple Newton), but is currently too large to run on the PalmPilot. Therefore, we will use the Remote Commander mechanism so the recognizer can run on the PC and the writing can be performed on the PalmPilot, and the recognized words can then be sent back to the PalmPilot for display. This would also allow handwriting to be used as input to arbitrary PC applications.

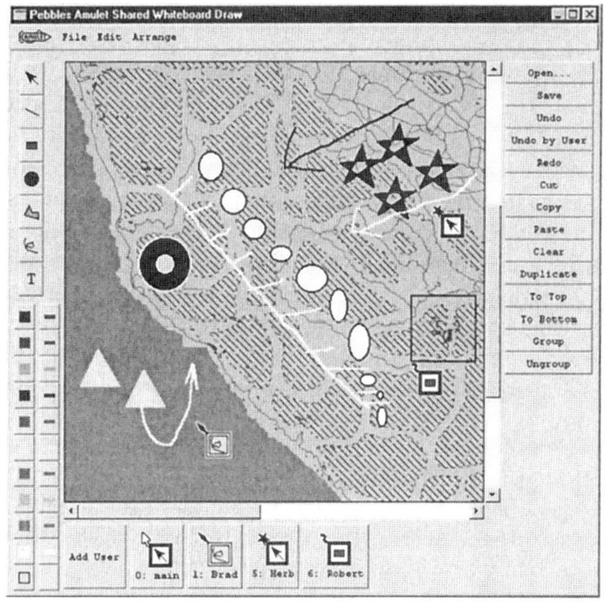

Figure 10. Multiple users can concurrently be annotating and setting up the map.

Some new mice, like the "IntelliMouse" from Microsoft and the "ScrollPoint" mouse from IBM, have an extra input device between the two buttons which can be used for scrolling. In earlier work, we found that it is more effective to use the *other hand* for scrolling, since then the user will naturally operate both input devices at the same time [6]. We will explore using the PDA as the other input device, so it can be used with the other hand for scrolling.

Instead of having the users' current modes shown in the cursor as in PebblesDraw, they might be shown on each person's PDA screen. Then, the user could easily see and choose the desired mode. The PDA can also be used as the user's "private space," if they want to compose content before sharing it with the group. Another idea is to use the PDA to hold items temporarily, like the Pick-and-Drop pens [20] that make it easy to transfer information from one computer to another. Once there is a protocol for applications to download their controls onto the PDA, this could be extended to allow the PDA to be a general-purpose controller for *any* device, not just a PC program. For example, the PDA could control house-hold appliances, light switches and thermostats.

Of course, we want to explore many other applications of these ideas to new domains. The CSCW literature contains many interesting programs designed for multiple computers, such as "Electronic Brainstorming" and "Structured Idea Generation Process" from Univ. of Arizona [16] and Xerox PARC's Cognoter [21]. We want to see which of these will be effective if used with PalmPilots and a single PC display.

CONCLUSIONS

We have developed applications to investigate many interesting uses for multiple PDAs connected to a PC. The Remote Commander application allows multiple co-located users to take turns controlling the mouse and keyboard of a PC without leaving their seat. The PebblesDraw application demonstrates interaction techniques that allow multiple users to work on the same display simultaneously. These tools can be useful for formal and informal meetings, and even for a single user. Using PDAs in this way takes advantage of technology that people already have and have already learned, and does not require changes in work habits. We are excited about the potential of this approach and the positive response we have received from initial users.

ACKNOWLEDGMENTS

For help with this paper, we would like to thank Saul Greenberg, Lauren Bricker, Andrew Faulring, Richard McDaniel, Robert Miller, Bernita Myers, Jason Stewart, and Bernhard Suhm.

This research was partially sponsored by NCCOSC under Contract No. N66001-94-C-6037, Arpa Order No. B326. The views and conclusions contained in this document are those of the authors and should not be interpreted as representing the official policies, either expressed or implied, of the U.S. Government.

REFERENCES

1. Abowd, G.D., *et al.* "Investigating the capture, integration and access problem of ubiquitous computing in an educational setting," in *Proceedings SIGCHI'98: Human Factors in Computing Systems.* 1998. Los Angeles, CA: pp. 440-447.

2. Bederson, B., *et al.* "Local Tools: An Alternative to Tool Palettes," in *Proc. UIST'96: ACM Symposium on User Interface Software and Technology.* 1996. Seattle, WA: pp. 169-170.

3. Berlage, T. and Genau, A. "A Framework for Shared Applications with a Replicated Architecture," in *Proceedings UIST'93: ACM SIGGRAPH Symposium on User Interface Software and Technology.* 1993. Atlanta, GA: pp. 249-257.

4. Bier, E.A. and Freeman, S. "MMM: A User Interface Architecture for Shared Editors on a Single Screen," in *Proceedings UIST'91: ACM SIGGRAPH Symposium on User Interface Software and Technology.* 1991. Hilton Head, SC: pp. 79-86.

5. Bricker, L., *Cooperatively Controlled Objects in Support of Collaboration.* PhD Thesis, Department of Computer Science and Engineering University of Washington, 1998, Seattle, WA.

6. Buxton, W. and Myers, B. "A Study in Two-Handed Input," in *Proceedings SIGCHI'86: Human Factors in Computing Systems.* 1986. Boston, MA: pp. 321-326.

7. Davis, R.C., *et al., NotePals: Lightweight Note Taking by the Group, for the Group.* CS Division, EECS Department, UC Berkeley, Report #CSD-98-997, 1998, Berkeley, CA.

8. Elrod, S., *et al.* "LiveBoard: A Large Interactive Display Supporting Group Meetings, Presentations and Remote Collaboration," in *Proceedings SIGCHI'92: Human Factors in Computing Systems.* 1992. Monterey, CA: pp. 599-607.

9. Goldberg, D. and Richardson, C. "Touch Typing with a Stylus," in *Proceedings INTERCHI'93: Human Factors in Computing Systems.* 1993. Amsterdam, Netherlands: pp. 80-87.

10. Greenberg, S. "Personalizable groupware: Accomodating individual roles and group differences," in *Proceedings of the ECSCW '91 European Conference of Computer Supported Cooperative Work.* 1991. Amsterdam: Kluwer Academic Press. pp. 17-32.

11. Greenberg, S., Gutwin, C., and Roseman, M. "Semantic Telepointers for Groupware," in *OzCHI '96 Sixth Australian Conference on Computer-Human Interaction.* 1996. Hamilton, New Zealand: pp. 24-27.

12. Landay, J.A. and Myers, B.A. "Extending an Existing User Interface Toolkit to Support Gesture Recognition," in *Adjunct Proceedings INTERCHI'93: Human Factors in Computing Systems.* 1993. Amsterdam, The Netherlands: pp. 91-92.

13. Manke, S., Finke, M., and Waibel, A. "NPen++: A Writer Independent, Large Vocabulary On-Line Cursive Handwriting Recognition System," in *Proceedings of the International Conference on Document Analysis and Recognition.* 1995. Montreal, Canada: IEEE Computer Society.

14. Myers, B.A. and Kosbie, D. "Reusable Hierarchical Command Objects," in *Proceedings CHI'96: Human Factors in Computing Systems.* 1996. Vancouver, BC, Canada: pp. 260-267.

15. Myers, B.A., *et al.*, "The Amulet Environment: New Models for Effective User Interface Software Development." *IEEE Transactions on Software Engineering*, 1997. **23**(6): pp. 347-365. June.

16. Nunamaker, J.A., *et al.*, "Electronic Meeting Systems to Support Group Work." *CACM*, 1991. **34**(7): pp. 40-61. July.

17. Olson, J., *et al.* "A Room of Your Own," in *Adjunct Proceedings of SIGCHI'98: Human Factors in Computer Systems Summary.* 1998. Los Angeles, CA: pp. 279-280.

18. Pederson, E., *et al.* "Tivoli: An Electronic Whiteboard for Informal Workgroup Meetings," in *Proceedings INTERCHI'93: Human Factors in Computing Systems.* 1993. Amsterdam, The Netherlands: pp. 391-398.

19. Quatech, "QSP-100 Four Channel Asynchronous RS-232 PCMCIA Adapter," 1997. Quatech, Inc., 662 Wolf Ledges Parkway, Akron, OH 44311. (330) 434-3154: http://204.210.192.4/public/qsp100.htm.

20. Rekimoto, J. "Pick-and-Drop: A Direct Manipulation Technique for Multiple Computer Environments," in *Proceedings UIST'97: ACM SIGGRAPH Symposium on User Interface Software and Technology.* 1997. Banff, Alberta, Canada: pp. 31-39.

21. Stefik, M., *et al.*, "Beyond the Chalkboard: Computer Support for Collaboration and Problem Solving in Meetings." *Communications of the ACM*, 1987. **30**(1): pp. 32-47.

22. Stewart, J., *et al.* "When Two Hands Are Better Than One: Enhancing Collaboration Using Single Display Groupware," in *Adjunct Proceedings of SIGCHI'98: Human Factors in Computer Systems.* 1998. Los Angeles, CA: pp. 287-288.

23. Stewart, J.E. "Single Display Groupware," in *SIGCHI'97 Adjunct Proceedings: Human Factors in Computer Systems, Extended Abstracts.* 1997. Atlanta, GA: pp. 71-72.

24. Want, R., *et al.*, "An Overview of the ParcTab Ubiquitous Computing Experiment." *IEEE Personal Communications*, 1995. pp. 28-43. December. Also appears as Xerox PARC Technical Report CSL-95-1, March, 1995.

Tailorable Domain Objects as Meeting Tools for an Electronic Whiteboard

Thomas P. Moran, William van Melle, and **Patrick Chiu***

Xerox Palo Alto Research Center, 3333 Coyote Hill Road, Palo Alto, CA 94304

{moran,vanmelle}@parc.xerox.com, chiu@pal.xerox.com

ABSTRACT

Our goal is to provide tools to support working meetings on an electronic whiteboard, called Tivoli. This paper describes how we have integrated structured "domain objects" into the whiteboard environment. Domain objects represent the subject matter of meetings and can be exchanged between Tivoli and group databases. Domain objects can be tailored to produce meeting tools that are finely tuned to meeting practices. We describe the facility for tailoring and managing domain objects and the user interface techniques for blending these into the whiteboard environment. We show examples of both specific and generic meeting tools crafted from domain objects, and we describe a long-term case study in which these tools support an ongoing work process.

Keywords: whiteboard metaphor, pen-based systems, freeform interaction, implicit structure, informal systems, recognition-based systems, list structures, meeting support tools, gestural interfaces, user interface design, tailorability, customization, object-oriented user interfaces

1. INTRODUCTION

Our goal is to provide computational support for working meetings, in which small groups of people collaborate in real time. By "working meeting" we mean group interactions that work with a large set of knowledge material (assessing, discussing, organizing, negotiating about the materials, creating new materials, etc.). Group interaction in such situations is freewheeling and fluid. Further, such meetings are usually part of a larger work process in which there is a knowledge base of materials that is used between meetings. During a given meeting, only a relevant "working set" of materials is needed to effectively conduct the meeting.

Groups often use whiteboards in meetings to provide a shared visual surface to represent the materials they are working with and to preserve a shared context. Pen-based computational systems that allow scribbling and gesturing on wall-size displays can support a whiteboard metaphor for working meetings.

We have been working for several years on a program of research to provide computational meeting tools based on a whiteboard metaphor. Our idea is to allow freeform creation and manipulation of materials on the whiteboard and to provide facilities to easily organize and structure the materials as needed by the group.

Our program of research is based on the LiveBoard [3], a large, shared, pen-based electronic (rear-projected) display. This provides a whiteboard-size interactive display that allows us to experience and experiment with "group-computer interaction" in a way not possible with smaller displays, such as workstations. We have developed a software application, called *Tivoli* [16], that simulates whiteboard functionality on the LiveBoard (or any other display). Tivoli provides basic pen-based scribbling and editing with pen-based gesturing and wiping techniques. In this paper, we use the term "board" to refer to an interactive electronic whiteboard.

We extended Tivoli [12] to allow "implicit structuring" of the material on the board. Material is created on the board in a freeform manner, which means that anything can go anywhere without constraint. However, the user can indicate by certain gestures that the material is to be regarded as temporarily structured in some manner, e.g., as handwritten text. Tivoli will then apply editing operations in accordance with the conventions of that structure, such as opening and closing space where needed when moving words around.

We then extended Tivoli by developing a set of simple and natural techniques for helping users spatially organize material on the board [11]. The most important is to provide ways to group materials into regions on the board. We provide for both rectangular regions and for freeform en-

CSCW 98 Seattle Washington USA

*Current Address: Patrick Chiu, FX Palo Alto Laboratory, 3400 Hillview Avenue, Palo Alto, CA 94304. At the time of the work reported in this paper, Patrick Chiu was with Liveworks, Inc., A Xerox Company, working at Xerox PARC.

closures of any shape. Tivoli can thus limit structured operations to the regions in which they are invoked.

These gestural pen-based techniques result in a fluid, graceful user interface that integrates the informality and flexibility of the whiteboard metaphor with the power of a graphical editing system.

In this paper, we build on the user interface and structuring features of Tivoli by adding a facility for handling new kinds of objects, *domain objects*, in Tivoli. Before this, all of the materials on the Tivoli board have merely been graphical objects, whose interpretation or relationship to other data exists only in the minds of the users. For example, suppose a group's current action items were exported from a workflow system as a prioritized list and read (as simple text) onto the Tivoli board; then users in a meeting edited, erased, added, and rearranged the action items on the board. The resulting board image would bear no relationship to the action item entities in the workflow system. However, by representing the action items as domain objects, these entities can be imported into Tivoli, manipulated *in a gestural whiteboard style* during a meeting, and then the results (annotated and rearranged priorities) can be exported back to the workflow system. Thus, domain objects represent the subject matter (i.e., domain of knowledge) of meetings. We use domain objects as the medium of exchange with repositories of work knowledge. We are able to tailor specialized domain objects as meeting tools that are tuned to particular contents and processes of meetings.

This paper proceeds by first focusing on our own work, motivating and describing our design of the domain object facility. We present an example of a working meeting that motivates our approach (Section 2), which we generalize to a set of objectives for the facility (Section 3). We contrast our approach with others (Section 4) and then describe the domain object facilities in detail (Section 5). We show how domain objects can be tailored to support different types of meetings (Section 6). Then we show how we have incorporated domain objects into a longitudinal case study of a real work process (Section 7). Finally, we step back and discuss several issues of our approach and compare it to other work (Section 8).

2. EXAMPLE OF A WORKING MEETING

Consider an actual working meeting at PARC (in May 1995). It was the fifth in a series of meetings. In the first four, different groups brainstormed a set of 34 scenarios for a system being designed. The goal of the fifth meeting was to select a few scenarios for further study. In the previous meetings, scenario descriptions were captured on Excel spreadsheets, which were consolidated into a single list. In the fifth meeting, however, the group quickly abandoned the spreadsheet, since it was too difficult to see the overall picture and too awkward to manipulate.

Instead the list of scenario names was imported into Tivoli, in a four-column format, so that all the scenario names could be seen at once (see Figure 1a). The group spent 50 minutes discussing the various scenarios, moving the names around to group them into categories by similarity, and then selected six of them for further work. The result of this work (Figure 1b) is a complete rearrangement of the items, plus scribbled annotations.

The group faced a challenging task, and the method of accomplishing it was not understood at the beginning of the meeting. Once they started moving items in Tivoli, the strategy and process came naturally, which involved a lot of physical manipulation (over 50 item moves). Several critical features of the tools made this meeting effective:

- A representation of previous work was needed as a starting point.
- The materials needed to be easily and freely manipulated on the 2D surface of the board in order to discover a satisfactory categorization.
- Handwritten annotations were intermixed with the initial textual materials.
- The items and annotations were spatially arranged into regions of similar items. The circled numbers were used to indicate when clustered items made sense.

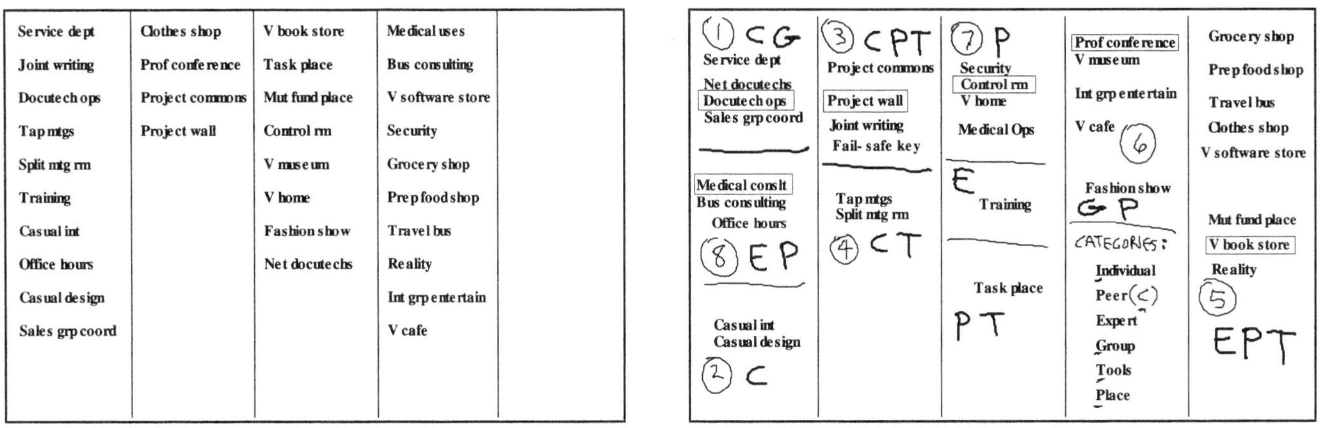

Figure 1. Tivoli Board for the Scenarios Meeting: (a) initial state; (b) final state.

- Category annotations were used to help articulate the similarities and differences among the groups.
- Representative items were selected by coloring them red (shown as boxed items in Figure 1b), and the overall pattern of the selections was assessed.

Note that the materials on the board were treated as a set of objects to be arranged and annotated and that this was the medium for carrying out the work that had to be done.

3. OBJECTIVES FOR MEETING TOOLS

From this example and other experiences with Tivoli in different meetings, we formulated objectives for the design of a facility for meeting tools on an electronic whiteboard:

1. The system must be able to represent the *semantic content* of meetings, the things meetings are about. We encoded these "things" as *domain objects*, i.e., objects that represent meaningful entities in the subject matter domain that end users think about and consciously work with.
2. The domain objects must be *connected with the "workbase"* (e.g., database, document management repository, workflow system) used outside of meetings.
3. The domain objects must be incorporated into a *whiteboard style of interaction* (rapid, easy, pen-based and gesture-based) to support, and not inhibit, the way meetings work.
4. The whiteboard representation must include informal scribbled *annotations* as well as domain objects, since meetings never stay within the confines of a formal representation. The main user interface issue is to effectively accommodate the *blending of structured and freeform* materials on the board.
5. The system must be able to *interpret the 2D spatial arrangement* of the domain objects on the board, for the spatial arrangement is the visible shared representation meeting participants use to develop a shared understanding.
6. The format and behavior of the domain objects must be *tailorable* to the special needs of different meetings. Meetings are not isolated events, but are part of a larger work context. While there are generic aspects to meetings, most efficient meetings are characterized by adopting practices that are tuned to the work to be done in the particular work context.

4. APPROACHES

There are several different approaches to the design of a meeting tools facility:

1. Use standard *desktop-style software tools*. While users are familiar with these tools, annotations are difficult to do. The tools are rigid and usually not adaptable to unexpected turns that take place in meetings.
2. Import *snapshots* from standard tools under a freeform drawing layer, such as can be done with MeetingBoard.[1] This makes annotations easy, but the contents of the snapshots are not manipulable.
3. *Embed* the desktop applications within a freeform whiteboard environment using an object embedding technology such as OLE or ActiveX [2]. The workbase objects are manipulable and editable within the embedded application, and annotations can be made around it. However, this can result in a confusing mix of user interfaces (different UIs for different applications); and the whiteboard's freeform manipulation techniques cannot be used within the embedded applications.
4. Use *domain objects* in a freeform whiteboard environment. The difference from the previous approach is that semantic data is packaged into objects in the whiteboard application. Thus the domain objects are treated as whiteboard graphic objects, and the whiteboard user interface is extended by tailoring the domain objects to have specialized behaviors appropriate to their use.

Note that in this paper we use the unmodified term "object(s)" to refer to domain object(s).

5. THE DOMAIN OBJECT APPROACH

We have implemented domain objects as tailorable graphic objects in Tivoli. Domain objects are significant at two levels: (1) as a part of an architecture that allows Tivoli to participate in a larger collaborative support system and (2) as new user interface techniques in the Tivoli whiteboard environment.

Architecture of Domain Objects

The architecture is illustrated in Figure 2. We assume some kind of workbase (e.g., Lotus Notes) to persistently store the materials of a collaborative work process. People can interact with this workbase with various client applications on their desktop workstations, thus providing asynchronous coordination of individual work through the workbase. However, desktop applications are not effective in meeting settings; Tivoli is a more appropriate user interface. While we can put and get Tivoli files (containing editable page images) from the workbase, these files are a separate representation from the other data in the workbase. The issue is how to use the Tivoli user interface with this other data.

The strategy we follow is to provide a script to import data from the workbase and translate them into a set of domain objects and page layouts in a markup file, which can be read into Tivoli. The meeting participants interact with Tivoli, manipulating the objects with the whiteboard user interface. The altered objects are then exported and trans-

[1] MeetingBoard (LiveWorks, Inc.) is the whiteboard product based on Tivoli.

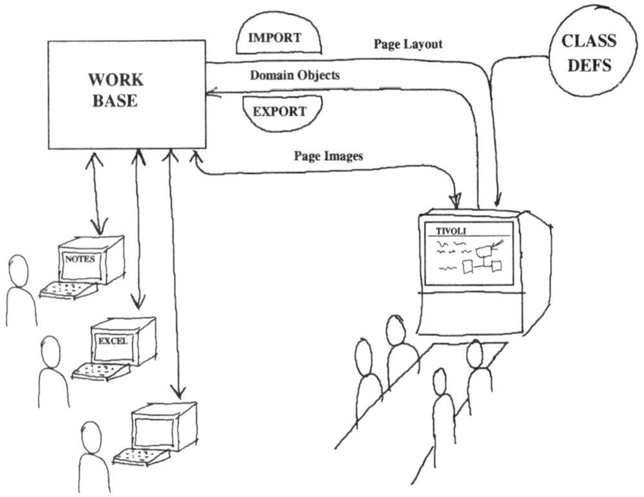

Figure 2: Architecture of Domain Objects

lated back to the workbase representation. Thus, the results of meeting activities are fully integrated into the workbase.

Tivoli has facilities for representing, defining, and managing domain objects. A domain object is a cluster of data representing a work entity (a document, an action, a person, an idea, a proposal, a note, etc.). Each object has a class and a property (attribute-value) list. There is a class definition language for specifying the structure, appearance, behavior, and interpretation of objects of each class and a markup language for laying out domain objects and other graphic objects on Tivoli pages. Thus, to fully tailor Tivoli to a particular style of meeting, one has to create domain class definitions plus import and export scripts.

For example, consider how domain objects might be used in the meeting in Section 2. There would be object classes for the scenarios and for group and category labels. Scenario objects would be imported from the spreadsheet. Participants would manipulate the scenario objects and create label objects in the meeting. The labeled and selected scenarios would then be exported back to the spreadsheet.

Domain Object Definitions

We illustrate the way domain objects are defined and used by an example shown in Figure 3. Four domain object classes are defined in Figure 3a: Label, Task, RegionSum, and LinkedSum. The simplest is a Label object, which just has a name. A Task object has four properties: id, duration, name, and assignee. Domain objects appear on the Tivoli board as graphic objects, called *views*, whose appearances are defined in view layouts in their classes. A Task has two view layouts: view1 shows just its id and duration, whereas view2 also shows its name. Figure 3b shows 22 Task objects. They are all displayed as view1s, except for T8, which is displayed as a view2. The figure also shows four Label objects in four regions. Note that the fourth label, in the freeform region, has a scribbled name.

Figure 3a. Domain Object class definitions

```
class Label (name)
    view1: name
class Task (id, duration, name, assignee)
    view1: id duration
    view2: id duration name
    computed value of assignee:
            get name of Label in my region
    actions:
        right in view1 → change to view2
        left in view2 → change to view1
        up on duration → duration = duration + 1
        down on duration → duration = duration – 1
class RegionSum (sum)
    view1: "RSum=" sum
    computed value of sum:
            add up durations of Tasks in my region
class LinkedSum (sum)
    view1: "LSum=" sum
    computed value of sum:
            add up durations of Tasks linked to me
```

Figure 3b. Domain Object instances on a Tivoli board.

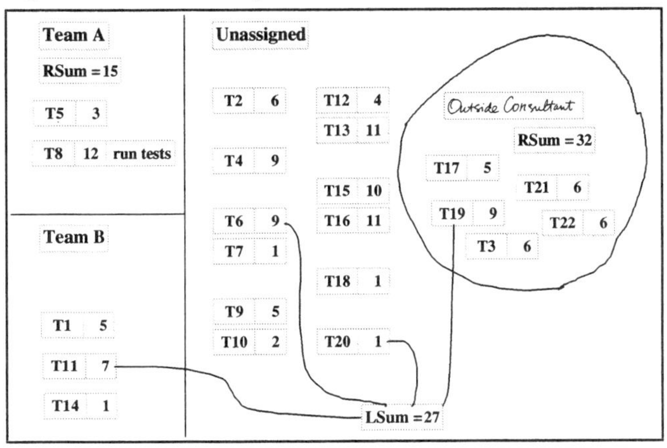

Task objects have specialized behaviors in response to gestures on them[2], as defined in the *actions* in Figure 3a. By making leftward or rightward gestures on Task views, the user can control how they are displayed. In Figure 3b, the user has "expanded" the view of Task T8 by a rightward gesture. Also, by gesturing upward or downward, the user can change a task's duration value. Note that the first two gestures work on specific views, while the other two gestures work only on the duration field (i.e., gesturing up on the id field has no affect). The general form of an action rule in Tivoli class definitions is:

view, field, gesture → action

[2] Actually, on their views. It is often natural to refer to a view as if it were the object itself, and we do so frequently in this paper.

Objects for summing up durations are also defined in Figure 3a. A RegionSum object has a sum property, which is computed dynamically by a formula, which says to add up the duration values of all the Task objects in the local region. This computation is spatially localized to be relative to the spatial position of the RegionSum object. For example, there are two RegionSum objects in Figure 3b, one in the region labeled "Team A" and one in the region labeled "Outside Consultant." The computed sums change dynamically as the user moves objects on the board between regions. For example, if Task T4 were dragged to the Team A region, the RegionSum there would jump to 24; and if the RegionSum object in the Team A region were dragged to the Team B region, it would show 13.

Tivoli supports computations based on spatial relationships — such as containment, location, relative position, and linkage — on a freeform whiteboard environment. For example, a LinkedSum object is shown in Figure 3b, which adds together the durations of Tasks linked to it. (More details about the mechanisms of spatial computation are presented in [14].)

Note that computations based on spatial relations *interpret the significance of the spatial arrangement of objects* on the board and encode them as values of object properties. A better example of this is the assignee property of Task objects, which is computed dynamically by finding a Label object in the same local region and getting its name property (see Figure 3a). For example, the assignee value of T5 is "Team A"; if T5 is dragged to the region below, its assignee value will change to "Team B". If the name of any Label object is changed, then the assignee properties of Task objects in the same region are also changed. If these Tasks had been imported from a project management system, then these assignments could be exported back to the project management system.

The value of these mechanisms will be seen as we consider how this facility is used to create meeting tools.

6. MEETING SCENARIOS

We used meeting scenarios to drive the design and development of the domain object facilities. Based on years of experience in observing and supporting meetings with Tivoli, we chose several specific meeting scenarios. These meetings involved budgeting, decision making, presenting, reviewing, interviewing, and brainstorming. We created specialized meeting tools out of domain objects to support these scenarios. We also built tools to support generic meeting activities, such as managing agendas and timing, taking attendance, notetaking, recording actions, etc.

In this section we present a sampling of these to illustrate how domain object meeting tools can be integrated into the activities of a meeting.

Budget Meeting Scenario

The tools for this kind of meeting are easiest to understand, because the behavior is like a "freeform spreadsheet." This domain consists of cost items organized into budget centers, which are both represented by objects. The goal is to arrange the cost items to fit the budgets. See Figure 4.

Cost item objects have a succinct view, showing only a (truncated) name and cost. These are distributed among different regions, which are labeled with budget center objects. Doing a hold gesture on a budget center pops up an overlay view that documents the class. Figure 4 shows an overlay for the GIR budget center. It shows the four parts of a budget center object: a name, a computed sum of cost items in its region, a target budget, and a computed variance from the budget. It also shows that gestures can alter the target budget.

The meeting proceeds by manipulating cost item objects to eliminate the variance. Cost items can be moved between budget center regions and the lower row of regions, where they are not charged to any budget center. Note also that scribbled annotations are allowed, and they do not affect the computations.

There are additional computations that interpret the arrangement of objects. Each cost item has a budget-center property, which is computed by getting the name of the budget center object in the same column, and a charge-to property, which is computed by getting the name of the budget center in the same local region. Moving cost items to the lower row of regions result in a charge-to of nil, since there are no budget center objects in those regions.

Decision-Making Meeting Scenario

Decision-making meetings are concerned with evaluating and choosing among alternatives of some type. In this scenario, the alternatives are projects; and the goal is to choose a subset of the projects to fund within the budget (the units are percentages of headcount).

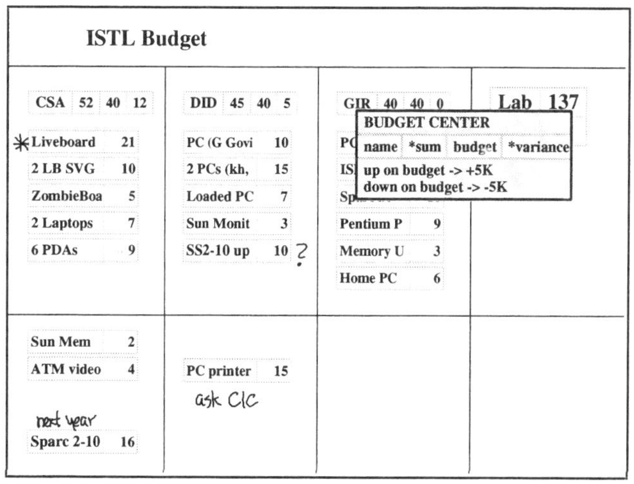

Figure 4. Tivoli Board for the Budget Meeting Scenario.

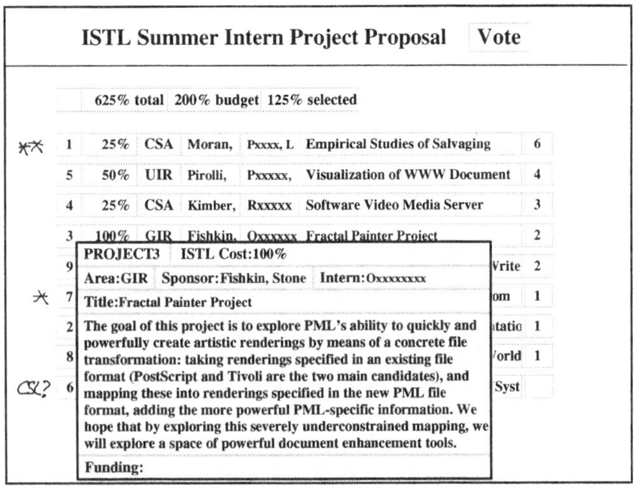

Figure 5. Tivoli Board for the Decision-Making Meeting Scenario.

A project object contains several properties. The list view of a Project object is a wide one-liner showing many of these properties. These can be arranged in a vertical list. See Figure 5. This meeting involves first reviewing the projects. A double-tap gesture on the list view of an object creates an overlay with an expanded view of the project object's data, as shown.

Freehand annotations can be made on the board, such as the stars marking certain projects in Figure 5. The project objects in the list can be manually rearranged: one simply taps on a project object to select it and drag it up or down. When released, the objects will adjust (opening and closing space) to keep it a neat list. The annotations move with the objects, because the implicit structure mechanisms in Tivoli work with *all* graphic objects on the board (see [14] for details).

It is sometimes useful to sort the projects. An up-down gesture on any field of a project causes the project list to be sorted according to that field. This sorting is animated so the users can better comprehend the action; and, again, the annotations are sorted with the project views.

In this scenario, meeting members vote on the projects. This is supported by vote objects. The "Vote" button at the top of Figure 5 is scripted to create a set of vote objects and place them to the right of each of the project objects, as shown. Votes are recorded by gesturing on the vote objects to increment (or decrement) the vote counts. Gesturing up-down on a vote object causes them to be sorted, carrying the project objects and annotations with them.

Finally, the choice of particular projects is recorded by gesturing on them. An up gesture on a project selects it, a single action that results in its status property being set to "selected", its view changed to red to visually distinguish it, and its cost added to the budget summary object at the top of the page. (Similarly, a down gesture deselects a project.)

Generic Meeting Tools

The scenarios above illustrate that meeting tools vary from the specific to the generic (e.g., from project objects to cost item objects to vote objects). There are many generic elements to most meetings, and so we found it useful to define generic objects for these: agenda items, action items, people, notes, votes, labels, etc.

Usually the most specialized element of a meeting is the specific subject matter being discussed, such as the projects in the decision-making meeting or the scenarios in the meeting in Section 2. At the extreme level of generality we found it interesting to create a "thing" object that can represent any kind of thing being discussed. The generic thing object is useful, for example, in a brainstorm meeting where things get created by scribbling on the board. Scribbles can be encapsulated into a thing object by a box gesture. The things can then be arranged, marked with label objects, assigned to people objects, voted upon, etc.

Another generic element in meetings has to do with timing. We have a clock object that holds the current time. Our generic agenda items can be simple or timed. A timed agenda item has a planned time (which the user can set and adjust) and an actual time (which is computed by using the clock object). The agenda item object warns the users (with an audio action) when the actual time approaches the planned time.

Another use of the clock is in proportional timing. In a meeting that has to process a number of items (e.g., a conference program committee meeting), a timing summary object keeps track of how many items have been processed and computes and displays a prediction of when the meeting will end based on the current rate of processing.

Generic tools can be useful by themselves in some meetings, but they are probably more useful as starting points for tailoring. We next present a case study, where we started with generic tools and evolved a much more specialized and finely tuned set of meeting support tools.

7. CASE STUDY: IP REVIEW MEETINGS

For several years, we have been supporting the intellectual property process at PARC by providing Tivoli meeting support, plus audio capture, indexing, and salvaging tools [10, 13]. The central activity in this process (documented in [10]) is an ongoing series of meetings that review *invention proposals* (IPs) by rating and ranking them. After the domain object facilities were sufficiently complete and we had some experience designing both specialized and generic meetings with them, we designed a set of tools for the IP review meetings. These meetings have a rich structure and practice, which will become apparent as we describe the tools (also see [10]).

The workbase for intellectual property is Lotus Notes. We wrote a script that imports from Notes the working set of information needed for a given review meeting, defines a set of domain objects, and lays them out onto several Tivoli pages. There is a page of attendees, an agenda page, pages for recording notes and ratings for each IP reviewed, a page for ranking IPs (called a *ladder*), and provision for dynamically creating new pages for notes on IPs not on the agenda. Being able to easily navigate within and between these pages is crucial, and Tivoli has a jump action that can be triggered by gestures (usually down and up for forward and backward jumps).

The main subject matter in these meetings are IPs, represented as IP objects, which consist of a dozen properties (about a page of textual information for each IP). The set of IPs need to be worked with in a number of different ways, and so many different views are defined: agenda views, title views (on review pages), small ladder views, plus larger views for displaying all of an IP's information on overlays (similar to Figure 5). Another reason for multiple views per object is that it makes it easy to propagate changing information, such as the ratings, to different pages.

The agenda page is simply a list of IP agenda views (similar in appearance to the list of project views in Figure 5). The agenda can be edited, e.g., by making scribbled annotations or dragging IPs around to reorder the list; the navigation gestures follow the edited order. Gesturing down on an IP in the agenda jumps to a page for reviewing that IP.

An IP review page (Figure 6) contains four regions: a title region, a button region, an action item region for generating final actions, and a notes region for collecting notes and actions. The title region contains an IP title-view, which shows the rating value, and buttons to jump to the agenda and ladder pages. The rating is set by tapping on the various objects in the button region.

The main activity in the meetings is the discussion of each IP. The notes region supports the collecting of notes during the discussion. Notes can be scribbled in this region and converted to note objects. However, the preferred method is to take notes on a laptop and to beam them into Tivoli, which then creates note objects and appends them to the list of notes in the notes region. Notes can also be re-beamed if they have been further edited at the laptop. An interesting feature is that the beamed notes contain the times they were created (which is used later to control playback of the recorded audio [13]), and the note objects have a property for these times, shown as the little clocks in Figure 6.

The action item region is used at the end of the discussion to create any actions to follow up. Actions are recorded by scribbling in this region. Tapping on the Action Item label causes all scribbles in this region to be scooped up into a new action item object, which is appended to the notes region. The notes region is typically long and not visible on the board when actions are scribbled; thus a tiny view is also created in the Action Item region (see action "16" in Figure 6); gesturing on this view causes a full overlay to pop up in the Action Item region. An action item object has

Figure 6. Tivoli Board with an IP Review Page. Some text is "encrypted" to mask proprietary data.

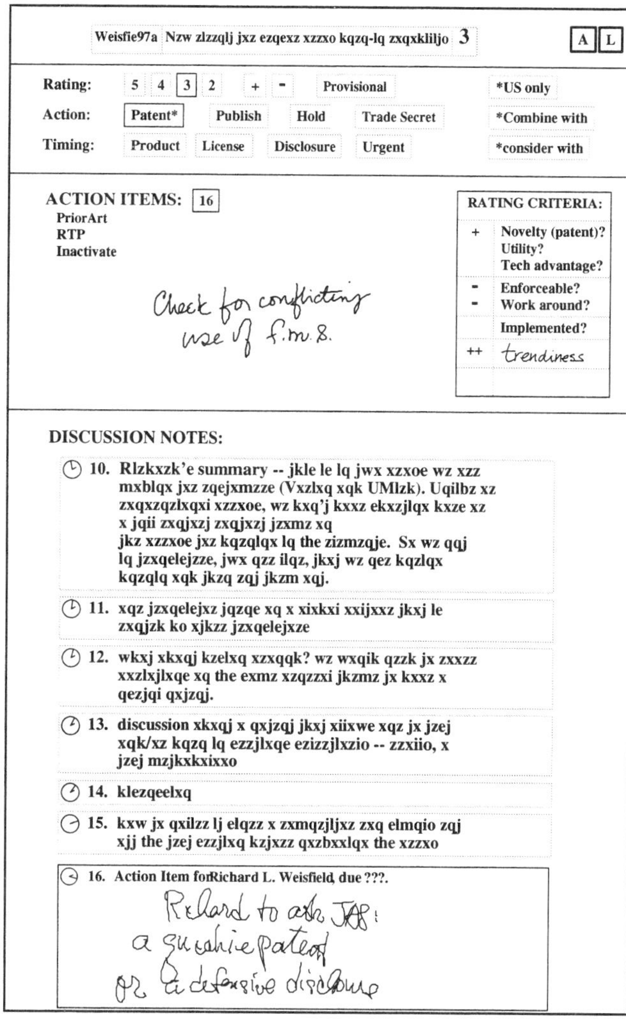

a field for the "assignee." Tapping on this field brings up a menu of people to assign the action to. Alternatively, a person's name can be scribbled on the side and dragged onto the assignee field (which also causes a new person object to be created).

At the end of the meeting, it is often useful to gather all the action items generated during the meeting into one place to review them. The natural place for this is the Attendees page (Figure 7), which contains a list of person objects (the possible attendees). Gestures on these allow people to be marked as present. The names of unanticipated attendees can be scribbled and converted to person objects. A "Show Actions" button causes the current action items from the various review pages to be displayed as tiny views arranged next to the people they are assigned to. Gesturing on one of these causes an overlay to pop up (see Figure 7). An action can be reassigned by simply dragging it onto another person object (the action item object then automatically scoots to the end of the person object's row).

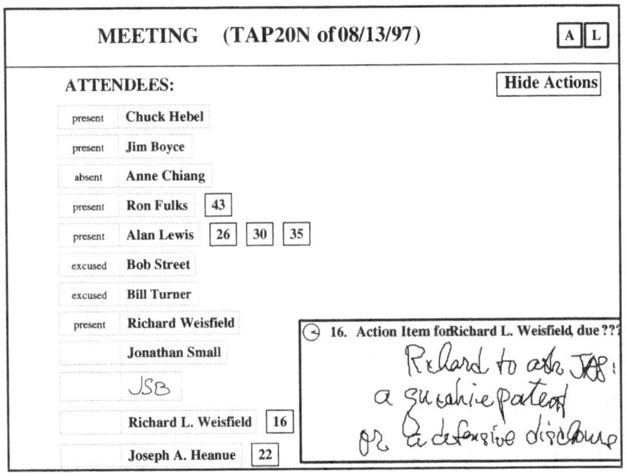

Figure 7. Tivoli Board with an IP Attendees Page.

Finally, there is the ladder page (Figure 8), which is a map of all current IPs in a particular technology area (not just the IPs being reviewed in the meeting). Small IP views are used so that an overview can be seen. Gesturing on an IP view brings up a full display of the IP on an overlay. The page is divided into regions with *ranking* label objects ("A", "B", "New", "Hold", etc.). IP views can be moved around by dragging, and Tivoli's implicit structure mechanism maintains the list structure. An IP's ranking is computed dynamically, as explained previously, from where it is positioned on this page (using both its region's label and its position in the list). Scribbled annotations can be made anywhere on the page. Gesturing down on an IP causes a new page to be created, where notes on that IP can be taken, action items can be created, and/or its rating changed.

These tools were designed and evolved over a half dozen IP meetings starting in October 1996, and they have been in continual use since then, during which time only minor changes have been made. The tools are finely tuned to the practices of these meetings. Further changes would involve changes in the practices. For example, we thought it would be useful to be more explicit about rating criteria, and so we experimented with a "Rating Criteria" object (shown in Figure 6); while useful in a couple of cases, it is not used most of the time.

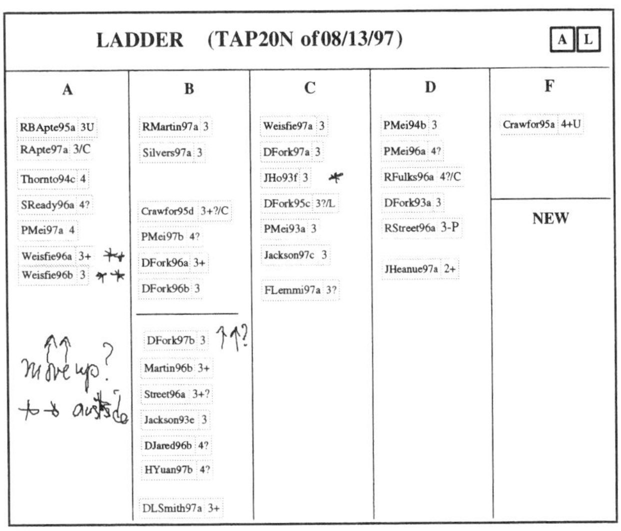

Figure 8. Tivoli Board with an IP Ladder Page.

These tools were developed in an "evolutionary engagement" [10] with the participants in the IP review meetings. Observations of the meetings and discussions with the participants show that the tools have resulted in several improvements in the meeting processes:

- The relationship among large sets of items is easily manipulated and explored, while all present can see and participate. Prioritizing IPs on the ladder is a qualitatively better activity. The rearrangable agenda enables a better-planned meeting.
- Information is retrievable when needed without being in the way when not needed. The details of older IPs can easily be popped up in the ladder page as needed.
- Information created or altered in one location is propagated to other locations. The ratings can be seen on several different pages; the action items can be gathered together for a final review.
- Notes can be taken and indexed on old IPs that are not on the agenda for the day. New review pages can be easily created from the ladder as the discussion spontaneously focuses on old IPs.

While all of these activities are supported with the tailored meeting tools, they exist in a whiteboard environment, where the meeting can always revert to scribbled notes when the specialized tools are not appropriate.

8. DISCUSSION

Now that we have described the domain object facility and how domain objects are used as meeting tools, we can step back and reflect on our objectives (listed in Section 3) in designing this facility.

Connecting to the Workbase at the Semantic Level

Our first two objectives were to represent the semantic content of meetings and to connect to the workbase at this level of content.

It is apparent, as we show in Figure 2, that Tivoli can connect to the workbase by simply putting and getting files with editable page images. The problem is that this representation is not compatible with other file representations in the workbase, and thus any information has to be manually transcribed between representations. The connection is at the document (or page) level and not the object (or "item" or "field") level of information. Tivoli has always been capable of having text elements on the board that can be freely moved around on the board. The problem is that the significance of this 2D arrangement is lost in converting it back into a textual representation (a string of characters).

Other systems, such as Lotus Notes, allow interaction with the workbase at the "field level" by having a database of "objects" that can be presented in different interactive views. But Notes does not offer a whiteboard-style view that can be used in meeting settings. The system that is closest to ours is Dolphin [18], which also uses the LiveBoard. Dolphin offers a neat solution integrating the synchronous work in a meeting with the asynchronous work outside of meetings, but does this within a particular hypermedia model of nodes and links.

Our approach is to integrate with a variety of different workbases and to present a whiteboard-style user interface in the meeting setting. We do this by translating the data at an object level for presentation and by providing a facility to interpret the spatial arrangements created in the meeting. In this way, we can connect with any workbase that has an appropriate API at the level of objects.

Designing Finely Tuned Tools

Our third and fourth objectives were to provide in the meeting setting a freeform whiteboard user interface that blends informal scribbling and annotations with structured domain objects. We have explored a variety of user interface techniques to integrate domain objects into Tivoli's whiteboard environment, and we have developed some design principles for tailoring meeting tools with the domain object facility.

Domain objects behave fully like any other graphic objects on the board in Tivoli. In addition, they are responsive to special gestures. In tailoring such gestures we employ standard user interface design principles. Gestures are invisible and thus must be remembered. We found it helpful to use certain gestures consistently, e.g., the hold gesture for bringing up documentation of an object's class behavior (as in Figure 4) (cf. [6]) and the double-tap gesture for bringing up further information about the contents of the particular object (as in Figure 5). To make gestures feel natural, the principle of "gesture compatibility" is relevant, such as an up gesture invoking an increment action, a right gesture invoking an expansion of the view in a rightward direction, or an up-down gesture invoking a sorting operation, where the objects in the list shuffle up and down as the sort is animated.

Scribbles and domain objects are well integrated. Users can, of course, scribble anywhere on the board around domain objects (as in Figures 4, 5, and 8). These objects and scribbles work together in Tivoli's implicit structure mechanism. For example, the scribbled annotations in Figure 5 move with the project views when the project list is sorted. Scribbles made on the board can be incorporated into domain objects in various ways. Any set of scribbles can be converted to an object by a box gesture around the scribbles (the same technique as used in Dolphin [18]). Domain objects can be tailored to "absorb" scribbles that are dragged onto their views and to "pull" scribbles in their spatial regions (which other systems cannot do). All these techniques allow users in meetings to easily shift between loose and structured modes of expression.

Our overall design strategy for using domain objects as meeting tools was to stress the use of board pages containing overviews of sets of data. This relies on the flexibility of the domain object view mechanism, allowing multiple views of differing detail. The principle for information presentation is to get as much information as possible on a page using smaller views (but allow users to pop up more information as needed), to use different pages for different arrangements of information for different purposes, and to allow easy navigation between these pages. The IP Review case study provides evidence that this is an effective strategy.

Using and Interpreting 2D Spatial Arrangements

Our fifth objective was to allow the free use and interpretation of 2D spatial arrangements on the board.

Our strategy of providing overviews of information allows users to see the interrelationships among objects. By providing easy ways for them to rearrange and organize objects on the board they can explore new relationships. 2D spatial relationships — containment, adjacency, relative position, alignment, clustering, etc. — are the medium of expression and exploration. Our ability to have the system interpret some of these spatial relationships allows us to capture and encode semantic relationships that would otherwise be implicit. In doing this we are building on and integrating with the previously-developed spatial interpretation mechanisms in Tivoli [12, 11].

A distinguishing characteristic of our approach is the use of a range of 2D spatial relationships, as opposed to node-link structures. Dolphin [18] allows users to create relationships by expressing them in node-link structures and graph representations. This follows in the hypertext tradition, which stresses *explicit* links.[3] Indeed, in our own experience, from NoteCards [4] to Viki [8], it took us several years of experience and exploration to fully appreciate that 2D layout was usually a more expressive and more compact representation than node-link graphs and to understand that 2D spatial arrangements could be usefully interpreted [17], even though the relationships are more implicit and subtle.

Tailoring Specialized Meeting Tools

Our final objective was to provide facilities for tailoring specialized meeting tools. We provide a scripting language for defining the structure, appearance, and behavior of domain object classes. Our language has most of the elements of the Oval [7] system (objects, view, agents, links), but in a much simpler form. Yet, in a similar way, we find

[3] So-called "idea processing" applications also focus on explicit node-link representations, e.g., the "mind maps" of Inspiration [5].

that this language allows for the creation of quite a broad range of meeting tools. Our facility is much more specialized than Oval in being integrated with a sophisticated whiteboard environment with spatial organization, manipulation, and interpretation capabilities.

Tailoring is a costly activity. It is possible to craft meeting tools from scratch. Our view is that one would begin with some generic meeting objects, such as those in Section 6 we used to create the IP Review tools (Section 7). We have identified a few generic objects, but there is a lot more to do to attain a polished set of meeting building blocks.

Most meeting support tools are geared to a particular task or process, such as gIBIS [1] for issue discussion, or a suite of different processes, such as GroupSystems [15] or MeetingRight [9]. These tools tend to be intentionally quite restrictive, so as to guide a normative process. Our philosophy is that tools are better adopted if they can be tuned to existing practices, at least initially. Building tools on a tailorable foundation provides the flexibility to do this. In our facility, tailoring must be done by reworking class definition scripts, which must be done between meetings; that is, tools are iteratively refined over a series of meetings. We have not provided any interfaces to allow class definitions to be edited in a meeting. Though this is a possible course of investigation, we do not think this is a good use of meeting time. Instead, we provide the flexibility in the user interface for working around the immediate limitations of the tools in a meeting by informal scribbling, thus providing an experiential basis for improving the tools. Our long-term experience in the case study in Section 7 has shown that this is an effective way to evolve both the tools and the meeting practices [10].

9. CONCLUSION

We have shown how to integrate structured domain objects into a freeform whiteboard user interface. This integration is useful, because it allows us to work in meetings in a whiteboard style with data from structured workbases. Further, these domain objects are tailorable so that they can be tuned to specific meeting practices. This increases the amount and quality of work that is possible in a meeting, as shown, for example, in our case study. These kinds of improvements are possible when tools can be tailored to well understood and predictable meeting practices. When meetings take unanticipated turns, users can slide into familiar informal methods of scribbling. The ability to do this depends on the smooth blending of structured and informal user interface techniques (which are discussed in more detail in a companion paper [14]).

Acknowledgments. We thank our colleagues in the Collaborative Systems Area of PARC for many discussions over the course of this work. Chuck Hebel worked closely with us in creating and evolving the tools for the IR review process. Thanks also to Beverly Harrison for critiquing this paper.

REFERENCES

1. Conklin, E. J. & Begeman, M. (1988). GIBIS: A hypertext tool for exploratory policy discussion. *Proceedings of CSCW'88*, 140-152.
2. Denning, A. *ActiveX Controls Inside Out*, 2nd ed., Microsoft Press. 1997.
3. Elrod, S., Bruce, R., et al. (1992). LiveBoard: A large interactive display supporting group meetings, presentations, and remote collaboration, *Proceedings of CHI'92*, 599-607.
4. Halasz, F. G., Moran, T. P., & Trigg, R. (1987). NoteCards in a nutshell. *Proceedings of CHI'87*.
5. *Inspiration: the thought processor*. (1990). Ceres Software, Inc.
6. Kurtenbach G., Moran, T. P., & Buxton, W. (1994). Contextual animation of gestural commands. *Proceedings of Graphics Interface'94*, 83-90. Canadian Information Processing Society.
7. Malone, T., Lai, K., & Fry, C. (1992). Experiments with Oval: a radically tailorable tool for cooperative work. *Proceedings of CSCW'92*, 289-297.
8. Marshall, C. C., Shipman, F. M., & Coombs, J. H. (1994). VIKI: Spatial hypertext supporting emergent structure. *Proceedings of ECHT'94*.
9. *MeetingRight software user's guide*. (1994). Rochester, NY: Xerox Quality Solutions.
10. Moran, T. P., Chiu, P., Harrison, S., Kurtenbach, G., Minneman, S., & van Melle, W. (1996). Evolutionary engagement in an ongoing collaborative work process: a case study. *Proceedings of CSCW'96*, 150-159.
11. Moran, T. P., Chiu, P., & van Melle, W. (1997). Pen-based interaction techniques for organizing material on an electronic whiteboard. *Proceedings of UIST'97*, 45-54.
12. Moran, T. P., Chiu, P., van Melle, W., & Kurtenbach, G. (1995). Implicit structures for pen-based systems within a freeform interaction paradigm. *Proceedings of CHI'95*, 487-494.
13. Moran, T. P., Palen, L., Harrison, S., Chiu, P., Kimber, D., Minneman, S., van Melle, W., & Zellweger, P. (1997). "I'll get that off the audio": A case study of salvaging multimedia meeting records. *Proceedings of CHI'97*, 202-209.
14. Moran, T. P., van Melle, W., & Chiu, P. (1998). Spatial interpretation of domain objects integrated into a freeform electronic whiteboard. *Proceedings of UIST'98*.
15. Nunamaker, J., Dennis, A., Valacich, J., Vogel, D., & George, J. (1991). Electronic meeting systems to support group work. *Communications of the ACM*, 34(7), 40-61.
16. Pedersen, E., McCall, K., Moran, T. P., & Halasz, F. (1993). Tivoli: An electronic whiteboard for informal workgroup meetings. *Proceedings of INTERCHI'93*, 391-389.
17. Shipman, F. M., Marshall, C. C., & Moran, T. P. (1995). Finding and using implicit structure in human-organized spatial information layouts. *Proceedings of CHI'95*.
18. Streitz, N., Geissler, J., Haake, J., & Hol, J. (1994). Dolphin: integrated meeting support across local and remote desktop environments and liveboards. *Proceedings of CSCW'94*, 345-358.
19. Trigg, R., Moran, T. P., and Halasz, F. G. (1987). Adaptability and tailorability in NoteCards. *Proceedings of Interact'87*.

Mobility in Collaboration

Paul Luff
WIT Research Group, King's College
Campden Hill Road
London, W8 7AH, UK
+44 171 333 4289
Paul.Luff@kcl.ac.uk

Christian Heath
WIT Research Group, King's College
Campden Hill Road
London, W8 7AH, UK
+44 171 333 4496
Christian.Heath@kcl.ac.uk

ABSTRACT
This paper addresses an issue that has received little attention within CSCW - the requirements to support mobility within collaborative activities. By examining three quite different settings each with differing technological support, we examine the ways in which mobility is critical to collaborative work. We suggest that taking mobility seriously may not only contribute our understanding of current support for collaboration, but raise more general issues concerning the requirements for mobile and other technologies.

Keywords
mobile communications, augmented reality, object-centred interaction

INTRODUCTION
It is a strange irony that given the promise of new spaces and novel environments for collaboration, current technologies appear so rigid. Tools for remote collaboration, such as desktop conferencing, groupware, and more innovative technologies like Clearface [14] and CVEs [3], are available on devices which are static and tied to the desk. Systems designed for co-present collaborative activities (e.g. [16]), such as meetings and decision support, although they are concerned with providing new and innovative environments, are similarly typically located on inflexible workstations. Even attempts at expanding the workspace through the novel use of multiple or roving cameras have quite inadvertently severely restricted the movement of individuals both within their own environments and those with which they connected [5, 11].

The ways in which mobility features in collaborative work has largely been overlooked within CSCW (but see [2, 20] for exceptions). It has neither formed the focus for developing innovative mobile technologies nor featured in empirical studies of work and communication. In this paper, we report on studies of communication and collaboration in three very different settings and discuss the implications of the observations for supporting mobility and more generally enhancing collaborative work. The three settings consist of: primary health consultations; construction sites; and stations on London Underground. In exploring work and communication in these different environments, we consider how individuals rely upon their own mobility, and the mobility of particular artefacts, to support collaboration, and consider resources which might enhance their current tasks and responsibilities.

CSCW 98 Seattle Washington USA

BACKGROUND
Within the field of CSCW considerable attention has been paid to the types of technology that could support remote collaboration between individuals. The development of these technologies, often in prototype form, have both informed and been informed by recent debates concerning the possible changing character of organisations and organisational activities. For example, it is widely accepted that we are witnessing the emergence of new forms of organisation, in particular the fragmented or disaggregated organisation which consists of dynamic networks of firms which temporarily coalesce to produce a particular product or service [1]. It is suggested that the emergence of new communication technologies provide the relevant support for these flexible and contingent organisational forms. For example, mobile technologies, whether these are mobile telephones or more sophisticated devices, seem to support such transformations, allowing organisational activities not to be so focused within a particular office or at a particular desk.

In a rather different way, it is also argued that new technologies play an important part in recent attempts to 're-engineer' business processes, to focus on 'core activities' and to facilitate developments such as 'hot desking', where the organisation is less centred on individual members, and more on the activities they have to perform [6]. Systems for collaborative work, would appear to correspond with and facilitate such developments, offering the kind of support for geographically dispersed individuals only previously available within a setting.

For example, some CSCW prototypes provide novel environments in which individual users, or representations of them, can not only have access to distributed colleagues, but can move through, or reconfigure a shared spatial environment [5, 3]. More conventional systems provide participants with visual and audible access to each other, as well the ability to share and exchange documents and the like. However, despite the contribution of such systems to supporting distributed activities, the technologies are unwieldy and, rather than enhancing an individual flexibility within his or her immediate environment, tie participants to tightly circumscribed regions within their setting. The physical configuration of the technology may appear to be of minor consequence if the system can provide unprecedented access to remote individuals. However, the trend to make particular devices, routinely workstations, increasingly complex, has important consequences for the sorts of activity and collaboration that such technologies can support. By constraining the movement of individuals, and burdening the user with a complex, yet inflexible technology, we run the risk of undermining an important resource in collaboration, namely, an individual's ability to reconfigure him or herself with regard to ongoing demands of the activity in which he or she is engaged. CSCW runs the danger of localising activities, enhancing the facilities available to the individual 'user' whilst undermining flexible and contingent collaboration.

The trend in CSCW to enhance collaboration by providing increasingly complex support on conventional workstations, would appear to run counter to the findings of many workplace studies. Whilst not concerned with mobility *per se*, it is interesting to note how a range of studies of various settings have demonstrated how participants, as a matter of coordinating their activities with others, rely upon their own mobility and the mobility of artefacts. For example, our own studies of the control rooms of London Underground, demonstrate how peripheral awareness and participation is dependent upon the ability of particular individuals to ongoingly configure their spatial relationships to enable them to overhear and oversee the contributions of others, whilst rendering their own activities visible. Similarly studies of air traffic control, of offices, of news rooms, of ship navigation, of printing processes and of financial institutions, all in various ways reveal how the mobility of personnel and artefacts is critical to communication and collaboration. And yet many of us, including ourselves (cf. [8, 12, 13]) have been principally concerned with enhancing the shared facilities for individuals on fixed workstations.

By considering, in a little detail, the ways in which personnel in conventional working environments rely upon their own mobility and the mobility of artefacts in accomplishing their work, we may learn a little about how we might enhance support for collaboration. The settings in question raise rather different issues and pose rather different problems for computer support. In the first case, we reconsider the introduction of computer based records into the medical consultation, and explore how the technology has undermined a critical resource in collaboration; the ecological mobility of traditional, paper record. In considering the use of the paper record, we consider how professional medical practice articulates the document to support reading and writing in concert with the real time contributions of the patient. The construction site raises rather different issues. It provides a brief glimpse of how documents can be manipulated and transported within a domain to support coordination and collaboration. Observation of these indigenous practices, practices which both rely upon and enhance mobility, begin to reveal how system support for mobility can fail, and can fail by virtue of the technology's ability to support the sorts of collaboration afforded by the original document. Finally, we consider London Underground, and a project concerned with supporting mobile station staff. Its aim is to provide supervisors with access to the facilities of a fixed command and control centre wherever they may be around large stations with complex interconnections. By considering how staff coordinate their activities with each other, we can begin to explore the issues that arise in providing multimedia support for mobile collaboration, and in particular in reconfiguring the environment to support awareness, communication and cooperation.

MICRO-MOBILITY: MEDICAL CONSULTATIONS

In the first study we explore the range of ways in which the mobility of a simple paper document is critical to the work and communication of the medical practitioner. The document in question is the medical record in primary health care; a document which is increasingly being enhanced and replaced by computerised records. We note that the paper record supports both synchronous and asynchronous collaboration, and collaboration between both doctors and other professionals, and between the patient and the doctor. In particular we suggest that the medical consultation, like other activities which are largely office bound, points to a form of mobility not normally associated with new technologies, that is 'micro-mobility'; the way in which an artefact can by mobilised and manipulated for various purposes around a relatively circumscribed, or 'at hand', domain.

Consider, for example the medical consultation. Over a number of years we have undertaken successive studies of primary health care and shown the various ways in which the record card is critical to professional practice and the interaction between patient and doctor [7, 10]. The paper medical record consists of a small A5 (7" x 5") envelope containing various pieces of paper and card, including discharge letters, referral notes and test results (see Figure 1).

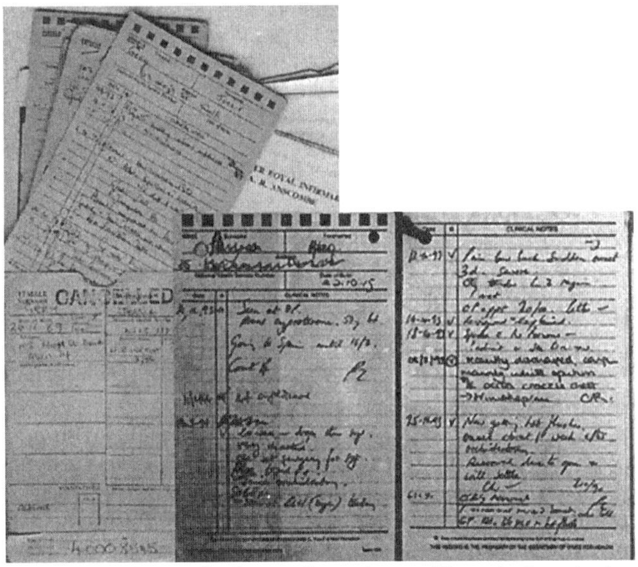

Figure 1: the medical record envelope with typical contents (left), and a detail from a record card (right)

For members in a practice, the paper medical card serves as an important resource for (asynchronous) communication and collaboration. It is transported around the practice or clinic, and even the local region, and some trouble is given to make it available when and wherever patient and practitioner meet. Despite the introduction of computerised systems, the paper record remains an important resource in professional medical practice. Its portability is a critical part of its success, as it passes between the hands of different professionals, is carried around the practice, and located in different parts of the office and clinic.

However, it is perhaps in the dealings between patient and doctor, during the consultation, that the mobility of the paper record, becomes critical. For example, the record is read and written in various locations on the desk: it is placed on the knee, held in the hand, and even passed to the patient to read or help decipher the odd entry. It is propped on the desk, whilst the doctor talks to the patient, it can become the focus of gestures and remarks. The ecological flexibility of the record is a resource in a range of activities, and assists the communicative flexibility of the doctor. For example, whilst talking to the patient, the record can be positioned and manipulated so as to avoid interrupting the free flow of the conversation, or on occasions 'foregrounded' so as to give the doctor time to read or enter information. Or consider for example, how a doctor can position the record so as to invite the patient to view the materials; the text itself becoming the focal medium through which the talk is produced and interpreted. The record can even be dismantled, letters removed, or reassembled in different ways; once again the separate mobility of the record's contents exploited for various ways of acting and interacting with the patient.

Unfortunately, this ecological dexterity is not found with conventional computer systems; indeed, even portables, laptops and the like, are still cumbersome and rigid. It is difficult to position a workstation, both keyboard and monitor in such a way that the doctor can maintain a principal orientation towards the patient whilst reading of entering information, and the physical separation of the area where text is entered from where it is seen, undermines the doctor's ability to momentarily enter data. The system clutters the desk, and cannot be easily pushed to the rear or brought forward, and whilst a monitor can be swung towards the patient, it is difficult to configure a suitable framework around the desk to allow the participants equal access to the information (5). The system is indeed part of the furniture, and as part of the furniture it demands an orientation from the participants, rather than allowing the participants themselves the ability to ongoingly configure the artefact with regard to the shifting demands of the activity.

The relevance of the micro-mobility of artefacts to the accomplishment of workplace activities is not solely found within medicine or general practice. Indeed, our observations of a broad range of workplace activities in various domains, including news rooms, travel agencies, financial institutions, control rooms, even universities, point to the ways in which the micro-mobility of paper documents is a critical resource in, and feature of, collaboration and interaction. Indeed, with the recent discussions concerning the advantages of paper, the simple yet critical fact that the record is handlable, manipulable, portable, dismantlable and can easily be reordered and reassembled for particular purposes, are critical features of the ways in which the document supports the work and interaction between colleagues, and colleagues and their clients. Unfortunately the desk top metaphor, and its influence on the design of digital technologies, fails to take seriously how more traditional artefacts and tools can be reconfigured on the desk with regard to ongoing demands of the work and interactions with others.

REMOTE MOBILITY: A CONSTRUCTION SITE

In the construction site we find a more conventional sense of mobility; individuals who move around different physical locations who require access to information and colleagues. In the case at hand, a mobile system was developed and deployed to support the work of foremen, who as a matter of their daily responsibilities, have to monitor the work of gangs based in different locations around the construction site.

At first glance, the document used by a foreman is not unlike the medical record card. The 'allocation sheet' is a paper record of the work which is done by each gang. It records what activities have been undertaken, the time spent, and any problems which have been found and managed (see Figure 2). The record is completed everyday and is used by a range of personnel to monitor the progress of work, to identify problems, and coordinate activities. The document therefore is both a record of, and a resource in the organisation of work. It is used and referred to by, amongst others, engineers, accountants, surveyors, clerks, and managers.

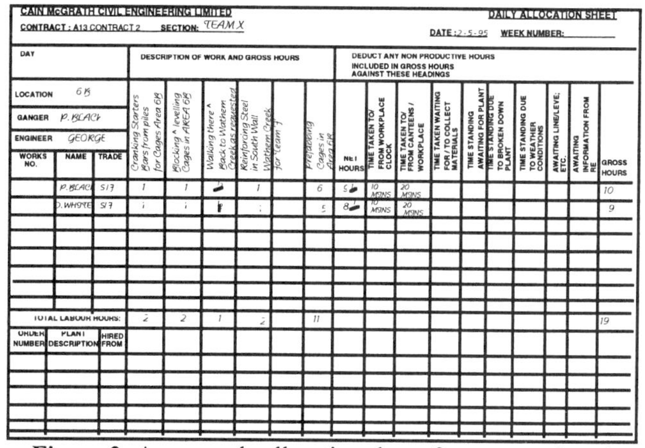

Figure 2: An example allocation sheet, for a gang of steel fixers (S/F).

Allocation sheets record the work of all the gangs of manual workers out on site and are filled in by those responsible for each gang – the gangers. The completed sheets are then used by a range of personnel within the site hut. Hence, they are a resource for asynchronous and remote communication between those out on site and those in the hut. A foreman, responsible for several gangs typically collects these sheets, checks what has been filled in and then passes them on to the appropriate individuals in the hut. The sheets therefore are mobile; they move around the construction site and are exchanged and assembled within the site hut. Unfortunately, like other paper documents, the traditional allocation sheet is regarded as an outmoded artefact, and it is generally believed that new technologies can provide enhanced support for the documentation, evaluation and management of work on site. These reservations and ambitions informed an exercise undertaken by system developers in the construction company to replace the paper sheets with an electronic system.

In general, it was assumed that a new mobile system would not only fulfil many of the functions currently covered by the paper allocation sheets, but also help document information more quickly and make it more accessible to the various interested personnel. It was also believed that documenting data on a mobile system would allow foremen, where necessary, to discuss various details with gang members and others, wherever they might be located. In a sense therefore, it was believed that a mobile system would enhance communication and collaboration, as well as making more bureaucratic activities more efficient. Finally, it was also hoped that the system itself, would provide a resource to foreman to become more proactive; to anticipate problems and difficulties and put solutions into place before trouble emerged.

The allocation sheet is a fairly conventional form that records on what, and for how long, each individual worker has been working. At the end of each day the ganger writes the entries for that day and passes it to the foreman. Once within the site hut the form is the resource for a complex series of activities by various personnel both within the ganger's team and elsewhere in the organisation. So, for example, time-keepers use the allocation sheets for assessing the number of hours worked by particular personnel, engineers and team managers use the sheet for checking on what (and for how long) they have been engaged, and accountants and bonus surveyors use them to estimate how much each activity is currently costing.

The system designers decided that a Fujitsu 500 Stylistic notepad computer would be an appropriate device to replace the paper allocation sheet. An interface was developed that replicated, as far as possible, the actions accomplished on the paper form. Communication from the device to the site hut was through a mobile phone via a modem.

Needless to say, there were difficulties associated with the introduction of the initial version of the technology. Nevertheless, the system was in continuous use for six months until the team completed work on the construction site. It was then used by other teams for another six months until the completion of the entire construction project. It was used in the everyday work of the project and produced information that was of relevance for the management of the team. For example cost data, useful for planning work to be done on the site, was produced for the appropriate weekly team meeting rather than a week late, as usually happened with the paper based system.

Despite the success of the system, there were some interesting differences between the aims of the project and the way in which the technology was used. In particular, when it was put into regular service, it was found that it was necessary to employ an additional person whose sole responsibility was to deal with the system, enter the allocation information and transform it into the form required by other members of staff. This work was not undertaken as envisaged out on site, in cooperation with the gangers, but rather in the site hut itself. In other words, despite the design of system it was neither used as a mobile device nor as a communication tool; rather it remained in a fixed location and was principally used to document data.

This was a consequence of the experiences when the system was tried out in earnest by the foreman during his everyday work around the site.

As mentioned, rather than gangers entering the information for each team, with the introduction of the system these data would be inputted by the foreman for all of the gangs. This would appear to make more efficient use of the technology, particularly as a critical feature of the foreman's work is to roam around the site to monitor problems as they occur. The mobility of the technology could then also provide a resource for discussions between foremen and gangers about problems occurring on the site.

In some ways, the foreman's mobility around the site is critical for both his work and is relied on by colleagues. In going around the site, the foreman can monitor the activities in various areas and engage in interactions with participants responsible for them concerning the problems which they are facing. Indeed, these movements appear to be relied on by other participants; that he will be around at some time, at a particular location or passed when travelling around the site. Such 'serendipitous' contact, or at least the frequent accessibility of the foreman is a critical feature of his work, both for himself and for others on the site.

However, although the allocation system was mobile and eventually could be operated at some speed out on the site, its use tended to transform the ways the foreman worked. Not only did the technology become an explicit topic in the talk between gangers and foreman, but the activity of filling in the allocation sheets became a focus of the work whilst out on site. What had been a brief handover of paper documents, and a transient interaction between ganger and foreman became an extensive activity. Instead of being a resource for talking about the ongoing problems on the site, using the technology actually impeded such discussions. Indeed, in trying to use the system on the site, the foreman would either not be able deal with problems in a particular area or would remain tied to one location. Rather than becoming a resource for mobile collaboration, the technology actually appeared to hinder it.

Following some initial use with the system around the site, the foreman began to use it only in the site hut. He would collect the allocation information from the gangers in a notebook, or even on the old paper allocation sheet and then type all the gangs' information into the system. In this way he could enter the information undisturbed, but this further undermined his routine work of travelling around the site. Rather ironically, the introduction of the mobile system made the user less mobile, less able to monitor the ongoing work and less available to engage in activities with others on site. Hence, after a few weeks it was decided to transform how the technology was to be deployed; another individual would be responsible for entering the information into the system.

These difficulties suggest some misunderstandings by the proponents of the system concerning the nature of the collaborative activities on the site and the technology required to support them. In particular it suggests a misapprehension as to the mobile nature of the work. Because the individuals were mobile it would appear that a mobile technology would be most appropriate. However, the activity it is designed to support does not require the kind of mobility the system provides. Paper allocation sheets are frequently filled out at home, or off site, by gangers. Allowing for the transformation of the activity so actually filling out the sheets can take place around the site requires attention to be paid to how their collaborative production can be supported. In this regard it is unclear whether the technology chosen is the most appropriate one. Indeed, its size, shape and the low intensity of the lighting of the screen made it problematic for items displayed on it to become topics of discussion. It did not even offer the interactional support of the paper allocation sheet.

If this support was considered then attention would have to be paid to the nature of the interactions around the objects and artefacts, the sketches, notes and work schedules, currently utilised within discussions between foremen and gangers. At present it is these that appear to be a resource for collaboration. As in the medical consultation, it may be that a different set of resources are required to support such interactions. Rather than just allowing information to be entered in a range of geographical locations the mobility required may be more in terms of the moment-to-moment accomplishment of the collaborative activities – the micro-mobility of the activity. It may then be necessary to see how delicate shifts in the accessibility of information, from the individual to the collaborative can be supported during co-present interactions, wherever these may be.

It is also unclear whether the device was appropriate with regard to the more general aim of transforming the activity of the foreman through the use of new technologies. As mentioned, the foreman does have a general concern with the items entered into the allocation sheet, with respect to, for example, retrospectively monitoring the activities which are recorded as having happened. But, his main concerns are with the ongoing occurrences on the site. It is unclear how getting a foreman to fill in the data would help him be more prospective. Indeed, it was curious, that in the initial use of the system, rather than transforming the foreman's task to be more proactive and involve more planning and management, the foreman became more involved in bureaucratic activities, keying in data and coding the information against cost categories.

It is not surprising, therefore, that the team decided to continue using the paper sheets and employ someone else to enter and code the information from them. In this way, the foreman could remain mobile around the site, the gangers continued entering the information onto the paper sheets and data were available in an electronic form for a range of personnel in the site hut. The use of the computer system, even with the mobile phone connection, remained situated in the hut. Luckily the flexibility of the deployment process, the use of prototyping and the involvement of staff allowed such a transformation in the objectives and design of the system and a technological solution to remain appropriate.

It is a shame that the ambitious aims of the proponents of the system did not quite match the way it was eventually used. But the individuals in the site hut did get the information, by and large, they required in an electronic form and the foreman was not unduly overburdened with an additional and largely irrelevant task. Despite the identification of an individual who needed to be mobile, activities that appeared cumbersome and redundant, and a resource that seemed to require mobile support, the original focus of the exercise appears to have been chosen without paying enough attention to the nature of the activity that the system was intended to replace. This itself did not require mobile support, or at least not of the kind provided; the kind offered on a small. individual system. Even the more radical aim of transforming the work of the foreman, getting him to be involved in planning and more focused discussions about work on the site was hampered rather than supported by the technology.

The development of a mobile technology for foremen may have seemed straightforward. It was focused on individuals who move around a fairly large domain, who need access to remote information and colleagues and it was based on an everyday artefact that was similarly mobile. Nevertheless, the technology, and more specifically the ways in which it could be used, though mobile was not sensitive in the appropriate ways to the practical concerns of those who were meant to use it. Even though critical features relating to mobility were identified, these seemed too crude when the practices of the individuals for which the technology was intended were considered in more detail. To support the mobility required by the foremen appears to require more than transforming a paper document into an electronic one. Serious attention has to be paid to the ways in which personnel interact with colleagues whilst out on site and use various objects and artefacts to accomplish their work with others.

REMOTE AND LOCAL MOBILITY: LONDON UNDERGROUND

Unfortunately therefore, the design and deployment of a mobile system to support the work of foremen and others, largely failed to enhance the production or coordination of the various tasks and responsibilities. In part, the failure of the system derived from the ways in which the designers had conceived of the work of foreman and others, and in particular their disregard for the interactional nature of many of the activities. In a sense, whilst the designers recognised the importance of cooperation, they failed to take into account how the documents themselves could form a basis for real-time collaboration and communication. They also, quite understandably, paid less attention to seemingly latent aspects of particular activities, the way for example foremen's contact with gangs provided a vehicle for more general discussion of site work and its management. In part therefore, the design and deployment of the system misconceived collaboration, and in particular supported asynchronous cooperation whilst disregarding real-time interaction between personnel. In considering mobility, we need to examine the activities in which people engage, with others, when they are 'mobile', and how various tools and artefacts, feature in those activities.

To explore some of these issues, it may be helpful to consider a rather different domain, a domain in which the mobility of staff is critical to the accomplishment and coordination of a range of everyday actions and activities. The case to point is London Underground, and in particular large interchange stations, such as Oxford Circus, Liverpool Street or Waterloo. These stations are very complex 'spaces'; they include platforms at different levels serving different lines, networks of interconnecting passageways (some of which include escalators and lifts), foyers both over and underground, ticket halls and barriers, inter-connecting shopping areas, and multiple entrances and exits. These stations can be dealing with well over a hundred thousand passengers a day, and staff have to oversee these complex ecologies and deal with problems and emergencies when they arise.

The organisational hub of the station is the operations room, commonly known as the 'Ops room'. In the Ops room personnel are provided with radio with which to contact other station staff, a public address system with which to make announcements to passengers, direct lines to Line Control Rooms and the police, switches to open and close gates to the station, and devices to set and reset alarms. Staff are also provided with a bank of CCTV monitors which cover principal areas of the station including the platforms, foyers, escalators and platforms (see Figure 3). The Ops room is normally staffed by one of the duty station supervisors, or in rare cases a suitably trained station assistant.

Figure 3: The technology in the Station Ops room

It is widely recognised amongst both staff and management on London Underground, that severe problems derive from the fact that the bulk of information and communication resources are based in one location, namely the Ops room. For example, when a member of staff such as a station supervisor leaves the Ops room, he or she no longer has access to deal with or overhear incoming calls from the line control rooms, which provide information concerning problems and emergencies, is unable to view areas beyond his/her line of site in the station, or even make announcements to passengers. To have a flavour of the seriousness of this 'resource isolation' of station staff once outside the control room, it is worthwhile referring to the official report on the fire at King's Cross Station [4]. It is startling to read how station staff, by virtue of their lack of access to other areas of the station, inadvertently instructed passengers to follow particular routes which were already encased in fire. Moreover, emergency services such as the London Fire Brigade also not only had limited knowledge of the station, but also could not access the detailed paper plans of the domain during the fire. More than thirty people died in the incident.

It is perhaps worth briefly describing the sorts of problems which arise in stations and which reveal the necessity for support for mobile staff.

When trains are delayed, especially during peak hours, stations can become severely congested, and because of the increasing number of people on a platform passengers can be pushed towards the edge. Such congestion can require 'station control', where the gates at the entrance of a station are closed to stop more passengers entering. Such a solution requires station staff, preferably a station supervisor, to have access to what is going on in each area of the station and to be able to communicate directly with passengers. Unfortunately, a station supervisor located on the platform has no visual access to what is happening in an entrance hall, and *vice versa*. He may well have to rely on a colleague's description of the extent and areas of the congestion, and moreover is unable to speak directly to passengers in particular locales. Members of staff require remote access to domains which will be changing moment-to-moment, access which is currently only available in the Ops room. They also need the ability to discuss and co-ordinate solutions with colleagues, and to make announcements to passengers in particular locations.

A second example, illustrates how staff in fixed locations, may require variable access to mobile staff and events. A common problem on London Underground, as we have discussed elsewhere, (cf. [8, 9]) are 'suspect packages'. These are packages of any sort, over a certain size, large enough to take a small bomb or incendiary device. It is of course, difficult to tell whether a package, such as briefcase or plastic bag, does indeed contain a device, and in general, staff are required to evacuate the station or at least take part of the decision about what course of action is to be taken. Despite relatively strict guidelines as to when an evacuation should take place, the discovery and identification of a suspect package routinely involves discussion between staff, and sometimes staff, police and specialist bomb disposal teams. In such circumstances various problems arise. Staff in the area of the potential problem are unable to share images of the package and discuss with colleagues based in the Ops room and elsewhere, and staff in the area of risk are unable to remain aware of the build up of passengers or other traffic problems. They are also unable to make specific or general announcements to passengers, or have direct contact with the Line Control Room which can make any necessary alterations to traffic flow.

Such information need not just be required by individuals in isolation. When critical incidents occur staff with a range of different roles and responsibilities may not only need access to real-time information but may need to collaborate with others in their immediate vicinity. For example, members of the emergency services need to have information concerning the detailed layout of the station, to see the current status of the incident and its consequences around the domain, and also discuss these with members of London Underground staff at the scene. In less critical circumstances, engineers and maintenance staff not only need visual access to an area where a problem has occurred, but also to discuss possible solutions with station staff. Even in more routine situations staff are frequently faced with having inadequate information when dealing with others in their local vicinity. Station staff whether mobile supervisors or station assistants are continually having to deal with passenger enquiries and yet either do not have the real-time information necessary to answer these or the information given them is available in an inappropriate form. For example. problems and delays on the line, at other stations or on the network as a whole are typically either announced publicly or broadcast to staff through the radios. Hence, there is no (semi-) permanent record to refer to, when later these matters seem relevant to particular queries asked by passengers. It would be useful, for example, if station staff could have real-time information that they could at least be used to show to passengers when suggesting the alternatives routes for their journeys or when explaining current problems on the network.

These very brief examples, raise some rather interesting issues with regard to the design of mobile systems. In the first instance, there are a range of facilities that different staff need to access across various locations, including CCTV pictures, information concerning the current state of traffic, audio communications with various personnel, both in and outside the station, and with passengers, gate and alarm operation, and in some cases, access to more general data such as station diagrams, maps of the region and such like. Secondly, different personnel require access to different sorts of information and communication facilities, and in some cases these facilities need to be accessed in different ways. So for example, whilst station assistants need to be able to open and close gates remotely, it may not be necessary for them to be able to make announcements throughout the station, or have general access to CCTV. Perhaps most importantly however, a mobile system needs to support a range of different types of cooperation and collaboration, ranging from simple spoken exchanges through to sharing and discussing images of, say suspect packages, in real time, both with co-present and remote colleagues.

In supporting mobile personnel therefore, a critical consideration is not simply the character of the tasks and responsibilities of the individuals users, but rather how access to such information requires, and engenders cooperation and collaboration. In a sense, supporting station staff on London Underground brings together, requirements for both micro-mobility and synchronous collaboration with more conventional considerations for support for asynchronous, cooperation between distributed personnel.

Mobile station staff on the London Underground then both need what might be considered conventional support for mobility – communication and information resources which can be available around the domain – as well as support for micro-mobility – ways of providing and receiving information whilst co-present with others. Examining the requirements in this case may then provide a foundation for a more general consideration of the kinds of mobility which need to be supported in collaborative work.

POTENTIAL TECHNOLOGIES FOR SUPPORTING MOBILITY ON LONDON UNDERGROUND

In the light of the issues outlined, we are collaborating with London Underground, several radio research and development organisations and other transport-related organisations to explore ways of utilising high bandwidth wireless communication systems to support station staff. In particular, the project is examining the ways in which new technologies can provide access to information and communication resources that are sensitive to both the location and circumstances of the users.

Hence, the project is exploring ways of utilising high bandwidth wireless communication systems to extend the current capabilities of station radio, so that it can support the transmission of graphic and textual information about what is happening on the line and the network, access to controls, communication and announcement systems and even CCTV images. With such capabilities it is possible to provide mobile station supervisors with many of the resources available in the Ops room whilst they move around the setting.

In considering the design of the technology however, we have increasingly realised that it may well be a mistake to place access to all necessary resources on the device itself. It is critical for example that the system remains portable, and becomes one of the various tools that station staff carry about with them as part of their normal duties. Moreover, while it may be sensible to provide access to limited textual and diagrammatic information on the device itself, for certain purposes a small CCTV image is of little use.

Consider for example, attempting to discuss the features of a small suspect package on a screen large enough to fit in a pocket, or making a sensible judgement about passenger congestion from a similarly small display. More importantly, it would be difficult to support even the most basic forms of collaboration, such as discussions concerning timings of trains along the line, let alone a plan of the station in the case of a fire or a video image of a suspect package, on a small mobile device designed for an individual user. Hence, to provide for more flexible forms of collaboration, allowing for mobility around the domain as well as micro-mobility around the artefact requires a reconsideration of the kind of support a mobile device can provide.

One approach would be to consider the mobile system as not just the destination of information whilst on the move but also the means through which location-specific information is made available on other devices: devices such as fixed displays that not only are more suitable for the task-at-hand, but also support co-present collaborative activities. The support for mobile personnel would thus be through a heterogeneous combination of technologies, for example a mix of small mobile devices and larger fixed systems.

So in the case of station supervisors the mobile wireless devices could be used in combination with fixed systems spread around the domain. In some cases this could utilise displays that are currently available, for example at the gate-lines of many stations or at the end of most platforms. In others additional fixed displays could be used which are more ordinarily for other purposes, such as providing passenger information. When in the proximity of such displays it would then be possible for the station supervisors to transform the use of such fixed devices making them active so that information specific to their needs could be displayed.

So, taking a case mentioned earlier, when a 'suspect package' has been reported the mobile device would allow the supervisor to see the status of various alarms, communicate with members of staff both in the station and elsewhere and also make public announcements. Although some access to video would be available on the device, but when used in conjunction with a fixed display full CCTV video images could be made available. Such a resource would not only be more suitable to the supervisor's own requirements, but would also provide for shared viewings with other members of London Underground staff and personnel from other organisations. So, for example, a suspect package and the surrounding domain could be viewed with members of the police and other services. Similarly, in the case of a fire, detailed plans of the station could be displayed and used as a resource in discussions with individuals from the emergency services.

Such a configuration can also support other kinds of collaborative activity. In response to a passenger query, for example, relevant network and line information could be brought up on the mobile system and if necessary shifted over to the fixed device. Or, in the case where two members of staff are remotely collaborating over a problem, the fixed display could provide access to a common resource, say, a CCTV image of a particular domain. So when stations are being controlled staff around the gate-line can see and discuss what is happening down on the platform and *vice versa*.

In each of these, the mobile system in combination with fixed devices, provides resources that not only become active and available around the setting, but also support different forms of collaboration. More importantly, they allow for participants to shift from moment-to-moment, given the circumstances at hand, from the individual and private, to the collaborative and public. They provide, to some extent, for micro-mobility within co-present collaborative activities. Moreover, such resources are not tied to any particular location, but available in various locations around a complex setting.

These suggestions currently form the basis for the development of a prototype technology to be used in a trail within London Underground stations. Needless to say, extensive technological testing and design is required to transform this envisionment into a working prototype. The project will have to consider a range of complex design issues, particularly the allocation of functions between fixed and mobile resources, how information can be made readily visible and accessible and how any enhanced communication or collaborative resources relates to existing roles and responsibilities of personnel. Moreover, we will also have to consider ways in which the shift between the private and the public can be facilitated, so that such transformations do not themselves become too intrusive to the demands of the co-participants co-present in the local environment. The London Underground case provides a useful starting point for considering such issues as the technology may have to be utilised within various quite different kinds of activity and between differing forms of collaboration. For example, the ways in which a resource is made available to a co-located member of staff may differ from how it is distributed to remote participant(s), and these in turn may be different from the ways in which members of staff make available items of information to one or more members of the public. In each case not only the resource but the way it is made available – the shift towards the collaborative – needs to be sensitive to the ongoing activities of the participants.

IMPLICATIONS FOR TECHNOLOGIES TO SUPPORT MOBILITY IN COLLABORATION

Although the requirements of London Underground staff may appear rather unusual and particular to that setting, this case raises more generic issues with respect to the design and development of new technologies.

For example, in distributing technologies around the environment, developing support for station supervisors would appear to be a prototypical case of 'ubiquitous computing' or 'augmented reality' (cf. [18]). However, although typical developments in these areas aim to support tasks and activities by augmenting everyday artefacts with computational capabilities it is not all that clear which artefacts are most relevant for such enhancement, or what capabilities should be augmented. As the case study on the construction site suggests, the apparent ubiquity, mobility or affordances of an artefact may not lead directly to an appropriate device or activity on which to base a design. One way of focusing the augmentation of artefacts and environments, particularly if such developments are to move outside the laboratory, would be to consider how everyday artefacts can be resources for collaborative activities in real-world settings. This need not just be concerned with augmenting everyday tools and devices with access to remote individuals, Indeed, in the cases considered here, it would appear enough of a challenge to support co-present collaborative activities around a domain. In doing so, it would be important to examine how such technologies might be sensitive to the local situated activities of participants, the ways in which, in real-time, participants delicately shift their orientations to one another, the relation of these to the ongoing talk and the different ways objects are used and moved during an interaction - that is, the micro-mobility of objects.

Such an orientation may also be relevant in settings where participants would not seem to require the use of mobile technologies, say in an office environment like that of the medical consultation. Even here, exploring the micro-mobility of documents, could suggest ways in which everyday objects, such as the medical record, could be augmented [15]. As in the case of London Underground, supporting the micro-mobility of such a document, may not just require a mobile device, like a PDA or a notepad computer, but a combination of these with fixed displays, so that, for example, items and objects could be moved between the individual and private to the collaborative and public. In this case, during a consultation, a doctor could, when appropriate, make items visible to a patient which could become a resource for more focused collaborative activities.

Such possibilities are quite distinct from those typically considered in relation to mobile technologies. The potential of mobile devices is usually regarded in terms of their capacity to receive and transmit information when the individual using them is moving between or situated in a range of locations. Even wireless communications aimed at supporting activities in offices are considered in terms of the ease by which the mobile devices can be connected to local networks and communicate information. Though important, such considerations neglect the potential of mobile technologies to support more fine-grain collaborative activities, moving documents, information and objects between devices with different capabilities from moment-to-moment.

Of course, developments such as these require careful consideration of a range of conventional issues with respect to the design of the technology. For example, it is important to consider how such capabilities are presented through the user interface. The need to manipulate objects within an interaction across different platforms, places demands on the underlying architecture, particularly with respect to the persistence of objects and how consistency can be maintained between the various devices. Moreover, the heterogeneous use of mobile technologies with fixed devices may require the capabilities, at any time, to be sensitive to the actual location of the device, for example information may need to be displayed on the 'nearest' appropriate fixed display to the mobile device. One of the typical features of system architectures, particularly within CSCW, is that the location of devices, applications and, even users, is transparent. Applications such as those for the London Underground require the architecture to be location-sensitive.

Nevertheless, it appears from the studies considered in this paper that the micro-mobility of objects may be critical when considering how to support co-present, collaborative activities. To provide for this may require not only both mobile and fixed devices, but quite novel support for mobility that focuses on the moment-to-moment manipulation of objects. It may be then that such mundane details as the movement of a document around a desk, the orientations of the participants in a setting, how a document is made visible within the talk of participants in an interaction and how it makes apparent aspects of that talk, could all be relevant for the design of new technologies. These details may not just be of relevance to technologies designed to support similar activities between remote participants, as typically found in CSCW, but for devices that can be used locally when co-participants are co-present. An orientation towards the detailed interactional work which surrounds artefacts may thus bring together contributions from several quite distinct concerns including those of researchers in CSCW, those concerned with innovations in augmented reality and ubiquitous computing and developers of mobile devices and wireless communications.

SUMMARY

When we examine workplace activities in a range of settings, not only those considered here, but others including control rooms, financial dealing rooms and architectural practices, we see how individuals' orientations towards objects are continually shifting and being transformed with respect to the ongoing interactions and activities of participants [12]. If we take these apparently mundane activities seriously it may be possible to suggest some ways in which they could be relevant for the design of novel technologies.

Each of the studies discussed here have focused on different aspects of mobility within collaborative work. In the medical consultation the use of existing devices, both paper and electronic, suggested some of the ways in which the mobility of an artefact not only supports collaborative activities in and around the wider environment, but also within co-present interaction between doctors and patients. In the construction site, the introduction of a novel mobile technology was examined. This revealed the different ways in which mobility may be relevant for participants in a setting. What may seem an obvious resource to support with a mobile technology may not actually be sensitive to the practical concerns of the participants. In the London Underground observations of the communication and collaboration between staff have revealed a range of ways in which access to information may be relevant to mobile staff. These also suggest some considerations that have to be taken when attempting to provide this information through new technologies.

These cases, and several related workplace studies, have revealed how the use of objects-in-interaction are delicately interweaved within the interaction and activities of others [19, 12] By attending to the resources through which objects are made relevant from moment-to-moment we can see how their mobility is critical in the accomplishment of collaborative activities. Although there have been a few pioneering studies that have explored mobility in the workplace (e.g. [2, 20]). these have tended to focus on tracking individuals who move and roam around a setting. Local mobility in these studies concerns the movements of individuals around a domain and technological support for them is then considered in terms of providing them with the awareness of others and others of them. This is a quite different kind of local mobility to that which surrounds the fine-grained use of artefacts and provides a real-time resource for moment-to-moment collaboration between participants.

Though technologies have been developed that allow a certain amount of fluidity between individual and collaborative activities and between various forms of collaboration, these means, such as providing different ways of displaying representations or images of participants, have been largely provided on fixed devices. The technology may allow for different views of a document or object and even various types of orientation to a remote participant, but they constrain the user within his or her own local domain; the device through which these capabilities are provided usually being cumbersome and unwieldy for use even within its immediate setting. Particularly within interactions, the ways in which a user needs to be mobile have largely been ignored within CSCW.

Developments in augmented reality, at least, focus attention on the object through which computational capabilities are provided. However, such technologies largely ignore how they may be used to support collaborative activities.

Although these oversights might be curious, it may be not so surprising that micro-mobility within collaboration has been ignored by developers of CSCW systems. The local and detailed uses of objects-in-interaction are still relatively unexplored within the social sciences. Indeed, even less subtle ways of individuals, artefacts and activities being mobile within and around a domain have been largely neglected. For example, there has been a tendency for workplace studies, including many of the ones we have been involved in, to focus on 'centres of coordination' [17]. It may be that this focus has led to a tendency to also conceive of technologies to support workplace activities as constrained to particular locales and thence to particular fixed devices. This would be unfortunate, as the very richness of these studies is in their uncovering of the fluid, contingent and situated nature of collaborative work. It may be that we not only need to pursue an examination of the situated use of objects and artefacts, but also augment the corpus of workplace studies, so that more open environments are considered.

In considering the requirements for, and development of, more flexible and mobile technologies to support collaborative work, it may be that we need to explore in more detail how objects are used in interaction and forms of work where the mobility of participants is critical to that work. Such an examination may not only provide resources for developers of innovative collaborative technologies, but may suggest ways in which conventional personal workstations, mobile devices and systems for ubiquitous computing might be shaped so that they fit the local demands of the participants in the setting. Such analyses may also form the foundation for a more fundamental reconsideration of the uses of artefacts in everyday, social interaction.

ACKNOWLEDGEMENTS

The work reported here was undertaken through the support of the ESRC and DTI through the jointly funded PORTRAIT Project, as well as other projects supported by the EC ACTS Programme and the EPSRC. We would also like to thank Jon Hindmarsh for his comments on an earlier version of this paper.

REFERENCES

1. Barnatt, C., *CyberBusiness: Mindsets for a wired age.* Chichester, Wiley, 1995.

2. Bellotti, V. and Bly, S. *Walking Away from the Desktop Computer: Distributed Collaboration and Mobility in a Product Design Team.* in *Proceedings of CSCW '96.* (Cambridge, MA) ACM Press, 209-218, 1996.
3. Benford, S. and Fahlén, L. *A Spatial Model of Interaction In Large Visual Environments.* in *Proceedings of ECSCW'93.* (Milan) Kluwer, 109-124, 1993.
4. Fennell, D., *Investigation into the King's Cross Underground Fire.* Department of Transport, HMSO, (Cm 499) November 1988.
5. Gaver, W.W., Smets, G. and Overbeeke, K. *A Virtual Window on media space.* in *Proceedings of CHI '95*) ACM Press, 257-264, 1995.
6. Hammer, M. and Champy, J., *Reengineering the corporation: A manifesto for business revolution.* New York, Harper Collins, 1993.
7. Heath, C.C., *Body movement and speech in medical interaction.* Cambridge, Cambridge University Press, 1986.
8. Heath, C.C. and Luff, P. *Collaborative Activity and Technological Design: Task Coordination in London Underground Control Rooms.* in *Proceedings of ECSCW'91.* (Amsterdam, Netherlands) Kluwer, 65-80, 1991.
9. Heath, C.C. and Luff, P., *Convergent Activities: Line Control and Passenger Information on London Underground,* in *Cognition and Communication at Work,* Y. Engeström and D. Middleton (eds.), Cambridge University Press, Cambridge, 96-129. 1996.
10. Heath, C.C. and Luff, P. *Documents and Professional Practice: 'bad' organisational reasons for 'good' clinical records.* in *Proceedings of CSCW '96.* (Boston, MA) ACM Press, 354-363, 1996.
11. Heath, C.C., Luff, P. and Sellen, A. *Reconsidering the Virtual Workplace: Flexible Support for Collaborative Activity.* in *Proceedings of ECSCW'95.* (Stockholm, Sweden) Kluwer Academic Press, 83-100, 1995.
12. Heath, C.C. and Luff, P.K., *Technology in Action.* Cambridge, Cambridge University Press, in press.
13. Hindmarsh, J., Fraser, M., Heath, C.C., Benford, S. and Greenhalgh, C. *Fragmented Interaction: Establishing mutual orientation in virtual environments.* in *Proceedings of CSCW'98.* (Seattle) ACM Press, 1998 forthcoming.
14. Ishii, H. and Kobayashi, M. *Clearface: a seamless medium for sharing drawing and conversation with eye contact.* in *Proceedings of CHI 92.* (Monterey, CA) ACM Press, 525-532, 1992.
15. Luff, P., Heath, C.C. and Greatbatch, D. *Tasks-in-interaction: Paper and screen based documentation in collaborative activity.* in *Proceedings of CSCW '92.* (Toronto, Canada) ACM Press, 163-170, 1992.
16. Stefik, M., Foster, G., Bobrow, D.G., Kahn, K., Lanning, S. and Suchman, L., Beyond the Chalkboard: Computer Support for Collaboration and Problem Solving. *Communications of the ACM, 30, 1,* 32-47, 1987.
17. Suchman, L., *Technologies of Accountability: On Lizards and Aeroplanes,* in *Technology in Working Order,* G. Button (ed.), Routledge, London, 113-126. 1993.
18. Weiser, M., The Computer for the 21st Century. *Scientific American, September 1991.*
19. Whalen, J., *A Technology of Order Production: Computer-Aided Dispatch in Public Safety Communications,* in *Situated Order: Studies in the Social Organisation of Talk and Embodied Activities,* P. ten Have and G. Psathas (eds.), University Press of America, Washington, 187-230. 1995.
20. Whittaker, S., Frohlich, D.M. and Daly-Jones, O. *Informal Workplace Communication: What is it like and how might we support it?* in *Proceedings of CHI '94.* (Boston, Mass) ACM Press, 1994.

Just Talk to Me: A Field Study of Expertise Location

David W. McDonald and Mark S. Ackerman
Department of Information and Computer Science
University of California, Irvine
Irvine, CA 92697-3425
{dmcdonal, ackerman}@ics.uci.edu
http://www.ics.uci.edu/CORPS/dmcdonal
http://www.ics.uci.edu/CORPS/ackerman

ABSTRACT
Everyday, people in organizations must solve their problems to get their work accomplished. To do so, they often must find others with knowledge and information. Systems that assist users with finding such expertise are increasingly interesting to organizations and scientific communities. But, as we begin to design and construct such systems, it is important to determine *what* we are attempting to augment. Accordingly, we conducted a five-month field study of a medium-sized software firm. We found the participants use complex, iterative behaviors to minimize the number of possible expertise sources, while at the same time, provide a high possibility of garnering the necessary expertise. We briefly consider the design implications of the identification, selection, and escalation behaviors found during our field study.

Keywords
Expertise networks, knowledge networks, computer-mediated communications, expert locators, expertise location, expertise finding, information seeking, CSCW, computer-supported cooperative work.

INTRODUCTION
Wayne is a support rep for a software company. Today, a client sent Wayne a problem, one he hadn't seen before. Wayne spent several hours trying to diagnose the problem and eventually realized that he could not solve it alone. Now Wayne has another problem — deciding whom he will ask to help him. Unfortunately, this is not simple; Wayne is not sure of the problem's exact cause. Is the problem related to user training? Or, is the problem the result of a recent customization by the developers? Will Wayne need to resort to just asking around?

Wayne must find the expertise needed to solve his client's problem. He needs to find the people who are most appropriate to ask and get their help.

CSCW 98 Seattle Washington USA

Systems that assist users with finding others who have specific, desired information are increasingly interesting to organizations and scientific communities. However, as we begin to construct such systems, it would be useful to determine the social, cognitive, and informational aspects we are trying to augment before constructing these systems. It is our goal to guide the construction of information systems that facilitate finding expertise within organizations. We believe that one can do so best with a field study of existing practice. Accordingly, we conducted a five-month field study, using a socially distributed cognition viewpoint, of how people in a medium-sized software firm find the expertise to construct, maintain, and support their software systems.

We begin with an overview of the literature covering expert-locator systems and several key studies of the collaborative aspects of expertise. We then detail the field site, the data, and the site's work and information needs. Following, we describe the site's mechanisms for identifying and selecting people with required expertise, as well as show how the organization prevents or recovers from breakdowns. Finally, we conclude with implications for future systems.

CSCW AND COLLABORATIVE INFORMATION SEEKING
The CSCW and adjacent literatures have numerous attempts to facilitate finding information through social networks. Several systems have explicit models of expertise.[1] The Answer Garden [2] and Answer Garden 2 [3] systems, designed to facilitate informal flows of information and their capture, have a naive view of expertise. Answer Garden allowed only a few levels of expertise in answering questions for users. While Answer Garden 2 had an explicit expertise-location engine and provided computer-mediated

[1] In this paper, the term *expertise* assumes the embodiment of knowledge and skills within individuals. Our definition distinguishes expertise, which is a range, from expert. An individual may have different levels of expertise about different topics. Expertise can be topical or procedural and is arranged and valued within social and institutional settings.

communications mechanisms to find others with a range of expertise, the mechanisms were not very elaborated.

Two other systems help find people knowledgeable about a topic. Referral Web [12] helps find research experts. Referral Web assumes a topical expertise among all co-authors, and therefore identifies expert individuals by their participation in co-author relationships. Yenta [7] creates and shares personal profiles based on text content analysis. It can then route messages along a network of inferred common interest (based on keyword or other indexing techniques). Both of these systems not only assume a single level of expertise, but also that one can determine a list of experts through merely textual analysis.

While collaborative filtering systems [9, 13] can help find other people, they generally do not distinguish levels of expertise. A related system, Phoaks [10], can be used to identify who contributed information. This distinction among contributors allows a user to make judgements about the contributors' expertise, but these must be inferred.

None of these systems have very sophisticated models of expertise and information seeking. The social world is far more complex. Studies of collaborative problem-solving make this clear. For example, Allen [4] noted that engineers differentiate whom to ask with great nuance. Information seekers weigh the psychological cost of asking, including loss of status, expected reciprocity (i.e., likelihood of returning the favor), and social equity (i.e., how well they know the person socially).

Cicourel's study [5] of medical diagnosis provides ethnographic detail about the social complexity surrounding information seeking in organizations. Cicourel demonstrates that the expert's knowledge, organizational status, and day-to-day interactions contribute to the attribution of expertise and authority by those who work with the expert. This complex set of reinforcing mechanisms supports and enhances the status of an expert as an expert. Additionally, Cicourel noted that both information seekers and experts make judgements about the validity of the information they receive. The specific structure of the organization in Cicourel's study (i.e., a teaching hospital) led him to examine the structured interchange of expertise within daily face-to-face meetings.

Orr's study [14] of copy repair technicians provides additional ethnographic detail about the social complexity of expertise. In the technicians' work, learning by doing and through stories are the main mechanisms for displaying, sharing, and propagating expertise. Idiosyncrasies of the customer and their equipment, incomplete information about the state of a breakdown, and the relatively independent nature of the technician lead to expertise that cannot be formally codified or categorized. Like Cicourel's doctors, the service technicians in Orr carefully weigh the selection and quality of information sources. As well, their use of their expertise in a diagnostic situation is constrained by many organizational and social factors. However, Orr's major concern is the use of narrative in diagnosis and information sharing; he is only peripherally concerned with seeking expertise per se.

Within this study, we extend Allen's work in identifying potential sources of information. We have adopted Cicourel's and Orr's general point of view to examine finding expertise in technical support, bug tracking, and similar software activities. These work processes occupy a middle ground between the life-critical and highly personally interdependent medical work in Cicourel and between the relatively independently accomplished service work in Orr. We believe that the type of work processes we examined are common within workplaces, and our emphasis is on locating expertise within daily work.

Next we turn to a description of the study and site.

THE STUDY SITE AND DATA

The study took place at Medical Software Corporation[2] (MSC), a company that builds, sells and supports medical and dental practice management software. MSC sells its software pre-installed on a high performance Unix server as a turnkey system. MSC has been in this business for almost 20 years and they have a large share of the group medical and group dental markets. MSC is a medium-sized company, with just over 100 employees.

Practice management software provides functions distinct from clinical management software. Practice management is primarily concerned with appointment scheduling, treatment planning, patient recalls, insurance billing, patient billing, and payment reconciliation. These functions are often considered the business side of medicine. These functions are closely related to the clinical management (treatment) of the patient.

The majority of the participants in the study worked in three departments, Technical Development, Technical Support, and Technical Communications. Each department provided access to entry-level, senior, and management employees. Additionally, we observed and interviewed several people in Human Resources and Client Relations.

The first author was on-site for 5 months and conducted follow-up interviews for another 4 months. Data were collected through participant observation, semi-structured interviews, and informal open-ended interviews. In total, we conducted 37 formal interviews and more than 50 informal interviews; formal interviews were taped and transcribed. Additionally, we had access to various internal communications including memos, internal and client oriented electronic bulletin board systems, and a large number of online historical files.

We analyzed the data using standard ethnographic techniques [17]. We approached the data using Socially Distributed Cognition (s-dcog) theory [11, 16], since it considers the expert within the social context of the information

[2] All names and identifiers have been changed in this paper.

seeker. S-dcog provides a useful view of the cognitive as well as the social aspects of the organization and its knowledge resources. Following the common s-dcog framework, the socially cognitive aspects are observable through processes that translate cognitive states among levels of representation or where representations are effectively externalized in some form. Viewing asking for help as an externalized representation that becomes shared among multiple participants through time afforded a fresh perspective on information seeking activity.

THE NATURE OF THEIR PROBLEMS

The types of problems which MSC employees face stem from the complexity of the software and the expansive feature set. An appreciation of the complexity that these informants face on a day-to-day basis is important to understanding why they work so hard to find just the right person to answer their question or help with a problem. The medical system is a good example of the complexity of MSC's systems.

The medical system has a text based interface and is often used with text only terminals. The top level menu of the medical program has over 100 specifically identifiable features, and it is common for there to be sub-menus. There are even sub-menus attached to what are primarily data entry screens. The software is written entirely in a proprietary version of BASIC that supports chaining.[3] The features are spread through more than 200 medical system specific programs. There are numerous programs that are shared by the medical and dental system. As well, many files are client specific customizations. The standard application is highly customizable. For many clients customization is handled with a large number of customization flags that are not always mutually compatible.

The software is in a relatively constant cycle of new feature development and maintenance. New feature development is often the result of requests from existing clients. When enough new features have been added to the software they are integrated into a complete system and that new system is declared to be the next version. This new version is then offered to any client for minimal cost. A client is never forced to upgrade to a new version of the software.

The integration of new features leads to problems when the new features conflict with existing customizations or pre-existing default behavior. The solution to the conflict is to create a customization flag that can be set or unset in a customization file. The code then executes one of several incompatible features by reading the customization flags and branching as appropriate. The most difficult part of upgrading a client is setting the flags in the configuration file.

This development strategy means that many different versions with different customizations are in the field and supported all at the same time. Developers and technical support staff must be especially sensitive to the version and the customizations that have been applied when helping a client, fixing a bug, or adding a feature. In this world, in this software, what appears to be a very simple problem could turn out to be a very complex interaction.

As a relatively simple example, a client had paid for a new feature which worked for a couple weeks and then mysteriously stopped working. Kelly, the client manager, was providing support and needed to solve the client's problem. She checked the documentation and found that it described two possible behaviors for this section of code. Neither behavior covered the new feature created for this client. Kelly asked the Support manager if he knew anything about the two customization flags. The Support manager told Kelly that Brad had made the change and that she should check the work order for the change. She saw that Brad was the appropriate developer and that he had described a new setting for the flag. Kelly then went to Brad's office and asked him whether the third setting described in the work order was correct. Brad examined the code and verified that for this specific client there were now three possible flag settings and the third was correct. He apologized that this was not in the authorized documentation and pointed out that this feature was not yet part of the standard version.

The problem and solution process described above is typical around MSC. They rely on artifacts and people in the environment to help them find the expertise necessary to complete their work.

EXPERTISE LOCATION

In the following sections, we distinguish two steps in finding expertise within organizations, separating finding into identification and selection phases. *Expertise identification* is the problem of knowing what information or special skills other individuals have. The above example highlighted the problem of figuring out who has what knowledge or special skills. *Expertise selection* is appropriately choosing among people with the required expertise. If there are multiple potential experts or people with the requisite expertise, it is necessary to select one (or more) to ask.

We make this distinction analytically, recognizing that it does not hold all of the time or for all participants. We wish to emphasize that expertise identification and expertise selection are iterative, interwoven behaviors at MSC and most likely in general work life. Yet, this distinction has grounding in theory, data, literature, and design criteria:

- From the perspective of s-dcog theory, solving many problems collaboratively requires first identifying the necessary resources in the environment and then obtaining them (although this may be done iteratively). Some-

[3]In this version of BASIC, chaining is an overlay technique that allows two BASIC programs to share variables. This whole approach can be considered similar to a procedure call, but without the ability to automatically return to the prior execution context.

times, participants will do these two activities consciously; at other times, the activities will have become routinized.

- Many, but not all, of our informants separated identification and selection. Many informants appeared to separate out, most of the time, how they knew people had expertise from the act of picking people they wished to approach. Informants did so spontaneously over several interview questions and in informal interviews. Even those participants who were somewhat inarticulate about identification had noticeably nuanced and articulated selection criteria.
- Paepcke [15] suggests this separation in his description and analysis of contact brokers.
- As well, a separation such as this holds promise for the design and implementation of potential systems.

The distinction between the two is valuable analytically and will prove useful in the following discussion. We cover expertise identification and expertise selection in turn.

EXPERTISE IDENTIFICATION

Identifying people who have expertise to share is a crucial first step in solving many problems at MSC. Expertise identification is a difficult problem. The nature of expertise itself, what it is and how it is used, as well as the fact that people grow and change over time, make solving this problem difficult. This is the first problem with which information seekers must deal before they can hope to get information they need.

Everyday Expertise

Many people at MSC, especially those who are senior, have difficulty articulating how they know who has knowledge about system components, diagnostic methods, business practices, and the like. For many people, "experience" is the primary guide in identifying others with specific expertise. Senior employees mention "experience" regularly in interviews and cannot articulate more detailed steps:

> You learn who's [the] most experienced in what areas. ...You just know. - Sherry.

At the time, this programmer had been with the organization for more than eight years. For Sherry and others, their knowledge of what others know is part of their everyday understanding of MSC. It stems from performing work and the large gamut of social interaction, both formal and informal, that is part of that work over time.

However, junior people do not yet have this implicit understanding of who knows what. In addition, even senior people cannot track everything in even a company this small. There are, then, mechanisms that some interviewees articulated and some that we observed for identifying the right people to ask. Some of these have been observed in other studies, such as judging professional experience, organizational tenure, and geographical proximity. We describe below two mechanisms which people use at MSC, but that have not been reported in the literature. The first is how people use artifacts to gain information about who does what in the organization and the second is a specialized role that helps people find the right person.

Historical Artifacts

One mechanism for identifying potential sources is to use historical or archival data that the organization maintains. At MSC, programmers and support staff use the change history records to identify potential experts. This program change history is modified for every change made to a file in the system for as long as that file exists. Maintaining the program history is a requirement of the developer who modifies the source code, and this change history can be used to identify possible experts for technical support. Within MSC, this is sufficiently important that it has been given a name, the "line 10 rule".

> ...you can simply look on the system at the program history. And we keep an on-line history of every change that's made to a program, and it shows the programmer who made that change. And so I can look at a program and I can not only see who was the last person who worked on the program was, but I can see who the last 10 people or 20 people or whatever who have worked on it. - Ian.

Developers use the change history similarly. Faced with modifying a program or file which they did not "know," developers use the change history to see who had made previous changes. The rationale is very simple. The developers use the program history to identify the person who most likely has the "freshest" memory of the code. In the following quote, line 10 contains the "mnemonics" of the programmer who last changed the code. In MSC, "mnemonics" (or "mnemonic") are constantly used as identifiers; they are roughly people's initials.

> When a programmer makes a change in a program he is supposed to add his mnemonic to the line and update the date. This is how we know who last changed the program. Whoever made the last change in the program is the default expert in that program. ... It's close enough. The logic is that the person who spent time on it last has it freshest in memory and so they are the best person to ask a question. - Brad

However, the generic rule upon which support and development rely is not always correct. Making a small change can mark a developer as the expert even in the case where the small change was really insignificant:

> It's not always the right way because sometimes someone makes a one byte change on a program. Because you make that change you put your mnemonics on the program and then, say someone comes to you and, I don't know the program, I just made this one byte change. Go see this person, someone else. - Joey

There are other uses of historical data in MSC as well. In Technical Support, they create and maintain informal documents to which any support representative can contribute. Often individual contributions to these informal documents are marked by the contributors' mnemonics. This informal information is often scattered and incomplete, so one informant's final recourse is again to use the mnemonics as a means of guiding her identification.

The use of historical data for expertise identification may seem logical, common, even simple. But historical data presents several problems for expertise identification. For example, the use of the change history as an expertise identification technique is a very simple, effective rule of thumb that can fail. The quote by the developer above demonstrates a major problem: It is very difficult to detect the difference between small changes and larger changes with the change history. This problem can lead to falsely identifying another person as a possible expert.

Relying on the change history can result in other problems when identifying possible experts. A developer is sometimes interested in identifying other developers who have worked with a larger portion of the code. Because the change history does not effectively convey the size of a change and because the history is organized on a file by file basis, the developers must rely on some other identification technique when they are going to make a large scale change that will affect several files.

MSC staff use the line 10 rule and other sources of online information because they are the most current and accurate representations of what people are doing. They are not perfect, but they are the best available. Mechanisms such as these must be either consciously maintained or be created as an ongoing byproduct of the organization's work activity. Online information at MSC that is not constantly updated, and therefore accurate, is eventually ignored. For example, a problem solution index that was used by Technical Support fell into disuse because, in the words of one interviewee, "I don't know if someone is validating the solutions."

Similarly, in 1990 MSC experimented with the development of a formalized experts directory. The directory was generated by providing department managers with an open-ended list of topics specific to MSC technologies. A manager then filled in the mnemonics of individuals who the manager felt knew something about the topic. By most accounts this formal directory was not maintained and not frequently used. At the time of our study, the directory was seven years old, had never been updated, and was not in use.

Expertise Concierges

Organizations often have key people who have very strong very elaborated social networks. Allen's [4] discussion of the technological gatekeeper presented a highly connected organizational role which specifically served to bring new technically relevant information to potential information seekers.

The technological gatekeeper is an important organizational role that mediates many requests for information. Other researchers have found variants of the gatekeeper. Ehrlich and Cash [6] found an information mediator who facilitates access to relatively local corpus of documents and similar information. Paepcke [15] found a role similar to that of Allen's gatekeeper; Paepcke's contact broker knew people in other parts of the organization. We would expect many variants of gatekeeping, since according to s-dcog theory, this role should become specialized as it becomes adopted in specific organization's work processes.

At MSC we found another variant, critical to the information processes at MSC, the *expertise concierge.* The expertise concierge is a critical identification resource for individuals who are seeking expertise. The expertise concierge facilitates the exchange of information by referring people looking for information to those who are most likely to have that information. The expertise concierge maintains a sophisticated map of the individuals in the organization and what they know. When a person who is looking for expertise asks the concierge about people who may be able to help, the concierge shares a portion of this expertise map, identifying possible candidates. Concierges can do this because they have a high level of technical competence, allowing them to make appropriate judgements about the topics and ranges of others' expertise. Concierges both maintain their map and share their map through the social interaction of making technical referrals.

In the following quote, one expertise concierge is emphatic about his role. He considers himself an expert at knowing who knows and who does not know the answers. In the quote an explicit example is made of a particular piece of code, but the expertise that this concierge had was not just with respect to code.

> ... And what I, I am the expert in, I am the expert in knowing, I'm the one that knows who has the answers. ... Because I worked with these people from day one. And I know what they know, what they don't, what they worked on, and I can, and I see a program and I see this line of code and I look at it and I say, come on, Mary wrote this in 1992. I *know* that [emphasis in the original]. - Eyal

The quote illuminates another dimension of the expertise concierge. The type of knowledge, which these people dispense, is also a specific type of expertise. This concierge specifically considers himself an expert at this. For him, there is a type of domain expertise which people leverage to solve their problems and a type of social expertise that he dispenses to help people find those domain experts.

There were two different people at MSC who performed the role of the expertise concierge.[4] Through our observations and interviews, we came to the conclusion that the roles of expertise concierge, information mediator, and technological gatekeeper are distinct, but they share many

[4]In fact, our use of the term is derived from one interview where the informant used the term "concierge" to describe the behavior and role of one of these expertise concierges.

of the same characteristics. People in these roles were technically sophisticated, had relatively long tenure with the organization, and had high-status positions in MSC.

Identification in Design

We observed varying identification mechanisms at MSC; yet, it is clear that no system can hope to implement all of them. The expertise concierge is clearly beyond current system capabilities. However, some of the identification mechanisms may form the basis for a user assistance strategy. For example, one mechanism reported here, the reliance on historical artifacts, seems promising. Historical artifacts are used in a particular style at MSC, but clearly historical artifacts vary among organizational cultures, work processes, and system goals. An assistance strategy may wish to consider the types of historical artifacts that are employed by local users as resources and then incorporate use of those within a system.

EXPERTISE SELECTION

Identifying people with expertise is not sufficient to solve one's problem or answer one's question. A person must then go to one or more people to get help. This leads to the next phase, expertise selection.

Given several different methods of identifying possible sources of expertise, the next problem is that of selecting one or more appropriate sources. It is unlikely that any single individual will have complete understanding of a very complex system. Any view of expertise that results in only one possible expert on any given topic is not very elaborate nor realistic. Information seekers are often faced with choosing from among several possible experts, each of whom possibly has the necessary expertise. Additionally, with a complex problem, seekers will likely query more than one person, collecting important insight into both the problem and the developing solution with each social interaction.

Through our interviews and observations, we were able to identify three general expertise selection mechanisms: organizational criteria, the load on the source, and performance. Informants were surprisingly detailed and nuanced about these mechanisms (especially considering their reliance on "experience" in identification). The nuance results in a long list of behaviors, each of which fit in one of the general categories.

The many variants which we found testify to the social and psychological complexity of expertise selection in practice. Selection cannot be distilled down into one or two behaviors, as will be seen in the following description. Instead, expertise selection is achieved through combinations of many, slightly different, behaviors each adding to an individual's judgement about the appropriateness of one or more expertise candidates.

The following section describes the many selection behaviors observed at MSC. While this list represents the common behaviors at MSC, we do not believe that this is an exhaustive list of all possible expertise selection behaviors.

Organizational Criteria

Organizations have norms about which they structure their members' activities. In choosing people to ask in MSC, participants kept to a standard set of rules-of-thumb. Senior personnel tended to ignore these more frequently than did junior staff, either because they had more sophisticated selection criteria or because they were "grandfathered" into an earlier and less restrictive organizational structure.

Keeping it local

The first rule-of-thumb is to keep the problem as close to the place where it originated. At MSC, as in many hierarchically-structured organizations, people prefer to stay within the organizational lines as long as possible. Developers attempt to keep within the development department, and support representatives attempt to keep within the support department.

This rule-of-thumb results in the selection of people who are most likely to understand and relate to the context of the problem. In many cases these are relative peers or immediate supervisors.

Cross department

When a problem comes to the person and he cannot solve it, the next step is to cross departmental boundaries. The following quote shows a two-step process. If the problem was primarily one concerning a support problem, this technical support person stays within Support. A peer or manager is completely acceptable. If the problem concerns the programming of the system, he goes to Development.

> ... And if it's related to the project itself I go straight to the project manager [in my department] first. ... [Instead] say it's a programming question that is also related to the project, but is more a programming issue, I'll ask one of the programmers that's available ... - Mario

This process is echoed by the Technical Support manager:

> If you're asking me that, then depending upon what in particular, in this case we're talking about something that looks like it's program related, I would go generally to the expert in that program. - Ian

Note that the Support manager goes directly to the person in the other department whom he thinks is the expert in the specific area. During the interview Ian was asked why he did not go to the other manager. He replied that the Development manager would probably not have the immediate knowledge of the program to facilitate a solution and that using the chain of command would only slow down obtaining a solution.

The last resort

At MSC, there is a final place for all technical questions. Above we have discussed the expertise concierge. One of these is assigned the position of internal technical consultant, with the expectation that this consultant will get an answer or develop a solution if there is no available expertise:

> … Because people ask me question every time I have to have an answer. … Right. See, I have no where to go. I have no where to go. … The code, yeah, that's it, you see. … - Eyal

Eyal often ends up reading the code to find solutions to problems. The internal consultant represents the last resort for all technical questions and problems.

Load on the Source

When selecting a person our informants often considered the person's workload. This load results from both regular day-to-day work activities and the added burden of serving requests for expertise. It seems that both the immediate workload and the workload over time are important criteria in selecting a person to pursue for help.

Selection based on regular workload

Rarely is it the case that an organization allows a person to sit idle waiting to be asked questions. Organizations hope to get the most out of each employee. It is likely that when looking for information, an information seeker will find some experts busier than others. At MSC, one criteria used in selecting is the workload that the expert must handle in the performance of their day-to-day duties. A junior level developer stated his rationale for careful preparation and selection this way:

> ... The people you ask have work to do too. They aren't just sitting around waiting for you to ask them questions. - Han

Technical Support has an institutionalized mechanism to estimate one another's workload. An in-house help management application maintains a "call list." The call list tracks all recent support requests made by all clients assigned to a specific support representative. Any support representative can view any other's call list by simply entering the mnemonics of the desired representative.

The length of an individual's call list is important shared information. A junior support representative, who frequently relies on the expertise of her senior colleagues, put it this way:

> … And I also, sometimes I look at their list, I go who's busy today, who has the most calls. … - Baht

This support representative uses shared information that indicates the general workload of other support representatives to decide who will be approached first. The lower the workload the more likely she is to approach them for help.

Developers do not have a similar system to compare the day-to-day workload of the individual developers. The development group has a system that pairs individual developers with specific work orders, but this system cannot be easily used to compare the workload of different developers. Instead the amount of load on any given developer is largely gained through word-of-mouth, closed office doors, and co-workers' assessment of one another's workload.

Selection based on workload over time

Day-to-day workload is not the only consideration. People also select an expert based on the workload imposed over time. That is, a person wanting help will try to disperse the questions among the possible experts in an attempt to distribute the effort, so as not to be seen as a pest, annoyance, or worse. The same junior support representative not only considers how busy her senior colleagues are on the given day, but how many times she has approached them for help:

> …I don't want to bug them too much. … - Baht

At MSC, assigning senior personnel to train new people for approximately three months ameliorates this issue.

Performance

The way experts share their expertise influence how and why they are picked, or not picked, by people who want their expertise. Sharing expertise is a type of performance [8, 14]. For the MSC participants, different experts have different strengths and weaknesses, and people choose experts based on the nature of the problem and an expert's performance characteristics. As well, within MSC, performance is often visible, and other employees note the personal and professional characteristics that are made visible as someone communicates and interacts with those who ask for help.

Problem comprehension

Problems that require expert help are often difficult problems. The very nature of the problem may itself be difficult to describe. In the best situations, an expert will engage in a dialog with the person seeking help to get a rich, fuller understanding of the nature of the problem. This does not happen all of the time. There are times when a problem is difficult to explain to the expert because of cultural differences, language problems, or a lack of experience in a related but necessary discipline.

The following quote is from a technical support manager who had worked at MSC for many years. In the quote he is quite clear that he feels that a certain developer is "the expert in Program SUMIO" which relates to processing insurance claims. He describes his difficulty explaining to the developer the impact that a problem with Program SUMIO has on a client's business:

> Um, Kumar is a good example. Kumar, his first language is not English and he has communication problems. … I would say he's the expert in Program SUMIO, in the medical, but sometimes to sit down and explain something to him doesn't work very well, and from our perspective it's important. … And he doesn't necessarily always understand the impact to the client and to their business and running their business. And part of that is the communication skills and so forth. - Ian

To work around Kumar's difficulty in comprehending the business-related problem, he instead goes to MSC's internal consultant. The manager explains the business problem to the consultant who then translates and explains the problem in technical details to the developer.

> And so sometimes I will go to Eyal and explain in a procedural manner or in a business manner, here's what it means to the client, here's what they are trying to accomplish and then he can translate technically to him (laughs) what he needs Kumar to go into the program and do or fix or, or whatever. - Ian

Communication and language skills are only part of the difficulty that the support manager has with this expert. It seems that Kumar also does not have an understanding of the nature of the client's business. In this case, Ian cannot use the expertise of Kumar easily.

Providing a suitable explanation

Some experts are just better at providing explanations of the problem and the solution [1]. That is, the way in which an expert provides the explanation is another performance criterion which people use when selecting an expert:

> ... There's certain people where, um, they, every time, they explain things very well to me and it just takes one shot and its explained; I understand it. But, um, you know those people sometimes are really busy and it's hard to get a hold of them. ... Those times I go to others where, um, I can go any time but sometimes ... I have trouble understanding the way they explain things to me. - Baht.

Like others, she prefers to pick people who provide clear, understandable, explanations. When a preferred source is overloaded, Baht reluctantly goes to people who do not share or explain effectively.

Attitude

Problem comprehension and solution explanation are not the only performance criteria people use when selecting an expert. People who look for help often mention the attitude of the expert. In informal discussions people are clearly reluctant to go to an expert who has a "bad attitude":

> ... there are people that you know that know a lot of stuff, but they won't give you information ... its just they're that type of person ... - Terry

Often this bad attitude is accompanied by an example where the problem or the person seeking help from the expert was belittled, treated with contempt, or even made into a joke.

The fact that a person cannot easily understand the problem, is poor at diagnosis, cannot explain the solution, or is labeled as having a "bad attitude" does not completely rule them out as a possible source. The expertise is still desirable, and in some cases it is essential. In these cases people who need the expertise will still pursue (perhaps reluctantly) the person with the needed expertise.

Selection in Design

Like identification, it is not likely that all selection strategies can be automated. In fact some selection strategies (e.g., considering an expert's attitude) will be very difficult to automate. Strategies like observing workload or following organizational structure that guide selection and reselection look like promising candidates for possible designs, since they can be estimated computationally by obtaining work data. Even still, workload is difficult to measure directly and social norms, like closing one's door, provide powerful cues to information seekers. Selection assistance should minimally consider alternative, implicit representations of workload as well as a mechanism for the individual to mark himself as busy. Again, we note the utility of augmentative systems; these would help users identify and *narrow* (rather than completely select) potential candidates for expertise.

ESCALATION

There are times when a person will make a selection, approach an expert for help, and not get any help. The identification or selection mechanisms have failed in some way. Escalation is the way in which people repair failures in identification and selection.

A simple example of escalation occurred when Mike, a support representative, helped a client with "payment aging" (used to handle late and deferred payments). MSC's software supports two aging methods, and "nearly all" of MSC's clients use the same one. This client called Mike because payment aging had apparently ceased to work. Using diagnostics, Mike determined that the client was trying to switch from the standard to the non-standard aging method. Mike could not figure out why aging was not working, so he checked the change history. He saw that Han had recently worked on that code and went to Han for help. However, Han had made only minor changes to the code and was not sure why the client was having a problem. Han and Mike then went to ask Eyal for help, but Eyal was on vacation and the problem languished waiting for Eyal's return. When Eyal returned, Han went to him with the problem. Eyal quickly emphasized that that client with that configuration should use the standard method, closing the problem.

The above example shows two different breakdowns and a simple escalation that eventually solved the problem. In the first breakdown, Mike used the change history to identify Han as a likely candidate for the necessary expertise, but the change history was misleading in this case. This was a breakdown in identification. In the second breakdown, Han correctly identified Eyal as having the expertise to solve the problem (Eyal being a concierge). But the selection failed because Han did not know or had forgotten that Eyal was on vacation and unavailable.

As a generalization of this example, expertise identification can fail in three ways: over-identification, under-identification, and misidentification. Over-identification provides a set of candidate sources that is entirely too large. The set includes people who have the necessary expertise but it also includes a large number of people who do not. Or, it may include people who are truly experts when this level of expertise is not required. Over-identification is likely to result in the selection of a person without the proper level of expertise.

Under-identification provides a set that is too small. With under-identification, all of the identified candidates have some expertise in the necessary topic, but the set excludes at least one person who is necessary for the problem to be solved.

When only one or two people are required, under-identification is the same as misidentification. A misidentification breakdown identifies a set of people, but none of these people has the required expertise, at a sufficient level, to solve the problem or answer the question.

Expertise identification is not the only place where a failure might occur; a breakdown may also occur in the selection phase. For example a breakdown in the load balancing strategy may result in selecting someone who is actually too busy to respond. Alternatively, a breakdown in using performance criteria may result in the selection of a candidate who just cannot understand the nature of the problem.

Escalation provides a way to either adjust the set of candidates initially identified or to reselect from among those candidates utilizing information gained in the initial attempt. (We note that just as identification and selection are occasionally only analytically separable in the initial search, this is also true in escalation.) The term escalation is used here to describe an increase in the intensity with which a possible solution is pursued. Escalation does not always mean that a problem is pushed up or down the organizational hierarchy. Within MSC, people seeking information may go to less desirable sources (e.g., to people with less expertise or to ill-maintained documents), sources with a higher psychological cost (e.g., to objectionable people), or cross departmental or even organizational boundaries.

In practice, breakdowns and their repairs are fluid. The following example shows how breakdowns in identification and selection, as well as their repairs, are interwoven and fluid. Although this was an unusual event, it highlights critical features of escalation at MSC.

The Server Crisis

MSC had been having problems with a high-speed dedicated line between their headquarters and a machine across town that was their gateway for all outside connections. Late one Friday afternoon, the substitute system administrator ("sysadmin") decided to work on the problem, the normal system administrator being on vacation. The substitute changed a few fields of the network configuration file, ran a test, and saw that the throughput between the warehouse and headquarters had not changed. Since his attempted fix had not changed the problem, he reset the configuration back to what it was when he started. Thinking that everything was working, the substitute sysadmin left for the weekend.

Monday morning a senior developer, Karl, was called at home by a client who asked why the system was down. The senior developer logged on and checked the processes on the network server. He quickly decided that this was a serious problem:

> At that point I got on my PC at home and tried to get in. I could see there was a problem. Well, I telneted and I could see, no processes, that nobody could get in. I decided that the problem must be critical so I paged Daniel [V.P. of Development]. I had Laurie call or page Andreas and Craig. - Karl

The call to Daniel is an example of tightly-tied identification and selection. Daniel is very knowledgeable, but in this case Daniel's organizational status was more important. Karl called Daniel first, not to get explicit help, but to get recognition that the problem was critical and would require additional resources.

At the same time, Karl requested assistance from Craig and Andreas. Karl requested that they both come to work early. In this step, Karl specifically marshaled expertise resources that he wanted at his disposal: Craig, an expertise concierge, was a manager, and Karl was hoping that Craig would decide to come in earlier than normal. In effect, Karl identified Craig as having important expertise if Karl and Andreas were to fail in their initial attempts.

Andreas was already at MSC when Karl arrived. Together Karl and Andreas, both programmers, tried various diagnostic routines. They checked the router link, called their dedicated line provider for a line diagnostic, and even checked the network card in the server. Lastly, they restarted the server. Everything checked out, but the server was still not accessible from the outside. Karl then turned to Craig for help.

As mentioned, the identification of Craig occurred earlier, but his selection had been deferred. Craig was not consulted immediately because Craig was in a different part of the organization. Instead, Karl selected Andreas because of Karl's desire to "keep it local." This turned out be fruitless; Karl and Andreas exhausted everything they knew to try. An escalation then occurred where Craig was explicitly used as a concierge to suggest others who could help. In the escalation, Craig suggested the substitute sysadmin and an off-site employee who was very knowledgeable about Unix. In this second escalation, the substitute sysadmin was quickly selected. This provided the solution:

> We got on a phone conference with a guy out in the Edinger building [across town]. He used the Unix setup program. I was unaware that Unix had a setup program. Among all the options, one was changed. I don't know what these options do, but I noticed that something was missing. The default gateway was missing. I don't know what it was but it's not workable this way. The guy ... had a screen shot from last Friday and he confirmed that it was missing. I don't know why he had a screen shot. But putting that [the default address] back fixed the problem. - Andreas

This example shows escalation as a standard repair technique at MSC. In simpler cases, like the first example, the escalation would likely end with an expertise concierge, Craig or Eyal. Indeed, in the end, the substitute sysadmin was finally included at Craig's recommendation. The example also shows how participants sometimes separate identification and selection of the necessary expertise: Karl reserved the use of Craig. As well, the substitute sysadmin was selected in the second escalation, after two potential candidates were identified.

Escalation in Design

The above example demonstrates that breakdowns occur naturally. Expert-locator systems are likely to have breakdowns too. As with identification and selection, escalation behaviors may be too difficult to support fully. It is not clear that the reservation of expertise, as Karl did with Craig above, can be supported through a system.

Escalations, except in the simplest cases, will have multiple iterations. Multiple iterations require mechanisms for tracking a problem and its state, both social and informational. On any iteration, an expert-locator system will need mechanisms to understand what a user has previously attempted so that suggestions can be modified to fit the severity and situation of the problem. This argues for at least two types of feedback and modification techniques; one that can handle the escalation of a single problem over a short period of time and one that can tailor itself to the preferences and needs of an individual user.

SUMMARY

Our field study of information sharing at a medium sized software company focused on the expertise that is leveraged through social interactions by the participants. We observed participants solving two general finding problems through social mechanisms: expertise identification and expertise selection. We believe that these are two crucial problems that must be solved for individuals to satisfy their need for expertise. We believe that the escalation behavior that we describe here also represents an important expertise location mechanism.

Our goal with this field study was to provide the broader research community and ourselves a rich, empirically based description of expertise sharing that can be the basis for new expertise sharing information systems. The next step in our research agenda will be to pursue the development of new systems based on these results from our field study.

Acknowledgements

This project has been funded, in part, by grants from National Science Foundation grant (IRI-9702904) and the University of California MICRO program. This project benefited from the reviewers' comments and from conversations with John King, Jonathan Grudin, Kate Ehrlich, Fernando Olivera, Stephanie Teasley, Loren Terveen, Christine Halverson, Tom Gruber, Clark Turner, Suzanne Schaefer, the ICS Graduate Student Advancement Colloquium, and many others. Our research group, Jack Muramatsu, Wayne Lutters, and Keri Carpenter, contributed to this understanding of expertise and organizations. We would also like to thank the participants at MSC for their insights and assistance.

References

1. Ackerman, M. S. Answer Garden: A Tool for Growing Organizational Memory. Ph.D. Thesis, MIT, 1993.
2. Ackerman, M. S. Augmenting the Organizational Memory: A Field Study of Answer Garden. Proceedings of CSCW '94, 1994: 243 - 252.
3. Ackerman, M. S. and D. W. McDonald. Answer Garden 2: Merging Organizational Memory with Collaborative Help. Proceedings of CSCW '96, 1996: 97-105.
4. Allen, T. J. Managing the Flow of Technology. MIT Press, Cambridge, 1977.
5. Cicourel, A. V. The Integration of Distributed Knowledge in Collaborative Medical Diagnosis. In Galegher, J., R. E. Kraut and C. Egido (ed). Intellectual Teamwork. Lawrence Erlbaum, Hillsdale, NJ, 1990.
6. Ehrlich, K. and D. Cash. Turning Information into Knowledge. Proceedings of Digital Libraries '94, 1994: 119 - 125.
7. Foner, L. N. Yenta: A Multi-Agent, Referral-Based Matchmaking System. Proceedings of Agents'97, 1997:
8. Goffman, E. The Presentation of Self in Everyday Life. Anchor-Doubleday, New York, 1961.
9. Goldberg, D., D. Nichols, B. M. Oki and D. Terry. Using Collaborative Filtering to Weave an Information Tapestry. Communications of the ACM, 1992, 35(12): 61 - 70.
10. Hill, W. and L. Terveen. Using Frequency-of-mention in Public Conversations for Social Filtering. Proceedings of CSCW '96, 1996: 106 - 112.
11. Hutchins, E. Cognition in the Wild. MIT Press, Cambridge, MA, 1995.
12. Kautz, H. A., B. Selman and M. Shah. Referral Web: Combining Social Networks and Collaborative Filtering. Communications of the ACM, 1997, 40(3): 63 - 65.
13. Konstan, J. A., B. N. Miller, D. Maltz, J. L. Herlocker, L. R. Gordon and J. Riedel. GroupLens: Applying Collaborative Filtering to Usenet News. Communications of the ACM, 1997, 40(3): 77 - 87.
14. Orr, J. E. Talking About Machines: An Ethnography of a Modern Job. Cornell University Press, Ithaca, 1996.
15. Paepcke, A. Information Needs in Technical Work Settings and Their Implications for the Design of Computer Tools. Computer Supported Cooperative Work, 1996, 5: 63 - 92.
16. Resnick, L. B., J. M. Levine and S. D. Teasley (ed). Perspectives on Socially Shared Cognition. American Psychological Association, Washington DC, 1991.
17. Strauss, A. L. Qualitative Analysis for Social Scientists. Cambridge University Press, New York, 1987.

Sustaining mentoring relationships on-line

D. Kevin O'Neill
Ontario Institute for Studies in Education
University of Toronto
252 Bloor St. W.
Toronto, Ontario M5S 1V6 Canada
(416) 923-6641 x2531
dko@acm.org

Louis M. Gomez
School of Education and Social Policy
Northwestern University
2115 N. Campus Dr.
Evanston, IL, 60208 USA
(847) 467-2821
l-gomez@nwu.edu

ABSTRACT

CSCW systems and research aim to sustain productive relationships over barriers of time and space. For the most part, however, the CSCW literature has focused on short-term relationships or collaborative episodes. Here, we examine in depth 26 lengthy email relationships between students in grades 7 to 12 and volunteer scientists who advised them on science projects. We illustrate the unique dynamics of these relationships, consider their technical and social demands, and discuss the potential for CSCW systems to help sustain long-term help relationships by better accommodating their needs.

Keywords

CSCW, help, long-term relationships, mentoring, telementoring

INTRODUCTION

The central goal of CSCW systems and research is to sustain productive relationships over barriers of time and space. Recent research in the field has examined the short-term help exchanges that can be supported by CSCW systems, revealing a critical interplay between the dimensions of the helping task, its associated roles, and the technical affordances which keep these exchanges socially viable [1]. Despite a growing interest and investment in the longer-term helping relationships which can be supported by CSCW systems, however, little attention has so far been paid to them in the research literature. We will begin filling this void with an analysis of data from an in-depth study of email-based mentoring relationships.

The relationships under study here took place between 90 teen-aged and pre-teen science students and volunteer scientists from across the United States and Canada. Each relationship continued for a period of up to nine weeks and revolved around an ill-structured intellectual task: designing, carrying out and reporting a science project. As we will discuss below, the email-based mentoring that we have documented shares some of the influences discussed by Ackerman et. al., but has unique dynamics of its own which present unique technical and social demands. Using several examples from telementoring dialogues, we will elucidate these demands and discuss the potential for CSCW systems to better sustain long-term help relationships by accommodating them.

CSCW 98 Seattle Washington USA

Mentoring Relationships

While successful people often point to the importance of mentoring relationships in their development [2], these relationships are quite sensitive to time and space constraints. Since they often arise out of informal communications, they can be hampered by a variety of incidental factors such as office locations [3], preventing people who might excel as mentors from serving in this capacity. Where the spatial organization of the workplace is not an obstacle, mentoring activities may be hampered by daily schedules and organizational surroundings. Thus, while programs do exist which link school and work settings [4, 5], these programs have not become widespread because the different schedules on which schools, corporations and universities operate make it difficult to maintain relationships across these organizations.

From Mentoring to Telementoring

In response to the problems described above, researchers have begun actively orchestrating mentoring relationships on-line. Over the past three years, "telementoring" has become an active field of development in which a significant financial investment is being made [6-8]; however, reporting on the dynamics of these relationships and their implications for CSCW has been sparse.

Our research began in response to the practical challenges of providing students with sufficient guidance for ambitious, long-term science projects [9]. For the past five years, a teacher collaborator of ours has taught a project-based high school Earth Science class which attempts to motivate traditional science avoiders by offering them greater freedom to study phenomena that interest them. In this class, small teams of students conduct lengthy investigations into any natural phenomena they please, "so long as they are not living — that's Biology." The teacher imposes strict requirements on the methods and reporting of students' research, but the coverage of particular content is not required.

While the teacher may be familiar with most of the phenomena that his students choose to study, he may not always be up-to-date on the current state of research in the field or the latest Internet resources available for study. During the year that this research was conducted, for instance, a group of young women became intrigued with the controversy over the swimming motions of an aquatic dinosaur called the plesiosaur. Other challenging project ideas that year included differentiating black holes from other radiation sources in space. While these were clearly worthwhile subjects for study, the teacher's own intellectual resources were insufficient to provide for his students' needs. In each case, volunteer telementors recruited via the Usenet ".sci" hierarchy were able to help guide the projects to satisfying conclusions.

Over a period of three years, we have helped hundreds of volunteer scientists, including university faculty, graduate students and a variety of applied scientists, offer guidance to high school and middle school science students for just a few minutes each week, entirely via email. News of our work sometimes meets with a skeptical reaction from those wondering where we could possibly be finding a sufficient number of qualified people to volunteer their time. For those skeptics, Table 1 presents a profile of our mentor pool, broken down by profession.

Profession	%
Professional (engineer, consultant)	34
Master's student	31
University faculty	23
Doctoral student	7
Undergraduate student	3
Postdoc	2

Table 1: Professions of a sample of 90 volunteer telementors

Census data on voluntarism [10, 11] and conservative estimates of the number of college graduates with access to email at home [12] suggest that the available volunteer workforce for telementoring in the U.S. and Canada could be as large as 2.9 million people. This number is small by comparison to the number of K-12 students in the two countries, but the ratio (1 potential volunteer to every 17 students) is promising when one considers that telementoring is inappropriate for many ages of students, subject-matters and styles of teaching.

RESEARCH QUESTIONS AND METHODS

With additional development, we hope to see telementoring become a widespread application of CSCW in K-12 education. However, as our analysis below will make clear, this cannot occur with the present state of know-how in the field.

The question of whether any particular implementation of telementoring "works" in an educational sense is too complex to be addressed within the scope of this paper (it is explored at length in [13]). Here we will concern ourselves solely with the social-technical design issues surrounding how telementoring can be made satisfying enough for all participants to ensure their continued involvement.

As mentioned earlier, one of our teacher collaborators has been carrying out telementoring on an ongoing basis for a number of years, with little external support. Through close study of his mature implementation and attempts to reproduce it, we hoped to answer the following questions:

- What personal motives and social dynamics govern telementoring activity?

Understanding what people desire from this activity and the ways in which they may be prevented from getting it will help determine the practicality of sustained telementoring activity in other settings and on a larger scale.

- How feasible is it to organize telementoring for many people at a time (rather than as a boutique program)?

Many people find telementoring an enticing idea, but doubt its practicality at a large scale. Greater knowledge of the dynamics which govern telementoring activity will help establish reasonable expectations for more widespread use.

- What social and technological supports are most needed to sustain telementoring?

Having understood the motives of the participants in telementoring and the dynamics which govern it, we may be able to identify bottlenecks which specifically designed or tailored CSCW systems may alleviate.

Given these questions and concerns, our research followed a diagnostic strategy which capitalized on the natural variation in the development of telementoring relationships to tease out the most limiting social and technical factors. Our data collection began with broad-based surveys of the 90 students for whom we had orchestrated telementoring relationships. A survey instrument based on classroom observations and preliminary interviews by O'Neill was used to assess the degree of students' satisfaction with their telementoring relationships and the factors leading to it. This instrument was administered at the completion of each telementored project: a total of three times in the high school class, and once in the middle school.

Using these data, we constructed a stratified sample of relationships judged to be satisfying, mediocre and unsatisfying. For every project, 4-6 teams of target students were interviewed in their project groups for roughly 45 minutes apiece. Interviews were also conducted with a number of telementors involved in relationships at all three strata. These data assisted in the interpretation of automatically generated email logs, coded according to an inductively-developed scheme representing the topics raised in the messages.

ORCHESTRATING TELEMENTORING

Unlike the ephemeral help exchanges examined by Ackerman et. al., telementoring is very difficult to achieve without purposeful orchestration. In the two classrooms involved in this research, orchestration work was primarily performed by the teacher. As the first step, students are assigned to work in research teams of 1 to 5 when conducting their long-term science projects. In both settings, students had a high degree of control over the domains they studied and/or the research emphases they chose. This created a strong need for the guidance that telementors can provide. In the high school environment, students conducted three projects in a row, each seven weeks or more in length, and each with a different mentor. In the middle school, students did one lengthy project in which they had the flexibility to craft a specialty within a larger piece of research designed by the teacher.

Once the student teams identified their research domains and/or emphases, they were matched by their teacher with a volunteer mentor with some expertise in this area. For the most part, these volunteers were recruited through postings to Usenet groups such as sci.astro, sci.geo, and sci.environment. A typical recruiting posting read:

> Mentors Needed for Research Based Earth Science Class
>
> I am a high school Earth Science teacher. Our school is involved in a NSF grant project at Northwestern University....
>
> I am looking for oceanographers, astronomers, meteorologists and geoscientists (and grad students) to act as "Mentors" for various student projects. These mentors would assist my students in their explorations, not by giving answers and spending lots of time explaining basics, but by asking questions about the research, the data collection, and/or the methods. They might provide insight to data collection or interpretation. Basically, to help keep the kids on the track that I am laying down for them, and hopefully providing professional expertise/insights when appropriate. We're sort of modeling this on the graduate type of thesis research project, which is familiar to all of you in some form anyway. I'm hoping this will not be a time intensive kind of involvement.
>
> If you are at all interested in helping, please respond by email, and I will send you more detailed information.

Respondents to these postings received lengthier messages describing the teacher's school and students, the nature of the projects for which volunteers were needed, the sorts of difficulties students typically faced in this work, and the time commitment expected of volunteers. If they were ready to participate at that point, the teacher matched them with a team of students, and the relationship began.

While we had developed our own educational groupware product [14], we chose the low-tech approach of email in our initial experiments because the wide variety of computing platforms in use by our volunteers necessitated a lowest-common-denominator strategy. However, this approach had the collateral advantage of bypassing the introduction of software formalisms at an early stage [15], allowing for careful requirements-gathering. In fact, the only nonstandard piece in our technological setup was a custom-built email routing process which circulated messages reliably amongst all the members of a research team and their mentor, sent copies to the teacher if needed, and archived copies for later analysis. This mail router was later incorporated into a larger web-based application designed to streamline the management of telementoring for teachers. We will discuss this system and its functions at a later point in the paper.

As one might expect given the ill-structured nature of the task, both telementors and students needed substantial guidance concerning the kinds of help they should provide and expect. The guidance provided in our designs took several forms, including a limited amount of direct instruction to students about courteous email and the bounds of reasonable requests. However, the most important form of guidance we provided to both students and telementors consisted of "activity structures" describing the intellectual products expected from students (research questions, data sets, data analysis plans, etc.), the schedule on which they were due, and the responsibilities of all participants with respect to these. The activity structures played an important role in shaping and bounding the on-line relationships, ensuring that to the greatest degree possible, they contributed to classroom work rather than devolving into unproductive chat.

A SAMPLE RELATIONSHIP

A brief example will illustrate the nature of these telementoring relationships. This example does not represent the best relationship we have studied, nor the worst; but it highlights some of the important general influences on telementoring in an economical fashion. These influences include:

- The types of *utility* provided by telementoring (an important part of which is *timeliness*)
- The *visibility* of protégés' work to their mentors
- Participants' sensitivity to their *roles* and the *limits* of those roles.

Three high school students (2 male, 1 female) had decided to conduct a research project on forest fires started by lightning. Like all the students in their class, they were required to formulate a nontrivial research question about this phenomenon which could be addressed through some form of numerical data analysis, rather than simply by consulting references. Having chosen their general topic, however, the students quickly got bogged down in a fruitless web search for numerical data that would allow them to pose a more specific research question. As a result, they missed their deadline to propose a research question to their teacher. Finding themselves in crisis, they urgently looked to their mentor, Bruce, for advice:

> Dear Bruce,
>
> We tried to contact the lady that has all the information relating to lightning and forest fires, but she did not write us back. Our situation is now pretty brutal: we don't really have a specific question (because we can't find any data), our paper is due in a little over a week, and if this lady doesn't talk to us, we have no more leads to follow and we will have to start from scratch. If there is any way possible for you to think of another aspect of lightning to study and write about, we are in desperate need. We especially could use something that won't take a month

to gather all the research on. Thanks for all your help and effort.

Note that from the beginning, the students' relationship with Bruce focused on a practical problem of some intellectual depth. The students were not simply asking for answers to factual questions or "information" about lightning which they might locate elsewhere, but were appealing for suggestions toward a viable research agenda. Since it was clear that expertise, not information, was the critical bottleneck to their performance, they could see the *productive utility* of the relationship with their mentor and were willing to invest effort in developing it.

The students' candid report of their predicament was also vital to the success of this relationship, providing needed *visibility*. In fact, in nearly every successful relationship we observed, mentors appeared to rely upon regular, honest status reports to provide the grist they needed to size up their protégés' current goals and the difficulties they were facing. Without this knowledge, it was difficult (if not impossible) to formulate the subtle mid-course corrections that constitute the core of telementoring activity. Bruce's next messages illustrate this type of advice.

Bruce responded to his protégés' request in a very *timely* fashion the following day, suggesting two possible research agendas and data sources appropriate to them. His message illustrates some of the most important kinds of advice that a telementor can offer, given sufficient knowledge about a students' project:

> Good morning,
>
> Did you look at the web site I mentioned in my last message? It contains the 1995 fire statistics, noting cause and state. That's about the best data you can get on-line, I suspect. If you can then find data on either the acres of forest in each state (should be relatively easy to find) or the population density in each state, you can look at some comparison of the % of fires started by lightning and the population density, or the forested area.
>
> Taking the population density issue, you should be able to get state populations from either an atlas or the U.S. Census Bureau (I'm pretty sure they have a web site). State areas should also be easy to find. With this info. and the fire statistics, you could easily calculate 50 (x,y) pairs of coordinates where x and y are the population density and the % of fires started by lightning. (Which of these would be the dependent and which the independent variable?)
>
> Do you know about least-squares fit, or linear regression? Do you expect to find that % lightning fires increases as pop. density increases, or should %LF decrease when pop. density increases? Does a linear regression agree with what you expect?

With his assertion that the web site he recommended had about the best relevant data on-line, Bruce immediately saved his protégés a lot of fruitless web searching. The *productive utility* of this advice was very clear to the students, and probably helped keep them involved in the relationship. Bruce also offers direction by presenting not one, but two reasonable research agendas concerning the empirical relationship between variables associated with forest fires. One of these agendas (concerning the percentage of lightning fires in an area and its population density) was apparently a favorite of his, and he described an elaborate plan for pursuing it. This plan would still take considerable initiative for students at this level to carry out, so Bruce was not simply "giving answers away".

At this point, days passed with no further communication. Then the team committed to a research question and reported its decision to Bruce. Surprisingly, they had not chosen to follow the research agenda that he had so clearly laid out for them; instead, they focused their attention on the relationship between lightning fires and the forested area in a state. Bruce's response shows his clear regard for his *role* and its *limits*. Far from being irritated by their choice, Bruce reinforced it and did his best to help them follow through on their new plan. He did, nonetheless, remind them of other avenues of investigation still open:

> Glad you've got a topic, finally! I checked a couple of sites that I thought would list the acres of forest for the 50 states, but neither panned out. I have three options for you:
>
> 1. Call the Forest Inventory and Analysis office of the Forest Service at (202) 205-1343 and ask if the data is on-line. If it is, they should know.
>
> 2. Email me again with a fax number and I can fax you some pages that will list "acres protected" of forest and rangeland, which is a column that normally appears next to those on the lightning-data web page
>
> 3. Do population density, not forested area. I suspect there'll be a stronger correlation, and the population of the U.S. states should be quite simple to find (look in a road atlas if you can't find the Census Bureau's web page).

In an important way, *visibility* is at play in this message, too. Bruce's advising strategy of presenting options and standing back is adaptive for someone who is knowledgeable about students' project goals and their research domain, but has limited knowledge of their full capabilities, their commitment to their work, or the resources available to them. As the forest fires team moved forward with its project, Bruce presented options and expressed informed opinions, but did not attempt to issue commandments or usurp the teacher's role as the ultimate arbiter of worthy project ideas. In other words, he respected the *bounds* of his role. His protégés appreciated his advice and took advantage it, yet they did not follow it slavishly.

PATHS OF TELEMENTORING RELATIONSHIPS

The forest fires project was, of course, just one of many telementoring relationships that have occurred in the two participating classrooms, and cannot be taken as representative. As in other instances of electronic help exchanges, including the Zephyr help instance [1] and Usenet news, our telementoring relationships varied considerably in their helpfulness to the participants, and at times they failed altogether. The CSCW design challenge is to understand the various paths that long-term telementoring relationships can take, and find ways to maximize the positive outcomes. In this section, we will provide a brief overview of the various paths that our telementoring relationships followed, and why. Later sections will discuss possible design solutions to the problems described below.

The simplest measure of telementoring activity is, of course, the number of messages exchanged by the participants in a relationship. Figure 1 shows the total volume of email messages exchanged by 59 student teams in the two classes and their assigned mentors. As is obvious, the majority of these relationships did not involve a large quantity of correspondence. While the total number of messages was over 40 in one case, the median number of messages per relationship was only 9.

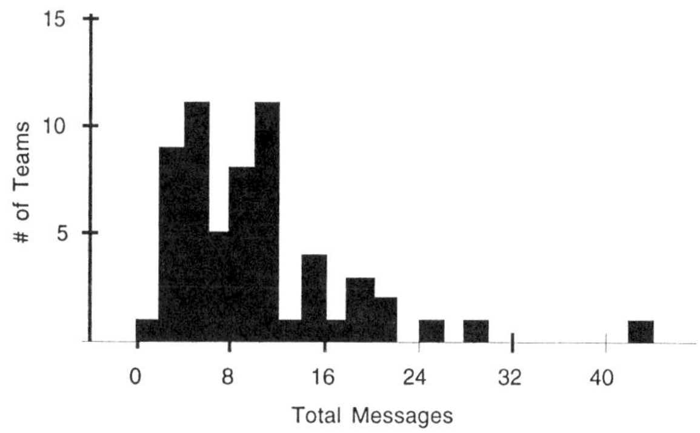

Figure 1: Volume of messages exchanged by 59 student teams and their mentors

While large and small volumes of email are one useful indicator of students' and mentors' engagement, however, they do not correspond in any reliable way to the success or failure of those relationships. It can be the case, for instance, that a student team only needs one crucial piece of advice to launch its project, which is taken care of in an exchange of four or five messages with a telementor. Alternatively, messages can be fewer in number but very involved. For instance, one of the deepest student-mentor research collaborations of 1995/96 (detailed in [13]) involved the exchange of only 15 email messages, spread over a period of 9 weeks.

To get a clearer sense of the variety of relationships we orchestrated, a detailed topical coding of all the logged email (representing 26 relationships) was produced using QSR NUD*IST [16], a qualitative data-analysis software package. This coding became quite detailed, with a total of 32 hierarchical categories. Among the high-level topics of dialogue that emerged from the coding were:

- students' project ideas (questions to answer, hypotheses to test, or simply topics to learn more about)
- the status of students' work (what students have done, how far along they think they are in their projects)
- domain phenomena under study (e.g. earthquakes)
- specialized terminology
- learning resources (books, journals, web sites, etc.)
- research methods (including choice and analysis of data)
- scientific practice in general

On the basis of this coding, we characterized three broad categories of telementoring dialogues: abortive, perfunctory, and interest-driven partnerships. Below, we will briefly discuss each of these categories, their prevalence, and their implications for the design of technical and social systems for sustainable telementoring.

Abortive dialogues

While nearly all of the telementoring dialogues we analyzed (92%) involved some mention of students' ideas for their science projects, many fewer (65%) progressed as far as raising specific domain-related phenomena for deeper discussion. We characterize the balance of the dialogues (35%) as "abortive" because they were apparently abandoned by the participants. Interviews suggested a variety of causes for this abandonment. In a few cases, the telementor was simply unresponsive to the students: often due to an absence from work. In other cases, students were unable to articulate their needs well enough to get the dialogue started, contacted their telementors too late for them to provide timely guidance, or failed to invest any effort in the relationship because it seemed to them to be a waste of time.

In any sustainable model of telementoring, the frequency of abortive relationships must be kept below a certain threshold; though this threshold will be unique to circumstances and participants. While our volunteer mentors generally appreciated that not all students are well motivated to study science, and that each volunteer received "the luck of the draw" when matched with students, abortive relationships generate frustration for telementors and waste the teachers' administrative effort. The greatest concern about these relationships from the designer's standpoint is that too many might cause substantial attrition from the volunteer pool, thus threatening the viability of telementoring in the long term.

Perfunctory dialogues

A step up from abortive dialogues were topic-driven ones in which students treated their assigned mentors essentially as research librarians. As in a brief consultation with a librarian, students' contributions to the perfunctory dialogues consisted primarily of factual questions or requests for references to data or articles. If telementors satisfied these requests routinely and failed to build a deeper form of participation in students' work (such as an influence over the research agenda or the methods employed in pursuing it), they could be left with little control over how the relationships developed, or whether they continued. In the worst case, students might decide to "take the goods and run". Take, for instance, this exchange between two young men and a geologist at the U.S. Geological Survey:

> Subject: flood help
>
> Hi, Richard, We are two students doing a project on floods. We are looking for some concrete data to observe. Our teacher said that you might be able to help. We have

access to the web, so if you know of any good web cites we would love that. Thanks for your time.

Sincerely, Ken and Cody

Subject: Re: flood help

If you are interested in studying Illinois floods, the web site you will want to look at is "http://wwwdilurb.er.usgs.gov/pub/floodinfo/", which maintains both historical and real-time flood (and other streamflow) data for Illinois rivers.

You will also want to browse the US Geological Survey homepage, which is at "http://www.usgs.gov/". Note the link at that page to water resources, which will lead you to a wealth of flooding information for sites and events all over the country.

Let me know how else I can help, especially with your study design and/or interpretation of the field data.

Richard

While Richard was clear in his desire to offer advice on the study design and data interpretation, his protégés' next and final message was simply to inform him that their project was finished:

Subject: final paper

Richard,

Cody and I would like to thank you for all of your help on our floods project. We also apologize for a lack of keeping in touch. The net sites that you told us about, the USGS ones, were absolutely great and helped a lot. thanks again. We also thought you might want a copy of our paper so here it is.

Thanks,

Ken and Cody

Despite his clear interest in the students' work, Richard was simply shut out of the bulk of the project activity. Even if he had wanted to take a proactive role in the project, he could not have, because he simply had no idea what the students were up to (i.e. zero *visibility*). Thankfully, the case described above is the *only* recorded instance in which students discussed resources to the total exclusion of other matters important to their shared work with their mentor, such as constraints like project deadlines, time on-line, their background knowledge, etc. These issues were raised in 31% of the dialogues.

Like abortive dialogues, these perfunctory dialogues are of concern to the designer because they are not likely to provide the rewards that bring volunteers back to telementoring. They may, however, offer utility to students and teachers in the short term, and this makes them especially dangerous to the long-term sustainability of telementoring.

Interest-driven partnerships

Looking only at the above types of relationships, one might get a poor impression of telementoring. However, a considerable proportion of the relationships we studied developed beyond a simple focus on resources for study, broaching topics such as specialized terminology (42%) or broader issues of scientific practice (15%). These dialogues more closely approached the ideal of a research partnership. As an example, below are excerpts from an exchange between a telementor and a research team beginning a project on sea surface temperatures. As the conversation begins, the students are relatively directionless in their work, having already begun and abandoned a project on riverbeds:

Subject: Re: Hi

Dear Byron and Vanessa,

> We are two high school students in an earth
> science class researching sea surface temperatures.
> We, if we can find any data, are going to research
> the question: How do the temperatures in
> the Northern Atlantic and Northern Pacific compare?
> And try to find a reason for this. If you have any
> questions, comments, pointers, or anything else, we
> would be grateful to hear about it!

You have chosen an interesting topic. Where are you in your research now?

A lot of data exist on sea surface temperatures (SSTs). Compiled data sets of historical measurements from ships are one data source. Another data source is satellite data. An introductory textbook on general oceanography (e.g., Grant Gross's _Oceanography:_A_ View_of_the_Earth_) would be a good place to do some of your initial research.

Regards, David

We should note that in his first message, David contributes to the team's productivity without being merely compliant. While he provides some reinforcement of the students' research agenda and offers a pointer or two, he also makes a bid for greater *visibility* by asking Byron and Vanessa immediately for a report of their progress to date. Not only does he get this report, but his mentees actually defer to his judgement as to how they should continue:

Subject: We are...

Hey David, currently we are working on finding places on the web where we can find out data about oceans and their temperatures. One site I found to be useful was a site from a Japanese company (not that I remember the name or anything...). But I found it very helpful. We need to re-write our Background Information (on oceans/their temperatures and how they are controlled). But this can wait until next week (unless you think we should do it now). So thanks a lot,

Byron and Vanessa

Subject: Re: We are...

Dear Byron and Vanessa:

I would start writing ASAP. Writing often takes longer than you think it will.

> The Levitus `94 data set has global ocean temperatures and salinities as a function of latitude, longitude, and depth. You can access it at:
>
> http://ingrid.ldgo.columbia.edu/SOURCES/.LEVITUS94
>
> Another site that may be helpful to you is (perhaps it's the Japanese site you mentioned?):
>
> http://dpo.ori.u-tokyo.ac.jp:81/ocean/toolmap/Levitus-map.html
>
> It not only has a link to the Levitus `94 data set, it allows you to specify what parts of it you want to look at (e.g., only North Pacific SSTs).
>
> Enjoy, David

It took Byron and Vanessa several more messages to settle on a research question they were content with, but throughout this time they remained engaged in their relationship with David. This sustained conversation gave David natural opportunities to offer advice on writing reports ("start ASAP"), and guidance to data sources and analytical tools. Because the students made much of their progress and their thinking visible to David, he was able to offer a greater variety of guidance than mentors in perfunctory relationships.

Arguably, the most highly developed relationships were those that involved the discussion of research methodology (27%). For example, one student team which had been attempting to grow several varieties of crystals sought advice on how to recover from the apparent failure of their experiments. In order to secure advice from their telementor, they found it necessary to explain what they had done, and their reasons for doing it, in considerable detail:

> Dear Kevin,
>
> We tried to make crystals using powdered sugar, regular white sugar, brown sugar, and salt (we couldn't get epsom salt) we mixed 2 tablespoons (30 mL) of all the solids with 150 mL of tap water 'till all the solid was dissolved. Then we tied string to a popsicle stick and put it on the glass so that the string was hanging in the liquid. This was about four days ago, but there are only crystals in the salt and it looks like there's mold or something in the powdered sugar and in the regular sugar. Did we use too much water? I used that much water so that there would be a lot of string in liquid. Should we try again or wait 'till all the water evaporates? we're also going to do the same thing only put the beakers in shade, light, cold, and on a hot plate to see if darkness, heat, etc. has any effect on crystal growth. I know that the crystals on the hot plate will grow faster but do you have any suggestions on what we should do with the beakers we've already mixed? should we use less water for the other experiments? --Katie

Katie's message is a nice example of a circumstance in which students engaged their telementors as a helpful and critical audience. Katie invests effort in making her team's work visible to her mentor, not because she was compelled by her teacher to do so or was trying to impress anyone, but because she needed her mentor to understand the team's predicament in order to secure informed advice.

SUSTAINING FORCES

As we mentioned above, one of the teachers involved in this research has been orchestrating telementoring relationships for several years now on a largely independent basis. As other teachers become involved in similar efforts, it is worth considering the sustaining forces behind such early, successful implementations of telementoring.

Productive Utility

First and most obvious, telementoring relationships have *productive utility* for students, often helping them "get into position to think" about their research and steering them toward more manageable investigations. This is a substantial benefit, since settling on a research agenda is frequently the most time-consuming and least productive stage of project work. Without their mentors' attention and advice, it is clear that a greater number of teams would flounder or languish in their work for longer periods.

From a whole-classroom perspective, students avoiding unproductive floundering also has *motivational utility* that is of particular value to the teacher. Since the teacher's time is at a premium during the agenda-formation stage of students' projects, students are most likely to be frustrated in their demands for advice and guidance at this time. A scarcity of timely guidance not only reduces students' productivity, but generates frustration which in turn might threaten the viability of the whole project-based approach to teaching. Thus, the additional support of telementors is of value to the teacher in maintaining students' motivation to participate in projects.

Altogether, though a proportion of telementoring relationships always fizzle or fail (depending upon the implementation and the participants' expectations), volunteers' effort allows both teachers and students to channel their efforts more selectively. The time and effort that telementors save the teacher in offering guidance and searching for resources to support students' work can be reinvested in guiding other students who need additional help. The quality of guidance provided to the class as a whole is therefore improved.

Lightweightedness

Like Zephyr help exchanges, telementoring relationships are typically "lightweight" for the volunteers: often requiring as little as fifteen minutes of time invested each week. All the same, these brief moments can provide volunteers with unique opportunities to break from their routine work and contribute something worthwhile to the future of their chosen field. Students' projects can also present opportunities for mature practitioners to stretch themselves beyond their customary job roles or expertise in a way that can be quite stimulating. As a Physics graduate student explained after guiding three students through their project on black holes:

> I really enjoyed it, and for me it was great. I'd be sitting down, coding all day, writing [computer] programs, and I'd be able to take [a] break every couple of days to answer this email and look up something that I wanted

> to learn about. ....The main thing was that it was something that I could use when I needed a break. I mean, that's really the way I looked at it. ...You know, I can go spend a half an hour learning about something else I enjoy.

LIMITING FACTORS

What path a telementoring relationship will follow cannot be predicted in advance, even by teachers familiar with both their students' capabilities and their volunteers' expertise. However, several issues discussed above and raised repeatedly in interviews with students and telementors offer explanations for the failure of specific relationships and point to key design considerations.

Low Visibility

As we discussed above, it is difficult for a rich telementoring relationship to develop under conditions of low visibility. One enthusiastic volunteer who had been faced with uncooperative protégés suggested that advising students via email could be "very much working in a black box." This sentiment was shared by her protégés, who complained that telementors:

> ...have no idea what you're doing, what you've been doing, what you've gone through, what you haven't gone through. They've got no clue. ...personally the way I see it is if they're not stepping through the project with you, they've got no idea what you've already done, and I don't like repeating myself very much.

Telementors clearly suffer by comparison to the relatively instant gratification that is provided by classroom teachers when they are readily available. As the same pair of students complained:

> A: It's like one thing if you've got like a teacher, but it's another thing if you're trying to talk to someone...
>
> B: Over the computer. And it's like you wait for the response. And by that time you did something else! And then you know, it's like writing about what you did in the past, and when you get the response it's already done.

These students were not the most dedicated in their class, but they do point to a tough design problem for telementoring. If a mentor's guidance is to be helpful, it must be *timely*; and timely, pertinent advice relies on the kind of visibility that can only be based on routine review of students' work, such as a teacher does when circulating in a classroom.

Since email-based telementoring relationships do succeed, it is clear that some students are capable of furnishing adequate visibility even in as unsupportive a medium as email. Teachers assist this effort indirectly through the activity structures and daily shepherding they provide. In the ideal case, however, telementoring would not rely quite so much on students' facility as regular correspondents. Instead, visibility would be produced by a more supportive electronic discourse environment and a classroom culture that honors the production of status documents in electronic form. We will revisit this possibility in the "Design Implications" section below.

Concern with "Too Much Help"

The lack of visibility endemic to email-based mentoring not only makes offering guidance difficult, but it can exacerbate volunteers' natural concerns with providing "too much help" to their protégés. Detailed case studies of individual telementoring relationships [13] revealed the important influence that both mentors' and students' concerns over this issue had on the development of both successful and unsuccessful telementoring relationships. In some instances, mentors' worries led to an unfortunate "teasing" dynamic in which the students made what they believed to be reasonable requests, only to be rebuffed with the assertion that "I know the answer to your question, but I don't think I should tell you." In such cases, students may suspect their telementors of egotism or simple mean-spiritedness, wondering: "if he didn't want to help us, why did he volunteer in the first place?"

Sociability and Developmental Readiness

While the relationships we are discussing here are meant, first and foremost, to contribute toward curriculum goals, our interviews with volunteers make it clear that they derive greater satisfaction from their efforts by "getting to know the kids". In a roundabout way, sociability also contributes to the productivity of the relationships by helping participants' build confidence in one anothers' good intentions, and by opening doors to collateral learning opportunities. In both of the classrooms discussed here, we have seen volunteers present students with an "insider's view" of a field of work which would be rare for students to encounter at school.

In the middle school classroom, dialogues turned much more frequently to students' non scholastic interests and telementors' hobbies or home lives (67%) than it did in the high school classroom (17%). In part, this difference was a consequence of the different activity structure implemented in the middle school, which required the exchange of personal biographies as a first step to establishing the relationship. However, interview data make it clear that our high school students would likely have presented resistance to this strategy. In the quotation below, two young women express their confusion over the motives of volunteer mentors:

> A: I don't see why they would want to [volunteer]. I mean personally, it's not like you're going to make a new friend. I have some weird feeling that our mentor expected us to be friendly.
>
> B: Buddy-buddy.
>
> A: Yeah, 'cause we were fairly businesslike. They were like, "give a brief description of yourself." And we were like, "students, this school, this age. Anyway, back to what we really need."

While this is not a representative attitude, differences in the sociability of students present serious concerns about how to most sustainably implement telementoring. As the cases discussed above illustrate, no telementoring relationship can succeed without students' active engagement; yet because mentoring relationships are developmental in nature [2] students may simply not be equipped to anticipate or appreciate the potential benefits of telementoring as they begin it. We might refer to this as the "developmental catch-22".

Survey data collected at the end of each of the three high school projects in 1995/96 shed some light on the implications of the developmental catch-22, showing that it is not necessarily fatal. With more experience of telementoring, students' expectations appear to become more reasonable.

Among the items on our closing survey was a 7-point Likert scale on which students rated their satisfaction with the telementoring experience. Figure 2 shows project-to-project changes in the distribution of these satisfaction ratings for 22 students who had a mentor for every project. For clarity, these ratings are grouped into three categories: "Happy" (5 to 7), "Neutral" (4), and "Unhappy" (1 to 3).

Note that the number of "unhappy" respondents, the largest single group at the end of Project 1, drops steadily throughout the year. This change in project-to-project satisfaction suggests, as do our interview data, that students developed substantially more reasonable expectations of telementoring over the course of a year. Alternative designs discussed in the next section may make it possible to "bootstrap" students into more reasonable expectations even more quickly.

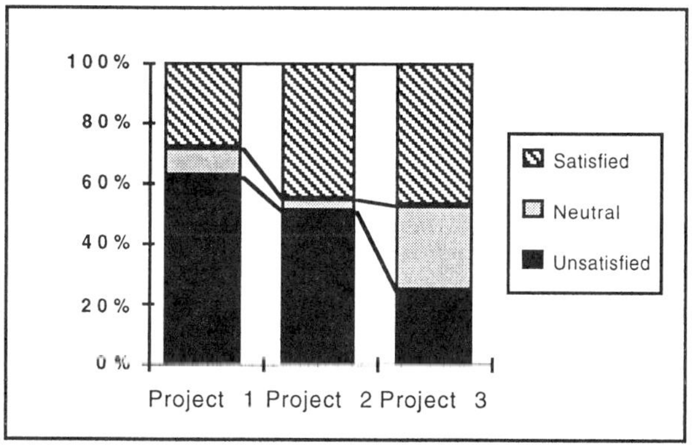

Figure 2: Students' agreement with the statement, "Overall, the mentoring was a success for me"

DESIGN IMPLICATIONS

This research points to several needs for sustained telementoring, associated with both CSCW systems and routines for their use in classrooms.

Developing understanding of mentoring

Because of the developmental catch-22, understanding the nature and potential rewards of mentoring is not a trivial matter, even when it is connected to practical tasks. And, while students and telementors can benefit from some up-front preparation for their roles, nothing will better enable them to make the most of the opportunities presented by telementoring than more experience of it.

In the best design, students and mentors would have the opportunity to be involved in several telementoring relationships per year. Another, less demanding approach is to provide opportunities for participants to observe other mentoring relationships while building their own. In a recent design experiment in three high school classrooms in Toronto, an educational groupware product called Knowledge Forum [17] was used to orchestrate telementoring relationships in a public discourse space. While formal matches were made between students and mentors, and compartments were set up within the environment to separate project topics, participants were encouraged to (and did) read the dialogues between all the mentors and students.

While one might have expected participants to resist the lack of privacy involved in this arrangement, both mentors and students responded positively to the opportunity to self-monitor their performance relative to others and emulate the best practices they observed. This type of arrangement therefore holds promise for reducing the proportion of relationships which are aborted by students who simply cannot anticipate the potential benefits of investing effort in the relationship.

Increasing visibility

As we made clear above, an important requirement of sustainable telementoring is that volunteer mentors see enough of their protégés' work to provide informed advice. It is also important for mentors' satisfaction that they understand how they contributed to students' work. As one volunteer put it, "I would have been more gratified to know what problems the students had that I was helping them to solve. It's kind of like if you're tutoring math, you want to know how the kid did on the exam afterward."

One way to address the visibility problem is through the use of groupware products like Knowledge Forum which might make more of students' routine work accessible to telementors. However, if the system is not to be seen as creating extra work, the curriculum and classroom culture must privilege the production of literate records of learning to assist local tasks, as well as sharing them with external collaborators.

Minimizing management and preserving goodwill

Observation of the teaching practice surrounding telementoring [13] suggests that if it is to be practical for more teachers, the greatest technical need is for services to streamline teachers' effort, make maximum use of volunteers' available time, and preserve volunteers' goodwill. In the long run, Usenet will not be a feasible way to locate large numbers of volunteer telementors, and organizing their effort will be too organizationally intensive for most teachers without new tools.

In response to this problem, we have built a Web-based application to serve the needs of teachers seeking telementors, mentors looking for volunteer opportunities, and students involved in telementoring relationships. This system, called "the CoVis Mentor Database", performs several functions:

- It provides a centralized database of volunteers (recruited by a school board or local community organization), which teachers can search by mentors' expertise, teaching experience, and other criteria.

- It offers an expedient way for teachers to solicit a large number of potential volunteers from the database at once. Forms prompt teachers for the details of a project which have most often been requested by volunteers in the past.
- When volunteers agree to participate in a particular project, they are "checked out" of the database, to prevent them from receiving further requests until their current mentor relationship ends. They can also log in at any time to make themselves temporarily unavailable for mentoring.

A more sophisticated and customizable version of the system is under development at OISE/UT. We hope to make this system inexpensive enough and simple enough to use that corporations and school boards will be able to run their own "mentor databases" to support a variety of community-based telementoring projects.

CONCLUSION

In our experiments, telementoring has served as a practical means to support ambitious project-based science learning in grades 7-12, and cost-effective staff development and educational outreach in adult workplaces. For this CSCW practice to reach more settings and be sustainable, however, two key social-technical requirements must be met. First, students' work needs to be made more visible to volunteer mentors than seems likely with email alone. Mature tools already exist to fill this need, and further experiments are needed to test their appropriateness for telementoring. Second, teachers must have appropriate organizational tools to reduce the management overhead that telementoring now requires. These tools, which we have begun to develop, can not only make telementoring more practical for teachers, but help preserve volunteers' goodwill as well.

ACKNOWLEDGMENTS

Rory Wagner of New Trier High School in Winnetka, Illinois and Judith Lachance-Whitcomb of Jordan Community School in Chicago were invaluable collaborators in this research. We thank them and their students for their contributions. We also gratefully acknowledge the support of the National Science Foundation under grant #RED-945729 and the Illinois State Board of Education. This research continues in collaboration with the CSILE/Knowledge-Building team at the Ontario Institute for Studies in Education of the University of Toronto, with support from the James S. McDonnell Foundation and the Natural Sciences and Engineering Research Council of Canada.

REFERENCES

1. Ackerman, M.S. and L. Palen. *The Zephyr help instance: Promoting ongoing activity in a CSCW system*. in *CHI 96: Conference on human factors in computing systems*. (1996), New York: Association for Computing Machinery.
2. Kram, K.E., *Mentoring at work: Developmental relationships in organizational life*. (1985), New York: University Press of America.
3. Fish, R.S., Kraut, R. E., Root, R. W. & Rice R. E., *Video as a technology for informal communications*. Communications of the ACM (1993) 36(1): p. 48-61.
4. Waltner, J.C., *Learning from scientists at work,. Educational Leadership* (1992) p. 48-52.
5. EDC, *Industry volunteers in the classroom: Freeing teachers' time for professional development*. (1994) Educational Development Center, Inc., 55 Chapel Street, Newtonville, Mass., 02158-1060.
6. Bennett, D.T., *et al. Telementoring: Designing on-line mentoring environments for high school women in science and technical courses*. in *Joint National Conference of the Women in Engineering Program Advocates and the National Association of Minority Engineering Program Administrators*. (1997) Washington, DC.
7. Harris, J., *The Electronic Emissary*. (1997) [on-line]: http://www.tapr.org/emissary/
8. Neils, D., *The Hewlett-Packard e-mail mentor program* (1997) [on-line]: http://mentor.external.hp.com/
9. Wagner, R., *Expeditions to Mount Everest*, in *Tales from the electronic frontier: First-hand experiences of teachers and students using the Internet in K-12 math and science*, R.W. Mayumi Shinohara, Art Sussman, Editor. (1996) WestEd: San Francisco.
10. Ross, D.P. and E.R. Schillington, *A Profile of the Canadian volunteer: A guide to the 1987 Survey of Volunteer Activity in Canada*. (1988, November) National Voluntary Organizations: Ottawa, Canada.
11. Hayghe, H.V., *Volunteers in the U.S.: Who donates the time?* Monthly Labor Review. (1991, February) p. 17-23.
12. Anderson, R.H., *et al.*, *Universal access to e-mail: Feasibility and societal implications*. (1995) Santa Monica, CA: RAND.
13. O'Neill, D.K., *Engaging science practice through science practitioners: Design experiments in K-12 telementoring*. (1998) Unpublished doctoral dissertation, Northwestern University.
14. O'Neill, D.K. and Gomez, L.M. *The Collaboratory Notebook: A networked knowledge-building environment for project learning*. in *Ed-Media '94: World Conference on Educational Multimedia and Hypermedia*. (1994) Vancouver, BC, Canada.
15. Bowers, J., *The politics of formalism*, in *Contexts of computer-mediated communication*, M. Lea, Editor. (1992), Harvester Wheatsheaf: New York. p. 232-261.
16. QSR, *NUD*IST*. (1997), Scolari: Thousand Oaks, CA.
17. Learning in Motion, Inc., *Knowledge Forum*. (1997) Learning in Motion: Santa Cruz, CA.

Cooperative Knowledge Work and Practices of Trust: Sharing Environmental Planning Data Sets

Nancy A. Van House, Mark H. Butler, Lisa R. Schiff
School of Information Management and Systems
102 South Hall #4600
University of California, Berkeley, CA 94720-4600
{vanhouse, markhb, lschiff} @ sims.berkeley.edu

ABSTRACT
Knowledge communities of all kinds have social and material practices for deciding what is known and who is to be trusted. In this paper, we address a specific kind of knowledge work, environmental planning, and a particular form of collaboration, the sharing of measurement data sets. We are interested in how trust is created; how trustability is assessed in the arm's-length collaboration of sharing data sets; and how changes in technology interact with those practices of trust. We look at several elements of scientific practice that facilitate this sharing -- communities of practice, boundary objects, and assemblages -- and discuss the implications for CSCW, digital libraries, and other information-sharing applications.

Keywords
Knowledge work, environmental planning, boundary objects, assemblages, communities of practice, data sets, digital libraries, UC Berkeley Digital Library

INTRODUCTION

Technology designed to support work has to be consonant with actual work practices. CSCW is explicitly concerned with the socially-organized practices of users, as well as with technological support for those practices.

Much CSCW research and design has been directed at small, stable, heterogeneous groups with on-going organizational and/or task connections [e.g. 18, 16; 4, et al]. Even when membership in the group is fairly large, it is, or is assumed to be, limited and/or known: e.g. people working on a project, within an organization, or as part of a professional community. However, much cooperative work is performed by large, heterogeneous, shifting, transient groups, distributed in time and space, with permeable boundaries.

CSCW 98 Seattle Washington USA

Among the tasks supported by CSCW applications is the sharing of information. In some cases, the information is a resource in a cooperative task. In other cases, what Schmidt and Bannon [18] call the joint construction of a common information space is the task itself. Creating such a shared information space is no simple task. Decisions have to be made about what to include, how to present it, how to interpret and use it, what accompanying information to include, and when to purge it; and about who decides. These are the practical manifestations of the larger questions of deciding what is known and who is to be believed.

The tasks of establishing the content and interpreting the meaning of a shared information space is, of course, not unique to the kinds of work with which CSCW has generally been concerned. Nor is CSCW the only area in which technology to support such work is at issue. CSCW and the growing area of digital libraries [24] have in common a concern with designing technology to support shared knowledge work.

A major function of knowledge communities is negotiating what is known and the methods of agreeing on what is known, what counts as evidence, and who speaks. Knowledge communities of all kinds have social and material practices for inscribing, transporting, evaluating, and using information; for bridging local and global, private and public; for coordinating work across space and time; and defining what Star, following Becker, calls hierarchies of credibility [22]. Although we actually know little about the social practices of credibility, value, and trust [16], these are perhaps most studied in science and technology studies (STS). STS contends that scientific knowledge is socially-produced, not discovered, and studies the ways in which communities decide what is known, what counts as evidence, and who speaks [e.g. 8, 6, 21, 10] -- seeking to understand " the political and relational aspects of what we call knowledge" [22 p. 1].

Changes in technology change the material bases of work and make possible new forms and methods of work, which often foregrounds previously taken-for-granted practices. The World Wide Web is one such change. Among its many effects is a blurring of the boundaries between private and public, published and unpublished, closed and open. It allows people to by-pass, or at least alter, the established channels by which communities have decided to what and to whom it pays attention. It opens up the collaborative process in ways both intentional and unintentional. And it is being used increasingly for CSCW applications, Digital Libraries, and other forms of cooperative work and information sharing.

This paper examines practices of credibility and trust in the development of shared information resources. We are interested in how trust and credibility are created; how credibility is assessed in the arm's-length collaboration of sharing information among people who may not know one another; and how changes in technology interact with those practices of trust. We look at several elements of scientific practice that facilitate this sharing -- communities of practice, boundary objects, and assemblages -- and discuss how a Web-based Digital Library might affect these elements and the knowledge work that they support. We don't have all the answers to how design of Web-based cooperative information resources can address these issues. Instead, this discussion is aimed at highlighting the importance of issues of credibility and trust in the adoption and use of CSCW and Digital Library applications, the critical role of local practices, and the need for new applications to understand and support existing social practices.

In this paper, we address a specific kind of knowledge work, environmental planning, a particular form of collaboration, the sharing of measurement data sets, and the possible changes in social arrangements of deciding what is known and who is to be trusted brought about by a shift to Web-based distribution of data.

THE PROJECT

The UC Berkeley Digital Library project, part of the NSF/NASA/ARPA Digital Library Initiative, is creating a digital library in support of environmental planning. Our goal is to develop technologies that support "work-centered" digital library services, oriented to the mission of the work group. Work groups require sophisticated digital library services and collaborative support to effectively utilize massive, distributed repositories of multimedia information. The technologies provide integrated, seamless access to bodies of new and old information via the network.

We are creating a digital library testbed of environmental information, consisting of a substantial and diverse collection of many kinds of textual documents, photo images, botanical data sets and various kinds of map data including aerial photos, digital ortho-photoquads, and digitized topographic maps. Our testbed currently holds 58,000 photo images plus 1,000 aerial photographs. We have botanical data sets of 8,300 recognized plants in California and 82,000 other plants worldwide. We have scanned and processed about 2,300 documents comprising about 251,000 pages of text.

We have made research progress in the areas of image retrieval, new document models, natural language processing, and Web-based geographic information systems. We have constructed Web-accessible Java prototype systems of our research achievements to access our collections. The digital library, as well as added documentation about it, is publicly accessible at http://www.elib.cs.berkeley.edu.

A major goal of the user needs assessment and evaluation part of the project has been to better understand the practices of environmental planning, particularly those of information use and production; the information artifacts used and produced; and the possible effects of a Web-based digital library (DL) on planning practices. More generally, our goal is to understand distributed, collaborative cognitive work, the role of information and information practices and artifacts, and the social context, uses, and nature of DLs. The work described in this paper is a part of our on-going research on knowledge work and DLs.

METHOD

The focus of the research reported here is the work of a group of people engaged in environmental planning in California, particularly water and watershed planning. Our participants included professionals employed by state, local, and federal agencies, representatives of environmental organizations and industry, concerned residents, and landowners. This analysis is based, in particular, on discussions with (1) people engaged in two interagency (state, federal, and local) programs for sharing data sets; (2) state employees whose responsibilities included collecting, analyzing, and distributing data about various aspects of the environment; and (3) a group of local stakeholders, including local agency employees, landowners, residents, and representatives of environmental organizations engaged in planning for a specific, contentious watershed.

We conducted approximately 65 interviews, primarily in people's own workplaces, observed meetings, and examined reports and other information artifacts used and produced by our participants. Although we had also hoped to observe people going about their work, this was feasible only to a very limited extent. First, while some respondents' work consists primarily of collecting and analyzing data, for many others generally only a small part of their work consists of visibly using or producing this kind of data. Furthermore, we found that many aspects of their work were politically sensitive. We were asked not to videotape public meetings, for example, because our informants feared that the presence of a video camera, however thoroughly we explained our purpose, would affect the already-contentious debate.

In this paper we only discuss the part of the study that had to do with sharing data sets. We did not begin by targeting this as an important concern for DLs. Rather, as we talked with people engaged in environmental planning about their work, their information production and use, and the possible uses of DLs, respondents immediately targeted data sets as an area of great concern where a DL could be useful.

ENVIRONMENTAL PLANNING

Environmental planning is often done by professionals employed by government agencies. It is frequently a collaborative, multi-disciplinary activity undertaken by people trained in scientific and technical disciplines (e.g. engineering, biology) and in planning, a social science-based discipline. In California, environmental planning often also involves community-based groups representing the major stakeholders, including, in addition to government agencies, resource-based industries such as agriculture and timber, other environmentally-based industries such as recreation, residents, landowners, and non-governmental environmental groups. The goal is for a wide range of stakeholder groups to come to a limited shared understanding of the current state of their geographical area, the threats to it, and the likely outcomes of various future actions, and to reach a loose and perhaps shifting agreement on actions to be taken by the various parties.

The work that we have studied generally does not consist of a single project with a fixed group of participants and a defined beginning, end, and product. Instead, we find a dynamic, on-going, overlapping array of programs and projects, with participants recombining in various subsets, coming and going as the issues and personnel change. Planning issues and projects cross multiple levels, for example, state, regional, and local planning efforts interact in various ways. The process is often crisis-driven: such events as winter floods or a proposed listing of a fish species as endangered will mobilize action.

It is also explicitly, overtly political. Water is extremely important in California. Its availability, cost, and quality has enormous implications for land use and development, agriculture, industry, recreation, and for the citizens, who need a reliable source of water, as well as for ecological systems and environmental quality. Generally, data collection and analysis is instigated by some proposed change in policy, land development, possible endangered species listing, or the like. As one respondent said: "Remember, the policymakers pay the bills."

The stakeholder groups have diverse and often-competing interests. Relations among the various actors may be delicate, strained, and litigious. The political and economic stakes are high. As are the environmental stakes: many of these decisions have serious long-term environmental consequences that would be difficult or impossible to reverse.

The result of planning is often not a blueprint but a shared understanding. Participants often do not need to -- and generally will not -- come to an all-embracing agreement, only to a negotiated shared understanding, "cooperation without consensus" [18]. In the watershed that we studied, for example, most of the land is privately-held. The likely actions are not so much regulatory as voluntary. The state of the watershed is a function of people's day-in and day-out practices; a major goal of environmental planning is to ensure that participants engage in practices consonant with the health of the watershed. The shared understanding becomes invisibly embedded in people's interpretations and practices [7].

INFORMATION IN ENVIRONMENTAL PLANNING

Environmental planning is collaborative, not just in the planning process itself, but in the creation and use of information. Environmental planning is characterized by uncertainty and disagreement. The usual first step in watershed planning, for example, is to infer from limited evidence the current state of the watershed, its problems, threats, and trends. Possible causes and solutions are considered and disputed.

A wealth of information and information artifacts are used and created: data sets, reports, maps, tables, memos, newsletters, and so on. Information is used, not just for making decisions, but for defending points of view and persuading and educating others. Information is highly political. As one respondent said, "Activists from every end of the spectrum will access the information, twist it, and use it for their own purposes -- that's a given." It is an ally, in Latour's terms [10,11]. It serves interests. It is contested. Different groups use and privilege different information and uses of it: engineers, for example, are somewhat contemptuous of the "soft" data of biologists, and both are suspicious of the social science approaches of professional planners.

MEASUREMENT DATA

In this paper, we focus on one kind of information that is used heavily in environmental planning: measurement data. Much of what we learned applies to other kinds of information, as well, but we will concentrate primarily on this kind of information, how it is used, the concerns expressed by our respondents, and the implications for collaborative work.

Examples include indicators of water quality, population samples of fish species, the distribution of plant species, and reports on water supply. These data are used to describe past and present, to uncover trends, to test hypotheses of causality, and to forecast the future.

Data are collected using measurement devices and/or human observers, often at the same locations over a period of time, with a fixed or variable frequency. Some are on-going, decades-long time series; some are collected once or for a short time for a specific project.

Data collection is often expensive and time-consuming. It requires skill. The data go through a complex chain of transformation and representation from raw data to summarization, analysis, and interpretation, creating a cascade of representations [10].

Data are collected at varying levels of granularity, ranging from satellite photos to a person walking the ground and mapping each individual plant representing an endangered species. The level of granularity often correlates with the organizational level: the federal government may be the source of satellite photos, local residents may walk an area and map individual elements. This means that cooperation across levels is necessary.

A current concern may result in people going back through old data sets looking for evidence, e.g., if a fish species seems to be declining, historical data on its population and on possible correlating factors may suddenly become useful. Long time series and data on multiple variables for the same site and/or period of time are particularly useful for tracking trends and assessing causal links. A major concern among many of our participants was tracking down unpublished data from a variety of sources. A recurring assumption was that a wealth of potentially-useful data was buried in file cabinets around the state.

Analysts may combine data from a variety of sources, often collected by different observers at different times using different methods and definitions. Combining data from multiple sources is difficult, requiring an understanding of the similarities and differences among multiple sources and how to appropriately combine them.

SHARING DATA

Until recently, data were collected and published primarily by government organizations and large non-profits. The unanalyzed data were available to only a few people, usually only directly from the owner of the data. Most users had to be satisfied with published summaries, analyses, and graphical representations.

For many users, that suffices. The volume of data available (collected as often as every 15 minutes) and the time and expertise required to deal with it is beyond most users. When people do want access to the underlying data, however, often it is because of litigation or strong contentiousness, such as a highly-contested decision. Without access to the underlying data set, users' abilities to re-interpret or re-use the data or challenge analyses are limited.

In the past, much data collected by nongovernmental (and some governmental) organizations were simply not available. Other data were available only by means of personal contact. This contact allowed the data supplier to advise the user about the nature of the data, conditions under which it was collected, and so on. And it allowed the user to query the provider and get insight into the data. Our respondents, who were mostly "insiders" to the water planning community, generally found this satisfactory. They described the community as "tight" and "close-knit" and had few problems getting the data they needed, once they had discovered its existence, which was often a problem. The difficulty is the time and labor required of both supplier and user.

Other respondents, however, outside the state government, often reported suspicion and distrust of the state (and federal) agencies, the power that this system gives them, and their data, analyses, and forecasts. Some felt that political appointments, funding, and policy objectives inevitably biased the data and analyses.[1] They pointed out the many decisions, assumptions, and judgment calls that go into any such enterprise. One person, for example, said of the state water agency:

> For example, their estimates of water reclamation levels and urban conservation capabilities are exceedingly low and in direct contrast with reclamation firms and conservation groups. This is because [the agency] wants to build the peripheral canal[2], and they can't justify it with high reclamation and conservation levels.

Such critics want the agencies' data and analyses open for criticism and re-analysis, and they want other groups' data and analyses more widely available.

Others argued for the valuable contribution to be made by local and other groups, collecting new data, running different analyses, and bringing fresh viewpoints. And, finally, others simply said, "The taxpayers pay for that data, it belongs to the public. The public should have access to it."

MAKING DATA AVAILABLE ON THE WEB

Computing and telecommunications are changing the means by which data are distributed. In California, a variety of efforts are underway to identify and share environmental data sets. File transfer protocols have been used to share data among agencies. More recently some groups are experimenting with using the Web to distribute data to all comers. When we began talking with people in the environmental planning community about our Digital Library, they raised the issue of using our DL as a means of distributing and analyzing data. Some were enthusiastic, others much less so.

The enthusiasts included those who saw this as a means of gaining wide distribution for their own work. Of the concerns raised, in this discussion we will focus on what many respondents loosely called "quality control." These

---

[1] We should note that respondents differed considerably as to which agencies they trusted and distrusted.

[2] A highly-controversial proposal that has been publicly debated periodically for at least 20 years.

concerns were of two sorts: misuse of data, and the distribution of poor quality data.

Misuse of Data

Many professionals were concerned that making unanalyzed data – data early in the process of transformation and representation -- accessible via our Web-based DL could result in inappropriate use of the data or incorrect interpretations, with potentially-serious consequences. (One agency respondent spoke of "having our data used against us.") For example, one source of data on fish populations is boat trips that net fish and measure their catch. The time of year and day, the stage in a species' spawning cycle, weather conditions, type of net, the depth at which the net is trolled, and many other factors affect the catch. A comparison with "last year at this time" and conclusions about trends in the fish population that did not account for these factors could be seriously misleading.

"Bad" Data

Another major concern was the ease with which data collected by untrained individuals using inappropriate protocols or differing definitions of data elements and methods could be promulgated. Professionals worried about untrained users' inability to evaluate such information or the source.

PRACTICES OF TRUST

To better understand these concerns, we looked to several socially-organized practices that, in the past, helped environmental planners to collaborate. We have found several concepts that are current in the literature on CSCW and Science and Technology Studies useful in understanding the issues around Web-based access to environmental data sets: communities of practice, boundary objects, and assemblages. Together they give us a way to talk about the concerns of the professional environmental planning community around the increased openness of the Web.

Scientific Practices

Scientific practices are aimed at ensuring objectivity, the "view from nowhere" that establishes a fact as a fact, at closing the black box on how a statement became a fact [9, 12, 15]. These are practices of what counts as evidence, logic, and proof, who speaks, and whose judgment counts. Whether or not we believe that the view from nowhere is possible [6] is irrelevant for our discussion here; scientific practices are designed to translate local knowledge into global, personal into universal [25].

The Publishing System and Libraries

Another contributor to the coordination of the work of people who are distant in space and time is what Chartier calls the "order of the book" [2, 14] -- which includes the publishing system and libraries. It makes accessible the work of people who may be unknown to one another in a form that is transportable and reliable -- Latour's "immutable mobiles." [10]. Publication and libraries act as a multi-stage system of filtering and reduction: creating inscriptions, then determining which will be made available and preserved. Each step is an exercise of cognitive authority, in which someone decides what is worth sharing and preserving, and makes linkages among data, documents, authors, and ideas.

Communities of Practice

A community of practice is a group (e.g., work group, profession, or discipline) that shares practices, understandings, technology, artifacts, and language [13]. Communities of practice are where professionals learn the methods, attitudes, values, and interpretations of their community. What is learned is not simply a body of knowledge but a mode of action, an ability to improvise appropriately. People learn not only how to practice their profession but also how to be a professional and how to understand the world. Communities of practice are about, among other things, what is known, what counts as evidence, and who speaks; and how it is decided what is known, what counts, and who speaks. "A community of practice is an intrinsic condition for the existence of knowledge, not least because it provides the interpretive support necessary for making sense of its heritage" [13, p. 98].

Lave and Wenger's [13] model is apprenticeship. The apprentice learns, not only from the master, but by doing, watching, listening, and from other members of the community, including other apprentices. The master too learns continually in this process. And not just the apprentices and the masters but also the skills and knowledge are changed in this process.

The boundaries of communities of practice are permeable. A person typically belongs to several: a botanist who works for the State doing research on a particular species in a particular geographical area may belong, with varying degrees of centrality, to several intersecting communities of practice – botanists, people working for that agency, researchers in that geographical area, to name a few. The interaction among communities of practice as they recombine around problem areas to create emergent, fluid new communities is part of the tension between change and stability.

Communities of practice are sources of credibility. One way that users judge whether work is to be trusted is to look at its source: is he or she a part of our community of practice? Can he or she be trusted to have used accepted methods to collect, analyze, and interpret the data? Do we speak the same language? Do they see the world the same way that we do?

Boundary Objects

Collaboration takes place in environmental planning both within and across groups. Environmental planning is not unique in needing to reconcile multiple viewpoints and create solutions that are coherent across groups without necessarily reaching complete consensus. Star suggests that one tool used by scientists (and, we would argue, other knowledge communities) is what she calls "boundary objects" [19, 20]. Boundary objects are shared by multiple communities. They are both plastic enough to adapt to local needs and have different specific identities in different communities, and robust enough to maintain a common identity across sites, and thus to be a locus of shared work.

Star identifies a non-exhaustive list of four types of boundary objects, which are helpful in fleshing out the meaning of the term:

- Repositories, which are "ordered piles of objects indexed in standardized fashion" [19, p. 48]. They are modular (that is, users can lop off subsets), and the units of analysis are heterogeneous. Examples include libraries and museums.
- The ideal type or platonic object, which, being abstracted from all domains, doesn't describe any one of them in detail but whose vagueness allows it to cross domains. Her example is early atlases of the brain, which in fact described no specific brain but communicated across the research and clinical worlds.
- Terrain with coincident boundaries and different internal contents; e.g., the state of California was a boundary object for the people who collected specimens, funded, managed, and did ecological research using the Museum of Vertebrate Zoology [20]. All the participants were in natural science within the boundaries of California.
- Forms and labels, such as standardized forms filled out in one site and passed on to another for further work.

Assemblages

Another approach to the question of how local knowledge gets "rendered equivalent, general, and cohesive" in science and in other knowledge systems is that of Watson-Verran and Turnbull [25]. They define an assemblage as "the amalgam of places, bodies, voices, skills, practices, technical devices, theories, social strategies, and collective work that together constitute technoscientific knowledge/practices." They say that no other term – including boundary objects – quite gets at the entirety of what is referred to. They find the term useful in that it connotes:

> ...the ad hoc contingency of a collage in its capacity to embrace a wide variety of incompatible components. It also has the virtue of connoting active and evolving practices rather than a passive and static structure. It implies a constructed robustness without a fully interpreted and agreed-upon theoretical framework.... Assemblages constitute connections and contrive equivalencies between locales in knowledge systems....Here the relations of power and knowledge are understood as invested in the material, social, and literary practices of discourse and representation, discipline and resistance. [25, p. 117].

Their examples of assemblages include those of Gothic cathedral builders (who designed and built large, complex, innovative structures without architects or plans over hundreds of years), the Incas (who coordinated the work of and fed 5 million people in an arid environment without reading and writing), and the knowledge system of Pacific navigators that was likewise embedded in an oral culture. All are presented as examples of the melding of quite heterogeneous and disparate practices to form stable "assemblages that connect"..."disciplining life at the local level in constituting a knowledge system." [25 p. 126]. In other words, assemblages are collages of disparate elements that coordinate local actions in such a way that the local knowledge becomes global.

SHARING DATA SETS

Now let us reconsider environmental planning and our respondents' concerns about sharing of data sets via the Web. Environmental planning is distributed knowledge work engaged in by people from multiple communities of practice, separately and together. We see a major goal of a planning project or group as creating a new (limited and temporary) community of practice among the people concerned with a particular geographical area and/or issue; in their interdisciplinarity, crossing the boundaries of existing communities of practice. The group, in working together and making collective sense of the evidence about their area and issue, forges a shared set of practices and understandings about who they are, what they are doing, and about their area of common concern; and about what evidence they will use and how they interpret it. Part of the tension in environmental planning is the conflict among communities of practice – people with not only different disciplinary bases and ways of working (e.g., engineers and biologists) but with different priorities and ways of seeing the world (e.g., local residents and state agency representatives).

To share data sets is to grant them the status of boundary objects: to determine that they are sufficiently robust to be used across sites, and malleable enough to be adapted to local needs. It is to understand them enough to know when and how to use them.

We then need to consider how our respondents determine the trustability of a data set. A fundamental requirement is for those whose work it represents to have followed the appropriate scientific practices. However, this is not sufficient. Choices are continually made in what data to collect, represent, and analyze, and how, and in interpretation. Choices introduce bias. These biases range from professional (engineers see the world differently than biologists) to economic (timber harvesters have different interests from environmentalists) to political (local agencies and organizations have different priorities than the state).

Similarly, the publishing system, a source of trust in other scientific work, is only minimally useful here. Most of the data at issue comes from agency reports, technical reports, and other sources outside of the controls of the publishing system. Instead, trustability has to be assessed and continually re-assessed by the user. It is rooted in the community of practice and the assemblage of environmental planning.

Our respondents rely on knowing the organization's reputation, knowing the individual, personally or by reputation, and making personal contact. They repeatedly emphasized the "close-knit" nature of the community. When professionals expressed concern about the work of non-professionals, they didn't know that the non-professionals failed to follow accepted protocols, but they couldn't be sure that they did. Their uncertainty extended beyond the methods of data collection to the whole assemblage of the collection, use, manipulation, representation, and interpretation of environmental data.

This kind of work is not simply a matter of following instructions: Goodwin [5] for example, shows how archaeology students on a dig are taught to see what an archaeologist sees in the dirt. The seeing is learned through situated practices in relevant settings. To say that the data need to be understood in context, while true, understates the complexity, richness, and dynamism of the assemblage.

People define and master assemblages, and assemblages continually evolve, in communities of practice. Our respondents relied heavily on both organizational and personal reputations in determining what data -- what sources -- to trust. Personal and organizational reputation was the marker, in a way, for membership in a community of practice and mastery of an assemblage.

Now we can look again at the concerns expressed about provision of poor quality data, and inappropriate use of data by means of a Web-based Digital Library. It is our contention that the concerns that we heard expressed anxiety about the increased permeability of the boundaries of communities of practice, the dissociation of data sets from the assemblages within which they are created and are intended to be used, and therefore the questioning of their status as boundary objects.

In other words, making data available to and accepting it from a wide, possibly unknown and unknowable, group via the Web may violate, or at least bring into question, the practices aimed at ensuring the credibility of the data sets as boundary objects. Opening up the shared information space has broken (or threatened to break) the way in which the practice of environmental planning was framed and the participants in the construction of the shared information space vetted.

IMPLICATIONS

The sharing of information is critical to cooperative work and to the construction of knowledge and understanding, which is ultimately a social, not individual, task. Changes in information technology substantially impact people's information and work practices. The Web is being used increasingly for CSCW applications. "Knowledge management," which entails, among other things, using technology to make an organization's distributed knowledge resources available within an organization and to its clients and collaborators, is currently a major concern in organizations [3]. Massive efforts are devoted to digital libraries [e.g., 24]. The National Science Foundation has a major initiative on Knowledge and Distributed Intelligence [9]. These are just a few examples of the ways in which technology is being used to make information more available to a wide range of people.

The design of technology to support the sharing of knowledge needs to be based on an understanding of the existing social practices by which communities decide what they know, how they know, and who they believe. Important among these are practices of trust and credibility, which may be threatened by unthinking technological design. We found communities of practice, assemblages, and boundary objects helpful in understanding these practices. Communities of practice are where practices and interpretations are learned and developed, where knowledge is constructed, and trust and credibility defined. Assemblages are the fluid, ad hoc collages of people, practices, artifacts, rules, strategies, and so forth by which communities do their work. Boundary objects coordinate and carry work within and across communities of practice.

CSCW and digital library applications that are open to unregulated, possibly unidentified and unidentifiable, users and even contributors may open the social and technical boundaries of communities of practice, dissociate work from its assemblages, and undermine socially-organized practices. They may cast doubt upon the trustability of boundary objects. We suspect that problems of trust and credibility are potentially major factors in the non-use of CSCW applications and digital libraries.

Schmidt and Bannon [18] make three recommendations for creating shared information spaces for cooperative work involving a large and indefinite number of people, from different perspectives, over a protracted period of time. They recommend identifying the originator of information as a means of assessing its validity; identifying its context of production and use; and identifying the politics of data. Data, they say, "are not innocent and neutral. Our environmental planners would heartily agree. But how do we do this?

Much as we would like to offer global solutions, we believe that ultimately there are none. Instead, we recommend increased understanding of current social practices of credibility and trust. We further suggest a highly participatory role for the user community.

One place to look for a better understanding of the social processes of knowing is science studies -- and not just for environmental planning. Science is in many ways the exemplar of rationality in our society, and many in STS are critically examining our assumptions about how science works. One key element is that there is no single, indisputable truth to be "discovered." Rather, it is important for a shared information space to have available a range of evidence and interpretations. Users need to be able to examine, use, refute, and build upon the available evidence. Data needs to be linked with analytical tools that will help users make their own sense. And a range of voices needs to be represented. In our DL, for example, we provide a range of GIS capabilities for users to graphically represent and link geographical data sets in a variety of ways.

In the design of specific applications, local concerns and practices of trust and credibility should be investigated in order to better support, or at least not undermine, current practices. These practices vary. In environmental planning, for example, we found a practice of deliberately fudging geography so as to be vague about such things as locations of endangered species - not only to protect the individual specimens, but to gain the cooperation of landowners by avoiding finger-pointing, described as "protecting their privacy."

The community of practice is a key element. Our respondents evaluate information using their knowledge of its source, which indicates (to the insider) the other's practices and perspective. We could never provide enough or the most appropriate contextual information to satisfy all users (and suppliers). The identity of the source and linkages to its other work, however, is critical information.

Our findings reinforce the need for participatory design in content as well as functionality and interface. The librarians' and computer scientists' definitions of themselves as experts on information divorced from ideology and institutions, from users, uses, and interpretations, is not sustainable [1]. While collecting documents to support watershed planning in one contentious geographical area, for example, we worked with a committee representing a variety of local groups. They designated one trusted person to act as clearinghouse for documents to be scanned into the digital library. This was much better than having the DL staff, outsiders to the process and the participants, make those decisions.[3] In other areas, we found highly collegial, interagency groups of mid-level governmental agency staff hammering out solutions to the complex problems of data sharing across agencies, platforms, disciplines, and ecological regions. What they needed from us was technical expertise and resources. What they could provide us was unmatched expertise in the content and uses of their databases.

Finally, we may not always want to make information widely available -- just because we can, that doesn't mean we should. Given the sensitivity of some kinds of data, password-protected web pages and other means of providing users with ways to safeguard their data are needed.

ACKNOWLEDGEMENTS

This work was supported in part by the NSF/NASA/ARPA Digital Library Initiative under contract # IRI-9411334, Robert Wilensky, Principal Investigator.

REFERENCES

1. Agre, Philip E. Institutional circuitry: Thinking about the forms and uses of information. *Information Technology and Libraries 14*, 4 (Dec 1995), 225-230.
2. Chartier, R. *The order of books: readers, authors, and libraries in Europe between the fourteenth and eighteenth centuries.* Trans. by L. Cochrane. Stanford University Press, 1994.
3. Cole, R. (ed.). Special Issue on Knowledge and the Firm. *California Management Review 40* (1998), (entire issue).
4. Crow, D., Parsowith, S., and Wise, G. The Evolution of CSCW: Past, Present, and Future Developments. *SIGCHI Bulletin 29,* 2 (1997), 20-26.
5. Goodwin, C. Professional Vision. *American Anthropologist 96,* 3 (1994), 606-633.
6. Haraway, D. J. *Modest_Witness@Second_Millenium. ©FemaleMan_Meets_Oncomouse™: Feminism and Technoscience.* Routledge, NY, 1997, 23-39.
7. Innes, J. Introduction to the Transaction Edition: Understanding the Alliance of Knowledge and Policy, in: *Knowledge and Public Policy: the Search for Meaningful Indications*, 2nd expanded edition, Transaction Books, New Brunswick, NJ, 1990.
8. Jasanoff, S., et al, (eds.). *Handbook of Science and Technology Studies,* Sage, 1995, 115-139.
9. Knowledge and Distributed Intelligence. Available at http://www.nsf.gov/pubs/1998/nsf9855/nsf9855.htm .
10. Latour, B. *Science in Action.* Harvard University Press, Cambridge, MA, 1987.

[3] This group did not make all the decisions about the DL's content. Rather, they represented the community engaged in watershed planning in that area. For other parts of the DL, we worked with other groups.

11. Latour, B. Visualization and Cognition: Thinking with Eyes and Hands, in *Knowledge and Society: Studies in Sociology of Culture Past and Present*, 6, (1986) 1-40.

12. Latour, B. and Woolgar, S. *Laboratory Life: the Construction of Scientific Facts*. Princeton University Press, Princeton, NJ, 1991.

13. Lave, J. and Wenger, J. *Situated Learning: Legitimate Peripheral Participation,* Cambridge University Press, Cambridge, England, 1991.

14. Levy, D.M. Cataloguing in the Digital Order in *Proceedings of Digital Libraries '95* (Austin TX) Hypermedia Research Laboratory, Texas A&M University, 1995.

15. Potter, T. Information, power, and the view from nowhere, in Bud-Frierman, L. (ed.), *Information Acumen: The Understanding And Use Of Knowledge In Modern Business,* Routledge, London and NY, 1994, 217-230.

16. Ruhleder, K. and King, J. Computer Support for Work Across Space, Time, and Social Worlds. *Journal of Organizational Computing* 1 (1991) 341-355.

17. Schiff, L., Van House, N. and Butler, M. Understanding Complex Information Environments: a Social Analysis of Watershed Planning. *Digital Libraries '97: Proceedings of the ACM Digital Libraries Conference*, (Philadelphia, PA, July 23-26, 1997), ACM Press, 161-186.

18. Schmidt, K. and Bannon, L. Taking CSCW Seriously: Supporting Articulation Work. *Computer Supported Cooperative Work, 1*, 1992, 7-40.

19. Star, S. L. The Structure of Ill-Structured Solutions: Boundary Objects and Heterogeneous Distributed Problem Solving, in Gasser, L. and Huhns, M., etc. *Distributed Artificial Intelligence 2*, Pitman Publishing, 1989, 37-54.

20. Star, S. L. and Griesemer, J. Institutional ecology, translations, and boundary objects: amateurs and professionals in Berkeley's Museum of Vertebrate Zoology, 1907-39, *Social Studies of Science, 1,* 1989, 387-420.

21. Star, S. L. (ed.). *Ecologies of Knowledge: World and Politics in Science and Technology.* State University of NY Press, 1995.

22. Star, S. L. (ed.). Introduction to *Ecologies of Knowledge: World and Politics in Science and Technology,* State University of NY Press, 1995, 1-35.

23. Suchman, L. Centers of Coordination: A Case And Some Themes, to be published in Resnick, L., (ed.) *Discourse, Tools and Reasoning*, forthcoming.

24. Third ACM Conference on Digital Libraries, (Marriott City Center, Pittsburgh, PA, June 24-27, 1998). Available at http://www.ks.com/d198/ .

25. Watson-Verran, H. and Turnbull, D. Science and Other Indigenous Knowledge Systems, in Jasanoff, S. et al, (eds.), *Handbook of Science and Technology Studies*, Sage, 1995, 115-139.

Using Filtering Agents to Improve Prediction Quality in the GroupLens Research Collaborative Filtering System

Badrul M. Sarwar*, Joseph A. Konstan*†, Al Borchers*, Jon Herlocker*, Brad Miller†, and John Riedl*†

*GroupLens Research Project
Dept. of Computer Science and Engineering
University of Minnesota
Minneapolis, MN 55455

†Net Perceptions, Inc
11200 West 78th Street
Suite 300
Minneapolis, MN 55344-3814

{sarwar,konstan,borchers,herlocker,riedl}@cs.umn.edu; bmiller@netperceptions.com

ABSTRACT

Collaborative filtering systems help address information overload by using the opinions of users in a community to make personal recommendations for documents to each user. Many collaborative filtering systems have few user opinions relative to the large number of documents available. This sparsity problem can reduce the utility of the filtering system by reducing the number of documents for which the system can make recommendations and adversely affecting the quality of recommendations.

This paper defines and implements a model for integrating content-based ratings into a collaborative filtering system. The filterbot model allows collaborative filtering systems to address sparsity by tapping the strength of content filtering techniques. We identify and evaluate metrics for assessing the effectiveness of filterbots specifically, and filtering system enhancements in general. Finally, we experimentally validate the filterbot approach by showing that even simple filterbots such as spell checking can increase the utility for users of sparsely populated collaborative filtering systems.

Keywords

Collaborative filtering, information filtering, content analysis, recommendation systems, social filtering, GroupLens Research, information filtering agents.

INTRODUCTION

Each day, more books, research papers, television programs, Internet discussion postings, and web pages are published than any individual human can hope to review, let alone read and understand. To cope with information overload, we try different approaches to separate the interesting and valuable information from the rest.

Historically, this process was placed in the hands of editors and publishers—people given the responsibility for reviewing many documents and selecting the ones worthy of publication. Even today, we rely heavily on newspaper editors, moderators of discussion lists, journal editors and review boards. We also often read the opinions of movie, restaurant, and television critics to decide how to spend our finite time and money.

Professional human reviewers do not solve all problems, however. Often, individuals' information needs and tastes differ enough to make a small number of editors ineffective. Also, the number of documents in the web, in research libraries, and in archives of discussions has grown so large as to defy systematic editing by individual editors. Accordingly, researchers have developed a wide range of systems that bring the power of computation to the problem of selecting, for each individual, the information he or she considers valuable from the enormous amount of available information.

Information retrieval (IR) systems allow users to express queries to select documents that match a topic of interest. IR systems may index a database of documents using the full text of the document or only document abstracts. Sophisticated systems rank query results using a variety of heuristics including the relative frequency with which the query terms occur in each document, the adjacency of query terms, and the position of query terms. IR systems also may employ techniques such as term stemming to match words such as "retrieve," "retrieval," and "retrieving." [15] IR systems are generally optimized for ephemeral interest queries, such as looking up a topic in the library. [3] In the Internet domain, popular IR systems include AltaVista (www.altavista.digital.com) for web pages and DejaNews (www.dejanews.com) for discussion list postings.

Information filtering (IF) systems use many of the same techniques as IR systems, but are optimized for long-term information needs from a stream of incoming documents. Accordingly, IF systems build user profiles to describe the documents that should (or should not) be presented to users. Simple examples of IF systems include "kill files" that are used to filter out advertising or flames (i.e., attack messages) and e-mail filtering software that sorts e-mail into priority categories based on the sender, the subject, and whether the message is personal or sent to a list. More complex IF systems provide periodic personalized digests of material from sources such as news wires, discussion lists, and web pages [3]

One embodiment of IF techniques is software *agents*. These programs exhibit a degree of autonomous behavior, and attempt to act intelligently on behalf of the user for whom they are working. Agents maintain user interest profiles by updating them based on feedback on whether the user likes the items selected by the current profile. Research has been conducted in various feedback generation techniques, including probabilistic models, genetic algorithms and neural network based learning algorithms [2]. *NewT* is a filtering agent for Usenet news based on genetic algorithm learning techniques [8]. It performs full text analysis of articles using vector-space technique. *Amalthaea* is a multi-agent system for personalized filtering, discovery and monitoring of information sources in the *World Wide Web* domain [11].

IR and IF systems can be extremely effective at identifying documents that match a topic of interest, and at finding documents that match particular patterns (e.g., discarding e-mail with the phrase "Make Money Fast" in the title). Unlike human editors, however, these systems cannot distinguish between high-quality and low-quality documents on the same topic. As the number of documents on each topic continues to grow, even the set of relevant documents will become too large to review (e.g., who has time to read every technical report with CSCW in the keyword list?). For some domains, therefore, the most effective filters must incorporate human judgements of quality.

Collaborative filtering (CF) systems recommend documents to a user based on the opinions of other users. In their purest form, CF systems do not consider the content of the documents at all, relying exclusively on the judgement of humans as to whether the document is valuable. In this way, collaborative filtering attempts to recapture the cross-topic recommendations that are common in communities of people.

Tapestry [4], one of the first computer-based collaborative filtering systems, was designed to support a small, close-knit community of users. Users could filter all incoming information streams, including e-mail and Usenet news articles. When users evaluated a document, they could annotate it with text, with numeric ratings, and with boolean ratings. Other users could form queries such as "show me the documents that Mary annotated with 'excellent' and Jack annotated with 'Sam should read.'" A similar approach is used in Maltz and Ehrlich's *active collaborative filtering* [9], which provides an easy way for users to direct recommendations to their friends and colleagues through a *Lotus Notes* database.

Collaborative filtering for large communities cannot depend on each person knowing the others. Several systems use statistical techniques to provide personal recommendations of documents by finding a group of other users, known as *neighbors*, that have a history of agreeing with the target user. Once a neighborhood of users is found, particular documents can be evaluated by forming a weighted composite of the neighbors' opinions of that document. Similarly, a user can request recommendations for a set of documents to read and the system can return a set of documents that is popular within the neighborhood. These statistical approaches, known as *automated collaborative filtering*, typically rely upon *ratings* as numerical expressions of user preference.

Several ratings-based automated collaborative filtering systems have been developed. The GroupLens Research[1] system [6,13] provides an pseudonymous collaborative filtering solution for Usenet news and movies. *Ringo* [16] *and Video Recommender* [5] are email and web systems that generate recommendations on music and movies respectively, suggesting collaborative filtering to be applicable to many different types of media. Indeed, commercial applications of ratings-based collaborative filtering now exist in a variety of domains including books, music, grocery products, dry goods, and information.

While collaborative filtering has been a substantial success, there are several problems that researchers and commercial applications have identified:

The early-rater problem. A collaborative filtering system provides little or no value when a user is the first one in his neighborhood to enter a rating for an item. Current collaborative filtering systems depend on the altruism of a set of users who are willing to rate many items without receiving many recommendations. Economists have speculated that even if rating required no effort at all, many users would choose to delay considering items to wait for their neighbors to provide them with recommendations [1]. Without altruists, it might be necessary to institute payment mechanisms to encourage early ratings.

The sparsity problem. The goal of collaborative filtering systems is to help people focus on reading documents (or consuming items) of interest. In high-quantity, low-quality environments, such as Usenet news, users may cover only a tiny percentage of documents available (Usenet studies have shown a rating rate of about 1% in some areas; we can

[1] GroupLens™ is a trademark of Net Perceptions, Inc., which holds exclusive rights to commercialize the results of the GroupLens Research project. Net Perceptions allows the University of Minnesota to use the name GroupLens Research to avoid name discontinuity in the project.

estimate that few people will have read and formed an opinion on even 1/10 of 1% of the over two million books available through the largest bookstores). On the one hand, this sparsity is the motivation behind filtering: most people do not want to read most available information. On the other hand sparsity poses a computational challenge as it becomes harder to find neighbors and harder to recommend documents since few people have rated most of them.

Efforts have been made to overcome these problems in collaborative filtering system:

- **partitioning**. The GroupLens Research project showed that partitioning the ratings database by Usenet newsgroup resulted in somewhat higher accuracy and density, since not all users subscribed to all newsgroups. Even with partitioning, however, sparsity was still a problem.
- **dimensionality reduction**. Several researchers have been examining statistical techniques for compressing the dimensionality of the database. These techniques, which include general clustering, singular value decomposition, factor analysis, and others appear promising, but none has yet been demonstrated to solve the sparsity problem.
- **implicit ratings**. Several systems attempt to increase the number of ratings entered by observing user behavior. The GroupLens Research system determined that time spent reading a Usenet news article was an effective rating measure [10]. PHOAKS found that URLs mentioned in Usenet postings could be filtered to detect recommendations [17]. Other systems have examined user history or watch user behavior[14,12]. At the extreme, the MovieLens system was able to reduce start-up sparsity somewhat by incorporating several million pre-existing ratings.

We should point out that content-based approaches used in IF and agent systems are less directly affected by these problems because they use content analysis techniques that apply across all documents. For example, a filter that gives high scores to articles with the word "baseball" in them, can give a score to a new article before anyone has rated it. To exploit the advantages of content analysis, Fab implements a hybrid content-based collaborative system for recommending Web pages [2]. In Fab user profiles are maintained by using content analysis. The profiles are directly compared to determine similarity between users to support collaborative recommendation.

In this paper, we investigate another hybrid approach to addressing the rating sparsity and early rater problems. This approach incorporates semi-intelligent filtering agents called filterbots into a ratings-based collaborative filtering system.

RESEARCH APPROACH: THE FILTERBOT CONCEPT

Our approach to addressing the ratings sparsity and early rater problems is to incorporate non-collaborative information filtering techniques into a collaborative filtering system. We introduce these techniques through the creation of *filterbots*—automated rating robots that evaluate new documents as soon as they are published and enter ratings for those documents. We chose this model because we found that it is appealingly simple from both the collaborating filtering system's and the filterbot author's point of view.

The **collaborative filtering system** treats a filterbot as another ordinary user, albeit a prolific and generous one that enters many ratings but doesn't request predictions. The collaborative filtering engine need not even know whether users are filterbots or humans.

The **filterbot author** writes a filterbot just like an information filtering agent. This agent is called whenever new documents arrive, and it returns a numeric rating (1 through 5 in our system). The filterbot author need not be concerned with the use of the filterbot in a collaborative filtering system.

There are other approaches to merging content filtering with collaborative filtering, including the "communicating agents" model proposed by Maes [8] and the correlating profiles model in Fab [2]. We found the filterbot model more appealing than alternative models of integrating information filtering techniques with collaborative filtering ones because the collaborative filtering engine already includes a filter to personalize the weight assigned to each filterbot. If a user agrees consistently with a filterbot, that filterbot is accorded a high weight for the user. If a user's ratings do not correlate well with a filterbot's, that filterbot is not used in generating recommendations and predictions for that specific user.

An implication of this design is that we can employ a wide range of algorithms in filterbots without concern that an algorithm would have a detrimental effect on individual users. By comparison, a system that employs a filter across all users (e.g., system-level advertisement detection and kill files) indiscriminately filters out content for both those who are annoyed by advertising and those interested in learning about new products.

In this work, we report on a set of filterbots using very simple algorithms such as spelling correctness and article length. By demonstrating the value of the filterbot concept on simple algorithms, we hope to encourage people who have insight into factors related to user preferences in collaborative filtering systems to build their own filterbots. Authors don't need know anything about collaborative filtering; they just need an idea for a strategy to automatically rate items. Write it; throw it in; and watch people benefit!

We also recognize, but have not yet implemented, the potential for incorporating learning agents as filterbots in a collaborative filtering system. The collaborative filtering system might receive ratings from one or several filterbots per user, and the users would benefit from having access to the learned preferences of each agent, again relying upon only those filterbots with whom they have agreed individually over time. Agents researchers can further this process by creating a community of agents under natural selection rules, so agents that are ineffective are eliminated to create resources for variants of effective ones.

The rest of this paper presents our research design for assessing the value of filterbots in a collaborative filtering system, presents the results of the experiment, and discusses the limitations of our work and the implications for other researchers in collaborative filtering and information filtering.

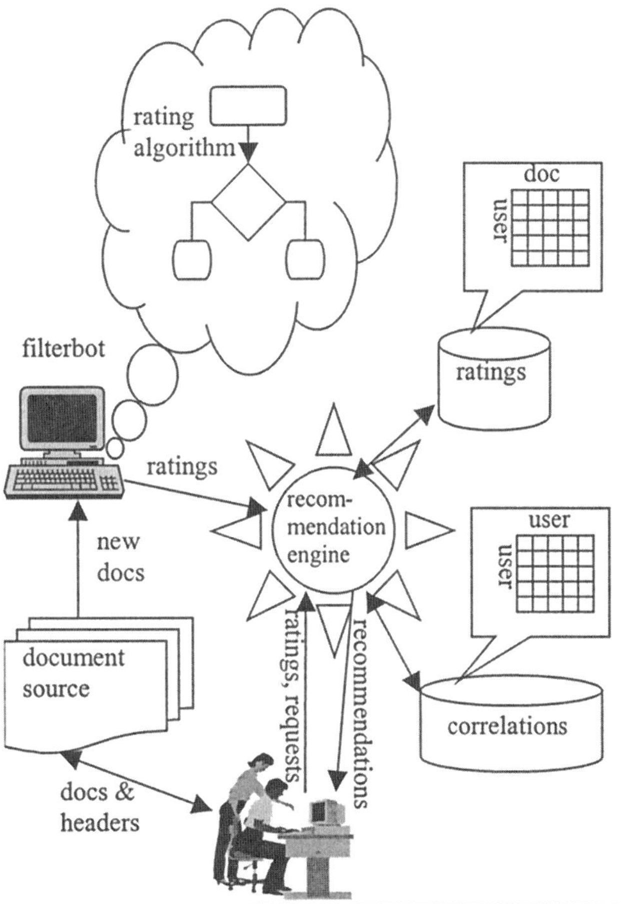

Figure 1. System architecture for a collaborative filtering system with live users and filterbots.

RESEARCH DESIGN

Architecture

The basic idea of collaborative filtering system is to help people collaborate to find items of interest from a large collection of items. In this section, we describe the architectural framework of a collaborative filtering system that can support the incorporation of filterbots. This architecture is based on using the GroupLens Research Recommendation Engine, but a similar architecture would work with any collaborative filtering engine that works using ratings. An overview of this architecture is shown in figure 1.

In general, collaborative filtering systems employ a client-server architecture. CF clients are programs that present the user with an interface for browsing documents. Example clients include news readers and web browsers. These client applications communicate with document servers to retrieve documents for the user (e.g., news servers, web servers, databases). The clients use a well-known document server API to request these items (e.g., NNTP, HTTP). Clients also communicate with a *recommendation engine* server through its API. Calls are provided to enter ratings for particular documents, to request recommendations for documents to request, or to evaluate a set of useful documents.

In the original GroupLens Research trial, the clients were Usenet news readers that had been specially modified to connect to the GroupLens Research server. The readers, which included gnus, xrn, and tin, were adapted to request predicted values from the GroupLens Research server before displaying article subjects to each user. As the user read a newsgroup, she could enter ratings. Those ratings were stored by the reader and sent to the server at the end of the newsgroup.

The GroupLens Research engine stored two sets of data: user ratings of news articles and user-user correlation information. From the correlation table, the recommendation engine can quickly identify the neighborhood of similar users for prediction purposes. A prediction is calculated by returning a weighted average of normalized ratings, as reported in [13].

Filterbots are incorporated into this framework as follows:

- They request (or subscribe to) new items from the document source.
- They apply the rating algorithm to each document that arrives.
- When the algorithm returns a rating, they submit that rating to the recommendation engine.

As we implemented them, the filterbots poll the Usenet news server to request new items. News clients already have mechanisms for detecting which articles are new (a file that stores the range of read items for each newsgroup). The ratings algorithms, which are described below, perform simple content analysis and produce ratings for all articles.

Hypothesis

Because of the ratings sparsity and early rater problems, collaborative filtering systems are often only able to offer users predictions and recommendations for a small subset of the documents available. The filterbot framework provides an augmentation that should improve the value of collaborative filtering systems. By integrating content filtering into collaborative filtering, filterbots should increase the utility of the system for users who agree with the filterbots while not affecting other users. Accordingly, we propose the following hypothesis:

H1: *Adding content-based filterbots into a collaborative filtering system improves utility for human users.*

We should clearly state that we are not evaluating the value of filterbots *without* human ratings, for the simple reason that human ratings are necessary for computing the agreement among the users and between users and filterbots.

Experiment Design

We implemented three different filterbots: SpellCheckerBot, IncludedMsgBot and LengthBot. We conducted our experiments by incorporating these filterbots individually into the GroupLens Research collaborative filtering system. The filterbots fetch and analyze articles from the *Usenet news* server and send the ratings directly to the *GroupLens* recommendation engine using the *GroupLens client library API.* Our filterbots were applied to five different newsgroups selected to be representative of many of the different types of newsgroups on Usenet. The newsgroups are: (1) *rec.humor*, a low-quality high-volume entertainment newsgroup, (2) *rec.food.recipes,* a moderated newsgroup with no discussion, (3) *mn.general,* a local discussion newsgroup, (4) *comp.lang.perl.misc,* a technical discussion group (5) *comp.os.linux.announce,* a technical announcement group.

Next we describe the design of each filterbot.

SpellCheckerBot rates articles based on the proportion of spelling errors present in the article text. It uses the *spell* utility of the *unix* system as its spell-checking engine. *Spell* uses its own dictionary to check the words in a document and dumps the words not found the dictionary as misspelled words. As a result, any correctly spelled word that is not present in *spell*'s dictionary will be taken as a misspelled word. Such words include widely used colloquial expressions, word abbreviations, acronyms, technical terms, proper nouns and so on. Using *spell*'s internal dictionary will incorrectly count these words as spelling errors. The addition of an *auxiliary dictionary* solves this problem. This auxiliary dictionary contains a list of known correct words and is used by *spell* in addition to its own dictionary. Since Usenet newsgroups carry discussions on different topics, an auxiliary dictionary intended for a particular newsgroup will not, in general, be applicable to another newsgroup. For example, the word *gzipped* is added to the auxiliary dictionary for *comp.lang.perl.misc* newsgroup but is not a suitable entry into the auxiliary dictionary for the *rec.food.recipes* newsgroup, where the word *canola* would be suitable.

We created the auxiliary dictionary for each newsgroup by running the *spell* program on the message bodies of each article, collecting the set of words that spell did not recognize. We then hand-reviewed all of the terms that were frequently misspelled to determine whether they should be added to the dictionary, or were instead simply common misspellings (the word "receive" was commonly misspelled, for example). For real-world use, this start-up phase would be performed once, with an incremental process that could add new words to the dictionary as they come into use in a newsgroup.

Once the dictionary was created, the filterbot processed each message by:

1. stripping off headers, signatures, and included text from prior messages ,
2. running the *spell* program to count the number of misspelled words,
3. counting the number of words in the message body,
4. converting the percentage of misspelled words into a rating on a scale of 1 through 5, and
5. submitting the rating to the recommendation engine.

To avoid confounding variables in the experiment, we chose to establish a mapping between misspelling percentage and rating that would result in a ratings distribution that closely approximated the human ratings distribution for that newsgroup. Prior experience suggests that correlation-based collaborative filtering algorithms are not very sensitive to individual differences in rating distribution, but keeping the distribution the same allowed us to avoid depending on those experiences. The same mapping strategy is used in the other filterbots.

IncludedMsgBot rates each article based on the percentage of text quoted from other articles. Replies to discussion threads often include some or all of the message being replied to. In some cases, as a thread continues the amount of included text grows substantially. Our experience and discussion with users suggested that many users dislike long messages with little new content.

IncludedMsgBot searches for this type of message, giving low ratings to articles with large amounts of included text and high ratings to articles with little included text. The filterbot:

1. separates out lines with a prefix of ">" -- most news posting software uses this convention to mark included text, and a hand inspection of the text confirmed that it was a useful heuristic for these newsgroups;
2. counts lines of new text and lines of included text;
3. computes the ratio of included text lines to total lines, and coverts that ratio to a rating on the scale of 1 through 5; and
4. submits the rating to the recommendation engine.

LengthBot rates articles based on the hypothesis that Usenet readers value brevity. After stripping off headers, signatures, and included text, LengthBot counts the number of words in the article body and converts the length into a rating on the scale of 1 to 5. Shorter articles receive higher ratings and longer ones receive lower ratings.

Analysis of Metrics

In our hypothesis, we use the concept of "improved utility." Given the goal of collaborative filtering systems—helping users more effectively identify the content they want—we define utility to include two dimensions: *coverage* and *accuracy*.

Coverage is a measure of the percentage of items for which a recommendation system can provide recommendations. A low coverage value indicates that the user must either forego a large number of items, or evaluate them based on criteria other than recommendations. A high coverage value indicates that the recommendation system provides assistance in selecting among most of the items.

A basic coverage metric is the percentage of items for which predictions are available. This metric is not well-defined, however, since it may vary per user, depending on the user's ratings and neighborhoods. To address this problem, we use a usage-centric coverage measure that asks the question: "Of the items evaluated by the user, what percentage of the time did the recommendation system contribute to the evaluation process?" More formally, for every rating entered by each user, was the system able to make a recommendation for that item immediately prior to it being rated? We compute the percentage of recommendation-informed ratings over total ratings as our coverage metric.

Accuracy has been measured in many different ways in prior research. The two general approaches used are *statistical recommendation accuracy* and *decision-support accuracy*. [16]

Statistical recommendation accuracy measures the closeness between the numerical recommendations provided by the system and the numerical ratings entered by the user for the same items. Three common metrics used are *Correlation*, *Mean Absolute Error* (MAE), and *Root Mean Squared Error* (RMSE).

Correlation is a statistical measure of agreement between two vectors of data. We use the standard Pearson correlation coefficient as a measure of linear agreement between the two vectors. A higher correlation value indicates more accurate recommendations.

MAE is a measure of the deviation of recommendations from their true user-specified values. The lower the *MAE*, the more accurately the recommendation engine predicts user ratings.

RMSE is a measure of error that is biased to weigh large errors disproportionately more heavily than small errors. The intuition behind RMSE is that many recommendations that are off by .25 on a scale of 5 are better than a few ones off by 3 or 4. Like *MAE*, lower *RMSE* also indicates better accuracy.

Decision-support accuracy measures how effectively recommendations help a user select high-quality items. They are based on the observation that for many users, filtering is a binary process. The user either will or will not read the document or consume the article. In the Usenet news case, users make rapid decisions about whether to read an article, and the difference between a recommendation score of 4.0 and 4.5 is irrelevant if the user reads everything rated 4 and above. Similarly, the difference between 1 and 2 is irrelevant if either article will be skipped. Three measures of decision-support accuracy are *reversal rate*, *ROC sensitivity*, and *PRC sensitivity*.

Reversal rate is a measure of how often the system makes big mistakes that might undermine the confidence that a user has in the recommendation system. Low reversals refer to cases where the user strongly dislikes an item (i.e., gives a rating lower than a threshold *L*) and the system strongly recommends it with a high recommendation score (i.e., above a threshold *H*). High reversals are cases where the user strongly likes the item, but the system recommendation is poor (i.e., user rating > *H*, system recommendation < *L*).

ROC sensitivity is a measure of the diagnostic power of a filtering system. Operationally, it is the area under the receiver operating characteristic (ROC) curve—a curve that plots the sensitivity and specificity of the test [7]. Sensitivity refers to the probability of a randomly selected good item being accepted by the filter. Specificity is the probability of a randomly selected bad item being rejected by the filter. The ROC curve plots sensitivity (from 0 to 1) and *1 – specificity* (from 0 to 1), obtaining a set of points by varying the recommendation score threshold above which the article is accepted. The area under the curve increases as the filter is able to retain more good items while accepting fewer bad items. For use as a metric, we must determine which items are "good" and which are "bad." For that task, we use the user's own ratings. A rating of 4 or 5 is deemed to be a good item (signal), a rating of 1, 2, or 3 is deemed to be a bad item (noise). The ROC sensitivity measure therefore is an indication of how effectively the system can steer people towards highly-rated items and away from low-rated ones. Particularly important values are 1.0, the perfect filter, and 0.5, a random filter.

PRC sensitivity is a measure of the degree to which the system presents relevant information. In fact, it is the area under the precision-recall curve. Precision measures the percentage of selected documents that are relevant; recall measures the percentage of relevant documents that are selected. Hence, precision indicates how selective the system is, and recall indicates how thorough it is in finding valuable information. [15] We use as the domain of our metric the set of articles on which the user has recommendation-informed ratings. We plot a curve of different precision-recall pairs for different recommendation score thresholds, and take the area under that curve as a metric of PRC sensitivity. A higher value is more accurate, and a low value is less accurate.

For these experiments, we use ROC and PRC sensitivity as our primary accuracy metrics because they most closely match the goals of our experiments. We are more interested in whether adding filterbots to the GroupLens Research system helps users decide whether to read articles than in minimizing errors in areas that do not affect user decisions. Large reversals, the other decision-support metric, were too infrequent in this data set to use with confidence. As a sanity check, we did analyze our results using MAE and RMSE; results were similar, which is in line with the finding of prior work that accuracy improvements tend to be reflected across the spectrum of metrics.

EXPERIMENTS WITH FILTERBOTS

Data

The data we used for these experiments is from the GroupLens Research trial of Winter 1996. During that seven-week trial, described in [10], we collected 47,569 ratings from over 250 users across many newsgroups. The newsgroups used for these experiments are a cross section of technical and recreational, moderated and unmoderated.

Procedure

To test our hypothesis *H1* we need to get predictions from the *GroupLens* server both with and without filterbot ratings. For each newsgroup we created four files of data: one with user ratings only, and one each with the ratings of the three filterbots. Each record contained a user ID, newsgroup, message ID, and rating. To obtain base statistics for user-only recommendations, we followed this procedure:

1. Create an empty GroupLens database.
2. For each rating in the ratings file:
    a. request a recommendation for that user/newsgroup/message;
    b. record the returned recommendation or lack thereof; and
    c. submit the rating.
3. Compute coverage and accuracy statistics.

For the filterbot experiments, after step #1, we loaded all filterbot ratings into the database, and then proceeded with steps #2 and #3.

The experimental configuration uses Net Perceptions' commercial GroupLens Recommendation Engine version 2.2.2.5 configured to use a neighborhood size of 50 and no neighbor correlation threshold.

RESULTS

H1 hypothesizes that that adding filterbots into a collaborative filtering system will improve utility for users. To test this hypothesis, we look at experiments with several different Usenet newsgroups and several different filterbots. Since utility is a function of both item coverage and accuracy, we examine coverage, ROC sensitivity, and PRC sensitivity metrics in each newsgroup with each filterbot and without filterbots. If the coverage and accuracy both increase, then we can accept **H1**. If coverage increases and accuracy is unchanged, or accuracy increases with no change in coverage, we can also accept **H1**. However, if either coverage or accuracy decreases, we will be unable to accept **H1**. Because the effectiveness of filterbots may vary by newsgroup, we present the results separately for each newsgroup. Then we look at the value of each filterbot overall, and evaluate the hypothesis in general.

Results by Newsgroup

mn.general

This newsgroup is a local unmoderated newsgroup with discussion and announcements on all topics from local events to finding reliable or inexpensive Internet service. We had 17 users who rated an average of 65 of the 559 articles in the newsgroup (for an average of 1.98 ratings per article). As table 1 shows, coverage improved somewhat for the newsgroup with each filterbot, but accuracy either decreased slightly or was inconclusive. Accordingly, we were unable to accept **H1** for **mn.general**.

Table 1 : Results for mn.general newsgroup

Filterbots	Coverage (%)	ROC Sensitivity	PRC Sensitivity
No filterbot	40.670	0.6937	0.2295
SpellChecker	43.155	0.6779	0.2075
IncludedMsg	46.056	0.7044	0.2180
Length	44.609	0.6719	0.2110

comp.lang.perl.misc

The newsgroup comp.lang.perl.misc is an unmoderated technical discussion group focused on the scripting language Perl. The *.misc* suffix indicates that this group receives primarily articles that do not fit into one of the other Perl newsgroups. We had 10 users who rated an average of 70 of the 627 articles in the newsgroup (for an average of 1.66 ratings per article). As table 2 shows, coverage and accuracy improved dramatically for the spell checking filterbot. Coverage increased by 85% for the other filterbots, with the included message algorithm having no significant effect on accuracy and the length algorithm having a very small positive effect. Given the success of the spell checking filterbot, we are able to accept **H1** for **comp.lang.perl.misc**.

Table 2 : Results for comp.lang.perl.misc newsgroup

Filterbots	Coverage (%)	ROC Sensitivity	PRC Sensitivity
No filterbot	7.010	0.6523	0.4698
SpellChecker	42.775	0.7448	0.6030
IncludedMsg	13.017	0.6400	0.4694
Length	13.180	0.6770	0.4981

comp.os.linux.announce

The newsgroup comp.os.linux.announce is a moderated technical discussion group that is used to make announcements to developers and users of the Linux operating system. We had 23 users who rated an average of 24 of the 421 articles in the newsgroup (for an average of 1.33 ratings per article). As table 3 shows, the length and spell checking filterbots both provided dramatic increases in coverage with moderate increases in accuracy. The included message filterbot increased coverage somewhat, but decreased accuracy. Given the success of the spell checking and length filterbots, we are able to accept **H1** for **comp.os.linux.announce**.

Table 3 : Results for comp.os.linux.announce group

Filterbots	Coverage (%)	ROC Sensitivity	PRC Sensitivity
No filterbot	14.874	0.6619	0.3234
SpellChecker	46.319	0.6822	0.3643
IncludedMsg	20.430	0.6117	0.3146
Length	48.745	0.7046	0.3686

rec.food.recipes

The newsgroup rec.food.recipes is a moderated recreational group where contributors post recipes and occasional requests for recipes. We had 7 users who rated an average of 22 of the 92 articles in the newsgroup (for an average of 1.66 ratings per article). As table 4 shows, the spell checking filterbot greatly increased coverage and accuracy, with a particularly strong increase in PRC sensitivity. The included message filterbot provided a much smaller increase in coverage, but similarly impressive accuracy improvements. The length filterbot provided inconclusive accuracy results (worse ROC, better PRC) with an in-between increase in coverage. Based on the strength of the spell checking filterbot, we are able to accept **H1** for **rec.food.recipes**.

Table 4 : Results for rec.food.recipes newsgroup

Filterbots	Coverage (%)	ROC Sensitivity	PRC Sensitivity
No filterbot	22.222	0.6181	0.3902
SpellChecker	71.710	0.6601	0.6254
IncludedMsg	27.451	0.6667	0.5937
Length	42.763	0.5687	0.4570

rec.humor

The newsgroup rec.humor is an unmoderated recreational group where contributors are expected to post jokes and other humorous material. It is a well-known high-noise newsgroup that is commonly cited as an example of a group where filtering is useful. We had 19 users who rated an average of 92 of the 1367 articles in the newsgroup (for an average of 1.27 ratings per article). As table 5 shows, all three filterbots provided dramatic increases in accuracy, and two of them also increased coverage by more than 200%. Accordingly, we are able to accept **H1** for **rec.humor**.

Table 5: Results for rec.humor newsgroup

Filterbots	Coverage (%)	ROC Sensitivity	PRC Sensitivity
No filterbot	15.384	0.4604	0.1253
SpellChecker	50.258	0.8081	0.3638
IncludedMsg	50.373	0.7228	0.3915
Length	16.657	0.7188	0.2487

Since rec.humor was the group with the largest combination of effect size and number of users, we decided to look more closely at the degree to which individual users agreed with the filterbots. Figure 2 shows rating correlations between the three filterbots and the twelve

Figure 2: Correlations between users and filterbots

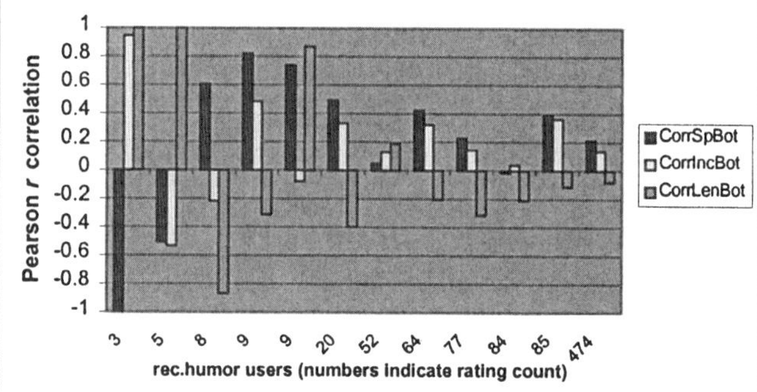

users who had rated enough articles to have correlations. The extreme correlations for five users reflect their small number of ratings, rather than any systematic agreement. Several users with large numbers of ratings have fairly high correlations, particularly with the spell checking filterbot. Of six users with more than 50 ratings: four have correlations greater than 0.2 with SpellCheckerBot (two at or above 0.4), two have correlations above 0.3 with IncludedMsgBot, and three have negative correlations stronger than –0.2 with LengthBot. Even the least-correlated user (the one with 52 ratings) had a correlation of 0.19 with one of the filterbots. We can use the user-filterbot correlation to determine which filterbots are most useful for a given set of users. Filterbots that are not valuable for a set of users can be turned off, to save computation. From the above diagram we see that our notion of "long messages are bad" may not be suitable for the users in the rec.humor newsgroup. A possible reason for the poor performance of this filterbot is that users actually prefer long messages in this newsgroup. We had disabled negative correlations for our study, since in previous work they led to worse results [16]. To rule out this possibility, we also tested a filterbot that rated using the rule "short messages are bad", but that filterbot performed even more poorly. Our conclusion is that length is not a good predictor of quality in rec.humor.

Results by Filterbot

SpellCheckerBot shows very promising results. It provided both improved coverage and improved accuracy in four of the five newsgroups we tested. It appears that Usenet readers prefer articles with correct spelling. This does not necessarily imply that they care about spelling *per se*, but that something that they care about correlates well with spelling. For example, readers may value careful writing, simple vocabularies, etc.

IncludedMsgBot shows mixed results, providing improved coverage in all groups but accuracy improvements only in the recreational groups. One interpretation is that the nature of a group determines whether included content is good, bad, or neutral. Technical groups (and mn.general) often have discussions where readers appear to value the context provided by included text. In these group, the best amount of included text is neither "more" nor "less" but simply "the right amount." Neither the recipe nor the humor group is supposed to have much included text at all. Rec.food.recipes is not to be used for discussion of recipes and rec.humor is not to be used for discussion of jokes. Accordingly, results in these groups may mostly reflect identifying and giving low ratings to out-of-place postings (for rec.food.recipes, the periodic "request for recipes" collection).

LengthBot showed benefits for rec.humor and comp.lang.perl.misc, and showed the best results by all measures in comp.os.linux.announce. Length was not useful in mn.general or rec.food.recipes. As with included text, this suggests that readers of different newsgroups value different attributes. Indeed, much of LengthBot's value in rec.humor came from negative correlations—people who apparently preferred longer articles.

Overall Results

Based on all of the results presented above, we accept the hypothesis that content-analysis filterbots can improve user utility. In four of the five newsgroups, we found at least one filterbot that improved both coverage and accuracy, measured both by ROC and PRC. We analyzed statistical significance of the ROC values at 95% confidence level. SpellCheckerBot showed statistically significant improvements compared to the corresponding values obtained without using filterbots in three newsgroups, but in the mn.general and comp.os.linux.announce newsgroups the ROC values were not significantly different. IncludedMsgBot showed significantly higher ROC values in rec.humor and significantly lower ROC values in comp.os.linux.announce newsgroup. In the rest of the newsgroups ROC values did not change significantly. LengthBot provided significantly better results in two newsgroups and worse ROC values in rec.food.recipes. In mn.general and comp.lang.perl.misc newsgroups differences in ROC values were not statistically significant.

DISCUSSION

These experiments demonstrate that simple content-analysis filterbots can help improve the coverage and accuracy of a collaborative filtering system. We recognize that there are several important limitations to this work, but also many exciting applications of it. In this section, we discuss both, along with some of our ideas for future work.

Limitations

This study is one of the first on combining collaborative filtering techniques with syntactic filtering techniques. We therefore focussed on very simple syntactic techniques, to gain some understanding of how these two filtering techniques can be combined successfully. It is possible that more sophisticated filterbots would have performed much better than the simple filterbots we studied. However, the results are important in showing that even simple filterbots add value to user ratings.

Our results were based on a collaborative filtering dataset from the GroupLens Research public trial. While this trial is still one of the largest trials conducted on streams of discussion data, the ratings density in the data is very low. Newsgroups such as rec.humor would require hundreds or thousands of users to achieve an average of even ten ratings per article, in part because the newsgroup has so many unfunny articles that there is substantial incentive to skip any article that doesn't have a strong recommendation.

Possible consequences of low rating density include:

- Less personalization within the recommendation process, since there are too few ratings for the algorithm to be "fussy" about matches.
- Lower accuracy and coverage in the "no filterbot" case than would be the case otherwise.

At the same time, low rating density is a real-world condition that presents the problem that filterbots are intended to solve.A related limitation is the small number of users studied. We had 76 users who rated articles that overlapped the filterbot ratings. Of these users, many rated only a few articles and therefore contributed little to the analysis. Even though this study should be replicated with a larger user set, we believe it reflects the largest study of its type, and therefore can serve as a basis for additional experimentation.

Finally, we recognize that Usenet News is, in general, a high-noise information stream. We selected two moderated newsgroups to ameliorate that effect, but should caution those trying to generalize the work to low-noise environments that very simple filterbots may not add enough value to be useful.

Applications of this Work

There are several interesting applications of our architecture and results. A number of real-world collaborative filtering systems recommend objects from immense sets (e.g., books in print, web pages) where filterbots could help address ratings sparsity.

A particularly exciting idea is the use of the filterbot framework as a mechanism for increasing the utility of agent software. Few agents today are sufficiently powerful and general to merit individual use, so integrating them into a framework with collaborative filtering and other agents can help them reach the threshold of utility. Also, individual filtering agents aren't inherently god or bad; they are more useful to some users and less useful to others. Integrating them into a collaborative filtering framework helps match users to agents. It also helps address the case where a particular agent has no information to communicate—a feature that may have helped our filterbots.

Future Work

Our results represent only a first step in understanding the ways in which content filtering can be successfully integrated into collaborative filtering. Among the issues we would like to study in the future are:

- the interaction of sets of filterbots in the same system.
- the process of selecting proper filterbots for an application domain; we clearly could not know in advance which algorithms would work for the newsgroups, and indeed certain cases resulted in a drop in overall accuracy.
- the use of more complex filterbot algorithms, including algorithms that learn.
- a "personal filterbot" system where each user has "agent filterbots" attempting to learn her tastes.
- the value of filterbots for users with few ratings. Should the engine only phase in filterbots after users have a certain number of ratings and established correlations?

In addition to these questions, we have a large number of particular filterbots and applications that we'd like to explore, including filterbots for movies and other non-textual media.

CONCLUSIONS

This paper makes three contributions to the field of collaborative filtering.

First, it defines and implements a model for integrating content-based ratings into a collaborative filtering system. This filterbot model allows collaborative filtering systems to address sparsity and early-rater problems by tapping the strength of content filtering techniques. Second, it identifies and evaluates metrics for assessing the effectiveness of filterbots specifically, and filtering system enhancements in general. Third, it experimentally validates the filterbot approach by showing that even simple filterbots such as spell checking can increase the utility for users of sparsely populated collaborative filtering systems.

ACKNOWLEDGEMENTS

The authors gratefully acknowledge the contributions of all the members of the GroupLens Research team, and the support of Net Perceptions Inc. and the National Science Foundation under grant IRI-9613960. We also thank the anonymous reviewers for their valuable comments.

REFERENCES

1. Avery, C. and Zeckhauser, R. Recommender Systems for Evaluating Computer Messages. *CACM.* 40(3), pp. 88-89, March 1997.
2. Balabanovic, M. and Shoham, Y. Fab: Content-Based, Collaborative Recommendation. *CACM.* 40(3), pp. 66-72, March 1997.
3. Belkin, N. J. and Croft, B. W. Information Filtering and Information Retrieval: Two Sides of the Same Coin? *CACM.* 35(2), December 1992.
4. Goldberg, D., Nichols, D., Oki, B. M. and Terry, D. Using Collaborative Filtering to Weave an Information Tapestry. *CACM.* Dec. 1992.
5. Hill, W., Stead, L., Rosenstein, M., Furnas, G. Recommending and Evaluating Choices in a Virtual Community of Use. *Proceedings of CHI '95.*
6. Konstan, J. A., Miller, B. N., Maltz, D., Herlocker, J. L., Gordon, L. R. and Riedl, J. GroupLens: Applying Collaborative Filtering to Usenet News. *CACM.* 40(3), March 1997.
7. Le, C. T. and Lindgren, B. R. Construction and Comparison of Two Receiver Operating Characteristics Curves Derived from the Same Samples. Biom. J. 37(7), pp. 869-877, July 1995.
8. Maes, P. Agents that Reduce Work and Information Overload. *CACM.* July 1994.
9. Maltz, D. and Ehrlich, K. Pointing the Way: Active Collaborative Filtering. *Proceedings of CHI '95.*
10. Miller, B., Riedl, J. and Konstan, J. Experiences with GroupLens: Making Usenet Useful Again. *Proceedings of the 1997 Usenix Technical Conference.*
11. Moukas, A. and Zacharia, G. Evolving a Multi-agent Information Filtering Solution in Amalthaea. In *Proceedings of Autonomous Agents 97.*
12. Resnick, P. and Varian, H. R. Recommender Systems. *CACM.* 40(3), pp. 56-58, March 1997.
13. Resnick, P., Iacovou, N., Suchak, M., Bergstrom, P. and Riedl, J. GroupLens: An Open Architecture for Collaborative Filtering of Netnews. *Proceedings of CSCW '94.* Chapel Hill, NC. 1994.
14. Rucker, J. and Polano, M. J. Siteseer: Personalized Navigation for the Web. *CACM.* 40(3), March 1997.
15. Salton, G. and McGill M. J. *Introduction to Modern Information Retrieval.* McGraw-Hill, Inc. 1983.
16. Shardanand, U. and Maes, P. Social Information Filtering: Algorithms for Automating "Word of Mouth". In *Proceedings of the CHI '95.* Denver, CO. May 1995.
17. Terveen, L., Hill, W., Amento, B., McDonald, D. and Creter, J. PHOAKS: A System for Sharing Recommendations. *CACM.* 40(3), pp. 59-62, March 1997.

Evaluating Emergent Collaboration on the Web

Loren Terveen
AT&T Labs - Research
180 Park Avenue
Florham Park, NJ 07932
+1 973 360-8343
terveen@research.att.com

Will Hill
AT&T Labs - Research
180 Park Avenue
Florham Park, NJ 07932
+1 973 360-8342
willhill@research.att.com

ABSTRACT

Links between web sites can be seen as evidence of a type of *emergent collaboration* among web site authors. We report here on an empirical investigation into emergent collaboration. We developed a webcrawling algorithm and tested its performance on topics volunteered by 30 subjects. Our findings include:

- Some topics exhibit emergent collaboration, some do not. The presence of commercial sites reduces collaboration.
- When sites are linked with other sites, they tend to group into one large, tightly connected component.
- Connectivity can serve as the basis for collaborative filtering. Human experts rate connected sites as significantly more relevant and of higher quality.

Keywords

Social filtering, collaborative filtering, computer supported cooperative work, human computer interaction, information access, information retrieval

INTRODUCTION

The field of CSCW sees collaboration as involving people who *know* they are working together, e.g., to edit a document, to carry out a software design review, or to play a role-playing game. CSCW research then focuses on understanding the nature of collaboration and developing computer support to enhance collaboration.

Our focus is different. We have been inspired by the example of a path through the woods. A path results from the decisions of many individuals, united only by where they choose to walk, yet still reflects a rough notion of what the walkers find to be a good path. The path both reflects history of use and serves as a resource for future users. We look for analogous situations in the computational world, attempting to turn implicit "paths through the woods" of particular user communities into explicit, shared resources. We seek situations where groups of people already are producing computational records (such as documents, Usenet messages, or web sites and links) as part of their normal activity. We then identify potentially useful information implicit in these records and invent computational techniques to harvest the information and make it explicit. Finally, we create interfaces to distribute the information both to the original group members and to a wider community.

The work reported here investigates links between web sites as a potential ground for emergent collaboration. Links from a single web site tell us what the site author thinks are topically relevant, high quality sites. However, we hypothesize that patterns of links among a group of web sites can tell us what a (usually implicit) community of web site authors, united only by their interest in a common topic, think are relevant, high quality sites. This paper reports on an empirical test of this hypothesis.

EMERGENT COLLABORATION: OUR PERSPECTIVE AND RELATED WORK

Our first line of work that took the emergent collaboration approach was history-enriched digital objects [4, 5, 13]. This work was based on the observation that objects in the real world accumulate wear over the history of their use, and that wear — such as the path through the woods or the dog-eared pages in a paperback book or the smudges on certain recipes in a cookbook — informs future usage. *Edit Wear* and *Read Wear* were terms used to describe computational analogues of these phenomena. Statistics such as time spent reading various parts of a document, counts of spreadsheet cell recalculations, and menu selections were captured and then used to modify the appearance of documents and other interface objects in accordance with prior use.

Recently other researchers have begun to explore the use of capturing and visualizing history. Seligman [11] takes the metaphor of paper documents literally, visualizing web pages as if they were paper documents, showing information about their access history as smudges, stains, fingerprints, etc. Wexelblat's Footprints system [14] captures the history of access to sets of web pages and creates visualizations based on this history to aid navigation. Alexa (http://www.alexa.com) keeps track of the links users follow from one web page to another and uses this information to recommend the most popular links.

Our second attempt at harvesting information from group records was PHOAKS (People Helping One Another Know Stuff)[6, 12]. PHOAKS is a collaborative filtering system, based on the premise that an effective way of finding good items of information about a given topic is to ask the experts. One problem is that one often does not know any experts for a particular topic. PHOAKS looked to Usenet news for the solution: it searches messages in thousands of newsgroups for mentions of web pages. It then applies a set of rules to identify those mentions that were done for the purpose of recommending a web page. Web pages are ranked within a topic by the number of different individuals who recommended them. We showed that Usenet messages are an abundant source of recommendations of web pages, that recommendations could be recognized automatically with high accuracy, and that there was some correlation between the number of recommenders of a web page and other metrics of web page quality.

There is a significant amount of ongoing research aimed at extracting useful information from the structure of web links. Two projects related to ours are those of Kleinberg and Carrière & Kazman. Kleinberg [7] defines algorithms that identify *authoritative* and *hub* pages within a hypertext. Authorities and hubs are mutually dependent: a good authority is a page that is linked to by many hubs, and a good hub is one that links to many authorities. An equilibrium algorithm is used to identify hubs and authorities in a hypertext collection. Carrière & Kazman's WebQuery system [2] sorts pages into equivalence classes based on their total degree (number of other pages in the collection they are connected with), and displays the pages in a "bullseye" layout, a series of concentric circles each containing pages of equal degree.

Pirolli, Pitkow, and colleagues at Xerox PARC have done a great deal of work that analyzes web structure and usage data, attempting to categorize and cluster web pages. Pitkow and Pirolli [10] describe clustering algorithms based on co-citation analysis [3]. The intuition is that if two documents, say A and B, are both cited by a third document, this is evidence that A and B are related. The more often a pair of documents is co-cited, the stronger the relationship. They applied two algorithms to Georgia Tech's Graphic Visualization and Usability Center web site and were able to identify interesting clusters. Pirolli, Pitkow, and Rao [9] defined a set of functional roles that web pages can play, such as "head" (roughly the "front door" of a group of related pages), "index", and "content". They then developed an algorithm that used hyperlink structure, text similarity, and user access data to categorize pages into the various roles. They applied these algorithms to the Xerox web site and were able to categorize pages with good accuracy.

Botafogo et al [1] present interesting algorithms for analyzing hypertexts. Although much of their focus was on the analysis and improvement of (navigation through) a single hypertext, some of their techniques undoubtedly could be used to analyze collections of hyper-linked documents.

In summary, our approach is to harvest information that emerges from patterns of individual activity, where the individuals involved may not be communicating explicitly, but are bound by common artifacts and interests — documents they edit, topics they care about, web sites they maintain and visit, newsgroups they read and post to. Like others, our concern is with deriving useful information from links between web sites. The unique contribution of the work we report here is that it investigates empirically how individual decisions to link to other sites knit topic areas together and how the connectivity of sites within a topic correlates with human judgements about the relevance and quality of sites.

THE DATA

We invited members of our laboratory to supply us with topics they were interested in. We asked that topics be represented by a Yahoo™ category; for example, astronomy is represented by the Yahoo category Science:Astronomy. Yahoo categories offer a convenient means of obtaining a set of web pages for a given topic.

30 people responded to our request, 26 with a Yahoo category, and 4 with either a single links page or a set of web sites that they selected to represent their interest. (Since we simply needed sets of sites on specific topics for this experiment, we were happy to accept the 4 submissions that were not Yahoo categories.) In addition, for reasons that we discuss below, we selected another 15 Yahoo categories randomly, 5 from the Business and Economy hierarchy, 10 from elsewhere in the hierarchy. Table 1 shows how the topics are distributed across the Yahoo hierarchy (we were easily able to classify the 4 topics that were not represented as Yahoo categories). Some examples of the topics users selected include Palm Pilots, slide rules, Frank Herbert's "Dune" series, interactive fiction, astronomy, and computer electronics.

Table 1: Topic areas in the experiment

Category	*User-supplied*	*Selected randomly*
Arts and Entertainment (A)	11	3
Science (S)	6	4
Recreation (R)	6	0
Business and Economy (B)	5	5
Computers and Internet (C)	1	
Education (E)	1	
Health (H)		3
Totals	30	15

We applied our web-crawling algorithm (described in [13]) to the set of sites for each topic to construct the inter-site graph. The nodes of this graph are the sites, and there is an edge from one site's node to another if and only if (some page of) the first site links to (some page of) the second.

Our algorithm heuristically aggregates pages into sites ([13] gives details). For example, if it encounters a link to the URL http://a/b/c/page1.html, and http://a/b/c/index.html is a known site, it records this URL as part of the site. Further, if the link was encountered while analyzing the site http://x/y/z/, a link is recorded from the site http://x/y/z/ to the site http://a/b/c/index.html. We ran our webcrawler to fetch and analyze 25 pages for each site. The primary reason to fetch a significant number of pages per site is to maximize the chance of obtaining the links page of each site (if there is one; if not, we still have a better chance of getting links that are distributed across the site's pages) so that we construct the inter-site graph accurately. In addition, the algorithm constructs a profile of site content, collecting and counting links to images, audio files, html and text files, and the more pages fetched, the more accurate the profile. The content profile aids both user comprehension and automatic classification of sites.

As we analyzed the data, we noticed important differences between Business and Economy (B&E) topics and the other topics (see below for details). However, since users had supplied only 5 B&E topics, we wanted to obtain a larger sample; therefore, we randomly selected 5 additional B&E topics, as well as 10 other topics to further increase our sample size.[1] Thus, we ended up with 45 topics, which contained an average of 79 sites.

After we built the graph for a topic, we carried out two types of analysis. First, we analyzed the connectivity of the graphs; the goal was to determine whether topics on the web are marked by emergent collaboration (as indicated by significant linking between sites). Second, we investigated whether the connectivity of a site could serve as the grounds for collaborative filtering, i.e., could it allow us to identify high quality sites. To answer this question, we selected 20 sites at random from each topic and presented the sites to the person who suggested the topic for rating. Sites were presented in an HTML form; subjects followed hot links to sites to investigate their content, then used menus to rank site relevance and quality on a scale of 1 to 5. 23 of the people rated at least some of the sites for their topic.

We discuss each of these analyses in turn.

CONNECTIVITY OF TOPIC GRAPHS: COLLABORATION OR COMPETITION?

We first checked each graph to see how many of the sites were isolated, that is, neither linking to nor linked to by any other sites on their common topic. We were surprised to find a large number of isolated sites: on average, 43% of the sites on a topic were isolated. While the web raises the possibility of creating a multi-author, inter-related, cross-referenced knowledge base for a topic, a large proportion of sites do not follow this ideal. We did two things to follow up on the finding of a large number of isolated sites. First, we analyzed the structure of the non-isolated sites; next, we tried to understand why so many sites were isolated. We will discuss each of these analyses in turn; however, first let us consider two topic graphs.

Figure 1 shows a fairly densely connected graph for an Arts & Entertainment category, "Beat Poets". Of the 32 sites in the topic, only 8 are isolated. There are 44 links, giving a *density* of 0.044 (density is defined below). Even the coarse presentation of Figure 1 reveals some patterns, e.g., a few sites with many outgoing links and one site with many incoming links.

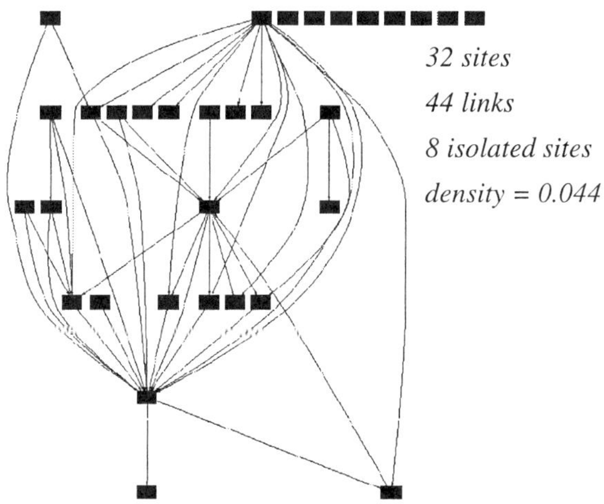

Figure 1: Densely connected graph ("Beat Poets")

Figure 2 shows a more sparsely connected graph for the topic of travel to Italy. The most striking feature is that 42 of the 58 sites are isolated. The density is 0.0048 (an order of magnitude less than the previous graph). We discuss this topic more later.

[1] We should note that there were no significant differences between the topics supplied by our subjects and those we selected at random on any of the measures we report here.

Figure 2: Sparsely connected graph ("Italian travel")

Connected Sites: Giant Components, High Density, Short Paths

We first examined the component structure of connected sites — a component is a subset of the nodes in a graph such that there is a path from any node in the component to any other node and no paths between nodes in different components.[2] It is completely plausible that the sites could be fairly evenly distributed across a set of components. For example, a topic with 50 non-isolated sites could consist of components of size 20, 15, 9, and 6. However, this was not the case: if sites were not isolated, they tended to be part of one giant component. On average, there were just under 2 components per graph, and the largest component contained 90% of all the non-isolated nodes.

Another metric for measuring the connectivity of nodes in a graph is *density*. Density is simply the number of links that do exist divided by the number of links that could exist (if the graph were fully connected). For a directed graph of size N, a total of N * (N-1) links are possible. Clearly, the Web as a whole is a very sparse graph; the probability that there is a link between any two sites selected at random is nearly 0. However, the graph defined by a particular topic area is much denser: the average density of the 45 graphs we analyzed was 0.056. This means that a graph of size 50 would contain about 138 links.

Another useful way to characterize the structural connections of the non-isolated sites is to examine the *lengths of paths* among them. We applied the following test to each topic with at least 25 non-isolated sites (this gave us 20 topics). We selected 20 different random subsets of size 1, 2, ... , 10 of the non-isolated sites to use as a "seed". (We proceeded only if at least 20 non-isolated sites remained once we made the selection.) For each set of seed sites, we counted the number of other non-isolated sites that could be reached via a path of length 1 or 2. Figure 3 shows the results. For a seed set of size 2, 71% of the other sites were reached, for a seed set of size 5, 85% were reached, for a seed set of size 10, 92% were reached, etc.

To understand this experiment thoroughly, let us consider the case of 5 randomly selected seeds in a bit more detail. The topic graphs in this experiment contained an average of 126 sites, of which 40 sites (32%) were isolated. Once we selected 5 sites at random to serve as a seed, this meant that 81 sites (126 – 40 – 5) were potentially reachable. 85% (69/81) of these sites were reached by following 1 or 2 links from one of the seed sites.

This experiment shows how tightly topically related sites are knit together by inter-site links. It also has interesting consequences for site discovery, showing that one can start with a small set of seed sites known to be on a topic and find a large majority of related sites by following just one or two links. We discuss this point in more detail later.

Non-collaborative Topics: It's Money That Matters

We examined the data further to better understand the large number of isolated sites — were all topics roughly the same in this respect, or were there differences based on the type of topic? We immediately observed a striking difference between Business and Economy topics, such as lawn and garden companies, consumer electronics, and year 2000 software organizations, and other types of topics. For 10 B&E topics, 79% of sites were isolated, for the other 35 topics, only 32% of sites were isolated. (This was a significant difference, using a standard two sample t-Test, $t(43) = -6.02$, $p < 0.0001$.) There was also a large difference in density: the average density for B&E topics was 0.004, and for the other topics it was 0.071. (However, this difference was not significant at the 95% level: using a standard t-Test, $p(43) = 1.87$, $p = 0.068$.) Again, to be concrete, in a graph of 50 sites, this is the difference between 10 links and 174. To sum up, topics dominated by merchants who are competing for the same customers do not exhibit collaboration.

[2] For the purposes of component analysis, we treated the graph as symmetric; that is, sites **a** and **b** were considered connected if there was a link from either **a** to **b** or from **b** to **a** (or both). And **a** and **c** are part of the same component if there is some (undirected) path between them, e.g., from **a** to **b** and **b** to **c**, even if **a** and **c** do not link directly to each other.

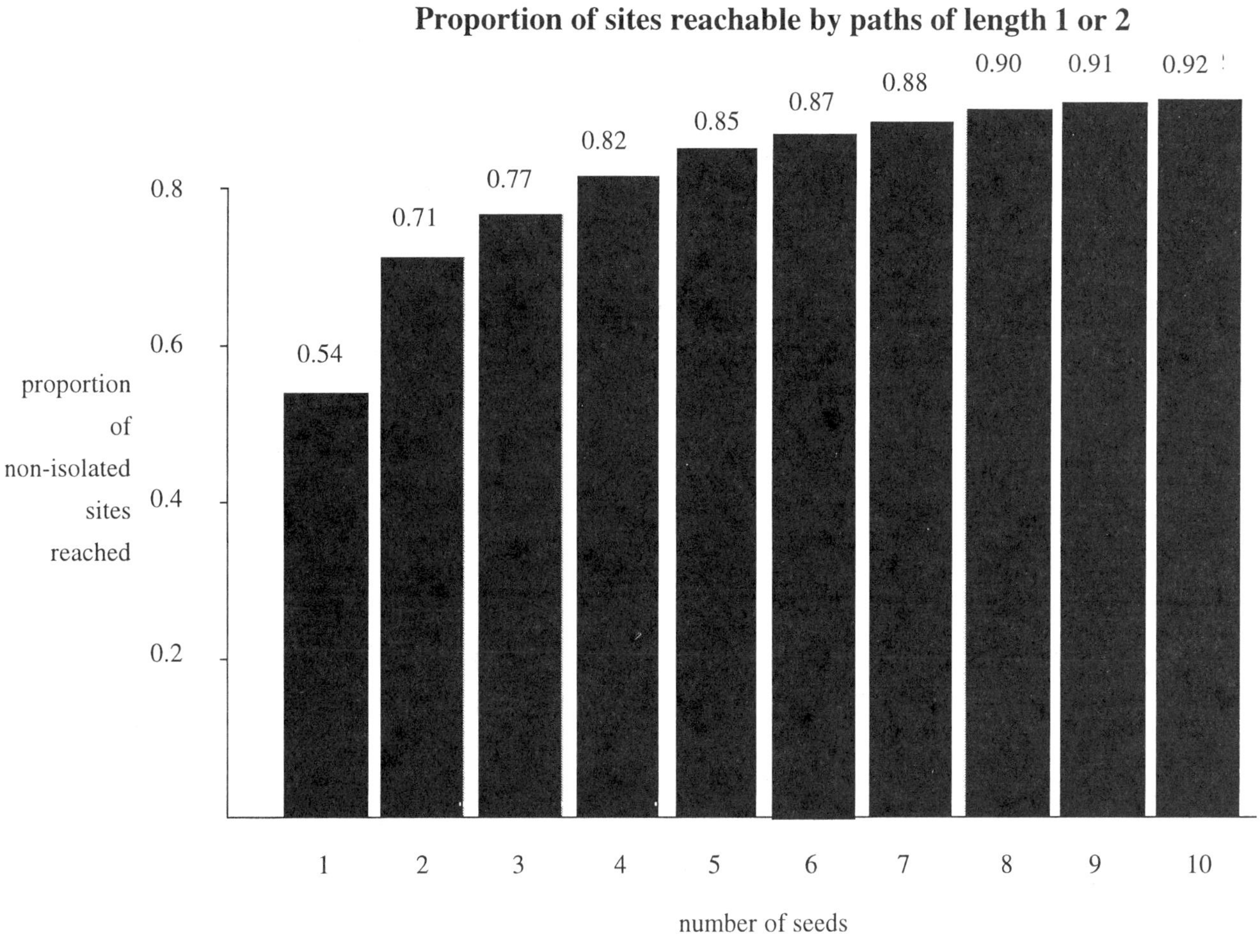

Figure 3: Reachability of sites by paths of length 1 or 2

Figure 4 (see also Color Figure 1) summarizes our findings concerning isolated sites and components. Each bar represents one topic. The gray upper block in each bar represents the number of isolated sites. Lower blocks show the number of sites in each component of the graph. The labels on the X axis indicate the type of each topic (see Table 1 — "A" is Arts and Entertainment, "S" is Science, etc.) For example, the bar with the label "NLP, which represents the topic Natural Language Processing, has one component of size 16 (the lowest block), then components of size 3, 2, and 2, and 22 isolated sites.

Some of the bars in the plot appear to be exceptions to our generalization about Business and Economy topics being non-collaborative. It is worth discussing several cases individually since, upon closer examination, they shed more light on the generalization. "Coin collecting" is a B&E topic, yet has a very small proportion of isolated nodes. Although the majority of the sites are commercial and do not link to each other, there are a few index sites that link to many of the other sites and thus knit them together into a large connected component. However, the overall density of the graph is still low (190 links in a topic of 149 sites = 0.0086), which shows that very little linking between sites actually is occurring.

Two Recreation topics have a large proportion of isolated nodes. As discussed earlier, in the "Italian travel" topic, 42 of the 58 sites were isolated, and the density was only 0.0048. This was because the topic contained a large number of sites for travel agencies and official city and regional information bureaus, which do not link to each other. The "interactive fiction" topic contained a large number of sites for computer games and software companies, and it is these sites which tend to be isolated from the rest. (108 of 176 sites were isolated, and there were 120 links, for a graph density of 0.004.) Thus, we see that some topics may have a "mixed" nature, containing both commercial sites, which do not link, and sites maintained by enthusiasts or hobbyists, which do.

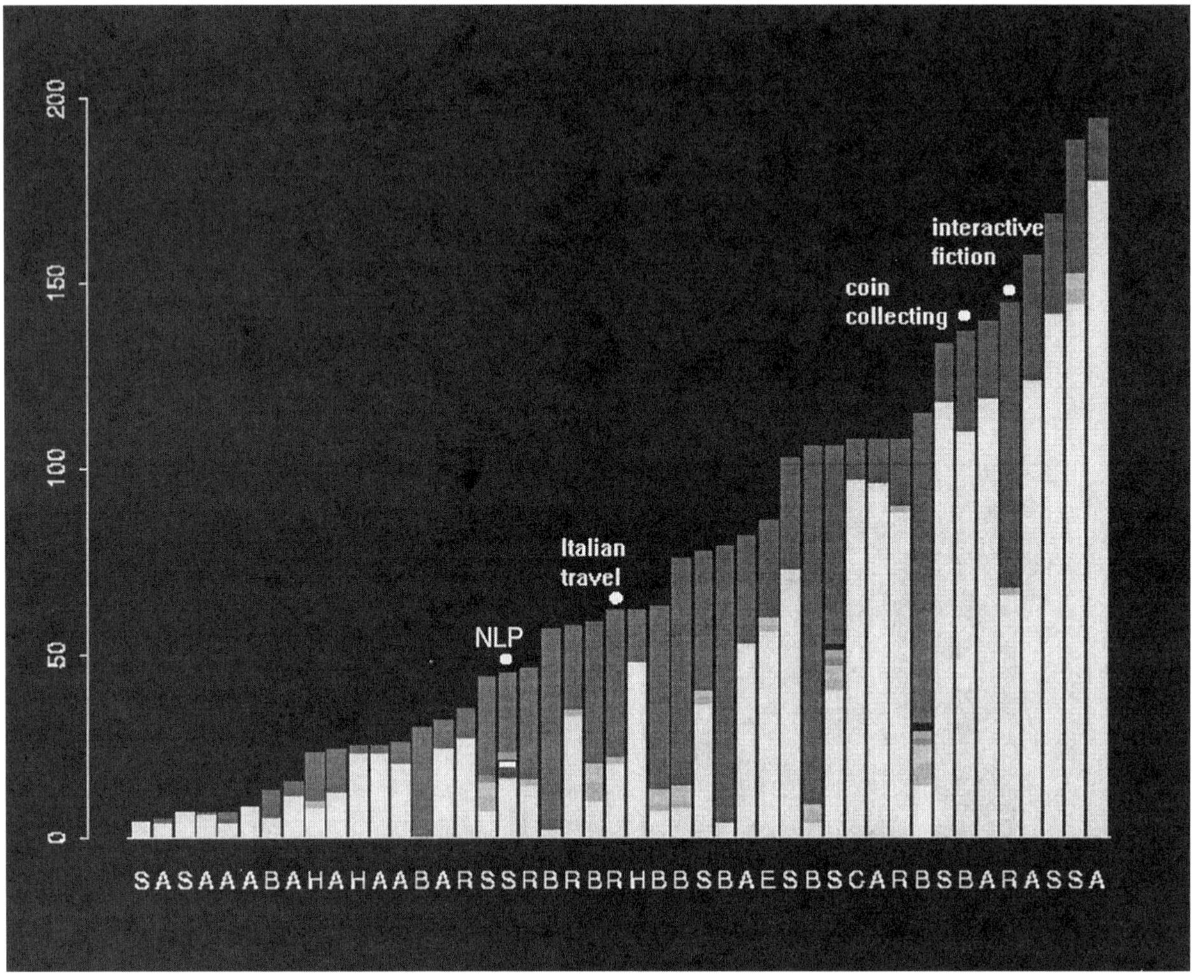

Figure 4: Components and isolated sites

We see two major implications of our findings. First, link-based collaborative filtering can work only for topics with a significant number of inter-site links. We have identified one large topic area where such links are extremely rare and have suggested that it is because commercial sites that are in competition with one another do not link. We will look for other topic areas that are especially collaborative or non-collaborative as we continue our investigations.

Second, we found that nearly all (90%) the sites for a topic that are not isolated group into one large component, and that nearly all of the non-isolated sites are within 2 links of a small, randomly selected subset of "seed" sites. The patterns of connection that emerge from the implicit collaboration among web site authors are potentially useful in two ways. First, connectivity may be used as an estimate of relevance and quality, e.g., in ordering the presentation of sites in an interface. Second, site discovery algorithms can find a vast majority of sites related to a set of seed sites by following just 1 or 2 links from the seeds. We discuss each of these points in detail in the next two sections.

DO LINKS BETWEEN SITES CORRELATE WITH HUMAN RELEVANCE AND QUALITY JUDGEMENTS?

The 23 people who rated topics collectively rated the relevance and quality of 346 sites. The mean relevance of these sites was 3.99, and the mean quality was 3.16 (both relevance and quality were rated on a scale of 1 to 5, with 1 being least relevant/lowest quality and 5 being most relevant/highest quality).

We investigated the relationship of site connectivity to relevance and quality judgements. It was our hypothesis that connectivity would influence these judgements, and the data support this hypothesis. Of the 309 sites, 88 were isolated, and 258 were connected to other sites in their topic. The mean relevance of connected sites was 4.09 and of isolated sites was 3.70. (This was a significant difference, using a standard two sample t-Test, $t(344) = 2.96$, $p < 0.005$). However, there was a much larger difference in the quality of connected and isolates sites. The mean quality of connected sites was 3.33 and of isolated sites was 2.66. (This was a significant difference, using a standard two sample t-Test, $t(344) = 4.36$, $p < 0.0001$). And there was a modest positive correlation between the in-degree of a site (the number of other sites that linked to it) and its quality of 0.23 ($r(344) = 0.23$, $p < 0.001$). Table 2 summarizes these results.

Table 2: Relevance and Quality

	All sites	Connected sites	Isolated sites
Relevance	3.99	4.09	3.70
Quality	3.16	3.33	2.66

The difference in quality between isolated and connected sites is quite large and worth exploring in more detail. One way we did this was by forming three subsets of sites: isolated sites, those with exactly one in-link, and those with multiple in-links. (Our intuition was that in-links should be a better quality estimator than out-links, since they show that a site's peers found it worth linking to; in-links did in fact prove to be more correlated with quality than were out-links) For each of these sets, we then computed the proportion of low quality (quality ≤ 2) and high quality sites (quality ≥ 4). As the connectivity increases, the proportion of low quality sites decreases, and the proportion of high quality sites increases. For the 88 isolated sites, 39 were bad (44%) and 24 were good (27%). For the 49 sites with just one in-link, 14 were bad (29%) and 18 were good (37%). For the 155 sites with multiple in-links, 39 were bad (25%) and 81 were good (52%). Figure 5 shows how the proportion of good sites increases with connectivity.

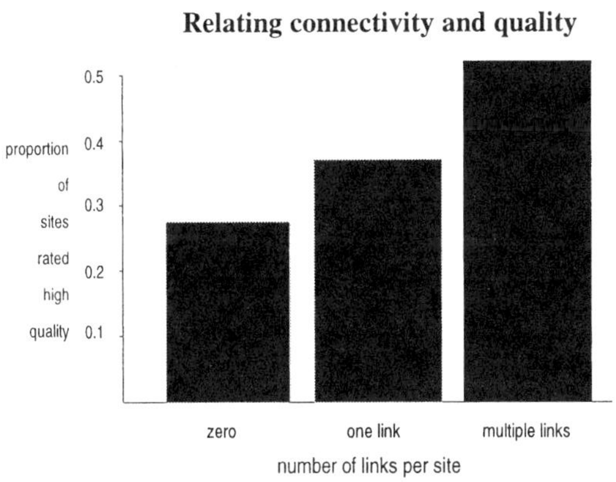

Figure 5: Quality and connectivity

Another way to see the power of connectivity is to consider the correlation between the density of a topic graph and the mean quality rating the subject assigned to sites for that topic. There was a fairly strong correlation between density and mean quality of 0.51 ($r(21) = 0.51$, $p < 0.05$). Therefore, topics that are collaboratively bound together by links tend to contain higher quality information.

These data show that using connectivity data could significantly boost the quality of sites contained in index sites, whether Yahoo or specialized indices maintained by someone who is interested in a particular topic. For example, it would be a reasonable strategy to order sites by their degree or in-degree, so the proportion of high quality sites will be highest at the top of the list.

We also can observe how manual collaborative filtering can be enhanced by computational techniques. A person might construct an initial index, then apply algorithms to both order the items in the initial index and suggest new items for addition to the index. We discuss this topic of site discovery briefly in the next section.

FROM RANKING TO DISCOVERY: NK CLAN GRAPHS

We have focused so far on analysis of a given set of sites which can be assumed to be at least somewhat relevant to a topic, since they were included in a manually constructed index page. We also mentioned the companion problem of discovering additional sites related to a given set of sites. We want to discuss our approach to this problem briefly in light of the results presented here.

Our webcrawler is part of a more comprehensive system that constructs the *NK clan graph* [13] relative to a set of "seed" sites. The NK clan graph for a seed set S is {(v,e) | v is in an N-clan with at least K members of S}. An N-clan [8] is a graph where (1) every node is connected to every other node by a path of length N or less, and (2) all of the connecting paths only go through nodes in the clan. We are interested primarily in 2-clans, that is, the 2K clan graph. The indicated subgraph of Figure 6 shows an example of a 2-clan contained within a larger graph.

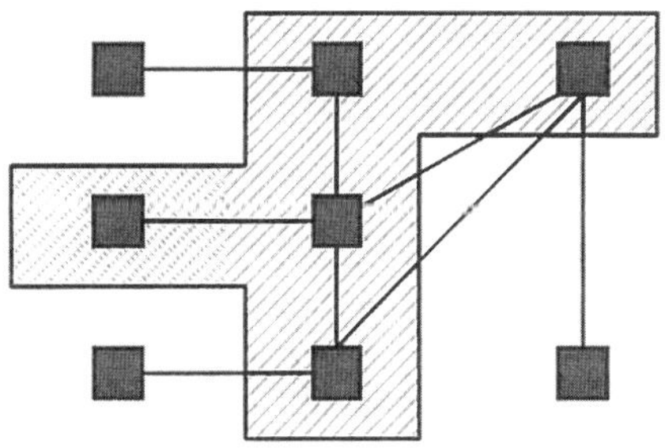

Figure 6: An example 2 clan

We proposed the NK clan graph as a useful formalization of the notion of a topically related locality of web sites (or, more generally, of documents in a hyper-linked collection). Thus, we claimed, if you know of a few sites on a particular topic, our system can construct the NK clan graph for you, and the sites it discovers and adds to the graph are quite likely to be on topic. Our argument in favor of this claim was purely analytic: we pointed out that any documents in a 2-clan also would participate in either collaborative filtering, co-citation, or citation transitivity relationships. Since these relations all group together related items, we claimed that the NK clan graph would tend to do so, too.

This paper adds an empirical argument for the use of the 2K clan graph. We showed that the vast majority of sites known to be on a topic (known because they occurred in the same index page) can be generated by following 1 or 2 links from a small set of seed sites for the topic. This is precisely how far we look when building the 2K clan graph.

In information retrieval terms, what the empirical evidence shows so far is that the NK clan graph is likely to offer good recall, i.e., it is likely to include the vast majority of web sites related to the seed sites. We still need to prove that it shows good precision, i.e., that it does not discover many irrelevant sites along with the relevant ones. That is the focus of another experiment that we are conducting in parallel with the one reported here.

Finally, we discuss briefly one promising way the resource discovery and ranking techniques we have presented here can be used. Index pages exist for many, if not most, topics. However, indices have at least two problems. It is difficult for them to be comprehensive and up-to-date, and, paradoxically, the more comprehensive they are, the harder it may be to focus in on just the high-quality sites. Our techniques can address both problems. A person who is maintaining an index can apply our techniques to follow links from the current index and discover new sites that may be relevant. The discovered sites can be presented to the index maintainer who then can decide which ones to add to the index. And site connectivity information can be used as an aid in ordering sites within the index.

This process is collaborative in two ways. First, over time the index becomes a product of emergent collaboration, since it contains sites because they were linked to by sites from earlier incarnations of the index. Second, this also is a human-computer collaboration process, with the webcrawling algorithm continuously suggesting new sites to the index maintainer based on their relevance to sites already in the index, with the maintainer retaining the final decision over what sites to include.

CONCLUSIONS

We reported on an empirical investigation into patterns of collaboration emergent from links between web sites. We both presented novel algorithms and offered empirical evidence of their utility. We showed that topics dominated by commercial sites are not collaborative at all, but that, in other topics, most sites are knit together into large, closely connected components. We also showed that connectivity is related to human relevance and quality judgements: sites from more densely connected topics receive higher overall quality ratings, and individual sites that are linked with their peers receive higher ratings than isolated sites. Finally, we argue that these findings suggest a promising approach to discover new web sites related to an initial set of seeds.

ACKNOWLEDGEMENTS

We are deeply grateful to all the members of our laboratory who supplied us with topics and spent the time to give us relevance and quality judgements.

REFERENCES

1. Botafogo, R.A., Rivlin, E., and Shneiderman, B. Structural Analysis of Hypertexts: Identifying Hierarchies and Useful Metrics. *ACM Transactions on Information Systems 10, 2* (April 1992), 142-180.
2. Carrière, J., and Kazman, R. WebQuery: Searching and Visualizing the Web through Connectivity, in *Proceedings of WWW6* (Santa Clara CA, April 1997).
3. Garfield, E. *Citation Indexing*. ISI Press, Philadelphia, PA, 1979.
4. Hill, W. C., Hollan, J. D., Wroblewski, D., and McCandless, T., Edit Wear and Read Wear, in *Proceedings of CHI'92*. (Monterey CA, May 1992), ACM Press, 3-9.
5. Hill, W.C., Hollan, J.D. History-Enriched Digital Objects: Prototypes and Policy Issues. *The Information Society, 10, 2* (1994), 139-145.
6. Hill, W. C. and Terveen, L. G. Using Frequency-of-Mention in Public Conversations for Social Filtering. in *Proceedings of CSCW'96* (Boston MA, November 1996), ACM Press, 106-112.
7. Kleinberg, J.M. Authoritative Sources in a Hyperlinked Environment, in *Proceedings of 1998 ACM-SIAM Symposium on Discrete Algorithms* (forthcoming).
8. Mokken, R.J. Cliques, Clubs and Clans. *Quality and Quantity 13*, (1979), 161-173
9. Pirolli, P., Pitkow, J., and Rao, R. Silk from a Sow's Ear: Extracting Usable Structures from the Web, in *Proceedings of CHI'96* (Vancouver BC, April 1996), ACM Press, 118-125.
10. Pitkow, J., and Pirolli, P. Life, Death, and Lawfulness on the Electronic Frontier, in *Proceedings of CHI'97* (Atlanta GA, March 1997), ACM Press, 383-390.
11. Seligman, D.D. http://medusa.multimedia.bell-labs.com/LWS/
12. Terveen, L.G., Hill, W.C., Amento, B., McDonald, D., and Creter, J. Building Task-Specific Interfaces to High Volume Conversational Data, in *Proceedings of CHI'97* (Atlanta GA, March 1997), ACM Press, 226-233.
13. Terveen, L.G., and Hill, W.C. Finding and Visualizing Inter-site Clan Graphs, in *Proceedings of CHI'98* (Los Angeles CA, April 1998), ACM Press, 448-455.
14. Wexelbat, A. History-Rich Tools for Social Navigation, in submission to Communityware'98,. See also http://footprints.media. mit.edu.
15. Wroblewski, D., McCandless, T., Hill, W. Advertisements, Proxies and Wear: Three Methods for Feedback in Interactive Systems, in *Dialogue and Instruction*, Beun, R., Baker, M., and Reiner, M. (eds.), 1994, Springer-Verlag.

MusicFX: An Arbiter of Group Preferences for Computer Supported Collaborative Workouts

Joseph F. McCarthy
Theodore D. Anagnost

Center for Strategic Technology Research
Andersen Consulting
3773 Willow Road
Northbrook, IL 60062 USA
+1 847 714 {2260,2021}
{mccarthy,anagnost}@cstar.ac.com

ABSTRACT

Environmental factors affecting shared spaces are typically designed to appeal to the broadest audiences they are expected to serve, ignoring the preferences of the people actually inhabiting the environment at any given time. Examples of such factors include the lighting, temperature, décor or music in the common areas of an office building. We have designed and deployed MusicFX, a group preference arbitration system that allows the members of a fitness center to influence, but not directly control, the selection of music in a fitness center. We present a number of empirical results from our work with this intelligent environment: the results of a poll of fitness center members, a quantitative evaluation of the performance of a group preference arbitrator in a shared environment, and some interesting anecdotes about members' experiences with the system.

Keywords

Intelligent environments, ubiquitous computing, shared spaces, human-computer interaction, social behavior, social interactions, empirical studies, evaluation, audio, audio spaces.

INTRODUCTION

We spend much of our time in shared environments – spaces in which two or more people are in close proximity and are mutually affected by tactile, olfactory, visual, and aural factors such as temperature, scents, lighting, and background noise. These factors are increasingly under the control of computers embedded in our environments. Combined with a growing variety of sensors that can detect people and their activities, these new capabilities allow for the design of intelligent environments. This new paradigm results in a shift of perspective: from viewing people as *users* of computers to a view of people as *inhabitants* of environments. One way that an intelligent environment can respond to its inhabitants is by adjusting itself to better suit the inhabitants' needs or preferences.

Traditionally, environmental factors in the common areas of a workplace are affected in one of the following manners:

- They may be held fairly constant, e.g., the décor in a hallway or entrance area.
- They may be varied based on a clock, e.g., lowering the temperature late at night.
- They may be controlled by a single person, e.g., turning on the lights in a conference room.

In each case, some thought is typically given to the expected preferences of the people affected by the environmental factors, and one can imagine instances in which explicit preferences might be sought ("Does anyone mind if I open a window?"). However, the growing proliferation of embedded computers provides an opportunity to explore the prospect of a more systematic way of taking explicit preferences into account.

MusicFX is a system that adjusts the selection of music playing in a fitness center to best accommodate the musical preferences of the people working out at any given time. The system has a database of fitness center members' preferences for a wide range of musical genres, a mechanism for identifying who is working out at any given time, and an algorithm for selecting a musical genre that will promote members' listening pleasure.

This research grew out of the juncture of two concurrent threads in the authors' experience. One is a perception that most of the research in ubiquitous computing has focused on ways that an environment might respond to a single individual rather than a group of people. The other is a

CSCW 98 Seattle Washington USA

frustration with the "lowest common denominator" music typically played in a fitness center on a daily basis.

The group preference agent embodied in MUSICFX is not limited to selecting music in a fitness center, however. It is applicable to any shared environment in which people gather for an extended period of time. For example, a restaurant provides another type of environment that might benefit from a group preference agent, however an elevator would not be a good candidate. Furthermore, the approach is applicable to environmental factors beyond music or other auditory input: visual, olfactory and tactile factors could also be adapted to the set of people assembled in a particular location. Finally, the set of preferences for each individual might either be explicitly specified by each person, or inferred based on knowledge of the person's behavior, e.g., a shopper's purchase history.

In the sections that follow, we will describe the fitness center environment in which MUSICFX operates, provide an overview of how the system works, present the results of a poll we have conducted to assess the popularity of MUSICFX among fitness center members, describe a quantitative evaluation of the performance of the system based on comprehensive logs of all events of interest, and conclude with some interesting interactions we have observed between members and the system.

THE FITNESS CENTER ENVIRONMENT

The music played in a fitness center provides for an ideal laboratory in which to experiment with a group preference agent. People are gathered together in a common location, each performing separate (though related) activities that do not typically require much attention. Since the foreground activities are not engrossing, background environmental factors become more important. Most people want to hear *some* music while they are working out; the problem for the staff of a fitness center is to decide which music to play.

The fitness center at the Andersen Consulting Technology Park (ACTP), called the Fitness Xchange (FX), is located in the lower level of our Northbrook facility, and is open to all ACTP residents from 6:00 a.m. through 8:00 p.m. each weekday. The FX has 24 cardiovascular machines (treadmills, stationary bikes, stair climbing machines, and so on), 14 strength-training machines and an assortment of free weight equipment. The number of people working out ranges from a high of around 25 at peak times (before work, lunchtime, and after work) to one or two people during mid-morning and mid-afternoon hours.

ACTP subscribes to the PrimeStar™ direct broadcast satellite service, which includes the Digital Music eXpress (DMX ©) music service, providing 91 stations of commercial-free music, each representing a different musical genre. The variety of genres includes Album Rock, Classic Jazz and Symphonic, as well as Flamenco Music, German Oldies and Beach Party. Prior to the installation of MUSICFX, the FX staff manually selected DMX stations; this manual selection process was complicated by the fact that the room containing the satellite receiver is located in another part of the building, resulting in relatively infrequent station changes.

The FX is the most popular service at ACTP, with over 600 members among the Park's 1500 residents. However, despite the general popularity of the FX, the music played in the FX was a source of controversy, accounting for 50% of the verbal complaints made by members to the FX staff and 25% of the written "suggestions" submitted anonymously by members. There are a small number of members who are quite willing to express their preferences for (or, more often, against) different types of music, and in the absence of input from the less vocal members, there tended to be a "squeaky wheel syndrome" where the complainants got their way. This factor, combined with the inconvenience of physically changing stations, resulted in only three stations – the ones that generated the fewest complaints – being played, out of the set of 91 possible stations.

The primary research goal of MUSICFX is to explore the social ramifications of a group preference agent in a shared environment, i.e., whether a system that controls an environmental factor based on people's preferences can prove socially acceptable. Related to this research goal, our more pragmatic goals for the MUSICFX system are to:

- *Democratize the music selection process.* Accommodate the silent majority rather than the vocal minority, resulting in greater listening enjoyment for FX members. The more vocal members may not be pleased as often, but the less vocal members will now have their voices "heard".
- *Increase the variety of music played.* Provide airtime for the stations outside of the lowest common denominator set. Members who work out at off-peak hours may now be able to listen to music that would never be played when larger numbers are present.
- *Offload the music selection task from the FX staff responsibilities.* Enable the staff to spend more time attending to fitness related matters rather than acting as disc jockeys.

While these goals focus on the issue of music selection in the context of a fitness center, they have broader applicability. The idea of democratizing the control of a common environmental factor could be applied to lighting or temperature levels. While people probably would not enjoy rapidly fluctuating lighting and temperature levels, increased variety in the décor of common areas might be a welcome change. Finally, any person who shoulders the burden of controlling a highly controversial environmental factor could benefit from a system that arbitrates among diverse preferences.

Having described the environment in which the MUSICFX system operates, let us now turn to a description of the system itself.

THE MUSICFX SYSTEM

The MUSICFX system runs on two Windows 95™ computers that are linked via the ACTP local area network. One computer, which we call the DMX computer, is located in the room that houses the DMX satellite receiver: it has an infrared (IR) remote control device attached to its serial port. The other computer, the FX computer, is located in the FX: all the software modules described below reside on this computer. When the system selects a new station, it sends a command from the FX computer to the DMX computer, which translates it into a channel change signal sent to the IR remote control device.

MUSICFX provides two interfaces accessible on the FX computer. The *FX member interface* allows members to login to the system, to update their preferences for any station, and to provide us anonymous feedback about the system. The *FX staff interface* allows the staff to monitor the system, manually select new stations and to adjust certain parameters that will be described below.

Underlying these interfaces, the FX computer hosts three components that enable the operation of the system: a database of FX members' musical preferences, a mechanism for identifying who is working out in the FX at any given time, and an algorithm for selecting one among the 91 genres of music that will promote members' listening pleasure. This algorithm is invoked each time an event occurs, e.g., a member enters the FX to begin a workout. Each of these components is described in greater detail below.

Preference Database

In order for a group preference agent to make an informed decision about how to affect environmental factors, it must know something about what the current inhabitants prefer. In MUSICFX, each FX member specifies his or her preference for each musical genre. The preference rating for a genre is represented by a number ranging from +2 to –2; Figure 1 provides an interpretation for each of these levels of preference.

Rating	Interpretation
+2	I *love* this music
+1	I *like* this music
0	I *don't mind / don't care about* this music
-1	I *dislike* this music
-2	I *hate* this music

Figure 1. Rating Scale for Musical Genres

A member submits an electronic MUSICFX enrollment form upon first joining the fitness center; the FX member interface also contains an update screen that permits a member to enter or update his or her musical preferences in the fitness center at any time.

Presence Detection

A group preference agent must know the composition of the group – who are the current inhabitants? – in order to make decisions about how to adjust environmental factors. Members login to MusicFX by swiping their ACTP badges across a proximity badge reader. In case a member loses his or her badge, the system also permits members to login manually, using the same login ID they use for logging their fitness activities at a separate computer maintained by the FX staff.

Group Preference Arbitration Algorithm

The group preference arbitration algorithm takes as input an M x N table of integer-valued preferences ranging from –2 to +2, where M is the number of categories being rated (musical genres) and N is the number of inhabitants (FX members who are currently working out). For each category i, and each member j, that member's individual preference for that category ($IP_{i,j}$) is used by the algorithm to compute the overall group preference for that category (GP_i) using the following summation formula:

$$GP_i = \sum_{j=1}^{N} \left(IP_{i,j} + 2\right)^2$$

The formula first converts all individual preference ratings to non-negative numbers, so that we can later apply a weighted random selection operator (described below). These values are then squared in order to widen the gap in selection probabilities between the more popular categories and the less popular categories.

Once this group preference value is computed for each category, the list of values is sorted in descending order, such that the most popular category is first and the least popular is last.

We considered the policy of always selecting the top category, but since most people typically workout at the same time each day, they would tend to hear the same music under this scheme (unless they update their individual preferences). The second most popular station might be the favorite among a few of those people, but it may never be played. Therefore, the system uses a weighted random selection policy for selecting one of the top m stations (we call this the *candidate set*), where m is a parameter whose value is set by the FX staff.

Figure 2 depicts a set of sample preferences for five people (A through E) and ten musical genres. The group preference value calculated for each genre (GP_i) is shown in the second column from the right. Assuming that m=3, i.e., the candidate set is limited to the three most popular genres, the probability of selecting each genre (Pr_i) is shown in the rightmost column. The sum of the GP values for the three most popular genres is 141, so the probability of selecting the most popular genre, Alternative Rock, is 0.48, nearly twice the probability of selecting the third most popular genre, New Music.

i	*Genre* *Person*	A	B	C	D	E	GP_i	Pr_i
1	Alternative Rock	2	2	0	2	2	68	0.48
2	Hottest Hits	1	1	2	0	-2	38	0.27
3	New Music	1	1	1	0	0	35	0.25
4	Hot Country	2	0	0	0	-2	28	0.00
5	Dance	2	-1	1	-1	-1	28	0.00
6	World Beat	0	1	-1	1	-2	23	0.00
7	Traditional Country	1	0	0	-2	-2	17	0.00
8	50's Oldies	0	0	0	-1	-1	14	0.00
9	Heavy Metal	-1	-1	-1	-1	-2	4	0.00
10	Polka	-1	-1	-2	-2	-2	2	0.00

Figure 2. Sample Preferences

Note that if these five people were to work out at the same time each day, simply choosing the most popular station would mean that person C would always listen to music that he or she does not particularly like (nor dislike). Using the weighted random selection algorithm would allow this person to listen to music that he or she likes (New Music) or loves (Hottest Hits) some of the time.

Events

There are five events that trigger the execution of the group preference arbitration algorithm:

- Member Entrance
- Member Exit
- Individual Preference Update
- System Parameter Adjustment
- Maximum Station Play Time Elapsed

Each time one of these events occurs, the algorithm is run, and if the currently playing station is no in the candidate set, a new station is selected.

Member Entrance

As mentioned earlier, members either swipe their ACTP badges or manually login at the computer. When a new member enters the FX, his or her preferences must be added to the pool of preferences used in the group preference calculation, so this login process triggers the Member Entrance event.

Member Exit

We decided not to require explicit logouts to trigger Member Exit events, for fear that people might forget to logout at the end of their workout sessions; another consideration was that the music plays both in the fitness center and the adjacent locker rooms, and we wanted members' preferences to still be considered while they are in the locker rooms. A survey revealed that the average duration of a workout, including locker room time, is 70 minutes, with a standard deviation of 20. We decided it was better to continue to include some members' preferences after they finish working out than to exclude some members' preferences while they are still working out; therefore, we set a default time of 90 minutes for the duration of a workout session. After this time, a Member Exit event is triggered, and that member's preferences are removed from the pool of preferences considered in the group preference calculation.

Individual Preference Update

Whenever a member updates his or her preferences, the pool of preferences (the set of individual preferences associated with the group of people currently working out) considered during the previous invocation of the algorithm is no longer valid. Such an update often occurs when a member decides he or she dislikes or even hates the currently playing station, even though he or she had previously specified a more positive rating for that station. After the individual preference update, the group preference value for the currently playing station would then decrease, possibly so far as to cause the current station to fall outside the candidate set. Since we don't want the current station to continue playing in this case, we trigger an Individual Preference Update event to force the algorithm to run again.

System Parameter Adjustment

When the FX staff changes a system parameter, e.g., narrowing the range of top-rated stations to be considered, the currently playing station may or may not remain in the candidate set, so a Parameter Adjustment event is triggered.

Maximum Station Play Time Elapsed

Due to the diverse, and sometimes conflicting, musical tastes of the FX members working out at any given time, we recognize our inability to please all the people all the time. One situation that we endeavor to avoid is "starvation" – one or more members never hearing music they enjoy due to the differences between their music preferences and those of the majority of people with whom they regularly workout. The weighted random selection operator is one strategy we use to reduce the likelihood of starvation. Another strategy used is to limit the period of time that any one genre will play – regardless of how popular it is – before the selection algorithm is invoked in order to select a new station. A Maximum Station Play Time Elapsed event is triggered when the specified period of time elapses.

System Parameters

The FX staff can constrain the operation of the MUSICFX system by adjusting any of the following three parameters:

- Individual Preference Filter

- Group Preference Filter
- Maximum Station Play Time

Each of these is discussed in more detail below.

In addition to a set of controls for the parameters listed above, the interface for FX staff also provides the capability to manually select new stations to play at the press of a button (rather than having to walk down the hallway to another room). The FX staff interface also includes a button to turn off the algorithm, requiring manual intervention by the FX staff for all subsequent station changes.

Individual Preference Filter

A primary motivation behind MUSICFX is to increase the listening pleasure of the FX members working out at any given time. This can be accomplished by playing more of the music that members want to hear or by playing less of the music that members do not want to hear (ideally, both). One way to ensure that the system plays less music that people do not want to hear is to prohibit the system from playing any station for which anyone present has specified a low rating. The system provides the FX staff a way to specify an individual preference filter threshold between 2 and –2; any station for which a present member has specified a preference value below the threshold is eliminated from consideration by the algorithm. For example, a threshold setting of –1 prohibits any station for which anyone currently working out had specified a rating of –2 (i.e., at least one member hates this kind of music).

Group Preference Filter

The group preference filter parameter (the variable m in the group preference formula listed above) allows the FX staff to specify how many of the top-rated stations are considered candidates for the weighted random selection procedure. The possible values range from 1 to 91, where 1 forces the system to select the top choice each time and 91 permits the system to select any station (though selection of popular stations would be more probable than selection of less popular stations). This parameter was included to give the staff some control over the variability of the music being played. Most FX members follow fairly regular workout schedules, e.g., Monday, Wednesday and Friday from 7:00 to 8:00 in the morning; thus, many of the same people work out at the same time each day. If the system always chose the top-rated station, then members would be likely to hear the same station every time they work out. While we still permit this policy – with a group preference filter setting of 1 – we also allow the music selection to vary among the set of most popular stations.

A group of stations with the same group preference value forms an equivalence class. The group preference filter threshold may arbitrarily partition such an equivalence class: some members of equivalence class will be included in the candidate set, while the rest are excluded. If there were a fixed ordering within an equivalence class, the stations that occur earlier in the ordering would tend to be played more often than those that occur later in the ordering. Therefore our sorting routine ensures that stations within an equivalence class are randomly distributed within each segment of the sorted list. This is especially important since, as noted before, the regularity of member workout times combined with a constant group preference filter would result in the same stations being prohibited each day.

Maximum Play Time

The period of time that any one genre can play without interruption is limited by the maximum play time parameter, which varies between 1 and 60 minutes. We have used an initial setting of 30. Coupled with our estimate of workout sessions lasting 90 minutes, on average, this results in at least three genre changes – for a total of at least four genres that will be played for any one member's workout

POLL RESULTS

Six weeks after we installed MUSICFX, we conducted a survey to find out how well the members liked the music being played in the fitness center. We asked members whether they thought the music being played was better, worse or the same, compared to before the system was installed. We also asked them to tell us the things they liked most, and the things they liked least, about the system.

We received a total of 71 responses, which represents more than 25% of the members considered active[1] at the time we conducted our poll. The responses are summarized in Figure 3.

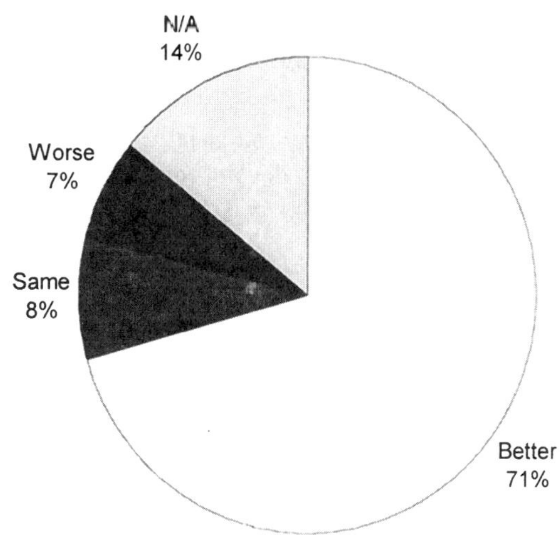

Figure 3. Popularity of MusicFX

[1] A member is "active" if he or she has worked out at least once in the preceding month.

The vast majority of the respondents (71%) said they like the music selected by MUSICFX better than the music that had been played prior to the installation of the system, and only a small fraction of the people (7%) thought the music is worse. A few people (8%) thought the music was about the same, and there was a final group of people (14%) who had joined the fitness center after MUSICFX was installed, and thus were unable to answer that question.

Nearly half of the respondents told us that they enjoyed the increased variety of music played by MUSICFX. A third of those responding told us that they liked having some influence in the selection of music. One fourth told us that they liked the "good music" played by the system. Other popular aspects of the system include exposure to new music, being subjected to "bad music" less often, and the elimination of disputes over the music since the system was installed.

MUSICFX currently has no mechanism for detecting song boundaries, so it often changes stations abruptly in the middle of songs; this shortcoming was cited by a third of the respondents as one of the least popular features. The "occasional" selection of "bad music" was a complaint among fifteen percent of our survey participants, a side effect of the greater variety of music played. Eight percent of the respondents told us that MUSICFX did not exhibit *enough* variety in its selection. Three people said the stations changed too often, while one said they didn't change often enough, and three people complained about the offensive lyrics heard on the Rap station.[2]

QUANTITATIVE EVALUATION

We are encouraged by the apparent popularity of MUSICFX, based on the results of our poll. However, we also wanted to take advantage of the extensive logs being kept by the system, and undertake an in-depth evaluation of how well the music played by the system corresponds to members' stated preferences.

In this section, we describe the data we used in the evaluation, the metrics we developed to measure the performance of the system, and the results of this evaluation.

Evaluation Data

MUSICFX maintains three log files:

- An *event log* that is updated for each of the five system events listed above (member entrance, member exit, individual preference update, system parameter adjustment, and maximum station play time elapsed).
- A *preference log* that is updated each time a member makes changes to his or her ratings for any of the 91 stations.
- A *feedback log* that is updated each time a member submits anonymous feedback through the member interface.

The data we used for the evaluation was drawn from the first two log files, which are described in more detail below. The feedback log is a text file into which comments typed in by members on a special pop-up window are anonymously written. It has only been used a few times, and the comments are similar to those mentioned above in the section on poll results.

Event Log

Every event that has some potential effect on the system is tracked in the event log. Over 5000 events were logged during the initial six-week period. Each entry in the event log includes several fields:

- *Date* and *time.*
- *Type* of event, e.g., member entrance.
- *Member IDs* of the people present, in the order of their arrival.
- *System parameter values*: settings for the individual preference filter, group preference filter and maximum play time.
- *Station* currently playing.
- The *status of each station*, including the station ID, the group preference value (GP_i) for that station, and a prohibited flag that indicates whether the station is currently a member of the candidate set or prohibited (based on the individual preference filter or group preference filter).
- *Reason* for station change (if applicable), e.g., to distinguish between station changes due to a timeout (based on the maximum play time parameter) from those due to the currently playing station falling out of the candidate set (based on a change in group preference values due to the entrance or exit of a member).

Preference Log

Each preference log entry includes the date and time of the entry, the member ID and name of the person updating his or her preferences, the new set of ratings for each station, and a flag indicating whether this is a new member enrolling in the system with an initial set of preferences or an existing member updating an established set of preferences.

[2] Due to the nature of some of the Rap lyrics, which were deemed inappropriate in a business setting, we were asked to disable the selection of this station by MUSICFX, leaving us with 90 candidate stations. Since this change occurred after the evaluation period covered by this paper, we will continue to refer to 91 stations.

Evaluation Metrics

The data collected in the MUSICFX log files provides us with the opportunity to evaluate a broad range of issues concerning the behavior of the system – especially with respect to its selection of stations – and its effect on people.

Statistics Gathered about People

Our primary goal in evaluating the data contained in the logs is to quantitatively assess the satisfaction of members, by comparing their preferences to the stations to which they were listening while in the fitness center. However, we are also interested in the distribution of ratings for different musical genres, and how that distribution changed over time.

To compute the satisfaction of members over the first six weeks, we extracted information from both the event and preference logs. For each member entrance event, we tracked the stations that were selected for that member during that 90-minute *session*, and how long those stations played during the session. We then determined the member's rating (-2 to +2) for each station at that time, and multiplied the member's rating by the length of time the member listened to that station. Dividing this number by the duration of that session gives us the *session satisfaction* for that member on a scale of –2 to +2. The average satisfaction for that member over the entire six-week period can be found by simply taking the average of all session satisfaction values. The average satisfaction for the 170 members who logged into the system during the six-week period is shown in Figure 4.

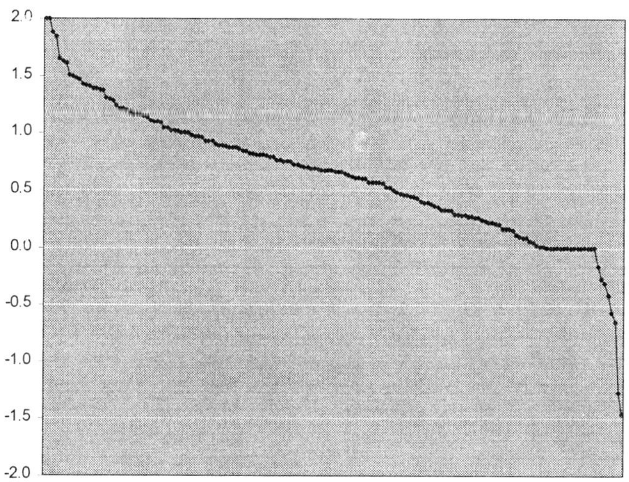

Figure 4. Average Satisfaction of FX Members

All but eight members have non-negative satisfaction values, and the vast majority of members have positive satisfaction values. Of the eight members who appear dissatisfied, i.e., have negative satisfaction levels, five had logged in fewer than five times, and can reasonably be expected to achieve higher levels of satisfaction over time. The other three members each specified a rating of –2 for 88 out of 91 stations, and therefore might be considered difficult to satisfy, with respect to their musical tastes.

We computed the overall satisfaction with MUSICFX as the average of all per-session average satisfaction values for all member sessions. For the six-week period we examined, the overall satisfaction rating was 0.64 (again, on a scale of –2 to +2). Prior to the installation of the system, the selection of music was fairly evenly distributed among three stations (Hottest Hits, Power Hits and Dance); based on our logs, we estimate that the overall satisfaction of members would have been 0.44 during this period had the previous distribution been in effect. It is interesting that what appears to be a modest gain in our satisfaction scale is still significant enough that the vast majority of people polled report that the selection of music is better than before.

We are also interested in the distribution of people's musical preferences, i.e., how many stations people generally love, like, dislike and hate. We computed the average preference for each person by multiplying each preference rating (-2 to +2) by the number of stations with that rating, and taking the average of those values. The distribution of average members across all members is shown in Figure 5 (the dashed lines indicate changes in preferences).

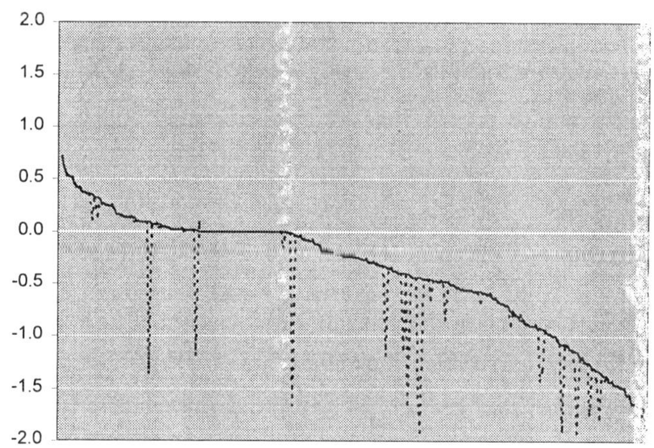

Figure 5. Average Preferences of FX Members

For the initial preference database, the average preference for all members was –0.38, confirming our hypothesis that people tend to hate or dislike more types of music than they love or like, at least while they are working out. Over the six week period, fitness center members tended to lower their ratings for various stations: 103 individual preference update events were logged, and the average preference for all members decreased to –0.44 at the end of this period. The three dissatisfied individuals mentioned above have the three lowest average preference levels of all members.

Statistics Gathered about Stations

The primary focus of our evaluation was on how the behavior of MUSICFX affected people working out in the fitness center. However, we were also interested in which stations were being played, and how well these stations were liked by the people listening to them. Therefore, we also collected statistics about the individual stations.

The first thing we wanted to find out was how often different stations were being played. Figure 6 shows the top 10 most frequently played stations, along with the percentage of time those stations were played.

Station	Percent of Total Airtime
Alternative Rock	14.3
Album Rock	9.0
Power Hits	8.6
Classic Rock	7.9
Hit Sweep	7.7
80's Music	7.6
Hottest Hits	7.5
Dance	6.5
New Music	4.4
Adult Contemporary	3.6

Figure 6. Top 10 Stations

The three stations previously played – exclusively – in the fitness center are among the top 10 stations most often selected by MUSICFX (these are italicized in Figure 6). However, it is interesting to note that the two most popular stations had not been played before, there are five stations more popular than two of the three "old" stations, and the three "old" stations are only played 23% of the time now that MUSICFX is selecting music.

In the first six weeks of operation, 77% of the airtime in the fitness center has been devoted to these top 10 stations. However, the system has played a variety of music, selecting 66 of the available 91 stations at least once during this period. This greatly increased variety is enjoyed by many, though not all, of the members, as shown in the features cited by members responding to our poll. It has also led to a variety of interesting situations that we have observed (or heard about) in the fitness center since MUSICFX was installed.

EXPERIENCES WITH MUSICFX

The community of people who work at ACTP, and who workout at the fitness center, is a technology-savvy crowd. Most members in the fitness center are quite at ease with using the MUSICFX member interface, and several have shown great interest in attempting to manipulate the system to get "their" music to play.

When we first installed the system, we recommended that the fitness center staff set the Individual Preference Filter to –1 so that the system would never select a station that was hated by one or more members present at any given time. Unfortunately, on the first day, each author separately observed a different member – at different times – who learned that whenever someone changed the rating for the currently selected station to –2, the system would change the station immediately. We therefore recommended that the Individual Preference Filter be set to –2 (essentially, turned off). One of the aforementioned individuals was observed the next day showing off his newfound manipulative capabilities, only to be frustrated by the system no longer responding to his preference changes.

Since then, the staff has experimented a few times with setting the Individual Preference Filter to –1, but this nearly always resulted in the candidate set dwindling to one or two stations, and sometimes to zero[3], whenever the number of members present approached ten. Given the heavy negative bias of members' musical preferences, it appears that the Individual Preference Filter is best not used (set to –2).

Another example of members' efforts to manipulate the system was a situation in which two members decided to see if they could cause the system to select the Polka station (Polka and Opera are tied for least popular station among fitness center members). Both members changed their ratings for the Polka station from –2 to +2. However, since there were seven other people working out at that time, most of whom [presumably] had a rating of –2 for the Polka station, two people increasing their ratings was not sufficient to put Polka into the candidate set of stations considered by MUSICFX. In fact, Polka is among the 25 stations that have not yet been selected by the system.

One member, with rather broad musical tastes, and who tends to work out during off-peak hours, has been surprised by the responsiveness of the system. He has been treated to Brazilian Music, Flamenco Music, Hawaiian Music, and a variety of other stations that are not commonly played in the fitness center. However, when other people are present, he has in some cases changed his rating on some of these stations so that stations that are more widely popular could be played instead.

Another member observed a situation in which Chinese Music was selected during a time when few people were working out. While this genre might not normally be considered workout music, one of other people present commented favorably on the music, and expressed an

[3] The system has a default station, which can be set by the fitness center staff, that determines what station is selected when the candidate set is empty, a situation that arises whenever the fitness center is empty.

interest in learning more about this type of music. MUSICFX thus has increased members' awareness of the variety of musical genres.

In addition to the members' experiences, the FX staff has also had positive experiences with the system. One FX staff member reports that complaints she has received about the music have decreased from several per day to a couple per week. Another staff member says the complaints she has received have declined from five to ten per week down to a total of three since the system was installed. Although we provided several parameters through which the staff could influence the operation of the system, the two staff members with whom we spoke reported changing system parameters only a few times, and that our default settings appear to work quite well.

The FX staff members have been enthusiastic supporters of the system since we began our initial discussions regarding plans for MUSICFX. Arbitrating among the diverse musical preferences of the fitness center members was one of the most dreaded aspects of their jobs; the increased satisfaction of the FX members has translated into a big increase in the job satisfaction of the FX staff.

RELATED WORK

A number of researchers [Hill and Terveen, 1996; Shardanand and Maes, 1995] have explored the idea of collaborative filtering, which involves inferring preferences of a user based on the preferences of other, similar, users. This inference is used to make a selection that typically affects only a single user directly. MUSICFX differs from these systems in that our system uses explicit preferences of all inhabitants to make a selection that will directly affect everyone who is present.

Other researchers have explored how environments might sense and respond to inhabitants, but most of them have focused on single inhabitants.

The Olivetti Active Badge™ system [Hopper, *et al.*, 1993; Want, *et al.*, 1992] provides a mechanism for locating and tracking individuals throughout a building using infrared badges and a network of transceivers. The system, as originally designed, did not include a representation of preferences, and was primarily focused on how artifacts (computers, doors, or telephones) might respond to an individual rather than a group. However, this kind of technology could be quite useful in the MUSICFX system, since it would eliminate the need for a manual login or a preset timeout to trigger entrance and exit events – the system could simply poll periodically for the presence of active badges in the fitness center and locker rooms.

The Xerox PARCTAB system [Want, *et al.*, 1995] also provides a mechanism for locating and tracking people who are carrying a handheld device. One application allows individual inhabitants of a room to vote on the quality or pace of a presentation using their PARCTABS; the presenter can then respond to this feedback, but the environment itself does not respond to voting. A PARCTAB could be used to control the lighting or temperature of a room – much as we can change channels with a television remote control device – but it does not appear that the designers were concerned with using this functionality in rooms with multiple inhabitants.

The Responsive Environment Project at Xerox [Elrod, *et al.*, 1993] explored how an environment might conserve energy by adjusting the lighting and temperature, based on an awareness of who was present (or scheduled to be present) in offices and common areas within a building. This work differs from MUSICFX in that it was basically a two-state system – an office or common area was either empty or non-empty – and the preferences of the inhabitants was not considered in its control strategy.

The Intelligent Room at MIT [Coen, 1997] is able to track multiple inhabitants in the room, and supports a number of methods for inhabitants to give commands to the room. While it has some capability for noting individual preferences (e.g., not playing Mozart as someone is dozing), it has no explicit mechanism for arbitrating among preferences of a group of people.

The Reactive Room [Cooperstock, *et al.*, 1997] is a shared telepresence environment which responds to its inhabitants, and has a mechanism for storing preferences for videoconference equipment usage. This work focuses on a very difficult problem – how a shared *virtual* environment might better adapt to its inhabitants, where the inhabitants are distributed across multiple physical sites. One way that the room reacts is to adjust a remote camera based on someone leaning left or right; however, it is not clear how the room would react to different people leaning in different directions simultaneously.

Cooperstock, *et al.* [1997], posit four important factors that affect any intelligent environment: the invisibility of the technology, the capability of manually overriding the system, a mechanism for providing feedback to users, and an ability to adapt to the preferences of users. MUSICFX meets all four of these criteria: other than requiring manual login, the system does not require conscious interaction on the part of the FX members, e.g., requiring people to input their preferences each time (or voting on each song); the FX staff can manually override the station selected by the system at any time; the primary feedback that the system provides is in the selection of music played, but the system also provides some feedback to each member with respect to how well the member's preferences align with those of the current group; finally, the system's primary purpose is to continually adapt to the preferences of a changing group of people working out in the FX.

CONCLUSION

Our experience with MUSICFX has shown that an intelligent environment can sense and respond effectively to the preferences of its inhabitants. The vast majority of fitness center members who are affected by the actions of MUSICFX are happy with the system, both by their own account and according to a quantitative assessment of what they have been listening to. People appreciate the ability to influence their environment, and we expect that this appreciation will extend to other environmental factors.

Fitness centers are not the only environments where adaptation to personal preferences might be beneficial. Any environment in which groups of people are gathered for significant periods of time – say, more than 15 minutes – and in which it would be preferable to listen to or watch something rather than nothing is a candidate for this approach. For example, restaurants might more effectively cater to their customers by playing music that the customers really want to hear, rather than music that the staff thinks the customers want to hear (or music that the restaurant staff wants to hear). Perhaps the issuance of frequent diner's [smart] cards could include musical preferences, as well as culinary preferences and other factors that might help make the restaurant's atmosphere and service more personalized.

Music is not the only environmental factor that could beneficially adapt to a group of inhabitants. Visual displays might adapt to a group of shoppers in a store, or perhaps in a region of a store, promoting items that are likely to be of interest to the current group. User preferences in this case might be inferred from the purchase history of the shoppers rather than explicitly requested, since shopping goals vary more frequently than music preferences. In fact, shoppers might be encouraged to identify themselves to such a system – using smart cards or some special courtesy card – by the prospect of a MUSICFX system that will play the music that they want to hear while shopping.

ACKNOWLEDGMENTS

The authors wish to thank: Chirag Patel for contributing both ideas and code toward the initial development of MUSICFX; Kelly Dempski and Eric Meidel for their assistance with the networking and hardware for the system; Madeleine Milan, Sharon Kordik and Fran Scott for their help in pushing this project out of the research lab and into the real world; and Andy Fano, Bruce Gotteiner, Mark Jones, Naghi Prasad, Annamaria Cherubin and the CSCW '98 reviewers for helpful comments on earlier drafts of this paper.

REFERENCES

1. Michael H. Coen. 1997. Building Brains for Rooms: Designing Distributed Software Agents. in *Proceedings of the Ninth Conference on Innovative Applications of Artificial Intelligence (IAAI '97)*. 971-977. Menlo Park, CA: AAAI Press.
2. Jeremy R. Cooperstock, Sidney S. Fels, William Buxton, and Kenneth K. Smith. 1997. Reactive Environments: Throwing Away Your Keyboard and Mouse. *Communications of the ACM* 40(9):65-73.
3. Scott Elrod, Gene Hall, Rick Costanza, Michael Dixon, and Jim Des Rivieres. 1993. Responsive Office Environments. *Communications of the ACM* 36(7):84-85.
4. Andy Harter and Andy Hopper. 1994. A Distributed Location System for the Active Office. *IEEE Network* 8(1):62-70.
5. William Hill and Loren Terveen. 1996. Using Frequency-of-mention in Public Conversations for Social Filtering. In *Proceedings of the ACM 1996 Conference on Computer Supported Cooperative Work (CSCW '96)*. 106-112.
6. Upendra Shardanand and Pattie Maes. Social Information Filtering: Algorithms for Automating "Word of Mouth." In *Proceedings of the 1995 Conference on Human Factors in Computing Systems (CHI '95)*. 210-217.
7. Roy Want, Andy Hopper, Veronica Falcao, and Jonathon Gibbons. 1992. The Active Badge Location System. *ACM Transactions on Information Systems* 10(1): 91-102.
8. Roy Want, Bill N. Schilit, Norman I. Adams, Rich Gold, Karin Petersen, David Goldberg, John R. Ellis, and Mark Weiser. 1995. An Overview of the PARCTAB Ubiquitous Computing Experiment. *IEEE Personal Communications* 2(6):28-43.

Designing Groupware for Congruency in Use

Wolfgang Prinz, Gloria Mark, Uta Pankoke-Babatz
GMD - FIT
Schloß Birlinghoven
53754 Sankt Augustin, Germany
{wolfgang.prinz, gloria.mark, pankoke}@gmd.de

ABSTRACT

In this paper, we present experiences from long-term groupware development, introduction, and use in an organization. We report lessons learned concerning how a complex design process operates and how its components interact. Our experiences suggest that the processes of requirement analysis, system development, and user support need to facilitate the merging of individual work patterns into congruent system usage. We confirm the changing nature of groupware use by reporting empirical results describing different learning phases.

Keywords

Cooperative design, user advocacy, groupware requirements, group work, system introduction, prototyping.

INTRODUCTION

Observing the process of groupware use as it unfolds over time can reveal a number of subtle and important factors that influence how progress is made. A longitudinal observation also enables the reconstruction and evaluation of decisions concerning the design process and system development.

Despite the widespread use of groupware systems, the process of groupware design and use is still not well understood. From the perspective of system development, observation over time has provided some valuable insights, e.g. in identifying a time frame for system changes [26]. From the perspective of system use, several important studies have identified factors that groupware practitioners should be aware of when implementing systems: e.g. the extra burden imposed on some group members through groupware participation [21], the imbalance in costs and benefits [7], unanticipated overhead [3], as well as the potential for innovating work practices [15]. Only by observing within a long timeframe could such lessons be learned.

Designing groupware requires an acknowledgement of the interplay between the tasks of gaining design requirements, system use, and system development. These processes interact and evolve over time, each aspect exerting influences on the other components. One of the main lessons learned from our experiences is that these processes need to be directed toward the goal of supporting system usage by group members so that their actions are congruent with each other. Congruency refers to all members having the same assumptions of how the system is to be used in performing their work. This cannot be accomplished unless the design team and users achieve a common understanding of the users' tasks, work processes, and system design. Thus from our view, most importantly what we gain by observation over time is the capability to better understand the dynamics of these processes in order to identify lessons and establish guidelines for future practice.

In this paper we contribute towards understanding groupware use and design by presenting empirical results from different phases involved in groupware adaptation and development. The results are based on work in the POLITeam[1] project [8] in which a groupware system was used in the course of daily work in a government ministry. From the beginning of the project to the present, we have had the opportunity to observe the users (and ourselves) through three years of system use, from introduction, through initial growing pains, through coordination difficulties, to the point where the users can report that in retrospect, the work to learn the system has paid off: groupware use has increased the efficiency of their work. As the users developed and improved their understanding of system use, and of their group, so did the design team as well improve its understanding of how the design process and the system itself affects the adaptation and learning process. To this end, in this paper we report lessons learned from the various perspectives involved in groupware implementation, and offer our experiences on what fosters and hinders system use.

This paper begins with a description showing how coordination with groupware use is related to the process of group development. We then outline our particular design approach explaining how we tried to achieve a common understanding between the design team and users, and how we tried to account for user group development. In the following section we present empirical results on the actual use of the system in the work setting, illustrating how the group strived to achieve congruent conventions.

CSCW 98 Seattle Washington USA

[1] POLITeam is funded by the German research ministry in the framework of the POLIKOM initiative.

Finally, we outline the lessons we have learned during four years of groupware system development in close cooperation with users, including three years of practical use.

ACHIEVING CONGRUENT USE OF GROUPWARE

When we first consider the process of learning groupware, we must take into account not only understanding the system functionality, but as many researchers in CSCW have pointed out, there must also be reflection on how members need to develop procedures to coordinate their work and the use of the functionality [10, 12, 20]. Developing coordination practices goes hand-in-hand with enabling various social processes in the group to develop, e.g. the building of communication networks, role adoption, resolving status and hierarchies, and articulation, to name only a few.

During the course of a group's development, group members slowly merge their different attitudes, behaviors, and social norms, gradually moving towards a congruency in the group [14]. Karl Weick [27, p. 46] describes this development as organizing a collective structure which exists "when behaviors of two or more persons become interstructured". The process of electronic group formation operates in a similar way, with some important differences. The electronic interaction of group members often occurs while members are remote. We refer to achieving congruency with groupware use as involving two processes: first, the group must develop appropriate communicative behaviors, and secondly, group members must merge different perspectives to reach common agreements about cooperation.

Communicative behaviors are the means through which group members can influence each other and create standards of behavior: e.g. by observing each other's actions, or by explicit and implicit communication [28]. The difficulty that electronic groups face during system use is that they lack the social information that groups generally gain through formal and informal interaction. This social information helps group members to evaluate each others' actions and observe discrepancies. Through this, members gradually accommodate themselves to the group (as the group accommodates to individual styles), developing commitments along the way [13]. It is in this accommodation process in which conventions are formed by the group for using the system in cooperative work. The conventions that must be formed are not static; they evolve with the group, must be robust, yet at the same time must be flexible to adapt to local contingencies [12].

In general, in groupware design, the group process and the technical system cannot be considered separately [5, 16]. Because of this interdependence, the design of the system, and the process used to support users and gain design requirements, should function together to facilitate the development of congruent behaviors in an electronic group. Two ways of achieving this are by supplementing user-user communication, and by supporting the process of establishing and maintaining conventions. Above all, the congruency process cannot be supported unless the design team and the users have a common understanding of goals and of the work to be supported.

While it is now more clear for us how the design process and groupware learning can influence each other, in the next sections we report on our design approach which aimed to achieve a common understanding between the design team and users so as to develop adequate user system support and facilitate congruent use of the system.

THE DESIGN APPROACH

The aim of our approach was that concepts and systems for the support of group work need to be developed in a situated manner [23], such that the technical system, the work practice and the users' working habits can progress together. None of these elements could be improved separately. Our technical design was guided by the idea of providing a medium that could adapt to the local contingencies of situated work, as opposed to implementing mechanisms that prescribe actions for work.

The Setting

The idea for POLITeam emerged as a result of the decision of the German parliament in 1992 to move the capital from Bonn to Berlin and to split a large number of government ministries between these locations. This decision increases the need for technological support for intra-ministerial cooperation over a distance of 600 km. The German research ministry launched the POLIKOM program in 1994 to investigate technologies to support cooperation, and to develop appropriate design and introduction methods. The focus of the POLITeam project is on the support of ministerial procedures and coordinated document processing.

Within a German ministry, there exists a ministerial organizational handbook, the GGO (a common set of organizational procedures) which prescribes the cooperation processes via hierarchical lines (department, subdepartments, units) as strongly regulated paper-based processes. However, the representation of these rigidly defined processes into electronic cooperation support systems would not be adequate, due to the situated nature of real work [19, 23].

Most cooperative work in the ministry is performed at the Unit level. Therefore, three representational Units of two departments were selected in which to implement the system: two located in Bonn, and one in Berlin. One Unit in Bonn is a central writing office, the other two Units support political decision and management processes. The tasks for these users include speech writing, program development, administration of public institutions and accounts, and correspondence with citizens. Accordingly, the majority of working time is devoted to paper-work. This includes the individual or cooperative production of documents or responding to incoming documents.

To support these tasks, the POLITeam system provides an electronic desktop that integrates standard office applications, email, and shared workspaces [17] to share documents for the support of unstructured document production processes, and electronic circulation folders [18] for the support of structured, sequential cooperation processes along hierarchical lines. The technological infrastructure used for POLITeam is LinkWorks, a groupware platform by Digital.

POLITeam is used by the members and heads of the three Units on a daily basis for individual and cooperative document production. Occasional users of POLITeam are managers and their offices at the department and subdepartment level above the unit level.

Shared workspaces were used cooperatively by two different groups in the ministry: typists in a writing office and members of the ministry Units. The members use the workspace to exchange documents with each other. The electronic circulation folders were used occasionally for the transport of bundles of documents between the Units in Bonn and Berlin, for initiating procedures along the hierarchy and for the individual structuring and organization of the electronic desktop.

Designing the user-designer cooperation process

The Scandinavian school developed methods for design at work [9]; this approach enables users to evaluate system prototypes in work-like situations. We based the POLITeam design process on this idea, but went further to enable users to evaluate a system in real work practice. We could then base further system development on these user experiences. We realized that our goal was ambitious and required responsible and careful modes of cooperation with the users since their primary goal, even when involved in a system development project, is to get their work done. Thus, we had to develop methods to involve the users in the design process, yet at the same time ensure that they will benefit in their work from their participation.

Three means helped achieve this goal: the introduction of a groupware system as a means for the articulation of requirements, the establishment of a permanent communication channel through the role of user advocates, and regular workshops for the exchange of feedback between the users and designers. The groupware system, provided to users almost from the very beginning, gave the users a tangible artifact enabling them to experience its usability and to articulate further needs.

To support the communication and cooperation between the design team and users, we developed a new role, the user advocate, which became the interface between the users and the designers. The user advocate had the following tasks:

- to support the users in working with the system, during regular site visits
- to help the users to coordinate their work and to adapt work-habits
- to observe where the system fits and where improvements were required
- to feed the user requirements back into the design process

To support user-user communication, and user-design team communication, workshops were held at regular intervals. The roles of the workshops were:

- to provide feedback on usage and to articulate further needs within the user group and between users and designers
- to give designers feedback to improve their understanding of the users' work
- to demonstrate and discuss new system functionalities
- to discuss and find conventions for the cooperative use of the system

We have augmented these communication channels with regular interviews which allowed the users to rethink and describe their actual work.

Medium vs. mechanism as technical design guideline

Although the GGO procedures appeared at first as a constraint, users revealed in interviews that they did not consider deviations from the standard GGO procedures as exceptions. This led to providing cooperation support based on the provision of flexible cooperation media instead of prescribed cooperation mechanisms. The result of that approach is a set of combinable cooperation tools. Users can coordinate their work using these tools; the tools themselves do not incorporate a priori any representation of the cooperation process [1, 19].

With a media approach, an analysis of cooperation processes in work practice must focus not only on the overall cooperation, but it must also consider individuals' actions with the shared artifacts. The electronic circulation folder has been realized as a medium to express and modify plans for work sequences in the course of their execution. The shared workspace, as a medium, stores and provides the material for cooperation. Appropriate metaphors were used to express the function of the media to the users and to guide designers during the design process [11]. The presentation and functions of the electronic media were related to their counterparts in the real world. In addition, these media had to be combinable with each other, e.g. it should be possible to store a circulation folder in a shared workspace or to forward an alias to a shared workspace by an electronic circulation folder. Similarly, switching actions between different media had to be easy. The exchange of objects, e.g. documents, between different media had to be easy and should not result in a loss of process-relevant meta-data. Additional aspects that are more related to the configurability of a cooperation media can be found in [1].

Cycles of system development

Improvement of the system occurred in cyclic processes: longer outer cycles where communication occurred between the design team and users, and shorter inner cycles contained within, where communication occurred among the design team members.

Outer Cycle

There were four outer cycles, each of which took about one year. The components of the cycles consisted of installing the system (or a new version), and the presence of user advocates at first on a daily basis, and then weekly, with the purpose to train, observe, support, and gather requirements. The cycle continued with workshops, interviews, the development of a new system version, and then installation of that version at the users' site.

During site visits, the user advocates actively solicited problems and requirements. They examined alternative ways to perform tasks with the system. They also detected different and conflicting user habits and supported the coordination of individual work styles. These discrepant workstyles were discussed at regular user workshops which served as the means to find conventions for system use. They also served to raise new user needs and to discuss new solutions between designers, users, and user advocates, which was important feedback used in the design process of the inner cycle.

Inner Cycle

The inner cycle took place within the design team. In this process, the user advocates argued from the perspective of the users, explaining their requirements, and whether they would possibly benefit from a planned feature. The designers proposed potential solutions. The design was done through prototyping, enabling us to recognize the interdependencies between the different system components. In addition, this allowed the user advocates to make a first evaluation of the features and experiment with them, using typical examples from the users' work. This very often led to another redesign cycle. Thus the design procedure was highly incremental. The inner cycle was completed with laboratory workshops where some users could try the new version, sometimes leading to another redesign. This cyclic procedure reduced the risk of disrupting work practice with an unsuitable system version. We never had to withdraw a version once introduced, although sometimes features needed to be redesigned after some use.

Stages of system development

The continuous system development yielded three consecutive POLITeam versions. The characteristic of each version mirrors the evolutionary stage of user requirements in the course of system use. We introduced the first version of POLITeam in February 1995, the second version in February 1996, the third one in December 1996, and the final one was ready in December 1997.

The first POLITeam version provided a technically stable and functionally sufficient system. In a simple way it provided most of the functionality needed by the users to start with the requirement analysis in the work setting. The functionality of that version was derived from initial user interviews. This version included a personal electronic desktop, email, an electronic circulation folder, and a shared workspace. At the beginning, this version was mainly used for the support of individual work and thus the majority of requirements targeted additional support for individual work.

The second version refined existing functionality and added new functions for a user-specific document processing.

The main requirement for the third version was the integration of the POLITeam system with the organization specific IT-infrastructure. This abolished the situation of the POLITeam users as being on an "island" within the organization. To enable the use of the POLITeam system along hierarchical lines, new functions were included that focused on the specific requirements of managerial users.

As described in the next section, in the course of time the users' understanding of groupware increased and more mature group work occurred based on the growing congruency of individual work patterns. This led to more elaborated requirements for a smoother cooperation and means for an informal coordination of work. e.g. for the support of conventions in shared workspaces, informal substitution regulations, and cooperative use of institutional mail inboxes. These needs were addressed in the final version.

POLITEAM USE

In this section, we present empirical results showing the use of the system over three years which points to different phases in groupware learning leading to congruent usage.

Method

The method used for identifying the phases in groupware learning was in-depth field research, supplemented with user interviews and protocols from five design team-user workshops. User interviews were conducted at three points during the project: before the system was installed, in order to determine work requirements, midway through the project, and at the close of the project after three years.

The site visits were documented in logbooks. The user advocates recorded where users had problems in system use and user requirements, along with some general observations. In order to track the process by which group members merge their individual work patterns into congruent system usage, user experiences were categorized into three categories using content analysis. The coding was checked by a second person. Where a few discrepancies were found, they were discussed and recategorized. The categories were:

- *General System Understanding:* Problems that concerned understanding single-user system functionality, e.g. Word, Excel, icon views, etc.
- *Individual Use Events:* Problems and experiences that concerned system handling of all aspects that do not concern shared objects, e.g. setting up individual document templates, organizing personal directories.
- *Group Use Events:* Problems and experiences that concerned system handling and understanding of shared objects.

Phases of system use

As a result of this categorization, rough phases of group development with the system were identified, and are shown in figure 1. The events in General System Understanding were so few that they were combined with Individual Use Events for the description. The six month divisions seemed to be a reasonable amount of time in which to characterize system use; smaller time categories had less data, and time frames longer than six months lowered the precision. We can describe these phases qualitatively as follows.

Initially, we see by far in the first six months that most of the group events concerned setting up group functionality, by the typist and Unit leader: shared folders, assigning colors for editing in Word, and new access rights profiles for common document templates. A few requirements emerged at this point concerning awareness: the typist wanted automatic notification to inform her clients when documents were completed, and the Unit leader wanted to know who made changes to a shared object. Also, the users discovered that they needed file codes for the common documents. In terms of individual events, here we see users setting up their own information structures. We also see a lot of "growing pains", i.e. problems with general system understanding: the Word menu, enlarging icons, formatting, etc.

In the second six months, we see more setting up of group functionality, mostly by the Unit leader: an address list, shared calendar, and internal shared folder. A few groupware requirements emerged: different access rights for different groups, and changing the date of the shared folder to reflect changes in the contents. Single-user events also concerned mainly general system understanding.

During the third six months, no new functionality has been set up, but it is now being refined. This concerns mainly the document template collection, since the users and typists are now established in a group work pattern and are now exchanging a variety of documents quite regularly. For example, the typist wanted access to a Unit member's document templates to ease her work. Single-user events show that users are beginning to customize features of the system, e.g. setting up personal document template collections, and creating email directories.

After one and a half years of system use, the group events are similar to the last phase: functionality is continuing to be refined in minor ways. A few requirements occur: the Unit leader wants to be able to establish shared templates for circulation folders, and employees should be identified in shared document printouts. Interestingly, two (new) users report that the naming conventions for documents is not clear to them. Single-user events also continue with minor understanding problems.

After two years of system use, we see a definite change to the events that are occurring. Many users are now reporting problems that they are having as a result of other users' actions: users are concerned that files are taken out of the shared folder and are lying on others' personal desktops, and there is confusion reported in how addresses in the shared address book are organized. First trials of electronic circulation folders were initiated by the newly-connected managers of the Units which led to the report of stalled folders (as with paper folders). Single-user events are minor, generally dealing with small problems with Word.

In the last six months of the project, again we see more problems reported that concern other users' actions: e.g. only owners can erase documents. The Berlin users want to identify only changes from specific users in Bonn, not all users. Also, Berlin and Bonn Unit leaders need specific colors assigned for editing. In addition, we see refinements for the awareness feature, e.g. reporting changes made on objects within a shared folder, and showing changes between Bonn and Berlin users. In addition, important requirements emerged concerning establishing a registry for documents. Single-user events continue as minor adjustment problems.

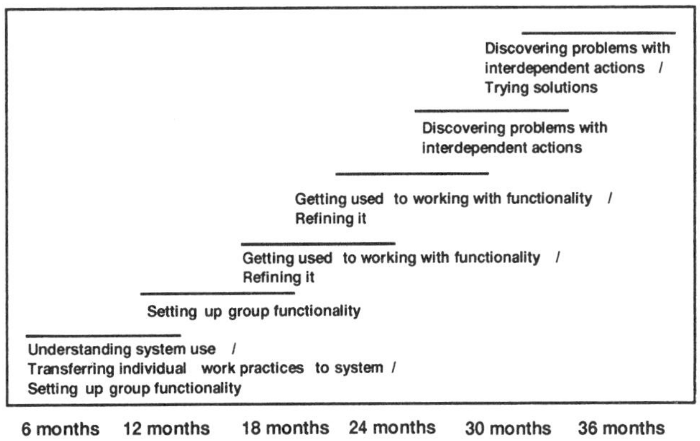

Figure 1. Approximate stages of groupware learning.

What is interesting for us, is that we see the group going through a process of developing congruent actions. We especially see a number of events that suggest that after about two years, now that group functionality has been set up, and work patterns seemingly firmly established, the group members now report problems that concern coordinating their work patterns. We interpret that at this point the group members are beginning to recognize the consequences of their interdependencies. We have some evidence that shows that the same types of problems with interdependencies occurred very early on in the system use, yet were not considered by users to be due to the actions of other members. For example, in the first three months of system use, the typist complained that an icon which usually turned blue was now turning black due to a system problem. Yet the typist did not make a connection that the color change was caused by a status change due to another user's action. This suggests that only with continued system use, the users gradually became aware of how others' actions were affecting their own system use, and they adjusted and accommodated their behaviors accordingly.

We see the workshops as playing an important role in facilitating users' recognition of how their work patterns interacted. In the first workshop, the users already began discussing basic conventions concerning naming, storing, and deletion of objects. In the second workshop, the users discussed categorization of shared documents through the assignment of file codes, as well as common structuring of the folders. In the third workshop, which took place after one and one half years, conventions for new situations were discussed, e.g. for cases of substitution, or when a member leaves the team. Also, conventions were elaborated concerning the appropriate technical means for a cooperative task, and general system use behaviors, e.g. starting the system in the morning, and checking mail regularly.

Although conventions were discussed heavily at the workshops, particularly the latter ones, the work to make the conventions work was actually delegated by the users to the design team, as opposed to being self-regulated. This was not our intent; our intention was to facilitate thinking about conventions, and we had expected that the users would take the responsibility. This was an indication to us that following conventions requires overhead and that technical support may be needed.

LESSONS LEARNED

At this point we have presented an overview of our experiences with the design approach and POLITeam use. During this process of designing a system in tight cooperation with users, we have learned a number of lessons with respect to group work practices, as well as on design issues for groupware. In the following, we have selected those that we feel best portray the challenges of continually integrating design with system use.

Lesson 1: Opening windows of opportunity

Research has shown that during the introduction of a groupware system, there appears to exist a limited timeframe in which modifications to a system can opportunistically be made [26]. Beyond this frame, changes are difficult to introduce since work patterns with the system become routinized, making system changes harder to be accepted.

In our view, windows of opportunity refer not only to system modifications but also to enabling the development of the appropriate group dynamics involved in groupware use. Group work requires a continual adaptation process to changing situations and tasks. This requires that group members are willing to continually reflect on their working habits, and on what is needed for their work. Windows of opportunity must therefore exist and be kept open (or reopened) to insure flexible adaptations of work patterns. Otherwise, the willingness for adaptation decreases, as does the potential for improvements of individual usage and cooperative processes. However, our experience has shown this window to be influenced by specific events, as well as the course of time.

The workshops became a forum in which events occurred to reopen windows; in fact the users themselves took the initiative. Although the designers intended the workshops for discussing design issues, the users took over and discussed their individual and group work contexts and practices. For example, a shared folder containing public information, which had been neglected, increased in use after the users discussed it (although curiously, the discussion concerned defending why it was not used). The user advocates also served to keep the window for change open. When problems with the integration of the house email system occurred (stage 3 of the system development), the user advocates stimulated the usage of the email by raising awareness of the external email functionality after the problem was solved.

Lesson 2: Lengthening the acceptance and tolerance window through user trust and resilience

Long term cooperation requires a trustful relationship between users and the design team. We have learned that the foundations for that relationship are laid in the first phase after system introduction and that serious consideration and immediate reactions to the user requirements are factors for building this relationship.

In the initial interviews, the impression of the design team was that the users viewed the introduction of the POLITeam system with a mixture of expectation and skepticism, motivation and anxiety. Common reactions from users were that they would need a lot of teaching, and in fact, they requested it. To achieve a trustful relationship and increase acceptance of the system, the user advocates stayed full-time for two weeks in the users' working environment. In this way, the advocates could immediately spot new requirements and feed them directly back to the design team in order to find a quick solution that could be realized on-site. For example, urgent requirements such as a reconfiguration of access rights, interface terminology, and document templates could be fulfilled directly on-site by adaptations and configurations of the system platform. For more complex problems, e.g. awareness, workspace administration, and integration of a registry, the designers came up with proposals for solutions which were discussed with the users at workshops or at site visits. The Ministry location in Bonn was closely located to the designers' site. In case of technical problems, site visits were possible within one hour.

Later during the project, users often mentioned that the immediate reaction to their needs contributed to the feeling that they were taken seriously as an important factor in the design process; they were not just treated as guinea pigs. By experiencing that their requirements were taken up and realized in new system versions, users became more tolerant to system functionality that was insufficient or lacking. They believed that these issues would be solved in the future and continued the system use instead of becoming frustrated. This relationship was later put to a test when the installation of a new version led to a dramatic setback of system performance at the client-PCs. Although users complained, system use did not drop since they expected that soon a solution would be found based on their previous experiences. However after the problem was solved by increasing the system memory in each PC, the users made it clear that again the fast reaction was important.

This observation adds a new dimension to the "windows of opportunity". Whereas the technologies studied in Tyre and Orlikowski [26] already passed the test of technical and organizational feasibility, POLITeam actually was the test for the technical and organizational feasibility of a groupware system in a ministerial setting. It was crucial to keep the tolerance window open to make the technology work for the users, and to do this, it was necessary to create a situation in which users felt that their problems and requirements were taken seriously and fulfilled within a foreseeable time-span. Our experience thus shows that the events that keep the window of acceptance open are immediate feedback on users' needs and a quick inclusion of urgent requirements in new system versions.

Lesson 3: Users cannot always predict their own system needs

Only after some time of system use, could the users gain a deeper understanding of how groupware could support their work. We discovered that what users may judge as attractive for their work practice at the outset may not be what they actually use. One user expressed this as, "Now we know how we work". In all of our discussions with potential users, the electronic circulation folders were judged to be the most attractive feature, even when they were tried during a laboratory workshop. Although improved during the course of the project, electronic circulation folders turned out not to be suitable for the particular tasks of the users. The users could not have predicted that: 1) they would use workspaces as the means for the permanent organization of their cooperative work; and 2) joint text production would be done in the shared workspace, instead of email exchange as the typists used before the groupware introduction. Not using the electronic circulation folders may be due to the horizontal cooperation of the users; a different finding may occur when hierarchical cooperation exists. At the end of the project, it was occasionally used in the cooperation with the Unit leader's superior.

Another finding for us was that something that appears theoretically reasonable for users may turn out quite different in practice. For example, the users requested that the system should ask for a file code upon document creation. However in use, most users did not obey the command, specifying a dummy code, and some complained that they felt "dominated by the system". This made it especially clear to us for the need to carefully understand the work process underlying system use [4].

Lesson 4: Supporting users in real work provides better feedback for system development

By gathering user requirements in the course of real work, we were able to learn many needs that were not articulated during interviews; this is due to both observing and supporting users in their situated work environment [23, 25]. The user advocates were external to the group; for this reason they were able to discover discrepancies among group members in their real work. They could develop an overview, seeing the whole cooperative network which the users themselves had trouble seeing. For example, it was discovered that different user groups adopted different naming conventions for the same documents. Also, some users worked on shared documents inside the shared workspaces whereas other users pulled the shared documents onto their personal desktops. The writing office manager complained that she no longer had access to the documents when she needed them. Removing documents from the shared workspace reduced the transparency and visibility of the cooperation.

Yet the user advocates also changed the way that users worked by presenting others' viewpoints, mediating, and discussing with users alternatives or limitations of the system. This support provided high quality requirements, e.g. membership administration, awareness, and conventions, since they were expressed in a situated context, often immediately, using the POLITeam system as the expressive medium.

Lesson 5: Conventions are eased with technical support

We learned that for a group to become congruent in its groupware behavior, a variety of conventions are needed. One can differentiate between conventions which can only be enacted through social means, and others that need technical support. For example, conventions that require extra actions on particular objects can be ideally supported technically by flexibly attaching configurable enablers that perform these actions automatically [24]. In POLITeam, a convention was established that removal of an object from a folder should leave an alias in the folder. This was supported technically with the option of applying it to particular folders. By applying a technical implementation that supported the user in applying the convention without enforcing it, it was easier for the users to follow the convention of not removing objects from the shared folder. Our lesson in this case is that designers need to give special consideration to conventions that require extra cognitive or manual overhead by the users.

Lesson 6: A medium approach requires awareness

The medium approach enabled a self-organization of cooperative work within the group instead of prescribing a sequence or turn-taking of cooperative actions. We learned that it requires the provision of awareness features to make the cooperation transparent and to avoid additional overhead for the coordination of situated activities. In the first system version, we excluded all functions that had the potential of being misused for purposes of controlling other users' system behavior, e.g. notification of changes of documents. We had the fear of getting in trouble with the union and many users during the initial interviews mentioned their concern about being controlled. However, the extensive use of shared folders led to a number of requirements for a notification functionality for the actions of users on shared objects. Users were tired of sending notification emails to inform others who were dependent on their results. Thus, it was necessary to provide notifications to make cooperative actions visible and to inform partners about intermediate actions or the completion of a task.

The user advocates discovered that awareness notifications were useful for understanding the system behavior in asynchronous work processes. In particular, it can aid users in attributing system behavior to another user's action, thus facilitating the users in thinking of a cooperative system use model, as opposed to a model for individual system use. Before awareness facilities were introduced, one typist misunderstood the disappearance of a document from a folder not as a consequence of another user's action, but as a failure of the system.

It became clear that the awareness mechanisms need to be tailorable to different user groups, different contexts, and individual preferences. For the Bonn users, identifications of all authors of text modifications were relevant. However, what was not foreseen was that for Berlin users, only the final changes made by the two Bonn leaders would be relevant. Seeing all changes was confusing and created overhead for the Berlin users.

Lesson 7: Prototypes are design specifications

Prototypes are a valuable tool for cooperative prototyping studies [2] and as a "proof of concept". We have learned that during the design process they serve also as the design specification. In the early project phase, many prototypes have been developed to evaluate the practicality or realizability of the different requirements. These initially quite simple prototypes were quickly extended and revised in several versions, as more requirements and design proposals and ideas were born. However, many versions were abandoned and thrown away by a frustrated designer after it was evaluated within the design team, until we reached a stable version that was released for a new system version at the users' site. We often asked ourselves if we could have done a better job, by a more detailed system specification in advance in contrast to quickly implementing ideas in a prototype. However, our lesson learned that groupware cannot be evaluated prospectively on a theoretical basis answers that question. In most discussions concerning a design decision, the design group was fairly confident that we would have found a good solution. But when experimenting with the resulting prototype, immediately new perspectives on the problem, as well as the interplay of the new component with other functionalities were revealed. The different perspectives of the designers and the users, represented through the user advocates, allow only an iterative approach to the final system design. Our experiences show that instead of a theoretical paper-based design specification, it is the prototype that plays the role of the design specification in the inner cycle of our cooperative design approach.

Lesson 8: The potential and limitation of off-the-shelf groupware platforms

An off-the-shelf groupware platform proved to be a good basis for a cooperative design in work practice, but it needs to fulfill a number of requirements to enable an adaptation to the work setting and to allow sophisticated developments.

The LinkWorks groupware platform provided the basic tools for the realization of the POLITeam system components. It offers an object-oriented API (Application Programmers Interface) for a functional extension and integration of external applications. Our experiences with this platform led us to the following general requirements:

- The integration of external applications is important for embedding the groupware platform into the existing IT-infrastructure.
- The platform must support an adaptation to the specific terminology of the work setting to support the mapping of real-world artifacts to their electronic counterparts.
- The initial introduction of POLITeam required a reduction of the overall functionality: to reduce complexity, to exclude functionality that could be misused for controlling purposes, and to support the building of shared usage and cooperation patterns.
- Prototyping tools should be provided either by the platform itself, e.g. through scripting languages, or must be capable of being integrated.
- The programming interface should not only provide methods for an extension of the functionality, but also for a modification of the behavior of basic functionality, i.e. access control mechanisms, listing events of user actions, presentation methods at the graphical user interface, and system consistency [6].

Although these experiences are based on a particular platform, we believe that they are general enough to be applicable to other platforms too. In fulfilling these requirements, a groupware platform possesses a high potential for cooperative design in work practice, since it frees the design team from investing too much effort in building and dealing with the technological infrastructure. It enables concentration on the fine tuning of specific aspects of cooperation support. However, the limitation comes to pass, when the last requirement is not accomplished. In our case the realization of awareness features [22] and a group-based tailoring functionality [24], was neither supported on the client nor server side of the platform. As a result, the realization of these functionalities in a new client made a reimplementation of the standard groupware-client necessary which required 50%-60% of the whole development effort. Unfortunately, it is almost impossible to anticipate these development problems, since a user-driven approach makes it difficult to foresee upcoming user requirements.

SUMMARY AND CONCLUSIONS

In this paper we presented our experience from four years of system development including three years of users' work practice. Our goal was to support group work with appropriate technology, within the constraints of a ministerial setting. We discovered this to be a continual and dynamically changing development process. What contributed to these dynamics were the interactions and influences between the system development, design process, and system use. Interestingly, the rates of change in these components were not constant, but rather fluctuated over the course of the project. Sometimes we observed many effects occurring rapidly, e.g. an increase in requirements after a new POLITeam version was introduced, or increased system usage after a workshop. In these cases, the events that opened the "windows of opportunity" (e.g. workshop discussions) were valuable because they lengthened the timeframe in which system features could be accepted, and they increased the openness of the users towards experimentation.

Both the design process and system design must support the congruency process of a group. This involves observing whether users have the same assumptions about their cooperative work with the system, and helping users to become aware of, and to find methods to coordinate their interdependencies. Interdependencies may arise through planned cooperation and use of the functionality, but there also exist interdependencies in a group of users who are simply using the same shared objects without explicit intent to cooperate with these objects. Experiencing and understanding the implicit dependencies of groupware use requires learning over time as well, as does the use of groupware features for intentional cooperation. An important factor for achieving this is the technical support of awareness that can make people's actions and the group context visible, and therefore facilitates the management of interdependencies. User conventions appear to be necessary to adjust different work patterns among a group. However, obeying conventions may involve enough extra effort so that they are not followed. Technological solutions can ease the following of conventions, yet the challenge is that they remain flexible to adapt to the local contingencies of situated work.

The design process should function to keep windows of opportunity open so that users are open to new features of the system. Routinized system use can lead to the danger of preventing users from being open to change, particularly change which may benefit them. With the media approach we used, system use is not very predictable. Therefore, it is especially important that users do not become routinized too quickly in their system usage, which would hinder the potential for emergent change in their work patterns. The design approach must also react flexibly to emerging collaboration patterns.

Perhaps one of the strongest lessons that we have learned in the course of the project is that the design process itself must take the situated nature of group work into account. The well-elaborated four-year project plan used for funding was soon relegated backstage as we became aware that we needed to adapt our methods to new situations in the group's work as they arose. Formal business process analyzing of workflows, formal object-oriented specification of system functionality, and formal project plan milestones were abandoned, and instead scenario-based understanding of situated work processes, rapid prototyping, and user-driven priorities were adopted.

Although we hope that the POLITeam system will remain in the user organization after the project is over, it is not yet clear. At the time of this writing, the IT-department is still in the decision phase whether or not POLITeam becomes the organization-wide strategic groupware system. Discussion of the worst case scenario with the pilot users reveals that although the technical system may be withdrawn, the ideas and concepts will survive. The pilot users will look for ways in how to apply the cooperation patterns they developed in POLITeam to the standard organization-wide system, which supports simple file sharing and email. Furthermore, the IT-department involves some of the pilot users in the decision process. We were glad to hear that all users are willing to participate again in such a pilot test. The reasons for this are that they felt that they became a valuable partner who influenced and determined the design process, and that they have achieved an increased competence in technical, organizational, and social aspects of groupware. It was not just us who learned a list of lessons, but also the users as well.

ACKNOWLEDGMENTS

Many thanks to Wolfgang Gräther and our anonymous reviewers for comments on this paper, to all other members of the POLITeam project and especially to all POLITeam users for their motivated participation in the project.

REFERENCES

1. Bentley, R. and P. Dourish. Medium versus mechanism: Supporting collaboration through customization, in *Proc. of Fourth European Conference on Computer Supported Cooperative Work (ECSCW '95)*, Stockholm, Sweden, H. Marmolin, Y. Sundblad, and K. Schmidt (eds.), Kluwer, 1995, 133-148.
2. Bødker, S. and K. Grønbæk. Cooperative Prototyping Studies - Users and Designers Envision A Dental Case Record System. In *Studies in Computer Supported Cooperative Work - Theory Practice and Design,* J.M. Bowers and S. Benford (eds.), North-Holland, Amsterdam, 1991, 315-332.
3. Bowers, J. The Work to Make the Network Work: Studying CSCW in Action, in *Proc. of Conference on Computer Supported Cooperative Work,* Chapel Hill, NC, USA, R. Furuta and C. Neuwirth (eds.), ACM Press, 1994, 287-298.
4. Button, G. and R. Harper. The relevance of "Work Practice" for Design, *Computer Supported Cooperative Work: The Journal of Collaborative Computing 4,* 4, 1996, 263-280.

5. Button, G. and W. Sharrock. The Production of Order and the Order of Production: Possibilities for Distributed Organisations, Work and Technology in the Print Industry, in *Proc. of Fifth European Conference on Computer Supported Cooperative Work,* J.A. Hughes, *et al.* (eds.), 1997, 1-16.

6. Dourish, P. The Parting of the Ways: Divergence, Data Management and Collaborative Work, in *Proc. of Fourth European Conference on Computer-Supported Cooperative Work: ECSCW '95,* Stockholm, H. Marmolin, Y. Sundblad, and K. Schmidt (eds.), Kluwer Academic Publishers, 1995, 215-230.

7. Grudin, J. Why CSCW Applications Fail: Problems in the Design and Evaluation of Organizational Interfaces, in *Proc. of CSCW '88,* Portland, Oregon, ACM, 1988, 85-93.

8. Klöckner, K., P. Mambrey, M. Sohlenkamp, W. Prinz, L. Fuchs, S. Kolvenbach, U. Pankoke-Babatz, and A. Syri. POLITeam: Bridging the Gap between Bonn and Berlin for and with the Users, in *Proc. of ECSCW '95,* Stockholm, Kluwer, 1995, 17-32.

9. Kyng, M. Experience with Participative Application Development, in *Proc. of IFIP 13th World Congress,* K. Brunnstein and E. Raubold (eds.), Elsevier Science B.V. (North Holland), 1994, 107-119.

10. Malone, T.W. and K. Crowston. What is Coordination Theory and How Can it Help Design Cooperative Work Systems, in *Proc. of CSCW '90,* Los Angeles, USA, ACM Press, 1990, 357-370.

11. Mambrey, P. and A. Tepper. Metaphors and System Design. In *Computers As Assistants. A New Generation of Support Systems,* P. Hoschka (eds.), Lawrence Erlbaum Assoc., Mahwah, New Jersey, 1996, 269-280.

12. Mark, G., L. Fuchs and M. Sohlenkamp. Supporting groupware conventions through contextual awareness, in *Proc. of Fifth European Conference on Computer Supported Cooperative Work,* Lancaster, U.K., J. Hughes, *et al.* (eds.), Kluwer Academic Publishers, 1997, 253-268.

13. Moreland, R.L. and J.M. Levine. Newcomers and Oldtimers in Small Groups. In *Psychology of Group Influence,* P. Paulus (eds.), Lawrence Erlbaum, Hillsdale, NJ, 1989, 143-186.

14. Newcomb, T.M. Interpersonal Balance. In *Theory of Cognitive Consistency - A Sourcebook,* R.P. Abelson (eds.), McNally, Chicago, 1968, 10-51.

15. Orlikowski, W.J. Improvising Organizational Transformation Over Time: A Situated Change Perspective, *Information Systems Research 7,* 1, 1996, 63-92.

16. Paetau, M. Configurative Technology: Adaptation to Social Systems Dynamism. In *Adaptive User Support - Ergonomic Design of Manually and Automatically Adaptable Software,* R. Oppermann (eds.), Lawrence Erlbaum Associates, Hillsdale, 1994, .

17. Pankoke-Babatz, U. and A. Syri. Collaborative Workspaces for Time Deferred Electronic Cooperation, in *Proc. of GROUP'97: International ACM SIGGROUP Conference on Supporting Group Work,* Phoenix, AZ, S. Hayne and W. Prinz (eds.), ACM Press, 1997, 187-196.

18. Prinz, W. and S. Kolvenbach. Support for Ministerial Workflows, in *Proc. of Conference on Computer Supported Cooperative Work (CSCW'96),* Boston, MA., M.S. Ackermann (eds.), ACM Press, 1996, 199-208.

19. Robinson, M. and L. Bannon. Questioning Representations, in *Proc. of ECSCW '91,* Amsterdam, Netherlands, L. Bannon, M. Robinson, and K. Schmidt (eds.), Kluwer, 1991, 219-234.

20. Rogers, Y. Coordinating Computer Mediated Work, *Computer Supported Cooperative Work: The Journal of Collaborative Computing 1,* 4, 1993, 295-315.

21. Rogers, Y. Exploring Obstacles: Integrating CSCW in evolving organizations, in *Proc. of Conference on Computer Supported Cooperative Work,* Chapel Hill, NC, USA, R. Furuta and C. Neuwirth (eds.), ACM Press, 1994, 67-77.

22. Sohlenkamp, M., L. Fuchs and A. Genau. Awareness and Cooperative Work: The POLITeam Approach, in *Proc. of HICCS'97,* Maui, Hawaii, IEEE Computer Society Press, 1997, 549-558.

23. Suchman, L.A. *Plans and situated actions. The problem of human-machine communication,* Cambridge University Press, Cambridge, 1987.

24. Syri, A. Tailoring Cooperation Support through Mediators, in *Proc. of ECSCW'97: Fifth European Conference on Computer Supported Cooperative Work,* Lancaster, UK, H. Hughes, *et al.* (eds.), Kluwer Academic Publishers, 1997, 157-173.

25. Twidale, M., D. Randall and R. Bentley. Situated Evaluation for Cooperative Systems, in *Proc. of CSCW'94: Conference on Computer Supported Cooperative Work,* Chapel Hill, NC, USA, R. Furuta and C. Neuwirth (eds.), ACM Press, 1994, 441-452.

26. Tyre, M.J. and W.J. Orlikowski. Windows of Opportunity: Temporal Patterns of Technological Adaptation in Organizations, *Organization Science 5,* 1, 1994, 98-118.

27. Weick, K.E. *The Social Psychology of Organizing,* Addison-Wesley, Reading, MA, 1969.

28. Williams, J.S., J.D. Martin and L.N. Gray. Norm formation or conditioning, *Small Group Behaviour 6,* 1975, 141-150.

Representing Fieldwork and Articulating Requirements through VR

James Pycock[1], Kevin Palfreyman[2], Jen Allanson[2] and Graham Button[1]

[1]Xerox Research Centre Europe,
61 Regent Street,
Cambridge.
CB2 1AB
U.K.
{pycock, button} @xrce.xerox.com

[2]Computing Department,
Lancaster University,
Lancaster
LA1 4YR
U.K.
{kev, allanson}@comp.lancs.ac.uk

ABSTRACT

Virtual Reality has attracted much attention in CSCW as a means for providing 'Collaborative Virtual Environments'. In this paper an alternative use is made of VR for CSCW. Our work focuses not upon VR as an actual interface to CSCW systems but as a means for providing a rich environment in which to, firstly, represent the results of ethnographic study and, secondly, to explore requirements for a collaborative system by envisioning new work arrangements. We report on our use of VR in this way and what it offers for supporting the transition between ethnographic fieldwork and system design. We also report on the transition from a 3D envisionment to designing a 2D system intended for real world use.

Keywords

Ethnography, Virtual Reality, Envisionment, VRML, Workspaces, Process simulation.

INTRODUCTION

In recent years a number of CSCW researchers have explored the use of emerging virtual reality (VR) technology as a means to support cooperative work [1, 10, 11]. The development of these 'Cooperative Virtual Environments' (CVEs) represents a radical shift away from single user VR systems. Such single user VR technologies are typically oriented towards supporting the manipulation of complex objects rendered in 3D, disembedded from any context and indeed often displayed floating in 'black space'. CVEs, on the other hand, are characterised by the rendering of virtual places (meeting rooms, theatres, marketplaces and so on) which are inhabited by multiple distributed users who are mutually represented to each other in order to support cooperative action and interaction within a shared virtual space. A number of CSCW applications of this technology have been reported such as virtual conferencing [10] and collaborative information retrieval [1]. Such 'mutual reality' applications attempt to utilise CVE technologies to provide arenas in which social interaction may take place and through which cooperative work may be supported.

For many in CSCW these virtual environments offer a new form of interface technology not only for interacting with computational resources such as database systems or Computer-Aided Design applications but for cooperating with other users [9]. The recent emergence of internet-based CVEs [8] and the development of standards such as VRML [18] has further heightened the interest in these technologies. The increased accessibility of such internet-based CVE technologies has significantly extended their user base and resulted in the rapid 'colonization' of large virtual spaces. That CVEs offer this potential for providing a new form of interface technology for CSCW has led some to explore the worth of social science contributions to the design and evaluation of such systems. Issues such as social interaction within CVEs have been studied [5, 6] while contributions from ethnography have included empirical studies of real world activities and settings in order to inform the design of CVE systems which may be inserted in support of the work in these settings [3] as well as scoping the applicability of CVE technology relative to the requirements of the work they seek to support [12]. This paper, however, provides a different use of virtual reality technology for CSCW. It focuses not upon the technology as an actual interface to a system, but upon the potential for using virtual environments as a means of exploring and articulating requirements for collaborative systems. Our emphasis has not been upon making VR into a CSCW environment through developing CVE functionalities, but upon the use of VR as a tool for addressing a number of specific problematics within CSCW concerning social science contributions to system design. In this way, the paper offers an alternative relation between ethnography and VR technology in CSCW. This is achieved through the development of VR models which are grounded in

CSCW 98 Seattle Washington USA

empirical studies of real world settings and are oriented towards CSCW design but which are nevertheless not CVEs nor themselves intended as interfaces through which cooperative work will be conducted.

The Cross-over Between 2D and 3D

Before describing our work in detail it is worth noting a further difference between this work and previous research in CSCW. The development of CVEs has been informed by a background of concepts identified over the years through the experience of attempting to produce effective 2D CSCW systems. Well established notions in CSCW such as 'awareness' and 'shared context' helped scope the rationale for much of the first CVE work. More recently a number of researchers have derived insights through explicitly considering this cross-over between 2D and 3D collaborative environments. Smith [16], for example, has transferred concepts developed in the course of designing 2D multi-user interfaces to 3D CVEs. In particular, he extends the provision of 'subjective views' for different participants to CVEs. Rodden [13], on the other hand, has explored the applicability of representations such as graph theory for describing both 2D and 3D cooperative systems. Additionally, Benford et al's [2] staging of artistic events using 3D CVE technology has suggested orientations to such occasions and their 'event management' which may be equally applicable to some 2D multi-user sessions. The research reported here also addresses the transitions between 2D and 3D collaborative environments, though in different ways to those described above. This previous work has considered *general* concepts developed in one technology for their applicability in another technology. Existing concepts from 2D CSCW systems have been applied to 3D CVEs and issues discovered through the development of rich 3D worlds have been transferred to 2D cooperative systems. Our work has, however, involved the use of VR in the articulation of requirements for a *specific* cooperative system and the transfer of particular features of a design *solution* from a 3D envisionment to a 2D platform. This use of VR has taken place within the context of a larger project aiming to develop specific system solutions for use in the near term as commercial products for particular work settings.

AN ETHNOGRAPHY OF LARGE-SCALE DOCUMENT PRODUCTION

The background to this research has been work carried out within the Studies of Technology, Organisations and Work group (STOW) in the Cambridge Laboratory of the Xerox Research Centre Europe (XRCE). A major focus for the group is to understand the impacts which network technologies have upon the ways in which organisations do business and coordinate activities. Work place studies are used to investigate the impacts of network technologies upon work practices and work processes and to understand, for a specific work setting, what opportunities are enabled by these technologies and what barriers exist to their effective use.

One such study within STOW has investigated large-scale document production through observations of the ways in which factory production printing is managed and organised [7, 4]. The organisation studied — Establishment Printers (EP) — has multiple print sites geographically dispersed throughout the UK. Typically each site may manage on any one day the production of over a million documents. One of the topics of this study has been an attempt to understand the impacts of networking together these sites so as to allow distributed document production (DDP) across sites. The focus has been upon understanding the work practice and business issues involved in DDP rather than technical issues of bandwidth, file format compatibility and the like. The study has been able to identify some of the enablers and barriers to DDP that exist. Networking for DDP offers clear advantages in terms of providing the capability for load balancing across sites, for making available specialist resources previously only accessible at one site to the whole organisation, for allowing production at the site nearest the customer or the customer's customer and so on. A distributed production environment would mean though that certain problematics would be systematically encountered and, unless addressed, these could constitute serious barriers to making DDP work in practice. For example, effective load balancing requires knowledge of the production capacity utilization across sites. There is little point distributing a print job to another site for production if that site lacks the capacity (of the right sort at the right time) for producing the job. However, at present the only mechanism for obtaining this information about spare capacity, and hence the only means to identify which sites to collaborate with in distributed production, is to telephone around all of the sites. This is a 'hit and miss' process that would be unable to cope with the demands of regularly engaging in DDP.

Moving Towards Design

This ethnography of large-scale document production had produced a detailed understanding of factory production printing and had isolated some of the central issues that would effect a move towards networking production environments. The challenge for STOW was to move from this ethnographic fieldwork towards informing system design through a process of conveying what had been observed at EP sites about how work was done there and by presenting supporting fieldwork materials (photographs, videos and so on) in a manner which could inform the design of systems to support DDP. In addressing this challenge we faced a number of problems, problems which have occupied many in CSCW for some time. That is, having spent long periods of time at a work place attempting to understand in detail how work there is undertaken there, nevertheless, remains a need to, firstly, effectively convey the rich details of what is observed at a work site to those who are not able themselves to visit the site and, secondly, to represent the mass of materials which are collected during fieldwork in a form which is most useful for design purposes.

Within CSCW such concerns have motivated the development of tools which are not so much aimed at supporting the traditional activities of the ethnographer in structuring and organising fieldwork data for analysis purposes, but which are aimed at assisting in the *presentation* of ethnographic accounts for the specific purposes of informing system design. Hence, in addition to existing qualitative data analysis applications such as Nudist [14] and The Ethnograph [15], which support tasks such as data coding and indexing, ethnographers in CSCW have explored the use of new tools such as the Designers' Note Pad (DNP) [17] in an attempt to also make the results of their analyses more readily available in forms which may be more suitable for system design purposes. By supporting diagrammatic representations, tools such as DNP attempt to allow the presentation of ethnographic accounts in forms other than traditional natural language and relatively unstructured text. However, a third challenge faced our project as it sought to move from ethnographic fieldwork to systems design. This concerned a desire not only to provide intelligence on the work practices within a print production environment but also to convey ideas which had emerged from the project for orders of solution to the problems of DDP based upon a need to overcome anticipated barriers to DDP. That is, our intention was not to only provide accounts of work as it is presently undertaken nor to only provide critiques of existing systems such as that reported in [4] (interesting though they may be), but to begin a constructive engagement with system design. We required a means for moving from detailed observations of present work practices to the development of requirements for future technologies and orders of design solutions to existing or foreseeable problems for the work. Again, in having to address this topic, we orient towards a persistent issue for ethnographic work within CSCW. That is, according to some, ethnography suffers from being overly focused upon present work practices which is problematic given that new systems are inevitably transforming of the ways in which work is done. While we do not necessarily agree with the formulation of this criticism, our work on this project has involved finding a way to develop and articulate requirements for future DDP systems on the basis of fieldwork.

Articulating a 'Lightweight' Solution

In particular we sought a way to convey an alternative order of solution to the problems of DDP to that which was commonly assumed to be the best way forward within the industry and indeed within parts of our own organisation. We wanted to suggest that a 'lightweight' solution to supporting collaboration between sites was possible. Our ideas for a lightweight solution were 'multi-dimensional' and there were a number of different elements that we needed to convey.

Firstly, such a solution had an *organisational* element to it in that it aimed to preserve the present status of EP sites which operate as independent business units with their own customers, targets, accounts, charging and so forth. This autonomy of the sites provided them with the essential ability to compete in local markets with locally determined prices and locally based customers. In addition, it also allowed local control over the ordering of production as described in [7] which, given the massively contingent nature of their work, was vital for effective production management. Our ideas for a 'lightweight' solution for DDP sought to avoid the need for organisational restructuring and to avoid the formation of some centralised 'command and control' unit to automatically dispatch jobs to what would then become satellite units.

Additionally, our notion of a 'lightweight' solution had *work practice* and *work process* elements to it in that we wished to extend rather than replace existing ways of working. These existing practices were not only successful but, given that DDP was likely to add to rather than replace existing single site production, such practices would remain necessary even in a fully networked environment. In other words, print work that arose from jobs received over a DDP network would have to be smoothly interwoven with locally sourced jobs being managed through the established work practices in these sites. We sought, then, a DDP system that left these practices intact and enabled new procedures for DDP to be folded into existing ways of working.

Finally, we also sought to build upon the *artefacts* and *devices* that were presently used to coordinate and manage production within single sites by making these artefacts available in a distributed networked environment. These devices included the production schedules (or 'Forward Loading Boards') and production monitoring devices (or 'Load Monitors') described in [7]. Our focus at this stage was not so much on the improvement of these devices with the addition of extra features and functionality (though this was clearly possible and desirable); instead we were concerned initially to see these artefacts as evolved and locally constructed solutions to making manageable the 'calculus of production' [7] in a print site. Our 'lightweight' approach sought to comprehend the *order* of solution that these devices presented. For example, it sought to understand how they displayed 'at a glance' the status of production, how they were instantly revisable in the light of unfolding circumstances, how they formed the focus for collaborative decision making in production management, how they enabled managers to keep the order of work 'in their heads' and so forth. Our 'lightweight' solution attempted to draw upon the nature of these devices but to extend their usefulness to address the barriers that would arise from networking for distributed production. In seeking to show how they could be made available within a networked environment in ways which would address these barriers we also sought to articulate a 'lightweight' solution which allowed the use of existing practices and stock-in-trade competencies in the interpretation of these artefacts. In other words, our intention was that the skills used in interpreting these artefacts as they presently existed within single sites could, in a DDP scenario, be deployed in interpreting similar artefacts made available by other sites through a networked production management system.

(In fact our notion of a 'lightweight' solution also had *technological* elements to it in terms of avoiding the need for a homogeneous technological infrastructure and so as to allow more flexible collaborations between 'loosely coupled' sites. However, as these issues mainly concern the development of an actual system for DDP rather than the VR envisionment described in this paper, then they are not elaborated upon here).

The challenge for us, however, was to find a way to give some form to our alternative order of solution and, in so doing, to unpack some of its details.

MODELING WORK PLACES

In this context of seeking to move from ethnographic fieldwork to system design, we have turned to using VR not as an actual interface to support the work observed but as a mode of representation for fieldwork *and* as a means for visualising future ways of working. We draw upon the powerful modeling capabilities of VR in order to develop models of real world work environments and to build on these to produce visualisations of future workspaces which are nevertheless firmly grounded in a detailed understanding of specific ways of working. For us this is the key to using VR to articulate system requirements on the basis of work place studies. In this way, the models which we build are not rapid prototypes of early versions of an actual system interface, but rather provide an environment which visualises an order of solution to work problems. Furthermore, it was necessary for us to convey elements of the 'lightweight' solution which were not only technological but involved new work processes, work practices and particular organisational operational structures. These elements can be at best implicit when the level of a specific user interface design has been reached and we were concerned to use an envisionment environment in which they too could remain visible. Finally, much of what we wanted to convey concerned the temporal and spatial nature of existing and future work processes and, as we shall describe, 3D VR offered a less static medium than floor plans, photographs or process models in this regard.

VIRTUAL WORKSPACES FOR DISTRIBUTED DOCUMENT PRODUCTION

We have then developed comprehensive VR models of EP print factories in order to articulate and provide access to our fieldwork materials as well as to provide an environment in which future scenarios for DDP can be visualised (for example, Figures 1, 2 and 3). We have used the VRML language in order to make our models navigable through a web browser and hence readily accessible to our globally distributed system design teams. The models we have built convey a range of features of the work settings and contain a number of components worth describing.

Figures 1, 2 and 3: Models of EP print factories

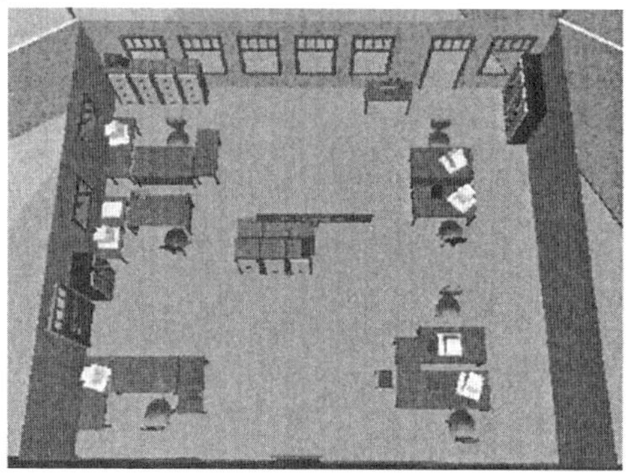

Conveying Spatial Layout

Firstly, we have built models of all the departments (Administration, Origination, Digital Print and so forth) within EP sites. These are the locations where all of the various print production processes take place (order entry, scheduling, proofing, plate making and so on). The 3D models allow a viewer to gain a sense of the layout of EP sites, their departments, work areas, machines, desks, artefacts and the like. Conveying spatial layout in this way is oriented towards presenting aspects of the work arrangements that are socially significant and significant for the work rather than purely presenting an architectural model. For while architects do use 3D models precisely because 2D floor plans can be notoriously hard to interpret when seeking to gain a sense of a site, our concerns extend to include the role of spatial arrangements in the organisation of work. For example, it is possible to see in these models how the production schedule in EP does not reside on someone's computer screen but is a public display in the work place and is visible 'at a glance' from the desks within the Administration Department which are themselves allocated to particular role incumbents. In this way, VR has proved to be a useful medium for displaying how the everyday activities of 'looking and seeing' and the practices of 'using your eyes' are supported by the arrangements of the work environment. (As we shall discuss, this has been important for us when seeking to show how these practices, which are presently restricted to a local site, might be extended to a distributed environment through technology and hence form the basis of a lightweight solution to some of the potential problems of DDP).

Animations of Work Process

Secondly, in addition to the free navigation of these models, an animated simulation of the work processes that a print job goes through has been built. This shows the movement of artefacts through the work place, the transformation of artefacts and the operations of associated machines upon those artefacts. The simulation utilizes the functionality of VRML 2.0 to provide a dynamic component to the model of the work site (something that we have noted is missing in other representations such as floor plans or static process diagrams utilized in tools such as DNP). The simulation is under the user's control and is stepped through by clicking arrow objects placed at points within the model. These arrows trigger the stages in the process simulation. They also change the user's viewpoint onto the world so that their view moves from, for example, one desk to another while the movements of the objects of the work at that point (typically documents) are animated (Figure 4). In this way, they allow a user to 'follow the job' as it moves through production in the print factory. The workflow is visualised and contextualised within the spatial layout of the workplace. Transformations of the physical materials of a print job are also animated. For example, the models visualize the placement of metal printing plates on to EP's large traditional print presses and show the subsequent production of printed paper coming off the presses.

Simulations of Coordination Devices

Thirdly, specific production management artefacts (such as 'Forward Loading Board' schedules and 'Load Monitors' [7]) have also been built in a form which end-users can directly manipulate and consequently use to simulate operations of the corresponding real world artefacts.

In the screen shot shown in Figure 5, we see the Administration Manager's desk during the order entry process. Data is entered from the 'Customer Order Form' into a database through the manager's PC. From this a 'Job Ticket' is printed off. Above the manager's desk is the 'Forward Loading Board' which displays the production

Figure 4: Snapshots of an animated work process

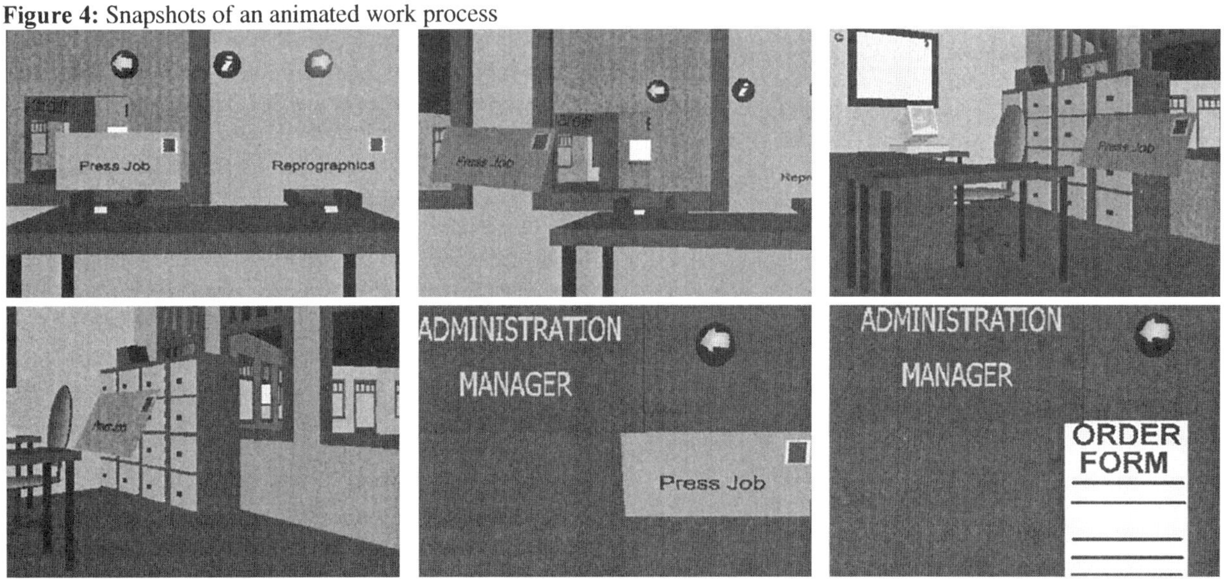

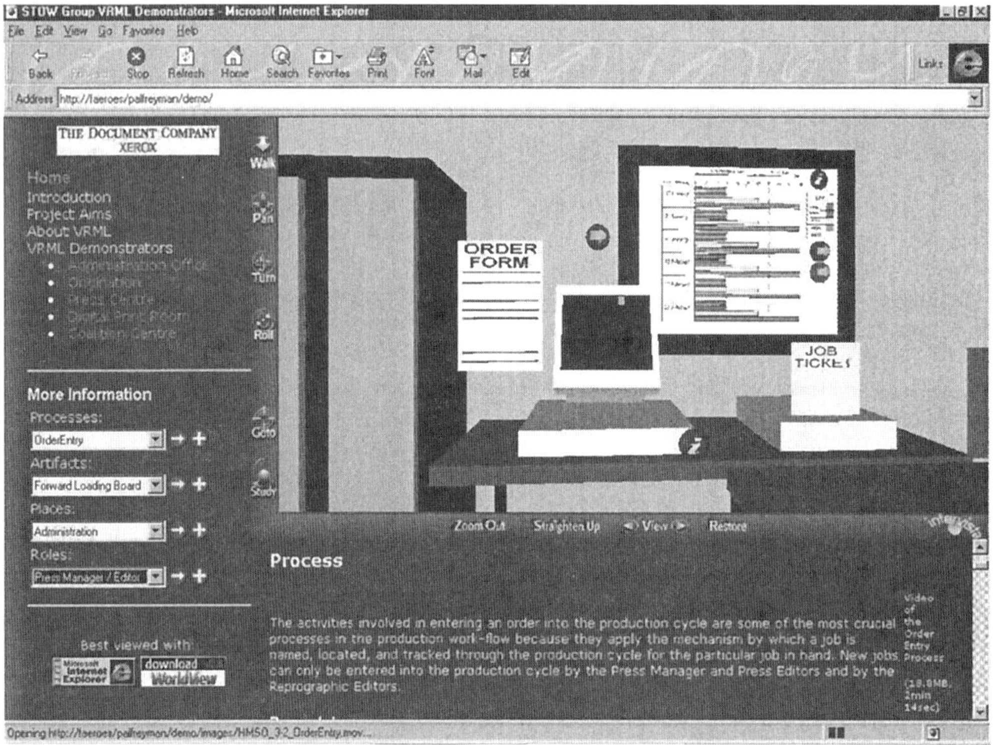

Figure 5: The Administration Manager's desk

schedule. The order entry process is animated within this VRML model and the 'Forward Loading Board' is directly manipulable in ways in which the real world artefact is (for example, by placing the cursor over the device and dragging one of the columns to 'block out' allocated capacity on a printing press). This VRML model is presented within one frame of a web browser. The frame underneath the model is used to present descriptions and information derived from fieldwork and which are relevant to the process stage being viewed at the time.

Providing Detail on Demand

Fourthly, further 'information nodes' are included within the models using an '*i*' icon. These provide 'detail on demand' by allowing users to access (if they wish) additional multi-media presentations of fieldwork materials which have been segmented into information on roles, artefacts, places and processes and which are relevant to the point where these information nodes are placed. These provide not only access to additional descriptive information, but also to further results of the analysis work of the project concerning the work practices of large-scale document production. In the screen shot shown in Figure 6, an information node has brought up a video of the real world activities involved in order entry. Process diagrams, photographs, scanned documents and the like can also be accessed in this way. (Additionally, this information can be directly accessed at any point through menus that are permanently displayed in the left-hand frame of the browser).

The VRML model acts, then, as a persistent top level representation from which further information and representations can be accessed as required or according to the context provided by the 3D model. This allows us to utilize the strengths of the VR representation (spatial context, free navigation and so on) while also linking to other representations such as process diagrams or video clips which may better convey certain forms of information such as process overviews or fine details of work activities. The model may then augment rather than replace text based accounts, process models and so forth.

Figure 6: Information node for the Order Entry process

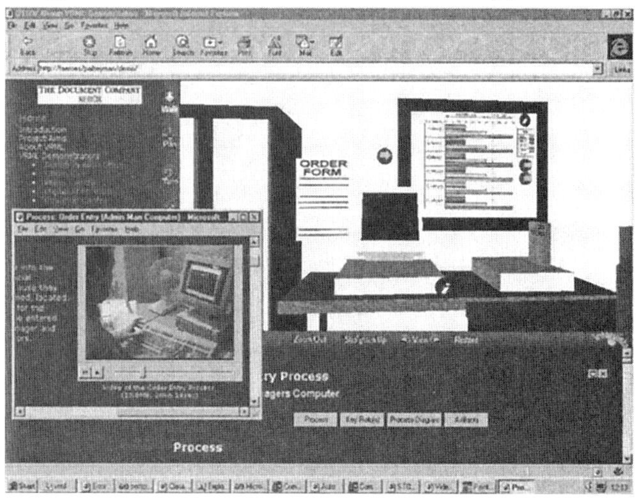

VISUALISING FUTURE WAYS OF WORKING

As well as providing an innovative way of presenting fieldwork materials derived from workplace studies, VRML offers a rich modeling environment in which new collaborative work arrangements can be envisioned. In this way it was possible for us to begin to move beyond representations of how things are now to how they may be. For example, in the case of DDP there is a transition from locally based single site document production to multi-site distributed production through the use of network technologies.

Conceiving of Future Spaces

In order to begin to give some form to our alternative 'lightweight' approach to DDP, we developed a model of a virtual centre that was accessible from all the distributed sites we had modeled. This gave us a starting point for considering how an electronically generated centre could support DDP collaborations without requiring an organization to restructure to provide a physical centre. From this starting point it has been possible to articulate further DDP requirements by addressing questions such as 'what would this space be used for?', 'why is it needed?', 'who would go there and when?' and 'where would they go when leaving the space?'.

Populating Spaces with Artefacts

It has also been possible using this model to show how a 'lightweight' order of solution to DDP barriers could build upon the existing production management devices in use in EP sites. By addressing the questions of 'what would need to be in this space to enable DDP?' and 'what artefacts would people take with them to conduct DDP?' in terms of the possible uses of existing devices, then we have been able to further articulate our 'lightweight' alternative solution.

Figure 7: The Coalition Centre

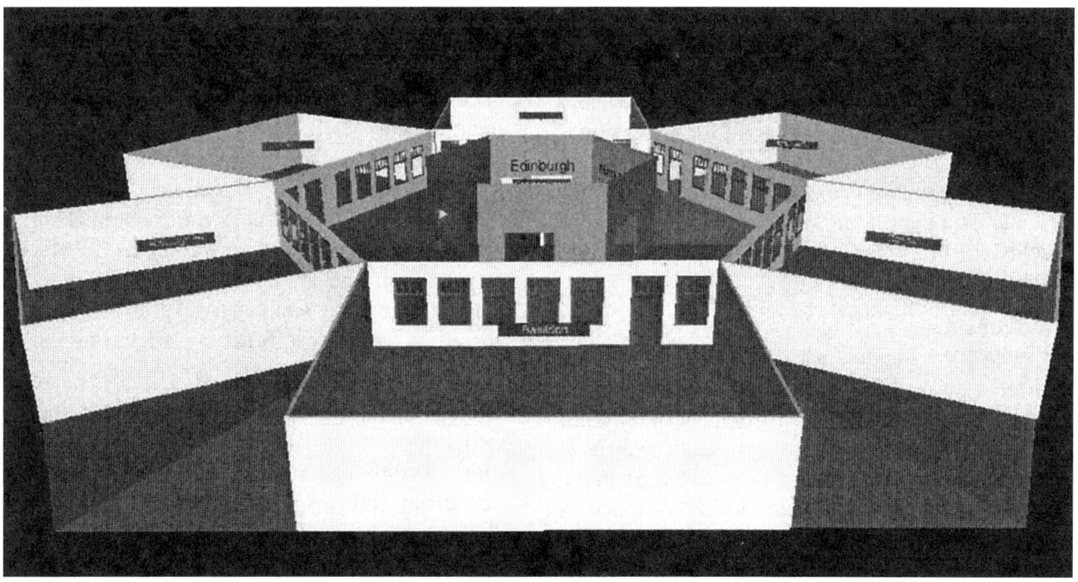

Consequently, in the screen shot shown in Figure 7, we see a virtual 'coalition centre' model which acts as a 'hub' which can be visited from multiple EP sites. This virtual centre acts as a meeting place for autonomous sites, not a command and control centre. Within the centre are displays of the different sites' production management devices, the relevance of which has been determined by the fieldwork analysis. For example, multiple Forward Loading Boards from different sites are displayed within the centre. As each of these represent the planned production capacity utilization of a site, then the visual juxtaposition of the collection of such devices within the same electronically generated space may enable human schedulers to use their existing skills in 'looking and seeing' to identify 'at a glance' spare capacity across sites rather than just within a single site. In this way, we are able to envision elements of a 'lightweight' solution to one of the identified barriers to effective load balancing in DDP. Such an order of solution relies upon the visual display of existing production management artefacts and hence contrasts with alternative 'heavyweight' systems that either require the technical integration and exchange of data between distributed scheduling engines for the purposes of automating job allocations or the centralisation of production control into the hands of some 'command' centre. Furthermore, such a persistent graphical display offers advantages over the temporary audio connections available at present through telephoning around sites.

Mapping Future Processes

Additionally, because this new virtual place can be modeled along side the facsimile models of real world places (Administration, Origination, Digital Print and so on) in *continuous* space, then it is possible to show in the model movements in and out of these places and the transportation of artefacts across the organizational boundaries which are visualized in the models.

New work processes required in a future DDP scenario can be modeled and can include those which cross traditional site boundaries and which in our 'lightweight' solution utilize an electronically generated 'coalition centre'. For example, previous screen shots showed models in which the Forward Loading Board is visualized on display in the Administration department of a site (Figures 5 and 6). Attached to this artefact in the model are two arrow nodes, one of which triggers a simulation of present work processes for single site production while the second triggers a step through of possible future work processes needed for DDP. These two routes are then visualized in the same environment and the simulation of future work processes is able to convey the need to transport particular artefacts and materials from one site to another. Locating these two arrows on the Forward Loading Board is also used to indicate one of the results of the project's analysis — that it is at scheduling time that a decision can be made between local or remote DDP production and that it is at this point that new work processes for DDP will have to be folded into existing ways of working.

DISCUSSION

Within CSCW, ethnography has been pioneered as a method which seems to hold potential for informing system design. To realise this potential it is essential that means for bridging between fieldwork and design be found. It has, however, long been recognized that moving from one to the other is not necessarily an easy matter. This work seeks to add to the toolkit of methods available to support this transition by providing a novel presentation of fieldwork materials. The presentation we have developed *augments* traditionally text based fieldwork accounts with other media and segments accounts by separating some of the threads which may be interwoven in conventional descriptions as well as using hypermedia to change the linearity and accessibility of these accounts. VRML is used to provide a persistent top-level *orienting* representation from which further purpose specific representations, such as process diagrams, can be accessed on demand. In addition, VR provides a rich environment for articulating requirements for orders of solution to work problems and for conveying a range of spatial and temporal dimensions of present and future work arrangements. To conclude, we wish to briefly reflect upon the experiences of using this tool in moving from our fieldwork to system design and outline some of the further directions we are pursuing.

'Gearing into' Design

It has been our experience that using VR in this way has facilitated the rapid and effective leveraging of a fieldworker's knowledge of a work environment in deriving potential contributions for system design. Using VR as a mode of representation meant that we were able to move quickly from debriefing sessions with an ethnographer to iteratively building up facsimile models of the workplaces that were so familiar to the fieldworker as a result of their studies. This account of the workplace could be developed using 'primitives' which the fieldworker could instantly relate to. The fieldworker could easily 'gear into' the development of a model being produced in terms of graphical representations of existing spaces, artefacts and devices — rooms, desks, Forward Loading Boards and so forth. Once the geometry of the spaces was in place, the models could then be augmented with spatial and temporal information on the movements, transitions and transformations that result from the activities of the work. (However, while such models have many useful features that provide us with powerful resources for conveying fieldwork materials and design concepts, it is clearly the case that additional effort is required to construct such virtual reality models. Currently, in order to build the type of 3D VR model that we have portrayed in this paper, it is necessary to have an in-depth understanding of VR toolkits. The problem is not one of simply constructing a geometric model to represent a building, but that in order to 'bring the model to life', the developer must construct a complex network of interlinked behaviours. Exactly how much effort is involved, however, is dependent upon just what tools are available. It is already possible, for example, to download libraries of common geometric objects (desks, chairs and the like) from the internet and in creating the models presented here we also generated a small library of useful behaviour objects, enabling more rapid future development through the re-use of existing components. More sophisticated and higher-level creation tools such as 'key frame editors' are also becoming available all the time. Consequently, it is already the case that building the models presented here would be a very different order of endeavor today to what it was when we were engaged in developing them).

It is important to stress, though, that the models we have developed are *analytic* models. We mean by this that they embody an analysis of the setting and the organisation of the work encountered in it. Thus, the models are not the presentation of 'raw data' but rather what has been made of such data by the ethnographer. What is modeled in the VR environment is, consequently, not simply domain knowledge or surface characteristics of the setting. (In fact, VRML is in many ways particularly poor for conveying surface detail with any degree of photorealism). In part the effort involved in developing complex VRML models such as ours from the ground up, object-by-object, surface-by-surface using the simple geometric primitives of VRML forced us to give careful consideration to just what it was that was important to convey and present.

In this sense the represented world of a virtual model may perhaps offer certain advantages over photographic or video records of the work environment when what one is concerned with is conveying an account of particular features of the work for system designers. The reason for this is that merely presenting a setting in visual form using, for example, video recordings will still require the designer to attempt to formulate an understanding of the setting and the organisation of the work they are designing for but without equipping them with the situated and contextual resources with which to understand and find that organisation in what they see. The designer would have little more than a partial view of the situation and gain little more than a 'tourist' perspective upon the scenes of a print site. On the other hand, the traditional purely text based ways of presenting an analysis of the setting and the organisation of the work, although indeed presenting the results of an ethnographic study, are often unable to present much of the data the analysis is based upon and do not provide the means with which to make the analysis more flexible. The VR model then has the advantage of presenting an analysis of the setting and the work based upon ethnographic research while also providing some of the data and a flexible method of organising it. In this way it does not completely tie the designer to what the ethnographer wishes to convey.

Additionally, the model provides the opportunity to understand different configurations of working and organising processes, neither of which is available through traditional forms of representing ethnography in design. The ability to construct hypothetical new functionalities in the form of, for example, new spaces for interaction and cooperative work also, in this case at least, facilitated the process of idea generation and stimulated ethnographers and designers in working together to imagine new possibilities. Utilizing such rich VR environments can 'kick start' the design process by allowing all participants to 'gear into' designing envisionments which start from the familiar and extend to the novel. It provided a context within which to address the requirements for distributing information between sites by addressing the issues in terms of questions about what would be in these spaces, what would be transported across existing organisational boundaries and so on. Furthermore, as we always viewed the VR environment very much as an envisionment and not a system for deployment in support of the actual conduct of the work, then it had the additional benefit of encouraging us not to narrow down too much too soon the design possibilities being explored.

Collaborative Virtual Envisionments

In considering the future directions that this work may take, we are considering revisiting some of the multi-user capabilities offered by CVE technology. For though we only set out to provide a means through which requirements for a cooperative system could be articulated using VR, the development of these virtual models does present further interesting possibilities for developing a CVE version. Producing a multi-user version of the model could enable the telepresentation of the fieldwork and the envisionment of orders of solution for DDP. Remote designers and ethnographers may be able to cooperatively explore the models, simulating roles and interactions if they wish. The ability to 'inhabit' a role could, for example, be particularly useful when it is important to not only be able to follow a job through a work environment but to be able to take the perspective of a role within a workflow. We are already exploiting the abilities for remote viewing of the VRML models through standard web browsers in our distributed development efforts and are looking to explore a CVE version of the models in the future.

Migrating Understandings to 2D Platforms

Effectively conveying an alternative lightweight solution has enabled us to inform high-level product visions and market strategies. However, our final challenge has been to also migrate the understandings developed using this modeling environment to the design of less 'exotic' technologies which are more likely to be deployed in the near term as means for actually supporting DDP. Our concern has been to facilitate the migration of specific features of the envisionment from 3D to 2D system design. This work is already well underway, and the VR models we have developed have enabled those designers with whom we are working most closely on developing prototypes and who have never visited the field sites to gain a sense of the fieldwork environment, to rapidly understand the order of solutions we envisage and to see the grounding and sense of these solutions within the work of factory production printing. Such results might have been achieved through other means, such as handing over fieldwork reports, but our ability to augment such representations with a rich 3D environment provides us with a range of extra resources for conveying field work and design concepts. For example, within one environment we can present the spatial and temporal dimensions of work such that workflows are visualised within the context of a 3D navigable model of the work setting, we can construct new workspaces as extensions to models of existing real world places, we can model possible work processes in and through these various spaces and so forth.

Our approach in developing a 2D prototype has been to exploit the fact that a number of CSCW technologies, which, while not VR based, nevertheless, create shared workspaces. We are using 2D shared and persistent workspace technologies to develop electronically generated 'coalition centres' and other spaces designed to support DDP 'in anger'. Having articulated design requirements initially in this rich VRML environment (and in terms of modeling places, the movements of artefacts, boundaries and so on rather than user interface issues of menus, buttons and the like) it is proving possible to develop corollaries of these VRML models on other platforms as prototypes of potential actual systems. We have been able, for example, to reproduce in 2D the means to identify spare capacity across a coalition of sites through the visual juxtaposition of existing production management artefacts made available in a shared space provided by a networked environment. That is not to say, however, that the development of the actual system with which we are presently engaged does not itself involve a whole range of further decisions, further refinements of requirements, further reflections upon the fieldwork and so on. Similarly it is not the case that our analytic VR model then simply becomes a design model for many of the elements of the VR envisionment convey aspects of the multi-dimensional lightweight solution which are not and need not be translated into user interface buttons, menus and the like. For example, the new work flows and their points of intersection with existing work processes are explicitly visualised in the VR envisionment but need not then be built as widgets in a user interface though the interface provides features to support those processes. It is the case, though, that our progress in developing this 2D system owes a great deal of direction and form to the VR envisionment described in this paper and is oriented towards providing fundamentally the same order of solution as that envisioned through the use of VR.

This work has taken place within the context of a group examining the impacts of network technologies upon work and has concerned the networking of geographically distributed sites for the purposes of distributed document production. Our needs were, for example, to convey spatial and temporal dimensions of organisational and inter-organisational processes, to convey a multi-dimensional solution involving organisational, work process, work practice and coordination device elements and to further the aims of the larger project to develop commercial products for a particular work setting. In this context, VR gave us resources to convey what we needed to convey. We hope that in the context of different studies and different projects others find VR similarly useful as a means to represent fieldwork and articulate design requirements.

ACKNOWLEDGMENTS

We wish to thank Bob Anderson, Dik Bentley, Marge Eldridge, Kenton O'Hara and our reviewers for comments on earlier versions of this paper.

REFERENCES

1. Benford, S., Snowdon, D., Greenhalgh, C., Ingram, R., Knox, I. and Brown, C. VR-VIBE: A Virtual Environment for Co-operative Information Retrieval. In *Proceedings of Eurographics'95*, Maastricht, The Netherlands, 1995.
2. Benford, S., Greenhalgh, C., Snowdon, D. and Bullock, A. Staging a Public Poetry Performance in a Collaborative Virtual Environment. In *Proceedings of ECSCW'97*, Kluwer Academic Publishers, 1997.
3. Benford, S., Snowdon, D., Coleborne, A., O'Brien, J. and Rodden, T. Informing The Design of Collaborative Virtual Environments. In *Proceedings of Group '97*, ACM Press, 1997.
4. Bowers, J., Button, G. and Sharrock, W. Workflow From Within and Without: Technology and Cooperative Work on the Print Industry Shopfloor. *Proceedings of ECSCW'95*, Kluwer Academic Publishers, 1995.
5. Bowers, J., Pycock, J. and O'Brien, J. Talk and Embodiment in Collaborative Virtual Environments. In *Proceedings of CHI'96*, ACM Press, 1996.
6. Bowers, J., O'Brien, J. and Pycock, J. Practically Accomplishing Immersion: Cooperation in and for Virtual Environments. In *Proceedings of CSCW'96*, ACM Press, 1996.
7. Button G. and Sharrock, W. The Production of Order and the Order of Production. In *Proceedings of ECSCW'97*, Kluwer Academic Publishers, 1997.
8. Contact Consortium http://www.ccon.org
9. Damer, B. and Bruckman, A. Peopled Online Virtual Worlds: A New Home for Cooperating Communities, a New Frontier for Interaction Design. In *Proceedings of CSCW'96*, ACM Press, 1996.
10. Greenhalgh, C. and Benford, S. Massive: A Virtual Reality System for Tele-conferencing. In *ACM Transactions on Computer Human Interfaces*, 1997.
11. Nakanishi, H., Yoshida, C., Nishimura, T. and Ishida, T. FreeWalk: Supporting Casual Meetings in a Network. In *Proceedings of CSCW '96*, ACM Press, 1996.
12. Pycock, J. and Bowers, J. Getting Others To Get It Right: An Ethnography of Design Work in the Fashion Industry. In *Proceedings of CSCW'96*, ACM Press, 1996.
13. Rodden, T. Populating the Application: A Model of Awareness for Cooperative Applications. In *Proceedings of CSCW'96*, ACM Press, 1996.
14. Richards, T. and Richards, L. The NUDIST Qualitative Data Analysis System. In *Qualitative Sociology*, 14: 3. New York: Human Sciences Press, 1991.
15. Seidel, J. and Clark, J. The Ethnograph: a computer program for the analysis of qualitative data. In *Qualitative Sociology*, 7 (1/2). New York: Human Sciences Press, 1984.
16. Smith, G. Cooperative Virtual Environments: Lessons from 2D Multi User Interfaces. In *Proceedings of CSCW'96*, ACM Press, 1996.
17. Twidale, M., Rodden, T. and Sommerville, I. The Designers' Notepad: Supporting and Understanding Cooperative Design. In *Proceedings of ECSCW '93*, Kluwer Academic Publishers, 1993.
18. VRML http://www.vrml.org/

Recomposition: Putting It All Back Together Again

Rebecca E. Grinter
Bell Labs, Lucent Technologies
263 Shuman Boulevard, 2F-309
Naperville, IL 60566 USA

beki@research.bell-labs.com
http://www.bell-labs.com/~beki

ABSTRACT
Design and development work have become increasingly interesting to CSCW researchers. This paper introduces a new perspective for examining that work: recomposition. Recomposition focuses on the activities required to coordinate the assembly of an artifact. Using examples drawn from a study of three software development organizations, I show how recomposition is a form of articulation work. I describe how that articulation work influences the product produced, and how the product itself influences the coordination required. I discuss the implications of a recomposition view for CSCW research.

Keywords
Software design studies, articulation work, recomposition.

INTRODUCTION

In the last few years there has been an increasing interest in design among CSCW researchers. First, design is the activity that studies of work intend to inform [23]. As discussions about the relationship between studies of work and systems development continue, design will remain a focus of attention within the community. Second, design is a highly collaborative activity. It provides a good opportunity to study issues that are relevant to CSCW concerns.

This paper follows the tradition of examining the collaborative aspects of developing software. Development work includes design activities, because the process of shaping software never ends during development. However, this study differs from many other investigations of development work to date, that have focused on work that occurs in meetings [4, 18], or how individuals reflect on the problem [26]. It is also different from the smaller pool of studies of coding work, the development of the software itself [7]. Finally, it does not take the broader perspective of those studies that examine the overall project organization of development work [8, 12].

This paper takes a different perspective, one that looks at the process from its conclusion, a reassembled artifact. Specifically, I examine the process of designing and building software from the perspective of the coordination issues it creates when the product is put back together. I call this process of reassembling the product *recomposition.*

The paper begins with an examination of the process of decomposition, where the overall problem to be solved is divided into components. The process of recomposition is then defined. I discuss three different kinds of recomposition work, and the coordination they require after describing the methods and sites where this work was conducted. Finally, I outline the implications this perspective has for CSCW research. Specifically, considering the construction of software systems from this perspective yields two important findings for the CSCW research community. First, it grounds articulation work in the technical realities of assembling products. Second, it offers insights into the character of intergroup and interorganizational coordination.

DECOMPOSITION IMPLIES RECOMPOSITION

That software development involves coordination work is not a new observation. In 1968 North Atlantic Treaty Organization (NATO) convened a meeting in Garmisch, Germany that drew researchers from industry and academia. At this meeting the name software engineering was picked as the title for the emerging research discipline investigating the complexities of software development [19]. Already, the topic of coordinating the development of software was being discussed as one of their challenges.

Around the same time, Conway was writing an explanation of why this was the case [11]. Conway's thesis — subsequently this has become known as Conway's Law — was that the structure of the code mirrored the structure of the committee that had designed it.

By the mid-70's, the coordination involved in software development work was becoming increasingly important to researchers. Brooks observed that adding more people to a software development project does not make the process happen quicker [3]. Specifically, he argued that the coordination overhead of adding new people would slow down the project.

Like Brooks, David Parnas also recognized the importance of coordination in software development. Like Conway, Parnas recognized a relationship between the people working on the software and the product built. His attention was focused on the process of modular decomposition.

Modular decomposition is the process of dividing the software problem into smaller tractable pieces to work on. Once those pieces have been defined, and the relationships among the components specified, the work of development commences. What was not well understood were the criteria to guide the decomposition itself. Parnas recognized that this process was not only a technical division of the product, but a division of labor among individuals [21]. Specifically, the smaller pieces typically would be assigned to the different individuals on the project, who would then know how their code fitted into the bigger software problem being addressed.

Parnas argued that the advantages of doing a good modular decomposition of a software problem were more than simply technical they were also managerial. Specifically he thought that good modular decomposition could reduce the communication required among different developers by eliminating some of their relationships with others.

Despite the widespread use of modular decomposition, recent studies of software developers suggest that they still spend over 50% of their time communicating with others [22]. Clearly, relationships exist among developers that need to be articulated. There are at least three reasons why these relations may exist. First, some relationships are defined at decomposition time. Second, legacy code complicates the decomposition process. The initial decomposition of new problems onto an existing base of code is analogous to retrofitting or extending an existing house rather than building a new residence. Some relationships may be maintained simply because it is easier in terms of putting new features on to the existing code base. Third, it is well known that requirements change during the development life cycle, and so as features are deleted, added and modified, those relationships are all subject to change.

This last reason is particularly significant when trying to understand how relationships in code affect coordination. Specifically, understanding the relationships among developers and the code that they produce in the decomposition phase provides only a limited insight into the social relationships that evolve and disappear during development. Instead, I chose the more unusual perspective of examining these relationships from the perspective of putting the system back together. I call the aggregate of activities seen from this perspective *recomposition*. This builds on the work of Tellioglu and Wagner [29], who observe that the relations among developers play a critical role in how products are assembled. It also follows in the spirit of Button and Harper [6] who argue that studies of work should go beyond theoretical and abstract notions of work, and examined the lived work of those studied.

Software recomposition occurs whenever the pieces of code are put together. Obviously the software is recomposed once to be released to the customer. However, the software needs to be recomposed many times before that, for testing purposes. Therefore, recomposition occurs far more times than the initial decomposition, and it is because it happens over and over again, I call it recomposition. It includes basic configuration management practices, release management work, and other integration work. The recomposition perspective focuses on the work that it takes to reassemble the product from its pieces.

It is at the point of recomposition when the relationships among the different system components become critical. The technical relationships among modules are known as dependencies, and they can take a number of forms. For example, if module A passes a variable to module B, then module B depends on A to give it that information. Another kind of dependency occurs if module A contains information that B needs in order to compile. Then A must be compiled before B. One of the hardest kinds of dependency to find is when module A generates a certain behavior during program execution which module B needs to function. This last case is known as a run-time dependency, and is hard to see because there may be scant evidence of this relationship in the written code itself.

Dependencies become interesting from a sociological perspective because of the potential division of labor among the components. When two modules are owned by different developers and share a dependency relationship then the individuals find themselves needing to maintain enough communication about the state of their work with the other person. If the communication fails the result is often that the modules will not work together — either at all or as intended. It is at the point of recomposition when developers are focused on making their code work, not only with other pieces they wrote, but with yet more components written by others' that these relationships become the acts by which software is recomposed. The strength of those relationships also becomes the ability of the developers to put all the pieces back together and make them work. In other words it is at the point of recomposition when a dependency among modules must be understood by all the developers that own the pieces involved.

The next section introduces the sites and methods used in this study. Then I describe three kinds of recomposition work that I discovered formed a routine part of development: module, subsystems, and institutional. Throughout the discussion I want to draw attention to the intimate link between the social and technical aspects of development that the developers find themselves managing. It is more than just grappling with an organizational context of design work but that social relationships are embedded into the software itself, and furthermore, can be driven and dictated by the technology.

SITES AND METHODS

I used two criteria for selecting sites for this study. First, and foremost I wanted the organization to be successful. I defined success simply as the ability to produce working software and sell it to their customers. Second, they also needed to be willing to host a researcher, sometimes for extended periods of time.

Tool Corp. is the vendor of a configuration management (CM) tool. At the time they were finishing a new release of the product as well as an upgrade to an existing version.

Both products contained code from prior systems. During my time there Tool Corp. grew from 14 to 18 developers and their product consisted of 1 million lines of code (LOC). I spent three months on site and conducted over 100 interviews there.

Computer Corp. is a large computer company that produces a real-time operating environment. They employ 700 developers who are distributed across a number of sites in the US and other continents. Their product suite consists of around 10 million LOC. I conducted 14 interviews with developers and spent three days on site.

Flow Corp. is the vendor of a suite of office technologies. The company employs over 1000 people spread out across different sites around the world. As a result of their product diversity it is hard to estimate the size of their code base. I conducted 6 interviews with one group working on one product within the suite.

Methods...

A qualitative approach was used to gather and analyze the data. In particular I used grounded theory, a method of developing substantive formal theories from qualitative data [14]. Grounded theory calls for a continual interaction between data gathering and analysis. As the researcher gathers new data they analyze it to see how it extends, modifies, or contradicts the existing theory being constructed. The result of grounded theory is an explanation of a set of practices.

Data were collected using observation and interviewing techniques. At all three sites I conducted non-participant observation, by watching people at work and maintaining diaries. I also used participant observation data gathering strategies at Tool Corp. and Computer Corp. Participant observation involves working in the environment being studied. The researcher learns — by doing — about the participants' work.

Two interview protocols, unstructured and semi-structured, were employed at the three sites. Unstructured interviews have little if any interview guide and present opportunities to gather information about the concerns of the participants. These were used extensively at the beginning of the study of Tool Corp. and towards the end to fill in any gaps in the theory.

Semi-structured interviews make use of an interview guide. The guide consists of a number of questions to ask the interviewee. The contents of the guide changed over the course of the study as the theory developed; however, I was careful to revisit old questions every so often to insure that the answers remained consistent among different developers and organizations.

Data analysis consists of three stages known as open coding, axial coding, and selective coding. Open coding consists of reducing raw data to categories that explain the behaviors reported. A category is a classification drawn from the field notes that describes an event. These categories have properties that can vary along dimensions. An example would be the category of pain, that can vary on the dimension of how intense the pain was. Axial coding involves developing these categories further, finding the conditions that lead to their emergence, and the consequences of their occurrence. Selective coding involves picking one category as the core category that forms the center of the theory. The three coding steps take individual cases of action reported and generate a formal theory that can be tested and revised in other settings. The value added in this approach is distilling what the people in the setting know and presenting it in an organized way.

...and Practice

The data were collected from the three sites using the techniques described above. Initially my interests focused on the coordination involved in the production of software. This led very naturally to the recomposition work. Specifically, I began examining configuration management practices in place.

Initial interviews and observations focused on the formal procedures and tools that developers used to perform configuration management activities. I have written about these practices and tool support elsewhere [15, 16]. However, the interviews soon broadened to encompass other activities described by developers: talking with people, the use of meetings, and diagrams. My interests also broadened to the sum of all the activities involved in reassembling software, from configuration management to larger integration efforts, and final release management techniques. This usually meant re-interviewing the initial participants in the study to find out whether they were using informal methods of coordinating work, and whether they were involved in integration and release management work. The advantage of qualitative interviewing is that it allows for this on-going revision of the study during the data gathering period.

The process of generalizing about how developers manage dependencies in their work involves making a shift from what Strauss calls substantive to formal theory [28]. This was accomplished in two ways. First, I used and refined the concepts generated at Tool Corp. in the organizations I subsequently visited. The discoveries at Tool Corp. helped to shape and refine the interviews and the observations that I made in the other organizations. Second, in each subsequent organization I revisited a set of core questions asked at the earlier organizations. This combination of refining parts of the interviews while holding other questions constant allowed me to extend the theory through the collection of new facts and data, while insuring the reliability of previous data collected. Thus, the process of generalization consists not of counting instances of occurrence, but through systematic collection of data that elaborates on the patterns of behavior found in multiple organizations, both extending and refining previous understandings. Finally, I took the results of my fieldwork and presented them to some of the developers I had interviewed and asked them for comments.

MODULE RECOMPOSITION

The division of labor in software development work usually means that small teams of developers — often collocated — work on related parts of the system. Within large subsystems, this division is further applied until small groups have established responsibility for a small component. Recomposition work at this level involves assembling modules into pieces of the subsystem. In this section I describe three kinds of recomposition work: merging, single module over time, and change sets.

Merging

When two or more developers work on the same piece of code simultaneously it is known as parallel development. When this happens the first stage of recomposition involves making a unified module out of the versions that exist. Tools exist that automatically merge code; however, in many cases the developers find that they need to get together with their colleagues and manually merge the versions.

Tools fail to support merging well as the complexity of what has to be merged increases [15]. Most tools manage to merge versions automatically if the components do not depend on each other in any way. For example, one person changed the comments and another altered a fragment of the code in an unrelated part of the module. However, some changes can not be handled automatically because they involve unraveling and sorting out dependencies between the multiple versions of the module.

Some developers related their merging difficulties with the process of decomposition itself. As one developer put it:

> Perhaps the module itself needs to be broken up ... usually this set of functionality belongs to me, other people working on the project are working on a different functionality in the same module, therefore the modules doing too much.

The complexity of merging increases when the developers have simultaneously altered the same lines of code or algorithm to address different problems. There are now technical dependencies among the different changes that need to be understood and combined to produce one aggregated version of the module. Consequently, developers have to find everyone else, discuss what changes they each worked on, and how they altered the code. They work together to develop a shared understanding of all the versions, and determine the functionality of the merged module. This activity often takes place as a joint merging effort. The developers sit around one terminal and select the lines that should go into the final merged module.

Parallel development involves multiple developers working on the same module at the same time. The developers depend on the same module for the work that they need to be done, and they end up depending on each other. Merging is the resolution of the technical dependencies that exist between the versions of the module. It also involves managing the social dependency among the developers working on that module.

Single Module Over Time

Merging focuses on the relations among multiple versions of a module that coexist at the same point in time. Another set of dependencies exists among versions of the same module over time. At all the sites I noticed that developers often examined the previous versions of a module before making decisions about how to proceed.

Developers described this behavior as necessary as part of the process of designing the best solution for their current problem. Previous versions of a module represent an evolution of implementation decisions and a set of technical constraints and opportunities for future work. One developer justified why he went back to previous versions of code as seeing:

> why this particular change was made um how it does or doesn't affect this next set of changes or you understand why this person made this change and hadn't considered this other problem and that sort of thing.

The developer is clear about the technical implications of changing the module without considering what has happened previously. However, he also identifies another person, the individual who made those changes in the past.

Dependencies with code in the past involve individuals who previously worked on that code. These kinds of relationships can get very complicated in established organizations. As the software and organization grow older, more employees move among projects. Other developers leave the company, and new people arrive to take their place. Consequently, many developers become responsible for code they did not originally design and the person who did is not available to explain how it evolved. The new owners are left trying to understand the character of the software from the code itself. New developers described situations where they needed to learn about what problems previous developers had been trying to fix and the reasons behind the choice of solution.

Some configuration management tools provide information that forms a kind of organizational memory, giving developers some clues about who changed code, and why. The more readily this information is available the more likely developers are to use it in their work, because without it tracking down documentation or other people who remember the person and their development work is a time consuming and sometimes inconclusive activity.

When developers do choose to ignore the past they are not in any doubt of the potential problems that it could cause:

> If you have to go through a lot of steps to figure out the history and do comparisons and things like that you tend not do that. You know cause I don't have time to do this, I'll just kind of blast ahead and cross my fingers and hope that I haven't screwed up.

Historical dependencies arise because the approach to changing the present version of a module may depend on how a developer changed that module in the past. This becomes challenging when the module has changed ownership, and one developer needs to understand the work of another. When the previous developer can not be contacted, then the current developer depends on information stored inside tools, organizational repositories and people who remember that development time.

Change Sets

The previous two cases have focused on relationships that exist between versions of the same module. Another relationship developers manage derives from the fact that their work involves changing the behavior of the system. One logical change — a request for a new, enhanced or corrected feature — often results in more than one module being altered. Making the logical change involves aligning all the physical changes to the components so that the desired outcome is produced. The modules involved in the logical change are known as a change set. They depend on each other to produce the feature requested. Furthermore, usually the change set must be introduced into the system when all the physical changes have been made otherwise any system build will probably fail.

A consequence of change sets is that the developers responsible for making the necessary alterations to their code become involved in a relationship with the others working on the same logical change. Synchronizing all the alterations and putting the updated versions of the change set back into the main line development requires coordination. At all the organizations I studied coordinating change sets was a combination of manual and automated procedures.

Developers at all the sites had access to some systems —often problem tracking facilities — that supported some of this change set work. The developers would usually begin by identifying who they were working with on the change set, which involved extrapolating back from the physical change to the statement of the logical problem to be fixed. Typically the systems provided some clues about who was working on related parts of the problem.

Then the developers would get together and discuss how they were going to implement the change as a group. Finally, one person would take responsibility for tracking how all the physical changes were progressing, with the view to informing the person responsible for the system build when that change set was ready to be compiled.

This sequence of events is managed more or less formally depending on the size and span of the change to be made. A small change involving two or three developers from the same team was usually handled informally with the developers organizing themselves. When a change spans a number of subsystems and involves more developers then some levels of management may formally orchestrate the process to ensure that the work remains aligned.

Change sets begin with the dependencies among modules as they are simultaneously altered to meet new system requirements. The technical component of the dependency involves ensuring that all the altered code functions together, produces the desired behavior, and works with the rest of the system. At the same time, the individuals responsible for the physical changes, and sometimes their management, need to form and maintain relationships to ensure that everyone's efforts are synchronized.

SUBSYSTEM RECOMPOSITION

The previous section described the coordination required to align a few modules together. This section focuses on the work necessary to assemble collections of modules into parts of the product — subsystems — and the entire system. This kind of recomposition work also involves modules of code, but because it involves increasingly more parts of the system so the processes required by an organization to coordinate and accomplish this work become increasingly formalized and complex. I begin by examining the complexities of recomposing a subsystem: the build. Then I discuss managing multiple builds of a single subsystem, and finally describe the processes behind assembling the entire system.

Build

Groups of developers working on a subsystem often want to test their changes — before submitting them to an official test group — against a working version of the subsystem. A build is process for pulling together all the modules and components that make up the subsystem. The build gives developers something to test their next changes against, and provides them with feedback on the changes that they made that are inside the build.

I have described the advantages of using a tool to automate this process elsewhere [16]. Instead, I want to describe how the technical dependencies among the pieces of code form social relationships that have to be maintained, in varying degrees, by the person responsible for the build. This person is known as the build manager.

The three organizations varied considerably on their automated support for build management. Among the organizations where there were manual procedures in place the role of the build manager involved maintaining important relationships that allowed them to build the code. Specifically, the build manager needs to know about at least three things.

First, they must be aware of any change sets in development. A person responsible for managing a change set needs to coordinate with the build manager to let them know when to put all the revisions of a module into the build. Second, the build manager also needs to know about any compile-time dependencies that exist among pieces of code. Compile-time dependencies specify that one module must be processed before another because it provides information to the latter one. Third, they need to understand the dependencies that exist among the components in the subsystem as they were defined at decomposition and have evolved. By this I mean that they need to know how the subsystem produces its functionality and what kinds of run-time dependencies exist among the code within the system. This piece of information becomes particularly useful when the build breaks and they need to identify the source of the problem.

For these reasons build managers try to have close communications with all the members of the development team. Depending on the degree of tool support for the build process, build managers interact with their colleagues to find out what code the developers are working on, what impacts that has on the subsystem, and where the components reside. The work of the build manager involves maintaining up to date information about all the technical dependencies in a subsystem; consequently, they find themselves sustaining relationships with everyone involved in the development effort.

The degree of formalization of the build manager role varied among the three organizations. At Tool Corp. and in the part of Flow Corp. I studied, the role of build manager was an additional responsibility on top of one developer's work. The build managers at these sites were responsible for doing build work within fairly small teams of developers. Computer Corp. was a much bigger organization, and some of the subsystems were big enough that they had full-time staff that would perform the build function for their systems. Computer Corp. also had some teams that were small enough to provide their own build function internally, in much the same way that Tool Corp. and Flow Corp. did.

Platforms Creating Multiple Life Cycles

The need to compete for market share creates another dependency. It is only applicable to those development efforts that span multiple hardware and software platforms. It is a dependency when code is shared and developed for multiple platforms simultaneously.

When the companies I studied made a decision to offer their product on a new platform they did not double the development effort. Often parts of the code remain the same across platforms and new platform-specific pieces are created in the development environment to accommodate the differences. This approach means that the system now depends on the platform-specific components to provide the functionality of the product to the new platform. At all the companies I studied, some developers become responsible for working on the platform-specific pieces of code in the system.

Typically with a new development effort, some initial work needs to be done before anything is ready to compile. One solution the developers used was to copy a version of the system into their workspace and develop the variants from that. As changes carried on to the main development effort, the copied code became increasingly misaligned to the main development effort. So, at some point the new platform variants need to join the main development effort and be realigned.

The technical dilemma faced is that if they are introduced too early then they are unstable and under tested and as a consequence likely to break the build. However, if the developers wait too long the main system will have changed so significantly that the build may break due to the fact that the platform variant modules assume a set of behaviors that the system no longer produces. One solution developers used was to recopy the system to their private workspace with increasing frequency as they approached the point when they wanted to put their platform-specific changes into the central development effort. This prevented the gross misalignment from occurring towards the latter stages of platform variant development.

By reusing as much of the system as possible, the developers created a dependency between their platform specific code and the rest of the modules. They had also created an important relationship that they needed to maintain, one that allowed them to time when their pieces would go into the system. The relationships would need to provide them with enough information to plan how to prepare to fit their work into the development effort. This coordination requires working with people who are familiar with the current state of the system and can suggest when to put certain pieces back into the system.

Who these individuals happen to be is highly contingent on the specific arrangement of work within the development organization. I found that the developers sought out people who had detailed knowledge of the current state of the system development. In some cases that was the person responsible for managing the integration of the code. In other cases, developers turned to managers for help finding out when introducing their code would not do too much harm to others. The common feature here is that developers who create relationships between platform-specific components and the main system find themselves needing to maintain strong ties to the rest of development or risk mistiming the introduction of their work into the central effort.

Assembling the Entire System

The product also needs to be integrated as a whole, which involves making sure all the subsystems work together. At Tool Corp. assembling the entire system was equivalent to assembling two groups' work, as the organization was small. The coordination work involved in assembling the system was much greater for larger organizations such as Computer Corp.

At the sites studied, systems assembly work consisted of two stages. First, the individual teams needed to align their work with other groups with whom they shared dependencies. Once that was done the entire system needed to be assembled. At the time of the study, neither organization had any tools that automated the entire function. Instead, the companies used a combination of technical and organizational solutions to making the product work as a whole.

Tool Corp. was able to align the two subsystems it had fairly easily. Experts for each team were well known to all the developers there so they could check individual problems throughout development. The build managers for each system also worked closely to maintain alignment.

Computer Corp. used two strategies to manage the alignment issues. Some pieces of the system are more central than others. Changes to those pieces of code had impacts across the organization because many subsystems depended on that code behaving a certain way. Computer Corp. had established a repository and an organizational defined unit — the shared resources group — to manage the problems of commonly used code. The shared resources group had the responsibility of maintaining the code in a publicly accessible repository.

The shared resources group also standardized ways of accessing the common code. They categorized the code by what part of the system it came from, and then informed all the teams where the code could be found inside the repository. This process formalized the ways that other teams accessed the code by removing the individual communication required and replacing it with a formal procedure. It also helped to prevent the problems of having multiple versions of a single piece of common code being used by different teams in their development work.

However, not all code was managed by the shared resources group. In the absence of the shared resources group taking care of their code, teams had to find out who was using their code. One mechanism some developers used was to broadcast information about their systems electronically, in the hope that people who were dependent on their code would reply. The weakness of this approach was that the dependency relationships were identified by the individuals who owned each component. When the developer who owned the remote code left or moved on to a new project the connection was lost. If the relationship spanned large sections of the organization the developer who needed to reestablish contact with the other side of their dependency would likely not know anyone to ask.

Computer Corp. was in the process of implementing technology that would sit on top of the CM tools and store versions of subsystems that other groups could access. Part of the functionality of the system was to depersonalize the code, remove individual's names from the modules that they worked on, and replace it with the team name. In this case depersonalization was an effort to make the subsystems more recognizable by assigning ownership at a higher level of abstraction.

At Computer Corp. the actual act of systems assembly was handled by another separate organizational unit responsible for releases. All the groups working on the product suite would hand over a copy of their code to the release group at fixed points in the development life cycle. The release group would then test to see whether the code from different groups worked together as expected.

Assembling the entire system is a coordination intensive activity. It is the time when all the subsystems must work with each other. This drives a complex set of relationships among developers and other people responsible for elements of this process. The management of this relationship requires the construction and maintenance of complex documented procedures, organizational units, and some technologies.

INSTITUTIONAL RECOMPOSITION

The development environments I have described have appeared relatively autonomous. Most of the dependencies and relationships discussed so far have been created by decisions taken within companies. However, outside influences also create complex relationships that managers and developers have to manage as part of their work. In this section I will describe just one of those relationships brought about by open systems.

Open Systems

The dependencies created by platforms I described earlier focused on fitting development efforts in different stages of being finished together. However, platforms and other kinds of software create another set of dependencies that forced all the companies I studied to create and maintain more complex relationships with vendors of other hardware and software products. All of the companies I studied, built products that needed to work with other systems and as a consequence found themselves managing these relationships.

One way that other vendors influence the development strategies followed by these companies is through their own releases. For example when a company released a new version of its operating system, Tool Corp. found itself having to make important development decisions. Specifically, Tool Corp. had to decide whether enough potential and existing customers of their tool would upgrade to the new operating system and whether that warranted starting a new development effort to make their own product compatible.

Sometimes the companies I studied wanted a tighter integration between their products and those of other vendors. Then some code must be shared between two independent vendors. At Computer Corp. I found developers that work with other companies' code, and who find themselves dependent on how those companies choose to make their own system revisions.

I spoke to one developer who was hired into the organization particularly for his experiences with a software package that Computer Corp. wanted to integrate with their software. His own development, the integration between the two products, was routinely impacted by changes made to the vendor code, as he explained:

> basically you have to take their base and compare it to what they've given you now and see the differences there and then you have the choice of either implementing it from their new code or putting their changes into your new code.

These vendors change their code, not only in terms of functionality of individual modules, but at higher levels, in the architecture of the overall product, over time. However, software development organizations who depend on other vendors, pay a high price for that dependency. The development organization must adjust their code every time a vendor's code changes. Quite frequently, the development organizations need to ensure that they support both new and older versions of the vendor's code, allowing customers the option of upgrading or not.

Developers who have code that depends on other vendors' systems find themselves spending time reworking their own modules to accommodate new changes from other vendors. Sometimes the connections between vendors let developers interact with their counterparts in the other organization; sometimes managers meet and negotiate for information about product changes. Critically, for these developers part of the job of making their code work depends on maintaining enough of a connection to the other vendor.

IMPLICATIONS FOR CSCW RESEARCH

In the last three sections I have described specific instances of the coordination work required to produce software. Studying the coordination from the recomposition perspective has helped to identify the occasions that create coordination work, and what work individuals and organizations have to do. Although I have focused on the recomposition work necessary to assemble software systems from their parts, recomposition work occurs in other settings.

Studies that include hardware design suggest that the same issues arise there [5, 20]. For example, in his studies of engineering design, Bucciarelli notes that synthesis of the product even at early stages of design is not simple. It also seems probable that this kind of work exists in the assembly of other artifacts, such as large documents written by multiple participants. In their study of the IMF, Harper and Sellen [17] observe that professionals working on documents spend time corroborating their sections with their colleagues to make sure that they fit together. In this section, I examine what the recomposition perspective has to offer for our understandings of coordination work and organizational CSCW.

Recomposition as Articulation Work

Recomposition work is a specific form of the broader concept of articulation work. Articulation work is all the coordination and negotiation necessary to get work done [27]. Recomposition work is the coordination required to assemble artifacts from their parts. Schmidt and Bannon [25] have argued that articulation work focuses on work practices that reach beyond small group settings and provides a useful conceptual tool for broadening the scope of CSCW. Recomposition work includes local work practices, but must also span the entire organization, and even brings different companies together.

This study has illuminated four features of this kind of articulation work. First, dependencies among the pieces — in this case system components — create a host of complex social relationships that need to be articulated and coordinated over long periods of time. Furthermore the strength of these relationships influences the organizations' ability to assemble its artifact. In other words, if these relationships can not be maintained then it is likely that the artifact will not fit together, as pieces will drift away and become increasingly misaligned.

Second, these relationships change over time as the product changes its technical character and the organization changes its social makeup. Knowing what they were when the artifact was originally designed is not enough, because the requirements change, the people change, and so the product is transformed. People need to revise their understandings of where the artifact is headed continually in order to understand what it has become.

Third, any existing artifacts — in this case code — creates even more complications. It creates difficulties for the initial decomposition effort in ways that potentially create more dependencies among various pieces than desired. For example, the choice not to create an entirely new and separate product for each platform means that all new development must fit with all the existing work going on.

Fourth, these dependencies are not entirely under the control of the organization. If another organization — a company, a federal agency, or regulatory body — makes revisions that impact the organization's work, the organization must realign their efforts again. In other words, the recomposition perspective situates the production of artifacts in a broader institutional context.

In summary, this study ties the coordination work required to produce objects to the artifact that is developed. Specifically, recomposition grounds one type of articulation work in the technical details of what is produced. This study demonstrates the importance of articulation work, the variety of types that occur simultaneously during the production of an artifact, and clarifies the character that these relations take during the process.

Button and Sharrock [9] observe that a relationship exists between technology and an organization. In this case, it is a relationship between the technology under production and the organization shaping it. Recomposition work provides a mechanism for understanding how coordination influences the outcome of any artifact produced, and in turn how that artifact directs the coordination required. Furthermore, it suggests that there is a three way relationship: among the artifact — whether it be a technology or not — produced, the organization building it, and any technology introduced to facilitate the development process.

Organizational CSCW

Recently, CSCW researchers have begun to explore intergroup and interorganizational forms of coordination [2]. This study shows that many of the technical solutions that support recomposition work exist for small groups trying to coordinate their development efforts locally. The amount of technical support decreases when multiple teams or organizations are involved. At the same time, and not unsurprisingly, the number of organizational "fixes" increases. The establishment of departments, steering committees, and other policies, all step in to address the coordination needs that their current technologies do not [10, 24].

This study has outlined some of the ways that organizations coordinate their development efforts. However, the relationship between the artifact and organization that I have identified also offers opportunities for examining potential organizational and technological solutions for organizational CSCW. In the rest of this section I discuss two occasions when recomposition provides insight into organizational CSCW issues.

Loosely Coupled Work and Architectures

Olson and Teasley [20] describe one organizational solution to the challenges of aligning geographically distant design work. The solution that two teams — one in the USA and the other in France — took involved slowly uncoupling their work over time. Initially they had an architecture that required them to work closely. As the project evolved it became easier to redivide the work in ways that reduced the coordination required. They call this kind of work loosely coupled.

This study suggests that when work is redivided to accommodate distance then a corresponding change in the architecture of the artifact built must also occur (which Olson and Teasley suggest happened in their study). Work can still proceed in a loosely coupled fashion without changing the architecture of the artifact, but serious difficulties will arise. Although it may save time initially, allowing different groups to proceed more independently, if they have to reassemble their product and the dependencies have gotten misaligned, it will take longer, and require reestablishing the lost connections, and forgotten context.

This suggests that the architecture constrains the ability of developers to choose tight or loose coupling independently of the artifact. So, the artifact itself can provide a source of information about what kinds of work can be distant and uncoupled, and those which if loosely coupled create recomposition problems. This information could be used to determine opportunities for groupware, and other settings where those same technologies would be less helpful. Furthermore, by comparing the architecture with charts that identify whether work is loose or tightly coupled we can find places where work has become loosely coordinated when it should not be. Finally, the recomposition perspective provides insight into the specific activities that developers will find hard if the work has been loosely coupled while the architecture demands tight coordination.

Organizational Awareness

In their study of design work Bellotti and Bly [1] describe how individuals watched and talked with their colleagues as a way of maintaining enough awareness of what others were doing. This study confirms that developers engage in the same practices to maintain this information about what their team mates are working on. In these activities, developers associate information about other software components with the individuals building them.

Much of the awareness literature to date makes this tie between individuals and artifacts. The three types of awareness mechanisms Dourish and Bellotti [13] describe all connect information about work states with an individual responsible. Informational awareness allows individuals to describe what they did and role restrictive awareness lets other deduce what work has happened based on the role of the individual. Their shared feedback approach provides awareness of others within a commonly shared electronic workspace. Changes to an artifact are associated with the individual that made them in all these approaches.

This study suggests that awareness at an organizational level is subtly different. Awareness — what people need to be aware of — changes when organizations attempt to assemble artifacts that span many divisions of the company. In the organizations I studied, people involved in subsystems and systems recomposition work found it more useful to have components associated with the team that produced it. In fact, developers at all of the companies I studied often referred to subsystems by the name of the team that built them. Often the subsystem name was the team name (i.e., the kernel group built the kernel). For systems development this means providing ways to aggregate and display awareness information about teams. Furthermore, it raises questions about how to represent abstractions of team activity.

The notion of awareness changes radically when companies create alliances with other vendors. Companies are interested in making their products compatible, but not giving away proprietary information. What it means to be aware, to maintain enough context to align products, becomes the discussion of management meetings and the content of legal documents.

CONCLUSIONS

The predominant way of thinking about design and development work focuses on the work to break the problem into smaller components. This view permeates the literature about design as well as the techniques for organizing project activities. Systems assembly seems to play a minor role in this view.

Reversing our thinking from decomposition to recomposition places systems assembly at the center of the development effort. For CSCW researchers it highlights how critical and just how difficult individuals find maintaining congruency among all the parts. Furthermore, it establishes a foundation for explaining exactly how coordination work directly impacts the artifact produced, and in turn how that artifact affects the coordination work required. The recomposition perspective also situates this coordination in the local and global contexts of production. Finally, it offers some insights into technological and social solutions for organizational CSCW. Recomposition provides a new tool for CSCW researchers to explore the coordination involved in the production of large collaborative artifacts.

ACKNOWLEDGMENTS

This study is a product of the collective wisdom of those who manage these dependencies in their daily work. Mark Ackerman, Lisa Covi, Jonathan Grudin, Jim Herbsleb, John L. King, Tom Rodden, and Larry Votta provided support and helped me to articulate these ideas. I thank the reviewers for their comments. None of this would have been possible without the financial support of the Engineering and Science Research Council of the United Kingdom.

REFERENCES

1. Bellotti, V. and S. Bly. Walking Away from the Desktop Computer: Distributed Collaboration and Mobility in a Product Design Team. In *Proceedings of ACM Conference on Computer Supported Cooperative Work CSCW '96* (Cambridge, MA, November 1996), ACM Press, 209-218.

2. Bowers, J., G. Button, and W. Sharrock. Workflow from Within and Without: Technology and Cooperative Work on the Print Industry Shopfloor. In *Proceedings of European Conference on Computer-*

Supported Cooperative Work ECSCW '95 (Stockholm, Sweden, September 1995), Kluwer Academic Publishers, 51-66.

3. Brooks Jr., F. P. The Mythical Man-Month. *Datamation. 20*, 12 (1974), 44-52.
4. Bucciarelli, L. L. An Ethnographic Perspective on Engineering Design. *Design Studies. 9*, 3 (1988), 159-168.
5. Bucciarelli, L. L., Designing Engineers MIT Press, Cambridge, MA, 1994.
6. Button, G. and R. Harper. The Relevance of 'Work-Practice' for Design. *Computer Supported Cooperative Work: The Journal of Collaborative Computing. 4*, 4 (1996), 263-280.
7. Button, G. and W. Sharrock, The Mundane Work of Writing and Reading Computer Programs. In *Situated Order: Studies in The Social Organisation of Talk and Embodied Activities*, P. ten Have and G. Psathas, Editors. 1992, The University Press of America: Washington D.C.
8. Button, G. and W. Sharrock. Project Work: The Organisation of Collaborative Design and Development in Software Engineering. *Computer Supported Cooperative Work: The Journal of Collaborative Computing. 5*, 4 (1996), 369-386.
9. Button, G. and W. Sharrock. The Production of Order and the Order of Production. In *Proceedings of Fifth European Conference on Computer-Supported Cooperative Work ECSCW '97* (Lancaster, UK, September 1997), Kluwer Academic Publishers, 1-16.
10. Carstensen, P. H. and C. Sørensen. From the Social to the Systematic: Mechanisms Supporting Coordinating in Design. *Computer Supported Cooperative Work: The Journal of Collaborative Computing. 5*, 4 (1996), 387-413.
11. Conway, M. E. How Do Committees Invent? *Datamation. 14*, 4 (1968), 28-31.
12. Curtis, B., H. Krasner, and N. Iscoe. A Field Study of the Software Design Process for Large Systems. *Communications of the ACM. 31*, 11 (1988), 1268-1287.
13. Dourish, P. and V. Bellotti. Awareness and Coordination in Shared Workspaces. In *Proceedings of ACM Conference on Computer-Supported Cooperative Work CSCW '92* (Toronto, Canada, October 31 - November 4, 1992), ACM Press, 107-114.
14. Glaser, B. G. and A. L. Strauss, The Discovery of Grounded Theory: Strategies for Qualitative Research Aldine de Gruyter, Hawthorne, N. Y., 1967.
15. Grinter, R. E. Supporting Articulation Work Using Configuration Management Systems. *Computer Supported Cooperative Work: The Journal of Collaborative Computing. 5*, 4 (1996), 447-465.
16. Grinter, R. E. Doing Software Development: Occasions for Automation and Formalisation. In *Proceedings of Fifth European Conference on Computer-Supported Cooperative Work ECSCW '97* (Lancaster, UK, September 1997), Kluwer Academic Publishers, 173-188.
17. Harper, R. and A. Sellen. Collaborative Tools and the Practicalities of Professional Work at the International Monetary Fund. In *Proceedings of ACM Conference on Human Factors in Computing Systems CHI '95* (Denver, CO, May 1995), ACM Press, 122-129.
18. Herbsleb, J. D., *et al.* Object-Oriented Analysis and Design in Software Project Teams. *Human-Computer Interaction. 10*, 2-3 (1995), 249-292.
19. NATO Science Committee. *Working Conference on Software Engineering*. NATO Scientific Affairs Division. 1969.
20. Olson, J. S. and S. Teasley. Groupware in the Wild: Lessons Learned from a Year of Virtual Collocation. In *Proceedings of ACM Conference on Computer Supported Cooperative Work CSCW '96* (Cambridge, MA, November 1996), ACM Press, 419-427.
21. Parnas, D. L. On the Criteria to be Used in Decomposing Systems into Modules. *Communications of the ACM. 15*, 12 (1972), 1053-1058.
22. Perry, D. E., N. A. Staudenmayer, and L. G. Votta. People, Organizations, and Process Improvement. *IEEE Software. 11*, 4 (1994), 36-45.
23. Plowman, L., Y. Rogers, and M. Ramage. What Are Workplace Studies For? In *Proceedings of Fourth European Conference on Computer-Supported Cooperative Work ECSCW '95* (Stockholm, Sweden, September 1995), Kluwer Academic Publishers, 309-324.
24. Schmidt, K. Of Maps and Scripts: The Status of Formal Constructs in Cooperative Work. In *Proceedings of International ACM SIGGROUP Conference on Supporting Group Work GROUP '97* (Phoenix, AZ, November 1997.), ACM Press, 138-147.
25. Schmidt, K. and L. Bannon. Taking CSCW Seriously: Supporting Articulation Work. *Computer Supported Cooperative Work (CSCW): An International Journal. 1*, 1-2 (1992), 7-40.
26. Schön, D. A., The Reflective Practitioner: How Professionals Think in Action Basic Books Inc., New York, NY, 1983.
27. Strauss, A. Work and the Division of Labor. *The Sociological Quarterly. 26*, 1 (1985), 1-19.
28. Strauss, A., Qualitative Analysis for Social Scientists Cambridge University Press, New York: N.Y., 1987.
29. Tellioglu, H. and I. Wagner. Negotiating Boundaries: Configuration Management in Software Development Teams. *Computer Supported Cooperative Work: The Journal of Collaborative Computing. 6*, 4 (1997), 251-274.

Panel
An Internet Paradox: A Social Medium That May Undermine Sociability

Sara Kiesler (Chair), Robert Kraut, *Carnegie Mellon University, USA,* Judith Donath, *MIT,* USA, Barry Wellman, *University of Toronto, Canada,* and Howard Rheingold, *Independent consultant*

Is the current Internet leading people to have strong connections to others or is it working against this? New empirical results suggest that using the Internet leads to less social involvement, more loneliness, less communication within the family, and more depression. The panel will assess whether these results are believable, and if so whether new services on the Internet can be designed to support strong social ties. The second goal of the panel is to outline these good designs.

CSCW 98 Seattle Washington USA

Panel
Everyone is Talking About Knowledge Management

Irene Greif, *Lotus Research, USA* (Chair)

Everyone is talking about Knowledge Management (KM). At least, everyone in the commercial world who used to buy or sell groupware. Some debate whether it's real or a fad. Others claim it's the next step in evolution from email, through groupware and on to what everyone *really* needs. Still others say it is exactly groupware, no more no less, but with a new marketing spin. It's captured the attention of vendors, customers, analysts and reporters. We believe it merits the attention of the CSCW community.

This panel will take a look at the KM frenzy, with an eye towards identifying open research questions that could be addressed by CSCW research. CSCW has been described as the science behind groupware. If the commercial world has moved on to KM, is there a message for CSCW? Can taking a look at the business world reinvention of groupware expand our vision of the scope of CSCW research? Or, as experts in collaboration, might we offer insight to the business world on how best to incorporate groupware technology into KM solutions?

The panel will include representatives of two or three (non-research) views of what constitutes Knowledge Management as well as one or two voices from research on the substantive underlying issues. No doubt, additional research issues will emerge in the open discussion with audience participation.

Questions for the panelists will lead them to address some of the following topics.

Framing the Problem

When software vendors talk with their customers, they hear cries for help. Their problems range from ones that seem to have been created by the technology – "How can I find what's in my thousands of Lotus Notes databases?" – to ones that they always may have faced – "How do I capture information in the heads of people who may leave my company?"

In between are a number of variants: "How can we accelerate learning for new employees and retraining for whole teams?" "What does our organization 'know'?" "Can we measure the value of our knowledge assets?" "How can our organization learn (or increase its knowledge assets)?" "Shouldn't I be fostering collaboration among people in my organization?"

The KM label gets applied at various times to some of these problems. Occasionally it seems to be used as a promised panacea for all of these problems. Nevertheless, as you look at some of the specific problems, you can see substance – there are people feeling real pain and looking to technology for solutions. What's more, there is a clear relationship to CSCW, both in the widespread belief that groupware technologies play a significant role in KM, and in the rich interplay between technological and social issues raised by KM.

The intersection of search and groupware

The first problem – managing the information overload – lends itself to technological solutions, including better information retrieval and new forms of collaboration. In fact, looking just at the problem of managing large repositories of information one can take the position that KM is no more than a combination of search and groupware. Groups are producing more and more information in sharable repositories. This increase in information stresses requirements for better search capabilities.

Once search is elevated to a major activity it becomes something you spend a fair amount of time doing, and something that you might do better in teams or with the support of occasional expert intervention. Collaborative search, collaborative filters, joint browsing, are all technologies that begin to leverage people's combined skills at finding things in this sea of information. Hence, KM as intersection of search and groupware.

Leveraging Expertise (or is it just expert systems, again?)

But search, whether collaborative or not, just helps you find information of one sort – information that has already been made explicit in the form of online files, published for sharing. What about the information in people's heads? Or the information typically found only in informal conversation and networking? Or information transferred only through apprenticeship and experience. Does technology play a role?

One approach is to get more information out of people's heads into the system, for search engines to grovel over. Put their expertise on line, and then others can leverage it at their leisure. This offers the promise of freeing people from needing to find each other, and may meet the corporate goal of providing some protection against loss of key people. The panel will discuss the feasibility of this quest: what kinds of information can be stored this way?; how hard (and expensive) is it to really capture all that one expert knows?; when is the cost higher than the benefit?; didn't we learn from expert systems that it isn't easy to capture an expert's knowledge?

Networking and Communities

An alternative approach – one that places higher value on people and collaboration – is to use technology to bring people together so that they can learn from each other. Technology can be used to facilitate networking, but once again, only at the expense of making some information explicit. With information about people stored on line, you can use search engines to find other people, and then talk with them. You don't have to get their expertise out of their heads, but you do need "meta-data" descriptions of their areas of expertise and interests.

Beyond networking, some people find themselves in sustained relationships with a group they come to see as a community. Many communities arise naturally through shared interests and serendipitous meetings, enabling people to "leverage the expertise" of other community members. Technologies such as news groups and on-line chats have been used successfully to build and sustain on-line communities. Increasingly, people talk about augmenting these technologies with more meta data and matchmaking technology to put on-line communities to use as part of KM. The panel will include at least one person experienced in the development of on-line communities who will address the viability of this approach.

Is this CSCW?

Trade-offs between technology and social interventions are at the core of the discussion of KM, just as they always have been in CSCW. Can an organization shape its culture so that people will network and share expertise, making knowledge explicit whenever possible, rather than just whenever convenient? What incentives have to be put in place? How do you address the trade-offs between cost and benefits, so often misjudged in earlier CSCW and groupware systems? On this dimension, CSCW and KM seem aligned.

But, CSCW, as well as most groupware products, tend to address small group needs. Even in the context of large enterprise deployments of products, the emphasis has until recently been on having a common infrastructure for many uses of many smallish groups. It may well be that the issue of scaling up from groupware to enterprise wide solutions is the primary impetus for the recognition of KM as a problem and product category.

Although CSCW research is very grounded in user experience and field studies, it could still be out of touch with the scaling issues of "real world" deployments of groupware. We expect that the panel will uncover research questions of scale in organizational systems that are as yet unanswered – the question for all of us will be whether they suggest a new research agenda to the assembled CSCW community.

CSCW 98 Seattle Washington USA

Panel
Six Readings of a Single Text: A Videoanalytic Session

Timothy Koschmann, *Southern Illinois University, USA* (Chair), Anne Anderson, *University of Glasgow, UK,* Rogers Hall, *University of California, Berkeley, USA,* Christian Heath, *Kings College,* London, UK, Curtis LeBaron, *University of Colorado at Boulder, USA,* Judith Olson, *University of Michigan, USA,* Lucy Suchman, *Xerox Palo Alto Research Center, USA*

The purpose of this special session will be to illuminate some of the possible ways in which we, as observers and researchers, can come to understand collaboration and how it is achieved within the context of joint activity. Historically, collaboration has been studied in a variety of ways, both quantitative and qualitative, drawing on the research traditions of both the psychological and the social (i.e., Anthropology, Sociology, Linguistics, Communications) sciences. Our goal here is to highlight some of these methodological differences while at the same time demonstrating how different approaches can each contribute to a richer and more fully elaborated view of the collaborative process. In preparation for this session six researchers with extensive experience in studying collaboration were asked to analyze a common piece of data – a pre-selected segment of videotaped interaction, involving three architects engaged in the design of a building. Each will summarize their findings followed by a discussion intended to highlight the complementarities and incommensurabilities among the six analyses.

A transcript of the video segment will be distributed to the audience and the video segment will be played. Each of the panelists will then be given 10 minutes to describe how they would go about analyzing this segment. The remainder of the session will be devoted to an open discussion exploring differences and commonalities among the analyses presented.

Questions to be discussed include: How does the analytic approach applied constrain the types of claims that might made about what is observed? What are the limits of what can be learned by micro-analytic studies of single settings? What guidance for the design of artifacts can be obtained from studies of this kind?

Anne H. Anderson

University of Glasgow

Psychologists working in the field of CSCW have traditionally conducted laboratory studies of the impact of various CSCW technologies such as video conferencing on shared problem solving tasks. My own research in CSCW followed this tradition where with colleagues I investigated the nature of collaboration, communication and task performance where pairs of participants either worked in a co-located face-to-face setting or supported by various communication technologies. The analytical techniques which we applied involved detailed analysis of the structure and content of the resulting task dialogues.

The dialogue analysis involved exploring the amount of speech required to complete the tasks in each communicative context and the nature of the turn taking among speakers such as the frequency of interruptions. Studies using these kinds of analyses, combined with user satisfaction questionnaires have shown characteristic differences in the way people commnicate and collaborate when engaged in face-to-face interaction, when supported by off-the-shelf videophones, and when using various qualities of videoconferencing tools (see Anderson et al, 1996,1997).

We have also combined such measures with very detailed analysis of the content of the dialogues. The nature of this content analysis was based on a technique called Conversational Games Analysis (Kowtko, Isard & Doherty-Sneddon, 1991) which involves assigning a communicative function to each utterance based on its position in the sequence of the dialogue, its verbal content, and its prosody, combined with the analyst's knowledge of the stage of the problem solving task which has been reached at the time of the utterance. The categories of Conversational Games include such functions as instructing, questioning, eliciting and providing feedback. The dialogue is divided into a sequence of these Conversational Games which can contain several constituent utterances and even can contain embedded conversational games. This system of analysis can be used reliably by different judges and can be applied to a range of problem solving tasks, such as shared route finding tasks and lab simulations of a range of service encounters such as travel booking and financial services. The system has illuminated how the differences in the lengths of dialogues which we observed in earlier studies of video-supported and face-to-face collaboration. Visual signals in face-to-face interactions seem to be used to substitute for a considerable amount of verbal feedback between participants but even high quality conferencing systems do not seem to support such visual interchanges between participants in a the same way as face-to-face interactions (Doherty-Sneddon, Anderson et al, 1997).

More recently we have moved from laboratory simulations of shared work, to work place studies of cross- company virtual teams of engineers collaborating supported by videoconfernceing and various shared graphical tools. In analyzing these work place meetings we have had to devise news forms of communication analysis. Although this analytical work is still in development, early studies of how the interaction is distributed across co-present and remote participants, how the content of the discussion can be assigned to problem-solving talk, social talk, technology talk, are already revealing interesting aspect about the impacts of technology and virtual team working (Carletta, Anderson & McEwan, 1998).

References

Anderson, A.H., Newlands, A, Mullin, J., Fleming, A, Doherty-Sneddon, G. & Van der Velden, J. (1996) *Impact of video-mediated communication on simulated service encounters.* Interacting with Computers, 8(2), 193-206.

Anderson, A.H., O'malley, C., Doherty-Sneddon, G., Langton, S., Newlands, A., Mullin, J., Fleming, A., Van der Velden, J. (1998) *The impact of VMC on collaborative problem solving.* In Finn, K., Sellen, A., & Wilbur, S. (eds) Video Mediated Communication . LEA New Jersey.

Carletta, J., McEwan, R. & Anderson, A.H. (1998) *Communication in virtual supply chain teams.* Proceedings of Prolamat 98, Trento, Italy.

Doherty-Sneddon, G., Anderson, A.H., OÌMalley, C., Langton, S., Garrod, S. & Bruce, V. (1997) *Face-to-face and video-mediated communication:a comparison of dialogue structure and task performance.* Journal of Experimental Psychology: Applied, 3(2), 105-125.

Kowtko, J., Isard, S. & Dohert-Sneddon, G. (1991) *Conversational games in dialogue.* In A. Lascarides (ed) Proceedings of the ESPRIT/DAWDI Workshop on Discourse Coherence, University of Edinburgh.

How to Follow Learning in the Coordinated Assembly of Representational States?

Rogers Hall, *University of California, Berkeley*

A central feature of collaborative learning is participating in the coordinated assembly of representational states (C. Goodwin, 1995; Hall, 1996; Hutchins, 1995a, 1995b; Ochs, Jacoby, and Gonzales, 1994; Saxe, 1991). Much of my recent research focuses on this type of activity in ongoing, multi-party interaction around shared tasks, drawn from middle school mathematics classrooms and adult workplaces where people design things (Hall, in press, 1995; Hall and Stevens, 1995, 1996). From an empirical perspective, assembling representations is a densely present, emergent, and mundane activity in school and professional settings where people work together. But giving an adequate account of this activity poses several theoretical problems:

- How do people bring talk, embodied activity, and various forms of inscription into coordination as they work (i.e., how do they assemble representational states)?
- How should we distinguish between making and using representational forms, including differences in the prevalence of these activities and their developmental trajectories?
- How is access to participation in these activities organized in different settings, both as a problem for adequate description and as an issue in instructional design?
- How can different perspectives on "competence" be aligned in studying, designing, or participating in these activities?

My contribution to the proposed panel would be to foreground the work of representational assembly and then to return to the theoretical/methodological issues raised above.

References

Goodwin, C. (1995). *Seeing in depth.* Social Studies of Science, 25, 237-274.

Greeno, J. G. and Hall, R. P. (1997, January). *Practicing representation: learning with and about representational forms.* Phi Delta Kappan, 361-367.

Hall, R. (in press). *Following mathematical practices in design-oriented work.* In C. Hoyles and R. Noss (Eds.) Mathematics for the new millennium. London: Falmer Press.

Hall, R. (1996). *Representation as shared activity: Situated cognition and Dewey's cartography of experience.* Journal of the Learning Sciences, 5, 209-238.

Hall, R. and Stevens, R. (1996). *Teaching/learning events in the workplace: A comparative analysis of their organizational and interactional structure.* In Proceedings of the Eighteenth Annual Conference of the Cognitive Science Society (pp. 160-165). Hillsdale, NJ: Lawrence Erlbaum Associates.

Hall, R. and Stevens, R. (1995). *Making space: a comparison of mathematical work in school and professional design practices.* S. L.. Star (Ed.) The cultures of computing (pp. 118-145). London: Basil Blackwell.

Hutchins, E. (1995a). *Cognition in the wild.* Cambridge, MA: The MIT Press.
Hutchins, E. (1995b). *How a cockpit remembers its speeds.* Cognitive Science, 265-288.
Ochs, E., Jacoby, S., & Gonzales, P. (1994). *Interpretive journeys: How physicists talk and travel through graphic space.* Configurations 1, 151-171.

Curtis D. LeBaron
University of Colorado at Boulder

My approach to analyzing videotaped data is best described as micro-ethnographic, which in my case involves a convergence of two competencies:

1. Methods that focus on talk, especially Conversation Analysis ;
2. Methods that focus on embodied action, such as Context Analysis.

Conversation Analysis and Context Analysis are easily combined because both are detailed, descriptive, structural, and naturalistic approaches. Both methods help account for the relationship between form and meaning, which is basic to structuralism. Behavior is not regarded as an external display of internal meaning, but as a form out of which people create meanings. Most forms (whether linguistic or embodied) are under-specified but become meaningful for participants as they constitute their context.

Conversation Analysts describe the role of spoken utterances within strips of interaction. Utterances are treated as social actions. Special attention is given to the ongoing orderliness of talk, because the sequential placement of an utterance helps to determine its social action. Utterances are shaped by their particular context (utterances have no meaning outside context); utterances register their context (participants display situational relevances to one another); and utterances constitute a context of subsequent social interaction (cotext). In sum, people make sense of their world, ascribe meaning to their world, and create structure for their world—through talk. Conversation Analysis is unabashedly microscopic, because, as Oliver Sacks has written, a "detailed study of small phenomena may give an enormous understanding of the way humans do things".

Context Analysts study how people move their bodies and occupy space in orderly ways. Pioneered by Ray Birdwhistell and Erving Goffman, this approach regards face-to-face interaction as a spatial process. Participants move so as to see and hear each other, arranging themselves in ways that show their mutual involvement and their understanding of the current activity. Behaviors such as head movements or postural shifts have no intrinsic meaning; rather, they are social actions to be understood through their relationship with other embodied behaviors, occurring within a context that participants construct.

Altogether, the present method involves four sets of related activities:

- Recording natural talk and embodied action.
- Repeated observing.
- Transcribing and digitizing.
- Composing descriptions and reporting findings.

Panel
Cooperative Buildings – Integrating Information, Organization and Architecture

Norbert A. Streitz, *GMD-IPSI,* Germany (chair), Volker Hartkopf *Carnegie Mellon University,* USA, Hiroshi Ishii *MIT Media Lab,* USA, Simon Kaplan, *University of Queensland,* Australia, Thomas P. Moran, *Xerox PARC,* USA

INTRODUCTION

Future work, cooperation, and organizations will be characterized by a high degree of dynamics, flexibility and mobility — substantially more so than today. Realizing this goal has profound implications for information and communication technology as well as architecture because virtual and physical spaces have to be designed in an integrated fashion in order to provide equally flexible cooperative work environments. The notion of "Cooperative Buildings" [6] provides a framework to focus and merge a number of currently still parallel approaches and developments in different disciplines contributing to the design of the workspaces of the future.

The purpose of this panel is to introduce the CSCW audience to a challenging generation of new problems and issues which are likely to shape research in CSCW and architecture in the foreseeable future.

Cooperative Workplaces and Buildings

Volker Hartkopf, *Center for Building Performance and Diagnostics, Carnegie Mellon University,* Pittsburgh, USA

(vh02+@andrew.cmu.edu)

As manufacturing and marketing of products have become global with the need to be, at the same time, local in meeting the needs of demanding customers, research, design and engineering activities of global companies are increasingly being decentralized. This poses significant challenges to create collaborative environments. Such environments must support many forms of collaboration one on one, one to many, many to many, asynchronously and synchronously. This raises the following questions:

What kind of characteristics must the places possess in which literally hundreds of different forms of collaboration and individual work will be conducted? How do we enable individuals and organizations to be productive, creative, innovative and reliable? How are the systems integrated that make a building: structure, facade, heating, ventilating, air conditioning and cooling (HVAC), lighting, furniture, Computer Supported Cooperative Work Systems (CSCW)? Four major characteristics of such workplaces will be exemplified: individual comfort, organizational flexibility, technological adaptability, energy and environmental effectiveness.

Architectural Space as an Interface Between People and Bits

Hiroshi Ishii, *MIT Media Laboratory,* USA

(ishii@media.mit.edu)

We envision that the architectural spaces we inhabit will be an interface between humans and online digital information. We call it "Tangible Bits" [3]. First, I will introduce the ambientROOM project [4, 7], which was designed to explore how an architectural space could be used to convey information to a user and have that information smoothly transition from the user's center of attention (foreground) when needed and fade into the periphery (background) when not in use. We constructed a special room equipped with embedded ambient displays and sensors. The ambientROOM lead us to the design of standalone ambient fixtures which include Water Lamp and Pinwheels [7]. The Water Lamp projects water ripple shadow created by a "rain of bits." The Pinwheels spin in a "bit wind." These ambient fixtures present information within an architectural space through subtle changes in light, sound, and movement, which can be processed in the background of awareness. In this panel, I will describe the conceptual framework of Tangible Bits, present several design examples, and discuss design issues.

Blending Virtual and Physical Space

Simon Kaplan, *Department of Computer Science and Electrical Engineering; The University of Queensland,* Australia

(s.kaplan@dstc.edu.au)

It is clear to anyone who thinks about this that as a community we need to support a blending of 'physical' and 'virtual' space in our collaboration support. Thus we might be able to support collaborations that span from a group of people sitting around a table, or wandering around, to remote participants at their desktops, to immersive interfaces. This raises questions of what it means to work across physical and virtual space, how we should understand such work, etc. In my part of the panel, I will outline some ways we might go about modeling and understanding what all this means, drawing on our own work on Locales Framework, and Alexander's work on patterns and centers [1].

Physical/Virtual Collaborative Environments

Thomas P. Moran, *Xerox PARC,* USA (moran@parc.xerox.com)

Collaborative work takes place in physical, as well as virtual space. With the rapid advances of networks, the web, and wireless communication, virtual space is rapidly being tied together. Work is physically distributed over multiple workplace sites, as well as the home. CSCW has traditionally focussed on the issues of distributed work and how to link people, synchronously and asynchronously. Within a physical site, work is distributed throughout complex architectural spaces. The artifacts of working are spread over desks, tables, walls, and floors, as well as in organized filing cabinets. Dealing with the reality of the physical workspace and its relation to the virtual information space is a new challenge for CSCW. Inherent in the physicality of work activity is its informal nature: conversations and encounters are casual, and even formal meetings are largely freewheeling. Further, the everyday products of work practice are informal, such as scribbled notes (personal, shared) and annotations on artifacts. The informal aspects of work have traditionally been a focus of PARC research: media spaces, pen-based tools, multimedia meeting capture, ubiquitous and "calm" computing.

Recently, PARC has been turning to the issues of the physical/virtual boundary: how to coordinate the simple physical artifacts and architectural spaces of work into the virtual knowledge spaces. PARC's approach is based on trying to understand work practice while trying to exploit several technologies:

Sensors attached to physical work artifacts (e.g., to be able to identify paper documents).

Sensors embedded into the physical architecture (e.g., to identify physical locales to guide people through them)

Cameras to capture work surfaces (e.g., large whiteboard images).

Recognition techniques on video data sources (e.g., to identify information artifacts or to interpret human gestures)

Integrative architectures to pull together heterogeneous sensed event data to provide context-based services.

Some of the issues we are facing involve:

understanding what is "natural" work activity

understanding personal vs shared information

keeping user interfaces invisible

built-in vs mobile technologies

cheap/ubiquitous vs expensive/sophisticated techno-logies

interpreting imperfect sensory data

graceful embedding of displays in the physical environemnt

the role of traditional physical artifacts (books to whiteboards)

synchronizing virtual information with physical reality

aligning virtual representations with the physical world

Roomware for Cooperative Buildings

Norbert A. Streitz, *GMD-IPSI,* Germany (streitz@darmstadt.gmd.de)

As part of my introduction to the panel, I will also present the i-LAND environment [5]. It constitutes an example of our vision of the workspaces of the future in so called "cooperative buildings" [6]. i-LAND supports cooperative work of dynamic teams with changing needs addressing the implications of new work practices. It is based on an integrated design of information and architectural spaces and related to augmented reality and ubiquitous computing. The design results in so called "roomware" components [5], i.e. computer-augmented objects integrating room elements with information technology. They require and provide new forms of human-computer interaction and enable the composition and decomposition of teams and subgroups in new ways. Besides the theoretical framework, the design of i-LAND was informed by the results of a requirements study investigating so called "creative teams" in major companies. I will present a brief overview of the current realization of i-LAND [2] in terms of the following roomware components: an interactive wall (DynaWall), an interactive table (InteracTable), and two computer-augmented chairs (CommChairs). They are complemented by the Passage mechanism which allows for an intuitive physical transportation of digital information.

References

Fitzpatrick, G., Kaplan, S., Parsowith, S. (1998). Experience in Building a Cooperative Distributed Organization: Lessons for Cooperative Buildings. In: Streitz et al. (Eds.), *Proc. of CoBuild '98*, pp. 66-79.

Holmer, T., Lacour, L., Streitz, N. (1998). i-LAND: An Interactive Landscape for Creativity and Innovation In: *Video Proceedings of ACM conference CSCW'98.*

Ishii H., Ullmer, B. (1997). Tangible Bits: Towards Seamless Interfaces between People, Bits and Atoms. *Proceedings of CHI '97* (March 1997), ACM, 234-241.

Ishii, H., Wisneski, C., Brave, S., Dahley, A., Gorbet, M., Ullmer, B., and Yarin, P. (1998). ambientROOM: Integrating Ambient Media with Architectural Space (video). In: *Conf. Summary of CHI '98*, ACM, 1998.

Streitz, N., Geissler, J., Holmer, T. (1998). Roomware for Cooperative Buildings: Integrated Design of

Architectural Spaces and Information Spaces. In: Streitz et al. (Eds.), *Proc. of CoBuildí98*, pp. 4-21.

Streitz, N., Konomi, S., Burkhardt, H. (Eds.), *Cooperative Buildings - Integrating Information, Organization, and Architecture. Proceedings of CoBuild'98*, Darmstadt, Germany. Lecture Notes in Computer Science 1370. Springer.

Wisneski, C., Ishii, H., Dahley, A., Gorbet, M., Brave, S., Ullmer, B., Yarin, P. (1998). Ambient Displays: Turning Architectural Space into an Interface between People and Digital Information. In: Streitz et al. (Eds.), *Proc. of CoBuild '98*, pp. 22-32.

CSCW '98 Workshop Program

Paul Dourish, *Xerox PARC, USA (dourish@parc.xerox.com)*, Mike Robinson, *University of Jyväskylä, Finland (mike@cs.jyu.fi)*

W1: Methodologies for Evaluation
Jean Scholtz, *NIST, USA*

Laurie Damianos, *MITRE, USA*

Andrew Greenberg, *TASC, USA*

Robyn Kozierok, *MITRE, USA*

This workshop will discuss different approaches used to evaluate CSCW systems. Our goal is to produce a taxonomy of evaluation methodologies for CSCW systems, identifying the type of systems for which a technique is most useful, the stage of development in which a methodology is appropriate, the resources needed to conduct an evaluation, and the appropriate measures for the various techniques. We plan to discuss various methods of data collection for collaborative work and identify the evaluation methodologies for which various types of data collection are most appropriate. Other issues we hope to discuss during the workshop include sharing and comparing collected data, the usefulness of standardized component tests, and the organization of evaluation results to make them more accessible to the development community.

Contact: jean.scholtz@nist.gov

W2: Towards Adaptive Workflow Systems
Mark Klein, *MIT, USA*

Chrysanthos Dellarocsa, *MIT, USA*

Abraham Bernstein, *MIT, USA*

Today's business environments are characterized by dynamic, uncertain and error-prone environments. To effectively support business processes in such contexts, workflow systems must be able to adapt themselves when deviations from the "ideal" process (i.e., "exceptions") occur. The goal of the workshop is to draw together researchers on adaptive workflow systems and help identify the breadth of current work, commonalities, gaps, potential collaborations and future research directions. Relevant topics include, but are not limited to methodologies and tools for detecting, understanding and resolving exceptions; infrastructures for dynamically modifiable process models; semi-prescriptive process models for dynamic environments; and empirical studies of exception handling in collaborative work settings

Contact: m_klein@mit.edu

W3: Identifying Constraints in Design
Todd Cherkasky, David Levinger, *Rensselaer Polytechnic Institute, USA*

Scoping out constraints and possibilities is an important task for any designer or consultant. This workshop focuses on improving collaborative design and consulting interventions by better charting technological and organizational constraints. In participatory design and computer supported collaborative work, practitioners and participants must attend to numerous constraints if they are to discover productive possibilities. For example, software is designed on the terrain of hardware capabilities, building configuration and use arise amidst zoning restrictions, and organizations identify and tap sources of legitimacy. Constraints include tools, knowledge, organizational support, social and cultural conventions, time, and others. Making conflicts explicit between different sets of design constraints is productive as it encourages new and creative ways to solve design problems. How do consultants make these conflicts explicit? We will consider experiences in which design practice was improved by explicitly examining constraints. Workshop participants will develop a draft guide including various methods for mapping out constraints to design processes.

Contact: cherkt@rpi.edu

W4: Understanding Professional Work and Technology in Domestic Environments
Jon O'Brien, *Lancaster University, UK*

Konrad Tollmar, Stefan Junestrand, *Royal Institute of Technology,Sweden*

Many technologies such as the PC, Internet access, new digital media and advanced telephony are now found in the home and are changing (or seeking to change) the ways in which people are entertained, informed and interpersonally connected in domestic environments. The goal of the workshop is to understand and experience the practice of professional work and the use of advanced communication technology in domestic environments. This will be accomplished through collaborative exploration into the territory of empirical research in CSCW and its increasingly important focus on technological change.

Of special interest for the workshop will be to identify where (and where not) already known methods and practices could be applied in domestic environments.

Contact: konrad@nada.kth.se

W5: Changing Work Practice in Technology-Mediated Learning Environments
Toni Robertson, Sue Fowell, *University of New South Wales, Australia*, Penny Collings, *University of Canberra, Australia*

The theme of this workshop is the relations between the rhetoric of choice, opportunity, and market advantage that surround the introduction of information technology into learning environments and the practice of those whose work includes the development and facilitation of courses in these environments. We encourage participation by those interested in clarifying the dynamics between economic arguments for increasing the use of information technology teaching and learning environments; the very real educational potentials that technology-mediated environments offer; the industrial relations and work practice implications of developing and facilitating courses in these environments; and the changing opportunities for students in terms of access and participation in their education programs.

Contact: t.robertson@unsw.edu.au

W6: Internet-based Groupware for User Participation in Product Development
Monica Divitini, Babak A. Farshchian, *NTNU, Norway*, Tuomo Tuikka, *University of Oulu, Finland*

This workshop will focus on the adoption of Internet-based groupware for promoting user participation in collaborative development of both software and non-software products. We invite participation of both practitioners and academics. We aim to provide a forum for gaining better understanding of user participation in the product development process through the Internet, as well as of the support that can be provided through groupware systems. We therefore welcome position papers describing tools and prototypes, reporting on experiences, and identifying open problems in this area.

Contact: igroup@idi.ntnu.no

W7: Designing Across Borders: The Community Design of Community Networks
Doug Schuler, *Evergreen State College, USA*

The workshop explores the current state and possible futures of networked (geographic) community communication and information systems ("community networks"). We are especially interested in how participatory design techniques can be integrated into public democratic design approaches and systems. We also believe that input from citizens as "lay designers" will provide an invaluable infusion of insight into the development of effective systems in civic and other realms. Finally, since these communication systems are becoming global in nature, we feel that issues about localism and globalism are extremely appropriate in the context of CSCW and geographically-based community systems. We will examine four main community design themes: (1) Looking at Innovative Regional Systems; (2) Theorizing About New Systems; (3) Recommendations and Future Directions; and (4) Critical Issues.

Contact: douglas@scn.org

W8: Handheld CSCW
Hans-W. Gellersen, *University of Karlsruhe, Germany*

The workshop investigates the application of handheld and wearable computers to support collaborative work. Participation is sought both from the collaborative work research community and handheld computing research areas such as ubiquitous computing, wearable computing, personal digital assistants, and mobile computing. Specific objectives are to analyse handheld CSCW systems and applications, to review handheld technologies with respect to their application in CSCW, and to inform handheld computing development from analysis of collaborative work. More general goals are to promote an awareness of handheld computing in the CSCW community, to stimulate a shift from single-user to multi-user application of handhelds and wearables, and to foster a community for handheld CSCW research.

Contact: hcscw@teco.edu

W9: Collaborative and Cooperative Information Seeking in Digital Information Environments
Elizabeth Churchill, *FX Palo Alto Laboratory, USA*, Dave Snowdon, *Xerox Research Center Europe, France*, Gene Golovchinsky, *FX Palo Alto Laboratory, USA*

We will discuss current conceptions of collaborative and cooperative information seeking activities, and identify potential areas for future research on the design and use of digital information spaces. We wish to explore different kinds of collaboration, including asynchronous recommendation systems and synchronous collaborative search and browsing activities by non-collocated participants. Our concern is that in the absence of such a debate, systems will be designed embodying assumptions about information seeking as a solitary activity. This workshop will be of interest to researchers concerned with the design of user interfaces and systems for supporting information exploration and information seeking activities. This includes user-centered aspects of design of systems for public use (e.g. public digital libraries, the WWW) and systems for use by more focused work groups.

Contact: churchill@pal.xerox.com

W10: Connectivity: Human and Technical

Jolene Galegher, *Carnegie Mellon University, USA*

As opportunities for technological connectivity increase – between people and people, between people and organizations, and between organizations and organizations – new social forms are arising, and new opportunities for research are appearing. Examples include uses of the Internet by journalists, connections between marketers and systems designers in banks, and fully automated transactions within or between organizations. CSCW scholars of every stripe – from system builders to behavioral scientists – are invited to present theoretical, experiential or research papers, as well as examples of prototypes, either the real thing or a videotape. People from business with interesting or unusual examples to present or questions to ask of the research community are also invited to prepare short "hands on" papers describing issues or problems in their organizations.

Contact: galegher@andrew.cmu.edu

W11: Designing Virtual Communities for Work

Lori Toomey, *FX Palo Alto Laboratory, USA*, John C. Tang, *Sun Microsystems, Inc., USA*, Gloria Mark, *GMD-FIT, Germany*, Lia Adams, *Lia Adams Consulting, USA*

While the popularity of networked virtual communities has been growing, their use has remained primarily social. Given the necessity of communication and collaboration among distributed workers, it seems natural to consider how these spaces might be used to support work and the surrounding social interactions. This workshop will focus on understanding how organizations are currently using virtual communities, and how they could be enhanced to better support the needs of collaborative workers. By "virtual communities" we are thinking primarily of MUDs, MOOs, and other collaboration software involving text, graphics, and/or other media. We will explore how to take advantage of the inherently engaging attributes of virtual communities to accomplish work, preserve organizational memory, promote corporate culture, and encourage professional networking. We will identify issues that are common to groups exploring work-based virtual communities and share the design approaches that are being tried to address them.

Contact: toomey@pal.xerox.com

W12: User-Centered Design in Practice - Problems and Possibilities

Jan Gulliksen, *Uppsala University, Sweden*
Ann Lantz, *Royal Institute of Technology, Sweden*
Inger Boivie, *Enator AB, Sweden*

Approaches in User-Centered Design (UCD) vary from Participatory Design to model-based engineering. No matter what the approach, UCD is not a simple, clear-cut way to develop uccessful systems. The purpose of this workshop is to discuss the problems encountered in practice and possible solutions, focusing on case studies in real systems development projects. Problems in this area include communication problems or lack of communication between system developers and users, between management and users, and between individuals in a team; and conflicting goals between the different groups in the process. Does UCD require certain attitudes in the organization and in individuals in order to bring success? Do UCD and requirements engineering conflict? What is the role of management and authority in a project in order to be able to make the decisions that are required for a project to succeed? Is UCD appropriate for every type of work activity?

CSCW '98 Doctoral Colloquium

Judith S. Olson, Gary M. Olson, *Collaboratory for Research on Electronic Work (CREW), USA. {jsolson, gmo}@umich.edu*

The Doctoral Colloquium at CSCW'98 is a forum in which Ph.D. students meet and discuss their work with each other and a panel of experienced CSCW researchers and practitioners. This year's panel of researchers and practitioners include Judy and Gary Olson, chairs, Atul Prakash, Carl Gutwin, Joerge Haake, and Yvonne Waern. Ten participants were accepted from the disciplines that form CSCW, including computer science, cognitive science, sociology, etc. The abstracts of their work appear below. During the colloquium, participants give a short informal presentation of their work, followed by an open discussion of their work. At the end of the session is a general discussion of career issues and research in CSCW.

The Effect of Proxemic Information in Video Mediated Communication

David Grayson

Multimedia Communications Group
University of Glasgow
52 Hillhead Street
Glasgow G12 9BH UK
david@mcg.gla.ac.uk

Proximity is arguably the most basic form of non-verbal communication and is known to affect the way that an interaction occurs, influencing factors such as dialogue, persuasion, trust and length of an interaction. So far it is unknown however whether proximity can have similar effects in Video Mediated Communication (VMC).

To investigate the possible effects of a stranger appearing close or far away, an experiment was devised simulating a financial advice transaction using a multimedia banking kiosk, where the financial advisor appeared either very close or far away. The experiment showed that when the financial advisor appeared very close, interactions were longer, with the customer saying more, making more interruptions, and having more turns than if the advisor appeared far away.

While this research indicates that perceived proximity may indeed have behavioral implications for interacting across a video link, future research aims to investigate further the precise nature both of the consequences and the reasons behind them. As part of this, Conversational Games Analysis (CGA) is used to examine the functional differences in the dialogue as well as the structural. Other issues raised by the research include the nature of familiarity and social presence.

Computer mediated communication across divergent research networks

Jenny Fry

University of Brighton
School of Information Management
Watts Building
Lewes Road
Brighton, East Sussex
BN2 4GL
England
j.fry@bton.ac.uk

Developments in electronic networks, such as the Internet, provide the potential to alter scholarly communication patterns and work organisation radically. The focus of this study is the mutual interaction between electronic networks and disciplinary culture and the consequences of cultural differences for the uptake and use of such networks. Knowledge domains within academia are not homogenous, each discipline has a distinctive social and epistemological structure which leads to variations in the communication system which underpins academic research. These domains can be categorised into four general types: Pure science; applied science; arts and humanities; and social science. A number of authors have devised typologies that outline the social and epistemological processes which span the disciplines within each group. The relationship between these differential cultures and electronic networks will be explored using in-depth interviews with networks of researchers from several divergent specialisms. Analysis of pilot interviews has revealed domain differences in the purpose, frequency, and perception of electronic network use.

A comparison of video-mediated, face-to-face and audio-only group communications

Emma France

Multimedia Communications Group
University of Glasgow
52 Hillhead Street
Glasgow G12 9BH UK
emma@mcg.gla.ac.uk

Few studies of technology mediated group communication exist. This paper describes a laboratory-based information exchange task comparing the communication and task performance of 36 three-person groups in face-to-face, audio-only, and video-mediated communication (VMC). Analyses revealed no statistically significant differences in dialogue length or performance between the three conditions. However, VMC conversations tended to have most words and speaking turns and those in face-to-face communication the least. This trend was explored using Conversational Games Analysis (Kowtko, Isard & Doherty-Sneddon, 1991), an exhaustive form of coding of the functional use of utterances. The content of 12 face-to-face and 12 video-mediated dialogues was coded. This showed that significantly more interactive work tended to be required in VMC to complete the task. It is proposed that impoverished visual feedback cues, novelty and remoteness in VMC make it more difficult for the participants to reach mutual understanding, and hence more difficult to complete the task.

Communication and co-ordination through public representations

Christer Garbis

Department of Communication Studies
Linköping University
581 83 Linköping
Sweden
christer.garbis@tema.liu.se

In my thesis work I am investigating the way in which teams of operators engage in co-operative process management, such as nuclear power plant control, use 'public representations', i.e., the artifacts representing information in such a way that it is commonly accessible and available to all team members at the same time (for example, a wall mounted electronic display). I am particularly interested in the role that these representations play for the operators' collective assessment and awareness of the state of the system that they are responsible for operating. In addition, I am researching the differences between accessing information through a 'public representation,' such as a fixed line diagram in the underground line control, and through 'private representations,' such as a single-user computer screen. It is my belief that the role and function of 'public' and 'private' representations in the above settings should be carefully studied so they can be designed in a more tightly coupled and integrated way in order to provide the operators with a sufficient and flexible mode of information.

An investigation of multi-user design tools for collaborative 3-D modeling

Tek-Jin Nam

Interaction Design Research Group
Department of Design
Brunel University
Egham, Surrey, TW20 0JZ UK
Tek-Jin.Nam@brunel.ac.uk

The objective of this research is to help designers working in teams by providing an improved collaborative design environment. The focus is on the investigation into specific issues and requirements for the development of multi-user CAD systems for collaborative 3-D modeling. By examining means for incorporating shared design workspace into conventional design workspace, we propose new mechanisms to transform existing CAD tools into collaboration-aware systems. From an initial experimental study of the team design process and a series of prototype development of collaborative CAD systems, a theoretical framework has been proposed and applied to the new collaboration-aware design systems. The result of the research will lead to the new generation of design tools to support team design tasks improving efficiency and effectiveness of team working.

EVOLVE: EVOLutionary aspects of Videoconferencing Explored

Marike Hettinga

Telematica Instituut
P.O. Box 589
7500 AN Enschede
The Netherlands
hettinga@telin.nl

The EVOLVE project focuses on evolutionary processes that take place after the introduction of videoconferencing in medical teleconsultation sessions. Evolution refers to what happens with patterns of work, including patterns of using a technology for particular purposes. As these patterns often divert from the patterns initially expected by designers, we believe that evolutionary processes are an important factor for the successfulness of the introduction of new technology. EVOLVE aims at yielding design guidelines for a better support of these evolutionary processes. These guidelines concern the technology (the "technical system"), as well as the organization of the use of the technology (the "social system"), and the relation between the technical and social system.

Concurrency control for real-time diagramming

Jeffrey D. Campbell

Department of Information Science and Telecommunications
University of Pittsburgh
135 North Bellefield Avenue
Pittsburgh, PA 15260 USA
jeffc@sis.pitt.edu

Diagrams represent a design, concept or object. Multiple users working together simultaneously to create a diagram can interfere with each other's work. At a minimum this results in lost productivity. If undetected, the interference can cause inconsistencies or errors in the diagram greatly reducing its value. A concurrency control mechanism is needed to maintain integrity for collaborative diagramming. The method described here focuses on identifying logical units of work for collaborative diagramming. These units are analogous to transactions in a database system. This emphasis on transaction identification is a key distinction between this technique and prior CSCW concurrency control approaches. The improvement in transaction identification along with an implementation of split transactions reduces resource blocking, a problem generally found in applying locking techniques from database to CSCW applications.

Supporting dynamic recommendations in organi-zational information systems

David McDonald

Computing, Organizations, Policy and Society (CORPS)
Information and Computer Science, CS 444
University of California, Irvine
Irvine, CA 92697-3425 USA
dmcdonal@ics.uci.edu

This work explores how information systems can be augmented to assist users in finding other individuals who are likely to have specialized, expert information that they need. In particular, this work considers the social and cognitive mechanisms that people use to find candidate sources of expertise. I recently completed a field study of information finding and sharing in a software development organization. The social and cognitive mechanisms identified during the study will be used to design and implement a system that can assist users with finding potential experts. The design and implementation of a system concomitant with an analysis of subsequent data are work in progress.

Designing the *DomeCity* MOO Collaboratory: A multi-user simulation in a text-based networked virtual environment that supports non-scripted interactions toward intercultural understanding.

Elaine M. Raybourn

Sandia National Laboratories
P.O. Box 5800
Albuquerque, New Mexico 87185 USA
emraybo@sandia.gov

This proposal argues that designing a multi-user social-process simulation in a shared virtual environment offers unique opportunities to explore intercultural issues such as identity, power, , and prejudice because its collaborative environment is much less threatening than face-to-face. In the proposed Text-Based Networked Virtual Environment (TNVE) also known as a Multi-User Dimension Object Oriented (MOO), players' narratives and experiences provide the basis for discovery and exploration in a virtual "collaboratory." The *DomeCity*MOO environment is unique in that it advances our state of knowledge of the effects of designing a non-scripted collaborative social process simulation which supports both group and individual intercultural learning in a shared virtual space.

High level requirements analysis for systems in complex work settings

Mark Bergman

Information and Computer Science
University of California, Irvine
Irvine, CA 92697 USA
mbergman@ics.uci.edu

Large scale intra- and interorganizational information systems development has failed to yield useful systems ~50% of the time. It appears that one cause of these failures is the misunderstanding or overlooking of organizational and institutional requirements in the design of these systems. High-level requirements analysis is being created as one way to start to address this problem. It is a new methodology that can be used to gather organizational, institutional as well as technical information system requirements. Research is being performed to determine how to build a high-level requirements analysis framework. Then, research will continue in applying the framework to identify critical individual or combinations of technical, organizational, institutional requirements for a "real life" project that have been misunderstood or overlooked. Beyond this, high-level requirements analysis should allow for increased insights in (1) requirements analysis, (2) complex system design which contains technological, organizational, and institutional factors, (3) how technology, organizations, and institutions co-evolve over time, (4) policy creation in the development and governance of these types of systems, and (5) how to build, maintain, and improve a high-level requirements extraction and analysis system. Altogether, this sets up a research framework that may eventually yield solutions to become much more successful at either implementing large scale intra- and interorganizational information systems or knowing when not to build them.

CSCW 98 Seattle Washington USA

CSCW '98 Video Program

1. A demonstration of awareness driven video quality of service

Gail Reynard, Chris Greenhalgh and Steve Benford
Computer Science Department,
University Park,
University of Nottingham,
NG7 2RD, UK.
Contact: Gail Reynard
+44 115 951 4277
gtr@cs.nott.ac.uk

We present a combined conferencing/mediaspace application that extends previous work on texture mapping video streams into virtual environments by introducing awareness driven video Quality of Service (QoS). This uses movements within a shared virtual world to activate different video services as defined by their frame-rates. Three different services are supported: portholes, providing 1 frame of video per 5 minutes; glance, 1 frame per second and full frame rate video. Our application uses awareness driven video for facial expressions and for views into remote physical environments. This enables seamless shifts in mutual involvement and makes underlying QoS mechanisms more visible and malleable. The video gives a guided tour through the mediaspace, demonstrating the different video services. This work was published as: "Awareness Driven Video Quality of Service in Collaborative Virtual Environments", Gail Reynard, Steve Benford, Chris Greenhalgh and Christian Heath, Proceedings CHI '98, April, 1998, Los Angeles, pp. 464-471.

2. iLAND: An Interactive Landscape for Creativity and Innovation

Torsten Holmer, Laurent Lacour and Norbert Streitz
GMD-IPSI,
German National Research Center for Information Technology,
Dolivostr. 15, D-64293,
Darmstadt, Germany.
Contact: Torsten Holmer
+49 6151 869921
holmer@darmstadt.gmd.de

i-LAND constitutes an example of our vision of the workspaces of the future employing "roomware" components in so called "cooperative buildings". It provides an innovative work environment supporting cooperative work of dynamic teams with changing needs resulting from new work practices, such as ad hoc, and on-demand, teams. We propose an integrated design of digital information spaces and real architectural spaces enabling new forms of human-computer interaction and support for cooperative work. The approach is related to augmented reality and ubiquitous computing. The central concept presented in the video is the notion of "roomware" components, i.e. computer-augmented objects integrating room elements with information technology. We present the current realization of i-LAND in terms of an interactive wall (DynaWall), an interactive table (InteracTable), and two computer-enhanced chairs (CommChairs). They are complemented by the Passage mechanism which allows for an intuitive physical transportation of digital information. The concept and the usage of the roomware components are demonstrated with several sample scenarios.

3. Insight Lab: a Team Workspace

James Meyers, Beth Lange and Mark Jones
Center for Strategic Technology Research,
Andersen Consulting,
3773 Willow Rd.,
Northbrook, IL,
60062-6212, USA.
Contact:James Meyers
+1 847 714 3338
meyers@cstar.ac.com

The Insight Lab is an environment in which teams come together to analyze complex situations. The lab is particularly valuable when teams are studying large amounts of qualitative data, including videotapes, audio recordings, photos or documents. In addition to utilizing a three monitor large-screen display, the lab takes advantage of electronic whiteboards, linked sticky notes, and linked printed reports to bring information out of the computer box and into the physical world. By linking pieces of paper to the digital world via barcodes, the lab turns its walls into a huge computer desktop. The Insight Lab utilizes electronic whiteboards and linked sticky notes to capture critical team interactions, thereby documenting the rationale behind a group decision. Working "out-of-the-box" and maintaining a group memory provides a truly immersive environment, thereby creating a next generation team workspace.

4. The Mirror: reflections on inhabited TV

Andrew McGrath, Amanda Oldroyd and Graham Walker
BT Labs,
British Telecom,
MLB G PP13,
Martlesham Heath,
Ipswich, Suffolk, UK
Contact: Andy McGrath
+44 1473 606759
andy.mcgrath@bt-sys.bt.co.uk

Inhabited TV is a vision of future television services in which multi-user 3D virtual environments deliver unprecedented levels of audience participation. Social chat and interaction are mixed with professional content and programming to create on-line communities. The Mirror was a groundbreaking collaborative experiment in Inhabited TV, created by BT, Sony, Illuminations and the BBC. Six on-line worlds were available to over 2000 viewers of the BBC2 series "The Net" in January and February 1997, and this video provides a flavour of the project.

5. GestureLaser: Supporting Hand Gestures in Remote Instruction

Hideaki Kuzuoka, Shinya Oyama
Institute of Engineering Mechanics,
1-1-1 Tennoudai, Tsukuba,
Ibaraki 305,
University of Tsukuba, Japan
Hiroshi Kato, Hideyuki Suzuki
C & C Media Research Laboratories,
NEC Corporation,
1-1, Miyazaki 4-chrome,
Miyamae-ku, Kawasaki,
Kanagawa 216, Japan
Keiichi Yamazaki, Akiko Yamazaki
Faculty of Liberal Arts,
Saitama University,
255, Shimo-Ookubo,
Urawa, Saitama, 338, Japan
Hiroyuki Miki
Media Laboratories,
Oki Electric Industry Company,
550-5 Higashiasakawa-cho,
Hachiouji 193-8550, Japan.
Contact: Hideaki Kuzuoka
+81 298 53 5258
kuzuoka@kuzuoka-lab.esys.tsukuba.ac.jp

GestureLaser is a remote controlled laser pointer which allows an instructor to gesture at real world objects over distances. To control the position of the GestureLaser's spot, a laser beam is reflected by two mirrors each rotated by a stepping motor. The remote instructor controls the motion of the laser's spot using a computer mouse in the same way an ordinary mouse pointer is controlled. The instructor can thus show position, rotation and direction by moving the spot. The laser's low illumination mode is used to indicate transitions between gestures while still allowing operators to track the spot. We have already undertaken a few experiments in order to understand how users can effectively use the laser's spot as a substitute for real hand gestures.

6. Hypermirror: mirror reflections representing users as if they are all in the same room

Osamu Morikawa
National Institute of Bioscience and Human Technology,
Higashi, Tsukuba,
Ibaragi, 305-8566, Japan
Takanori Maesako
Faculty of Human Sciences,
Osaka University, 1-2
Yamadaoka, Suita,
Osaka 565-0871, Japan
Contact: Osamu Morikawa
+81 298-54-6775
morikawa@nibh.go.jp

HyperMirror is a new video communication system which realizes video WISIWYS (What I See Is What You See). We create an attractive, highly understandable communication environment, rather than imitating face-to-face communication. Like telephones, this system is intended to have easily understood limitations. Each site has a large screen which displays not only the remote participants image, but also the overlaid mirror image of the local participants. In this way, participants can share exactly the same video space. Thus they can use gestures and pointing to indicate background objects or images. There are several ways to synthesize the HyperMirror image. In this video, we present an optical synthesis and an electronic synthesis uses "chroma-keying".

7. Crisis in Ragan: Orbit at work

Richard Taylor, Tim Mansfield, and Geraldine Fitzpatrick
Distributed Systems Technology Centre,
University of Queensland,
St. Lucia 4072,
Brisbane, QLD, Australia
Contact: Richard Taylor
+61 7 3365 4310
taylor@dstc.edu.au

How can an overworked editor in head office and an unprepared reporter in the far away land of Ragan get a breaking story to press in less than a day? We follow these journalists as they use the WORLDS project's collaboration environment, Orbit, integrated with other prototype tools developed at the DSTC, to accomplish their task. Orbit is based on the notion of software locales or "group-zones" to provide contexts for shared work. A navigator provides access to all the group-zones to which one of the journalists currently belongs. Users can dynamically change their view of each of these group-zones to match their changing needs, and the currently selected documents and folders from all zones are shown in a desktop-style workspace. They can also use integrated audio and video conferencing to communicate with each other. As well as Orbit, the video shows the intrepid team using other integrated DSTC tools including a backwards recovery workflow system, group awareness, and information filtering, to work together to make the 5pm bulletin.

8. GAZE: Visual-Spatial Attention in Communication

Roel Vertegaal,
Cognitive Ergonomics Department,
Twente University,
The Netherlands
Contact: Roel Vertegaal
+31 53 4893324
roel@acm.org

This video illustrates the importance of conveying visual attention in multiparty mediated systems. In terms of multiparty turntaking efficiency, current-day video-conferencing systems do not seem to provide the expected added value over telephony. We attribute this to a lack of Conversational Awareness: knowing who's talking to whom. The visual attention of participants directly relates to their auditory and articulatory attention, i.e., their gaze direction indicates whom they listen or speak to. Conveying gaze direction seems to ease turn-taking by allowing more rapid speaker switches and more efficient use of deictic verbal references (e.g., "What do YOU think?"). This video exemplifies the differences between face-to-face, traditional video-mediated, and attention-based conferencing. It features an early simulation of the GAZE Groupware system, a multiparty mediated system which metaphorically conveys gaze direction. Using an eyetracker, the system measures where participants look inside a 3D virtual meeting room, and rotates their video images to align with their gaze.

9. The SubCam: An insight into the phenomenal flow of office life

Anne-Laure Fayard and Saadi Lahlou
EDF R&D Division,
1, Avenue du general de Gaulle,
92241 Clamart, France
Contact: Anne-Laure Fayard
+33 1 47 65 36 23
Anne-Laure.Fayard@notes.edfgdf.fr

This video presents the SubCam perspective and the methods used to analyze the video data it provides. We study office work in a large industrial research center and focus on the interactions of office workers with their social and spatial environment. Current research methods (observations, interviews, ethnographic studies with video) provide interesting data, but fail to identify some key phenomena on the situated nature of the work. In order to determine the affordances of the environment, we design a new observation tool: the Subjective camera or SubCam. It is composed of a pair of glasses on which a miniature video camera and a microphone are clipped. The Sub Cam gives a rather good indication of what the subject sees, although it does not track eye gaze. It provides an insight in the phenomenal flow in which subjects are immersed and a subjective view of subjects' movements and interactions. The SubCam provides a very large and rich set of data. To focus our investigation, we have chosen 6 foci of analysis grounded on previous results and a first perusal of the data: 1. Interruption; 2. Feeling lost; 3. Navigation in the Workspace; 4. Artifacts; 5. Peripheral Awareness; 6. Cooperation.

10. Enabling personal tele-embodiment

Eric Paulos and John Canny
Computer Science Department,
University of Berkeley,
387 Soda Hall, Berkeley,
CA, 94720-1776, USA.
Contact: Eric Paulos
+1 510 642 8149
paulos@cs.berkeley.edu

Current internet applications fail to interface to the real physical world in which we live, work, and play. This video illustrates the development of several simple, inexpensive, internet-controlled, untethered tele-robots or PRoPs (Personal Roving Presences) that provide the sensation of tele-embodiment in a remote real space. These devices range from small helium filled tele-operated air-borne blimps to more recent ground based systems with longer ranges, battery life, and abilities. All PRoPs support at least video and two-way audio as well as mobility through the remote space they inhabit. The physical tele-robot serves both as an extension of its operator and as a visible, mobile entity with which other people can interact. ProPs enable their users to perform a wide gamut of human activities in the remote space, such as exploring, conversing with people, hanging out, wandering around, pointing, examining objects, reading, and making simple gestures. The goal is to identify and distill a small yet sufficient number of traits that are vital to human communication and interaction and to physically implement them on PRoPs. For more information please visit www.prop.org.

11. Focus and Awareness in Groupware

Carl Gutwin
Computer Science Department,
University of Saskatchewan,
1c101 Engineering Building,
Saskatoon, SK, S7N 5A9, Canada
Saul Greenberg
Computer Science Department,
University of Calgary,
Calgary, Alberta,
T2N 1N4, Canada

Contact: Saul Greenberg
+1 403 220 6087
saul@cpsc.ucalgary.ca

Medium-sized shared workspaces present two design goals to groupware designers: first, people need to focus on the details of their work; second, people need to stay aware of others working elsewhere in the workspace. This video presents and compares four different visualization techniques for achieving these goals. The techniques are part of a system for building and editing concept maps, visual languages for representing ideas and relationships. When people use concept maps, they often need to work in different parts of the map. Since a groupware workspace can only show a small part of the map at one time, this means that staying aware can become a problem. We present four different visual approaches to supporting both detail and awareness. All approaches extend the earlier versions illustrated in our CSCW '96 videos, and (for ease of comparison) all work within the concept map editor. The radar view splits the interface into detail and awareness windows. The fisheye view uses distortion to integrate detail and awareness in a single window. The dragmag view lets people selectively magnify a portion of a large overview. The two-level view overlays a full-screen overview onto a detail view.

CSCW 98 Seattle Washington USA

Tutorials

Tom Finholt, *University of Michigan, USA*

Mark S. Ackerman, *University of California, Irvine, USA*

T1. A Grand Tour of CSCW Research

Jonathan Grudin, *University of California, Irvine, USA*
Steven E. Poltrock, *The Boeing Company, USA*
John Patterson, *Lotus Development Corporation, USA*

Goals and content: An introduction to Computer Supported Cooperative Work research for those unfamiliar with the field. We provide a framework for understanding CSCW as a research domain, a development opportunity, and a management challenge. We present a taxonomy of CSCW technologies, explain the computing architectures of CSCW technologies, and analyze successes and obstacles to success.

This tutorial balances the social and technical issues that thread through this conference. It also identifies the conference events that expand on this social and technical framework.

About the instructors: Jonathan Grudin has worked as developer, researcher and consultant on CSCW and groupware. Steven Poltrock introduces, evaluates, and deploys groupware systems. John Patterson is developing architectures for synchronous groupwork. The first two instructors are the co-chairs of CSCW 98.

T2. A Technical Overview of CSCW

Presun Dewan, *University of North Carolina - Chapel Hill, USA*

Goals and content: In the past decade, a variety of systems (applications and infrastructures) have been developed to support collaboration. These systems have been developed in diverse fields including user-interfaces, multimedia, operating systems, database systems, programming languages, networking, computer hardware, distributed systems, and hypermedia. This tutorial will take the audience on a tour of these systems, discussing technical issues that arise in their design and implementation.

About the instructor: Presun Dewan is an Associate Professor of Computer Science at the University of North Carolina. His research interests are in infrastructure for implementing groupware, collaborative software engineering, object-oriented database systems, and distributed operating systems. He is also Associate Editor of ACM Transactions on Information Systems and a member of the IFIP-WG2.7 group on Engineering for Human Computer Interaction.

T3. Activity Theory: Basic Concepts and Applications

Victor Kaptelinin, *Umeå University, Sweden*
Bonnie Nardi, *AT&T Research, USA*

Goals and content: This tutorial introduces participants to Activity Theory, a conceptual approach that provides a broad framework for describing the structure, development, and context of computer-supported activities. The tutorial will consist of lectures, discussion and small group exercises. A Web community will be established so attendees will be able to continue to learn about and use activity theory.

About the instructors: Victor Kaptelinin is a Research Associate at the Department of Informatics at Umeå University and has written several articles on the relationship between activity theory and human-computer interaction. Bonnie Nardi is a member of the Human Computer Interface Department at AT&T's Information Systems and Services Research Lab and is the author of Context and Consciousness: Activity Theory and Human-Computer Interaction (1996, MIT Press).

T4. The Theory and Practice of Fieldwork for System Development

Dave Randall, *Manchester Metropolitan University, U.K.*
Mark Rouncefield, *Lancaster University, U.K.*

Goals and content: This tutorial has the objective of developing an appreciation of the various theoretical perspectives utilized by CSCW practitioners and the practical issues that arise during the conduct of "naturalistic" inquiry. A number of competing theoretical perspectives will be examined, compared, and contrasted, including "grounded theory," "soft systems," distributed cognition, ethnomethodology, participatory design, "business-led" perspectives, and activity theory. The tutorial will draw from the instructors' experiences working with design and management teams to illustrate many of the practical problems associated with doing fieldwork.

About the instructors: Dave Randall is a senior lecturer at Manchester Metropolitan University and has done work on air traffic control systems and retail financial systems. Mark Rouncefield is a researcher at the CSCW center at Lancaster University who has conducted fieldwork in the financial services sector.

T5. Contextual Inquiry: Gathering Customer Data for System Development

Karen Holtzblatt and **Hugh Beyer,** *InContext Enterprises, USA*

Goals and content: This tutorial, taught by the originator of contextual inquiry, presents a practical introduction to the use of field research in designing computer systems that support and extend people's work. Contextual inquiry is a technique for interviewing and observing users in their own workplace as they work. The tutorial will develop skills in data collection, analysis, and use through hands-on examples of how to apply contextual inquiry throughout the system development cycle and how to adapt the approach to different situations.

About the instructors: Karen Holtzblatt has designed products and processes in the computer industry for the past ten years. She has led teams in customer-centered design to develop products, strategies, internal systems, and organizational structures. The techniques she pioneered are used and taught internationally. Hugh Beyer has worked in the industry as programmer, architect and consultant. He has designed and developed object-oriented repositories and integrated CASE systems, and has developed processes for using customer data to drive object-oriented design. They are co-founders of InContext Enterprises Inc., a consulting firm leading design and management teams in using customer-centered approaches in their organizations.

T6. Virtual Humans in Collaborative Virtual Environments (CVEs)

Nadia Magnenat Thalmann, *University of Geneva, Switzerland*

Daniel Thalmann, *Swiss Federal Institute of Technology, Switzerland*

Goals and content: The merging of recent developments in virtual reality, human animation and CSCW has led to new fields of research: the integration of virtual humans in collaborative virtual environments; the interaction of humans with virtual humans; and the representation of humans in virtual worlds. This tutorial will emphasize real-time animation techniques, real-time motion tracking, and communication among humans and virtual humans, using examples of social behavior, group behavior, and crowd behavior. The course will also discuss facial animation techniques for virtual actors and communication with them. Finally, the interaction among humans and autonomous virtual humans inside the virtual space will be illustrated with applications in telecooperative work.

About the instructors: Nadia Magnenat Thalmann is the founder of Miralab at the University of Geneva and was previously on the faculty of the University of Montreal. Daniel Thalmann is a professor and director of the Computer Graphics Laboratory at the Swiss Federal Institute of Technology in Lausanne.

T7. Computer Support for Community Work: Designing and Building Systems for the "Real World"

Doug Schuler, *The Evergreen State College, USA*

Goals and content: This tutorial is designed to introduce CSCW researchers and implementers to the rapidly growing field of public CSCW applications, services, and institutions ("Computer Supported Community Work"). It is the goal of this tutorial to present several examples of this work along with the major challenges and opportunities involved in this endeavor and to engage all the participants in a dialogue as to the future of these new systems. Each participant should, after attending this tutorial, have a much clearer idea what systems might be developed, what research questions are involved, and what they themselves can do to make them happen.

About the instructor: After working in the computer industry for over 15 years, Doug Schuler now teaches Computers and Society studies at The Evergreen State College. He is one of the founders of the Seattle Community Network, a free, public computer network with over 12,000 registered users. Doug is also the author of New Community Networks: Wired for Change (1996, Addison-Wesley).

T8. Building Computer-Based Shared Information Systems

John Mariani, *Lancaster University, U.K.*

Goals and content: This tutorial compares and contrasts the use of real-world information artifacts and their electronic counterparts in traditional database systems, provides an understanding of the problems facing designers and implementers of shared information systems, and indicates how such systems can present awareness information to end-users. The tutorial will produce an understanding of the nature of shared information spaces, of the techniques used to realize shared information spaces, and of case studies about the design and development of shared information spaces.

About the instructor: John Mariani of the Computing Department and CSCW Center at Lancaster University has been part of national and international research teams working on shared information spaces, including the COMIC Shared Object Service.

T9. Avoiding Damn Lies: Understanding Statistics

Alan Dix, *Staffordshire University, U.K.*

Goals and content: Many practitioners and researchers in CSCW have to use statistics. However, many people, despite their ability to run a statistics package or calculate simple statistics, remain uncertain about what the numbers mean.

This tutorial will produce an understanding of key statistical concepts enabling understanding and interpretation of statistical analyses.
For more information, see:
http://www.hiraeth.com/alan/tutorials/stats/.

About the instructor: Alan Dix is Professor of Computing and Associate Dean at Staffordshire University. Before moving into CSCW research, he was a mathematician and professional statistician.

T10. Working through Collaboration: A Framework for Designing Technology Support

John L. Bennett, *Independent consultant, USA*
John Karat, *IBM T.J. Watson Research Center, USA*

Goals and content: As we design computing technologies to support collaboration face to face and at a distance, it is important to have a basic understanding of what makes collaboration work. This tutorial focuses on distinctions among types of collaboration; the roles of conversations in establishing and maintaining collaboration; the importance of partnership in successful collaboration; and the role of culture in supporting collaboration. Examples of software support using a commercial product (Lotus Notes/Domino) and the World Wide Web will illustrate strengths and weaknesses of existing systems. Cases will be drawn from the papers review process for CHI'98 and from a longitudinal study of a customer service group.
After completing the tutorial, attendees should be able to formulate plans for designing, evaluating, installing, and bringing into practice technological support for collaboration.

About the instructors: John Bennett specializes in work with design teams developing systems that support effective human-computer interaction. While at IBM Research he served as an IBM Research Staff Member, project leader, manager, and consultant to development divisions. At several ACM SIGCHI annual conferences he taught (with people from Digital Equipment Corporation) tutorials on "Usability Engineering" and on "Contextual Inquiry" methods. He collaborated in producing the book Bringing Design to Software, edited by Terry Winograd. He contributed "Building relationships for technology transfer" to the feature articles in the September, 1996, Communications of the ACM.
John Karat's current research is focused on improving the design process for usable systems. He is a member of the ACM SIGCHI Advisory Board, is the United States representative to IFIP TC 13 (Human-Computer Interaction) and a member of the Board of Directors of the Federation on Computing in the United States (FOCUS). He and John Bennett co-presented tutorials at CSCW94, CSCW96, and ECSCW97. He has been an instructor for the University of Michigan Summer Schools in Human-Computer Interaction since 1996. He organized workshops at CHI'91, CHI'94 and CSCW92, and built on the results of the CHI'91 workshop to produce an edited book outlining the area (Taking Software Design Seriously: Practical techniques for human-computer interaction design).

T11. Developing Collaborative Applications on the World Wide Web

Andreas Girgensohn, *FX Palo Alto Laboratory, USA*
Alison Lee, *IBM T.J. Watson Research Center, USA*

Goals and content: Building collaborative applications from the ground up is a challenging task; one that requires balancing social, user interface, and technical concerns. The Web facilitates this task by providing building blocks that make it easy to rapidly develop collaborative applications. Using the Web helps lower the technical hurdles in the task and allows researchers, designers and developers to focus on exploring and understanding the sociological and HCI concerns. This tutorial demonstrates, with fragments of program and pseudo code, how the Web building blocks can be used to develop typical collaborative applications consisting of components such as awareness, shared objects, and conversational tools. Also, the tutorial highlights ways to address issues (e.g., interactivity, customization, data and tool integration, control, synchronization, firewall support, and security) related to using the Web as a development platform. The goal of the tutorial is to provide insights into and understanding of the Web building blocks and how to use the Web as a rapid prototyping platform for collaborative applications. At the end of the tutorial, participants will be able to begin developing Web-based collaborative applications.

Intended audience: This tutorial is intended for researchers, designers, and developers working on building CSCW applications or interactive Web content. Familiarity with Web browsers and at least one C-like programming language (e.g., C++, Java, Perl) is recommended.

About the instructors: Andreas Girgensohn and Alison Lee have backgrounds and experiences in computer science and human-computer interaction. They have developed tools and methodologies to support distributed group work. In the last four years, much of that development work has been carried out using the Web technologies.

T12. An Introduction to Distributed Cognition: Analyzing the Organizational, the Social, and the Cognitive for Designing and Implementing CSCW Applications.

Christine Halverson, *IBM T.J. Watson Research Center, USA*
Yvonne Rogers, *University of Sussex, U.K.*

Goals and Content: To introduce the theory of distributed cognition and elucidate its application to design and evaluation using real examples, and to provide experience to the participants by providing a hands-on example to work through. We will explain the importance of adopting multiple perspectives when designing and evaluating CSCW systems and groupware, and describe the analytic framework provided by distributed cognition. We will provide a detailed outline of the micro-methodology, a step-by-step walkthrough of analysis, and a guided hands-on analysis of a collaborative setting.

About the instructors: Christine Halverson received her Ph.D. in Cognitive Science from the University of California, San Diego. For the last 3 years she has been a research staff member at IBM. Yvonne Rogers has a Ph.D. from the UK and is an associate research professor at the University of Sussex, where she teaches HCI, CSCW and cognitive science. Both instructors have used the distributed cognition methodology in many domains.

T13. Behavioral Evaluation of CSCW Systems

Tom Finholt, *University of Michigan, USA*

Goals and content: Evaluating CSCW systems is much more difficult than evaluating single-user systems because of the additional group and organizational factors. Behavioral evaluation consists of having people use CSCW technologies under appropriate conditions and gathering either qualitative or quantitative information about their behavior. We will examine a variety of methods, including case studies, large scale field studies, surveys, and laboratory studies.

About the instructor: Tom Finholt is the director of the Collaboratory for Research on Electronic Work at the University of Michigan. His current research interests include collaborative science over the Internet and geographically distributed development teams in the automobile and telecommunications industries.

T14. XML: Modeling Data and Metadata

Rohit Khare, *University of California, Irvine, USA*

Adam Rifkin, *California Institute of Technology, USA*

Goals and content: Designers of computer-supported cooperative work systems have long sought a portable information delivery format to share knowledge. Extensible Markup Language (XML) provides an effective solution for communicating across time, space, and communities. This tutorial introduces the family of Extensible Markup Language specifications to CSCW researchers and practitioners: XML, Namespaces, XSL (Styles), Xlink, Xpointer, RDF (Resource Description Format), and Schemas, as well as XML's interaction with other Web standards such as HTML, CSS, URI, and HTTP.

About the instructors: Rohit Khare was a member of the technical staff of the World Wide Web Consortium and was Editor-In-Chief of the World Wide Web Journal. Adam Rifkin works with the Infospheres Project on the composition of distributed active objects. His work on Infospheres has received two conference best paper awards.

T15. Workflow Management: Concepts, Architecture, Implementation and Deployment

Christoph Bussler, *The Boeing Company, USA*

Goals and content: This tutorial allows attendees to understand and characterize the field of workflow management and workflow management technologies in general. The tutorial will present and discuss the current state of workflow research, workflow standardization, and workflow products from a "neutral" viewpoint (i.e., independent of a specific philosophy or technology). The approach will be an overview of workflow concepts, architectures, and implementations-as well as references to current literature on workflow issues.

About the instructor: Christoph Bussler is project manager of a Workflow Management project. He is co-author of Workflow Management: Modeling Concepts, Architecture and Implementation.

T16. Using Social Network Analysis to Study Computer Networks: Theory, Methods and Substantive Findings

Barry Wellman, *University of Toronto, Canada*

Laura Garton, *Nortel, Canada*

Goals and content: When a computer network connects people or organizations, it is a social network. This tutorial will demonstrate the usefulness of a social network approach for the study of computer-mediated communication. Attendees will learn the principles, methods, and substantive findings of social network analysis, including: how to design social network research; how to collect social network data, and how to use standardized packages to analyze social network data.

About the instructors: Barry Wellman, a Professor of Sociology at the University of Toronto, founded the International Network for Social Network Analysis. He is currently studying the use of computer-mediated communication in loosely-coupled organizations and how residents of a highly-wired suburb use 100 Mb Internet access, and he is the Virtual Community Focus Area Advisor for SIGGROUP. Laura Garton is a a researcher at Human Resources at Nortel who has been using social network analysis to study organizations for 8 years.

T17. Theoretical Foundations of CSCL: How Do We Learn in Collaborative Settings?

Timothy Koschmann, *Southern Illinois University, USA*

Goals and content: CSCL (Computer Support for Collaborative Learning) is an emerging area of research in educational technology. Given that learning is a ubiquitous feature of all joint work, it follows that designers of applications meant to support cooperative work should develop at least a rudimentary understanding of existing theories of how people come to learn in these settings. This tutorial is designed for CSCW researchers and developers interested in exploring such issues. No prior background in educational theory will be assumed. The tutorial will begin by surveying five prominent, socially-motivated theories of learning (i.e., Neo-Piagetian, Cultural-Historical Activity Theory, Distributed Cognition, Bakhtinian, and Social Practice Theory). Following this overview, the group of attendees will be divided into smaller working teams which will undertake a task designed to deepen the participants' understanding of the five theories. As a result, tutorial participants will not only learn about collaborative learning, but will also have an opportunity to experience it.

About the instructor: The presenter is currently an Associate Professor at Southern Illinois University. He is an active member of the CSCL research community and was editor of a recently published book on this topic (CSCL: Theory and Practice of an Emerging Paradigm, Lawrence Erlbaum Associates, 1996). He was Program Chair for CSCL '95 (Indiana University) and Conference Co-Chair for CSCL '97 (University of Toronto). He has presented tutorials on CSCL at numerous past conferences.

T18. The World Wide Laboratory: Conducting Experiments on the Internet

Daniel B. Horn, Elena Rocco, and **Paul Resnick,**
University of Michigan, USA

Goals and content: Behavioral experiments have traditionally been done within the walls of a lab. Studies of this type have many advantages (e.g., high degree of experimental control), but they have costs and limitations (e.g., use of participants from a limited geographic area). The Internet provides new avenues to conduct research, creating new opportunities for scholars and practitioners. This tutorial examines traditional and new kinds of studies that can be conducted on the Internet. Covered topics include recruiting participants, identity verification, data management, on-line payment, experimental design, and the design of experiment Web sites.

About the instructors: Daniel B. Horn and Elena Rocco work at the Collaboratory for Research on Electronic Work at the University of Michigan. Paul Resnick was one of the developers of GroupLens, an early collaborative filtering system, and of PICS (Platform for Internet Content Selection), a set of technical specifications for the interoperation of Internet labeling and filtering systems.

Index of Paper Authors

NOTES

NOTES